ESSENTIALS
OF SPORTS LAW

ESSENTIALS OF SPORTS LAW

Fourth Edition

GLENN M. WONG

 PRAEGER

AN IMPRINT OF ABC-CLIO, LLC
Santa Barbara, California • Denver, Colorado • Oxford, England

Copyright 2010 by ABC-CLIO

Library of Congress Cataloging-in-Publication Data

Wong, Glenn M.
    Essentials of sports law / Glenn M. Wong. — 4th ed.
      p. cm.
    Includes bibliographical references and index.
      ISBN 978-0-313-35675-9 (hard copy : alk. paper) — ISBN 978-0-313-35676-6
(ebook)   1. Sports—Law and legislation—United States.   I. Title.
    KF3989.W66 2010
    344.73'099—dc22   2010021794

ISBN: 978-0-313-35675-9
EISBN: 978-0-313-35676-6

14   13   12   11   10   1   2   3   4   5

This book is also available on the World Wide Web as an eBook.
Visit www.abc-clio.com for details.

Praeger
An Imprint of ABC-CLIO

ABC-CLIO, LLC
130 Cremona Drive, P.O. Box 1911
Santa Barbara, California 93116-1911

This book is printed on acid-free paper (∞)

Manufactured in the United States of America

CONTENTS

Preface to the First Edition   xix
Preface to the Second Edition   xxi
Preface to the Third Edition   xxiii
Preface to the Fourth Edition   xxvii

CHAPTER 1
Introduction   1

1.1. The Sports Industry   2
1.2. Professional Sports Leagues   3
    1.2.1. A Brief Economic Overview   4
    1.2.2. Impact of Broadcast Contracts   6
    1.2.3. Attendance   9
    1.2.4. Luxury Suites   10
    1.2.5. Personal Seat Licenses   10
    1.2.6. Sponsorships, Licensing, and Merchandising   11
    1.2.7. Commissioners   13
    1.2.8. Single-Entity Leagues   15
1.3. Intercollegiate Athletics   16
    1.3.1. Organizational Structure   17
    1.3.2. Economic Overview   19
       1.3.2.1. Revenues   20
       1.3.2.2. Expenses   21
    1.3.3. The Institutions   22
    1.3.4. Institution Case Study: University of Michigan
       Athletic Department   23
    1.3.5. Knight Foundation Commission on
       Intercollegiate Athletics   25

1.4. The Olympics   27
     1.4.1.   Organizational Structure   27
     1.4.2.   International Federations and National
           Governing Bodies   31
     1.4.3.   Economic Overview of Olympic Bodies   33
     1.4.4.   International Olympic Committee Responses
           to Prevailing Legal Issues   34
1.5. Interscholastic Athletics   35
1.6. Individual Sport Issues   36
1.7. Facilities, Agency Firms, and Media   37

CHAPTER 2
The Court and Legal System in the United States   39

2.1. The Federal Court System   41
     2.1.1.   U.S. Supreme Court   41
     2.1.2.   U.S. Courts of Appeals   43
     2.1.3.   U.S. District Courts   44
     2.1.4.   Administrative Agencies   44
2.2. The State Court System   47
2.3. Civil Legal Process   48
     2.3.1.   The Complaint   48
     2.3.2.   The Parties   49
     2.3.3.   Court Jurisdiction   49
     2.3.4.   The Summons   49
     2.3.5.   The Answer   49
     2.3.6.   Discovery   50
     2.3.7.   Pretrial Motions   50
     2.3.8.   The Type of Court   50
     2.3.9.   The Trial   51
     2.3.10. The Judgment   52
     2.3.11. The Appeals Process   52
2.4. Sources of Legal Information   53
     2.4.1.   Legal Reference Materials   53
           2.4.1.1.   Legal Dictionaries   53
           2.4.1.2.   Legal Research Guides   53
           2.4.1.3.   Annotated Law Reports   54
           2.4.1.4.   Legal Encyclopedias   54
           2.4.1.5.   *Restatements of the Law*   54
           2.4.1.6.   Treatises   54
           2.4.1.7.   Legal Indexes   55
           2.4.1.8.   Law Review Articles   55
           2.4.1.9.   *Shepard's Citations*   56
           2.4.1.10. Legal Computer Services   56
           2.4.1.11. Sports Law Newsletters   57
           2.4.1.12. Sports Law Web Sites   58
     2.4.2.   Constitutions   58
     2.4.3.   Legislation   59
     2.4.4.   Federal Administrative Rules and Regulations   59

2.4.5. Case Law   60
    2.4.5.1. U.S. Supreme Court   60
    2.4.5.2. U.S. Courts of Appeals   60
    2.4.5.3. U.S. District Courts   61
    2.4.5.4. State Courts   62

CHAPTER 3
Legal Principles in Tort Law   63

3.1. The Tort of Negligence   65
    3.1.1. Duty of Care Owed   65
       3.1.1.1. Reasonable Person Standard   67
       3.1.1.2. Standard of Care for Children   68
    3.1.2. Breach of Duty Owed   69
       3.1.2.1. Violation of a Statute, Negligence *Per Se*   70
       3.1.2.2. *Res Ipsa Loquitur*   70
    3.1.3. Actual and Proximate Causation   71
    3.1.4. Damages   73
    3.1.5. Defenses for Negligence   74
       3.1.5.1. No Negligence   74
       3.1.5.2. Contributory Negligence   75
       3.1.5.3. Comparative Negligence   75
       3.1.5.4. Assumption of Risk   76
       3.1.5.5. Statute of Limitations   79
       3.1.5.6. Immunity and Good Samaritan Statutes   79
    3.1.6. Wrongful Death Statutes   81
3.2. The Tort of Reckless Misconduct (Gross Negligence)   82
3.3. Intentional Torts   83
    3.3.1. The Tort of Assault   83
    3.3.2. The Tort of Battery   84
    3.3.3. Defenses for Assault and Battery   85
       3.3.3.1. Consent   85
       3.3.3.2. Privilege   86
    3.3.4. Tortious Interference with Contractual Relations   87
    3.3.5. The Tort of Intentional Infliction of Emotional Distress   88
    3.3.6. Damages for Intentional Torts   89
3.4. Harm to Economic and Dignitary Interests   89
    3.4.1. Defamation Law   89
       3.4.1.1. Libel   90
       3.4.1.2. Slander   90
    3.4.2. The Tort of Invasion of Privacy   92
3.5. Products Liability Law   94
    3.5.1. Products Liability Based on Intent   94
    3.5.2. Products Liability Based on Negligence   94
    3.5.3. Products Liability Based on Strict Tort Liability   95
    3.5.4. Products Liability Based on Implied and Express Warranties   97
3.6. Vicarious Liability   97
    3.6.1. Exception: Independent Contractors   98
3.7. Workers' Compensation   99

CHAPTER 4
Application of Tort Law to Sports   105

4.1. Liability of Participants   106
4.2. Liability of Coaches and Teachers   110
    4.2.1. Failure to Provide Adequate Supervision   111
    4.2.2. Failure to Provide Proper Instruction and Training   113
    4.2.3. Failure to Provide Prompt and Capable Medical Assistance   115
4.3. Liability of Administrators, Schools, and Athletic Organizations   117
    4.3.1. Failure to Provide Supervision of Athletic
         Activities and to Hire Qualified Personnel   118
    4.3.2. Failure to Provide Proper Medical Assistance   120
    4.3.3. Failure to Provide Safe Equipment   121
    4.3.4. Vicarious Liability for Actions of Fans and Players   123
4.4. The Defense of Immunity   124
    4.4.1. Sovereign Immunity   124
    4.4.2. Charitable Immunity   126
    4.4.3. Civil Liability Immunity Legislation   127
4.5. Liability of Facility Owners and Possessors   128
4.6. Liability of Medical Personnel   138
4.7. Liability of Officials, Referees, and Umpires   142
4.8. Application of Legal Principles to Defects in Equipment   147
4.9. Liability Insurance   150
4.10. Waiver and Release of Liability   151

CHAPTER 5
Athletic Associations   157

5.1. Voluntary Athletic Associations   160
    5.1.1. Introduction   160
    5.1.2. The U.S. Olympic Committee   161
    5.1.3. National Collegiate Athletic Association (NCAA)   165
    5.1.4. Other Athletic Associations   170
    5.1.5. High School Athletic Associations   172
5.2. Legal Principles Pertaining to Amateur Athletic Associations   178
    5.2.1. Introduction   178
    5.2.2. Judicial Review   178
    5.2.3. Standing   182
    5.2.4. Injunctive Relief   182
5.3. Association Enforcement Authority   184
    5.3.1. Introduction   184
    5.3.2. NCAA Enforcement Procedure   185
        5.3.2.1. Committee on Infractions   186
        5.3.2.2. Infractions Appeals Committee   189
        5.3.2.3. NCAA Infractions Process   192
    5.3.3. The Knight Commission   193
    5.3.4. Interscholastic Enforcement Procedures   195
    5.3.5. Olympic Enforcement Procedures   198
    5.3.6. Court of Arbitration for Sport   201

5.4. Public Responsibility of Athletic Associations 205
    5.4.1. Disclosure 205
    5.4.2. Funding of Public Facilities 208
    5.4.3. The Buckley Amendment 209

CHAPTER 6
The Athlete and Constitutional Law 213

6.1. Athletic Associations and Constitutional Issues 215
    6.1.1. State Action Requirement 215
    6.1.2. Due Process 219
        6.1.2.1. Procedural Due Process 220
        6.1.2.2. Substantive Due Process 222
    6.1.3. Equal Protection 226
6.2. Definitions of Eligibility 229
6.3. Eligibility Requirements: College and High School 234
    6.3.1. Academic Eligibility Rules 236
        6.3.1.1. Initial Eligibility: National Collegiate
            Athletic Association (NCAA) 236
        6.3.1.2. Grade Point Average: High School 239
        6.3.1.3. Academic Progress: NCAA 240
        6.3.1.4. Academic Progress: High School 242
    6.3.2. Participation Rules 244
        6.3.2.1. Redshirting 244
        6.3.2.2. Longevity 247
        6.3.2.3. Transfer Rules 249
    6.3.3. Amateurism Rules 252
        6.3.3.1. NCAA Rules Regarding Scholarships,
            Financial Assistance, and Expenses 252
        6.3.3.2. Employment: NCAA 257
        6.3.3.3. Summer Camps and Independent Teams 258
        6.3.3.4. Olympic Eligibility Requirements 260
6.4. Athlete's Challenge of Rules 263
    6.4.1. Freedom of Expression 263
    6.4.2. Discipline 268
    6.4.3. Alcohol, Drug, and Conduct Rules: High School 273

CHAPTER 7
Drug Testing and Policies 275

7.1. Legal Principles in Drug Testing 277
    7.1.1. Constitutional Law 278
    7.1.2. Contract and Labor Law 281
7.2. Drug Policies and Legal Challenges 282
    7.2.1. Interscholastic Athletics 283
        7.2.1.1. *Vernonia School District v. Acton* 283
        7.2.1.2. Performance-Enhancing Drug Policies 285
        7.2.1.3. Considerations in Enacting Drug Testing Programs 285

7.2.2. Intercollegiate Athletics 287
    7.2.2.1. NCAA Policy and Legal Challenges 287
    7.2.2.2. College Conferences and Schools: Policies
        and Legal Challenges 291
7.2.3. Olympic and International Sports 293
7.2.4. Professional Sports 300
    7.2.4.1. National Football League 301
    7.2.4.2. National Basketball Association 304
    7.2.4.3. Major League Baseball 306
    7.2.4.4. National Hockey League 310
    7.2.4.5. Professional Golf Association 311
    7.2.4.6. Women's National Basketball Association 312

CHAPTER 8
Gender Discrimination in Athletics 315

8.1. Legal Theories in Gender Discrimination Cases 321
    8.1.1. Title IX 323
        8.1.1.1. Legislative History of Title IX 323
        8.1.1.2. Office of Civil Rights (OCR) Policy
            Interpretation of Title IX 323
        8.1.1.3. OCR Analysis and Method of Enforcement 326
    8.1.2. The Equal Rights Amendment and State Equal
        Rights Amendments 330
    8.1.3. Equal Protection Laws 334
8.2. Legal Challenges to Title IX 337
    8.2.1. Legality and Scope of Title IX 337
    8.2.2. Post–Civil Rights Restoration Act Litigation 342
8.3. Gender Discrimination Cases Involving Individual Athletes 349
    8.3.1. Men's Team, No Women's Team 350
        8.3.1.1. Contact Sports 350
        8.3.1.2. Noncontact Sports 353
    8.3.2. Women's Team, No Men's Team 356
    8.3.3. Women's Teams and Men's Teams 360
        8.3.3.1. Separate but Equal 360
        8.3.3.2. Contact Sports 361
        8.3.3.3. Noncontact Sports 363
    8.3.4. Same Sport, Different Rules 363
        8.3.4.1. Contact Sports 363
        8.3.4.2. Noncontact Sports 364
    8.3.5. Same Sport, Different Seasons 365
    8.3.6. Varsity Sport versus Club Sport 367

CHAPTER 9
Contract Law 369

9.1. Principles of Contract Law 370
    9.1.1. Formation of a Contract 371
        9.1.1.1. Offer 371

9.1.1.2. Acceptance	373
9.1.1.3. Consideration	374
9.1.1.4. Legality	377
9.1.1.5. Capacity	379
9.1.1.6. Drafting a Contract	379
9.1.2. Mistakes in Contracts	380
9.1.3. Parol Evidence Rule	381
9.1.4. Conditions of a Contract	381
9.1.5. Statute of Frauds	382
9.1.6. Assignment and Delegation of a Contract	383
9.1.7. Breach of Contract	383
9.1.8. Remedies for a Breach of Contract	386
9.2. Types of Athletic Contracts	388
9.2.1. Standard Player Contract	388
9.2.1.1. Reserve or Option Clause	389
9.2.1.2. Unique Skill Provisions	390
9.2.1.3. Hierarchy of Contracts	391
9.2.1.4. Player Exclusivity	392
9.2.1.5. Assignability	392
9.2.1.6. Bonus Clauses	393
9.2.1.7. Health Regulations	395
9.2.1.8. Full Performance	396
9.2.1.9. Example of a Standard Player Contract: National Football League	398
9.2.2. Defenses to Standard Player Contract Breaches	398
9.2.3. Tortious Interference with Contractual Relations	408
9.2.4. Marketing, Endorsement, and Sponsorship Contracts	410
9.2.4.1. Impact of League Rules	412
9.2.4.2. Sponsorship Rights	412
9.2.4.3. Indemnification	413
9.2.4.4. Right to Terminate	414
9.2.4.5. *Force Majeure* and Work Stoppage	414
9.2.4.6. Sponsorship Litigation Cases	415
9.2.5. Coaches' Contracts: Professional and Collegiate Sports	416
9.2.6. Coaches' Contracts: High School	432
9.2.7. Physicians' Contracts	434
9.2.8. Officials' Contracts	435
9.2.9. Facility Contracts	435

CHAPTER 10
Antitrust Law — 451

10.1. Overview of Antitrust Law	452
10.1.1. Sherman Act, Section 1: Restraint of Trade	453
10.1.2. Sherman Act, Section 2: Monopolization	455
10.1.3. Clayton Act	457
10.1.3.1. Treble Damages	457
10.1.3.2. Statutory Labor Exemption	457

10.2. Application of Antitrust Law to Professional Sports 458
    10.2.1. Player Restraints and Antitrust Theory 458
        10.2.1.1. Football 462
        10.2.1.2. Hockey 463
        10.2.1.3. Basketball 465
    10.2.2. Ownership Restraints and Antitrust Theory 466
        10.2.2.1. Existing Owners v. Existing Owners:
            Raiders v. NFL 468
        10.2.2.2. *Raiders v. NFL* Revisited 469
        10.2.2.3. Prospective Owners versus Existing Owners 471
            10.2.2.3.1. *Piazza v. MLB* 471
            10.2.2.3.2. *Morsani v. MLB* 471
            10.2.2.3.3. *MLB v. Crist* 471
    10.2.3. Interleague Antitrust Challenges 472
        10.2.3.1. *USFL v. NFL* 473
        10.2.3.2. *NASL v. NFL* 474
    10.2.4. Antitrust Litigation in Professional Tennis and Golf 476
        10.2.4.1. Age Restrictions 476
        10.2.4.2. Equipment Rules 477
        10.2.4.3. Blacklisting: *Blalock v. LPGA* 478
        10.2.4.4. Hosting Tournaments and Conflicts
            of Interest 478
10.3. Defenses to Antitrust Challenges 479
    10.3.1. The Baseball Exemption 479
        10.3.1.1. History of the Reserve System 479
        10.3.1.2. Creation of the Baseball Exemption:
            Federal Baseball 480
        10.3.1.3. Baseball Exemption Reaffirmed: *Toolson* 486
        10.3.1.4. Baseball Anomaly Upheld: *Flood* 487
        10.3.1.5. The Curt Flood Act 488
    10.3.2. The Nonstatutory Labor Exemption 489
    10.3.3. Early Uses of the Nonstatutory Labor Exemption:
        Philadelphia, *Mackey*, and *McCourt* 490
    10.3.4. Exemption after Expiration of Collective
        Bargaining Agreement: *Bridgeman* and *Powell* 493
    10.3.5. Exemption after Decertification: *McNeil* 495
    10.3.6. Nonstatutory Labor Exemption after *White*: *Brown* 496
    10.3.7. The Nonstatutory Labor Exemption in *Clarett* 497
    10.3.8. Single-Entity Defense by the Big Four 498
    10.3.9. Single-Entity Leagues: *Fraser v. MLS* 500
10.4. Antitrust Law and International Soccer: *Bosman* 502
10.5. Antitrust Law and the National Collegiate
    Athletic Association (NCAA) 504
    10.5.1. Decisions before *Board of Regents* (1984) 505
    10.5.2. The NCAA's Reduced Power over Television:
        NCAA v. Board of Regents 505
    10.5.3. Coaches' Salaries: *Law v. NCAA* 506
    10.5.4. Tournaments: *MIBA v. NCAA* 507
    10.5.5. The Bowl Championship Series 508
    10.5.6. Other Decisions after *Board of Regents* 509

CHAPTER 11
Labor Law   513

11.1. Development of Labor Law   515
    11.1.1.   History of Labor Law   516
    11.1.2.   National Labor Relations Act (as Amended in 1947) 517
    11.1.3.   National Labor Relations Act, Section 7   518
    11.1.4.   National Labor Relations Act, Section 8   518
    11.1.5.   Unfair Labor Practice Procedures   520
        11.1.5.1. Interference with Organizing or
               Bargaining Collectively   520
        11.1.5.2. Domination and Assistance   520
        11.1.5.3. Discrimination   521
        11.1.5.4. Retaliation   521
        11.1.5.5. Duty to Bargain in Good Faith   521
        11.1.5.6. Protection from Unions   522
    11.1.6.   National Labor Relations Board   523
    11.1.7.   Certification of a Union   524
11.2. Collective Bargaining   525
    11.2.1.   The Collective Bargaining Process   525
    11.2.2.   Mandatory and Permissive Subjects
           of Bargaining   527
    11.2.3.   Ratification   528
    11.2.4.   Decertification   528
11.3. Collective Bargaining in Professional Sports   529
    11.3.1.   The Players Associations in Professional Sports   530
    11.3.2.   National Hockey League Players Association   530
    11.3.3.   National Football League Players Association   531
    11.3.4.   National Basketball Players Association   533
    11.3.5.   Major League Baseball Players Association   534
    11.3.6.   Other Players Associations in North America   535
        11.3.6.1. Women's National Basketball Association   535
        11.3.6.2. Major League Soccer   535
        11.3.6.3. Arena Football League   536
        11.3.6.4. Canadian Football League
               Players Association   537
        11.3.6.5. Potential Unionization of Minor League
               Baseball and College Athletics   538
    11.3.7.   Collective Bargaining Agreements in
           Professional Sports   539
        11.3.7.1. Labor Disputes in Professional Sports   539
             11.3.7.1.1. Strikes   540
             11.3.7.1.2. Lockouts   543
             11.3.7.1.3. Impasse   544
             11.3.7.1.4. Baseball Collusion Cases   553
    11.3.8.   Outline of a Professional Sports Collective
           Bargaining Agreement   555
    11.3.9.   Free Agency   556
    11.3.10. Salary Caps   559
    11.3.11. Calculation of Salary Cap   561

11.3.12. Hard Cap versus Soft Cap 561
11.3.13. Arbitration 562
11.3.14. Grievance Procedures in Professional Sports 564
11.3.14.1. Unlawful Discharge 567
11.3.15. Salary Arbitration 569

CHAPTER 12
Agency Law 573

12.1. Agency Law 577
12.2. Player Agents 578
12.2.1. Functions of the Player Agent 578
12.2.1.1. Negotiating 581
12.2.1.2. Counseling 582
12.2.1.3. Managing 583
12.2.1.4. Marketing 583
12.2.1.5. Resolving Disputes 584
12.2.1.6. Planning 584
12.3. Players Associations and Agents 585
12.3.1. Salary Information 586
12.3.2. Union-Agent Relationships 590
12.3.3. Agent-Athlete Agreements 592
12.3.4. Agent-Athlete Dispute Resolution 593
12.3.5. Agent-Agent Grievance Arbitration 597
12.4. Agent-Agent Litigation 597
12.5. Government Regulation 598
12.5.1. Uniform Athlete Agent Act 598
12.5.2. Sports Agent Responsibility and Trust Act 609
12.5.3. State Regulations 609
12.5.4. Ethical Constraints 610
12.5.5. National Collegiate Athletic Association
(NCAA) Regulations 611
12.6. Team Sports Player Drafts 615
12.6.1. National Football League Draft 616
12.6.1.1. Draft Eligibility 616
12.6.1.2. Draft Retention Rights 616
12.6.1.3. Impact on NCAA Eligibility 621
12.6.2. Major League Baseball Draft 622
12.6.3. National Basketball Association Draft 625
12.6.4. National Hockey League Draft 626
12.6.5. Single-Entity League Drafts 626
12.6.5.1. Major League Soccer 627
12.6.5.2 Women's National Basketball
Association 627
12.7. Standard Player Contract 628
12.8. Endorsement Contracts and Financial Planning 633
12.9. Individual Performer Sports 647
12.10. Foreign Leagues 647

CHAPTER 13
Intellectual Property Law   663

13.1. Trademark Law   665
       13.1.1. The Lanham Act of 1946   667
       13.1.2. Service Marks and Collective Marks   667
       13.1.3. Identification Function of a Trademark   668
       13.1.4. Secondary Meaning   669
       13.1.5. Trademark Infringement   672
       13.1.6. Ambush Marketing   680
       13.1.7. Licensing Programs for Intercollegiate Athletics   682
                13.1.7.1. Litigation Involving Intercollegiate
                           Licensing Programs   684
                13.1.7.2. Trademark Law and Nicknames   687
       13.1.8. Trademark Law and the Olympics   689
13.2. Copyright Law   693
       13.2.1. Copyright Law and the Internet   696
13.3. Patent Law   700
13.4. The Right of Publicity   703

CHAPTER 14
Broadcasting and Multimedia   707

14.1. Legal Foundation: Establishing the Property Right,
       History, and Laws   710
       14.1.1. Case Law   710
       14.1.2. Copyright Laws   712
       14.1.3. Federal Communications Commission
                (FCC) Regulations   713
       14.1.4. Other Legislation   714
14.2. Broadcast Contracts   717
       14.2.1. Rights Granted   717
       14.2.2. Broadcast Rights of a Professional League   718
                14.2.2.1. Broadcast Rights of a Professional Team   720
       14.2.3. Broadcast Rights of the National Collegiate
                Athletic Association (NCAA)   723
                14.2.3.1. Broadcast Rights of the NCAA Championships   723
                14.2.3.2. Broadcast Rights of the Bowl
                           Championship Series   724
       14.2.4. Broadcast Rights for Conferences and Schools   724
                14.2.4.1. Antitrust Issues in Broadcasting for Colleges   728
       14.2.5. Broadcast Rights of Individual Sports   733
       14.2.6. Broadcast Rights for the Olympics   734
       14.2.7. Broadcast Rights of Individual Players   735
14.3. Other Important Issues in Sports Broadcasting   736
       14.3.1. Restrictions on Sports Broadcasting   736
                14.3.1.1. Restrictions on the Use of Advertising   736
                14.3.1.2. Restrictions on the Use of Replays   737

14.4. Internet Rights for Sports Broadcasts   737
       14.4.1. Home Recording of Copyrighted Events   739
       14.4.2. Domestic and International Piracy of Satellite
                and Cable Transmissions   740
       14.4.3. Blackouts of Scheduled Programming   741
       14.4.4. Satellite Distribution   742
       14.4.5. FCC and Indecency   743
14.5. A Broadcasting Checklist   744

CHAPTER 15
Business Law: Business Structures, Tax Laws,
and Employment Law   745

15.1. Business Structures   746
       15.1.1. Sole Proprietorships   747
       15.1.2. Partnerships   747
       15.1.3. Limited Partnerships   748
       15.1.4. Corporations   749
                15.1.4.1. C Corporations   749
                15.1.4.2. S Corporations   750
                15.1.4.3. Limited Liability Corporations   751
                15.1.4.4. Publicly Traded Corporations   752
15.2. Tax Issues   753
       15.2.1. Nonprofit Organizations   754
       15.2.2. Unrelated Business Income   755
                15.2.2.1. Facility Rentals   758
                15.2.2.2. Broadcast Receipts   759
                15.2.2.3. Sponsorship Revenue   759
       15.2.3. Scholarships   760
       15.2.4. Charitable Contributions, Luxury Box Rentals,
                and Entertainment Expenses   760
       15.2.5. Professional Sport Franchise Tax Issues   761
       15.2.6. Franchise Depreciation Issues   763
       15.2.7. State Tax Issues for Player Salaries   765
15.3. Employment Law   766
       15.3.1. Employment-at-Will Contracts   766
       15.3.2. Employment Discrimination Statutes   767
                15.3.2.1. Equal Pay Act   767
                15.3.2.2. Equal Employment Opportunity
                           Commission Coaching Pay Guidelines   770
                15.3.2.3. Title VII of the Civil Rights Act of 1964   772
                15.3.2.4. Gender Discrimination Cases under Title VII   772
                15.3.2.5. Gender Discrimination Cases under Title IX   775
                15.3.2.6. Race Discrimination Cases under Title VII   776
                15.3.2.7. Age Discrimination in Employment
                           Act of 1967   778
                15.3.2.8. State Discrimination Laws   780
       15.3.3. Sexual Harassment   780

CHAPTER 16
Additional Legal Concerns   785

16.1. Athletes, Violence, and Criminal Law   786
    16.1.1. Defining a Crime   788
    16.1.2. Player-against-Player Violence   791
    16.1.3. Player and Fan Violence   795
    16.1.4. Player-against-Official Violence   797
    16.1.5. Off-the-Field Criminal Conduct   799
    16.1.6. Solutions to the Problem of Sports Violence   801
        16.1.6.1. Governing Body Control   801
        16.1.6.2. Government Regulation   802
16.2. Illegal Gambling   803
    16.2.1. Intercollegiate Athletics and Gambling   803
    16.2.2. Professional Sports and Gambling   807
    16.2.3. Internet Gambling   810
    16.2.4. Fantasy Sports and Office Pools   810
16.3. Disabilities   812
    16.3.1. Federal Laws Affecting Persons with Disabilities   812
        16.3.1.1. The Rehabilitation Act   813
        16.3.1.2. Individuals with Disabilities
               Education Act (IDEA)   814
        16.3.1.3. The Amateur Sports Act   815
        16.3.1.4. Americans with Disabilities Act (ADA)   816
            16.3.1.4.1. Title I: Employment   817
            16.3.1.4.2. Title II: Public Services   817
            16.3.1.4.3. Title III: Public Accommodations
                   Operated by Private Entities   818
    16.3.2. Application to Athletic Organizations   819
        16.3.2.1. Youth Sports   819
        16.3.2.2. High School   820
        16.3.2.3. Colleges, Universities, and the National
               Collegiate Athletic Association   822
        16.3.2.4. Professional Sports   824
        16.3.2.5. Sports Facilities   825
16.4. Athletes with AIDS and Testing for HIV   826

Glossary of Legal and Sports Terms   827

Essentials of Sports Law Case Index
(Sorted Alphabetically by Plaintiff)   855

Index   885

PREFACE TO THE FIRST EDITION

In my several professional roles as attorney, teacher, and consultant, I meet frequently with individuals and groups active in amateur sports. Athletic administrators and others around the country have repeatedly expressed a need for a "practitioner's" book because sports law has become such an integral part of their day-to-day operation. They want to have a background on sports law before they deal with attorneys on legal issues. Even more important, they want to attempt to avoid litigation. The interest and concerns of these people motivated the writing of this book.

I started with the concept that the book should be written for those affected by sports law issues who are not necessarily lawyers, including college or high school athletic administrators or coaches, student-athletes, school board members, institutional representatives, and those involved in amateur sports organizations. There is, for example, a chapter on the court system, a glossary, and sample forms that can be used by practitioners as starting points for developing their own forms. The major intercollegiate and interscholastic amateur sports organizations, such as the U.S. Olympic Committee and the National Collegiate Athletic Association, are described in detail. All new legal concepts and issues are discussed, as are basic tort law, contract law, trademark law, and constitutional law. Each of the chapters has been designed as a self-contained unit that can be used as a quick reference. Case citations and brief summaries of cases (rather than lengthy discussions) have been included in the notes. The notes also include law review articles, names and addresses of relevant organizations, and other information that can lead the reader to additional sources of information.

I would like to thank some of the many people who have been instrumental in assisting me with *Essentials of Amateur Sports Law*. First, Margaret M. Kearney, the editor, helped express the thoughts and principles in this book. In addition, she kept the project moving and made sure that legalese was eliminated. As for research and writing, I would like to thank and acknowledge the work of Professor Richard J. Ensor of the University of Massachusetts, Amherst. He coauthored Chapter 13 (on trademark law) and Chapter 14 (on sports broadcasting). His numerous reviews of the manuscript and comments were invaluable in that he provided the perspectives of a sports lawyer and an experienced athletic administrator. I also acknowledge the contributions of several research assistants: David Knopp, William Hubbard, Scott Proefrock, and Scott Zuffelato. The many drafts of the manuscript were typed by Susan McBride, to whom I am grateful. Several others, too numerous to mention individually, also contributed in various ways to this project. Finally, I would like to thank Professor Robert Berry of Boston College Law School for getting me started in sports law.

PREFACE TO THE
SECOND EDITION

How much has changed since 1988, when the first edition of *Essentials of Amateur Sports Law* was published? The Knight Commission has been formed, disbanded, and reinstated; Dick Shultz has resigned as executive director of the National Collegiate Athletic Association (NCAA); and the impact of the passage of the Civil Rights Restoration Act is being felt and has even spawned a new term: *gender equity*. The first edition of this book does not mention idiopathic cardiomyopathy (Hank Gathers's form of heart disease); Jerry Tarkanian was still head basketball coach at the University of Nevada, Las Vegas; and there is another new term: *ambush marketing*. The first Proposition 48 (now Propositions 48/42/26) student-athletes have graduated, but it has not stopped the debate over academic requirements for NCAA initial eligibility. Butch Reynolds has a judgment in hand for $27.3 million, and a new law is coming into place: the Americans with Disabilities Act.

These are only some of the significant changes in the constantly changing area of sports law. Many of the changes since 1988 have further clouded the line between professional and amateur athletics: a case-decision ruling that a college football player was an employee of the university, the 1992 Men's Olympic basketball team dominated by professional basketball players from the National Basketball Association, and proposal to pay Olympic athletes for performance in the 1994 Olympics.

As you can see from this brief overview, there have been significant changes and important litigation that continue to shape athletics. Some will be discussed in a global manner in Chapter 1 and then discussed in more detail throughout the book. In all, there are approximately 165 new cases in this edition. The title of the book, however, remains the same. The reason for this is analogous to baseball's antitrust exemption—it is done for precedent reasons and not because it is the most appropriate title in 1994. The number of chapters and major topical areas covered in the book have not changed, but they have been updated.

For me, a major reason for putting together a second edition was the positive, strong, and encouraging responses I received from the audience. I would like to thank them. Many of these people have provided comments that have been incorporated into the second edition.

The second edition has been a challenge. While trying to finish the revision, I served for several months in 1992–1993 as director of athletics and dean of the School of Physical Education at the University of Massachusetts. Also, I was appointed as faculty athletics representative to the NCAA. While these positions made completion of the second edition more difficult, they also served to provide me with different insights and to confirm on a firsthand basis some of my thoughts and ideas. In addition, a second son, Gary, arrived. I dedicate the second edition to him, to my first son, Glenn, and to my wife, Paula.

There were many people who assisted in seeing this project through. Carol Barr, my research assistant, kept this project going, and my colleague, Lisa Pike, assistant professor, provided invaluable assistance with the manuscript, including feedback from the use of the book in her Sports Law course.

Other students and research assistants who assisted in the production of this second edition include Jack Woodbury, Jesse Wilde, Peter Carton, Leslie Keast, Margaret Driscoll, Steve Hilliard, Jeff Craig, and Burke Magnus. All these students and research assistants have already moved on to their careers in the sports industry.

For those of you who know publishing, you are well aware that there are several months' lag time between submission of the final manuscript and the published book. By the time you read this, my files will already include cases for the third edition. I anticipate many new cases involving discrimination issues (and also reverse discrimination), litigation or arbitration regarding eligibility for the Olympics, changes in NCAA enforcement procedures, drug testing and contractual rights, conference contract issues, additional litigation relative to medical issues, and a host of new issues that no one can predict. These new issues will continue to make sports law a constantly changing, interesting, and varied discipline and will certainly provide cause for a third edition of *Essentials of Amateur Sports Law*.

PREFACE TO THE THIRD EDITION

This is the third edition of *Essentials of Sports Law*. It has been eight years since the second edition, *Essentials of Amateur Sports Law*, was published. Over the course of these eight years, there have been significant changes in sports law.

The preface to the second edition mentions the passage of the Americans with Disabilities Act, and the third edition contains the court decision in *Casey Martin v. PGA Tour*, in which the U.S. Supreme Court ruled in favor of Martin and allowed him to participate on the PGA Tour while using a golf cart. There have been significant developments in the gender equity area, including the important cases of *Cohen v. Brown University*, which dealt with participation opportunities for women student-athletes. Other important gender equity decisions involved *Pederson v. Louisiana State University* and *Boucher v. Syracuse University*. A recently filed court case should be followed. The National Wrestling Coaches Association (NWCA) filed a lawsuit in 2002 challenging the U.S. Department of Education's Title IX regulations interpreting proportionality. If the NWCA is successful in its case, it will have significant ramifications for Title IX. In the tort liability area, the litigation continues, and more supervision cases and waiver cases were litigated. Courts have had to deal with injuries from higher risk activities such as "adventure sports" and injuries caused by team or school mascots. The National Collegiate Athletic Association (NCAA) has again faced the antitrust challenge and was on the losing end of the coaches' restricted earnings case *Law v. National Collegiate Athletic Association*. This resulted in a significant damages settlement by the NCAA and led to further litigation against the NCAA based on antitrust theory.

In the area of agents, there are continued abuses by some player agents. The Uniform Athlete Agents Act, which is model state legislation, was passed and has been adopted by several states. If this is done, it will create some uniformity in state legislation. The National Football League Players Association has adopted regulations regulating financial advisors of players. In the constitutional law area, freedom of expression reached the U.S. Supreme Court in *Sante Fe Independent School District v. Doe*, and drug testing cases continue to be litigated. The Olympic

movement made significant changes in its drug testing procedures and dispute res-
olution system. There have been several important court cases, including *Slaney v.
The International Amateur Athletic Federation and the United States Olympic
Committee*, and many arbitration decisions. There was also a significant amend-
ment to the 1978 Amateur Sports Act, the "Ted Stevens Olympic and Amateur
Sports Act," which was passed in 1998.

In addition to including the aforementioned developments, the third edition of
Essentials of Sports Law incorporates professional sports law issues; hence *Amateur* has been removed from the title. This reflects feedback from sports lawyers,
sports managers, and students who suggested that professional sports law issues
be included. Furthermore, the line between professional and amateur sport has
become blurred over the years. There is no better example than the Olympic
movement. When the first edition of *Essentials of Amateur Sports Law* was written in 1988, the Olympics were only for amateurs. Now professional athletes are
commonplace and (mostly) accepted as part of the Olympic Games. There are
many who believe that college athletics can no longer be properly characterized
as amateur athletics and point primarily to Division I football and basketball.
While certainly the NCAA clings to its notion that the student-athlete should not
be paid, the commercialism of the games, the broadcasts, the price of tickets, the
salaries of coaches, and many other aspects closely parallel professional sports.
There are some in college sports who no longer talk about amateurism but refer to
a different and unique model from professional sports. The changes and additions
to this third edition reflect both the interests of the audience and the changing
landscape of sports.

These are these new chapters in *Essentials of Sports Law*: Chapter 10, "Antitrust
Law"; Chapter 11, "Labor Law"; Chapter 13, "Intellectual Property Law" (copyright
law and patent law have been added to trademark law); Chapter 15, "Business Law:
Business Structures, Tax Laws, and Employment Law"; and Chapter 16, "Additional Legal Concerns" (disabilities law has been added). In these chapters, some
of the recent developments include the continued contentious labor situation in
Major League Baseball that led to the cancellation of the 1994 World Series.
Management and labor are currently involved in another bitter round of labor
negotiations, in which management has tried the new approach of contraction of
two teams. Whether contraction is successful remains to be seen, but this attempt
has led to much new litigation. Two interesting discipline cases were decided in
arbitration involving Latrell Sprewell and the National Basketball Association and
John Rocker and Major League Baseball. In new professional sports leagues, the
"single-entity" form of league ownership and operation has been implemented. In
Fraser v. Major League Soccer, the players were unsuccessful in challenging this
form of ownership based on an antitrust theory. In the intellectual property area,
the Internet and other forms of new technology have led to new revenue streams
and new terminology such as the Web, domain names, and cybersquatting, but
this has also led to disputes concerning ownership of the properties. There have
also been numerous employment law cases in sports, mostly involving gender
discrimination claims but also racial and age discrimination claims.

Sport and the law have changed significantly in the last eight years. There was
also a significant amount of change in the six years between the first and second
editions. Since I expect the litigation and legislation to continue, there is a need to
keep the reader of *Essentials of Sports Law* current on new litigation, legislation,
and agreements. Therefore the third edition of *Essentials of Sports Law* will be

supported by supplements. For those who teach a course using *Essentials of Sports Law*, an instructor's manual will be available. A case book, with edited court and arbitration decisions, is planned for 2003. Finally, a Web site will be available to provide information on the book, updates, and information for instructors.

I would like to thank all the people who have read previous editions of *Essentials of Amateur Sports Law*. Sports lawyers and sports managers have made numerous suggestions. The students in my sports law classes at the University of Massachusetts have also provided significant feedback. I have also received suggestions from people in the sports industry who have attended the seminars I have presented on various sports law issues. I have tried to incorporate my work experiences, both as a lawyer and sport administrator, into the book. I have considered all these experiences and comments and have tried to address many of them in the third edition of *Essentials of Sports Law*.

Law students, law school professors, and lawyers will see that this is not a typical law school case book. The book is written in a narrative style. The accompanying case book will be important and helpful to law students, professors, and lawyers. The third edition of *Essentials of Sports Law*, it is hoped, will be a starting point, with the case references in the book and the casebook providing the resources you need. The note sections in the text contain brief case summaries of leading cases and important and different fact situations but do not cover every case decision on the particular topic. *Essentials of Sports Law* is not designed to provide legal advice but rather to provide a starting point for sports lawyers and students.

For sports management students and professors, the book can be used as a textbook for sports law courses. It has been used in both undergraduate- and graduate-level courses. At the University of Massachusetts, it is used in Introduction to Sport Law, a required course in the sports management program. For graduate-level programs, *Essentials of Sports Law* can be used in conjunction with edited court and arbitration decisions.

Many people have contributed to this book. Four sports management graduate students who helped bring the manuscript to the finish line are John Shukie, Dominic Rivers, Stephanie Tryce, and Tim Cohane. And since this has been a work in progress for many years, there are many other students who contributed, including Mario Garcia, Steve Condrin, Karen Skinner, Karen Duncan, Doron Azrialy, Matthew Clark, John Clark, Vincent Dolan, and Luke Flockerzi.

Two colleagues made significant contributions: John T. Wolohan, attorney and faculty member at Ithaca College, and Lisa Pike Masteralexis, attorney and faculty member at the University of Massachusetts. I would like to thank Robert C. Berry and Harold J. Vanderzwaag for their continued guidance and support. Other people have supported this project with information, ideas, and support and include Richard J. Ensor, Herb Rudoy, Mike Gibbons, Gene Bailey, Steve Abbott, Barbara Morgan, Burke Magnes, Elsa Cole, Diane Morse, Kevin Kelly, Ethan Orlinsky, and Selin Dixon-Wheeler.

I would also like to thank three deans at the University of Massachusetts who have supported my research efforts and particularly this book: Cleve Willis, Robert Helgeson, and David Bischoff.

I would like to thank John Harney of Book Consultants of Boston, who started me on my journey into the publishing world almost 20 years ago and has always provided me good and sensible counsel along the way.

I would like to thank Dr. James T. Sabin, director of academic research and development, Greenwood Publishing, who has supported and guided this project from the beginning. Beth Wilson did an excellent job with the copyediting. And a thank-you also to these Greenwood Publishing people who worked on the project: Liz Leiba, Nicole Cournoyer, Michelle Scott, Margaret Maybury, and Paulette Chase.

Finally, I would like to thank my wife, Paula Nassif, and our two sons, Glenn and Gary, for their support.

PREFACE TO THE FOURTH EDITION

I am pleased to be able to write and publish the fourth edition of *Essentials of Sports Law*. It has been eight years since the publication of the third edition in 2002. The last eight years have shown a continuation of litigation from both the previous eight years (1994–2002) and the initial publication date (1988).

Following is the history of *Essentials of Sports Law*:

First Edition:	1988
Second Edition:	1994
Third Edition:	2002
Fourth Edition:	2010

There have been several significant sports law developments since the third edition, and these have been included in the fourth edition. Following are some examples:

- In *Stringer v. National Football League*, CV-0065-JDH-MRA (S.D. Ohio July 10, 2009), the court ruled that a helmet maker had a duty to warn football players of the risks of overheating caused by wearing a helmet following the death of Minnesota Vikings defensive lineman Korey Stringer.

- In *Brown ex rel. Brown v. Oklahoma Secondary School Activities Ass'n*, 125 P.3d 1219 (Okla. 2005), a high school football player sought an injunction of his suspension for kicking an opponent. The court issued an injunction and forced the postponement of the state semifinals and championship game. The Supreme Court of Oklahoma vacated the injunction and held that deference should be given to the internal affairs of a voluntary membership association.

- Beginning with the 2006–2007 school year, the state of New Jersey and the New Jersey Interscholastic Athletic Association became the first to institute a statewide performance-enhancing drug-testing policy for all high school athletes.

- In *Equity in Athletics, Inc. v. U.S. Department of Education*, 291 Fed. Appx. 517 (4th Cir. 2008), EIA claimed that JMU was intentionally discriminating against male athletes in violation of the U.S. Constitution and Title IX. The Fourth Circuit denied EIA's request for an injunction. In weighing the balance of hardship, the court noted that none of the student-athletes had lost their eligibility, were free to transfer to other colleges offering their chosen sport, and would not lose their scholarship funding if they stayed at JMU, while JMU would suffer enormous administrative and financial difficulties in reinstating and maintaining the programs.

- In *White v. National Football League*, 533 F. Supp. 2d 929 (D.Minn. 2008), the court ruled that the Atlanta Falcons could not recover $16.22 million of bonus money paid to imprisoned former quarterback Michael Vick. The judge ruled that the roster bonuses were "other salary escalators" and were already earned.

- In *White v. NCAA*, CV06-0999 (C.D. Cal. January 29, 2008), three former student-athletes filed a class action lawsuit alleging that National Collegiate Athletic Association (NCAA) bylaws that capped the amount of financial aid a student-athlete may receive constituted an unlawful agreement in restraint of trade in violation of Section 1 of the Sherman Act. The suit was settled in January 2008 when the NCAA agreed to make an additional $10 million available to qualifying student-athletes to reimburse them for "bona fide educational expenses hereafter incurred, such as tuition, fees, books, supplies and equipment."

- The National Basketball Association (NBA) established new age restrictions, which went into effect beginning with the 2006 draft. Domestic players must be 19 years old to be eligible, and international players must have had at least one NBA season pass since their high school graduation. This has resulted in numerous "one and done" players who play one year of college basketball before declaring for the draft.

- In *C.B.C. Distribution and Marketing, Inc. v. Major League Baseball Advanced Media, L.P.*, 443 F. Supp. 2d 1077 (E.D. Mo. 2006), *aff'd*, 505 F.3d 818 (8th Cir. 2007), the court agreed, ruling that the names and statistics of players lacked the originality required for copyright protection and that the First Amendment rights of C.B.C. took precedence over the players' right to control publicity. As a result of the ruling, ESPN opted out of a seven-year, $140 million licensing deal with MLBAM in January 2008.

As people who follow and/or practice sports law know, there will be enough developments for a fifth edition. These future developments, some already in the early stages of litigation, include the following:

- *American Needle v. NFL Properties*: an antitrust claim questioning the legality of the National Football League's group licensing policy
- *Gilpin v. Stinson*: a civil action in the death of a high school football player
- *Mansaurian v. University of California Davis*: a Title IX claim looking to clarify the participation of multisport student-athletes
- *O'Bannon v. NCAA*: a suit brought by former NCAA athletes looking for compensation for the use of their likenesses
- Labor agreements: each of the U.S. major professional leagues will have its CBA expire in 2011

But for the time being, my focus will be on finishing the fourth edition, not planning the fifth edition. As I have continued to use *Essentials of Sports Law* in my classes at the University of Massachusetts and for other speaking engagements to outside groups, I have developed PowerPoint slides and an instructor's manual. Please do not hesitate to contact me directly if I can help with these instructional materials (gwong@sportmgt.umass.edu). The instructor's manual contains sample questions, exam questions, course syllabi, grade rosters, and other material.

There have been, as in the past, several undergraduate and graduate sports management majors who have made contributions to the fourth edition of *Essentials of Sports Law*: Mark Bergeron, Bill Carmany, Vivian Chan, Chris Deubert, Sam Ehrlich, Corey Farrell, Matt Finlayson, Luke Flockerzi, Steve Gibbs, Mike Goldstein, Melissa Hylton, Ryan Jonas, Keijii Kawaii, Kevin Kristoff, Melissa Maxwell, Barbara Morgan, Joshua Nadreau, David Quinn, Brian Reed, Dominic Rivers, Emmanuel Rohan, Mark Scialabba, Brian Sharkey, Ted Sherburne, Teresa Skelly, and Jeff Wagner.

I would like especially to acknowledge two people who made multiple-year contributions: Christ Deubert and Mark Scialabba.

Finally, I would like to thank my editor, Dan Harmon, for his time, efforts, and persistence in working on the fourth edition. I would also like to thank Anthony Chiffolo, editorial director at Praeger, for his efforts to bring us to the finish line. Thank you to the copyeditors and reviewers.

I would like to reaffirm my appreciation to all those people I thanked in the preface of the first three editions of *Essentials of Sports Law*. There have been a lot of significant changes in each new edition, but the foundation of the book was established in previous editions with the help of many people. There are two constants through the four editions. The first is John Harvey, the original publisher, who has become a good friend and continues to provide his knowledgeable counsel to me. The second is my family: my wife, Paula, and my two sons, Glenn and Garry. Our two boys, born in 1987 and 1990, have grown up during the various editions of the book. Pretty amazing!

Thank you for considering *Essentials of Sports Law*, fourth edition. I have met many people during my travels who have read *Essentials of Sports Law*, and they have always provided me with terrific feedback. I encourage you to contact me by e-mail to let me know your thoughts, comments, and suggestions on *Essentials of Sports Law*. This will help me plan and work on the fifth edition, which I promise will be published in a shorter time frame (less than eight years). The people at Praeger and I both share this commitment.

Best in sports law!

Chapter 1

INTRODUCTION

1.1. The Sports Industry

1.2. Professional Sports Leagues

    1.2.1. A Brief Economic Overview
    1.2.2. Impact of Broadcast Contracts
    1.2.3. Attendance
    1.2.4. Luxury Suites
    1.2.5. Personal Seat Licenses
    1.2.6. Sponsorships, Licensing, and Merchandising
    1.2.7. Commissioners
    1.2.8. Single-Entity Leagues

1.3. Intercollegiate Athletics

    1.3.1. Organizational Structure
    1.3.2. Economic Overview
        1.3.2.1. Revenues
        1.3.2.2. Expenses
    1.3.3. The Institutions
    1.3.4. Institution Case Study: University of Michigan Athletic Department

1.3.5. Knight Foundation Commission on Intercollegiate Athletics

1.4. The Olympics

    1.4.1. Organizational Structure
    1.4.2. International Federations and National Governing Bodies
    1.4.3. Economic Overview of Olympic Bodies
    1.4.4. International Olympic Committee Responses to Prevailing Legal Issues

1.5. Interscholastic Athletics

1.6. Individual Sport Issues

1.7. Facilities, Agency Firms, and Media

INTRODUCTION

Athletic organizations have grown tremendously since the 1970s in terms of their scope, power, and financial status. In the United States alone, athletic organizations envelop the lives and athletic experiences of people from their early school years (e.g., Pop Warner football and Little League baseball), through high school years (e.g., the National Federation of State High School Associations), through college (e.g., the National Collegiate Athletic Association), and beyond (e.g., the U.S. Olympic Committee and professional sports leagues). Sports law has shaped the operations of those organizations and continues to have a pervasive impact on everyone involved, from ticket managers to public relations directors to team doctors to the athletes themselves.

Sports law helps to explain why sport businesses are structured the way they are. Oftentimes, court decisions have had a significant impact on sports leagues, associations, and entities. Thus, the purpose of this chapter is to give the reader an overview of the structure and involvement of these organizations, an understanding of those who are involved in rule making, and examples of the types of litigation involving these athletic organizations. The chapter begins with an introduction to the sports industry. Next, it presents information on the various segments of the sports industry, and finally shows how the rules and regulations of the organizations affect their constituencies.

1.1. THE SPORTS INDUSTRY

This chapter will first explore the segments or organizations of the sports industry. It will discuss various organizations' structure, rules and procedures, internal power and authority, and relationships with other organizations. The sports industry segments have been broken down into six groups. Below is an outline of the six groups, in order of appearance.

1. Professional leagues in the United States

   a. Big Four leagues: the National Basketball Association (NBA), the National Football League (NFL), the National Hockey League (NHL), and Major League Baseball (MLB)

   b. Single-entity leagues, which include Major League Soccer (MLS) and the Women's National Basketball Association (WNBA)

2. Intercollegiate athletics (which will primarily cover the National Collegiate Athletic Association)

3. The Olympics (which will investigate the U.S. Olympic Committee, the International Olympic Committee, the international federations for sports, and the national governing bodies for sports)

4. Interscholastic athletics (such as umbrella organization the National Federation of State High School Associations and state governing bodies such as the Massachusetts Interscholastic Athletic Association); this designation also includes leagues for youths that are not "interscholastic" per se such as Little League, Knothole, and Pop Warner

5. Public/private associations for professional and recreational sports

   a. Professional Golf Association (PGA), Ladies Professional Golf Association (LPGA), and Association of Tennis Professionals (ATP)

b. Country clubs, fitness clubs, recreation centers, and other places of leisure athletic participation

6. Facilities, agency firms, and media

These six groups have become increasingly interconnected as sport has evolved as a business. This is especially true as it relates to the law. Exhibit 1.1 illustrates how common legal concerns unite the six groups by minimal degrees of separation. Consequently, it may be beneficial for participants in one area (e.g., college athletics) to possess a working knowledge of the legal and business aspects of another area (e.g., high school athletics).

NOTES

1. Information on the sports business industry can be found in *Street and Smith's Sports Business Journal* (*SBJ*), a weekly publication dedicated to the business issues of sport. *SBJ* provides the critical news and information that sports industry leaders need to stay competitive and successful. Every issue features in-depth information on the deals, contracts, and power plays that shape the industry. Regular columns cover every aspect of the industry from media and marketing to finance and facilities. Subscription information can be found at http://www.sportsbusinessjournal.com. An additional resource is *Street and Smith's Sports Business Daily*, a daily publication that covers similar topics to their *SBJ*. However, *Sports Business Daily's* articles typically contain less depth and detail due to the fact that the reporting is on a daily basis.

2. For more information on the sports business industry, see Glenn M. Wong, *The Comprehensive Guide to Careers in Sports* (Sudbury, MA: Jones and Bartlett, 2009), and Lisa Pike Masteralexis, Carol Barr, and Mary Hums, *Principles and Practice of Sport Management*, 3rd ed. (Sudbury, MA: Jones and Bartlett, 2009).

1.2. PROFESSIONAL SPORTS LEAGUES

Professional sports leagues make up a large share of the more than $213 billion sports industry in the United States, transforming sports into an increasingly businesslike field since the 1970s. Because of the large amounts of money involved in professional sports leagues, industry professionals must understand a wide range of legal issues, including but not limited to: labor and antitrust, merchandising, television, drug testing, contracts, and employment law.

This section will focus on legal issues indigenous (but not exclusive) to the professional sports segment of the sports industry. It will include a brief economic overview of professional leagues and team operations, move to an overview of league office structure, and finish with a closer look at specific problems facing individuals who practice in the professional sports setting. Since the Big Four are the best-known and lucrative leagues, many other professional and amateur sports entities try to mimic their operations. Likewise, newer leagues, such as the WNBA and MLS, have learned from the legal histories of the Big Four and have structured themselves accordingly. Thus, persons involved in the sports industry may find issues covered in this chapter that pertain to topics outside their field of specialization. Each professional league, team, or association has unique legal issues surrounding its operation. While this chapter cannot possibly cover each specific problem, it will provide a foundation for a better understanding of the professional sports industry.

1.2.1. A Brief Economic Overview

The basic agreements of the Big Four leagues allow for all types of *private* franchise ownership, including sole proprietorships, partnerships, and corporations (see section 15.1, "Business Structures"). Sole proprietorships are decreasing due to the dramatic increase in franchise costs. Therefore, ownership groups must generally choose between the lower tax rates of a partnership and the decreased financial risk of a corporation (see note 1). The NFL prohibits public and corporate ownership of teams, requiring one person to hold at least a 30% ownership share. The one NFL exception is the founding member Green Bay Packers, who own a grandfather-clause exemption. However, public ownership has occurred increasingly in the other leagues such as the Atlanta Braves (MLB) and Toronto Raptors (NHL) (see note 3). Aside from certain regulations to ensure competitive balance (e.g., the draft, salary caps), teams may compete against one another as rival companies, just as they would in any other business.

As stated previously, the finances of professional sports have grown exponentially in recent years. Expenses such as player salaries have increased considerably in all Big Four Leagues. While the million-dollar salary was once the benchmark for the highest-paid athlete, it is common today for the top professional athletes to earn over $10 million annually (see exhibit 1.2). In fact, Alex Rodriguez's contract (2008–2017) with MLB's New York Yankees pays him an astronomical average annual salary of $27.5 million (see exhibit 1.3).

Franchise owners also benefit from the increased demand for professional sports. Teams generate millions of dollars per year from ticket sales, sponsorships agreements, the leasing of luxury suites, merchandise sales, and national and local broadcast agreements. Teams that own their stadium, or teams that have a beneficial lease agreement, also earn revenue from concession sales, parking, signage, and non-franchise-related events held in their arena, such as concerts and skating revues. The high price of player salaries notwithstanding, these potential streams of revenue have resulted in an exponential increase of franchise values and expansion fees for franchise owners.

Despite these gains, a league's governing documents (collective bargaining agreement, league constitution, and bylaws) may not prevent franchises in a larger market from earning a disproportionate amount of revenue compared to franchises in smaller markets. For example, in 2007, the New York Yankees had MLB's highest opening-day payroll of $189.6 million, and while they earned total operating revenue of $327 million, they suffered an operating loss of $47.3 million (see note 1). Meanwhile, the Florida Marlins maintained one of the league's lowest payrolls at $30.5 million but earned a profit of $35.6 million. Newer leagues, such as MLS and the WNBA, have largely shielded themselves from large market–small market competitive imbalances by constructing single-entity models. However, much more disparate revenue earnings occur in the more established leagues, especially MLB. The great disparity in MLB in revenue earning comes primarily from differing local broadcast contracts.

NOTES _____

1. *Forbes* magazine releases annual reports on the projected values, revenues, and expenses for teams in the NFL, NBA, NHL, MLB, NASCAR, and European soccer. The reports are available from the *Forbes* Web site at http://www.forbes.com/business/sports money/.

Exhibit 1.1
Legal Issues Connecting the Sports Industries

Constitutional law cases at the collegiate level, such as due process and discrimination cases, may also apply at the high school level, and vice versa.

Interscholastic & Little League

In his dissent against the decision *PGA Tour v. Casey Martin*, U.S. Supreme Court Justice Antonin Scalia worried that Little League hitters with attention deficit disorder might obtain court orders forcing umpires to grant them four strikes instead of three.

Intercollegiate Athletics

College eligibility, student-athlete compensation, and the regulation of agents all affect the inflow of talent to professional sports. Likewise, collective bargaining and litigation concerning amateur drafts may accelerate the exodus of high school and college players into the pros.

The Olympics

Olympic athletes must undergo drug testing. However, collective bargaining agreements in professional sports leagues often shield players from drug testing.

Associations, Country Clubs, Recreational

With the trend toward vertical integration, it is now possible for a corporation to own a sports team, the team's arena, the agents who represent the players, and the radio stations that broadcast the games. This creates potential antitrust issues and conflicts of interest for sport managers.

Professional Sports Leagues

Facilities, Agency Firms, & Media

Legal decisions and legislation affecting major arenas may pertain to smaller organizations. Even private clubs may be considered public when certain criteria are met.

2. MLB salaries are available from the *USA Today* Salaries Database at http://content.usatoday.com/sports/baseball/salaries/default.aspx.

3. Public ownership of sports teams has some inherent disadvantages for investors. Unlike other public stocks that increase in value when the company either buys other companies or expands, it is difficult for a single sports team to grow or expand. Likewise, when a sports team is part of a larger public company (e.g., the Atlanta Braves are owned by Liberty Media), it is difficult for these teams to contribute to the growth of that stock. Investors will typically exert pressure on the board of directors to dump or streamline their sports holdings. This largely explains the NFL's stance against public ownership. The NFL's constitution and bylaws from 1960 state in Article V, Section 4(a), that "new members must pledge that their organization is primarily for the purpose of operating a football team."

4. For further information on the economics of sports, see Andrew Zimbalist, *The Bottom Line: Observations and Arguments on the Sports Business* (Philadelphia, PA: Temple University Press, 2006), and James Quirk and Rodney Fort, *Pay Dirt: The Business of Professional Team Sports* (Princeton, NJ: Princeton University Press, 1997).

5. The *Journal of Sports Economics* is a leading resource on the sports industry and is available at http://jse.sagepub.com. In particular, see Herbert F. Lewis, Thomas R. Sexton, and Kathleen A. Lock, "Player Salaries, Organizational Efficiency, and Competitiveness in Major League Baseball," 8 *Journal of Sports Economics* 266 (2007), and Rodney Fort and James Quirk, "Owner Objectives and Competitive Balance," 5 *Journal of Sports Economics* 20 (2004).

6. For increased information about public ownership of teams, see Ryan Schaffer, "A Piece of the Rock (or the Rockets): The Viability of Widespread Public Offerings of Professional Sports Franchises," 5 *Virginia Sports and Entertainment Law Journal* 201 (2006), and Genevieve F. E. Birren, "NFL vs. Sherman Act: How the NFL's Ban on Public Ownership Violates Federal Antitrust Laws," 11 *Sports Lawyers Journal* 121 (2004).

1.2.2. Impact of Broadcast Contracts

All the Big Four professional leagues have national television contracts, which are divided equally among member teams. For example, the NFL signed contracts covering 2006 through the 2012 Super Bowl with FOX Sports ($4.275 billion), CBS Sports ($3.735 billion), NBC Sports ($3.9 billion), and ABC/ESPN ($6.6 billion). The contracts make those networks the exclusive broadcasters of regular season and postseason league games. In addition, the NFL has a deal with DirecTV through 2014 providing $1 billion annually in exchange exclusive multichannel television rights. The total annual revenue received ($4.735 billion) is divided equally among league teams (see note 1) over the length of the contract. Individual teams are allowed to negotiate their own local television contracts for pre-season contests (not part of the national package) and local radio broadcasts for all games.

It is the absence of an equitable sharing of these *local* broadcast contracts in MLB that creates a wide gap between the large-market and small-market franchises. For example, the New York Yankees, like all other MLB teams, receive a 1/30th share of MLB's national television contract with FOX Sports and ESPN. However, in 2002 the Yankees launched their own regional sports network (RSN), the Yankees Entertainment and Sports (YES) Network. Showing primarily Yankees games as well as New Jersey Nets games, the YES Network has been of the most successful and profitable RSNs ever: when the investment bank Goldman Sachs considered selling its 40% share in the YES Network in 2007, *Fortune*

Exhibit 1.2
The Big Four Salaries, 1990–2010

		1990	1995	2001	2010
MLB	**Minimum Salary**	$100,000	$109,000	$200,000	$400,000
	Average Salary	$597,537	$1.07 million	$2.26 million	$3.27 million
	Highest Paid Player	Robin Yount	Cecil Fielder	Alex Rodriguez	Alex Rodriguez
	His Salary	$3.2 million	$9.2 million	$22.0 million	$33.0 million

		1990–1991	1994–1995	2001–2002	2009–2010
NBA	**Minimum Salary**	$120,000	$150,000	$316,969	$457,588
	Average Salary	$825,000	$1.47 million	$3.20 million	$5.85 million
	Highest Paid Player	Patrick Ewing	David Robinson	Kevin Garnett	Tracy McGrady
	His Salary	$4.25 million	$7.3 million	$19.6 million	$23.2 million

		1990–1991	1994–1995	2001–2002	2010–2011
NFL	**Minimum Salary**	$50,000	$110,000	$209,000	$325,000
	Average Salary	$350,000	$716,000	$1.17 million	$1.8 million
	Highest Paid Player	Joe Montana	John Elway	Drew Bledsoe	Eli Manning
	His Salary	$3.2 million*	$4.6 million	$8.5 million	$16.25

NFL "Highest Paid" and "Average Salary" includes bonus prorations. *Montana's salary represents the average annual salary from his then four-year contract.

		1990–1991	1994–1995	2001–2002	2009–2010
NHL	**Minimum Salary**	$100,000 Canadian	$125,000 U.S.	$150,000 U.S.	$500,000 U.S.
	Average Salary	$271,000	$733,000	$1.6 million	$2.0 million
	Highest Paid Player	Wayne Gretzky	Wayne Gretzky	Jaromir Jagr	Vincent Lecavalier
	His Salary	$3.0 million	$6.5 million	$11.0 million	$10.0 million

magazine speculated that the YES Network could be worth $3–3.5 billion. This local revenue gulf between large market teams such as the Yankees, Baltimore Orioles, Los Angeles Dodgers, and Chicago Cubs and small-market teams (Pittsburgh Pirates, Minnesota Twins, etc.) leads directly to the ability to spend more money on player salaries. Hence, disparity and competitive imbalance, as argued by some who follow Major League Baseball. The more money a franchise earns, the more it will be able to spend on retaining its talented free agents as well as acquiring free agents from other teams. The wealthier franchises in Major League Baseball earn a disproportionate amount of their revenue from local broadcasting contracts. This topic is discussed further in Chapter 14, "Television and Broadcasting."

Exhibit 1.3
Top Big Four Salaries by Position

League	Player	Position	Team	2010 Salary
MLB	Alex Rodriguez	Third Base	New York Yankees	$33,000,000
MLB	C.C. Sabathia	Starting Pitcher	New York Yankees	$24,285,714
MLB	Joe Mauer	Catcher	Minnesota Twins	$23,000,000
MLB	Derek Jeter	Shortstop	New York Yankees	$22,600,000
MLB	Manny Ramirez	Left Field	Los Angeles Dodgers	$22,500,000
MLB	Mark Teixeira	First Base	New York Yankees	$20,625,000
MLB	Carlos Beltran	Center Field	New York Mets	$19,401,569
MLB	Ichiro Suzuki	Right Field	Seattle Mariners	$18,000,000
MLB	Mariano Rivera	Relief Pitcher	New York Yankees	$15,000,000
MLB	Chase Utley	Second Base	Philadelphia Phillies	$12,142,857

League	Player	Position	Team	2009-2010 Salary
NBA	Tracy McGrady	Small Forward	New York Knicks	$23,238,561
NBA	Kobe Bryant	Shooting Guard	Los Angeles Lakers	$23,034,375
NBA	Jermaine O'Neal	Power Forward	Miami Heat	$22,995,000
NBA	Shaquille O'Neal	Center	Cleveland Cavaliers	$20,000,000
NBA	Gilbert Arenas	Point Guard	Washington Wizards	$16,192,080

League	Player	Position	Team	2009-2010 Salary
NHL	Vincent Lecavalier	Center	Tampa Bay Lightning	$10,000,000
NHL	Alex Ovechkin	Left Wing	Washington Capitals	$9,000,000
NHL	Wade Redden	Defender	New York Rangers	$8,000,000
NHL	Marian Hossa	Right Wing	Chicago Blackhawks	$7,900,000
NHL	Roberto Luongo	Goaltender	Vancouver Canucks	$7,500,000

League	Player	Position	Team	2009-2010 Salary
NFL	Phillip Rivers	Quarterback	San Diego Chargers	$25,556,630
NFL	Kelvin Hayden	Defensive Back	Indianapolis Colts	$17,480,000
NFL	Julius Peppers	Defensive Line	Carolina Panthers	$16,683,000
NFL	Greg Jennings	Wide Receiver	Green Bay Packers	$16,251,300
NFL	Jason Brown	Offensive Line	St. Louis Rams	$15,007,150
NFL	James Harrison	Linebacker	Pittsburgh Steelers	$13,357,280
NFL	Maurice Jones-Drew	Running Back	Jacksonville Jaguars	$13,100,000
NFL	Heath Miller	Tight End	Pittsburgh Steelers	$7,216,240
NFL	Shane Lechler	Kicker/Punter	Oakland Raiders	$6,401,560

NFL numbers include prorated signing bonuses and performance bonuses.

NOTE

1. In some cases, new franchises entering a league, or franchises willing to relocate, will cede their portion of the television revenue for a set period of time. This issue can be a source of contention between owners because there is no set criterion for imposing this forfeiture of broadcasting revenue.

1.2.3. Attendance

Another major stream of revenue is generated through ticket sales. Ticket revenue depends on the amount of available seating, cost per ticket, local population size and demographics, presence of "superstar" or celebrity players, and the team's performance. Franchises in the Big Four leagues are constantly building or lobbying to build new stadiums in hopes of improving the seating inventory they have to sell. New stadiums are being built with additional amenities such as luxury suites, expanded club seating, children's areas, restaurants, and merchandise stores with the hope that the franchise will be able to generate more revenue. Franchises owning their own facility or franchises that receive concession, merchandise, and parking revenue may reduce ticket prices to fill their stadium to capacity in hopes of recuperating lost ticket revenue through concession sales, merchandise sales, and parking. Yet as players' salaries continue to increase, franchises adjust ticket, concession, parking, and merchandise prices upward. For example, prior to the 2001 season, the Boston Red Sox raised ticket prices 27.4% to an average of $36.08. The ticket price increase equated to approximately $20 million in additional ticket revenue each year, assuming that attendance averages near capacity. Coincidentally (or not) $20 million is equivalent to the average annual salary of Manny Ramirez, who was the Red Sox's high-profile free agent signee during the 2000–2001 off season.

The distribution of ticket revenue between franchises differs between leagues. In the NFL, 60% of non-luxury-box gate receipts are retained by the home team, and the remainder is channeled into a general fund. In the NHL, NBA, and MLB, gate receipts are not divided among the competing franchises. Teams with more seating than the market demands have shifted more focus to marketing efforts to fill empty seats. But teams that consistently sell out their stadium must seek alternative revenue streams to keep up with the continuously rising cost of franchise operation.

NOTES

1. For detailed information about the price of tickets, concessions, parking, and other related game-day fan expenses, see Team Marketing Report's Fan Cost Index survey, which can be sampled and ordered at http://www.teammarketing.com. The Fan Cost Index is intended to show the average cost for a family of four to attend a game, including four tickets, four soft drinks, two beers, four hot dogs, two programs, parking, and two caps.

2. For reasons likely related to the increase in the price of MLB tickets, attendance has increased at Minor League baseball games. According to a *Business Week* article titled "For the Love of the Game—and the Cheap Seats" (May 28, 2001, p. 46), Minor League baseball regular season attendance increased from approximately 20 million in 1986 to nearly 40 million in 2000. Minor league baseball has broken its own attendance record each year since 2004, and in 2007 the league drew more than 42.6 million fans; see Associated Press, *Minor league baseball sets attendance record for fourth straight year*, http://www.usatoday.com/sports/baseball/2007–09–05–644109086_x.htm (last updated September 5, 2007).

1.2.4. Luxury Suites

One attempt to find alternative revenue streams is the leasing of luxury suites. Luxury suites are often sold by franchises to corporate clients, who lease the suites for the course of the season. Franchises that have this type of seating in their inventory realize far greater revenues from luxury suites than they earn from regular seating sales. Franchises that do not control the sale of suites, or that play in stadiums without luxury suites, are at a marked disadvantage in generating revenue. Luxury suites are viewed by some leagues and teams as a more important revenue stream than that of regular seating.

1.2.5. Personal Seat Licenses

As of 2010, 25 professional franchises, and a number of Division I-A college programs, have resorted to charging a fee for a spectator to have the right to purchase tickets to the home contests over the course of a season. These personal seat licenses (PSLs) are sold to fans who pay a predetermined amount to reserve the preferred seat location before they actually buy tickets to the event. The individual is then considered the owner of the seat and usually (see note 1) is able to resell that particular seat. This concept is similar to owning a condominium. A person can purchase a condominium and, when he or she decides to move, has the right to sell the unit to the highest bidder. The individual taking out a PSL then must buy season tickets for the team's home games. Failure to do so results in a forfeiture of the seats and the money paid to reserve the seats. PSLs are another attempt by franchises to inject revenue into their operation from an otherwise stagnant or sold-out marketplace. Personal seat licenses can range from around $1,000 per seat for seats farther from the field to several thousand dollars for the best seats in the facility. In 1993, the Carolina Panthers NFL expansion franchise began selling PSLs to help fund the building of Ericsson Stadium. By the time the stadium opened in 1996, the Panthers had sold 61,000 PSLs, which cost between $750 and $5,400. These sales helped raise more than $150 million for the franchise, which helped finance the stadium, player contracts, and other general improvements. The case of the Panthers is an excellent example of how PSL revenue can help a new franchise. In 2008, PSLs were sold by 11 NFL teams, 3 MLB teams, 2 NHL teams, and 1 NBA team.

NOTES ———————————————————————————————

1. Personal seat licenses also affect Division I-A college sports. Demand for PSLs is so high at certain institutions that they no longer allow patrons to resell their seats. For example, at Ohio State University's Jerome Schottenstein Center and Value City Arena, the home of the men's and women's basketball teams as well as men's ice hockey, patrons must purchase PSLs for a 40-year term. During that term, they may not resell their seats to other patrons, but may sell their seats back to the university, which in turn sells the PSL to someone on a waiting list. Ohio State raised over $15 million, almost 10% of the total cost of construction, from the sale of PSLs, which cost fans anywhere from $1,000 to $15,000. Given the high demand at certain professional sporting events, it is likely that pro teams will adopt this policy in the future in order to finance new stadiums.

2. For more information on stadiums, see Danette R. Davis, "The Myth and Mystery of Personal Seat Licenses and Season Tickets: Licenses or More?" 51 *Saint Louis University Law Journal* 241 (2006), and Martin J. Greenberg, "Sports Facility Financing and Development Trends in the United States," 15 *Marquette Sports Law Review* 93 (2004).

1.2.6. Sponsorships, Licensing, and Merchandising

After the escalating value of television contracts and luxury suite revenues, licensing and merchandising have been the areas in professional sports that have seen the most revenue growth. Professional sport franchises receive revenue from team and league wide sponsorship agreements. These agreements allow an organization to license the team and/or league logo for commercial use in marketing efforts. Legal issues often revolve around or include a facet of these economic influences. For example, some owners have entered into agreements on an individual franchise level that are incongruous with league wide deals negotiated by the properties arms. Such was the case in *NFL Properties Inc. v. Dallas Cowboys Football Club, Ltd.* (see note 1).

Licensed products such as hats, jerseys, shorts, and T-shirts are prevalent throughout the world, but licensed apparel is not the only category from which the Big Four have reaped profits. They have put their league and team logos on items such as trading cards, publications, backpacks, pencils, sporting goods, and even food! Manufacturers of these items believe that their company and products will benefit from the association with a particular sport and its league through increased awareness and brand equity, and thereby contribute to their bottom line. The companies pay an up-front fee plus a percentage of each unit sale to be an official licensee of a particular league. Another way that Big Four properties departments generate income is by the licensing of teams and/or franchises for use in the marketing of logoed merchandise, or in advertising, or promotional programs on the part of the licensee. For example, Sprite is the official drink of the NBA, and Wilson makes the official ball for the NFL. The revenue from these agreements is distributed among the league and its member franchises.

Corporations will enter into licensing agreements with sport entities for the right to associate with a particular event, better known as sport sponsorships. Corporate sponsors pay a fee to the controlling entity in exchange for having their company or product name prominently associated with an event. A distinct example of this practice can be seen in the names of the Bowl Championship Series. The Allstate Sugar Bowl, the Fed Ex Orange Bowl, and the Tostitos Fiesta Bowl are three such examples of a corporation's becoming the title sponsor for a sporting event. The Big Four professional leagues have thus far restricted the sponsoring of major events like the Super Bowl and World Series to protect the integrity of the event. However, top-flight sponsors of these events are given prominent presenting sponsorships. The Big Four leagues will allow title sponsors for lesser events like Major League Baseball's State Farm Home Run Derby.

A final prominent form of sponsorship that has developed and grown in recent years is the practice of selling naming rights to a team facility or arena. Sponsors pay large sums of money to have their name on the stadium or arena of a franchise for the duration of the sponsorship agreement. As a result, we have witnessed the Hoosier Dome in Indianapolis change its name to the RCADome; Comiskey Park in Chicago to U.S. Cellular Field; the SkyDome in Toronto to the Rogers Centre; and Jacobs Field in Cleveland to Progressive Field. Many franchises have taken naming rights one step further. Before ground is even broken, many franchises enter into agreement with a sponsor to name the facility. The benefit of this practice is that it gains capital which can help finance construction of the facility. The benefit to the sponsor is that it may capitalize on the publicity associated with construction of the facility before the team even plays a game (see exhibit 1.4).

Lawsuits stemming from the area of licensed merchandising often involve the reproduction of league or team logos by manufacturers without proper consent

Exhibit 1.4
Top Stadium Naming Rights Deals

League	Venue	Major Tenant(s)	City	Years	Price
MLB	Citi Field	Mets	New York	2009–2029	$400 million
	Minute Maid Park	Astros	Houston	2003–2030	$168 million
	Citizens Bank Park	Phillies	Philadelphia	2004–2029	$95 million
Primarily NBA	Barclays Center	Nets	Brooklyn	2010–2030	$400 million
	FedEX Forum	Grizzlies	Memphis	2004–2024	$90 million
	AT&T Center	Spurs	San Antonio	2002–2022	$42 million
NFL	Reliant Stadium	Texans	Houston	2002–2032	$300 million
	FedEx Field	Redskins	Washington, D.C.	1999–2026	$207 million
	University of Phoenix Stadium	Cardinals	Phoenix	2006–2026	$154 million
Primarily NHL	Nationwide Arena	Blue Jackets	Columbus	Unknown	$135 million
	Prudential Center	Devils	Newark	2007–2027	$105.3 million
	RBC Center	Hurricanes	Raleigh	2002–2022	$80 million
Combined Use	American Airlines Center	Mavericks (NBA), Stars (NHL)	Dallas	2001–2031	$195 million
	Philips Arena	Thrashers (NHL), Hawks (NBA)	Atlanta	1999–2019	$181.9 million
	Staples Center	Lakers (NBA), Clippers (NBA), Kings (NHL)	Los Angeles	1999–2019	$100 million
NCAA	Papa John's Cardinal Stadium	Louisville Football	Louisville	1998–2040	$210 million
	Engelstadt Arena	North Dakota Men's and Women's Hockey	Grand Forks	In perpetuity	$104 million one time donation
	TCF Bank Stadium	Minnesota Football	Minneapolis	2009–2034	$35 million
	Kohl Center	Wisconsin Basketball and Hockey	Madison	In perpetuity	$25 million

from the governing organization. This unlicensed or "pirated" merchandise is a billion-dollar industry throughout the world. To combat the production of these types of goods, leagues warn customers to look for the official logo that indicates that the product is an endorsed product of the league. While the Big Four attempt to curtail the flow of this pirated merchandise, they are somewhat limited in their effectiveness by the wide scope of such illegal activity. The benefit to the merchandise pirates is that they can confuse the consumers into thinking that their product is endorsed or associated with a particular player, team, or league. This "likelihood of confusion" argument is often at the core of the trademark violation lawsuits. For a more complete description of trademark violation issues and cases, see section 13.1, "Trademark Law."

The area of licensing also extends to individual professional athletes. For example, NBA players, in addition to being obligated per the collective bargaining agreement to make appearances on behalf of the teams they play for, are also obligated to make appearances for the league's properties division. These appearances require the player to wear the official NBA-licensed apparel of the team they represent. The NBA Uniform Player Contract states that a player has fulfilled this duty if "during each year of the period covered by such Contract, the Player makes five individual personal appearances and five group appearances for or on behalf of or at the request of the Team by which he is employed and/or the NBA" (see exhibit 12.2 and section 12.8, "Endorsement Contracts and Financial Planning").

Players can use their own likeness for promotions and receive all the funds they are paid. In this case, the player may not appear wearing any items that would associate him with his team or the league. A player who is well known (such as LeBron James) is not hampered by this limitation, but a lesser known player may not be recognized without his or her uniform on.

NOTES

1. Various theories were asserted by the NFL in the *Dallas Cowboys* case, including violation of joint contract, violation of Lanham Act, breach of good faith, tortious interference, misappropriation of funds (nine counts in all). See Chapter 9, "Contract Law."

2. For a case involving individual team broadcasting agreements incongruous with league limitations, see *Chicago Professional Sports Limited Partnership v. NBA*, 95 F.3d 593 (7th Cir. 1996). See also Chapter 14, "Broadcasting and Multimedia."

3. For more information on professional sports sponsorships and merchandising, see Richard L. Irwin, William A. Sutton, and Larry M. McCarthy, *Sport Promotion and Sales Management*, 2nd ed. (Champaign, IL: Human Kinetics, 2008), and Stephen Hardy, Bernard J. Mullin, and William A. Sutton, *Sport Marketing*, 3rd ed. (Champaign, IL: Human Kinetics, 2007).

1.2.7. Commissioners

Perhaps the most visible individual in these leagues is the commissioner. In many ways, the commissioner is an *employee* of the owners. For example, the owners hire the commissioner, and possess mechanisms to terminate him when his decisions are adverse to their interests (see note 1). In other ways, the commissioner is a *boss* of the owners. He may stringently discipline owners and other team employees if their behavior is detrimental to the integrity of the sport. For example, after it was discovered that the New England Patriots had been videotaping opponent's defensive signals against league rules in September 2007, NFL Commissioner Roger Goodell fined the organization $250,000, fined head coach Bill Bellicheck $500,000, and revoked the Patriots first-round draft pick in the 2008 NFL draft. Also, NBA Commissioner David Stern has fined Dallas Mavericks owner Mark Cuban over $1.5 million for derogatory gestures, berating officials, and courtside misbehavior, including a $500,000 fine for his continuous derogatory public comments regarding NBA officials in January 2002. In MLB, New York Yankees owner George Steinbrenner endured two unrelated yearlong suspensions for illegal political contributions in the 1970s and involvement with gambler Howard Spira in the 1980s. In 2010, the commissioners for the Big Four were Bud Selig (MLB), David Stern (NBA), Roger Goodell (NFL), and Gary Bettman (NHL).

However, commissioners may not arbitrarily utilize this power of discipline over the owners. Owing to the diversity of owners' interests, an effective commissioner must politic in order to have a successful and lengthy tenure in office. Owners' interests are often split along big-market and small-market lines, especially in relation to issues of revenue sharing. Sometimes owners differ over whether to take a hard line in collective bargaining negotiations. Depending on the team's financial position, an owner may or may not be prepared for a long work stoppage (i.e., strike or lockout). A commissioner must weigh all such interests while simultaneously representing his sport as a chief ambassador and guarding the sport's long-term interests.

The commissioner's office also deals with issues involving players. The commissioner or his representatives may discipline or expel players. However, the commissioner's power (and the owners' power, for that matter) over the players is regulated by a sport's three main governing documents: the league's basic agreement, the uniform player contract, and the collective bargaining agreement (CBA). When there is a conflict between the documents, arbitrators and judges normally yield to the CBA because the CBA is negotiated by both employees (via the union) and management. The players in each of the four major professional leagues have a union, otherwise known as a player's association. In 2010, the heads of each players association were Michael Weiner (MLBPA), Billy Hunter (NBPA), and DeMaurice Smith (NFLPA) while the NHLPA was still looking to fill the vacancy created when Paul Kelly was fired in August 2009. (For more on the role of unions in professional sports, see Chapter 11, "Labor Law.") As a hypothetical example, a commissioner might suspend a player for life for beating up a referee during a game, citing a code of conduct in the Basic Agreement and Uniform Player Contract. However, the player might bring legal action against the commissioner, citing a clause in the CBA that all discipline cases must go to arbitration. In such a case, the courts are likely to favor the player because the CBA trumps the other governing documents.

Clearly, then, the existence and content of the CBA (whether it is pro-management or pro-player) is pivotal in determining a commissioner's, owner's, or player's likelihood of success in a legal dispute. For more details on this issue, see section 11.3, "Collective Bargaining in Professional Sports." A CBA (even after expiration) also can shield a league from most antitrust litigation brought by individual players or the union. For more details on this issue, see section 10.3.5, "Exemption after Decertification: *McNeil*."

NOTES

1. MLB owners forced commissioner Fay Vincent from office after Vincent made certain decisions that were contrary to many owners' interests. For a detailed account of this and other MLB commissioners' tenures, see John Helyar, *Lords of the Realm* (New York: Ballantine Books, 1994).

2. For real-life examples of legal challenges leading to the clarification or reduction of the commissioner's powers, see *Atlanta National League Baseball Club Inc. v. Kuhn*, 432 F.Supp. 1213 (N.D. Ga 1977), and *Chicago National League Ball Club Inc. v. Vincent*, No. 92C 4398, 1992 U.S. Dist. LEXIS 11033 (N.D. Ill. July 23, 1992).

3. For more on the authority of commissioners in professional sports, see Robert I. Lockwood, "The Best Interests of the League: Referee Betting Scandal Brings Commissioner Authority and Collective Bargaining Back to the Frontcourt in the NBA," 15 *Sports Lawyers Journal* 137 (2008), and David C. Weiss, "How Terrell Owens, Collective Bargaining, and Forfeiture Restrictions Created a Moral Hazard That Caused the NFL Crime Wave and What It Meant for Michael Vick," 15 *Sports Lawyers Journal* 279 (2008).

1.2.8. Single-Entity Leagues

While the Big Four leagues have shown an ability to generate significant revenues, they have also generated their share of problems. One of these problems has been competitive imbalance between large- and small-market teams (see section 1.2.1, "A Brief Economic Overview"). A second problem has been spiraling operating costs brought about by competitive bidding for players. Were it legal, owners of the Big Four teams would gladly work cooperatively in order to keep player salaries, and thus expenses, artificially low. However, Section 1 of the Sherman Antitrust Act forbids such conspiracy as do collective bargaining agreements such as Major League Baseball's, which prevents collusion. Nevertheless, the systems established in the collective bargaining agreements do prevent a true free-market for player services when compared to a typical American labor market but because the systems are agreed to by the players' union they are exempt from antitrust scrutiny (see section 10.3.2, "The Nonstatutory Labor Exemption").

Beginning as a single-entity league is an apparently legal way for new leagues to avoid some of the problems faced by the established Big Four leagues. Logically, one cannot conspire with oneself. Therefore, players who sue their single-entity league on the basis of conspiracy are unlikely to succeed.

The two preeminent single-entity leagues in the United States are Major League Soccer (MLS) and the Women's National Basketball Association (WNBA). MLS was established in 1996 as a limited liability corporation organized under Delaware law. Instead of team owners, the league has operator-investors. Some of these operator-investors may run more than one of the league's 14 teams. For example, Anschutz Entertainment Group owned six teams for a period around 2005. Players are hired by MLS, sign a contract with the league, and then are assigned to the various teams rather than being direct employees of a team. Furthermore, MLS distributes profits and losses to the operator-investors in a way similar to distribution of dividends to shareholders of a corporation. Players have challenged this structure as a "sham" to subvert Section 1 of the Sherman Act. However, the courts have so far held that the MLS structure is legally viable in *Fraser v. Major League Soccer* (see note 1). Therefore, while owners and commissioners of leagues like the NBA and NFL must bargain for salary restraints like a "cap," single-entity leagues like MLS can impose such restraints unilaterally.

The WNBA's structure is similar to that of MLS, the main difference being that the operator-investors are owners of *NBA* franchises or agents of the NBA itself. In fact, the WNBA offices are housed within the NBA building in New York City. Instead of a commissioner, the league has a president, much as one would see in a standard corporation. Furthermore, the marketing goals of the NBA and WNBA are closely aligned. The leagues attempt to attract common sponsors and have showcased events featuring both NBA and WNBA players. All but 2 of the 14 WNBA teams share arenas with their NBA counterparts. The Connecticut Sun are the only team to not play in a city with an NBA team.

Finally, the short-lived XFL structured itself similarly to the WNBA, an eight-team single-entity league owned by World Wrestling Entertainment, Inc. (WWE). The league folded in April 2001 due to disappointing television ratings and pressure from investors (WWE is a public company). Nevertheless, the XFL's decision for a single-entity structure, such as the MLS and WNBA, suggests that American start-up leagues will continue to adopt single-entity structures unless the courts prevent them from doing so.

NOTES

1. The legal test of the viability of single-entity leagues is *Fraser v. Major League Soccer*, 284 F.3d 47 (1st Cir. 2002). In addition to the Section 1 conspiracy complaints, the plaintiffs alleged Section 2 monopolization. Section 2 antitrust complaints do not require existence of conspiracy (see section 10.1, "Overview of Antitrust Law").

2. For more on the single-entity structure in professional sports, see Marc Edelman, "Why the 'Single Entity' Defense Can Never Apply to NFL Clubs: A Primer on Property-Rights Theory in Professional Sports," 18 *Fordham Intellectual Property, Media and Entertainment Law Journal* 891 (2008); Nathaniel Grow, "There's No 'I' in "League": Professional Sports Leagues and the Single Entity Defense," 105 *Michigan Law Review* 183 (2006); and Lacie L. Kaiser, "The Flight from Single-Entity Structured Sport Leagues," 2 *DePaul Journal of Sports Law & Contemporary Problems* 1 (2004).

3. Major League Lacrosse (MLL) and arenafootball2 (af2) are additional examples of single-entity leagues. MLL began play in 2001 with a six-team, 14-game regular season schedule and procured television coverage on regional networks such as FOX Sports New England and MSG. Additional information is available at http://www.majorleaguelacrosse.com. The af2 began play in 1999 to serve as a minor league feeder system for the Arena Football League. In 2010, the league consisted of 27 teams. More information is available at http://www.af2.com.

1.3. INTERCOLLEGIATE ATHLETICS

The governance of intercollegiate athletics consists primarily of five national organizations: (1) the National Collegiate Athletic Association (NCAA); (2) the National Association of Intercollegiate Athletics (NAIA), which governs four-year institutions; (3) the National Small College Athletic Association (NSCAA), which governs four-year colleges with enrollment of fewer than 500 male and/or female undergraduates; (4) the National Christian College Athletic Association (NCCAA), which comprises more than 100 members and is open only to four-year Christian institutions that are willing to subscribe to a "Statement of Faith"; and (5) the National Junior College Athletic Association (NJCAA), which encompasses men's and women's junior college athletic programs. The NCAA is the largest organization and it is the primary governing body for about 1,200 institutions of higher education in the United States. It serves a diverse constituency encompassing all sizes of athletic programs. Because of this diverse membership base, the NCAA faces unique challenges in the administration of collegiate athletics. This section will focus primarily on the NCAA.

This section will examine three areas of the NCAA that persons involved in the sports industry need to be familiar with in order to better understand legal issues involving the NCAA and its member institutions. This section will begin by discussing the organizational structure of the NCAA and how legislation is enacted. Next, a brief economic analysis of the NCAA, including revenues and expenses, will be covered. Finally, we will examine one member institution's finances. This section will focus primarily on the Football Bowl Subdivision (formerly Division I-A) athletics with brief mentions of Football Championship Subdivision (formerly Division I-AA), Division II, and Division III. A more detailed description of the four intercollegiate associations other than the NCAA can be found in section 5.1.4, "Other Athletic Associations."

1.3.1. Organizational Structure

The NCAA is a not-for-profit educational entity that was founded in 1906 to provide institutions of higher education an opportunity to administer athletic issues on the national level. Each member institution joins the NCAA voluntarily and theoretically can withdraw at any time (see note 1). Since 1906, its membership has grown from 62 institutions to comprise colleges and universities, conferences, organizations, and individuals totaling over 1,200 members.

The NCAA is headquartered in Indianapolis, Indiana, and comprises nine main departments staffed by full-time employees. These departments are the following:

Executive

Championships

Governance, Membership Services, Research and Education Services

Branding and Communications

Administrative Services

Enforcement

Office for Diversity and Inclusion

Eligibility Center, LLC

NIT, LLC

These central office employees carry out the day-to-day duties necessary to execute strategies and programs decided upon by the governance structure of the NCAA.

On August 1, 1997, the NCAA altered its governing structure to allow for more self-determination by individual divisions on specific division-level matters. Issues facing Division I member institutions are not necessarily the same issues facing Division II and Division III institutions. The new structure implemented by the NCAA gives divisional presidents and athletic administrators the ability to make decisions on certain issues separate from other divisions. In the past, Division II and III administrators had the ability to veto decisions that affected the NCAA membership as a whole. However, the balance of power has now shifted to the major Division I conferences, and with the new governance structure, Division II and III schools no longer have this impact. As exhibit 1.5 illustrates, the new governance structure is headed by the Executive Committee. This committee is the leading decision-making entity of the NCAA and comprises eight members from the Division I Board of Directors, two Division I-AA and I-AAA members each from the Division I Board of Directors, and two members from both the Division II and Division III Presidents Council. These members are the chief executive officers of member institutions (usually college or university presidents). In addition, the executive director of the NCAA and the chairs of the Division I, II, and III Management Councils serve on this committee in a nonvoting capacity. The Executive Committee rules on and enacts legislation that is brought to it by the lower councils and committees from the respective divisions.

The next tier of the governance structure is the Division I Board of Directors, the Division II Presidents Council, and the Division III Presidents Council. These

Exhibit 1.5
National Collegiate Athletic Association (NCAA) Governance Structure

bodies are also manned by CEOs of member institutions who review proposed legislation from the respective division's Management Council and related sub-committees. Division specific legislation can be approved and enacted at this level.

The next level of this structure is the Division I, II, and III Management Councils, made up of athletic administrators and faculty athletics representatives from the respective division's member institutions. In the Management Councils, athletic issues relating to the particular division are researched and discussed, and potential legislation is forwarded to the next higher level in the governance structure for approval. Often subcommittees are formed and assigned particular issues to research in order for them to return to the Management Council with a recommendation for action. It is important to understand that all legislation enacted by the NCAA governance structure is designed and approved by administrators from member institutions. Particularly sensitive issues, such as Proposition 48 and the revocation of freshman eligibility rules, are often discussed at the annual NCAA convention in an attempt to gauge membership support for the legislation. Ideally, all legislation passed by the NCAA is in the best interest of the student-athletes and member institutions; however, due to the large constituency of the NCAA, an ever-increasing amount of litigation faces the association (see Chapters 5 and 6).

NOTES

1. More information on NCAA rules, regulations, and bylaws can be found in the NCAA Manual, available at http://www.ncaa.org under "Legislation and Governance."

2. The NCAA publishes reports on a wide range of topics, including gender equity, finances, playing rules, gambling, drug testing, and more, available at http://www.ncaapublications.com.

3. In *Bloom v. NCAA*, 93 P.3d 621 (Colo.App. 2004), the court upheld the NCAA's decision to bar University of Colorado football player Jeremy Bloom from intercollegiate competition after having received paid endorsements related to his skiing career. Citing the NCAA's role as the guardian of amateur sport, the court found the NCAA's rules and decision to be reasonable and fair.

4. In *Law v. NCAA*, 134 F.3d 1010 (10th Cir. 1998), "entry-level" assistant basketball coaches challenged an NCAA rule that restricted their salaries to $16,000 annually. The court found that the compensation limit was an unlawful restraint of trade.

5. In *Tarkanian v. NCAA*, 511 U.S. 1033 (1994), the plaintiff alleged that the NCAA was not a voluntary association and that its member institutions had no viable alternatives in intercollegiate athletics. The court eventually ruled for the NCAA, holding that the association was not a state actor but a private organization.

6. For more on the varying issues that confront the NCAA, see Bradley S. Pensyl, "Whistling a Foul on the NCAA: How NCAA Recruiting Bylaws Violate the Sherman Antitrust Act," 58 *Syracuse Law Review* 397 (2008), and James Potter, "The NCAA as State Actor: Tarkanian, Brentwood, and Due Process," 155 *University of Pennsylvania Law Review* 1269 (2007).

1.3.2. Economic Overview

Despite its not-for-profit designation, the NCAA does generate substantial revenues and incur considerable expenses throughout the course of its operations. Most of the NCAA's operating revenue is generated from a few revenue-producing sports. The Division I men's basketball championship, in particular, is essential to the financing of NCAA operations, and is ultimately responsible for the NCAA's financing of the majority of intercollegiate championships. Concerns about the lucrative nature of certain aspects of intercollegiate athletics, led the Committee on Ways and Means of the U.S. House of Representatives to formally request answers to a variety of questions related to the NCAA's status as a tax-exempt organization from NCAA President Myles Brand. In particular the committee was concerned with the amateur status of student-athletes and the large sponsorship and rights agreements for NCAA events, in particular the men's basketball postseason tournament. Brand held off further inquiry by pointing out that in the 2004–2005 academic year, only 23 of over 1,000 Division I institutions athletic departments operated at a profit. This section will briefly examine such sources of revenues and expenses within the NCAA.

NOTES

1. Information on the finances of the NCAA can be found at http://www.ncaa.org under "About the NCAA."

2. For a review of some of the issues involving the economics of the NCAA, see John D. Colombo, "The NCAA, Tax Exemption, and College Athletics," 2010 *University of Illinois Law Review* 109 (2010), and Christian Dennie, "White Out Full Grant-in-Aid: An Antitrust Action the NCAA Cannot Afford to Lose," 7 *Virginia Sports and Entertainment Law Journal* 97 (2007).

3. For a more detailed understanding of the accounting of NCAA athletic programs, see Mitchell H. Raiborn, *Revenues and Expenses of Intercollegiate Athletics Programs* (Overland Park, KS: National Collegiate Athletic Association, 1994).

1.3.2.1. Revenues

The major source of revenue for the NCAA is the money it receives from its television contracts. For example, in fiscal year 2006–2007, television and marketing revenue accounted for approximately 81.9% of the NCAA's total revenue. Exhibit 1.6 lists six-year revenues for the NCAA and the corresponding year's revenues earned from the television contract.

It is easy to see how dependent the NCAA is on its television contract for revenues, much the way the Big Four professional sports leagues are dependent upon their broadcasting contracts. As long as networks are willing to pay large rights fees for premier events, the NCAA will be able to continue growing this particular revenue stream.

The premier revenue-generating event for the NCAA is the NCAA Division I men's basketball championship, which in 2001 brought in an estimated $276.1 million from television and ticket sales alone—nearly 85% of the association's total revenue. In 2010 the NCAA and CBS reached a 14-year deal for $10.8 billion, providing the NCAA with an average of over $740 million per year through 2024.

Recognizing its dependence on one main revenue stream, the NCAA had undertaken efforts to generate new sources of revenue. The association entered into an agreement with a private company that gave radio broadcast rights, television show, and publication rights to the company in exchange for a royalty fee. In 1998, the NCAA received $11.5 million from this agreement and expects that figure to grow annually. This corporate partnership program allows the sponsoring partner to develop promotions to help its business in conjunction with NCAA-sponsored events.

Exhibit 1.6
NCAA Total Revenues and Television Revenues, 2001–2007

Year	Total Revenue	Television Revenue
2004–2005	$507,740,614	$436,609,819
2005–2006	$558,162,620	$470,766,380
2006–2007	$621,791,807	$509,376,034
2007–2008	$633,453,000	$529,000,000
2008–2009	$701,900,000	$69,700,000
2009–2010	$710,000,000	$638,980,000

Another source of revenue for the NCAA is the championship events themselves. Gross receipts from championship events such as the College World Series (baseball) and the women's Division I basketball championship accounted for an estimated $80.8 million of the NCAA's total revenue in 2007–2008.

Although football is one of the largest revenue generators for its member schools, the NCAA does not benefit financially from the enormous popularity of college football. There is no postseason NCAA tournament for football; instead qualified teams play in individually sponsored bowl games, with the top 10 teams playing in five bowls run by the Bowl Coalition Series (BCS). The BCS is not affiliated with the NCAA but essentially equates to determining a national champion and is run by the major Division I Football Bowl Subdivision (formerly Division I-A) football conferences. The champions of the Atlantic Coast, Big East, Southeastern, Pac-10, Big Ten, and Big 12 Conferences are given automatic berths in one of the four bowls, while the other slots are filled by the two teams with the highest ranking according to the "BCS Formula." In addition, independent Notre Dame receives an automatic berth if it finishes in the top eight of the BCS rankings. The BCS computer formula takes into account the polls of the writers and coaches, computer rankings, strength of schedule rankings, and team record. Beginning with the 2006–2007 season, in addition to the four traditional and prestigious bowls, a National Championship game was added intended to determine the National Champion.

1.3.2.2. Expenses

The expenses of the NCAA are concentrated in two major areas, one being the expenses the organization needs in order to operate, pay its staff, and manage championships. However, because of the NCAA's nonprofit status, the majority of the remaining money is distributed to member institutions. Since Division I institutions provide the majority of the contests from which the NCAA generates revenue, they receive the majority of the revenue distributed. For instance, the total dollars of revenue distributed to Division I institutions in 2008–2009 was $388,901,094. Division II institutions received $28,246,989 in revenue distribution, and Division III institutions received $19,047,135. The bulk of the money distributed to Division I institutions is based on team and/ or conference participation in the men's Division I basketball championship. The distribution of the revenue to Division I conferences is based upon their performance in the tournament over a six-year period. For example, the money distributed in 2009–2010 is based upon a conference's performance over the period 2004–2009. The total dollars distributed by the NCAA in 2008–2009 for this fund was approximately $167.09 million. It also distributes funds to Division I institutions for academic enhancement, special assistance for student-athletes, conference grants, and a broad-based distribution based on the number of varsity sports a Division I institution sponsors and the number of athletic scholarships the institution offers.

The NCAA also must pay the lease for its offices and the salaries of its employees from the revenue it generates. In addition, it incurs the normal expenses for its full-time employees such as a pension plan and other benefits.

Another significant expense for the NCAA is litigation. For example, in 2004, the organizers of the postseason NIT tournament brought suit against the NCAA, alleging that the NCAA rule requiring member institutions to accept invitations to only the NCAA tournament and not any other postseason tournament was an antitrust violation; see *Metropolitan Intercollegiate Basketball Association (MIBA) v. NCAA*, 339 F.Supp.2d 545 (S.D.N.Y. 2004). Just as the case was coming to trial, the parties reached a settlement whereby the NCAA purchased the NIT for a period of 10 years for a total of $56.5 million. This, and other cases, could be a large expense to the NCAA and upset the distribution of its revenues to member institutions. NCAA antitrust issues are further investigated in Chapter 10.

NOTE

1. For more information on the business of the NCAA, see the following resources:
    a. http://www.ncaa.org > About the NCAA > Budget and Finances
    b. Gabriel A. Morgan, "No More Playing Favorites: Reconsidering the Conclusive Congressional Presumption That Intercollegiate Athletics Are Substantially Related to Educational Purposes," 81 *Southern California Law Review* 149 (2007).
    c. Lindsay J. Rosenthal, "From Regulating Organization to Multi-Billion Dollar Business: The NCAA Is Commercializing the Amateur Competition It Has Taken Almost a Century to Create," 13 *Seton Hall Journal of Sports and Entertainment Law* 321 (2003).

1.3.3. The Institutions

As mentioned earlier, the NCAA serves member institutions belonging to Divisions I, II, and III. Shortly we will examine the athletic operation of a single Division I institution. But first, we will examine the differences among the three divisions.

Division I member institutions are required by NCAA guidelines to sponsor at least seven varsity sports for men and women (or six for men and eight for women), with two sports being sponsored for both men and women (i.e., basketball and track and field). Every playing season must have a sport sponsored for each gender. Each Division I school has contest minimums and participant minimums that must be met in each sport. In addition, each member institution must be within the guidelines for granting athletic scholarships. The biggest difference in Division I is that Division I Football Bowl Subdivision football institutions must meet minimum attendance requirements, while Division I Football Championship Subdivision (formerly Division I-AA) institutions need not (see note 1).

Division II institutions also have sport sponsorship requirements to meet. For an institution to be classified as Division II, it must sponsor at least five sports for men and women (or four for men and six for women), with two of those sports being the same for men and women, and each sex being represented for each season. Division III institutions also must meet contest and participant requirements, as well as stay within approved guidelines for offering financial aid.

Division III institutions also must sponsor five sports for men and women with at least three sports per gender and each gender must be represented in every season. Minimum contest and participant requirements also apply to Division III institutions. The biggest difference between the other two divisions is that Division III institutions do not offer athletic scholarships—only financial aid based upon need.

NOTES _____

1. In 2002, the NCAA voted to implement a new standard that would drop football programs that do not meet a minimum attendance requirement from the Football Bowl Subdivision (formerly Division I-A) to Football Championship Subdivision (formerly Division I-AA).

2. In August 2007, the Division I Board of Directors enacted a four-year moratorium on permitting institutions to begin the process of moving from either Division II or the Football Championship Subdivision to the Football Bowl Subdivision. The moratorium did not affect 20 institutions that had already begun the five-year provisional membership process but meant no new schools could apply to make the move until August 2011.

1.3.4. Institution Case Study: University of Michigan Athletic Department

The athletic programs of many Division I-A colleges and universities have emerged as big businesses. Budgeting pressures have forced athletic administrators at these institutions to make some difficult decisions. Here is one example demonstrating the big-business, tight-budget environment of Division I-A athletics. This atmosphere at the micro level (at *one* NCAA institution) is both an outgrowth and an explanation of the complex compliance regulations imposed by the NCAA.

The University of Michigan Athletic Department was chosen to illustrate the budgetary concerns of all Division I programs. Michigan is a high-profile Division I-A athletic program and a member of a major conference, the Big Ten. In addition, since it is a public institution, financial information is made available to the public. Despite large inflows of revenue, nearly all athletic departments run a deficit. According to a letter from NCAA President Myles Brand to Congress in November 2006, only 23 Division I institutions' athletic programs generated a net profit. Michigan, one of the few exceptions, projects a $4.7 million surplus for the 2011 fiscal year, after an $8.8 million surplus in 2010 (see exhibit 1.7).

Michigan's revenues exceed $90 million annually, about one-third of which comes from the sale of football tickets. This is an unusually high percentage for a school, attributable to Michigan's 107,501-seat stadium that is sold out for every game. Also unusual is that the Athletic Department does not receive state funding or funding from student fees. Instead, additional revenues are gained from booster donations, sponsorships, licensing (such as merchandise bearing Michigan logos), shared earnings from the NCAA and Big Ten, and local broadcast deals. Michigan cited greater-than-expected annual gifts and licensing revenues as the key to the surplus.

The surplus represented years of hard work, as Michigan had lost about $2 million annually at the turn of the century. At the time, Michigan suffered through a sudden decrease in the sale of items bearing Michigan logos (accounting for $1.35 million in lost revenue alone), decreasing ticket sales to men's basketball games, a terminated radio contract, and less than anticipated donations. One key factor in determining the profitability of an athletic department is a school's generous offering of sports options. Michigan maintains 25 varsity sports and claims to offer the most scholarship dollars in the Big Ten (over $14 million). In particular, Michigan added women's soccer and crew in the 1990s in order to comply with Title IX (for more information, see Chapter 8).

Exhibit 1.7
Michigan Athletic Department 2010 Operating Budget (FY 7/1–6/30)
(in thousands)

REVENUES	
Spectator Admissions	$38,193
Conference Distributions	20,226
Corporate Sponsorship	14,021
Priority Seating and Other Annual Gifts	20,972
Licensing Royalties	4,100
Concessions and Parking	2,280
Facilities	1,748
Other Income	798
Investment Income	2,700
TOTAL	**$105,038**
EXPENSES	
Salaries, Wages, and Benefits	$35,703
Financial Aid to Students	16,206
Team and Game Expense	16,925
Facilities Expenses	8,148
Deferred Maintenance Fund Transfer	4,500
Operating and Administrative Expenses	6,342
Contingency	1,500
Debt Service Transfer to Plant Fund	10,983
TOTAL	**$100,307**
NET SURPLUS	**$4,731**

Athletic directors at universities and colleges have several options for dealing with their deficit problems. They may cut some men's teams, they may continue to raise ticket prices for demand-friendly sports like basketball and football, and they may dip into the reserves of their school's or department's endowments. The first two options may endanger the school's goodwill with alumni donors and the last cannot be sustained forever.

NOTES _____

1. Public records, budgets and reports from the University of Michigan are available at http://www.umich.edu/~urecord. For more on the current state and success of the Michigan Athletic Department, see Joe Nocera, "Skybox U," 6 *New York Times* P38 (October 28, 2007).

2. In recent years numerous universities have been forced to cut athletic teams for both financial reasons as well as Title IX compliance: after the 2006–2007 academic year, James Madison cut seven men's teams and three women's teams in order to comply; affected players and coaches sued, claiming the termination of the teams was unconstitutional. However, the court determined that no due process right, equal protection right, or First Amendment right had been violated; see *Equity in Athletics, Inc. v. Department of Educ.*, 504 F.Supp.2d 88 (W.D.Va. 2007). Also, in 2007, Rutgers cut five men's teams and one women's team; Ohio University announced plans to cut men's swimming and diving, men's indoor and outdoor track, and women's lacrosse; and in 2006, the University of New Hampshire cut women's crew, men's swimming and diving, and men's and women's tennis.

3. For more information on the effects of increased dollars entering intercollegiate sports, consult John Fizel and Rodney Fort, *Economics of College Sports (Studies in Sports Economics)* (New York: Praeger, 2004), and Andrew Zimbalist, *Unpaid Professionals* (Princeton, NJ: Princeton University Press, 1999).

4. For information on the financial and athletic turnaround of a university athletic department, see Rick Telander, *From Red Ink to Roses: The Turbulent Transformation of a Big Ten Program* (New York: Simon and Schuster, 1994).

5. For new perspectives on the place of athletics in an educational setting, see John R. Gerdy, *Air Ball: American Education's Failed Experiment with Elite Athletics* (Jackson: University Press of Mississippi, 2006); James L. Shulman and William G. Bowan, *The Game of Life: College Sports and Educational Values* (Princeton, NJ: Princeton University Press, 2001); and James J. Duderstadt, *Intercollegiate Athletics and the American University: A University President's Perspective* (Ann Arbor: University of Michigan Press, 2000).

1.3.5. Knight Foundation Commission on Intercollegiate Athletics

The John and James L. Knight Foundation is an American nonprofit foundation generally dedicated to journalistic causes. In 2006, the Foundation sponsored 191 new grants and funded over $104 million in research on media, journalism, and their role in our communities.

The Knight Commission, cochaired by Reverend Theodore M. Hesburgh, president of the University of Notre Dame, and William C. Friday, former president of the University of North Carolina, first began investigating intercollegiate athletics after a series of recruiting scandals in the late 1980s. The commission issued a three-volume report in 1993 that helped lead to the restructuring of the NCAA in 1996. Concerns about abuses in college sports inspired the reconvening of the John and James L. Knight Foundation on Intercollegiate Athletics in

2000 and 2001. The meeting culminated in a report offering the following 15 recommendations for the NCAA and its member institutions:

1. Athletes should be filtered through "the same academic processes as other students," including admission standards and degree requirements.

2. By 2007, teams that do not graduate at least 50% of their players should be banned from postseason play (180 of the 321 colleges with Division I basketball teams failed to meet that standard in 2000).

3. "Scholarships should be tied to specific athletes until they (or their entering class) graduate."

4. The length of playing seasons, practice seasons, and postseasons must be reduced.

5. The NBA and the NFL should be encouraged to develop minor leagues. (This would present an alternative for athletes who are not interested in or are unqualified for higher education.)

6. Football and basketball expenditures should be reduced, including the total number of scholarships that are awarded in Division I-A football.

7. Compliance with Title IX and support of women's athletics should be ensured.

8. Coaches' salaries should be reduced and "brought into line with prevailing norms across the institution."

9. Agreements for coaches' outside income should be negotiated with institutions, not individual coaches, because "advertisers are buying the institution's reputation no less than the coaches.'"

10. The NCAA plan for distribution of revenue from the CBS contract should be revised so that it is based on academic performance and gender equity compliance rather than on winning and losing.

11. Institutions alone should determine when games are played, how they are broadcast, and which companies are permitted to advertise.

12. Institutions should be discouraged from signing commercial contracts that violate "traditional academic values."

13. In-arena and in-stadium advertising should be minimized.

14. The NCAA should ban corporate logos on uniforms. (This presumably would include bowl game sponsors.)

15. Federal legislation to ban legal gambling on college sports in Nevada should be supported, and college presidents should address illegal gambling on their campuses.

Some of the Knight Commission's 2001 recommendations have been addressed: the NCAA has increased penalties for schools with low graduation rates for student-athletes, typically by revoking scholarships (see note 2). In addition, the NBA has collaborated with the NCAA on age restrictions and created the National Basketball Development League in 2001. In general, the other concerns of the Knight Foundation have most likely only been exacerbated, as schedules have remained constant or increased, the coaches' salaries and endorsement packages have increased, the NCAA and member institutions revenues have increased, and alcohol-related advertising is at an all-time high (see note 3).

For detail on the history and composition of the Knight Commission as well as its recommendations, see section 5.3.3, "The Knight Commission."

NOTES

1. In 2004, the Knight Foundation Commission issued a report titled *Challenging the Myth: A Review of the Links among College Athletic Success, Student Quality, and Donations*, challenging the assumption that winning teams attract more applicants and, in turn, better students. All Knight Commission reports are available from its Web site: http://www.knightfdn.org.

2. For a review of some of the issues the Knight Commission has attempted to address, see Josephine R. Potuto, "Academic Misconduct, Athletics Academic Support Services, and the NCAA," 95 *Kentucky Law Journal* 447 (2006–2007), and Symposium, "Are We Playing by the Rules? A Debate over the Need for NCAA Regulation Reform," 7 *Vanderbilt Journal of Entertainment Law and Practice* 439 (2005).

3. The NCAA tracks the Academic Progress Rate annually and penalizes teams failing to meet certain academic criteria. The Academic Progress Rate for individual schools and sports is available at http://www.ncaa.org/wps/ncaa?ContentID=276.

4. Days after the 2007–2008 men's basketball NCAA Championship game, over 100 college presidents and athletic directors sent a letter to NCAA president Myles Brand urging him to reconsider the prevalence of alcohol advertisements during the tournament. For more information, see Thomas O'Toole and Steve Wieberg, "NCAA Says It Followed Self-Limit on Final Four Beer Ads," *USA Today* 2C (April 25, 2008).

1.4. THE OLYMPICS

The Olympic Games have been a part of sports history since ancient Greece; however, while the underlying concept to the games may still be intact, the organizational structure of the games is greatly different today compared to the early games. The Olympic Games have become a business, much like other sporting events. For individuals working in or with Olympic contests, a thorough understanding of the modern Olympic movement is imperative in order to effectively manage Olympic-related entities. Issues such as drug testing (see section 7.2.3, "Olympic and International Sports"), eligibility of athletes, and boycotts of Olympic Games by countries have been sources of litigation for the International Olympic Committee (IOC). This section will review the structure and briefly examine the economics of the Olympic Games.

1.4.1. Organizational Structure

Created in 1894 to revive the ancient Greek games, the IOC is an international, nongovernmental, not-for-profit organization located in Switzerland. Its main duty is to oversee all aspects of the Olympic movement, but its most visible role is that of supervisor for the summer and winter Olympic Games. As the highest governing body of the Olympics, the IOC owns all of the rights to the Olympic symbol, anthem, flag, and motto.

The international nature of the Olympics complicates its study from a legal perspective since the countries in the Olympic movement have different laws, judicial systems and decisions, and different individual rights. The International Olympic Committee (IOC), International Federations (IFs), National Olympic

Committees (NOCs), and National Governing Bodies (NGBs) all have their own by-laws or charters. However, the IOC Charter is the ultimate governing document for all such organizations. Likewise, the IOC is the "supreme authority" on all matters pertaining to the Olympic Games. Exhibit 1.8 shows the organizational structure of the IOC.

The highest ranking body in the IOC hierarchy is the Executive Board. The Executive Board is elected by delegates of each organizational member in an annual meeting. This group of delegates who serve a one-year term is called a session. The session elects a president of the IOC (current president Jacques Rogge was elected in 2001), who serves an initial eight-year term and thereafter can be elected to one four-year term. The session also elects four vice presidents and six other members of the Executive Board who all serve four-year terms. The vice presidents and six other members can be re-elected, but not in the same year that their original term expires, unless they are elected by the president. The Executive Board meets either when the president orders a meeting or when a majority of its members request a meeting.

The Executive Board's main functions are the following:

- To attend to the observance of the Olympic Charter
- To assume responsibility for the administration of the IOC
- To approve the IOC's internal organization and all internal regulations relating to the organization
- To be responsible for the management of the IOC's finances

Exhibit 1.8
Olympic Structure

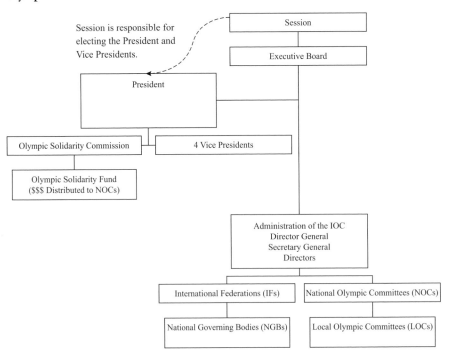

- To report to the session on any proposed rule changes
- To submit to the session the names of persons it recommends for election to the IOC
- To establish the agenda for the sessions
- To appoint the director general (on recommendation from the president)
- To keep records of the IOC
- To pass legislation and policy to ensure proper adherence to the Olympic Charter and the proper organization of the Olympic Games
- To perform any other duties assigned to it by the session (see http://www.olympic.org)

Beneath the Executive Board is the administration of the IOC. The administration is led by the director general and directors. The director general is similar to a chief operating officer of a corporation in that under the direction of the president of the IOC, he or she directs the day-to-day operations of the organization. The individual directors in the administration control specific areas of the IOC such as international cooperation, Olympic Games coordination, finance, marketing, legal affairs, technology, operations, communications, medical, and relations with the International Federations, National Olympic Committees, and Organizing Committees of Olympic Games (OCOG). The main duties of the administration are as follows:

- Implementing decisions made by the session, the Executive Board, and the president
- Implementation and follow-up of work from all commissions
- Serve as a liaison with all IFs, NOCs, and OCOGs
- Coordinate the preparation of all Olympic Games and other Olympic events
- Disseminate information within the Olympic movement
- Consult candidate cities on their bids to host the Olympic Games
- Promote sport, education, and culture with international governmental and nongovernmental agencies
- Execute tasks assigned by the president and the Executive Board (see http://www.olympic.org)

Beneath the IOC administration are the individual international federations (IFs). The IFs are nongovernmental bodies given the authority by the IOC to administer specific sports on the international level. IFs must adhere to the Olympic movement rules and regulations regarding fair play, humanitarian efforts, environmental concerns, and elevating the status of women in sport, but they maintain their independence as far as establishing and enforcing rules governing their respective sports. They set their definitions of "amateur" and decide whether or not professional athletes will be allowed to compete in the Olympic Games in their particular sports. IFs are also responsible for the organization and execution of their sport at all Olympic Games and any other games affiliated with the IOC such as the PanAm Games. For example, the international federation for the sport of basketball is known by the acronym FIBA (for Fédération Internationale de Basketball). Since the IFs are responsible for individual sports on an international level, they are directly above the national governing bodies of each sport. As an example, the NGB of basketball in the United States is called USA Basketball. As such, USA Basketball works with FIBA and must adhere to

FIBA's rules and regulations. To be eligible to participate in the Olympic Games, an individual must be deemed eligible by the particular IF and NGB presiding over the sport. Rule 45 of the Olympic Charter explains how Olympic athletes become eligible for competition:

> To be eligible for participation in the Olympic Games, a competitor must comply with the Olympic Charter as well as with the rules of the IF concerned as approved by the IOC, and must be entered by his NOC. He must notably:
>
> • Respect the spirit of fair play and nonviolence, and behave accordingly on the sports field
> • Refrain from using substances and procedures prohibited by the rules of the IOC, the IFs, or the NOCs
> • Respect and comply in all aspects with the World Anti-Doping Code (see http://www.olympic.org)

In addition, the bylaw to Rule 45 describes the role of the IFs and obligations of athletes when participating in the Olympic Games:

• Each IF establishes its sport's own eligibility criteria in accordance with the Olympic Charter. Such criteria must be submitted to the IOC Executive Board for approval.
• The application of the eligibility criteria lies with the IFs, their affiliated national federations, and the NOCs in the fields of their respective responsibilities.
• Except as permitted by the IOC Executive Board, no competitor who participates in the Olympic Games may allow his person, name, picture, or sports performance to be used for advertising purposes during the Olympic Games.
• The entry or participation of a competitor in the Olympic Games shall not be conditional on any financial consideration (see http://www.olympic.org).

Therefore, the eligibility rules for each sport are determined by the IF of that sport—an issue that came under international scrutiny when more professional athletes were allowed to participate in the Olympic Games.

The National Olympic Committees administer Olympic programs for a particular nation. For example, the United States Olympic Committee (USOC) is the NOC for all activities related to the Olympics in the United States. Despite the nonpolitical ideals of the Olympics, most governments exert a high level of influence over their countries' NOCs. The United States is no different, as witnessed by the political 1980 boycott of the Moscow games and various legislation devoted to the Olympics. In particular, Congress passed the Amateur Sports Act in 1978 and amended it in 1998, establishing the USOC's authority over international amateur sports competition (as opposed to the Amateur Athletic Union [AAU] or NCAA).

A responsibility of the National Olympic Committees is to establish training programs and funds so athletes have a competitive opportunity to earn a spot on the Olympic roster. The NOCs also supervise any attempt by a city in their country to host an Olympic Games. If there is more than one city from a country vying to host the games, then that country's NOC must decide which city will represent the country in the selection process in front of the IOC. In addition, the NOCs implement any rule changes passed by the IOC in their national Olympic programs. It is this structure that theoretically maintains a uniform playing field from country to country.

When a city is chosen to host an Olympic Games by the IOC, a managing body from that city is formed to coordinate all the operations undertaken to stage the games. These bodies are known as local organizing committees (LOCs). For example, the Salt Lake Organizing Committee (SLOC) was the organizing body for Salt Lake City, Utah, when it hosted the 2002 Winter Olympics. The LOCs are responsible for developing infrastructure, facilities, transportation, athlete housing, and any other elements deemed necessary by the IOC to ensure a successful Olympiad. Most countries' LOCs receive some funding from their national government to stage the games; the United States is the only country that *does not* grant any federal government subsidies to a city hosting the Olympic Games. Thus, the host city is burdened with providing additional revenue from the games in order to offset the expenditures undertaken in hosting the games. This topic will be covered in more depth later.

NOTES

1. For more information on the structure and rules of the International Olympic Committee, see http://www.olympic.org.

2. For more information on the U.S. Olympic Committee, see http://www.usoc.org.

3. The Olympic Games hold a unique place in international sports, and as a result there are often many issues with which they must deal; for more information see Robyn A. Goldstein, "An American in Paris: The Legal Framework of International Sport and the Implications of the World Anti-Doping Code on Accused Athletes," 7 *Virginia Sports and Entertainment Law Journal* 149 (2007); Christopher T. Murray, "Representant Les Etats—Unis D'Amerique: Reforming the USOC Charter," 7 *Vanderbilt Journal of Entertainment Law and Practice* 233 (2005); Jason Kroll, "Second Class Athletes: The USOC's Treatment of Paralympians," 23 *Cardozo Arts and Entertainment Law Journal* 307 (2005); and R. Jake Locklear, "Arbitration in Olympic Disputes: Should Arbitrators Review the Field of Play Decisions of Officials?" 4 *Texas Review of Entertainment and Sports Law* 199 (2003).

1.4.2. International Federations and National Governing Bodies

As mentioned earlier, the IFs are the governing bodies for a specific Olympic sport worldwide. They determine eligibility rules, game rules, and other procedures related to a particular sport. Let us return to our example of FIBA, the IF for the sport of basketball. FIBA is responsible for the overall management of all Olympic-related basketball activities, contests, and regulations. Operating from its statutes and laws, FIBA governs the NGBs to safeguard the game against corruption, to grow the game worldwide, and to foster competition between member nations.

Since FIBA is an IF, the rules of play differ from collegiate or professional rules to which most Americans are accustomed. For example, the size of the lane in FIBA rules is 19', 8.2" × 19', 0.3"; in the NBA the lane is 16' × 19'; and in NCAA competition the lane is 12' × 19'. FIBA also passes rules on eligibility of players. For instance, starting with the 1992 Barcelona Summer Olympics, FIBA allowed professional basketball players to participate in Olympic competition. Until that time, all the teams, including those from the United States, comprised amateur players. As a result of FIBA's rule change, the United States sent to the 1992 Olympics a team largely composed of NBA players, who routed all of their opponents. This "Dream Team" was met with great anticipation from around the world as the

United States showcased its best athletes. However, these players were selected instead of amateur collegiate players, the population who had represented the United States until then.

USA Basketball is the NGB for international basketball in the United States. As an NGB, USA Basketball is subject to the rules and regulations set forth by FIBA. However, within this framework, USA Basketball governs all basketball-related activities undertaken by the United States as it pertains to FIBA-sanctioned international competition and to national competition that falls under the Olympic umbrella. USA Basketball comprises 26 members of differing levels—active, associate, and affiliate. Active members are national sport organizations, such as the NCAA, AAU, and NBA, that operate a nationally active basketball program. Associate members, such as Athletes in Action and the Harlem Globetrotters, also conduct active basketball operations but do not qualify for active membership. Affiliate members like Basketball Travelers, Inc., and Sport Tours International, Inc., are basically for commercial groups that are involved in basketball in their businesses.

USA Basketball operations are derived from the Constitution of USA Basketball, which sets forth the organizational hierarchy, jurisdiction, grievance procedures, membership criteria, selection processes, and all other functions of the entity (see note 1). Of particular interest is the authority of USA Basketball as indicated in Article 4 of the Constitution. This article reads as follows:

Authority. This Association shall exercise the following powers:

4.1 Represent the United States in FIBA.

4.2 Establish national goals and encourage the attainment of those goals in the sport of basketball.

4.3 Serve as the coordinating body for amateur athletic activity in the sport of basketball in the United States.

4.4 Exercise jurisdiction over international amateur athletic activities and sanction international amateur athletic competition held in the United States and sanction the sponsorship of international amateur athletic competition held in the United States in the sport of Basketball, in accordance with the provisions of the Constitution.

4.5 Conduct amateur athletic competition in the sport of basketball, including national championships, and international amateur athletic competition in the United States, and establish procedures for the determination of eligibility standards for participation in such competitions, except for restricted competition referred to in the provision here below.

4.6 Recommend to the USOC individuals and teams to represent the United States in the Olympic Games and the Pan American Games in the sport of basketball.

4.7 Designate individuals and teams to represent the United States in international amateur athletic competition (other than the Olympics and Pan American Games) in the sport of basketball and certify, in accordance with the rules of FIBA, the amateur eligibility of such individuals and teams; provided that any amateur sports organization which conducts amateur athletic competition, participation in which is restricted to a specific class of amateur athletes (such as high school students, college students, members of the Armed Forces, or similar groups or categories) shall have exclusive jurisdiction over such competition.

As stated in the USA Basketball Constitution, USA Basketball has the authority to choose the players who represent the United States and the coaches who lead these teams. It also gives USA Basketball the authority to promote, coordinate, and regulate amateur athletic participation in basketball by many U.S. organizations. Owing to this broad field of responsibility, the Board of Directors for USA Basketball boasts a constituency from a diverse group of basketball-related organizations. The organizations represented on the board are Amateur Athletic Union (one member); National Association of Intercollegiate Athletics (one member); National Basketball Association (four members); National Collegiate Athletic Association (four members); National Federation of State High School Associations (one member); National Junior College Athletic Association (one member); and the U.S. Armed Forces (one member).

USA Basketball uses internal mechanisms to determine membership and eligibility issues as well as sanctioning of competition. In the case of declaring a participant ineligible, the association must inform the individual in writing and offer a hearing before the Board of Directors. The board's decision is not subject to appeal. However, if the internal mechanisms fail to satisfy either party, they may petition for a binding arbitration process following the rules and regulations of the American Arbitration Association.

NOTES

1. Information about the NGB for basketball in the United States, USA Basketball, can be found at http://www.usabasketball.com.

2. A list and link to all of the U.S. NGBs can be found on the USOC Web site at http://www.teamusa.org/ngb/sports.

3. The Summer Olympics sports IFs constitute a group known as the Association of Summer Olympic International Federations (ASOIF). More information can be found on the group's Web site at http://www.asoif.com.

4. A list and link to all IFs can be found on the IOC Web site at http://www.olympic.org/en/content/The-IOC/.

5. For more on the role of NGBs, see A. Jerome Dess, "Bring Back the Crowd? How Governing Bodies for Sports Should Provide Victims of Athlete Doping a Better Remedy," 9 *Florida Coastal Law Review* 179 (2008).

1.4.3. Economic Overview of Olympic Bodies

While the Olympic movement was originally designed to promote goodwill and international competition, it has since become a multimillion-dollar enterprise. Funding must be procured to finance the staging of the Olympic Games. Athletes need funding for equipment, training, travel, and competition. Full-time employees in the IOC, IFs, NOCs, and NGBs are all usually paid salaries and benefits, and offices for the organization and employees must be provided. Therefore, the modern Olympic Games have needed to rely on fundraising, donations, and commercialism in order to sustain their existence for the past 100 years. However, it was not until the 1984 summer games, when the IOC developed a comprehensive plan for marketing the Olympic Games called "controlled commercialism," that Olympic revenues began to grow substantially. The IOC designed this plan to stabilize the finances of the Olympic organizations; to build an ongoing marketing program for all LOCs, instead of starting over with every Olympic Games; to distribute revenues earned equally throughout the Olympic organizational hierarchy; to control broadcasts of the Olympics enabling the world to view the games; and to control commercialism and promote the Olympic ideals throughout the world.

The IOC marketing efforts fall under the control of the IOC Marketing Department, which works with sponsors, broadcasters, national organizing committees, and local organizing committees to develop new and creative ways to develop revenue in each organization's respective territory. One program, the Olympic Partners (TOP) program, began in 1985 in an effort to secure more sponsorship dollars and provide sponsors with greater return on their investment, is organized in four-year increments (called quadrenniums) surrounding an Olympic Game. Sponsors pay a sum of money to associate their brand name with the Olympics and be able to conduct promotions and run advertising utilizing the Olympic logo. This revenue has decreased the dependence the IOC had in previous years on the revenue received from selling broadcast rights. For example, in the 2001–2004 quadrennium, TOP revenue was approximately 34% of the total revenue received by the IOC, while television revenue was only 53%, down substantially from the 90% share television revenue accounted for 19 years earlier (see note 1).

NOTES

1. The quadrennium and other details regarding Olympic marketing revenues can be found from the IOC Web site at http://www.olympic.org/uk/organisation/facts/introduction/index_uk.asp

2. Olympic documents, including those related to revenue generation and distribution, can be found from the IOC Web site at http://www.olympic.org/en/content/The-IOC/Financing/Revenues/.

3. For a review of some of the problems associated with marketing and sponsorship at the Olympic Games, see Stephen McKelvey and John Grady, "An Analysis of the Ongoing Global Efforts to Combat Ambush Marketing: Will Corporate Marketers 'Take' the Gold in Greece?" 14 *Journal of Legal Aspects of Sport* 191 (2004).

1.4.4. International Olympic Committee Responses to Prevailing Legal Issues

The awarding of the Olympic Games to a host city has become an increasingly competitive and controversial process. In 1995, the IOC awarded the 2002 Winter Olympics to Salt Lake City. In subsequent years, the IOC faced the largest corruption scandal in its history. Ten IOC members resigned or were expelled in cases allegedly involving fraud, conspiracy, and bribery. Investigators determined that IOC members accepted more than $1 million in cash, improper gifts, and favors from backers of Salt Lake City's LOC in order to influence their votes.

Prior to the 2008 Summer Olympics in Beijing, China, there was a large amount of scrutiny and criticism around the world for China's hosting the Games despite what many considered to be a poor human rights record. Traditionally, the Olympic torch travels from Olympia, Greece, around the world and finally to the host city during the opening ceremonies. However, during the 2008 relay, the runners and the route were routinely met with protests and security issues, particularly in North America and Europe. As a result, the relay was often rerouted without notice and security was significantly increased. IOC President Jacques Rogge described the situation as a "crisis" and threatened to sanction any athlete who engaged in excessive propaganda during the Games. In addition, groups around the world called on their respective nations to boycott the Games but to no avail (see note 2).

Doping has been another point of controversy for the IOC. The term refers to the use of performance-enhancing drugs in athletic competition. After a failure to establish standardized regulations and procedures, the World Anti-Doping

Agency (WADA) was created in 2004 as the ultimate authority on doping and drug testing in international competition (the topic is covered in more detail in Chapter 7). Sometimes an athlete is disqualified for a positive drug test immediately prior to his or her Olympic event. When this occurs, it does not afford much time for the athlete to obtain due process. In order to handle disputes over matters such as a positive drug test, the Court of Arbitration for Sport (CAS) was created in 1983 (see note 1). It also allows disputes that arise during (or right before) the Olympic Games to be settled quickly and relatively inexpensively by the CAS Ad Hoc Division (AHD) (see notes 3 and 4).

It is important to point out that CAS arbitration can be used to settle disputes over matters other than doping. For example, it can be used to settle conflicts between IFs and NGBs and disputes involving sponsorship or television rights contracts. Athletes, sports federations, clubs, sponsors, suppliers, and television companies all have access to CAS.

NOTES

1. For additional information on CAS, see section 5.3.6, "Court of Arbitration for Sport (CAS)."

2. See Julie H. Liu, "Lighting the Torch of Human Rights: The Olympic Games as a Vehicle for Human Rights Reform," 5 *Northwestern University Journal of International Human Rights* 213 (2007).

3. At the 2004 Athens Summer Olympic Games, only one athlete, Kenyan boxer David Munyasia, took advantage of the CAS AHD. A urine sample taken upon Munyasia's arrival at the Games tested positive for cathine, a stimulant. Appearing before the CAS AHD, Munyasia did not dispute that a doping violation was found but claimed that he took it unknowingly or that the analysis was erroneous. In affirming the IOC Executive Board's decision to bar Munyasia from the Games, the CAS AHD stated that its authority was not to order additional laboratory analysis but simply to determine whether or not a doping violation had been found.

4. For further information on Olympic dispute resolution, see Jason Gubi, "The Olympic Binding Arbitration Clause and the Court of Arbitration for Sport: An Analysis of Due Process Concerns," 18 *Fordham Intellectual Property, Media and Entertainment Law Journal* 997 (2008), and Richard McLaren, "The CAS Ad Hoc Division at the Athens Olympic Games," 15 *Marquette Sports Law Review* 175 (2004).

1.5. INTERSCHOLASTIC ATHLETICS

High school athletics is governed at the national level by the National Federation of State High School Associations (NFSHSA) and at the state level, in all 50 states, by bodies such as the Massachusetts Interscholastic Athletic Association (MIAA). The legal issues involving high school athletic administrators are covered throughout the text, including injury liability (Chapter 4), the powers of athletic associations (Chapter 5), constitutional law rights of high school athletes (Chapter 6), drug testing (Chapter 7), hiring issues (Chapter 8), contracts (Chapter 9), and employment discrimination (Chapter 15).

Considerable tort litigation has been directed toward employees and volunteers of non-scholastic youth sports organizations (such as Little League and Pop Warner). The Youth Sports Volunteer Coalition (YSVC) was established to protect volunteers from what the YSVC calls "frivolous" lawsuits (see section 4.4.3, "Civil Liability Immunity Legislation"). However, this protection varies by region, and thus a thorough knowledge of state laws is important for volunteers of youth sports.

Finally, such volunteers should be aware of lawsuits involving gender discrimination that have occurred in nonscholastic sports. Even private organizations can be held liable for discrimination claims when certain criteria are met (see notes 1 and 2).

NOTES

1. In *Perry v. Ohio High School Athletic Association (OHSAA)*, 2006 WL 2927260 (S.D. Ohio October 11, 2006), a student-athlete sued OHSAA and Columbus Public Schools (CPS) after he transferred within the CPS system but was denied athletic eligibility. OHSAA rules permit a student to transfer within the same system without jeopardizing his eligibility with the approval of the OHSAA commissioner. In this case, the athletic director at the plaintiff's new school realized that he had failed to send the necessary paperwork, and subsequently, the school was forced to forfeit all games in which the plaintiff had participated, including the entire 2004–2005 basketball season and state championship. Also, the plaintiff had his MVP award revoked. The plaintiff had contended that the rules of the OHSAA were overly broad and violated his freedom of association rights under the First Amendment. In granting summary judgment for the defendants, the court explained that there is no constitutionally protected property interest in participating in interscholastic athletics.

2. In *Brown ex rel. Brown v. Oklahoma Secondary School Activities Ass'n*, 125 P.3d 1219 (Okla. 2005), a high school football player was granted an injunction preventing the enforcement of his two-game suspension for unsportsmanlike misconduct. Brown, a quarterback, was ejected from the quarterfinal game for kicking an opponent in the helmet while he was on the ground during a fight between the teams. As a result of the injunction, the association postponed the semifinal and state championship games. The Supreme Court of Oklahoma vacated the injunction 20 days after the incident, ruling that the suspension was reasonably applied; the association did not act arbitrarily or capriciously in postponing the next rounds of the playoffs and stated that deference should be given to the internal affairs of a voluntary membership association.

1.6. INDIVIDUAL SPORT ISSUES

The courts in the United States have sometimes faced the question of whether to respect the autonomy of private organizations or to accommodate the public good. The sports world has increasingly emerged as an epicenter of this debate. Even private recreational organizations, such as country clubs, can be susceptible to significant financial damages by engaging in discrimination (see note 2). Furthermore, the PGA's lost legal battle with Casey Martin demonstrates how even the highest profile sport organizations can be compelled to alter their established regulations (see note 1). Industry professionals working in these or similar associations can better understand laws of equal protection and the Americans with Disabilities Act after reading Chapters 8 and 16, respectively.

Professional athletes in sports governed by associations such as the PGA, LPGA, and ATP may not find the level of advocacy in their organizations that occurs in the unionized sports. As a result, athletes in these individual sports are on their own. One reason for this is because of the broad scope and goals of these organizations. For example, the PGA claims 28,000 members and a dedication to the promotion of the *game* of golf. By contrast, the National Basketball Players Association (a union) represents fewer than 500 active NBA players and states goals that are solely geared toward the promotion of *player* interests (see Chapters 11 and 12 for more information on players' unions). Furthermore, athletes in sports such as tennis and golf are not guaranteed income merely by participating in professional athletic competitions. Generally, such athletes earn income in two ways, tournament prize money and product endorsements. Owing to the latter, the player agent becomes especially vital for athletes in these sports (see section 12.2, "Player Agents").

NOTES _____

1. In the majority decision of *PGA Tour Inc. v. Casey Martin*, 532 U.S. 661 (2001), the U.S. Supreme Court determined that granting a disabled plaintiff a golf cart would not fundamentally alter the character of competition. Title III of the Americans with Disabilities Act (ADA) requires that a private business which accommodates the public must make "reasonable modifications … to individuals with disabilities, unless the entity can demonstrate that making such modifications would fundamentally alter the nature of such … accommodations." For more on the ADA and its potential impact on sports, see section 16.3.2, "Application to Athletic Organizations," and Maureen A. Weston, "The Intersection of Sports and Disability: Analyzing Reasonable Accommodations for Athletes with Disabilities," 50 *Saint Louis University Law Journal* 137 (2005).

2. In *Borne v. The Haverhill Golf and Country Club, Inc.*, 791 N.E.2d 903 (Mass.App. Ct. 2003), a jury in Massachusetts awarded $1.9 million to female plaintiffs who accused the private club of not extending full benefits of membership to women. For more on gender issues in golf, see Barbara Osborne, "Gender, Employment, and Sexual Harassment Issues in the Golf Industry," 16 *Journal of Legal Aspects of Sport* 25 (2006).

1.7. FACILITIES, AGENCY FIRMS, AND MEDIA

Corporate mergers at the turn of the 21st century began to unite the three formerly distinct industry segments of facilities, agency firms, and media. The development of the agency business can largely be traced to the growth of International Management Group (IMG). IMG was created by Mark McCormack, who became the first modern sports agent in 1960 via a handshake agreement with then 31-year-old golfer Arnold Palmer. IMG evolved to have a prominent role in nearly all facets of nearly all sports; it has represented athletes, broadcasters, events, and institutions while also having subsidiaries involved in marketing, television, and media. The resulting vertical integration raised potential legal and conflict-of-interest issues (see note 1).

To address these concerns, IMG sold off its baseball, football, and hockey representation divisions to Creative Artists Agency (CAA) in 2005. CAA, who also purchased SFX's football portfolio, has emerged as one of the leading representation agencies in the world, blending its sports clientele with clients working in music, TV, film and art, and literature. CAA represented all the NFL MVPs from 2003 to 2007 and David Beckham in the $250 million deal that brought the English soccer star to the MLS (see note 2). Some agencies, like the Bonham Group, have developed a strong niche by focusing its representation on corporate and property clients like facilities, convention centers, universities, and entertainment properties.

Two of the most important revenue-producing avenues for sports teams and leagues are stadium naming rights and broadcasting rights (see note 3). Consequently, practitioners in these sectors should become cognizant of the antitrust issues in professional sports (Chapter 11). At the same time, there are legal issues pertaining directly to facility owners (Chapter 4), agency firms (Chapter 12), and media (Chapter 14). Chapter 9 is directly relevant to all three sectors.

NOTES

1. For more on the potential conflicts of interest for sports agencies, see Scott B. Rosner, "Conflicts of Interest and the Shifting Paradigm of Athlete Representation," 11 *UCLA Entertainment Law Review* 193 (2004), and Stacey B. Evans, "Sports Agents: Ethical Representatives or Overly Aggressive Adversaries?" 17 *Villanova Sports & Entertainment Law Journal* 91 (2010).

2. For more on the legal and financial effect of Beckham's arrival, see Robert M. Bernhard, "MLS' Designated Player Rule: Has David Beckham Single-Handedly Destroyed Major League Soccer's Single-Entity Antitrust Defense?" 18 *Marquette Sports Law Review* 413 (2008).

3. For more on these issues, see Jack F. Williams, "The Coming Revenue Revolution in Sports," 42 *Willamette Law Review* 669 (2006), and Christian Maximilian Voigt, "What's Really in the Package of a Naming Rights Deal? Service Mark Rights and the Naming Rights of Professional Stadiums," 11 *Journal of Intellectual Property Law* 327 (2004).

SUMMARY

This chapter has provided background on the organizations involved in the sports industry. The discussion included information on the structure, rules and procedures, power and authority, and types of litigation that can involve these organizations. The rest of the chapters provide further detail on areas of the law and types of litigation that occur. Case decisions will be discussed in more detail with additional description of the constituency group involved and the type of complaint, the legal arguments, and the court decisions. The reader should refer to this chapter if questions arise about the organizations and constituencies involved in the litigation discussions presented in the rest of the chapters.

Chapter 2

THE COURT AND LEGAL SYSTEM IN THE UNITED STATES

2.1. The Federal Court System

    2.1.1. U.S. Supreme Court
    2.1.2. U.S. Courts of Appeals
    2.1.3. U.S. District Courts
    2.1.4. Administrative Agencies

2.2. The State Court System

2.3. Civil Legal Process

    2.3.1. The Complaint
    2.3.2. The Parties
    2.3.3. Court Jurisdiction
    2.3.4. The Summons
    2.3.5. The Answer
    2.3.6. Discovery
    2.3.7. Pretrial Motions
    2.3.8. The Type of Court
    2.3.9. The Trial
    2.3.10. The Judgment
    2.3.11. The Appeals Process

2.4. Sources of Legal Information

    2.4.1. Legal Reference Materials
        2.4.1.1. Legal Dictionaries
        2.4.1.2. Legal Research Guides

        2.4.1.3. Annotated Law Reports
        2.4.1.4. Legal Encyclopedias
        2.4.1.5. *Restatements of the Law*
        2.4.1.6. Treatises
        2.4.1.7. Legal Indexes
        2.4.1.8. Law Review Articles
        2.4.1.9. *Shepard's Citations*
        2.4.1.10. Legal Computer Services
        2.4.1.11. Sports Law Newsletters
        2.4.1.12. Sports Law Web Sites
    2.4.2. Constitutions
    2.4.3. Legislation
    2.4.4. Federal Administrative Rules and Regulations
    2.4.5. Case Law
        2.4.5.1. U.S. Supreme Court
        2.4.5.2. U.S. Courts of Appeals
        2.4.5.3. U.S. District Courts
        2.4.5.4. State Courts

INTRODUCTION

Directors of athletic organizations need a fundamental understanding of the legal system of the United States to deal effectively with the wide variety of legal matters they face today. While the overview given in this chapter is brief and general in nature, the reader can consult the notes for source materials that provide greater detail.

The purpose of the judiciary is to decide cases and controversies between parties by functioning as the neutral finder of fact (judge or jury). The judicial system in the United States is an adversarial one; that is, the parties, usually represented by lawyers, take opposing sides when they appear before the judge or jury. It is thought that the adversarial approach to resolving legal disputes is the most effective way for the finder of fact to arrive at the truth and reach a fair decision.

The American legal system is based primarily on the common law traditions established in England. The law in every state has its roots in common law, except Louisiana, whose law is based on the French Civil Code. *Common law* is established when judges apply previous decisions (precedent) to present cases with similar facts or issues. It is to be distinguished from statutory law. The written decisions, called opinions, are binding on future decisions of lower courts within the same jurisdiction (*binding authority*). In addition, opinions may serve to function as *persuasive authority*, that is, advice for consideration to courts outside the deciding court's jurisdiction that are adjudicating a case with similar facts or issues.

Predictability and stability in the law are major objectives of the legal system. Parties should be able to regulate their behavior and enter into relationships with reasonable assurance of the governing rules of law. The principles of *stare decisis* (to abide by or adhere to decided cases) and precedent (an adjudged case which serves as the authority for identical or similar cases or questions of law that subsequently arise) serve to provide this continuity. In addition, each court (except the U.S. Supreme Court) is bound by the decisions of courts of higher authority. The ruling of a court sets precedent that may be altered only by a court of higher authority.

The court system in the United States is generally viewed as having three functions: (1) administering state and national laws, (2) resolving disputes among parties, and (3) interpreting the legislative intent of a law in deciding a case. These functions are generally related to providing remedy to a party that has been unlawfully affected. Two forms by which remedy can be provided are civil and criminal legal proceedings. Civil law is between private parties only, and provides individuals with a cause of action by which they may be compensated through the recovery of damages. Criminal law is between private parties and society. It is designed to protect the public from harm through the punishment of conduct likely to cause harm. The state is a party to criminal action whereby the state attempts to protect society.

There are two basic legal systems in the United States: the federal system and the state system. Chapter 2 begins with a description of the federal court system, which includes the U.S. Supreme Court, U.S. courts of appeals, U.S. district courts, and several administrative agencies. The chapter next discusses the state legal system, which consists of the primary sources of law in each state's constitution and court decisions. Naturally, there is variation among state legal systems.

As important as understanding the legal system in the United States is knowing how to find legal information. The next section identifies and describes numerous legal sources that coaches and administrators may find useful. Section 2.3, "Civil Legal Process," describes the steps in a civil lawsuit. This information will assist the athletic administrator in understanding the trial process.

2.1. THE FEDERAL COURT SYSTEM

The federal court system in the United States consists of the Supreme Court, 13 courts of appeals, 94 district courts, certain specialized courts, and administrative agencies (exhibit 2.1). Federal cases usually are first heard in a district court, although certain cases are initiated in the courts of appeals or in the Supreme Court. Cases that are appealed after being heard in the district courts usually go to a court of appeals or, in rare cases, directly to the Supreme Court. The 13 courts of appeals (representing 11 judicial circuits, the District of Columbia, and the Federal Circuit) also review orders issued by administrative agencies such as the Securities and Exchange Commission, the Federal Trade Commission, the Internal Revenue Service, and the National Labor Relations Board.

The special federal courts include the U.S. Claims Court, the U.S. Court of International Trade, the U.S. Court of Military Appeals, the U.S. Tax Court, the U.S. Bankruptcy Court, and the Temporary Emergency Court of Appeals. The jurisdiction of these courts is rather narrow. For example, the U.S. Claims Court hears only cases in which individuals have a claim against the federal government, and the Court of International Trade hears civil actions against the United States arising from federal laws governing import and trade transactions. These courts generally are not of concern to athletic administrators.

2.1.1. U.S. Supreme Court

The U.S. Supreme Court is the highest court in the nation and the ultimate dispute arbitrator. Once the Supreme Court decides an issue, all other federal courts must interpret the law by its lead. The Supreme Court has two types of jurisdiction: original and appellate.

Original jurisdiction covers two types of cases: those involving ambassadors, ministers, and consuls and those involving a state as one of the parties to a lawsuit. The Supreme Court hears very few cases under original jurisdiction. An example of a case heard under original jurisdiction is *Kansas v. Colorado*, 533 U.S. 1 (2001), which deals with a violation of the Arkansas River Compact relating to development of the Arkansas River basin.

Appellate jurisdiction covers cases tried or reviewed by the individual states' highest court involving federal questions, including those bearing on the U.S. Constitution, congressional acts, or foreign treaties. It also covers cases tried or reviewed by the federal courts of appeals or the district courts. *Federal Baseball Club of Baltimore, Inc. v. National League of Professional Baseball Clubs*, 259 U.S. 200 (1922), is an example of a case heard under appellate jurisdiction; this case deals with the applicability of the antitrust laws to professional baseball.

A chief justice and eight associate justices sit on the U.S. Supreme Court. The nine justices are appointed by the president of the United States and confirmed by the U.S. Senate. They serve lifetime tenures. The chief justice receives a salary of $223,500, and the associate justices receive $213,900 each (2010).

The U.S. Supreme Court has broad discretion in determining whether to hear an appeal, with few exceptions. A person or party that wants a case to be heard

Exhibit 2.1
The U.S. Court System

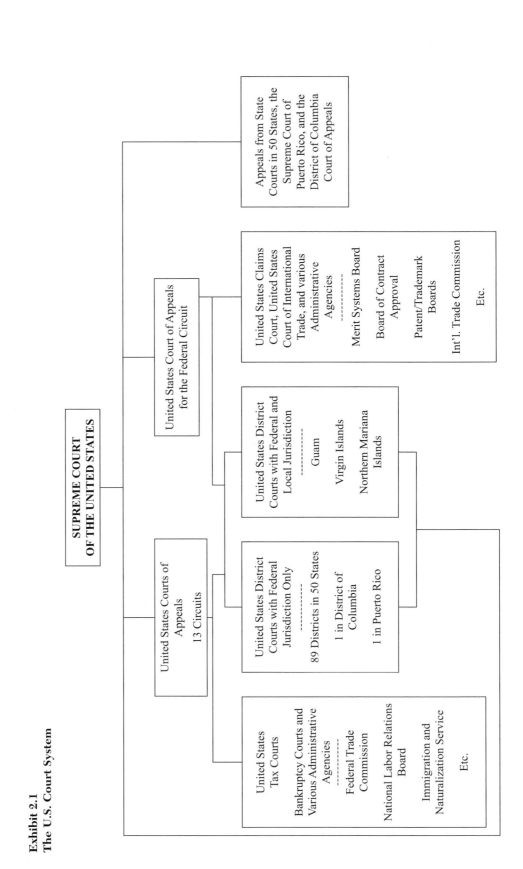

by the Supreme Court must ask in an application for a *writ of appeal* where jurisdiction is mandatory or a *writ of certiorari* where jurisdiction is discretionary. When the Supreme Court grants a writ, that case comes before the Court. A *writ of appeal* applies only to decisions made by three-judge federal district court panels that grant or deny injunctive relief. A *writ of certiorari* allows the Court to hear cases not covered by the writ of appeal. It is a written order to call up for review a case from a lower court. Four of the nine justices have to vote to review a case under a *writ of certiorari*. Certiorari gives the Supreme Court broad discretion in deciding which cases to review. It can be employed by the Court to review the following:

1. Any civil or criminal case from the federal court of appeals
2. Any state supreme court decision where the constitutionality of a federal or state statute or a treaty is questioned
3. Any state Supreme Court decision that rules a state statute violates federal law

The Supreme Court hears oral arguments from the attorneys for the parties when it decides to hear a case. Prior to oral arguments, the parties submit *briefs*, or written arguments, to the Court. Sometimes the Court allows a brief termed *amicus curiae*, or "friend of the court," to be submitted by third parties who believe that they (or the organization they represent) may be affected by the Court's decision in a case. For instance, in a 2001 Supreme Court case, *Casey Martin v. PGA Tour*, 532 U.S. 661 (2001), World Team Sports, an organization that creates and operates events that integrate athletes with disabilities with nondisabled athletes, was one of nine disabled sport organizations allowed to file an amicus brief.

Supreme Court decisions are made after the justices have heard the oral presentations and reviewed the briefs from both parties. Each justice renders an opinion on why a certain decision should be made, and then the justices vote in order of seniority. After a decision has been reached by majority vote, a justice is chosen to write the *opinion of the Court*. A justice who disagrees with the opinion and who did not vote with the majority may write a *dissenting opinion*. A justice who agrees with the majority opinion but not with the reasoning by which it was reached may write a *concurring opinion*. Other justices may join a dissenting or concurring opinion.

Some of the reasons that the overwhelming majority of cases filed at the trial level never reach the U.S. Supreme Court or the courts of appeals are the following: cases are settled; parties do not believe they will be successful on appeal; costs can be prohibitive; and appellate courts have discretion to refuse to hear an appeal. Cases that the appellate courts do review are those in which there may have been an error at the trial court level, those which involve novel legal issues, and those where the lower courts have been inconsistent in their decisions.

2.1.2. U.S. Courts of Appeals

There are 13 U.S. Courts of Appeals. In addition to the 11 judicial districts, there are the District of Columbia and the U.S. Court of Appeals for the Federal Circuit (exhibit 2.2). The appeals courts have one type of jurisdiction, *appellate*. That means they review cases tried in the federal district courts and cases heard and decided by the federal regulatory commissions mentioned earlier.

Exhibit 2.2
U.S. Court of Appeals Locations

Circuit	Location	States and Territories
District of Columbia	Washington, D.C.	
1st	Boston, San Juan	Maine, Massachusetts, New Hampshire, Rhode Island, Puerto Rico
2nd	New York	New York, Connecticut, Vermont
3rd	Philadelphia, Virgin Islands	Delaware, New Jersey, Pennsylvania, U.S. Virgin Islands
4th	Richmond	Maryland, North Carolina, South Carolina, Virginia, West Virginia
5th	New Orleans, Fort Worth, Houston, Jackson	Louisiana, Mississippi, Texas
6th	Cincinnati	Kentucky, Michigan, Ohio, Tennessee
7th	Chicago	Illinois, Indiana, Wisconsin
8th	St. Louis, Kansas City, Omaha, St. Paul	Arkansas, Iowa, Minnesota, Missouri, Nebraska, North Dakota, South Dakota
9th	San Francisco, Honolulu, Los Angeles, Portland, Seattle	Arizona, California, Hawaii, Idaho, Montana, Nevada, Oregon, Washington, Alaska, Guam and Northern Mariana Islands
10th	Denver, Wichita, Oklahoma City	Colorado, Kansas, New Mexico, Oklahoma, Utah, Wyoming
11th	Atlanta, Jacksonville, Miami, Montgomery, West Palm Beach	Alabama, Florida, Georgia
Federal	Washington, D.C.	

2.1.3. U.S. District Courts

The district courts are the trial courts of the federal court system. Each state has at least one district court, and some of the larger states have as many as four.

A total of 94 district courts cover the 50 states, the District of Columbia, the Commonwealth of Puerto Rico, Guam, the Virgin Islands, and the Northern Mariana Islands (see exhibit 2.3). Each district court has at least one federal district judge, and some have as many as 27.

2.1.4. Administrative Agencies

Rulings made by federal agencies such as the Federal Trade Commission, the Internal Revenue Service, and the National Labor Relations Board fall into the category of administrative law. For a number of reasons, notably specialization, efficiency, and flexibility, Congress and the state legislatures decided to grant certain judicial powers to administrative agencies such as those

Exhibit 2.3
U.S. District Court Locations

Alabama	3 districts (Northern, Middle, and Southern)
Alaska	1 district
Arizona	1 district
Arkansas	2 districts (Eastern and Western)
California	4 districts (Northern, Eastern, Central, and Southern)
Colorado	1 district
Connecticut	1 district
Delaware	1 district
District of Columbia	1 district
Florida	3 districts (Northern, Middle, and Southern)
Georgia	3 districts (Northern, Middle, and Southern)
Guam	1 district
Hawaii	1 district
Idaho	1 district
Illinois	3 districts (Northern, Central, and Southern)
Indiana	2 districts (Northern and Southern)
Iowa	2 districts (Northern and Southern)
Kansas	1 district
Kentucky	2 districts (Eastern and Western)
Louisiana	3 districts (Eastern, Middle, and Western)
Maine	1 district
Maryland	1 district
Massachusetts	1 district
Michigan	2 districts (Eastern and Western)
Minnesota	1 district
Mississippi	2 districts (Northern and Southern)
Missouri	2 districts (Eastern and Western)
Montana	1 district
Nebraska	1 district
Nevada	1 district
New Hampshire	1 district
New Jersey	1 district
New Mexico	1 district
New York	4 districts (Northern, Southern, Eastern, and Western)
North Carolina	3 districts (Eastern, Middle, and Western)
North Dakota	1 district
Northern Mariana Islands	1 district
Ohio	2 districts (Northern and Southern)
Oklahoma	3 districts (Northern, Eastern, and Western)

**Exhibit 2.3
(continued)**

Oregon	1 district
Pennsylvania	3 districts (Eastern, Middle, and Western)
Puerto Rico	1 district
Rhode Island	1 district
South Carolina	1 district
South Dakota	1 district
Tennessee	3 districts (Eastern, Middle, and Western)
Texas	4 districts (Northern, Southern, Eastern, and Western)
Utah	1 district
Vermont	1 district
Virgin Islands	1 district
Virginia	2 districts (Eastern and Western)
Washington	2 districts (Eastern and Western)
West Virginia	2 districts (Northern and Southern)
Wisconsin	2 districts (Eastern and Western)
Wyoming	1 district

**Exhibit 2.4
A Typical State Court System**

named in exhibit 2.1. These agencies are authorized to formulate rules for the administrative area they regulate, enforce the rules, hold hearings on any violations, and issue decisions, including penalties. This delegation of power to adjudicate controversies has been generally held to be constitutional, although the agencies must follow specific guidelines in their administration of these delegated powers. On the federal level, Congress has enacted the Administrative Procedure Act, which sets guidelines for the agencies to follow. Many states have similar state statutes. A party to an administrative law decision can appeal such decisions and sometimes obtain judicial review, depending on the nature of the dispute and whether all administrative remedies have been exhausted. It should be noted that absent of abuse of discretion, courts give great deference to the decisions of administrative agencies. An example of administrative agencies involving themselves with sports is the proposed broadcasting rights deal between DirecTV and Major League Baseball. In 2007, MLB and DirecTV tentatively agreed to a $700 million exclusive television deal for MLB's Extra Innings package, where fans can watch any out of market game, no matter where they live. The Extra Innings package was offered to baseball fans before 2007 on various cable and satellite providers. The proposed deal would force current cable and satellite costumers not with DirecTV to be forced to service their homes with DirecTV if they want the Extra Innings package. About 75 million non-DirecTV costumers have the Extra Innings package, while only 15 million DirecTV costumers own the package. Senator John Kerry (D-Mass.) spoke out against the proposed deal and asked the Federal Communications Commission to investigate the deal. Kerry stated that the proposed deal would deny as many as 5,000 baseball fans from watching their teams since DirecTV cannot reach every American home. FCC Chairman Kevin Martin announced that an investigation would take place in order to determine whether the deal harms television consumers. The deal was later modified in order to allow cable companies to access the baseball package as well.

2.2. THE STATE COURT SYSTEM

In general, state courts are similar in structure to the federal courts; the more important the court, the fewer there are in number. State courts, however, vary widely in nomenclature. In most states there is a three-tiered court system: a trial court level, an appellate level, and a Supreme Court level of review (see exhibit 2.4).

The lowest level of state courts, often referred to as inferior courts, may include the following: magistrate court, municipal court, justice of the peace, traffic court, and county court. Such tribunals handle only minor civil and criminal cases.

The superior courts are general jurisdiction trial courts, which hear the more serious offenses. Most jury trials occur here. Typically, these courts are organized by counties. They hear appeals from the inferior courts and have original jurisdiction over major civil suits and serious crimes. The highest state court, called either the appellate court, state court of appeals, or state supreme court hears appeals from the state superior courts and in some instances has original jurisdiction over particularly important cases. Some of the larger states, such as New York and Pennsylvania, also have intermediate appellate courts.

Each state judicial system hears cases and reviews the law on the basis of its state constitution, state statutes, and court decisions. In addition, a state court often must interpret the federal constitution and/or federal statutes in terms of how they impact state criminal or civil laws that are reviewed under its jurisdiction.

2.3. CIVIL LEGAL PROCESS

For many nonlawyers, a group that includes most athletic administrators, the threat of litigation is a very upsetting proposition, with the potential of great expense. However, with some basic information about how the trial system works, the athletic administrator will be better able to assist counsel.

An athletic administrator should follow these basic guidelines when there is a possibility of a lawsuit:

1. Know your organization's attorney and insurance carrier. If some event occurs that may lead to litigation, inform them immediately so that they can take steps to protect your organization's interests.

2. In preparing for litigation, it is imperative to be completely honest and open about the facts of the case. Be prepared to supply any information or records that are needed for trial.

3. Do not talk to outsiders, especially the media, about the pending litigation.

4. If possible, review any alternatives for possible settlement of the case before it goes to trial.

The civil legal process can be broken down into three major components: pretrial, trial, and posttrial:

I. Pretrial

    a. The Complaint

    b. The Parties

    c. Court Jurisdiction

    d. The Summons

    e. The Answer

    f. Discovery

    g. Pretrial Motions

II. Trial

    a. The Type of Court

    b. The Trial

    c. The Judgment

III. Posttrial

    a. The Appeals Process

2.3.1. The Complaint

The plaintiff files the *complaint*, the initial pleading in a trial, in a civil case, as does the prosecutor (e.g., attorney general, district attorney) in a criminal case.

Clarett v. National Football League, 369 F.3d 124; 2004 U.S. App., is an example of a civil case. The plaintiff, Maurice Clarett, filed a civil complaint against the National Football League (NFL) for violating U.S. antitrust law by preventing him from entering the NFL draft after his sophomore season of college. To illustrate an example of a criminal case, in 2004, the British Columbia attorney general's office issued a criminal complaint against Todd Bertuzzi, a professional hockey player, for assault causing bodily harm. Bertuzzi delivered a blow to Steve Moore's head with his fist and then repeatedly punched Moore's face into the ice once he had fallen

2.3.2. The Parties

The *plaintiff* is a person or party that initiates a legal action by bringing a lawsuit against another person or party. The *defendant* is the person or party against whom relief or recovery is sought in a legal action or lawsuit. The defendant does the defending or denying of the charges brought by the plaintiff. Sometimes another party will be joined in litigation as a *third-party defendant* when its involvement is such as to make its presence at trial imperative. Athletic associations such as the National Collegiate Athletic Association (NCAA) are often named as third-party defendants. For instance, a student-athlete who is suing the school over an eligibility matter often names the NCAA (or athletic governing organization) as a third-party defendant because the NCAA implements or oversees the regulations being enforced by the school against the student-athlete.

2.3.3. Court Jurisdiction

Two types of jurisdiction must be satisfied before a court can hear a case: personal and subject matter. *Personal jurisdiction* means that a court must have sufficient contact with the defendant to bring the defendant into its jurisdiction.

Simply stated, the defendant must have some contact within the boundaries of that court's jurisdiction to be eligible to be brought in for a trial. Some criteria that would be considered by a court to establish personal jurisdiction would be residency, voter registration, driver's license, or business activity. *Subject matter jurisdiction* means that the court must have authority to hear the subject matter that is being tried. For instance, a state court would not be the correct jurisdiction in which to bring a suit involving a federal law, which is within the subject matter jurisdiction of the federal courts.

2.3.4. The Summons

When filing a complaint, the plaintiff must make sure that notice of the legal action being instituted against the defendant is served. The *summons* is the actual serving of notice. The plaintiff (or prosecutor) serves a summons on the defendant ordering the defendant to answer the charge by a certain date. Often the summons is served by a process server or officer of the court, such as a sheriff. Until a complaint is lawfully served to the defendant, a court has no jurisdiction to review the dispute.

2.3.5. The Answer

The *answer* is the defendant's initial pleading on the alleged violation of criminal or civil law. The defendant may deny or admit to the allegations made by the plaintiff and state his or her own facts about the matter in dispute. In some instances, a defendant may file a *counterclaim* against the plaintiff, which essentially means the defendant admits no guilt and, in fact, has been injured by the plaintiff.

2.3.6. Discovery

Discovery is a pretrial procedure by which each party to a lawsuit obtains facts and information about the case from the other parties in order to assist the party's preparation for trial. Discovery is designed to do the following:

1. Discover facts and evidence concerning the case. It apprises the parties to the lawsuit of the nature of the claim to be litigated.
2. Bind the other party to a legal position. It is advantageous for the litigant to have the other party's legal position clearly stated in advance so as to anticipate what legal arguments are likely to be argued and what witnesses and evidence will be introduced at the trial.
3. Seek out weaknesses in the other party's legal position.
4. Preserve testimony that may become unavailable at trial.
5. Narrow the issues in contention.

A party can ascertain information about the case being litigated from the other party to the lawsuit by using a number of methods. The three most common discovery techniques are depositions, interrogatories, and requests for production of documents. A *deposition* is an out-of-court examination of a witness to a lawsuit, under oath, during which questions and answers are recorded by a notary public or court official. An *interrogatory* is a set of written questions sent by one party involved in a lawsuit to another party involved in the litigation. The questions must be answered under oath and must be returned within a specific period. A *request for production of documents* is a request by one party involved in a lawsuit to the other to produce and allow for the inspection of any designated documents. The documents produced must be returned within a specific period.

2.3.7. Pretrial Motions

Pretrial motions are proposed by either side concerning any number of legalities—for example, a motion to dismiss. In a motion, one of the parties to the suit is attempting to gain a better strategic position for the upcoming trial, or trying to have certain procedural matters settled prior to trial. For instance, a defendant may try to make a motion to dismiss because of a lack of sufficient grounds for the suit. Often, a judge will hold a pretrial conference in the judge's chambers in an effort to resolve the dispute or elements of the dispute before trial.

2.3.8. The Type of Court

The *trial court* is the court of original jurisdiction where all issues are brought forth, argued, and decided on by either a judge or a jury. The *appeals court* is the court of review where issues decided at trial are reviewed for error. No new evidence or issues may be entered. Generally, in order to be reviewed, an issue must have been objected to and put on the record at trial.

In the federal court system, original jurisdiction is limited to all criminal cases involving a federal law and civil cases that fall into the following categories:

> Federal Question: Title 28, Section 1331 of the United States Code (a) All civil actions arising under the Constitution, laws, or treaties of the United States Diversity of Citizenship; Amount in Controversy; Costs: Title 28, Section 1332 of the United States Code (a) All civil actions where the amount in controversy exceeds the sum or value of $75,000, exclusive of interest and costs, and is between

1. Citizens of different states
2. Citizens of a state and citizens or subjects of a foreign state
3. Citizens of different states, and citizens or subjects of a foreign state are additional parties
4. A foreign state as plaintiff and citizens of a state or different states

In the state court system, original jurisdiction exists for all state law matters, including disputes among the state's citizens and disputes between one of its citizens and a citizen of another state when the out-of-state party has made itself amendable to the jurisdiction of the suing party's state courts. For example, the NCAA, which is located in Indiana, is often a party in state court actions because it is a national organization with members in all the states and therefore has the requisite contact with each state to make it amenable to each state's jurisdiction.

2.3.9. The Trial

Trials can involve a jury or they can take place without a jury present. Whether a trial will be a jury or a nonjury trial depends on the nature of the trial. Federal criminal cases require a trial by a jury of 12 persons. State criminal cases generally require a jury of no fewer than six persons. If a defendant pleads guilty or waives the right to a jury trial, a jury is not required. In civil cases, a trial by jury is not always required and may be waived. Jury size in civil cases may vary. The state prosecutor in a criminal case or the plaintiff in a civil suit gives the *opening statement* to the court; then the defendant may do the same. The opening statement is designed to alert the triers of fact (either the judge or the jury, depending on the type of trial) to the nature of the case and to the types of evidence that will be presented during trial. Such statements set expectations and, when delivered correctly, can serve as the basis for a persuasive argument that will be presented during the trial.

After the opening statements have been made, the plaintiff (or the prosecutor) presents the case first. The plaintiff calls witnesses and examines them; the witnesses are cross-examined by the defendant (or the defense attorney), redirected by the plaintiff, and recrossed by the defendant. The defendant then presents his or her case and repeats the whole process—that is, the defense calls and examines its witnesses, and these witnesses are cross-examined by the plaintiff. After the witnesses are redirected by the defendant and recrossed by the plaintiff, both parties are allowed to call rebuttal witnesses. At the conclusion of the trial, the defendant (or defense attorney) gives a closing statement first. Then the plaintiff (or prosecutor) gives a closing statement.

2.3.10. The Judgment

After the closing statements when a trial is being argued before a jury, the judge instructs the members of the jury on their options in reaching a decision based on the applicable state and/or federal law or laws. These instructions can be quite involved and are often a subject of appeal by the losing party. Case law and precedent are noted in the instructions. If any statutes are involved, they are read to the jury. After deliberation, the jury renders a decision. In a trial without a jury, the judge can either recess the court while reaching a decision or render a decision immediately on completion of closing statements. Some decisions are given orally; others are written.

2.3.11. The Appeals Process

Many judgments by trial courts are *appealed*—that is, the party who lost the case requests that the trial proceedings be reviewed by a higher court in the hope that the decision will be reversed. Among the reasons allowed for an appeal are the following:

1. The plaintiff did not have an opportunity to state his or her case at trial.
2. Evidence was incorrectly allowed into or disallowed at the trial.
3. The judge interpreted the law incorrectly.

The party who takes an appeal from one court to another is called the *appellant*. The party in a case against whom an appeal is taken—the winning party at trial—is called the *appellee*. In an appeals procedure, no new jury, no new witnesses, and no new facts are allowed to be introduced. The basis for appeal is the record, which may include copies of the testimony, exhibits, and any other evidence introduced at trial.

Attorneys for the appellant and the appellee may appear before the court, argue their cases, and submit briefs. An appeals court may *reverse* (disagree with) a lower court's ruling totally or in part. It may *remand* (return) the case back to the lower court for further proceeding or it may *affirm* (agree with) the lower court's decision. After a decision has been rendered, the case may be appealed again to either a state supreme court or the U.S. Supreme Court, depending on what court system is involved. (State supreme court cases involving a federal question—for example, a constitutional law claim—may in some circumstances be appealed to the U.S. Supreme Court.)

NOTES

1. The glossary in this book contains a list of some of the legal and sports-related abbreviations used frequently in this text and in reported case decisions.

2. In any research involving a legal issue, or in preparation for litigation, an athletic administrator should attempt to answer some basic questions, including the following:

- Who are the plaintiffs in the case?
- Who are the defendants in the case?
- What are the legal theories of the plaintiffs?
- What are the defenses raised by the defendants?
- Is it state or federal court?
- Is it an administrative agency?
- Is it a decision on a pretrial motion?

- Is it a trial or appellate-level decision?
- What issue or issues did the judge have to decide in the case?
- For whom did the judge rule?
- What was the rationale for the judge's ruling?
- What is the impact of the case?
- Does the decision set any case precedent?

2.4. SOURCES OF LEGAL INFORMATION

It may be helpful for someone to locate legal information to supplement certain legal concepts. The following are different sources for locating legal information: legal dictionaries, research guides, annotated law reports, restatements, *Shepard's Citations*, computer services, directories, encyclopedias, indexes, treatises, guides, law reviews, state and federal constitutions and legislation, federal administrative rules and regulations, and case law.

2.4.1. Legal Reference Materials

2.4.1.1. Legal Dictionaries

Legal dictionaries contain definitions of words and functions that are commonly used in the legal system in the United States and other common law jurisdictions such as Great Britain, Canada, and Australia. The following are three useful legal dictionaries:

1. *Black's Law Dictionary*, 9th ed. (St. Paul, MN: West Group, 2009)
2. *Oran's Dictionary of the Law*, 9th ed. (Albany, NY: West Legal Studies, 2009)
3. *Webster's New World Law Dictionary* (Hoboken, NJ: John Wiley, 2006)

2.4.1.2. Legal Research Guides

Legal research guides are texts that explain how to conduct legal research. They include instruction on different sources of law and how best to utilize the sources. The following are legal research guides that will be helpful:

1. Miles O. Price and Harry Bitner, *Effective Legal Research* (Buffalo, NY: William S. Hein, 1999). This guide is considered to be the most comprehensive, basic manual on legal research methods. It is clear and concise while providing in-depth descriptions of legal research sources.
2. Steven M. Barkan, Roy M. Mersky, and Donald J. Dunn, *Fundamentals of Legal Research*, 9th ed. (Mineola, NY: Foundation Press, 2009)
3. Morris C. Cohen and Kent C. Olson, *Legal Research in a Nutshell*, 8th ed., Nutshell Series (St. Paul, MN: West/Wadsworth, 2003). A condensed guide that briefs the reader on how to perform legal research. This book may be most appropriate for the athletic administrator's introduction to legal research material.
4. Stephen Elias and Susan Levinkind, *Legal Research: How to Find and Understand the Law*, 13th ed. (Berkeley, CA: Nolo Press, 2005)
5. Amy E. Sloan, *Basic Legal Research Tools and Strategies*, 3rd ed. (New York, NY: Aspen, 2006)

2.4.1.3. Annotated Law Reports

The *American Law Reports* (*ALR*) gives comprehensive annotations on legal subject matters. It consists of five series. An *annotation* is a commentary on how a particular legal subject developed and the current status of the law on that subject. The annotations in the *ALR* often include a list of cases that have discussed the point of law that the annotation explains. For a good example of an *ALR* annotation, see "Tort Liability of Public Schools and Institutions of Higher Learning for Accidents Occurring during School Athletic Events," 68 *ALR* 5th 663.

2.4.1.4. Legal Encyclopedias

Legal encyclopedias are texts designed to give the reader a broad view of the law on any given legal subject. The following are two of the best:

1. *Corpus Juris Secundum* (*CJS*) (St. Paul, MN: West, 1936–current date). *CJS* was initially intended to be a compilation of the entire body of American law; however, its new subtitle, *A Contemporary Statement of American Law as Derived from Reported Cases and Legislation*, indicates that it no longer references every case. There are over 150 actual volumes of this text.
2. *West's Encyclopedia of American Law* (St. Paul, MN: West, 2005)

2.4.1.5. Restatements of the Law

The *Restatements of the Law* are produced by communities of distinguished judges, law professors, and lawyers and provide the reader with a "black letter" rule in specific legal areas such as torts, agency, contract, trusts, and property. In addition, the *Restatements* provide case authority and cross-reference to *ALR* annotations. The following in an example of a *Restatement of the Law: Restatement of the Law, Agency* (St. Paul, MN: American Law Institute, 1958–1999).

2.4.1.6. Treatises

Sport law books are texts designed to give the user legal information on one particular legal subject. Some sport law books are as follows:

1. Michael J. Cozzillio and Mark S. Levinstein, *Sports Law: Cases and Materials*, 2nd ed. (Durham, NC: Carolina Academic Press, 2007)
2. Doyice Cotten and John Wolohan, *Law for Recreation and Sport Managers*, 4th ed. (Dubuque, IA: Kendall/Hunt, 2007)
3. Linda Sharp, Anita Moorman, and Cathryn Claussen, *Sports Law: A Managerial Approach* (Scottsdale, AZ: Holcomb Hathaway, 2007)
4. Raymond Yasser, James McCurdy, C. Peter Gopeland, and M. Arellano Weston, *Sports Law Cases and Materials*, 6th ed. (Newark, NJ: Lexis, 2006)
5. Matthew Mitten, Timothy Davis, Rodney Smith, and Robert Berry, *Sports Law and Regulation*, 2nd ed. (New York: Aspen, 2009)

6. Walter Champion, *Fundamentals of Sports Law*, 2nd ed. and suppl. (Eugan, MN: Thompson West, 2004, 2010)

7. Paul Weiler and Gary Roberts, *Sports and the Law*, 3rd ed. (St. Paul, MN: West Group, 2003)

8. *Understanding Business and Legal Aspects of the Sports Industry* (New York: Practicing Law Institute, 2000)

9. Michael E. Jones, *Sports Law* (Upper Saddle River, NJ: Prentice-Hall, 1999)

10. Martin Greenberg and James Gray, *Sports Law Practice*, 2nd ed. and suppl. (Charlottesville, VA: Lexis Law, 1998, 2000)

11. Aaron Wise and Bruce Meyer, *International Sports Law and Business*, vols. 1–3. (Boston, MA: Kluwer Law International, 1997)

12. Doyice Cotten and Mary Cotten, *Legal Aspects of Waivers in Sport, Recreation, and Fitness Activities* (Canton, OH: PRC, 1997)

13. Robert C. Berry and Glenn M. Wong, *Law and Business of Sports Industries*, vols. 1 and 2 (Westport, CT: Praeger, 1993)

14. Berry, Robert C., William B. Gould, and Paul D. Staudohar, *Labor Relations in Professional Sports* (Dover, MA: Auburn House, 1986)

15. John C. Weinstart and Cym H. Lowell, *The Law of Sports* (Indianapolis, IN: Bobbs, 1978)

2.4.1.7. Legal Indexes

Legal indexes are lists of articles that contain information on legal subjects, case decisions, and general legal information that has been published in law reviews and other legal periodicals. The following are legal indexes:

1. *Index to Legal Periodicals* (Bronx, NY: H. W. Wilson, 1908–current date). Includes periodicals published in the United States, Canada, Great Britain, Ireland, Australia, and New Zealand and is therefore comprehensive in nature. The index is available in print, on Wilson Web, on Wilson Disk, and on CD-ROM.

2. *Index to Periodical Articles Related to Law* (Dobbs Ferry, NY: Glanville, 1958–current date). Contains articles that appear to be of value and are not covered by the *Index to Legal Periodicals.* This index is useful in locating newly developing areas of law.

3. *Current Law Index (CLI)* (Foster City, CA: Information Access, 1980–current date). This index is issued monthly and provides access to over 900 legal and law-related periodicals.

4. *Legaltrac* (Farmington Hills, MI: Gale Group, 1980–current date) is a CD-ROM database that indexes approximately 875 legal periodicals published in the United States, Canada, the United Kingdom, Australia, and other major English-speaking countries and is updated monthly.

2.4.1.8. Law Review Articles

Law reviews, published by law schools and administered by a student editorial board, contain current or historical articles that relate to the study of law and lawmaking (e.g., legal, legislative, entertainment, and sport law). A school usually publishes a general law review (e.g., *Boston College Law Review*) and many opt to publish additional reviews of specific areas of the law (e.g., *Seton Hall Journal of Sports and Entertainment Law*).

Law reviews are designed to add to the process of developing a better understanding of law and the legal process. This is accomplished by reviewing cases and the impact of decisions, analyzing the legal reasoning behind court decisions, reviewing legislative enactments, proposing reforms, and reviewing legal writings through book reviews. The following notes are examples of general law review articles and sport specific articles in sports law review journals (see notes 1–4 and 5–8).

NOTES

Law Review Articles

1. Richard L. Aynes, "Unintended Consequences of the Fourteenth Amendment and What They Tell Us about Its Interpretation," 39 *Akron Law Review* 289 (2006).

2. Daniel P. O'Gorman, "Looking Out for Your Employees: Employers' Surreptitious Physical Surveillance of Employees and the Tort of Invasion of Privacy," 85 *Nebraska Law Review* 212 (2006).

3. Honorable William G. Young, "Vanishing Trials, Vanishing Juries, Vanishing Constitution," 40 *Suffolk University Law Review* 67 (2006).

4. Alex Geisinger and Michael Ashley Stein, "A Theory of Expressive International Law," 60 *Vanderbilt Law Review* 77 (2007).

Sports Law Journal Articles

1. Benjamin A. Tulis, "Final-Offer 'Baseball' Arbitration: Contexts, Mechanics, & Applications," 20 *Seton Hall Journal of Sports & Entertainment Law* 85 (2010).

2. Matheieu Fournier and Dominic Roux, "Labor Relations in the National Hockey League: A Model of Transnational Collective Bargaining?" 20 *Marquette Sports Law Review* 147 (2009).

3. Glenn M. Wong and Chris Deubert, "The Legal and Business Aspects of Career-Ending Disability Insurance Policies in Professional and College Sports," 19 *Villanova Sports and Entertainment Law Journal* 101 (2010).

4. Diane Heckman, "Title IX and Sexual Harassment Claims Involving Educational Athletic Department Employees and Student-Athletes in the Twenty-First Century," 8 *Virginia Sports and Entertainment Law Journal* 193 (2009).

2.4.1.9. Shepard's Citations

Citators are used to research reported case decisions to determine whether the case being researched has been cited as authority by another court or whether a reported case has been overruled, modified, or questioned in a later decision.

They provide a complete history of any case since it was first reported. *Shepard's Citations* are available in print or online via Lexis-Nexis, a legal computer service (see later). KeyCite is the other major citation service. It is only available online through Westlaw, another legal computer service (see later).

2.4.1.10. Legal Computer Services

Legal computer services offer subscribers access through remote terminals to federal and state court decisions, annotated reports, statutes, law reviews, and so forth. They generally are the most up-to-date source for legal information. While students, professors, and administrators may have access to Lexis-Nexis through the school library, unfortunately, the services are not readily available to the layperson. Furthermore, they are expensive and require some training to use. The two major legal computer services are Lexis-Nexis (New York: Mead Data Central) and Westlaw (St. Paul, MN: West).

The use of the Internet has emerged as a powerful tool for conducting legal research. The following are some resources that may be useful to access federal and state-related information:

1. The Federal Judicial Center: http://www.fjc.gov/
2. U.S. Court Finder: http://www.uscourts.gov/courtlinks/
3. Federal Agencies Directory: http://www.lib.lsu.edu/gov/fedgov.html
4. State Court Web Sites: http://www.ncsc.org

2.4.1.11. Sports Law Newsletters

Sports law newsletters are publications that discuss various sports law legal concepts. The newsletters may discuss recent cases in the sports law industry or current events that are affecting sports legislation and policy. Other newsletters may discuss a specific aspect of sports law such as risk management or facility management. These newsletters are products of various legal sources including bar associations and other legal organizations. Many newsletters are available on-line and in print as well. The following are some of the most popular and useful sports law newsletters:

1. The National Sports Law Institute of Marquette University Law School publishes several sport law newsletters:

    a. *For the Record*: A quarterly print newsletter that discusses current events in sports law

    b. *Sports Facility Reports*: A semiannual online newsletter regarding sports facility legal issues

    c. *You Make the Call*: A biannual newsletter that examines the most recent sport law cases; for more information, see http://law.marquette.edu

2. *From the Gym to the Jury*: A bimonthly online newsletter that examines sports risk management concerns; for more information, see: http://www.gym2jury.com

3. *The Sports Lawyers*: An online newsletter produced by the Sports Lawyers Association regarding items that affect lawyers specializing in sport; for more information, see http://www.sportslaw.org/publications/newsletter.cfm

4. *Entertainment and Sports Lawyer*: A quarterly print newsletter by the American Bar Association that includes articles by current authorities on various legal concepts affecting sports attorneys; for more information, see http://www.abanet.org/forums/entsports/publications/home.shtml

5. *SRLA Newsletter*: An online newsletter published six times per year by the Sport and Recreation Law Association pertaining to general sports law issues; for more information, see http://law.marquette.edu/cgi-bin/site.pl?2130&pageID=1687

6. *Hackney Publications:* Online publications that explore the legal side of sports, including *Legal Issues in College Athletics, Sport Litigation Alert, Legal Issues in High School Athletics* and *Professional Sports and the Law.*

2.4.1.12. Sports Law Web Sites

Sports law Web sites are online tools that can help find specific information regarding sports law issues and current events. These Web sites can be professional sport league player associations that provide information on athlete management and the most current collective bargaining agreement. Other sport law Web sites are created by different legal associations and organizations that are devoted to studying and exploring sports law concepts. Some important sport law Web sites follow:

1. American Bar Association Forum on the Entertainment and Sports Industries: http://www.abanet.org/forums/entsports/home.html
2. Steroid Law: http://www.steroidlaw.com
3. Centre for Sport and the Law: http://www.sportlaw.ca
4. International Association of Sports Law: http://www.iasl.org
5. Marquette University Law School National Sports Law Institute: http://law.marquette.edu/cgi-bin/site.pl?2130&pageID=160
6. Sport and Recreation Law Association: http://srlaweb.org
7. Sports Lawyers Association: http://www.sportslaw.org
8. Sports Law Blog: http://sports-law.blogspot.com
9. Court of Arbitration for Sport: http://www.tas-cas.org
10. NFL Players Association: http://www.nflpa.org
11. MLB Players Association: http://mlbplayers.com
12. NBA Players Association: http://www.nbpa.com
13. NHL Players Association: http://www.nhlpa.com

2.4.2. Constitutions

A constitution is the written instrument that serves as the ultimate source of legal authority by which a government and the courts derive their power to govern and adjudicate. The courts in the United States use the federal Constitution or a state constitution as the source for interpreting whether enacted laws are constitutional and whether individual rights granted to citizens are legal. The laws and actions of a government must be consistent with the constitution of that government to be considered legal. A constitution may not always contain language that specifically covers every governmental action, and in such instances, the courts must interpret the constitution broadly to include certain governmental actions that are not specifically covered in the constitution. Constitutions can be amended. The following are online resources for exploring federal and state constitutions:

1. Constitution of the United States: http://www.gpoaccess.gov/constitution/index.html
2. U.S. state constitutions: http://www.constitution.org/cons/usstcons.htm

2.4.3. Legislation

Legislation is the process by which laws are enacted. Laws created by this process are also referred to as *statutes*. Federal legislation is enacted by the U.S. Congress. Very little federal legislation is geared specifically to amateur athletics.

One notable exception is the Ted Stevens Olympic and Amateur Sports Act (36 U.S.C. §§ 220501–220529 Supp. IV 1998), which governs some of the operation of amateur athletics, especially the U.S. Olympic efforts, in the United States. It should be noted that non-sport-specific legislation may be applied to athletics.

An example is Title IX, which governs education and applies to athletics because athletics pertains to the educational mission of an institution. Bills can be introduced by individual representatives or senators or groups of commissioned representatives or senators. Copies of pending legislation can be obtained by writing to the following addresses (enclose a self-addressed, gummed return label):

Senate Document Room	House Document Room
B04 Hart Senate Office Bldg.	B18 Ford House Office Building
Washington, DC 20510	Washington, DC 20515
(202) 228-2815	(202) 226-5200
http://www.senate.gov	http://www.hdocs@hr.house.gov

The public may receive up to six different items per request, but only one request will be filled per day. Also, only one copy of an individual item will be distributed at a time. When legislation is enacted and first issued, it is called a *slip law*. Once a session of Congress ends, all the slip laws are published as a group and called *U.S. Statutes at Large*. This is a chronological list of legislation that has been enacted. Every six years, the *U.S. Statutes at Large* is codified—that is, arranged by subject—and published as the *United States Code* (U.S.C.). The *United States Code* includes the public and permanent laws in effect, arranged alphabetically under 50 different titles. The annotated codes are also published by private firms; for example, the *United States Code Annotated* (U.S.C.A.) is published by West Group, and the *United States Code Service* (U.S.C.S.) is published by Lexis Law.

State legislation is enacted by the legislature in each state. As with federal legislation, very little state legislation is geared specifically to athletics. However, one example is Utah's Uniform Athlete Agents Act (15-9-101), which regulates athletes or sports agents. On the state level, bills are also introduced by individual legislators or groups of legislators. Copies of legislation can usually be obtained from the legislators or from the state office that handles legislative services. Each state publishes all the laws that it has passed in a given year. These are called *session laws*. Session laws are compiled into statutes, which may be single or multivolume editions. Annotated editions are usually available from private publishing companies.

2.4.4. Federal Administrative Rules and Regulations

Federal administrative rules and regulations attempt to translate enacted laws into practices that must be followed in order to comply with the law. For instance, when Congress enacted Title IX of the Education Amendments of 1972—a federal statute that prohibited gender discrimination in education (see Chapter 8)—the Department of Health, Education, and Welfare had to develop rules and regulations to be followed in order to comply with the new law.

2.4.5. Case Law

Although this book is not written as a case law text, case law is often cited to give the athletic administrator a better understanding of a legal point in sports law by providing an actual set of circumstances tried before a court. In the notes sections, case law is provided to give the athletic administrator a source for further information on a sports law subject.

A case law citation consists of a case title and a case citation. The case title explicitly identifies the persons or parties involved. The case citation includes the publication in which the decision can be found, the volume and the page number in the corresponding reporter, the court that made the decision, and the year the case was decided.

The best reference for checking the correct form for legal decisions or writings is the *Blue Book: A Uniform System of Citation*, 18th ed. (Cambridge, MA: Harvard Law Review Association, 2005). Case decisions and opinions are reported in different legal sources depending on the jurisdiction of the court that decided the case, as is illustrated later.

2.4.5.1. U.S. Supreme Court

All opinions that result from a Supreme Court case are reported in the following print and online publications:

1. *United States Reports* (official reporter), Washington, USGPO; cited U.S.
2. *Supreme Court Reporter* (St. Paul, MN: West, 1939–1957), cited S.Ct. Replaced by *United States Supreme Court Reports*.
3. *United States Supreme Court Reports*, lawyers' edition (Rochester, NY: Lawyers Cooperative Publishing, 1956–1997), cited L.Ed. or L.Ed.2d. Replaced by *United States Reports*. *Supreme Court Reporter* and *United States Supreme Court Reports* are unofficial reporters. Most lawyers and researchers use the unofficial sets because they include editorial features known as annotations, which are explanatory comments about the issues and holding of the opinion.
4. *United States Law Week* (Washington, DC: Bureau of National Affairs), cited U.S.L.W. The publication is composed of two loose-leaf volumes; one contains the current opinions of the U.S. Supreme Court and the other volume deals with matters that do not relate to the U.S. Supreme Court.
5. FindLaw (Thompson, 1994–2010), http://www.findlaw.com/casecode/supreme. html. This online research tool displays Supreme Court opinions from 1893 to the present.

2.4.5.2. U.S. Courts of Appeals

Decisions of the appeals courts (also called appellate courts) are reported in the *Federal Reporter* (Minneapolis, MN: West) and are cited F., F. 2d, or F. 3d,

Exhibit 2.5
Regional Reporters

Pacific Reporter (P. or P.2d)	Alaska, Arizona, California, Colorado Hawaii, Idaho, Kansas, Montana, Nevada, New Mexico, Oklahoma, Oregon, Utah, Washington, and Wyoming
North Western Reporter (N.W. or N.W. 2d)	Iowa, Michigan, Minnesota, Nebraska, North Dakota, South Dakota, and Wisconsin
South Western Reporter (S.W. or S.W. 2d)	Arkansas, Kentucky, Missouri, Tennessee, and Texas
North Eastern Reporter (N.E. or N.E. 2d)	Illinois, Indiana, Massachusetts, New York, and Ohio
Atlantic Reporter (A. or A. 2d)	Connecticut, Delaware, Maine, Maryland, New Hampshire, New Jersey, Pennsylvania, Rhode Island, Vermont, and District of Columbia Municipal Court of Appeals
South Eastern Reporter (S.E. or S.E. 2d)	Georgia, North Carolina, South Carolina, Virginia, and West Virginia
Southern Reporter (So. or So. 2d)	Alabama, Florida, Louisiana, and Mississippi

Exhibit 2.6
Case Citation

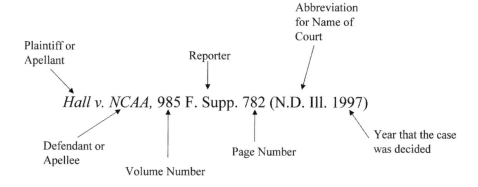

depending on the date of the court decision. The *Federal Reporter* has now limited the number of published opinions because of the caseload.

2.4.5.3. U.S. District Courts

Select decisions of the district courts are reported in the *Federal Supplement* (Minneapolis, MN: West) and are cited F. Supp. or F. Supp. 2d. In a district court opinion, the district involved is always included as a part of the citation. For example, D.N.J. 2001 is the citation for District of New Jersey, 2001. When there is more than one federal district court in a state, the particular district involved in the decision is cited. For example, S.D.N.Y. 2001 is the citation for Southern District of New York, 2001, which differentiates it from the Northern District of New York, 2001, or N.D.N.Y. 2001.

On the trial level of review, a case citation usually notes the plaintiff first and the defendant second. For example, in *Rodriquez v. Topps Co.*, 104 F. Supp. 2d 1224 (S.D.Cal. 2000), Rodriquez is the plaintiff and Topps Co. is the defendant.

2.4.5.4. State Courts

State court decisions can be reported (although only a small percentage are) in a state or regional collection of reports called a *reporter*. A regional reporter groups decisions from a number of states in one publication. The regional reporters as a group are termed the *National Reporter System*, which is published by West and includes West's federal law reports and some additional special court reporters. The *National Reporter System* provides a quick method of making the opinions of the state courts known to the public. The seven regional reporters are listed in exhibit 2.5. The main components of a case citation are illustrated in exhibit 2.6.

Chapter 3

LEGAL PRINCIPLES
IN TORT LAW

3.1. The Tort of Negligence
    3.1.1. Duty of Care Owed
        3.1.1.1. Reasonable Person Standard
        3.1.1.2. Standard of Care for Children
    3.1.2. Breach of Duty Owed
        3.1.2.1. Violation of a Statute, Negligence *Per Se*
        3.1.2.2. *Res Ipsa Loquitur*
    3.1.3. Actual and Proximate Causation
    3.1.4. Damages
    3.1.5. Defenses for Negligence
        3.1.5.1. No Negligence
        3.1.5.2. Contributory Negligence
        3.1.5.3. Comparative Negligence
        3.1.5.4. Assumption of Risk
        3.1.5.5. Statute of Limitations
        3.1.5.6. Immunity and Good Samaritan Statutes
    3.1.6. Wrongful Death Statutes

3.2. The Tort of Reckless Misconduct (Gross Negligence)

3.3. Intentional Torts
    3.3.1. The Tort of Assault
    3.3.2. The Tort of Battery
    3.3.3. Defenses for Assault and Battery

3.3.3.1. Consent
3.3.3.2. Privilege
3.3.4. Tortious Interference with Contractual Relations
3.3.5. The Tort of Intentional Infliction of Emotional Distress
3.3.6. Damages for Intentional Torts

3.4. Harm to Economic and Dignitary Interests
    3.4.1. Defamation Law
        3.4.1.1. Libel
        3.4.1.2. Slander
    3.4.2. The Tort of Invasion of Privacy

3.5. Products Liability Law
    3.5.1. Products Liability Based on Intent
    3.5.2. Products Liability Based on Negligence
    3.5.3. Products Liability Based on Strict Tort Liability
    3.5.4. Products Liability Based on Implied and Express Warranties

3.6. Vicarious Liability
    3.6.1. Exception: Independent Contractors

3.7. Workers' Compensation

INTRODUCTION

Tort law is an important area of sports law. There has been an increase in the number of cases filed based on intentional or unintentional tort theories over the past several decades. There are many reasons for this increase, including the astronomical rise in medical costs that injured athletes or other plaintiffs are unable to meet, along with a prevailing notion that one who injures deliberately or negligently should pay for such actions when he or she creates serious harm.

Civil law provides injured individuals with a cause of action by which they may be compensated or "made whole" through the recovery of damages. This cause of action comes under the general heading of torts. A *tort* is a private (or civil) wrong or injury, suffered by an individual as the result of another person's conduct. Tort law deals with the allocation of losses via monetary compensation of the individual for injuries sustained as a result of another's conduct.

Civil law and criminal law share the common end of inducing people to act for the benefit of society by preventing behavior that negatively affects society and by encouraging behavior that has a positive effect. Civil law and criminal law differ, however, in their means of achieving this common end. Criminal law seeks to protect the public from harm through the punishment of conduct likely to cause harm. Civil law, on the other hand, aims to compensate an injured party for the harm suffered as a result of another person's conduct.

Criminal actions emphasize the immorality or bad intentions of the defendants. Tort actions, on the other hand, seek to achieve desirable social results by resolving the conflicting interests of individuals. Society tends to distinguish criminal wrongs by condemning or judging the morality of the criminal more severely than that of the tortious wrongdoer. Once a crime has been discovered, the state or a subdivision of the state (e.g., county), in its capacity as protector of the public interest, brings an action against the accused. In a tort action, however, the injured party institutes the action as an individual in an effort to recover damages to compensate for the injury.

Several common problems are involved in the majority of sports-related tort cases. The first is the difficulty of determining exactly what a tort is in an athletic context. The second is that a public policy consideration is also involved, since it has been suggested in several court decisions that court interference with sports will destroy athletics and unreasonably restrict the free play of sports. The third common problem is that litigation may discourage participation in the more dangerous sports. For these reasons, athletic administrators must be aware of the legal principles involved in tort liability relating to sports so that they can be better prepared to take preventive measures that will minimize the adverse effects of such litigation.

For this purpose it is important to distinguish between intentional and unintentional torts. The responsibility of distinguishing between intentional and unintentional torts lies with the court because the court determines the manner in which it will assess the case. The degree of the defendant's intent toward the plaintiff (intent of harm) can be differentiated on the following three levels:

1. Intentional tort (e.g., assault and battery): intent to commit the act and intent to harm the plaintiff

2. Reckless misconduct or gross negligence: intent to commit the act but no intent to harm the plaintiff

3. Unintentional tort or negligence: no intent to commit the act and no intent to harm the plaintiff but a failure to exercise reasonable care

Reckless misconduct (also called gross negligence) falls somewhere between intentional torts and ordinary negligence. It differs from negligence in degree rather than in substance. The court may view a single act either as negligent or as grossly negligent, depending on the state of mind of the actor.

Unintentional and intentional torts are the most common tort actions in the sports setting. *Negligence*, an unintentional tort; *reckless misconduct*, somewhere between intentional and unintentional torts; and *assault and battery*, intentional torts, are therefore emphasized in the first part of the chapter. The section on intentional torts includes a discussion of *tortious interference with contractual relations*, a tort that recognizes a cause of action against one who intentionally induces another to breach a contract. The less common torts of *invasion of privacy* and *intentional infliction of emotional distress* are followed by a discussion of defamation law and the issues of *libel* and *slander*. The chapter then discusses *products liability law*, a growth area in sports because it allows a party who has been injured by a product (e.g., sports equipment) that is defectively designed, manufactured, or distributed to recover damages. The doctrine of *vicarious liability*, often used in tort cases to sue an employer for the negligence of employees, is presented next. Finally, the chapter concludes with an examination of *workers' compensation* issues present in amateur athletics.

3.1. THE TORT OF NEGLIGENCE

Negligence is an unintentional tort that focuses on an individual's conduct or actions. Accordingly, negligence is distinguished from intentional torts, which focus on the individual's state of mind or intent. *Negligent conduct* is defined as the failure to use ordinary care and caution, as would be expected by a prudent person, for the protection of others against an unreasonably great risk of harm. The ability of the injured party to sue and to recover damages for negligence is based on the idea that one who acts should anticipate the consequences of those actions that might involve unreasonable danger to others.

A person must take precautions only against unreasonable risks of harm. Unreasonable risks are those whose danger is apparent or should be apparent to one in the position of the actor. The law, however, does not seek to burden the freedom of human action with excessive or unreasonable demands and restraints.

Therefore, one is not expected to guard against situations or occurrences that are unlikely. The reasonable person standard measures the standard of care required. The reasonable person is one who selects a course of action that would be selected by an ordinary, prudent person residing in the affected community under the same conditions. The law excuses all persons from liability for accidents that are either unavoidable or unforeseeable. The following four elements must be proven by the plaintiff in order to sustain a negligence claim:

1. Duty of care owed by the defendant
2. Breach of that duty by the defendant
3. Actual and proximate causation
4. Damages

3.1.1. Duty of Care Owed

The plaintiff in a negligence case must initially establish the duty of care owed to him or her by the defendant. Duty is divided into two categories: a duty to act and a duty not to act in an unreasonable manner. A *duty of care* is an obligation, recognized by law, that requires an individual or a group to conform to a particular standard of conduct toward another. A general duty of care governs all activities. A person engaged in an activity has a legal duty to act as an ordinarily, prudent, reasonable person and thereby take precautions against creating unreasonable risks of injury to other persons. A person need only take precautions against foreseeable risks of injury. Other factors, such as statutes or status of the parties (e.g., doctor or coach), may limit or extend this general duty.

The duty of care required of an individual is established by reference to any special qualifications. In the case of a professional (e.g., doctor or trainer), a duty of care is determined by uniform requirements that establish minimum standards of behavior. All professionals are judged not as individuals in society at large but as members of a specified class. When acting in a professional capacity, the professional person will be judged by the standards of the profession in the same or similar communities.

The concept of *legal duty* is based on the relationship that exists between the parties involved. Certain relationships, such as employer-employee, principal-agent, teacher-student, and coach-athlete, establish a legal duty to act. An employer, for example, has the duty to render aid and assistance to an employee who is injured during the course of employment. However, absent a duty imposing relationship, an individual is not liable for an omission to act.

A moral obligation to act does not create a legal duty to act and hence the individual who failed to act cannot be held liable for negligence. If one without a duty to act does undertake to act, however, that person may be held liable if he or she acts negligently. By acting, one can create a duty between oneself and another that may not have previously existed. For example, a person who undertakes to rescue another may not abandon the rescue attempt if it becomes inconvenient. By acting, the would-be rescuer has created a duty to continue to aid the person in trouble.

In sports cases the duty is often described as the "reasonable care" necessary to avoid creating risks that may result in injuries to players or spectators. For example, Peter Perry suffered a serious neck injury in a high school football practice. Coach Foot attempted to provide medical assistance. In doing so, he became responsible for causing further damage that left Peter paralyzed. Peter may prevail in a negligence suit against the coach if the court finds that Coach Foot had a duty to act and breached that duty by not acting as a "reasonable football coach" would have acted in this situation, causing actual damage.

The determination of a legal duty will rest on whether the court designates the act or non-act as misfeasance, nonfeasance, or malfeasance. *Misfeasance* is the term applied to lawful conduct that is improperly done. *Nonfeasance* is an omission of an action that ought to be taken. *Malfeasance* is the doing of an act that is wholly wrongful and unlawful.

NOTES _____

1. In *Kavanagh v. Trustees of Boston University*, 795 N.E.2d 1170 (Mass. 2003), the Supreme Judicial Court of Massachusetts found that a university's duty to protect its own recruited scholarship athletes from harm does not extend to student-athletes from other schools. Consequently, Boston University owed no duty of care to protect a Manhattan College basketball player from a punch thrown by a Boston University player when the latter had previously shown no violent tendencies.

2. In *Allen v. Dover Co-Recreational Softball League*, 807 A.2d 1274 (N.H. 2002), the Supreme Court of New Hampshire ruled that the defendants, including the sponsors of a recreational softball league, team sponsors, an insurance company, the field owner, and an infielder on one team, owed no duty to protect a player on another team from the ordinary risks of participation in the game. As a result, the plaintiff could not recover for brain damage caused by an errantly thrown softball.

3. In *Davidson v. University of North Carolina at Chapel Hill*, 543 S.E.2d 920 (N.C. Ct. App. 2001), the Court of Appeals of North Carolina ruled that a special relationship existed between the University of North Carolina and its school-sponsored junior varsity cheerleading squad. This relationship imposed an affirmative duty of care on the university to provide for the cheerleaders' safety during practice, when the plaintiff suffered severe head injuries resulting from a 13 foot fall.

4. In *Boyd v. Texas Christian University, Inc.*, 8 S.W.3d 758 (Tex. App. 1999), a student at a private university and his parents sued the university after the student was seriously injured in a fight at an off-campus bar with four football scholarship athletes attending the same university. The Court of Appeals held that the university owed the student no duty to control student-athletes during an off-campus event that was not organized or sponsored by the university, and the university did not have a duty to protect students at an off-campus bar.

5. In *Kleinknecht v. Gettysburg College*, 989 F.2d 1360 (3rd Cir. 1993), the litigants confront the issue of a college's duty of care to recruited college athletes who become injured during participation in their sports. The issue of reasonable care is relevant because an institution has a greater duty of care for recruited athletes who are engaging in their recruited activity than it has to students under normal circumstances. The appellate court reversed the district court's holding that the college acted reasonably and also dismissed the district court's holding that the college was entitled to immunity under the Good Samaritan law.

3.1.1.1. Reasonable Person Standard

Even if a particular relationship does not exist between parties, a person owes to others the duty of exercising reasonable care in his or her activities. The courts "measure" the conduct in each negligence case against the "reasonable person" standard—that is, how a person of ordinary sense, using ordinary care and skill, would react under similar circumstances. It is important to note that the conduct of the "reasonable person" is not necessarily "perfect" conduct but is that of a prudent and careful individual. As employed by the courts, the standard of reasonableness takes into account the risk apparent to an actor, the capacity of the actor to meet the risk, and the circumstances under which the person confronts that risk.

The "reasonable person" possesses the level of knowledge common to the community in which the injury occurs. A negligent defendant who possesses superior knowledge, skill, or intelligence will be held to a greater degree of care—that is, conduct that conforms to that of others with similar knowledge and/or skill. For example, a team doctor performing a procedure on an athlete on the playing field would be held to the same standard of skill and conduct exhibited by other team doctors in the same specialty performing a similar procedure.

When the reasonable person standard entails a degree of skill or knowledge higher than that of a judge or layperson sitting on a jury, qualified expert testimony is utilized to establish the proper standard of care for the defendant.

Again, using the case of a team doctor sued for negligence, both parties would probably call as witnesses other qualified team doctors to testify as to how the procedure is usually performed and what precautions or steps are taken under normal circumstances. This expert testimony would help establish the appropriate standard of care. The jury would then determine whether the defendant doctor met that standard of care.

The reasonable person is deemed to possess physical characteristics identical to those of the defendant. If the actor is exceptionally strong, for example, the standard of care demands that the person exhibit conduct which parallels that of a reasonably prudent person of comparable strength under similar circumstances. However, the reasonable person standard does not take into account the temperament or emotions of the individual actor. The law seeks an objective standard, not a subjective one based on a person's mental attributes. There are several reasons for this. First, it would be extremely difficult, if not impossible, to prove what was in an individual's mind at the time of the particular conduct. Second, the harm caused by a negligent act is not changed by the actor's particular thoughts or feelings.

Finally, the courts have determined that a person must learn to conform to the standards of the community and to pay for violating those standards. In extreme cases of mental deficiency, the actor cannot comprehend the danger inherent in certain conduct. In the past, the courts applied the reasonable person standard when dealing with insane defendants. This was based on the public policy consideration of promoting the responsibility of guardians for those in their care. Recently, courts have held that insane persons are not negligent if their mental state prevented them from understanding or avoiding the danger. A "greater degree of care" may be required when dealing with an inherently dangerous object or an activity in which it is reasonably foreseeable that an accident or injury may occur.

NOTES _____

1. In addition to the subsequent notes, the standard of care for persons working in the sports industry, such as that for sports facility owners, is described in greater detail in Chapter 4.

2. In *Moulas v. PBC Productions, Inc.*, 570 N.W.2d 739 (Wis. Ct. App. 1997), a spectator at a hockey game who was struck by a puck sued the owners of the team and the arena. The court of appeals ruled that the arena had exercised reasonable care in installing high plastic protective barriers. The court adhered to the precedent set in baseball cases, which absolves facility owners from liability for injuries sustained by patrons who are hit with flying objects (balls and bats).

3. In *Beckett v. Clinton Prairie School Corporation*, 504 N.E.2d 552 (Ind. 1987), the Supreme Court of Indiana expressed the widely followed rule that high schools and their employees must exercise ordinary and reasonable care for the safety of their students. A student-athlete, who was injured in a collision with another student during baseball practice, claimed that his harm was caused by an assistant coach's failure to exercise reasonable care in giving safety instructions for chasing fly balls during windy conditions. While the court agreed that the coach owed the players such a degree of care, the school district successfully mounted a defense based on the principles of assumption of the risk (see section 3.1.5.4, "Assumption of Risk").

3.1.1.2. Standard of Care for Children

Children as defendants in a negligence case present an important exception to the reasonable person standard. Children are not held to the same objective standard of duty that is applied to adults. The courts recognize that at young age levels there exists a wide range of mental capabilities and experiences. The law attempts to accommodate for this range by viewing the reasonable child as one who exercises in his or her actions a degree of care that is to be expected of children of like age, intelligence, and experience. For example, in a baseball game, an 11-year-old boy swung at a pitched ball and missed it; the bat slipped from his hands, struck his teammate in the head, and caused serious injuries. The court held that there was no negligence because the batter exercised a reasonable degree of care for a person of his age, intelligence, and experience.

However, under this more subjective standard, it follows that if the 11-year-old boy has intelligence vastly superior to that of his peers, the child will be held to the standard of care encompassing his superior knowledge. Several states have established age brackets that purport to distinguish childhood from adulthood. This method has been criticized, however, because of the problems inherent in setting an accurate age level guideline regarding mental capabilities. An exception to the application of this subjective standard for children occurs when a child engages in an activity normally reserved for adults such as driving an automobile or hunting with a gun. In cases such as these, the courts in many jurisdictions will apply the reasonable standard for adults without any special consideration of the fact that the individual is a child.

3.1.2. Breach of Duty Owed

Once a plaintiff has demonstrated that the defendant owed the plaintiff a duty of care, the plaintiff must prove the defendant violated this duty by establishing that the defendant's conduct imposed an unreasonable risk of harm on the plaintiff. There are three methods by which the plaintiff may sustain this burden of proof:

1. Direct evidence of negligence
2. Violation of a statute
3. Res ipsa loquitur

Direct evidence of negligence is evidence tending to establish negligence through firsthand proof of actual factual occurrences. A prime example of direct evidence is eyewitness testimony. For instance, Larry Lacrois suffered an injury to his back in a high school lacrosse game. The athletic trainer told Coach Winatallcosts not to allow Larry to play. Coach Winatallcosts, ignoring the trainer's warning, coerced Larry to play the last 10 minutes because the state championship was on the line. As a result of further play, Larry was more severely injured. Coach Winatallcosts breached the duty of care he owed Larry. If Larry sued, the trainer's testimony would constitute direct evidence of negligence.

When direct evidence is not available, a plaintiff may still prove his or her case by certain procedural devices. One such device is a presumption. A *presumption* is a legal fiction that requires the judge or jury to assume the existence of one fact on the basis of the existence of another fact or group of facts. It is used in the absence of sufficient direct evidence to prove the fact itself. The classic example is the common legal presumption that a person who has been missing seven years without explanation is dead. Other presumptions include negligence per se and res ipsa loquitur.

NOTE _____

1. In *Rose v. Diocese of Bridgeport*, No. CV92–0293727, 1993 Conn. Super. LEXIS 880 (Apr. 16, 1993), the plaintiff was injured during a long jump event at a track meet.

Plaintiff alleged that the high school athletic conference and its president were negligent in that they "(a) failed to inspect the landing pit to insure that it did not contain foreign objects; (b) failed to adequately supervise the track meet; (c) failed to adequately train its employees and staff in the care and maintenance of the track facilities; (d) used large rocks around the landing pit and allowed these rocks to be in the pit; (e) failed to provide adequate regulations to provide for the care, maintenance, and supervision of the athletic facilities." Since the plaintiff had alleged the defendants owed her a legal duty of care, and direct evidence of her claims could establish breach of that duty, the court denied the defendants' motion to strike the complaint.

3.1.2.1. Violation of a Statute, Negligence Per Se

Violation of a statute is sometimes referred to as *negligence per se*. Negligence per se means that upon finding a violation of an applicable statute, there is a conclusive presumption of negligence. This conclusive presumption requires that a jury find for the plaintiff, although the plaintiff still has to prove the amount of damages. It does not allow the jury to weigh all the evidence and independently determine the relative liabilities of the parties. Although in some states, the violation of a valid statute may be considered negligence per se, in other states, the violation of a statute, ordinance, or administrative regulation is deemed only evidence of negligence.

In order for a statutory violation to provide evidence of negligence, the complaining party must establish two points. First, the statutory violation must be causally related to the plaintiff's harm and second that the statute protects against the particular harm for which the plaintiff seeks to recover. If an individual's taillights are out in violation of a statute, that violation may be used to establish negligence only when the failure of the taillights causes an accident. However, if the driver of one car rear-ends another car, it is of little or no significance that the rear-ending car's taillights do not work in violation of a motor vehicle safety statute. A statute requiring working taillights was most likely not meant to prevent a car without working taillights from rear-ending another car. It was probably meant for the exact opposite. Therefore, evidence that the rear-ending car's taillights did not work is not particularly relevant in determining whether or not the rear-ending car driver was negligent in the operation of his vehicle when he rear-ended another car.

When a violation of a statute is treated as evidence of negligence and not negligence per se, it is accorded a different weight. A jury will not be required to conclude negligence; instead, a violation merely establishes an inference of negligence that may or may not be accepted by the jury.

3.1.2.2. Res Ipsa Loquitur

The last method of establishing the negligence of the defendant is through the use of the legal doctrine of *res ipsa loquitur* ("the thing speaks for itself"). Res ipsa loquitur permits the fact finder to infer both negligence and causation from circumstantial evidence. It is, in effect, another type of presumption which enables the plaintiff to establish that more likely than not, the harm to the plaintiff was a result of the defendant's negligence. In order to defeat the application of this doctrine, the defendant must establish that there is another, equally believable explanation of the injury to the plaintiff.

The most common types of cases utilizing res ipsa loquitur involves airplanes and elevators. When those machines fail, it is almost always because of the operator or supervisor's negligence. The possibility that the operator or supervisor can rebut this presumption by demonstrating "another, equally believable explanation" of plaintiff's injuries is obviously minimal.

Res ipsa loquitur is strictly a procedural device designed to allow a plaintiff to establish an otherwise unprovable case. In negligence cases, direct evidence of the defendant's negligence may not be available. This doctrine allows a plaintiff to recover on the basis of what probably happened. The following three requirements must be met before the doctrine will be applied:

1. The event ordinarily does not occur except through the negligence of someone.

2. The plaintiff must show that the instrument which caused plaintiff's injury was in the exclusive control of the defendant at the relevant time.

3. The plaintiff must show that his or her injury was not due to plaintiff's own action.

NOTES

1. In *Hale v. City of Jefferson*, 6 S.W.3d 187 (Mo. Ct. App. 1999), a child suffered severe jaw injuries after he caught his tooth on an allegedly defective waterslide at a public pool. "The court barred the use of res ipsa loquitur to determine whether a 1/4" raised lip on the waterslide was the proximate cause of the plaintiff's injuries, as other reasonable explanations for the injury existed.

2. In *Grauer v. State of New York*, 181 N.Y.S.2d 994 (N.Y. App. Div. 1959), the plaintiff successfully raised the doctrine of res ipsa loquitur, when the ski lift chair that he attempted to sit on swung or was tipped such that it struck the back of his leg, fracturing it. The court held for the plaintiff, as the elements of res ipsa loquitur were satisfied and the defendants presented no other reasonable causes for the plaintiff's injury.

3.1.3. Actual and Proximate Causation

The primary issue in the area of causation is that of proximate cause, that is, whether the defendant's negligent act is sufficiently closely related to the plaintiff's harm that liability should attach, which means that the injury is reasonably foreseeable. Before the defendant's actions will be deemed the proximate cause of plaintiff's injury, the defendant's conduct must be shown to be the actual "cause in fact" of the plaintiff's harm. If the same harm would have resulted if the negligent act had never occurred, then the act is not the actual cause of the harm. This is sometimes referred to as the "but for" test: the particular harm in question would not have been suffered "but for" the defendant's negligent act.

Two other tests are sometimes used to determine actual cause in cases where more than one act or event may have caused an injury. The first test is called the *substantial factor test*. It is used in cases where two individual acts contributed to the injury. This substantial factor test precludes liability for inadvertent or minor causation factors. The second test is known as the *alternative causes approach*. This test applies when there are two acts, only one of which causes the injury, and it is not known which one caused the injury. The burden of proof shifts from the plaintiff to the defendant to prove that he or she did not cause the injury.

After establishing the existence of actual causation between the plaintiff's harm and the defendant's act, the plaintiff's harm that the defendant's act also *proximately* caused the plaintiff's injury. Proximate cause is determined by establishing whether or not the harm to the plaintiff was a reasonable, foreseeable consequence of the defendant's act. To demonstrate proximate cause, it is sufficient to show that the probable consequence of the defendant's act was harm of the same general character as that which befell the plaintiff. It is not necessary to show that the defendant should have foreseen the harm to the plaintiff in its precise form or particular manner. For example, Jerry Janitor, in cleaning a spot off the basketball court, used a cleaning substance that left the floor extremely slippery. During the game later that day, Ralph Rocket slipped on the spot and seriously injured his knee. Jerry's use of the improper cleaning substance was the proximate cause of Ralph's injury because it was foreseeable that someone would slip on the slick surface of a basketball court.

One last problem of determining causation occurs when there is more than one cause of injury. When a combination of causes leads to the damage, a defendant can defeat liability claims by demonstrating that an unforeseeable intervening act caused the injury. An *intervening cause* is one that comes into existence after the defendant's negligent action and contributes to that negligence in bringing about the plaintiff's injury. The intervening cause will relieve the defendant of liability if the defendant could not have foreseen either that the intervening cause might occur or that the plaintiff would suffer such great harm.

NOTES

1. In *Vaillancourt v. Latifi*, 840 A.2d 1209 (Ct. App. Ct. 2004), the Connecticut Appellate Court found that neither the umpire of a softball game nor the organizers of the event proximately caused harm to the plaintiff, who was knocked over in violation of league rules while playing catcher. Since the umpire could not have foreseen the violent act of another competitor, the umpire's failure to eject that competitor was not the legal cause of the plaintiff's injury.

2. In *Ascher v. Scarsdale School District*, 700 N.Y.S.2d 210 (N.Y. App. Div. 1999), the court determined that a teacher's failed supervision was not the proximate cause of injuries suffered by a child after the child attempted a back-flip dismount from a moving playground swing.

3. In *Reagan v. State of New York*, 654 N.Y.S.2d 488 (N.Y. App. Div. 1997), the court determined that the field's abnormal slope was not the proximate cause of the paralysis of an experienced rugby player, since several other factors contributed to the injury and paralysis was not a reasonable and foreseeable consequence of the field's slope.

4. In *Thomas v. United States Soccer Federation, Inc.*, 653 N.Y.S.2d 958 (N.Y. App. Div. 1997), the court determined that a soccer referee's inexperience was not the proximate cause of one participant biting off another participant's ear during a match. Since the attack occurred "suddenly and without warning," no referee of any experience level could reasonably have foreseen the possibility of harm to the plaintiff.

5. In *Singerman v. Municipal Serv. Bureau, Inc.*, 455 Mich. 135, 565 N.W.2d 383 (Mich. 1997), a hockey coach, acting as goalie without protective gear, claimed that poor lighting in the arena caused him to not see the puck that injured him. The Supreme Court of Michigan granted summary judgment to the defendant arena owners, overturning the appellate court decision. The Supreme Court reasoned, "Plaintiff was an adult and an experienced hockey player. The lighting in the rink is alleged to have been consistently inadequate, not subject to unexpected fluctuations or other changes. There was nothing to prevent plaintiff from realizing that the rink was inadequately lighted. Nor was there any chance that he would forget the potentially hazardous condition, because the condition was constantly before him. Finally, plaintiff was not compelled to use the rink for work, or profit, or any other overriding or substantial motivation. He chose to participate in a dangerous sport under conditions that he knew to be dangerous." The court found poor lighting had not proximately caused the plaintiff's injury.

6. In *Shorten v. City of White Plains*, 637 N.Y.S.2d 791 (N.Y. App. Div. 1996), the court refused summary judgment to a city-owned skating rink. A teenage boy, after skating recklessly for about an hour, injured the plaintiff. According to the court, the defendant could have prevented the injury with adequate supervision.

7. In *Sanders v. Kuna Joint School District*, 876 P.2d 154 (Idaho Ct. App. 1994), the Court of Appeals of Idaho ruled that the alleged failure of an athletic instructor to provide adequate instruction and supervision did not cause the injury of a high school student under his care. Assuming that the instructor did not advise against wearing running shoes to play softball or give specific instructions about the sport, the plaintiff still could not show that such omissions caused him to break his ankle while sliding into a base.

8. In *Wertheim v. U.S. Tennis Ass'n*, 540 N.Y.S.2d 443 (N.Y. App. Div. 1989), the New York Supreme Court Appellate Division reversed the lower court finding for the plaintiff who sought recovery for the wrongful death of a tennis umpire who died after being hit in the groin by a served tennis ball. The court ruled that even if the tennis tournament operator breached a duty of care owed to the umpire, it was unlikely that this breach of duty was the proximate cause of the umpire's death. The umpire had chronic cardiovascular disease and eyewitness testimony was consistent with the opinion of appellant's expert that the umpire suffered a stroke upon being hit by the ball.

9. In *Gehling v. St. George University School of Medicine*, 705 F. Supp. 761 (E.D.N.Y. 1989), plaintiff's family sued the medical school for his death, which resulted from his running in a student-sponsored road race. The school was found not to be the proximate cause of the plaintiff's death, because the participant, a medical student, was aware of the dangers of running the race in tropical weather, being 75 pounds overweight, suffering from high blood pressure, and having ingested an amphetamine-like drug prior to the race.

10. In *Locilento v. Coleman Catholic High School*, 523 N.Y.S.2d 198 (N.Y. App. 1987), the court found in favor of a student injured in an intramural football game in a suit against the school. The court held that the evidence sustained a finding that the school's failure to provide the student with proper equipment during an intramural tackle football game was a proximate cause of the shoulder injury and that the student's voluntary participation was merely an implied assumption of risk which did not preclude all recovery.

11. In *Burkart v. Health and Tennis Corporation of America*, 730 S.W.2d 367 (Tex. Ct. App. 1987), plaintiff brought suit against a health club for injuries received when he fell from a machine (Gravity Gym) which allows its user to hang upside down. Plaintiff alleged that the club failed to supervise his activities properly, that the club failed to inspect the Gravity Gym properly, and that the club's negligent failure to instruct its employees in the correct manner of using the Gravity Gym was the proximate cause of his injuries. The Texas Court of Appeals affirmed the lower court's decision in favor of the defendant, stating that the plaintiff's injuries were not the reasonable and foreseeable result of the club's actions.

3.1.4. Damages

Damages are monetary compensation given to any person who suffers an injury through the unlawful act, omission, or negligence of another. Damage is an essential element of a negligence claim; therefore actual injury or harm must be proven. Unlike intentional tort claims, harm will not be presumed; thus nominal damages are not available in a negligence claim.

Damages may be either compensatory or punitive. *Compensatory damages* consist of money given to the injured party that is measured by the amount of actual injury incurred: past, present, and prospective. A plaintiff may be compensated for medical expenses, lost earnings, pain and suffering (including mental distress), and impaired future earning capacity. In negligence cases, compensatory damages are the only sort of damages that are available. For example, Suzie

Slowpitch suffered an injury as a result of the negligence of the school district in not properly maintaining the softball field. She was hospitalized and missed work at her part-time job for three weeks. The court instructed the school district to compensate her for hospital costs and lost wages.

Punitive damages are awarded to an injured party to punish the defendant for intentional, reckless, willful, or wanton conduct. In addition, punitive damages also serve to punish the defendant and to set an example for other wrongdoers.

They are awarded to a plaintiff in an amount over and above the amount given to compensate for the actual loss, where the wrong done was aggravated by violence, oppression, malice, fraud, or excessively wicked conduct. Since punitive damages are not available in cases of ordinary negligence they will be discussed in greater detail below.

In a negligence action, the plaintiff may seek recovery of damages, past, present, and prospective, in any or all of the following three areas:

1. Economic loss: medical expenses, lost or diminished earning capacity
2. Physical pain: pain and suffering
3. Mental distress: fright, anxiety, humiliation, depression caused by the inability to lead one's previous life

In addition, the spouse of an injured plaintiff may bring a separate cause of action for loss of consortium, which is the right to a spouse's companionship. Similarly, some courts allow children of an injured plaintiff to bring a cause of action against a negligent defendant for loss of companionship and guidance.

3.1.5. Defenses for Negligence

The defendants in such lawsuits can employ a number of defenses once the plaintiff has proven the elements essential to a negligence action. The following are the most common defenses employed by defendants in tort actions for negligence:

1. No negligence
2. Contributory negligence
3. Comparative negligence
4. Assumption of risk
5. Statute of limitations
6. Immunity and Good Samaritan statutes

3.1.5.1. No Negligence

The defendant usually attempts to prove first that his or her behavior did not constitute negligence. This can be approached in two ways. The defendant can dispute the negligence claim either by attacking one or more of the four previously discussed elements of negligence or by proving that he or she exercised reasonable care in his or her actions. Thus, a defendant may defend against a claim of negligence by asserting that he or she had no duty toward the plaintiff.

The defendant may assert that if the defendant had a duty toward the plaintiff, he or she did not breach that duty. Therefore, any harm to the plaintiff would not be actionable negligence on the part of the defendant.

3.1.5.2. *Contributory Negligence*

The common law doctrine of contributory negligence provides that a plaintiff who is negligent and whose negligence in any way contributes to the proximate cause of his or her injury is totally barred from recovery. Contributory negligence, in essence, holds plaintiffs to the standard of reasonableness required of all people. The plaintiff need not actually appreciate the risk involved. There need only be a risk that is known or would be known, and would be avoided by a reasonable person. A plaintiff also has a duty to exercise ordinary care. Without such care, the plaintiff is at least to some degree contributorily negligent.

This doctrine is considered by most U.S. jurisdictions to be inordinately harsh since its effect is to prevent plaintiffs from recovering damages even if they are found to be just 1% at fault. Consequently, only the District of Columbia and four states—Alabama, Maryland, North Carolina, and Virginia—still adhere to the common law doctrine of contributory negligence. The success of the defense of contributory negligence rests on the defendant's ability to prove that the plaintiff failed to exercise due care for his or her own safety and that the lack of due care was the proximate cause of the plaintiff's injury.

In contributory negligence theory, as in negligence theory, the standard of care for children is reasonableness. The child's age, intelligence, and experience, however, are relevant to the issue of whether reasonable care was exercised. With respect to both negligence and contributory negligence, there are situations in which the negligent conduct of one party may be imputed to a second party under the doctrine of *respondeat superior*, which means "let the superior reply" (see section 3.6, "Vicarious Liability").

3.1.5.3. *Comparative Negligence*

The remaining 46 states have adopted some version of the comparative negligence doctrine to alleviate the harshness of the contributory negligence doctrine. Comparative negligence provides a basis for recovery to an injured plaintiff while still apportioning fault to each side for the determination of damages.

Where both the plaintiff and the defendant are negligent, comparative negligence statutes seek to divide the responsibility between the two negligent parties. Under a comparative negligence statute, the jury or fact finder determines the proportionate degree of negligence that will be attributed to all parties involved. The damages are then assessed pro rata.

In states that have adopted the doctrine of comparative negligence, contributory negligence on the part of the plaintiff is not necessarily a complete bar to recovery. In some states, the rule that is applied under the theory of comparative negligence is as follows: if the plaintiff's negligence, as compared with total negligence of all defendants, is greater than 50%, plaintiff is totally barred from recovery. For example, a plaintiff who is determined to be 60% at fault will not be able to recover against the defendant. If the plaintiff's negligence, as compared with the total negligence of all defendants, is 50% or less, plaintiff's damages are reduced in proportion to his or her negligence. For example, a plaintiff who suffers $100,000 in damages and whose negligence is determined to be 40% recovers

$60,000 ($100,000 total damages less 40% of $100,000, the plaintiff's proportion of negligence).

NOTES _____

1. Christo Lassiter, "Lex Sportiva: Thoughts Towards a Criminal Competitive Contact Sport," 22 *St. John's Journal of Legal Commentary* 35 (2007).

2. In *Bennett v. City of New York*, 303 A.D.2d 614 (N.Y. App. Div. 2003), the appellate court ruled that since the negligence of a 13-year-old athlete contributed to the injury she suffered while attempting to jump over a hurdle, the jury should have used the doctrine of comparative negligence to apportion fault between the plaintiff and the organizers of the event.

3. In *Nunez v. Recreation Rooms and Settlement, Inc.*, 645 N.Y.S.2d 789 (N.Y. App. Div. 1996), the court denied summary judgment to an ice skating rink after a nine-year-old first-time skater fell and broke her arm. The nine-year-old plaintiff testified that she had fallen while trying to skate away from a group of children who were pushing and playing in a rowdy fashion. No other child actually touched the plaintiff. Therefore, the defendants argued that the plaintiff's inexperience, not their failure to supervise, was the proximate cause of the plaintiff's injury. However, the court stated: "New York's comparative negligence statute allows for consideration of plaintiff's culpability in determining liability and apportioning damages.... [P]laintiff's admission that she did not know how to skate does not preclude a finding that Midtown is also liable for her injuries."

3.1.5.4. Assumption of Risk

Assumption of risk means that the plaintiff has voluntarily consented to take chances that harm will occur. To use this defense, the defendant must show that the plaintiff knew of the risk and voluntarily chose to assume it. This consent effectively relieves a defendant's obligation to a certain standard of conduct toward the plaintiff. There is no longer any legal duty existing between the two. When there is no duty, there is no negligence. The general rule in athletics is that participants assume the normal and reasonable risks of activities in which they participate, where those activities do not rise to the level of recklessness. There are two major exceptions to the general rule. First, there is no assumption of risk when something occurs that is not normal or reasonable for the activity. Second, the assumption of the risk defense will be unsuccessful when the participant is unaware of the risk. In addition to knowing and appreciating the risk, the plaintiff must also carefully and reasonably agree to assume whatever risk is involved.

There are two types of assumption of risk. The first is an *express assumption of risk*, which arises when a plaintiff gives advance consent to relieve a defendant of a legal duty and to take his or her chances from a known risk. The second is *implied assumption of risk*, which arises when a plaintiff's reasonable conduct in encountering a known risk creates an inference that he or she has agreed to relieve the defendant's duty of care.

The defense of assumption of risk may be utilized in those states which have not passed a comparative negligence statute to supplement the contributory negligence statute. In such states, the defendant may claim that the plaintiff, by assuming the risk of injury, is barred from any recovery. Under the comparative negligence statute, however, partial recovery is allowed in many situations in which the plaintiff's negligence proximately contributed to his or her injury. This does not reconcile with the legal interpretation under which no recovery is allowed to a plaintiff who is found to have assumed the risk, even when such assumption of risk was considered reasonable under the circumstances.

Many states distinguish between *primary* and *secondary* assumption of risk. In these states, primary assumption of risk generally means what has been described previously, that is, that the plaintiff cannot recover because he or she voluntarily encountered known risks inherent to a particular activity. Secondary assumption of risk refers to situations where the plaintiff is aware of somebody else's negligence but chooses to take part in an activity anyway. For example, if a golfer was aware of steering problems with a negligently maintained golf cart, but nonetheless drove the cart over the speed recommended by golf course personnel, the golfer may be found to have secondarily assumed the risk of any resulting harm. In states that use this doctrine, a defense of secondary assumption of risk will not result in a total bar to the plaintiff's recovery but instead in the application of comparative fault principles (see section 3.1.5.3, "Comparative Negligence").

NOTES

The following represent cases where the defendant raised a successful assumption of the risk defense.

1. In *Avila v. Citrus Community College District*, 41 Cal. Rptr. 3d 299 (Cal. Ct. App. 2006), the appellate court ruled that the possibility of being struck by a pitched ball during a game constitutes a risk inherent to the sport of baseball. Since the plaintiff knew of that risk when he stepped into the batter's box, he could not recover for injuries that resulted from being struck in the head by a pitch.

2. In *Harris v. Cherry Valley-Springfield School District*, 760 N.Y.S.2d 768 (N.Y. App. Div. 2003), the court ruled that a high school baseball player who was struck in the right eye by a baseball from a mechanical pitching machine had assumed the risk of that type of harm. The plaintiff was an experienced baseball player who had used the same kind of machine before and was aware of the possibility that the machine would miss its target.

3. In *Thurmond v. Prince William Professional Baseball Club*, 574 S.E.2d 246 (Va. 2003), the Supreme Court of Virginia ruled that a fan who was struck by a foul ball at a Minor League baseball game assumed the risk of such injuries. The plaintiff had chosen not to sit in the screened area behind home plate and had observed many baseballs flying into the stands before the incident occurred in the eighth inning.

4. In *Lee v. Maloney*, 704 N.Y.S.2d 729 (3 N.Y. App. Div. 2000), the court ruled that an experienced weightlifter assumes the risk that he may lose control of a 565-pound object, even with the help of spotters. In this case, the plaintiff had entered bench press competitions for 14 years prior to the incident and was well aware of the risks involved.

5. In *Bouchard v. Smile Bros.*, 685 N.Y.S.2d 289 (2 N.Y. App. Div. 1999), the court ruled against the estate of a deceased hiker, saying that the hiker had assumed the risk that she might lose her footing and fall off a cliff to her death. She had hiked the area at least 10 times previously, and the risk of falling was open and obvious.

6. In *Shelly v. Step*, 73 Cal. Rptr. 2d 323 (Cal. Ct. App. 1998), the appellate court ruled that those who exercise racehorses assume the risks of injury inherent in such a potentially dangerous activity, even if such injuries are caused by the negligence of fellow exercise riders.

7. In *Sandler v. Half Hollow Hills West High School*, 672 N.Y.S.2d 120 (N.Y. App. Div. 1998), a high school field hockey player assumed risks of injury that were clearly foreseeable consequences of her voluntary participation in athletic competition, despite her relative inexperience in the sport.

8. In *Davis v. Sayona Central School District*, 675 N.Y.S.2d 269 (N.Y. App. Div. 1998), a high school student was injured after striking an unpadded portion of school gymnasium wall during an interscholastic basketball game. The student sued the school district,

architects, contractor, and athletic equipment company. The Supreme Court, Appellate Division, held that the student assumed the obvious risks inherent in playing basketball in the school gymnasium.

9. In *Morgan v. State*, 685 N.E.2d 202 (N.Y. 1997), bobsledders assumed the risk of injuries that occurred when their bobsled crashed into a wall and continued through an opening. The court found that the opening did not add to the inherent and commonly appreciated risks of bobsledding, which were well known to the plaintiff after more than 20 years of experience in the sport.

10. In *Capello v. Village of Suffern*, 648 N.Y.S.2d 699 (N.Y. App. Div. 1996), a basketball player assumed the risk of playing on a slippery court. The court was covered with a dusty substance, but the player continued to play even though he was aware of the substance.

11. In *Swan v. Town of Grand Island*, 652 N.Y.S.2d 166 (N.Y. App. Div. 1996), a softball player assumed the risk of playing on a wet field. Although the condition of the field was poor, the player continued to play despite the fact that it was obvious the conditions were hazardous.

12. In *Fortier v. Los Rios Community College District*, 52 Cal. Rptr. 2d 812 (Cal. Ct. App. 1996), plaintiff brought suit against a community college as a result of a "no tackling" football class. The plaintiff suffered severe facial injuries during a collision with another participant. The court reasoned, "Plaintiff's injuries were the result of his voluntary participation in a sport in which the risk of injury due to accidental collision is known, acknowledged and accepted. Plaintiff's injuries could have occurred in the most benign forms of football, i.e., touch or flag ... or even in other sports considered to be non-contact e.g., baseball (collision of two defensive players trying to catch a fly ball) or basketball (collision between offensive and defensive rebounders or between offensive player driving for the basket and defender)." The appellate court affirmed the judgment for the defendant community college.

13. In *Ford v. Gouin*, 266 Cal. Rptr. 870 (Cal. Ct. App. 1990), plaintiff was injured when, while waterskiing on a narrow river channel, he collided with a tree limb overhanging the waterway. As a result, plaintiff suffered severe head injuries. At the time of the accident, plaintiff was skiing backward and barefoot and the boat towing the plaintiff was driven by the defendant. Evidence showed the plaintiff had skied in this area over 50 times before and was well aware of the channel and branches hanging over the waterway. Thus, the court held that the plaintiff reasonably assumed the risks inherent in the activity because of his extensive experience as a water skier in the area where his injuries occurred.

14. In *Wertheim v. U.S. Tennis Ass'n*, 540 N.Y.S.2d 443 (N.Y. App. Div. 1989), plaintiff executrix sought recovery for the wrongful death of a tennis umpire who died after being hit in the groin by a served tennis ball. In reversing the lower court finding for the plaintiff, the New York Supreme Court held that the umpire had assumed the risk of being struck by a served tennis ball.

15. In *Novak v. Lamar Insurance Co.*, 488 So. 2d 739 (La. Cir. Ct. App. 1986), plaintiff softball player brought action against a second softball player, the homeowner's insurer of that player's father, and the insurer of the church which sponsored the defendant softball player's team. Plaintiff sought recovery for injuries sustained when the two collided as defendant softball player ran to first base. The court held that the defendant softball player was not acting in a reckless or unsportsmanlike manner. The court reasoned that the risk of collision was a foreseeable risk which the plaintiff had assumed.

The following are cases where the defense of assumption of the risk failed.

1. In *Shin v. Ahn*, 141 Cal. App. 4th 726 (Cal. Ct. App. 2006), the court ruled that the risks inherent to the sport of golf were increased when one golfer teed off without knowing the location of another golfer in his party. Therefore, the injured golfer had not assumed the risk of such harm.

2. In *Livshitz v. Unites State Tennis Association National Tennis Center*, 761 N.Y.S.2d 825 (N.Y. Civ. Ct. 2003), the court ruled that a person who had paid for specialized

instruction did not fully assume the risk of being injured by a tennis ball during a drill. The plaintiff had suffered a serious injury to her eye when a tennis instructor hit a ball toward her before she was ready. The defendant tennis facility and its instructors owed the plaintiff a duty of care, and the court allowed a jury to determine whether the plaintiff appreciated the risk that she may be injured by "an alleged ballistic missile of great speed [launched] at her if the instructor saw or had reason to know that she was unaware that it was coming at her."

3. In *Kane v. North Colonie Central School District*, 708 N.Y.S.2d 203 (N.Y. App. Div. 2000), plaintiff was injured during an indoor track practice, which took place in the hallway of the high school building. The plaintiff argued that "the risk of contact and falling is unreasonably increased where the runners do not maintain a safe and appropriate distance, typically a stride, from one another." The appellate court held that the testimony of Kane and her expert witness was sufficient to "raise a question of fact as to whether the defendant's supervision was inadequate and resulted in the failure to exercise reasonable care to protect Kane from an unreasonably increased risk."

4. In *Kevan v. Manesiotis*, 728 A.2d 1006 (Pa. Commw. 1999), a defendant school district's poorly lit gym prevented its successful use of the assumption of risk defense in a motion for summary judgment. The plaintiff had been struck by a batted ball, hit at a high velocity. The court noted that baseball players typically assume the known risks associated with the game, but those risks were increased by poor lighting.

5. In *Sauray v. City of New York*, 690 N.Y.S.2d 716 (N.Y. App. Div. 1999), a mountain biker, injured when he struck a chain over a path in a city park, did not assume risk of injury from such collision. The court found that the chain posed a greater risk than the plaintiff assumed by taking part in the sport.

6. In *Calhanas v. South Amboy Roller Rink*, 679 A.2d 185 (N.J. Super. Ct. App. Div. 1996), the Superior Court of New Jersey had ruled that the plaintiff was precluded from recovering damages from a skating rink after an unidentified rowdy skater caused the plaintiff to fall and break a bone. According to New Jersey law (N.J.S.A. 5:14–16), "the assumption of risk ... shall serve as a complete defense to a suit against an operator by a roller skater." However, the appellate court ruled that the provision only covered the inherent risks of rolling skating and directed a jury to decide whether the rink operator's poor supervision had increased those risks.

Also see the following law review articles.

1. Keya Denner, "Taking One for the Team: The Role of Assumption of the Risk in Sports Torts Cases," 14 *Seton Hall Journal of Sports and Entertainment Law* 209 (2004).

2. David Horton, "Extreme Sports and Assumption of Risk," 38 *University of San Francisco Law Review* 599 (2004).

3. Gil Fried and Robin Annon Jr., "Baseball Spectators' Assumption of the Risk: Is It 'Fair' or 'Foul'?" 13 *Marquette Sports Law Review* 39 (2002).

3.1.5.5. *Statute of Limitations*

Statute of limitations prescribes the periods within which certain causes of action may be brought or certain rights enforced. Statute of limitations may begin at the time of the negligent act or at the time of its discovery. Today, statutes and case law apply the "time of discovery" rule. If a plaintiff does not institute a lawsuit within the time period prescribed by the statute of limitations, he or she will lose the right to sue.

3.1.5.6. *Immunity and Good Samaritan Statutes*

Immunity is a condition that protects a possible defendant against a tort action. It exists because of a position of the defendant, not because of any action taken by the defendant. This defense may exist either because of a relationship between the plaintiff and the defendant, or because of the capacity of the defendant.

Examples of the relationships that in some states permit a defense of immunity in intentional torts include those between husband and wife or between parent and child. Other immunity defenses that may be raised when appropriate are those of sovereign immunity, charitable immunity, and Good Samaritan statutes. The same type of immunity that can be raised in assault and battery cases—that stemming from relationships between the parties or the capacity of the parties—can also be applied to negligence actions. The trend, however, is to move away from an immunity defense based solely on the relationship of the parties.

Sovereign immunity developed in English common law. It was otherwise known as immunity of the king, which was expressed as "the king can do no wrong." This English rule was applied by early American courts to mean that the United States and states themselves could not be sued without consent. Today, by statute and judicial decision, this immunity is considerably limited.

By virtue of the Federal Tort Claims Act, Title 28 U.S.C., the United States has waived immunity for tortious acts and can be held liable to the same extent as a private individual when its employees are negligent within the scope of their employment. There are still circumstances where the immunity will apply: intentional torts; discretionary acts at the planning or decision-making level; and independent contractors, who may assert the immunity where the government had authority and control and exercised substantial supervision of the activities.

Like the U.S. government, most states have substantially waived their immunity from tort claims. Again, the immunity still attaches for discretionary acts and for legislative and judicial decisions. This applies to the government and governmental agencies. At least half of the states have abolished municipal tort immunity by statute or judicial decision to the same extent that they have waived their own state immunity.

Charitable immunity emerged from common law and provides charitable organizations with immunity from lawsuits. The rationale for such protection is as follows: (1) charities can be allowed to provide services without fear of bankruptcy resulting from potential lawsuits, (2) the donors have not given funds to the charitable organization for use to pay tort claims, and (3) the beneficiary of the charity has waived his or her right to raise a tort claim, simply by virtue of having accepted the benevolence. Most states have restricted charitable immunity on the following bases: the availability of liability insurance, the view that liability should not be determined based on whether or not a charity can satisfy a judgment and the existence of a category of people for whom it is not possible to waive their right to sue (such as children and unconscious victims).

Another statutory defense involves the Good Samaritan doctrine. Good Samaritan statutes, as a matter of law, preclude negligence liability for one who sees and attempts to aid another person who has been placed in imminent and serious peril due to the negligence of a third person. States that have adopted Good Samaritan statutes will impose a lesser standard of care for doctors and other individuals trained in first aid when they gratuitously render medical assistance to a sick or injured person. Good Samaritan statutes generally protect medical personnel rendering aid from liability, unless the treatment provided is grossly negligent or actually worsens the condition of the person in need of treatment.

NOTES

1. In *Yanero v. Davis*, 65 S.W.2d 510 (Ky. 2002), the Kentucky Supreme Court ruled that sovereign immunity did not protect a public high school baseball coach from liability for neglecting to ensure that one of his players wore a helmet. Although creation of the rule requiring helmets was a discretionary function that would enjoy sovereign immunity, enforcement of the rule was merely a ministerial function. Thus, the plaintiff was able to recover damages for the injury he sustained when hit in the head by a baseball.

2. In *Eneman v. Richter*, 577 N.W.2d 386 (Wisc. Ct. App. 1998), employees of the University of Wisconsin were sued for negligence after fans charged the football field to celebrate a victory and knocked over the goal posts, injuring more than 70 spectators. The appellate court dismissed charges of negligence against officers of the state because plaintiffs could not refute the fact that such officers were entitled to immunity. A lower court had already dismissed a claim against the university itself, which had been named as a codefendant in the suit under the theory of vicarious liability.

3. In *Evans v. Oaks Mission Public School*, 945 P.2d 492 (Okla. 1997), defendant school board was found to be statutorily immune from liability for injuries occurring as a result of a physical education wrestling match.

4. In *Home v. North Kitsap School District*, 965 P.2d 1112 (Wash. Ct. App. 1998), a junior high football coach who was injured when he attempted to protect player from a raised curb that separated the field from a surrounding running track, and was then struck by a second player, sued the school district, which owned the field. The court of appeals held that (1) the district was not protected by immunity under recreational land use statute because the field was not open for public use at the time of the scheduled school football game during which coach was injured and (2) the fact issue as to whether the coach had no reasonable alternative but to stand in front of curb in order to protect his players, and thus could not be said to have voluntarily assumed the risk created by the curb, precluded summary judgment.

Also see the following law review articles.

1. Timothy Davis, "Tort Liability of Coaches for Injuries to Professional Athletes: Overcoming Policy and Doctrinal Barriers," 76 *UMKC Law Review* 571 (2008).

2. Andrew F. Breach, "Dying to Play: School Liability and Immunity for Injuries That Occur as a Result of School-Sponsored Athletic Events," 10 *Sports Lawyers Journal* 275 (2003).

3.1.6. Wrongful Death Statutes

Wrongful death statutes exist in all states. They provide a statutory cause of action in favor of certain of the decedent's personal beneficiaries (e.g., a spouse, parent, or child) against the person who negligently caused the death. The provision changes the common law rule that the tort action was extinguished with the death of the person who was negligently injured by the defendant. The cause of action is for the wrong to the beneficiaries and for their loss of companionship and suffering—not for the harm done to the decedent. The majority of the statutes award compensatory damages. The award of these money damages is based on an evaluation of the monetary worth of the decedent to the plaintiffs. The damages awarded are greater for injuries inflicted intentionally or recklessly as opposed to those inflicted negligently. A few states employ a combination of the two methods to determine damages.

3.2. THE TORT OF RECKLESS MISCONDUCT
(GROSS NEGLIGENCE)

Reckless misconduct, or gross negligence, falls between the intentional torts of assault and battery and the unintentional tort of negligence. Behavior constituting reckless misconduct is characterized by defendant's *intent to commit the act*, but not the *intent to harm the plaintiff*. Reckless misconduct occurs when the actor intentionally performs an act while disregarding a risk known to him, and that risk is so great as to make the harm highly probable. It must usually be accompanied by a conscious disregard of the circumstances. For example, Frankie Fieldevent, after a high school track practice, was throwing the javelin at some of his teammates who were running around the track. While Frankie fully intended to throw the javelin, he had no intention of hitting any of his friends. Unfortunately, Mikey Marathon fell while running, and the javelin pierced him in the shoulder. Mikey successfully brought suit against Frankie for reckless misconduct.

Reckless misconduct is particularly important in the area of participant-against participant tort cases. Only since the 1970s have courts found a duty of sports participants to refrain from reckless misconduct toward another player. To constitute reckless misconduct, an action must be more than ordinary inadvertence or inattention but less than conscious indifference to the consequences. Reckless misconduct is defined as an action that is willful, wanton, or reckless; while there is no intent to harm, the degree of the care exercised is so far below the usual standard that in effect, it is treated as an intentional action. Reckless misconduct encompasses action that evidences an extreme departure from the ordinary degree of care required from the actor in the particular circumstances. Owing to the potentially harmful nature of such action, defendants found liable for reckless misconduct may be forced to pay punitive damages as well as compensatory damages. Punitive damages are based on entirely different policy considerations than are compensatory damages, which merely reimburse a plaintiff for any actual loss suffered. For example, Kenny Kicker, after failing to successfully complete a football drill in practice, was forced by Coach Haze to push a football back and forth in front of the school fifty times with his nose during school hours. Kenney sued Coach Haze and the school and was awarded punitive damages for suffering mental anguish, shame, and degradation.

NOTES

1. In *Gray v. Girous*, 730 N.E.2d 338 (Mass. App. 2000), after a golfer struck another golfer in the head with a misplaced shot, the injured party sued for negligence. The appeals court ruled against the plaintiff, stating that golfers cannot be held liable for injuries to other participants unless their actions are willful, wanton, or reckless. The defendant's actions did not constitute any of these.

2. Courts in most states will follow the general rule that a sport participant may not recover damages from a negligent coparticipant, unless the coparticipant acts willfully, wantonly, or recklessly (see case of *Nabozny* in note 3). However, courts will sometimes make exceptions to this rule when the negligence occurs during breaks in the action, immediately after competition, or at other periods when the court believes that the injured party did not assume the risk of injury. An example is the Wisconsin Supreme Court's decision in *Lestina v. West Bend Mutual Insurance*, 501 N.W.2d 28 (Wis. 1993). In this case, defendant was sued for violating a "no slide tackling rule" during an "Old Timers Soccer League Game" and injuring the plaintiff. The court ruled that defendant's

actions constituted ordinary negligence but still allowed for the plaintiff's recovery of damages.

3. In *Nabozny v. Barnhill*, 334 N.E.2d 258 (Ill. App. Ct. 1975), plaintiff soccer player filed suit for injuries received when he was kicked in the head by an opponent during an amateur soccer game involving two teams composed of high school age players. The defendant, David Barnhill, was playing a forward position for one team, and the plaintiff, Julian Nabozny, was the goaltender for the other team. Barnhill kicked Nabozny in the head while Nabozny was in possession of the ball. Contact with the goaltender while he is in possession of the ball is a violation of International Association Football Federation—soccer's international governing body—rules, which governed the contest. The resultant injury left the plaintiff with permanent skull and brain damage. Nabozny brought suit, and the trial court directed a verdict in favor of the defendant. On appeal, the court noted that it did not wish to "place unreasonable burdens on the free and vigorous participation in sports by our youth" but also stated that "athletic competition does not exist in a vacuum." Therefore, in reversing the trial court decision, the court held that a player is charged with a legal duty to every other player on the field to refrain from conduct proscribed by a safety rule. The court held that when athletes are engaged in athletic competition, all teams involved are trained and coached by knowledgeable personnel; a recognized set of rules governs the conduct of the competition; and a safety rule is contained therein which is primarily designed to protect players from serious injury. Thus, a reckless disregard for the safety of other players cannot be excused.

4. Erica K. Rosenthal, "Inside the Lines: Basing Negligence Liability in Sports for Safety-Based Rule Violations on the Level of Play," 72 *Fordham Law Review* 2631 (2004).

3.3. INTENTIONAL TORTS

Assault and battery can be both criminal and civil offenses. Most people associate assault and battery with criminal law because most state statutes broadly define criminal assault to include both attempted and actual battery. This differs from civil law, where assault and battery constitute two separate and distinct torts. Further elaboration clarifies the distinction between the criminal and civil law definitions of assault and battery.

A *civil law assault* is any intentional act that creates reasonable apprehension of immediate harmful or offensive contact, while a *civil law battery* is an intentional harmful or offensive contact with another person. For civil assault and battery, as for all intentional torts, there does not have to be harm to the plaintiff to establish a claim of assault and/or battery. The mere fact that a person has done and intended to do a proscribed action will suffice to provide at least nominal damages, but the degree of harm will be important in assessing monetary damages.

3.3.1. The Tort of Assault

For an action to constitute civil assault, each of the following three elements must be proven:

1. Any act that creates a reasonable apprehension in plaintiff of immediate harmful or offensive contact with plaintiff
2. Intent by defendant to cause harm or cause plaintiff's apprehension
3. Causation, defendant's act brought about the apprehension

Words alone are not enough to create an apprehension of immediate harm. Some sort of action on the part of the defendant must accompany the words. Courts rely upon the apparent ability to carry out a threat rather than the actual ability in determining assault. The defendant who claims he or she had no actual ability to carry out a threat will not be successful if he or she had the apparent ability to do so. For example, a defendant's claim that the gun pointed in the direction of the plaintiff was not loaded is not a successful defense against a reasonable person's being placed in apprehension of immediate harm by the defendant. The plaintiff had no way of knowing whether or not the gun was loaded. The apprehension of immediate harm by the plaintiff must be reasonable.

In determining whether the apprehension is reasonable, the courts will apply the *reasonable person standard*. An unusually timid plaintiff may not recover for an assault where a normal person would not have apprehended the harmful or offensive contact. However, the defendant will be held responsible if the defendant knows of the plaintiff's timidness.

Actual contact between the defendant and the plaintiff need not have occurred for assault to be committed; however, the plaintiff must be aware of the possibility of contact. The distinction between actual physical contact and its mere apprehension marks the dividing line between assault and battery. For example, in a high school baseball game, the pitcher threw a pitch that unintentionally got away from him and passed dangerously close to an opponent's head. The opponent took offense at the closeness of the pitch, charged the mound, and intentionally threw his bat in the direction of the pitcher. The pitcher saw the opponent throw the bat toward him. The bat missed the pitcher. Nevertheless, the pitcher could bring suit against the batter for assault. Regarding the intent element, the plaintiff prove either that the defendant intended to inflict bodily harm, or that the defendant intended to bring about plaintiff's apprehension of an immediate harmful or offensive contact. Causation exists where the plaintiff's apprehension was brought about by a direct or indirect act by the defendant. An indirect act includes that which the defendant sets in motion.

3.3.2. The Tort of Battery

For an action to constitute civil battery, three elements must be proven:

1. A harmful or offensive act by the defendant toward the plaintiff
2. Intent by defendant to bring about the harmful or offensive contact to plaintiff
3. Causation; defendant's action brought about the harmful or offensive contact

With regard to the first element, the plaintiff must prove that a *harmful* or *offensive contact occurred*. Mere apprehension of contact is neither sufficient nor necessary to show battery has occurred. An act is construed as harmful or offensive by the reasonable person's standard, that is, a person of ordinary sensibilities. The plaintiff's awareness of the contact at the time of the battery is not essential. For example, plaintiffs have made successful battery claims in cases in which the contact occurred when they were asleep or under anesthesia. Contact does not necessarily have to be "harmful"; it may instead be "offensive," such as spitting at another person. Contact is considered offensive if the plaintiff did not consent to it. For the purposes of determining whether a battery has been committed, anything connected to the plaintiff is considered a part of the plaintiff's person (e.g., clothing or an object held by the plaintiff). Similarly, the contact by the defendant need not be direct (with the plaintiff's body); it may be indirect, such as making contact with an object such as a bat or ordering a dog to attack the plaintiff.

The second element of *intent* requires that the plaintiff prove that the defendant intended to bring about a harmful or offensive contact with the plaintiff. The plaintiff does not have to prove that the defendant intended the specific harm incurred by the victim. The rationale is that the defendant is presumed to have intended the natural and probable consequences of the act. A touching that results from a reflex action is not considered intentional.

The third element required is causation. The defendant is liable for direct and indirect contact. The plaintiff need only prove that the defendant set in motion a force that brought about the harmful or offensive contact with the plaintiff. In contact sports, participants are expected to use force because it is one of the necessary terms and conditions of the game. The contact is justified if it is reasonable under the circumstances. Many contacts that occur in the sports setting would be considered battery in a non-sports setting. However, the key distinction in sports battery is whether the participant has consented to a particular contact. If the court concludes that consent was given and the contact was reasonable, a plaintiff will not be successful in a claim of battery. For example, during a basketball game, Bully Smith was guarding Tommy Timid as Tommy was about to receive a pass. Without provocation, Bully intentionally pushed Tommy from behind and punched him in the back of the head. As Tommy fell, Bully hit him again, knocking Tommy unconscious. The acts of Bully are not of the type to which Tommy would consent in a game of basketball. Thus, Tommy can bring suit against Bully for battery because there was an intended harmful contact caused by Bully. However, Tommy cannot bring an action for assault; there was no apprehension of harm because Tommy did not see the punch coming.

3.3.3. Defenses for Assault and Battery

The defenses that a defendant may raise against a plaintiff's claim of an intentional tort fall into two broad categories: (1) consent and (2) privilege, imposed as a matter of law, not the result of the investigation of facts. Under privilege, the defendant's actions that would otherwise constitute a tort are excused because the action furthers an interest of social importance deserving of protection.

3.3.3.1. Consent

Consent is a voluntary yielding to an invasion of one's interests by another. It is an act of reason, accompanied by deliberation, that is made by an individual possessing sufficient mental capacity to make an intelligent choice. To be effective, consent must be made without fraud or duress. Consent may be expressed or it may be reasonably implied by the circumstances surrounding the situation.

The defense of consent presents a special problem in the realm of sports in general and for athletic participants in particular. The traditional interpretation in many assault and battery cases in the sports setting has been that the athlete, by participating in a given event, consents to the degree of contact commonly found within the rules of the sport. A special problem arises in sports because it is often difficult to determine the extent or scope of the implied consent given.

Consent implied by participation in athletic events is not a blanket consent protecting athletes from the consequences of their actions under all circumstances. Instead, many plaintiffs argue that the scope of consent is limited to acts that occur in the ordinary and normal conduct of the game. The difficulty arises from the determination of what is "ordinary and normal conduct" in a particular game. For example, the consent defense may be raised in a sports-related assault and battery action. The defendant could claim that no tort was committed, given the nature of the relationship with the plaintiff. The defendant could further argue that the plaintiff, by his or her participation in the sport contest, consents to a certain degree of contact. The court must then determine when or how a tort occurs.

3.3.3.2. Privilege

A privilege is a particular, limited benefit enjoyed by an individual or class of individuals that extends beyond the common advantages of other citizens. In certain situations, a privilege is more appropriately classified as an exemption from a burden rather than as a benefit to be enjoyed. A privilege is commonly enjoyed in situations in which the defendant has acted in defense of his or her person or property. The defendant bears the burden of proof to establish that a privilege existed and that the force used pursuant to the privilege was reasonable under the circumstances. The defense will be denied and the defendant will be held liable if the force used is found to be excessive or unreasonable. The defendant must argue and bear the burden of proving the privilege. Privilege includes the following:

1. Self-defense
2. Defense of others
3. Defense of property
4. Recapture of chattels (personal property)
5. Necessity
6. Arrest
7. Discipline

Self-defense is the most commonly used privilege in sports cases. The self-defense privilege rests upon the public policy that allows a person being attacked to come to his or her own defense. The privilege arises when danger exists or there is a reasonable belief that danger is imminent. It is limited to the use of force that is reasonably necessary or appears to be necessary to repel an attack. There is never any privilege to use force when immediate danger is past.

Another viable legal defense against an intentional tort such as assault or battery is the *defense of others*. In order for the defense to be effective, certain requirements must be met. First, the privilege extends only to the reasonable force necessary to defend another from imminent harm. Second, the defense must occur in reaction to events as they exist at the time of the threat. There is no privilege for physical reactions to future threats or past attacks.

This privilege is available to anyone who reasonably defends another. No special relationship between the defender and the victim need exist. The view of the majority of courts is that the defender "steps into the shoes" of the victim. Jurisdictions are split as to whether or not someone can make a mistake in the defense of others. Historically, if the victim would not have been privileged to use force in self-defense, neither would the defender. Accordingly, the defender would be liable even if he or she acted upon a reasonable mistake as to the victim's right to self-defense. However, there is a substantial modern trend that permits the defender to use force whenever he or she reasonably believes the victim would have the privilege of self-defense.

3.3.4. Tortious Interference with Contractual Relations

Tortious interference with contractual relations occurs where a third party, without justification, intentionally induces one person not to perform a contract with another person. The third party is liable to the person with whom the original contract was signed or going to be signed. This type of tort liability protects the rights of a party to a contract from third-party interference. The plaintiff in such a suit bears the burden of proving that the defendant intentionally interfered with the plaintiff's contractual relationship such that the performance of the contract was either prevented or made difficult. The defendant must have actual knowledge of the contract or pending contract and have the intent to interfere with it. The defendant can rebut or justify the interference by showing that the conduct was not "improper."

The *Restatement (Second) of Torts* sets forth the following seven factors to be considered in determining whether the conduct was improper:

1. The nature of the actor's conduct
2. The actor's motive
3. The interests the actor seeks to advance
4. The interests sought to be advanced by the actor
5. The social interests in protecting the freedom of the action of the actor and the contractual interests of others
6. The proximity or remoteness of the actor's conduct to the interference
7. The relations between the parties

This theory has been used when a player or coach signs a contract with a rival team while already under contract with his or her present team. Often, the temptation to obtain a player or a coach already obligated to another team is too difficult to resist, and a player or coach will be induced to breach a current contract to sign with a new employer. In such a situation, the party injured by the breach of the contract may sue the new party for intentionally interfering with the previous contract. Recently, universities have used the doctrine of tortious interference with contractual relations against agents who have interfered with their players' eligibility.

NOTE _____

1. In *Bauer v. Interpublic Group of Companies*, 255 F. Supp. 2d 1086 (N.D. Cal. 2003), the plaintiff alleged that the defendant athlete agents and their associates had interfered with plaintiff's contract to represent David Carr, a college quarterback who was eventually selected first overall in that year's NFL draft. The defendants were granted summary judgment because the plaintiff could not prove that they had the intent to interfere with an existing contract nor that they had actually interfered. Carr did not enter

negotiations with the defendants until he had already decided to terminate his contract with the plaintiff.

3.3.5. The Tort of Intentional Infliction of Emotional Distress

The tort of intentional infliction of emotional distress protects a person's emotional tranquility. Simple minor disturbances and infringements are not actionable. The provoking conduct must be outrageous for the plaintiff to have a viable action. An increasing number of states are recognizing intentional infliction of emotional distress as an independent tort. To establish a claim for intentional infliction of emotional distress, the following elements must be proven by plaintiff:

1. There must be extreme and outrageous conduct by the defendant.
2. The defendant's intention was to cause the plaintiff to suffer severe emotional distress or the defendant recklessly disregarded the high probability that emotional distress would occur.
3. The defendant's conduct must be the cause of emotional distress.
4. Damages; the distress must be severe.

The conduct required is outrageous and extreme. The plaintiff has an initial burden of showing enough evidence for reasonable persons to find extreme and outrageous conduct. The plaintiff is required to show that he or she actually suffered severe emotional distress.

The necessary mental state of the defendant is broader than that of other intentional torts. For other intentional torts, the required intent includes the defendants' desire to cause a certain result and the defendant's knowledge to "substantial certainty" that a particular result will occur. In an intentional infliction of emotional distress claim, the mental state of the defendant can be either the intent to cause the emotional distress, knowledge with a substantial certainty that emotional distress would occur, or reckless action in disregard of the high probability that emotional distress would occur. For example, if the defendant is joking and informs the plaintiff that her son has been killed and the plaintiff suffers emotional distress, the defendant will be liable. Or if a doctor falsely or recklessly makes it known to a person that he or she is suffering from a fatal disease, then the doctor will be liable.

A leading case in the area of intentional infliction of emotional distress is *Chuy v. Philadelphia Eagles Football Club*, 431 F.Supp. 254 (E.D. Pa. 1977), *aff'd*, 595 F.2d 1265 (3d Cir. 1979). Chuy, a professional football player, brought suit against the Eagles and the National Football League, seeking to recover the balance of his salary allegedly due on his contract and for damages for defamation and intentional infliction of emotional distress. Chuy had suffered a serious injury while playing football. Chuy's claims for emotional distress were based on a statement made by a team physician who was being interviewed by the press. The doctor falsely reported that Chuy had contracted a rare blood disease that would prevent him from ever playing football again. Chuy, having no prior knowledge of the existence of such a condition, claimed that upon hearing the report, he was put under incredible emotional anguish and anticipated death.

The court held that the doctor's conduct was sufficiently outrageous. The court found that the doctor intentionally told reporters that Chuy was suffering from a blood disease, knowing that this was in fact not true. Chuy recovered $10,000 in compensatory damages for this infliction of emotional distress. He also recovered $60,000 in punitive damages, an amount affirmed on appeal as not being excessive.

Athletic administrators must also be on their guard about statements made by members of an organization's staff that could lead to litigation such as that in *Chuy*. The following are examples of instances in which such statements to the media could lead to similar litigation:

1. A coach's statement about the playing ability of a student-athlete, including professional career aspirations
2. An administrator's statement about the employment tenure of a coach
3. A trainer's announcement about the playing ability or injury of a student-athlete
4. A sports information director's comments about student-athletes and coaches

In any of these situations, if the statement was "extremely outrageous" and injured the individual about whom it was made, an athletic administrator might anticipate that litigation will be filed.

3.3.6. Damages for Intentional Torts

In a case involving intentional torts, the plaintiff may recover compensatory damages for lost earning capacity, medical expenses, pain and suffering, and for the loss of consortium (i.e., affection, assistance, and marital fellowship). These damages are sometimes termed *actual damages*. In an intentional tort case, it is not necessary to prove actual damages in order to recover. The plaintiff may recover damages without proving specific bodily injuries. Furthermore, torts involving intentional harm allow for recovery of damages for emotional suffering (i.e., humiliation, indignity, injury to feelings), as long as this suffering was proximately caused by the defendant's conduct.

Certain conduct by the plaintiff that is not sufficient to constitute a defense to the action may be considered in mitigation of damages. For example, although provocative words by the plaintiff do not justify the defendant's use of force, these words may be considered to mitigate the amount of damages awarded to the plaintiff.

In addition to actual damages, a plaintiff may recover *punitive damages*. Punitive damages are awarded to penalize a defendant who has acted willfully or has exhibited outrageous conduct. These damages are awarded on the theory that they may help to deter future wrongful conduct.

3.4. HARM TO ECONOMIC AND DIGNITARY INTERESTS

3.4.1. Defamation Law

Defamation law protects a person's reputation. The focus of a defamation action is on the alleged defamatory statement and its impact on third persons.

The elements that must be proven to establish liability for defamation are the following:

1. A false statement concerning the plaintiff
2. The publication (communication) of the false statement by the defendant to a person(s) other than plaintiff
3. Fault, amounting to at least negligence, on the part of the defendant
4. Damage or injury to the reputation of the plaintiff

A defamatory statement exposes the plaintiff to public hatred, shame, contempt, or ridicule. A statement may be oral or written, a photograph, a cartoon, or any other form of communication. The plaintiff must show that his or her reputation was injured in the eyes of the community.

Defamation is divided into two categories: libel and slander. *Libel* is the publication of a defamatory statement in writing. There are three classes of libel: (1) libel per se, which includes materials that are obviously defamatory by community members; (2) materials that could be taken as defamatory; and (3) materials that are not by themselves defamatory but when combined with other facts become libelous. *Slander* is the publication of defamatory matter through spoken words.

In some cases, libel or slander may be considered *defamation per se*. In such cases, an injury to the reputation is presumed without proof of special damages if it falls into one of the following categories:

1. It accuses the plaintiff of a crime involving moral turpitude.
2. It adversely affects plaintiff's abilities in his or her profession, business, or trade.
3. It accuses the plaintiff of having a loathsome disease.
4. It accuses the plaintiff of sexual misconduct.

3.4.1.1. Libel

The basic elements of libel are a defamatory statement, its publication, fault and damages. Truth is an absolute defense to a libel action. The defendant has the burden of proving the truth of the communication if his or her defense is truth. If the statement is false, the plaintiff has the burden of proving the appropriate level of fault on the part of the defendant. To prove fault, the plaintiff must prove that the statement was made with hatred, ill will, malevolent intent, or negligence as to the truth or falsity of the statement. The plaintiff must prove that a third person was exposed to the publication. Finally, the plaintiff must prove actual damages.

In libel cases, it is critical to recall the distinction between compensatory and punitive damages. As with any tort, a plaintiff who can prove a case for libel will be able to recover whatever compensatory damages he or she can demonstrate. But the plaintiff will not be limited to such recovery: since defamation is an intentional tort, punitive damages will also be available to successful plaintiffs.

3.4.1.2. Slander

Slander is publication of defamatory matter by spoken words. There must be a publication, and the plaintiff must be held up to scorn and ridicule as a result of the defamatory statement. Truth is an absolute defense to a slander action. Again, however, the plaintiff must show that the statement was heard and understood by a third person. Unlike libel, the injury to reputation is not presumed. Therefore, the plaintiff must prove special damages, usually required to be of a pecuniary nature, unless it is slander per se.

The U.S. Supreme Court has established standards that apply in libel and slander situations. In its decisions, the Court has balanced the competing interests of protecting the reputation of an individual against freedom of the press.

In the first of its decisions in 1964, the Court held that the constitutional guarantee of a free press requires a public official to prove actual malice in the publication of a defamatory falsehood in order to recover for defamation (*New York Times Company v. Sullivan*, 376 U.S. 254 (1964)). In 1967, the Court extended the constitutional privilege to public figures as well as public officials. Finally, in *Gertz v. United States*, 418 U.S. 323 (1974), the Court extended the "actual malice" standard. A public official or public figure who has been defamed must prove that the defendant published the statement with actual malice, that is, knowing that the material was false or in reckless disregard as to whether it was false or not.

Defamation should be distinguished from both intentional infliction of emotional distress and invasion of privacy. *Intentional infliction of emotional distress* is classified as an intentional tort and is concerned with the impact on the individual plaintiff without regard to third persons. *Defamation* involves the element of publication to third persons as well as the requirement that the material be taken by these third persons as damaging. Defamation must also be distinguished from the tort of invasion of privacy. An action for *invasion of privacy* concerns one's right to peace of mind and comfort, while an action for defamation involves the plaintiff's character or reputation. Invasion of privacy can also be distinguished from defamation in that truth is an absolute defense to the defamation action, but truth is not a defense to an invasion of privacy action.

A leading sports case in the area of defamation law is *Curtis Publishing Co. v. Butts*, 388 U.S. 130 (1967). Curtis Publishing Company had printed an article alleging that Wallace Butts, while the athletic director at the University of Georgia had supplied to Paul Bryant, the head football coach at Alabama, information concerning Georgia's game plan for an upcoming game against Alabama. The article was based on a phone conversation between Butts and Bryant, supposedly overheard by an insurance salesman.

Butts filed a libel suit against Curtis in federal court and the court awarded compensatory and punitive damages. Curtis appealed the decision to the Supreme Court. Curtis argued that Butts was a public figure and thus needed to prove that a public figure who is not a public official may recover damages for a defamatory falsehood obviously damaging to his reputation. Curtis claimed that such a figure must show that the conduct of the publisher was highly unreasonable and constituted an extreme departure from the standards of investigation and reporting ordinarily adhered to by responsible publishers. The Supreme Court affirmed the trial court's decision.

Sports are played in public settings and are coached and administered in what often seems like "the heat of battle." Thus, athletic administrators have to be extremely cautious that what began as a sporting event does not erupt into litigation involving defamation—either libel or slander. The passions of the contest should not be allowed to evolve into inappropriate statements about an individual to the media or the general public. Athletic administrators always have to be on guard for such possibilities and must instruct their staff about the potential litigation any such statement could cause for the organization or individuals involved.

NOTES

1. In *Knievel v. ESPN*, 393 F.3d 1068 (9th Cir. 2005), the Ninth Circuit ruled that ESPN did not defame daredevil Evel Knievel when it posted online a picture of him with his wife on one arm and another woman on the other with a caption reading "Evel Knievel proves that you're never too old to be a pimp." Knievel claimed that the caption accused him of the crime of soliciting prostitution and accused his wife of being a prostitute. The court found that the totality of circumstances, including the context of the "extreme sports website" EXPN.com, made clear that the "loose, figurative language" used by the defendants would not be taken literally by anyone who read it.

2. In *Cobb v. Time, Inc.*, 278 F.3d 629 (6th Cir. 2002), the Sixth Circuit considered a defamation suit filed by Randall "Tex" Cobb, a professional boxer, against a publishing company. The defendant owned *Sports Illustrated*, which had published an article asserting that Cobb had knowingly participated in a fixed boxing match and that he had used cocaine with his opponent and the promoter of the event. The court ruled as a matter of law that Cobb, a public figure, could not prove actual malice with respect to any of the details in the article. *Sports Illustrated's* story, based largely on statements from Cobb's opponent in the fight and on corroborating evidence where possible, contained no reckless disregard for the truth nor intentional falsehoods.

3. In *Riggs v. Clark County School District*, 19 F.Supp. 2d 1177 (D. Nev. 1998), a former high school volleyball coach sued the district and a district official for defamation for remarks allegedly made to parents of students following coach's termination. On defendants' motion to dismiss, the District Court held that under Nevada law, the statement that coach "was being replaced for the betterment of the program" constituted pure opinion.

4. In *Moore v. University of Notre Dame*, 968 F. Supp. 1330 (N.D. Ind. 1997), a former football coach alleged that he was defamed by his head coach who stated that the plaintiff only could coach for one or two more years and that he was no longer physically capable of putting in long hours like his coaching colleagues. Under Indiana law, this was deemed to be not defamatory per se. Furthermore, the plaintiff coach failed to demonstrate actual damages or establish actual malice as required for claim of defamation. The defendant's motion to dismiss was therefore granted.

5. For information on an athlete's right of publicity, or his or her exclusive ability to control and profit from the use of his or her name, likeness, and persona, see section 13.4, "The Right of Publicity." Using a person's name, likeness, or persona without his or her permission can amount to misappropriation, a state law tort claim.

Also see the following law review articles:

1. Pamela C. Laucella and Barbara Osborne, "Libel and College Coaches," 12 *Journal of Legal Aspects of Sport*, 183 (2002).

2. Mark Gatto, "An Athlete's Statements Regarding the Conduct of His Agent Can Be Actionable Under State Defamation Laws," 9 *Seton Hall Journal of Sports and Entertainment Law* 263 (1999).

3.4.2. The Tort of Invasion of Privacy

An action for invasion of privacy is designed to protect against unreasonable interferences with a person's solitude or "right to be let alone." Although some intrusions into a person's life are expected and must be tolerated in society, when the intrusions become excessive or unjustified, then a cause of action will exist for invasion of privacy.

One can invade the privacy of another in four distinct ways:

1. Intrusion by the defendant upon plaintiff's affairs or solitude
2. Publicly disclosing private facts about the plaintiff by the defendant
3. Publication by defendant of facts that put plaintiff in a false light in the public eye
4. Appropriation by defendant of plaintiff's picture or name for defendant's commercial gain

In an action for invasion of privacy, the intrusion must be substantial and must be into an area for which there is an expectation of privacy. For example, simply staring at a person would not generally amount to an intrusion; wiretapping, on the other hand, would amount to an intrusion.

The plaintiff must also show that the publication of private matters involved a matter that in fact was truly private. Newsworthy public interest matters or public facts are not considered to be of a purely private nature. Court records, for example, are open to the public and are therefore not viewed as private facts.

The U.S. Supreme Court in *Time, Inc. v. Hill*, 385 U.S. 374 (1967) held that the First Amendment to the U.S. Constitution protects reports of newsworthy matters. These matters can be publicized unless, as was discussed in the previous section, actual malice is shown. The actual malice standard may be applied even though a plaintiff was a private person who did not want the publicity.

In *Bilney v. Evening Star Newspaper Co.*, 406 A.2d 652 (Md. Ct. App. 1979), a leading case in the area, members of the University of Maryland basketball team brought suit against two newspapers. The newspapers published an article concerning certain players whose academic standing was threatening their eligibility. The players based their action, in part, on the theory of invasion of privacy. The court, basing its decision on the *Restatement (Second) of Torts*, Section 652, held that the players were public figures. The court found that there was widespread public interest in Maryland basketball. When the players' academic standing threatened their eligibility, the privacy of those facts lessened. The court stated that "the publication of their eligibility-threatening status was not unreasonable and did not trample community mores" of what is legitimate public interest.

The court relied primarily on the reasoning of the *Restatement (Second) of Torts*, Section 652D. This section explains that a public figure cannot complain when given publicity that was sought, even though it may be unfavorable. The *Restatement (Second) of Torts* also holds that the publicity of public figures "is not limited to the particular events that arouse the interests of the public" (Section 652D, comment). The legitimate public interests of these figures extends into some of their private matters. The court also held that the right to make public the private facts of a public figure is not an unlimited right and that the limit is determined by community mores: "The line is to be drawn when the publicity ceases to be the giving of information to which the public is entitled and becomes a morbid and sensational prying into private lives" (Section 652D, comment).

The *Bilney* case typifies the difficult burden an athlete has in winning an invasion of privacy action. The Maryland players were unsuccessful because the news article did not invade a "private" area. The opinion reflects how difficult it is for a person classified as a public figure to recover for invasion of privacy. Public figures must put up with more publicity concerning their private lives than those who are not public figures. Since most pro athletes and the majority of big-time college student-athletes would probably be classified as public figures, it remains difficult for them to recover under the theory of invasion of privacy.

3.5. PRODUCTS LIABILITY LAW

Products liability is an expansive area of tort law that allows a party who has been injured by a product defectively designed, manufactured, or distributed to recover under several possible causes of action. The causes of action in products liability cases are intent, negligence, strict liability, and breach of implied warranty of merchantability and fitness and representation theories (express warranty and misrepresentation).

The class of possible defendants in a products liability action is broad. Everyone in the chain of distribution of a product is potentially liable, from the manufacturer to the seller or lessor of the product to those who service or install the product. A product is any item of personal property, most commonly consumer goods, including the container in which it is sold. Even vacant land that has been altered by earth-moving equipment to be made into a baseball diamond can be a "product," so that the manufacturer (earth mover) could be liable for injuries caused by holes or bumps in the surface.

The plaintiff in a products liability case must show that a defect existed at the time the product left the control of the defendant and that the injury was caused by the defect. Courts have most frequently applied a definition of defect from the *Restatement (Third) of Torts*, Section 402A, which states that a product is in a defective condition if it is "unreasonably dangerous to the user." Comment (i) of Section 401A further defines a defect: the article sold must be dangerous to the extent beyond that which would be contemplated by the ordinary consumer who purchases it, with the knowledge common to the community as to its characteristics.

In the amateur sports setting, an athletic administrator has to be particularly aware of potential product liability problems. Sports involve the participation of individuals and their use of equipment, both of which are factors in a product liability lawsuit. Ultimately, such litigation leads to increases in a sports organization's insurance premiums, a subject discussed in section 4.9, "Liability Insurance."

3.5.1. Products Liability Based on Intent

A defendant is liable to a plaintiff injured by an unsafe product if the defendant intended the consequences or knew with substantial certainty that they would occur. Liability based on an intentional tort is uncommon in products liability cases. It is more likely that such a case would be brought to court as a battery claim.

3.5.2. Products Liability Based on Negligence

In products liability law, a manufacturer of a product has the duty to meet legal standards of safety and care in the product's design, manufacture, and use. The product supplier and seller may additionally be liable for negligence if they have not exercised reasonable care. The courts generally balance the probability and gravity of the potential harm against the social value of the product and the inconvenience and expense of taking precautions in determining whether or not a duty of care has been breached. The standard of care involved in manufacturing is one of reasonable care in both the manufacture and the design of the product to ensure that it will be reasonably safe when used in the manner intended. Where a product may be dangerous even when properly used, the manufacturer may have an additional *duty to warn* the product's users of the hazard. However, the manufacturer is not required to make the safest or best possible product, although the product will be compared to similar products. The similar products will be used to help determine what is a "reasonably" safe product. Suppliers, the wholesalers of a product, must also exercise reasonable care.

First, a supplier has a duty to use reasonable care to make a product safe. If the supplier knows or has reason to know that the product is dangerous and that the user is not likely to realize the danger, the supplier must additionally exercise reasonable care to *notify* the user of the potential dangers. For example, the Flybynight Company was contracted to replace a drainage system at a high school soccer field. After completion of the job, the ground around one of the drainpipes settled, leaving the pipe exposed. Kenny Keeper dived to make a save; he fell on the pipe and suffered severe injuries. The Flybynight Company was negligent for its failure to ensure the safety of the field and failure to warn of the potential hazard. The school would also be a potential defendant for negligently hiring an incompetent contractor to install the new drainage system.

Sellers of a product are also subject to liability for negligence in some circumstances. A seller who knows a product is dangerous has a duty to warn a purchaser, who has no knowledge of the dangerous nature of the product. A seller may also have a duty to inspect a product manufactured by another if the seller knows or has reason to know that it is likely to be hazardous.

Advertisers and marketers of a product also have a duty to exercise reasonable care. When a product appears on the market, a warning about the dangers associated with the product must accompany it. This warning must disclose the dangers from an improper use as well as dangers that are possible even when the product is properly used. The warning must also be sufficient to protect third parties who might reasonably be expected to come into contact with the product.

NOTE

1. In *Ford v. Nairn*, 717 N.E. 2d 525 (Ill. App. Ct. 1999), a minor trampoline user who injured her knee when jumping on the trampoline sued the trampoline's owners and manufacturer on theories of negligence and products liability. The Circuit Court of Jersey County granted summary judgment for defendants. Plaintiffs appealed, and the owners also appealed. The appellate court held that (1) a reasonable 14-year-old would appreciate the open and obvious danger of jumping on a recreational trampoline and thus there was no duty to warn and (2) warnings issued by the manufacturer were adequate in any event.

3.5.3. Products Liability Based on Strict Tort Liability

The theory behind strict liability is that when the seller markets its product for use and consumption by the public, it assumes a special responsibility to any member of the public for any injury caused by the product. The public has the right to expect that the seller will provide a reasonably safe product. There is a strong public policy supporting the demand that the burden of accidental injuries caused by a seller's products be placed on those who produced and marketed them. The theory is that the cost inherent in the assumption of responsibility can be insured; it will be treated as a cost of production and added to the cost of the item. Therefore, the consumer is given the maximum possible protection from unreasonably dangerous products in that the people in the best position to provide this protection are those who market and profit from the products.

The strict tort liability definition states that one who sells a product which is unreasonably dangerous to the user or consumer because of a defect—whether in design or in manufacture—is held liable for any physical harm to the ultimate user or consumer, or that person's property, proximately caused by use of the product. The following elements must be proved to establish a strict tort liability claim:

1. Strict duty owed by a commercial supplier

2. Breach of that duty by the defendant

3. Actual and proximate causation

4. Damages

The seller must be engaged in the business of selling such a product and not merely a causal seller. This would include manufacturers, retailers, assemblers, or wholesalers. The plaintiff need not prove that the defendant was at fault or negligent in selling or producing a defective product—only that the product, in fact, is defective, causing it to be "unreasonably dangerous." This strict liability standard applies even if a seller exercised all necessary and appropriate care in the preparation and sale of the product.

The seller will be liable if the defective product was the actual cause of plaintiff's harm, provided that the product has not been changed from its initial state or condition upon leaving defendant's control. The same concepts of proximate causation governing general negligence claims are applicable to strict tort liability for defective products. Damages under a product liability claim are the same as those recoverable in negligence, that is, personal injury and property damage. For defendants facing a strict tort liability claim, ordinary contributory negligence is *not* a defense. Assumption of the risk for voluntarily and knowingly risky behavior on the part of the plaintiff, however, is a valid defense. Note that liability can be found only if the product has been used in the manner that could be foreseen by the seller. Accordingly, a seller will not be liable for harm resulting from unforeseeable, abnormal use of the product.

NOTE _____

1. In *Bourne v. Marty Gilman, Inc.*, 452 F.3d 632 (7th Cir. 2006), the Seventh Circuit ruled that a student who was rendered paraplegic by a falling football goalpost could not prevail against the goalpost's manufacturer on a theory of strict products liability. The plaintiff had joined a crowd in rushing the field after the game and was severely injured after turning his back to the goalpost before other members of the crowd brought it down. The court held that since the danger posed by the goalpost was obvious, it was not an unreasonably dangerous product.

3.5.4. Products Liability Based on Implied and Express Warranties

A cause of action for product liability may be based on a breach of warranty claim against a manufacturer. This is basically an adaptation of contract law to tort problems. First, the plaintiff must establish that there was an express or implied warranty. The plaintiff must then prove that the defendant breached the warranty causing harm to the plaintiff. The advantage to a claim based on warranty principles is that the plaintiff does not have to prove that the product was defective in its design.

An *express warranty* is an affirmation of material fact concerning the nature and fitness of a particular product upon which the buyer might reasonably rely. An *implied warranty* does not arise from any words of the seller, either oral or in writing, but is a rule of law in every state. The rule is embodied in Section 2-314 of the Uniform Commercial Code, which states: "A warranty that the goods shall be merchantable is implied in a contract for their sale if the seller is a merchant with respect to goods of that kind." Merchantable goods are fit for the ordinary purposes for which such goods are ordinarily used.

3.6. VICARIOUS LIABILITY

The doctrine of vicarious liability imposes liability for a tortious act upon a person who is not personally negligent but is held liable because of the relationship between the parties. The most typical relationships that give rise to vicarious liability are master-servant (employer-employee) and principal-agent. Vicarious liability is also known as the doctrine of *respondeat superior*. The most frequent situation in which vicarious liability exists is within the relationship of employer-employee. If A, an employee of C, negligently causes an injury to B, vicarious liability imposes liability for the negligent act by A upon C if the negligence occurs within the scope of that employment relationship. Under the doctrine of vicarious liability, C is liable to B, the party injured by A, even though C was not himself negligent, did not aid or encourage the negligence of A, and did everything he could to prevent harm to B. For example, if a player was injured due to the negligence of the groundskeeper, the employer of the groundskeeper (jointly with the groundskeeper) may be held vicariously liable to the injured player if the tortious act occurs within the scope of the groundskeeper's employment.

The rationale behind the doctrine rests on public policy considerations. Since the servant is furthering the master's enterprise, any accident that arises directly or indirectly from the enterprise should be paid for by the enterprise (owner). Such costs are considered as a cost of doing business. This places an increased burden on the master, but the master is in a better position to bear the risks of injuries to others by obtaining insurance against work-related accidents. This doctrine allows an innocent plaintiff to recover from the master, who is said to have "deep pockets," while the employee may be judgment proof. Vicarious liability causes the employer to be held responsible when the employer exercises control and direction over the employee, and the employee is negligent while acting within the scope of his employment. Vicarious liability is usually not imposed on the employer for intentional torts committed by the employee.

An intentional tort is usually considered beyond the scope of authority and control of the employer and not in the furtherance of the employer's business. For example, if a coach assaults a bartender after work, the school district will not be held liable under a vicarious liability theory. However, an employer may be held responsible for an intentional tort committed by an employee if the employee was under the authority and control of the employer and the employee is in a position where such torts may be encouraged or expected in furtherance of the employer's business. These same general rules apply to principal-agent vicarious liability situations in sports-related cases.

The doctrine of vicarious liability is widely applicable to tort actions for negligence in the sports setting. For example, a coach may be held liable for the actions of his players, a school district may be held liable for the actions of a coach or a teacher, or an athletic administrator may be held liable for the actions of a coach. In order for an employer to be held liable in these situations, the employee must first be found negligent under the primary standard of reasonable care, and then the action must be determined to have been within the scope of the defendant's employment.

In a case (sport or nonsport) involving a monetary award for damages, it is common practice to sue in the alternative, that is, to sue each party involved in the alleged incident of negligence. This practice serves three primary purposes:

1. It allows the plaintiff to determine exactly who is liable for the particular injury.

2. It allows the plaintiff to determine which party involved in the suit has money sufficient to pay the damages award ("deep pockets").

3. It allows judicial efficiency by preventing multiple suits on the same cause of action against various defendants.

Thus, in some cases, an employer may be sued both on a theory of vicarious liability and for negligent hiring if the employee had a history of unreasonable conduct at the time of hiring.

NOTES _____

1. In *Myricks v. Lynwood Unified School District*, 74 Cal. App. 4th 231 (1999), the appellate court ruled that a city employee was not acting within the scope of her job with the recreation and parks department when she volunteered to drive the plaintiffs to a basketball tournament. During the trip, the city employee fell asleep and the van rolled over, killing one student and injuring several others. Since it had exercised no control over the planning or execution of the trip, the city could not be found liable for the driver's negligence.

2. Chapter 4, "Application of Tort Law to Sports," discusses the ways that the doctrine of vicarious liability is applied to various persons in the sports industry such as facility owners, university presidents, directors of athletic organizations, and owners of professional sports franchises. Also see the following law review article: Vered Yakovee, "Legal Aspects of Big Sports Event Management," 25 *Entertainment and Sports Lawyer* 1 (2007).

3.6.1. Exception: Independent Contractors

The existence of independent contractors raises an important issue in understanding the scope of the doctrine of vicarious liability. An independent contractor is a person who, although in some way connected to the employer, is not under the employer's control and thus vitiating vicarious liability.

To determine the status of any person, the law examines the degree of control that the employer has over the employee's actions. A person hired for a specific, limited purpose, with no direct supervision, who works without allowing the employer to have control over his or her actions, is most likely an independent contractor. If the person is an independent contractor, the employer may not be liable for negligence committed by that independent contractor. However, officials remain liable for any negligent acts of their own.

As a general rule, a doctor who is provided by a school that is hosting a football game is considered to be an independent contractor. Here, although paid by the school district, the doctor is not in any way under its control when making medical decisions. Thus, the doctrine of vicarious liability would not be applicable and the school would not be liable for the doctor's medical negligence.

Another group classified as independent contractors are officials and referees. In most cases, the referee has been determined by the courts to be an independent contractor (see section 4.7, "Liability of Officials, Referees, and Umpires").

NOTES

1. In *Rostai v. Neste Enterprises*, 138 Cal. App. 4th 326 (Cal. Ct. App. 2006), the court of appeal affirmed the trial court's summary judgment against a vicarious liability claim. The plaintiff had suffered a heart attack while working out at the gym under the supervision of a personal trainer who was not a gym employee. Since the gym exercised no control over the workout and the plaintiff assumed the risks associated with physical training, the gym was not liable for the harm to the plaintiff.

2. In *Harvey v. Ouachita Parish School Board*, 545 So. 2d 1241 (La. Ct. App. 1989), an injured football player sued the state high school athletic association for negligence for injuries suffered as a result of excessively rough behavior. The court held for the defendant on the basis that the association was not responsible for the referees' failure to remove football players who were displaying excessively rough behavior. The court reasoned that though the association had registered the referees, the referees were neither agents nor servants of the association.

3. In *Classen v. Izquierdo*, 520 N.Y.S.2d 999 (N.Y. County Sup. Ct. 1987), plaintiff widow brought action against ringside physicians and the proprietor of the sports facility to recover damages for the death of her husband, a boxer. The proprietor did not participate in the selection of the referee or ringside physicians and did not provide them with training, instruction, or supervision. Consequently, the court held that the proprietor was not vicariously liable for any negligence of the referee in the boxing match for allowing the contest to continue since the referee was an independent contractor.

Also see the following law review articles:

1. Michael Mayer, "Stepping in to Step Out of Liability: The Proper Standard of Liability for Referees in Foreseeable Judgment-Call Situations," 3 *DePaul Journal of Sports Law & Contemporary Problems* (2005).

2. Darryll M. Halcomb Lewis, "After Further Review, Are Sports Officials Independent Contractors?" 35 *American Business Law Journal* 249 (Winter 1998).

3.7. WORKERS' COMPENSATION

Workers' compensation is a statutorily created method for providing cash benefits and medical care to employees and their dependents when employees suffer personal injuries or death in the course of employment. The purpose of the benefits is to provide employees and their dependents with greater protection than afforded by the common law remedy of a suit for damages. Each state has its own workers' compensation act that provides a system of monetary payments for the loss of earning capacity to an employee, according to a scale established by the state. The act may also have provisions for paying burial, medical, or other expenses incurred by the employee.

Workers' compensation acts differ as to where the funds are derived and the method of payment used in compensating claims. Some acts require the employer to make payment directly to the employee. Other acts provide payment out of a fund to which many different employers contribute. In other acts, the employer's private insurer makes payments.

The primary reason for passage of workers' compensation statutes was to eliminate the inadequacies of the common law remedies that resulted from the injured party having to show that the employer was negligent. Proving negligence was often difficult for the employee because of defenses available to the employer such as contributory negligence, assumption of the risk, and coworker negligence. Under a workers' compensation act, the injured employee need only show that the employer was subject to the act, that he or she was an employee under the act's definition, and that the injury occurred during the course of employment. Fault or employer negligence is not a prerequisite to receiving workers' compensation benefits. Payments are made at intervals, when the injured party and his or her dependents need money most, instead of waiting until the completion of costly litigation. To claim a right to compensation, an employee need only fall within the terms of the statute. This theory of compensation shifts the burden of economic loss from the employee and the employee's dependents under common law to the employer under the act. While the employer considers workers' compensation benefits part of its production cost, consumers may bear the economic cost of the benefits if the employer adds the costs to its products or services.

Although each jurisdiction varies in the details of its act, the various acts have some general similarities. For example, in all jurisdictions there is a short waiting period during which the employee must be either totally or partially incapacitated. This is to avoid small and insignificant claims. When the period ends, the worker is eligible for compensation beginning from the date of the injury. Every jurisdiction sets its own rate schedule prescribing minimum and maximum compensation amounts for total disability, partial disability, or permanent and total disability. These amounts are determined by each state's legislature and may be revised yearly. An additional benefit, separate from weekly compensation, is added for every person wholly dependent on the injured provider.

Workers' compensation issues affect college athletic administrators in significant ways, as scholarship student-athletes who suffer injuries may seek to establish their eligibility for benefits. Although a limited number of such claims have succeeded, most courts to confront the issue have ruled that scholarship agreements differ from employment contracts, thus exempting colleges and universities from the requirements of workers' compensation statutes.

This issue was raised in *Rensing v. Indiana State University Board of Trustees* (see note 10) and in *University of Denver v. Nemeth* (see note 6). In these cases, the courts were divided as to whether the student-athlete was eligible to receive workers' compensation benefits. In finding that the student-athlete was an employee of the institution, and thus eligible for benefits, the court in *Nemeth* ruled that the continued receipt of a job, free meals, or scholarship money was conditioned on the student-athlete's participation in football, thereby creating a contract for employment. With the employment contract established, workers' compensation benefits were paid to the employee-athletes injured or killed during the course of their employment.

In the majority of other cases involving student-athletes, however, courts did not find that employment contracts existed, and benefits were denied (see notes 7–11). In two such cases, it was found that football was not an integral moneymaking part of the university's educational function. Therefore, while the student-athlete was employed because of the receipt of an athletic scholarship, that employment was not in the institution's usual trade or business.

When considering the issue of whether an athletic department or institution's employee who was injured while participating in employer-sponsored athletic activities is entitled to workers' compensation benefits, the courts attempt to determine whether the injury occurred in the course of employment. Factors the courts will consider include whether the event occurred on the employer's property and during working hours; whether the employer provided financial support, awards, and/or equipment; the level of encouragement to participate expressed by the employer; and any benefits derived by the employer as a result of the employee's participation in the event. For instance, if the employer required employees to participate in athletic activities with prospective clients as a means of increasing business and income, an employee injured in such activities may prove that the injury occurred while he or she was acting in the course of his or her employment. In addition, injuries sustained while participating in a local school system's basketball league to promote better public relations have been found compensable under workers' compensation statutes (see note 2).

Workers' compensation claims filed by injured student-athletes against their institutions increased during the early 1980s. In response to this trend, the National Collegiate Athletic Association (NCAA) in 1985 instituted a catastrophic injury protection insurance plan that could be purchased by member institutions. The NCAA's insurance policy provides benefits to catastrophically injured student-athletes regardless of fault. In many cases, the NCAA program may be more attractive than a successful workers' compensation claim because the student-athlete may obtain benefits immediately and avoid the time delays, costs, and uncertainties of litigation involved in filing for workers' compensation benefits. Yet because the scholarship athlete/employee issue had not been firmly resolved, injured student-athletes may still bring workers' compensation cases. However, the NCAA program has met its objectives. The NCAA would rather have the costs of the benefits to the injured student-athlete covered by an insurance policy than paid for through the more costly and more tenuous method of workers' compensation. The catastrophic injury protection plan is paid for by the NCAA and its member institutions and benefits the institutions by protecting them against the sudden and substantial costs of injury benefits.

NOTES

The following are cases where the court granted workers' compensation.

1. In *Dubinsky v. St. Louis Blues Hockey Club*, 229 S.W.3d 126 (Mo. App. E.D. 2007), the court granted Steven Dubinsky workers compensation for injuries sustained in an NHL game. However, in accordance with Missouri statutes, the court did grant the Blues a credit

against the amounts owed to Dubinsky because they continued to pay him his salary until his contract expired.

2. In *Pro-Football, Inc. v. Paul*, 569 S.E.2d 66 (Va. Ct. App. 2002), the court of appeals upheld a workers' compensation award to Tito Paul, a former member of the Washington Redskins who had suffered a knee injury while playing against the Pittsburgh Steelers. The Redskins argued that since Paul had originally signed a contract with the Denver Broncos in Colorado before being traded, his contract had not been "made in Virginia." The court ruled that since Paul's trade to the Redskins was only completed when he passed a physical exam administered by the team in Virginia, the contract had in fact been made in the state.

3. In *Dozier v. Mid-Del School System*, 959 P.2d 604 (Okla. App. Div. 1998), a teacher sought award of workers' compensation benefits for injury he sustained while playing in a charity basketball game to raise funds for a school athletic program. The Court of Civil Appeals held that the school district derived substantial direct benefit from the teacher's participation in the basketball game, and thus the teacher was entitled to award of benefits.

4. In *Connery v. Liberty Northwest Insurance Corp.*, 929 P.2d 222 (Mont. 1996), the Supreme Court of Montana posed the question of whether an injury that occurred in a warm-up run for an employee ski instructor immediately prior to her class is compensable. The court held that a "warm-up run" was a prescribed duty of her employment as a ski instructor so that her injury occurred during the course and within the scope of her employment.

5. In *McCarthy v. Quest International Co.*, 667 A.2d 379 (NJ Super. Ct. App. Div. 1995), plaintiff was injured while participating in a tug-of-war during company picnic. Compensation was allowed because her attendance was mandatory; she was urged to enter the tug-of-war by her company's president against her own desires; and the employer so involved the plaintiff in the activities of the picnic as to make the activity an incident of her employment.

6. In *University of Denver v. Nemeth*, 257 P.2d 423 (Colo. 1953), Nemeth, a student-athlete injured during football practice, was found eligible for workers' compensation. Since Nemeth was given meal money and a job on campus only if he performed well on the football field, he fulfilled the workers' compensation act's requirement that the injury arise out of an act in the course of employment.

The following are cases in which the court denied workers' compensation.

1. In *Waldrep v. Texas Employers Insurance Association*, 21 S.W.3d 692 (Tex. Ct. App. 2000), the Texas Court of Appeals let stand a lower court ruling that an injured college football player was not an employee of the school at the time of his paralyzing injury 26 years earlier, and therefore, he could not claim workers' compensation benefits.

2. In *Dandenault v. Workers' Comp Appeals Bd*, 728 A. 2d 1001 (Pa. Commw. 1999), a professional hockey player sought benefits for injury he sustained while playing summer hockey in order to remain in shape during the off season. The court held that the player's injury did not arise in the course of his employment so as to be compensable.

3. In *Brighton School District v. Lyons*, 873 P.2d 26 (Colo. Ct. App. 1993), the court denied workers' compensation to a high school referee who broke his leg while working a football game. Since the referee worked part-time for the school district and was free from the district's control and direction while performing his duties, he was not an employee of the district but an independent contractor.

4. In *Rensing v. Indiana State University Board of Trustees*, 444 N.E. 2d 1170 (Ind. 1983), the court noted a number of factors that suggested that the scholarship did not constitute an employment contract: (1) Rensing had not reported his benefits on his income tax returns; (2) NCAA regulations are incorporated by reference into the scholarship agreement, and since these regulations prohibit payment for athletic participation, the scholarship cannot be a job contract; and (3) the employer's right to dismiss Rensing on the basis of poor performance was conspicuously absent. Finally, the court also found that neither of the parties had the intent to enter into an employment contract.

5. In *Coleman v. Western Michigan University*, 336 N.W.2d 224 (Mich. Ct. App. 1983), the Michigan State Court of Appeals found that an injured college football player was not entitled to workers' compensation benefits. According to the court, the plaintiff was not an "employee" under the meaning of the Michigan workers' compensation act. The Michigan act, unlike that of some other states (the Court named California's as an example), places the burden of proof in establishing employment on the plaintiff. In other states, the burden of proof is placed on the *employer* to disprove an employer-employee relationship. The court was also persuaded by the language of a dissenting Indiana Court of Appeals judge in *Rensing* (see note 10). Quoting Judge Young of Indiana: "[Plaintiff's] participation in football may well have benefited the university in a very general way. That does not mean that [plaintiff] was in the service of the Trustees. If a student wins a Rhodes scholarship or if the debate team wins a national award that undoubtedly benefits the school, but does not mean that the student and the team are in the service of the school. [Plaintiff] performed no duties that would place him in the service of the university."

Also see the following law review articles.

1. Casey N. Harding, Nick and Dimed: North Carolina Court Blocks Carolina Panthers' Attempt to Avoid Payment of Workers' Compensation Benefits to Injured Athletes," 28 *North Carolina Central Law Journal* 241 (2006).

2. Nathan McCoy and Kerry Knox, Comment, "Flexing Union Muscle—Is It the Right Game Plan for Revenue Generating Student-Athletes in Their Contest for Benefits Reform with the NCAA?" 69 *Tennessee Law Review* 1051 (2002).

3. Eric D. LeBeau and Thomas H. Sawyer, "Worker's Compensation and Scholarship Athletes: Are They Protected?" 10 *Journal of Legal Aspects of Sports* 18 (2000).

4. Sean Alan Roberts, "College Athletes, Universities, and Workers' Compensation: Placing the Relationship in the Proper Context by Recognizing Scholarship Athletes as Employees," 37 *South Texas Law Review* 1315 (October 1996).

5. David W. Woodburn, "College Athletes Should be Entitled to Workers' Compensation for Sports-Related Injuries: A Request to Broaden the Definition of Employee under Ohio Revised Code Sec. 4123.01," 28 *Akron Law Review* 611 (Spring 1995).

Chapter 4

APPLICATION OF TORT LAW TO SPORTS

4.1. Liability of Participants

4.2. Liability of Coaches and Teachers

    4.2.1. Failure to Provide Adequate Supervision

    4.2.2. Failure to Provide Proper Instruction and Training

    4.2.3. Failure to Provide Prompt and Capable Medical Assistance

4.3. Liability of Administrators, Schools, and Athletic Organizations

    4.3.1. Failure to Provide Supervision of Athletic Activities and to Hire Qualified Personnel

    4.3.2. Failure to Provide Proper Medical Assistance

    4.3.3. Failure to Provide Safe Equipment

    4.3.4. Vicarious Liability for Actions of Fans and Players

4.4. The Defense of Immunity

    4.4.1. Sovereign Immunity

    4.4.2. Charitable Immunity

    4.4.3. Civil Liability Immunity Legislation

4.5. Liability of Facility Owners and Possessors

4.6. Liability of Medical Personnel

4.7. Liability of Officials, Referees, and Umpires

4.8. Application of Legal Principles to Defects in Equipment

4.9. Liability Insurance

4.10. Waiver and Release of Liability

INTRODUCTION

Chapter 4 is organized according to possible defendants in sports tort cases. The chapter begins with a discussion of the potential liabilities of a *participant* in a sporting event. It then focuses on the potential liabilities of *coaches and teachers* in the areas of supervision, instruction and training, medical assistance, and vicarious liability for actions of fans and players. The legal theory most commonly used in this area is negligence. The chapter next covers the potential liabilities of *administrators*, *schools*, and *universities*. Administrators may be found negligent in hiring personnel (an employee such as a coach or teacher) or in supervising personnel. Administrators may also be found vicariously liable for the negligence of an employee in rendering medical assistance. Finally, administrators may be found negligent for not providing equipment, or vicariously liable if an employee did not furnish equipment or furnished ill-fitting or defective equipment. Schools and universities may also be sued under a vicarious liability theory for the negligence of any of their employees in the areas of supervision and personnel, medical assistance, and equipment. For public school or university administrators, sovereign immunity may provide a defense.

The next topics presented in Chapter 4 are those of charitable immunity and civil liability immunity legislation, followed by the liability of *facility owners* and *possessors*, which may include liability for defects in a building or negligent supervision of a crowd and the liability of *medical personnel* for negligent treatment of an injured athlete or fan. The chapter continues with a discussion of the potential liabilities of *officials*, *referees*, and *umpires*. Some officials have been sued for injuries to athletes that have allegedly resulted from officials' failure to take corrective action to remedy the injury-causing situation. Examples include failing to stop a game during inclement weather or allowing objects or spectators to be too close to the playing area. Officials, referees, and umpires have also been sued for the incorrect application of game rules and making incorrect judgment calls.

The next section sets forth cases involving defects in equipment. It is followed by a discussion of liability insurance, waivers, and releases of liability. High school athletic associations and high schools have purchased insurance to combat the rising number of tort claims being made by those associated with sports activities. (The National Collegiate Athletic Association has maintained a disability insurance program since the 1985–1986 academic year.)

4.1. LIABILITY OF PARTICIPANTS

The liability stemming most directly from sports activity is that for injuries to participants. At one time, most sport-related injuries were viewed as a natural outgrowth of the competitive and physical nature of sports. This attitude was supported by the traditional belief that a participant assumes the dangers inherent in the sport and is therefore precluded from recovery for an injury caused by another participant. Although this theory has some merit, it fails to address injuries that occur during a game that are not necessarily an outgrowth of competitive spirit.

This traditional attitude has been strictly scrutinized in decisions, beginning with *Nabozny v. Barnhill*, 334 N.E.2d 258 (Ill. App. Ct. 1975), that clearly establish that a player does not necessarily assume the risk of all injuries resulting from the gross recklessness of another player (see note 1f), nor does the player necessarily consent to intentional attacks falling outside the recognized rules of the sport. Thus, the defenses of assumption of the risk or of consent must be reviewed on a case-by-case basis to determine their applicability (see section 3.1.5, "Defenses for Negligence").

This change in attitude has occurred in part because of the increasing number of serious injuries to sports participants. The increased volume of sports participation resulting from the involvement of boys and girls, and men and women, in unprecedented numbers has produced a corresponding increase in the number of sports-related injuries, leading to efforts by governing bodies to reduce injury risks. For example, the National Collegiate Athletic Association (NCAA) attempts to survey injuries resulting from participation in intercollegiate games through the NCAA Injury Surveillance System. The 2004–2005 survey indicated that football posed by far the highest risk to student-athletes, with 39.1 injuries per 1,000 athlete exposures. For more information, see http://www.ncaa.org.

A second reason for the change in attitude is that professional sports, and to some extent intercollegiate and Olympic athletics, are now viewed as businesses. Because of this, people are more inclined to consider lawsuits to be viable responses to sports injuries. Many athletic organizations have greater revenues and may have deep pockets to pay large awards. A third reason is that legal precedents have been established which allow injured athletes to recover. Finally, the rise in sport-related lawsuits is a result of society becoming increasingly reliant on the judicial system for the resolution of disputes.

An increase in claims of negligence and other tortious conduct has paralleled the rising number of sports injuries in recent years. One factor behind the rise in participant versus participant lawsuits is the steady erosion of the athlete's traditional reluctance to sue fellow participants. The increasing recognition of the dangers involved in playing a game against an opponent who does not follow an accepted safety rule has increased the likelihood of a lawsuit. Players are refusing to accept injury-provoking actions of opponents when the actions are not sanctioned by the rules of the game. There are legal precedents that recognize that each player has a legal duty to refrain from unreasonably dangerous acts (see section 3.2, "The Tort of Reckless Misconduct (Gross Negligence)").

Courts have found that many sports, including soccer, softball, football, and golf, have created safety rules to help define the often unclear line between legal and illegal behavior on the field. A safety rule is one that is initiated to protect players and to prevent injuries. The existence of safety rules mandates that in many situations a player be charged with a legal duty to every other player involved in the activity. In cases involving the alleged violation of a safety rule, the courts have held that a player is liable for tort action only if his or her conduct displays deliberate, willful, or reckless disregard for the safety of other participants and results in injury to another participant. Thus, a participant may recover either for an intentional tort or for gross negligence, but ordinarily will not be able to recover based on a negligence theory. However, case law indicates that there are situations in sports for which the commonly accepted defenses of assumption of risk and contributory negligence are not adequate to bar recovery by the plaintiff.

NOTES

The courts discussed the liability of participants in sports in the following cases.

1. In *Noffke ex. rel Swenson v. Bakke*, 760 N.W.2d 156 (Wis. 2009), the Supreme Court of Wisconsin ruled that cheerleading falls within the contact sports exception, which grants

immunity from liability to those participating in a recreational activity that includes physical contact between persons in a sport involving amateur teams. In *Noffke*, a female high school cheerleader, Brittany Noffke, sued Kevin Bakke, a male cheerleader, for failing to prevent her from falling from a raised position as part of the cheerleading squad's performance.

2. In *Thompson v. Park River Corporation*, 830 N.E.2d 1252 (Ohio Ct. App. 2005), the appellate court considered a lawsuit filed by the parents of a boy who was injured when another boy shoved him into a pool during a swimming class. The court held that in a recreational sports activity such as swimming lessons, coparticipants should be found liable only if they have acted in a reckless or intentional manner. In this case, one of the defendants was an eight-year-old boy whose "childish prank" resulted in an unforeseeable injury to the plaintiffs' son. The injury, which occurred when the plaintiffs' child's foot became caught on a handrail in the pool, was the first of its kind to occur since the pool had been opened. Therefore, it was impossible that the defendant intended the injury as a consequence of his act or consciously disregarded the risk that such an injury might occur.

3. In *Mark v. Moser*, 746 N.E.2d 410 (Ind. Ct. App. 2001), the plaintiff triathlete was injured when a competitor veered into her path, causing a collision that resulted in serious injuries. The defendant was disqualified from the competition for violating a safety rule, although the competition's judge made no finding as to the defendant's intent. The appellate court held that the plaintiff had assumed the risk of dangers inherent to participation in a triathlon. Therefore, she could prevail only if she produced evidence of recklessness or intentional conduct on the defendant's part. The court directed the lower court to determine whether the defendant's actions had been intentional or reckless or whether they merely posed risks inherent to triathlons.

4. In *Kiley v. Patterson*, 763 A.2d 583 (R.I. 2000), a second baseman, filed a lawsuit seeking damages for injuries she suffered as a result of a collision with a base runner during a recreational game of softball. The Supreme Court of Rhode Island held that the duty of care owed by participants in team athletic events to each other is not measured by ordinary negligence. Instead, in order for a participant plaintiff to prevail, he or she must prove willfulness or recklessness on the part of the other participant. The court remanded the case to the trial court to allow the plaintiff to attempt to prove recklessness by the defendant, who had caused the plaintiff's injury when he slid into second base with his foot raised high in the air.

5. In *Gauvin v. Clark*, 537 N.E.2d 94 (Mass. 1989), plaintiff hockey player sued the defendant for injuries sustained when the defendant "butt-ended" the plaintiff in the abdomen with his stick. The supreme judicial court held that the defendant was not liable for injuries caused by his violation of a safety rule where he did not act in reckless disregard of the plaintiff's safety.

6. In *Novak v. Lamar Insurance Co.*, 488 So. 2d 739 (La. Ct. App. 1986), plaintiff softball player brought action against a second softball player, the homeowner's insurer of that player's father, and the insurer of the church that sponsored the defendant softball player's team. Plaintiff sought recovery for injuries sustained when the two collided as defendant softball player ran to first base. The court held that the defendant was not acting recklessly or in an unsportsmanlike manner when he crashed into the plaintiff at the base, causing facial injuries to the plaintiff. The defendant's intention was solely to reach first base, and in doing so he did not violate any game rules. Since the possibility of such a collision was foreseeable, the plaintiff had assumed the risk of the harm that resulted.

7. In *Nabozny v. Barnhill*, 334 N.E.2d 258 (Ill. App. Ct. 1975), plaintiff soccer player filed suit for injuries received when he was kicked in the head by an opponent during an amateur soccer game involving two teams composed of high school age players. The defendant, David Barnhill, was playing a forward position for one team, and the plaintiff, Julian Nabozny, was the goaltender for the other team. Barnhill kicked Nabozny in the head while Nabozny was in possession of the ball. Contact with the goaltender while he is in possession of the ball is a violation of International Association Football

Federation—soccer's international governing body—rules, which governed the contest. The resultant injury left the plaintiff with permanent skull and brain damage. Nabozny brought suit, and the trial court directed a verdict in favor of the defendant. On appeal, the court noted that it did not wish to "place unreasonable burdens on the free and vigorous participation in sports by our youth" but also stated that "athletic competition does not exist in a vacuum." Therefore, in reversing the trial court decision, the court held that a player is charged with a legal duty to every other player on the field to refrain from conduct proscribed by a safety rule. The court held that when athletes are engaged in athletic competition, all teams involved are trained and coached by knowledgeable personnel; a recognized set of rules governs the conduct of the competition; and a safety rule is contained therein which is primarily designed to protect players from serious injury. Thus, a reckless disregard for the safety of other players cannot be excused. Although the defendant's violation of the safety rule could be considered *evidence* of recklessness, it was not sufficient to establish recklessness.

8. In *Griggas v. Clauson*, 128 N.E.2d 363 (Ill. App. Ct. 1955), Griggas, a 19-year-old member of an amateur basketball team, brought suit for injuries received during a game. During that game he was guarded by La Verne Clauson. While Griggas had his back to Clauson and was about to receive a pass from a teammate, Clauson pushed him and then struck him in the face with his fist. As Griggas fell, Clauson struck him again and knocked him unconscious. Clauson began to swear profusely and made statements to the effect that he was going to teach Griggas a lesson and that one of the two was going to play in the city and the other was not. Griggas was hospitalized for about three weeks. The Appellate Court of Illinois supported a trial court decision for Griggas. It held that the evidence in the record supported the finding that Griggas was subjected to a wanton and unprovoked battery.

The liability of participants has also been a subject of much judicial scrutiny on the professional sports level. The following cases examine this area of sports law.

1. In *McKichan v. St. Louis Hockey Club*, 967 S.W. 2d. 209 (Mo. Ct. App. 1998), plaintiff, a professional hockey goaltender for a minor league affiliate of the NHL's Vancouver Canucks, was injured during a game. Plaintiff sued the opposing player who charged into him, as well as the offending player's team owners. About three weeks before trial, the plaintiff and defendant players settled their claims and counterclaims against each other. However, the case proceeded against the team under vicarious liability theory, and a jury awarded the plaintiff $175,000. The state appellate court overturned the jury award, however, stating, "We find that the specific conduct at issue in this case, a severe body check, is a part of professional hockey. This body check, even several seconds after the whistle and in violation of several rules of the game, was not outside the realm of reasonable anticipation. For better or for worse, it is 'part of the game' of professional hockey. As such, we hold as a matter of law that the specific conduct which occurred here is not actionable."

2. In *Hackbart v. Cincinnati Bengals*, 435 F. Supp. 352 (D. Colo. 1977), *rev'd*, 601 F.2d 516 (10th Cir. 1979), Charles Clark, a running back with the Cincinnati Bengals, was sued for reckless misconduct by Dale Hackbart, a defensive back for the Denver Broncos. Clark had struck Hackbart in the head, an action outside the rules of the game of football. The trial court had ruled that there was no duty between the players. However, the appeals court found enough justification for a retrial on a reckless misconduct theory before a jury to determine the liability of defendant Charles Clark. The case was settled before trial for a reported $200,000.

In 2002, Chicago Cubs pitcher Ben Christensen settled his portion of a battery claim filed against him and several other defendants by former University of Evansville player, Anthony Molina. An incident occurred in 1999 while Christensen was a student at Wichita State University. Molina was standing about 24 feet from home plate when he was hit in the left eye by a Christensen fastball. Molina said Christensen deliberately hit him after being warned about "timing" Christensen's pitches. The case against the university and members of the coaching staff is pending in Sedgwick County (Kansas) District Court.

For further information on participant liability in sports, see the following law review articles.

1. Denise M. Yerger, "High Risk Recreation: The Thrill That Creates a Statutory and Judicial Spectrum of Response and Drives the Dichotomy in Participant and Provider Liability," 38 *Suffolk University Law Review* 687 (2005).

2. Keya Denner, "Taking One for the Team: The Role of Assumption of the Risk in Sports Torts Cases," 14 *Seton Hall Journal of Sports and Entertainment Law* 209 (2004).

3. Robert Carroll, "Determining Duty of Care between Sports Co-Participants in Light of the Indiana Comparative Fault Statute," 11 *DePaul University Journal of Sports and Entertainment Law* 425 (Fall 2001).

4.2. LIABILITY OF COACHES AND TEACHERS

Coaches and teachers, as individuals, are always responsible for any intentional torts they commit in their capacity as coaches or physical education teachers. They are generally not shielded from liability by virtue of their positions through the defenses of consent, privilege, and immunity (see section 3.3.3, "Defenses for Assault and Battery").

The coach is judged by the standard of a "reasonable coach" and the teacher by the standard of a "reasonable teacher." There are some limited exceptions in which coaches and teachers are held to a lower standard of care and will not be held liable unless they are deemed to be grossly negligent. One situation involves coaches or teachers who are considered to be in loco parentis—that is, the coach or teacher is placed in the position of the parents of the student-athlete. A coach or teacher may, however, have a number of defenses available (see section 3.1.5, "Defenses for Negligence").

Since minors are often involved in these cases, note should be taken that certain defenses, such as contributory negligence, comparative negligence, and assumption of the risk, may be affected by the different standard of care for children (see section 3.1.1.2, "Standard of Care for Children"). The defense of sovereign immunity is frequently important for coaches and teachers. Generally, the coach or teacher cannot be sued individually when the school district is protected under sovereign immunity as discussed in section 4.4.1. However, this protection may not cover the coach who is acting outside the scope of employment or who has performed his or her job in a clearly improper manner (acted with misfeasance). The sovereign immunity protection is also limited to coaches at public institutions, as opposed to coaches at private institutions.

Until recently, very little litigation was brought against coaches and teachers as a result of the sovereign immunity protection and the reluctance of potential plaintiffs to bring lawsuits. This was especially true in the case of coaches and teachers, who were often members of the community and highly respected for their work. However, the coach and teacher are increasingly likely to be sued due to the greater likelihood of injured student-athletes filing lawsuits and the erosion of the sovereign immunity doctrine.

In many cases, the institution is sued under the doctrine of *respondeat superior* (also called vicarious liability) for the individual coach's or teacher's negligence, although the individual is also named as a defendant. In future cases, the coach and teacher may be sued individually more often. Areas of responsibility for which a coach or teacher may be successfully sued include supervision, instruction and training, and medical assistance. Coaches and teachers have also been sued under the theory of vicarious liability for the actions of fans and players, but these lawsuits usually have not been successful.

Prior to addressing those areas individually, certain important points are beneficial for institutional administrators to remember regarding the liability of coaches and teachers. Those include the following:

1. Coaches and teachers must be aware of safety issues when coaching and instructing.
2. Coaches and teachers must be careful with punishment-type drills.
3. In terms of risk management, administrators need to know the activities of the coaches and teachers.
4. Also in terms of risk management, coaches and teachers need to be aware of liability issues.
5. Coaches and teachers must be aware of school district and athletic association rules.

Adherence to these key points may prove tremendously valuable in eliminating potential liability of coaches and teachers as well as subsequent institutional liability under vicarious liability theories by minimizing potentially injurious situations.

4.2.1. Failure to Provide Adequate Supervision

Although coaches and teachers are not regarded as insurers of everyone under their care, they are responsible for providing reasonable supervision to the student-athletes under their direction. Examples of failure to provide adequate supervision include negligent supervision at a football game and failure to provide the proper equipment for the game. Examples may also include improperly supervising an off-season weight training program or encouraging an injured student-athlete to play. An additional responsibility for the coach or teacher is to check the playing area to make sure it is in proper condition and that nothing is on or near the playing area that could cause injury, including benches, other participants, and spectators.

Finally, the coach or teacher also may be sued for nonplaying field activities such as supervising student-athletes who are going to or from the playing field. The coach or teacher is responsible for providing reasonable supervision. Any supervisory capacity carries with it the responsibility to exercise due care—that is, the care of a "reasonable supervisor" (see section 3.1.1, "Duty of Care Owed"). This due care must be provided for the safety of anyone who is likely to or actually does come into contact with the area under supervision. The duty entails using reasonable care in either rectifying dangerous situations or warning those who may encounter them of the possible hazards.

A supervisor generally is not liable for any *intentional* acts of his employees unless the supervisor directed the action and the employer benefited from it. A school district or supervisor is liable in such instances only if the institution, or one to which the district or supervisor is legally responsible, breaches the requisite standard of care. The school district and/or supervisor will only be liable if the employee and the action taken satisfy the requirements of vicarious liability (see section 3.6, "Vicarious Liability"). Also, the doctrine of sovereign immunity may bar the action depending on the state where the action took place (see section 4.4.1).

A supervisor is not, however, an insurer of everyone's safety; rather, the supervisor needs only to exercise reasonable care. Unless there is information or notice to the contrary, the supervisor is entitled to assume that all under his or her supervision will exercise due care. Thus, a spectator who is injured by another spectator may not enforce a claim against a school district or its administrators unless the school district or administrator, having notice that the other spectator was likely to cause an unreasonably dangerous condition, failed to take steps to prevent the injury. Past experience, moreover, will be considered when assessing liability. For example, if the same spectator appeared at a later contest and injured a fellow spectator, the school district might be held liable for negligent supervision because the first situation provided warning of the person's potentially dangerous nature. The duty of care required may depend on the type of event. Hockey games, for instance, may require more security and precautions than track and field events. The general rule is that the coach has no duty regarding the matching up of participants. Yet the prudent athletics administrator would ensure reasonable matchups in order to minimize risk of litigation in this area, as well as decrease the potential for injury to the participant.

NOTES

1. In *Santho v. Boy Scouts of America*, 857 N.E.2d 1255 (Ohio Ct. App. 2006), the appellate court affirmed a summary judgment against a claim filed by the parents of a boy who had suffered a head injury during an ice skating event. During the skate, the plaintiffs' son, an experienced skater, had participated in a relay race. While looking backward over his shoulder to determine where his competitor was, the boy crashed headlong into the boards surrounding the ice, suffering a fractured skull and concussion. His parents alleged that the Boy Scout den leader's failure to enforce the rules of the event by ensuring participants wore helmets had proximately caused their son's harm. However, the court ruled that the boy and his parents had assumed the risk of any negligent supervision and that the den leader and the Boy Scouts had not recklessly increased the risk of the activity.

2. In *Koffman v. Garnett*, 265 Va. 12 (Va. 2003), a middle school football player sued his football coach for negligence, assault, and battery after the coach thrust his arms around the player's body, lifted him off his feet, and slammed him to the ground to display proper tackling technique. The coach weighed approximately 260 pounds compared to the boy's 144 pounds. The force of the tackle broke the humerus bone in the boy's left arm. In finding for the boy, the Supreme Court of Virginia held that the boy consented to physical contact with players of like age and experience but that he did not expect or consent to his participation in aggressive contact tackling by adult football coaches.

3. In *Fintzi v. New Jersey YMHA-YWHA Camps*, 765 N.E.2d 288 (N.Y. 2001), the New York Court of Appeals reviewed a claim for negligent supervision filed by the parents of a 10-year-old boy who had broken his arm during a relay race at summer camp. The plaintiffs alleged that the decision of camp counselors to allow the race to proceed on a damp field had caused their son's injury. The Court of Appeals directed that summary judgment be entered for the camp and its counselors, finding that "merely allowing children to play on wet grass does not constitute negligent supervision." By allowing the race to take place, the counselors did not increase the risk associated with an obviously damp field.

4. In *Prejean vs. East Baton Rouge Parish School Board*, 729 So. 2d 686 (La. Ct. App. 1999), a fifth grade student was injured on an outdoor basketball court while practicing basketball with other fourth and fifth graders. A volunteer basketball coach was actively playing on one of the teams when the plaintiff lost the ball out of bounds. The coach pushed a student, who fell on the plaintiff's leg, causing his injury. The coach immediately called for paramedics, who promptly transported the plaintiff to the hospital. The appeals court, in reversing the decision of the trial court, held that the volunteer basketball coach did not breach the duty he owed students by participating in a basketball

scrimmage. The court reasoned that all team sports involve a risk of injury as a result of physical contact, and that the other students could have provided a risk just as great as that of the coach.

5. In *City of Miami v. Cisneros*, 662 So. 2d 1272 (Fla. Dist. Ct. App. 1997), during a city-sponsored football game, a 70- to 75-pound participant broke his leg in his attempt to tackle a 128-pound opponent. The appellate court disallowed the assumption of the risk defense because the coach had promised the participant's parents he would not wrestle the boy against anyone over 90 pounds. The coach had a responsibility to instruct the boys in football techniques and to supervise them while they were playing. Although the boy and his parents may have assumed the risks inherent to participation in football, the court found that "those risks did not include negligent supervision, the claim at issue herein."

6. In *Searles v. Trustees of St. Joseph's College*, 695 A.2d 1206 (Me. 1997), plaintiff college basketball player sued his coach for repeatedly playing him in games despite the fact that the coach knew he had a serious knee injury. The player sought damages for his injuries and reimbursement for related medical expenses and also alleged intentional infliction of emotional distress and sought punitive damages. While the superior court granted summary judgment to the coach, the Supreme Judicial Court of Maine remanded the question to a jury, stating that the coach was charged with a duty to exercise reasonable care for his players and that questions of material fact existed as to whether the coach had exercised such care. The plaintiff asserted that he had repeatedly advised the coach of his pain and that the coach demonstrated his knowledge of the plaintiff's injury by holding the plaintiff out of practices so he would be ready for games.

7. In *Edelson v. Uniondale Union Free School District*, 631 N.Y.S.2d 391 (N.Y. App. Div. 1995), a high school wrestler received injuries during a match against an opponent in a higher weight classification than plaintiff's normal category. The appellate court granted summary judgment, finding the school district's duty of care "limited to exercising ordinary reasonable care in protecting the plaintiff from unassumed, concealed or unreasonably increased risks." The plaintiff was an experienced wrestler who could properly calculate the risks involved in the match, and the court deemed the ultimate cause of his injury was the way he received a wrestling move, not the size of his opponent.

8. In *Lynch v. Board of Education of Collingsville Community School District*, 390 N.E.2d 526 (Ill. App. Ct. 1979), parents of a junior in high school brought a negligence suit on her behalf against the school district for damages she received as a result of an injury suffered in a powder puff intramural football game. Plaintiffs alleged ordinary negligence on the part of the defendant in failing to provide adequate equipment and willful and wanton misconduct in failing to adequately supervise the game. An appeals court, in affirming the trial court's decision for the parents, held that since the teams' coaches were teachers and the field on which the contest was played was fenced and could have been locked to keep students out, there was sufficient evidence for the jury to conclude that the game was authorized by the school. The court also held that the presence of the plaintiff's parents at the game site did not obviate the school's duty to provide adequate equipment.

For more information, also see the following law review articles.

1. Marc J. Dobberstein, "'Give Me the Ball Coach': A Scouting Report on the Liability of High Schools and Coaches for Injury to High School Pitchers' Arms," 14 *Sports Law Journal* 49 (Spring 2007).

2. Brad Colwell and Brian Schwartz, "Coaches' Liability for Injury to Student Athletes," 194 *West's Education Law Reporter* 765 (March 2005).

4.2.2. Failure to Provide Proper Instruction and Training

Coaches and teachers are responsible for providing proper instruction and training to the student-athletes, and they should be qualified to teach the particular activity involved. The coach additionally must properly instruct the student-athletes on the activity, the safety rules, and the proper method of playing. It is imperative that coaches exercise care in providing instruction on safe play in order to minimize the risk of injury to student-athletes. In a number of cases, injured players allege that the coach or teacher did not provide proper instruction and training. A proper preseason conditioning program should also be provided, although such programs become an issue where football practice begins in August and some players experience fatal injuries related to heat exhaustion.

Coaches and teachers should keep detailed records of their instruction and training sessions. They should also be aware of any new developments in their sport. Some companies have started producing instruction and training films to assist coaches and teachers in preparing their student-athletes. Another area of potential liability for the coach or teacher is a claim by a student-athlete of assault and battery. Several issues are raised in this area. Is there a defense of privilege? Is the standard of care "reasonable care" or "gross negligence"? Does sovereign immunity protect the coach and teacher? Can force be used to bring about compliance with commands and to punish prohibited conduct? Can force be used when the player has not performed adequately? There has not been a great deal of litigation in this area, but coaches and teachers should be aware that cases may be brought.

NOTES

1. In *Karas v. Strevell*, 860 N.E.2d 1163 (Ill. App. Ct. 2006), the appellate court considered a case in which the plaintiff's son had been seriously injured at an ice hockey game as a result of being checked in the back in violation of league rules. Among other claims, the plaintiff argued that the hockey league and its officials had failed to provide proper instruction regarding rules against hitting from behind. The appellate court reversed the trial court's dismissal of this claim in order to allow the plaintiff to present evidence that the league's lack of proper instruction had contributed to the cause of his son's injury.

2. In *Wu v. Shattuck-St. Mary's School*, 393 F. Supp. 2d 831 (D. Minn. 2005), the federal district court considered a case in which a high school student suffered brain damage after being struck in the temple with a golf ball during practice. The defendant school argued that the plaintiff assumed the risk of harm when she stepped into a netted area near another student who was practicing his swing. The court ruled that the plaintiff's claim constituted an assertion of negligent supervision or instruction and that the plaintiff had not assumed the enhanced risk caused by lack of supervision and instruction.

3. In *Schultz v. Foster-Glocester Reg'l School Dist.*, 755 A.2d 153 (R.I. 2000), the plaintiff, a cheerleader, was injured at cheerleading practice while practicing a basket toss. The basket toss required two cheerleaders to toss the plaintiff into the air and catch her in their interlocking arms; however, they failed to catch her, and she missed the safety mat. The plaintiff badly injured her elbow. The plaintiff filed a negligence suit against the school, alleging that it failed to properly train, supervise, and instruct the plaintiff and her teammates. She further alleged that they failed to provide proper equipment and proper postinjury treatment. The Supreme Court remanded the case to a Superior Court trial on the question of whether the minor assumed the risk of this injury.

4. In *Taylor v. Massapequa International Little League*, 689 N.Y.S.2d 523 (N.Y. App. Div. 1999), a 10-year-old participant in a youth baseball league brought personal injury action against the league for injuries he sustained upon sliding into a base at the coach's direction. The 10-year-old alleged that he had never slid into a base before and that his coach offered no instruction to him or his teammates on the proper technique. There were factual questions as to whether the plaintiff was aware of, appreciated, and voluntarily assumed the risks of sliding into a base. The court therefore denied the defendant's motion to dismiss the complaint.

5. In *Hammond v. Board of Educ.*, 639 A.2d 223 (Md. Ct. Spec. App. 1994), Tawana Hammond, the first female high school football player in Carroll County, Maryland, history, was injured in her team's initial scrimmage. Her family filed suit in the Circuit Court for Carroll County against the Board of Education of Carroll County, seeking $1.25 million in compensatory damages. The Hammonds claimed that the high school authorities negligently failed to warn them of the potential risk of injury inherent in playing football and that if they had been so warned, Tawana would not have chosen to play football and her mother would not have permitted her to do so. After the parties conducted discovery, the board moved for summary judgment, which the circuit court granted and the appellate court subsequently affirmed. The appellate court reasoned that the danger of football was "ordinary and obvious" and that the school board, therefore, had no duty to warn the Hammonds of the danger.

6. In *Thompson v. Seattle Public School District* (unpublished decision 1985), plaintiff high school football player sought to recover damages for injuries sustained during a high school football game. The plaintiff was injured after lowering his head to ward off tacklers. The court decided in favor of the plaintiff on the basis that the player was not properly warned of the dangers of lowering his head while carrying the football.

7. In *Vendrell v. School District No. 26C, Malheur County*, P.2d 406 (Or. 1961), plaintiff, a freshman football player who had played two years of junior high football, brought suit against the school district for damages for the neck injury he sustained while playing in a high school game. The plaintiff suffered a fractured neck when he lowered his head and collided with two opposing players. The plaintiff contended that he was an inexperienced player and had been improperly trained. The court of appeals ruled against the plaintiff, holding that the plaintiff was not inexperienced in that he had played for two years in junior high school and during those years had received substantial football training from competent coaches. The court held that the game of football is an inherently rough sport in which body contact and some degree of injury are inevitable and that no player should need to have this explained.

8. In *Pirkle v. Oakdale Union Grammer School Dist.*, 253 P.2d 1 (Cal. Sup. Ct. 1953), an eighth grade student brought an action against the school district for injuries received from being blocked during a touch football game that was played without supervision. The court held for the defendant on appeal, ruling that the players had been properly selected and instructed. The court also held that plaintiff's injuries could not have been readily apparent to a layperson and that no further damage resulted from a delay in receiving medical treatment.

4.2.3. Failure to Provide Prompt and Capable Medical Assistance

A common risk encountered in the area of sports is that of serious injury. There are two important points for the coach's attention regarding medical assistance. First, the coach should know what medical personnel are present. Second, if medical personnel are not present, their accessibility should be determined in advance. When an injury to an athlete or spectator appears to be serious, those in charge of the activity are under a duty to use reasonable efforts to obtain reasonably prompt and capable medical assistance. At the same time, there is a duty to refrain from actions that might aggravate an injury when a reasonable person would know of the risk. The coach and teacher are held to a standard of "reasonable care" when rendering medical assistance to an injured student-athlete. They are not expected to provide the assistance of a doctor or one with medical training. In fact, some of the obligations of the coach and teacher have been shifted to others. For example, many states have passed statutes requiring that medical personnel be in attendance at games. Such laws may reduce the liability exposure for the coach and teacher.

The institution may be the responsible party if medical personnel have not been provided. In addition, the institution may be responsible for having medical personnel "reasonably" available, even when it is not statutorily mandated. With medical personnel available, the care of the injured student-athlete may not be undertaken by the coach or teacher. Therefore, in most situations, the main responsibilities of the coach and teacher are twofold. First, they may have to render assistance before the medical personnel arrive. First-aid training may be helpful to prevent a situation in which, for example, the coach improperly moves an injured student-athlete. The second responsibility is to exercise reasonable care in sending an injured athlete for medical treatment. Coaches and teachers may be found liable for negligence if they fail to fulfill either of these duties. In addition, some jurisdictions have also sought criminal charges against coaches for their actions or omissions resulting in a student-athlete's death (see note 1).

NOTES

1. In January 2009, a Louisville grand jury indicted high school football coach Jason Stinson for reckless homicide. Stinson conducted a high school football practice in late August when 15-year old sophomore Max Gilpin suffered heatstroke and later died. The prosecution claimed that a reasonable person should have understood that a death could happen and that Stinson failed to perceive that risk. In September 2009, Stinson was found not guilty of all charges. Medical experts testified that the combination of the heat, the use of the dietary supplement creatine, and the attention-deficit disorder drug Adderall all contributed to Gilpin's accidental death.

In summer 2001, two highly publicized legal cases resulted following football players' deaths during preseason training camp.

2. In *Stringer v. Minnesota Viking Football Club, LLC*, 705 N.W.2d 746 (Minn. 2005), the Supreme Court of Minnesota reviewed a wrongful death suit filed by the widow of Vikings offensive lineman Korey Stringer, who had died of heatstroke after collapsing at football practice. Members of the Vikings' training staff were among the defendants. The court ruled that since Stringer had been a coemployee of those defendants, his widow could prevail only if she demonstrated that the defendants owed Stringer a personal duty and were grossly negligent in performing it. Since the defendants were acting within the scope of their job duties when they attempted to treat Stringer at the Vikings' practice facility, they owed him a professional duty but not a personal one. The summary judgment in the defendants' favor was affirmed. For more on this case, see section 4.8, "Application of Legal Principles to Defects in Equipment," note 1.

3. On February 26, 2001, 18-year-old Florida State University football player Devaughn Darling collapsed and died during a workout prior to spring football practice. His family members sued for wrongful death, alleging that the university had failed to provide adequate fluids during the drills and had failed to make prompt and capable medical assistance available to participants in the workouts. The medical examiner found that Darling's sickle-cell anemia, of which he was aware, also contributed to his demise. The family and Florida State settled for $2 million. See details on CSTV Online at http://www.cstv.com/sports/m-footbl/stories/062804aai.html. However, the story did not end there. The amount of the settlement exceeded the maximum ($200,000) that Florida law permitted to be levied against the state and its agencies. The approval of the state legislature was thus required, but it was not forthcoming. The legislature did not approve the claim in its 2005 or 2006 sessions. As a result, Darling's family has collected only $200,000 of the settlement amount.

4. In *Myers v. Friends of Shenendehowa Crew, Inc.*, 31 A.D.3d 853 (N.Y. App. Div. 2006), the father of a 14-year-old rower alleged that a coach's negligent supervision of a training program had caused harm to the plaintiff's daughter. The 14-year-old fainted during

an exercise drill intended to increase endurance, and again after the coach had escorted her to the nurse's station and left her there alone.

5. In *Gahan v. Mineola Union Free School District*, 241 A.D.2d 439, 660 N.Y.S.2d 144 (N.Y. App. Div. 1997), coaches may have exacerbated a high school softball player's injury by moving her before medical personnel arrived, creating an additional risk. The question was remanded to a jury for consideration.

6. In *Kleinknecht v. Gettysburg College*, 989 F.2d 1360 (3rd Cir. 1993), the court held that when a college or university recruits an athlete to play a particular sport, a special relationship arises which imposes a duty of reasonable care. In this instance, the college has a duty to provide prompt medical care for an athlete injured while engaged in a school-sponsored athletic activity.

7. In *Stineman v. Fontbonne College*, 664 F.2d 1082 (8th Cir. 1981), plaintiff was a deaf student-athlete whose softball coaches were aware of her handicap. Plaintiff had signed an authorization for emergency medical treatment in the event of an injury. During the course of practice, plaintiff was struck in the eye with a ball. A coach applied ice and advised her, despite the great amount of pain she was experiencing, to go to her room and rest and she would be all right. Neither coach who was present suggested that she seek medical attention. No immediate professional medical attention was given, even though the school infirmary was across the street. Permanent eye damage resulted from the injury. The trial court found negligence of the college in failing to provide the proper medical assistance. The appeals court affirmed the decision; however, it reduced the damages from $800,000 to $600,000.

8. In *Mogabgab v. Orleans Parish School Board*, 239 So. 2d 456 (La. Ct. App. 1970), an action brought by parents for the wrongful death of their son, a high school football player who died as a result of heatstroke and exhaustion following a practice. The plaintiffs sued the coach, the school principal, and the school district on the theory that the school was negligent in not making sure the coach was properly trained. They argued also that the school was negligent in making arrangements for the proper care of sick and injured players. The court held that the coach who actively denied the student-athlete access to medical treatment for two hours after symptoms of heatstroke and shock appeared was guilty of negligence. However, the court did not find negligence attributable to the principal, school district, physical education supervisor, or school superintendent because they were unaware of the events.

4.3. LIABILITY OF ADMINISTRATORS, SCHOOLS, AND ATHLETIC ORGANIZATIONS

Sports-related injuries that occur within the confines of an educational institution raise the issue of legal accountability of the institution itself. From the perspective of the seriously injured plaintiff, it may be more desirable to obtain a judgment against an institution rather than an individual coach or instructor because the institution is much more likely to have a deep pocket from which the plaintiff bringing suit can receive monetary damage awards.

If an administrator or institution is subject to liability, the standards to which it will be held are the same as in similar areas of tort law. The administrator and institution are required to exercise reasonable care to prevent reasonably foreseeable risks and to make foreseeably dangerous conditions safe by repairing or warning. If the institution fails to maintain a reasonable standard of care, it may be liable for negligence. For example, the administrator or institution should establish rules for the safe use of facilities, provide supervision of athletic activities, hire qualified personnel, provide proper medical assistance, and provide proper equipment. Institutions cannot guarantee the safety of students, but they are subject to liability when the institution or someone for whom the institution is legally responsible does not meet the standard of care required by the law.

The administrator, school, or university may also be sued under the theory of vicarious liability for the alleged negligence of an employee in the performance of his or her job duties. An administrator may be sued in his or her role as the supervisor of a coach or teacher. The institution may also be sued in its role as the employer of the administrator, coach, teacher, referee, or doctor or as the owner or lessor of a facility.

One roadblock in the path of the potential plaintiff, however, is the sovereign immunity doctrine (see section 4.4.1, "Sovereign Immunity"). This doctrine is a rule of law, which in many states exempts public schools and universities from private suit. Sovereign immunity has existed for centuries, but more recently the doctrine has eroded out of concern for injured plaintiffs. In states where sovereign immunity has been partially eliminated, there are usually special rules of procedure that the plaintiff must carefully follow.

Vicarious liability and sovereign immunity issues may substantially overlap with the liability of facilities, where administrators, schools, and universities are often the facility owners and possessors. In these cases, the administration needs to be careful about the duty to control crowds at athletic events such as when fans rush to tear down goalposts. In 1993, more than 70 spectators were injured at a University of Wisconsin football game when fans rushed onto the field after an upset victory over Michigan, forcing those at the front of the crowd against a chain-link fence. A state appeals court dismissed a suit filed by eight injured students in 1998, finding they could not sue school officials due to sovereign immunity. However, in many other states, sovereign immunity would not have raised a total bar to recovery, and in no state would the doctrine cover a *private* school.

4.3.1. Failure to Provide Supervision of Athletic Activities and to Hire Qualified Personnel

The administrator is the supervisor of the coach or teacher and as such may be held liable in negligence for failing to exercise reasonable care in fulfilling this responsibility. Many of the administrator's duties and responsibilities are similar to the supervisory duties of the coach or teacher in dealing with student-athletes.

In dealing with personnel, administrators may be held liable if they have not exercised reasonable care in hiring coaches and teachers with proper skills and qualifications and in ensuring that properly qualified personnel are supervising. Similarly, if evidence shows that an administrator hired a coach or teacher with a previous history of substandard safety practices, the administrator may be vulnerable to liability for negligent hiring.

In other cases, schools and universities may be sued on a vicarious liability theory, meaning that the negligence of their employee is imputed to the employer. The negligent individual may be an administrator, a teacher, a coach, a substitute teacher, a student teacher, or even a referee. Again, any of these individuals, and the school or university, may be immune from lawsuit based on sovereign immunity (see section 4.4.1, "Sovereign Immunity").

NOTES _____

1. In *Hemady v. Long Beach Unified School District*, 143 Cal. App. 4th 566 (Cal. Ct. App. 2006), a seventh grade student sought damages from a physical education teacher,

school, and school district after a classmate accidentally struck her in the face with a club during golf class. Attendance at the class was mandatory to fulfill the school district's physical education requirements. The plaintiff argued that the coach had failed to ensure that students maintained a safe distance from one another during the lesson and that this failure had caused her injury. The court held that school districts take responsibility for any injuries to their students that are caused by school officers' or employees' lack of ordinary care. Under the circumstances of this case, the facts alleged by the plaintiff therefore precluded summary judgment on behalf of the defendants.

2. In *Duffy v. Suffolk County High School Hockey League, Inc.*, 289 A.D.2d 368 (N.Y. App. Div. 2001), a high school student alleged negligent supervision by his high school hockey team and its league after he was struck in the head by a puck during practice for interscholastic competition. The plaintiff had been skating behind the goal when he was hit with a teammate's errant shot. The appellate court ruled that the plaintiff had assumed the ordinary risks of participation in ice hockey, including the possibility of the type of injury he suffered. The plaintiff had participated in the same drill before and was familiar with its risks, and the defendants' supervision did nothing to increase the risk unreasonably. Therefore, summary judgment in favor of the defendants was affirmed.

3. In *Kane v. North Colonie Central School District*, 708 N.Y.S.2d 203 (N.Y. App. Div. 2000), a high school student sued the school district, alleging inadequate supervision by the school stemming from injuries sustained by the plaintiff during an indoor track practice. The coach directed the plaintiff and her teammates to run up and down the hallway of the high school for thirty minutes. The plaintiff tripped and sustained injuries. She sued the school district, alleging inadequate supervision. On appeal, the plaintiff offered evidence that "the risk of contact and falling is unreasonably increased where the runners do not maintain a safe and appropriate distance, typically a stride, from one another." The appellate court held that there was sufficient evidence "to raise a question of fact as to whether the defendant's supervision was inadequate and resulted in the failure to exercise reasonable care."

4. In *Scott v. Rapides Parish Sch. Bd.*, 732 So. 2d 749 (La. Ct. App. 1999), the court held that the school district breached its duty to a student who was injured while attempting a long jump in physical education class. The appellate court affirmed the trial court's ruling that the track coach breached his duty to the plaintiff by failing to provide adequate supervision in safe long jumping technique, thereby causing the harm that the plaintiff suffered when he landed improperly. The school board was held vicariously liable for the coach's negligence.

5. In *Phillipe v. City of New York Board of Education*, 678 N.Y.S.2d 662 (N.Y. App. Div. 1998), a student was killed in a pickup football game that took place in a school yard. The survivors of the decedent filed suit against the city board of education. The Supreme Court, Appellate Division, reasoned that since the game occurred prior to the start of the school day, the defendant school board had no duty of supervision.

6. In *Moose v. Massachusetts Institute of Technology*, 683 N.E.2d 706 (Mass. App. Ct. 1997), a university was held liable for injuries a pole-vaulter sustained when he fell off the back edge of a landing pit and hit his head. Evidence was provided indicating that the length of the landing pit and its closeness to the hard track surface did not provide a safe environment. This was exacerbated by the fact that the pole-vaulter was using a pole that was too light for his weight and that he was running too fast on his approach. The court determined that the risk of this type of harm was reasonably foreseeable to experienced track-and-field coaches and refused to overturn a jury verdict against the defendants.

7. In *Giovinazzo v. Mohawk Valley Community College*, 617 N.Y.S.2d 90 (N.Y. App. Div. 1994), a softball player injured her foot while playing in muddy conditions on the softball field and filed suit against her college for negligence, specifically in the maintenance of the playing conditions but also for failure to provide adequate supervision. The defendant institution was found not liable under a successful assumption of the risk defense. The plaintiff's awareness of the poor field conditions, and voluntary participation nevertheless,

sufficiently established her assumption of the risk. Therefore, the court found no failure in the duty of care by the defendants.

8. In *Schiffman v. Spring*, 609 N.Y.S.2d 482 (N.Y. App. Div. 1994), a college varsity soccer player brought suit against the athletic director and coach after being injured on a wet, mud-soaked playing field. Although the plaintiff and several teammates had complained to the coach about the conditions of the field, they nonetheless voluntarily elected to participate in the game. Since they did so with full awareness of the muddy surface and the risk of injury, the appellate court found that they had assumed the risk of the type of harm suffered by the plaintiff. The court therefore ordered that summary judgment be entered for the defendants.

9. In *DeMauro v. Tusculum College, Inc.*, 603 S.W.2d 115 (Tenn. 1980), plaintiff brought suit for injuries he received in a golf class. Plaintiff was injured when a teaching assistant, an inexperienced golfer who was assigned to supervise the plaintiff's class, was attempting to demonstrate how to hit a golf ball. The teaching assistant shanked the shot, which struck the plaintiff in the face. The court allowed the plaintiff to sue the college under the doctrine of vicarious liability.

10. *Brahatcek v. Millard School District*, 273 N.W.2d 680 (Neb. 1979), was a suit involving an action for the death of a ninth grade student who was accidentally struck by a golf club during physical education class. The court held that the school district and instructors were negligent in not providing supervision and that the lack of supervision was the proximate cause of the student's death. It held that the instructors should have foreseen the intervening negligent act of the student who fatally struck the other student. If there had been proper supervision, the death would not have occurred, and therefore, intervening negligence of the classmate did not preclude the district from liability for the death.

11. In *Carabba v. Anacortes School District*, 435 P.2d 936 (Wash. 1967), the plaintiff, a high school wrestler, brought suit against the defendant school district to recover injuries sustained in a match. The plaintiff was injured when the referee's attention was diverted and his opponent applied an illegal full nelson hold. The plaintiff was paralyzed below the neck due to substantial severance of his spinal cord. The court held that because the referee was an agent for the school district, the school could be held vicariously liable for the referee's negligence.

For more information, see the following law review article: Janis K. Doleschal, "Managing Risk in Interscholastic Athletic Programs: 14 Legal Duties of Care," 17 *Marquette Sports Law Review* 295 (Fall 2006).

4.3.2. Failure to Provide Proper Medical Assistance

Administrators, schools, and universities are generally not responsible for providing direct medical treatment to an injured student, student-athlete, or spectator. However, the administrator, school, or university may be sued on the doctrine of vicarious liability if an employee improperly provided medical treatment. The administrator, school, or university generally will not be held responsible for the medical malpractice of a doctor since in most cases the doctor is held to be an independent contractor and not an employee. However, the administrator, school, or university may be held responsible for the negligent selection, supervision, or hiring of medical personnel. For example, school administrators will be expected to ensure a doctor or trainer is qualified to provide on-field assistance to injured players. Potential liability also exists if the administrator, school, or university was negligent by not providing medical personnel at a game or practice. Many schools and universities have rules that require medical personnel at certain events such as football or basketball games. Many states, including Massachusetts, require a physician or person trained in emergency medical care to be assigned to all interscholastic football games; See Mass. Gen. Law Ann. Ch. 71, Section 54A (see note 1). Finally, the school or university may be held responsible on the theory of vicarious liability if the administrator is found to be negligent.

NOTES

1. Mass. Gen. Law Ann. Ch. 71, Section 54A, reads: "A physician employed by a school committee or a person who has completed a full course in emergency medical care as provided in section six of chapter one hundred and eleven C shall be assigned to every interscholastic football game played by any team representing a public secondary school in the commonwealth, and the expenses of such physician or person shall be paid by the school committee of the city, town or district wherein such football game is played."

2. In *Orr v. Brigham Young University*, 960 F. Supp. 1522 (D. Utah 1994), a former college football player sought damages for harm allegedly caused by medical negligence on the part of the defendant university. The plaintiff had suffered recurring back pain during his time playing football at Brigham Young University (BYU). He regularly apprised his position coach of his condition and was frequently treated by university training staff. After playing two seasons, the plaintiff was diagnosed with three herniated discs in his spine. The court denied the defendant's motion for summary judgment against the medical negligence claim, finding that a jury should determine whether BYU employees had exercised the degree of care required for their profession.

3. In *Kleinknecht v. Gettysburg College*, 989 F.2d 1360 (3rd Cir. 1993), a 20-year-old student-athlete died of cardiac arrest while participating in a practice session of the intercollegiate lacrosse team at Gettysburg College. His parents brought a wrongful death suit against Gettysburg College, claiming that the school breached the duty of care it owed their son by failing to provide proper medical services at the time of his death. The student-athlete was participating in a drill when suddenly he stepped away from the play and dropped to the ground. There was no trainer on the field during the practice because the practice session was held during the nontraditional fall practice season and the school did not require trainers to be at these practices. The practices were being held on the softball fields outside the football stadium. The nearest telephone was in the football stadium's training room, which required scaling an eight-foot fence in order to get inside the stadium. The head trainer was the first to administer CPR, but 5–12 minutes passed before he was summoned and arrived on the field. It was also estimated that another 10 minutes elapsed before the first ambulance arrived at the scene. The district court ruled for the defendant, stating that even though the parents had presented evidence showing that severe and life-threatening injuries can occur and are not out of the question during contact sports, the college still had no duty to the student-athlete because it could not foresee that a young athlete who had no previous history of medical trouble was likely to suffer cardiac arrest during a practice or game. The court of appeals, however, ruled that the district court's definition of foreseeability was too narrow and felt that the parents had produced ample evidence that a life-threatening injury occurring during participation in an athletic event such as lacrosse was reasonably foreseeable. The college, therefore, owed the student-athlete a duty, which required the college to have measures in place at the lacrosse team's practice in order to provide prompt treatment in the event that any member of the lacrosse team suffered a life-threatening injury.

4.3.3. Failure to Provide Safe Equipment

The failure to provide equipment or the failure to provide satisfactory equipment has been the basis for a number of lawsuits brought against administrators, schools, and universities. The individuals who are responsible for equipment vary from institution to institution. They include the coach, teacher, and equipment manager; business managers who purchase the equipment; the athletic director;

and/or other administrators. All these individuals are employees of the institution, and the institution may be responsible for their negligent acts under the theory of vicarious liability.

Although many lawsuits filed against institutions regarding equipment have been unsuccessful, they indicate potential liability areas. The first consideration is the purchase of appropriate equipment for the athletic activities offered. The second consideration is the purchase of equipment that is of satisfactory quality. For example, with respect to football helmets, the institution should adhere to guidelines established by the National Operating Committee on Standards for Athletic Equipment (NOCSAE). Its Web site is http://www.NOCSAE.org. The third consideration is the provision of equipment for the athletic activities in which equipment is necessary. For example, a plaintiff may allege that a defendant school or school district was negligent in not providing sufficient padding for a tackle football game. The fourth consideration is the provision of properly fitting equipment. For example, a football player may allege that shoulder pads did not fit properly and that poor fit was the proximate cause of the resulting injuries. The fifth and last consideration is the periodic inspection of the equipment and reconditioning or replacement when necessary. The NOCSAE guidelines will again be useful.

NOTES

1. In *Kelly v. McCarrick*, 841 A.2d 869 (Md. Ct. Spec. App. 2004), the plaintiff was a junior high school softball player who suffered a fractured ankle in a collision at second base during an interscholastic competition. The plaintiff sued the school that hosted the competition, alleging among other things that her injury had been partially caused by the school's negligent failure to install breakaway bases on the field of play. The school argued that the plaintiff had assumed the risk of playing with stationary bases that did not break away, and the appellate court affirmed the trial court's summary judgment in favor of the school. The plaintiff had routinely played on fields with stationary bases, and she and her parents were aware of the risks such bases posed.

2. In *Elledge v. Richland/Lexington School District Five*, 534 S.E.2d 289 (S.C. Ct. App. 2000), the mother of a nine-year-old girl sued the defendant school district for injuries her daughter sustained in a fall from monkey bars on school property. The girl had sustained a spiral fracture of her right femur when she fell from the bars, which the school had previously modified in an effort to make them safer. The plaintiff sought to introduce evidence of industry guidelines on safe playground equipment in order to prove that the defendant's alterations to the monkey bars had been negligently performed. Although the school district had not adopted the industry guidelines, the appellate court ordered the guidelines admitted as evidence that was relevant to establish the appropriate standard of care.

3. In *Palmer v. Mount Vernon Township High School District 201*, 169 Ill.2d 55, 662 N.E.2d 1260 (Ill. 1996), the plaintiff, a star high school basketball player who had previously injured his cheekbone under his left eye, was told by his coach not to use his protective eye goggles because someone else might get hurt. The plaintiff lost the vision in his left eye after he was hit in the eye by another player's finger. The Illinois Supreme Court held that the school district has a duty of ordinary care to provide adequate safety equipment for students' use during athletic activities but did not impose a separate duty to warn students to wear safety equipment and the duty to allow students to provide their own safety equipment.

4. In *Baker v. Briarcliff School Dist.*, 613 N.Y.S. 2d 660 (N.Y. App. Div. 1994), the appellate court reviewed a case filed by the father of a high school student who was injured during field hockey practice. The plaintiff's daughter had been struck in the mouth by a field hockey stick while not wearing her mouth guard. The plaintiff alleged that the defendant school district was negligent in failing to ensure the use of proper

safety equipment; the school district argued that the plaintiff's daughter had assumed the risk of this type of harm when she practiced without a mouth guard. The court denied the defendant's motion for summary judgment, ruling that a jury should decide whether the school district and its employees had adequately informed student-athletes of the importance of using safety equipment.

4.3.4. Vicarious Liability for Actions of Fans and Players

The coach and teacher may be sued under a vicarious liability theory for either the unintentional or the intentional tort of a fan or player. However, plaintiffs generally have difficulty in winning cases based on a vicarious liability theory.

For instance, in *Toone v. Adams*, an umpire was injured by a fan, and the umpire sued, among others, the manager for inciting the fan to act. The court held for the manager and found that the manager's actions were not the proximate cause of the umpire's injuries (see note 2).

The nexus between the coach and the injury may be more easily established in other fact situations that have occurred but have not resulted in litigation. For example, a coach who orders a player to fight or attempt to injure an opposing player may be liable under the vicarious liability theory if injuries occur.

NOTES

1. In *Lackner v. North*, 135 Cal. App. 4th 1188 (Cal. Ct. App. 2006), a skier sought recovery for severe injuries she suffered after a member of a high school snowboarding team collided with her while she stood at the bottom of a ski run. The court held that the school could be found vicariously liable for the student's actions only if the team's coach had negligently supervised the student by disregarding a known tendency for recklessness. The coach had instructed team members to "take it slow and easy" during practice and had no reason to suspect that the experienced and generally responsible student-athlete involved in the accident needed individual supervision. Therefore, the court affirmed the dismissal of the plaintiff's claim against the school district.

2. For a case involving coaches' vicarious liability for the actions of fans and players, see *Toone v. Adams*, 137 S.E.2d 132 (N.C. 1964). A baseball umpire brought suit against the manager and the owner of the team after being assaulted by a fan after a game. The umpire contended that the conduct of the manager, who had been ejected from the game, and the lack of adequate protection were the proximate causes of his injury. The court found that umpires are used to having their calls disputed and that disagreements, as such, are not a major problem. The plaintiff was well escorted on his way to the dressing room, and though the guards themselves could have been more diligent, lack of protection was not the proximate cause of the plaintiff's injury. The court asserted that the club and its manager did not actually intend, and could not have reasonably anticipated, that one or more persons would assault the plaintiff as a result of the manager's conduct.

For more information, see the following law review articles.

1. C. Peter Gopelrud III, "Allocation of Risk between Hockey Fans and Facilities: Tort Liability after the Puck Drops," 38 *Tulsa Law Review* 445 (Spring 2003).

2. Steven I. Rubin, "The Vicarious Liability of Professional Sports Teams for On-the-Field Assaults Committed by Their Players," 1 *Virginia Journal of Sports and the Law* 266 (Fall 1999).

For more information specifically for the athletic administrators, see the following book:

1. John O. Spengler, Dan Connaughton, and Andrew Pittman, *Risk Management in Sport and Recreation* (Champaign, IL: Human Kinetics, 2006).

4.4. THE DEFENSE OF IMMUNITY

Immunity is a condition that protects against tort liability regardless of the circumstances. Immunity is to be distinguished from a *privilege*, which operates to excuse the commission of an intentional tort under specific conditions (see section 3.1.5.6, "Immunity and Good Samaritan Statutes").

4.4.1. Sovereign Immunity

Sovereign immunity is the type of immunity most often encountered in a sports setting, although charitable immunity will be a consideration in some instances. Historically, all states had sovereign immunity laws. Recently, however, some state courts and legislatures have determined that states can be sued in certain situations for certain activities. To determine if an entity is immune from legal recourse, one must first determine whether it is a governmental entity.

Governmental entities may be federal, state, or local governments, municipalities, or any activity that is under the control of any of the aforementioned. Certain public policy considerations underlie the establishment of sovereign immunity. One rationale is that public agencies have limited funds and should expend them only for public purposes. To allow an individual to sue a public entity unfairly restricts the amount of funds available for public welfare. Another rationale for sovereign immunity is the traditional idea that the state can do no wrong. This is a vestige of the historical view that a monarch was infallible, and was the original basis for sovereign immunity.

Other reasons include the idea that the public cannot be held responsible for the torts of their government employees and that public bodies themselves have no authority to commit torts. Many believe that the aforementioned policy considerations are not compelling, and the trend in several jurisdictions is to repeal or limit the immunity granted to governments.

Sovereign immunity rests on the concept that a state must give consent to be sued. Most states have given such consent, either in the form of a statute, which authorizes an individual to sue, or by providing special courts (e.g., courts of claims) and procedures to be followed when an instrumentality of the state causes an injury. In addition, these statutes generally limit the amount a tort claimant may recover in an action against the government. The statutes generally are narrowly interpreted, but they have been extended to agencies related to, but not part of, the actual state government. Public high schools and high school athletic associations are usually included on the list of agencies whose traditional sovereign immunity may be limited by statutes of this kind.

In states with sovereign immunity statutes, the distinction between governmental and proprietary activities presents an important legal issue. A *governmental activity* is one performed only by the state and as such is commonly protected from lawsuits on the grounds of sovereign immunity. For example, education is a governmental activity. A *proprietary activity* is one that is done by the state but that could be undertaken by the private sector and is therefore not given the protection of sovereign immunity. An example is when a town leases a facility for a professional sporting event.

In any lawsuit brought against a government entity, it must first be determined whether the activity on which the plaintiff's case is based on governmental or proprietary activity. If the activity is found to be a governmental one, the action brought by the plaintiff will be dismissed on the basis of the sovereign immunity statute that protects the governmental body. A determination that the activity is proprietary in nature, however, permits continuation of the case and possible recovery of damages by the plaintiff. Naturally, then, in the initial stages of a case involving the state, the defendant commonly argues that the activity in question was governmental and the plaintiff claims it was proprietary.

The distinction between governmental and proprietary functions is very difficult to make. A sports facility may be conducting either a proprietary or a governmental function. In the case of a public school using its own sports facility, the courts have usually found that the holding of athletic contests is part of the educational function of the state and is therefore a governmental function protected by the sovereign immunity doctrine. If the facility is leased for use by the private sector, the courts have concluded that the school has conducted a proprietary activity (by leasing) and will therefore be liable for injuries sustained as a result of negligent maintenance or construction of the facility.

NOTES

1. In *Summy v. City of Des Moines*, 708 N.W.2d 333 (Iowa 2006), the Supreme Court of Iowa reviewed a case in which a golfer standing in the 18th fairway of a city-owned golf course was struck in the eye by a golf ball driven off the first tee. The city claimed immunity under an Iowa statute insulating municipalities from liability in the performance of certain public functions, including issuance of permits. The city argued that it was immune since the golfer who had struck the ball was admitted to the course using a permit issued to his employer. The court disagreed, ruling that the plaintiff's claim was based not on the issuance of the permit but on the city's failure to protect the plaintiff from a foreseeable hazard. A jury award in the plaintiff's favor was therefore affirmed.

2. In *Ilott v. University of Utah*, 12 P.3d 1011 (Utah Ct. App. 2000), a spectator was allegedly injured when a plank broke beneath her foot as she walked down bleachers during a university football game. She brought a negligence claim against the university. The district court granted summary judgment in favor of the university on the grounds that Utah's governmental immunity statute specifically retained sovereign immunity for (1) negligent inspections carried out by the state and (2) for latent defects in state-owned property. The appellate court reversed this judgment, finding that (1) branches of the state government could not claim immunity for inspections of their own property and (2) since the university had not shown its inspection of the bleachers was adequate, issues of material fact existed as to whether the defect in question was latent or patent.

3. In *Caldwell v. Griffin Spalding County Bd. of Ed.*, 503 S.E.2d 43 (Ga. Ct. App. 1998), a freshman on a varsity football team was beaten by members of the team in an apparent "initiation ritual" at the team's summer football camp. The victim's father, who alleged that the defendants should have known of the initiations and should have prevented the attack, filed a lawsuit against the board of education, head football coach, and principal. The trial court granted summary judgment to the defendants based on the board's sovereign immunity and the official immunity of the head football coach and the principal.

4. In *Singerman v. Municipal Services Bureau, Inc.*, 565 N.W.2d 383 (Mich. 1997), an experienced ice hockey player who had been struck in the face with a puck at a facility run by the city filed suit against the city, the company created by the city to run the arena, and arena managers. The plaintiff alleged that poor lighting in the arena was the cause of his injury. The trial court barred the city as a defendant based on governmental immunity. The state Supreme Court dismissed the case against the other defendants, reasoning that the danger of playing hockey in poor light was open and obvious to the plaintiff.

5. In *Carter v. New Trier High School*, 650 N.E.2d 657 (Ill. App. Ct. 1995), a tennis player who had injured his ankle on a poorly maintained high school court named the high school as a codefendant under the theory of vicarious liability. The immunity statute absolved state agencies from liability except in cases of "willful or wanton" conduct on the part of its employees. The high school was therefore dismissed as a defendant. On appeal, the plaintiff claimed that the trial judge erred in referring to the culpability attached to *willful and wanton* conduct as being similar to the culpability associated with *criminal* conduct. In fact, the immunity law in question defined willful and wanton conduct as "a course of action that shows an actual or deliberate intention to cause harm or which, if not intentional, shows utter indifference to or conscious disregard for the safety of others or their property." The appellate court agreed that willful and wanton conduct is different from criminal conduct and remanded the immunity question to a jury.

6. In *Acosta v. Unified School District*, 37 Cal Rptr. 2d. 171 (Cal. Ct. App. 1995), a high school gymnast was rendered quadriplegic and eventually died after being injured in the school gymnasium under the supervision of his coach. The school district argued that it should not be held vicariously liable for the negligence of the coach because Section 831.7 of the Government Code immunizes a public entity from liability for injuries resulting from participation in a "hazardous recreational activity." The appellate court ruled that as a matter of law, school-sponsored extracurricular activities supervised by school personnel are not hazardous recreational activities under the statute. Therefore, even though the incident occurred during an off-season workout, the school district could not claim governmental immunity.

7. In *Montgomery v. City of Detroit*, 448 N.W.2d 822 (Mich. Ct. App. 1989), the mother of a student who died of a heart attack after collapsing on a school's athletic field sued the principal, the teacher, and the operator of the emergency medical service telephone. The court found for the defendants, holding that (1) the principal was immune from liability; (2) the alleged failure of the teacher to learn to make emergency calls was immune as a discretionary decision; (3) the telephone operator was not negligent; (4) the statute that provided that school officials could be sued for discretionary acts constituting gross negligence did not apply; and (5) the student's civil rights were not violated by the schoolteacher's acts, which allegedly delayed the student's arrival at the hospital.

The availability of insurance will not eliminate immunity as a defense. See, for example, the following cases.

1. In *Weinstein v. Evanston Township Community*, 351 N.E.2d 236 (Ill. App. Ct. 1976), the court held that the purchase of liability insurance did not waive general immunity of the school district, and no damages were awarded to a junior high school student who was injured while exercising on the parallel bars.

2. In *Merrill v. Birhanzel*, 310 N.W.2d 522 (S.D. 1981), plaintiff sued the teacher who was in charge of a required wrestling class at the time of plaintiff's injury. During the match, the plaintiff was thrown to the ground and his left ankle was broken. The court failed to find any grounds for the district to be sued given its sovereign immunity. It noted that the "authority to purchase, and the purchase of liability insurance does not provide that permission.... We have consistently held that if there is to be a departure from the immunity rule, the policy must be declared and the extent of liability fixed by the legislature."

4.4.2. Charitable Immunity

Charitable immunity was developed to limit the liabilities of charitable organizations. The justifications for applying the charitable immunity laws are based on the following reasons:

1. Donations to charitable organizations constitute a trust fund that may not be used for an unintended purpose.

2. Since charities do not benefit financially from the activities of their employees and volunteers, the doctrine of vicarious liability cannot apply.

3. Those who accept services from charities should assume the risk of the charities' negligence.

4. A charity's ability to protect the public is protected by not diverting its money to pay damage claims.

The doctrine of charitable immunity, similar to sovereign immunity, has been eliminated or limited in most states. To the extent the doctrine still applies, it will generally not serve to insulate charities from liability for injuries suffered by their own volunteers (see note 1).

NOTES

1. In *Romanowski v. Township of Washington*, 2006 WL 1650967 (N.J. Super. A.D. June 16, 2006), a volunteer soccer coach sued a youth soccer association after he was injured while participating in a soccer license certification class. The court held that the coach was a beneficiary of the youth soccer association's charitable works, and thus the association was entitled to charitable immunity.

2. In *Roberts v. Timber Birch-Broadmoore Athletic Association*, 852 A.2d 271 (N.J. Super. Ct. App. Div. 2004), the court considered the limitations of New Jersey's charitable immunity statute. The plaintiff was injured at a concession stand while attending a soccer tournament sponsored by the defendant, a nonprofit organization covered by the statute. Both the plaintiff's children played in the tournament, and her husband coached one of the children's teams; the plaintiff assisted with team functions, including equipment, scorekeeping, and scheduling. The appellate court ruled that although the charitable immunity statute did apply to operating concessions which were integral to nonprofit goals, questions of material fact regarding the plaintiff's status as a volunteer precluded summary judgment in the defendant's favor. If the plaintiff could show she was a volunteer at the tournament, the charitable immunity statute would not apply to her suit. The court remanded the case for consideration by a jury.

4.4.3. Civil Liability Immunity Legislation

Increasingly, and for a number of reasons, governmental bodies have seen a need to institute regulations that govern certain aspects of sports. As litigation flourishes, state officials seek to balance injured participants' need for redress with the public policy of promoting physical activity. An area that has undergone particular legislative scrutiny is liability for sports coaches, administrators, and officials, especially in regard to youth sports organizations. Legislation has been proposed on both the federal and state levels of government and has been enacted in several states. The federal Volunteer Protection Act became law in 1997 (see note 2 below), and by the early part of the 21st century every state had passed immunity statutes covering volunteers at several sport and recreational events.

Proponents of civil liability immunity legislation that is directed to youth sport organizations contend that it is needed because of a proliferation of civil lawsuits that threaten to force many of those involved in sports, especially volunteers, from participating in sport organizations. It is reasoned that coaches and managers of youth sport organizations and other like groups cannot carry out their roles without fear of being sued for damages. For instance, during consideration of legislation in

New Jersey, the most frequently cited case involving Little League lawsuits was a complaint filed by a Camden County mother against the Runnemede Youth Athletic Association, seeking $750,000 in damages after her son misjudged a fly ball and was struck in the eye.

Another area that has drawn extensive focus from state governments is *recreational use immunity*. This doctrine holds that landowners who offer their property for public use with no expectation of financial benefit should enjoy immunity from suit by those who accept the offer. Although state statutes vary in the extent of immunity provided, every state in the country recognizes a measure of recreational use immunity in order to encourage wealthy landowners to allow the public to benefit from use of their land.

NOTES

1. In *Whooley v. Commonwealth*, 783 N.E.2d 461 (Mass. App. Ct. 2003), a woman who visited a state-owned ice rink to watch her grandson play hockey slipped and fell entering the arena's bleachers. She sued the state of Massachusetts in its capacity as owner of the facility, asserting that a layer of ice on a metal walkway had caused her fall. The state claimed it was immune under the existing recreational use statute, and the court agreed. Although her grandson was a member of a team that paid to rent the rink, the plaintiff herself had entered the premises free of charge. Since the state's alleged misconduct in maintaining the bleachers was at worst negligent and did not rise to the level of willful, wanton, or reckless conduct, the recreational use statute insulated the state from liability.

2. On June 18, 1997, the Volunteer Protection Act of 1997 was enacted into law by the U.S. Congress (42 U.S.C. §§ 14501–14505). The act states, with some noted exceptions, that "no volunteer of a nonprofit organization or governmental entity shall be liable for harm caused by an act or omission . . . on behalf of the organization." One stated purpose of the act was to encourage citizens to volunteer their services and to make people feel less deterred by the potential liability of doing so.

3. Also see section 4.7, "Liability of Officials, Referees, and Umpires," for legislation directly related to such persons.

4.5. LIABILITY OF FACILITY OWNERS AND POSSESSORS

The duty that the owner or possessor of a facility owes varies, depending on the status of the party who was injured while on the premises. Therefore, to establish the extent of duty for owners, operators, supervisors, or possessors of land, the status of the person injured must first be determined. Generally, there are two classes of persons: licensees and invitees.

A *licensee* is one who enters the property of another, with the owner's consent, for the licensee's own purposes. The occupier of the property owes licensees only a duty of ordinary care. There is no obligation to inspect the area to discover dangers that are currently unknown, nor to warn of conditions that should be obvious to the licensee. The occupier of the property owes a licensee a duty to warn only when a risk is known or should have been known by the occupier under the reasonable person standard, and when the licensee is unaware of the danger.

An *invitee* is someone who is invited onto the property and whose presence benefits the occupant. An invitee is owed a greater degree of care by the owner, operator, supervisor, or occupier of the property. There is an affirmative duty to make safe both known defects as well as those defects that should have been discovered by reasonable inspection. The basis of liability is the implied representation at the time of the invitation that the premises are safe to enter. The invitation does not have to be extended personally for an individual to be classified as an invitee. For example, an advertisement which invites people to buy tickets and enter a stadium is considered an invitation for this purpose.

The invitation implies that reasonable care has been exercised for the safety of the invitee. The owner or possessor of the property is not, however, an insurer of the safety of the invitee. That is, the owner does not guarantee safety under all possible circumstances. Instead, the owner or possessor must exercise only reasonable care for the invitee's protection.

The distinction between licensee and invitee is important because the different standards of care that may be applied can be decisive in determining the outcome of a lawsuit. An athlete or a spectator at a sports event is characterized as a business invitee. A *business invitee* is a visitor who brings a monetary benefit to the person in possession of the property. The business invitee is also a person whom the possessor encourages to enter onto the property. By such encouragement the possessor implicitly represents that the premises are safe to enter. The distinction between patent and latent defects is also important in any discussion of the liability of owners and possessors of sports facilities. Both types of defects are potentially injury-causing, but an owner or operator can only be held liable for defects which are discoverable.

A *patent defect* is one that is plainly visible or that could easily be discovered upon inspection. A facility owner or a lessee is liable for obvious defects, such as debris on steps that creates a hazard, if they cause an injury. A *latent defect* is a hidden or concealed defect that could not be discovered by reasonable inspection. It is a defect of which the owner has no knowledge or of which, in the exercise of reasonable care, the owner should not have knowledge. Owners and lessees are generally not liable for injuries caused by latent defects. In the eyes of the law, when a facility is leased, it is in effect sold for a period of time. Thus, the lessee—the person taking control of the property—assumes the responsibilities of the lessor—the person giving up control of the property—toward those who enter the property. The lessor still has a duty, however, to disclose any concealed or dangerous conditions—any known latent defects—to lessees, their guests, and others reasonably expected to be on the premises. For this duty to attach, the lessor does not have to believe that the condition is dangerous or to have definite knowledge of the defect. Instead, it is sufficient that the lessor be informed of facts from which a reasonable person would conclude that there is a possible danger. However, the lessor has no duty to warn about patent defects, which are defined as known, open, or obvious conditions. When a property is leased for a purpose that includes admission to the public, the lessor has an affirmative duty to exercise reasonable care to inspect and repair the leased property. This duty is imposed to prevent an unreasonable risk to the public. Liability will extend only to parts of the premises open to the public and to invitees who enter for the purpose for which the place was leased.

Facility owners and possessors also have a duty to exercise reasonable care in maintaining the premises and in supervising the conduct of others at the facility. They are, however, entitled to assume that participants will obey the rules and that employees will not be negligent, absent notice to the contrary. Thus, their duty does not include protecting consumers from unreasonable risks. An unreasonable risk is one in which the probability of injury outweighs the burden of taking adequate precautions.

The general rule is that facility owners and possessors are liable for conditions on their premises which cause physical harm if they know or should reasonably have known about the existence of the dangerous condition when such a condition poses an unreasonable risk to an invitee. The requirement of reasonable care is supported by the proposition that a spectator or a participant assumes all the ordinary and inherent risks of the particular sport. These inherent risks are those commonly associated with the sport. The application of this common knowledge rule will depend on the circumstances. No invitee, whether a player or a spectator, assumes the risk that an owner will fail to meet his or her duty of reasonable care.

Having considered the legal rules and responsibilities that apply to facility owners and operators, we turn now to practical implications for sport managers. A facility owner and possessor's duty of reasonable care can be divided into three areas. First is the duty to protect invitees from injurious or defective products. An owner and possessor must exercise reasonable care in the selection of equipment necessary for the operation of the facility. Second, owners and possessors must exercise reasonable care in the maintenance of the facility itself and any equipment in the facility. Standards of safety, suitability, and sanitation must be maintained. In addition, if an invitee uses any of the equipment and the facility owner or possessor supervises, then the facility owner or possessor is held to a standard of reasonable care. Third, an owner and possessor must guard against foreseeable harmful risks caused by other invitees. A breach of any of these duties may subject a facility owner or operator to liability for negligence.

In recent years, courts have examined whether a facility owner or operator's duty to guard against foreseeable risks of harm includes a requirement to have automated external defibrillators (AED's) on the premises. Although relatively few courts have considered the issue, those that have done so have thus far declined to impose a duty to maintain AED's on owner/operators.

Promoters and other sports event organizers often use a facility for only a day or a few days. They do not own the facility, and they are not in a long-term lease situation; therefore, they cannot be considered permanent tenants. Examples include mixed martial arts events, Harlem Globetrotter games, and ice shows. The promoter owes a duty of reasonable care in the maintenance and supervision of the facility.

With respect to maintenance, the owner is more likely to be responsible for patent defects that are uncorrected. With respect to supervision, the promoter is responsible for reasonable care in the running of the event, although the determination of reasonable care may differ depending on the type of event.

For example, the amount and type of necessary security may differ for a family event as opposed to a rock concert. The promoter, however, is not responsible for unique or unforeseeable events in the absence of notice that an injury is apt to occur. Therefore, courts have often refused to find liability for patrons' injuries caused by other spectators. Promoters are required only to exercise reasonable precautions. Nevertheless, to protect themselves in the event that an invitee is successful in a claim against a promoter, facility owners or possessors may require promoters to execute lease agreements (see section 9.2.9, "Facilities Contracts"). An agreement will usually require the promoter to obtain general liability insurance and agree to indemnify and hold harmless the facility owner or possessor.

At events where alcoholic beverages are sold, additional concerns will apply. Owners of facilities that allow alcoholic drinks to be consumed at athletic events have consequently instituted some of the following procedures:

- To purchase beer, customers must go to the concession stand. Beer vendors are no longer allowed to sell beer to customers in their seats. In addition, low-alcohol (3.2 beer) and no-alcohol beer are offered for sale.

- At football games, the sale of beer is discontinued at the beginning of the third quarter; at baseball games, beer sales may be ended at the seventh inning stretch or earlier.

- The largest container of beer sold is 20 ounces instead of 32.

- Season ticket holders can lose their ticket rights for subsequent seasons if they become involved in fights or other such rowdy behavior or even if they give their tickets to others who proceed to engage in such behavior.

- No-alcohol seating sections are designated.

Control of alcohol beverage sales in the facility, limiting or supervising the practice of tailgating in pregame and postgame situations, and ensuring that security is present inside and outside the facility are further examples of reasonable precautions taken by facility operators. At a minimum, sponsored activities require some type of increased safety measures, especially if there have been incidents of rowdiness or other disruptive behavior in the past. If such measures are undertaken, liability should be greatly reduced.

Another potential problem area for facility owners is tailgating, which has become a standard component of the traditional college football weekend. In fact, many colleges and universities have actively promoted the concept, seeking to capitalize on its popularity to market their intercollegiate athletic programs. In most cases, tailgating is a harmless afternoon's pleasure for fans, but on occasion it can lead to excessive drinking and rowdy behavior. In general, there has been an increasing concern by society and state legislatures and courthouses about excessive drinking and its impact on public safety. It is this aspect of tailgating that must concern facility administrators.

Sports administrators have also been concerned about drinking at intercollegiate events. The National Collegiate Athletic Association has long banned the sale of alcoholic beverages at NCAA tournaments and postseason championship events, and many campuses have policies that limit consumption of alcoholic beverages at on-campus athletic events.

In summary, the following checklist is offered to help facility owners protect themselves against possible litigation:

1. Anticipate any potentially injurious conditions in the facility (stadium, arena, pool, etc.) or event site (baseball field, soccer field, etc.) in order to identify and reduce risk.

2. Ensure that the facility is adequately maintained and perform regular inspections (with written reports) on the condition of the facility.

3. In designing a facility, make safety a top concern of the architects and planning committee. Ensure that safe materials are used throughout the facility (glass, padding, mats, etc.).

4. Designate an individual on the staff to serve as the safety expert.

5. Develop a clear, written policy concerning safety in the facility, institute a reporting procedure for potential problems, and document any mishaps in detail.

6. Develop policies for crowd management, including alcohol consumption at the facility.

7. Develop clear, written guidelines for management of crises.

8. Ensure that all personnel are trained in safety procedures; to the extent possible, include staff in identifying potential safety hazards.

NOTES

The following cases were brought against facility owners or possessors by spectators hit with flying objects.

1. In *Crespin v. Albuquerque Baseball Club, LLC*, 216 P.3d 827 (N.M.App. 2009), the Court of Appeals of New Mexico declined to adopt the "Baseball Rule," which generally provides that in the exercise of reasonable care, the owner of a baseball stadium need only provide screening for the area behind home plate and is otherwise generally not liable for injuries as a result of batted balls. In reversing a summary judgment decision, the court held there was a genuine issue of material fact as to whether the city and home club breached their duty of reasonable care under the circumstances. During pregame batting practice, Crespin, a four-year-old boy, was hit while seated in a picnic area in the left field stands.

2. In *Turner v. Mandalay Sports Entertainment, LLC*, 180 P.3d 1172 (Nev. 2008), the Supreme Court of Nevada affirmed a judgment of summary judgment on behalf of a Minor League baseball team. Kathleen Turner sued the team after she was struck in the face with a foul ball as she sat in the stadium's concession area, which had no protective screen surrounding it. The court stated that the team had a limited duty to Turner and that she failed to show that the concessions area posed an unduly high risk of injury.

3. In *Maisonave v. Newark Bears Professional Baseball Club, Inc.*, 881 A.2d 700 (N.J. 2005), a patron who suffered an eye injury while waiting in line at a mezzanine-level concession stand at a baseball park brought suit against the Minor League team that owned the stadium. The stadium included screened seating and concessions behind home plate, but there was no screening in the area where the plaintiff was harmed. The Supreme Court of New Jersey held that the state's limited duty rule for facility owners and operators applied only to injuries that occurred in the stands and therefore did not apply to the plaintiff's injury. The case was remanded to the trial court for application of the business invitee rule to the facts.

4. In a tragic accident in March 2002, a 13-year-old spectator at a National Hockey League game between the host Columbus Blue Jackets and visiting Calgary Flames was struck in the head by a puck that had flown over the protective Plexiglass surrounding the playing surface. Two days later, the young girl died as a result of a blood clot caused by the incident. The case never came to trial, but the girl's parents settled for $1.2 million from the arena owners and the National Hockey League (NHL). The NHL soon ordered the installation of protective nets above the Plexiglass at either end of all NHL rinks, thus attempting to obviate the risk of harm to spectators in areas of the stands that were most exposed to errant shots.

5. In *Marshall v. Heartland Park Topeka*, 49 P.3d 501 (Kan. 2002), the Supreme Court of Kansas considered the case of a drag racing spectator who was struck by a tire that flew into the grandstand after an accident on the track. The court held that since the possibility of tires and other debris entering the seating area constituted a known and reasonably foreseeable danger of drag racing, the defendant track operator had a duty to afford reasonable protection to spectators by building protective barriers. The defendant asserted they had fulfilled this duty by building a 40-inch-high concrete wall, the top of which the tire had struck before careening into the stands; the lower courts had agreed

and entered summary judgment for the defendant. The Supreme Court reversed however, finding that the adequacy of the wall was a material question of fact which a jury should decide based on expert testimony.

6. In *Benejam v. Detroit Tigers Inc.*, 635 N.W.2d 219 (Mich. Ct. App. 2001), a young girl was injured by a flying bat particle along the third base line. Although plaintiff was behind a protective net, a fragment of the bat curved around it. Plaintiffs sued the Tigers, claiming that the net was insufficiently long and that warnings about the possibility of projectiles leaving the field were inadequate. Plaintiff suffered crushed fingers as a result of the accident and a jury awarded plaintiffs noneconomic damages (past and future) totaling $917,000, lost earning capacity of $56,700, and $35,000 for past and future medical expenses. The appellate court overturned the verdict, holding that the Tigers had fulfilled their limited duty by making protected seating available and that the club had no duty to warn of open and obvious dangers.

7. In *City of Coral Springs v. Rippe*, 743 So. 2d 61 (Fla. Dist. Ct. App. 1999), plaintiff was watching her son play in a Little League game from park bleachers. For a better view of the game, she moved in front of the players' bench, where the fence was only four feet high. She was struck by a foul ball, knocked unconscious, and suffered injuries. A jury concluded that the plaintiff was 60% at fault and the city was 40% at fault and awarded the plaintiff a judgment of $130,000. The jury concluded that the city either negligently failed to warn of or correct a known dangerous condition. The appellate court affirmed the verdict based on the city's demonstrated failure to correct a known dangerous condition.

8. In *Jasper v. Chicago Nat'l League Ball Club*, 722 N.E.2d 731 (Ill. App. Ct. 1999), plaintiff sued the owner of Wrigley Field (the Chicago Cubs) after he was struck by a foul ball during a baseball game. The plaintiff alleged that before 1992, a net hung between the upper deck and a backstop behind home plate at Wrigley Field. However, in 1992, the club removed the net when it built skyboxes behind home plate just below the upper deck. Hence, the plaintiff alleged that the club had "willfully and wantonly, or negligently, removed the netting, failed to warn patrons of the increased risk, failed to offer safer seating, and allowed the sale of food and beverages in an area where vendors would distract patrons from approaching foul balls." The defendant sought protection for its conduct under the Illinois Baseball Act. That act provides that "the owner or operator of a baseball facility shall not be liable for any injury to the person or property of any person as a result of that person being hit by a ball or bat unless: (1) the person is situated behind a screen, backstop, or similar device at a baseball facility and the screen, backstop, or similar device is defective (in a manner other than in width or height) because of the negligence of the owner or operator of the baseball facility; or (2) the injury is caused by willful and wanton conduct, in connection with the game of baseball, of the owner or operator or any baseball player, coach or manager employed by the owner or operator" (745 ILCS 38/1; West 1996). The plaintiff argued that the Baseball Act was unconstitutional special legislation and that it therefore violated the equal protection guarantees of the Illinois and U.S. constitutions (see section 6.1.3, "Equal Protection"). The plaintiff reasoned that the act violated the principle of equal protection by conferring a special benefit or exclusive privilege on a person or class to the exclusion of others and specifically that "no legitimate state interest is reasonably served by providing special tort protection to owners who host baseball games solely to make a profit." The court disagreed, stating, "We believe the sport of baseball does have unique characteristics that would reasonably prompt a legislature to enact limited liability legislation." The court also stated that the act encourages the building and use of parks for recreational activity and that therefore professional teams were not the sole beneficiaries of the limited liability protection. Because the court found the act to be constitutional and the defendant's conduct to be neither wanton nor reckless, it affirmed the lower court's finding in favor of the Cubs.

9. *Benjamin v. State*, 453 N.Y.S.2d 329 (N.Y. Ct. Cl. 1982), was an action brought by an 11-year-old spectator who, in November 1979, was injured in a college hockey doubleheader at Romney Arena, a state facility on the campus of the State University of New York at Oswego. Plaintiff was seated behind the protective fence, 10–15 feet north of the nearest

players' bench. An errant puck found its way through the open area in front of the players' bench, passed behind the protective fence, and struck plaintiff on the left side of the forehead. Plaintiff brought action against the state alleging that the state failed to provide adequate protection for the safety of spectators seated in the arena. At the trial an expert testified that in similar facilities it was the usual and customary practice to protect the area around the players' bench. Absent such protection, it was the usual and customary practice to restrict seating in an arena without protection from the zone of danger. Since neither course of action was chosen, the court held that the state failed to provide plaintiff with adequate protection that evening. The court found that the failure of the state to provide for the safety of its patrons in the protected seating area constituted negligence and that such negligence was a substantial factor in bringing about the injuries.

In the following cases, spectators brought suit against facility owners or possessors for reasons other than flying objects:

1. In 2009, two lawsuits were brought against baseball clubs and stadium owners for allegedly forcing fans to stand during the playing of "God Bless America." Bradford Campeau-Laurion sued the New York Yankees, the City of New York, and the New York Police Department after he was ejected from a Yankees game for refusing to stand during the playing of the song. In *Gadye v. Bases Loaded Group, LLC*, three teenagers sued after they were forced from a Newark Bears Minor League baseball game after refusing to stand during the song. Both cases alleged that the teams had policies requiring fans to stand during the song, in violation of constitutional rights protecting the freedom of religion. Both cases were settled out of court.

2. In *Verni v. Harry M. Stevens, Inc.*, 903 A.2d 475 (N.J. Super. Ct. App. Div. 2006), the appellate court considered the liability of concession operators at Giants Stadium for injuries caused by a patron who had allegedly been served beer while visibly intoxicated. The plaintiffs had been seriously injured by the car driven by the patron, whose blood alcohol concentration at the time of the accident was found to be .266. The driver had consumed multiple beverages purchased from other vendors before and after visiting the stadium and also admitted to smoking marijuana purchased from an unidentified individual at the stadium. A jury had awarded the plaintiffs, a mother and her infant daughter, over $100 million in damages. The appellate court found "multiple errors in the course of the trial." For example, the court found that evidence concerning "a culture of intoxication" at games at Giants Stadium had been improperly admitted and was not relevant to the issue of whether the patron had been served alcohol while visibly intoxicated. In that context, the testimony of multiple witnesses regarding the rowdy atmosphere of the crowd at football games at the stadium had the clear capacity to mislead and inflame the jury. The appellate court reversed the verdict and remanded the case for a new trial.

3. In *Brisbin v. Washington Sports and Entertainment, Ltd.*, 422 F. Supp. 2d 9 (D.D.C. 2006), the court considered a claim against the operators of an arena by a spectator who had been injured by a fellow patron at a professional hockey game. The plaintiff was sitting in her seat when a member of the crowd who had been sitting several rows above her, having tripped and fallen, slid down the rows of seats, and landed on top of her. The plaintiff alleged that the defendants had failed to protect her from known dangers of which they were or should have been aware. In entering summary judgment in favor of the defendants, the court ruled that the plaintiff had failed to identify any course of action the defendants could have taken to reduce the risk of such an unlikely and unforeseeable accident.

4. During halftime of an NFL exhibition game on August 12, 2006, New Orleans Saints quarterback Adrian McPherson was struck by a golf cart driven by the host Tennessee Titans' mascot T-Rac, a performer in an armored raccoon costume. At the time of the accident, the mascot's attention was allegedly focused on the task of hurling items into the stands. The Titans were not disciplined by the NFL, though the league subsequently reminded all teams that mascots must stay at least six feet from the field at all times. McPherson, who suffered a deep bruise and was cut by the Saints before the start of the

regular season, filed a lawsuit in December 2006 alleging negligence and recklessness. He seeks $5 million in compensatory damages and $15 million in punitive damages from the Titans. The suit is pending.

5. In *Rogers v. Professional Golfers Association of America*, 28 S.W.3d 869 (Ky. Ct. App. 2000), the plaintiff, a spectator who suffered a leg injury when she slipped and fell on a hillside at the Professional Golfers' Association (PGA) Championship, brought suit against the PGA and the host golf course. The court ruled that the defendants' duty to business invitees such as the plaintiff did not include a duty to warn of open and obvious dangers that invitees would be expected to discover through the exercise of ordinary prudence. In this case, the plaintiff was aware of the heavy rain that fell the day before her accident. The court affirmed summary judgment in the defendants' favor.

6. In *Hayden v. University of Notre Dame*, 716 N.E.2d 603 (Ind. Ct. App. 1999), the plaintiff asserted that the defendant university should have acted to prevent the risks the risks posed to football spectators by the foreseeable actions of other spectators. The plaintiff was injured when a football entered the stands following a field goal attempt. Several spectators lunged for the ball, knocking the plaintiff over and injuring her shoulder. The trial court had held that Notre Dame owed the plaintiff no duty to prevent this kind of injury, but the appellate court reversed that judgment. The court ruled that Notre Dame had "a duty to take reasonable steps to protect [the plaintiff] from injury due to the actions of other fans in attempting to retrieve footballs which land in the seating area."

7. In *Daniels v. Atlanta National League Baseball Club, Inc.*, 524 S.E.2d 801 (Ga. Ct. App. 1999), the plaintiff sustained injuries when she slipped on either a cup or the liquid from the cup upon exiting the stadium. She filed suit against the Braves organization, alleging that they failed to exercise ordinary care. The court rejected the plaintiff's claim, holding that the "risk of a cup left on the aisle steps is not an 'unreasonable risk of harm' for one exiting a baseball stadium at the end of a game." To expect the defendant to inspect every aisle and walkway for debris before tens of thousands of people exit would be "unduly burdensome."

8. A spectator at a Miami Heat game brought claims for physical and emotional damages after Burnie, the Heat mascot, pulled her to the ground. The spectator had fallen to the ground while resisting Burnie's insistent tugging, as he urged her to come onto the floor and dance with him. In *Gil-De-Rebollo v. Miami Heat Ass'n*, 137 F.3d 56 (1st Cir. 1998), the U.S. Court of Appeals for the First Circuit affirmed a jury's $50,000 damage award to the plaintiff.

9. In *Bearman v. University of Notre Dame*, 453 N.E.2d 1196 (Ind. Ct. App. 1983), plaintiff sued the University of Notre Dame for injuries she suffered as she left a Notre Dame home football game. The injury occurred in the stadium's parking lot when a third party, who was tailgating and became involved in a fight, fell onto the plaintiff and broke her leg. Plaintiff claimed that the school had "a duty to protect her from injury caused by the acts of other persons on the premises" since she was a business invitee. The university argued that it could not be held liable for the act of a third person since it had no knowledge or notice of any danger to the woman. The Court of Appeals of Indiana, Third District, noted that the issue involved two different factors: An operator of a place of public entertainment generally "owes a duty to keep the premises safe for its invitees"; on the other hand, "an invitor is not the insurer of invitee's safety and before liability may be imposed on invitor, it must have actual or constructive knowledge of the danger." The court reasoned that Notre Dame was aware of the tailgate parties in the parking areas around the stadium and the fact that drinking occurs. It recognized that while Notre Dame did not have particular knowledge of any danger for the plaintiff, it was aware that intoxicated people pose a threat to the safety of patrons at the games. The appeals court therefore reversed the lower court's decision and held that Notre Dame had a duty to do all it could reasonably do to protect those people who attend the games from injury inflicted by the acts of third parties.

10. In *Guttenplan v. Boston Professional Hockey Ass'n*, No. 80-415, 1981 U.S. Dist. LEXIS 10434 (S.D. N.Y. 1981), four hockey fans sued nine individual Boston Bruin hockey

players, the Bruins, the New York Rangers, Madison Square Garden, Inc., the National Hockey League, and the city of New York for $7 million in damages for injuries suffered when a players' brawl on the ice spilled over into the stands in December 1979. The suit charged that the plaintiffs were "stomped" by the Bruins players while league and arena security personnel "merely observed and made no attempt to prevent or stop" the altercation. Criminal charges against individual Bruin players were dropped due to conflicting evidence and testimony that indicated fans had provoked the players. A federal judge dismissed the civil damage suit on jurisdictional grounds.

11. In *Woodring v. Board of Education of Manhasset*, 435 N.Y.S.2d 52 (N.Y. App. Div. 1981), plaintiff brought a wrongful death suit against the school district after a platform railing in the gymnasium gave way, throwing decedent to his death. In affirming the $1,400,000 award to plaintiff, the appeals court found evidence that the school district (1) lacked a preventive maintenance program, (2) improperly constructed the platforms, (3) failed to inspect its gymnasium facilities regularly, and (4) should have known—given the extensive use of the platforms by students—that injury was foreseeable if the railings were not properly maintained or constructed. The appeals court thus sustained the jury's determination of the defendant's negligence.

12. In *Townsley v. Cincinnati Gardens, Inc.*, 314 N.E.2d 409 (Ohio Ct. App. 1974), plaintiff, a minor, brought suit after being assaulted in a washroom by a group of boys while he was attending a Harlem Globetrotters exhibition at Cincinnati Gardens. The plaintiff, as a business invitee of the facility owner, sought damages for negligence on the part of the facility. The trial court held for the plaintiff, stating that "the defendant either knew, or, in the exercise of ordinary care, should have known of the danger which victimized the plaintiff." On appeal, the decision of the trial court was reversed. The appeals court ruled that there was no evidence to indicate that the defendant could have anticipated, or reasonably have known of, the danger to the plaintiff.

In the following cases, participants brought suit against facility owners or possessors.

1. In *Stelluti v. Casapenn Enterprises, LLC*, 975 A.2d 494 (N.J.Super.A.D. 2009), a new member of a fitness club fell from her bike during a spinning class and sued the club claiming the club ailed to maintain the bicycle properly, provide adequate warnings and instruction on its safe use, or adequately train and supervise its employees. The club was granted summary judgment based on the membership agreement.

2. In *Withers v. Bogus Basin Recreational Association, Inc.*, 156 P.3d 579 (Idaho 2007), the Supreme Court of Idaho reviewed a grant of summary judgment in favor of a ski area operator against a skier who had tripped over a rope separating a chairlift from an unloading ramp. The plaintiff alleged that the operator's negligence in placing the rope had proximately caused her injuries. The court disagreed, ruling that the defendant had fulfilled its duty under Idaho law by configuring the rope to lessen the inherent risk of skiers colliding.

3. In *Souza v. Squaw Valley Ski Corporation*, 138 Cal. App. 4th 262 (Cal. Ct. App. 2006), an eight-year-old skier injured her mouth when she collided with a "plainly visible" snowmaking hydrant. The plaintiff sued the operator of the ski resort, alleging that the hydrant was inadequately padded, that it had been negligently located in a high-traffic area, and that the defendant had failed to warn her of the danger posed by the hydrant. The trial court had entered summary judgment for the defendant, ruling that the plaintiff's collision had resulted from an inherent risk of skiing and that she had therefore assumed the risk. The appellate court agreed, reasoning that the danger posed by the hydrant was open and obvious; that there was ample room on either side of the hydrant for skiers to pass by; and that "the large metal plainly-visible snow-making hydrant served as its own warning."

4. In *Salte v. YMCA of Metropolitan Chicago Foundation*, 814 N.E.2d 610 (Ill. App. Ct. 2004), a health club member who suffered a heart attack at the club alleged negligence against the club operator. The plaintiff argued that the operator's failure to maintain a cardiac defibrillator on the premises, and to train a paramedic employed by the club to use a

defibrillator, had proximately caused the plaintiff's harm. The defendant argued that its duty to render first aid to business invitees did not include a responsibility to have a defibrillator on its property nor to use one on the plaintiff. The appellate court agreed, finding that the defendant was not required to foresee every kind of medical care that a patron might require. The defendant's duty was only to render whatever aid they were reasonably capable of providing under the circumstances.

5. In *Plotsker v. Whitey Ford's Grand Slam, Inc.*, 693 N.Y.S.2d 219 (N.Y. App. Div. 1999), the appellate court granted summary judgment to the defendant possessor of a basketball court after plaintiff blamed his injury on the "worn and uneven" court. Even if the plaintiff could have demonstrated that the court was the proximate cause of his injuries, he was precluded from recovery because the danger was "open and obvious."

6. In *Maddox v. City of New York*, 455 N.Y.S.2d 102 (N.Y. App. Div. 1982), 487 N.Y.S.2d 354 (N.Y. App. Div. 1985), a former New York Yankee center fielder brought suit against the owner, maintenance company, and designer of Shea Stadium for an injury that occurred when he slipped on the wet field in the stadium. In ruling for the plaintiff on defendant's motion for a summary judgment, the court found that Maddox did not assume the risk of playing on a dangerous field in that, as an employee, he was under the orders of his superiors. The appeals court reversed the lower court decision and held (1) that the doctrine of assumption of risk completely barred recovery; (2) that a professional baseball player did not fall within protected individuals under the statute governing general duty of the employer to protect health and safety of employees; (3) that even if eligible under the statute, the ballplayer failed to allege any fault by employer which resulted in the wet condition of the playing field; and (4) that player was not acting within the confines of the superior's instructions when he was injured.

7. In *Wilkinson v. Hartford Accident and Indemnity Co.*, 411 So. 2d 22 (La. 1982), plaintiff sued athletic coach, school board, and school's liability insurer to recover for injuries his son sustained when he crashed through a glass panel of the gymnasium foyer while engaging in an unsupervised race during physical education class. The Louisiana Supreme Court reversed a lower court's decision and held for the plaintiff, reasoning that the school board was negligent because several years previously a visiting coach had broken the glass panel when he walked into it. The glass panel was so close to spectator traffic that school authorities should have known of the hazard it created.

8. In *Eddy v. Syracuse University*, 433 N.Y.S.2d 923 (N.Y. App. Div. 1980), plaintiff sought recovery for injuries he received during a Frisbee game. Plaintiff was an ultimate Frisbee player for a team of college students. In March 1977, the team traveled to Syracuse University to play against a group of Syracuse students, although the latter team was neither officially recognized nor sponsored by the defendant. During the course of an ultimate Frisbee game played in the basketball gymnasium, the plaintiff crashed through a glass window in one door, severely lacerating his arm. The plaintiff sued the university for negligence in a personal injury action. The defendant argued that since it did not authorize use of the gym, had no foreknowledge of plaintiff's use, and could not have foreseen that students would use the basketball courts for an ultimate Frisbee game and that the gym was not defective in design or construction for its ordinary purposes, there was lack of evidence to even submit the issue of negligence. The trial court ruled for the plaintiff. In affirming the trial court verdict, the appeals court held: "Surely the jury could have concluded that ... on the campus of a large university ... some of its students, and their guests, might use the facility without express permission ... (in novel games)." Also properly left to the jury were the questions of whether the glass doors, located as they were in a building intended to be used for strenuous physical activity, constituted a dangerous condition and whether the risk presented by the glass doors could have been alleviated without imposing an undue burden on the university.

For more information, also see the following law review articles:

1. Kevin P. Polansky, "Parental Violence at Youth Sporting Events: Should Landowners be Liable?" 39 *Suffolk University Law Review* 561 (2006).

2. George D. Turner, "Allocating the Risk of Spectator Injuries between Basketball Fans and Facility Owners," 6 *Virginia Sports and Entertainment Law Journal* 156 (Fall 2006).

3. E. G. Hochuli, "Liability to Spectators at Sporting Events," 47 *Federation of Insurance and Corporate Counsel Quarterly* 209 (Winter 1997).

4.6. LIABILITY OF MEDICAL PERSONNEL

A person or an organization in charge of a sports activity has a duty to provide reasonable medical assistance to participants as well as to spectators. To determine if this duty has been met, both the quality and the speed of the treatment must be considered. The quality of the treatment will be assessed by looking at the qualifications of the provider and the type of treatment offered. The speed of the treatment may be determined by the response time and availability of medical personnel.

There are many different levels of health care providers within the American medical system. With respect to athletic events, these providers may be doctors or nurses; more often they are trainers or emergency medical technicians (EMTs). The standard of care required of each medical provider is based on the person's training and qualifications (see section 3.1.1, "Duty of Care Owed"). A higher standard of care is established if the class of medical personnel possesses skills and training beyond what is expected of the reasonable layperson. For example, the standard of care imposed on the medical profession is that the doctor must have met the level of skill and knowledge common to the profession and adhered to a uniform standard of conduct.

In the case of a specialist, however, the duty has increasingly become more stringent. A specialist must act with the skill and knowledge reasonable within his or her specialty. Thus, the growing ranks of doctors practicing sports medicine may eventually lead to widespread recognition of sports medicine as a distinct specialty, thus leading to a higher standard of care for doctors specializing in sports injuries in negligence lawsuits brought by injured athletes. In court, the relevant standard of care will usually be established by expert testimony.

Generally, medical personnel are considered independent contractors rather than employees, even though they may be paid by a school district, facility owner, or other supervisory body (see section 3.6.1, "Exception: Independent Contractors"). As independent contractors, even if medical personnel are found negligent, their negligence cannot be imputed to their employers under the doctrine of vicarious liability (see section 3.6, "Vicarious Liability"). To determine if a doctor or other medical person is an independent contractor, the court considers the degree of control exercised by the employee's supervisor over actual medical decisions. There have been cases in which the employer has been held liable under the doctrine of vicarious liability. In these cases, courts have found that the employer exercised control and direction over the medical personnel.

There are some special considerations for a doctor involved in the area of athletics. The first concerns the relationship between doctor and patient. Typically, the doctor is paid by the patient. However, in sports, the doctor is hired and paid by the athletic organization. Usually, there is a confidential relationship between doctor and patient. When the doctor is employed by a third party, however, the normal relationship is not established. In effect, then, team doctors have two masters to serve: the athletic organization for which they work and the players they treat. In addition, while both the organization and the player are concerned with restoring the player to full health, there are situations in which the team may seek a shorter rehabilitation program while the player may favor a more cautious time frame for recovery. The team doctor is placed in the middle. The doctor's dilemma is highlighted by suits involving the team doctor if the player believes the doctor has not placed his or her long-term recovery before the program's wishes.

In one case, a team doctor and athletic trainer allowed a college football player to play with a sprained neck, altering the player's equipment to restrict movement. The player was injured during the game and rendered quadriplegic. Such a case also raises the issue of the duty of a player to refuse to play with an injury after a team doctor has declared him or her healthy enough to participate. In addition to this potential conflict, the normal confidential relationship between a doctor and patient (the athlete) changes when a third party, the athletic organization, pays the doctor. The athletic organization typically has full access to the athlete's medical records and often discusses the appropriate treatment for the injured athlete with the doctor and patient.

In some situations, the athletic organization has access to the medical records and the athlete does not. The potential for abuse in this situation was demonstrated in *Kreuger v. San Francisco Forty-Niners*, 234 Cal. Rptr. 579 (Cal. App. 1st Dist. 1987). Kreuger, a player with the 49ers, sued team personnel for fraudulent concealment of medical information. The court found that due to the team's interest in keeping Kreuger on the field, he never received a full disclosure of the extent of his knee injury and thus continued to play when he should have retired from the game. As another example, Rafael Septien, a placekicker formerly with the Dallas Cowboys, sued the Cowboys for full access to his medical records. The confidential relationship between a doctor and a patient may also preclude a doctor's release of information to the athletic organization or anyone else without permission from the patient.

Another consideration concerns the prescribing of painkilling drugs to enable the athlete to continue playing for the benefit of the team but to the potential detriment of the player's career and postcareer activities. There have been situations on the professional level in which athletes—for example, Bill Walton and Dick Butkus—have brought lawsuits against their employers and team physicians for prescribing painkilling drugs that allowed them to play without informing them of the potential harm to their long-term careers. These cases could be applicable at the collegiate level given similar circumstances. Furthermore, they raise the issue of the responsibility a doctor has to his patient, the injured player, and the responsibility the doctor has to his or her employer, the team.

One final consideration is that even though doctors may be negligent in their handling of an injured player, they may not be legally liable under normal tort analysis. When a player is injured through intentional or negligent actions on the part of a coach, referee, player, spectator, or anyone else, subsequent negligent action will not usually relieve the original tortfeasor from liability created by the original action. Doctors may, however, be liable as an additional defendant if their conduct is found to be a substantial factor in the injury or if additional injuries occurred because of their negligence. Nevertheless, subsequent medical negligence is generally not an unforeseeable and unreasonable cause that would relieve the original party from liability.

NOTES

The duty to provide prompt medical services for recruited athletes injured on the playing field figures in the following cases.

1. In *Kelly v. McCarrick*, 841 A.2d 869 (Md. Ct. Spec. App. 2004), a minor softball player who had been injured during a game and her parents alleged that inadequate

training in postinjury care had contributed to the player's harm. The direct cause of the plaintiff's injury was a collision on the base paths. The appellate court upheld a lower court's ruling that no evidence had been adduced at trial to demonstrate that postinjury care worsened the plaintiff's condition. School personnel on the field had received adequate first aid training, and there was no evidence to indicate that awaiting emergency medical technicians would have improved the plaintiff's condition.

2. In *Campbell v. Shelton*, 727 N.E.2d 495 (Ind. Ct. App. 2000), a high school football player hit his head on a concrete track. The plaintiff alleged medical malpractice against a doctor whose diagnosis cleared the plaintiff to play football with a blood clot in his brain. As a result, the plaintiff suffered damages including permanent brain damage. The jury's verdict in the plaintiff's favor was affirmed.

3. In *State of Oregon v. Superior Court*, 29 Cal Rptr 2d 909 (Cal. Ct. App. 1994), a college basketball player who had previously suffered a stroke was instructed by the college medical staff to reduce his anticoagulation medication so that he could be eligible to compete. One month after his medication was reduced, the basketball player suffered a fatal stroke. The California appellate court denied the defendant's request to quash the case on jurisdictional grounds, finding that personal jurisdiction was warranted (see section 2.3.3, "Court Jurisdiction"). However, since the allegedly wrongful actions resulting in wrongful death had occurred in Oregon, the California courts were obliged to apply Oregon law to the wrongful death claim filed by the student-athlete's mother.

4. Boston Celtics star Reggie Lewis died suddenly on July 27, 1993, while practicing at Brandeis University. He had previously collapsed during a Celtics playoff game less than two months prior to his death. Following the playoff incident, Lewis received treatment by a team of New England Baptist Hospital doctors who told him he had a life-threatening heart condition that could end his career. Lewis was warned to restrict physical activity. However, Lewis sought a second opinion from Dr. Gilbert Mudge and two consulting physicians at Brigham and Women's Hospital. At a news conference on May 10, 1993, Mudge announced that Lewis had a neurological condition that caused fainting spells and that Lewis could likely return to professional basketball. After Lewis's death, his widow sued the insurance company of the Brigham and Women's doctors, Controlled Risk Insurance Company, claiming negligence. The hospitals were not named in the suit because Massachusetts law limits their liability under a charitable immunity law (see section 4.4.2, "Charitable Immunity"). After an initial 15-week trial, two of the physicians were found not negligent, while the jury was hung on the fate of the third physician, Dr. Gilbert Mudge. Lewis's widow then filed a second lawsuit against Dr. Mudge, which the insurance company defended and won. In his defense, Mudge testified that Lewis had confessed to him that he was a drug user. Allegedly, while the two were sitting in Mudge's car parked at Brandeis University just days before his death, Lewis said that he used cocaine. Mudge either testified or implied that Lewis's drug use rather than his misdiagnosis was the proximate cause of Lewis's death. For more information on this case, see the following law journal articles: (1) "CRICO of Vermont RRG Wins Celebrity Lawsuit after Two Trials," 14 *The Risk Retention Reporter* 9 (September 2000); (b) "Cardiologist Says Lewis Confessed," 13 *Workplace Substance Abuse Advisor* 15 (July 1, 1999).

5. On March 4, 1990, during an intercollegiate basketball game between Loyola Marymount University and the University of Portland, Hank Gathers, star of the Loyola Marymount team, collapsed and died as a result of a heart disorder known as cardiomyopathy. Shortly after his death, several members of Gathers's family filed suit, claiming that Gathers's death was a result of negligence of Gathers's physicians, the Loyola Marymount trainer, the head basketball coach, the athletic director, and the university itself. The lawsuit revolved around allegations made by the family about the treatment and information Gathers was given prior to his death. After passing out during a game earlier in the season, Gathers was examined by a number of doctors and underwent tests to discover the nature of his illness. Gathers was diagnosed with a syncope, a temporary suspension of respiration and circulation due to an obstructed

flow of blood to the brain, and cardiac arrhythmia, an alteration in the normal rhythm of the heartbeat. Gathers was started on medication to help regulate his heartbeat and cleared to rejoin the basketball team. The lawsuit claims, however, that doctors decreased the dosage of the medication because of its effect on Gathers's on-court performance. In addition, the school purchased a defibrillator, a machine used to help restore the rhythm of the heart, and kept it courtside during practices and games. The family alleged, however, that the defibrillator was not used within the required timeframe after Gathers had collapsed. In settlements reached with Loyola Marymount and Dr. Vernon Hattori, a cardiologist who treated Gathers, Lucille Gathers, Hank's mother, received $545,000 from the university and $350,000 from Hattori, while Aaron Crump, Gathers's eight-year-old son, received $855,000 from the school and $650,000 from Hattori. These settlements were a result of the wrongful death claims made against the involved parties. Earlier in the proceedings, Loyola Marymount athletic director Brian Quinn, head basketball coach Paul Westhead, former trainer Chip Schaefer, and four of the five named physicians were dismissed from the suit. The final lawsuit, a civil action brought by the family against two doctors who attended to Gathers on the night he collapsed, was dismissed September 9, 1992, after the plaintiffs did not appear in court to testify. The family members had contended that the doctors were negligent and caused the family emotional distress in the way they treated Gathers at courtside and outside the gym.

6. In *Krueger v. San Francisco Forty-Niners*, 234 Cal. Rptr. 579 (Cal. Ct. App. 1987), the court ruled in favor of a retired professional football player and held that he might be entitled to damages for fraudulent concealment of medical information by team personnel.

7. Former Citadel football player Marc Buoniconti sued Citadel team doctor E. K. Wallace, Jr., Citadel athletic trainer Andy Clawson, and Citadel, as employer, for injuries that rendered him a quadriplegic after he tackled an opponent in a 1985 football game. Buoniconti alleged that the doctor should not have allowed him to play in the game with a sprained neck. A major issue in the trial was the doctor's addition of a 10-inch fitted strap to Buoniconti's uniform, running from the face mask and hooked to the shoulder pads. Plaintiff's experts testified that the strap restricted movement and contributed to the injury, whereas the defense experts stated that the strap prevented hyperextension of the neck and did not cause the injury. The jury raised a question: If helmet manufacturers are held liable for faulty design or construction, should not the team doctor also be liable for a fault in the design or construction of his alteration of that equipment? The jury found no liability for the doctor. The athletic trainer and Citadel settled out of court for $800,000.

8. In *Wilson v. Vancouver Hockey Club* (1983), 5 D.L.R. (4th) 282, a doctor employed by the hockey club to treat players for hockey injuries failed to refer plaintiff hockey player to a specialist for a biopsy on a mole on plaintiff's arm. The plaintiff claimed that the doctor negligently failed to tell the player that he suspected cancer. Evidence indicated that the doctor made the final decision as to what treatment an injured player would have and whether an injured player would play, without advice from the management of the club, and therefore the doctor acted as an independent contractor and not as a servant of the hockey club. The court held that the club was not vicariously liable for the negligence of the doctor because he was an independent contractor.

9. In *Robitaille v. Vancouver Hockey Club*, 3 W.W.R. 481 (Ct. App. B.C. 1981), plaintiff professional hockey player brought suit against his club for injuries incurred while playing. A shoulder injury caused the plaintiff recurring problems, which the club's management and physicians attributed to mental rather than physical causes. The plaintiff was ordered to play while injured and sustained a minor spinal cord injury during a game. He requested medical attention but was ignored because he was perceived as having mental problems. Further play aggravated the minor injury, and the plaintiff suffered a spinal cord injury which left him permanently disabled. The appeals court upheld the award of damages to

the plaintiff and held that the club had breached its duty to ensure the fitness, health, and safety of its player. The club was also found to have exercised sufficient control over the doctors to make the doctors employees of the club. Therefore, the club was liable for the acts of the doctors.

10. In *Walton v. Cook*, Civil Case No. A8003-0165 (Or. 1981), professional basketball player Bill Walton filed suit against Robert Cook, the team doctor of the Portland TrailBlazers, and 20 other unnamed physicians of the Oregon City Orthopedic Clinic for $632,000 in lost income and medical expenses and $5 million in general damages. The complaint alleged negligence in the examination, diagnosis, and treatment of his left foot, along with failure to provide him with accurate information concerning the true nature of the injury. Drugs were prescribed and shots of steroids were given Walton, and he was advised to play in games. Three months later, Walton consulted other physicians and discovered that he had actually fractured a bone in his foot, which caused damage to the nerves, muscles, and tissues of the left foot as well as a permanent weakness in that foot and an increased chance of subsequent fractures. Furthermore, Walton could not continue to play basketball. The case was settled for an undisclosed amount prior to the trial.

11. In *Fish v. L.A. Dodgers Baseball Club*, 128 Cal. Rptr. 807 (Cal. Ct. App. 1976), plaintiffs sought recovery from defendant club and defendant physician for the death of their son, who died as a result of an allegedly negligent diagnosis after being struck by a foul ball. In reversing judgment, the court of appeals held for the plaintiffs, finding that negligence of the ballpark doctor in failing to ascertain decedent's symptoms necessitated the emergency surgery which resulted in death. This converted decedent from a patient who probably would have survived without emergency surgery to a patient who had little hope of recovery. The trial court's verdict in favor of the club was also reversed for consideration of the issue of the agency relationship between the parties.

For further information on the liability of medical personnel, see the following law review articles:

1. Barry R. Furrow, "The Problem of the Sports Doctor: Serving Two (Or Is it Three or Four?) Masters," 50 *Saint Louis University Law Journal* 165 (2005).

2. Matthew J. Mitten, "Emerging Legal Issues in Sports Medicine: A Synthesis, Summary, and Analysis," 76 *Saint John's Law Review* 5 (Winter 2002).

4.7. LIABILITY OF OFFICIALS, REFEREES, AND UMPIRES

Officials, referees, and umpires have sought recovery in civil litigation for injuries suffered in the course of employment. They may also be protected against violence, in certain states, by criminal statutes.

Game officials may incur tort liability as a result of their actions or inactions on the playing field. There have been two distinct areas in which suits against officials, referees, and umpires have been filed: the personal injury area, in which the official, referee, or umpire is sued for negligence, and judicial review of an official's, referee's, or umpire's decision. There have been a few reported cases in both of these areas since few cases have been filed and many of those have been settled. However, this area has the potential for increased litigation.

In the personal injury area, the official, referee, or umpire may be sued for negligence in a number of different situations. The first is when there has been a failure to inspect the premises. For instance, a plaintiff may contend that a referee should have inspected the field for holes or other dangerous conditions that could cause injury to players. In the second situation, the game official fails to keep the playing area free of equipment and/or spectators. For example, a ball or bat may be left on the playing field and a player may trip, fall, and be injured by the equipment. With respect to spectators, an injured spectator might contend that the official, umpire, or referee should have stopped play on the field and warned the spectators to move from the playing area. Similarly, a player who is injured by running into a spectator might contend that officials should have moved the spectator away from the playing area.

The third situation involves weather conditions. An injured player may contend that the official, referee, or umpire should not have started the game or that the game should have been stopped. The fourth situation involves equipment. It could be argued that the official, referee, or umpire has the responsibility to prevent a player from participating if the player's equipment is obviously ill fitting. A situation that may be more likely to result in successful litigation is when a referee does not enforce a rule, especially a safety rule requiring certain equipment (such as helmets) or banning dangerous items (such as earrings). The fifth and final situation involves a potential claim that the official, referee, or umpire did not properly enforce the rules of the games. For example, the plaintiff may allege that the basketball referees failed to control the game by not calling fouls or technical fouls and that this resulted in a much rougher game, proximately causing the injuries suffered by the plaintiff.

The area of judicial review of an official's, referee's, or umpire's decision is one that has been infrequently litigated. Generally, courts are reluctant to review playing field decisions, whether involving errors in judgment or misapplication of a rule. Plaintiffs have not been successful in this area, and the courts will continue to show their reluctance to become involved in decisions on the playing field unless fraud or corruption can be found.

A problem not related to the liability of referees, officials, and umpires, but one that an athletic administrator and the official should be aware of, is the type of relationships created by the association of referees, officials, and umpires. The official may be classified as an independent contractor or an employee. This distinction becomes important if an official is injured in the course of performing his or her duties. If acting as an independent contractor, the official will not be eligible for workers' compensation; but if classified as an employee, the official would be entitled to receive those benefits. In addition, the athletic administrator could be held liable for the actions of the referee under the legal theory of vicarious liability if the referee is deemed to be an employee. The athletic administrator will generally not be held responsible for the actions of the official if he or she is an independent contractor (see section 3.6.1, "Exception: Independent Contractors"). The interpretation of a referee's status differs from state to state on the basis of state laws and the legal relationship between the referees and the hiring institution. An examination of legal cases involving the question to determine a particular state's interpretation of the relationship is advised.

The following liability checklist will help officials, referees, and umpires protect themselves against possible litigation:

1. Inspect playing surface, including sidelines and end lines, for visible and potential hazards.
2. Determine if weather conditions are appropriate for competition and do not allow coaches or other athletic officials to influence the decision.
3. Inspect game equipment such as bases and goalposts.

4. Ensure that players wear safety equipment required by the rules of the league or athletic association.

5. Inspect players' equipment for safety and make sure that players are not wearing any potentially dangerous jewelry or accessories.

NOTES

1. In *Patton v. United States of American Rugby Football, Union, Ltd.*, 851 A.2d 566 (Md. 2004), a rugby player and his father, who had been a spectator at a tournament in which his son was participating, were struck by lightning during a game. The player was seriously injured and his father was killed. The plaintiffs alleged that the game referee, among others, was negligent in allowing players and spectators to be exposed to the dangers posed by the thunderstorm. The Court of Appeals of Maryland disagreed, finding that the relationship between the plaintiffs and the referee imposed no duty on the referee to protect the plaintiffs from inclement weather conditions which were "visible to all competent adults."

2. In 2001, former Cleveland Brown's offensive tackle, Orlando Brown, filed a $200 million lawsuit in Bronx, New York, state court against the National Football League. Brown suffered career-threatening impaired vision as a result of a penalty flag thrown by referee Jeff Triplette, which accidentally struck Brown in his right eye. Brown's complaint alleged that the league failed "to properly supervise and enforce rules that flags be properly weighted and thrown in a proper fashion." Brown, who was unable to play for three years following the incident, received a multimillion-dollar settlement from the NFL. NFL referees are likely to be considered employees by the courts rather than independent contractors because they are members of a union sanctioned by the National Labor Relations Board (NLRB). Section 11 of the National Labor Relations Act (NLRA) specifically states that independent contractors are not covered under the act. See Chapter 11, "Labor Law," for more information.

3. In 1999, Neal Goss, a 15-year-old captain of a Chicago-area high school hockey team, was paralyzed from the chest down after being slammed into the boards by an opposing player. Goss contended that the paralyzing hit occurred after the final buzzer of the game, thus making the hit an act of battery rather than an act that one assumes the risk of during the course of a hockey game. Criminal battery charges were filed against the opposing player, whose identity was kept anonymous under state law since he was a minor. The defendant subsequently plea-bargained to a lesser battery charge that carried a maximum penalty of one year in prison. Goss also filed a civil suit in December 2000 against the Illinois Hockey Officials Association, claiming that the officials failed "to adequately and ably control the game." Defendants in the civil suit also included the player who injured Goss, the opposing team's coach, the hockey league, the sponsors of the opposing hockey team, and the Amateur Hockey Association of Illinois. For more information, see Jason R. Schuette, "Adolescent Sports—Violence When Prosecutors Play Referee: Making Criminals Out of Child Athletes, but Are They the Real Culprits?" 21 *Northern Illinois University Law Review* 515 (2001).

4. In *Rolison v. City of Meridian*, 691 So. 2d 440 (Miss. 1997), during a softball game, which was supervised by the officials chosen and compensated by the city, a player negligently threw a baseball bat, causing plaintiff, who was running the bases, to be knocked unconscious and suffer the loss of 5% of his brain function. The plaintiff sued the city, alleging that the officials were negligently selected and inadequately trained and that the city allowed the game to be conducted in an unreasonably unsafe manner. The city responded by asserting an assumption of the risk defense. Furthermore, the city stated that the officials were independent contractors who were immune from liability by statute, and such immunity flowed to the city. The court granted summary judgment for the defendants. On appeal, the court held that a referee does not have the duty to protect a participant or a spectator from a thrown bat.

5. In *Santopietro v. City of New Haven*, 682 A.2d 106 (Conn. 1996), the court stated that umpires have a duty "to exercise reasonable judgment as umpires in order to maintain control of the baseball game so as to prevent an unreasonable risk of injury to others. ... The breach of this duty, however, must be proved, in the absence of exceptional circumstances, by expert testimony establishing that the allegedly negligent action or failure to act by the umpire constituted an abuse of the umpire's discretion to evaluate the particular circumstances and to take only such disciplinary action as the umpire deems appropriate. Moreover, the expert testimony must establish an abuse of that discretion sufficient to permit a jury to infer that the umpire's action or failure to act constituted such a loss of control of the game as to give rise to an unreasonable risk of injury to the plaintiff." In this case, the plaintiff was a spectator who had been hurt when a participant in the game threw a bat away in frustration after hitting a pop fly. The Supreme Court of Connecticut found that the umpires' actions did not lead to an unreasonable risk of injury and therefore affirmed the lower court's judgment in favor of the umpires.

6. In *Harvey v. Ouachita Parish School Board*, 545 So. 2d 1241 (La. Ct. App. 1989), an injured football player sued the state high school athletic association under negligence for injuries suffered as a result of excessively rough behavior. Although the association had registered the referees, the schools themselves were responsible for hiring the officials for each game. Thus, any negligence on the referees' part could not be imputed to the defendant. The court reasoned that though the association had registered the referees, the referees were neither agents nor servants of the association.

7. In *Bain v. Gillespie*, 357 N.W.2d 47 (Iowa Ct. App. 1984), plaintiff, a Big Ten basketball referee, filed suit for injunctive relief and damages against defendants who produced T-shirts with his likeness in a noose imprinted on them. Defendants had produced the T-shirts after a controversial call by the referee at an intercollegiate basketball game. The defendants filed a counterclaim, asserting that the plaintiff's performance of his job had cost the University of Iowa the Big Ten men's basketball championship and cost the defendants sales of T-shirts and other memorabilia. The court thoroughly analyzed the policy implications of judicial review of athletic officiating before affirming the grant of injunctive relief to the plaintiff and the dismissal of the defendants' counterclaim.

8. In *McHugh v. Hackensack Public Schools*, 483 A.2d 148 (N.J. 1984), plaintiff high school basketball referee was attacked by an unknown fan after a state tournament game and sought damages from the public school system because it did not provide a safe place to work, safe entry and exit before and at the conclusion of the game, or proper supervision of the crowd. The trial court granted summary judgment in favor of the school since the school was immune under the New Jersey Tort Claims Act. For another case involving intentional and negligent injury of officials, see *Toone v. Adams* in section 4.3.4, "Vicarious Liability for Actions of Fans and Players," earlier in this chapter.

9. In *Georgia High School Ass'n v. Waddell*, 285 S.E.2d 7 (Ga. 1981), the Georgia Supreme Court ruled that it does not possess authority to review the decision of a high school football referee. The high school referee admitted that he made the error—not awarding an automatic first down on a roughing-the-kicker penalty—which might have been determinative of the final outcome for the game. The trial court had overturned the referee's ruling based on a school's property right in the game of football being played according to the rules. The court ordered the game to be replayed from the point of the referee's error. The Georgia Supreme Court reversed, stating: "We now go further and hold that courts for equality in this state are without authority to review decisions of football referees because those decisions do not present judicial controversies."

10. In *Carroll v. State of Oklahoma*, 620 P.2d 416 (Okla. Crim. App. 1980), appellant challenged an Arizona statute under which he was convicted for assault. Appellant was an assistant coach for the losing team at a baseball tournament. After the game, the home plate umpire was at the trunk of his car in the parking lot changing uniforms in preparation for the next game. He was surrounded by a group of players from the losing team who were criticizing his calls. The assistant coach approached the group, exchanged words with the

umpire, and struck the umpire on the jaw with his fist. The assistant coach was convicted of "assault upon a sports officiary" under Oklahoma law. The appellant challenged the statute on the grounds that it was unconstitutionally vague. The court of criminal appeals, however, held that the statute clearly indicated which persons were covered and also apprised the public of what particular conduct was deemed punishable, for which reasons the court found the statute neither unconstitutionally vague and indefinite nor void for uncertainty.

11. In *Pantalone v. Lenape Valley Regional High School*, Docket No. L-40828-26, Sussex Co. (N.J. Sup. Ct. 1976), a New Jersey high school wrestling referee was sued for allegedly allowing a wrestler to continue an illegal hold on his opponent, which resulted in a paralyzing injury. The plaintiff averred that the referee's negligence had proximately caused his debilitating injury. The case was settled out of court.

12. In *Gale v. Greater Washington, D.C. Softball Umpires Ass'n*, 311 A.2d 817 (Md. Ct. Spec. App. 1973), the court ruled that an umpire is not an employee of an umpire association but an independent contractor, thereby precluding the umpire from receiving workers' compensation under Maryland law.

The National Association of Sports Officials (NASO) has drafted model legislation to encourage individual states to adopt some statutory protections limiting or preventing liability in regard to sports officials (see later). For more information, see NASO's Web site at http://www.naso.org. According to NASO, 16 states have currently adopted limited liability legislation for sports officials. Those states are Arkansas, Delaware, Georgia, Illinois, Louisiana, Massachusetts, Mississippi, Missouri, Nevada, New Jersey, North Dakota, Ohio, Pennsylvania, Rhode Island, and Tennessee. Here is the model legislation that was used to craft many of these state statutes:

> *Section 1:* Sports officials who officiate athletic contests at any level of competition in this State shall not be liable to any person or entity in any civil action for injuries or damages claimed to have arisen by virtue of actions or inactions related in any manner to officiating duties within the confines of the athletic facility at which the athletic contest is played.
>
> *Section 2:* Sports officials are defined as those individuals who serve as referees, umpires, linesmen, and those who serve in similar capacities but may be known by other titles and are duly registered or members of a local, state, regional or national organization which is engaged in part in providing education and training to sports officials.
>
> *Section 3:* Nothing in this law shall be deemed to grant the protection set forth to sports officials who cause injury or damage to a person or entity by actions or inactions which are intentional, willful, wanton, reckless, malicious or grossly negligent.
>
> *Section 4:* This law shall take effect immediately, and shall apply to all lawsuits filed after the effective date of this law, including those which allege actions or inactions of sports officials which occurred prior to the effective date of this law.

In addition, 23 states have passed legislation specifically targeting assault against game officials.

For more information, also see the following law review articles:

1. Jason A. Kuiper, "Sports Volunteer Protection Statutes: Moving toward Uniformity and Providing Volunteer Referees with Medical Training," 16 *Marquette Sports Law Review* 157 (2005).

2. Mark A. Grober, "Law and Sports Officiating: A Misunderstood and Justly Neglected Relationship," 16 *Constitutional Commentary* 293 (Summer 1999).

3. Shlomi Feiner, "The Personal Liability of Sports Officials: Don't Take the Game into Your Own Hands, Take Them to Court," 4 *Sports Lawyers Journal* 213 (Spring 1997).

4. Carole J. Wallace, "The Men in Black and Blue: A Comment on Violence against Sports Officials and State Legislative Reaction," 6 *Seton Hall Journal of Sports and Entertainment Law* 341 (1996).

4.8. APPLICATION OF LEGAL PRINCIPLES TO DEFECTS IN EQUIPMENT

In cases involving various types of sports equipment, plaintiffs have alleged "failure to warn" on the part of equipment manufacturers. This theory is established upon the finding of a manufacturer's duty to warn of known latent and potential injury-causing defects in the design or fabrication of equipment. The extent of the duty is based on the age and experience of the reasonably foreseeable users of the product.

In order to maintain a suit based on a products liability theory, the plaintiff must prove that the product is defective in design or manufacture. The test used by courts has two distinct prongs. The first prong involves looking at the product to see if it has failed to perform as safely as an ordinary consumer would expect. Whether it was used as intended, or was misused or tampered with, will be considered in making this determination. If the plaintiff cannot directly establish that the product failed to perform adequately, this part of the test may be satisfied by the second prong, which involves proving that the product's defective design proximately caused the injury and that the benefits of the challenged design do not outweigh the inherent risk of danger created by the design. To aid in its determination as to both defectiveness and resultant liability, the court will also consider factors such as the nature of the sport, the type of injury, the amount of use or foreseeable misuse, the degree to which the particular risk is greater due to the defect, and the current state of the art in designing an absolutely safe product (see section 3.5, "Products Liability Law").

NOTES

1. In *Stringer v. National Football League*, CV-0065-JDH-MRA (S.D. Ohio July 10, 2009), the court ruled that helmet maker Riddell had a duty to warn football players, notably Vikings defensive lineman Korey Stronger, of the risks of overheating caused by wearing a helmet. Stringer died of heat stroke during Vikings training camp in July 2001. For more on the case, see section 4.2.3, "Failure to Provide Prompt and Capable Medical Assistance," note 2.

2. In *Bostick v. Flex Equipment Company, Inc.*, 107 Cal. App. 4th 80 (Cal. Ct. App. 2007), a man who suffered severe, disabling injuries at a gym when a barbell fell on him brought a strict products liability action against the gym and the manufacturer of the weight lifting equipment. After the plaintiff settled with the gym, a jury found the manufacturer 90% at fault for the plaintiff's injury and awarded significant damages. The award was reduced based on the plaintiff's fault and on his settlement with the gym. The manufacturer nonetheless argued that the amount was grossly excessive and was a result of an improper instruction that led the jury to award punitive damages in the guise of compensation for pain and suffering. The appellate court affirmed the award.

3. In *Repka v. Arctic Cat, Inc.*, 20 A.D.3d 916 (N.Y. App. Div. 2005), a snowmobiler who was rendered quadriplegic in an accident alleged negligence, strict products liability, and breach of warranty against the manufacturer and retailer of the snowmobile that he was riding at the time of the incident. The appellate court rejected summary judgment for the defendants on all counts. Issues of material fact existed as to the allegedly defective design and manufacture of the snowmobile as well as to the defendants' failure to warn of

the risk of harm. The plaintiff had not assumed that risk since risks inherent to the sport of snowmobiling do not include those posed by unreasonably dangerous and concealed conditions.

4. In *Sanchez v. Hillerich & Bradsby Co.*, 104 Cal. App. 4th 703 (Cal. App. 2 Dist. 2002), Andrew Sanchez, a pitcher for Cal-State Northridge, brought suit against the maker of an aluminum bat after Sanchez suffered serious head injuries when he was struck by a ball hit off a bat made by Hillerich and Bradsby Co., better known as Louisville Slugger. The case was settled for an unspecified amount with no admission of liability. There have been several other aluminum bat cases brought but most have been settled out of court. See *Baggs v. Little League Baseball, Inc.*, 840 N.Y.S.2d 529 (N.Y. Sup. 2007), and also Steve Kallas, "'Metal Bat' Cases Resulting in Serious Injury or Death Being Brought to the Forefront in the Battle of Wood v. Metal," *Sports Plus by Steve Kallas*, http://skallas.wordpress.com/.

5. In *Breeden v. Valencia, Inc.*, 557 So. 2d 302 (La. Ct. App. 1990), a 12-year-old injured while riding a jet ski at camp claimed that the jet ski was unreasonably dangerous and contained inadequate warnings. The court found no evidence that a defect existed in the design or manufacture of the steering mechanism. It further found that warnings contained in the instruction manual were adequate to inform riders about the turning ability of the jet ski. Therefore, the court affirmed the trial court's conclusion that the accident had been caused "solely by the fault of the plaintiff."

6. In *King v. Kayak Manufacturing Corp.*, 387 S.E.2d 511 (W. Va. 1989), the plaintiff sued a manufacturer of an aboveground swimming pool under a product liability claim when he was rendered quadriplegic after diving into four feet of water. The trial court held the manufacturer strictly liable and directed the verdict for the plaintiff. The appellate court reversed and remanded the case to resolve the issues of whether the plaintiff was contributorily negligent and assumed the risk of injury on the dive. The court recognized that the defense of assumption of risk is available in a strict product liability case where there is evidence that the plaintiff had actual knowledge of the risk and accepted the chance of injury.

7. In *Everett v. Bucky Warren, Inc.*, 380 N.E.2d 653 (Mass. 1978), plaintiff hockey player claimed that his serious head injury resulted from the defective design of the helmet he wore. The team's hockey coach distributed to the team helmets that were of a three-piece design, consisting of three plastic pieces. One piece covered the back of the head, one the forehead, and one the top of the head. The pieces were attached to each other by elastic straps. The straps expanded, depending on the size of the wearer's head, leaving gaps as large as three-fourths of an inch. This design was somewhat unique; however, there were also available on the market helmets which were of a one-piece design with no gaps. During a game with the Brown University freshman team, plaintiff threw himself in front of a Brown player's shot in an attempt to block it. The puck struck Everett above the right ear, penetrating a gap in the helmet and causing a skull fracture. The injury required that a steel plate be inserted in his skull and caused recurring headaches. Everett then brought suit against the school, the manufacturer, and the retailer on the grounds of strict liability. The appeals court held that the manufacturer could be found strictly liable for producing a helmet with an "unreasonably dangerous design." Factors that the court weighed when determining whether a particular design is reasonably safe included "the gravity of the danger posed by the challenged design, the likelihood that such danger would occur, the mechanical feasibility of a safer alternative design, the ... cost of an improved design, and the adverse consequences to the product and the consumer that would result from an alternative design." The court held that the gravity of the danger was demonstrated by the injuries, that helmets of the one-piece design were safer than the model used and were in manufacture prior to the injury, and that, while more expensive than the helmets used, the one-piece helmets were not economically unfeasible.

8. In *Heldman v. Uniroyal, Inc.*, 371 N.E.2d 557 (Ohio Ct. App. 1977), a professional tennis player injured her knee during a tennis championship and brought suit for damages

against Uniroyal, Inc., which supplied the tennis court surface for the matches. Plaintiff claimed that the defendant made certain representations and warranties, both expressed and implied, concerning its court surface. An appeals court ruled that there was sufficient evidence to raise a jury question as to whether plaintiff assumed the risk by playing in the match. The court reached its conclusion based on the reasons that the plaintiff told all the members of her team that the court was in a dangerous condition, that she was a professional tennis player and is presumed to know the various risks attendant with playing on different types of surfaces, and that a higher degree of knowledge and awareness is imputed to professional tennis players than to average nonprofessional tennis players as to the dangers of playing on a synthetic tennis court having obvious bubbles on the playing surface.

9. In *Dudley Sports Co. v. Schmitt*, 279 N.E.2d 266 (Ind. Ct. App. 1972), a 16-year-old high school boy sought recovery for injuries received when he was struck in the face by the throwing arm of an automatic baseball pitching machine that was purchased in March 1965 by Danville High School. Designed and manufactured by Dudley, the machine consisted of a frame and an open extended metal throwing arm. No protective shield guarded the throwing arm. When the arm reached a 10 o'clock energized position and received a ball, energy was released from the coiled spring and transmitted to the arm; the arm passed through a clockwise pitching cycle at a high rate of speed and came to rest in a 4 o'clock position. The machine was capable of delivering a powerful blow in the 10 o'clock position, even if it was unplugged. When the machine was uncrated, it came with a parts list, assembly instructions, and a tool to deactivate the spring. The only warning instruction contained in the crate was a general warning tag that said: "Warning! *Safety First* STAY CLEAR OF THROWING ARM AT ALL TIMES." No operating instructions were included in the crate. The machine was stored, unplugged, behind locked doors in locker room no. 2. However, the two adjoining locker rooms, with inside entrances to locker room no. 2, were not locked from the outside hallway entrance. On the day he was injured, plaintiff student was sweeping in locker room no. 2, as he had done in the past at the request of the coaching staff. He said that as he approached the front of the machine he heard a whistling noise and a pop. He was hit in the face by the throwing arm and received extensive facial injuries. Plaintiff brought this action alleging negligence against the high school, the sporting goods company, and Dudley. The appeals court held that Dudley was negligent in the design, manufacture, and sale of the machine. The ability of the machine to operate while unplugged as a result of even a slight vibration was considered a latent danger, which could only be discovered through an examination of the machine combined with knowledge of the engineering principles which produce the action of the machine. Such knowledge is not ordinarily possessed by a 16-year-old high school boy who had never before seen the machine.

10. For a case in which liability for failure to warn was based on constructive knowledge, see *Filler v. Rayex Corp.*, 435 F.2d 336 (7th Cir. 1970). Plaintiff baseball player sued defendant sunglass manufacturer for negligence, strict liability, and breach of implied warranty of fitness for a particular purpose when the glasses shattered into his eye. The court of appeals, in affirming the district court in favor of the plaintiff, held that defendant, which advertised the glasses as providing protection against baseballs, had constructive knowledge of the danger and was liable for failure to warn and liable for breach of warranty of fitness for a particular purpose.

11. The National Operating Committee on Standards for Athletic Equipment (NOCSAE) was organized to research and test equipment, develop new standards, and improve existing ones. NOCSAE was founded in 1969 in an effort to reduce death and injuries through the adoption of standards and certification for athletic equipment. The NOCSAE continues to develop performance standards for equipment in a variety of sports. According to its Web site, http://www.nocsae.org, "By 1985 a significant downward trend in head injury fatalities was observed leading to zero deaths during the 1990 season for the first time since the beginning of annual fatality reports in 1931. Of even more fundamental importance, the incidence of serious head injuries, the leading cause of disability and death

in football, estimated to average 4.25/100,000 players in the 1964–68 era, immediately prior to the formation of NOCSAE, has averaged only 0.68/100,000 players during the 1987–90 season, an 84 percent drop."

For further information on the application of legal principles to defects in equipment, see the following law review articles:

1. Matthew R. Wilmot, "Baseball Bats in the High Tech Era: A Products Liability Look at New Technology, Aluminum Bats, and Manufacturer Liability," 16 *Marquette Sports Law Review* 353 (Spring 2006).
2. Russ VerSteeg, "Pole Vault Injuries: Product Liability and Commercial Law Theories," 5 *Texas Review of Entertainment and Sports Law* 237 (Spring 2004).
3. Gil B. Fried, "Punitive Damages and Corporate Liability Analysis in Sports Litigation," 9 *Marquette Sports Law Journal* 45 (Fall 1998).

4.9. LIABILITY INSURANCE

Liability insurance is a form of indemnity whereby the insurer undertakes to indemnify or pay the insured for a loss resulting from legal liability to a third person. It is based on contract law principles. Liability insurance protects an insured person against financial loss resulting from lawsuits brought against him or her for negligent behavior. Common subjects for liability insurance in athletics are risks from use of the premises, from faulty products, from use of vehicles, and from the practice of professions.

Insurance is effective even if the insured has committed a minor violation of the criminal law. A minor violation will not invalidate the insurance or deprive the defendant of protection. An insurance policy may be invalidated, however, if the insured's conduct was so outrageous that it would be against public policy to indemnify it. The policy may also be invalidated if the insured misrepresented a material fact at the time of the application for the policy.

One of the standard provisions in any insurance policy requires the insured to cooperate fully with the insurance company by providing full and accurate information about the accident. It may also require the insured to attend the trial, to take part in it if required, and to do nothing for the injured party that would harm the insurance company. A violation of any of the preceding requirements would relieve the insurance company of liability to the injured third party.

The term *subrogation* is often found in tort cases involving insurance claims. Subrogation is the right of the insurance company that has paid the legal obligation of the insured party to recover payment from the third party who was negligent. For example, a fan is injured at a baseball stadium by a foul ball that passed through a hole in the netting behind home plate, and the hole was there because of the negligence of a third-party contractor who damaged the screen during installation. If the liability insurer for the stadium pays the injured fan, it has the same right, under subrogation, to sue the installer for negligence as its insured, the stadium owner, had.

Typically, insurance policies contain a clause that explicitly entitles the insurer to be subrogated to his insured cause of action against any party who caused a loss that the insurer paid. The insurer can also be entitled to subrogation in the absence of an express contractual provision; this is called *equitable subrogation*. In some states, however, an insurance company must prove it was not a gratuitous payment in order to recover under equitable subrogation.

One response by institutions and sports associations to the increasing number of lawsuits brought under a tort liability theory is to use insurance. The National Federation of High School Associations and many state high school athletic associations and their member schools have adopted a liability/lifetime catastrophe medical plan. The plan covers the National Federation of State High School Associations, the state high school athletic/activity associations, their member schools and school districts, and member school administrators, athletic directors, coaches, and trainers. This type of insurance allows the student-athlete who suffers a catastrophic injury to waive suit and opt for medical, rehabilitation, and work-loss benefits for the rest of his or her life. The philosophy behind the insurance plan is to provide needed benefits to the injured student-athlete without the time, costs, and risks involved in litigation. If the injured student-athlete opts for the benefits provided by the insurance policy, the institution saves time, expense, and a possible award in favor of the plaintiff.

The NCAA instituted a similar catastrophic injury protection plan (see section 3.7, "Workers' Compensation"). The NCAA's plan accomplished two important objectives. First, by having this type of plan, it reduced—if not eliminated—the number of workers' compensation cases filed against NCAA member institutions. Second, the NCAA insurance policy assists the catastrophically injured student-athlete by providing benefits immediately, without time delays, without the costs of litigation, and without the uncertainties involved in litigation. The student-athlete who is catastrophically injured as a result of negligence of an institution or one of its employees retains the right to litigate the case and not collecting the benefits provided by the NCAA policy.

4.10. WAIVER AND RELEASE OF LIABILITY

In the law, there are often competing legal theories in a given situation. The resolution of this type of situation is usually based on the preeminent public policies existing at the time the conflict arises. In the area of waivers and releases of liability, the underlying principles of tort law and contract law conflict. *Waivers* or *exculpatory agreements* are contracts that alter the ordinary negligence principles of tort law. *Contract law* is based on the idea that any competent party should have the absolute right to make a binding agreement with any other competent party. The only limit to this right is that a contract is invalid if it violates public policy. For example, a contract in which the parties agree to commit a crime would violate an important public policy of protecting public order, and thus would be unenforceable.

Tort law, on the other hand, is based on the idea that all persons should be responsible for negligent or intentional actions that cause injury to other persons. Waivers, then, create a conflict between the right to enter into contracts and the policy that one should be held responsible for injury-causing negligent actions. This conflict has been resolved in favor of the general rule that waivers and releases of liability will be enforceable unless they frustrate an important public policy goal or unless the party getting the waiver is unfairly dominant in the bargaining process. This resolution is based on the general contract law principle that a party is bound by the signing of a contract unless there is evidence of fraud, misrepresentation, or duress.

In order to determine if fraud, misrepresentation, or duress exists, a court will consider whether the party waiving its rights knew or had an opportunity to know the terms. This does not mean that merely failing to read or to understand a waiver and release of liability will invalidate it; rather the language by which one party waives its rights must be conspicuous and not be hidden in fine print so that a careful reader is unlikely to see it. The waiver and release of liability must also result from a free and open bargaining process. Therefore, if one party forces the other to agree to a waiver, it will not be enforceable. Another consideration is whether the express terms of the waiver and release of liability are applicable to the particular conduct of the party whose potential liability is being waived. In other words, the language of the waiver must be clear, detailed, and specific. However, no waiver or release of liability will be enforceable if it attempts to insulate one party from wanton, intentional, or reckless misconduct. Therefore, only liability for negligent actions can be waived.

If the person signing the waiver and release of liability is a minor, other issues are raised. Under basic contract principles, a minor may repudiate an otherwise valid contract. A problem may also arise when parents sign waivers for their children. Courts are struggling with the issue of the rights of minors that may be waived by their parents.

For competent adult participants in sports activities, waivers and releases of liability are generally upheld unless the waiver or release of liability violates public policy. However, questions are frequently litigated in the area of auto racing. Courts have reasoned that a driver is under no compulsion to race; therefore, a driver has the ability to decide whether to race and to assume all the risks inherent in auto racing. This may include risks that arise as a result of negligence on the part of the event's promoters. Courts are generally more reluctant to enforce a waiver and release of liability signed by spectators, based on the theory that they may not be as familiar with the risks of auto racing and that they are entitled to assume that the premises are reasonably safe.

NOTES

1. In *Wagner v. SFX Motor Sports, Inc.*, 460 F. Supp. 2d 1263 (D. Kan. 2006), a motorcyclist who was severely injured during a race brought suit for negligence and wanton conduct against the racetrack operator and the race organizer. The plaintiff alleged that the defendants had taken inadequate measures to ensure the safety of participants, resulting in the harm he suffered from a crash during the race. The issue before the court was whether the waiver signed by the plaintiff precluded his claims. The court held that the relevant language in the waiver, which was capitalized so as to stand out from the rest of the text, was sufficiently clear and unequivocal to notify the plaintiff that he had surrendered any claim based on ordinary negligence. However, the defendants' alleged wanton disregard of a known and imminent risk could not covered by the waiver and remained a question for the jury.

2. In *Roane v. Greenwich Swim Committee*, 330 F. Supp. 2d 306 (S.D.N.Y. 2004), a swimmer alleged that event organizers, among others, were responsible for the harm he suffered when he was rescued during the event. The plaintiff had sustained injuries to his midsection during a failed attempt to bring him aboard a rescue vessel. The defendants argued that the waiver the plaintiff signed prior to the competition contained clear and unequivocal language that insulated them from liability for the plaintiff's harm. The court disagreed, noting that the language of the waiver did not include the word *negligence* nor any words to the same effect. Since the plaintiff had not agreed to expose himself to any risk of injury enhanced by the defendants' negligence, the court ruled that the waiver was unenforceable.

3. In *Holzer v. Dakota Speedway, Inc.*, 610 N.W.2d 787 (S.D. 2000), a pit crew member was struck and severely injured by a detached car wheel during a stock car race. The

coguardians of the injured pit crew member brought suit against the racetrack owner (and the liability insurer), alleging negligence, reckless disregard for life, safety and health, negligent inspection, and breach of duty to third parties. The Supreme Court of South Dakota held, among other things, that the release signed by the crew member was enforceable. The conduct of which the plaintiff complained was neither willful nor wanton and was covered by the clear language of the release. Thus, application of the release to bar the plaintiff's claim did not violate public policy.

4. In *Lund v. Bally's Aerobic Plus, Inc.*, 93 Cal. Rptr. 2d 169 (Cal. App. Ct. 2000), a member of a health club alleged that the personal trainer was negligent in his instruction on how to use an inclined bench press. The club member sued the club for her personal injuries. The Court of Appeals of California held that the waiver and release of liability served a written assumption of the risk, effectively barring recovery. The waiver applied "clearly, unambiguously, and expressly" to the sort of harm which befell the plaintiff.

5. In *Covert v. South Florida Stadium Corp.*, 762 So. 2d 938 (Fla. App.Ct. 2000), a holder of a club-level seat sued the stadium owner for personal injuries sustained as a spectator of a professional football game. The plaintiff sustained injuries as a result of allegedly intoxicated fans beating him up. The district court overruled the circuit court's decision to enter judgment on the pleadings for stadium owners. The district court held that the contract signed by club level season ticket holders, which relieved the stadium of liability for negligence, was ambiguous and therefore did not support judgment on the pleadings.

6. In *Hiett v. Lake Bancroft Community Ass'n*, 418 S.E.2d 894 (Va. 1992), the plaintiff was competing in a triathlon when he dove into the water during the swim portion and struck his head on the bottom or some unseen object beneath the surface. The injury left Hiett a quadriplegic. Prior to competing in the triathlon, each participant had been required to sign an entry form which included a waiver releasing the event's organizers and sponsors from liability "for any and all injuries" suffered in the event. Hiett cited a Virginia Supreme Court decision from 1890, *Johnson's Adm'x v. Rich Danville R.R. Co.*, 11 S.E. 829 (Va. 1890), in which the court found that an agreement with the railroad company excusing them from liability for any injuries or death resulting from any cause whatsoever was in violation of public policy and therefore invalid. Hiett argued that this precedent still stands, and Virginia law has voided any preinjury agreement releasing a party from liability for negligence. The Supreme Court agreed with this argument and found that the release of liability on the entry form for the triathlon violated public policy and was therefore invalid.

7. In *Childress by Childress v. Madison County*, 777 S.W.2d 1 (Tenn. Ct. App. 1989), a mentally handicapped student and his parents sued a county and its board of education, alleging negligence in supervision of the student, who was taken to a public pool for training for the Special Olympics. The court found the county negligent in failing to supervise the student adequately and also found that the release signed by the student's mother relieved the county of liability to the mother but in no way waived the rights of the student or the father to sue the county for negligence.

8. In *Doyle v. Bowdoin College v. Cooper International, Inc.*, 403 A.2d 1206 (Me. 1979), an action was brought by plaintiffs on behalf of their son Brian, who was injured while playing floor hockey at a clinic sponsored by the defendant college and directed by the school's agents. Plaintiffs alleged that the defendant's negligence resulted in their son's injury when a plastic hockey blade flew off the end of another boy's stick, hitting Brian in the eye, shattering his glasses, and damaging his retina so as to leave him partially blind. The case was tried before a jury which concluded that the negligent conduct of defendants Bowdoin College and its agents proximately caused plaintiffs' son's injuries. The defendants appealed this judgment, contending that the trial court erred in holding (1) that certain documents were *not* releases relieving defendants of all liability for future injuries Brian might suffer as a result of defendants' negligent conduct and

(2) that another document was not a contract of indemnification obligating the injured child's mother to reimburse defendants for any liability they might incur regarding injuries sustained by him at the clinic. The appeals court denied the defendants' appeal. It noted that courts have traditionally disfavored contractual exclusions of negligence liability. The court found that the documents executed by the child's parents contained no express reference to defendants' liability for their own negligence: "Though the documents state that Bowdoin College will not 'assume' or 'accept' any 'responsibility' for injuries sustained by participants unless the waiver violates public policy." The court held that the contract signed by the plaintiff was valid.

9. Releases are not valid if they are not clearly stated. For example, in *Hertzog v. Harrison Island Shores Inc.*, 251 N.Y.S.2d 164 (N.Y. App. Div. 1964), plaintiff beach and yacht club member sought recovery for injuries received in a fall from the gangplank leading to the dock on club premises. The court held for the plaintiff, despite the fact that the plaintiff signed a release of liability. The court reasoned that a provision of the membership application, providing that, if accepted as a member, plaintiff would waive his claim for any loss to personality or for personal injury while a member of club, was not sufficiently clear or explicit to absolve club of its own negligence in regard to the plaintiff's fall.

For more detailed analysis of the viability of waivers in sports, see Doyice J. Cotton and Mary B. Cotten, *Legal Aspects of Waivers in Sport, Recreation and Fitness Activities* (Canton, OH: PRC, 1997). This book identifies particular U.S. states as "lenient," "moderate," or "rigorous" with respect to allowing waivers to stand up in court. Furthermore, the book provides specific examples of waivers that were upheld or disregarded by the courts.

The following are examples of waivers and releases of liability:

1. The following is an NCAA Ticket Release of Liability Statement: Dear College Basketball Season Ticket Holder: Enclosed are your NCAA tickets. Please safeguard your tickets; lost tickets will not be replaced. °°Please note there will be no drop-off of tickets at the Reservations Window for the rest of the season or NCAA games. Tickets *Will Not Be Accepted* under any circumstances. Please distribute any tickets prior to day of game.

THIS TICKET IS A REVOCABLE LICENSE USER ACCEPTS RISK OF INJURY

The holder of this ticket voluntarily assumes all risks of property loss and personal injury arising during its use. Management may revoke the license and eject or refuse entry to the holder by refunding the stated purchase price. Tickets reported as lost or stolen may not be honored. If lost or stolen, this ticket will not be replaced nor the price refunded. Holder may not solicit contributions or distribute literature on the premises. Every person, regardless of age, must have a ticket to enter the facility. Holder may not bring alcoholic beverages, bottles, cans or containers, irritants (e.g., noise makers), videotape cameras, cups, shakers or strobe lights onto the premises without the written permission of the NCAA. Large signs, flags or banners are not permitted. It is the tournament manager's responsibility to confiscate all prohibited articles. No signs, flags or banners of any size may be affixed to the facility. Items that reflect good sportsmanship that can be held by one individual and do not block the view of other ticket patrons may be permitted. Unless specifically authorized in advance by the NCAA, this ticket may not be offered as a prize in a sweepstakes or contest. No readmittance.

2. The following waiver was considered by the court in the case of *Brown v. Racquetball Centers Inc.* (see note 7): I, LeRoy F. Brown, voluntarily enter the Westend Racquet Club, ... to participate in the athletic, physical and social activities therein. I have inspected the premises and know of the risks and dangers involved in such activities as are conducted therein and that unanticipated and unexpected dangers may arise during such activities. I hereby and do assume all risks of injury to my person and property that may be sustained in connection with the stated and associated activities in and about those premises.

In consideration of the permission granted to me to enter the premises and participate in the stated activities, I hereby, for myself, my heirs, administrators and assigns, release, remise and discharge the owners, operators and sponsors of the premises and its activities and equipment and their respective servants, agents, officers, and all other participants in those activities of and from all claims, demands, actions and causes of action of any sort for injury sustained to my person and/or property during my presence on the premises and my participation in those activities due to negligence or any other fault.

Chapter 5

ATHLETIC ASSOCIATIONS

5.1. Voluntary Athletic Associations

    5.1.1. Introduction

    5.1.2. The U.S. Olympic Committee

    5.1.3. National Collegiate Athletic Association (NCAA)

    5.1.4. Other Athletic Associations

    5.1.5. High School Athletic Associations

5.2. Legal Principles Pertaining to Amateur Athletic Associations

    5.2.1. Introduction

    5.2.2. Judicial Review

    5.2.3. Standing

    5.2.4. Injunctive Relief

5.3. Association Enforcement Authority

    5.3.1. Introduction

    5.3.2. NCAA Enforcement Procedure

    5.3.2.1. Committee on Infractions

    5.3.2.2. Infractions Appeals Committee

    5.3.2.3. NCAA Infractions Process

    5.3.3. The Knight Commission

    5.3.4. Interscholastic Enforcement Procedures

    5.3.5. Olympic Enforcement Procedures

    5.3.6. Court of Arbitration for Sport

5.4. Public Responsibility of Athletic Associations

    5.4.1. Disclosure

    5.4.2. Funding of Public Facilities

    5.4.3. The Buckley Amendment

INTRODUCTION

So far, this book has considered in some detail the legal system within which athletic associations operate, including certain legal duties they are charged to fulfill. We turn now to the manner in which these associations govern themselves, from the authority they possess and their ability to assert it to their need to comply with other relevant legal principles and constitutional requirements. The organizations that govern athletics are collectively referred to in this chapter as athletic associations.

This chapter will examine athletic associations, including (1) high school and college athletic associations such as statewide high school organizations, the National Federation of State High School Associations (NFSHSA), the National Collegiate Athletic Association (NCAA), the National Association of Intercollegiate Athletics (NAIA), and the National Junior College Athletic Association (NJCAA); (2) high school and college athletic conferences such as the California Interscholastic Federation (CIF) and the Pac-10; and (3) national and international governing bodies such as the International Olympic Committee (IOC), U.S. Olympic Committee (USOC), the International Amateur Athletic Federation (IAAF), and USA Track and Field.

The organizations mentioned are usually set up as nonprofit associations, with their own constitutions and bylaws. A constitution and bylaws are generally drafted by the members of the organization, and can be modified only by a vote of the association members and/or their representatives. In general, associations comprise a board of directors, chief operating officer (i.e., president, executive director), various other association officers (depending upon the size of the association), and representatives from the association members (i.e., athletic directors, athletes, faculty representatives, etc.). While this organizational model is a typical one, each association may vary its structure, depending upon its members' needs. Larger organizations, for example, the NCAA, elect their officers and/or board of directors. Often, however, organizations hire people from outside their membership to run the day-to-day activities of the association.

These officials, whether elected or hired, comprise the association office. The association office discharges many responsibilities. Among these obligations, association offices are generally responsible for decisions concerning the eligibility of athletes, the implementation and administration of drug testing programs, and imposing disciplinary sanctions upon association members and athletes when warranted. They generally are not responsible for formulating the rules that govern their particular association. Instead, the governing body of the particular association generally controls the process of creating rules and policies.

Collegiate and high school athletic association rules have historically provoked frequent scrutiny under the U.S. Constitution. A key component in such cases is whether the defendant association is considered public or private by the court: Only *public* organizations, known by the judiciary as "state actors," are required to consider constitutional issues, although courts also recognize certain duties which even private organizations owe to their members (see section 5.2.2, "Judicial Review"). For an association to be found guilty of violating the Constitution, the association must be deemed a "state actor" or public corporation (see section 6.1.1, "State Action Requirement"). Court decisions about what constitutes "state action" in athletics have varied, but since the mid-1980s, the Supreme Court has issued two decisions on this topic that have clarified the issue.

First, in the case of *NCAA v. Tarkanian*, 488 U.S. 179 (1988), the U.S. Supreme Court decided by a 5–4 vote that the NCAA cannot be construed as a state actor for purposes of constitutional law. Tarkanian brought a case against the NCAA stating that the association had violated his due process rights under the U.S. Constitution by sanctioning his program for NCAA violations. The Supreme Court disagreed, stating:

> The Nevada state university's actions with respect to the coach, in compliance with the rules and recommendations of the association of which the university was a member, did not turn the association's conduct into such state action, or action under color of state law, because it would be more appropriate to conclude that the university conducted its athletic program under the color of the policies adopted by the association, rather than that those policies were developed and enforced under color of the law of Nevada.

In other words, since the NCAA, and not Nevada, had made the relevant decisions, no state action had occurred. As a result of this decision, the NCAA is never considered a state actor.

However, in the case of *Brentwood Academy v. Tennessee Secondary School Athletic Association*, 531 U.S. 288 (2001), the U.S. Supreme Court decided that the *high school athletic association* for the state of Tennessee was a state actor and therefore subject to litigation for violations of the 1st and 14th Amendments. The court believed that members of the state government were so involved in the association that the association must be considered a state actor: "The Association's regulatory activity is state action owing to the pervasive entwinement of state school officials in the Association's structure, there being no offsetting reason to see the Association's acts in any other way." The consequence of this decision is that *all* high school athletic associations nationwide are considered state actors. These influential cases will be discussed further later in the chapter because the debate over whether athletic associations are private or public entities has been a pervasive issue in athletics (see section 5.4, "Public Responsibility of Athletic Associations").

Associations can be challenged legally by both their members and outside groups. For example, the NCAA has found itself involved in litigation over antitrust issues with member schools (*NCAA v. Board of Regents, Univ. of Oklahoma*, 468 U.S. 85 (1984); see section 14.2.4.1, "Antitrust Issues in Broadcasting for Colleges") as well as with coaches (*Law v. NCAA*, 134 F.3d 1010 10th Cir. (1998); see section 10.1.3, "Clayton Act"). Also, the sportswear manufacturer Adidas challenged the association because NCAA rules limited the size of the logos allowed on member institutions' uniforms (*Adidas v. NCAA*, 40 F. Supp. 2d. 1275 (D. Kan. 1999); see section 14.3.1.1, "Restrictions on the Use of Advertising"). Historically, the NCAA and other associations were not frequently challenged in terms of legal accountability, but their pervasive influence in the world of athletics has now led to increasing legal scrutiny. Some argue that this scrutiny has resulted in better protection of individual rights from arbitrary or unfair actions of governing organizations, institutions, schools, or coaches and teachers. Others argue that this increased judicial presence is an unwarranted intrusion into athletics.

In addition to the organizations considered earlier, three other groups are involved in the governance of interscholastic and intercollegiate athletics in the United States: educational institutions (represented by presidents, chancellors, and principals), athletic directors, and coaches. These groups, together with the athletic associations, operate in a pyramid-like fashion: Athletic associations set certain minimum standards and requirements for eligibility and participation; conferences and educational institutions may impose stricter obligations on their student-athletes; and athletic directors and coaches may demand further stringent requirements that they judge to be necessary for successful performance in their individual sport or for proper functioning of the educational department as a whole. Schools, coaches, and athletic directors who seek to skirt or avoid the rules may find themselves on the receiving end of associations' regulatory authority. Since educational institutions and coaches must act within the scope of the association and conference regulations, our focus within this chapter will be primarily on the activities, rules, and governance of athletic associations and conferences.

In this context, Chapter 5 analyzes the impact of the law on athletics and notes the growing power of the organizations that govern athletics. The chapter begins with a description of influential athletic associations. It next discusses significant legal principles that must be understood within the context of athletics. The third segment of the chapter involves the authority that is vested in these associations, and how they enforce their rules and regulations. The next section deals with the effect that constitutional law has had upon athletic associations, and how athletes have been able to argue for their constitutional rights through the court system. The final portion of the chapter deals with the responsibility that athletic associations have to the public.

NOTES

For further information on the emergence of intercollegiate athletics as big business, see the following:

1. Lindsay A. Oliver, "NCAA: A Lesson in Cartel Behavior and Antitrust Regulation," 8 *Transactions: Tenn. J. Bus. L.* 7 (2006).

2. Paul Fellin, "The Commitment to Participate Rule: The NCAA Fights to Keep the March Madness Ball in Its Court," 20 *St. John's J. Legal Comment.* 501 (2006).

3. Erin Guruli, "Commerciality of Collegiate Sports: Should the IRS Intercept?," 12 *Sports Law. J.* 43 (2005).

4. Jodi M. Warmbrod, "Antitrust in Amateur Athletics: Fourth and Long: Why Non-BCS Universities Should Punt Rather Than Go for an Antitrust Challenge to the Bowl Championship Series," 57 *Okla. L. Rev.* 333 (2004).

5. Lindsay J. Rosenthal, "From Regulating Organization to Multi-Billion Dollar Business: The NCAA Is Commercializing the Amateur Competition It Has Taken Almost a Century to Create," 13 *Seton Hall Journal of Sports and Entertainment Law* 321 (2003).

5.1. VOLUNTARY ATHLETIC ASSOCIATIONS

5.1.1. Introduction

Fundamental legal principles apply to athletic associations of every type. Although athletic associations and conferences, such as the National Federation of State High School Associations, the NCAA, and the Big Ten, are private and voluntary in character, courts nevertheless examine their affairs for two reasons: (1) large numbers of public institutions form the membership of these organizations and (2) these organizations perform public functions which were traditionally reserved to the government.

In this vein of serving the public, over more than a century, many organizations have been created to serve different groups of individuals in a variety of athletic activities. For example, the Amateur Athletic Union (AAU) has, for 120 years, dedicated itself to the development of amateur sports and physical fitness for amateur athletes of all ages. Similarly, the NCAA has taken upon itself the role of coordinator and overseer of college athletics, in the interest of individuals and their educational institutions. As these organizations increasingly become a part of the public domain in the eyes of the judicial system, it becomes imperative to understand the nature and composition of these "private" associations.

As mentioned in the introduction, a major issue surrounding athletic associations has been the categorizing of associations as either private or public entities for purposes of litigation involving constitutional law. For the purposes of discussion within this chapter, the focus will be upon traditionally "amateur" associations.

The constitutional issues covered in this chapter do not apply to professional leagues for two reasons. First, professional sports franchises and associations are generally private entities. While some professional sports franchises have public aspects, sometimes including publicly held shares in the franchise, they are *not* public in the sense that they are funded by the state or any state entity. Second, through their collective bargaining agreements, professional athletes waive many of their legal rights relative to litigation (see Chapter 11, "Labor Law").

There are a few rare instances, however, where professional athletes may litigate on constitutional law grounds, which will be discussed in Chapter 6. For now, we will maintain our focus on amateur athletic associations. These athletic organizations are often distinguished on the basis of sport (e.g., USA Track and Field, the national governing body (NGB) for track and field in the United States), educational level (e.g., National Junior College Athletic Association), or geographic location (e.g., the California Interscholastic Federation). Some amateur sports organizations govern institutions (e.g., the NCAA) and some govern individual athletes (e.g., national governing bodies such as USA Track and Field). Belonging to one such organization does not preclude membership in another. In fact, most educational institutions belong to an allied conference (e.g., Big East Conference) in addition to being members of a national association with a broader constituency (e.g., NCAA). Allied conferences, a subset of the larger amateur sports associations, usually consist of a number of schools that share educational goals and geographic ties. These schools compete against each other in a number of sports and often vie for conference championships in each of the sports.

5.1.2. The U.S. Olympic Committee

In 1978, the U.S. Congress passed the Amateur Sports Act (36 U.S.C. 371–396) ("the ASA") in order to recognize and coordinate amateur athletics in the United States and to encourage and strengthen participation of U.S. amateurs in international competition. This act focuses on two primary areas: (1) the relationship between athletes eligible for international amateur competition and the ruling bodies that govern these competitions and (2) the relationship between the ruling bodies themselves. The ASA recognizes the U.S. Olympic Committee (USOC) as the principal mechanism for attaining these goals. One of the law's major objectives is to allow the USOC to make its own decisions concerning matters of eligibility without the outside interference of the court system.

The ASA creates a governing structure for the USOC by empowering it to select one NGB for each Olympic or Pan-American sport (see exhibits 5.1 and 5.2). The act enumerates specific responsibilities for an NGB, including the determination of eligibility rules for participation, team selection, drug testing, and eligibility status. NGBs also do the actual organizational work of developing athletes, organizing teams, instructing coaches and officials, and scheduling events. The ASA details explicit requirements for sports organizations to become NGBs and provides a mechanism for the resolution of disputes between two organizations wishing to be recognized as the sole NGB. In order to be selected, NGBs must have the backing of the sport's participants in the United States. International governing bodies must also recognize these associations as official national bodies for the particular sport.

Although the USOC has chosen to concentrate on Olympic and Pan-American sports, its control in this area is not exclusive. Not only must international governing bodies approve the NGBs, but the USOC itself must contend with and conform to the policies and regulations of the International Olympic Committee (IOC). Furthermore, the Amateur Sports Act specifies that "any amateur sports organization which conducts amateur athletic competition, participation in which is restricted to a specific class of amateur athletes (such as high school students, college students, members of the Armed Forces or similar groups or categories), shall have exclusive jurisdiction over such competition." It is only when such groups wish to become involved in international competition that the USOC may play a role

Exhibit 5.1
Organizational Chart Showing Regulatory Power of Amateur Sport Governing Bodies

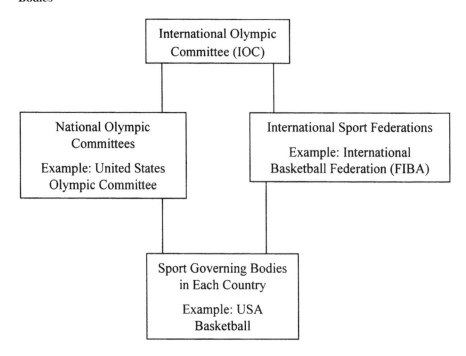

Exhibit 5.2
U.S. Olympic Committee Organizational Structure

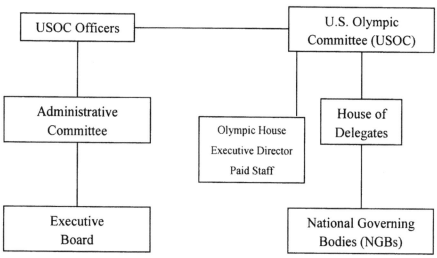

through the granting of a sanction or "certificate of approval issued by an NGB," which is required for such international competition.

Even in international competitions it helps to organize, the USOC does not have exclusive control. For instance, when the United States hosts the Olympic or Pan-American Games, the USOC must work in concert with local and state governments and in conjunction with the organizing committee of the host city.

Moreover, the USOC's authority has recently been affected by changes to the ASA. The Ted Stevens Olympic and Amateur Sports Act Amendments (36 U.S.C. §§ 220501–220529 (1998)) were passed into law in 1998, expanding both the USOC's authority and responsibilities in several ways: (1) The USOC was charged to become more inclusive of disabled athletes, among other things by serving as the national Paralympic representative to the International Paralympic Committee; (2) athletes were given a bigger role in USOC governance, including the right to elect a minimum of one fifth of voting members of all USOC legislative bodies; (3) the USOC was required to report every four years on participation data for women, racial and ethnic minorities, and disabled athletes; (4) the USOC was protected from injunctive relief in any suit concerning the "right to participate" by an athlete within 21 days of the beginning of the Olympic Games; and (5) the position of "athlete ombudsman" was created to provide free, independent advice to athletes about the Amateur Sports Act, the USOC bylaws and regulations, and rules of the NGBs with respect to the resolution of any right to compete dispute.

For the most part, the judiciary has been reluctant to tinker with the ASA in general and with the authority of the USOC and NGBs in particular. However, courts have intervened in questions involving the act when they believe that the USOC or NGBs have incorrectly applied their own rules (see notes 3, 5, and 6). Significantly, in *Reynolds v. International Amateur Athletic Federation*, 505 U.S. 1301 (1992), the Supreme Court ruled that an amateur athlete could pursue state law claims even after exhausting administrative remedies offered by the relevant NGB and international federation. The athlete's state law claims ultimately foundered over jurisdictional issues, thus making little impact on the judiciary's deferential posture toward NGBs and their international partners.

NOTES

1. In *Jacobs v. USA Track & Field (USATF)*, 374 F.3d 85 (2nd Cir. 2004), Regina Jacobs petitioned the courts to compel the USATF, the NGB for track and field in the United States, to arbitration regarding a doping suspension. Jacobs, who at the age of 39 in February 2003 became the first woman to ever break four minutes in the indoor 1,500 meters, tested positive for THG, a banned substance, in June 2003. Jacobs contended that American Arbitration Association (AAA) Commercial Rules applied. The USATF stated that arbitration was controlled by the Supplementary Procedures of the AAA. AAA ruled in favor of the USATF. While the District Court recognized conflicting regulations within both the USATF about which rules should apply, it ruled it did not have jurisdiction because both the Commercial Rules and Supplementary Procedures provide that an arbitrator is to rule on the matter. In affirming the decision, the Second Circuit stated arbitration cannot be compelled when the USATF has not refused to arbitrate.

2. In *Slaney v. USOC*, 244 F.3d 580 (7th Cir. 2001), Olympic runner Mary Decker Slaney brought suit against the USOC after she tested positive for drug use after Olympic trials in 1996. She was found to have a high enough ratio of testosterone to epitestosterone in her body to be consistent with blood doping (for more information on drug testing of Olympic athletes, see section 7.2.3, "Olympic and International Sports"). In her complaint against the USOC, Slaney alleged that the testing discriminated against women and was not scientifically valid. The Seventh Circuit concluded that the Amateur Sports Act provides the USOC with complete jurisdiction over decisions concerning an athlete's eligibility. The court reasoned that the USOC was the most qualified body for determining questions of eligibility. The court went on to state that the USOC could be held liable in questions of eligibility if they do not follow their own stated rules.

3. In *Lindland v. U.S. Wrestling Ass'n Inc. (USAW)*, 227 F.3d 1000 (7th Cir. 2000), two wrestlers sued to be included on the U.S. wrestling team at the 2000 Olympics. Matt Lindland wrestled Keith Sieracki in the finals of the Olympic trials and Sieracki won by a score of 2–1. Lindland protested the match, claiming Sieracki tripped him against the rules of Greco-Roman wrestling. USAW denied his protests but Lindland filed for arbitration under the Amateur Sports Act. An arbitrator ordered a rematch, which Lindland won 8–0. After the second match, Sieracki also commenced arbitration to substantiate his original victory and the appeals procedures of USAW. Only Sieracki and USAW appeared at this arbitration hearing, and the arbitrator ordered USAW to ignore the first arbitration hearing. USAW and the U.S. Olympic Committee (USOC) refused to honor the rematch, and Lindland then sought confirmation of the original arbitration award under the Federal Arbitration Act. USAW finally agreed to recognize the arbitration award, but the USOC still refused, saying Sieracki's name had already been give to the International Olympic Committee (IOC). The District Court ordered the USOC to substitute Lindland's name, which they did but also appealed. In affirming the decision, the Seventh Circuit noted the rules of the AAA do not allow arbitrators to redetermine the merits of any claim already decided. Lindland won a silver medal at the 2000 Olympics and has since become a successful mixed martial artist.

4. In *Floyd v. USOC*, 965 S.W.2d 35 (Tex. Ct. App. 1998), a runner tested positive for amphetamines after using a carbohydrate supplement named Sydnocarb. She believed that she could use the supplement without worrying about testing positive because when her husband had called the USOC to see if Sydnocarb was a banned substance, the USOC operator had responded that it was not. The operator did not say, however, that the supplement was safe to use or provide any other assurances. After Floyd tested positive she brought a claim of negligence against the USOC, alleging that it had provided her with false information regarding the supplement. The court ruled that under the Amateur Sports Act, no athlete has a right to a private cause of action against the USOC and dismissed Floyd's claim.

5. In *Foschi v. United States Swimming Inc.*, 916 F. Supp. 232 (E.D. N.Y. 1996), the court concluded that while the USOC has jurisdiction concerning eligibility determinations, courts have the ability to intervene to make sure that the USOC is following its own rules for determining eligibility. The federal district court granted the plaintiff's motion to remand back to New York state court the question of whether she was wrongfully suspended from United States Swimming. However the court stopped short of granting the plaintiff injunctive relief, due to its lack of jurisdiction.

6. In *Harding v. United States Figure Skating Association*, 851 F. Supp. 1476 (D. Or. 1994), the court enjoined the defendant association from proceeding with a disciplinary hearing because the association had violated its own bylaws by scheduling a disciplinary hearing too early for Harding to prepare her defense. The ruling in this case, allowing a court to intervene with an amateur athletic association, was limited by the judge's opinion, which stated, "Intervention is appropriate only in the most extraordinary circumstances, where the association has clearly breached its own rules, that breach will imminently result in serious and irreparable harm to the plaintiff, and the plaintiff has exhausted all internal remedies. Even then, injunctive relief is limited to correcting the breach of the rules. The court should not intervene in the merits of the underlying dispute."

7. For further information on the USOC and its powers, see *DeFrantz v. United States Olympic Committee*, 492 F. Supp. 1181 (D.D.C. 1980), *aff'd* without opinion, 701 F.2d 221 (D.C. Cir. 1980). The federal district court held that the Amateur Sports Act of 1978 did not establish a cause of action for 25 designated Olympic athletes who sought to prohibit the USOC from barring them from participating in the 1980 Olympic Games in Moscow. The court noted:

We...conclude that the USOC not only had the authority to decide not to send an American team to the summer Olympics, but also that it could do so for reasons not directly related to sports considerations.

We...find that the decision of the USOC not to send an American team to the summer Olympics was not state action, and therefore does not give rise to an actionable claim for the infringements of the constitutional rights alleged.

For further information on the politics and history of the modern Olympic Games, see the following:

1. Scott Rosner, "The Efficacy of Olympic Bans and Boycotts on Effectuating International Political and Economic Change," 11 *Texas Review of Entertainment & Sports Law* 27 (2009).

2. Richard W. Pound, *Inside the Olympics: A Behind-the-Scenes Look at the Politics, the Scandals and the Glory of the Games* (Hoboken, NJ: Wiley, 2006).

3. Andrew Jennings and Clare Sambrook, *The Great Olympic Swindle: When the World Wanted Its Games Back* (New York: Simon and Schuster, 2000).

4. Helen Jefferson Lensky and Varda Burstyn, *Inside the Olympic Industry: Power, Politics and Activism* (Albany: State University of New York Press, 2000).

5.1.3. National Collegiate Athletic Association (NCAA)

As discussed in section 1.3, "Intercollegiate Athletics," the NCAA is a voluntary association that comprises colleges and universities, conferences, organizations, and individuals totaling over 1,200 members.

Member schools agree to be bound by NCAA rules and regulations and are obligated to administer their athletic programs in accordance with the NCAA rules. Over half of the NCAA's members are state universities and nearly all receive some form of federal financial assistance. The NCAA does not offer membership to individual student-athletes. Instead, it operates under the principle of institutional control. In essence, this means that the NCAA deals only with a school administration, and the school is responsible for individual student-athletes.

When a violation that concerns a student-athlete is discovered, the NCAA informs the school of its findings and requests that the school declare the student-athlete ineligible. If the school does not comply with the request, the NCAA may invoke sanctions against all or any part of the institution's athletic program.

The purposes of the NCAA are stated in its constitution:

(a) To initiate, stimulate and improve intercollegiate athletic programs for student-athletes and to promote and develop educational leadership, physical fitness, athletics excellence and athletics participation as a recreational pursuit;

(b) To uphold the principle of institutional control of, and responsibility for, all intercollegiate sports in conformity with the constitution and bylaws of this Association;

(c) To encourage its members to adopt eligibility rules to comply with satisfactory standards of scholarship, sportsmanship and amateurism;

(d) To formulate, copyright and publish rules of play governing intercollegiate athletics;

(e) To preserve intercollegiate athletics records;

(f) To supervise the conduct of, and to establish eligibility standards for, regional and national athletic events under the auspices of this Association;

(g) To cooperate with other amateur athletics organizations in promoting and conducting national and international athletics events;

(h) To legislate, through bylaws or by resolutions of a Convention, upon any subject of general concern to the members related to the administration of intercollegiate athletics; and,

(i) To study in general all phases of competitive intercollegiate athletics and establish standards whereby the colleges and universities of the United States can maintain their athletic programs on a high level. (*2009–10 NCAA Manual*, Bylaw 1.2)

In addition, the NCAA proclaims its basic purpose as follows:

> The competitive athletics programs of member institutions are designed to be a vital part of the educational system. A basic purpose of this Association is to maintain intercollegiate athletics as an integral part of the educational program and the athlete as an integral part of the student body and, by so doing, retain a clear line of demarcation between intercollegiate athletics and professional sport. (*2009–10 NCAA Manual*, Bylaw 1.3.1)

Although the NCAA wields considerable authority over its members, the organization is structured so as to delegate significant regulatory responsibility. For example, the NCAA is divided into conferences, based primarily on geographic location. Each conference is responsible for regulating its member institutions and ensuring that the minimum standards, as outlined in the *NCAA Manual*, are not violated. Each conference has a detailed set of rules and regulations and a mechanism to enforce those rules.

Most NCAA member institutions are part of one conference or another, and some institutions belong to more than one. Institutions need not be part of a conference to participate in college athletics. For example, Notre Dame is part of the Big East Conference for all of its athletic programs except football; in Division I football, Notre Dame is considered an "independent." Nonetheless, because most institutions belong to a conference, it is important to analyze briefly the structure and organization of these conferences.

Today, conferences are an extension of the NCAA structure. Originally formed to foster regional rivalries among universities, conferences bring the governance of institutions to a more local level. However, the trend in conference expansion since 1990 has not necessarily been dictated by geography. While regional rivalries still exist, especially in older and well-established conferences, the priority in conference expansion has changed drastically in the past 20 years. For example, former Big East Conference members Boston College, Virginia Tech University, and the University of Miami (Florida) moved to the powerful Atlantic Coast Conference, creating a conference that stretches from south Florida to New England. The schools were motivated by the Atlantic Coast Conference's higher profile in revenue producing sports, especially football. Meanwhile, spots in the traditionally northeast-based Big East were eagerly claimed by the University of Louisville, the University of Cincinnati, and the University of South Florida, who sought to increase their own exposure and revenues.

The trend of conference realignment in the NCAA's top division has reached much farther west. The adaptability of the Western Athletic Conference, headquartered in Colorado, is another example of the diverse geographic trend in conference membership. After losing half of its members to the fledgling Mountain West Conference in 1999, the Western Athletic Conference survived in part by looking beyond its traditional regional boundaries. Despite losing other members to Conference USA (which had lost several of its own members to the Big East), the Western Athletic Conference now stretches from the University of Hawaii to Louisiana Tech University.

Each conference, which is commonly made up of 10–12 institutions, has its own constitution and bylaws, which contain the rules by which all members must abide. These regulations cover eligibility standards, dispute resolution mechanisms, sportsmanship rules, championship guidelines, and player/coach conduct. It is important to remember that each conference is still governed by the NCAA; therefore, no conference rule may contradict an NCAA rule.

The conferences that make up the NCAA were historically split into geographic or regional units. For example, as of June 2010, the Pac-10 is made up of the University of Arizona, Arizona State University, the University of California at Berkeley, UCLA, the University of Oregon, Oregon State University, the University of Southern California, Stanford University, the University of Washington, and Washington State University. Regional rivalries and comparable levels of competition encourage fans to travel from one city to another and reduce travel expenses for the institutions. In addition, some conferences are made up of teams with similar philosophies and comparable academic ideals, such as the Ivy League, which includes Yale, Harvard, Princeton, and Brown.

The role of the conference is similar to that of the NCAA, except on a more local level. The purposes section of the Southeastern Conference (SEC) Constitution reads as follows:

Constitution, Article 1

°1.2 PURPOSES

The purpose of the Southeastern Conference shall be to assist its member institutions in the maintenance of programs of intercollegiate athletics which are compatible with the highest standards of education and competitive sports. To this end, through the orderly establishment and enforcement of legislation, the Conference aims:

(a) to encourage sound academic practices for student-athletes;

(b) to foster strong competition among the teams of its member institutions in a broad spectrum of amateur sports and championships;

(c) to assure proper emphasis on the funding of athletic activities;

(d) to stimulate good sportsmanship;

(e) to provide leadership and a voice in the development of public attitudes toward intercollegiate sports generally; and

(f) to address the future needs of athletics in a spirit of cooperation and mutual benefit of the member institutions.

Each conference has an institutional framework that allows it to enforce league and conference rules, plan championships, and publicize conference games. Each conference has a commissioner who is the chief administrative officer of the conference and is responsible for its day-to-day operation. For example, the responsibilities of the commissioner in the Colonial Athletic Association include, but are not limited to, the following:

1. To act as the principal enforcement officer of the association rules

2. To present an annual operational budget to the executive committee for approval

3. To develop and conduct a continuous educational program aimed at the development of scholarship, sportsmanship, and understanding of the values of competitive athletics

4. To have jurisdiction over all questions of student eligibility

A commissioner is also generally responsible for maintaining the fiscal health of the conference. This objective is accomplished in part by marketing the conference, using methods such as selling sponsorships to local and national corporations and negotiating television contracts with broadcast networks. Meanwhile, conference offices will employ various people serving under the commissioner. For example, a conference office will typically employ an assistant commissioner for championships or an assistant commissioner for NCAA compliance. Employees of a conference office may also include a marketing staff, media relations specialists, and employees to coordinate the operations of conference tournaments.

All conferences have established formal governance structures. For example, the Pac-10 Conference Constitution reads in part, "The management of the Conference shall be vested in the Council. The powers of the Council in relationship to the Chief Executive Officers Group are set forth in Bylaw 1-1" (Bylaw 4-1). Bylaw 1-1 reads, "The Council shall be the operating body for the administration of the Pac-10 conference, under the direction of the Chief Executive Officers Group as provided herein. The Chief Executive Officers Group may propose actions by the Conference, and such proposals shall immediately be referred to the Council for appropriate recommendations unless eight members of the Chief Executive Officers Group vote to take action without referral to the Council. It is recognized the Chief Executive Officers Group bears the ultimate responsibility for governance of the Conference." Each institution in the conference is entitled to three representatives on the council; they are also part of council committees, including structural committees (Championship, Officiating, Revenue-Sharing, Television) and standing committees (Budget and Finance, Executive, Legislative, and Selection).

Each conference in the NCAA has a set of rules and regulations that cannot contradict what is established in the *NCAA Manual*. Conference regulations may be stricter than the NCAA's, but they may not be more relaxed. For example, each conference must have eligibility requirements that meet the minimum standards set forth by the NCAA. The Pac-10 handbook reads:

> Student eligibility and participation rules for Pac-10 teams and individuals are the NCAA rules of eligibility, except where the Pac-10 has a more strict rule or where special exceptions are made and recorded in the Pac-10 Handbook. (Article 7(1)(a), *Pacific-10 Conference Constitution*)

One of the more rigid eligibility rules concerns intraconference transferring. Historically, the Pac-10 maintained rigid eligibility rules concerning intraconference transferring. While the conference formerly charged such transfers with two years of eligibility, in 2004 it cut the residence requirement in half. (See note 4 for discussion of a case involving other aspects of the Pac-10 intraconference transfer rule.)

Each institution, before it permits a student who has transferred directly from another Pac-10 member institution to compete in intercollegiate athletics, shall require the student to fulfill a residence requirement of one full academic year (two full semesters or three full quarters) and shall charge the student with one year of eligibility in all Pac-10 sports, and during the period of ineligibility shall not offer, provide, or arrange directly or indirectly any athletically related financial aid (Article 7(3)(b), *Pacific-10 Conference Constitution*).

Conferences also have the ability to amend conference rules and regulations through legislation. Each conference has procedures that govern these practices. For example, in the Pac-10 Conference, 8 of the 10 members must vote in favor of a constitutional amendment. In terms of amendments to the bylaws, seven affirmative votes are required; in the area of enlarging the membership of the conference, a unanimous vote is necessary. The annual budget of the conference and selection and employment of the commissioner are based on a majority vote of the member institutions (*2009–2010 Pac-10 Handbook*, Bylaw 2).

NOTES ───

1. In *Hispanic College Fund, Inc. (HCF). v. NCAA*, 826 N.E.2d 652 (Ind. App. 2005), the HCF, a private nonprofit organization whose mission is to aid Hispanic students, brought suit against the NCAA, of which it had been a sponsoring member since early 1999. Prior to 1999, the NCAA adopted a policy that D-I schools could only play 11 games and an "exempted" pre-season game, certified by the Championships/Competition Cabinet, every four seasons that

would not count toward the 11-game limit. In 1999, the NCAA adopted a policy that starting in 2002 teams could play 12 regular season games; however, if a team played in a certified preseason game, that would count toward the 12-game limit. In 2002, HCF and other sponsors of preseason games sought to have their games be classified as exempt. However, the NCAA only granted exemptions to organizations that had TV broadcasting contracts prior to the 1999 change. HCF and other organizations were granted exemptions in 2002 but not in 2003 and 2004. The trial court held that the NCAA is a voluntary membership organization and absent allegations of fraud or illegality, the court would not interfere. The Court of Appeals affirmed.

2. In *Bloom v. NCAA*, 93 P.3d 621 (Colo. App. 2004), University of Colorado wide receiver Jeremy Bloom brought suit against the NCAA for a declaratory judgment that he could continue to receive paid endorsements associated with his professional skiing career that had begun before he entered Colorado. Bloom competed at the 2002 Olympics but never skied for Colorado. Bloom contended that the rules prohibiting his endorsements were arbitrary and capricious and constituted an unreasonable restraint of trade. In denying Bloom's requested relief, the court noted the unfair advantage Bloom's professional skiing status might provide over wholly amateur student-athletes. In addition, the court recognized the important role of the NCAA in protecting amateurism and the difficulty in discerning whether payments to Bloom were associated with his skiing rather than football. Bloom was drafted in the fifth round of the 2005 NFL draft by the Philadelphia Eagles.

3. In *Cohane v. NCAA*, 215 Fed. Appx. 13 (2nd Cir. 2007), the former men's basketball coach at SUNY Buffalo sued the NCAA after he was forced to resign. The NCAA Committee on Infractions had investigated Cohane for major rules violations and suggested to SUNY Buffalo that he be forced to resign. The Second Circuit reversed a summary judgment determination that the NCAA could not be shown to have been a "willful participant in joint activity with the State" because of accusations of abusing its power in its investigation of Cohane. Cohane alleged that the NCAA was actively involved in hearings held by the Mid-American Conference, intimidated student witnesses into giving false statements and suborned perjury at the NCAA hearing.

4. In the case of *Tanaka v. University of Southern California*, 252 F.3d 1059 (9th Cir. 2001), a former female soccer player for the University of Southern California brought an antitrust claim against USC and the Pac-10 Conference, charging that the conference rule on intraconference transfers was a violation of the Sherman Antitrust Act because the rule was an unreasonable restraint on her ability to transfer to her school of choice, UCLA. Tanaka charged that this rule was applied to her only because, before leaving the university, she had charged the university and athletic department with academic fraud. She believed that the rule was employed in her case as retaliation for her allegations against the athletic department. The court decided in favor of the university and the Pac-10, stating, "Tanaka has failed to identify a relevant market for antitrust purposes. If the relevant market is national in scope, the Pac-10 transfer rule could not have a significant anticompetitive effect, because by its own terms the rule does not apply to interconference transfers. Moreover, even if the relevant market is limited to the Pac-10 itself, Tanaka characterizes the Pac-10's imposition of sanctions against her for her intraconference transfer as an isolated act of retaliation. Tanaka simply has no antitrust cause of action" (see Chapter 10, "Antitrust Law").

5.1.4. Other Athletic Associations

In addition to the NCAA, several other athletic organizations play roles in governing collegiate sports in the United States. One of these is the National Association of Intercollegiate Athletics (NAIA), an organization composed of four-year institutions. The NAIA was formed in 1940 as the National Association of Intercollegiate Basketball and changed its name in 1952 as it expanded into more sports. The NAIA quickly grew from a small organization to one with over 500 members, though by May 2008, membership had declined to 284 schools. Many former members had moved to the NCAA. A good description of the NAIA is contained in *Williams v. Hamilton*, 497 F. Supp. 641 (D.N.H. 1980):

> [The] NAIA is a voluntary association of 512 four-year colleges ranging in size from small (500) to moderate (1100), whose primary purpose as set forth in its constitution is "to promote the development of athletics as a sound part of the educational offerings of member institutions." The member institutions of NAIA pay dues to the Association, which are scaled by enrollment. Among other things, NAIA sets standards for recruiting and eligibility, and it sponsors post-season national championships in various collegiate sports, including soccer.

NAIA is divided into several districts, each of which is governed by a District Executive Committee. Each district has voting representation at NAIA's Annual National Convention, at which time policy decisions are made. Also at the National Convention delegates vote for new members of the National Executive Committee, the overall governing body of NAIA.

The NAIA is open to any four-year, degree-granting college or university in the United States or Canada as well as certain two-year schools that offer bachelor's degrees or their equivalents. Those institutions belonging to the NAIA must operate their intercollegiate athletic programs according to the association's regulations and rules; of course, member institutions and conferences may establish even stricter standards than those of the association. The NAIA's eligibility regulations are very similar to those of the NCAA, except that the NAIA's eligibility rules govern all play in sports recognized by the association, whereas the NCAA has special rules for postseason tournaments.

Several other organizations govern competition among colleges that share defining characteristics ranging from size to shared educational missions. For example, the U.S. Collegiate Athletic Association conducts regional and national championships for colleges with enrollments under 1,500. The USCAA has 60 members from coast to coast. The National Christian College Athletic Association (NCCAA) is composed of 98 members that are willing to sign to a Statement of Faith in Christian principles. The NCCAA offers championships for both genders to teams from four-year schools.

The National Junior College Athletic Association (NJCAA), which has approximately 436 members as of 2008, performs ATHLETIC functions similar to those of the USCAA and NCCAA for junior colleges. It was described in *State ex rel. National Junior College Athletic Ass'n v. Luten*, 492 S.W.2d 404 (Mo. Ct. App. 1973) as

> a not-for-profit corporation which coordinates the scheduling and playing of intercollegiate athletics among its member schools. . . . who agree to "supervise and to control athletics sponsored by this corporation so that they will be administered in accordance with the eligibility rules . . . set forth in the . . . Bylaws." Among its functions it issues and enforces rules relating to the eligibility of students at its member schools participating in intercollegiate athletics.

Like the NCAA, all of these organizations perform functions related to education, raising the question of whether they might be considered state actors. With the exception of the NCCAA, they comprise both private and public institutions.

Therefore, the reasoning behind the *Tarkanian v. NCAA* decision (see the introduction to this chapter) indicates that associations of this type cannot be construed as state actors.

NOTES _____

1. In *Manuel v. NAIA*, 833 P.2d 288 (Okla. Ct. App. 1992), the appellate court considered the extent of the NAIA's governing authority. The plaintiff Manuel had obtained an injunction that prevented the NAIA from interfering with his scholarship to participate on the Oklahoma City University basketball team. The NAIA appealed this decision even though Manuel had already graduated, to make OCU and Manuel subject to retroactive penalties. Manuel had previously been declared ineligible under NCAA rules at the University of Kentucky, and the NAIA immediately declared Manuel ineligible upon his entrance at an NAIA member school, although this rule had not been applied in other cases with similar fact patterns. The appellate court upheld the injunction against the NAIA, stating, "The manner in which the NAIA chose to interpret its own rules with regard to Manuel appears, from the evidence, to be contrary to the way it has interpreted them in the past as to other student athletes.... The hard reality is that a college education is outside the reach of many students without the assistance of athletic scholarships. Once a student is fortunate enough to receive one, it should not be revoked through an arbitrary exercise of authority vested in a voluntary association such as the NAIA."

2. For more information on the NAIA, visit the organization's Web site at http://naia. cstv.com.

3. For further information on the NJCAA's governing authority as viewed by the courts, see *State ex rel. National Junior College Athletic Ass'n v. Luten*, 492 S.W.2d 404 (Mo. Ct. App. 1973).

4. For more information on the NJCAA, visit their Web site at http://www.njcaa.org.

5. For more information on the USCAA, visit the organization's Web site at http://www. theuscaa.com.

6. For more information on the NCCAA, visit the organization's Web site at http:// www.thenccaa.org.

5.1.5. High School Athletic Associations

High school athletic associations are voluntary associations consisting of all high schools within a state that wish to participate in association events, agree to abide by the rules of the association, and meet membership requirements. High school associations often derive their authority from state legislation, which in effect creates a private corporation to perform a quasipublic function. Each of the 50 states has its own high school athletic association to govern interscholastic athletics, and several states have more than one.

Generally, the need for multiple associations has arisen in two situations. First, the geography or population of the state makes it infeasible for one central state association to conduct all tournaments and other administrative duties. In these cases, states will form regional associations to administer the association rules. Second, separate athletic associations may be set up for schools in urban environments and schools in nonurban settings. Nevertheless, most state associations are set up so that all schools that wish to abide by association rules will be allowed entry. One example of a state with multiple subassociations is California (California Interscholastic Federation; CIF), which comprises the following regions:

1. Northern

2. North Coast

3. Sac-Joaquin

4. San Francisco

5. Oakland

6. Central Coast

7. Central

8. Los Angeles City

9. Southern

10. San Diego

In most cases, membership in an association is open to all high schools in the state that are approved by the appropriate state department of education, secondary education, or public instruction. Generally, the association's purpose is to promote, develop, direct, protect, and regulate amateur interscholastic athletic relationships among member schools and to stimulate fair play, friendly rivalry, and good sportsmanship among contestants, schools, and communities throughout the state.

On occasion, state interscholastic athletic associations have faced litigation claiming that association rules are unconstitutional or that the sanctions imposed on schools or athletes are discriminatory or unjust. Historically, athletic association rules have been vulnerable to litigation because they have been written unclearly or have been applied in an arbitrary and capricious manner. In the majority of these cases, the courts have found that the state athletic association has the responsibility to enforce its rules and that the student-athlete's participation in interscholastic athletics is a privilege, not a right. However, the courts have found that association rules cannot be arbitrarily or irrationally. In general, state high school athletic associations are subject to all the standards of judicial review covered in section 5.2.2, "Judicial Review."

Although no organization concerned with high school athletics possesses the sort of authority that the NCAA wields in college sports, the National Federation of State High School Associations (NFSHSA) provides support services for state and local organizations all over the country. While high school athletic associations are funded by dues and state budgets and control their own rule making and membership procedures, they often rely on NFSHSA publications for game rules and other aspects of high school sports. Founded in 1920, the federation is based on the belief that strong state and national high school organizations are necessary to protect the integrity of interscholastic programs and to promote healthy growth of these programs (see exhibit 5.3).

NFSHSA services include a press service subscribed to by editors of local, state, and national publications; a video library; playing rules publications for 17 sports; a national high school sports record book; sanctioning of applications for interstate and international events among schools; quarterly magazines for coaches, game officials, and administrators; and a monthly news magazine on high school activities. The NFSHSA membership serves over 20,000 high schools, 500,000 coaches and sponsors, and 500,000 officials and judges as well as 51 state associations and eight associations from Canada.

Exhibit 5.3
Organizational Structure of the NFSHSA

The above-mentioned CIF provides a good example of a high school association. Its members include public and private secondary schools as well as technical and vocational schools. Applicant schools must be approved by the Federated Council. This council has representatives from each of the 10 regions, including principals, superintendents, coaches, and athletic director as well as a representative from the California Department of Education and other CIF officials. Among the responsibilities which Article 3 of the CIF Constitution confers on the Federated Council are the following:

1. Determine the credentials of its own membership.
2. Exercise jurisdiction over all interscholastic athletic games, events, and meets involving CIF member schools. The Federated Council delegates jurisdiction to each CIF section for all interscholastic athletic games, events, and meets in which only CIF member schools of that particular section participate.
3. Be responsible for state and regional CIF playoff contests.
4. Act as a final court of appeals in protests.
5. Establish and enforce penalties for any violation of the constitution, bylaws, or other rules of the federation. Schools, leagues, and sections may establish and enforce penalties, provided that such penalties are not in conflict with penalties that have been established by higher authority.
6. Determine which athletic activities shall be conducted by the federation.
7. Prescribe ways and means by which standards of eligibility shall be met.
8. Elect its own officers.
9. Institute and conduct impeachment of officers of the federation or sections thereof.
10. For any matter of appeal not covered in the constitution and bylaws, an appeal to the Federated Council will be heard by the council's Appeals Committee.

Further details of the council's responsibility for playoff contests and for matters of appeal are also spelled out.

It is important to reiterate that state associations have the final decision in all matters of eligibility, discipline, and rules. For example, the CIF has set up a system where one official within each sport is designated as that sport's rules interpreter. For matters of eligibility and discipline, the sectional bodies are in charge of managing disputes in light of the CIF regulations. Only when these disputes cannot be resolved will the CIF Federated Council become involved in the dispute process (see section 5.3.4, "Interscholastic Enforcement Procedures").

State high school associations are usually nonprofit corporations per the guidelines of the Internal Revenue Service. Most associations generate revenue through gate receipts and membership dues. For example, the CIF generates much of its revenue via gate receipts from championship competitions, preseason games and tournaments, and sanctioned invitational tournaments and meets. Other revenue sources for associations include membership dues, officials' registration fees, media contracts, corporate sponsorship, licensing, and royalties. As nonprofit organizations, state associations enjoy tax-exempt status. For example, CIF declares its tax-exempt status within its constitution (Article 1, Section 13):

The property of this organization is irrevocably dedicated to charitable and educational purposes, meeting the requirements for exemption provided by Section 214 of the Revenue and Taxation Code. No part of the net income or assets of this organization shall ever inure to the benefit of any director, officer, or member thereof nor to the benefit of any private persons. Upon the dissolution or winding up of the organization, which is dedicated to charitable and educational purposes meeting the requirements for exemption provided by Section 214 of the Revenue and Taxation Code, its assets remaining after payment, or provision for payment, of all debts and liabilities of this organization, shall be distributed to a non-profit fund, foundation, or corporation which is organized and operated exclusively for educational purposes and which has established its tax exempt status under Section 501C(3) of the Internal Revenue Code.

As mentioned in the beginning of the section, the majority of states have one high school association that is open to public, private, and parochial schools. However, some states have three or four different governing associations defined by geographic boundaries. For example, the cities of New York and Philadelphia have separate associations that govern the city schools that do not compete for state titles.

State associations also differ in their approach to mixing or separating public and private schools. For example, in the state of Connecticut, the Connecticut Interscholastic Athletic Conference (CIAC) is open to "any public school whose application by the Chief Officer of the School District certifies that the school meets the statutory and regulatory requirements of the State Board of Education, and any non-public school which has been approved by the State Board of Education according to the Board's 'Criteria and Procedures for Non-Public School Approval.'" In the state of Texas, membership in the state association, the University Interscholastic League (UIL), is open to open enrollment charter schools and public schools that have paid their dues. Private schools may join only upon meeting certain conditions, including showing there is no comparable private association which they may join.

The question of whether to allow private schools to compete against public schools has generated some litigation. A leading case in this area of high school association governance is *In the Matter of Kellenberg Memorial High School et al., Appellants, v. Section VIII of the New York State Public High School Athletic Association*, 679 N.Y.S.2d 660 (N.Y. App. Div. 1998). Two high schools, Kellenberg Memorial High School and Chaminade High School, were refused enrollment into the New York State Public High School Athletic Association by a vote of the members of the association, in part due to the fear that these private, not-for-profit schools would be able to recruit players to enhance their athletic teams. The court decided that the private schools failed to demonstrate a constitutionally protected interest in membership in the association and denied their petition for membership (see notes 2 and 3 for a discussion of other cases involving participation in high school associations).

While cases involving school membership in an association have increased, much of the litigation that has involved high school associations has concerned their eligibility rules. The courts have commonly allowed associations to maintain restrictive rules and regulations so long as they follow their own rules and apply the rules in a reasonable and consistent manner. For example, in the case of *Brown ex rel. Brown v. Oklahoma Secondary School ActivitiesAss'n*, 125 P.3d 1219 (Okla. 2005), a high school football player had won an injunction preventing the enforcement of his two-game suspension for unsportsmanlike misconduct.

Brown, a quarterback, was ejected from the quarterfinals for kicking an opponent who was on the ground in the helmet. The injunction forced postponement of the state semifinals and championship game. The Supreme Court of Oklahoma vacated the injunction, ruling that the suspension had been reasonably applied, the association had not acted arbitrarily or capriciously, and that deference should be given to the internal affairs of a voluntary membership association.

The courts will, however, rule against high school athletic associations if the rules they maintain are unreasonable. For example, in *Davis v. Massachusetts Interscholastic Athletic Association*, No. 94–2887, 1995 Mass. Super. LEXIS (Mass. Jan. 18, 1995), the MIAA was attempting to block a young girl who was home-schooled from participating in interscholastic athletics for her local high school. The plaintiffs received an injunction allowing her to play on the high school softball team, and the court ruled that the MIAA regulation distinguishing between home-schooled students and others "creates varying treatment of students based on in-school and home-school status and the classification and varying treatment are not rationally related to a legitimate State purpose." Therefore, the MIAA could not provide a rational basis for its rule (see section 6.1.3, "Equal Protection"). It is also important to note that an association's rules and regulations can be challenged if they violate athletes' constitutionally protected freedoms. In particular, much litigation has been initiated in the areas of drug testing and freedom of expression. Chapter 6 considers such cases, as well as others involving eligibility rules, in greater detail.

NOTES

1. For further information on the high school athletic associations mentioned in this chapter visit the following Web sites: http://www.nfhs.org (National Federation of State High School Associations), http://www.cifstate.org (California Interscholastic Federation), http://www.casciac.org (Connecticut Interscholastic Athletic Conference), http://www.uil.utexas.edu (University Interscholastic League).

2. In *Christian Heritage Academy v. Oklahoma Secondary School Activities Association (OSSAA)*, 483 F.3d 1025 (10th Cir. 2007), Christian Heritage, a private religious school in Oklahoma, sued after it was denied membership to OSSAA twice. Christian Heritage failed to receive approval from a majority of the 471 OSSAA schools, 459 of which were public. In denying their application it became apparent some public schools were concerned with the advantages a private school may have, such as the ability to offer scholarships, larger geographic areas from which to draw student-athletes and more relaxed transfer restrictions. In its second application Christian Heritage decreased its proposed geographic area but was still denied. Christian Heritage brought suit alleging violations of the equal protection and due process clauses of the 14th Amendment and the free exercise clause of the First Amendment. The district court granted OSSAA summary judgment, but the 10th Circuit reversed and remanded. The 10th Circuit ruled that the membership process, conducted by a majority vote of existing members, was not rationally related to a legitimate purpose, as required by equal protection jurisprudence.

3. In *Suburban Scholastic Council v. Section 2 of the New York State Public High School Athletic Association (NYSPHSAA)*, 803 N.Y.S.2d 270 (2005), an athletic league consisting of 12 high schools sued the NYSPHSAA, of which the league and schools were members, after the NYSPHSAA announced plans to govern regular season football schedules based on the size of the schools. Plaintiff league stated that the classification was made in disregard of the NYSPHSAA constitution and arbitrary and capricious. In affirming the state Supreme

Court's summary judgment ruling, the appeals court stated the importance of courts not interfering with the internal affairs, proceedings and rules of a high school athletic association unless there are acts of an arbitrary, capricious nature or abuse of discretion.

4. In *Archbishop Walsh High School v. Section VI of the New York State Public High School Athletic Association, Inc.*, 660 N.E.2d. 521 (N.Y. 1996), a New York court held that it was not unconstitutional for a high school athletic association to restrict its membership to nonpublic high schools. The association could provide a rational basis for its restrictive rule: that they wanted to make sure that competition between schools within its membership was even. The association feared that allowing entry to nonpublic schools increased the possibility of uneven competition.

5.2. LEGAL PRINCIPLES PERTAINING TO AMATEUR ATHLETIC ASSOCIATIONS

5.2.1. Introduction

This section explores the principles of law which pertain to amateur athletic associations, examines the structures of the organizations themselves, and further analyzes litigation involving them. Three legal concepts are particularly important to this discussion: limited judicial review, standing, and injunctive relief.

The concept of *limited judicial review* rests on the assumption that courts should defer to voluntary organizations' decisions concerning their own rules and membership. As a general rule, the judiciary intervenes only when an association's actions violate rights guaranteed by law, by the Constitution, by basic notions of fairness, or rights granted by the association itself. It should be noted that federal courts will only hear cases involving certain constitutional or federal issues, leaving most other controversies in the hands of state courts. The federal courts may thus refuse to review cases that are subject to review at the state court level. However, a case in which state action violates a federal constitutional right usually triggers judicial review at the federal level.

The concept of *standing* refers to a party's right to be in court, and the plaintiff must demonstrate it prior to the initiation of any lawsuit. The requirement of standing is based on the theory that all cases brought before the legal system must be part of an ongoing controversy, involving the actual interests of those at the bar. Academic curiosity or contrived situations are not sufficient requisites for a plaintiff to demonstrate standing.

The type of relief granted in cases concerning athletic associations is the third important legal concept. Two types of relief are commonly sought: monetary damages and injunctive relief. Since monetary damages do not always give the plaintiff appropriate or adequate relief, the equitable remedy of injunctive relief is available. *Injunctive relief* is a fair, nondiscriminatory form of judgment to redress a wrong or an injury. Injunctive relief consists of a court order to one party either to do or refrain from doing a specific action. This type of relief is particularly important in sports in cases of eligibility and participation. Time is often of the essence, and injunctive relief may be critical to the student-athlete since it allows him or her to continue competing.

5.2.2. Judicial Review

College and high school administrators make decisions and take actions regarding rules and regulations every day, and it is important to stress that the courts can review some of these decisions. Prior to the 1960s, courts had refused to intervene in the internal affairs of organizations that govern any aspect of a school's athletic program. However, beginning in the early 1960s, student-athletes began to challenge the authority that was delegated to directors of athletic programs because, in some instances, these administrators were regulating personal behavior, including marriage and physical appearance. Courts accepted jurisdiction over these cases and invalidated rules that interfered with constitutional rights of individual participants. Since the 1980s, however, rules concerning physical appearance and marriage have not been frequently challenged, and consequently cases in these areas have not frequently reached the court system.

However, there have been numerous challenges involving athletic eligibility and team eligibility. As a general rule, the courts will review a voluntary association's rules only if one of the following conditions are present:

1. The rules violate public policy because they are fraudulent or unreasonable.
2. The rules exceed the scope of the association's authority.
3. The organization violates one of its own rules.
4. The rules are applied unreasonably or arbitrarily.
5. The rules violate a law.
6. The rules violate an individual's constitutional rights.

Even if a rule is subject to review, the role of the court is very limited. A court will not usually review the merits of the rule involved. It will only determine whether the rule or the enforcement of the rule is invalid by virtue of the six standards. If a violation is found, the court will order the association to take corrective action consistent with the court's decision. Constitutional violations that require judicial intervention are based on either due process or equal protection considerations. Due process involves infringements on life, liberty, or property; equal protection involves the fair application of laws to individuals. Both of these constitutional standards require that state action be present prior to judicial review (see sections 6.1.1–6.1.3).

Athletic associations can guard against judicial scrutiny by reviewing and updating rules and regulations so that they (1) protect the health and welfare of athletes and serve to protect a justifiable public interest and (2) are consistent with court decisions in the state, region, or nation regarding similar rules. If a case is brought, the court is then more likely to defer to the judgment of the athletic administrators who created these rules and are best equipped to decide controversies concerning them. Absent violation of existing law or of the Constitution, only evidence of fraud, collusion, or unreasonable, arbitrary, or capricious action will cause a court to intervene on behalf of an athlete concerning the interpretation of a rule.

NOTES

In the following cases, courts used judicial review to examine cases involving voluntary athletic associations:

1. In *Thomka v. Massachusetts Interscholastic Athletic Association, Inc. (MIAA)*, 2007 WL 867084 (Mass. Super. February 12, 2007), a female high school golfer brought suit claiming that she should be allowed to compete in the boys' individual state championship during the fall season. The boys' championship had a higher level of competition and greater attendance by college coaches and recruiters and may have given Thomka a better chance to showcase her golfing talents, as she contended. Thomka participated on a

mixed-gender team that played only in the fall. By 2007, Thomka was a three-time runner-up in the girls' individual championship that occurred in the spring but was at a disadvantage because she was not participating while in season like other girls. As a sophomore, Thomka shot 74 from the front tees in the team regional tournament, which would have qualified her for the boys' individual championship had she been allowed to compete. Her request for an injunction was granted and she participated in the 2005 boys' individual championship from the back tees. She did not qualify in 2006. Following the injunction, the Superior Court of Massachusetts declared that the rule violated the Massachusetts Equal Rights Amendment by unfairly discriminating on the basis of sex and enjoined the MIAA from enforcing the rule. In sum, the court felt that the spring tournament was not an equal opportunity for girls playing on mixed-gender teams in the fall.

2. In *Indiana High School Athletic Association v. Durham*, 748 N.E.2d 404 (Ind. Ct. App. 2001), the Indiana High School Athletic Association (IHSAA) argued that the trial court should not have been able to issue a permanent injunction to the athlete, Durham, because the court "failed to apply the deferential standard of review afforded to its administrative rulings in granting Durham's request for a permanent injunction." The appellate court agreed with the trial court's issuance of the injunction and use of judicial review, stating, "Given the evidence in this case, the trial court did not abuse its discretion in overturning the IHSAA's denial of full eligibility and refusal to grant a hardship exception. While it may be true that in other cases we have recognized the IHSAA's broad discretion in refusing to grant a student a hardship exception, this discretion is not unreviewable and is subject to the arbitrary and capricious standard upon review."

In the following cases, the court deferred to decisions of voluntary associations.

1. In *Rodriguez v. New York State Public High School Athletic Association*, 809 N.Y.S.2d 483 (Table) (2005), after the State Wrestling Protest Committee refused to overturn a referee's penalty assessed against a high school wrestler, Rodriguez, during a State Wrestling Championship match, the wrestler brought suit. At the conclusion of the 135-pound state championship match that Rodriguez had won 7–6, Rodriguez threw his headgear 20–30 feet in the air, and it landed near the scorer's table. As a result, Rodriguez was penalized for unsportsmanlike conduct, giving his opponent the necessary two points to beat him and claim the title. It was determined that Rodriguez's behavior constituted in-match behavior because he had not yet shook hands with his opponent as required by state rules. In dismissing the case, the court stated the importance of courts not interfering with the internal affairs, proceedings, and rules of a high school athletic association unless there are acts of an arbitrary, capricious nature or abuse of discretion.

2. In the case of *Hart v. NCAA*, 550 S.E.2d 79 (W. Va. 2001), the NCAA appealed a preliminary injunction that was awarded to Hart, a wrestler at Appalachian State University, which allowed him to participate in a fifth season of eligibility under NCAA rules. The appellate court overturned the injunction, deciding that the circuit court had abused its discretion in ordering the injunction for Hart. The district court made an erroneous decision in granting the preliminary injunction because Hart did not possess a right to participate in intercollegiate wrestling that merited protection by an issuance of an injunction.

3. In *Phillip v. Fairfield University*, 118 F. 3d 131 (2nd Cir. 1997), Fairfield University and the NCAA appealed the decision of a trial court to issue a preliminary injunction allowing a student-athlete to compete although he had not satisfied NCAA initial eligibility requirements. The appellate court overturned the decision of the trial court, concluding that the trial court had erred in assessing that the NCAA had arbitrarily not granted Phillip a waiver. The appellate court stated, "The district court purported to find without adequate explanation that some sort of a contractual duty was owed by the NCAA to Phillip as a result of the contracts between Fairfield and the NCAA and Phillip and the NCAA. We express no view of whether such a duty did exist. However, we think it clear that the district court erred in finding that the NCAA evidenced bad faith simply by acting arbitrarily."

For the proposition that harshness by itself is not grounds for judicial review, see the following cases.

1. In *Dempsey v. State*, WL 3933737 (Del. Ch. December 21, 2006), a Delaware state court upheld the Delaware Interscholastic Athletic Association's (DIAA) refusal to grant the plaintiff a "hardship" waiver that would have given him a fifth year of eligibility. Dempsey claimed that as a result of his mother's debilitating car accident, he was forced to take on extraordinary tasks to care for her and his siblings during ninth grade, the 2002–2003 academic year. The extra duties negatively affected his school work to the point where he was forced to repeat ninth grade. In ruling against Dempsey, the DIAA noted that he had failed to produce any witnesses or evidence of his mother's condition or accident. Also, the DIAA could not find a causal connection between the alleged hardship and his academic struggles, finding it was his failure to attend summer school and his poor academic performance during 2004–2005 that delayed his graduation. The court refused to grant a temporary restraining order because there was no evidence that Dempsey would suffer substantial and irreparable harm and he had failed to exhaust his administrative remedies.

2. In *Florida High School Athletic Association (FHSAA) v. Marazzito*, 891 So.2d 653 (2005), the FHSAA appealed an injunction that granted a high school baseball player an extra year of eligibility. The appellate court reversed, holding that there were no exceptional circumstances which justified interfering with the internal affairs of a voluntary membership association such as the FHSAA.

3. In *Indiana High School Athletic Association v. Vasario*, 726 N.E.2d 325 (Ind. Ct. App. 2000), a student in a foreign exchange program of study in the state was denied participation in interscholastic athletics. The ISHAA rule stated that all exchange programs must be approved programs if a student wished to participate in athletics. The plaintiff's program had lost its official approval, and therefore he was not able to participate. The court, reversing a trial court ruling, held that the rule was not arbitrary or capricious, and did not violate any of the plaintiff's rights.

Certain federal statutes are commonly cited in an effort to obtain federal court jurisdiction in athletic cases. Among them are the following:

(a) 28 U.S.C. section 1343—Civil Rights and Elective Franchise.

The district courts shall have original jurisdiction of any civil action authorized by law to be commenced by any person:

(1) To recover damages for injury to his person or property, or because of the deprivation of any right or privilege of a citizen of the United States, by any act done in furtherance of any conspiracy mentioned in section 1985 of Title 42;

(2) To recover damages from any person who fails to prevent or to aid in preventing any wrongs mentioned in section 1985 of Title 42 which he had knowledge were about to occur and power to prevent;

(3) To redress the deprivation, under color of any State law, statute, ordinance, regulation, custom or usage, of any right, privilege or immunity secured by the Constitution of the United States or by any Act of Congress providing for equal rights of citizens or of all persons within the jurisdiction of the United States;

(4) To recover damages or to secure equitable or other relief under any Act of Congress providing for the protection of civil rights, including the right to vote.

For purposes of this section—

(1) the District of Columbia shall be considered to be a State; and

(2) any Act of Congress applicable exclusively to the District of Columbia shall be considered to be a statute of the District of Columbia.

(b) 42 U.S.C. section 1983—Civil Action for Deprivation of Rights.

"Every person who, under color of any statute, ordinance, regulation, custom, or usage, of any State, Territory, or the District of Columbia, subjects, or causes to be subjected, any citizen of the United States or other person within the jurisdiction thereof to the deprivation of any rights, privileges, or immunities secured by the Constitution and laws, shall be liable to the party injured in an action at law, suit in equity, or other proper proceeding for redress, except that in any action brought against a judicial officer for an act or omission taken in such officer's judicial capacity, injunctive relief shall not be granted unless a declaratory decree was violated or declaratory relief was unavailable. For the purposes of this section, any Act of Congress applicable exclusively to the District of Columbia shall be considered to be a statute of the District of Columbia."

5.2.3. Standing

In order to establish standing in court, the plaintiff must satisfy three criteria. First, the plaintiff must demonstrate that the action in question did in fact cause an injury. Second, the plaintiff must establish that the interest to be protected is at least arguably within the zone of interests protected by the Constitution, relevant laws, or other legal principles. Finally, the plaintiff must be the party whose interest was infringed upon; that is, the plaintiff must be an interested party or be otherwise directly involved. If the plaintiff has only a peripheral interest, there will be no standing. This often applies in the case of an amateur association and one of its member institutions. An individual student-athlete is not directly involved in the controversy because the individual is not a member of the amateur association. Consequently, a student-athlete who brings suit must show actual harm that has occurred to him or her. An example is the NCAA, whose membership consists of colleges and universities, and not of individual student-athletes.

NOTES _____

1. In *Pelletier v. Maine Principals' Association (MPA)*, 261 F. Supp. 2d 10 (D.Me. 2003), parents of home-schooled children requested injunctive relief that would allow their children to participate in interscholastic athletics at a local Christian school, Seacoast, rather than the local public school as provided by Maine law. The Pelletiers contended that the MPA's refusal to allow them to compete at Seacoast violated their constitutional rights to due process and freedom of religion and also violated the equal protection rights of Seacoast. In denying the injunction, the court ruled among other things that the Pelletiers had no standing to bring a constitutional argument on behalf of Seacoast because Seacoast was more than capable of making the argument if it so chose.

2. In *Hairston v. National Collegiate Athletic Association*, 101 F.3d 1315 (9th Cir. 1997), former and current University of Washington football players brought action against the Pac-10 Conference and the NCAA for sanctions that the football program received after findings of recruiting violations. The majority opinion does not touch upon the issue of standing because it does not see it as relevant; however, in a concurring opinion, the concurring judge states, "The practical consequences of allowing the players to bring this lawsuit after their university—which has suffered enormous economic losses—has agreed to the sanctions, demonstrates that the players are not the proper antitrust plaintiffs. If we were to hold that these four players had antitrust standing to alter the sanctions against the UW, we would invite numerous groups of indirectly injured parties to bring antitrust lawsuits and argue that the Pac-10 should have imposed different sanctions or remedies."

5.2.4. Injunctive Relief

Provided the plaintiff has established standing and the court has decided to review the case, the next step is to request relief. When enforcement of an athletic association's rules prohibits an athlete from competing, of the preferred relief is an injunction that forces the association to allow the student-athlete to participate. Efforts to keep the student-athlete eligible may be critical to the high school athlete hoping to obtain a college scholarship, to the collegiate athletic program striving for a profitable and prestigious winning team and possibly to the student-athlete's eventual professional career. Injunctive relief is critical to a student-athlete because it allows the athlete to compete for his or her school pending trial. In many cases, by the time a trial on the merits of a case and an appeal take place, the situation becomes moot because the player has completed his or her season(s) of play.

An injunction is a court order for one of the parties to a lawsuit to behave in a certain manner. Injunctive relief is designed to prevent future wrongs—not to punish acts. Injunctive relief is also applied to prevent current wrongs from being perpetuated. It is used only to prevent irreparable injury, which is suffered when monetary damages cannot be calculated because money will not adequately compensate the injured party. Irreparable injuries include the risk of physical harm or death, the loss of some special opportunity, or the deprivation of unique, irreplaceable property. For example, a high school football star who may have violated a school rule may request an injunction to compete in the all-star game because an inability to do so would cause irreparable harm such as jeopardizing his chances of obtaining a college scholarship.

Thus, the injunction is a form of equitable relief that can be used to force an athletic association to engage in or refrain from an action that affects an institution, an individual student-athlete, or a staff member. There are three types of injunctive relief: a *temporary restraining order*, a *preliminary injunction*, and a *permanent injunction*. A *temporary restraining order* is issued to the plaintiff in emergency situations only and is usually effective for a maximum of 10–20 days. The defendant is not bound by the injunction until actual notice is received, although the plaintiff may obtain a temporary restraining order without notice to the defendant if irreparable harm appears certain and imminent. After receiving notice, the defendant can immediately ask the court for a review. A *preliminary injunction* is granted prior to a full hearing and disposition of a case. The plaintiff is obligated to give the defendant notice and also to post a bond. The defendant is usually present at the preliminary injunction hearing. A hearing on the issuance of a preliminary injunction is granted only under urgent circumstances and only if the plaintiff shows a likelihood of winning the case on the merits. Temporary restraining orders or preliminary injunctions may also be granted during the course of a trial to preserve the status quo until the rights of the litigants can be determined. A *permanent injunction* may be issued after a full hearing, and if it is issued, it remains in force indefinitely.

The issuance of any injunctive relief requires the exercise of sound judicial discretion. A judge generally considers three factors before granting or denying any form of judicial relief: the nature of the controversy, the objective of the injunction, and the comparative hardship or inconvenience to both parties. The judge then weighs these factors on a sliding scale before making a determination, for example, the more likely a plaintiff is to succeed on the merits at trial, the less harm the plaintiff needs to show to obtain relief. However, if the prospects of success on the merits of the case are not as strong, a plaintiff would have to show a far greater degree of potential harm before relief would be granted.

An example of the use of the preliminary injunction by a student-athlete is the case of *Pagnotta v. Pennsylvania Interscholastic Athletic Association*, 681 A.2d 235

(Pa. Commw. Ct. 1996). Pagnotta, a high school wrestler in the Methacton School District, was disqualified from continuing to participate in the state wrestling tournament as a result of being suspended for striking an opponent with his open hand after the opponent allegedly bit his finger during the match. Pagnotta was awarded a preliminary injunction from the trial court and was allowed to participate in the remainder of the state tournament. By the time the PIAA was able to have its appeal heard, the tournament had been completed, and the case before the court was dismissed as moot, thus dismissing the claims that association's rulings should not be subject to judicial review.

NOTES

1. In *Brown ex rel. Brown v. Oklahoma Secondary School Activities Ass'n*, 125 P.3d 1219 (Okla. 2005), a high school football player was granted an injunction preventing the enforcement of his two-game suspension for unsportsmanlike misconduct. Brown, a quarterback, was ejected from the quarterfinal game for kicking an opponent in the helmet while he was on the ground during a fight between the teams. As a result of the injunction, the association postponed the semifinal and state championship games. The Supreme Court of Oklahoma vacated the injunction 20 days after the incident, ruling that the suspension was reasonably applied, the association did not act arbitrarily or capriciously in postponing the next rounds of the playoffs, and deference should be given to the internal affairs of a voluntary membership association.

2. In *NCAA v. Yeo*, 171 S.W.3d 863 (Tex. 2005), a swimmer on the Singapore Olympic team followed her college coach from the University of California, Berkeley to the University of Texas, Austin. Yeo challenged the NCAA rule requiring an athlete transferring from one four-year institution to another to sit out one full academic year. Yeo swam in the Olympics during the fall of 2000 and took no classes at Texas. After sitting out the spring 2001 semester, Yeo and Texas believed she was free to swim for Texas in the fall of 2002. UC Berkeley complained, and the NCAA ordered Yeo to sit out the remainder of the fall 2002 season and four events in the spring 2002 season because she had swam four events in the fall. Texas then added three events to the beginning of the spring season that Yeo sat out and one regularly scheduled event. UC Berkeley again complained, and the NCAA ruled that the added events could not be counted toward the one-year restriction. Yeo filed for and was granted a temporary injunction to perform at the NCAA championships. A trial court subsequently determined that Texas had deprived Yeo of a protected liberty and property interest for disqualifying her from the event. Yeo argued that because of her unique reputation and earning potential, she was entitled to a full hearing before the NCAA. In reversing the lower courts, the Supreme Court of Texas held that Yeo's reputation is entitled to protection but denied that it was due any greater protection than that of the average athlete.

3. In *Cruz v. Pennsylvania Interscholastic Athletic Association*, 157 F. Supp. 2d 485 (E.D. Pa 2001), the court granted a permanent injunction to allow the plaintiff, Luiz Cruz, to participate in interscholastic athletics after the age of 18 due to learning disabilities. The association rule did not allow Cruz to participate. The court, taking a very active stance in this case, ordered not only that Cruz receive the permanent injunction but also that the association should adopt a waiver procedure to deal with Cruz and other students in similar situations.

5.3. ASSOCIATION ENFORCEMENT AUTHORITY

5.3.1. Introduction

The authority of athletic associations to regulate their membership derives from two sources. First, as corporate bodies, athletic associations must be recognized as entities of the state. Associations, once formed, create rules to govern their members. After those rules are created, the association takes on the role of enforcing those rules, similar to the functions of the state government. Second, in order for the association to govern effectively, members must agree to be so regulated. When, for example, a school chooses to enter an association, it voluntarily agrees to abide by the rules that the association sets forth.

At the collegiate level, the stakes of revenue-producing sports such as football and basketball have made it necessary to police a university's athletic programs strictly for rules violations. At the interscholastic level, often there is pressure to produce high-quality athletes and win, and this pressure can lead to violations of academic eligibility as well as recruiting violations.

5.3.2. NCAA Enforcement Procedure

The NCAA is a voluntary association whose members agree to honor certain conditions and obligations of membership, including the obligation to conduct their institutional athletic programs in a manner consistent with NCAA legislation. The enforcement procedure rules, as well as the NCAA rules, are published annually in the *NCAA Manual*, which is available to every member of the association. It is important to note that *schools* are the members of the NCAA and not individual athletes and coaches. Athletic directors, faculty athletic representatives, and college/university presidents represent the institutions in the NCAA proceedings.

The first NCAA enforcement program was enacted by the association in 1948 and was designed to address recruiting abuses. The NCAA created a Constitutional Compliance Committee to interpret the new code and investigate violations. The Constitutional Compliance Committee was replaced in 1951 by the Committee on Infractions, which was given broader investigative powers. In 1973, the NCAA membership voted to divide the responsibilities between the Enforcement Staff (investigations) and the Committee on Infractions (hearings).

As a result of a perceived integrity crisis in the early 1980s, the NCAA called a special summer convention (only the fifth in its history) and enacted stronger enforcement and penalty procedures for member schools that violate NCAA regulations. The "death penalty" was created, allowing an institution found in violation of a major NCAA rule twice in five years to be suspended from play for up to two years. Southern Methodist University (SMU) received the NCAA's death penalty due to a multitude of serious football recruiting violations, culminating in a finding that alumni boosters had paid athletes more than $60,000 during the 1986 season. SMU was forced to suspend play in football for the 1987 season and voluntarily chose to opt out of the 1988 season. The penalty so weakened the program that it has enjoyed only one winning season in twenty years since the lifting of the suspension. Stiff penalties against programs such as the UNLV men's basketball program (see the introduction to this chapter) were attempts by the NCAA to send a message of intolerance for lack of control over athletic programs.

Notwithstanding the two-year bowl ban and five-year probation handed to the University of Alabama's football program in 2002, the NCAA has been more lenient in its penalty enforcement since giving the death penalty to SMU, although some institutions' actions have arguably rivaled those of SMU. As will be seen in the following sections, the NCAA now asks athletic programs to conduct institutional reviews of their own athletic programs, and penalties have gradually become less harsh for academic, recruiting, and institutional control violations.

5.3.2.1. Committee on Infractions

The creation of the Committee on Infractions over 50 years ago demonstrates the NCAA's long-standing concern about issues that continue to arise today. In the early 1950s, there were a series of gambling-related scandals involving some of the top men's basketball teams of the time, including the City College of New York (CCNY), Manhattan College, and the University of Kentucky. Numerous players and gamblers were imprisoned, CCNY was banned from playing in Madison Square Garden, and Kentucky was forced to cancel its 1952–1953 season. As a result of the scandal, the NCAA was compelled to create the Committee on Infractions (COI). Since 1953, the COI has been an adjudication arm of the NCAA, responsible for administrating the NCAA enforcement program. The NCAA enforcement program is designed to "eliminate violations of NCAA rules and impose appropriate penalties should violations occur" (*2009–2010 NCAA Manual*, Bylaw 19.01.1).

The COI consists of 10 members, at least 7 of whom must be from NCAA member institutions and at least 2 of whom must be members of the general public with no affiliation with any institution or sports organization. In addition, at least two members of the committee must be women and two must be men. Committee members are elected to three-year terms but cannot serve more than nine years on the committee (*2009–2010 NCAA Manual*, Bylaw 19.1.1). It is the COI's duty to consider complaints filed by the NCAA enforcement staff, determine the facts, and find possible violations of NCAA rules and requirements. If a violation is found, the COI can impose the appropriate penalty (*2009–2010 NCAA Manual*, Bylaw 19.1.3). Self-disclosure, cooperation, and voluntary corrective measures by an institution often serve as mitigating factors. In addition, the COI may grant limited immunity to cooperative student-athletes who have important information (*2009–2010 NCAA Manual*, Bylaw 32.3.8).

There are two types of violations, secondary and major; a secondary violation is one that is "isolated or inadvertent in nature, provides or is intended to provide only a minimal recruiting, competitive or other advantage and does not include any significant recruiting inducement or extra benefit" (*2009–2010 NCAA Manual*, Bylaw 19.02.2.1). Major violations are all others, "specifically including those that provide an extensive recruiting or competitive advantage" (*2009–2010 NCAA Manual*, Bylaw 19.02.2.2). Penalties for secondary violations range from something as small as a letter in the school's file to suspensions, fines, reduction in scholarships and vacation of wins (*2009–2010 NCAA Manual*, Bylaw 19.5.1). Major penalties can prohibit certain recruiting activities, require termination of involved individuals, and ineligibility for regular season or postseason events (*2009–2010 NCAA Manual*, Bylaw 19.5.2). There have been over 600 major infractions cases since 1953.

The harshest penalty possible is the so-called death penalty, only given twice in the history of the NCAA. The death penalty is the NCAA's ability to eliminate an institution's scholarships or prohibit certain institutions from not participating in certain sports for a period of time. Institutions can receive the death penalty if they are found guilty of a major violation within five years of the starting date of a previous major penalty (*2009–2010 NCAA Manual*, Bylaw 19.5.2.3). The first time the death penalty was used was on the previously mentioned 1952–1953 Kentucky men's basketball team. The second and more famous use of the death penalty was on the Southern Methodist University (SMU) football team from 1986 to 1988. After having been placed on three years' probation in 1985, it was determined in 1986 that 21 players of the football team had been paid a total of approximately $61,000. SMU officials compounded the violation by lying about it to NCAA officials. As a result SMU was banned from playing football in 1987, banned from playing home games in 1988, and banned from bowl games through 1989, and its probation was extended to 1990. In addition, the team was limited to how many assistant coaches it could hire, and it lost 55 scholarships over four years. Unable to field a competitive team in 1988, that season was voluntarily canceled by SMU.

The Division I COI meets approximately six teams each year to conduct hearings. At the hearings, the NCAA enforcement staff will present the allegations and then the relevant parties of the institution, whether they are athletic directors, coaches, athletes, or their legal counsel, will have a chance to present a defense. At the conclusion of the hearing, the COI will determine the facts and impose penalties when appropriate. Six to eight weeks later, the COI will issue a Public Infractions Report laying out the penalties and the committee's rationale used in making its decisions.

In June 2003, University of Washington football coach Rick Neuheisel was fired after it was revealed that he and three friends had participated in past NCAA men's basketball tournament pools and won over $11,000 (see note 2). NCAA rules do not allow coaches, athletes, or staff members to gamble on college sports, although the rules do not specifically address such pools. The COI cited Washington for impermissible gambling activities, failure to monitor, and unrelated recruiting violations. Noting Washington's self-corrective action in firing Neuheisel, the university was given probation and the amount of allowable paid visits for recruits was reduced. It was not the first time Neuheisel ran afoul of NCAA violations (see note 6).

In 2003, Division II Morehouse College found the violations of its men's soccer program so egregious that it voluntarily disbanded the team permanently. From 1999 to 2001, it was found that former professional soccer players, players not yet cleared by the NCAA, and players not enrolled at the institution participated in NCAA matches. In addition, the head coach provided improper benefits, helped change the grades of a player, and financially rewarded players for accumulating red cards. In addition to the violations of amateurism and eligibility, Morehouse was cited for failure to monitor and lack of institutional control. As a result, the entire athletics program was given five years' probation.

From 1995 to 2000, the University of Alabama football program was involved in a string of serious and egregious violations, including recruiting inducements, violation of salary controls, and impermissible extra benefits, among others. One of the violations involved former assistant coach Ronnie Cottrell borrowing over $56,000 from a booster, failing to repay any portion of the loan for almost three years, and failing to make full disclosure of the loan to the NCAA. Cottrell and another assistant, Ivy Williams, sued the NCAA for defamation, alleging that it had made and published false statements about their activities while at Alabama. The Supreme Court of Alabama ruled for the NCAA, determining that Cottrell and Williams were limited-purpose public figures and that the NCAA did not publish the statements with actual malice (see *Cottrell v. NCAA*, 975 So.2d 306 (Ala. 2007)).

One of the boosters involved in the scandal was Ray Keller, from whom the university voluntarily disassociated itself during the NCAA investigation. Keller also sued the NCAA for defamation, citing the COI report which labeled certain boosters "rogue representatives [who] are the parasites of intercollegiate athletics." Although the report did not mention Keller by name, it was obvious from news reports that the NCAA was referring to Keller. A jury determined that Keller, a timber businessman, was not a public figure and awarded him $4.5 million.

NOTES _____

1. All COI decisions can be found from the NCAA Major Infractions Database, available at https://web1.ncaa.org/LSDBi/exec/homepage. IAC decisions can be found in the same database by checking the "Search for Appealed Cases" option.

2. Neuheisel sued the university for breach of contract, claiming he was fired without cause. Neuheisel also sued the NCAA claiming that NCAA investigators interviewed Neuheisel about the gambling accusations without being given proper notification of the purpose of the interview, as required by the NCAA bylaws. After five weeks of trial, in March 2005, the University and the NCAA settled the lawsuit for approximately $4.5 million.

3. In Baylor University Public Infractions Report (June 23, 2005), the men's basketball team was involved in "multiple, intentional and serious violations of NCAA rules" that former head coach Dave Bliss himself described as "despicable." Following the murder of Baylor basketball player Patrick Dennehy by teammate Carlton Dotson, Bliss lied to NCAA investigators and tried to get other student-athletes to also lie. In addition, it was determined that Bliss and his staff paid tuition bills for players; provided meals, cash, and transportation to players; and failed to properly report failed drug tests by student-athletes. The COI compared the case to the SMU football team given the death penalty in the late 1980s but differentiated the situation by noting Baylor's "decisive and meaningful action to stop the violations and to punish itself and the involved individuals." For findings of impermissible benefits, impermissible inducements, impermissible financial assistance, failing to follow procedures for reporting banned drug use, impermissible tryouts, extra benefits, impermissible contacts, unethical conduct, lack of institutional control, failure to monitor, and academic fraud, the university was given five years' probation, the men's basketball team's schedule was limited to conference games only in the 2004–2005 season, and there was a reduction in scholarships and limitations on recruiting activities. Bliss received a 10-year show cause order, while one assistant received a 7-year show cause order and two others received 5-year show cause orders.

4. In University of Missouri, Columbia Public Infractions Report (November 3, 2004), the COI found that the Missouri men's basketball coaches, led by head coach Quin Snyder, engaged in impermissible contact and provided impermissible benefits to 11 different recruits from 1999 to 2003. Specifically, Quinn provided junior college transfer Ricky Clemons gifts, transportation, and food and facilitated the payment of his $1,000 bail bond after he was arrested for battery. As a result, the university was cited for violations of recruiting legislation and honesty standards, impermissible contacts, impermissible extra benefits, and failure to monitor. Missouri was given three years' probation, scholarships were reduced, and the men's basketball team was prohibited from off-campus recruiting for one year. Snyder was given a letter of admonishment and his salary was frozen, but he kept his job, until he resigned following the 2005–2006 season.

5. In St. Bonaventure University Public Infractions Report (February 19, 2004), the men's basketball team was given three years' probation, a one-year postseason ban, a reduction in scholarships, and vacation of records and was forced to repay the Atlantic 10 Conference $115,943 for inappropriately certifying the eligibility of an ineligible player, changing his grade, and permitting him to participate in the 2002–2003 season. At the request of men's basketball coach Jan van Breda Kolff, university president Robert Wickenheiser certified the eligibility of junior college transfer Jamil Terrell, who only held a

certificate in welding, insufficient to meet NCAA junior college academic requirements. When the scandal broke, the team voted not to play its final two A-10 games, resulting in fines, and Van Breda Kolff was fired. St. Bonaventure was cited for failure to properly certify a student-athlete, extra benefits, impermissible academic arrangements, lack of institutional control, and unethical conduct.

6. In *University of Colorado, Boulder Public Infractions Report* (October 8, 2002), the Colorado football team was found to have committed a number of violations related to recruiting from 1995 to 1999. Head coach Rick Neuheisel and his staff were found to have had impermissible recruiting contacts with at least 26 prospective student-athletes. They also provided impermissible recruiting inducements, impermissible recruiting publicity, and excessive recruiting expense reimbursements. Colorado was cited for failure to monitor. For the self-described "creative" recruiting methods, Colorado football was put on two years' probation, lost five scholarships for one season, and the amount of expense paid visits was decreased. Neuheisel left Colorado for the University of Washington in 1999 and was given a two-year ban on off-campus recruiting.

7. In *University of Minnesota, Twin Cities Public Infractions Report* (July 2, 2002 and October 24, 2000) the Minnesota men's and women's basketball programs were involved in a series of scandals that resulted in a postseason ban, probation, reduction in scholarships and official visits, vacation of records, show cause orders, and other penalties. From 1994 to 1998, a secretary in the athletics academic counseling office partially or completely did approximately 400 pieces of course work for at least 18 men's basketball players, including papers, homework, and take-home exams. Minnesota men's basketball head coach, Clem Haskins, paid for a trip to Hawaii and gave $3,000 to the secretary for her work. The Committee on Infractions called the violations "among the most serious academic fraud violations to come before it in the past 20 years." Minnesota was found guilty of academic fraud, unethical conduct, extra benefits, failure to comply with eligibility requirements, lack of institutional control, and other violations. For his complicity in the scheme Haskins was given a seven-year show cause order, a penalty affirmed by the IAC. Haskins originally denied knowledge of the arrangement and accepted a buyout of his contract for $1.5 million. When Haskins later admitted lying to investigators, Minnesota sued. An arbitrator ordered Haskins to repay $815,000, and the award was upheld by the Hennpein County District Court, *University of Minnesota v. Haskins*, File No. 00-12750 (2002).

While on probation from the men's basketball scandal, members of the women's basketball team met with the athletic director with concerns about possible NCAA violations by head coach Cheryl Littlejohn. Minnesota alerted the NCAA and, after an internal investigation, fired Littlejohn. During 1998 and 1999, Littlejohn arranged for impermissible reduced-cost housing, provided extra benefits to recruits and athletes, such as transportation and cash and other violations warranting findings of recruiting inducements and violations, extra benefits, violation of off-campus recruiting contact legislation, unethical conduct, and lack of institutional control. As a repeat violator, the COI extended Minnesota's probation, reduced scholarships available to the women's basketball team, limited the number of official visits, and delayed the start of practice. Littlejohn was given a two-year show cause order.

5.3.2.2. Infractions Appeals Committee

Prior to 1992, all decisions by the COI were final and binding. However, in 1977, when the COI found that the UNLV men's basketball team was alleged to have committed 38 violations, 10 by head coach Jerry Tarkanian, Tarkanian brought suit in Nevada state court alleging that he had been deprived of his 14th Amendment due process rights. The team had been placed on two years' probation, and UNLV was given a show cause order, requiring it to show cause why the NCAA should not impose further penalties if it did not sever ties with Tarkanian. Ultimately, the Nevada Supreme Court granted Tarkanian injunctive relief and awarded him attorney's fees (*Tarkanian v. NCAA*, 103 Nev. 331 (Nev. 1987)). The Nevada Supreme Court held that the action of the NCAA was state action, requiring procedural due process. Furthermore, it was determined that Tarkanian had a due process property and liberty interest in keeping his coaching position. The U.S. Supreme Court reversed, holding that the disciplinary actions of UNLV in compliance with NCAA rules and recommendations was private conduct by the NCAA and was not performed "under color of" state law (*NCAA v. Tarkanian*, 488 U.S. 179 (1988)). Although the NCAA won the most important battle, enough scrutiny of its methods had occurred eventually prompting the creation of the Infractions Appeals Committee (IAC).

An institution or individual may appeal penalties imposed by the COI to the IAC by giving written notice to "the NCAA President not later than 15 calendar days from the date of the public release of the committee's report" (*2009–2010 NCAA Manual*, Bylaw 32.10.1). A penalty may not be set aside unless the IAC determines the penalty to be excessive or inappropriate based on all the evidence and circumstances (*2009–2010 NCAA Manual*, Bylaw 32.10.2). Determinations of fact and violations arrived at by the Committee on Infractions shall not be set aside on appeal, except on a showing that

1. The Committee on Infractions finding clearly is contrary to the evidence presented to the committee
2. The facts found by the Committee on Infractions do not constitute a violation of the Association's rules
3. A procedural error affected the reliability of the information that was used to support the Committee on Infractions' finding (*2009–2010 NCAA Manual*, Bylaw 32.10.2)

The IAC consists of five members, including at least one person from the general public. Members are elected to three-year terms, and no member can serve more than nine years on the committee (*2009–2010 NCAA Manual*, Bylaw 19.2.1). Since the establishment of the IAC in 1992, 42 cases have been appealed. When a case is appealed, the COI files a response, detailing the facts, violations and penalties of the case. A hearing is then held where each side is able to present its case after which the IAC makes its final decision. "Any decision in an infractions case by the Infractions Appeals Committee shall be considered final" (*2009–2010 NCAA Manual*, Bylaw 32.11.4).

In March 2006, the COI cited former Ohio State men's basketball coach Jim O'Brien for illegal recruiting inducements, impermissible extra benefits, violation of ethical conduct principles, and failure to monitor. O'Brien admitted to having given $6,000 to Alex Radojevic, a recruit that had signed a national letter of intent to attend Ohio State in 1999. O'Brien contended the money was a loan to aid Radojevic's family in war-torn Yugoslavia. Nevertheless, O'Brien was given a five-year show cause order by the COI.

O'Brien appealed his penalty to the IAC claiming that the findings were contrary to the evidence presented, that procedural error affected the reliability of the information used by the COI, and that his acts did not violate NCAA rules because he knew Radojevic was ineligible, having been paid to play in Yugoslavia. Ultimately, the IAC reversed the ruling with regard to Radojevic because the four-year statute of limitations had expired. On remand, the COI reduced O'Brien's show cause order to two years. O'Brien sued the university, claiming he was fired without cause (see note 2).

NOTES

1. In *Florida State University Infractions Appeals Report* (January 5, 2010), Florida State was placed on four years' probation, forced to vacate records, and forced to reduce scholarships in 10 men's and women's sports as a result of a widespread academic fraud scandal. The case got most of its attention because former Florida State football coach Bobby Bowden was forced 14 wins from his 389 career total, second most in college football history. The IAC ruled that the penalties imposed by the COI were not excessive and were not an abuse of discretion.

2. O'Brien was fired in April 2004 after he told Ohio State athletic director Andy Geiger about the 1999 loan, who reported the violation to the NCAA. Although the court found that O'Brien had reasonable cause to believe that he had committed an NCAA infraction in breach of his contract, the court ruled that O'Brien's failure to report the infraction was not a material breach that would give Ohio State cause for termination. O'Brien was awarded $2,253,619.45; see *O'Brien v. The Ohio State Univ.*, 2006 WL 571043 (Ohio Ct.Cl. February 15, 2006), *aff'd*, 2007 WL 2729077 (Ohio App. 10 Dist. Sep. 20, 2007).

3. In *University of Michigan Infractions Appeals Report* (September 25, 2003), Michigan argued that a ban on postseason play for its men's basketball team for the 2003–2004 season was excessive and inappropriate. The COI determined that from 1992 through 1999, booster Ed Martin gave over $600,000 in cash, clothing, jewelry, transportation, lodging, meals, and other benefits to Michigan basketball players Chris Webber, Maurice Taylor, Robert Traylor, and Louis Bullock. The IAC agreed with Michigan, reducing the postseason ban to the original one-year self-imposed, noting that only 29.4% of postseason bans have been multiyear bans. According to the IAC, three factors to be considered when determining a ban on postseason play are whether (1) the involved individuals remain active in the program, (2) a significant competitive advantage results from the violations, or (3) the violations reflect a lack of institutional control. The IAC ruled that none of these factors was present in this case.

4. In *University of Alabama, Tuscaloosa Infractions Appeals Report* (September 17, 2002), Alabama appealed a finding that a football recruit had received $20,000 and that another player had received $100 four separate times. In addition, Alabama contended that the penalties received, including five years' probation, a two-year ban on postseason competition, reduction in scholarships, and prohibitions against noninstitutional athletic representatives, were excessive and inappropriate. Alabama was found guilty of numerous other violations that it did not appeal, such as recruiting inducements, impermissible recruiting contacts, recruiting inducements through high school coaches, violation of honesty standards, violation of employment and salary controls, recruiting violations, impermissible extra benefits, and excessive entertainment during a recruiting visit. Alabama contended that the findings about a player receiving $20,000 were barred by the statute of limitations. The violations occurred during the 1995–1996 and 1996–1997 academic years, but Alabama did not receive notice of an inquiry until February 21, 2001. NCAA rules require that the school receive notice of an inquiry within four years of the violation. However, the IAC ruled that these violations constituted one of three exceptions to the statute of limitations: that they were part of "a pattern of willful violations...[that] continued into the four-year period." In affirming the penalties, the IAC cited the amount and level of the violations, including that the university was a two-time repeat violator.

5. In *University of Kentucky Infractions Appeals Report* (September 17, 2002), Kentucky appealed an order of three years' probation, a 2002 postseason ban, and a reduction in scholarships as excessive and inappropriate in conjunction with a former football recruiting coordinator having provided numerous impermissible recruiting inducements to high school student-athletes. The IAC noted a number of factors to be considered in reviewing penalties: nature, number, and seriousness of the violations; conduct and motives of the individuals

in the violations; corrective actions taken by the institution; comparison of the penalty or penalties imposed; institutional cooperation in the investigation; impact of penalties on innocent student-athletes and coaches; NCAA policies regarding fairness in, and equitable resolution of, infractions cases. Although only a few of the prospective student-athletes actually enrolled at Kentucky, the IAC still found that Kentucky had obtained a significant recruiting advantage as a result of its conduct. Kentucky was commended for its cooperation in the investigation, but the IAC found that the ban was consistent with similar cases and provided an important deterrent effect.

5.3.2.3. NCAA Infractions Process

The processing of a typical NCAA infractions case is a lengthy process intended to draw out all the relevant facts and provide the involved parties a sufficient means to present their side of the story (see note 1). Using the context of the University of Oklahoma football case from 2007–2008 will, it is hoped, illuminate the process. On March 3, 2006, Oklahoma and the NCAA received an anonymous email alleging that three football players were paid for work they did not perform from a car dealership during 2005. Having received information indicating a possible violation, the NCAA enforcement staff sets out to substantiate and confirm the violation.

In May 2006, after discussing the allegations with two of the football players and the owner and two employees of the auto dealership, the NCAA notified Oklahoma of its investigation and received a summary of Oklahoma's internal investigation into the allegations. Over the next six months, the NCAA interviewed over a dozen people, including student-athletes, their parents, employees at the auto dealership, and Oklahoma officials. Believing the violations confirmed and finding them to be major in nature, the NCAA sent a notice of allegations to Oklahoma in February 2007. Oklahoma responded a month later, accepting some of the allegations and denying others. In an attempt to mitigate the potential penalties handed down by the COI, since learning of the allegations, Oklahoma dismissed the players in question from the team, including starting quarterback Rhett Bomar; voluntarily prohibited students from working at the auto dealership in question; and placed an increased emphasis on student-athlete employment issues to its coaches, student-athletes, and boosters.

Refusing to accept all of the findings, Oklahoma and the NCAA's enforcement staff each presented its side of the case to the Division I Committee on Infractions on April 14, 2007. Oklahoma was cited for impermissible extra benefits and failure to monitor. On July 11, the COI issued Public Infractions Report No. 270 detailing its findings and penalties. Among the penalties imposed were probation, reduction in scholarships for two seasons, vacation of the football team's 2005 record, and disassociation from the auto dealership's manager for five years.

Less than 15 days after the public release of the COI report, Oklahoma notified the Infractions Appeals Committee, in writing, of its intention to appeal certain findings and/or penalties. Within the requisite 30 days, Oklahoma filed its appeal. The COI Coordinator of Appeals was then given a 30-day period in which to respond to the appeal, to which the university was given a 14-day rebuttal period. Specifically, Oklahoma appealed the findings that the university failed to follow established institutional procedures for the monitoring of student-athletes' employment and to detect that football players were working at the auto dealership. In addition, Oklahoma claimed the penalty requiring the team to vacate all wins during the 2005 football season, an 8–4 campaign including a Holiday Bowl victory over Oregon.

The IAC can either review hold another hearing or simply review the case based on the written record, as it did in the Oklahoma case on December 15, 2007. On February 22, 2008, the IAC released its report, affirming that the university failed to follow the necessary procedures to monitor student-athlete employment but vacating the finding that the university was at fault for failing to detect that student-athletes were working at the auto dealership. As a result, the IAC also vacated the penalty requiring the vacation of Oklahoma's 2005 football record.

NOTES

1. In *Tarkanian v. NCAA*, 511 U.S. 1033 (1994), it was ruled that the NCAA is not a state actor but a private, voluntary organization. Consequently, the NCAA is not subject to the due process requirements of the U.S. Constitution. However, on its Web site, the NCAA notes that its enforcement process "contain a multitude of traditional due-process protections" (available at http://www.ncaa.org/enforcement/faq_enforcement).

2. For more on NCAA infractions cases and processes, see Glenn M. Wong, Kyle Skillman, and Chris Deubert, "The NCAA's Infractions Appeals Committee: Recent Case History, Analysis and the Beginning of a New Chapter," 9 *Virginia Sports and Entertainment Law Journal* 47 (2009); Richard R. Hilliard, Angel F. Shelton, and Kevin E. Pearson, "An Update on Recent Decisions Rendered by the NCAA Infractions Appeals Committee: Further Guidance for NCAA Member Institutions," 28 *Journal of College and University Law* 605 (2002); and Kenneth J. Martin, "The NCAA Infractions Appeals Committee: Procedure, Precedent and Penalties," 9 *Seton Hall Journal of Sports and Entertainment Law* 123 (1999).

5.3.3. The Knight Commission

In 1989, trustees of the John and James L. Knight Foundation (a philanthropic organization established by newspaper moguls in the 1950s) created a commission in order to study and reform college sports. The Knight Foundation was concerned that abuses in college athletics were threatening the integrity of higher education. The recommendations of this commission over the years have had a significant effect on NCAA rules and their enforcement, especially with regard to academic standards and progress.

The Commission on Intercollegiate Athletics began as an independent panel of 22 leaders from the fields of education, business, and sports. While this commission had no formal authority over intercollegiate athletics, the NCAA would adopt approximately two-thirds of its recommendations by 1996 (see note 1). The most significant recommendation adopted by the NCAA in the 1990s was to alter the governance structure of college athletic departments so that college presidents, not athletic departments, were placed in charge of all policy and budgeting decisions. This change has led to the application of considerably stricter academic standards to student-athletes once they are enrolled in college.

The Knight Commission reconvened in 2000 and 2001 in order to assess the impact of the NCAA's adopted changes in the 1990s. The 2000–2001 meeting included "NCAA representatives, university presidents, a trustee board chair, faculty, conference commissioners, athletic directors, coaches, athletes, authors, professional sports executives, television officials, a sports apparel representative, a gambling lobbyist, leaders of national higher education associations, and a U.S. senator," and in June 2001 produced a report titled *A Call to Action: Reconnecting Sports to Higher Education*. The language of the 2001 report is largely conciliatory, citing NCAA and university sincerity in adopting the commission's recommendations of the 1990s. However, the report makes it clear that the institutional effort in the 1990s failed to reduce corruption:

> [In the 1980s] 57 out of 106 Division I-A institutions (54 percent) had to be censured, sanctioned or put on probation for major violations of NCAA rules....In the 1990's, 58 out of 114 Division I-A colleges and universities (52 percent) were similarly penalized. In other words, more than half the institutions competing at the top levels continue to break the rules. Wrongdoing as a way of life seems to represent the status quo.

In addition to "wrongdoing," the report also noted a "financial arms race," poor graduation rates, problems of increased commercialism, and the decaying of amateur ideals: "There is no question about who is winning this open, ever escalating war between the academic and athletic cultures. In too many places, the tail already wags the dog." The report therefore crafted the following 15 recommendations for the NCAA and its member institutions:

1. Athletes should be filtered through "the same academic processes as other students," including admission standards and degree requirements.
2. By 2007, teams that do not graduate at least 50% of their players should be banned from postseason play (180 of the 321 colleges with Division I basketball teams failed to meet that standard in 2000; see note 2).
3. Scholarships should be tied to specific athletes until they (or their entering class) graduate.
4. The length of playing season, practice season, and postseason must be reduced.
5. The NBA and the NFL should be encouraged to develop minor leagues. (This would present an alternative for athletes who are not interested in or are unqualified for higher education.)
6. Football and basketball expenditures should be reduced, including the total number of scholarships that are awarded in Division I-A football.
7. Compliance with Title IX and support of women's athletics should be ensured.
8. Coaches' salaries should be reduced and "brought into line with prevailing norms across the institution."
9. Agreements for coaches' outside income should be negotiated with institutions, not individual coaches, because "advertisers are buying the institution's reputation no less than the coaches.'"
10. The NCAA plan for distribution of revenue from the CBS contract should be revised so that it is based on academic performance and gender equity compliance rather than on winning and losing.
11. Institutions alone should determine when games are played, how they are broadcast, and which companies are permitted to advertise.
12. Institutions should be discouraged from signing commercial contracts that violate "traditional academic values."

13. In-arena and in-stadium advertising should be minimized.

14. The NCAA should ban corporate logos on uniforms. (This presumably would include bowl game sponsors.)

15. Federal legislation to ban legal gambling on college sports in Nevada should be supported, and college presidents should address illegal gambling on their campuses.

While many of these recommendations have had limited practical effects, others continue to influence NCAA rules, especially in the area of academic progress of student-athletes and academic compliance of institutions (see section 6.3.1.3, "Academic Progress: NCAA"). The Knight Commission's role in pressing the NCAA to live up to its professed ideals assures its continued relevance in the future.

NOTES

1. The report of the Knight Foundation Commission on Intercollegiate Athletics, *A Call to Action: Reconnecting College Sports and Higher Education*, can be found at the Knight Foundation's Web site: http://www.knightfdn.org.

2. In June 2010, the Knight Commission released a report making financial reform recommendations for college sports. The recommendations are intended to help guide leaders in higher education and college athletics to restore balance in an era when growth in athletics spending outpaces growth in academic investment at institutions with major-college athletics programs.

5.3.4. Interscholastic Enforcement Procedures

The National Federation of State High School Associations lacks the regulatory authority of the National Collegiate Athletic Association or the International Olympic Committee. Though it does set standards for competition and write high school contest rules for the majority of sports in its jurisdiction, the NFSHSA does not have enforcement procedures like those of the NCAA and IOC. Instead, the regulatory responsibilities fall to the state associations described earlier in the chapter. Each state association has a dispute resolution procedure that handles all conflicts that may arise between student-athletes, coaches, officials, and institutions. Each institution also has its own internal mechanisms, but if the disputes are not resolved at the local level, they are referred to the state associations.

The California Interscholastic Federation (CIF) is the state association for the state of California. Concerning the issue of dispute resolution, the CIF's constitution states that "the CIF is limited to facilitating the establishment of these regulations and minimum standards and to the application of appropriate sanctions when failure to meet these standards, rules, and regulations comes to the attention of the CIF." The CIF has two separate procedures: one for eligibility appeals and one for all other matters.

The student eligibility appeals and review procedure at the CIF state level reads as follows:

1100. CIF Section Student Eligibility Appeals Procedures

Each CIF section shall establish appellate procedures which incorporate the following requirements in final Section determination of student eligibility questions.

Upon written appeal, the Section shall cause the appointment of either:

A. A hearing panel, or
B. A single hearing officer.

Said panel or hearing officer shall be empowered to hear the matter under consideration and rule on the eligibility status of the appellant under Section and State CIF eligibility requirements. Neither members of the hearing panel, nor a single hearing officer can have been directly associated with the matter under consideration or directly associated with the schools involved in the matter or have any other interest, personal or professional, that would preclude a fair and impartial hearing. If it is apparent from the facts that the panel or the hearing officer have no authority to adjudicate the matter under the rules, the section may find the appeal to be without merit and deny a hearing. All business and deliberations of the appeal process must be conducted in public, except for those deliberations by a single hearing officer or when matters declared by law to be confidential are being reviewed. The section hearing need not be conducted according to the rules of evidence and those related to witnesses. Any relevant evidence including hearsay evidence shall be admitted. All testimony shall be given under oath or affirmation administered by hearing officer (a member of the panel or a single hearing officer). (Revised February 2000, Federated Council.)

1101. State CIF Student Eligibility Appeals and Review Procedure

Appeals of final decisions determined through the CIF section appeals procedure concerning student eligibility may be presented to the State CIF Executive Director's office after the CIF section decision has been made in accordance with the following, if the appellant believes that the Section violated one or more of the following procedural guidelines:

A. Was the section's decision or action lawful; i.e., did the decision or action violate

Title V, the Education Code, etc. and did it extend appropriate due process to the parties?

B. Was the section's decision or action fraudulent?

C. Did the section act arbitrarily?

(1) Did the section have rules and criteria by which it reached its decision?

(2) Were the section's rules and criteria reasonable, i.e., do the section's rules reasonably relate to a legitimate objective?

(3) Did the section follow its own rules and criteria?

(4) Does the section's action or decision have a basis in reason, or in other words, a reasonable basis? The test to be employed in the application of this criterion is whether responsible people, acting in a thoughtful manner, could reasonably have reached the same decision as the section and not whether others might personally believe the decision. The Executive Director, upon receiving such an appeal, may review the section's decision based on the above guidelines to determine whether their action was a violation of any of the above. If, in his or her judgment, this is the case, the Executive Director may return this matter to the section for further review or, if necessary, set aside the decision and take jurisdiction consistent with Bylaw 1108 A.

The California Interscholastic Federation also has a set of procedures that address matters other than student eligibility or section playoffs. Like the eligibility appeals process, these procedures include separate section and state appeals processes. If a decision at the section level is appealed to the state level, the appeals procedure is similar to the eligibility appeals procedure at the state level in that the same questions are asked: was the decision lawful? Did the section act arbitrarily? and so on. If a dispute concerning matters other than eligibility is not resolved at this level, the dispute will go to arbitration. The CIF constitution reads, "Each member school, by becoming or remaining a member of the CIF, and each CIF section agrees that in the event of a dispute with a fellow member school, or with a CIF section or CIF, such a dispute shall be submitted to binding arbitration." As with all private associations, the CIF derives its authority in such matters from the voluntary nature of its members' decisions to join.

NOTES

1. In *St. Patrick High School v. New Jersey Interscholastic Athletic Association*, 2010 WL 715826 (D.N.J. March 1, 2010), the court rejected a high school's petition for injunctive relief that would have permitted the school to play in the state basketball tournament. The NJSIAA banned the school from participating after finding two players improperly transferred to the school. The Court determined that the NJSIAA's procedures were sufficient to provide due process to St. Patrick and its student-athletes.

2. In *DelBuono v. Massachusetts Interscholastic Athletic Association (MIAA)*, 2006 WL 1345563 (Mass. Super. March 13, 2006), a state court denied a request to enjoin the MIAA from enforcing its suspension against Nicholas DelBuono and Kyle Murphy for the remainder of the Central Massachusetts Hockey Tournament. Nicholas was suspended for being the "third man in" in a fight, and Kyle was suspended for a spearing penalty. In denying the injunction, the court noted that no irreparable harm would be suffered because no scholarships would be lost or college play forfeited. In addition, the court stated that it was not the appropriate forum to contest "bad calls."

3. In *Florida High School Athletic Association (FHSAA) v. Melbourne Central Catholic High School*, 867 So.2d 1281 (Fla. App. 5 Dist. 2004), the FHSAA appealed a temporary injunction granting Robert Morris, a student at Melbourne, athletic eligibility. Morris transferred from Melbourne to Palm Bay in spring 2003, after the first semester of his junior year, only to return for the fall of his senior year. During summer 2003, Morris went to a camp where Tim Lester, a former NFL player, was a coach. Lester was to become the new coach at Melbourne starting that fall. The FHSAA ruled Lester's contact with Morris violated its restrictions on recruiting for athletic purposes and ruled Morris ineligible. The FHSAA's sectional appeals committee upheld the ruling and advised Morris to appeal to the FHSAA Board of Directors, which he failed to do. In reversing the injunction, the appellate court ruled that Morris was required to exhaust his administrative remedies and that Morris did not have a fundamental right in interscholastic athletic participation subject to due process protection.

4. In *Somerville School Committee v. Massachusetts Interscholastic Athletic Ass'n*, No. 00-01042B, 2000 Mass. Super LEXIS 109 (Mass. Mar. 15, 2000), the Somerville High School girls' basketball team was the victim of an incorrect call made by a referee during a tournament game. If the correct call had been made, the Somerville squad would have won the game. The committee was seeking an injunction to stop the finals of the tournament from occurring until this error could be resolved. The court issued a decision in favor of the MIAA, stating, "The court is not unmindful of the harm to plaintiff's team. Were it to be balanced only with the potential harm to the MIAA, the balance may be in the plaintiff's favor. However, the plaintiff's harm should also be balanced with the harm to innocent third parties, i.e. the Methuen and Brockton (the two teams scheduled to play in the championship game) team members. In light of the impact of

the order sought on those third parties and questions concerning the appropriateness of the court's intervening in a matter such as this, the court declines to enter the order requested."

5. In *Ruiz v. Massachusetts Interscholastic Athletic Ass'n*, No. CV00-68, 2000 Mass. Super LEXIS 213 (Mass. Feb. 7, 2000), the plaintiff, Rafael Ruiz, was seeking an injunction that would allow him to compete on the varsity basketball team for the remainder of the season. Ruiz had transferred to his current school, Canton High School, from Thayer Academy (a private school where he had a scholarship) because he had lost his scholarship due to non-maintenance of a satisfactory grade point average. The court decided in favor of Ruiz, citing his particular circumstances as extraordinary and not applicable under the MIAA transfer law. The court found that Ruiz met all requirements of obtaining an injunction. The court stated, "Ruiz is likely to prevail in establishing that the MIAA rule concerning ineligibility is not applicable as a matter of law to his involuntary transfer from a private school back into the public school system of his hometown."

Interscholastic federations, since the 1990s, have seen an increase in the cases involving eligibility enforcement and the Americans with Disabilities Act. For more information, see the following cases that have been heard in court:

1. *Kanongata'a v. Washington Interscholastic Activities Association (WIAA)*, 2006 WL 1727891 (W.D. Wash. June 20, 2006)

2. *Baisden v. West Virginia Secondary Schools Activities Commission (WVSAC)*, 568 S.E.2d 32 (W. Va. 2002)

3. *Cruz v. Pennsylvania Interscholastic Athletic Ass'n*, 157 F. Supp. 2d 485 (E.D. Pa 2001)

4. *Washington v. Indiana High School Athletic Ass'n*, 181 F.3d 840 (7th Cir. 1999)

5. *Dixon v. Ohio High School Athletic Ass'n*, No. C-1-99-827, 1999 U.S. Dist. LEXIS 21388 (S.D. Ohio Nov. 4, 1999)

6. *McPherson v. Michigan High School Athletic Ass'n*, 119 F.3d 453 (6th Cir. 1997)

7. *Johnson v. Florida High School Activities Ass'n*, 102 F.3d 1172 (11th Cir. 1997)

8. *Frye v. Michigan High School Athletic Ass'n*, Case No. 95-1266 (6th Cir. 1997)

9. *Rhodes v. Ohio High School Athletic Ass'n*, 939 F. Supp. 584 (N.D. Ohio 1996)

The NCAA has been faced with many cases concerning enforcement of eligibility requirements in light of the Americans with Disabilities Act. For more information, see the following cases that have been heard in court:

1. *Bowers v. NCAA*, 130 F. Supp. 2d 610 (D. N.J. 2001)

2. *Matthews v. NCAA*, 79 F. Supp. 2d 1199 (E.D. Wash. 1999)

3. *Ganden v. NCAA*, No. 96 C 6953 1996 U.S. Dist. LEXIS 17368 (N.D. Ill. Nov. 21, 1996)

5.3.5. Olympic Enforcement Procedures

Chapter 1 discussed in some detail the relationship between the International Olympic Committee, the International Federations, the National Olympic Committees, and the National Governing Bodies. Each level of organization has a set of rules and regulations that cannot be violated by those it serves.

The highest authority is, of course, the IOC, which is a private institution that is the apex of international sport regulation. The IOC is guided by the Olympic Charter, the supreme document that gives the IOC sole authority over decision making. In recent years, the IOC has given more authority to the International Federations to regulate their respective sports, but the IOC remains the highest governing authority.

The IOC's Ethics Commission is charged with responsibility for, among other things, alleged violations of the IOC's ethical procedures. In the context of the

Olympic movement, the Ethics Commission can request sanctions against IOC members and honorary members, International Federations, National Olympic Committees, and host cities. For example, possible sanctions against National Olympic Committees include (1) withdrawal of the right to enter competitors into the Olympic Games, (2) suspension, (3) provisional or permanent withdrawal, (4) and withdrawal of the right to organize a session or an Olympic Congress.

In the context of the Olympic Games, the Ethics Commission possesses authority to discipline individual competitors and teams, officials, managers, referees, and all other accredited persons. The charged party retains important due process rights, which require the IOC to comply with the following:

> The Ethics Commission will bear in mind the Olympic Charter as they build on the Olympic Movement to promote positive ethics and ensure transparency and accountability. The commission will also establish standards and rules that are understandable and applicable in the forthcoming IOC Code of Ethics, as well as verify that the response to ethical issues is active, comprehensive, and effective. (http//www.olympic.org)

It is important to review the role of the International Federations (IFs):

> The International Sports Federations (ISF) are responsible for the integrity of their sport on the international level. These organizations establish the playing and eligibility rules, set the schedule of events and select the referees, judges and other officials to "run" their respective sports at the Olympic Games as well as other international competitions. (http://www.olympic.org)

Thus, the IFs have the power to establish and enforce rules and regulations that consist with the Olympic Charter. Therefore, if there is a dispute in the area of figure skating concerning eligibility standards, the aggrieved party would go through the procedure set forth by the International Federation responsible for figure skating, the International Skating Union.

Earlier in this chapter, we looked at the U.S. Olympic Committee as an example of a National Olympic Committee (NOC). An NOC is responsible for representing the interest of its respective country with respect to the Olympic Games and for assuring compliance with the rules and regulations as defined by the IOC.

National Olympic Committees have extensive arbitration procedures that apply when disputes arise. For example, the USOC has an "Arbitration of Challenge" section in its constitution that deals with all disputes between an athlete and a NGB. It states:

(a) RIGHT TO REVIEW.—A party aggrieved by a determination of the corporation under section 220527 or 220528 of this title may obtain review by any regional office of the American Arbitration Association.

(b) PROCEDURE.—

   (1) A demand for arbitration must be submitted within 30 days after the determination of the corporation.

   (2) On receipt of a demand for arbitration, the Association shall serve notice on the parties to the arbitration and on the corporation, and shall

immediately proceed with arbitration according to the commercial rules of the Association in effect at the time the demand is filed, except that—

(A) the arbitration panel shall consist of at least 3 arbitrators, unless the parties to the proceeding agree to a lesser number;

(B) the arbitration hearing shall take place at a site selected by the Association, unless the parties to the proceeding agree to the use of another site; and

(C) the arbitration hearing shall be open to the public.

(3) A decision by the arbitrators shall be by majority vote unless the concurrence of all arbitrators is expressly required by the contesting parties.

(4) Each party may be represented by counsel or by any other authorized representative at the arbitration proceeding.

(5) The parties may offer any evidence they desire and shall produce any additional evidence the arbitrators believe is necessary to an understanding and determination of the dispute. The arbitrators shall be the sole judges of the relevancy and materiality of the evidence offered. Conformity to legal rules of evidence is not necessary.

(c) SETTLEMENT.—The arbitrators may settle a dispute arising under this chapter before making a final award, if agreed to by the parties and achieved in a manner not inconsistent with the constitution and bylaws of the corporation.

(d) BINDING NATURE OF DECISION.—Final decision of the arbitrators is binding on the parties if the award is not inconsistent with the constitution and bylaws of the corporation.

(e) REOPENING HEARINGS.—

(1) At any time before a final decision is made, the hearings may be reopened by the arbitrators on their own motion or on the motion of a party.

(2) If the reopening is based on the motion of a party, and if the reopening would result in the arbitrators' decision being delayed beyond the specific period agreed to at the beginning of the arbitration proceedings, all parties to the decision must agree to reopen the hearings. (*USOC Constitution*, Article VIII, Section IV)

After the filing of a complaint, the USOC must first determine whether the complainant has exhausted available remedies with the NGB. If it is shown that the complainant did not exhaust all such remedies, the USOC will direct the parties to follow applicable NGB procedures before coming back to the USOC. If the USOC finds that the NGB in question is not in compliance with Article 4, Section [c] and Article 7, Sections 1 and 2, the USOC shall have two options of punishment:

A. Place the National Governing Body on probation for a specified period of time, not to exceed 180 days, which the corporation considers necessary to enable the national governing body to comply with those sections.

B. Revoke the recognition of the National Governing Body.

Another conflict that Article 7 of the USOC Constitution addresses is when an organization seeks to replace an existing national governing body for a particular sport. When this arises, the applicant sports organization must establish by a preponderance of the evidence that it meets the criteria for recognition as a national governing body and that the current NGB does not meet the criteria. After hearings, the USOC shall make one of four decisions:

1. Uphold the right of the NGB to continue as the NGB for its sport

2. Revoke the recognition of the NGB and declare a vacancy in the NGB for the sport

3. Revoke the recognition of the NGB and recognize the applicant as the NGB

4. Place the NGB on probation for a period not exceeding 180 days, pending the compliance of the NGB, if the NGB would have retained recognition except for a minor deficiency in one of the requirements of Section 220522, 220524, or 220525 of this title, and notify such NGB of such probation and of the actions needed to comply with such requirements (USOC Constitution, Article VII, Section 3(d))

If either party is not satisfied with the decision of the USOC, they may file an appeal within 30 days and the matter will go to binding arbitration with the American Arbitration Association. The arbitration panel will make a final and binding decision on the matter.

NOTES

For more information, see the following law review articles.

1. Susan Zuckerman and Matthew Hauptly, "When Disputes Arise about Who Is Eligible to Participate on the U.S. Olympic Team, or a Positive Drug Test, the AAA Provides a Forum to Resolve Them," 63 *Dispute Resolution Journal* 44 (October 2008).

2. Jason Gubi, "The Olympic Binding Arbitration Clause and the Court of Arbitration for Sport: An Analysis of Due Process Concerns," 18 *Fordham Intellectual Property, Media & Entertainment Law Journal* 997 (2008).

3. R. Jake Locklear, "Arbitration in Olympic Disputes: Should Arbitrators Review the Field of Play Decisions of Officials?" 4 *Texas Review of Entertainment & Sports Law* 199 (Spring 2003).

4. James A. R. Nafziger, "Dispute Resolution in the Arena of International Sports Competition," 50 *American Journal of Comparative Law* 161 (Fall 2002).

5.3.6. Court of Arbitration for Sport

To deal with the increase in the number of international legal disputes in the sports industry, former IOC president Juan Antonio Samaranch began the process of creating an international court that would deal exclusively with international sports-related disputes. The Court of Arbitration for Sport (CAS), which began operation in 1984, was composed of 60 members appointed by the IOC, the International Federations, the National Olympic Committees, and the IOC president.

Between 1984 and 1991, the CAS was involved in cases pertaining to the nationality status of athletes, television rights, sponsorship, employment contracts, and licensing. In order to avail themselves of the CAS's ability to provide final and authoritative decisions, several international federations inserted a clause into their statutes and regulations that read: "Any dispute arising from the present Statutes and Regulations of the Federation which cannot be settled amicably shall be settled finally by a tribunal composed in accordance with the Statutes and Regulations of the Court of Arbitration for Sport to the exclusion of any recourse to the ordinary courts. The parties undertake to comply with the said Statutes and Regulations, and to accept in good faith the award rendered and in no way hinder its execution."

In 1992, a member of the International Equestrian Federation (FEI) appealed to the CAS to overturn an FEI judgment. The CAS decision partly overturned the FEI decision but still levied a judgment against the rider. The rider appealed the decision to the Swiss Federal Tribunal, claiming that the arbitration panel did not meet the conditions of impartiality needed to be considered a proper arbitration court. The tribunal found in favor of the CAS.

However, the tribunal did criticize the relationship between the IOC and the CAS and noted that should the IOC ever come before the CAS, the court may not be able to perform independently or impartially. The result of the decision was threefold:

1. The International Council of Arbitration for Sport (ICAS) was created to look after the running and financing of the CAS, thereby taking the place of the IOC.

2. Two arbitration divisions were created. The first deals with issues concerning decisions made by federations, commonly involving concerns over things such as television rights and sponsorships. The second division handles disputes characterized as last instance disputes, where the bylaws of certain athletic federations state that the ICAS will be the court of final jurisdiction if a satisfactory decision can't be reached within their own proceedings.

3. The reforms were outlined in a Code of Sports-Related Arbitration, which details the procedures that must be followed during all arbitration proceedings conducted by the council.

Due to its resulting independence from the IOC, the CAS is now structured in a more impartial fashion. In 2003, the Swiss Federal Tribunal found that this impartiality was sufficient to allow the CAS to sit in judgment of the IOC. Consequently, the CAS is now truly the final arbitrator in international sporting disputes (see notes).

Beginning in 1996, the ICAS began the practice of establishing ad hoc divisions in order to hear disputes at the Olympics within 24 hours. At the 1996 Olympic Games in Atlanta, the division dealt with six cases during the Games, with disputes ranging from disciplinary actions to a late entry. Due to the success of the ad hoc division, the precedent was duplicated in 1998 at the winter Olympic Games at Nagano, Japan, where the division handled four cases. At the 2000 summer Olympics in Sydney, Australia, the CAS decided a record number of 15 cases, with a range of issues including nationality, doping, and disputes over close finishes (see notes for a discussion of cases from the 2000 Sydney Olympics).

It is important to note that although these ad hoc committees of the CAS operate at the location of the Olympics while they are taking place, the CAS's permanent location in Lausanne, Switzerland, means that even ad hoc CAS proceedings are governed by Swiss law. This allows the CAS to treat all cases arising at the Olympics in as uniform a manner as possible.

NOTES

1. In *Hamilton v. United States Anti-Doping Agency (USADA) & Union Cycliste Internationale (UCI)*, the CAS upheld a two-year ban by UCI against American cyclist Tyler Hamilton after he tested positive for a blood transfusion. The positive test came only days after Hamilton won gold at the 2004 Olympics. Hamilton contended that the presence of two different types of blood cells in his system was because his twin sibling died in utero and that Hamilton had received his twin's stem cells. The CAS rejected Hamilton's story and concluded that the test was reliable.

2. In *World Anti-Doping Agency (WADA) v. United States Anti-Doping Agency (USADA), United States Bobsled & Skeleton Fed'n (USBSF) & Lund*, WADA appealed USADA's sanction against American bobsledder Zach Lund as being too light. During the 2005 World Cup, Lund tested positive for the prohibited substance Finasteride, but it was known that he had been using medication that included the substance for over five years. The medication, Propecia, is used to combat baldness. Lund included the substance on his Doping Control Forms but did not have a Therapeutic Use Exemption (TUE). The USADA only gave Lund a public warning and disqualified his World Cup results. Lund's doctor filed a TUE, and the USBSF selected Lund for the 2006 Olympics. The CAS ruled in WADA's favor, concluding that Lund was responsible for checking the prohibited substance list and for the presence of the drug in his system. The CAS said that a suspension must be included in the USADA's sanction but lessened the requested suspension from two years to one because Lund had no significant fault or negligence and the antidoping organizations were aware Lund was using the substance. Lund returned to win the 2006–2007 overall World Cup title.

3. In *United States Anti-Doping Agency (USADA) v. Montgomery*, the CAS upheld the USADA's ban against American track and field star Tim Montgomery for doping even though Montgomery never tested for any prohibited substance. The USADA charged Montgomery with doping after receiving evidence regarding his involvement with BALCO, an American athletic laboratory allegedly involved with providing steroids and other illegal substances to a various high profile athletes. Ruling in June 2005, the CAS stated that the USADA's authority extended to all cases of possible doping violations, not just drug testing. Although the CAS had evidence of abnormal blood tests from Montgomery, it relied heavily on testimony from American track athlete Kelli White. White, who had already accepted a two-year ban for doping, testified that Montgomery admitted using a prohibited substance known as "the Clear." Montgomery was banned for two years, he was ordered to repay approximately $1 million in earnings, and his record was expunged dating back to March 2001, including his 100-meter dash record of 9.78 seconds set in 2002.

4. In *Cañas v. ATP Tour*, Argentinean tennis player Guillermo Cañas challenged his two-year suspension from the ATP. During a February 2005 tournament in Acapulco, Mexico Cañas tested positive for hydrochlorothiazide, a diuretic and masking agent for other performance enhancing substances. Cañas says he was given the prescription drug by ATP doctors at the tournament. The CAS found that Cañas was responsible for the drug's presence in his body but bore no significant fault or negligence. Cañas was required to forfeit his prize money from the Acapulco tournament, but his suspension was reduced to 15 months, and he returned to the tour in September 2006. In March 2007, Cañas beat ATP #1 ranked Roger Federer twice in a row, becoming the only player other than Rafael Nadal to beat Federer twice in a row since 2003.

5. In *Yang and Korean Olympic Committee v. International Gymnastics Federation (FIG)*, the CAS upheld the FIG's ruling that the results of the 2004 Olympics men's individual gymnastics all-around final could not be changed. Yang was incorrectly given a starting value of 9.9 and received the bronze medal. The correct starting value of 10.0 would have given Yang the gold medal instead of American Paul Hamm. The CAS ruled that the score protests occurred after the event was over, not valid under FIG rules. In addition, the scoring could not be changed after the event because the judging is a "field of play" decision. The three judges responsible were suspended, and Yang was awarded a symbolic gold medal by his country.

6. In *Cole v. Football Association Premier League (FAPL)*, the CAS rejected an appeal by Arsenal defender Ashley Cole who was fined for talking with rival club Chelsea while under contract with Arsenal. The FAPL fined Cole 100,000 pounds ($240,700), Chelsea manager Jose Mourinho 200,000 pounds ($481,300), and Chelsea 300,000 pounds ($722,000) for violating Premier League rules prohibiting such contact without the approval of Arsenal. Cole alleged that it was an unfair restraint of trade. In January 2006, the CAS ruled that it did not have jurisdiction to rule on the dispute, which was subject to a collective bargaining agreement between Premier League players and clubs.

7. In *Dal Balcon v. Comitato Olimpico Nazionale Italione (CONI) & Federazione Italiana Sport Invernali (FISI)*, the CAS ruled that Italian snowboarder Isabella Dal Balcon met the selection criteria identified by CONI and FISI and must be added to the 2006 Italian Olympic team. Dal Balcon competed for Italy at the 2002 Olympics and was told that the criteria for making the 2006 team would be based on the World Cup and three other races prior to the 2006 Olympics. The criteria were later changed and Dal Balcon did not make the team, although she would have under the original criteria. Dal Balcon contended that the change was unfair and arbitrary. The CAS agreed, adding that the change was not properly communicated. Dal Balcon failed to medal at the 2006 Games.

8. In the arbitration case of *United States Olympic Committee (USOC) and USA Canoe/Kayak v. International Olympic Committee*, the USOC brought its case to the arbitration panel of the CAS at Sydney because the IOC was not going to allow Mr. Angel Perez to participate on the U.S. kayaking team in the Olympic Games. Mr. Perez had competed for Cuba in the 1992 Olympic Games in Barcelona, then had fled from his native country, and received full citizenship in the United States in 1999. Although he had competed for the United States in the world championships in 1997–1999, the IOC rules state that three years must pass before a newly nationalized citizen can compete in the Olympic Games for his or her new country. The USOC disagreed with the IOC, stating that Perez had achieved permanent residence status as a "resident alien" in 1995, and therefore should have been eligible for competition as a U.S. citizen. The CAS sided with the IOC, stating, "On the basis of a straightforward reading of Bylaw 2 of Rule 46 of the Olympic Charter, . . . Mr. Perez acquired his new nationality less than three years ago, and . . . the Cuban Olympic Committee did not agree to a reduction of this period."

9. In *Andrea Raducan v. International Olympic Committee (IOC)*, the CAS handled one of its most controversial cases to date. Andrea Raducan was a gold-medal-winning gymnast in both the team and the all-around competition for the Romanian national team. While competing for the all-around title, after winning the team gold medal, Raducan complained to the team doctor that she was not feeling well. The doctor gave her a Nurofen Cold and Flu tablet, which she took in his presence on two different occasions. After winning the all-around title, she was sent to supply a urine sample in accordance with Olympic Doping Control. The tablets she received were found to be in violation of the doping rules, and the CAS ruled in favor of the IOC decision, stripping the medals that she received, testing positive for the banned substance. The court stated, "The Panel is aware of the impact its decision will have on a fine, young, elite athlete. It finds, in balancing the interests of Miss Raducan with the commitment of the Olympic Movement to drugfree sport, the Anti-Doping Code must be enforced without compromise."

10. In *Bernardo Segura v. International Amateur Athletic Federation*, Segura was a racewalker for the Mexican national team. He was disqualified, under sport rules, because he had committed three infractions during the course of the race. There was a question as to whether Segura had seen the warnings and cautions that the judges of the event had issued to him. It is definite that he had seen the first warning, unclear whether he had seen the second warning, and most likely that he had not seen the third warning. Segura crossed the finish line believing he was the gold medalist and was not informed of his disqualification until 15 minutes after the end of the race. Segura did not question the infractions but said that because he had not been made aware of the disqualification immediately, the IAAF should not be able to strip him of his gold medal. The CAS

decided in favor of the IAAF, stating, "The IAAF Rules do not provide that disqualifications are invalid if they are not communicated 'immediately.' The Panel believes that it would be intolerable to disregard the unchallenged finding that on three occasions three separate judges found the Applicant to have infringed the rules."

11. For more information on the ICAS, visit its Web site at http://www.tas-cas.org. This site provides information concerning the history and purpose of the court as well as addresses and published court opinions.

5.4. PUBLIC RESPONSIBILITY OF ATHLETIC ASSOCIATIONS

As legally incorporated bodies, athletic associations have certain duties to fulfill to the public as a condition of their corporate existence. Public responsibilities can include broadcast rights (see Chapter 14), access to records, antitrust liabilities (see Chapter 10), and disclosure and funding of public facilities. Even a voluntary association that considers itself a private organization may have a responsibility to the general public. For example, the NCAA is responsible to the public for maintaining amateurism in college athletics, providing competition in intercollegiate sports for both male and female student-athletes, and allowing greater access to televised football.

Generally, any athletic organization that is public or quasipublic in nature is a potential defendant in a public responsibility case. A case that dealt with the public responsibilities of athletic associations was *Greene v. Athletic Council of Iowa State University*, 251 N.W.2d 559 (Iowa 1977). In *Greene*, the Iowa Superior Court ruled that an amateur college association, although private in name, is quasipublic in character. The Iowa court discussed the specific statute and decided that the controlling issue was whether the athletic council was a "council" as authorized by the laws of the state. The record showed that the Iowa State University (ISU) athletic council was an entity established by officials of ISU to manage and control its intercollegiate athletic program. After a discussion of specific powers, the court found that the athletic council exercised powers that clearly made it a governmental entity. The court went on to rule that the athletic council was authorized by state law, which allowed the university's board of regents to delegate responsibility to it. Considering all these factors, the court held that the council was subject to the Iowa open-meeting law.

Distinguishing itself from many of its members, the NCAA has argued that only through confidentiality can it investigate itself properly and thereby maintain its public responsibility to ensure amateur integrity. It argues that opening confidential investigation files compromises the NCAA's cooperative principles, to which all member institutions agree to adhere when they join the association. The NCAA is a voluntary association whose members, by joining the organization, agree to follow certain conditions and obligations of membership, including the obligation to conduct their individual institutional athletic programs in a manner consistent with NCAA legislation. In addition, member institutions agree to oversight by the NCAA's enforcement staff. The key to the NCAA investigative process is the cooperative principle—that is, the accused member institution and the NCAA's enforcement staff work together to ascertain the truth of alleged infractions.

5.4.1. Disclosure

Disclosure cases concern the question of how much of an organization's proprietary information, including meetings, should be a matter of public record.

Designation as a governmental or other public body may subject an agency to the Freedom of Information Act (5 U.S.C. § 552) or to state "sunshine laws." Thus, a quasipublic association may have to open its records for public inspection, while a private organization may not. The degree of disclosure that a quasipublic institution may be required to give varies from state to state. For example, under the state of Florida's public record laws, interviews related to searches for new coaches or athletic directors at state institutions are open to the media. For the media and the public, such laws provide factual accounts of who is competing for the job, where the interviews are conducted, what is being asked, and how those being interviewed are responding.

For athletic administrators and institutions, these laws create pressure to be unbiased, fair, and judicious in selecting candidates for vacant positions. Disclosure cases illustrate conflicts that arise concerning the right of the public to be accurately informed by athletic organizations against the need of an organization to protect the confidentiality of its files. In *Kneeland v. NCAA*, 850 F.2d 224 (5th Cir. 1988), a reporter sought to gain disclosure of information from the NCAA and the Southwest Conference about a recruiting scandal at Southern Methodist University. The U.S. Court of Appeals for the Fifth Circuit concluded that the NCAA and Southwest Conference were not governmental bodies and thus were not subject to the Texas Open Records Act. However, in *Hansberry v. Massachusetts Interscholastic Athletic Ass'n*, No. 95-6807-B 1998 Mass. Super LEXIS 706 (Mass. Super. Ct. Oct. 21, 1998), the plaintiff Hansberry was not allowed under MIAA regulations to participate in interscholastic athletics because he had exhausted his eligibility. Upon appeal, his application for a waiver was denied. Hansberry brought a claim against the MIAA because he had not been informed of the meeting to review his case, asserting that the MIAA was a de facto governmental body and therefore subject to open meeting laws.

The court agreed and decided that his disqualification from participation was moot because his case had been decided in violation of open meeting laws. The outcomes of these two cases call to mind the Supreme Court's recent rulings on state action in the context of decisions made by the NCAA and state high school athletic associations.

NOTES

1. In October 2009 a Florida state court ordered the NCAA to turn over documents related to the NCAA's investigation into violations within the Florida State athletic department. The records included almost 700 pages in interview transcripts with Florida State personnel. See 5.3.2.2. Infractions Appeals Committee note 1.

2. In *U.S. Dept. of Educ. v. NCAA*, 481 F.3d 936 (7th Cir. 2007), the appeals court ruled the NCAA does not have privilege that would protect it from being forced to turn over documents and information discovered by its investigators. Following the 2004–2005 basketball season, the University of the District of Columbia (UDC) self-reported violations, including the misuse of federal funds, to the NCAA. The Inspector General of the Department of Education began its own investigation and subpoenaed the material provided to the NCAA by UDC. The NCAA contended that forcing it to turn over materials voluntarily provided to it by member institutions would undermine its ability to effectively investigate and enforce possible rules violations. In rejecting the NCAA's argument, the court noted that not even investigative reporters have a privilege to conceal the identity of their sources from the government under federal law.

3. In *Dillman v. Trustees of Indiana University*, 848 N.E.2d 348 (Ind. App. 2006), the appeals court affirmed a ruling that a gathering of less than the majority of the nine trustees

did not violate Indiana's open door law requiring that meetings of public bodies be open to the public. Indiana President Myles Brand had been meeting with members of the board of trustees regarding the eventual dismissal of men's basketball coach Bobby Knight. However, Brand was careful to make sure that he never discussed the situation with more than four of the trustees present, avoiding a quorum that would have subjected such a meeting to the open door law.

4. In *University System of Maryland v. Baltimore Sun Co.*, 847 A.2d 427 (Md. 2004), the University of Maryland appealed a decision by a Maryland Circuit Court granting the *Baltimore Sun* salary and employment information of University of Maryland head coaches under the Maryland Public Information Act (MPIA). Originally Maryland was only willing to reveal that head football coach Ralph Friedgen's salary was $183,920 but would not release copies of his contracts, including bonuses, incentives, and other terms and conditions of Friedgen's employment and compensation. Maryland contended that it did not have the right to release certain aspects of Friedgen's personnel file, but in an attempt to avoid a lawsuit, Friedgen voluntarily submitted information stating that he made an additional $762,000 for competitive achievements and endorsements. Maryland then also supplied that Gary Williams, the men's basketball coach, had a salary of $202,991 but also earned an additional $540,400 in competitive achievement and endorsements; however, the university still refused to turn over copies of his contract and other records. Maryland contended that it was only required to release information related to how much the coaches were being paid from public funds, not the coaches' private, personal finances. The Supreme Court of Maryland ruled that the employment contracts did fall under the MPIA and must be turned over but remanded to the trial court to reevaluate whether third-party contracts were subject to disclosure.

5. In *Breighner v. Michigan High School Athletic Association, Inc. (MHSAA)*, 683 N.W.2d 639 (Mich. 2004), the parents of a disqualified skier brought suit under the Freedom of Information Act (FOIA) to force the MHSAA to turn over information regarding the MHSAA's criteria for sanctioning ski races. Breighner was disqualified from high school competition for participating in a nonsanctioned race. The trial court found for the parents but the Court of Appeals reversed. The Michigan Supreme Court affirmed, holding that MHSAA, an independent nonprofit corporation, is not a public body within the meaning of FOIA because it is not primarily funded by or through state or local authority. Approximately 90% of the MHSAA's revenues were gate receipts from postseason tournaments for football and basketball.

6. In *State, ex rel. Cincinnati Enquirer v. Krings*, 758 N.E.2d 1135 (Ohio 2001), Hamilton County had agreed to fund the building of a stadium for the Cincinnati Bengals. The Supreme Court of Ohio ruled that all records concerning the funding and building were public information. Therefore, the county commissioners had no right to preclude the plaintiff newspaper from access to this information. The court held that the records of the construction were public records even if they were in the possession of the private construction companies.

7. In *M.G. v. Time Warner, Inc.*, 89 Cal. App. 4th 623 (Cal. Ct. App. 2001), the defendant magazine publisher and television producer used a team photograph including the plaintiffs in both print and television stories about the molestation of child athletes. The team manager had plead guilty to molesting five of the children, including the children in the photograph. The plaintiffs survived a motion to dismiss the claim brought by defendant because the court believed that the plaintiffs had a reasonable chance of success on an invasion of privacy claim. The court reasoned that it was important that the team or players had never been revealed in previous media coverage of the scandal. The journalistic importance clearly did not outweigh the importance of maintaining the anonymity of the victims.

8. In *Smith v. Plati*, 56 F. Supp. 2d 1195 (D. Co. 1999), the plaintiff was an independent Web site operator who maintained a Web site about the University of Colorado athletics. When he first began coverage of the athletic programs on his site, he received the same treatment as members of the press concerning access to sports information. However, the

media relations department of the university reduced his access to only published material in order to limit his access to "publishable information." The court found that the university could claim sovereign immunity and that the defendant media relations director did not have a duty to give the plaintiff press access because the plaintiff had not been deprived of a protected right and he had no right to be qualified as "press."

9. In *Kirwan v. The Diamondback*, 721 A.2d 196 (Md. Ct. App. 1998), the Court of Appeals of Maryland ruled that parking tickets received by persons affiliated with an institution are not personnel records and therefore are open to the public. *The Diamondback*, a school newspaper, had alleged that basketball players on the University of Maryland campus were parking illegally, and coaches for the team were paying their parking tickets. The court rejected the school's argument that the parking tickets were financial records and therefore should remain confidential.

5.4.2. Funding of Public Facilities

Another development with respect to public responsibilities of athletic associations concerns challenges to the way public funds are spent. Challenges have been made to the building of sports facilities by faculty governing bodies concerned that funds would be diverted from other educational areas. In *Lester v. Public Building Authority of County of Knox*, No. 78491 (1983), a case settled out of court, the issues raised shed light on potential problem areas in financing athletic facilities. This suit was brought by faculty members of the University of Tennessee against the university in order to block its planned funding and construction of a $30 million assembly center and sports arena. The faculty was successful in placing pressure on school officials and, in return for not delaying the construction of the arena, won the right to be involved in the approval process when projects would affect faculty members.

Funding of facilities may raise other concerns regarding athletic organizations' responsibilities to the public. Universities differ over the propriety of sponsorship by companies involved in alcohol sales; while some schools decline such funding, others eagerly accept. For example, the University of Louisville's construction of a new football stadium was assisted by a $2 million contribution from Anheuser Busch. Should institutions of higher learning accept funding from sources whose products cannot legally be consumed by the majority of their undergraduates? This issue is certain to be hotly debated in coming years.

NOTES _____

1. In *Moschenross v. St. Louis County*, 188 S.W.3d 13 (Mo. Ct. App. 2006), the appellate court affirmed a declaratory judgment sought by the developers and financiers of the St. Louis Cardinals new stadium. The judgment ruled that the recently passed legislation requiring any financial assistance for the development of a professional sports facility to be approved by a majority of voters could not apply retroactively against the county's obligation to commit public funds towards the construction of the stadium.

For more information on the funding of public facilities, see the following law review articles.

1. Christopher B. Carbot, "The Odd Couple: Stadium Naming Rights Mitigating the Public-Private Stadium Finance Debate," 4 *FIU Law Review* 515 (2009).

2. Philip Weinberg, "Eminent Domain for Private Sports Stadiums: Fair Ball or Foul?," 35 *Envtl. L.* 311 (2005).

3. Frank A. Mayer III, "Stadium Financing: Where We Are, How We Got Here, and Where We Are Going," 12 *Vill. Sports & Ent. L.J.* 195 (2005).

4. Martin J. Greenberg, "Sports Facility Financing and Development Trends in the United States," 15 *Marq. Sports L. Rev.* 93 (2004).

5. Zachary A. Phelps, "Stadium Construction for Professional Sports: Reversing the Inequities through Tax Incentives," 18 *St. John's J. Legal Comment.* 981 (2004).

The courts will often be very protective of a perceived public interest. A key question is how much of the amateur athletic organization's power can be delegated. For an examination of this subject in regard to the Boston Marathon, see the following cases.

1. In *Boston Athletic Ass'n v. International Marathons, Inc.*, 467 N.E.2d 58 (Mass. 1984), the board of directors of the Boston Athletic Association (BAA) brought a lawsuit against International Marathons, Inc. (IMI) to prevent it from representing itself to the public as the association's agent. The hearing examiner found that the contract which set up the agency relationship and was signed by the president of the BAA violated state law and that the president had exceeded his authority in entering into the agreement.

2. In *International Marathons, Inc. v. Attorney General*, 467 N.E.2d 55 (Mass. 1984), IMI appealed the hearing examiner's decision in *BAA v. IMI*, but the court refused to review the decision because it was a moot question. The hearing examiner had disapproved the contract between IMI and BAA because it was violative of state law.

5.4.3. The Buckley Amendment

As we have seen, an integral aspect of the NCAA's enforcement program is the compilation of information regarding alleged infractions and the operation of institutions' athletic departments. Access to student-athletes' records concerning academic and financial aid information is critical. But in conducting their investigations, the NCAA and member institutions must be mindful of their public responsibility to student.

In order to protect against an invasion of a student's privacy and to prevent the use of such information in a way that hurts the student, Congress enacted the Family Educational Rights and Privacy Act, which regulates the release and review of such records. Consequently, the NCAA and other third parties can be restricted and sometimes prevented from accessing or publishing certain types of student-athlete information. The Family Educational Rights and Privacy Act of 1974 is often referred to as the Buckley Amendment.

The Buckley Amendment was designed to enhance comprehensive civil rights protections with two objectives in mind: (1) to assure parents of students, and students themselves, if they are attending an institution of postsecondary education or are 18 years old, access to their education records and (2) to protect the students' right to privacy by restricting the transfer and disclosure of information in their records without prior consent. The procedures established for accomplishing these objectives apply only to public or private educational agencies or institutions that receive funds, directly or indirectly, from a program administered by the secretary of education (e.g., Basic Educational Opportunity Grant, Guaranteed Student Loan, or National Direct Student Loans). The agency or institution is obligated to establish a written policy and procedure for the access, disclosure, and challenge of education records. The secretary of education has the power to withdraw federal funding from any educational agency or institution that does not comply with the Buckley Amendment.

This law primarily involves release of information concerning a student-athlete's education records, including academic rank, biographical material, and injury and health records. Since this type of information is often used in athletic department publications and media releases, sports information directors should especially be aware of the provisions and limitations enacted by the Buckley Amendment.

Two basic rights created under the Buckley Amendment are particularly important to athletic administrators. First, students have the right to challenge any information in their education record that they or their parents believe is inaccurate, misleading, or otherwise in violation of the student's rights. The student can bring the challenge in a hearing; if the institution still refuses the challenge, the student can note his or her concerns on the educational record. Second, the Buckley Amendment protects a student's right to prevent personally identifiable information from being disclosed, with some exceptions, in the absence of prior written consent of the parent or student. A school official with a "legitimate educational interest" may have access without consent.

As a general rule, information concerning student-athletes should not be disclosed unless the student has filled out and signed a consent-disclosure statement form. These consent-disclosure statements protect both the student-athlete and the institution. Therefore, the NCAA has student-athletes sign Buckley Amendment consent disclosure statements as part of student-athlete statements. Written consent-disclosure statements must include the following:

1. A specification of the records to be disclosed
2. The purpose or purposes of the disclosure
3. The party or class of parties to whom the disclosure may be made

In addition, the form should contain language that allows for the disclosure of unforeseen events, such as academic ineligibility, injury reports, and sudden illness affecting athletic involvement.

Another section of the Buckley Amendment deals with specific parties who do not have to receive a prior written authorization from the student to see the student's education files. Athletic department personnel fall into the school official exemption category and can review student-athlete files as needed to evaluate grade point average qualifiers, academic eligibility, and other matters that affect eligibility. However, athletic administrators should be aware that some states offer additional protections to students' privacy interests. However, these state statutes may not pre-empt the Buckley Amendment.

High school student-athletes' education records are also covered under the Buckley Amendment. A potential problem may arise when members of a community desire access to student records to determine the effectiveness of their educational system.

NOTES _____

1. The Buckley Amendment, introduced by Senator James Buckley, appeared as an amendment to the Family Educational Rights and Privacy Act of 1974. The bill extended the Elementary and Secondary Education Act of 1965, Pub. L. No. 93-380, 20 U.S.C. §1232g(a)(4)(A).

2. In *Unincorporated Operating Div. of Indiana Newspapers, Inc. v. Trustees of Indiana*, 787 N.E.2d 893 (Ind. App. 2003), the *Indianapolis Star*, the largest paper in Indiana, brought suit seeking documents involved with the firing of Indiana men's head basketball coach Bobby Knight in September 2000. The documents included notes from a private investigator hired by the university trustees to investigate Knight. During the investigation, the *Star* requested copies of all materials related to the investigation pursuant to the Indiana Access to Public Records Act (APRA). The trustees provided some materials but withheld the investigator's notes, claiming they were attorney work product. The *Star* subsequently

brought suit, but the trustees were granted summary judgment. The appeals court ruled that the Family Educational Right and Privacy Act forbade release of some documents because they included the educational records of Indiana students, including an ex-player Knight was accused of choking and a student Knight was accused of grabbing and scolding just prior to his firing. However, the appeals court remanded to determine whether the work of the investigators qualified as attorney work product; otherwise the information unrelated to student records could be released.

3. In *Doe v. Woodford County Board of Education*, 213 F.3d 921 (6th Cir. 2000), the defendant high school was cleared of violating the Buckley Amendment. In this case, the plaintiff student-athlete suffered from hemophilia and hepatitis B. The principal of the school, who was privy to this information, saw that the student was practicing with the basketball team. He approached the coach of the team during practice and told him that he should check the student's medical record. It was possible but not likely that this conversation was overheard by other students. The court believed that this did not violate the amendment for two reasons. First, the plaintiff, who was seeking summary judgment, did not show enough evidence that the other students heard the conversation of medical records, which might amount to a disclosure. Second, the court reasoned that the communication between the administrator and the coach was protected by the amendment because "an educational institution also 'may disclose personally identifiable information from an educational record to appropriate parties' if it is necessary to protect the health or safety of the student or others."

4. In *Kirwan v. The Diamondback*, 721 A. 2d 196 (Md. 1998), the Court of Appeals of Maryland ruled that parking tickets received by an employee are not personnel records or educational records, and therefore, are open to the public. *The Diamondback*, a school newspaper, had alleged that basketball players on the University of Maryland campus were parking illegally and subsequently, coaches for the team were paying off their parking tickets. The court rejected the school's argument that the parking tickets were financial records and therefore personnel records. Therefore, the court allowed the disclosure of the records.

Chapter 6

THE ATHLETE AND CONSTITUTIONAL LAW

6.1. Athletic Associations and Constitutional Issues

   6.1.1. State Action Requirement
   6.1.2. Due Process
        6.1.2.1. Procedural Due Process
        6.1.2.2. Substantive Due Process
   6.1.3. Equal Protection

6.2. Definitions of Eligibility

6.3. Eligibility Requirements: College and High School

   6.3.1. Academic Eligibility Rules
        6.3.1.1. Initial Eligibility: National Collegiate Athletic Association (NCAA)
        6.3.1.2. Grade Point Average: High School
        6.3.1.3. Academic Progress: NCAA
        6.3.1.4. Academic Progress: High School

6.3.2. Participation Rules
        6.3.2.1. Redshirting
        6.3.2.2. Longevity
        6.3.2.3. Transfer Rules
6.3.3. Amateurism Rules
        6.3.3.1. NCAA Rules Regarding Scholarships, Financial Assistance, and Expenses
        6.3.3.2. Employment: NCAA
        6.3.3.3. Summer Camps and Independent Teams
        6.3.3.4. Olympic Eligibility Requirements

6.4. Athlete's Challenge of Rules

   6.4.1. Freedom of Expression
   6.4.2. Discipline
   6.4.3. Alcohol, Drug, and Conduct Rules: High School

INTRODUCTION

The previous chapter studied the various athletic associations that govern amateur athletes in the United States. Formerly, it was titled "Amateur Athletic Associations," but the changing definition of *amateur* has necessitated the deletion of that word from the title. While some associations hold to the traditional sense of the term, other associations, such as the International Olympic Committee, have modified their designation of *amateur* since the mid-1980s.

These questions of amateurism, along with other issues examined in Chapter 5, make good examples of issues athletic associations decide for themselves. However, as we learned in section 5.2.2, "Judicial Review," these associations must on occasion answer to the judiciary. Chief among such occasions are those where an individual's constitutional rights are affected. Therefore, this chapter begins with an extensive discussion of constitutional guarantees.

In order to understand when an athlete might challenge association rules based on the Constitution, we must understand what sort of rules are involved, from eligibility to participation. This chapter continues with a discussion on the interpretation of an eligible athlete, especially in the light of the official status of Olympic athletes, and then discusses individual eligibility requirements for student-athletes. Many of the requirements, such as academic requirements, participation rules, and amateur eligibility, will be considered at both the interscholastic and the intercollegiate levels. The key aspects of association rules include initial eligibility rules, continuing eligibility rules, and scholarship restrictions. Although this chapter primarily examines individual eligibility requirements for participation at the high school and collegiate levels, a brief section is devoted to eligibility requirements for Olympic competition. The significance of this topic is not confined to the Olympic arena because participation in Olympic competition may affect a student-athlete's participation in interscholastic or intercollegiate competition.

A significant portion of this chapter will deal with what avenues are available for a student-athlete who is unhappy with the decision or regulation of a governing association. First, the affected student-athlete should review the legal documents of the entity, especially rules and regulations relating to athletes. The importance of the organizational rule book cannot be overstated, no matter which organization the athlete is dealing with. While the scope and detail of a rule book will vary depending upon the organization, the rule book will lay out all rules and regulations, and outline the procedures for athletes to appeal decisions. Second, the athlete should assess whether there is recourse within the organization for solving the problem such as an arbitration or appeals process. If the affected athlete does not have recourse within the association, or if the recourse offered is insufficient, he or she may consider a court case against the organization.

If the athlete does decide to bring litigation against the association, it is imperative to determine the legal status of the organization: is it public or private? If it is determined that the association is not a state actor, the athlete should establish whether or not the organization receives federal funds. If so, the athlete should next examine whether any federal legislation may apply in the particular situation, such as Title IX.

If the organization is a state actor, the next step for the athlete is to evaluate constitutional law arguments such as due process and equal protection, will be successful. The court will then have to balance the individual rights of the athlete against the authority of the coach or administrator to govern a sport. For example, courts have had to balance a coach's authority against the censoring of an individual's freedom of expression in cases involving everything from hair length to pregame prayer (see section 6.4.1, "Freedom of Expression").

Finally, it bears mention that this chapter will *not* deal directly with the applicability of the Constitution to professional sports. These issues tend to intersect with other major legal issues facing professional leagues, from antitrust law to labor law. While professional leagues are not state actors, and thus not subject to the sort of constitutional requirements imposed on public organizations, they do face different dilemmas under the Constitution. These issues will be treated in subsequent chapters.

6.1. ATHLETIC ASSOCIATIONS AND CONSTITUTIONAL ISSUES

Athletic administrators at the high school and college levels sometimes lament the volume of claims directed against them alleging violations of a student-athlete's constitutional rights. Nonetheless, recent judicial decisions clearly illustrate that institutions or associations whose severe penalties impair or jeopardize an individual's career may be found to have violated the athlete's constitutional rights.

This fact need not preclude organizations from imposing penalties for violations of their rules. When courts analyze such cases, they will hesitate to intervene in the association's decision unless a rule has been applied unfairly or unreasonably. In making such determinations, courts consider whether such rules are related to legitimate principles or business purposes of the association.

In certain cases, the courts may decide to consider directly constitutional claims by student-athletes. In light of the problems of limited judicial review and standing, claims of due process and equal protection may be the only constitutional avenues available. In addition, a student-athlete may bring the case to a federal court and raise other federal questions. The plaintiff will have to show that (1) state action exists, (2) the claim is not frivolous, and (3) the claim concerns a right of sufficient importance to be litigated in federal court. If these three points can be established, the student-athlete can then proceed on an equal protection and/or due process challenge, in addition to any state constitutional arguments that may exist.

6.1.1. State Action Requirement

The protections of the 5th and 14th Amendments of the U.S. Constitution apply only to actions taken by the government. Thus, any action taken directly or indirectly by a state, local, or federal government is *state action* for constitutional purposes. In addition, action by any public school, state college, or state university, or any of their officials, can be construed as state action. Although state action is relatively clear in such cases, other examples are more complex. Action by strictly private parties does not constitute state action, but questions arise when such parties act in concert with the government or to promote governmental objectives. For instance, actions by private organizations that are deemed to be performing a public function or are authorized under the laws of the state (quasipublic institutions) may be construed as state action.

Therefore, if actions taken by high school and college athletic associations could be considered state action, it may be argued that private institutions acting in compliance with association rules are also engaging in state action. How do courts answer these questions? In general, they use two common methods of analysis: the public function theory and the entanglement theory.

The *public function theory* is somewhat limited, in that it is traditionally confined to essential governmental services that have no counterparts in the public sector. Under this theory, private actors who perform such services may be considered state actors. For example, in cases of great historical significance, political parties running their own primary elections and corporations owning and operating their own towns have been found to be state actors under the public function theory. Conversely, private schools providing education and private companies operating shopping centers have been ruled classified as purely private actors.

The *entanglement theory* focuses on the relationship between the government and the private entity in question. If the court finds a sufficiently close *nexus* between the two, the private entity will be treated as a state actor. While government regulation and funding are important factors, they are not enough to demonstrate entanglement between the government and a private actor. The state or federal government must have substantial influence over the association's activities, and state and association actions must be intertwined to the extent that the organization's actions are supported or sanctioned by the government.

During the 1970s, most case law held the NCAA's actions to be the equivalent of state action under this theory. In these cases, the rationale typically had been that over half of the NCAA's members were state-supported schools. In addition, most NCAA member schools received federal aid, and their students received federal financial aid (work study, National Defense loans). Therefore, albeit indirectly, the NCAA was supported by state and federal governments. The NCAA also provided a service that was beyond the competence or authority of any one state.

In the 1980s, judicial appraisals of the NCAA's statues began to change. Courts began to take a narrower view of what was a state actor, beginning with a federal appellate court in *Arlosoroff v. National Collegiate Athletic Ass'n* (note 3). In 1988, the U.S. Supreme Court settled the question. Its decision in *NCAA v. Tarkanian*, 109 S. Ct. 454 (1988), ruled that the NCAA was not a state actor. The NCAA's policies were determined by several hundred public and private member institutions independent of any particular state, and the NCAA enjoyed no governmental powers to facilitate its investigation of UNLV and Tarkanian. Therefore, the NCAA was not entangled with any branch of government, and no state action existed. High school associations similarly have had their actions scrutinized under the entanglement theory. Many high schools and high school associations receive financial assistance from the state; have public officials who make decisions concerning policies and procedures; and have a large portion of their membership consisting of public schools. In *Brentwood Academy v. Tennessee Secondary School Athletic Ass'n*, 531 U.S. 288 (2001), the Supreme Court decided that such circumstances constituted state action under the entanglement theory. In this decision, the court discussed exactly why the TSSAA was a state actor:

> The Association's nominally private character is overborne by the pervasive entwinement of public institutions and public officials in its composition and workings, and

there is no substantial reason to claim unfairness in applying constitutional standards to it. To the extent of 84% of its membership, the Association is an organization of public schools represented by their officials acting in their official capacity to provide an integral element of secondary public schooling, interscholastic athletics. There would be no recognizable Association without the public school officials, who overwhelmingly determine and perform all but the Association's purely ministerial acts. Only the 16% minority of private school memberships keeps the entwinement of the Association and public schools from being total and their identities totally indistinguishable. To complement the entwinement from the bottom up, the State has provided entwinement from the top down: State Board members sit ex officio on the Association's governing bodies and Association employees participate in the state retirement system. Entwinement to the degree shown here requires that the Association be charged with a public character and judged by constitutional standards.

While the *Brentwood Academy* case settles the question of state action with regard to high school athletic associations, the same question with regard to the schools themselves and their employees depends on the schools individual characteristics. Public high schools are clearly state actors, affording their students the protections of the federal Constitution. However, private high schools will only be classified as state actors if a court finds sufficient entanglement between them and the state.

By now, we have seen the critical difference between the judiciary's treatment of the NCAA and high school athletic associations. As we move ahead, the reader will see the great practical impact of this distinction.

NOTES

Readers interested in the historical development of public function and entanglement analysis in nonsports cases may wish to look up the following cases:

1. *Rendell-Baker v. Kohn*, 457 U.S. 830 (1982)
2. *Hudgens v. NLRB*, 424 U.S. 507 (1976)
3. *Burton v. Wilmington Parking Authority*, 365 U.S. 715 (1961)
4. *Shelley v. Kraemer*, 334 U.S. 1 (1948)
5. *Marsh v. Alabama*, 326 U.S. 501 (1946)
6. *Smith v. Allwright*, 321 U.S. 649 (1944)

Before the Supreme Court's decision in *Tarkanian*, many courts believed that the NCAA was a state actor:

1. In *Howard University v. NCAA*, 510 F.2d 213 (D.C. Cir. 1975), the court noted that state supported educational institutions and their members and officers play a substantial role in the NCAA's program and that such state participation is a basis for finding state action (entanglement theory).

2. In *Parish v. NCAA*, 361 F.Supp. 1220 (W.D. La. 1973), *aff'd*, 506 F.2d 1028 (5th Cir. 1975), the court found state action since over half the NCAA's members are state-supported schools and the NCAA performs a public function by regulating intercollegiate athletics (entanglement theory).

3. *Buckton v. NCAA*, 366 F.Supp. 1152 (D. Mass. 1973), was the first case to declare the NCAA to be engaged in state action under the public function theory. The public function theory has since been supplanted by other theories.

4. In *Regents of the University of Minnesota v. NCAA*, 422 F.Supp. 1158 (D. Minn. 1976), the court acknowledged that the action taken by the NCAA has generally been accepted as the equivalent of state action.

5. In *Associated Students, Inc. v. NCAA*, 493 F.2d 1251 (9th Cir. 1974), the court determined that the actions of the NCAA did constitute state action since the NCAA regulates schools and universities, at least half of which were public.

In the following cases, the NCAA's decisions were found not to have constituted state action. All cases since *Tarkanian* have used the logic employed in that case in their decisions:

1. In *Hall v. NCAA*, 985 F.Supp. 782 (N.D. Ill. 1997), the court found that the NCAA was not a state actor in a case dealing with Bradley University, a private university. The court concluded, "If the NCAA's relationship with UNLV, a public university, was insufficient to translate the NCAA's actions into state action, then the NCAA is clearly not a state actor by virtue of its relationship with Bradley, a private university. Since the NCAA is not a state actor, it is not subject to constitutional restraints and cannot be sued under §1983 for alleged equal protection violations."

2. In *McDonald v. NCAA*, 370 F.Supp. 625 (C.D. Calif. 1974), the court concluded that the NCAA is not sufficiently state supported to be considered state action, and it has an existence separate and apart from the educational system of any state. In the court's words, "If an institution is unable to concur with a voluntary organization without contravening the constitutional rights of its students, it must withdraw from the organization."

3. In *Arlosoroff v. NCAA*, 746 F.2d 1019 (4th Cir. 1984), the court stated that the "fact that NCAA's regulatory function may be of some public service lends no support to the finding of state action, for the function is not one traditionally reserved to the state."

In the following cases, state action was found in the actions of interscholastic athletic associations:

1. In *Tennessee Secondary School Athletic Association (TSSAA) v. Brentwood Academy*, 127 S.Ct. 2489 (2007), the TSSAA sanctioned Brentwood after its football coach sent eighth-grade boys letters that the TSSAA determined to be the exercise of "undue influence" in recruiting. Brentwood sued, stating that the enforcement of the antirecruiting rule constituted state action and violated the 1st and 14th Amendments. The Sixth Circuit had previously held that the antirecruiting rule was a content-based regulation of speech not narrowly tailored to serve its permissible purpose. In reversing the Sixth Circuit, the Supreme Court noted that the TSSAA is a voluntary association and that the antirecruiting rule is necessary to managing an efficient and effective league.

2. In the case of *Indiana High School Athletic Association v. Carlsberg*, 694 N.E.2d 222 (Ind. Ct. App. 1997), the court found that the IHSAA was a state actor. However, it is also found that the right to participate in interscholastic athletics was not a protected right and that the plaintiffs had to prove that they were being discriminated against because they were members of a suspect class.

3. In *Indiana High School Athletic Association v. Reyes*, 694 N.E.2d 249 (Ind. 1997), the court made the same decision as in *Carlsberg*, reasoning that the IHSAA constituted a state actor for questions of constitutional law.

For a case in which the court ruled that an Olympic organization was not acting under color of state law, see the following:

1. *DeFrantz v. United States Olympic Committee*, 492 F.Supp. 1181 (D.D.C. 1980), *aff'd. without decision*, 701 F.2d 221 (D.C. Cir. 1980). Twenty-five athletes sought an injunction to bar the USOC from boycotting the 1980 Moscow Olympics. Emphasizing that the USOC receives no federal funding and that it operates and exists independently of the federal government, the court found that the state was not in a position of interdependence with the USOC. The court also stated that the plaintiffs failed to prove that some form of control, or governmental persuasion or pressure, was behind the challenged action (see the introduction to Chapter 1).

For further information, see the following law review article: James Potter, "The NCAA as State Actor: Tarkanian, Brentwood, and Due Process," *155 University of Pennsylvania Law Review* 1269 (2007).

6.1.2. Due Process

State action, while a critical foundational issue, is only the first constitutional concept relevant to athletic associations. Once an organization has been classified as a state actor, the question arises of what rights it must respect. A primary concern of athletic administrators when imposing penalties that jeopardize an individual's career should be minimum standards of "due process of law."

Due process is an elusive concept. One definition for the term *due process* is "a course of legal proceedings which have been established in our system of jurisprudence for the protection and enforcement of private rights" (*Pennoyer v. Neff*, 95 U.S. 714 (1877)). The concept may vary, depending on three basic considerations: (1) the seriousness of the infraction, (2) the possible consequences to the institution or individual in question, and (3) the degree of sanction or penalty imposed.

The constitutional guarantee of due process is found in both the 5th and 14th Amendments to the U.S. Constitution. The Fifth Amendment, enacted in 1791, is applicable to the federal government. It states that "no person...shall be deprived of life, liberty, or property without due process of law." In 1868, the 14th Amendment was ratified, reading in part, "nor shall any state deprive any person of life, liberty, or property without due process of law." This amendment extended the applicability of the due process doctrine to the states. Therefore, both amendments apply only to federal or state governmental action and not to the conduct of purely private entities. While the Constitution extends these liberties to all persons, a person must demonstrate deprivation of life, liberty, or property to claim a violation of due process guarantees.

Since athletic associations and conferences rarely deprive a person of life, the major interests that trigger application of the due process clause in the athletic context are deprivations of liberty and property. Unless an athlete or other party can establish that he or she has been deprived of liberty or property, he or she will not be able to establish a deprivation of due process.

The due process doctrine presses two inquiries. The first is *procedural due process*, which refers to the procedures required to ensure fairness. The second is *substantive due process*, which guarantees basic rights that cannot be denied by governmental action. Procedural due process has as its focal point the questioning of the decision-making process that is followed in determining whether the rule or regulation has been violated and the penalty, if any, that is imposed.

Was the decision made in an arbitrary, capricious, or collusive manner? Was the accused given the opportunity to know what to defend against and to know reasonably well in advance what is thought to have been violated? Substantive due process involves the substance of the rule, regulation, or legislation being violated, namely, is it fair and reasonable? Does the rule or legislation have a purpose and is its enforcement clearly related to the accomplishment of that purpose? How does the rule impact the liberty and property interests of the plaintiff?

Although we will focus here primarily on the federal Constitution, due process claims may arise from other legal sources as well. Claims to due process protection may be based on protections guaranteed by state constitutions and by federal and state statutes and on the regulations and constitutions of athletic institutions, conferences, and other athletic governing organizations.

6.1.2.1. Procedural Due Process

As noted, procedural due process focuses on the method by which decisions affecting individuals' rights are made. The two minimum requirements of procedural due process are the *right to a hearing* and *notice* to concerned parties of the hearing's time, date, and content. The characteristics of the hearing, including the degree of formality required, depend on the nature of the right involved as well as on the circumstances. As a general rule, the more an individual has at stake, the more extensive and formal are the due process requirements. If the deprivation concerned is not that of a fundamental right, or if the challenged rule only marginally affects the right in question, only minimal due process requirements may be necessary. On the other hand, when a fundamental right is involved or when an infringement on personal freedom occurs, the hearing must be more formal, with additional safeguards. The full protections of due process include notice in writing and the right to a hearing in front of a neutral decision maker, with an opportunity to make an oral presentation, to present favorable evidence, and to confront and cross-examine adverse witnesses. In addition, there may also be a right to have an attorney present during the proceedings, a right to receive a copy of the transcript of the hearing, and a right to a written decision based on the record.

Since a number of factors are involved, administrative agencies must examine each case individually in order to determine what sort of due process is required. The Supreme Court has supplied a three-pronged inquiry to determine what due process is in a given case: the private interest that will be affected by the official action; the risk of an erroneous deprivation of such interest through the procedures used and the probable value, if any, of additional or substitute procedural safeguards; and the government's interest, including the function involved and the fiscal and administrative burdens that the additional or substitute procedural requirement would entail (*Mathews v. Eldridge*, 424 U.S. 319 (1976)). With these guidelines in mind, some have suggested that athletic organizations fashion a set of notice and hearing procedures that will withstand constitutional scrutiny. The benefits to establishing a set of procedures include the following:

1. Establishing procedures may be fairer to student-athletes, thereby leading to more consistent decisions and building goodwill.

2. Courts, which are already inclined to defer to athletic decision makers, will in most cases find the procedures adequate if they are well detailed, particularly if the procedures are originally fashioned in light of the *Mathews* case.

3. Provided that the procedures are basically fair and balance the factors outlined in *Mathews*, they are less likely to be challenged by the student-athletes themselves because some due process will already have been afforded the aggrieved party.

4. Establishing procedures would contribute some certainty to an area otherwise fraught with ambiguity.

Having a set of notice and hearing procedures thus benefits the organization as well as the athlete, thereby reducing the role of the courts in fashioning and implementing required procedures.

NOTES _____

For more on due process requirements, see the following: James A. Rapp, *Education Law* (New York: M. Bender, 2008), also available on Lexis Nexis. In the following cases, the courts ruled that there was no violation of due process rights:

1. In *Marsh v. Delaware State University*, WL 141680 (D. Del. January 19, 2006), a track and field athlete sued the school to enforce his scholarship. In January 2004, the plaintiff was arrested possession of illegal drugs and possession of a weapon after a gun and small bag of marijuana were found in his dormitory. He was expelled from the school a month later after a hearing and an appeals process were held. Plaintiff contended violations of his due process rights under the 5th and 14th Amendments, his right to a jury trial under the 7th Amendment, cruel and unusual punishment under the 8th Amendment, and discrimination based on his race under the Civil Rights Act. The court stated that there are two basic due process requirements: (1) notice and (2) an opportunity to be heard, both of which were satisfied in this instance. In denying the injunction, the court the plaintiff had not established a likelihood of success on the merits.

2. In *Richard v. Perkins*, 373 F.Supp.2d 1211 (D.Kan. 2005), a track athlete at the University of Kansas brought suit alleging violations of his 1st and 14th Amendment rights after his scholarship was not renewed for his sophomore year and he was removed from the team. Plaintiff claimed he was removed from the team in retaliation for exercising his right to free speech by appealing the scholarship decision, which amounted to a violation of procedural due process. The court dismissed the claim that removing him from the team violated substantive due process, holding that although there can be a protected interest in participating in school activities, the plaintiff's removal from the team did not shock the conscience. However, the court sustained his First Amendment claim for trial.

3. In *L.P.M. and D.J.T. v. School Board*, 753 So. 2d 130 (Fla. Dist. Ct. App. 2000), two students were not allowed to participate in extracurricular athletics after it was found that they had violated a school rule by drinking alcohol off campus. The students were given a full administrative hearing where they were represented by counsel. The court held that the students had no protected right to participate in extracurricular athletics and that they had been given full due process under the school board's system.

4. In *In Re University Interscholastic League*, 20 S.W.3d 690 (Tex. 2000), the Texas Supreme Court found that a constitutional right was not violated when a student-athlete is not allowed to participate in extracurricular activities. In this case, an entire baseball team was ruled ineligible to compete in a high school playoff tournament because one of its players was declared ineligible. The court did not believe that because the players might suffer immediate and irreparable harm that they could show a constitutional violation.

5. In *Mazevski v. Horseheads Central School District*, 950 F.Supp. 69 (W.D. N.Y. 1997), the court held that a high school student did not have protected property interest in participating in extracurricular activities. In this case, a student was dismissed from his school's marching band because of an unexcused absence at an event. The parents of the student, the plaintiffs, brought a claim of procedural due process violations. The court did not rule on the merits of the plaintiff's case because the plaintiff was not able to establish that membership in an extracurricular activity is a protectable property right. The court reasoned that the only right that the plaintiff had was the right to an education, not to extracurricular activities.

In the following cases, the courts ruled that there was a violation of due process rights:

1. In *Butler v. Oak Creek-Franklin School District*, 172 F.Supp.2d 1102 (E.D. Wis. 2001), a student-athlete was cited for possessing fireworks, intoxicants, and committing disorderly conduct. These were the student's fourth and fifth violations of the athlete conduct code, and the player was suspended for 12 months from competition. Although it was held that the student did not have a protected interest to participate in athletics, the court reasoned that he was not given his full due process rights because he was not given notice of the

hearing regarding his misconduct and that the hearing was not impartial because it involved the school's athletic director. The court refused to dismiss the plaintiff's due process claims and ordered that a status conference be held within 11 days.

2. In *Christ the King Regional High School v. Catholic High Schools Athletic Ass'n*, 624 N.Y.S.2d 755 (N.Y. Sup. Ct. 1995), the girls' basketball team at the plaintiff high school was suspended from postseason play for one season for violating a league rule concerning traveling to out-of-state games. Upon reviewing the penalty imposed by the association's Principals Committee, the court discovered that the penalty was arbitrary and capricious because it violated the rules of the association, which only allowed for the association's Infractions Committee to enact such penalties.

3. In *Diaz v. Board of Education, City*, 618 N.Y.S.2d 948 (N.Y. Sup. Ct. 1994), the court found that the due process rights of an entire high school soccer team had been violated when it was not allowed to compete for an entire season due to the actions of one of its players. The director of the Public School Athletic League (PSAL), in a letter dated November 2, 1993, had warned the members of the Newtown High School soccer team that if they received one more red card during the season the entire team would be withdrawn from competition in the league. Nine days later, one player started a fight after spitting in the face of a referee and subsequently received a red card. After a disciplinary hearing was scheduled, the Newtown team was deemed ineligible to participate on the varsity level for the 1994–1995 season. The court found that this decision was erroneous on two grounds. First, the court believed that the director of the PSAL was not in a position to promulgate such a penalty because under the bylaws of the PSAL, all such policy decisions must be adopted by committee. Second, the court found that even if the director had the authority to hand out the penalty, the ruling was arbitrary and capricious. The court argued that the entire soccer team should not be condemned for the actions of one of its players and also pointed to evidence that such rules had never been handed out to other teams, leading the court to believe that the imposition of the penalty upon Newtown was discriminatory.

6.1.2.2. Substantive Due Process

Whereas procedural due process concerns the means and methods of decision making, substantive due process concerns the *fairness* of laws and regulations and of their application to individuals. The due process clauses of the 5th and 14th Amendments guarantee that no one may be unfairly or arbitrarily deprived of life, liberty, or property. In sports cases, the interest most commonly cited is the property interest, although in some instances, the liberty interest is involved (see hair length cases in section 6.4.1). For the purposes of the due process clause, property is a broad category. Therefore, the first problem encountered in many of these cases is a determination of whether the interest involved constitutes property. Traditionally, *property* has been defined as all valuable interests that can be possessed outside oneself, which have an exchangeable value or which add to an individual's wealth or estate and which are recognized and protected by the government. Since 1972, in the Supreme Court's decision in *Board of Regents v. Roth*, 408 U.S. 564 (1972), property has been defined as all interests to which an individual could be deemed "entitled." Entitlements occur only if there is some form of current interest in or current use of the property.

For example, a holder of a scholarship has a property right because he or she is currently entitled to benefits derived from it. Due process protections are triggered only when there is an actual deprivation of the entitled rights. This "entitlement" standard does not encompass wishes that do not come true or expectations that fail to materialize; an entitlement to property must be more than an abstract need or desire for it.

The property right frequently involved in sports is the right to participate in athletic activities. The major controversy concerns the question of whether participation is an individual, protectable property right, or something less. This question is analyzed differently depending on whether the athletic activity is on the high school or the college level. On both levels, defendants (i.e., schools, conferences, and athletic associations) have argued that participation in athletics is a privilege or "mere expectation" and therefore falls outside the parameters of the due process clause (see *Walsh v. Louisiana High School Athletic Association*, 616 F.2d 152 (5th Cir. 1980)).

In the collegiate area, however, plaintiffs have sometimes been successful in claiming a property interest based on the proximity of monetary benefits currently or potentially available to the student-athlete. A property interest has been found in athletic participation because there exists a potential economic benefit to the student-athlete in the form of either a scholarship or a future professional contract.

A current holder of a scholarship who would be deprived of that scholarship has a well-defined property interest based on the present economic value of the award. A college student-athlete may also have a protectable interest in a future professional contract, as in *Behagen v. Intercollegiate Conference of Faculty Representatives*, 346 F.Supp. 602 (D. Minn. 1972). Some courts, however, by looking at a statistical analysis of the percentage of people who successfully enter professional sports, have discounted a legitimate property interest in a future professional contract as being too speculative. Also, at least one court has indicated that it would find a protectable property interest only if there were a professional league in that particular sport.

In the interscholastic area, a different analysis applies. A high school student-athlete with only the possibility of obtaining a scholarship generally has no present, demonstrable economic interest, and the possibility of obtaining a scholarship is too speculative to receive protection. Similarly, a high school student-athlete is usually considered to have an entirely speculative interest in a future professional contract.

In high school cases, the question of property interest involves the student-athlete's argument that he or she has a right to an education and that participation in interscholastic athletics is included in that right. The threshold issue is whether there is a right to an education. The Supreme Court has specifically denied a general constitutional right to education (see *San Antonio Independent School District v. Rodriguez*, 411 U.S. 1 (1973)). But even though the right to an education is not grounded in federal law, a state may grant a right to an education either explicitly or implicitly by requiring school attendance. Through either measure, the state effectively gives each child within its boundaries an interest in the education provided. This interest has been held to be a type of property interest protected by the due process clause (see *Pegram v. Nelson*, 469 F. Supp. 1134 (M.D.N.C. 1979) and *Goss v. Lopez*, 419 U.S. 565 (1974)).

Whether a right is stated explicitly or implicitly, once it has been established, it cannot be limited or removed without due process protections. After finding a right to education based on statutory attendance requirements, a determination must then be made as to whether or not that right includes participation in extracurricular activities. If the right to education means a right to the "total" educational process provided by a school, the courts may find participation in athletic competition to be a right protected by due process considerations. Most courts, however, interpret educational rights as encompassing only classroom learning and view all other activities as mere expectations.

NOTES

In the following cases, the court found no violation of due process rights:

1. In *Hadley v. Rush Henrietta Central School District*, 2007 WL 12321753 (W.D.N.Y. April 25, 2007), a high school lacrosse player claimed that the school district violated his constitutional rights by preventing him from playing lacrosse due to his refusal to receive a tetanus vaccination for religious reasons. Hadley was allowed to attend high school by being granted a vaccination waiver for religious purposes, and he contended that this waiver applied to school-sponsored extracurricular activities as well. In dismissing the complaint, the court noted there is no constitutional right to participate in extracurricular sporting activities. In addition, the rule requiring a tetanus shot was rationally related to the school district's interest in ensuring student safety.

2. In *Angstadt v. Midd-West School District*, 377 F.3d 338 (3rd Cir. 2004), the parents of a student enrolled in a cyber charter school appealed a ruling from the District Court denying their request for injunctive relief. Their daughter, Megan, wanted to play interscholastic basketball for Midd-West, the local public school, but they claimed she had not met the requirements. The Angstadt's alleged their refusal to allow her to participate on the team violated Megan's First Amendment right to freedom of association, due process, and equal protection. In affirming the decision, the Third Circuit noted that Megan's curriculum was not approved by the State Board of Education, that there is no constitutionally protected right to participate in interscholastic sports, and that cyber-schooled students are not a suspect classification.

3. In *Pelletier v. Maine Principals' Association (MPA)*, 261 F.Supp.2d 10 (D.Me. 2003), parents of home-schooled children requested injunctive relief that would allow their children to participate in interscholastic athletics at a local Christian School, Seacoast, rather than the local public school as provided by Maine law. The Pelletiers contended that the MPA's refusal to allow them to compete at Seacoast (1) violated their 14th Amendment substantive due process right of parental educational choice, (2) violated the equal protection rights of Seacoast, and (3) violated their First Amendment right to freedom of religion. In denying the injunction, the court ruled that there was no burden on parental educational choice or free exercise of religion requiring substantive due process analysis because the state opens public high school athletic programs to home-schooled children. Also, the Pelletiers had no standing to bring a constitutional argument on behalf of Seacoast because Seacoast was more than capable of making the argument if it so chose.

In the following cases, the court decided that there was not a property interest in intercollegiate athletics:

1. In *Hall v. NCAA*, 985 F. Supp. 782 (N.D. Ill. 1997), the plaintiff, a prospective collegiate student-athlete, did not meet the minimum academic standards to qualify for participation in the NCAA. He did not take an adequate number of core courses in high school and did not maintain a minimum grade point average (GPA). The court held that the right to participate in athletics was not a protected property interest and that hopes for a career in basketball were also too speculative to be a constitutionally protected right.

2. In *Knapp v. Northwestern University*, No. 95-C-6454 1996 U.S. Dist. LEXIS 12463 (N.D. Ill Aug. 23, 1996), a student that had received an athletic scholarship to play basketball at Northwestern University was not cleared to play by team doctors because of a heart condition. The player argued that he had a substantial interest in playing because of the hopes of a professional career. The court, however, found this theory to be speculative, stating, "While participation in intercollegiate basketball has been recognized as a training ground for a professional basketball career, the possibility of obtaining that professional basketball career is too speculative to even constitute a present economic interest."

In the following cases, the court decided that there was not a property interest in interscholastic athletics:

1. In *St. Patrick High School v. New Jersey Interscholastic Athletic Association*, 2010 WL 715826 (D.N.J. March 1, 2010), the court rejected a high school's petition for injunctive relief that would have permitted the school to play in the state basketball tournament. The NJSIAA banned the school from participating after finding two players improperly transferred to the school. The Court stated that no property interest exists in participation in extracurricular activities, including sports, as a general principle, under the United States Constitution.

2. In *Perry v. Ohio High School Athletic Association (OHSAA)*, 2006 WL 2927260 (S.D. Ohio October 11, 2006), a student-athlete sued OHSAA and Columbus Public Schools (CPS) after he transferred within the CPS system but was denied athletic eligibility. OHSAA rules permit a student to transfer within the same system without jeopardizing his eligibility with the approval of the OHSAA commissioner. In this case, the athletic director at the plaintiff's new school realized that he had failed to send the necessary paperwork, and subsequently, the school was forced to forfeit all games in which the plaintiff participated, including the entire 2004–2005 basketball season and state championship. Also, plaintiff had his MVP award revoked. Plaintiff had contended that the rules of the OHSAA were overly broad and violated his freedom of association rights under the First Amendment. In granting summary judgment for the defendants, the court explained that there is no constitutionally protected property interest in participating in interscholastic athletics.

3. In *Taylor v. Enumclaw School Dist. No. 216*, 133 P.3d 492 (Wash. App. Div. 1 2006), a high school football player brought suit alleging violations of his 14th Amendment rights after he was suspended from one football game and five wrestling matches for alcohol use. Taylor had been questioned for drinking at a school dance, other players testified that he was under the influence of alcohol during a football game and school administrators found an empty beer case in his car. The plaintiff contended that he had a property interest in athletic participation as part of the larger educational process for which a property interest is recognized. The court denied such a premise and affirmed summary judgment for the defendants.

4. In *Ryan v. California Interscholastic Federation*, 94 Cal. App. 4th 1048 (Cal. Ct. App. 2001), a student enrolled in a high school after completing the 12th grade in a high school in Australia. He was found to be ineligible for athletic participation in California under CIF bylaws. The court held that California law did not provide a protected property right to participate in interscholastic athletics, and that participation was only a privilege.

In the following cases, the court determined that there was a property interest in interscholastic or intercollegiate athletics:

1. In *Puchalski v. School District of Springfield*, 161 F.Supp. 2d 395 (E.D. Pa. 2001), a football coach that had been fired by a public school brought, among other allegations, a claim that he had been deprived of a property interest by being fired and not being evaluated before his termination. The court disagreed, holding that property interest in public employment did not exist and that he had no right to evaluation unless made explicit by the employment contract.

2. In *Boyle v. Pennsylvania Athletic Ass'n*, 676 A.2d 695 (Pa. Commw. Ct. 1996), the Athletic Association denied eligibility to a student that had transferred from a public school to a Catholic school within the same association. The association was not swayed to change its decision even though the student transferred because of an altercation with his former coach at the public school. The student was seeking an injunction that would allow him to play on the Catholic school team. The court conceded that the plaintiff did not have a property interest in interscholastic athletics and that its right to interfere with the decisions of the Association was limited. Nevertheless, the court held that the plaintiff was entitled to the injunction. The court analyzed the purpose of the Pennsylvania transfer rule, which was to prevent transfers and recruiting done for athletic purposes. The court held that ruling that the student should be ineligible for competition was arbitrary and capricious and

therefore that the association violated his right to equal protection. There was no evidence to show that the student transferred because he was recruited or for any athletic purpose.

3. In *Lesser v. Neosho County Community College*, 741 F. Supp. 854 (D. Kan. 1990), the plaintiff was cut from his college baseball team shortly after receiving a scholarship. During his tenure on the team, he was subject to fines for violating a team appearance standard. The court analyzed claims of both property and liberty interest violations. The court held that he did not have a liberty interest to participate in intercollegiate athletics. Nevertheless, the court held that the plaintiff did have a property interest in the money that he was fined during his time with the team. It was clear that the athletes were not afforded their due process rights before punishment if they violated the team's grooming policies.

6.1.3. Equal Protection

So far, we have studied certain interests which may not be deprived without due process of law. *Equal protection* concerns something else. This independent constitutional guarantee governs all federal, state, and local laws that classify individuals and impact on individual rights. It derives from a clause found in the 14th Amendment of the U.S. Constitution, which reads, "No state shall…deny to any person within its jurisdiction the equal protection of the laws." It is specifically applicable only to the states, but the federal government is held to similar standards under the due process clause of the Fifth Amendment. Equal protection requires that no person be singled out from similarly situated people, or have different benefits bestowed or burdens imposed, unless a constitutionally permissible reason for doing so exists. Thus, in the equal protection clause of the 14th Amendment, student-athletes and coaches find the means to challenge rules and regulations of a discriminatory nature.

When considering equal protection claims, courts use three standards of review. The highest standard of review is that of *strict scrutiny*. Application of strict scrutiny by the court means that the challenged rule will be invalidated, unless the defendant can demonstrate that the rule is supported by a compelling state interest and that the rule is narrowly tailored to advance that interest. When a rule abridges a fundamental right or makes a distinction based on suspect criteria, the defendant bears the burden of proof. This standard tests only whether a classification is properly drawn, not whether an individual is properly placed within that classification. In the equal protection context, this type of review is triggered by the use of either a suspect classification, or the unequal deprivation of fundamental rights.

The Supreme Court has identified three suspect classifications: alienage, race, and national origin. Any time a rule discriminates directly or indirectly on the basis of these classifications, courts will apply strict scrutiny. Thus, in such cases, the relevant state actor will bear the burden of defending its rule and will have to show that the rule is the least restrictive means of achieving a compelling state objective. On the other hand, as we have seen in the due process context that courts usually find participation in athletics to constitute an expectation and not a constitutionally based right. In general, some interests have been specifically found to be nonfundamental; these include subsistence and welfare payments, housing, government employment, and education. The fact that education has been deemed a nonfundamental interest is particularly important in cases involving high school or college athletic associations.

This designation makes it difficult for the student-athlete plaintiff to establish athletic participation as a fundamental interest. Therefore, claims alleging the unequal deprivation of such opportunities are far less likely to provoke strict scrutiny than claims based on suspect classifications.

The second standard of review under the equal protection guarantee is the *rational basis* test. This standard is used when no suspect classifications or fundamental rights are at issue. Rational basis review requires only that the rule have some rational relationship to a legitimate organizational or governmental purpose; the plaintiff bears the burden of proving otherwise. Rules reviewed under this standard are difficult for a plaintiff to challenge successfully because the defendant is generally able to present some rational relationship between the restriction and a legitimate governmental objective. Consequently, when courts decide to use this standard, the defendants nearly always prevail.

The third standard of review or category of classes imposes an *intermediate scrutiny* test, which falls between the strict scrutiny and rational basis tests. It requires that rules classifying certain groups demonstrate an "important" but not necessarily a "compelling" interest and that the rules in question be "substantially related" to that interest. Two quasisuspect classifications have been established: gender and legitimacy. Therefore, use of either gender- or legitimacy-based classifications will trigger this intermediate standard of review. Although the difference between a compelling interest and an important interest frequently seems unclear in court decisions, it is at least clear that the state actor bears the burden of demonstrating that its important interest is advanced by the rule in question. In practical terms most—but not all—laws using quasisuspect classifications are struck down. As equal protection jurisprudence continues to evolve, the issue of what other classifications may qualify as quasisuspect will take on great importance.

The equal protection guarantee relates to classifications and distinctions inevitably drawn whenever a legislative body makes rules relating to specific groups. One method typically employed to challenge a rule under the equal protection clause is to claim either under- or overinclusiveness. *Overinclusiveness* means that the legislative classification includes many people to whom the rule in question lacks a rational relationship. In other words, at least some of the affected individuals are not part of the problem addressed by the rule and the rule as applied to these people has no relationship to its purpose. A rule's validity depends not on whether classifications differ but on whether the differences are pertinent to the subject with respect to which the classification is made. Whereas overinclusiveness exists when a rule creates a class more extensive than necessary to effectuate the purpose of the rule, *underinclusiveness* exists when a class does not contain all the members necessary to effectuate the rule's purpose.

It is possible for a rule to be both over- and underinclusive. For example, consider the following rule, aimed at preventing high school students from transferring for athletic purposes: "All transfer students from public high schools will be ineligible for interscholastic play for one year from date of entry." This rule is overinclusive with respect to public school transfers that were made for reasons unrelated to athletics. It would be underinclusive, however, if it permitted immediate eligibility for transfer students from private schools who might be transferring for solely athletic reasons. How a plaintiff might challenge a rule would depend on the specific classifications involved.

To draw perfect classifications that are neither over-nor underinclusive is extremely difficult. In light of this, when no important constitutional rights are involved, the courts can and do uphold both over- and underinclusive categories as long as they can find a rational relationship between the rule and its purpose. Courts wish to allow athletic associations to deal with problems on an objective basis and do not expect perfect solutions prior to attacking specific problems.

However, if constitutionally protect rights are involved, over- or underinclusive regulations are likely to be invalidated. In some cases, the court will not decide whether the rule itself is invalid but will conclude that its application to a specific individual violates the person's constitutional rights. The court can therefore defer to the legislative judgment supporting the rule while simultaneously upholding the rights of the individual.

Where does all this leave us in terms of equal protection analysis in sports-related cases? While athletes have long faced obstacles to the recognition of athletic participation as a fundamental right, they retain the right to compete free of discrimination. The manner in which a court will analyze a claim of discrimination depends upon the nature of the classification being challenged. As we will see in the rest of the chapter, discrimination is just one of many issues that arise in the context of eligibility and participation rights. And as we will see later, the spirit underlying equal protection claims also buttresses the application of federal laws to discrimination in athletics.

NOTES _____

1. In *Christian Heritage Academy v. Oklahoma Secondary School Activities Association (OSSAA)*, 483 F.3d 1025 (10th Cir. 2007), Christian Heritage, a private religious school in Oklahoma, sued after it was denied membership to OSSAA twice. Christian Heritage failed to receive approval from a majority of the 471 OSSAA schools, 459 of which were public. In denying their application it became apparent some public schools were concerned with the advantages a private school may have such as the ability to offer scholarships, larger geographic areas from which to draw student-athletes, and more relaxed transfer restrictions. In its second application, Christian Heritage decreased its proposed geographic area but was still denied. Christian Heritage brought suit alleging violations of the equal protection and due process clauses of the 14th Amendment and the free exercise clause of the 1st Amendment. The district court granted OSSAA summary judgment, but the 10th Circuit reversed and remanded. The 10th Circuit ruled that the membership process, conducted by a majority vote of existing members, was not rationally related to a legitimate purpose, as required by equal protection jurisprudence.

2. In *Thomka v. Massachusetts Interscholastic Athletic Association, Inc. (MIAA)*, 2007 WL 867084 (Mass. Super. February 12, 2007), a female high school golfer brought suit claiming that should be allowed to compete in the boys' individual state championship that occurs in the fall season. The boys' championship had a higher level of competition and greater attendance by college coaches and recruiters and may have given Thomka a better chance to showcase her golfing talents as she contended. Thomka participated on a mixed-gender team that played only in the fall. By 2007, Thomka was a three-time runner-up in the girls' individual championship that occurred in the spring but was at a disadvantage because she was not participating while in season like other girls. As a sophomore, Thomka's 74 from the front tees in the team regional tournament would have been good enough to qualify for the boys' individual championship, but she was not allowed to compete because of her gender. Her request for an injunction was granted, and she participated in the 2005 boys' individual championship from the back tees. She did not qualify in 2006. Following the injunction, the Superior Court of Massachusetts declared that the rule violated the Massachusetts Equal Rights Amendment by unfairly discriminating on the basis of sex and enjoined the MIAA from enforcing the rule. In sum, the court felt that the spring tournament was not an equal opportunity for girls playing on mixed-gender teams in the fall.

3. In *Jones v. West Virginia State Board of Education*, 622 S.E.2d 289 (W.Va. 2005), the parents of a home-schooled student brought suit seeking injunctive relief so that their son, Aaron, could participate on the middle school wrestling team. The West Virginia Secondary School Activities Commission (WVSSAC) ruled that interscholastic athletic activities

were limited to student enrolled full-time in a WVSSAC school. In reversing the injunction, the West Virginia Supreme Court of Appeals prohibiting home-schooled children from participating interscholastic athletics does not violate equal protection because of the vast differences between being home-schooled versus receiving an in-school education. The court also recognized that participation in extracurricular activities is not a fundamental right.

4. In *Fusato v. Washington Interscholastic Activities Ass'n*, 970 P.2d 774 (Wash. Ct. App. 1999), the court found that the WIAA had violated Fusato's equal protection rights by not allowing her to play interscholastic athletics. Under their transfer rule, student-athletes who transfer to a high school are not allowed to compete immediately unless they move with the entire "family unit." In Fusato's case, she moved from Okinawa by herself to live with her aunt and uncle in Washington and was not allowed to play immediately for her high school due to the transfer rule. The court decided for Fusato because it believed that she was being discriminated against due to her nation of origin, which is a suspect class in questions of equal protection. The court stated, "We hold the trial court did not err applying the strict scrutiny test when deciding the WIAA residence and transfer rules violated Ms. Fusato's equal protection rights under the 14th Amendment. Although Ms. Fusato cannot prove a fundamental right is threatened, she established she was a member of a suspect class based upon national origin or alienage. Upon her showing of disparate impact, together with discriminatory purpose or intent, the WIAA was required to meet the burden of showing a compelling state interest was served by the challenged rules. The WIAA failed to meet its burden and made no effort to demonstrate that the least restrictive regulatory means were used to accomplish the stated purposes of their rules."

5. In *Howard University v. NCAA*, 510 F.2d 213 (D.C. Cir. 1975), the court applied strict scrutiny in striking down the NCAA's "Foreign Student Rule" because the classification was based on alienage. Even though the court accepted the purpose of the rule, it held that the rule was not closely tailored to achieve its goal since it penalized foreign student-athletes for activities that citizens participated in without penalty.

6.2. DEFINITIONS OF ELIGIBILITY

Each athletic association has developed its own definition of an eligible athlete. Historically, most amateur organizations refused to allow athletes to receive any money at all in compensation for their time or expenses. In fact, this restriction was the basis for distinguishing the amateur athlete from the professional athlete.

Increasingly, however, athletes are allowed to receive compensation for certain living, training, and competition expenses. The amount and type of reimbursement allowed are determined by the governing athletic association. Furthermore, in the Olympics, there are still organizations, such as U.S. Rowing, that allow only amateur athletes to compete.

The National Collegiate Athletic Association's Bylaw 12.1.2. stipulates that a student shall lose his or her eligibility if the individual

a. uses his or her athletic skill (directly or indirectly) for pay in any form in that sport

b. accepts a promise of pay even if such pay is to be received following completion of intercollegiate athletics participation

c. signs a contract or commitment of any kind to play professional athletics, regardless of its legal enforceability or any consideration received

d. receives, directly or indirectly, a salary, reimbursement of expenses or any other form of financial assistance from a professional sports organization based upon athletics skill or participation, except as permitted by NCAA rules and regulations

e. competes on any professional athletics team per Bylaw 12.02.4, even if no pay or remuneration for expenses was received

f. after initial full-time collegiate enrollment, enters into a professional draft

g. enters into an agreement with an agent

The IOC allows its international federations (IFs) to make decisions concerning the eligibility status of the athletes within their sports. Bylaw 45 of the Olympic Charter specifies the following:

> To be eligible for participation in the Olympic Games a competitor must comply with the Olympic Charter as well as with the rules of the IF concerned as approved by the IOC, and must be entered by his NOC.
>
> • Each IF establishes its sport's own eligibility criteria in accordance with the Olympic Charter. Such criteria must be submitted to the IOC Executive Board for approval.
>
> • The application of the eligibility criteria lies with the IFs, their affiliated National Federations and the NOCs in the fields of their respective responsibilities.
>
> • Except as permitted by the IOC Executive Board, no competitor who participates in the Olympic Games may allow his person, name, picture, or sports performances to be used for advertising purposes during the Olympic Games.
>
> • The entry or participation of a competitor in the Olympic Games shall not be conditional on any financial consideration.

Like the IOC, the U.S. Olympic Committee (USOC) allows decisions concerning eligibility status to be determined by the governing bodies of the individual sports. Within Article VII, Section III of the USOC Constitution, the USOC authorizes its governing bodies to "conduct amateur athletic competitions, including national championships, and international amateur athletic competitions, in the United States, and establish procedures for the determination of eligibility standards for participation in such competitions." The California Interscholastic Federation's constitution outlines which athletes are eligible to compete in interscholastic competition and how eligibility may be lost. In rules 213 and 600-604, these regulations are explained:

213. AMATEUR STATUS

B. Reinstatement of Amateur Status

A student will become ineligible for CIF competition in a given sport if the student is determined to be a professional by the national sports governing body (NSGB) for the sport in question. A student may apply for reinstatement of his/her amateur status through the Section in which the student competes. Any request for reinstatement must include a statement from the NSGB for the sport in question that the student's amateur status has been reinstated by the appropriate NSGB.

D. Professional Tryout

A student shall become ineligible for CIF competition if he/she participates in any tryout for a professional team in any CIF-approved sport from September 15 to June 15 unless:

(1) His/her principal has given written approval to a request for such participation from a professional team; AND

(2) The tryout is limited to five students or less.

600. COMPETITION ON AN OUTSIDE TEAM

A student on a high school team becomes ineligible if the student competes in a contest on an "outside" team, in the same sport, during the student's high school season of sport (See Bylaw 511). The following exceptions apply:

A. If the outside team has half or more of the team members as stated in the National Federation rules book for that sport, it shall be considered the same sport. Examples: three on three basketball—outside team competition prohibited; two on two volleyball—outside team competition permitted.

B. FLAG FOOTBALL For purposes of this rule, touch football and flag football are considered to be a different sport than tackle football.

C. SOCCER In the sport of soccer, Bylaw 600 shall be in effect only during the winter high school soccer season. High school soccer programs that compete during the fall or spring season are not subject to Bylaw 600.

D. SWIMMING & DIVING Swimmers may compete for an amateur team during the season of sport in the USA Swimming Senior National Championship Meet, the USA Swimming Sectional Championship meets and the YMCA National Meet. Divers may compete for an amateur team during the season of sport in the USA National Diving Championships and the USA National Junior Diving Championships.

E. Bylaw 600 shall not be in effect for those sports conducted outside the State-adopted season of sport.

F. SPONTANEOUS RECREATIONAL ACTIVITY

It is permissible for a high school team member to participate in a spontaneous recreational activity or game in which sides or teams are chosen without regard to players representing any group or organization. Such participation would not cause loss of eligibility. (Definition of spontaneous: no prior planning or notice; an unplanned part of another activity which has a primary focus other than the sport.)

G. UNATTACHED COMPETITION IN INDIVIDUAL SPORTS

(1) An unattached athlete shall not represent any team. Points won by the athlete shall not be credited to any team. An unattached athlete shall not use a uniform which identifies a school or "outside" team. Any violation shall be considered an infraction of Bylaw 600.

(2) Unattached competition is permissible for a student in other than school contests during the season of sport provided the student enters in the individual sports of badminton (singles and doubles), cross country, golf, gymnastics, skiing, swimming and diving (including unattached entry on relays), tennis (singles and doubles), track and field (including unattached entry on relays) and wrestling. (Revised May 2003 Federated Council)

(3) CERTIFICATION OF UNATTACHED ATHLETES

No official recognition or certification on the part of the CIF-member school or personnel of the CIF-member school may be given in order that unattached athletes may participate in contests.

(4) REPRESENTATION IN CIF COMPETITION

Unattached competition is not permitted in any CIF competition (See Bylaw 302). Individuals or teams entered in CIF competition must represent a CIF-member school. No other form of representation shall be permitted in CIF competition.

601. PAN-AMERICAN OR OLYMPIC COMPETITION

During the high school season of sport, a high school student who has been selected or qualified for participation on the United States team, which will engage in Pan-American or Olympic competition, may participate on that team.

602. OLYMPIC DEVELOPMENT PROGRAMS

During their high school season of sport, a high school student who has been selected or qualified for an Olympic development program by the respective national governing body for that sport, shall be permitted to participate in such a program without loss of interscholastic eligibility, if the following conditions are met:

A. The Olympic development program is:

(1) Verified as such by the State CIF; AND

(2) a. Conducted or sponsored by the United States Olympic Committee; OR

b. Directly funded and conducted by the U.S. national governing body for the sport on a national level; OR

c. Authorized by a national governing body for athletes having potential for future national team participation; AND

B. The student informs the high school principal at least 30 days prior to participating in the program; AND

C. The principal verifies the authenticity of the program; AND

D. The student makes prior arrangement to complete missed academic lessons, assignments and tests before the last day of classes of the semester in which the student's absence occurs. E. This bylaw was written with the intent that only individual student-athletes that have been identified by the respective National Governing body for that sport, as having Olympic potential, would be eligible for this exemption of Bylaw 600. Individual student-athletes who are members of a club team(s) consisting in whole or part of high school age athletes, participating in any competitions (e.g. Super Y League events, championships, etc.), even if the competition itself is labeled as an ODP event, that occur during the high school student's season of sport are not eligible for this exemption. (Revised Federated Council May 2007)

603. INTERNATIONAL COMPETITION

Each Section may grant approval, upon individual petition, for an athlete to travel to a foreign country to participate in international competition sanctioned by the governing body for that sport in the United States and the international governing body. (Revised May 2003 Federated Council)

604. PENALTIES FOR VIOLATION OF BYLAW 600

A. Individual

   (1) First Offense in High School Career in Any Sport

     The student becomes immediately ineligible for participation with his/her high school team for a number of contests equal to twice the number of contests of outside competition in which the student participated.

   (2) Any Subsequent Offense in High School Career in Any Sport

     The student becomes immediately ineligible for one year (365 days) from the second infraction in all sports.

   (3) Appeals

     Upon written appeal to the Section commissioner, the student may petition his/her Section for reinstatement of his/her eligibility status.

B. Team

   (1) Games Forfeited

     Games in which a student participated on his/her high school team after violation of Bylaw 600 shall be forfeited.

   (2) Appeals

   Sections may establish rules and procedures to consider requests for waivers of game forfeitures.

The U.S. Tennis Association (USTA) is an example of sports association that allows members to be professionals and also allows professionals to compete in the Olympic Games. The association does, nevertheless, maintain a definition of an amateur within its constitution in order to conduct events involving solely amateur competitors (Part 3, Section XII, Art. A, *USTA Handbook of Tennis Rules and Regulations*):

1. An amateur shall not receive pecuniary advantage because of his skills as a tennis player. Any tennis player is an amateur if he does not receive and has not received, directly or indirectly, pecuniary advantage by the playing, teaching, demonstrating, or pursuit of the game except as expressly permitted by the USTA.

2. Definition of professional. All other tennis players who accept the authority of, and who are in good standing with, the USTA shall be designated as professionals.

3. An amateur remains an amateur throughout a tournament. A player starting play in a tournament as an amateur shall remain an amateur for the purposes of that tournament.

The changing definitions of an amateur have sparked intense debate because of the serious consequences of defining an amateur athlete. At the international level, in 1986, the International Olympic Committee endorsed a proposed rule change to eliminate the distinction between amateur and professional athletes.

After this IOC decision, international federations retain control over deciding who can compete at the Olympic level. In 1998, the National Hockey League decided to allow its players to play in the Olympic Games in Nagano, Japan, and even stopped play for two weeks to accommodate traveling athletes. In figure skating, a controversy erupted in 1998 when figure skaters who had been considered professional were allowed to compete at the Olympic level. Meanwhile, the National Basketball Association has allowed its players to compete in the Olympics since 1992.

High school and collegiate athletic administrators should familiarize themselves with the amateurism rules of various federations because athletes deemed professional by a federation may lose their eligibility under NCAA or high school regulations. Athletes who choose to compete as professionals must also be aware of the impact of their choice on their amateur status in other sports. For example, Renaldo Nehemiah, a former world-class hurdler who joined the San Francisco 49ers of the National Football League, lost his amateur track status for several years as a result of his professional status in football. He was reinstated after he retired from the 49ers and returned to amateur track and field.

Historically, if an association maintained a traditional definition of *amateur* for eligibility, it was generally true that a member athlete could not be a professional in any sport, including sports that he or she does not compete in on the amateur level. However, this rule has become increasingly more flexible. In the NCAA, for example, athletes that have participated in professional sports are allowed to play intercollegiate athletics as long as it is in a different sport than the one they played professionally. For example, 2000 Heisman Trophy winner Chris Weinke of Florida State University was allowed to participate in intercollegiate football after playing Minor League baseball; more recently, Tripper Johnson joined the University of Washington football team after eight years in baseball's minor leagues. Still, the NCAA maintains that an athlete cannot participate in collegiate athletics in the same sport that he or she played professionally (see note 1).

NOTE

1. In the case of *Lasege v. NCAA*, 53 S.W. 3d 77 (Ky. 2001), the NCAA appealed a decision to grant a preliminary injunction to a basketball player whom the association had deemed ineligible. Lasege was a basketball player at the University of Louisville, when it was discovered that he had received funds to play basketball professionally before he had arrived in the United States. Louisville requested a waiver of the eligibility rules because Lasege, a native of Nigeria, had been ignorant of the rules of the NCAA when accepting the money to play and was not aware that his eligibility could be jeopardized by such actions. Louisville was granted an injunction on the district court level, which was affirmed in the appellate court. The NCAA sought interlocutory relief in this action, which is granted only when the plaintiff can show "extraordinary" cause. The court, in a split decision, found that the NCAA was deserving of this interlocutory relief and granted the NCAA's motion to disallow Lasege from playing basketball. The court stated, "In this case, we find that the trial court abused its discretion by: (1) substituting its judgment for that of the NCAA on the question of Lasege's intent to professionalize; (2) finding that the NCAA has no interest in this case which weighs against injunctive relief; and (3) declaring NCAA Bylaw 19.8 invalid. This combination of clearly erroneous conclusions constitutes extraordinary cause warranting [interlocutory] relief."

6.3. ELIGIBILITY REQUIREMENTS: COLLEGE AND HIGH SCHOOL

Individual eligibility requirements are a major area of legal concern because of their impact on student-athletes, coaches, and institutions. For instance, intercollegiate athletics, especially football and basketball, are potentially financially lucrative for institutions and coaches and may lead to career advancement for coaches and athletes.

To capture financial benefits for their institutions, there are several ways athletic departments can be set up. Some departments operate under the university budget, with revenues going directly to the general fund and expenses covered as line items; others are operated like businesses; still others are separately incorporated and are responsible for covering the expenses of the department solely with revenues taken in by the department. As football and basketball have become more lucrative, the financial stakes in intercollegiate athletics have become higher and the pressure to be successful has become greater (see section 1.3.2, "Economic Overview"). Consequently, athletic excellence has been pursued in some instances at the expense of academic performance. College and high school athletic associations have tried to address this problem by establishing academic, amateur, and participation requirements. Athletic associations enact these requirements to protect student-athletes and institutions and to promote amateur athletics. Consistent with these objectives, individual eligibility requirements are established with regard to GPA, academic progress, transferring, age restrictions, years of athletic participation, professional pay, drug use, and full-time student status, among others.

Individual student-athletes must meet many standards in order to be eligible for intercollegiate and interscholastic practice and/or competition. Each school, conference, or association, such as the NCAA, has rules and regulations covering various areas of sports activities. For collegiate and high school student-athletes, there are usually academic standards, rules governing personal conduct, and rules for each individual sport. Individual institutions on the collegiate and scholastic level may also establish eligibility requirements that are stricter than the minimum standards imposed by that institution's conference or association. In addition, a conference may impose a stricter rule than its association.

Under the NCAA's principle of *institutional control*, member schools bear primary responsibility to determine which of its student-athletes meet, and do not meet, the eligibility standards. The process of determining eligibility for each student-athlete may be very time consuming for an institution's athletic department, depending on the number of student-athletes participating, the number of sports offered by the institution, and the complexity of institutional, conference, and association rules, regulations, and interpretations.

In some cases, an institution's conference may assist members in keeping track of the eligibility status of every student-athlete. The most a conference might do in this area is to recheck, confirm, and correct, when necessary, all institutional information. Conferences may aid in the complex process of eligibility determination because correct eligibility status may be the best, if not the first, prevention of rule violations.

An institution's athletic department is usually the primary governing body and is responsible for enforcing eligibility rules and regulations. Penalties or sanctions may be levied against a student-athlete and the team and/or institution for knowingly or unknowingly allowing ineligible student-athletes to compete. In addition to enforcement, college and high school athletic associations recommend changes in rules, make policy decisions, and interpret eligibility rules and regulations.

6.3.1. Academic Eligibility Rules

The purpose of academic eligibility rules is to ensure that student-athletes are able to perform adequately in the classroom as well as on the field. With the financial stakes for both schools and athletes increasing, athletic associations want to prohibit institutions from recruiting athletes who have no desire to pursue an education. It is important to remember that high schools and colleges are educational institutions whose primary responsibility is to give a student an education.

Academic eligibility rules are designed to encourage student-athletes to perform adequately in the classroom; a student who does not meet the requirements will be deemed ineligible. Thus, student-athletes, coaches, and athletic directors want to ensure that the academic requirements are met.

A delicate balance must be struck between the educational institution and the governing athletic association concerning which entity will develop academic eligibility rules. There is often a conflict between allowing institutional self-control over academic standards and the need for governing associations to set uniform minimum standards for their member institutions. After many academic scandals, associations have increased the number of minimum rules by which institutions must abide.

6.3.1.1. Initial Eligibility: National Collegiate Athletic Association (NCAA)

GPA has long been used and recognized as a measure of a student's academic achievement. Consequently, the NCAA and several conferences have employed GPA requirements to ensure that student-athletes are academically qualified to participate at the collegiate level. GPA calculations typically involve converting letter grades to a four-point scale.

To compute a student's GPA, the letter grade in each course is converted to the 4.000 scale (A = 4, B = 3, C = 2, D = 1, F = 0). Grade points are weighted according to the number of credits awarded for each class. The points are then totaled for the courses to be included in the computation, and that total is divided by the number of courses. A student's GPA is usually calculated for each academic term each year and cumulatively for the student's entire high school or college career. The method and the subjects to be considered in the computation of a student's GPA vary from school to school. The GPA is used both as a measure of initial eligibility at the interscholastic level and as an indicator of progress to maintain the athlete's eligibility at the collegiate level.

The NCAA, conferences, and schools can measure a student-athlete's success in the classroom by comparing that student-athlete's grade with a selected marker (i.e., 2.0, a C average). A student-athlete who is not able to maintain a grade above that marker can be deemed ineligible for athletic participation. Rules of this sort have sometimes been subjected to judicial review. Courts may consider which types of courses should be included in the computation of the grade point average.

For example, should physical education courses count? The NCAA has attempted to address these issues. In 1983, the NCAA passed Proposition 48 (hereinafter referred to as Prop 48), requiring all incoming first-year student-athletes to achieve both a GPA of 2.0 in a core curriculum of at least 11 academic courses and a score of at least 700 on the SAT test or a composite score of 18 on the ACT. Proponents of Prop 48 saw the core curriculum requirements as providing an athlete exposure to a solid base of academic work. It also eliminated the use of noncore curriculum courses, such as physical education, from being used to increase overall GPA. Meanwhile, the test score requirement provided some uniformity in standards among institutions. Prop 48 was a signal to high school athletes that they needed to play close attention to their academic preparation if they planned to participate in college athletics. It was designed to give admitted student-athletes a better chance of obtaining a college degree and to end the exploitation of talented athletes that had been commonplace at many Division I institutions.

In an attempt to ease the criticism of Prop 48 (see notes following this section), the concept of *partial qualifier* was introduced in 1991. A partial qualifier was a student-athlete who met some, but not all, of the requirements for first-year eligibility under Prop 48. A partial qualifier could still receive institutional financial aid, including an athletic scholarship, but could not play or practice with the team as a freshman. The student-athlete would have only three years of eligibility remaining.

In 1994, the NCAA created the Initial Eligibility Clearinghouse. This central clearinghouse determines the initial eligibility of all incoming freshman student-athletes. Under the new Proposition 16 (Prop 16), an "initial eligibility index" was established that used a *sliding scale* to determine the eligibility status of incoming collegiate freshman. For example, a student who carried a 2.50 GPA in high school core courses (see exhibit 6.1) needed to score only 820 on the SAT or a total score of 68 on the ACT. However, a student with a core GPA of 2.0 needed a 1010 SAT score or sum of 86 on the ACT. This provided some flexibility for students who did not score well on the tests yet were solid students in a classroom environment, while students who did not perform as well in the classroom could compensate with higher test scores. Despite intervening changes to SAT scoring, the NCAA continues to use this scale today by combining the scores of the critical reading and math sections of the test.

The NCAA divides incoming freshman into only two categories: qualifiers (as described earlier) and nonqualifiers. A qualifier is a student who has met all of the minimum academic eligibility standards set out by the association and institution.

Exhibit 6.1
Minimum Core Curriculum and Grade Point Average Requirements for Initial Eligibility

Course	Minimum Requirement
English	4 years
Mathematics (Algebra I or higher)	3 years
Natural or physical science	2 years
Additional courses in English, mathematics, or natural or physical science	1 year
Social science	2 years
Additional courses in any of the above areas or foreign language, philosophy, or nondoctrinal religion	4 years
Core curriculum grade point average	2.000

The other group of incoming student-athletes is known as nonqualifiers. These are students who either have not graduated from high school or have not met the GPA or SAT/ACT requirements to become a qualifier. Nonqualifiers are not allowed to practice or compete with the institution's team and are not allowed to receive any athletic scholarship monies.

NOTES

The following are cases where eligibility requirements concerning GPA were challenged by student-athletes:

1. In *Bowers v. National Collegiate Athletic Association (NCAA)*, 475 F.3d 524 (2007), the Third Circuit reversed the district court and reinstated a 1996 lawsuit by a New Jersey high school football player, Michael Bowers. In high school, Bowers was took primarily special education classes and untimed tests, the result of a learning disability diagnosis. During his senior year, Bowers was being recruited by the University of Iowa and Temple University football programs, but they stopped because they did not believe his academic transcript would meet NCAA requirements. Indeed the NCAA/ACT Academic Clearinghouse ruled Bowers did not qualify because his special education classes did not satisfy the NCAA's core course requirements, and he took an untimed SAT without sufficient documentation. Bowers nonetheless enrolled at Temple but missed the fall 2006 semester for back surgery. Bowers began at Temple in spring 1997 and achieved a 3.63 GPA that semester. However, at the time, Bowers began to abuse prescription painkillers related to his back injury. Bowers dropped out of Temple and was in and out of hospitals and mental health programs until he died of a drug overdose in June 2002. Bowers filed his initial lawsuit in the spring of 1997, alleging that the NCAA had violated the Americans with Disabilities Act (ADA). State law discrimination claims were also asserted against Temple and Iowa. All suits were eventually dismissed in March 2005. Bowers's estate appealed and the Third Circuit reversed and remanded for a new trial in February 2007. The Third Circuit ruled that the district court focused on the wrong time frame to determine whether or not Bowers qualified for protection under ADA. The appropriate time frame was Bowers's senior year of high school, not when the suit was filed, as contended by the district court.

2. In *Pryor v. NCAA*, 288 F.3d 548 (3rd Cir. 2002), the plaintiffs challenged the NCAA's Proposition 16, a 1992 rule that establishes scholarship and athletic eligibility criteria for incoming student-athletes. The plaintiffs alleged that the rule was designed to cause black student-athletes to lose their eligibility. The District Court dismissed the suit, but the Third Circuit reversed and remanded on the issue of whether or not the seemingly neutral rule unfairly discriminated against black athletes in violation of Title VI. In an interrogatory, the NCAA stated that one of the main reasons for the rule was to raise the graduation rate for black athletes and decreased the "black-white gap." The court determined it was a legitimate question whether or not the rule did this by eliminating or screening black athletes in the first place. The lawsuit was brought by the same lawyer in *Cureton* (see note d), after their motion to file an amended complaint was denied; see *Cureton v. NCAA*, 252 F.3d 267 (3rd Cir. 2001).

3. In *Cole v. NCAA*, 120 F.Supp.2d 1060 (N.D. Ga. 2000), a high school student who had been diagnosed with a learning disability was classified as a partial qualifier under NCAA rules after entering a waiver allowing him to qualify completely. Cole's high school grades did not qualify him as even a partial qualifier. He argued that the NCAA was violating the ADA by not allowing him to play in his freshman season of college. The court did not grant Cole an injunction to compete for two reasons (see section 16.3.1.4, "Americans with Disabilities Act"). First, the case had been rendered moot because Cole's one year of ineligibility as a partial qualifier had passed. Second, the court stated that "abandoning the eligibility requirements altogether for this or any athlete is unreasonable as a matter of law and is not required by the ADA. In addition, the NCAA's rules and decisions regarding

the concerns and challenges of student-athletes are entitled to considerable deference and this court is reluctant to replace the NCAA subcommittee as the decision-maker on private waiver applications."

4. In *Cureton v. NCAA*, 37 F.Supp.2d 687 (E.D. Pa. 1999), *rev'd*. 198 F.3d 107 (3rd Cir. 1999), two potential college student-athletes brought a suit against the NCAA, claiming that the association's initial eligibility rules violated Title IV of the Civil Rights Act of 1964 because the SAT test unintentionally discriminated against African Americans (see section 15.3.2.3, "Title VII of the Civil Rights Act of 1964"). The students had maintained A grade point averages on the high school level, yet both had not achieved the minimum SAT score to qualify for initial eligibility on the collegiate level. In fact, the students ranked 5th and 27th in a graduating class of 305 students. Although the students were able to achieve admission to college based on grades alone, they were not allowed to receive athletic financial aid or compete in athletics under NCAA rules. The federal appeals court ruled for the NCAA, deciding that although it did receive some federal financial assistance, the NCAA was not subject to this federal legislation as a private entity.

5. In *Tatum v. NCAA*, 992 F.Supp. 1114 (E.D. Mo. 1998), a student-athlete sought an injunction allowing him to play basketball although he had not qualified under initial eligibility standards adopted by the NCAA. The NCAA did not accept Tatum's ACT score that was received under nonstandard conditions. The court refused to award Tatum a preliminary injunction, stating that he did not have a likelihood of winning the case on the merits, and it was uncertain whether he would suffer irreparable harm as a result of not playing basketball.

For more information on NCAA initial eligibility requirements, see the following law review articles:

1. M. Tae Phillips, "Un-Equal Protection: Preferential Admissions Treatment for Student Athletes," 60 Alabama Law Review 751 (2009).

2. Doug Bakker, "NCAA Eligibility Requirements: The Case Law behind the Changes," 3 *DePaul J. Sports L. & Contemp. Probs.* 160 (2006).

3. Ellen J. Staurowsky and B. David Ridpath, "The Case for a Minimum 2.0 Standard for NCAA Division I Athletes," 15 *J. Legal Aspects Sport* 113 (2005).

4. Kelly M. Trainor, "The NCAA's Initial Eligibility Requirements and the Americans with Disabilities Act in the Post-PGA Tour, Inc. v. Martin Era: An Argument in Favor of Deference to the NCAA," 46 *B.C. L. Rev.* 423 (2005).

5. "Title VI—Third Circuit Upholds Viability of Standardized Test Scores as a Component of Freshman Athletic Eligibility Requirements—*Cureton v. NCAA*, 198 F.3d 107 (3d. Cir. 1999)," 114 *Harvard L. Rev.* 947 (January 2001).

6.3.1.2. Grade Point Average: High School

In an attempt to ensure academic achievement for their student-athletes, most high schools have adopted grade point average standards. These rules serve the dual purpose of assuring that student-athletes make sufficient academic progress during high school and are eligible for participation in intercollegiate athletics as incoming freshman. The rules also allow high schools to help their own student-athletes become strong candidates for scholarships and for admission to colleges and universities. A generally accepted rule concerning grade point average and eligibility on the high school level is the "no pass, no play rule."

For example, in 1985, legislators in Texas passed a rule requiring all students involved in extracurricular activities to maintain a minimum grade of 70 in each class to retain eligibility; scores below 70 during a six-week grading period resulted in ineligibility during the next six-week grading period. Like most high school eligibility rules, this one focused solely on GPA, as distinguished from the NCAA's inclusion of standardized test scored to determine initial eligibility. In most cases, courts have declined to review high school eligibility rules, preferring to leave these matters in the hands of the schools and associations.

NOTE

1. In *Hoot v. Michigan High School Athletic Ass'n*, 853 F.Supp. 243 (E.D. Mich. 1994), a student who had not achieved a satisfactory GPA to compete on the high school level (.981 out of 4.0) brought a case against the MHSAA alleging a violation of equal protection and the ADA because Hoot had been diagnosed with a learning disability. The MHSAA was denied a preliminary injunction dismissing the case, having not supplied sufficient information to the court. The court believed "that a genuine issue of material facts exists as to each count within the Complaint. While discovery and an answer may shed light on some of the factual issues, the MHSAA's Motion for Summary Judgment must be denied without prejudice."

6.3.1.3. Academic Progress: NCAA

At the intercollegiate level, the general rule for continued academic eligibility under NCAA rules (Divisions I and II) is that a student-athlete, after the first academic year, must maintain satisfactory progress toward a degree based on the member institution's academic eligibility rules, the NCAA rules, and the member institution's conference affiliation. Regulations for continuing eligibility are different than initial eligibility rules for two reasons. First, academic progress rules are set by the academic institutions or conferences in addition to those of the NCAA, which allows institutions to create standards that relate to their own academic programs. Second, rules for continuing eligibility generally deal solely with grade point average while at the institution and not standardized test scores, which are only used for initial eligibility. The purpose of these rules is to ensure that student-athletes are meeting certain academic standards. Like the GPA standard, academic progress standards were initiated to guarantee that student-athletes were receiving an education and were not at institutions solely to participate in athletics. Bylaw 14.4.1 of the *2009–2010 NCAA Manual* explains the academic progress rule:

> **Progress-Toward-Degree Requirements.** To be eligible to represent an institution in intercollegiate athletics competition, a student-athlete shall maintain progress toward a baccalaureate or equivalent degree at that institution as determined by the regulations of that institution. As a general requirement, "progress toward degree" is to be interpreted at each member institution by the academic authorities who determine the meaning of such phrases for all students, subject to controlling legislation of the conference(s) or similar association of which the institution is a member. (See Constitution 3.2.4.13 regarding the obligations of members to publish their progress-toward-degree requirements for student-athletes.)

NCAA bylaws concerning credit-hour requirements for eligibility are rather dense. To retain eligibility, student-athletes must complete 24 semester or 36 quarter hours of academic credit before beginning their second years; 18 semester or 27 quarter hours over succeeding two-semester or three-quarter periods; and 6 semester or 6 quarter hours during each individual semester or quarter (*2009–2010 NCAA Manual*, Bylaw 14.4.3.1). Academic progress in college also requires that a student-athlete be accepted into a degree-granting program by the beginning of the third year of enrollment and thereafter make satisfactory progress toward that specific degree (*2009–2010 NCAA Manual*, Bylaw 14.4.3.1.6). In addition, a student-athlete must have completed successfully at least 40% of the course requirements in the student's degree program when entering his or her third year of enrollment, 60% by the fourth year, and 80% by the fifth year (*2009–2010 NCAA Manual*, Bylaw 14.4.3.2).

Schools, instead of the NCAA, are generally handed the administrative duties of monitoring the satisfactory academic progress of their student-athletes. Cases involving academic progress have rarely reached the level of the courts. It has been the policy of most courts to uphold the ideal of institutional control and limited judicial review in cases involving these matters.

Nonetheless, in 2004, the NCAA exerted greater control over academic progress on a team-by-team basis. By instituting requirements that all teams achieve a certain *academic progress rate* (APR), with sanctions including scholarship reductions and eventual postseason bans for failure, the NCAA sought to ensure that only teams whose student-athletes remain enrolled and continue to make progress toward a degree would enjoy the full benefits of NCAA membership. Teams and schools achieving the highest APR scores receive public recognition awards from the NCAA.

Although APR rates and their application can seem quite complex, in essence, they require each individual team to achieve a 92.5% success rate (a 925 APR) in retaining student-athletes in school and on track to earn degrees. Teams that fail to make the grade annually and over a four-year period are subject to increased penalties for each year of noncompliance, with teams failing to make a 900 score subject to greater penalties. Teams that fall out of compliance may avoid further penalties by improving their four-year average, while schools with multiple teams with failing grades may face program-wide sanctions. For more information on APR rules and application, see http://www.ncaa.org/wps/ncaa?ContentID=276.

NOTES

1. In *Matthews v. NCAA*, 79 F.Supp.2d 1199 (E.D. Wash. 1999), the plaintiff was not allowed to play in intercollegiate competition because he did not qualify under the "75/25" rule requiring that a student-athlete earn at least 75% of the minimum credits during the academic year as opposed to the summer. The purpose of the rule is to ensure that student-athletes undertake a course load similar to other college students. Matthews requested a preliminary injunction allowing him to play but was denied by the court. Matthews argued that the application of the rule to him was in violation of the ADA because he had a diagnosed learning disability (see section 16.3.1.4, "Americans with Disabilities Act"). The court decided that the NCAA had sufficiently accommodated Matthews's disability by granting him two previous waivers. On a motion for summary judgment, the district court issued a stay pending the decision in *PGA Tour Inc. v. Casey Martin* (see section 16.3.2.4, "Professional Sports"). In Martin, it was determined that the ADA did apply to the PGA Tour and it indicated it would to the NCAA as well. As a result, the court in Matthews ruled that granting Matthews a waiver is a necessary and reasonable modification of NCAA bylaws and it would not fundamentally alter the NCAA's purpose. However, the case was deemed moot because Matthews eligibility had expired.

2. For a case in which the academic progress rule was challenged, see *Hall v. University of Minnesota*, 530 F.Supp. 104 (D. Minn. 1982). Hall, a former basketball player, brought suit against the University of Minnesota for its failure to admit him to a degree-granting

program, which resulted in his being declared ineligible to play basketball for his senior year. Big Ten Conference rules require a student-athlete to be enrolled in such a degree granting program to maintain eligibility. The court found in favor of Hall, stating that a constitutionally protected property interest in a potential professional basketball contract was involved; therefore, Hall's due process rights had been violated.

3. See the following law review article for a discussion of academic eligibility in the NCAA: Alfred Dennis Mathewson, "The Eligibility Paradox," 7 *Villanova Sports & Entertainment Law Forum* 83 (2002).

6.3.1.4. Academic Progress: High School

Academic progress rules are designed to ensure that student-athletes enroll in the type of courses required to obtain a high school diploma or college degree. At the interscholastic level, most state high school athletic associations do not set minimum academic progress rules. Instead, most state associations allow the individual schools to set the minimum standards for academic progress. The most common standard academic progress rule is a "no pass, no play" standard. This standard signifies that a student-athlete must maintain a minimum "passing" GPA in order to participate in interscholastic athletics. Depending on the preference of the institution, the passing standard can be set at a C or D level. Unlike colleges and universities, high schools are allowed a great amount of latitude when drafting and administering academic progress regulations. The Massachusetts Interscholastic Athletic Association (MIAA), for example, has the following regulations:

58. Student Eligibility: Academic Requirements

58.1 A student must secure during the last marking period preceding the contest (e.g., second quarter marks and not semester grades determine third-quarter eligibility) a passing grade, and full credit, in the equivalent of four traditional year long major English courses. A transfer student may not gain academic eligibility if he/she was not, or would not be, eligible at the sending school, unless transfer was necessitated by a move of parents and then eligibility would be determined by receiving school's eligibility standards.

58.2 A student cannot at any time represent a school unless that student is taking courses which would provide Carnegie Units equivalent to four traditional year long major English courses.

58.3 To be eligible for the fall marking period, students are required to have passed and received full credits for the previous academic year the equivalent of four traditional year long major English courses.

58.4 Academic eligibility of all students shall be considered as official and determined on the published date when the report cards for that ranking period are to be issued to the parents of all students within a particular class.

Note: The MIAA academic eligibility standards are designed to ensure that a student is fully enrolled in school and actively engaged in his/her academic life on a consistent basis throughout the school year. When utilizing a 4 × 4 block schedule, a student must pass at least two of the four required "major" courses (or equivalent) in each academic marking period.

The questions you must ask in determining equivalency are:

- How many minutes per day/week/semester does this course meet?
- How many credits toward graduation as approved in advance by school committee policy will be offered for this course?
- Is this equivalent to past academic requirements?

(If further clarification is necessary, principals and athletic directors are encouraged to contact a member of the MIAA executive staff.)

58.5. Incomplete grades may not be counted toward eligibility until they are made up following school policy.

58.6. A student who repeats work upon which he/she has once received credit cannot count that subject a second time for eligibility.

58.7 A student cannot count for eligibility any subject taken during the summer, unless that subject was pursued and failed during the immediately preceding academic year. (Part IV, Rule 58, 2009–2011 Rules and Regulations Governing Athletics, MIAA)

The academic progress rules of an interscholastic state association were addressed in *Ingram v. Toledo City School District Board of Education*, 339 F.Supp.2d 998 (N.D. Ohio 2004). A high school senior requested a preliminary injunction allowing him to participate in football after he was declared academically ineligible by the Ohio High School Athletic Association (OHSAA). Ingram had been diagnosed with a learning disability and as a result had an Individualized Education Plan (IEP) since third grade. OHSAA requires student-athletes to pass at least five core classes each quarter to be eligible. During Ingram's spring semester, he only took five classes and failed English by not turning in 9 out of 25 assignments. Ingram failed his English final but retook it after studying with his tutor and earned a B minus. The new grade allowed Ingram to pass English for the semester, but he still failed the quarter. Ingram contended that his teacher promised to change the grade to passing if he passed the final exam, but the teacher denied such a promise, and his high school ruled him ineligible. Ingram contended that his high school failed to provide him the proper testing accommodations and failed to construct a proper IEP program. The court agreed and Ingram was granted a temporary restraining order, allowing him to make up the missing work and improve his grade to a D. However, he was still ineligible because the OHSAA does not permit makeup work. The court then granted a temporary injunction placing the majority of the blame for Ingram's academic failures on the schools inability to properly implement his IEP.

NOTES

1. In *Baisden v. West Virginia Secondary Schools Activities Commission (WVSAC)*, 568 S.E.2d 32 (W. Va. 2002), the West Virginia Supreme Court of Appeals reversed a permanent injunction that granted a 19-year-old eligibility to play high school football. The WVSAC ruled that Jarrett Baisden was ineligible because he turned 19 prior to August 1, 2001. Baisden had repeated both first and sixth grade and had been diagnosed with a learning disability in eighth grade. Although Baisden had graduated, the court granted judicial review, noting that the issue will certainly be encountered by other students. The essential question was whether or not Baisden qualified under the ADA such that the WVSAC would be required to make reasonable accommodations. Although the court stated that waivers can and should be granted, it ruled that a waiver for Baisden would have been inappropriate, noting that he was 6'4", 280 pounds, ran a 40-yard dash in 5.3 seconds, and would possibly be competing against students five years younger.

2. In *Jordan v. Indiana High School Athletic Ass'n*, 16 F.3d 785 (7th Cir. 1994), Jordan was a high school student who had serious academic problems during his first two years at Marshall Metro, in Chicago. In his third year, Jordan was absent so many times that he was forced to withdraw from school. He did not receive any academic credit for that school year, and he was not allowed to participate on any athletic teams due to his substandard academic performance. Jordan then transferred to a school in Fort Wayne, Indiana,

where he began his junior year again and played for the high school basketball team. Jordan turned around his academic performance in Fort Wayne. However, before his senior year, the IHSAA decided that Jordan could not compete because he had already been eligible for eight semesters of competition. On the district court level, Jordan was granted a preliminary injunction allowing him to play in his senior season. The IHSAA appealed the decision, and the appeals court decided that the case was moot because Jordan had completed his senior year of competition, and he would not be affected by the outcome of the trial. The judgment of the district court was vacated and remanded with instructions to dismiss the case as moot.

6.3.2. Participation Rules

6.3.2.1. Redshirting

The practice of redshirting is a means by which to extend the playing career of a student-athlete by postponing or passing over a year of athletic participation, while not affecting the student-athlete's maximum allowable time for participating. In the NCAA, a student-athlete has five years from enrollment in a member institution to complete eligibility:

A student-athlete shall complete his or her seasons of participation within five calendar years from the beginning of the semester or quarter in which the student-athlete first registered for a minimum full-time program of studies in a collegiate institution, with time spent in the armed services, on official church missions or with recognized foreign aid services of the U.S. government being excepted. For foreign students, service in the armed forces or on an official church mission of the student's home country is considered equivalent to such service in the United States (*2009–2010 NCAA Manual*, Bylaw 14.2.1).

Any participation during a season in an intercollegiate sport, including a scrimmage with an outside opponent, counts as a season of competition toward the four-year total, as does any season of competition at the junior-college level. Redshirting rules are designed to allow delaying a student-athlete's eligibility on the basis of legitimate factors such as injury or academic difficulty, while preventing abuse by coaches and student-athletes seeking to gain a competitive advantage through an extension of a student-athlete's career. High school athletic associations and conferences, which do not allow redshirting, typically employ a four-year eligibility rule. Under most high school association rules, a student-athlete has eight consecutive semesters in which to participate in interscholastic competition, beginning with the student-athlete's entry into the ninth grade.

The practice of redshirting may be initiated for a number of reasons, including the following:

1. *Medical reasons.* Includes a serious injury or illness occurring in the off season or before the start of the season. The student-athlete might consider it advantageous to recover fully from such a problem by postponing for a year the resumption of athletic competition.
2. *Transfers.* The five-year rule also protects the playing career of first-time transfer students, allowing them the opportunity to switch schools once without eliminating one of their four seasons of playing time. The student-athlete must complete one full year of academic residence at the institution before being eligible to compete (Division I) (*2009–2010 NCAA Manual*, Bylaw 14.5.1).

3. *Coaching strategy.* The coach might ask a student-athlete to redshirt a season because the coach wants to use and schedule the player's eligibility to fit the long-term needs and requirements of the team.

At the interscholastic level, the practice of redshirting is not as commonplace as on the intercollegiate level, primarily because the rules do not allow the flexibility provided at the intercollegiate level. The only alternative at the high school level in many states may be keeping back a student-athlete for an extra year before the student-athlete enters high school. This allows a student-athlete another year to develop his or her body and playing skills before entering high school competition. However, the student-athlete who does this must be careful about maximum age restrictions. For instance, the MIAA does not allow students aged 19 and above to compete in high school athletics unless they turn 19 after September 1 of the school year (Part IV, Rule 60, 2009–2011 Rules and Regulations Governing Athletics, MIAA). The MIAA also restricts competition to four consecutive years after entering ninth grade (Part IV, Rule 59.1). However, although it occurs infrequently, the MIAA's executive director can authorize exceptions to the 12-consecutive-season rule because of injury or illness (Rule 59.2).

High school regulations prohibiting the practice of redshirting have been justified on the basis of preventing competition between individuals with vast differences in strength, speed, and experience. Such rules are designed to promote equitable competition and player safety as well as to prevent schools from abusing athletes by holding them back a grade or redshirting them to allow them to mature and develop athletically. However, high school rules may make exceptions for students who academically fail a grade since the retention was not related to athletics. Therefore, a student-athlete may be allowed to compete in the fifth year but not to compete for more than four seasons in total.

Disabled student-athletes have made notable inroads in interscholastic athletics since the passage of the ADA. Many state associations or individual institutions have made allowances for disabled athletes to compete athletically even if they are not able to finish their studies within the prescribed period allotted to nondisabled student-athletes (see section 16.3.1.4, "Americans with Disabilities Act").

NOTES _____

1. In *NCAA v. Brinkworth*, 680 So.2d 1081 (Fl. Dis. Ct. App. 1996), a football player for the University of Miami was redshirted his first year at Miami and proceeded to participate in three full years of competition. During his fourth year at Miami, as the starting fullback, Brinkworth was injured during the first game of the season. He was unable to compete for the remainder of the season due to the injury. Miami applied for an eligibility waiver on behalf of Brinkworth from the NCAA, and his application was denied. Based on this decision, Miami did not allow Brinkworth to compete until a resolution was made with the NCAA because Miami could have faced sanctions if they allowed him to play. Brinkworth initially received a preliminary injunction from a state court allowing him to play, and the NCAA appealed this decision. The appeals court sided with the NCAA, stating that the procedures for waivers and appeals were fair and not arbitrary; many student-athletes in Brinkworth's situation had been denied waivers in the past. The court found that it was not their place to interfere with how the NCAA interprets its own rules, concluding, "The issue Brinkworth seeks to raise is beyond our province to review. It is up to the NCAA to interpret its own rules, not the judiciary. The NCAA followed fair procedures in allowing the university the opportunity to state its case on behalf of the student athlete, including an appeal within the

NCAA when dissatisfied with the initial ruling. As the procedures were adequate and fair, there was no basis on which to intervene in the internal affairs of the NCAA." This decision demonstrates the reluctance that courts have in interfering with legitimate rules and regulations that the NCAA institutes.

2. In *Jones v. NCAA*, 679 So.2d 1337 (La. 1996), the student-athlete, Jones, was originally granted an injunction to allow him to play intercollegiate football despite running out of NCAA eligibility after his fourth year. The appellate court, in a short decision, overturned the lower court, stating, "Courts should not interfere with the internal affairs of a private association except in cases when the affairs and proceedings have not been conducted fairly and honestly, or in the cases of fraud, lack of jurisdiction, the invasion of property or pecuniary rights, or when the action complained of is capricious, arbitrary, or unjustly discriminatory."

3. The NCAA grants what it terms a *hardship waiver*, which is often confused with redshirting. A student-athlete may be granted an additional year of competition by the Eligibility Committee for reasons of *hardship*, which is defined as an incapacity resulting from an injury or illness that has occurred under all of the following conditions:

a. The incapacitating injury or illness occurs in one of the four seasons of intercollegiate competition at any two-year or four-year collegiate institution or occurs after the first day of classes in the student-athlete's senior year in high school

b. The injury or illness occurs prior to the first competition of the second half of the playing season that concludes with the NCAA championship in that sport and results in incapacity to compete for the remainder of that playing season

c. The injury or illness occurs when the student-athlete has not participated in more than three contests or dates of competition (whichever is applicable to that sport) or 30% (whichever number is greater) of the institution's scheduled or completed contests or dates of competition in his or her sport (*2009–2010 NCAA Manual*, Bylaw 14.2.4)

In the following cases, courts examined interscholastic association redshirt rules:

1. In *Bingham v. Oregon School Activities Ass'n*, 37 F. Supp. 2d 1189 (D. Or. 1999), a student-athlete was granted an injunction allowing him to participate in interscholastic athletics although he had been eligible for participation in athletics in eight previous semesters and therefore was not eligible under Oregon state rules. The student, Bingham, had not played in his freshman year of high school but did compete in his sophomore year. Bingham transferred to another school in Florida before the next school year, and due to academic and learning difficulties, he repeated his sophomore year while continuing in athletics. The family then moved to Oregon, where Bingham enrolled in high school and competed in athletics as a junior. As a senior, he was ruled ineligible under state association rules because he had completed eight semesters of high school. The court ruled for Bingham, deciding that because Bingham had repeated his sophomore year due to his disability, he was covered under the ADA, and the waiving of the eight-semester rule by the association would be a reasonable accommodation for Bingham, considering his disability.

2. In *Rhodes v. Ohio High School Athletic Ass'n*, 939. F. Supp. 584 (N.D. Ohio 1996), the court upheld the OHSAA's rule regarding eight semesters of play. The plaintiff, Rhodes, sought a preliminary injunction allowing him to play interscholastic athletics under the ADA (see section 16.3.1.4, "Americans with Disabilities Act"). Although the court found that there would be irreparable harm if the plaintiff was not allowed to compete, it found that the plaintiff did not have a likelihood of success on the merits, and therefore the injunction was denied.

3. In *Alabama High School Athletic Ass'n v. Medders*, 456 So.2d 284 (Ala. Sup. Ct. 1984), a student who had successfully completed but voluntarily repeated eighth grade was declared ineligible to play football on the high school team during his senior year under the eight semester rule. The court held that although the rule was susceptible to two interpretations, it had been interpreted in the same way as in the student's case for 35 years, and that interpretation fell short of fraud, collusion, or arbitrariness.

6.3.2.2. Longevity

The NCAA created a longevity rule to address concerns that some student-athletes, particularly in soccer and track, were gaining experience in amateur leagues in the United States and foreign countries before matriculating at NCAA member institutions. Consequently, the rule aims to prevent older, more experienced athletes from placing younger athletes at a disadvantage athletically and in competing for scholarship monies.

Bylaw 14.2.3.5 of the *2009–2010 NCAA Manual* reads:

> In sports other than tennis and swimming and diving, any participation as an individual or a team representative in organized sports competition by a student during each 12-month period after the student's 21st birthday and prior to initial full-time enrollment in a collegiate institution shall count as one year of varsity competition in that sport. Participation in organized competition during time spent in the U.S. armed services shall be excepted.

The NCAA succeeded in defending an earlier version of this rule in *Butts v. NCAA*, 751 F.2d 609 (3rd Cir. 1984) (see note 1), and later amended the rule to apply to students beginning at their 21st birthdays instead of their 20th.

High school athletic associations have adopted longevity rules for similar reasons. Such rules typically limit the age of participants in interscholastic athletic competition, usually to 19 years of age. Many associations also maintain rules concerning the total number of semesters during which a student may remain eligible following his or her initial enrollment (see section 6.3.1.3, "Academic Progress: NCAA"). While courts tend to give athletic associations broad leeway to craft their own eligibility rules, associations and their members must remain mindful of existing laws that might affect their discretion (see note 2b).

NOTES _____

An early version of the NCAA's longevity rule was upheld in the following cases:

1. The case of *Butts v. NCAA*, 751 F.2d 609 (3rd Cir. 1984), shows how the courts view the purpose of the NCAA longevity rule. Butts had played for the Frederick Military Academy basketball team after reaching the age of 20. When Butts entered LaSalle, a private university, it was feared that under NCAA Bylaw 5-1-(d)-(3), his post–high school experience would be counted against his four years of college eligibility. Bylaw 5-1-(d)-(3) stated that "any participation by a student as an individual or as a representative of any team in organized competition in a sport during each 12-month period after his 20th birthday and prior to his matriculation at a member institution shall count as one year of varsity competition in that sport." When the NCAA indicated that Butts would be ineligible to play basketball during his senior year, he filed suit against the NCAA and LaSalle, seeking declaratory and injunctive relief. Butts claimed that the bylaw violated 42 U.S.C. §2000d (1982), which states, "No person in the United States shall, on the grounds of race, color, or national origin, be excluded from participation in, be denied the benefits of, or be subjected to discrimination under any program or activity receiving federal financial assistance." The district court concluded that Butts had shown a strong likelihood that the bylaw had a racially disparate impact (affected some races more than others even though unintentionally); however, it also concluded that the NCAA had advanced a legitimate, nondiscriminatory reason for the bylaw: the bylaw is designed and intended to promote equality of competition among its members at each level so as to prevent college athletics and access to athletic scholarships from being dominated by more mature, older, more experienced players and to discourage high school students

from delaying their entrance into college in order to develop and mature their athletic skills. The district court held that Butts had the burden of showing that the bylaw was pretextual or that "some other, less intrusive, rule would accomplish the stated objects of the present rule." The district court found that Butts had not shown a reasonable likelihood of being able to meet this burden, and it upheld the rule and the NCAA's position and denied a preliminary injunction.

2. In *Spath v. National Collegiate Athletic Ass'n*, 728 F.2d 25 (1st. Cir. 1984), the plaintiff was a Canadian citizen who had played after his 20th birthday for a team in Canada prior to entering college in the United States. The plaintiff filed suit after he was deemed ineligible for the fourth season after playing three years of intercollegiate hockey. The court found that the rule was reasonable and the plaintiff's due process rights had not been violated.

The following cases considered state associations' longevity rules:

1. In *Dempsey v. State*, WL 3933737 (Del. Ch. December 21, 2006), a Delaware state court upheld the Delaware Interscholastic Athletic Association's (DIAA) refusal to grant the plaintiff a hardship waiver that would have given him a fifth year of eligibility. Dempsey claimed that as a result of his mother's debilitating car accident, he was forced to take on extraordinary tasks to care for her and his siblings during ninth grade, the 2002–2003 academic year. The extra duties negatively affected his school work to the point where he was forced to repeat ninth grade. In ruling against Dempsey, the DIAA noted that he had failed to produce any witnesses or evidence of his mother's condition or accident. Also, the DIAA could not find a causal connection between the alleged hardship and his academic struggles, finding it was his failure to attend summer school and his poor academic performance during 2004–2005 that delayed his graduation. The court refused to grant a temporary restraining order because there was no evidence that Dempsey would suffer substantial and irreparable harm, and he had failed to exhaust his administrative remedies.

2. In *Kanongata'a v. Washington Interscholastic Activities Association (WIAA)*, 2006 WL 1727891 (W.D. Wash. June 20, 2006), a high school football player sought relief allowing him to participate in athletics during his sixth year of high school at the age of 20. Plaintiff had been diagnosed with both ADHD and a learning disability and had suffered through the tragic death of his brother and being expelled from his family home. He had also been suspended from school multiple times for fighting, truancy, cheating, and failing grades. Also seeking damages, the plaintiff alleged violations of the ADA. The court ruled that the eligibility rule was arbitrarily and capriciously applied to the plaintiff because the WIAA contended that a year during which the plaintiff did not live in Utah because was ineligible due to a transfer rule counted toward his four years of eligibility. In addition, the plaintiff should have been granted a hardship waiver because of his situation and material issues of fact existed as to whether or not the rules of WIAA violated the ADA. However, the court did state that there is no recognized property interest in interscholastic athletics under the 14th Amendment's due process clause.

3. In *Kling v. Mentor Public School District*, 136 F. Supp. 2d 744 (N.D. Ohio 2001), a student-athlete who suffers from cerebral palsy and a hearing impairment was granted a preliminary injunction allowing him to compete in the public high school district's athletic competitions. The court granted the injunction because it believed that the disabled student had a probability of success of proving at trial that he would suffer irreparable harm in his development by not being allowed to participate in athletics.

4. In *Cruz v. Pennsylvania Interscholastic Athletic Ass'n*, 157 F. Supp. 2d 485 (E.D. Pa. 2001), the court granted a permanent injunction to allow the plaintiff, Luiz Cruz, to participate in interscholastic athletics after the age of 18 due to learning disabilities. The association rule did not allow Cruz to participate. The court, taking a very active stance in this case, ordered not only that Cruz receive the permanent injunction but that the association should adopt a waiver procedure to deal with Cruz and other students in similar situations.

5. In *Washington v. Indiana High School Athletic Ass'n*, 181 F.3d 840 (7th Cir. 1999), the court decided to affirm the granting of a preliminary injunction by the trial court to

allow the plaintiff, Washington, to participate in interscholastic athletics even though he had passed eight semesters of athletic eligibility. The court decided that IHSAA did not have any legitimate reason why it should not grant a waiver to Washington, stating, "Nor will the record support the argument that a waiver of the rule in Mr. Washington's case would place an undue administrative or financial burden on the IHSAA. The record indicates that Mr. Washington is the only student-athlete to seek a waiver because of a learning disability in more than a decade. The few case-by-case analyses that the IHSAA would need to conduct hardly can be described as an excessive burden."

6. In *McPherson v. Michigan High School Athletic Ass'n*, 119 F.3d 453 (6th Cir. 1997), the court decided that a rule allowing players to be eligible for only eight semesters of athletic competition was not crafted in order to discriminate against disabled students. The court stated, "The plaintiff has no evidence, and has not even suggested, that the formulation or implementation of the MHSAA's eight-semester rule has in any way been motivated by considerations of barring students with learning disabilities from play." The court dubbed the rule a "neutral" rule, meaning that it was nondiscriminatory in its intent. The court did not believe that MHSAA had an obligation to force the MHSAA to waive the eight semester rule in each case that it was faced with, stating, "To do so would amount to an improper delegation to the MHSAA of this court's responsibility to independently determine whether the rule is, in fact, necessary."

6.3.2.3. Transfer Rules

At the intercollegiate level of competition, the issue of student-athletes transferring from one institution to another often sparks controversy. For the student-athlete, the issue centers on freedom to attend school and compete in athletics wherever he or she wishes. For institutions, conferences, and the NCAA, the issue centers on stability of programs and on the schools' educational missions. Thus, NCAA rules seek to prevent continued recruitment of student-athletes who are already enrolled in college by limiting their ability to transfer freely between schools. In so doing, the rules also seek to forestall shopping around by student-athletes for institutions that seem to offer them the best opportunities to advance their athletic careers. Courts have generally upheld transfer rules, noting the absence of suspect classifications and fundamental rights in relevant cases. Under such circumstances, the transfer rules need only be rationally related to a legitimate state interest (see section 6.1.3, "Equal Protection").

A case in the area of student-athlete transfer rules in the NCAA is *NCAA v. Yeo*, 171 S.W.3d 863 (Tex. 2005). Yeo, a swimmer on the Singapore Olympic team, followed her college coach from the University of California, Berkeley to the University of Texas, Austin and subsequently challenged the NCAA rule requiring an athlete transferring from one four-year institution to another to sit out one full academic year. Yeo swam in the Olympics during the fall of 2000 and took no classes at Texas. After Yeo sat out the spring 2001 semester, she (and Texas) believed she was free to swim for Texas in the fall of 2002. UC Berkeley complained, and the NCAA ordered Yeo to sit out the remainder of the fall 2002 season and four events in the spring 2002 season because she had swam four events in the fall. Texas then added three events to the beginning of the spring season that Yeo sat out and one regularly scheduled event.

UC Berkeley again complained, and the NCAA ruled that the added events could not be counted toward the one-year restriction, meaning that Yeo would have to sit out succeeding events including the NCAA swimming and diving championships. Yeo was granted a temporary injunction to compete at the championships. A trial court and an intermediate appeals court subsequently determined that, in attempting to enforce the NCAA's ruling, Texas had deprived Yeo of protected liberty and property interests. In reversing the lower courts' rulings, the Supreme Court of Texas held that Yeo's reputation as an elite international athlete was entitled to protection but denied that it was due any greater protection than that of an average student-athlete. Therefore, the court ruled that Yeo had no protected property or liberty interests in intercollegiate athletic participation.

The court's decision in *Yeo* demonstrates again the judicial tendency to defer to reasonable rules concerning collegiate transfers, as the court specifically noted its desire not to intervene in disputes concerning student-athletes. Although courts may generally be expected to defer in high school cases also, such conflicts do raise some distinct issues of their own.

High school athletic associations usually restrict eligibility for student-athlete transfers through either blanket restrictions or complex transfer regulations. Some associations, in an effort to limit abuse, apply the blanket restriction approach on all students who change schools for any reason.

This approach is often overly restrictive and unduly harsh. Even so, such rules are often upheld by the courts against those bringing suit for monetary or equitable relief. The rules are frequently said to be reasonably related to alleviating recruiting problems, and courts remain reluctant to get involved with private voluntary organizations.

However, interscholastic transfer rules have come under scrutiny when the transfer is due to the movement of school boundaries or for family or religious reasons. A noteworthy case is *Indiana High School Athletic Association v. Durham* (see note 4). The court decided that Indiana's transfer rule was arbitrary and capricious because it did not take into account the fact that Durham's parents had separated, which had created his reason for transferring. Many court cases have challenged high school transfer rules on constitutional grounds, including equal protection, freedom of religion, right to travel, and due process (see notes 2, 3 and 6). In most cases, the courts have upheld such rules, except where the student-athlete established a violation of a constitutionally protected right or if fraud, collusion, or arbitrariness was found. Outside of the courtroom, states may adopt statutes preventing implementation of transfer rules that are deemed to be overly broad.

NOTE

1. In *Tanaka v. University of Southern California*, 252 F.3d 1059 (9th Cir. 2001), a federal appeals court upheld the NCAA's transfer rule. A former female soccer player for the University of Southern California (USC) brought an antitrust claim against USC and the Pac-10 conference, charging that the conference rule on intraconference transfer was a violation of the Sherman Antitrust Act because the rule was an unreasonable restraint on her ability to transfer to her school of choice, namely, University of California, Los Angeles. Tanaka charged that this rule was applied to her only because, before leaving the university, she had charged the university and athletic department with academic fraud. She believed that the rule was employed in her case as retaliation for her allegations against the athletic department. The court decided in favor of the university and the Pac-10, stating, "Tanaka has failed to identify a relevant market for antitrust purposes. If the relevant market is national in scope, the Pac-10 transfer rule could not have a significant anticompetitive effect, because by its own terms the rule does not apply to interconference transfers. Moreover, even if the relevant market is limited to the Pac-10 itself, Tanaka characterizes the

Pac-10's imposition of sanctions against her for her intraconference transfer as an isolated act of retaliation. Tanaka simply has no antitrust cause of action" (see Chapter 10 for more discussion of antitrust principles).

The following cases examined high school athletic associations' transfer rules.

1. In *Indiana High School Athletic Association, Inc. (IHSAA) v. Watson*, 913 N.E.2d 741 (Ind.App. 2009), the Court of Appeals of Indiana affirmed a preliminary injunction in favor of Jasmine Watson, a high school girls' basketball player, after she transferred to a different high school for her senior year. Despite the fact that the Watsons had moved because Valerie's mother had lost her job and their home had been foreclosed, the IHSAA found that the move occurred primarily for athletic reasons. In affirming the injunction, the court ruled that the IHSAA acted arbitrarily and capriciously in enforcing its transfer rules.

2. In *Perry v. Ohio High School Athletic Association (OHSAA)*, 2006 WL 2927260 (S.D. Ohio October 11, 2006), a student-athlete sued OHSAA and Columbus Public Schools (CPS) after he transferred within the CPS system but was denied athletic eligibility. OHSAA rules permit a student to transfer within the same system without jeopardizing his eligibility with the approval of the OHSAA Commissioner. In this case, the athletic director at the plaintiff's new school realized that he had failed to send the necessary paperwork, and subsequently, the school was forced to forfeit all games in which the plaintiff participated, including the entire 2004–2005 basketball season and state championship. The plaintiff also had his MVP award revoked. The plaintiff contended that the rules of the OHSAA were overly broad and violated his freedom of association rights under the First Amendment. In granting summary judgment for the defendants, the court explained that there is no constitutionally protected property interest in participating in interscholastic athletics.

3. In *Parker ex rel. Parker v. Arizona Interscholastic Association, Inc. (AIA)*, 59 P.3d 806 (Ariz. App. Div. 1 2002), the AIA declared Jason Parker ineligible for interscholastic athletics for one year after he voluntarily transferred high schools without moving. The trial court granted an injunction on behalf of Parker and also with regard to the AIA restitution rule. The restitution rule stated that if a student is permitted to participate pursuant to any kind of court order, and that order is subsequently vacated or reversed, the AIA may require the team and or individual victories or awards to be forfeited or vacated. The trial court ultimately ruled that the transfer rule was rationally related to a legitimate state interest in restricting the right to travel but that the restitution rule was unconstitutional. The appellate court affirmed that the transfer rule did not violate the equal protection clause of the 14th Amendment but did not address the restitution rule because Parker understandably did not appeal it.

4. In the case of *Indiana High School Athletic Ass'n v. Durham*, 748 N.E.2d 404 (Ind. Ct. App. 2001), the Indiana High School Athletic Association (IHSAA) argued that the trial court should not have issued a permanent injunction to the athlete, Durham, because the court "failed to apply the deferential standard of review afforded to its administrative rulings in granting Durham's request for a permanent injunction." Durham's parents had separated, and his mother was not able to afford the tuition for the private school he had attended in the past, forcing Durham to attend the regional public school, at which point, under IHSAA transfer rules, he was deemed ineligible for competition. The appellate court agreed with the trial court's issuance of the injunction and use of judicial review, stating, "Given the evidence in this case, the trial court did not abuse its discretion in overturning the IHSAA's denial of full eligibility and refusal to grant a hardship exception. While it may be true that in other cases we have recognized the IHSAA's broad discretion in refusing to grant a student a hardship exception, this discretion is not unreviewable and is subject to the arbitrary and capricious standard upon review."

5. In the case of *Missouri State High School Activities Ass'n v. Romines*, 37 S.W.3d 421 (Mo. Ct. App. 2001), the Missouri State High School Activities Association (MSHSAA) appealed a decision of the circuit judge to issue an injunction to allow a student-athlete to remain eligible despite breaking the association's transfer rule, which made him ineligible in the eyes of the association. The court ruled for the association, deciding that the judicial

review of the court was not necessary in this case, stating, "We are unable to find any basis upon which the Circuit Court could exercise its jurisdiction to enjoin the Association's decision. There was no allegation in the petition of lack of procedural due process, and no indication of malice, fraud or collusion."

6. In *Fusato v. Washington Interscholastic Activities Ass'n*, 970 P.2d 774 (Wash. 1999), the court found that the WIAA had violated Fusato's equal protection rights by not allowing her to participate in interscholastic athletics. Under the WIAA's transfer rule, student-athletes who transfer to a high school are not allowed to compete immediately unless they move with the entire family unit. In Fusato's case, she moved from Okinawa by herself to live with her aunt and uncle in Washington and was not allowed to immediately play for her high school due to the transfer rule. The court decided for Fusato because it believed that she was being discriminated against due to her national origin, which is a suspect class in questions of equal protection. The court stated, "We hold the trial court did not err applying the strict scrutiny test when deciding the WIAA residence and transfer rules violated Ms. Fusato's equal protection rights under the 14th Amendment. Although Ms. Fusato cannot prove a fundamental right is threatened, she established she was a member of a suspect class based upon national origin or alienage. Upon her showing of disparate impact, together with discriminatory purpose or intent, the WIAA was required to meet the burden of showing a compelling state interest was served by the challenged rules. The WIAA failed to meet its burden and made no effort to demonstrate that the least restrictive regulatory means were used to accomplish the stated purposes of their rules."

7. In *Kentucky High School Athletic Ass'n v. Hopkins County Board of Education*, 552 S.W.2d 685 (Ky. Ct. App. 1977), a high school student-athlete sought a permanent injunction to stop the Kentucky High School Athletic Association (KHSAA) from denying him eligibility to participate in interscholastic athletics. The student-athlete's parents were divorced, with legal custody awarded to the mother. After living with his mother and playing varsity sports at the high school where he was enrolled, the student-athlete decided to move to his father's home and enrolled in another school. The court of appeals found that the student-athlete was not compelled to change his residence but did so because of his own wishes, and therefore the transfer was not involuntary. The appeals court also found that the association did not act arbitrarily in applying the transfer rule to the student-athlete. The district court's issuance of an injunction was therefore reversed. After deciding the essential issue, the court discussed at length a particular problem illustrated by this appeal: in the court's mind, this case demonstrates why courts are a very poor place in which to settle interscholastic athletic disputes, especially since this type of litigation is most likely to arise at playoff or tournament time. If an injunction or restraining order is granted erroneously, it will be practically impossible to unscramble the tournament results to reflect the ultimate outcome of the case. In almost every instance, the possible benefits flowing from a temporary restraining order or injunction are far outweighed by the potential detriment to the association as well as to its member schools who are not before the court. Only in a rare instance should a temporary restraining order or preliminary injunction be granted.

6.3.3. Amateurism Rules

6.3.3.1. NCAA Rules Regarding Scholarships, Financial Assistance, and Expenses

The purpose of regulations relating to collegiate student-athletes' finances is to maintain the level of amateurism in intercollegiate athletics, while also discouraging institutions from recruiting players with the promise of pay. NCAA guidelines strictly regulate the amount of financial assistance that a student-athlete may receive from his or her institution or from outside sources.

Under the guidelines, athletic scholarships in Divisions I and II may not exceed commonly accepted educational expenses, including tuition, fees, room and board, and books. Schools may not pay expenses exceeding these (*2009–2010 NCAA Manual*, Bylaw 15.2). Student-athletes whose financial assistance exceeds a certain amount may lose their eligibility.

In addition, a team is limited to a certain number of full scholarships or total value of financial aid awards (equivalents) at one time in any given sport. For example, an intercollegiate baseball team may be allowed to divide 10 full scholarships among the members of its team, leaving the coach with options on how to divide the aid. For example, he may choose to carry 10 players on full scholarship. A more common practice is to divide the scholarship money among the players on the team; for example, 20 players on the team may receive half scholarships.

The maximum number of equivalent scholarships that can be granted per sport can be found in the *2009–2010 NCAA Manual*, Bylaw 15.5.3. A team may forfeit games or even an entire season if the number of full scholarships or equivalents exceeds the limits established by the NCAA for that particular sport. Other sports, referred to as "head-count sports," are subject to limits on the total number of student-athletes who may be receiving any portion of a scholarship (*2009–2010 NCAA Manual*, Bylaw 15.5.2).

The NCAA's concern for amateurism extends beyond financial assistance provided to student-athletes while they are enrolled in college. Under NCAA rules, a former professional athlete may receive institutional financial aid provided all of the following conditions are met:

1. The student-athlete is no longer involved in professional athletics

2. The student-athlete is not receiving any remuneration from a professional sports organization

3. The student-athlete has no active contractual relationship with any professional athletics team, although the student-athlete may remain bound by an option clause (i.e., a clause in the contract that requires assignment to a particular team if the student-athlete's professional athletics career is resumed)

Regarding payment for participation in collegiate level sports, the NCAA's policy is very clear. With few exceptions, acceptance of either payment or the promise of money for participation automatically categorizes the student-athlete as a professional and thus makes him or her ineligible. This restriction also covers payment for participation in events in which the student-athlete does not represent the institution and even unpaid participation in commercially sponsored events.

Student-athletes may not participate in any competition for cash or prizes, either for themselves or for a donation on their behalf, unless they are eligible to receive such monies under NCAA guidelines. For example, the NCAA does not approve of the granting of scholarship funds in a student-athlete's name if the person was selected as the most valuable player by a national advertiser or sponsor of an event.

The issue of expenses can provide a unique source of trouble for the NCAA student-athlete. In general, an athlete is allowed to receive money for expenses but prior to receiving such compensation should distinguish between those who are permissible to receive funds under NCAA rules, and, more important, those who are not (*2009–2010 NCAA Manual*, Bylaw 12.1).

The NCAA's rule of thumb on expenses provides that a student-athlete may not receive money that exceeds the actual and necessary expenses involved in any authorized activity. Examples of prohibited expense payments include travel expenses to a special location for an article and/or photographs of a student-athlete (unless in conjunction with the receipt of an established/authorized award at that location) and travel or other benefits paid by any person seeking to represent the student-athlete in the marketing of his or her athletic skills or by any registered agent (*2009–2010 NCAA Manual*, Bylaw 12.3.1.2). The courts have historically upheld the NCAA rules restricting excess financial assistance unless the regulations violate constitutionally protected rights (see notes 2 and 3).

A leading case in the area of excess financial assistance is *Wiley v. NCAA*, 612 F.2d 473 (10th Cir. 1979), *cert. denied*, 446 U.S. 943 (1980). An action was brought by Wiley, a student-athlete who was declared ineligible to compete because his financial aid exceeded the amount allowed by the NCAA. Wiley had been awarded a full Basic Educational Opportunity Grant in addition to an athletic scholarship. Taken together, these exceeded the financial limitations imposed on student-athletes under NCAA regulations and made Wiley ineligible to compete. The court applied a rational basis analysis, rejecting Wiley's appeal to apply strict scrutiny because poverty or wealth is not a suspect classification (see section 6.1.3, "Equal Protection"). The court refused to prohibit the NCAA from enforcing its regulations, holding that "unless clearly defined constitutional principles are at issue, suits by student-athletes against high school athletic associations or NCAA rules do not present a substantial federal question."

The NCAA's rules on expenses even extend to friends' and family's attendance at student-athletes' competitions. Under NCAA rules, a member school may allow a student-athlete a maximum of four complimentary admissions for each contest in his or her particular sport.

However, in Division I, the student-athlete's guest may only be admitted via a pass list and may receive no hard tickets (*2009–2010 NCAA Manual*, Bylaws 16.2.1.1, 16.2.1.2). Tickets are prohibited as a result of previous abuses by student-athletes who received money for selling their tickets for more than face value. NCAA rules regarding athletic scholarships are critical to athletic departments and to student-athletes themselves. Athletic scholarships are technically renewable each year, but after being granted, they cannot be increased, reduced, or canceled during the period of the award on the basis of the student-athlete's ability or contribution to the team. In addition, athletic scholarships cannot be withdrawn during the period of the award because of an injury to a student-athlete or for any other athletically related reasons (*2009–2010 NCAA Manual*, Bylaw 15.3.4.3). NCAA rules do not, however, prohibit all types of scholarship revision or rescission. Scholarship aid may be canceled or reduced during the period of the award for any of the following reasons:

1. The student-athlete's rendering himself/herself ineligible for competition
2. Fraudulent misrepresentation by the student-athlete on an application, letter of intent, or financial aid agreement
3. Serious misconduct by the student-athlete warranting substantial disciplinary penalty
4. Voluntary withdrawal by the student-athlete from a sport for personal reasons; however, the recipient's financial aid may not be awarded to any other

student-athlete in the academic term in which the aid was reduced or cancelled (*2009–2010 NCAA Manual*, Bylaw 15.3.4.2 (a–d))

Any gradation or cancellation of aid per the reasons mentioned earlier is permissible only if such action is taken for proper cause and the student-athlete has had an opportunity for a hearing (*2009–2010 NCAA Manual*, Bylaw 15.3.4.2.1).

NCAA rules also place responsibility on institutions and their employees (especially coaches) for any decision not to renew a scholarship award (*2009–2010 NCAA Manual*, Bylaw 15.3.5.1). When a scholarship is not renewed, care must be taken to provide due process in case the student-athlete chooses to request a hearing or file suit. The nonrenewal letter sent to the student-athlete should include the reasons for the action and a statement informing the athlete that he or she is entitled to a hearing. This letter should be kept on file in the athletic director's office and be available upon request to the student-athlete. When a hearing is requested, it may include a presentation of statements from both parties, cross-examination of witnesses, and the right to legal counsel.

Another important issue in the area of scholarships is the national letter of intent. The Collegiate Commissioners Association (CCA), through the commissioners of athletic conferences, administers the letter of intent program. An institution must be an NCAA member to belong to the program, and the national letter of intent applies only to four-year member institutions in Divisions I and II. Letters of intent were developed on the conference level in the late 1940s, during a period when intercollegiate athletics first gained national prominence. The program in its present form was started in 1964 with seven conferences and eight independent institutions joining for a total of 68 schools. In 1982, a women's letter of intent was added. In 2009, 610 institutions belong to the program.

The letter of intent is considered a preenrollment application by the CCA, although much of the language creates the possibility that it may be construed as a contract: signees are obligated to complete a full academic year at the institution to which they commit. The men's and women's letters of intent contain identical regulations and procedures; only the membership differs. Both have five signing dates based on sports categories of (1) midyear junior college football transfers, (2) football, (3) basketball (basketball has two signing dates—an early signing period in November and the traditional period beginning in April), (4) field hockey, soccer, cross country/track and field, and men's water polo, and (5) all other sports; as with basketball, this catch-all category has signing periods in both the fall and the spring.

The letter of intent aims to provide certainty and closure to the recruiting process for schools and student-athletes. Once the recruited athlete signs a national letter of intent, there are no further limits on contacting the student-athlete by the *signing* institution. After the signing, no other member institution subscribing to the program may make any effort to recruit the student-athlete. With the program's membership at over 600 institutions, coaches can feel secure that their recruits will not be bombarded with contact from other schools after signing the letter.

NCAA regulations prohibit members from publicizing a student-athlete's intent to enroll and permit only a single formal press conference to announce all National Letter of Intent Signings in a particular sport (*2009–2010 NCAA Manual*, Bylaws 13.10.7, 13.10.9.2). A student who signs the letter with one program participant but enrolls at another is barred from intercollegiate athletics until he or she completes one full academic year at the second school. The student-athlete also loses one year of eligibility in all sports.

However, the student-athlete remains free to enroll at any member institution to pursue his or her academic interests. The letter of intent also contains some strict regulations; for example, an athlete will lose one year of eligibility if he or she transfers within the first year of attendance at the institution.

A letter of intent becomes invalid if any of the following circumstances exists:

1. The player does not meet minimum academic standards to play as a freshman

2. The player attends and graduates from a junior college

3. The player does not enroll and the institution withdraws its scholarship offer the next year

4. The player serves in the armed forces or a church mission for at least 18 months

5. The institution discontinues the sport

6. The institution is later found to have violated conference or NCAA rules in the recruiting process, resulting in the player's need to seek eligibility reinstatement from the NCAA

For more information on the National Letter of Intent Program, visit the Collegiate Commissioners Association Web site at http://www.ncaa.org/wps/wcm/conn ect/nli/NLI/Home.

NOTES _____

1. The NCAA rules concerning pay were challenged in *Shelton v. NCAA*, 539 F.2d 1197 (9th Cir. 1976). Lonnie Shelton, a student-athlete at the time, was allegedly persuaded to sign a professional contract by the use of fraud and undue influence by an agent. After being declared ineligible by the NCAA, Shelton sued the NCAA, claiming that the rule should not be enforced against him since the misconduct of the agent rendered the contract voidable. The court, however, after examining the rule, upheld it because the NCAA goals of protecting and promoting amateurism, which were incorporated into the rule, were legitimate. Therefore, although the rule might, when applied in certain situations, produce unreasonable results, it did not violate the U.S. Constitution because the rule was rationally related to its goals.

2. A case in which a court *denied* a student-athlete's eligibility on the basis of his receipt of excess financial aid is *Jones v. NCAA*, 392 F.Supp. 295 (D. Mass. 1975). An American ice hockey player brought an action against the NCAA for a preliminary injunction to prohibit the NCAA from declaring him ineligible to compete and from imposing sanctions against his college if they allowed him to play because of excess financial aid he received. Prior to entering college, the student-athlete had been compensated while playing junior hockey in Canada. During one of those years, he was paid a weekly salary and received a signing bonus. The court denied Jones injunctive relief, finding that the NCAA's rules on financial aid were reasonable.

3. A court *granted* eligibility to a student-athlete in *Buckton v. NCAA*, 366 F.Supp. 1152 (D. Mass 1973), despite the NCAA's contention that the student-athlete received excess financial aid. Buckton and other Canadian ice hockey players were denied eligibility because they had received funding from Junior League Hockey teams in Canada rather than from high schools, as is the custom in the United States. The court prohibited the NCAA from enforcing ineligibility because the rule, in effect, discriminated against individuals on the basis of national origin.

4. Under NCAA regulations, a student-athlete remains eligible in a sport even though, prior to enrollment in a collegiate institution, he or she may have tried out with a professional team. However, the expenses paid by the team(s) are limited: a student-athlete remains eligible in a sport even though, prior to enrollment in a collegiate institution, the student-athlete may have tried out with a professional athletics team in a sport or received not more than one expense-paid visit from each professional team (or a combine including that team), provided such a visit did not exceed 48 hours and any payment or compensation in connection with the visit was not in excess of actual and necessary expenses. A self-financed tryout may be for any length of time (*2009–2010 NCAA Manual*, Bylaw 12.2.1.1).

6.3.3.2. Employment: NCAA

The prohibition on payment of student-athletes is predicated on the concept of amateurism and should not be confused with employment, which is permitted in certain situations under NCAA regulations. Since 1998, a student-athlete who is receiving a full athletic scholarship from an institution can be employed during the academic year. However, the student-athlete may not be compensated for any value to the employer accruing from the student-athlete's athletic ability and accomplishments. Rather, the student-athlete may only be compensated for work actually performed at the going rate in the institution's location (*2009–2010 NCAA Manual*, Bylaws 12.4.1, 15.2.7).

Student-athletes can hold campus jobs or employment through alumni of the institution, but once again, they must be paid only for the work actually done. Student-athletes who receive remuneration for work not performed lose eligibility to participate in intercollegiate athletics.

With some exceptions, any compensation received over commonly accepted educational expenses as set by the individual institution must be deducted from the financial assistance package received by the student-athlete (including athletic scholarships) or else the student-athlete will be ineligible to compete for the institution. There are other limits to the types of employment a student-athlete may obtain while maintaining amateur status and collegiate eligibility. For example, student-athletes are not permitted to be employed by their institutions as teachers or coaches in any sport for which they wish to remain eligible and may be employed by other organizations as teachers or coaches in their particular sport only under certain circumstances (*2009–2010 NCAA Manual*, Bylaw 12.4.2.1).

With all of the preceding in mind, monitoring a student-athlete's employment activities during the academic year is an important endeavor for an athletic administrator. Weekend jobs, jobs with friends, or odd jobs on and off campus, while seemingly insignificant to the casual bystander or to the student-athlete, may in fact be a threat to retaining eligibility to compete in intercollegiate athletics.

NOTE _____

1. Under NCAA regulations, a student-athlete who is preparing to compete or has competed in the Olympic Games is entitled to recover any financial loss occurring as a result of absence from employment to prepare for or participate in the Games only if authorized by the U.S. Olympic Committee. The period involved in recovering the losses must immediately precede and/or include actual Olympic competition (*2009–2010 NCAA Manual*, Bylaw 12.4.2.2).

6.3.3.3. Summer Camps and Independent Teams

Prospective student-athletes, with the exception of football players (*2009–2010 NCAA Manual*, Bylaw 13.12.1.2.1), are allowed to enroll in, participate in, or be employed at camps, schools, and clinics that are run by an NCAA member institution. However, this allowance comes with many regulations. In Division I, it is permissible to employ a prospective student-athlete, provided that the student-athlete is not a "senior prospective student-athlete." The NCAA defines a senior prospect as one who is eligible for admission to a member institution or who has started classes for the senior year of high school. A prep school or two-year college student is considered a senior prospect (*2009–2010 NCAA Manual*, Bylaw 13.12.1.2.1.1). While a senior prospect may attend a camp or clinic, he or she is not allowed to participate in any physical activities (*2009–2010 NCAA Manual*, Bylaw 13.12.1.2.1.2). These rules have been established to stop the use of summer camps as tryouts for prospective student-athletes.

High school athletic associations also employ regulations on the eligibility of student-athletes for summer camps. In the case of *Kite v. Marshall*, 661 F.2d 1027 (5th Cir. 1981), parents of high school student-athletes brought an action that challenged the constitutionality of the summer camp rule, which was adopted by the defendant University Interscholastic League (UIL), the high school athletic association in Texas. The rule stated that any person who attended a special athletic training camp would be ineligible for one year of competition. The rationale underlying the rule's adoption was that it ensured that high school athletes would compete on a relatively equal basis.

The Fifth Circuit found that "this case implicates no fundamental constitutional right" and that no suspect classifications were used by the UIL and therefore applied the rational basis test to the plaintiffs' constitutional arguments. The court held that the summer camp rule did not violate either the due process or the equal protection clause of the Constitution. This case shows again the reluctance of courts to overturn association rules that are reasonably related to a legitimate purpose or that have any rational purpose at all.

Many high school and college athletic associations also establish rules that prohibit student-athletes from participating on independent teams (YMCA, private clubs, church leagues, etc.) while the student-athlete is participating in the same sport as a member of a high school or college team. Like summer camp rules, these rules are intended to prevent players from obtaining unfair additional training and competition and to keep overzealous coaches from involving student-athletes in excessive athletic participation. Not all sports are subject to these rules, however. Specified exceptions for several sports are listed in Bylaw 17 of the *2009–2010 NCAA Manual.*

The courts have generally upheld independent team participation rules on the grounds that the restrictions do not violate any constitutionally protected rights. In one case, the court dismissed a student-athlete's complaint because the limitation on the student-athlete's participation created no circumstances violative of either state or federal constitutions.

There has been one successful challenge to an independent team rule. In the case of *Buckton v. NCAA*, 366 F. Supp. 1152, 1155 (D. Mass. 1973), two resident alien college hockey players brought suit against the Eastern College Athletic Conference (ECAC) and the NCAA to challenge an ECAC and NCAA regulation that declared them ineligible because they had competed as members of the Canadian

Amateur Hockey Association's major junior A classification. The challenged independent team rule stated, "Any student-athlete who participated as a member of the Canadian Amateur Hockey Association's major junior A hockey classification shall not be eligible for intercollegiate athletics" (NCAA Constitution, Article 3, Section 1, 0.I.5. (1973–1974); ECAC Bylaws, Article 3, Section 1, 0.I.5 (1972)). The court struck down the rule after finding that it violated the equal protection clause of the 14th Amendment by treating resident aliens differently from American citizens. The court ruled that the university must declare the student-athletes eligible, and the NCAA was prohibited from bringing sanctions against the university.

NOTES

1. In *Letendre ex rel. Letendre v. Missouri State High School Activities Association*, 86 S.W.3d 63 (Mo. App. E.D. 2002), a state appellate court ruled that association rule prohibiting a student-athlete from competing on both a school and a nonschool team in the same sport during the same season was legal. The student swimmer argued that the prohibition violated her First Amendment freedom of association rights. In holding that the rule was rationally related to the association's purpose of protecting student-athletes, the court stated that a court may only review the actions of a voluntary association when (1) there are inconsistencies between the association's charter and bylaws and any action taken in respect to them; (2) whether the member has been treated unfairly, that is, denied notice, hearing, or an opportunity to defend; (3) whether the association undertakings were prompted by malice, fraud, or collusion; and (4) whether the charter or bylaws contravene public policy or law.

2. In *Burrows et al. v. Ohio High School Athletic Ass'n*, 712 F.Supp. 620 (S.D. Ohio 1988), the plaintiffs brought action challenging the constitutionality of the defendant's bylaw which provided that no soccer squad member could participate in independent soccer and maintain eligibility for interscholastic soccer without approval of the commissioner of the association. The court held that high school students' association with others for the purpose of participating in independent spring soccer and out-of-season instruction was not private association or expressive association within the constitutional protection of freedom of association. Furthermore, the bylaw did not violate the equal protection guarantee because it did not apply to students who had not played interscholastic soccer the previous fall or because it did not apply to certain sports involving primarily individual rather than team competition.

3. In *Zuments v. Colorado High School Activities Ass'n*, 737 P.2d 1113 (Colo. Ct. App. 1987), student-athletes enrolled in various Colorado public high schools sued to enjoin the defendant from enforcing its outside competition rule, which prevented students from practicing with nonschool teams while participating in interscholastic athletics. The lower court granted a preliminary injunction to the students. On appeal, the court of appeals held that the association's enforcement of the outside competition rule was not arbitrary, capricious, or haphazard and that it rationally furthered legitimate state purposes so as not to violate the students' right to equal protection. Furthermore, the outside competition rule did not impermissibly burden the students' constitutional right of free association.

4. No athletics department employee may take part in a camp or clinic that provides any sort of scouting of prospective student-athletes (*2009–2010 NCAA Manual*, Bylaw 13.12.2.3.1). The bylaws also restrict participation in camps to certain dates and number of days for coaches in basketball and football: basketball coaches may only participate in their own institutions' summer camps, and football coaches are limited to two camps lasting a maximum of 15 days each during the summer months (*2009–2010 NCAA Manual*, Bylaws 13.12.2.3.2, 13.12.2.3.3).

5. The Florida High School Activities Association (FHSAA) has the following regulation regarding high school student-athletes who work at summer camps, clinics, or recreational programs:

Policy 27: The following guidelines govern participation of students of FHSAA member schools in coaching schools, camps, clinics or workshops for an interscholastic sport.

1. Individuals

    Students from FHSAA member schools may participate as individuals in coaching schools, camps, clinics or workshops at any time of the year without jeopardizing their interscholastic athletic eligibility, provided:

    (a) Students participating in the event do not, in any way, represent their school.

    (b) Fees for the students who participate in the event are not paid by the school, coach or school district.

    (c) Students provide their own transportation or are provided transportation by their own school. No student may be transported to or from the event by an employee, athletic department staff member or representative of the athletic interests of any school other than the school that the student currently attends. (*2009–2010 FHSAA Handbook*, Policy 27, http://www.fhsaa.org)

6.3.3.4. Olympic Eligibility Requirements

While many high schools or colleges are not fortunate enough to have a student-athlete of Olympic quality as a member of their athletic program, high school and college athletic administrators need to know how Olympic governing bodies view the student-athletes and their eligibility as well as how the courts view the governing bodies and their rules and regulations. The consequences of not understanding these relationships may affect a student-athlete's eligibility for interscholastic, intercollegiate, and/or Olympic athletic participation. As was discussed in section 6.2, "Definitions of Eligibility," the definition of who can participate in the Olympic games will differ depending upon the decisions of the governing body of each sport. It is in the best interest of the administrator and student-athlete to research the bylaws of the national and international governing bodies of their sports in order to understand what eligibility requirements exist.

The USOC has specific regulations that govern the eligibility of athletes who try out for a spot on the U.S. Olympic team. Any athlete who is a U.S. citizen at the time the team is selected and is eligible under the international rules of the IOC for selection for membership on the U.S. Olympic or Pan-American team is allowed to try out directly or indirectly under the authority of any national governing body. All members qualifying for the Olympic or Pan-American teams must pass the USOC medical examination before being accepted on the team as well as sign an oath attesting to their eligibility (USOC Constitution, Chapters XL, XLI). Although the specific eligibility rules and regulations are determined by the IOC and the international federations for each sport, the USOC does play an important role in serving to reconcile differences in eligibility requirements that exist among the various athletic organizations and Olympic governing bodies. For more information on the Olympics, see the following sections within the text: section 5.1.2, "The U.S. Olympic Committee," and section 5.3.5, "Olympic Enforcement Procedure."

NOTES

The following cases deal with the relationship between the athlete and Olympic governing bodies:

1. In *Hollonbeck v. United States Olympic Committee*, 513 F.3d 1191 (10th Cir. 2008), a paralympic athlete alleged that the USOC's policy of providing grants, tuition assistance and health insurance benefits only to Olympic team members violated the Ted Stevens Olympic and Amateur Sports Act (ASA). The court disagreed, finding that the policy was neither facially discriminatory or discriminatory by proxy.

2. In *Slaney v. United States Olympic Committee*, 244 F.3d 580 (7th Cir. 2001), the strength of the Amateur Sports Act received a judicial boost. In this case, Olympic runner Mary Decker Slaney brought suit against the USOC after she tested positive for drug use after Olympic trials in 1996. She was found to have a high enough ratio of testosterone to epitestosterone in her body to be consistent with blood doping (for more information on drug testing of Olympic athletes, see section 7.2.3, "Olympic and International Sports"). In her complaint against the USOC, Slaney alleged that the testing discriminated against women and was not scientifically valid. The Seventh Circuit upheld the strength of the Amateur Sports Act (see section 5.1.2, "The U.S. Olympic Committee" for more information on the Amateur Sports Act) when it concluded that the act provides the USOC with complete jurisdiction over decisions concerning an athlete's eligibility. The court reasoned that the USOC was the most qualified body for determining questions of eligibility. The court went on to state that the USOC could be held liable in questions of eligibility if they do not follow their own stated rules.

3. In *Floyd v. United States Olympic Committee*, 965 S.W.2d 35 (Tex. Ct. App. 1998), a runner tested positive for amphetamines after using a carbohydrate supplement named Sydnocarb. She believed that she could use the supplement without worrying about testing positive because when her husband had called the USOC to see if Sydnocarb was a banned substance, the USOC operator had responded that it was not. The operator did not say, however, that the supplement was safe to use or provide any other assurances. After Floyd tested positive, she brought a claim of negligence against the USOC, alleging that they had provided her with false information regarding the supplement. The court ruled that under the Amateur Sports Act, no athlete has a right to a private cause of action against the USOC and dismissed Floyd's claim.

4. In *Foschi v. United States Swimming, Inc.*, 916 F. Supp. 232 (E.D. N.Y. 1996), the court concluded that while the USOC has jurisdiction concerning eligibility determinations, courts have the ability to intervene to make sure that the USOC is following its own rules for determining eligibility.

5. In *Harding v. United States Figure Skating Association*, 851 F. Supp. 1476 (D. Or. 1994), the court enjoined the defendant association from proceeding with a disciplinary hearing because they had violated their own bylaws by scheduling a disciplinary hearing too early for Harding to prepare her defense. The ruling in this case, allowing a court to intervene with an athletic association, was limited by the judge's opinion, which stated, "Intervention is appropriate only in the most extraordinary circumstances, where the association has clearly breached its own rules, that breach will imminently result in serious and irreparable harm to the plaintiff, and the plaintiff has exhausted all internal remedies. Even then, injunctive relief is limited to correcting the breach of the rules. The court should not intervene in the merits of the underlying dispute."

6. In *Dolan v. United States Equestrian Team, Inc.*, 608 A.2d 434 (N.J. Super. Ct. App. Div. 1992), a horse rider brought a claim against the U.S. Equestrian Team, claiming that the team had violated the Amateur Sports Act with their procedure and criteria for selecting team members. The court held that Dolan had not exhausted her administrative remedies under the Amateur Sports Act, and until she had met that condition, she was not able to bring a private right of action. The court also held that requiring Dolan to exhaust her administrative remedies was fair and also consistent with the

purpose of the Amateur Sports Act to have jurisdiction over resolution of disputes in Olympic sports.

7. In *Martin v. International Olympic Committee*, 740 F.2d 670 (9th Cir. 1984), women runners and runners' organizations filed suit against the IOC and sought to require the IOC to institute 5,000-meter and 10,000-meter track events for women at the 1984 summer Olympic games in Los Angeles. The U.S. District Court (C.D. Cal.) denied a request for a preliminary injunction, and the U.S. Court of Appeals affirmed this decision. The two courts reasoned that the IOC's Rule 32, which was the process for adding new events, was not arbitrary. In addition, it was reasoned that state law should not be applied to alter the structure of Olympic events.

8. In *Michels v. United States Olympic Committee*, 741 F.2d 155 (7th Cir. 1984), a federal appeals court found that an individual athlete had no private cause of action (a reason or means by which to challenge the USOC's authority) against the USOC, under the Amateur Sports Act of 1978. In reversing a district court decision, the appeals court noted that the Supreme Court had emphasized congressional intent in ruling on cause of action suits and that "the legislative history of the Act clearly reveals that Congress intended not to create a private cause of action under the Act."

9. In *DeFrantz v. United States Olympic Committee*, 492 F.Supp. 1181 (D.D.C. 1980), *aff'd. without opinion*, 701 F.2d 221 (D.C. Cir. 1980), the district court held that the Amateur Sports Act of 1978 did not establish a cause of action for 25 designated Olympic athletes who sought to prohibit the USOC from barring these American athletes from participating in the 1980 Olympic Games in Moscow because of an American boycott of the event. The court concluded "that the USOC not only had the authority to decide not to send an American team to the summer Olympics, but also . . . could do so for reasons not directly related to sports considerations."

10. In *Behagen v. Amateur Basketball Association*, 884 F.2d 524 (10th Cir. 1989), the plaintiff, after having played professional basketball in the National Basketball Association, wanted to return to Italy and play for an amateur team for which he had played the year before. The Amateur Basketball Association had informed the International Basketball Association (FIBA) of Behagen's professional playing career; thus FIBA declared Behagen ineligible to compete for the Italian team. Behagen filed suit, claiming a violation of antitrust laws, through the formation of a boycott preventing him from competing in Italy, and a violation of his due process rights. The court of appeals held for the defendants, stating that the actions of the amateur basketball association, in refusing to reinstate plaintiff's amateur status, were exempt from the federal antitrust laws and that the association was a private rather than a governmental actor and thus not subject to due process requirements.

For a fuller discussion on the roles of the different governing bodies in the Olympic Games organization, see the following:

1. In *United States v. Wrestling Division of the AAU*, 545 F.Supp. 1053 (N.D. Ohio 1982), the federal court prohibited one national sports organization (the Amateur Athletic Union) from exercising any of the national governing body power and ordered it to sever all ties with the international governing body for that sport pursuant to the Amateur Sports Act of 1978 since the U.S. Olympic Committee had selected a competing national sports organization to be the NGB. The USOC was also ordered to terminate its recognition of the AAU group as the NGB and the U.S. representative to the international federation. See also the companion case *United States Wrestling Federation v. United States Olympic Committee*, Civil Action No. 13460-78, Superior Court, District of Columbia (1978), in which the USWF successfully filed suit against the USOC to compel it to recognize it as its national governing body and Group A member for amateur Olympic wrestling.

Another major purpose of the Amateur Sports Act of 1978 was to protect the USOC's ability to raise financial revenues to field American Olympic teams, which receive no direct government funding. In *United States Olympic Committee v. Interlicense Corporation*, 737 F.2d

263 (2nd Cir. 1984), the U.S. court of appeals affirmed the judgment of the district court, which ruled that, pursuant to the Amateur Sports Act, the USOC's consent is a prerequisite to marketing the Olympic symbol (five interlocking rings) in the United States.

6.4. ATHLETE'S CHALLENGE OF RULES

The authority of an athletic association and a coach to make rules regarding a student-athlete's private life is limited. As with rules of athletic associations and conferences, the rules of coaches and institutions are held to the standards of reasonableness and rational relationship to a legitimate purpose. Generally, the purpose of the rules must be reasonably related to the conduct of the sport itself. Without this relationship, the rule may be deemed impermissible on constitutional grounds by the courts.

Even when a rational relationship does exist, a rule may be impermissible if it infringes on the constitutional rights of life, liberty, and property, which are protected by due process guarantees (see section 6.1.2, "Due Process"). In other words, rules have been struck down when they affect personal choices and preferences in areas where the Constitution guarantees reasonable expectations of privacy and individual freedoms. In these cases, the courts have to weigh the personal freedoms of student-athletes against institutions' or coaches' regulation of athletics in the name of character building, fair play, and esprit de corps (see section 6.1.3, "Equal Protection").

The authority of a coach is limited to his or her position within the institution. One basis for a coach's authority is that the relationship between the coach or institution and the student-athlete may be analogous to that between parent and child; in legal terms, the coach or school is said to stand in loco parentis to the student-athlete. Although this principle would seem to give a coach virtually a free rein in disciplining players, its validity, particularly as it applies to college student-athletes, many of whom are adults in the eyes of the law, has not been absolute.

The sections that follow are broken down into three different areas. Section 6.4.1 will discuss freedom of expression and how institutions are allowed or prohibited from infringing upon an athlete's rights to self-expression, including such issues as tattoos, prayer, hair-length, and right to marriage. Section 6.4.2 will consider discipline within athletics and what rights student-athletes, coaches, and institutions possess. The third and final section, 6.4.3, will deal with the effects of alcohol and drug rules in high school athletics.

6.4.1. Freedom of Expression

Freedom of expression often arises in amateur athletics when an athlete's or coach's right to speak is impeded. Student-athletes, coaches, and others have alleged that they lost scholarships or jobs for engaging in expressive activity or speech that was unacceptable to their superiors. If the superior who limited the right to free expression is found to be engaged in state action, the student-athlete or coach may have constitutional grounds to sue the superior.

Freedom of expression is the cornerstone of the Bill of Rights and individual liberty under the First Amendment to the U.S. Constitution. The term *freedom of expression* is sometimes used rather than *free speech* because certain non-verbal types of communication are protected under the First Amendment—for example, carrying a sign with a written message. Therefore, while the First Amendment uses the words "Congress shall make no law ... abridging the freedom of *speech*" (emphasis added), a broader range of expression is protected.

In some cases, a student's claim of a right to free expression may create conflict with other parts of the First Amendment. For example, in *Santa Fe Independent School District v. Doe*, 530 U.S. 290 (2000), the Court decided that the recitation of prayers before a public high school football game was a violation of the requirement of the separation of church and state under the First Amendment. The players were therefore not allowed to read prayers before games, a practice they claimed was protected by the First Amendment. See note 1(c) for further details.

For purposes of analysis, expression must be broken down into two component parts. First is the physical element of speech or conduct, which is a necessary part of communicating a message. For example, a demonstration requires conduct by the demonstrators that can be either peaceful or violent. Violence is a noncommunicative aspect of speech that may be regulated because there are compelling government interests in peace and order involved. Second is the component that is the actual message or *content* of speech. This communicative aspect of speech, consisting of the thoughts or informational content of the communication, may be regulated only when there is a clear and present danger of imminent lawless action—for example, shouting "fire" in a crowded theater.

Some student-athletes, coaches, and athletic personnel have been successful in challenging the termination of scholarships or suspension from their jobs on freedom-of-expression grounds. In analyzing these situations, the courts have examined whether or not the individual's communication involved a public or a private concern. Courts are generally inclined to protect the individual's right to express his or her views, but this protection is not absolute: The courts must balance the speaker's interest against the other party's interest.

However, student-athletes have, on occasion, received some protection of First Amendment rights. A good example of a case in the area of freedom of expression concerning athletics is *Wildman ex rel. Wildman v. Marshalltown School Dist.*, 249 F.3d 768 (8th Cir. 2001). A high school basketball player alleged that the school district, principal, athletic director, and basketball coach violated her First Amendment rights by conditioning her continued participation on the team on her issuing an apology to the other team members. The plaintiff, disappointed in not playing for the varsity, had written a letter to team members to gauge their support of her negative feelings for the coach. The coach obtained a copy of the letter, and subsequently told the plaintiff she could not return to the team without first apologizing; the plaintiff refused and was suspended for the remainder of the season. The court ruled in favor of the defendants, stating that the right to free speech in a school environment is not absolute and that the plaintiff's use of a profanity in the letter constituted insubordination towards her coach for which she could be dismissed from the team.

While most litigation of athletic rules on constitutional grounds has been based on allegations of infringement upon a property interest, cases involving hair-length regulations have been attacked for infringing on personal liberty interests. Some courts have recognized a student-athlete's right to govern his or her personal appearance while attending public school, while other circuit courts see this liberty interest as too insubstantial to create a protectable interest. Because of shifts in culture and grooming style, issues of hair length have not been hotly debated topics within the courts in recent years (see notes 2 and 3 for cases involving hair length).

Rules relating to high school marriages also once resulted in much litigation. In the early cases, rules excluding married student-athletes from interscholastic competition were upheld under the rational basis standard (i.e., they bore a rational relationship to a legitimate objective). These rules were considered reasonable because it was believed that exclusion of married students from athletics was necessary to (1) protect unmarried students from bad influences, (2) encourage students to finish high school before marriage, and (3) give married students the opportunity for more time together to develop their family life.

More recently, however, such rules have been struck down as invalid and improper invasions of the right to marital property (i.e., the right to be married). Courts have also reasoned that such rules deprive student-athletes of a chance for a college scholarship and therefore infringe upon their property interest of obtaining a free education (see note 5(e) for the *Moran* case). Most courts have refused to accept the property interest found by *Moran*, noting that such an interest is too speculative at the high school level to merit legal protection as a property interest. However, the courts now typically hold that marital classifications are unconstitutional on equal protection grounds. Like grooming rules, high school rules regarding marriage have virtually disappeared due to changes in cultural norms (see below for cases involving marriage and interscholastic athletics).

NOTES

The following cases also involve freedom of expression:

1. In *Lowery v. Euverard*, 2007 WL 2213215 (6th Cir. August 3, 2007), high school students brought suit after they were dismissed from their high school football team claiming violations of their First Amendment rights. The players had made a petition that simply stated "I hate Coach Euvard [*sic*] and I don't want to play for him." The players alleged that Coach Euverard had struck a player in the helmet, threw away college recruiting letters to disfavored players, violated high school rules by instituting a year-round conditioning program, and generally degraded and humiliated players by using inappropriate language. Eventually 18 players signed the petition, which was planned to be held until after the season. However, Coach Euverard found out about the petition and demanded players apologize to remain on the team; the four players bringing suit refused. In ordering summary judgment for the defendants, the Court emphasized the importance of a coach's ability to discipline his team in order to maintain authority and unity. While emphasizing the voluntary nature of interscholastic athletics, the court also questioned the dissenting players' efforts when they so disliked their coach, which may have also threatened team unity.

2. In *Rottmann v. Pennsylvania Interscholastic Athletic Association, Inc. (PIAA)*, 349 F.Supp.2d 922 (W.D. Pa. 2004), a girls' basketball coach brought suit challenging PIAA's antirecruiting rule after she was suspended for one year for talking with a standout eighth grade basketball player. The rule provides for sanctioning schools or coaches for talking with a student or her parent, trying to convince them to transfer for athletic purposes. Rottmann contended the rule unconstitutionally infringed on her First Amendment freedom of speech by being vague and overbroad. In ruling for the PIAA, the court refused to apply a strict scrutiny test and stated that because the disputed speech is a private matter only, there is no constitutional protection.

3. In *Santa Fe Independent School District v. Doe*, 530 U.S. 290 (2000), the Supreme Court decided in a 6–3 decision that saying prayers before a public high school football game was a violation of the First Amendment separation of church and state. The school board had allowed students to read overtly Christian prayers at graduation ceremonies

and home football games. At the district court level, the court adopted a policy, the October policy, that allowed the school to deliver a nondenominational prayer and allowed the students to vote on whether they wanted to have a prayer, and who would deliver it. The appellate court found that this decision was erroneous because it still violated the establishment of religion clause in the First Amendment. On writ of certiorari, the Supreme Court found the following: "1) under the circumstances presented, a student invocation pursuant to the October policy violated the establishment of religion clause, as (a) such invocations were not private student speech, but rather public speech, (b) the student election did nothing to protect minority views, (c) the policy involved perceived and actual endorsement of religion, (d) the student election mechanisms did not insulate the school from the coercive element of the message, (e) the elections encouraged divisiveness along religious lines in a public school setting, and (f) even if every high school student's decision to attend a home football game were regarded as purely voluntary, the delivery of a pregame prayer had the improper effect of coercing those present to participate in an act of religious worship; and (2) the simple enactment of the policy was a facial constitutional violation, even if no student ever offered a religious message pursuant to the policy."

4. In the case of *Chandler v. Siegelman*, 230 F.3d 1313 (11th Cir. 2000), a similar fact pattern existed as in *Santa Fe Independent School District v. Doe*. In this case, a message with religious content was broadcast over a public address system in a public high school. The case was appealed to the Supreme Court, but the Court, after making the decision in *Santa Fe*, remanded the case to the appeals court for a decision that was consistent with the *Santa Fe* case, determining in fact that a violation of the First Amendment separation of church and state had occurred.

5. Although this case did not reach the trial court level, in 2001 a Cal-State Fullerton track runner was suspended from participating on the track and field team at the university because she maintained a part-time job as an exotic dancer. The coach of the team told her that her job as a stripper violated university athletic policies. Upon reconsideration of the decision, officials at the institution decided to reinstate the runner to the team if she was able to achieve the required academic eligibility standards. The university officials noted that stripping is a "constitutionally protected form of expression" and feared a lawsuit if the suspension were upheld.

6. A leading case in the area of freedom of expression concerning athletics is *Williams v. Eaton*, 468 F.2d 1079 (10th Cir. 1972). The plaintiffs were a group of 14 black football players for the University of Wyoming. In October 1969, prior to a game against Brigham Young University, the players had approached head football coach Lloyd Eaton about wearing black armbands to protest the beliefs of the Mormon Church. Coach Eaton dismissed them from the team for violating team discipline rules, which did not allow protests or demonstrations by players. The players brought suit in district court, but their action was dismissed. The players appealed, and the court of appeals affirmed the decision in part while sending the case back for further proceedings. Upon the second hearing, the lower court held that the players had been given a full and impartial hearing before their suspensions and that their procedural due process rights had not been violated. The court reasoned that Coach Eaton's rule had not been arbitrary or capricious, and up until their action, there had been no complaint concerning the rule by any of the players. In addition, Coach Eaton, acting as an agent of the University of Wyoming and the state of Wyoming, was compelled not to allow the players, under the guise of the First Amendment rights of freedom of speech, to undertake a planned protest demonstration against the religious beliefs of the Mormon Church and Brigham Young University. The demonstration would have taken place in a tax-supported facility, and had the officials of the university acceded to the demands of the players, such action would have been violative of Brigham Young University's First Amendment rights. The court held that the rights of the players to freedom of speech as guaranteed by the First Amendment could not be held paramount to the rights of others under the same amendment to practice their religion free from state-supported protest or demonstration.

7. In *Menora v. Illinois High School Ass'n*, 527 F.Supp. 637 (N.D. Ill. 1981), *vacated*, 683 F.2d 1030 (7th Cir. 1982), *cert. denied*, 103 S. Ct. 801 (1983), a federal district court ruled that an Illinois High School Association (IHSA) rule that prohibited student-athletes from wearing soft barrettes or yarmulkes during basketball games violated their right to freedom of religion guaranteed by the First Amendment. Orthodox Jewish students are required by their religion to keep their head covered at all times except when unconscious, immersed in water, or in imminent danger of loss of life. On appeal to the court of appeals, the decision was overturned. The court ruled that the students have no constitutional right to wear yarmulkes during the basketball games. It noted that Jewish religious law requires only that the head be covered, not specifically by yarmulkes.

8. In *Tinker v. Des Moines Independent School District*, 93 U.S. 503 (1969), student-athletes wearing politically motivated black armbands in a public high school were found to have a constitutionally protected right of expression. The court recognized that the student-athletes' First Amendment rights do not stop at the schoolhouse or gym door, and that constitutional protection extends to forms of expression other than speech or written communication.

The following cases viewed issues involving hair length warranted constitutional review:

1. In *Dostert v. Berthold Public School Dist. No. 594*, 391 F. Supp. 876 (D.N. Dak. 1975), a student-athlete sought relief from a rule regulating hair length. The court held that the school's interest in requiring uniformity was such a compelling part of its public educational mission as to outweigh the constitutionally protected interest of student-athletes in regard to personal appearance.

2. In *Long v. Zopp*, 476 F.2d 180 (4th Cir. 1973), a high school football player challenged the denial of his football letter because of his hair length. The court held unlawful the coach's regulation of the hair length of his players after the end of the football season. The holding was based on the analysis that it was reasonable for a coach to require short hair during a playing season for health and safety reasons. However, it was not reasonable to deny an athletic award or an invitation to a sports banquet when a student-athlete allowed his hair to grow long after the season.

In the following cases, the court found issues of hair length were too insubstantial to warrant constitutional review:

1. In *Davenport v. Randolph County Bd. of Education*, 730 F.2d 1395 (11th Cir. 1984), high school football student-athletes sought an injunction from the school board's decision that refused them participation in athletics unless they complied with the coach's clean-shaven policy for football and basketball team members. The district court denied the injunction. The court of appeals affirmed the decision.

2. In *Zeller v. Donegal School District*, 517 F.2d 600 (3rd Cir. 1975), a high school soccer player sought an injunction and monetary damages under the Civil Rights Act for his dismissal from the soccer team for noncompliance with the athletic grooming code, regulating length of hair. The district court dismissed the complaint, and the student-athlete appealed. The court of appeals held that the nature of the constitutional interpretation calls for the making of a value judgment in areas that were regulated by the state and in which the federal courts should not intrude, and it stated: "We hold that plaintiff's contention does not rise to the dignity of a protectable constitutional interest." The court based its decision on the concept that a student-athlete's liberties and freedoms are not absolute and stated: "We determine today that the Federal System is ill-equipped to make value judgments on hair-lengths in terms of the Constitution." The court concluded that the student-athlete hair-length case should be left to school regulation, "where the wisdom and experience of school authorities must be deemed superior and preferable to the federal judiciary's."

Rules barring married student-athletes from participation in extracurricular activities were held constitutionally *permissible* in the following cases:

1. An early case in the area of interscholastic athletic eligibility and marriage is *Estay v. La Fourche Parish School Board*, 230 So.2d 443 (La. Ct. App. 1969). In *Estay*, a married high school student challenged his exclusion from all extracurricular participation based on

a school board regulation. The court of appeals held that the school board had the authority to adopt the regulation. It found the regulation to be reasonable—not arbitrary or capricious—and concluded that enforcement of the rule did not deprive the student of any constitutional rights. The court reasoned that there was a rational relationship between the rule and its stated objective of promoting completion of high school education prior to marriage. The court held that the classification rested on a sound and reasonable basis and that the criteria were applied uniformly and impartially.

2. In *Board of Directors v. Green*, 147 N.W.2d 854 (Iowa 1967), an action was brought to prohibit enforcement of a school board rule barring participation in extracurricular activities by married pupils. Upon appeal, the Iowa Supreme Court held that engaging in extracurricular activities, such as basketball, is a privilege that may be enjoyed only in accordance with standards set by the school district. The student did not have a "right" to participate; therefore no violation of the equal protection clause occurred.

3. In *Starkey v. Board of Education*, 381 P.2d 718 (Utah Sup. Ct. 1963), the Utah Supreme Court held that the "rule against participation in extracurricular activities by married students bore a reasonable relationship to the problem of 'dropouts' and did not constitute an abuse of school board's discretion."

Rules barring married students from participation in extracurricular activities were held *impermissible* in the absence of a finding of a rational basis for the rules:

1. In *Beeson v. Kiowa County School District*, 567 P.2d 801 (Colo. Ct. App. 1977), the court of appeals ruled for the plaintiff, stating that the student had a fundamental right to marry and reasons given by the school board regarding a policy that prohibited married students from participating in extracurricular activities did not establish compelling state interest to justify violation of the plaintiff's fundamental right.

2. In *Indiana High School Athletic Ass'n v. Raike*, 164 Ind. App. 169, 329 N.E.2d 66 (Ind. Ct. App. 1975), a public high school rule that prohibited married students from participating in any extracurricular activities was held invalid. The court found the rule both over-inclusive because it barred married students of good moral character and underinclusive because it did not bar unmarried students of questionable character. The court concluded, therefore, that the rule did not have a substantial relationship to its goal, and thus it violated the equal protection clause.

3. In *Bell v. Lone Oak Independent School District*, 507 S.W.2d 636 (Tex. Ct. App. 1974), the court of appeals reversed a district court decision and held that a regulation prohibiting married high school students from participating in extracurricular activities was a violation of the equal protection clause of the 14th Amendment.

4. In *Hollon v. Mathis Independent School District*, 358 F. Supp. 1269 (S.D. Tex. 1973), the plaintiff sought a temporary injunction against the enforcement of a school district policy that prohibited married students from engaging in interscholastic league activities. The district court held that the policy was unconstitutional. The court decided "there was no justifiable relationship between the marriage of high school athletes and the overall dropout problem; nor does it appear that preventing a good athlete, although married, from continuing to play...would in any way deter marriages or otherwise enhance the dropout problem."

5. In *Moran v. School District, Yellowstone County*, 350 F. Supp. 1180 (D. Mont. 1972), a marriage rule was held invalid because it deprived a student-athlete of the chance for a college scholarship without showing any evidence that the presence of married students would result in a reasonable likelihood of imposing moral pollution on unmarried students. No rational basis on which to restrict participation existed.

6.4.2. Discipline

The topic of discipline of individual student-athletes is particularly important and sensitive since disciplinary action may precipitate an athlete's decision to pursue litigation. The high school or college that fails to carry out a disciplinary action against a student-athlete, as prescribed by an association or conference, risks forfeiting games and championships, returning television and championship money, and possibly losing its membership in the governing athletic organization. These unpleasant alternatives often place the high school or college athletic administrator in a precarious position between the student-athlete and the athletic association or conference.

Disciplined athletes will often bring claims that their rights are violated when they are not allowed to participate in athletics. Athletes may also raise issues of due process when they are not provided adequate hearings or appeals. The best way to illustrate these issues is to examine situations that have been litigated in the courts.

In the case of *Wooten v. Pleasant Hope School Dist.*, 139 F. Supp.2d 835 (W.D. Mo. 2000), a softball player was not allowed to participate on her high school team after she failed to appear for a game. The plaintiff alleged that she was denied her procedural due process rights because she was not given notice of her right to a hearing before her dismissal from the team.

It was true that Wooten had been dismissed from the team before she was able to plead her case to her coach. When she met with the coach, the coach told her that the players did not want her back on the team, and under this understanding, she told the coach that she did not want to be reinstated to the team. After a month away from the team, however, Wooten discovered that the coach was mistaken in his statement concerning the attitude of her teammates, and she applied to be reinstated to the team through an appeals board. The appeals board denied her a hearing, finding she had waived her right to one by voluntarily asking not to be reinstated.

The federal district court ruled against Wooten because it found she had no protected interest in playing softball. The court provided an eloquent discussion of the merits of allowing a coach to have discretion when disciplining its players:

> That Pleasant Hope encourages its students to participate in extracurricular activities does not mean that students have an unqualified right to be a member of specific team, club or group. Notably, none of the Handbook passages discussing disciplinary action limits a coach's ability to train or punish the athletes for whom he/she is responsible. The Court recognizes that coaches must have discretionary decision-making authority to act in the best interests of the team, even if that has a negative effect on an individual team member. Accordingly, without explicit Handbook language stating that students have a protected right to participate in extracurricular activities, the Court declines to find that such a right exists.

The decision in Wooten demonstrates the power that a court grants to a coach to exercise his or her right to discipline athletes. As long as a coach can offer legitimate reasons for their disciplinary actions, and is not acting with malice, courts will be likely to defer to their decisions.

Discipline of athletes may also cause disputes between institutions and governing associations. A leading case in this area is *Regents of University of Minnesota v. National Collegiate Athletic Association*, 422 F. Supp. 1158 (D. Minn. 1976). In this case, the University of Minnesota challenged an NCAA sanction placing all the university's athletic teams on indefinite probation when the university refused to declare three student-athletes ineligible for intercollegiate competition. The student-athletes had admitted to the NCAA violations, which consisted of (1) selling complimentary season tickets; (2) accepting an invitation to stay at a cabin with all meals, lodging, and entertainment provided by a member of the booster club; and (3) using a private line to place long-distance calls. After admitting to the violations, the student-athletes donated the proceeds from the sale of the tickets to charity to satisfy a university committee. However, the NCAA was not satisfied. The NCAA's proposed penalty for Minnesota's not declaring the student-athletes ineligible was a three-year probation and a two-year ban on postseason play and televised games. Additionally, the NCAA imposed a two-year restriction on the granting of athletic scholarships for basketball. Minnesota, in accordance with its policy for all students, had afforded the three basketball players a hearing before the Campus Committee on Student Behaviors and the Assembly Committee on Intercollegiate Athletics. These committees voted not to declare the student-athletes ineligible, despite the findings of the NCAA's Committee on Infractions.

The district court found that participation in intercollegiate athletics was a substantial property right entitled to due process guarantees. Thus a student-athlete had to be afforded due process rights before the right to an education or any substantial element of it could be adversely affected. Consequently, the court reasoned that the NCAA's action transgressed on the university's legal duty to afford due process hearings to student-athletes and to abide by the results of the hearings. The court concluded that the plaintiffs had demonstrated a strong possibility of success on the merits and that Minnesota would be irreparably harmed if a preliminary injunction was not issued, while the NCAA would not be harmed (see section 5.2.4). The court therefore directed the NCAA to lift the probation and temporarily prohibited the NCAA from imposing further sanctions pending a hearing on the merits.

The NCAA appealed the district court's decision to the Eighth Circuit in *Regents of University of Minnesota v. National Collegiate Athletic Ass'n*, 560 F.2d 352 (8th Cir. 1977). The appeals court dissolved the preliminary injunction. The court noted that, as a voluntary member of the NCAA, the university agreed to adhere to association rules, including Constitution 4-2-(a), which required Minnesota "to administer their athletic programs in accordance with the Constitution, the Bylaws and other legislation of the Association."

In another case concerning discipline of a student-athlete, *Carlton Walker v. NCAA*, No. El-C-916 (W.D. Wis. 1981), Walker, a starting guard for the University of Wisconsin football team, was declared ineligible to participate in the Garden State Bowl as a result of an investigation of recruiting violations. Previously, in July 1981, the NCAA had officially charged the university and its alumni with twenty violations of NCAA regulations and bylaws in connection with Walker's recruitment. Neither the NCAA nor the university charged Walker with any violation. Walker immediately filed a motion for a preliminary injunction to gain eligibility for the postseason bowl game. Walker contended that since athletic participation was a property right protected by the Constitution, he had not been afforded adequate due process in connection with the declaration of eligibility. The district court denied Walker's motion on the grounds that he failed to establish irreparable harm and thus was unlikely to succeed on the merits (see section 5.2.4, "Injunctive Relief"). Walker, who attended the University of Wisconsin from fall 1980 to spring 1982, then transferred to the University of Utah and enrolled as a full-time student. In August 1982, pursuant to NCAA Bylaw 5-3-(3), the University of Utah requested a waiver of Walker's one-year loss of eligibility due to his transfer

(NCAA Bylaw 5-1-[j]-[7]). The NCAA Committee on Infractions reviewed the waiver request by Utah.

The committee determined from the available evidence that Walker's involvement in the Wisconsin recruiting violations was not inadvertent or innocent and denied the waiver. Walker amended his initial complaint in November 1982 and claimed that the NCAA had tortiously and arbitrarily interfered with the contractual relations between Walker and the Universities of Wisconsin and Utah (see section 3.3.4), thereby depriving him of the opportunity to compete in collegiate athletics and damaging his ability to secure a professional contract. The NCAA moved for dismissal or summary judgment. Regarding Walker's due process claims, the NCAA stated that it was well settled that a student possesses no liberty or property interest in intercollegiate athletics. Therefore, the NCAA argued, the privilege of participating in intercollegiate athletics falls outside the parameters of the due process clause.

Of course, the situations exhibited in these cases will not arise if the student-athlete retains eligibility. This, obviously, can be accomplished if the athlete obeys the rules and regulations of the associations and conferences to which the institution belongs, but compliance may not always be within the athlete's control. An athlete may unknowingly violate eligibility rules or be deceived or coerced into rules violations by a third party. Other athletes may be declared ineligible as part of a larger sanction against their high school or college, as when a football team is placed on probation and suspended from post-season competition for recruiting violations.

A student-athlete who is declared ineligible can take a number of actions in response. First, the athlete should exhaust all remedies available under the school's or association's policies. These remedies may include the opportunity to appeal the decision, ask for a reconsideration, or initiate other procedures for reevaluating the initial ruling of ineligibility. If a person does *not* exhaust such remedies, he or she will have virtually no chance of success in court.

Once these procedures are exhausted, the athlete may then resort to a lawsuit against the governing body. Even though most such claims against the NCAA or other amateur athletic association rules have not succeeded, it may still be possible for student-athletes to obtain their objective—another season of competition. The student-athlete can achieve this objective by arguing that the applicable association rule is unenforceable, and that the plaintiff is entitled to a preliminary injunction. The student-athlete can argue that the rule violates the due process or equal protection clauses of the state and federal constitutions, violates federal antitrust and other federal laws, or represents a breach of contract. On these grounds, the student-athlete may ask for a court order prohibiting enforcement of the rule as applied to his or her individual case until the case goes to trial. Since this may be months or years later, the student-athlete can compete in the interim if he or she succeeds in obtaining a preliminary injunction. (These and other legal principles are discussed in Chapters 3, 4, and 13.)

NOTES

The discipline decisions of intercollegiate athlete associations were *upheld* in the following cases:

1. In *NCAA v. Gillard*, 352 So.2d 1072 (Miss. Sup. Ct. 1977), sanctions were imposed against a non-NCAA member player who accepted a 20% clothing discount. There was some evidence that this discount policy was not limited to student-athletes. The NCAA decided

there was a rule transgression. The Mississippi Supreme Court held that the player's rights were adequately protected by the NCAA's procedures and that the player's right to play intercollegiate football was not a property right protected by due process guarantees.

2. In *Samara v. NCAA*, 1973 Trade Cases (CCH) 74,536 (E.D. Va. 1973), the court upheld an NCAA decision that participation by a student-athlete in a noncertified track and field event resulted in ineligibility for further NCAA competition. The court stated that the NCAA rule and its subsequent sanctions were not illegal. This was true even though the event would have been certified if the Amateur Athletic Union (AAU) had requested the NCAA to provide such authorization.

For a case in which discipline decisions of intercollegiate athletic associations have been *struck down*, see the following:

1. *Hall v. University of Minnesota*, 530 F.Supp. 104 (D. Minn. 1982), also discussed in note 2 of section 6.3.1.3, concerned a conference academic progress rule. The court was quick to point out that the student-athlete had been recruited as "a basketball player and not a scholar" and that "his academic record reflects that he has lived up to those expectations as do the academic records of many of the athletes presented to this court." The court ruled that a constitutionally protected interest was involved and that Hall's due process rights had been violated. The court ordered the restoration of Hall's scholarship money and mandated his acceptance into a degree-granting program.

The following cases involve discipline issues relating to student-athletes in interscholastic athletics:

1. In *Brown ex rel. Brown v. Oklahoma Secondary School Activities Ass'n*, 125 P.3d 1219 (Okla. 2005), a high school football player was granted an injunction preventing the enforcement of his two-game suspension for unsportsmanlike misconduct. Brown, a quarterback, was ejected from the quarterfinal game for kicking an opponent in the helmet while he was on the ground during a fight between the teams. As a result of the injunction, the association postponed the semifinal and state championship games. The Supreme Court of Oklahoma vacated the injunction 20 days after the incident, ruling that the suspension was reasonably applied, that the association did not act arbitrarily or capriciously in postponing the next rounds of the playoffs, and that deference should be given to the internal affairs of a voluntary membership association.

2. In *In Re University Interscholastic League*, 20 S.W.3d 690 (Tex. 2000), the Texas Supreme Court found that a constitutional right was not violated when a student-athlete was not allowed to participate in extracurricular activities due to disciplinary reasons. In this case, an entire baseball team was ruled ineligible to compete in a high school playoff tournament because one of their players was declared ineligible. The court did not believe that because the players may suffer immediate and irreparable harm they could show a constitutional violation of their rights.

3. In *Mazevski v. Horseheads Central School District*, 950 F. Supp. 69 (W.D. N.Y. 1997), the court held that a high school student did not have protected property interest in participating in extracurricular activities. In this case, a student was dismissed from his school's marching band because of an unexcused absence at an event. The parents of the student, the plaintiffs, brought a claim of procedural due process violations. The court did not reach the merits of the plaintiff's case because the plaintiff was not able to establish that membership in an extracurricular activity was a protectable property right. The court reasoned that the plaintiff's right to an education should be protected, not his right to extracurricular activities.

The following cases overturned the disciplinary decisions of an interscholastic association:

1. In *Christ the King Regional High School v. Catholic High School Athletic Ass'n*, 624 N.Y.S.2d 755 (N.Y. App. Div. 1995), the girls' basketball team at the plaintiff high school was suspended from postseason play for one season for violating a league rule concerning traveling to out-of-state games. Upon reviewing the penalty meted out by the Association's Principals Committee, the court discovered that the penalty was arbitrary and capricious because it violated the rules of the association, which only allowed for the Association's Infractions Committee to dispense such penalties.

2. In *Diaz v. Board of Education*, 618 N.Y.S.2d 948 (N.Y. Sup. Ct. 1994), the court found that the due process rights of an entire high school soccer team had been violated when they were not allowed to compete for an entire season due to the actions of one of their players. The director of the Public School Athletic League (PSAL), in a letter dated November 2, 1993, had warned the members of the Newton High School soccer team that if they received one more red card during the season the entire team would be withdrawn from competition in the league. Nine days later, one player started a fight after spitting in the face of a referee and subsequently received a red card. After a disciplinary hearing was scheduled, the Newton team was deemed ineligible to participate on the varsity level for the 1994–1995 season. The court found that this decision was erroneous on two grounds. First, the court believed that the director of the PSAL was not in such a position to promulgate such a penalty because under the bylaws of the PSAL, all such policy decisions must be adopted by the committee. Second, the court found that even if the director had the authority to hand out the penalty, the ruling was arbitrary and capricious. The court argued that the entire soccer team should not be condemned for the actions of one of its players and also pointed to evidence that such rules had never been handed out to other teams, leading the court to believe that the imposition of the penalty upon Newtown was discriminatory.

6.4.3. Alcohol, Drug, and Conduct Rules: High School

Another set of rules frequently contested in the courts are those regulating the use of alcohol and other drugs. While acknowledging that a school and its coaches have a strong interest in the prevention of drug abuse (see Chapter 7, "Drug Testing and Policies"), the courts have consistently required that any rule established in this area be closely related to the problem of drug abuse.

Many high schools and high school athletic associations also have "good conduct" rules. These rules can be general in nature, as opposed to specific alcohol and drug rules, and usually require the student-athlete to adhere to some standard of conduct. If these rules, like the alcohol and drug rules, extend to a legitimate sports-related purpose, they will most likely be upheld. If, on the other hand, the rule is too broad and attempts to overly regulate an athlete's conduct, it may be struck down by the courts.

A case in this area is the case of *Butler v. Oak Creek Franklin School District*, 116 F.Supp.2d 1038 (E.D. Wis. 2000). A student-athlete sought an emergency preliminary injunction allowing him to play interscholastic football despite his suspension due to violations of the school's athletic code. The code required "student athletes to refrain from consuming, selling, buying, distributing, or possessing" any amount of alcoholic beverages, controlled substances, and drug paraphernalia. Rule 2 required student-athletes to refrain from using and possessing tobacco products. Rule 3 required students to refrain from violating any criminal law or local ordinance, and from being at any gathering where minors were partaking of alcohol or drugs. The code provided that a student who broke the code three times would be suspended from a year of competition. Butler had broken the athletic code five times before August 31, 2000. Butler did not receive the injunction because the court decided that it was unlikely he would be able to prove that his suspension was a violation of his rights under the U.S. Constitution or Wisconsin Constitution.

NOTES

1. In *D.N. v. Penn Harris Madison School Corp.*, 2006 LEXIS 70605 (N.D.Ind. September 18, 2006), a student was suspended from participating in extracurricular sports after being ticketed for minor consumption of alcohol, his second violation of the school's code of conduct. In dismissing the case, the court affirmed the view that students have no property

right in participating in an athletics program. Also, the case became moot as the plaintiff had graduated from high school.

2. In *Taylor v. Enumclaw School Dist. No. 216*, 133 P.3d 492 (Wash. App. Div. 1 2006), a high school football player brought suit alleging violations of his 14th Amendment rights after he was suspended from one football game and five wrestling matches for alcohol use. Taylor had been questioned for drinking at a school dance, other players testified that he was under the influence of alcohol during a football game, and school administrators found an empty beer case in his car. The plaintiff contended that he had a property interest in athletic participation as part of the larger educational process for which a property interest is recognized. The court denied such a premise and affirmed summary judgment for the defendants.

3. In *L.P.M. and D.J.T v. School Board*, 753 So. 2d 130 (Fla. Dist. Ct. App. 2000), two students were not allowed to participate in extracurricular athletics after it was found that they had violated a school rule by drinking alcohol off campus. The students were given a full administrative hearing where they were represented by counsel. The court held that the students had no protected right to participate in extracurricular athletics and that they had been given full due process under the school board's system.

4. In *Zehner v. Central Berkshire Regional School District*, 921 F. Supp. 850 (D. Mass. 1996), the plaintiff was suspended from school and his school soccer team after arriving at a school-sponsored dance in an obviously inebriated state. He was told the morning after the dance that he was not permitted to play on the soccer team for the rest of the season. The plaintiffs claimed that his participation in athletics was a protectable property interest and that he was denied his rights of due process before being suspended. The court agreed with the majority of federal courts when it decided that Zehner did not have a protected property interest in participating in athletics, only an expectation. Even though the plaintiff may have been an exceptional soccer player, this factor was irrelevant when determining whether a right had been violated.

Chapter 7

DRUG TESTING AND POLICIES

7.1. Legal Principles in Drug Testing

    7.1.1. Constitutional Law

    7.1.2. Contract and Labor Law

7.2. Drug Policies and Legal Challenges

    7.2.1. Interscholastic Athletics

        7.2.1.1. *Vernonia School District v. Acton*

        7.2.1.2. Performance-Enhancing Drug Policies

        7.2.1.3. Considerations in Enacting Drug Testing Programs

    7.2.2. Intercollegiate Athletics

        7.2.2.1. NCAA Policy and Legal Challenges

        7.2.2.2. College Conferences and Schools: Policies and Legal Challenges

    7.2.3. Olympic and International Sports

    7.2.4. Professional Sports

        7.2.4.1. National Football League

        7.2.4.2. National Basketball Association

        7.2.4.3. Major League Baseball

        7.2.4.4. National Hockey League

        7.2.4.5. Professional Golf Association

        7.2.4.6. Women's National Basketball Association

INTRODUCTION

Perhaps more than any other issue in sports, drug testing is complex and rapidly developing. A discussion of recent cases would most likely prove outdated in only a few months. In recent years, every major sporting league or association has been forced to address, reassess, and in some cases completely overhaul its approach to drug testing. In an age where the science of steroids and other performance enhancing substances is constantly evolving, concerns about the legitimacy of the on-field product are increasingly prevalent and have even drawn the attention of government officials and legislators (see notes). In addition, some teams and leagues have also attempted to proactively address the off-field conduct of its athletes (see section 16.1.5, "Off-the-Field Criminal Conduct"), including their use of recreational drugs. As the professional levels have been forced to address their drug testing policies and initiatives, many interscholastic, intercollegiate, and amateur associations have done the same.

Drug testing was first used by the U.S. military during the Vietnam War. Testing then slowly expanded to include all federal employees with potentially hazardous jobs and has since become the norm for nearly all government positions and many private companies. The first full-scale testing program in sports was implemented at the 1976 summer Olympic Games in Montreal. Sports organizations might enact a particular substance abuse policy for several reasons, including (1) the concern for the health/safety of the participants, (2) the concern that a player's substance abuse might affect a team's chance of winning, and (3) to gain the confidence of the public. The second reason particularly applies to athletes who abuse street, as opposed to performance-enhancing, drugs. A player who abuses street drugs is presumed not to play at his or her best, thereby depriving a team of its investment in him or her.

It is crucial to understand that an athletic organization does not always possess unilateral power to implement the drug policy that it believes is optimal. Organizations are limited by existing laws and court precedents and are typically (in the case of professional sports leagues) limited by the terms of a collective bargaining agreement. While no players union supports the use of illegal drugs by its member-players, it is important for the union to protect the rights of its players, or if nothing else, to use acquiescence to stricter drug testing policies as leverage in collective bargaining negotiations. While labor law controls many of the important aspects of drug testing in professional sports, the issues of interscholastic and intercollegiate athletics tend to be addressed in constitutional law. Some opponents of drug testing contend that the testing violates the privacy rights of student-athletes. Likewise, Olympic and international sports drug testing has been heavily involved in contract law as athletes tend to be viewed as independent contractors financially dependent on endorsement deals.

To ensure that athletic competitions are fair and equitable, as well as to protect the health and safety of the athletes, most athletic organizations at the interscholastic, intercollegiate, Olympic, and professional levels have implemented drug testing programs. The context of the testing is also important. Some sports, such as cycling and football have been far more susceptible to suspicions of illegal drug use while the PGA Tour has had much less scrutiny.

Chapter 7 takes a look at the general considerations that should be considered by any athletic organization or institution with athletic teams, especially those which implement a drug testing program. The chapter begins by examining the legal principles in drug testing, and then moves on to address the issues that are relevant to interscholastic sports, intercollegiate sports, Olympic sports, and professional sports. In each section, prominent cases and legislation are discussed.

NOTES

1. Following the release of the "Mitchell Report" (discussed in greater detail in section 7.2.4.3, "Major League Baseball"), the House Committee on Oversight and Government Reform held a hearing in January 2008 on the findings of the report. Questioned at the hearing where former Senator George Mitchell, the author of the report, MLBPA Executive Director Don Fehr, and MLB Commissioner Bud Selig. The stated purpose of the hearing and the report were "to bring to a close this troubling chapter in baseball's history and to use the lessons learned from the past to prevent future use of performance enhancing substances."

2. In March 2005, the House Government Reform Committee held a hearing on steroids in baseball. Commissioner Bud Selig and union chief Don Fehr were subpoenaed and present, along with sluggers Rafael Palmeiro, Sammy Sosa, and Frank Thomas. Also present was pitcher Curt Schilling, retired star Mark McGwire, and his former teammate Jose Canseco, an admitted steroid user. McGwire refused to answer questions regarding his suspected steroid use while Palmeiro vehemently denied having ever used steroids. The hearing was considered widely embarrassing for MLB and subsequently an impetus for the strengthening of its testing policies in November 2005. In August 2005, Palmeiro tested positive for a banned substance and was suspended for 10 days. McGwire, who had 583 career home runs, the eighth of all time, received only 23.5% of Hall of Fame votes in January 2007, far short of the 75% minimum.

3. A subcommittee of the House Energy and Commerce Committee subpoenaed the commissioners of MLB and the NBA, NHL, NFL, and MLS, along with the executive directors of the MLBPA, NBPA, NHLPA, and NFLPA to Washington in May 2005 to again discuss steroid use in sports. Both the House Government Reform Committee and the House Energy and Commerce Committee passed bills setting minimum steroid testing rules and penalties for professional sports in June 2005. The bills were never voted on in the House and did not become law.

4. For more on the debate over government's role in drug testing, see Joshua H. Whitman, "Winning at All Costs: Using Law and Economics to Determine the Proper Role of Government in Regulating the Use of Performance-Enhancing Drugs in Professional Sports," 2008 *University of Illinois Law Review* 459 (2008), and Joseph M. Saka, "Back to the Game: How Congress Can Help Sports Leagues Shift the Focus from Steroids to Sports," 23 *Journal of Contemporary Health Law and Policy* 341 (2007).

7.1. LEGAL PRINCIPLES IN DRUG TESTING

The three main legal areas governing drug testing of athletes are constitutional law, contract law, and labor law. The legal principle that will govern a particular complaint depends on the individual's circumstances. For example, the drug testing of high school or college athletes raises a number of constitutional issues concerning the athlete's right to due process, equal protection, and privacy as well as protection against illegal search and seizure and self-incrimination. Many of the same constitutional issues have applied to Olympic athletes, although the recent trend is to resolve disputes through the arbitration process. In professional sports, most of the issues and cases involving drug policy are governed by league rules and collective bargaining agreements, and are resolved through internal grievance and arbitration systems. The court system is likely to serve only as an appellate review of decisions made by an arbitrator or the *National Labor Relations Board* (NLRB), and the scope of judicial review will be limited (see section 11.3.13, "Arbitration," and its notes). However, while labor law will control most disputes in professional team sports, contract law may also apply.

For example, a team may negotiate a provision regarding drug testing into an individual player's contract if such clauses are allowed under the collective bargaining agreement. These clauses are usually inserted into the contracts of players who have already tested positive for drug use or who have had a drug-related problem in the past.

7.1.1. Constitutional Law

The first legal principle to be examined is *state action*. The due process, equal protection, and other safeguards of the U.S. Constitution apply only when state action is present. State action is defined as any action taken directly or indirectly by a state, municipal, or federal government. Therefore, while public high schools and colleges and their officials are state actors, professional sports leagues and their teams, for the most part privately owned, are not subject to the same array of constitutional restrictions. For example, in *Long v. NFL*, 870 F.Supp. 101 (U.S. Dist. 1994), a former football player sued the NFL in connection with his suspension pursuant to the league's policy after he tested positive for presence of anabolic steroids. The district court dismissed Long's claim, holding that there was insufficient evidence to find state action and support a constitutional law claim. In most cases, private entities are not subject to constitutional challenges. For a more detailed discussion on state action and when the actions of private organizations can be found to be state action, see section 6.1, "Athletic Associations and Constitutional Issues."

Another legal principle prevalent in drug testing cases is *due process*. Due process was reviewed in section 6.1.2, "Due Process." Some of the potential claims a plaintiff may argue under the due process theory are: an objection to the consent forms for drug testing to be signed by the student-athlete as prerequisite to participation; an appropriate hearing to rebut a positive test result as inadequate or denied; or an argument that penalties assessed on the grounds of evidence brought forth by an unreliable test were unfair. Under the due process clause, the plaintiff needs to show the deprivation of a significant liberty or property interest. Legal precedent in this area has most often found that a student-athlete does not have a liberty or property interest in athletics.

A third legal principle is *equal protection*. Student-athletes may argue under this principle that they are being singled out, through a student-athlete versus non-student-athlete class distinction. An institution or organization cannot discriminate against a group, such as student-athletes, in a drug testing program unless they can establish a rational relationship for the existence of this classification in order to justify the drug testing program.

The fourth constitutional law principle affecting the legality of drug testing programs is the Fourth Amendment to the U.S. Constitution. The Fourth Amendment states:

> The right of the people to be secure in their persons, houses, papers, and effects, against unreasonable searches and seizures, shall not be violated, and no warrants shall issue, but upon probable cause, supported by Oath or affirmation, and particularly describing the place to be searched, and the persons or things to be seized.

The fifth legal principle is the 14th Amendment, which is a guarantee against unreasonable searches and seizures by states.

In 1989, in the cases of *Skinner v. Railway Labor Executive Assn.* and *National Treasury Employees Union v. Von Raab*, the U.S. Supreme Court held that state compelled collecting and testing of urine constitutes a "search" subject to the demands of the Fourth Amendment (see note 5). In the 1995 case of *Vernonia School District v. Acton*, the U.S. Supreme Court held that "the legality of a search of a student should depend simply on the reasonableness, under all the circumstances, of the search" (see note 3). In determining whether a drug test is reasonable, the court balances the intrusion of the test on an individual's Fourth Amendment interests against its promotion of legitimate governmental interests. For example, if the intrusion is minimal and the state benefit is substantial, the test would not violate an individual's Fourth Amendment rights. If, however, the intrusion is substantial, and the state benefit is minimal, then the test would violate an individual's Fourth Amendment rights. In conducting this balancing test, the court examines three factors.

The first factor to be considered is the *nature of the privacy interest* upon which the search intrudes. The Fourth Amendment protects only those expectations of privacy that society recognizes as "legitimate." What expectations are legitimate varies, of course, with context, depending upon whether the individual asserting the privacy interest is at home, at work, in a car, or in a public park.

In addition, the legitimacy of certain privacy expectations vis-à-vis the state may depend upon the individual's legal relationship with the state. For example, in high school, athletes would have a lesser expectation of privacy than individuals in college or members of the general population. The reason that high school athletes would have lower privacy expectations is due to the fact that schools have a custodial and tutelary responsibility for the students. The Supreme Court also noted that high school athletes shower and change together before and after each practice or game. Therefore their privacy expectations are small.

The second factor to be considered is the *character of the intrusion*. In determining the character of the intrusion in a drug testing case, the court examines both how the sample is produced and what type of information is being collected.

In examining the intrusiveness of the drug test, the degree of intrusion will depend upon the manner in which the drug test is conducted. For example, the court will examine how the sample is collected and monitored. Is the individual required to give a blood or urine sample? The court may reject a drug test that called for blood samples since the collection and testing of urine samples is far less invasive. As for the type of information obtained by the test, the test should look only for illegal drug use and not HIV/AIDS or pregnancy. Also, test results should be disclosed only to those individuals who have a need to know and have been specified.

The final factor to be considered is the *nature and immediacy of the governmental concern* and the efficacy of the drug test in meeting that concern. In other words, the court must determine whether the state's interest in conducting the drug test is important enough to justify intruding upon an individual's genuine expectation of privacy.

The second part of the Fourth Amendment requires that before any search can be conducted, there must be probable cause. The Supreme Court, however, has recognized that a search unsupported by probable cause can be constitutional when the state has special needs. However, a school or athletic team will have a difficult time establishing that it has a "special need" to test athletes. Therefore, in most situations, a school or athletic team must show probable cause.

Finally, it is important to note that nearly all state constitutions include sections quite similar to the Fourth Amendment. In fact, some state constitutions may afford more protections to citizens with respect to search and seizure than the U.S. Constitution. The plaintiffs in *Hill v. NCAA* successfully invoked the state constitution before losing their case on appeal (see note 4). Article I, Section 1, of the California Constitution states:

> All people are by nature free and independent and have inalienable rights. Among these are enjoying and defending life and liberty, acquiring, possessing, and protecting property, and pursuing and obtaining safety, happiness, *and privacy*. (italics added)

As a result, it is possible for a state court to find that drug testing violates the state's constitution even if the program does not violate the U.S. Constitution. Athletic or school administrators should contact their state attorney general's office for an interpretation of their state's constitution or laws related to this matter. A plaintiff who is unable to show state action on the part of the organization conducting the drug testing or that the test violated constitutional rights, may be forced to rely on contract and/or labor law for possible legal theories.

NOTES

1. In *York v. Wahkiakum School Dist. No. 200*, 163 Wash.2d 297 (Wash. 2008), the parents of student-athletes at a pubic high school claimed that the school's policy of random and suspicionless drug testing of student-athletes violated the Washington State Constitution. The trial court ruled for the school district, stating that the policy was narrowly tailored to reach a compelling government end. On appeal, the Supreme Court of Washington began by noting that while the federal Fourth Amendment protects against "unreasonable searches and seizures," the Washington State Constitution states that "no person shall be disturbed in his private affairs, or his home invaded, without authority of law." In ruling that the policy violated the State Constitution, the court ruled that "there is no authority of law that allows a school district to conduct random drug tests."

2. In *Board of Education of Independent School District No. 92 of Pottawatomie County v. Earls*, 536 U.S. 822 (2002), middle school and high school students contended that the school district's policy requiring all students participating in extracurricular activities to submit to urinalysis drug testing violated the Fourth Amendment. Under the policy set in *Vernonia School District*, the District Court granted summary judgment. The 10th Circuit reversed, stating that before imposing a suspicionless drug testing program, a legitimate drug problem must be identified among those to be tested. The Supreme Court reversed, stating that the policy reasonably served the school district's interest in detecting and preventing drug use among its students.

3. In *Vernonia School District v. Acton*, 515 U.S. 646 (1995), a high school athlete sued the school district, challenging a requirement that student-athletes submit to random, mandatory drug testing. The U.S. Supreme Court, in upholding the constitutionality of the drug testing program, held that taking into account the decreased expectation of privacy, the relative unobtrusiveness of the search, and the severity of the need met by the search, the school district's policy was reasonable and constitutional.

4. In *Hill v. NCAA*, 7 Cal. 4th 1, 865 P.2d 633 (Cal. S.Ct. 1994), two private university students brought an action challenging the NCAA's drug testing program. The students argued that the program violated the privacy initiative of the California State Constitution. The plaintiffs not only objected to the invasiveness of a urine test but also resented a requirement to disclose medications such as those which indicate sexual activity. The California Supreme Court, in overturning the lower courts, held that the benefits of the NCAA

drug testing policy justified the invasion of privacy. In a 4–3 decision, the majority reasoned: "These kinds of disclosures are reasonably necessary to further the threshold purpose of the drug testing program—to protect the integrity of competition through the medium of accurate testing of athletes engaged in competition. The NCAA's interests in this regard adequately justify its inquiries about medications and other substances ingested by tested athletes." The majority also cited a diminished expectation of privacy on the part of the athletes in its rationale.

5. *National Treasury Employees Union v. Von Raab*, 489 U.S. 656 (1989), and *Skinner v. Railway Labor Executive Assn.*, 489 U.S. 602 (1989), were not sports-related cases. They pertained, respectively, to the testing of U.S. Customs officers in high-security positions and to the drug testing of train crews following accidents. However, these cases expressed the high court's approval of testing of state workers without suspicion, so long as "special needs" can be demonstrated. In *Von Raab*, the "special need" was safety; in *Skinner*, it was security.

6. For more on the constitutional concerns regarding federal legislation and drug testing, see Lindsay J. Taylor, "Congressional Attempts to 'Strike Out' Steroids: Constitutional Concerns about the Clean Sports Act," 49 *Arizona Law Review* 961 (2007), and Joshua Peck, "Last Resort: The Threat of Federal Steroid Legislation—Is the Proposed Legislation Constitutional?" 75 *Fordham Law Review* 1777 (2006).

7.1.2. Contract and Labor Law

Other legal areas that impact the ability of a sports organization to conduct drug testing are contract and labor law. In professional sports, the players' conduct is governed by a contract that is negotiated between the league, representing the owners, and the players' association, representing the players. This contract or collective bargaining agreement deals with any issue related to the players' hours of work, wages, and conditions of employment. Since a drug testing program effects athletes' conditions of employment, most of the issues and cases involving drug testing are resolved through internal grievance and arbitration systems set up within the league's collective bargaining agreement. However, state law issues can also play an important factor (see section 7.2.4.1, "National Football League").

The court system is likely to serve only as an appellate review of decisions made by an arbitrator or the NLRB, and the scope of judicial review will be limited. For example, in *Holmes v. NFL*, 939 F.Supp. 517 (N.D. Tex. 1996), a professional football player was involuntarily enrolled in the league's drug program and then suspended after testing positive for marijuana use. He sued the league, alleging that its actions constituted a breach of the collective bargaining agreement. However, the court upheld the ruling of the league, reasoning that constitutional rights do not apply to procedures of arbitration between league and players pursuant to the collective bargaining agreement. Collective bargaining and the sanctity of arbitration are discussed in greater detail in sections 11.3.7 and 11.3.13.

While the NFL and NBA Collective Bargaining Agreements explicitly prohibit the negotiating of any provision regarding drug use and testing into the standard player contract (see section 9.2.1, "Standard Player Contract"), MLB and the NHL do not. In 1986, when the owners' MLB Player Relations Committee attempted to add one of two clauses to individual players' contracts that would have required mandatory random drug testing. The Players Association filed a grievance, and arbitrator Thomas T. Roberts ruled that "the drug testing clauses . . . are in violation of the CBA [collective bargaining agreement]" and that "any such clauses must be negotiated with the Players Association."

Prior to the NBA's current collective bargaining agreement, such covenants were allowed. For example, the NBA banned Roy Tarpley in 1991 for cocaine use. As a condition of his reinstatement in 1994, Tarpley signed a contract that contained a provision requiring him to participate in the league's aftercare program, which included frequent drug testing. The contract also stated that his contract could be voided if he was found to be using alcohol or drugs.

NOTES

1. In *Foschi v. United States Swimming, Inc.*, 916 F.Supp. 232 (E.D.N.Y. 1996), a competitive swimmer brought a state court action against the national governing body for the sport of swimming (U.S. Swimming) and the U.S. Olympic Committee, alleging breach of "contractual due process" arising from her two-year suspension due to her failing a drug test. Defendants removed action to federal court. On the plaintiff's motion for remand to state court, the court held that Foschi's claims did not arise under federal law. The USOC's constitution and bylaws and U.S. Swimming's rules and regulations entitled Foschi to certain "due process" rights. Therefore, even though the case might at some point involve the interpretation of a federal statute, namely, the Amateur Sports Act of 1978, Foschi's claims were contractual in nature.

2. In *Dimeo v. Griffin*, 721 F.Supp. 958 (N.D. Ill. 1989), the Illinois Racing Board promulgated a substance abuse rule providing for random drug testing and individualized suspicion drug testing of licensees, including outriders, parade marshals, starters, assistant starters, drivers, and jockeys. A class action was brought against the board, alleging that various provisions of the rule violated the Fourth Amendment prohibition against unreasonable searches and seizures. The court granted an injunction with respect to random drug testing but held that individualized suspicion drug testing which granted limited discretion to stewards was justified by the board's interest in preserving the integrity and safety of the sport.

3. In *Shoemaker v. Handel*, 795 F.2d 1136 (3rd Cir. 1986), horse racing jockeys brought an action challenging the New Jersey Racing Commission regulations, which permitted a state racing steward to direct any official, jockey, trainer, or groom to submit to Breathalyzer and urine testing to detect alcohol or drug consumption. The jockeys claimed that this constituted an illegal search and seizure and was a violation of their Fourth Amendment rights. The court of appeals, in upholding the regulations, held that the commission's concern for racing integrity warranted the tests and that as long as the commission kept the results confidential, there was no violation of the jockeys' rights.

4. For more on the role of collective bargaining as it relates to drug testing in professional sports, see David M. Wachutka, "Collective Bargaining Agreements in Professional Sports: The Proper Forum for Establishing Performance-Enhancing Drug Testing Policies," 8 *Pepperdine Dispute Resolution Journal* 147 (2007), and Lisa Pike Masteralexis, "Drug Testing Provisions: An Examination of Disparities in Rules and Collective Bargaining Agreement Provisions," 40 *New England Law Review* 775 (2006).

7.2. DRUG POLICIES AND LEGAL CHALLENGES

Drug tests today are much more sophisticated and yield much more information than whether or not the athlete is on drugs. They can be used to identify the use of performance-enhancing drugs, street drugs, birth control pills, and any other medication an individual might be taking. This intrusion into the individual's privacy rights raises an issue for organizations wishing to test athletes.

Should an organization's drug policy include random mandatory testing? If so, what type of drugs should it test for? For example, should it test for illegal drugs like marijuana or for alcohol (illegal for those under 21), which are not considered performance enhancing? How about legal drugs, such as androstenedione, which is banned by most sports organizations as performance-enhancing but can be purchased by anyone? Performance-enhancing drugs are, quite simply, substances used by athletes to improve their performance, whereas illegal street drugs could harm an athlete's performance and threaten his or her ability to fulfill contractual obligations. Sports organizations have an interest in instituting drug testing policies to both protect the health of athletes and to ensure a fair playing field.

The rest of this chapter examines the drug policies and testing programs of high schools, the NCAA, intercollegiate athletic conferences and individual colleges, the Olympics, and professional sports. The following sections will also examine the rationale for the policies, the legal barriers to policies that include testing, the types of drugs that are tested for, the penalties imposed for testing positive, and the results of any subsequent litigation.

7.2.1. Interscholastic Athletics

To deter the use of performance-enhancing or recreational drugs, schools and state athletic associations may consider enacting a drug policy that includes testing. As the following case will demonstrate, the court in this case held that it is legal to test athletes for drugs, largely due to their diminished expectation of privacy. Both drug *education* and drug *testing* programs can be prohibitively expensive. While the former is unlikely to face legal scrutiny, a school implementing a drug testing program should first understand the legal issues involved. The leading case in drug testing of high school athletes is *Vernonia School District v. Acton*, 515 U.S. 646 (1995).

7.2.1.1. Vernonia School District v. Acton

In the middle to late 1980s, teachers and administrators in Vernonia, Oregon, began to observe a sharp increase in drug use and an increase in disciplinary problems. Not only were student-athletes among the drug users, they were the leaders of the drug culture. This caused administrators particular concern since drug use increased the risk of sports-related injury. In an effort to combat this trend, the school board approved a drug testing policy. The policy's expressed purpose was to prevent student-athletes from using drugs, to protect their health and safety, and to provide drug users with assistance programs. The policy applied to all students participating in interscholastic athletics.

In fall 1991, James Acton, then a seventh grader, signed up to play football at one of the district's grade schools. He was denied participation after he and his parents refused to sign the testing consent forms. The Actons filed suit, "seeking declaratory and injunctive relief from enforcement of the policy on the grounds that it violated the Fourth and Fourteenth Amendments to the United States Constitution and Article I, § 9, of the Oregon Constitution."

The U.S. Supreme Court held that the ultimate measure of the constitutionality of a governmental search under the Fourth Amendment is "reasonableness." Whether a particular search meets the reasonableness standard, the Supreme Court held, "is judged by balancing its intrusion on the individual's Fourth Amendment interests against its promotion of legitimate governmental interests." Taking into account the decreased expectation of privacy, the relative unobtrusiveness of the search, and the severity of the need met by the search, the Court concluded Vernonia's policy was reasonable and hence constitutional.

The first factor to be considered is the nature of the privacy interest upon which the search here at issue intrudes. The Fourth Amendment does not protect all subjective expectations of privacy but only those that society recognizes as "legitimate," as outlined in section 7.1.1, "Constitutional Law."

In examining the nature of the privacy interest, the Supreme Court held that 4th Amendment rights, no less than 1st and 14th Amendment rights, are different in public schools than elsewhere; the "reasonableness" inquiry cannot disregard the schools' custodial and tutelary responsibility for children. For their own good and that of their classmates, public school children are routinely required to submit to various physical examinations and to be vaccinated against various diseases. Therefore, with regard to medical examinations and procedures, "students within the school environment have a lesser expectation of privacy than members of the population generally." The Supreme Court further stated that "legitimate privacy expectations are even less with regard to student-athletes. School sports are not for the bashful. They require suiting up before each practice or event, and showering and changing afterwards. Public school locker rooms, the usual sites for these activities, are not notable for the privacy they afford. . . . There is an additional respect in which school athletes have a reduced expectation of privacy. By choosing to go out for the team they voluntarily subject themselves to a degree of regulation even higher than that imposed on students generally."

Finally, the Supreme Court examined the nature and immediacy of the governmental concern at issue and the efficacy of this means for meeting it. In determining whether drug testing in the absence of individualized suspicion "must demonstrate a 'compelling need' for the program," the court found that the phrase "compelling state interest" describes an interest that appears important enough to justify the particular search at hand, in light of other factors that show the search to be relatively intrusive upon a genuine expectation of privacy.

In *Vernonia*, the Supreme Court found that the school's interest in deterring drug use by schoolchildren was an important state interest. As to the efficacy of this means for addressing the problem, the Court concluded that a drug problem largely fueled by the "role model" effect of athletes' drug use, and of particular danger to athletes, is effectively addressed by the drug testing of athletes.

Since the Supreme Court's decision in *Vernonia*, a number of schools across the country have instituted similar drug testing policies for their interscholastic athletes in hopes of deterring drug use. Provided the drug testing program fulfills a compelling need and the "reasonableness" requirement, the objectives necessitating the implementation of a drug testing program will outweigh the potential invasion of privacy of the student-athletes. Institutions that implement testing programs should remain cognizant of the invasiveness of the test. The Court clearly stated that athletes can be compelled to produce a urine sample under the circumstances described. However, the Court did not give an opinion on the use of blood or hair as the testing medium. Are these procedures more invasive or less invasive than urinalysis? Furthermore, should technology produce a testing method that is clearly less invasive than urinalysis, it is uncertain whether the Supreme Court would continue to consider urinalysis drug testing to be a justifiable invasion of Fourth Amendment rights. While *Vernonia* stands as the leading case on the issue of drug testing of high school athletes, there have been several subsequent cases on the issue (see notes 2, 3, and 6).

7.2.1.2. Performance-Enhancing Drug Policies

Beginning in the 2006–2007 school year, the state of New Jersey and the New Jersey Interscholastic Athletic Association (NJISAA) became the first state to institute a statewide performance-enhancing drug testing policy for all high school athletes. Under the policy, any athlete or team that qualifies for the state playoffs is subject to random testing. Also, in order to participate in high school athletics in New Jersey, a student-athlete and a parent must sign a form consenting to random testing. The cost of each test is $150 to $200, with the state and the NJIAA each contributing $50,000 toward the cost. Sixty percent of the tests will be from the sports of football, wrestling, track and field, swimming, lacrosse, and baseball, where statistics suggest there are higher incidences of drug use. Any athlete who tests positive under the policy will forfeit one year of eligibility.

Since New Jersey's action, other states have passed or are attempting to pass similar legislation. Texas and its University Interscholastic League (UIL) passed a bill subjecting all high school athletes to random testing with approximately 40,000 to 50,000 students being tested each year. Texas pays The National Center for Drug Free Sport, a leading provider of drug-testing programs, $5.6 million annually to administer the program. However, due to the overwhelming costs, only about 30% of all schools are selected for testing. A first positive test results in a 30-day suspension from athletics; a second positive test results in suspension for the remainder of the school year and the student-athlete is permanently banned from high school athletics after a third positive test (see note 7). As of 2010, at least twenty-eight other states or state athletic associations have policies banning steroid use but do not require testing.

7.2.1.3. Considerations in Enacting Drug Testing Programs

When an association, institution, or organization considers implementing a drug testing plan for its athletes, a number of serious questions have to be answered:

- Should the organization implement a drug education program? If so, what type of program?
- Should the organization implement a drug testing program? If so, what type of program?
- If the organization has a drug testing policy, is it clearly defined and in writing?
- Does the organization's drug testing policy conform to conference and association rules and regulations?
- Who will conduct the tests?
- Who will be tested?
- Who will pay for the tests?
- Will the tests be random and mandatory, or only for probable cause or reasonable suspicion?
- What constitutes probable cause or reasonable suspicion?
- How much notice should be given before testing begins?
- What types of drugs are to be tested for, and how frequently?
- Should testing include street drugs, such as marijuana and cocaine, or just performance-enhancing drugs, such as steroids?

- What actions will be taken when an athlete tests positive?
- Will there be an appeal process for a positive test result?
- Is there a method for retesting when the initial results are positive?
- What confidentiality and constitutional law issues does drug testing raise?
- Do the sanctions to be imposed adhere to federal and/or state constitutional law and statutes?

The answers to these critical questions, and many others like them, should provide the basis for a carefully designed drug testing program. A meaningful program should, at the very least, consider the following components:

1. A *policy statement*. The purpose(s) behind the implementation of a drug testing program must be clearly stated from the outset.

2. *Notification of testing*. Before starting a drug testing program, it is imperative to give advance written notice to all who could be affected by its implementation. This information should include all policies and procedures utilized by the program as well as the voluntary consent form to be signed by the amateur athlete that allows for urinalysis testing and for the release of test result information.

3. *Identification of banned substances*. The organization needs to decide what types of drugs the athlete will be tested for and provide a comprehensive list of these banned substances to its athletes.

4. *A testing component*. The organization needs to decide whether the drug testing program will be random, in that all athletes are mandatorily required to submit to testing on a periodic basis, or based on reasonable suspicion, so that only athletes suspected of drug involvement are required to submit to testing.

5. *Accuracy of the tests*. No drug testing method is 100% accurate, so the organization needs to address the problem of "false positives" before implementing a testing program. One sound method of dealing with the problem of false positive results is to conduct a second, more sensitive test following any positive test result. Another possible concern relates to the actual collection process and "chain of custody" used in testing. Detailed security procedures regarding the sample need to be followed, and documented maintenance of the specimen needs to be assured.

6. *Sanctions*. Decisions must be made as to what action will be taken when an athlete tests positive.

7. *Due process considerations*. When implementing a program, consideration should be given to an athlete's right to have a hearing in response to a positive test result or to challenge penalties imposed as a result of a positive test.

8. *Confidentiality issues*. Steps should be taken to be sure that the procedures outlined in the program will not violate the privacy of the athlete.

NOTES

1. In *York v. Wahkiakum Sch. Dist. No. 200*, 178 P.3d 995 (Wash. 2008), the Washington Supreme Court concluded that the district's policy of conducting random and suspicionless drug testing of student athletes was unconstitutional and violated student athletes' rights under the Washington Constitution.

2. In *Dominic J v. Wyoming Valley West High School*, 362 F.Supp.2d 560 (M.D.Pa. 2005), a high school swimmer was accused of using narcotics and removed from the team and that if he wished to participate on the team he must pass a drug test. The court found that the compulsory drug screening did not constitute an unreasonable search and seizure under the Fourth Amendment and that the student did not have a due process protected property interest in participating in extracurricular activities such as swimming.

3. In *Joye v. Hunterdon Cent. Regional High School Bd. of Educ.*, 176 N.J. 568 (N.J. 2003), the parents of three high school students challenged a high school's policy of random suspicionless drug testing of students engaged in extracurricular activities as an unreasonable search and seizure under the state constitution. Relying on the three-part special needs analysis laid out in *Vernonia*, the New Jersey Supreme Court found no such violation.

4. In *Board of Education of Independent School District No. 92 of Pottawatomie County v. Earls*, 536 U.S. 822 (2002), the Supreme Court extended the holding of *Vernonia*. The Court refused to require that the school district demonstrate a preexisting drug abuse problem among students participating in extracurricular activities. The Court declared that it would be illogical "to require a school district to wait for a substantial portion of its students to begin using drugs before it was allowed to institute a drug testing program."

5. According to the Office of National Drug Control Policy, the price of a drug test varies according to the type of test and the drugs involved, but is generally between $10 and $30. For a school with 100 athletes who are all tested initially each season and then another 10% tested randomly each week for 35 weeks, the school can expect to pay from $4,500 to $13,500 annually.

6. According to the 2007 "Monitoring the Future" study conducted by the University of Michigan's Institute for Social Research, 46.8% of youths will experiment with illicit drugs before graduating high school, and 72.2% of students will consume alcohol before finishing high school. The rates for steroid use (not including legal supplements, such as andro, or times when taken legally, e.g., prescribed by a doctor) were 1.5%, 1.8%, and 2.2% in grades 8, 10, and 12, respectively.

7. In *Todd v. Rush County School*, 133 F.3d 984 (7th Cir. 1998), the court, in upholding the testing of all participants in any extracurricular activity or driving to school, citing *Vernonia*, held that the tests applied only to those students wishing to participate in these activities. This type of participation was voluntary and a privilege; therefore, the court held it was the student's choice whether or not to participate in the program.

8. For more information on interscholastic drug testing, see the National Federation of State High School Associations Web site: http://www.nfhs.org/sportsmed.aspx. More information on Texas' performance-enhancing drug testing policy can be found on the UIL Web site at http://www.uil.utexas.edu/ATHLETICS/health/steroid_information.html.

7.2.2. Intercollegiate Athletics

This section examines drug testing at the intercollegiate level. Most of the section focuses on the NCAA's policy. It then considers the policies of specific institutions and conferences. Relevant litigation is also discussed.

7.2.2.1. NCAA Policy and Legal Challenges

In January 1986, the NCAA membership at its annual convention agreed to begin a drug testing program for NCAA-sanctioned championships and other events such as football bowl games. The policy has since expanded to include all student-athletes, and in addition Division I and II student-athletes are subject to year-round testing.

The decision to implement a drug testing policy was not easily reached. Chief among the dissenting views of the policy was that it singles out the student-athlete, who may or may not be a scholarship athlete, to undergo urine testing that is not required of any other student who participates in student activities.

In other words, why should an athlete be treated any differently from a member of the band, drama society, or glee club? However, with the passage of a random mandatory drug testing policy, the NCAA made the mandatory signing of a consent form to allow testing a condition of athletic participation.

From 1986 to 2009, the NCAA has tested approximately 190,000 athletes. Clearly drug testing is an expensive proposition. When the policy first began in 1986–1987, the testing program cost $950,000 for approximately 3,000 tests. In 2009–2010, the NCAA spent approximately $5 million in drug testing and education. Prior to the 2004–2005 academic year, both Division I and Division II approved year-round drug testing for all sports. Under the revised policy, eight random student-athletes, plus 18 football players if the institution has a football program, are subject to drug testing each fall. In addition, at any time during the year the institution can be chosen for the same amount of random drug tests.

Critics of the NCAA's drug-testing program claim that it does not

1. safeguard student-athletes' procedural rights, especially in regard to the appeal process for a positive test
2. safeguard the student's privacy rights, especially when the media become aware of a test result
3. give the student-athletes sufficient information before they sign the mandatory consent form
4. ensure that the school will represent the student-athlete's interests and rights when an athlete tests positive

In addition, many coaches have criticized the plan for the effect it has on a team when team members must participate in drug testing after an NCAA tournament or a championship victory.

The NCAA drug testing plan is constantly evolving and being modified, but as it is offered, it presents the athletic administrator with the basic materials needed to make an informed decision when dealing with coaches, medical staff, student-athletes, and the NCAA about the plan.

The NCAA provides a list of banned substances to its membership. More than 90 drugs in seven different categories are included in this list. These are drugs that the NCAA considers to be "performance-enhancing and/or potentially harmful to the health and safety of the student-athlete." Student-athletes are required to sign a consent form prior to practice or the Monday of the institution's fourth week of classes, whichever date occurs first, may be deemed ineligible. Any student-athlete who tests positive will be subject to disciplinary action, including being declared ineligible for further participation in post-season and regular season competition during the period ending one calendar year after the student-athlete's positive drug test. A second positive tests for any drug other than a street drug, as defined in Bylaw 31.2.3.4, results in the loss of all future eligibility. If the student-athlete tests positive for a street drug, he or she will lose a minimum of one additional season of eligibility and will not be restored to eligibility until the student-athlete retests negative (*2009–2010 NCAA Manual*, Bylaw 18.4.1.5.1).

The NCAA bans seven different categories of drugs: psychomotor and central nervous system stimulants, anabolic steroids, some substances banned in specific sports, diuretics, street drugs, peptide hormones and analogues, and antiestrogen (see note 1). The NCAA bans these drugs for either of two reasons—because they illegally enhance performance or because they are potentially harmful to the student-athlete's health. The practice of blood doping—the intravenous injection of whole blood, packed red blood cells, or blood substitutes—and the use of growth hormone—human, animal, or synthetic—are also prohibited by the NCAA.

There are two general exceptions to the NCAA banned drug list. These exceptions involve the use of local anesthetics and asthma- or exercise-induced bronchospasm medications. As long as they are administered correctly and their use is medically justified, the NCAA approves them.

Almost since the inception of the NCAA drug testing program, student-athletes claiming that the test is a violation of their constitutional rights have challenged the program in the courts. Some lawsuits have been filed when a student refuses to sign a consent form and is therefore deemed ineligible to participate. Other times, a lawsuit occurs as the result of a positive test (see notes 2 and 3).

One of the most noteworthy cases is *Hill v. NCAA*, 865 P.2d 633 (Cal. 1994). Hill, a member of the swimming team at Stanford University, brought action challenging the NCAA's drug testing program. Hill argued that the program violated her privacy rights under the California State Constitution. In particular, Hill pointed to the NCAA's procedure for collecting urine samples and the consent form, which asked students to disclose medical and sexual information.

Although Hill was successful in the lower courts, the California Supreme Court, in overturning the lower courts, held that the NCAA's drug testing policy involving monitoring of urination, testing of urine samples, and inquiry concerning medication did not violate the students' constitutional right to privacy. In holding that the program was consistent with the privacy provisions of the state constitution, the California Supreme Court held that the NCAA's interest in protecting both the health and safety of the athletes and the integrity of the programs outweighed Hill's privacy interests.

In addition to claims that the NCAA's drug testing program is an invasion of the student-athlete's privacy rights, student-athletes have also challenged the sample collection and notification protocol in *Premock v. Montana*, Case 74947/40 (Mont. Dist. Ct. 1991) (see note 2) and the legality of the consent form signed by all students in *Bally v. NCAA*, 707 F. Supp. 57 (D. Mass. 1988) (see note 3).

Another criticism of the NCAA drug testing program is that it is ineffective and does not stop individuals from using performance-enhancing drugs. For example, during the 2004–2005 academic year, the NCAA conducted a total of 10,094 drug tests, but only 107 student-athletes (1.1%) failed the test (see exhibit 7.1). Since there are so few positive results each year, critics claim that the tests prove that there is no drug problem among college athletes. The NCAA, however, argues that the test is a success because it discourages student-athletes from using drugs.

NOTES

1. More information on the NCAA drug testing program, including the list of banned substances, can be found on the NCAA Web site: http://www.ncaa.org > Legislation and Governance > Eligibility and Recruiting > Drug Testing.

2. For information on NCAA drug testing results, visit http://www.ncaa.org/sports_sci ences/drugtesting/drug_testing_results_archive.html.

The following are examples of cases stemming from a student's positive drug test:

1. In *Brennan v. Board of Trustees for University of Louisiana Systems*, 691 So.2d 324 (La. Ct. App. 1 Cir. 1997), a student-athlete who had been suspended from intercollegiate athletic competition after testing positive for the anabolic steroid testosterone sued the university's board of trustees, seeking to enjoin enforcement of suspension imposed by the

Exhibit 7.1
NCAA Drug Testing Results (2004–2005) Year-Round Program

Sport	Number of Samples	Positive Test Results	Positive Test Rate
Division I Baseball	516	6	1.2%
Division I Men's Basketball	88	0	0%
Division I Football	4,622	33[a]	.7%
Division I Men's Track & Field	253	1[b]	.4%
Division II Football	1,828	15[c]	.8%
Division I Women's Basketball	72	0	0%
Division I Women's Track & Field	157	2[d]	.6%
All Division 1 Sports	**7,462**	**45[e]**	**.6%**

a) Includes 1 Protocol Violation and 6 Failed to Show
b) Includes 1 Failed to Show
c) Includes 6 Failed to Show
d) Includes 1 Failed to Show
e) Includes 1 Protocol Violation and 8 Failed to Show

NCAA Drug Testing Results (2004–2005) Postseason Program

Sport	Number of Samples	Positive Test Results	Positive Test Rate
Division I Baseball	48	0	0%
Division I Men's Basketball	64	1[a]	1.5%
Division I Football	205	7[b]	3.4%
Division I Men's & Women's Track & Field	96	1	1.0%
Division II Football	196	8[c]	4.1%
Division I Women's Basketball	64	1	1.5%
All NCAA Sports	**1,516**	**38[d]**	**2.5%**

a) Positive Test was for THC, the active compound in marijuana
b) Includes 1 Positive Test for THC and 3 for Amphetamines
c) Includes 5 Positive Tests for THC
d) Includes 2 Failed to Show

Source: *NCAA Drug-Testing Results 2004–05*, available at http://www.ncaa.org/wps/ncaa?
ContentID=485.

NCAA. The court of appeals, in rejecting the plaintiff's claim, held that the student-athlete had a diminished expectation of privacy, and the small compromise of privacy from a urine test was outweighed by the significant interest of the university and NCAA. The court also held that the student-athlete has no liberty or property interest protected by due process in participating in intercollegiate athletics.

2. In *Premock v. Montana*, No. 74947/40 (Mont. Dist. Ct. 1991), a student-athlete brought a complaint regarding the drug testing protocol that was used, which resulted in a positive result. The judge found that although the NCAA's "goal of drug-free sports is commendable,

their methods of achieving that goal are deplorable." The judge found that the drug testing area lacked the control required for a credible collection process (Premock had left the collection area for several minutes, and his urine sample was left unattended during that time); there were violations of the NCAA's chain-of-custody requirements (the NCAA could not account for the specimens from the time they reached the campus of UCLA, where they were to be tested, until they arrived at the drug-testing laboratory); the lab breached the protocol in the testing and retesting process (the urine analysis test on both samples was conducted by the same person and took more than 24 days to complete); and the NCAA failed to notify the university of Premock's test results until 33 days after the sample was collected. Premock won a restraining order from the district court judge restoring his eligibility, but Premock had already completed his eligibility and the case was settled out of court.

3. In *Barbay v. NCAA*, No. 86–5697 1987 U.S. Dist. LEXIS 393 (E.D. La. Jan. 20, 1987), the plaintiff, a football player at Louisiana State University, tested positive for steroids prior to the January 1987 Sugar Bowl and was thus prohibited from competing in the bowl game by the NCAA. The plaintiff sought a preliminary injunction preventing the NCAA from enforcing this penalty based on a violation of his 14th Amendment rights. The plaintiff stated that the NCAA penalty prohibiting student-athletes from competing in post-season competition after testing positive for drugs was instituted after he had taken steroids to help in his rehabilitation of a knee injury. He should not be punished, therefore, for taking steroids prior to the establishment of this penalty. The district court first found that there was no state action; thus the plaintiff had no claim against the NCAA. In addition, the plaintiff could not demonstrate an irreparable harm if a ruling in his favor was not granted; therefore the court denied the plaintiff's petition for a preliminary injunction.

4. In *Mira v. NCAA*, No. 87–55213 (Fla. Dist. Ct. 1988), the plaintiff sought a temporary and permanent restraining order preventing the NCAA from enforcing its drug testing program. The plaintiff argued that the drug testing program violated the plaintiff's constitutional rights. The district court ruled that there was no state action and therefore no claim upon which it could base relief.

The following are examples of cases stemming from students' refusals to sign a consent form or unwillingness to submit to testing:

1. In *Hill v. NCAA*, 865 P.2d 633 (Cal. 1994), the California Supreme Court held that the NCAA's drug testing policy involving monitoring of urination, testing of urine samples, and inquiry concerning medication did not violate the student's state constitutional right to privacy.

2. In *Bally v. NCAA*, 707 F.Supp. 52 (Mass. 1988), the Superior Court of Massachusetts ruled that the NCAA consent form did not infringe on any rights secured by the Massachusetts Civil Rights Act and that the consent form by itself does not subject the plaintiff to an illegal search and seizure or violate his or her right to privacy.

7.2.2.2. College Conferences and Schools: Policies and Legal Challenges

Although the NCAA conducts over 10,000 drug tests of student-athletes each year, its program is limited, given that over 400,000 athletes participate in NCAA sponsored events each year. To fill in any gaps in the NCAA's program, many athletic conferences have taken a position on the drug testing issue, from providing statements regarding drug usage in their handbooks to implementing their own drug testing program. The Big 12 Conference has established a drug testing program whereby each year, drug testing of student-athletes will be conducted at four randomly selected championship events sponsored by the conference. In addition, the conference will conduct on-campus drug testing at each member institution once each semester.

The conference also reserves the right to conduct a second drug test during a semester at a randomly selected institution. A total of 30 student-athletes from all intercollegiate sports sponsored by each member institution shall be selected at random to participate in each on-campus drug test. Member institutions are notified 24 hours in advance. The student-athletes, who are randomly selected to participate in the drug test, are notified two hours in advance. Beginning in 2007–2008, the Big Ten instituted a similar policy.

In addition to NCAA testing and conference testing, some schools conduct their own drug testing programs. The University of North Carolina at Chapel Hill adopted random, unannounced testing of its athletes in 1999. Banned substances include steroids, diuretics, and a variety of street drugs. An athlete testing positive for the first time may receive probation and required counseling, and his or her parents will be informed. A second positive test will result in permanent suspension from athletics and a possible termination of his or her scholarship.

Bowling Green State University requires its athletes to submit to "reasonable suspicion" testing for performance-enhancing and recreational drugs. A refusal to test, when confronted with reasonable suspicion, will result in a suspension of athletic participation and scholarship award for one year.

The NCAA has encouraged, but not mandated, that member institutions implement some type of drug testing program such as the ones described earlier. The 2007 NCAA Survey: Member Institution's Drug Education and Drug-Testing Program, which was conducted by the NCAA Committee on Competitive Safeguards and Medical Aspects of Sports, showed that 65% of the schools surveyed, responded that they had a drug/alcohol education program for student-athletes. An additional 10% of the institutions responded that they were actively planning to begin a program. The percentage of institutions that have instituted a drug testing program has increased dramatically, from 10% in 1984 to 42% in 1999 to 50% in 2007 (see note 1).

NCAA member institutions have taken a varied approach to the issue of drug testing. These approaches can be categorized as follows:

1. No drug testing or drug education programs
2. An educational program on the drug issue but no drug testing
3. Random mandatory testing only for street drugs such as marijuana and cocaine
4. Random mandatory testing only for performance-enhancing drugs such as steroids
5. Random mandatory drug testing for both street drugs and performance-enhancing drugs

A characteristic of the majority of conference and institutional drug testing programs is that there is mandatory testing for student-athletes but not for coaches and staff. The programs provide a specific written policy on testing to student-athletes and require the student-athlete to sign an institutional waiver or consent form. Institutional drug testing programs have come under scrutiny by student-athletes, much as the NCAA drug testing program has, for possible violations of the student-athlete's constitutional rights (see notes 2–4).

NOTES _____

1. The 2007 NCAA Survey: Member Institution's Drug Education and Drug-Testing Program can be viewed online at http://www.ncaa.org > Legislation and Governance > Eligibility and Recruiting > Drug Testing.

2. In *University of Colorado v. Derdeyn*, 863 P.2d 929 (Colo. 1993), student-athletes challenged the state university's mandatory drug testing program. The Colorado Supreme Court found that the program failed to meet the warrant and probable cause requirements of the Fourth Amendment of the U.S. Constitution and Article II, Section 7, of the Colorado Constitution. In years prior to the case, the university had modified the testing procedures to be less invasive to the athletes (in the 1980s, trainers had to watch the athlete urinate into a receptacle). Despite the less invasive procedure, the court cited the absence of voluntary consent on the part of the student-athlete and ruled the drug testing program to be an unconstitutional search.

3. In *Bally v. Northeastern University*, 532 N.E.2d 49 (Mass. 1989), a student-athlete challenged the university's drug testing program by claiming the policy of requiring student-athletes to consent to drug testing as a condition of participating in intercollegiate athletics was a violation of civil rights and the right to privacy and also constituted a breach of contract. The court ruled for the university and upheld the constitutionality of the drug testing program.

4. In *O'Halloran v. University of Washington*, 679 F.Supp. 997 (W.D. Wash. 1988), a student-athlete claimed that the NCAA and the school's drug testing program violated her privacy, and constituted an unreasonable search and seizure. The district court found that the collection of a urine sample was a "search" for the purposes of the Fourth Amendment but that the compelling interest of the university and the NCAA in implementing the drug testing program far outweighed the hardships on the student-athlete. The court ruled for the university.

7.2.3. Olympic and International Sports

Many argue that perhaps the greatest threat to the image, integrity, and even the continued existence of elite-level international competitions, from the World Cup to the Tour de France to the Olympic Games themselves, is the use of illicit performance-enhancing drugs. When a millisecond difference between gold and silver can amount to millions in endorsement contracts and appearance fees, some athletes are willing to risk using drugs to get that winning edge. With so much at stake, it is not surprising to see some athletes get caught testing positive for drug use.

The Tour de France, the world's premier cycling event, has a long history of suspicion of illegal drug use. A British cyclist died in 1967 after a stage in which he used amphetamines; in 1998 six teams were forced to drop out and the leading team, Festina, was disqualified because of suspected doping; American Lance Armstrong was constantly dogged by accusations and investigations of doping when he won seven straight Tour de Frances from 1999 to 2005, despite never having been found to have committed a violation; in 2006 American Floyd Landis, the declared winner of the 2006 tour, was stripped of his title after it was revealed he had tested positive for testosterone after a mountain stage (see note 4); 2007 prerace favorite Alexandre Vinokourov withdrew from the race after he tested positive for blood doping; lastly, the eventual 2007 winner, Alberto Contador of Spain, has been accused of being involved in a doping operation called Operación Puerto that kept his team out of the 2006 tour.

Drug use by Olympic athletes is nothing new. Ancient Greek athletes are reported to have used various substances to increase their strength and endurance. In the 1960 Olympic Games in Rome, two athletes died from overdosing on drugs they took before competing in their events. To protect the health of the athletes and to ensure fair and equable competition, the International Olympic Committee began to routinely perform drug tests at the 1968 summer Olympic Games in Mexico City, and began full-scale testing at the 1976 summer Olympic Games in Montreal.

To discourage drug use by athletes, any athlete caught doping faces the loss of medals and a suspension from competition. One of the more publicized case is that of Canadian sprinter Ben Johnson, who tested positive for steroids at the Olympic Games in Seoul in 1988 and was stripped of his gold medal and world record.

Despite all the actions of the IOC, some athletes may continue to use drugs to gain a competitive advantage. Therefore, to protect the future of the Olympic Games, the IOC held the World Conference on Doping in Sport in February 1999 at Lausanne, Switzerland. The purpose of the conference was to establish uniform policies under which all athletes and sports federations would be tested. The conference, which was attended by approximately 600 representatives of national Olympic committees, national governing bodies, government officials, and athletes, was held to establish an international anti-doping agency, develop penalties (including a proposed automatic two-year suspension for all doping offenses), and get the international governing bodies of sports such as swimming and track and field to agree to the same rules.

The end result was the creation of the World Anti-Doping Agency (WADA), financed by intergovernmental organizations, governments, and other public and private bodies. In 2004 over 1,000 delegates of sports organizations and governments gave their approval to the World Anti-Doping Code created by WADA. For the first time ever, the code created standardized antidoping rules and regulations for all sports and all countries. Although the code does not have the force of law, all international and national Olympic committees adopted the code and have the power to sanction non-compliant organizations. FIFA, the international governing body of perhaps the world's most popular sport, soccer, did not accept the code until 2006, before the World Cup in Germany, during which no positive tests were reported. Prior to accepting the code, WADA forced the Court of Arbitration for Sport (CAS) to issue a ruling that FIFA's testing did not comply with WADA rules and WADA threatened to advocate for soccer's omission from the Olympics until FIFA complied.

The current WADA Prohibited List prohibits nine different types of substances: anabolic agents, hormones and related substances, beta-2 agonists, hormone antagonists and modulators, diuretics and other masking agents, stimulants, narcotics, cannabinoids and glucocorticosteroids, as well as substances banned in particular sports (see note 1). In 2010, WADA had a budget of $28 million, with the IOC contributing almost $13 million and the member nations of the IOC contributing a matching amount. The United States was the largest contributor to the WADA budget at over $1.87 million (see note 1).

Although the IOC has adopted the WADA Code as its standard for drug testing, the IOC Executive Board is ultimately responsible for establishing the policies and procedures used in Olympic-related drug testing. While some believe that IOC drug sentences have been unduly harsh, many believe that the IOC has a conflict of interest in any drug testing program. The IOC, while wanting to ensure fair competition, also must be concerned with the impact a positive doping test could have on the Olympic image, resulting in the loss of corporate sponsorship and fans.

A major point of interest concerns unannounced or short-term testing. Canada, England, Sweden, and a handful of other countries have instituted frequent, random, out-of-competition testing for anabolic steroids. The purpose of this type of testing is to combat the use of performance-enhancing drugs taken during training. In many cases, the evidence of drug use has left the body by the time of the competition. However, the drugs' impact will have already carried over and given the athlete a possible advantage. For example, steroids are training drugs and are not used for a certain period of time before a competition, thereby avoiding a drug test which might occur during a competition.

The U.S. Olympic Committee (USOC) employs its own drug education program for events involving national team tryouts and competitions. This program helps the USOC to instruct its athletes about the vast international drug regulations and to support its program to deter drug use. In October 2000, the USOC turned over responsibility for testing of Olympic and Pan American athletes to the U.S. Anti-Doping Agency (USADA). Any athlete eligible to compete in events sanctioned by his or her sports federation or by the USOC will be subject to unannounced out-of-competition testing. The IOC has adopted the WADA Code and Prohibited List.

The testing process begins with the collection of two specimens (A and B). Specimen A is tested; if a positive result occurs, another sample from A will be tested. If this second test of specimen A results in another positive test, the athlete will be notified immediately by the USADA. This notification will also tell the athlete the time and date of the testing of specimen B. The athlete may witness this testing or a surrogate representative will be assigned to witness the testing of specimen B. If specimen B tests positive, the appropriate penalties will be imposed. The athlete has the right to request a hearing on the positive drug result. Penalties for positive tests vary, depending on the substance. A confirmed first positive test will result in a suspension ranging from three months to two years. A confirmed second positive test will result in a two-year suspension for some substances and a lifetime ban for other substances.

The USADA's strict policies were put into effect prior to the 2002 Winter Olympic games in Salt Lake City. Before the games, the USADA administered unannounced tests on most of the 2,500 athletes competing in the games. All athletes at the games carried a "doping passport" which showed when and how they were drug tested. During the games, the USADA administered postevent drug tests to athletes in the first four places of their respective events. A "doping escort" was assigned to each athlete and administered the test within an hour of the event's finish. If an athlete tested positive for any prohibited substance, a series of hearings decided if the athlete would be stripped of his or her medals and banned from future competition.

The USADA operates a 24-hour, toll-free drug hotline that athletes, coaches, trainers, doctors, and administrators can call for more information on banned drugs, drug testing procedures, and the drug education program. In 2008, the USADA spent over $2.76 million on research and education related to the deterrence of the use of performance-enhancing drugs in sports. About 87% of the agency's $13.3 million annual budget is funded by the federal government, while the USOC covers the rest.

In some cases, national governing bodies (NGBs) and international federations (IFs) will call for stricter penalties for positive tests than the USOC or IOC. For example, the NGB for the biathlon may recommend a four-year penalty for the use of a substance, whereas the USOC/IOC may recommend a two-year penalty. In that case, the governing body's sanction will take precedence over the USOC/IOC prescribed penalties.

Historically, due to several parties' being involved in international competition (IFs, NGBs, IOC, etc.), complications can arise over penalties after positive tests.

Prior to the creation and implementation of WADA standards, disputes over drug penalties often wound up in courts and before different governing bodies, creating confusion with regards to jurisdiction and testing standards (see note 14). The problem arises as to which organization and/or country has the final authority in disputes involving a drug testing program. By creating a uniform code and more streamlined appeals process, WADA has reduced many of these issues.

In order to handle disputes over matters such as a positive drug test or eligibility, the Court of Arbitration for Sport (CAS) was created in 1983. The CAS was designed to be an independent agency that could serve as a neutral and final arbitrator in sports disputes but also requires sports organizations to voluntarily subject themselves to its jurisdiction, as all Olympic IFs have done (for more on the role of the CAS, see section 5.3.6, "Court of Arbitration for Sport"). The option of the CAS allows disputes that arise during (or right before) the Olympic Games to be settled quickly and inexpensively. The CAS sets up ad hoc (nonpermanent) courts and sends representatives to the Olympic Games in the event that a situation arises where a hearing and ruling must be pronounced within twenty-four hours of the disputed claim. Athletes, NGBs, and IFs all have access to CAS (see note 16). As drug testing policies and penalties have become more stringent with the creation of USADA and WADA, the importance of the CAS as the ultimate authority in disputes has increased.

NOTES

1. More information on WADA, the code, the Prohibited List, and its budget can be found online at http://www.wada-ama.org/en/.

2. More information on the USADA, including USADA Arbitration Rulings, are available from its Web site at http://www.usantidoping.org/.

3. In November 2007, the World Conference on Doping in Sport was held to review the success of WADA and discuss proposed changes to the code and its standards. Members of all the major international sports organizations attended, including the IOC, NOCs, and NGBs, as well as members of the CAS and WADA Accredited Laboratories. The Conference was first held in 1999, when it tried to establish a working group of athletes, government representatives, sports governing body members, and IOC members to define the anti-doping agency's structure, mission, and funding. Leading to the creation of WADA, the original conference established the consensus that the antidoping agency should be independent of the IOC in order to avoid conflict-of-interest issues; that the new organization should have out-of-competition drug testing, coordinated research, promotion of preventive and educational programs; and that it should harmonize scientific and technical standards, procedures for testing, and equipment. The conference also proposed an automatic two-year suspension for all doping offenses, which has been adopted by WADA. The two-year sanction for a first offense was adopted with compromise wording that the suspension could be modified in "specific, exceptional circumstances" to be evaluated by international sports federations. Representatives from soccer, cycling, and tennis who wanted to retain autonomy over athlete suspensions opposed the proposal for uniform penalties.

4. During the 2006 Tour de France, American cyclist Floyd Landis staged an epic comeback during stage 17 on his way to winning the tour. However, just days after the race, it was announced that a Landis drug test taken immediately following stage 17 revealed an unusually high ratio of testosterone. The USADA suspended Landis for two years, finding that the scientific components of the test occurred properly. A dissent argued that there was not a proper chain of custody for Landis's sample, but in affirming the decision, the CAS determined that the lab results were in accordance with international standards. In 2010 Landis admitted using PEDs during his cycling career.

5. During the 2006 Kansas Relays, American sprinter and three-time Olympic medalist Justin Gatlin tested positive for testosterone or its precursors. In 2001, while at the University

of Tennessee, Gatlin had tested positive for amphetamine; however, it was stipulated by the IAAF that the positive test was the result of Gatlin's taking Adderall for attention deficit disorder (ADD) and he received a lessened suspension. Against Gatlin's protest, the USADA considered Gatlin's 2006 test his second positive test, subjecting him to a lifetime ban. Gatlin was given a four-year ban after appearing before the North American Court of Arbitration for Sport Panel, but a vigorous dissent stated that Gatlin should not be faulted for his first test and that the USADA was failing to comply with the Americans with Disabilities Act. After the CAS rejected Gatlin's appeal, Gatlin filed for a permanent injunction in the Northern District of Florida. After Gatlin was granted a temporary restraining order that would have allowed him to participate in the 2008 Olympic trials, the IOC stated that the court lacked jurisdiction and should Gatlin wish to appeal the CAS ruling he must do so to the Swiss Federal Court. Four days before the start of the trials, the court reversed, stating it lacked jurisdiction.

6. In 2006 WADA appealed USADA's sanction against American bobsledder Zach Lund as being too light. During the 2005 World Cup, Lund tested positive for the prohibited substance Finasteride but it was known that he had been using medication that included the substance for over five years. The medication, Propecia, is used to combat baldness. Lund included the substance on his doping control forms but did not have a therapeutic use exemption (TUE). The USADA only gave Lund a public warning and disqualified his World Cup results. Lund's doctor filed a TUE and the USBSF selected Lund for the 2006 Olympics. The CAS ruled in WADA's favor, concluding that Lund was responsible for checking the prohibited substance list and for the presence of the drug in his system. The CAS said that a suspension must be included in the USADA's sanction but lessened the requested suspension from two years to one because Lund had no significant fault or negligence and the antidoping organizations were aware Lund was using the substance. Lund returned to win the 2006–2007 overall World Cup title.

7. During a February 2005 tournament in Acapulco, Mexico, Argentinean tennis player Guillermo Cañas tested positive for hydrochlorothiazide, a diuretic and masking agent for other performance enhancing substances. Cañas was subsequently suspended by the ATP for two years. Cañas says he was given the prescription drug by ATP doctors at the tournament. The CAS found that Cañas was responsible for the drug's presence in his body but had no significant fault or negligence. Cañas was required to forfeit his prize money from the Acapulco tournament, but his suspension was reduced to 15 months, and he returned to the tour in September 2006.

8. In 2004, the CAS ruled that American sprinter Jerome Young should not have been allowed to race at the 2000 Olympics Games, where he won a gold medal as part of the American 4 × 400 relay team. Young tested positive for the banned substance nandrolone months before the 2000 Olympics but was cleared by a USATF appeals panel. In July 2005, the CAS ruled that Young's teammates could keep their medals. Three other members of the relay team (who had participated at varying times during the Olympics), twins Alvin and Calvin Harrison and Antonio Pettigrew later received drug related suspensions. As a result, Michael Johnson, another member of the team, voluntarily returned his gold medal. Young tested positive for another banned substance, EPO, a month after the 2004 CAS ruling, and he accepted a lifetime ban.

9. Days after winning gold at the 2004 Olympics, American cyclist Tyler Hamilton tested positive for a blood transfusion. The USADA suspended Hamilton for two years, a penalty upheld by the CAS. Hamilton contended that the presence of two different types of blood cells in his system was because his twin sibling died in utero and Hamilton had received his twin's stem cells. The CAS rejected Hamilton's story and concluded that the test was reliable.

10. In 2005, the CAS upheld the USADA's ban against American track and field star Tim Montgomery for doping even though Montgomery never tested for any prohibited substance. The USADA charged Montgomery with doping after receiving evidence regarding his involvement with BALCO, an American athletic laboratory found to have been involved with providing steroids and other illegal substances to a various high profile athletes. The CAS stated that the USADA's authority extended to all cases of possible doping

violations, not just drug testing. Although the CAS had evidence of abnormal blood tests from Montgomery, it relied heavily on testimony from American track athlete Kelli White. White, who had already accepted a two-year ban for doping, testified that Montgomery admitted using a prohibited substance known as "the Clear." Montgomery was banned for two years, was ordered to repay approximately $1 million in earnings, and his record was expunged dating back to March 2001, including his 100-meter dash record of 11.78 seconds set in 2002. For more on this case, see Paul Greene, "United States Anti-doping Agency v. Montgomery: Paving a New Path to Conviction in Olympic Doping Cases," 59 *Maine Law Review* 149 (2007).

11. Montgomery's then wife, sprinter Marion Jones, was also implicated in the BALCO investigation. Jones was originally married to American shot putter C. J. Hunter, who was suspended for using performance-enhancing drugs during the 2000 Olympics. Hunter later told a federal grand jury that Jones had been using performance-enhancing drugs for years during the BALCO investigation, charges that Jones denied on the stand. Jones later admitted lying to federal agents about her use of steroids and pled guilty to perjury. Jones was forced by the IOC to return her give Olympic medals and was sentenced to six months in prison beginning in January 2008.

12. In 1997, USA Track and Field, the NGB for track and field in the United States, suspended Mary Slaney after she allegedly tested positive for testosterone at the 1996 U.S. Olympic trials. Slaney had a testosterone-to-epitestosterone (T/E) ratio of 11.6:1, higher than the allowable 6:1. Slaney claimed that the reason her T/E ratio was high was because she was at the end of her menstrual cycle at the time, she was taking birth control pills for the first time, and she had had a glass or two of red wine the night before the test. All these are factors that can affect a woman's T/E ratio. After originally imposing its own suspension, the USATF submitted the case to a panel of the USATF doping hearing board, which, upon review, "concluded Mary Slaney committed no doping violation last year." The International Amateur Athletic Federation referred the case to arbitration in Monaco. In April 1999, an arbitration panel appointed by the *IAAF* concluded that Slaney had tested positive for excessive levels of the male sex hormone testosterone. Slaney failed to appear at the hearing and was tried in absentia. Slaney filed a lawsuit in Indianapolis against the International Amateur Athletic Federation, track and field's world governing body and the United States Olympic Committee. In *Slaney v. The International Amateur Athletic Federation*, 244 F 3d 580 (7th Cir., 2001), the court refused to overturn the decision of binding arbitration, stating, "Our judicial system is not meant to provide a second bite at the apple." The highest T/E ratio ever uncovered in an international sport drug test is the 42:1 that Britain's Diane Modahl registered when she tested positive in 1994. Modahl's lawyers were able to show that there must have been a mistake with the test, in particular how the sample was stored.

13. In *Walton-Floyd v. United States Olympic Committee*, 965 S.W.2d 35 (1998), an athlete banned from competition for failing a drug test brought an action against the USOC for breaching its duty of care. The athlete was issued a card that listed several banned substances and a phone number to call for a complete list of banned substances. The instructions on the card directed that it was the responsibility of the athlete to call the hotline and to be aware of all the banned substances included. The athlete called the number numerous times to check on a particular substance, Sydnocarb, and was told by the hotline operator that the substance was permitted. The drug test that disqualified the athlete indicated the presence of amphetamines that were produced by Sydnocarb. In the lawsuit, the athlete asserted that the USOC breached its duty by not keeping hotline officials up to date on the status of Sydnocarb. The USOC countered that the Amateur Sports Act, 36 U.S.C.A. 371–396, did not create any legal duty of care for the USOC to protect a governed athlete and that it was the athlete's responsibility to be aware of banned substances. The District Court, Harris County, granted summary judgment in favor of USOC. On appeal, the court held that (1) the Amateur Sports Act did not provide for implied private cause of action permitting athlete to recover monetary damages against USOC and (2) the act preempted claims asserted by an athlete against the USOC under state tort law.

14. In August 1990, Butch Reynolds, world record holder in the 400 meters and a 1988 Olympic silver medalist, allegedly tested positive for the anabolic steroid nandrolone after an international track and field meet in Monte Carlo. Shortly thereafter, the International Amateur Athletic Federation (IAAF), the NGB for track and field, suspended Reynolds from competition for two years. Reynolds immediately filed suit in U.S. District Court in Ohio, claiming that the testing procedure was flawed and that he had not used steroids. The court ruled, however, that Reynolds must first exhaust all administrative remedies. Reynolds next took his case before the American Arbitration Association, a procedure specified by the U.S. Amateur Sports Act and the USOC Constitution, and was exonerated. Both the IAAF and the Athletics Congress (TAC), however, refused to accept the decision because the USOC's administrative proceedings were inconsistent with the IAAF's adjudication process. In September 1991, however, TAC also exonerated Reynolds after finding clear and convincing evidence that the test results were tainted. Once again, the IAAF refused to accept the decision. In the three weeks preceding the 1992 U.S. Olympic trials, Reynolds once again turned to the courts in order to gain the right to compete for the U.S. Olympic team. The district court, in *Reynolds v. International Amateur Athletic Federation*, 841 F.Supp. 1444 (S.D. Ohio 1992), found that Reynolds had established a likelihood of success on the merits of his case, ruling that a breach of contract appeared to have occurred when evidence showed inconsistencies in the testing and that the IAAF, ignoring its own policy of confidentiality, released information that Reynolds had tested positive before granting him a hearing. The court issued a preliminary injunction on June 19, 1992, which allowed Reynolds to participate in all track and field competitions, including the Olympic trials and Olympic Games. TAC appealed the decision to the U.S. Sixth Circuit Court of Appeals, which overturned the lower court's decision, ruling that no U.S. court had the jurisdiction to allow Reynolds to compete in Barcelona. In addition, the court ruled that granting Reynolds an injunction would harm other athletes through the IAAF's threat to invoke the "contamination rule," which would bar from the Olympic Games any athlete who competed against Reynolds. Reynolds appealed to the U.S. Supreme Court. In 1992, Justice John Paul Stevens reinstated the injunction, claiming that the IAAF's threatened harm to other athletes could not dictate the disposition of Reynolds's claim. The issue of whether or not Reynolds could compete in the 1992 Barcelona Olympiad was rendered moot when he failed to qualify. On December 3, 1992, a U.S. District Court in Ohio awarded Reynolds $27.3 million ($6.8 million in compensatory damages and $20.5 in punitive damages) from the IAAF as a result of the lawsuit he filed against TAC and the IAAF, citing lost earnings and personal anguish. Judge Joseph P. Kinneary stated in his ruling that the IAAF had defamed Reynolds, had acted with "malice" and "a spirit of revenge," and had "purposefully avoided the truth" in the case. The IAAF maintained that no court in the United States had an legal jurisdiction over it. The IAAF even went so far as not to appear in court throughout the proceedings. The IAAF appealed, and in May 1994, the U.S. Sixth Circuit Court of Appeals reversed and remanded the district court's $27.3 million judgment. The Court of Appeals held that finding the IAAF amenable to suit in an Ohio court under the fact of the case comports with "traditional notions of fair play and substantial justice." Upon remand, the district court was ordered to dismiss the case for lack of personal jurisdiction over the IAAF. *Reynolds v. International Amateur Athletic Federation*, 23 F.3d 1110 (6th Cir. 1994).

For more information on WADA and Olympic drug testing, see the following:

1. Richard H. McLaren, "WADA Drug Testing Standards," 18 *Marquette Sports Law Review* 1 (2007), and Robyn R. Goldstein, "An American in Paris: The Legal Framework of International Sport and the Implications of the World Anti-doping Code on Accused Athletes," 7 *Virginia Sports and Entertainment Law Journal* 149 (2007).

For further information on Olympic dispute resolution, see the following:

1. Jason Gubi, "The Olympic Binding Arbitration Clause and the Court of Arbitration for Sport: An Analysis of Due Process Concerns," 18 *Fordham Intellectual Property, Media and Entertainment Law Journal* 997 (2008), and Kristin L. Savarese, "Judging the Judges: Dispute

Resolution at the Olympic Games," 30 *Brooklyn Journal of International Law* 1107 (2005). Also see the Court of Arbitration for Sport Web site at http://www.tas-cas.org/.

7.2.4. Professional Sports

Owing to the widespread media coverage of professional sports, the drug problems of many professional athletes are now exposed to anyone who reads the sports pages. This media attention has made drug abuse and the drug testing of players two of the most emotionally charged issues facing athletes, coaches, and fans of professional sports. Unlike interscholastic and intercollegiate sports organizations, professional sports organizations face a different set of legal concerns when trying to establish a drug policy.

The first distinction is state action. As mentioned in section 7.1.1, "Constitutional Law," professional sports teams are for the most part privately owned and therefore not subject to the same array of constitutional law arguments that face many interscholastic and intercollegiate sports organizations. Even when the state is involved in the drug testing of professional athletes, the courts have afforded wide latitude to such programs.

Another major distinction between interscholastic and intercollegiate sports organizations and professional sports is the fact that professional athletes are considered employees. As discussed in Chapter 11, the National Labor Relations Act (NLRA) grants all employees the right to organize and bargain collectively with their employer with respect to their wages, hours, and conditions of employment. Since many professional athletes in the United States are unionized, the leagues and clubs have a duty under the NLRA to bargain in good faith with the players regarding conditions of employment. Drug testing is a condition of employment. Furthermore, fines or suspensions for drug use affect a player's wages. Therefore a drug policy is a mandatory subject of bargaining between the leagues and the players. If a professional sports league wants to adopt a drug testing program, it must bargain for it. If a professional sports league wants to increase penalties for cocaine use, it must bargain for it.

In order to "bargain for" something, a side must give up something else. In other words, if a league asks a players' union if it may implement a drug testing program, the players' union may ask for an increased pension, an increased minimum salary, a reduction in free agency restrictions, or something else of benefit to the players. As the remainder of this chapter will illustrate, the strictness of a sport's drug policy is inversely proportional to the bargaining leverage of the league's players and the strength of the players' union.

This is not to suggest that players' unions will *always* fight for a more lenient drug policy. For example, an NFL player who has never used steroids might encourage his union to adopt a stronger policy against steroids. The job of the players' unions is to protect the players' (workers) right to work and their wages.

However, unions also have a duty to ensure that the players (workers) are able to perform their jobs in a safe work environment. The union must therefore balance these two obligations before agreeing to any drug policy.

To combat drug use by players and protect their investments, professional sports leagues began drug testing athletes in the 1980s. Even professional sports organizations that do not test for drugs have some type of substance policy. The following sections briefly examine and compare the drug policies of five prominent sports leagues as well as the Professional Golf Association.

NOTE

1. For more information regarding legal challenges to professional sport drug testing programs see Victor S. Broccoli, "Williams v. NFL: The Eighth Circuit Flags the NFL for Interference with State Drug Testing Laws," 17 *Sports Law. J.* 283 (2010).

7.2.4.1. National Football League

The National Football League has two separate policies, one for anabolic steroids and related substances, first established in 1993, and a policy for substances of abuse, created in 1986. The NFL's substance abuse policy prohibits but is not limited to, cocaine, marijuana, opiates, methylenedioxymethampetamine (MDMA), and phencyclidine (PCP). In 1994, in an addendum to the collective bargaining agreement, the NFL reduced the penalties for drug use and expanded its treatment program.

The NFL's drug testing policies underwent major judicial scrutiny in 2009. In 2008, several NFL players tested positive for bumetanide, a banned diuretic and masking agent. Two of the players, Kevin Williams and Pat Williams, both of the Minnesota Vikings, sued the NFL, claiming that the NFL and its doctor, Dr. Lombardo, knew that the banned substance was in StarCaps, a popular product, and failed to adequately warn the players under Minnesota drug testing law. In *Williams v. National Football League*, 582 F.3d 863 (8th Cir. 2009), the court found that the state law drug testing claims were not preempted by the NFL Collective Bargaining Agreement. The decision arose out of a complex case that called into question a sports league's ability to collectively bargain for a drug testing policy without having to consider each state's individual drug testing laws. A Minnesota state court later reinstated the suspensions, finding that the Williams were not harmed by the violation in state law.

The stated cornerstone of the NFL's drug program is intervention. Under the program, which prohibits the illegal use of drugs and the abuse of prescription and over-the-counter drugs, such as amphetamines or codeine, players are tested, evaluated, treated, and monitored for substance abuse. Every NFL player is subject to both random and mandatory drug tests (exhibit 7.2 outlines the NFL's substance abuse policy and the various penalties associated with multiple offenses).

Regarding illegal drugs *other* than steroids, *all* players must be tested once between April 20 and August 9, at a random time determined by the NFL's medical director. The medical director may choose to test an entire team at a time, or an entire position group at a time, but not on an individual-by-individual basis. In addition, draft-eligible players are tested prior to the draft. Also, a preemployment test may be administered to a free agent player (rookie or veteran) not under contract at the end of the preceding year, prior to the execution of a new NFL player contract. Regarding steroids, the league may test at random times throughout the season, "with limits on the number of times any given player can be tested to be negotiated between the Commissioner and the NFLPA."

Players submit one urine specimen that is split into two separate A and B specimens. If A tests positive, the player is notified and B is tested two days later. A player's refusal to produce a specimen constitutes a positive test. The first time a player is confirmed to test positive for illegal drugs other than steroids, he enters stage 1 of drug treatment. This treatment will involve more frequent tests, but the player is neither fined nor suspended.

When a player violates stage 1 of treatment (usually via a second positive test for drugs other than steroids), he is assigned to stage 2 of treatment. If a player is

Exhibit 7.2
NFL Substance Policy

Substance	First Offense	Second Offense	Third Offense	Fourth Offense
Steroids	4-game suspension	8-game suspension	1-year suspension	
Recreational drugs, via drug test	Enter program; fine of 3/17ths of base salary if noncompliant with program	Fine of 4/17ths of base salary and/or 4-game suspension	4- to 6-game suspension; forfeiture of proportionate amount of signing bonus	Banished 1 year or more
DUI, alcohol offense	1/2 of 1/17th of base salary, up to $20,000	Commissioner discretion	Commissioner discretion	Commissioner discretion
Violation of law (guilty/no contest)	Commissioner discretion	Commissioner discretion	Commissioner discretion	Commissioner discretion

determined to fail to comply with his treatment plan under stage 1, he is subject to a fine equal to 3/17 of his salary. Players in stage 2 are subject to testing 2–10 times per month. The first violation of the terms of stage 2 will result in a suspension of up to four regular season games without pay. A second violation of the terms of stage 2 will result in a suspension of up to 10 regular season games without pay, and the player moves to stage 3. Players who violate the terms of stage 3 will be banished from the NFL for no less than one year.

It will normally require three positive drug tests before a player is suspended from the NFL for at least one year. The NFL's policy and program also covers alcohol. The program states that when consumed abusively, alcohol not only produces or contributes to conduct that is unlawful and threatens the health and safety of players and other persons, but is also detrimental to the integrity of and the public confidence in the NFL. If a player is convicted of or admits to an incident involving alcohol, such as DUI, there is a maximum $20,000 fine for the first offense.

Interestingly, the penalties for illegal drug use or alcohol violations are harsher if they are discovered via a violation of law rather than via a positive drug test. In addition to the penalties proscribed by the substance abuse policy, the NFL commissioner reserves broad powers to fine and suspend players under the NFL's Personal Conduct Policy (see note 2). If a player is discovered to have violated the terms of the drug policy via a violation of law, he will normally be suspended without pay for four regular and/or postseason games (normally six games for a second violation of law). In addition, he will be admitted to the appropriate stage of treatment, depending on his history of positive tests. However, the commissioner reserves the right to impose more stringent penalties (suspensions and larger fines) for more egregious conduct such as drug trafficking. The commissioner's decisions may be appealed. However, the commissioner has the power to unilaterally decide that appeal in this instance.

The penalties for steroid abuse are a four-game suspension for the first positive test and an eight-game suspension for the second positive test. A third positive test results in a minimum one-year suspension. Players are not paid during suspensions. All players are tested at least once a year, for the first time during training camp and randomly thereafter during the pre-, regular, and postseasons. In addition, players are subject to up to six random tests during the off season. The testing is done in the same way as under the substance abuse policy. The NFL policy prohibits anabolic steroids, peptide hormones (hGH, hCG), beta-2 agonists, antiestrogenic agents, diuretics and other masking agents, ephedrine, amphetamines and other stimulants, dietary supplements containing prohibited substances, and other related substances. The NFL and the players' association did not always agree on how to handle drug testing. In 1986, NFL commissioner Pete Rozelle unilaterally implemented a new drug testing policy when he was unable to convince the NFL Players Association to agree to a stricter policy. The players' association filed for an arbitration hearing and the arbitrator ruled that since the new policy unilaterally changed the terms and conditions of the players' employment, provided for in the collective bargaining agreement, it was unenforceable (see note 8).

NOTES

1. The NFL's drug policy, steroid policy, and collective bargaining agreement are viewable online at http://www.nflplayers.com > Member Services > Rules & Regulations .

2. For more on the drug testing policy in the NFL, see Scott B. Shapiro, "Who Decides: Institutional Choice in Determining a Performance Enhancing Drug Policy for the NFL," 7 *Wyoming Law Review* 183 (2007).

3. Since Roger Goodell became NFL commissioner prior to the 2006 season, he has enforced the NFL's Personal Conduct Policy much more stringently. The following players have all been given suspensions ranging from six games to a full season or more for various types of illegal and inappropriate conduct: Michael Vick, Adam "Pacman" Jones, Plaxico Burress, Donte Stallworth, Chris Henry, Tank Johnson and Ben Roethlisberger.

4. During the 2007 season, it was reported that Denver Broncos running back Travis Henry had tested positive for marijuana. Rather than appeal the suspension through the collectively bargained process outlined in the drug testing policy, Henry sued the NFL in New York state court. When the NFL filed to remove the case to federal court, all proceedings against Henry were stayed. The NFL again argued that Henry's claims were preempted by the LMRA (see note 5), but Henry never missed any games during the 2007 season due to suspension.

5. In *Bryant v. National Football League, Inc.*, 2007 WL 3054985 (D.Colo. October 18, 2007), former NFL wide receiver Antonio Bryant filed for a temporary restraining order after the NFL told him that if he did not submit to drug testing, he could be disciplined by the NFL. Bryant was a member of the San Francisco 49ers during the 2006 season, when he was charged with DUI and other offenses after driving his Lamborghini over 100 mph. As a result of the incident, Bryant was suspended for the final two games of the 2006 season and the first two games of the 2007 season. Prior to the 2007 season, while not a member of any team, Bryant failed a drug test. Bryant contended that because he was not actively pursuing employment with an NFL team he should not have been subject to additional drug testing in the fall of 2007. Bryant's motion for a temporary restraining order was denied because he had failed to show he was at risk of suffering an immediate injury. The case was voluntarily dismissed by both parties soon after the NFL filed for a motion to dismiss, claiming that Bryant's claims were preempted by the Labor Management Relations Act (LMRA) which requires deference to collectively bargained grievance procedures.

6. In 1997, former Tampa Bay Buccaneer and Pittsburgh Steeler Steve Courson filed a damage suit against the NFL, claiming that the league had failed to enforce its steroid policy

against him. Courson contended that his steroid use caused him to develop a weakened heart condition, and that he had become an alcoholic by drinking to mask pain. Courson claimed that chronic alcoholism should be considered similar to an injury suffered during a game. Winning the suit would have entitled Courson to as much as $224,000 in benefits annually, instead of the $21,000 he was receiving. In 2000, Courson's claim was rejected by a three-judge panel of the U.S. Court of Appeals for the 3rd Circuit. "'While all of Courson's assertions linking alcohol consumption with league play may be true, they fall short of establishing that NFL teams actually condoned or encouraged the consumption of alcohol,' Judge Carol Mansmann wrote. 'If anything, the evidence shows that the league and member teams discouraged alcohol abuse.'" For more information, see Richard Willing, "Court: Courson's Alcoholism Not Football's Fault," *USA Today*, June 2, 2000, p. 18-C.

7. In *Long v. NFL*, 66 F.3d 311 (3rd Cir. 1994), Terry Long, a member of the Pittsburgh Steelers, failed a drug test when his urine tested positive for anabolic steroids. He was then suspended pursuant to the NFL's drug testing policy. Long sued the National Football League, the Pittsburgh Steelers, the city of Pittsburgh, and the Stadium Authority of Pittsburgh, claiming that the league's policy violated the 4th and 14th Amendments of the U.S. Constitution; Article I, Section 8, of the Pennsylvania Constitution; and various state laws. The court held that Long failed to show a sufficiently close nexus between the actions of the city and city officials and the decision of the NFL to establish an actionable constitutional claim based on his suspension for use of anabolic steroids. The court concluded that Long was suspended based on independent medical conclusions and NFL policy objectives over which the state had no influence.

8. The important aspect of Arbitrator Sam Kogel's 1986 decision is that he ruled that Commissioner Pete Rozelle had the authority, under the auspices of the "integrity of the game" clause, to augment the existing drug policy as long as it did not contradict the terms of the existing policy. Areas the commissioner could address were the definition of prohibited substances, a player's entitlement to get paid for the time spent in the hospital for drug treatment, and the extent to which the commissioner can discipline players for improper drug involvement. These topics were not addressed in the existing policy; therefore the commissioner could address them through his "augmented" program.

7.2.4.2. National Basketball Association

While other leagues' drug testing issues have dealt primarily with performance-enhancing drugs, the NBA's drug and drug testing issues have more often involved substances of abuse and street drugs. In the early 1980s, NBA commissioner David Stern was facing a drug problem with his league. Some estimated that 70% of NBA players were using cocaine and that such activity was contributing to the league's difficulty attracting top sponsors and broadcasting contracts. Consequently, the NBA sought mandatory testing of all players in 1982. The National Basketball Players Association (NBPA), however, resisted this type of testing. After negotiations, the NBPA agreed to allow testing only when there was reasonable cause and later made another concession in 1988, when it allowed rookies to be tested. Though credited with cleaning up the image of a league, the drug testing policy lacked some key provisions, from the NBA's perspective. For example, players were not tested for marijuana; teams were not required to report drug abusers to the NBA office; and veterans were not subject to random testing. By the late 1990s, the NBA was again facing a reputation for excessive drug use, culminating in Toronto Raptor Charles Oakley's claim that 60% of NBA players were using marijuana. Despite the residual labor strife from the preceding lockout, the NBA successfully negotiated a tougher drug policy into the collective bargaining agreement in 1999. Under the terms of the 1999 agreement, banned substances included amphetamine and its analogues, cocaine, LSD, opiates (heroin, codeine, and morphine), PCP, steroids—*and* marijuana. (Until the

1999 collective bargaining agreement, the only prohibited drugs were cocaine and heroin.) The 1999 agreement also extended testing to veteran players during training camp and included testing for steroids and other performance-enhancing drugs.

The testing mechanism (urine sample, hair, etc.) may be determined by the medical director, who is chosen jointly by the NBA and NBPA. A player may come forward voluntarily regarding his use of a prohibited substance and seek treatment in the program. There is no penalty the first time a player comes forward voluntarily, unless he fails to cooperate with treatment (see exhibit 7.3). Players submit a specimen, which is divided into A and B samples. If sample A tests positive, players can request that sample B goes to a different lab for testing.

If the NBA or NBPA receives information that provides reasonable cause for a player's use, they may request a hearing with the other party and the independent expert (hired jointly by the NBA and NBPA). If the independent expert believes there is reasonable cause, the NBA will arrange for testing of a player four times during the next six-week period. The 2005 agreement allowed for random testing of all players up to four times during the season for any prohibited substance.

The penalties for drug use in the NBA vary substantially, depending on the substance abused and the circumstances under which the offense is discovered. Similar to the NFL policy, penalties are stiffer if the offense is discovered via a violation of law. However, there is a clear difference in emphasis between the two policies. The NFL policy is tougher on steroids, while the NBA policy is tougher on street drugs such as cocaine and opiates. Here are the particulars of the NBA's penalties for substance violations:

1. Via a positive test

   a. Steroids: First offense (ten games without pay and player enters treatment program), second offense (twenty-give games without pay and enter program), third offense (one year without pay and enter program), fourth offense (disqualification from the NBA)

   b. Marijuana: First offense (enter program), second offense ($25,000 fine and enter program), third offense (5 games' suspension without pay and enter program), any subsequent violation the player shall be suspended for five games longer than his previous suspension

Exhibit 7.3
NBA Substance Policy

Substance	First Offense	Second Offense	Third Offense	Fourth Offense
Steroids	10-game suspension	25-game suspension	1-year suspension	Disqualification
Marijuana	No penalty; enter program	$25,000 fine; re-enter program	5-game suspension; reenter program	5-game suspension; reenter program
Others (Drugs of Abuse)	No penalty; stage 1 of program	Minimum 6-month suspension; stage 2 of program	Disqualification (see note 2)	Disqualification

    c. Drugs of Abuse (amphetamines and its analogs, cocaine, LSD, opiates and PCP): First offense (One year disqualification for first-year players, two-years for veterans)

2. If the grievance arbitrator determines that a player has used or possessed amphetamines and its analogues, cocaine, LSD, opiates, or PCP, *or has distributed any prohibited substance*, he will be dismissed and disqualified from the NBA in accordance with the provisions of a positive test.

3. A conviction or no-contest plea in criminal trial for either possession or distribution of banned substances (other than marijuana) will result in disqualification from the NBA.

4. Non-compliance with the drug program

    a. Fines and suspensions, which will be imposed until that player fully complies with the requirements of the program

    b. A player in the program for substances *other than steroids and marijuana* who fails to comply with his in-patient or aftercare treatment will automatically be suspended during his period of in-patient treatment and for at least six months of his aftercare.

        (1) Second offense will result in disqualification from the NBA.

NOTES

1. The NBA Collective Bargaining Agreement, including the drug policy and grievance procedure, is viewable online at http://www.nbpa.com.

2. In August 2009, Rashard Lewis of the Orlando Magic, a two-time NBA all-star, became the most prominent NBA player to be disciplined for a PED violation. Lewis was suspended the first 10 games of the 2009–2010 season after testing positive for the banned substance DHEA, frequently used to combat fatigue.

3. In January 2006, New Orleans Hornets forward Chris Andersen was disqualified from the NBA for violating the league's antidrug policy. He became the first player disqualified since Stanley Roberts in 1999. Andersen was in the first year of a four-year, $14 million deal when he tested positive for a drug of abuse. Pursuant to the collective bargaining agreement, the type of drug was kept confidential. Andersen applied for and was granted reinstatement in January 2008.

4. To clarify, a player who is disqualified is not necessarily expelled from the NBA forever. Any veteran player who is disqualified will be disqualified for a period of not less than *two* years. Any first-year player who is disqualified will be disqualified for a period of not less than *one* year. A player may be reinstated only with the approval of both the NBA and the NBPA, and such approval may be conditioned on random testing and other terms.

7.2.4.3. Major League Baseball

No sport's drug testing policies has undergone more scrutiny in the United States than baseball. Major League Baseball's program is unique in that it is not part of the collective bargaining agreement. Owing to the strength of the Major League Baseball Players Association (MLBPA), MLB was reluctant and incapable of negotiating stringent drug testing into the collective bargaining agreement.

Owing to the marked increase of drug-related problems in MLB in 1982–1983 and the resulting media fallout, the MLBPA and MLB adopted the Joint Drug Agreement (see note 8). Prior to the agreement, the MLBPA worked informally with MLB on drug-related issues involving players as they arise, such as in the case of Steve Howe (see note 6). The agreement established a joint review council consisting of three experts in the field of drug abuse who were to make recommendations on treatment and other issues. Not everyone was happy with the agreement, however. Ken Moffett, executive director of the MLB Players Association, was dismissed in November 1983 by the MLBPA, in part because of his willingness to work with MLB executives to develop a drug testing plan for players.

In 1985, the new commissioner of baseball, Peter Ueberroth, announced a plan under which Minor League players and nonplaying personnel in the major leagues would be randomly tested. Ueberroth sought the voluntary participation of Major League players in a similar program. However, unable to reach an agreement on random testing with the players' association, MLB terminated the Joint Drug Agreement in October 1985.

In 1986, in connection with the so-called Pittsburgh Drug Trial, Commissioner Ueberroth placed all drug testing under the control of the commissioner's office (see note 8). The drug testing program, which has been updated by later commissioners, has remained under the control of the commissioner's office.

In 1997, Commissioner Bud Selig distributed a memorandum to all clubs regarding the league's drug policy. The main points of the memorandum included no unannounced testing for Major League players, random unannounced testing for Minor League players, a program to help treat and rehabilitate individuals with a drug problem, as well as a new disciplinary code for positive test results and those engaging in the sale or distribution of illegal drugs or controlled substances (see note 7). As mentioned previously, these provisions were not achieved via collective bargaining. While the provisions pertaining to MLB employees and Minor League players can be considered binding, any provisions pertaining to Major League players are subject to the grievance procedure. This is because club fines exceeding $250 or commissioner suspensions or fines exceeding $500 are subject to the grievance procedure according to Article VII (Discipline) of the collective bargaining agreement.

In 2001, MLB unilaterally implemented testing for performance enhancing substances as well as drugs of abuse in the Minor Leagues. Only players not on the 40-man roster could be tested, otherwise the testing policy would have been subject to collective bargaining. Finally, after pressure from Congress (see note 6), MLB and the MLBPA agreed to anonymous "survey" testing for the 2003 season. During 2003, 1.438 players were tested anonymously, and because greater than 5% of players failed the test, penalties for positive tests were to begin in 2004 (see note 1). The original penalties were treatment for a first positive test, 15 day suspension or a fine up to $10,000 for a second positive, 25 days or up to a $25,000 fine for a third positive, 50 days or up to a $50,000 fine for a fourth test, and one year suspension or fine up to $100,000 for a fifth test. All suspensions would be without pay.

With continued speculation and government questioning (see note 4), MLB and the MLBPA altered the policy in January 2005, and the penalties were increased to 10 days for the first positive test, 30 days for the second, 60 days for the third, and one year for the fourth (see exhibit 7.4). After yet another government hearing (see note 5), the current and strongest penalties yet were implemented.

In December 2007, former Senator George Mitchell, as commissioned by MLB, released a 409-page report into the use of PEDs in MLB (see note 3). The report included the names of 89 former or current MLB players and included 19 recommendations for cleaning up the game of baseball. As a result, in May 2008, MLB

Exhibit 7.4
MLB Substance Policy

Substance	First Offense	Second Offense	Third Offense
Steroids	50 games	100 games	Lifetime ban
Recreational drugs, via drug test	Enter rehab program; failure to comply is 15–25 games	2nd failure to comply is 25–50 games	3rd failure to comply is 50–75 games
Stimulants/amphetamines	Increased testing	25 games	80 games
Conviction/no contest for possession of prohibited substance	60–80 games for PEDs; 15–30 for Drugs of Abuse	120 games to a year for PEDs; 30–90 for Drugs of Abuse	Permanent suspension for PEDs; one year for Drugs of Abuse

and the MLBPA agreed to institute nearly all of Senator Mitchell's recommendations, including increased testing and an independent administrator of the testing.

NOTES

1. Although the results of the survey testing were to be anonymous, a list was made containing the names of the players that had tested positive in 2003. For purposes related to ongoing government investigations (see note 2), the list was never destroyed. As a result, several high-profile players have been linked to positive tests from the 2003 survey testing, including Alex Rodriguez, David Ortiz, and Manny Ramirez.

2. In *U.S. v. Comprehensive Drug Testing, Inc.*, 473 F.3d 915 (9th Cir. 2006), the Ninth Circuit refused to quash a subpoena from government investigators for the names of the MLB players who had failed a drug test during the 2003 season. The government subpoenaed the names in relation to its investigation of BALCO, a San Francisco–based laboratory that was accused of supplying illegal performance-enhancing substances to many top-flight athletes, including baseball players Barry Bonds, Jason Giambi, and Gary Sheffield, runners Marion Jones and Tim Montgomery, and numerous members of the Oakland Raiders football team. The Ninth Circuit ruled that the subpoenas were reasonable, within the scope of a legitimate grand jury investigation, and did not constitute harassment. Bonds testified during the case that he never knowingly took any illegal substances and was subsequently indicted for perjury and obstruction of justice based on other evidence. In 2010 the 9th Circuit ruled certain evidence against Bonds inadmissible, making a conviction less likely.

3. Among the names in the Mitchell Report was seven-time Cy Young winner Roger Clemens. Clemens vehement denial of the accusations from his former trainer Brian McNamee led to a hearing before the House Oversight and Government Reform Committee and a defamation lawsuit against McNamee. The Mitchell Report can be found on MLB's Web site at http://mlb.mlb.com/mlb/news/mitchell/index.jsp.

4. In March 2005, the House Government Reform Committee held a hearing on steroids in baseball. Commissioner Bud Selig and union chief Don Fehr were subpoenaed and present, along with sluggers Rafael Palmeiro, Sammy Sosa, and Frank Thomas. Also present were pitcher Curt Schilling, retired star Mark McGwire and his former teammate Jose Canseco, an admitted steroid user. McGwire refused to answer questions regarding his suspected steroid use, while Palmeiro vehemently denied having ever used steroids. The hearing was considered widely embarrassing for MLB and subsequently an impetus for the strengthening of its testing policies in November 2005. In August 2005, Palmeiro tested

positive for a banned substance and was suspended for 10 days. McGwire, who had 583 career home runs, eighth of all time, received only 23.5% of Hall of Fame votes in January 2007, far short of the 75% minimum needed for induction.

5. A subcommittee of the House Energy and Commerce Committee subpoenaed the commissioners of MLB and the NBA, NHL, NFL, and MLS, along with the executive directors of the MLBPA, NBPA, NHLPA, and NFLPA, to Washington in May 2005 to again discuss steroid use in sports. Both the House Government Reform Committee and the House Energy and Commerce Committee passed bills setting minimum steroid testing rules and penalties for professional sports in June 2005. The bills were never voted on in the House and did not become law.

6. In June 2002, the Senate Commerce Committee held a hearing at which Senator John McCain (R-Ariz) and other Senators interrogated MLB Commissioner Bud Selig and MLBPA executive director Don Fehr on where there was not already a steroid testing policy in place, as there was in the NBA and NFL. The subcommittee holds legislative jurisdiction over sports in the United States and made insinuations that if MLB were not able to implement a steroid testing policy, the Senate could pass legislation requiring testing that would be binding on MLB.

7. In *In the Matter of the Arbitration Between Major League Baseball Players Association and the Commissioner of Major League Baseball*, Grievance No. 92–7; Suspension of Steven Howe, Nicolau, Chairman of Arbitration Panel, November 12, 1992, Commissioner Fay Vincent banned New York Yankee pitcher Steve Howe from baseball for life for violating the terms of his reinstatement in 1990 after being suspended during the 1988 and 1989 seasons. Between 1982 and 1988, Howe was hospitalized for drug-related treatment six times and was reinstated in 1990 on the condition that he refrain from using or selling drugs. However, the arbitrator found that there was no "just cause" for the lifetime ban because Vincent did not do all that was contractually required for Howe (periodic drug tests) prior to the total ban.

8. The Pittsburgh drug trial was held during the 1985 playoffs and the World Series. The trial involved Curtis Strong, a Philadelphia resident accused of selling cocaine to MLB players. In the first week of Strong's trial, Lonnie Smith of the Kansas City Royals described, under a grant of immunity, his introduction to cocaine in the Major Leagues and how the drug was purchased and distributed in MLB. In following days some of MLB's best-known players, including Keith Hernandez, Dale Berra, Enos Cabell, Dave Parker, and John Milner, also testified under immunity about drug use in baseball. While no MLB player was charged in the Pittsburgh case, by the time the trial ended in late September and Curtis Strong had been convicted and sentenced to 10 years in prison, it seemed to many fans that professional baseball had been judged guilty.

9. In 1983, MLB commissioner Bowie Kuhn, in response to the arrest and conviction of four Kansas City Royals players and the resulting media attention, the MLBPA and MLB adopted the Joint Drug Agreement. The agreement established a joint review council, consisting of three experts in the field of drug abuse, who were to make recommendations on treatment and other issues. Most owners considered the joint program too watered down, but Commissioner Kuhn felt otherwise. Kuhn stated that the program was a "dramatic breakthrough in labor relations and sports." The policy included the following provisions:

1. The program excluded marijuana, amphetamines, and alcohol. Players who were found to be abusing these substances would continue to be subject to action by the commissioner, and the union would continue to have the right to file grievances in such cases.

2. A cornerstone of the new agreement was a salary abatement procedure to penalize players who continued to use drugs. A player who asked for help with a drug program would receive full pay for the first 30 days of treatment and half pay for the next 30 days. Beyond 60 days, if kept on the roster by the club, the player would be paid at a rate of $60,000 a year, the minimum salary.

3. A club that suspected a player of drug involvement would ask the person to undergo examination. If the player refused, the evidence would be presented to a review council that included drug counselors. The members of this council were to be selected by a joint committee of owners and players. If the council recommended that the player undergo testing or treatment and the player refused, he would be subject to disciplinary action by the commissioner.

7.2.4.4. National Hockey League

After a prolonged lockout that resulted in the canceling of the NHL's 2004–2005 season, the NHL and NHLPA reached a new collective bargaining agreement that contained the first ever performance-enhancing drug policy. Like the NBA and NFL, the NHL, with the NHLPA, has a multiphased Substance Abuse and Behavioral Health Program. During phase 1, a player who tests positive for a drug of abuse is not suspended and begins treatment. More failed tests put the player in phases 2 and 3 of the program, during which the player is suspended and must seek reinstatement from the league. The more positive tests a player has, the more scrutiny he will face upon request for reinstatement. However, NHL commissioner Gary Bettman has also suspended or fined players involved in legal incidents as a result of substance abuse under the NHL's Personal Conduct Policy.

When NHL players began participating in the Olympics in 1998, there was controversy over whether or not they would be drug tested. During the 1998 games, NHL and NBA players were given an exemption from testing. However, owing to a compromise between the USOC and NHL Players Association, players are tested only for steroids or masking agents, *not* street drugs. Beginning with the 2002 Olympics, however, all NHL players playing in the Olympics must submit to random drug tests in order to participate in the Olympics (see note 1).

In the 2005 collective bargaining agreement, the NHL and NHLPA agreed to a jointly administered Performance-Enhancing Substances Program. The program initially adopted WADA's list of banned substances to be altered as necessary, through negotiation, for the sport of hockey. NHL players are subject to two random tests from the start of training camp through the end of the regular season. For the first positive test players are suspended for 20 games, without pay, and entered into the Substance Abuse and Behavioral Health Program. A second positive is a 60-game suspension, without pay, and enrollment in the program. A third test results in a permanent suspension without pay, and the player can apply for reinstatement after two years.

NOTES ————————————————————————————

1. Prior to the 2006 Olympic Games, the U.S. Anti-Doping Agency tested 100 prospective American hockey players and one tested positive: Columbus Blue Jackets defenseman Bryan Berard tested positive for nadrolene, an anabolic steroid. Berard, who was not selected for the Olympic team, blamed the positive test on a tainted supplement. Also, Jose Theodore, a Canadian goalie for the Colorado Avalanche, tested positive for a nandrolene masking agent and as a result was given a two-year suspension from international play, even though it was determined that the positive result was caused by Propecia, a hair loss drug Theodore had been legally taking. Because these tests were not administered by the NHL-NHLPA program, neither player was disciplined by the NHL.

2. The first player to test positive in an NHL administered test was Sean Hill, a 37-year-old defenseman for the New York Islanders, in April 2007. Hill denied knowingly taking a banned substance but served a 20-game suspension.

3. A mandatory drug testing program was proposed in 1986 by John Ziegler, the president of the National Hockey League, and Alan Eagleson, executive director of the NHL Players Association. The announcement was an apparent reaction to a published report in the May 12, 1986, issue of *Sports Illustrated* on cocaine problems among players in the NHL. Ziegler and Eagleson, in a joint news release, proposed the program as a means of cleaning up the league's image. The proposal, however, required the approval of a majority of the NHL Players Association members before it could be incorporated into the league's collective bargaining agreement. The players decided against the program.

7.2.4.5. *Professional Golf Association*

Golfers on the PGA tour are not unionized. They are not even employees. While widely considered to be independent contractors working on the PGA tour, the U.S. Supreme Court has suggested that their legal relationship may be more akin to *customers* of the PGA tour. In *PGA Tour Inc. v. Casey Martin*, 532 U.S. 661 (2001, U.S.), the court noted that golfers must pay a $3,000 fee to attend qualifying school before qualifying for the tour, making them, essentially, paying customers.

Regardless of the precise legal status of PGA golfers, they are not unionized, and therefore the PGA tour is under no obligation to bargain with them over the terms of a drug policy. Just as the commissioner of MLB was free to institute random drug testing over nonunionized Minor League baseball players (see section 7.2.4.3, "Major League Baseball"), the PGA commissioner *does* reserve the right to demand a urine sample from any suspected violator of the PGA substance abuse policy.

The PGA substance abuse policy is as follows:

1. Any member found to be using or selling illegal substances shall be considered to have engaged in conduct unbecoming a professional and shall be subject to a very significant penalty (minimum fine of $1,000 and multiyear suspension up to and including expulsion).

2. Any member found to have violated any of the following provisions relating to the use of alcohol shall be considered to have engaged in conduct unbecoming a professional and shall be subject to a significant penalty (a minimum fine of $1,000, suspension from play of no less than four weeks, and one year probation):

   A. Consuming an alcoholic beverage during any practice round or tournament round (whether a pro-am round or a tournament competition round), on the practice tee or putting green.

   B. Moderate, responsible consumption of alcoholic beverages after play or during social functions is permitted. But players should know that alcohol-related unprofessional incidents will carry the above minimum penalties.

3. A PGA tour member's responsibility to conduct himself in a professional manner and lend credit to himself and his organization extends beyond the time that the member is engaging in tournament play at a tournament site. Accordingly, the membership should be aware that, depending on the circumstances, being under the influence of alcohol at any time in a public place, whether at a tournament site or otherwise, may constitute conduct unbecoming a professional under the PGA tour alcohol and substance abuse policy, and may be subject to appropriate penalties.

4. The commissioner will conduct such inquiries and investigations as shall be appropriate (taking statements from witnesses, requiring urinalysis tests, etc.) to determine whether a member has violated the alcohol and substance abuse policy or any interpretations thereof (see note 1).

The policy of the PGA is stringent in relation to the policies of the Big Four leagues, all of which had to be negotiated with players' unions. The contrast is particularly revealing when one considers the paucity of substance-related incidents in the sport of golf. While John Daly and Notah Begay have experienced bouts with alcohol abuse (see note 3), few others are known to the public. There have been no legal challenges to the PGA substance policy, nor have there been any publicized instances of the PGA commissioner requesting a drug test.

With nearly every other professional sport receiving substantial public criticism for the use of performance-enhancing drugs, the PGA Tour announced it was beginning an Anti-Doping Program in 2008. The program was approved by the PGA Tour's Policy Board, which consists of four players and four independent directors, typically prominent businessmen. The program subjects golfers to unlimited random testing throughout the year. PGA Tour commissioner Tim Finchem can impose a variety of sanctions, including disqualification, ineligibility for a first violation, up to five years for a second violation, a lifetime ban for a third violation, and fines up to $500,000.

NOTES

1. For more information on the PGA Tour's drug testing policy, see Thomas Bonk, "PGA's Drug Plan Includes 1-Year Ban; a Second Violation Could Lead to a Five-Year Suspension. Program Calls for Testing at Any Time," *Los Angeles Times* D10 (November 14, 2007).

2. Prior to the 2008 U.S. Open, premier golf coach Butch Harmon told *Golf World* that the golf community would be "very naïve to say that someone has never tried [performance-enhancing drugs] in our sport." Comments with which Harmon's former pupil Tiger Woods wholeheartedly agreed. See Barker Davis, "Squeezing for Juice; PGA Can Begin Random Drug Tests July 1," *The Washington Times* C02 (May 29, 2008).

3. John Daly was suspended in 1997 after he "nearly drank himself to death" at the Players Championship. Notah Begay was not suspended in 2000, after serving seven days in jail for his second DWI offense. For more information, see Pete Herrera, "Begay Had Previous Drunken Driving Conviction in Arizona," *Associated Press* (January 21, 2000).

7.2.4.6. *Women's National Basketball Association*

WNBA players have managed to avoid the negative substance-abuse publicity that has plagued their male counterparts in the NBA. The WNBA players are represented by the same union as the NBA players: the NBPA.

While very similar to the NBA substance policy, the WNBA policy is slightly stricter in the area of penalties for marijuana use. WNBA players are suspended after their second positive marijuana test, while NBA players are suspended after their third marijuana test. Perhaps more important, veteran players can be tested *twice* per year in the WNBA (once in the preseason and once in the regular season). NBA veterans, after passing their initial random drug test in the preseason, are not tested for marijuana during the regular season.

It should be noted that drug-related fines in the NBA can be large, consistent with the NBA players' much higher salaries. Nevertheless, the fact that the NBA and WNBA policies are different demonstrates that the strictness or leniency of a league's drug policy is *not* always attributable to the scope of the league's drug problem, but instead is a product of the parties' bargaining leverage and other interests.

When the WNBA players negotiated their first collective bargaining agreement in 1999 (see section 11.3.6.1, "Women's National Basketball Association"), their demands were much more modest than those of the Big Four leagues. In a league where players average five-figure salaries, instead of seven-figure salaries, the players were fighting for such basic things as dental insurance and a 401(k) plan—demands that employees fight for in more typical (nonsports) unions. Consequently, WNBA players were not willing to play "hardball" on the drug issue when (1) they lacked the leverage of their male counterparts (e.g., lower television ratings) and (2) due to the "drug problem" not being a significant one, there was little reason to risk a loss of benefits to fight for a less crucial issue. The WNBA began testing for performance-enhancing drugs beginning with the WNBA's 2003 CBA. A player is suspended 2 games for a first offense, 5 games for a second offense, and 10 games for a third offense. To date, no player has been disciplined under the WNBA PED policy.

Chapter 8

GENDER DISCRIMINATION IN ATHLETICS

8.1. Legal Theories in Gender
Discrimination Cases

    8.1.1. Title IX
        8.1.1.1. Legislative History of
             Title IX
        8.1.1.2. Office of Civil Rights
             (OCR) Policy Inter-
             pretation of Title IX
        8.1.1.3. OCR Analysis
             and Method of
             Enforcement
    8.1.2. The Equal Rights Amend-
        ment and State Equal Rights
        Amendments
    8.1.3. Equal Protection Laws

8.2. Legal Challenges to Title IX

    8.2.1. Legality and Scope of Title IX
    8.2.2. Post–Civil Rights Restoration
        Act Litigation

8.3. Gender Discrimination Cases
Involving Individual Athletes

    8.3.1. Men's Team, No Women's
        Team
        8.3.1.1. Contact Sports
        8.3.1.2. Noncontact Sports
    8.3.2. Women's Team, No Men's
        Team
    8.3.3. Women's Teams and Men's
        Teams
        8.3.3.1. Separate but Equal
        8.3.3.2. Contact Sports
        8.3.3.3. Noncontact Sports
    8.3.4. Same Sport, Different Rules
        8.3.4.1. Contact Sports
        8.3.4.2. Noncontact Sports
    8.3.5. Same Sport, Different
        Seasons
    8.3.6. Varsity Sport versus Club
        Sport

INTRODUCTION

Since the 1970s, gender discrimination in sports has become a highly litigated topic. The initial development of athletic opportunities for women may be attributed, to a large extent, to Title IX of the Education Amendments of 1972, a federal statute that prohibits gender discrimination. Title IX gave women an important legal option to fight gender discrimination, and in turn the availability of legal options brought about an increased reliance on the legal system to redress gender discrimination. Women brought complaints about unequal treatment to court and were often successful in their litigation.

Throughout the mid-1980s, however, a series of setbacks besieged the women's athletic movement. The failure to enact the federal Equal Rights Amendment and limitations imposed on Title IX enforcement by the Supreme Court in *Grove City College v. Bell*, 465 U.S. 555 (1984), brought the opportunities for women to attack perceived gender discrimination through the court system and legislation at a virtual standstill throughout much of this period. With the passage of the Civil Rights Restoration Act by Congress in 1988 and, consequently, the resolution that athletic programs which did not directly receive federal funds were nevertheless bound by Title IX, the movement toward equality in athletics regained momentum. In 1992, the U.S. Supreme Court found, in *Franklin v. Gwinnett County Public Schools*, 503 U.S. 60 (1992), that victims of discrimination under Title IX could be entitled to monetary damages. This decision to make funds available for winners of Title IX lawsuits gave plaintiffs additional strength in Title IX cases, caused a proliferation of lawsuits by student-athletes, and forced many athletic departments to comply with regulations or settle pending litigation in fear of paying large settlements to plaintiffs. Today, Title IX, along with other legal options, are effective legal theories for increasing opportunities for women in athletics in the courtroom.

Participation in women's athletics has increased for many reasons. A major factor is the drastic change in social attitudes about women, including a new perception among women of their own athletic capabilities and interest in participation.

After the U.S. Women's National Soccer Team won the Women's World Cup in the summer of 1999, many credited Title IX for the victory. Title IX has enabled women to demand equality in sports, which in turn has given them the opportunity to compete. A generation later, U.S. women are seeing the results. In 2009, the United States is home to a professional women's basketball league (WBNA) and a professional women's soccer league (WPS). Also, women have had great success in individual sports such as tennis and golf for many years.

Before the passage of Title IX, women composed only 7% of the total number of athletic participants in high school and 16% in college. By 1992, 37% of all interscholastic participants and 35% of all NCAA intercollegiate participants were women. In a report released in 2009, the NCAA found that during the 2008–2009 academic year, there were 182,503 female athletes competing at NCAA member schools, which is nearly 43% of collegiate athletes, and the number of female participants in intercollegiate athletics increased 58% in the 1990s alone (see notes 1 and 2).

The Miller Lite Report in 1985 and the Melpomene Institute in 1995 concluded that women who were active in sports at a young age feel greater confidence and self-esteem in their physical and social selves than women who were sedentary as youths. The Women's Sports Foundation notes that women who participate in sports are more likely to experience academic success than women who do not participate in sports. Also, girls who participate in sports are more likely to do well in science courses. The NCAA reports higher graduation rates for female athletes than for women students in general (71% vs. 64% in 2006).

While participation in women's sports has increased dramatically since the passage of Title IX, other problems have emerged. According to the 2010 "Women in Intercollegiate Sport," report, by R. Vivian Acosta and Linda Carpenter of Brooklyn College, while the data show a near all time high for participation by women in our nation's intercollegiate athletics programs . . . the representation of females coaching men's teams remains remarkably low. Also, the number of women in administrative roles is roughly at the same level as the mid-1970s.

Most plaintiffs utilize Title IX as the primary legal theory in their gender discrimination lawsuits. However, some plaintiffs also use the constitutional law theory of equal protection and a state equal rights amendment if the state has enacted one. For employment discrimination cases involving gender, Title IX is often used, but plaintiffs also make use of Title VII, a federal antiemployment discrimination law, and the Equal Pay Act, a federal law that ensures equal pay for equal work and experience (see Chapter 16, "Additional Legal Concerns").

Title IX, however, has been the most important of the legal theories used in gender discrimination cases. The first type of Title IX cases involved participation rates of females in athletics. Plaintiffs were largely successful in these cases, and this type of litigation has consistently been decided in favor of increasing opportunities for women. The most important case on participation rates is *Cohen v. Brown University*, which is discussed in depth in section 8.2.2, "Post–Civil Rights Restoration Act Litigation." The second area being litigated under Title IX involves equitable financial assistance. In these cases, courts look at how men and women's teams are funded as well as the equivalent availability of athletic scholarships to men and women. The third area of potential litigation involves "other benefits" that schools provide to athletic teams. The area of "other benefits" involves topics such as equality of access to facilities; coaching staff and support staff; publicity for both men and women; and equal quality of facilities for both genders (see note 3).

Title IX, despite its generally favorable consequences for women, has not been without its many opponents. With the mandate to increase opportunities for women in athletics, athletic departments have taken varied approaches on how to address their particular situations and comply with the legislation. The most frequent downside to Title IX has been the elimination of men's athletic programs to compensate for the addition of women's programs. Many universities have not had the necessary funds to add women's programs while maintaining the same number of men's athletic programs. Athletic departments have been forced to cut men's sports such as wrestling, gymnastics, and baseball. In addition to cutting sports, departments have also reduced the number of scholarships available to men's athletic teams. The elimination of men's athletic programs has led to a number of lawsuits filed by male athletes, claiming reverse discrimination under Title IX. Generally, men have not been successful with their claims of reverse discrimination (see note 4).

Some athletic departments, albeit rarely, have been able to fully accommodate the interests of female athletes while not reducing participation opportunities for male athletes. These athletic programs generally are very well funded. The most common approach used to comply with Title IX in intercollegiate athletics has been to increase women's opportunities while reducing men's opportunities. Therefore Title IX has many opponents who believe that Title IX has unfairly taken away opportunities for male athletes.

Chapter 8 is organized into three major sections. The first part of the chapter discusses the various legal theories and principles utilized in gender discrimination cases in high school and intercollegiate athletics, and the legality, scope, and applicability of Title IX. The second part of the chapter discusses early legal challenges to Title IX and the evolution of the policy from the 1970s through the early 21st century. The final part of the chapter discusses gender discrimination cases involving individual athletes. The cases have been grouped according to the presence or absence of teams available for either gender and according to whether the sport involved is a contact or noncontact sport.

NOTES

1. At NCAA member institutions, the number of female participants in intercollegiate athletics increased from 32,000 in 1971–1972 to 91,000 by 1988–1989 and then rose to 182,503 in 2005–2006 (see exhibit 8.1). During that period, the number of NCAA member institutions that sponsored women's intercollegiate sports increased as follows.

2. On the high school level, prior to the enactment of Title IX in 1972, fewer than 300,000 girls took part in high school athletics. In 2009, this figure rose to 3,114,091 (compared with 4,422,662 boys participating). See www.nfhs.org.

3. In 1992, prompted by the immense impact of Title IX upon intercollegiate athletics, the NCAA established the NCAA Gender Equity Task Force to study how the NCAA could effectively accommodate female athletes under Title IX. Gender equity is defined as follows: "An athletics program is gender equitable when either the men's or women's sports program would be pleased to accept as its own the overall program of the other gender" (*NCAA Gender-Equity Task Force, 2000 Manual*). The task force was given the charge "to develop a definition of gender equity; to assure that no NCAA policy, practice or legislation could deter a member institution from compliance with Federal or state law relevant to gender equity; to examine the policies of the Association for gender bias; to attempt to correct any such policy; and to assist the member institutions in achieving gender equity" (*NCAA Gender-Equity Task Force, 2000 Manual*). In 1993, the task force released its findings/recommendations. Among these recommendations was the establishment of a manual that would serve as a guide to help member institutions to understand and implement Title IX. In addition, a yearly conference to discuss Title IX was proposed and adopted. Also adopted at the 1993 convention was a certification program for institutions to comply with Title IX. By 2001, all of these recommendations had become part of the NCAA's comprehensive efforts to maintain Title IX compliance within its member institutions.

Exhibit 8.1
Women's Teams at NCAA Member Institutions

Sport	1971	1991–1992	1998–1999	2008–2009
Basketball	307	810	1,001	1,054
Cross-Country	10	677	891	996
Softball	147	605	831	949
Swimming	140	394	458	510
Tennis	243	723	877	900
Track and Field	78	561	671	758
Volleyball	208	762	960	1,015

The first recommendation, the manual for complying with Title IX, has evolved since 1993. The most recent manual, *Gender Equity in Intercollegiate Athletics: A Practical Guide for Colleges and Universities*, which was published in 2006, involves seven main areas to help understand and comply with Title IX:

1. Sources of Law (provides legislative language)

2. Understanding Title IX Athletics Compliance (explains the relevant rules and tests, such as the three-part "Effective Accommodation Test")

3. NCAA Issues (discusses Division I Athletics Certification and Emerging Sports)

4. Harassment Issues Facing Colleges and Universities Under Title IX (discusses the applicability of Title IX to sexual harassment claims)

5. Employment Issues (discusses relevant federal laws regarding possible employment discrimination)

6. Gender-Equity Plans, Audits, Policies, and Training (provides direction for Title IX compliance)

7. Current Case Law (keeps members up to date on recent litigation involving Title IX)

The manual can be downloaded at the NCAA's Gender Equity Web site at www.ncaa. org > Research > Gender Equity

The NCAA sponsors an annual Title IX seminar for its members to assist institutions in complying with Title IX. Speakers such as athletic directors, representatives from the Office for Civil Rights, and attorneys with Title IX experience make presentations to the attendees at the seminar on varied aspects of Title IX.

The NCAA has maintained a program of certification of its member institutions under Title IX. A basic summary of the program areas to be reviewed is presented in the gender equity manual released by the NCAA. Each institution must go through two cycles of certification, and provide a plan of how gender equity is, or will be, achieved at the institution.

4. In 2005, then President George W. Bush, instituted a new policy that allowed schools to use a simple survey of women as an evaluation of whether females were being given equal opportunity to participate. The policy combined non-responses with negative responses. Critics said gave institutions an easy way to avoid providing equal athletic opportunities for females. In 2010 President Obama repealed the policy.

5. The Acosta-Carpenter study reveals that in 1972, 90% of women's athletic programs were run by female administrators, compared with only 19.3% in 2010. The report also states that women hold 34.9% of all administrative jobs in collegiate women's programs. However, in 23% of women's programs, no woman is involved in the administration. Among the intercollegiate coaching ranks, the percentage of women coaching women's teams has steadily dropped over the years. In 2010, 42.6% of women's teams are coached by women, while only 2% of men's teams are coached by women. While this problem may be, in part, a reflection of the limited experience of women in the coaching ranks, some claim it is also because women have a limited role in the governing procedures of the NCAA. The most startling of these statistics, however, is that the number of female administrators and coaches has been declining since 1995.

The following cases have been brought by male athletes charging reverse discrimination under Title IX:

1. In *Bukowski v. Wisconsin Interscholastic Athletic Association (WIAA)*, 726 N.W.2d 356 (Table) (Wis. App. 2006), a male public high school student requested an injunction after the WIAA would not allow him to participate on the girls' gymnastics team. Bukowski contended that the WIAA rule violated the Equal Protection Clause of the 14th Amendment and Title IX. In affirming the decision, the Court of Appeals of Wisconsin held that because the WIAA is not a state actor and does not receive federal funds, it is not subject to an equal protection or Title IX claim.

2. In *National Wrestling Coaches Ass'n v. U.S. Dept. of Educ.*, 263 F.Supp.2d 82 (D.D.C. 2003), the plaintiffs consisted of a number of groups intended to protect the interests of male intercollegiate athletes, coaches, and alumni. They sued to enjoin the Department of Education from enforcing Title IX, specifically the three-part accommodation test set forth in the 1979 Policy Interpretation and affirmed in the 1996 Clarification. The plaintiffs alleged that the three-part test violated the Constitution and Title IX and that the Department exceeded its rulemaking authority in violation of the Administrative Procedure Act. Even assuming that the plaintiffs suffered an injury in fact, that is, that men's teams had been eliminated or rosters reduced, the court found that the causation element of standing was tenuous and that it was not possible for a judicial decision to remedy the plaintiff's supposed harm. The court ruled that the three-part test was not a substantial factor in the alleged injury but rather the alleged injury was caused by the independent decisions of individual schools attempting to comply with Title IX. The D.C. Circuit affirmed the decision in 2004.

3. In *Miami University Wrestling Club v. Miami University*, 302 F.3d 608 (6th Cir. 2002), former members of men's wrestling, tennis, and soccer teams at Miami of Ohio claimed that the elimination of those teams violated Title IX. The Sixth Circuit affirmed the district court's summary judgment decision. Miami eliminated the programs as part of a six-year attempt to comply with Title IX. The court dismissed the plaintiff's 14th Amendment Equal Protection claim because the defendant's reason for discriminating based on sex was to conform to federal law. Last, the court stated that there is no constitutional right to participate in intercollegiate athletics and that Miami was within its Title IX power to eliminate men's programs in order to comply.

4. In *Chalenor v. University of North Dakota*, 291 F.3d 1042 (8th Cir. 2000), the court affirmed an August 2000 summary judgment decision in favor of the University. In June 1998, the university approved an Intercollegiate Athletic Committee's recommendation to eliminate the men's wrestling team. Members of the team filed suit in December 1999 after the school had already added three women's teams over the previous five seasons in an attempt to come in compliance with Title IX. The court ruled that the university was free to determine the best way to meet the first prong of the accommodation test, including eliminating men's teams. In addition, the fact that the program had the potential to use private funds was irrelevant because those funds must also be counted with regard to Title IX.

5. In *Neal v. Board of Trustees*, 198 F.3d 763 (9th Cir. 1999), a plaintiff wrestler at California State University-Bakersfield was unsuccessful in claiming reverse gender discrimination under Title IX after his sport was cut due to disproportionate participation rates between male and female athletes.

6. In *Boulahanis v. Board of Regents*, 198 F.3d 633 (7th Cir. 1999), plaintiff wrestlers and soccer players from Illinois State University claimed they were discriminated against based on gender because their teams were eliminated in order to comply with Title IX. Prior to their elimination, the ratio of male-to-female athletes was 65% male and 35% female, while the enrollment was 45% male and 55% female. After the changes, the rates were 52% female and 48% male, placing Illinois State in compliance. The plaintiffs were unsuccessful in their claim, the court stating, "The elimination of men's athletic programs is not a violation of Title IX as long as men's participation in athletics continues to be 'substantially proportionate' to their enrollment."

7. In *Kelley v. Board of Trustees, University of Illinois*, 35 F.3d 265 (7th Cir. 1995), the plaintiffs were members of the men's swimming team at the University of Illinois. Their program was cut from the athletic department, and they charged gender discrimination under Title IX as well as equal protection violations. The plaintiffs were unsuccessful in their claims; the court stated, "The University could, however, eliminate the men's swimming program without violating Title IX since even after eliminating the program, men's participation in athletics would continue to be more than substantially proportionate to their presence in the University's student body."

Many articles have been written criticizing Title IX for its negative consequences for male athletes. Refer to the following:

1. J. Chadwick Schnee, "Wrestling with Retaliation: Pinning Down the Burlington 'Dissuading' Standard Under Title IX," 17 *Sports Lawyers Journal* 223 (2010).

2. Victoria Langton, "Stop the Bleeding: Title IX and the Disappearance of Men's Collegiate Athletic Teams," 12 *Vanderbilt Journal of Entertainment and Technology Law* 183 (2009).

3. Welch Suggs, *A Place on the Team: The Triumph and Tragedy of Title IX* (Princeton, NJ: Princeton University Press, 2005).

4. Danielle M. Ganzi, "After the Commission: The Government's Inadequate Responses to Title IX's Negative Effect on Men's Intercollegiate Athletics," 84 *Boston University Law Review* 543 (2004).

5. Nicole Stern, "Preserving and Protecting Title IX: An Analysis and History of Advocacy and Backlash," 10 *Sports Lawyers Journal* 155 (2003).

6. George Will, "Extortion Holds a Nation Hostage," *Chicago Sun-Times* (February 26, 2000).

Administrators and coaches will find the following organizations' resources useful:

1. Women's Sports Foundation, located at Eisenhower Park in Nassau County, Long Island, New York. This organization publishes *Women's Sports and Fitness*, a monthly magazine. The foundation also created the Sporting Woman Exhibit, a traveling exhibit. The Women's Sports Foundation also has a Web site at http://www.womenssportsfoundation.org.

2. National Association for Girls and Women in Sport, 1900 Association Drive, Reston, VA 22091. The association regularly publishes official rulebooks for many women's sports. In addition, the National Association for Girls and Women in Sport has a Web site at http://www.aahperd.org/nagws/.

3. National Women's Law Center, 11 Dupont Circle, Suite 800, Washington, DC 20036. The National Women's Law Center has a Web site at http://www.nwlc.org.

4. National Organization for Women Task Force on Women's Sports, National NOW Action Center, 733 15th Street, NW, 2nd floor, Washington, DC 20005. NOW's Web site is at http://www.now.org.

5. Gender Equity in Sports, University of Iowa Gender Equity in Sport Project, 340 Carver-Hawkeye Arena, Iowa City, IA 52242. Doctors Christine H. B. Grant and Mary C. Curtis maintain a Web site at http://bailiwick.lib.uiowa.edu/ge/ that provides current information on the status of Title IX and gender equity.

8.1. LEGAL THEORIES IN GENDER DISCRIMINATION CASES

Gender discrimination in high school and intercollegiate athletics has been challenged using a variety of legal arguments, including Title IX of the Education Amendments of 1972, state equal rights amendments, and equal protection laws under the U.S. Constitution. Equal protection arguments are based on the 5th and 14th Amendments of the U.S. Constitution, which guarantee equal protection of the law to all persons within the United States. The law states, "No state shall...deny to any person within its jurisdiction the equal protection of the laws" (see section 6.1.3, "Equal Protection").

Title IX has had the greatest impact in attacking gender discrimination in athletics. Although the original legislation was passed in 1972, implementation was delayed for the promulgation of regulations and policy interpretations. Even with the delay, many have claimed that the rise in women's participation in athletics was directly related to the passage of Title IX. Title IX states, "No person in the United States shall, on the basis of sex, be excluded from participation in, be denied the benefits of, or be subjected to discrimination under any education program or activity receiving Federal financial assistance." A state equal rights amendment can also be used to attack alleged gender discrimination. However, not all states have passed such legislation (see note 6 of section 8.1.2). State equal rights amendments, and the proposed and defeated federal Equal Rights Amendment, were formulated to provide more protection from sex-based discrimination than the federal Constitution provides under the equal protection clause of the 14th Amendment. The goal of the legislation is to protect against all sex-based discrimination and to protect women's rights.

Most gender discrimination challenges have been based on either the equal protection laws or Title IX, or both. For example, in *Adams v. Baker*, 919 F.Supp. 1496 (D. Kan. 1996), a 15-year-old female plaintiff sought a preliminary injunction, alleging that the school district violated her equal protection rights *and* violated Title IX because it did not allow her on the school's all-male wrestling team. The court concluded that the school district's reasons for not allowing plaintiff on the wrestling team were either not "important governmental objectives" or "not substantially related" to its objectives and granted the preliminary injunction for Adams on the grounds of equal protection. However, if the plaintiff had only filed a complaint under Title IX, she would not have been successful; the court stated, "Because wrestling is a contact sport, Title IX does not require that Valley Center High School allow a female to try out for the boys wrestling team." The court ruled that plaintiff was not likely to succeed on the merits of her Title IX claim, and therefore an injunction was not warranted on those grounds. However, the plaintiff was still able to receive the injunction due to the violation of equal protection under the U.S. Constitution.

Regardless of whether plaintiffs employ a Title IX or an equal protection approach in a gender discrimination case, they generally will argue that they are being deprived of equality under the law. When a court deals with claims of equal protection or Title IX violations, there are three important factors that courts commonly will consider when analyzing whether there is actual discrimination.

The first factor that a court will consider is whether a sport is a contact sport. Total exclusion from sports, and especially noncontact sports, is generally considered a prima facie violation of equal education opportunities. However, Title IX provides for a "contact sport exception" that allows athletic programs to bar women from engaging in contact sports with men.

The second factor that the court will consider is the quality or quantity of available opportunities for each gender. The OCR in the Department of Education (formerly part of the Department of Health, Education and Welfare) monitors compliance with the dictates of the law. Under the OCR interpretation of Title IX, courts must look to see if the institution in question is meeting the interests of the underrepresented gender and whether equal treatment is given. Under an equal protection analysis, courts will determine if the regulations in place unfairly discriminate against one gender.

The third factor that a court will consider is the age and level of competition involved in the dispute. The younger the athletes involved, the fewer actual physiological differences exist. Without demonstrable physiological differences, the justification of inherent biological differences as a rational basis for the exclusion of one sex from athletic participation is negated. Courts are reluctant to enforce discriminatory practices at a young age, when there are only negligible physiological differences between the two sexes.

8.1.1. Title IX

Title IX, since its inception in 1972, has undergone a series of changes and revisions while remaining true to its original mission of abolishing discrimination based on gender in federally funded activities. From the original policy interpretation by the Department of Health, Education, and Welfare (HEW) through the decision in *Grove City College v. Bell*, the passage of the Civil Rights Restoration Act, and subsequent litigation, the history and effect of Title IX will be discussed within the following sections.

8.1.1.1. Legislative History of Title IX

Section 901 (a) of Title IX of the Education Amendments of 1972 contains the following language:

> No person in the United States shall, on the basis of sex, be excluded from participation in, be denied the benefits of, or be subjected to discrimination under any education program or activity receiving Federal financial assistance.

Title IX became law on July 1, 1972, as Public Law 92–318 (codified at 20 U.S.C. §§1681–1987). It specifically and clearly recognizes the problems of gender discrimination and forbids such discrimination in any program, organization, or agency that receives federal funds. Athletics and athletics programs, however, were *not* specifically mentioned in Title IX when it first became law in 1972. HEW, taking the position that sports and physical education were an integral part of education, specifically included athletics, despite strong lobbying efforts to exempt revenue-producing intercollegiate sports from the Title IX requirements. This specific inclusion of athletics into Title IX occurred in 1974 and extended from general athletic opportunities to athletic scholarships. The principles governing athletic scholarships included the idea that all recipients of federal aid must provide "reasonable opportunities" for both genders to receive scholarship aid. The existence of reasonable opportunities is determined by examining the ratio of male to female participants. Scholarship aid must then be distributed according to this participation ratio (see 45 C.F.R. §86.13 (c)).

A long process of citizen involvement preceded the first set of regulations. In July 1975, the Department of Health, Education, and Welfare issued the regulations designed to implement Title IX. These regulations are found in Title 45, Code of Federal Regulations (C.F.R.), section 86 A–F. The regulations were criticized by many as being vague and inadequate. In December 1978, HEW attempted to alleviate the criticism by releasing a proposed policy interpretation that attempted to explain but did not change the 1975 requirements. However, not until December 1979, seven years after the original passage of Title IX, did the Office for Civil Rights (OCR), the successor to HEW, release the policy interpretation for Title IX. These final guidelines specifically included interscholastic and intercollegiate athletics. Developed after numerous meetings and countless revisions, they reflected comments from universities, legislative sources, and the public.

8.1.1.2. Office of Civil Rights (OCR) Policy Interpretation of Title IX

The policy interpretation, finalized in 1979, focused on three areas that the OCR evaluates to determine whether an institution is in compliance with Title IX regulations with regard to athletics. In assessing compliance with Title IX, the OCR looks at several factors, including athletic expenditures and program components. Athletic expenditures need not be equal, but the pattern of expenditures must not result in a disparate effect on opportunity. Institutions may not discriminate in the provision of necessary equipment, supplies, facilities, and publicity for sports programs.

Another step that also was crucial to providing clear guidelines in the interpretation of Title IX legislation and what Title IX compliance involves was the publication of the *Title IX Athletics Investigator's Manual* in 1990 by the Office of Civil Rights. This manual superseded the *Interim Title IX Intercollegiate Athletics Manual 1980* and the memorandum "Guidance for Writing Title IX Intercollegiate Athletics Letters of Findings," issued in 1982. This manual set out three main areas that are involved in Title IX compliance and would be investigated by the OCR and the courts when ruling on whether an institution is complying with Title IX. The OCR also released a report in 1997, *Title IX: 25 Years of Progress*, which provides an overview of the impact of Title IX in improving educational opportunities for students (see note 1 for more information on the OCR). In 2003, the assistant secretary for the OCR issued further clarification in a "Dear Colleague" letter.

The first area that is identified in the *Investigator's Manual*, and that the OCR assesses, is the extent to which the institution has met the interests and abilities of male and female students. The policy interpretation requires that the school "equally and effectively" accommodate the athletic interests and abilities of both men and women. This determination requires an examination of the institution's assessment of the athletic interests and abilities of its students, its selection of offered sports, and its available competitive opportunities. The OCR evaluates the level of competitive opportunities in one of three ways:

1. Are intercollegiate competitive opportunities provided in numbers substantially proportionate to the respective enrollment of each gender?

2. Is the institution's current and historical practice of program expansion responsive to the athletic interests of the underrepresented gender?

3. Does the institution fully accommodate the abilities and the interests of the underrepresented gender in the current program?

In analyzing this area, the OCR and the courts must determine the extent to which the institution has met the interests and abilities of male and female students.

In other words, a determination must be made as to whether there are equal opportunities to participate for both men and women and whether the opportunities are at equivalent levels of competition (see note 2 in section 8.1.1.3). In analyzing this particular area, the OCR and the courts compare the ratio of male and female athletes to the ratio of undergraduate full-time students of each gender. The ratios should be equivalent. If the OCR determines that an institution complies with any one of these tests, the institution is judged to have effectively accommodated the interest and the abilities of its student-athletes.

Second, the OCR assesses the financial assistance that male and female athletes receive from the institution. This involves assessing whether an institution's athletic scholarships are awarded on a "substantially proportional" basis. In analyzing this area, the OCR and the courts determine the proportion of scholarship dollars that are spent on male and female athletes and compare this proportion to the proportion of athletes of each gender. However, if a disparity is explained by legitimate and nondiscriminatory factors, the OCR will find compliance. These proportions should be equivalent when an institution is complying with Title IX. For example, compare schools A, B, and C. At school A, 50% of the athletes are female, but only 25% of the total financial assistance goes to females. At school B, 50% of athletes are female, and 45% of the financial assistance goes to females.

At school C, 50% of the athletes are female, and 50% of the financial assistance goes to females. School A would not be in compliance with Title IX because the 25% assistance to females is significantly below the 50% participation rate. School C is clearly in compliance because the proportion of financial assistance equals the proportion of participation to females. School B's situation requires further analysis. Although if the disparity is unexplained and greater than 1% the OCR will presume discrimination is taking place, as explained in the 1998 OCR Letter on Financial Aid.

The policy manual also suggests certain nondiscriminatory factors that may explain disparities in financial assistance to men's and women's athletic programs. An example of a nondiscriminatory factor would be the difference between in-state and out-of-state tuition. Two students in a public institution may both have a scholarship for one year, but since one of the students is from out of state, his or her scholarship has a much higher price tag. Donations from private individuals to athletic programs do count when considering financial equity under Title IX.

The third area of assessment under the policy interpretation is the degree to which the institution provides equal treatment, benefits, and opportunities in certain program areas. Some areas considered by the OCR in evaluating equivalent treatment include equipment, coaching, and facilities. The OCR may use additional factors in determining whether an institution is providing equivalent opportunity for members of both genders in its sports program. However, some of these factors (publicity, academic tutoring, housing, and dining services) are relevant in intercollegiate programs but are not generally relevant in assessing a sports program in a secondary school.

The OCR has distinguished 11 program component areas that have been targeted when investigating this area (see note 3 in section 8.1.1.3):

- Provision and maintenance of equipment and supplies
- Scheduling of games and practice times
- Travel and per diem allowances
- Opportunity to receive academic tutoring and assignment and compensation of tutors
- Opportunity to receive coaching and assignment and compensation of coaches
- Provision of locker rooms and practice and competitive facilities
- Provision of medical and training facilities and services
- Provision of housing and dining facilities and services
- Publicity
- Provision of support services
- Recruitment of student-athletes

Title IX requires that both genders receive comparable or equivalent services in each of these program component areas. However, the *Investigator's Manual* identifies some potential differences that do not cause the institution to be out of compliance with Title IX. These differences are allowed if they are based on certain factors the OCR has identified as nondiscriminatory:

- Unique nature of the particular sport
- Special circumstances of a temporary nature
- The need for greater funding for crowd control at more popular athletic events
- Differences that have not yet been remedied but that an institution is voluntarily working to correct

In the area of compensation for men's and women's coaches, HEW assessed rates of compensation, length of contracts, experience, and other factors, while taking into account mitigating conditions such as nature of duties, number of assistants to be supervised, number of participants, and level of competition. As long as these differences in the program component areas are based on one of the non-discriminatory factors, the OCR and the courts have not found noncompliance with Title IX (see note 2 in section 8.1.3).

The major issues raised regarding Title IX revolve around the scope of the legislation and the programs to which it is applicable. The July 1975 policy regulations issued by HEW covered three areas of activity within educational institutions: employment, treatment of students, and admissions. Several sections of the regulations concerned with the treatment of students included specific requirements for interscholastic, intercollegiate, intramural, and club athletic programs.

Another section of the HEW Title IX regulations specifies requirements for athletic programs (see 45 C.F.R. §86.41(c)). Contact sports are subject to regulations distinct from those governing noncontact sports. The regulations in this section state that separate teams are acceptable for contact sports and for teams in either contact or noncontact sports in which selection is based on competitive skill. There is one exception to the rule forbidding separate teams when a selection is based on competitive skill: if a school sponsors a team in a particular sport for one gender, but not for the other, and if athletic opportunities for the excluded gender have been historically more restricted than athletic opportunities for the other gender, members of the excluded gender must be allowed to try out for the team. The exception does not apply if the sport is a contact sport.

For noncontact sports, if only one team exists, both sexes must be allowed to compete for positions on the team.

8.1.1.3. OCR Analysis and Method of Enforcement

The procedures for Title IX analysis are established in the regulations that list specific factors that should be examined in determining whether or not equality in athletics exists. The number of sports, the type of arrangements, and benefits offered to women competing in athletics are reviewed. When teams of one gender are favored in such areas as funding, coaching, and facilities, resulting in severely reduced opportunities for the other gender to compete, the courts will closely examine program expenditures, number of teams, and access to facilities to determine if the school is fulfilling the requirements of Title IX. Title IX does not require a sport-by-sport analysis but rather an overall program assessment. The

OCR has stated that the reduction or cutting of teams, male or female, is disfavored and not required for compliance with Title IX.

The final area of coverage within the regulations is the method of enforcement of Title IX. The procedure to be followed is initiated by the OCR, which makes random compliance reviews and also investigates complaints submitted by individuals. The first step in the process is to examine the records kept by the institution under investigation in order to review its attempt to comply with Title IX. Each institution must adopt and publish compliance procedures and designate one employee to carry out its Title IX responsibilities, including investigation of complaints. The institution must notify all students and employees of the designated employee's name, office address, and telephone number. After a preliminary review, the OCR has the option to conduct a full hearing or to drop the case.

If the OCR calls a full hearing, the institution has the right to have counsel present and to appeal an adverse decision; the complainant has neither of these rights. The affected individual is not a party involved in the hearing. Instead, the OCR becomes the complainant and pursues the claim. If the OCR finds that there has not been substantial compliance, it may turn its finding over to federal or local authorities for prosecution under the appropriate statutes (see note 5).

This section has provided the basic legislative history of Title IX legislation and the subsequent policy interpretation. For an in-depth discussion of the earliest cases involving Title IX, ensuing policy reinterpretations, review of recent cases involving Title IX, and the effect that Title IX has had upon intercollegiate athletics, refer to section 8.2.1.

NOTES

1. To view and order all of the information that has been released by the Office for Civil Rights, including *Equal Opportunity in Intercollegiate Athletics, Clarification of Intercollegiate Athletics Policy: The Three-Part Test, Title IX and Sex Discrimination, Title IX Grievance Procedures: An Introductory Manual*, and *25 Years of Title IX*, visit the following Web site: http://www.ed.gov/about/offices/list/OCR/publications.html#TitleIX.

2. There are three different definitions of participant to be used in gender equity analysis as listed in the NCAA Gender Equity Manual:

   a. For participation analysis under Title IX
   b. For purposes of Title IX financial aid analysis
   c. For Equity in Athletics Disclosure Act purposes

3. The 2007 NCAA Gender Equity Manual provides in-depth guidance on how schools can provide equitable program components and is available on the NCAA Web site at www.ncaa.org > Research > Gender Equity.

4. In 2006, James Madison University (JMU) decided to eliminate seven men's sports and three women's sports to comply with Title IX. Equity in Athletics (EIA) was formed by athletes, coaches and fans to prevent the cuts. In *Equity in Athletics, Inc. v. U.S. Department of Education*, 291 Fed.Appx. 517 (4th Cir. 2008), EIA claimed that JMU was intentionally discriminating against male athletes in violation of the U.S. Constitution and Title IX. The Fourth Circuit denied EIA's request for an injunction. In weighing the balance of hardship the court noted that none of the student-athletes had lost their eligibility, were free to transfer to other colleges offering their chosen sport, and would not lose their scholarship funding if they stayed at JMU, while JMU would suffer enormous administrative and financial difficulties in reinstating and maintaining the programs. The court also found that EIA was unlikely to prevail on the merits, noting that courts have consistently rejected EIA's underlying claim that equal opportunity in athletics should be tied to expressed interest rather than actual participation.

5. In *Miller v. University of Cincinnati*, 2008 WL 203025 (S.D. Ohio 2008), the court granted the University of Cincinnati's motion for summary judgment after members of the women's rowing team claimed the school violated Title IX and the 14th Amendment by failing to provide adequate facilities, equipment, coaching, or scholarship opportunities and then deciding to eliminate the program in favor of a women's lacrosse team. Using the three-prong compliance test, the court ruled that Cincinnati was in compliance, citing the fact that the duplicated number of intercollegiate athletic participants was 51.1% male and 48.9% female, while only 47.5% of the undergraduate student population was female.

6. In *Cobb v. U.S. Dept. of Educ. Office for Civil Rights*, 2007 WL 951688 (D.Minn. March 27, 2007), two Minnesota high school girls' hockey players alleged that the DOE and OCR violation of equal protection and unequal treatment and benefits under Title IX. Amelia Cobb and Diana Saly participated in the Minnesota State High School League (MSHSL) state hockey tournament but alleged that the MSHSL did not provide the girls with comparative facilities to that of the boys' tournament. Cobb and Saly filed complaints with the OCR, but the OCR approved the MSHSL's decision to hold the tournament at an inferior facility. The court denied the government's motion to dismiss the Title IX based on sovereign immunity because the "case fell within the narrow circumstances involving allegations that the agency has conspicuously and expressly abdicated its enforcement duties, that it acquiesced or actively participated in discriminatory practices, or that it has wrongly refused to pursue further action when efforts to achieve voluntary compliance have failed."

7. In *Barrett v. West Chester University of Pennsylvania of State System of Higher Educ.*, 2003 WL 22803477 (E.D. Pa. November 12, 2003), the court granted a preliminary injunction in favor of eight members of the former West Chester women's gymnastics team to reinstate the team. Announced in April 2000, the team was to be removed, along with men's lacrosse, while adding a women's golf team. The move would have created 9 men's teams and 12 women's teams. In May 2003, one parent filed a complaint with the OCR but withdrew the complaint when it was apparent that the complaint would not be addressed in a sufficient time to reinstate the team for the 2004 season. After defendant's rejected plaintiffs offer to settle the issue, the plaintiffs filed suit in September 2003. In 1998, West Chester formed a Sports Equity Committee to address compliance with Title IX. In 2001, this committee informed West Chester that they were badly noncompliant with Title IX. Both parties admitted that West Chester's proportional spending was noncompliant by 16.2%. The court noted the committee's comments and that the school had only added two women's teams in the last 24 years in finding that West Chester did not meet the second prong of the accommodation test. The court rejected a survey intended to judge the interests of its student body with regards to Title IX because only 39% of the student body responded; far less than the 60% recommended by the NCAA for validity. Entering the 2007–2008 academic year, West Chester had 9 men's teams and 14 women's teams, including gymnastics.

8. In *Beal v. Midlothian Independent School Dist. 070908 of Ellis County*, 2002 WL 1033085 (N.D.Tex. May 21, 2002), four girls participating in high school athletics contended that their school district violated Title IX by denying them an equal opportunity to participate and received unequal treatment. The girls claimed that the male athletes received better equipment and that the girls received less access to travel and practice sites, fewer coaches, and inferior facilities. The court dismissed the plaintiffs' Title IX effective accommodation claim for lack of standing because they did not demonstrate that they were ready and able to participate in an athletic opportunity not offered by the school district.

9. In *Grandson v. University of Minnesota*, 272 F.3d 568 (8th Cir. 2001), the court affirmed the district court's dismissal of the plaintiff's claims. In April 1997, the university and the OCR entered into an agreement to settle a 1996 Title IX complaint against the university. The agreement also called for annual reports, the last of which came in 2000. After the 2000 report, the OCR determined that the university had complied with the provisions of the agreement. The original lawsuit was filed by Grandson in February 1997 and more plaintiffs were added in June 1997. Both suits were dismissed in February 1999

because the plaintiffs had failed to complain in a timely manner to a university official about the alleged unequal treatment nor did they provide any support of unequal funding. Most important, the court noted that the first lawsuit was not sufficient to put the university on notice of the second group of plaintiffs' specific complaints. In addition, the plaintiffs lacked standing because three had exhausted their NCAA eligibility and another was no longer a student.

10. In *Landow v. School Bd. of Brevard County*, 132 F.Supp.2d 958 (M.D. Fla. 2000), high school softball players brought suit because four softball teams from two schools were forced to share a public field without lights or a scoreboard while the baseball teams at the respective schools had their own facilities on the schools' campuses. Using the 10-factor test to determine whether equal opportunities are available to both sexes, the court determined that the school board was not compliant with Title IX.

11. In *Daniels v. School Board*, 985 F.Supp. 1458 (M.D. Fla. 1997) and 985 F.Supp. 1394 (M.D. Fla. 1997), two members of the Merritt Island High School (MIHS) girls' varsity softball team sought an injunction against the school board for violations of Title IX and the Florida Educational Equity Act. The plaintiffs claimed that there were significant inequalities between MIHS baseball and softball facilities. Some of the differences included the following: an electronic scoreboard for the baseball field while the softball field had no scoreboard at all, the baseball team had a batting cage while the softball team did not, there was a sign advertising "Merritt Island Baseball" and not one for the softball team, and the baseball field had lights, but the softball field did not. The court concluded that there was enough evidence that plaintiffs were likely to succeed on the merits of the Title IX claim, and therefore an injunction was proper. The court allowed MIHS an opportunity to submit a plan to rectify the Title IX violations. The court determined that the plan was not sufficient. In fact, the court stated that it "is inclined to agree with Plaintiffs that many of the Board's proposals seem more retaliatory than constructive." The court granted the injunction ordering the school board to eliminate the inequalities.

12. In *Gonyo v. Drake University*, 879 F.Supp. 1000 (S.D. Iowa 1995), plaintiffs, former members of the Drake wrestling team, brought action against the university alleging Title IX and equal protection violations after the university dropped the wrestling program due to lack of funding for athletic scholarships. Male athletes at Drake received only 47% of the university's athletic scholarships even though they made up 75.3% of the university's athletes. This appears to be a violation of Title IX if participation rates are not considered. The court concluded that there was not a violation of Title IX and stated, "The court concludes that the participation test more comprehensively serves the remedial purposes of Title IX than does the scholarship test and therefore must prevail."

13. The Office for Civil Rights is responsible for conducting compliance reviews of Title IX. The OCR selects schools randomly for Title IX compliance reviews and will also review schools based on complaints brought by individuals. Educational institutions are required to keep and submit to the Department of Education accurate compliance reports to enable it to determine whether Title IX requirements have been satisfied. The educational institution is also required to permit access by the Department of Education to its books, records, accounts, other sources of information, and its facilities that may be pertinent to ascertaining compliance. The OCR begins its investigation by notifying the school and then collecting data on the overall athletic program. The information may include the number of teams, scheduling of games and practice times, travel and per diem allowances, compensation of coaches, provision of facilities, and amount of publicity (press releases, media guides, etc.). Aggrieved individuals may also sue an institution directly, without being required to rely on the enforcement mechanism of the Department of Education. On the basis of a review of the data, the OCR will determine whether or not equivalent treatment, benefits, and opportunities, as mandated by Title IX, have been afforded to both genders.

OCR officials will meet with the administrators of an investigated institution and review the OCR's proposed findings before a letter of noncompliance is issued. If the institution voluntarily adopts a plan to rectify its violations within a reasonable period, the institution will be granted a letter of compliance. The Department of Education is then responsible for monitoring the progress of the plan. If the plan is not implemented within the time specified or proves to be an inadequate remedy, the institution will be found in noncompliance and further legal action against the school could be taken.

If there is a failure to comply with Title IX, or a voluntary compliance agreement cannot be reached, or the violations cannot be corrected by informal means, compliance may be effected by the suspension or termination of, or refusal to grant or to continue, federal financial assistance. In addition, the Department of Education may refer the matter to the Department of Justice, with a recommendation that appropriate proceedings be brought to enforce any rights of the United States.

Prior to suspending, terminating, or refusing to grant or continue federal financial assistance, an institution must be afforded the opportunity for a hearing before an administrative law judge. If the educational institution does not request a hearing within the time allowed, the right to the hearing is waived and a decision will be made on the basis of the information then on file.

After a hearing is held, the hearing judge will either make an initial decision on the institution's compliance or certify the entire record, including his or her recommended findings and proposed decision, to the appropriate reviewing authority for a final decision. Both the Department of Education and the institution may appeal that determination to the department's reviewing authority. If the reviewing authority affirms the administrative law judge's decision, the institution may request a review by the secretary of education.

If the Department of Education decides to withdraw funding, it must report that decision to the appropriate congressional committees 30 days prior to the termination of funds. Having exhausted its administrative remedies, the institution could then seek judicial review of the department's actions. For more information on the Office for Civil Rights and its analysis and enforcement of Title IX, visit the OCR Web site at http://www.ed.gov/about/offices/list/ocr/.

8.1.2. The Equal Rights Amendment and State Equal Rights Amendments

Although there are many legal alternatives to allegations of gender discrimination, there has been a recent push for a nationwide comprehensive prohibition of gender discrimination. Supporters of the Equal Rights Amendment (ERA) argued that passage of a constitutional amendment would remedy the lack of such a general prohibition. In order to amend the U.S. Constitution, the proposed amendment must first be passed by a three-fourths vote of both the U.S. Senate and the House of Representatives. Then it must be ratified by at least 38 state legislatures. The ERA was passed in both houses of Congress in 1972, but it did not receive the necessary 38 ratifications from state legislatures by the required deadline of July 1, 1982 (see note 1 for a discussion of the proposed federal ERA).

While uniform prohibition of gender discrimination has not materialized, many states and the District of Columbia have enacted their own Equal Rights Amendments. Thus Equal Rights Amendments have impacted athletics at the state level but not at the federal level. Several cases have been decided in favor of the complainant on the basis of a state ERA. It is important to note that many of these cases, however, could have been brought on other arguments in states without ERAs. As of 2010, 22 states have included an Equal Rights Amendment within their constitution that provides more protection against sex-based discrimination (see notes 8 and 9).

Supporters of a constitutional amendment continue to argue that the effectiveness and importance of an Equal Rights Amendment can be demonstrated in *Commonwealth v. Pennsylvania Interscholastic Athletic Association* (see note 7). In *Commonwealth*, the court decided that the rule of the PIAA violated the Pennsylvania State Equal Rights Amendment, which states, "Equality of rights under the law shall not be denied or abridged in the Commonwealth of Pennsylvania because of the sex of the individual." Although the plaintiffs had also claimed a violation of the equal protection clause of the Constitution, the court did not have to consider this claim because it was found that the PIAA had violated the state ERA. Regardless of the precarious position in which protection against gender discrimination exists, the existence of an Equal Rights Amendment on the state level is often helpful and may even be crucial to the success of gender discrimination cases.

NOTES

1. In general, the proposed federal ERA absolutely prohibited discrimination based on gender and required that any law using gender as a basis for classification be subject to a strict scrutiny analysis by the courts. Supporters of the ERA argued that without proper enforcement, neither Title IX nor Title VII could alleviate the basic problems of gender discrimination. The weakness of Title IX, in particular, is its dependence on federal funding since reduction in funding can effectively diminish the OCR's enforcement capabilities. In addition to this financial vulnerability, gender discrimination statutes are also subject to congressional revisions, which may lessen or even negate much of the available protection. It has been argued that a constitutional amendment would be more sheltered from fluctuating political interests.

2. In *Thomka v. Massachusetts Interscholastic Athletic Association, Inc. (MIAA)*, 2007 WL 867084 (Mass. Super. February 12, 2007), a female high school golfer brought suit claiming that should be allowed to compete in the boys' individual state championship that occurs in the fall season. The boys' championship had a higher level of competition and greater attendance by college coaches and recruiters and may have given Thomka a better chance to showcase her golfing talents as she contended. Thomka participated on a mixed-gender team that played only in the fall. By 2007, Thomka was a three-time runner-up in the girls' individual championship that occurred in the spring but was at a disadvantage because she was not participating while in season like other girls. As a sophomore, Thomka's 74 from the front tees in the team regional tournament would have been good enough to qualify for the boys' individual championship but she was not allowed to compete because of her gender. Her request for an injunction was granted, and she participated in the 2005 boys' individual championship from the back tees. She did not qualify in 2006. Following the injunction, the Superior Court of Massachusetts declared that the rule violated the Massachusetts Equal Rights Amendment by unfairly discriminating on the basis of sex and enjoined the MIAA from enforcing the rule. In sum, the court felt that the spring tournament was not an equal opportunity for girls playing on mixed-gender teams in the fall.

3. In *Kemether v. Pennsylvania Interscholastic Athletic Association, Inc.*, 1999 WL 1012948 (E.D.Pa. November 8, 1999), a female basketball official claimed that the Pennsylvania Interscholastic Athletic Association (PIAA) violated the Civil Rights Act, Title IX, and the Pennsylvania Equal Rights Amendment for failing to consider her for the opportunity to officiate boys games. A jury found numerous incidents of intentional discrimination based upon Kemether's gender, and the PIAA was held vicariously liable under Title IX as a recipient of federal funds. As a result, the PIAA was ordered to change a number of bylaws and rules allowing for females referees to be considered for boys' games.

4. In *Blair v. Washington State University*, 740 P.2d 1379 (Wash. 1987), female athletes and coaches of female athletes brought a gender discrimination action under the state

Equal Rights Amendment. The trial court ruled for plaintiffs and awarded damages, injunctive relief, attorney fees, and costs. On appeal, the Washington Supreme Court affirmed the lower court's conclusion of gender discrimination but modified the lower court's calculations of comparative scholarships for male and female athletes and attorney fees.

5. In *MacLean v. First Northwest Industries of America*, 600 P.2d 1027 (Wash. Ct. App. 1979), a class action was brought against the city of Seattle and the corporation operating a professional basketball team that alleged "Ladies Night" price-ticketing policies were violations of the state's equal rights amendment that prohibited gender discrimination. The court of appeals reversed a lower court decision and found the ticket practice a violation of the amendment.

6. In *Darrin v. Gould*, 540 P.2d 882 (Wash. 1975), an action was brought by the parents of high school students Carol and Delores Darrin, who appealed a Washington Superior Court decision denying them relief in their class action claim of illegal discrimination against females in interscholastic football competition. The Washington Supreme Court found that the school board's denial of permission for the girls to compete on the boys' interscholastic contact football team constituted "a discrimination by state action based on ability to play." Under the due process clause of the 14th Amendment, "performers are entitled to an individualized determination of their qualifications, not a determination based on the qualifications of a majority of the broader class of which the individual is a member." The Supreme Court decided that the Darrin girls could participate, based on the provision of Washington's Equal Rights Amendment, which stated, "Equality of rights and responsibility under the law shall not be denied or abridged on account of sex."

7. In *Commonwealth v. Pennsylvania Interscholastic Athletic Ass'n*, 334 A.2d 839 (Pa. Commw. Ct. 1975), the state of Pennsylvania, acting through its attorney general, filed suit against the Pennsylvania Interscholastic Athletic Association (PIAA), charging that Article XIX, Section 38, of the PIAA bylaws, which states that "girls shall not compete or practice against boys in any athletic contest," was in violation of both the 14th Amendment of the U.S. Constitution and Pennsylvania's Equal Rights Amendment. Plaintiff claimed that the association's rule denied to female athletes the same opportunities to practice and compete in interscholastic sports that were afforded male athletes. Pennsylvania's ERA provided that "equality of rights under law shall not be denied or abridged in the Commonwealth of Pennsylvania because of the sex of the individual." The court found the association's rule to be "unconstitutional on its face under the ERA" and proclaimed, "None of the justifications for it offered by the PIAA, even if proved, could sustain its legality." The court found it unnecessary to consider whether or not the rule also violated the 14th Amendment.

8. As of 2010, the following 22 states had enacted their own individual equal rights amendments within their state constitutions: Alaska, California, Colorado, Connecticut, Florida, Hawaii, Illinois, Iowa, Louisiana, Maryland, Massachusetts, Montana, New Hampshire, New Jersey, New Mexico, Pennsylvania, Texas, Utah, Virginia, Washington, Wisconsin, and Wyoming.

9. An example of an equal rights amendment is Massachusetts Constitution Part 1, Article 1, Amendment Article 106:

Art. CVI, Article I of Part the First of the Constitution is hereby annulled and the following is adopted:

All people are born free and equal and have certain natural, essential and unalienable rights; among which may be reckoned the right of enjoying and defending their lives and liberties; that of acquiring, possessing and protecting property; in fine, that of seeking and obtaining their safety and happiness. Equality under the law shall not be denied or abridged because of sex, race, color, creed or national origin.

10. Title IX and educational equity laws, which have been passed on to the state level, parallel the intent and coverage of the federal Title IX legislation; 13 states (Alaska, California, Florida, Illinois, Maine, Montana, Massachusetts, Nebraska, New Jersey, Oregon, Rhode Island, Washington, and Wisconsin) have each enacted state laws that closely mirror the federal regulation. Another 20 states (Arizona, California, Colorado, Connecticut,

Hawaii, Idaho, Indiana, Iowa, Kansas, Louisiana, Maryland, Michigan, Minnesota, New Hampshire, New York, North Carolina, Pennsylvania, South Dakota, Vermont, and Wyoming) have enacted gender equity laws that incorporate various aspects of the federal regulation.

11. The State of Florida adopted legislation in 2001 (updating legislation from 1994) that consisted of a number of gender equity issues. Some of the topics covered in this legislation are the following:

(d) Students may be separated by gender for a single-gender program for any portion of a class that deals with human reproduction, or during participation in bodily contact sports. For the purpose of this section, bodily contact sports include wrestling, boxing, rugby, ice hockey, football, basketball, and other sports in which the purpose or major activity involves bodily contact.

(e) Guidance services, counseling services, and financial assistance services in the state public K-20 education system shall be available to students equally. Guidance and counseling services, materials, and promotional events shall stress access to academic and career opportunities for students without regard to race, ethnicity, national origin, gender, disability, or marital status.

(3) (a) No person shall, on the basis of gender, be excluded from participating in, be denied the benefits of, or be treated differently from another person or otherwise be discriminated against in any interscholastic, intercollegiate, club, or intramural athletics offered by a public K-20 educational institution; and no public K-20 educational institution shall provide athletics separately on such basis.

(b) Notwithstanding the requirements of paragraph (a), a public K-20 educational institution may operate or sponsor separate teams for members of each gender if the selection for such teams is based upon competitive skill or the activity involved is a bodily contact sport. However, when a public K-20 educational institution operates or sponsors a team in a particular sport for members of one gender but does not operate or sponsor such a team for members of the other gender, and athletic opportunities for that gender have previously been limited, members of the excluded gender must be allowed to try out for the team offered.

(c) This subsection does not prohibit the grouping of students in physical education classes and activities by ability as assessed by objective standards of individual performance developed and applied without regard to gender. However, when use of a single standard of measuring skill or progress in a physical education class has an adverse effect on members of one gender, the educational institution shall use appropriate standards which do not have such effect.

(d) A public K-20 educational institution which operates or sponsors interscholastic, intercollegiate, club, or intramural athletics shall provide equal athletic opportunity for members of both genders.

1. The Board of Governors shall determine whether equal opportunities are available at state universities.

2. The Commissioner of Education shall determine whether equal opportunities are available in school districts and community colleges. In determining whether equal opportunities are available in school districts and community colleges, the Commissioner of Education shall consider, among other factors:

a. Whether the selection of sports and levels of competition effectively accommodate the interests and abilities of members of both genders.

b. The provision of equipment and supplies.

       c. Scheduling of games and practice times.

       d. Travel and per diem allowances.

       e. Opportunities to receive coaching and academic tutoring.

       f. Assignment and compensation of coaches and tutors.

       g. Provision of locker room, practice, and competitive facilities.

       h. Provision of medical and training facilities and services.

       i. Provision of housing and dining facilities and services.

       j. Publicity.

Unequal aggregate expenditures for members of each gender or unequal expenditures for male and female teams if a public school or community college operates or sponsors separate teams do not constitute nonimplementation of this subsection, but the Commissioner of Education shall consider the failure to provide necessary funds for teams for one gender in assessing equality of opportunity for members of each gender.

(e) A public school or community college may provide separate toilet, locker room, and shower facilities on the basis of gender, but such facilities shall be comparable to such facilities provided for students of the other gender.

8.1.3. Equal Protection Laws

The basic analysis utilized for equal protection questions is discussed in section 6.1.3, "Equal Protection." Within the U.S. Constitution, the equal protection guarantee is found in the 14th Amendment. It states that "no state shall...deny to any person within its jurisdiction the equal protection of the laws." Under this clause, people are allowed to challenge laws, rules, and regulations that seem to unfairly classify and discriminate. Here we examine more closely the effects of using gender to classify persons for different athletic opportunities.

Historically, gender has been an acceptable category for classifying persons for different benefits and burdens under any given law. In 1873, the Supreme Court, in *Bradwell v. State*, 83 U.S. 130 (1873), opened with the statement that a woman's place was in the home. The Court went on to say that this was part of a "divinely ordained law of nature." In 1908, the Court stated in *Muller v. Oregon*, 208 U.S. 412 (1908), that a classification based on gender was a valid constitutional classification. Such a classification was not considered to be a violation of equal protection, regardless of whether it was based on actual or imagined physical differences between men and women. Modern equal protection theories have now gained preeminence, and the use of gender to classify persons is considered less acceptable.

A school's, conference's, or athletic association's rules prohibiting mixed-gender competition have typically been challenged on equal protection grounds. In a number of cases, women have been successful in asserting their right to participate on an equal basis with men, and one legal theory they have utilized on these occasions has been the equal protection clause.

Under traditional equal protection analysis, the legislative gender-based classification must be sustained unless it is found to be patently arbitrary and/or if it bears absolutely no rational relationship to a legitimate governmental interest. Under this traditional rational basis analysis, overturning discriminatory laws has been extremely difficult. The implication for gender discrimination sports litigation in high schools and colleges is that women may be excluded from athletic participation upon a showing of a rational basis for their exclusion. The rational reason must be factually supported and may not be based on mere presumptions about the relative physical athletic capabilities of women and men. It remains, however, a relatively easy standard for the defendant to meet as it invokes only the lowest standard of scrutiny by the court.

The court will apply its highest standard, that of strict scrutiny, if it finds that the classification restricts a "fundamental right" or if the rule involves a "suspect" classification. Under the standard of strict scrutiny, the institution seeking to uphold the regulation must show that the rule's classification is necessary to promote a compelling governmental purpose or interest. To date, most courts have not found gender to be a suspect class, which would elevate it to the status held by race, national origin, and alienage (see note 4 for a case that used strict scrutiny for gender classification). However, gender and other classifications may be deemed suspect under a state equal protection clause.

If the courts were, however, to decide that gender is a suspect class or athletic participation is a fundamental right, all rules that classify on the basis of gender would become subject to strict scrutiny analysis. If this were the standard, the rule makers would have to demonstrate that there are compelling reasons for the classification and that there is no less restrictive alternative. They would also have to prove that the classification was directly related to the constitutional purpose of the legislation and that this purpose could not have been achieved by any less objectionable means. Many rules and laws would fail to meet this high standard and hence would be judged discriminatory.

The Supreme Court has moved away from the broad interpretation of the rational relationship test by increasing the burden on the defendant. This intermediate test, between the rational basis and strict scrutiny tests, was first established in *Reed v. Reed*, 404 U.S. 71 (1971). The Supreme Court established therein that gender-based classifications must be "reasonable, not arbitrary, and must rest upon some ground of difference having a fair and substantial relation to the object of the legislation, so that all persons similarly circumstanced shall be treated alike." The Supreme Court again addressed this issue in *Frontiero v. Richardson*, 411 U.S. 677 (1973); in a plurality opinion, Justice Brennan stated, "What differentiates sex from such non-suspect statuses as intelligence or physical disability...is that the sex characteristic frequently bears no relation to ability to perform or contribute to society." Finally, in *Craig v. Boren*, 429 U.S. 190 (1976), and again in *Mississippi University for Women v. Hogan*, 458 U.S. 718 (1982), the Supreme Court held that a gender classification will fail unless it is substantially related to a sufficiently important governmental interest. Thus the Supreme Court has established the *intermediate* level of scrutiny to apply in gender-based discrimination cases.

A factual basis for any gender classification must exist. Mere preferences or assumptions concerning the ability of one gender to perform adequately are not acceptable bases for a discriminatory classification. The intermediate standard requires more than an easily achieved rational relationship but less than a strict scrutiny standard would demand. The class must bear a substantial relationship to an important but not compelling governmental interest. Also, the relationship between a classification and a law's purpose must be founded on fact, not on general legislative views of the relative strengths and/or abilities of the two genders.

Three key factors are commonly considered in an equal protection analysis of athletic discrimination cases. The first factor is state action. Before any claim can be successfully litigated, a sufficient amount of state action must be present. Without state action, an equal protection argument under the U.S. Constitution is not applicable. This factor has significant ramifications in cases in which the athletic activity is conducted outside the auspices of a state or municipal entity or a public educational institution. Examples include youth sport leagues such as Little League Baseball, Pop Warner Football, and the YMCA's youth basketball association.

The second factor is whether the sport involves physical contact. In contact sports, the courts have allowed separate men's and women's teams. This "separate but equal" doctrine is based on considerations of the physical health and safety of the participants. For example, in the case of *Mercer v. Duke University*, the football team had no obligation under Title IX to allow Mercer to try out for the football team because football is classified as a contact sport (see note 1 in section 8.3.1). In non–Title IX cases, when separate teams do not exist, both genders may have to be given an opportunity to try out and to meet the necessary physical requirements on an individual basis. A complete ban on the participation of one gender will not be upheld if it is based on generalizations about characteristics of an entire gender rather than on a reasonable consideration of individual characteristics.

The third factor to be considered is whether both genders have equal opportunities to participate. This "equal opportunity" usually requires the existence of completely separate teams or an opportunity to try out for the one available team. If there are separate teams, however, it is permissible for the governing organization to prohibit coed participation. Unlike classifications based on race, when gender is a determining factor, "separate but equal" doctrines may be acceptable.

The issue then often becomes whether the teams are indeed equal (see *O'Connor v. Board of Education of School District No. 23* in section 8.3.3). Other factors that have been taken into consideration are the age of the participant and the level of the competition. Physical differences between boys and girls below the age of 12 are minimal. Therefore health and safety considerations that might be applicable to older athletes have not constituted legitimate reasons for restricting young athletes' access to participation.

The legal analysis of any particular case also depends on the philosophy of the court and the particular factual circumstances presented (see *Alston v. Virginia High School League, Inc.* in section 8.3.5). Some courts are reluctant to intervene in discretionary decisions made by an association governing athletic events unless there are obvious abuses (see section 5.2.2, "Judicial Review"). Other courts have been reluctant to intervene in discretionary decisions because they do not believe they have the administrative knowledge or time necessary to oversee the administration of sports programs effectively.

Historically, challenging sex discrimination based on equal protection laws has been generally ineffective. Under the intermediate test used for gender classification, the defendant must show an important state interest for the rule in question (see notes 1 and 4). One disadvantage of the equal protection laws is that they constitute a private remedy. Therefore the plaintiff must be in a position to absorb the costs of litigation. This reduces the number of complaints filed and encourages settlement before judicial resolution of a number of equal protection claims. Previously it had been held that Title IX's implied private remedy was sufficiently comprehensive that a plaintiff could not also bring a constitutional equal protection claim at the same time. However, in *Fitzergald v. Barnstable*, 129 S.Ct. 788 (2009), the Supreme Court unanimously reversed this consensus, holding that Title IX does not preclude an action alleging unconstitutional gender discrimination in schools.

NOTES

1. In 1996, Congress passed the Equity in Athletics Disclosure Act (EADA), 20 U.S.C. § 1092 (1996), that stipulated that schools receiving federal financial assistance report annually to the Department of Education regarding athletics participation, staffing numbers, and revenues and expenses, separated by sex.

2. In *Adams v. Baker*, 919 F.Supp. 1496 (D. Kan. 1996), a 15-year-old female plaintiff sought a preliminary injunction, alleging that the school district violated her equal protection rights. Plaintiff was not allowed on the school's wrestling team. The court concluded that the school district's purposes in not allowing plaintiff on the wrestling team were either not "important governmental objectives" or "not substantially related" to its objectives. The court granted the preliminary injunction (see note 3 in section 8.3.1.1 for a discussion of the Title IX claim in this case).

3. In *Blair v. Washington State University*, 740 P.2d 1379 (Wash. 1987), female athletes and the coaches of female athletes brought a gender discrimination action under the state Equal Rights Amendment. The trial court ruled for plaintiffs and awarded damages, injunctive relief, attorney fees, and costs. On appeal, the Washington Supreme Court affirmed the lower court's conclusion of gender discrimination but modified the lower court's calculations on comparative scholarships between male and female athletes and attorney fees.

4. In *Ridgefield Women's Political Caucus, Inc. v. Fossi*, 458 F.Supp. 117 (D. Conn. 1978), girls and taxpayer parents brought claims against town selectmen, seeking to prohibit the town from offering public property at a nominal price to a private organization that restricted membership to boys. The district court found for the girls' parents, ruling that the town selectmen had no right to offer land at less than fair value to the private organization in question as long as this organization restricted membership and the town failed to offer girls recreational opportunities equivalent to those provided by the organization in question. Until such services were offered, any conveyance of the property at a nominal fee would constitute governmental support of gender discrimination in violation of the equal protection clause of the 14th Amendment.

5. In *Richards v. United States Tennis Ass'n*, 400 N.Y.S.2d 267 (N.Y. Sup. Ct. 1977), an action was brought by a professional tennis player who had undergone a sex-change operation against a professional tennis association that sought a preliminary injunction against the organization to prevent it from requiring the tennis player to undergo a sexchromatintest to prove she was a female and eligible to participate in a women's tournament. The court granted the injunction and held that the test was grossly unfair, discriminatory, and inequitable, and violated the tennis player's rights under the New York Human Rights Law.

6. In *Frontiero v. Richardson*, 411 U.S. 677 (1973), the Supreme Court applied strict scrutiny to strike down a rule requiring female, but not male, service members to prove spousal dependency in order to receive increased military allowance. Although this is not a case that involves sports, it is nevertheless an important case because it shows that a court has the power to use the standard of strict scrutiny in evaluating claims of equal protection violations. Despite the fact that all of the judges did not agree on the classification of gender as a suspect class, the majority opinion stated, "(1) statutory classifications based upon sex were inherently suspect and thus must be subjected to close judicial scrutiny, and (2) under such standard of judicial scrutiny, the challenged statutes were unconstitutional as constituting an invidious discrimination against servicewomen in violation of the due process clause of the Fifth Amendment, the sole purpose advanced for the statutory discrimination being mere administrative convenience."

8.2. LEGAL CHALLENGES TO TITLE IX

8.2.1. Legality and Scope of Title IX

The Title IX regulations and accompanying policy interpretations were promulgated by the Department of Health, Education, and Welfare (HEW) and were not finalized until July 1979, after the adoption of regulations and policy interpretations. The NCAA brought the first legal challenge to Title IX. The NCAA sought declaratory and injunctive relief for the invalidation of the Title IX regulations promulgated by the HEW in *NCAA v. Califano*, 444 F.Supp. 425 (D. Kan. 1978), *rev'd.*, 622 F.2d 1382 (10th Cir. 1980). The NCAA specifically sought relief for the invalidation of the Title IX regulations promulgated by HEW with respect to gender discrimination in athletics. Summary judgment was granted to HEW, the district court holding that the NCAA did not have standing as an association representing its member schools to pursue the suit. The NCAA appealed the district court decision. The appeals court reversed the lower court ruling and held that while the NCAA does not have standing to sue in its own right, it does have standing to sue on behalf of its members (see section 5.2.3, "Standing").

After the enactment of Title IX in 1972, a major point of contention had been whether the legislation applied only to the specific departments that received direct funding (commonly referred to as the "programmatic approach") or to the entire institution (referred to as the "institutional approach"). This dilemma had often been expressed in a debate as to whether Title IX was or was not program specific.

An integral factor in the resultant litigation had been the determination of what constituted federal financial assistance. In some cases, it had been argued that federal student loan programs constitute federal aid to an institution, while other interpretations defined federal aid as only those funds specifically earmarked or directly given to a particular program. Therefore, in terms of the scope of Title IX, the questions became very complex: what constituted federal aid? Was indirect aid or direct aid required by the statute? Once federal assistance was found, was only the particular program that benefited from the aid or the entire institution subject to Title IX regulation?

Judgments in many of the cases shortly after the enactment of Title IX had been contradictory on the issue of what constituted federal financial assistance. In *Othen v. Ann Arbor School Board*, *Bennett v. West Texas State University*, and *Hillsdale College v. Department of Health, Education, and Welfare*, the courts took a programmatic approach (see notes 6, 7, and 10). However, in the case of *Haffer v. Temple University*, the court took an institutional approach. The court found that the Temple athletic program should be subject to Title IX regulations even if it does not directly receive any federal funding for the athletic program. In the subsequent notes, the settlement of this case is outlined in great detail. The wording of the settlement, and its recommendations, mirror the wording in the OCR interpretation of Title IX (see notes 8 and 9).

However, the most important case decided during this era was *Grove City College v. Bell* (see note 4). Finally, the issue of "programmatic" versus "institutional" was decided by the Supreme Court in favor of the "programmatic approach." The Supreme Court determined that the language of Title IX should apply only to specific programs that receive direct federal financial assistance.

Until the passage of the Civil Rights Restoration Act of 1987, the *Grove City* case was the standard for judgment on Title IX. The next section will discuss how the Civil Rights Restoration Act of 1987 reversed the effect of *Grove City*.

NOTES

1. In *Roe ex rel. Callahan v. Gustine Unified School District*, 678 F.Supp.2d 1008 (E.D. Cal. 2009) a student, who attended football camp jointly coordinated by two high schools, brought an action against the school districts, high school football coaches, and numerous

other students and their parents for claims arising out of alleged student-on-student harassment which occurred at camp. In granting summary judgment for the school district, the court ruled that in order for a funding recipient to be subject to Title IX liability for sexual harassment, an official who at a minimum has authority to address the alleged discrimination and to institute corrective measures on the recipient's behalf must have actual knowledge of discrimination.

2. In *Bukowski v. Wisconsin Interscholastic Athletic Association (WIAA)*, 726 N.W.2d 356 (Wis. App. 2006), a male public high school student requested an injunction after the WIAA would not allow him to participate on the girls' gymnastics team. Bukowski contended that the WIAA rule violated the equal protection clause of the 14th Amendment and Title IX. In affirming the decision, the Court of Appeals of Wisconsin held that because the WIAA is not a state actor and does not receive federal funds, it is not subject to an equal protection or Title IX claim.

3. In *Smith v. National Collegiate Athletic Ass'n*, 266 F.3d 152 (3rd Cir. 2001), a female volleyball player claimed that by prohibiting her from participating in athletics while enrolled at a graduate school different from her undergraduate institution, the NCAA violated Title IX. On remand from the Supreme Court of the United States, the Third Circuit held that the NCAA is not subject to Title IX, because it does not exercise controlling authority over federally funded member institutions. However, if it could be proven that the NCAA indirectly received federal financial assistance from other programs, the NCAA would be subject to Title IX. The Supreme Court also ruled that the NCAA's receipt of dues from member institutions did not constitute federal assistance.

4. In *Johnny's Icehouse, Inc. v. Amateur Hockey Ass'n of Illinois, Inc.*, 134 F.Supp.2d 965 (N.D.Ill. 2001), a youth girls hockey team alleged that the Amateur Hockey Association of Illinois, amongst other complaints, violated Title IX for refusing to admit Johnny's 15 and Under team as a top tier team. The court granted summary judgment because the AHAI does not receive federal funding.

5. In *Grove City College v. Bell*, 465 U.S. 555 (1984), a private, liberal arts college refused to execute an "assurance of compliance" with Title IX. The Department of Education initiated proceedings to declare the college and its students ineligible to receive basic educational opportunity grants (BEOGs), and the college and four of its students filed suit after an administrative law judge ordered federal financial assistance terminated until Grove City met the requirements of Title IX. The U.S. Supreme Court ruled that the language of Title IX made it program-specific and that only those programs directly receiving federal funds were subject to the regulations of Title IX. This ruling applied to schools that participate in the BEOG program. Otherwise, one student receiving federal aid would trigger Title IX coverage of the entire institution, and this does not square with the program-specific language of the legislation.

6. In *Cannon v. University of Chicago*, 460 U.S. 1013 (1983), the Supreme Court held that Title IX granted an implied private right of action to individuals harmed by sex discrimination in federally funded educational institutions. Supporters of Title IX celebrated *Cannon* for providing victims of sex discrimination with the means to enforce their rights in the courtroom and for bolstering the efforts of overburdened administrative agencies. Following the Court's recognition of a private right of action in *Cannon*, another debate regarding the scope of Title IX's protections arose in the federal courts. Because of the sparse legislative history of Title IX, a question had existed since its enactment regarding whether Title IX compliance was specifically levied against individual programs within the institution that received federal funds or against the institution as a whole.

7. In *Othen v. Ann Arbor School Board*, 507 F.Supp. 1376 (E.D. Mich. 1981), aff'd., 699 F.2d 309 (6th Cir. 1983), a complaint was filed on behalf of female student-athletes, charging the Ann Arbor school board and its golf coach with gender discrimination in violation of Title IX. The father of the girls sought a temporary restraining order immediately restoring his daughters to the 1979 golf team and prohibiting discrimination "against women who want to play on the Pioneer golf team." The district court denied the motion for an injunction and found the father/daughters had failed to demonstrate a likelihood

of success on the merits. The school board responded to the amended complaint with a motion for summary judgment, stating that none of the athletic programs at Pioneer received federal financial assistance and therefore were not covered by the provisions of Title IX. The district court found the athletic programs at Pioneer received no direct federal assistance, and the indirect federal assistance from "impact aid" was "de minimus." The court's finding that "the clear language of Title IX and the intent of Congress require that the Act [Title IX] be applied programmatically" had important ramifications in the case. Since it was determined that the athletic programs and activities under the jurisdiction of the Ann Arbor School Board received no direct federal financial assistance, the school board was not obligated under the law to establish a golf team for girls. Therefore the daughters were not excluded from participation, denied, or discriminated against in violation of Title IX.

8. In *Hillsdale College v. Department of Health, Education and Welfare*, 696 F.2d 418 (6th Cir. 1982), HEW issued an order disqualifying students from participation in federal aid programs in response to the refusal of Hillsdale's officials to sign an "assurance of compliance" with Title IX. Hillsdale appealed the HEW order. The court reversed and held for Hillsdale, reasoning that because Congress failed to adopt proposals that would have prohibited all discriminatory practices by an institution that receives federal funds, it was clear that, as enacted, Title IX adopts a "programmatic as opposed to institutional approach to discrimination on the basis of sex in education." Even though the court found that Hillsdale was subject to Title IX regulations in those programs receiving federal financial assistance, the court believed that while HEW had been given the authority to promulgate regulations for Title IX enforcement, in this case the order imposed was in excess of statutory authority in that it would subject the entire college, rather than any one program, to the strictures of Title IX.

9. In *Haffer v. Temple University*, 524 F.Supp. 531 (E.D. Pa. 1981), *aff'd.*, 688 F.2d 14 (3d Cir. 1982), the defendant appealed the district court decision denying summary judgment to Temple University finding that Temple's athletic department was not exempt from Title IX regulation. Eight women undergraduates had filed a class action suit charging Temple University with gender discrimination in its intercollegiate athletic program in violation of Title IX. Temple had requested summary judgment, arguing that Title IX applied only to those educational programs or activities which received direct federal funding, and that the athletic department at Temple had received no such assistance. Temple appealed, questioning whether the court's inclusion of the athletic program under Title IX jurisdiction was consistent with the wording of the statute, which required that the education program or activity receive "federal financial assistance" as a prerequisite for its inclusion in the realm of Title IX authority. The appeals court affirmed the lower court's opinion and rejected the "program-specific" interpretation put forth by Temple, claiming that the entire institution should be considered the "program." In referring to *Grove City College* (appellate court decision), the court suggested, "The legislators [who enacted Title IX] did not contemplate that separate, discrete and distinct components or functions of an integrated educational institution would be regarded as the individual program to which section 901 . . . refer[s]." The court added that "if Temple University as a whole is to be considered the program or activity" for Title IX purposes, it follows that because the university as a whole receives federal monies, Title IX governs its intercollegiate athletic department. The court held that the district court's theory that federal monies received by the institution benefited the athletic program because it freed other university money for athletic program-related purposes was consistent with its finding that Title IX was applicable.

10. In *Haffer v. Temple University*, Consent Decree, Rollin Haffer et al. filed this lawsuit against Temple University, complaining that Temple violated the equal protection clause of the 14th Amendment of the U.S. Constitution, the Pennsylvania Equal Rights Amendment, and Title IX of the Education Amendments of 1972 by discriminating against women student-athletes and potential student-athletes at Temple on the basis of gender in the provision of opportunities to participate in intercollegiate athletics, athletic

financial aid, and athletic resources. While denying allegations, Temple entered into a consent decree dated June 9, 1988, settling the case. The parties agreed to the following conditions:

i. An increase in opportunities for women to participate in intercollegiate athletics that are comparable to the opportunities provided its men students.

   1. Temple will provide sufficient resources for its women's intercollegiate athletic crew team.

   2. Temple will establish a women's intercollegiate athletic swimming team.

   3. With respect to Temple's intercollegiate athletic teams which were in place during the 1986–87 academic year (that is, not including women's crew and swimming), certain other guidelines were established to deal with:

     a. Increases or decreases in participation.

     b. Discontinuance of teams.

   4. Temple will maintain the overall percentage of women participating in intercollegiate athletics equal to the percentage of men participating if a men's team is added.

   5. [T]o determine the percentage of women and men participating in the overall intercollegiate athletic program, women and men student-athletes who participate on more than one team will be counted separately for each team on which they participate.

ii. Temple will provide to its women student-athletes a percentage of athletic financial aid that, in the aggregate and averaged over three years, will not be less than two percentage points below the participate rate of women student-athletes in the overall intercollegiate athletic program, also averaged over those same three years, with certain other provisions.

iii. The percentage of money that Temple will spend on its women's intercollegiate athletic teams each year, in the aggregate, will be within 10 percentage points of the participation rate of women student-athletes in the overall intercollegiate athletic program in that year, provided that expenditures on home game events, coaches' salaries and benefits, and post season competition will be excluded from the aggregate percentage requirement (these will be treated under specific guidelines agreed to by the two parties).

iv. Temple will hire an additional full-time weight-training coach by February 1, 1989. Temple will provide to its women student-athletes weight-training coaching, facilities, and equipment comparable to the weight-training coaching, facilities, and equipment that it provides to its men student-athletes, consistent with the needs of each sport.

v. Temple will hire a full-time employee to promote Temple's women's intercollegiate athletics by February 1, 1989.

vi. Temple continues to recognize that its women student-athletes are entitled to treatment that is comparable to the treatment provided to its men student-athletes in the remaining aspects of the intercollegiate athletic program beyond those addressed in paragraphs 1 through 5 of this Consent Decree.

   1. Subject to the steps set forth in subparagraph B below, Temple will continue to provide treatment to its women student-athletes that is comparable to the treatment it provides to its men student-athletes in the following areas:

     a. Athletic administration, including the assignment of support staff.

     b. Locker rooms and practice, competitive, and other facilities.

     c. Athletic medicine, including medical and training services and facilities.

     d. Uniform and equipment managers and other uniform and equipment-related support, including laundry.

    e. Academic advising, including the provision of tutors to accompany teams on trips when both the academic advisor and head coach determine that it is necessary.

    f. Awards and honors.

    g. Practice and competitive schedule.

    h. Sports information.

    i. Fund-raising.

    j. Cheerleaders, band(s), and mascot(s).

2. Temple will:

    a. By November 1, 1988, carpet the women's locker room at Temple Stadium.

    b. Rearrange the awards in the intercollegiate athletic award display cases so that the women's awards are exhibited in a manner comparable to that of men's awards. By October 1, 1989, and by October 1 of each year thereafter, Temple will file with the Court and serve on plaintiff's counsel reports setting forth Temple's compliance with the terms of this Consent Decree for the immediately preceding academic year [these reports have extensive requirements which are outlined in detail in the Consent Decree].

    11. In *Yellow Springs Exempted Village School District v. Ohio High School Athletic Ass'n*, 443 F.Supp. 753 (S.D. Ohio 1978), *aff'd.*, 647 F.2d 651 (6th Cir. 1981), a suit was brought against the Ohio High School Athletic Association (OHSAA) and the Ohio Board of Education challenging the association's rule excluding girls from participation in contact sports. In 1974, two female students competed for and earned positions on the Morgan Middle School's interscholastic basketball team. The board excluded them from the team and then created a separate girls' basketball team. The district court held that the "Association's exclusionary rule deprives school girls of liberty without due process of law. Freedom of personal choice in matters of 'education and acquisition of knowledge' is a liberty interest protected by the due process clause of the Fourteenth Amendment." The appeals court upheld portions of the district court's decision and ruled that Title IX focuses on "recipients" of federal aid. Even though OHSAA was not itself a recipient of federal aid, it may not adopt a rule that limits the abilities of recipient schools to furnish equal athletic opportunities for girls and boys.

8.2.2. Post–Civil Rights Restoration Act Litigation

The passage of the Civil Rights Restoration Act in 1987 restored Title IX's applicability to athletic programs across the country. In March 1988, the U.S. Congress acted to clarify this issue when it voted to override President Ronald Reagan's veto of the Civil Rights Restoration Act of 1987 (see note 1). Enactment of this legislation served "to restore the broad scope of coverage and clarify the application of Title IX of the Education Amendments of 1972." Thus Congress returned Title IX applicability to the "institutional approach"; accordingly, athletic departments within institutions benefiting from federal assistance are subject to the Title IX strictures. Passage of the Civil Rights Restoration Act counteracted the effects of the Supreme Court's decision in *Grove City College* (see note 4 in section 8.2.1, "Legality and Scope of Title IX"). Therefore most colleges, both public and private, were subject to Title IX.

The passage of the Civil Rights Restoration Act also restored strength to the administrative enforcement of Title IX. The ability of the Office of Civil Rights (OCR) to effectively investigate possible Title IX violations by institutions has always been contingent upon the prevailing judicial sentiments and legislative enactments regarding Title IX at a particular time. While Title IX does not require the creation of athletic programs or the same sport offerings for both genders—for example, a football program for women or a volleyball program for men—it does require equality of opportunity in accommodation of interests and abilities, in athletic scholarships, and in other benefits and opportunities.

Another reason for the increased strength of Title IX occurred in 1992, with the decision in *Franklin v. Gwinnett County Public Schools* (see note 10). The court's decision in *Gwinnett* stated that monetary damages were a valid remedy for violations of Title IX. Now, an added incentive was available for athletes and attorneys to bring claims of Title IX violations: money. A large increase of Title IX cases was seen because student-athletes were able to pay for private attorneys, without relying upon the Office for Civil Rights or worrying about burdensome legal bills. This trend has continued, with private attorneys undertaking Title IX cases and reducing the number of cases brought by OCR.

As mentioned, there are three areas of Title IX compliance that institutions must meet: financial assistance, athletic benefits and opportunities, and effective accommodation of athletic interests and abilities. However, cases subsequent to the passage of the Civil Rights Restoration Act have focused most on the analysis of the accommodation of interests and abilities. This type of analysis is evident in *Cohen v. Brown University*, 101 F.3d 155 (1st Cir. 1993), *cert. denied*, 520 U.S. 1186 (1997); *Favia v. Indiana University of Pennsylvania*, 7 F.3d 332 (3d Cir. 1993) (see note 9); *Roberts v. Colorado State University*, 814 F.Supp. 1507 (D. Colo. 1993) (see note 8); and *Cook v. Colgate University*, 992 F.2d 17 (2d Cir. 1992) (see section 8.3.6, "Varsity Sport versus Club Sport").

In the *Cohen v. Brown University* leading case, plaintiff female student-athletes brought a Title IX complaint against the university after women's gymnastics and women's volleyball, along with men's golf and men's water polo, were dropped to club status in the spring of 1991 because of financial difficulties the university was experiencing. The plaintiffs claimed that Brown violated the "equal opportunity" provision for participation under Title IX and that the interests and abilities of the female student-athletes were not being effectively accommodated. The district court, 809 F.Supp. 978 (D.R.I. 1992), granted a preliminary in junction against Brown University, ordering the immediate restoration of the women's gymnastics and women's volleyball teams to their former status as fully funded intercollegiate varsity teams. The First Circuit Court of Appeals upheld the district court's preliminary injunction, stating that the ordering of Brown University to return the two women's sport programs to varsity status was a fair and lawful solution. Both courts applied a three-part test in determining the accommodation of interests and abilities issue:

1. Whether intercollegiate level participation opportunities for male and female students are provided in numbers substantially proportionate to their respective enrollments

2. Where the members of one gender have been, and are, underrepresented among intercollegiate athletes, whether the institution can show a history and continuing practice of program expansion that is demonstrably responsive to the developing interests and abilities of the members of that gender

3. Where the members of one gender are underrepresented among intercollegiate athletes, and the institution cannot show a continuing practice of program

expansion such as that cited, whether it can be demonstrated that the interests
and abilities of the members of that gender have been fully and effectively accommodated by the present program

The plaintiffs argued that Brown University did not meet any of these requirements because the female athlete proportion stood at 39%, compared to an undergraduate female enrollment of 48% to 49%, and no women's varsity sport had been
added since 1982. The university failed to meet the third part of the three-part
test because it had refused to elevate the women's fencing team to varsity status,
showing that the underrepresented sex had not been fully accommodated. Brown
University argued that the plaintiffs were not interpreting Title IX legislation accurately. Brown asserted that Title IX provisions explicitly recognize that equal
opportunity does not require proportionality, and that the interests and abilities
of the students, not the relative proportion of the genders, determine what participation opportunities must be offered to each gender. Brown argued that the
60% male to 40% female athletic participation ratio was merely a reflection of
the interests and abilities of the student body. Therefore Brown was effectively
accommodating the interests and abilities of the students through the participation opportunities it was providing. Brown University also argued that if Title IX
required full and effective accommodation of the underrepresented gender, then
this requirement would violate the Fifth Amendment's equal protection clause by
putting male athletes at a disadvantage.

The district court and court of appeals, in addressing both the plaintiff's and
the defendant's arguments, found that with the demotion of the four sports, two
women's teams and two men's teams, from varsity to club status, the percentage
of male and female athletes did not change. Thus women athletes at Brown still
constituted 39% of the total number of student-athletes. The courts went on to
say that this was not an example of effectively accommodating the interests and
abilities of the underrepresented gender because there were women interested
in competing and participating in additional activities, as the interest and talent
at Brown in women's gymnastics and volleyball teams demonstrated. This critical ruling by the court set a standard for women in that full accommodation of
the interests and abilities of the underrepresented gender must be met, and that
Brown's argument regarding its 60/40 participation proportion being appropriate will not hold when analyzing Title IX compliance. In addition, keeping the
percentage of female athletes at 39% does not effectively accommodate the equitable proportion of athletic opportunities available to each gender as required
by Title IX. Brown did not meet the full accommodation test, and therefore a
violation of Title IX was occurring. The court of appeals discussed the Fifth
Amendment argument and ruled that Brown supplied no evidence that showed
men were more likely to engage in athletics than women. In addition, the court
stated that in view of congressional and administrative urging that women, if
given the opportunity, will naturally participate in athletics in numbers equal
to those of men, the court did not find that the regulation offended the Fifth
Amendment.

The court of appeals upheld the district court's granting of a preliminary injunction, which ordered Brown University to restore the women's gymnastics
and women's volleyball teams to their previous varsity status. These rulings were
based on an analysis of one part of the three areas that Title IX policy interpretations state should be used when investigating Title IX compliance—effectively

accommodating the interests and abilities of the underrepresented gender. Other Title IX cases and court decisions have also used the analysis of the interests and abilities component to rule on Title IX compliance cases (see notes 2 and 3). The OCR has never established an acceptable percentage difference with regards to participation proportions. In examining the second prong of the accommodation test, the OCR focuses on records of adding intercollegiate teams by sex, records of upgrading teams to intercollegiate status by sex, records of increasing the number of participants of the underrepresented sex, and affirmative responses to requests by students or others to add or elevate sports. To determine whether an institution has a continuing practice of accommodation, the OCR considers whether there is a current implementation of a policy or procedure for requesting the addition of sports that includes the elevation of club or intramural teams, effective communication of that policy or procedure to students, the current implementation of a plan or program expansion that is responsive to developing interests and abilities of the underrepresented sex, and whether the institution has demonstrated efforts to monitor developing interests and abilities.

In the leading case of *Boucher v. Syracuse University* (see note 6), the university was able to find a safe harbor under Title IX by employing the defense that it had shown "a continuing practice of program expansion such as that cited, whether it can be demonstrated that the interests and abilities of the members of that gender have been fully and effectively accommodated by the present program." The university had plans to add three women's sports to varsity status in the near future, and therefore the court decided that although the women's needs were not being currently met, this plan would bring Syracuse under Title IX compliance. As of 2002, Syracuse is the only university that has been able to successfully defend against a Title IX claim in court by arguing that the program had shown a history of expansion for women.

In the case of *Pederson v. Louisiana State University* (see note 4), plaintiff female athletes at Louisiana State University (LSU) charged that they had not been offered equitable sports opportunities at the university. The Fifth Circuit court ruled against LSU, rejecting LSU's argument that women are less interested in participating in sports than men. The court went on to reprimand LSU for taking such a position, stating that "advancing this argument is remarkable, since of course fewer women participate in sports, given the voluminous evidence that LSU has discriminated against women in refusing to offer them comparable athletic opportunities to those it offers its male students." Courts have shown an unwillingness to accept the argument that women are less interested in sports than men are and therefore do not merit equal opportunity and funding. The parties in *Pederson* settled for $1.2 million in 2001.

To determine whether there is sufficient interest to sustain a varsity team, the OCR released an Additional Clarification in 2005 that said institution could not rely on a Web-based model survey supplied by the OCR. Schools may not use such a survey to eliminate a team but may use them to justify not starting a team. The Clarification allows the schools to count nonresponses by students as a lack of interest. In addition, the Clarification states that there is no minimum response level for the survey to be considered valid. In *Barrett v. West Chester*, 2003 WL 22803477 (E.D. Pa. November 12, 2003), the court ruled a survey was invalid because only 39% of students responded rather than the 60% recommended by the NCAA. The NCAA sent a resolution to the Department of Education disagreeing with the Clarification. The NCAA believed that the Clarification conflicts with a

1996 Clarification, does not support the general purpose of Title IX, fails to measure interest broadly, authorizes flawed survey methodology, shifts the burden to the female students to show there is interest, and fails to provide any way to monitor schools' implementation of the survey or the results.

As was mentioned in the introduction to this chapter, Title IX is not without its detractors in interscholastic and intercollegiate athletics. Athletic departments, traditionally male dominated, have been compelled to add opportunities for women in athletics, usually without increased budgets. This has led to tough financial decisions in most intercollegiate athletic departments and a real challenge to maintain scholarship levels for male athletes. In fact, many male athletes have felt that they have been discriminated against in the name of gender equity.

Many athletic departments have been forced to cut the number of scholarships that they offer to male athletes, cap rosters, and/or the number of men's varsity sports that are offered to ensure compliance with the OCR and Title IX. For more information on cases and articles concerning male backlash against Title IX and reverse discrimination, see note 4 in the introduction to this chapter.

NOTES

1. The following is language from the Civil Rights Restoration Act of 1987, which restores the impact of Title IX on athletic departments:

PUBLIC LAW 100–259-Mar. 22, 1988

Public Law 100–259 100th Congress

An Act To restore the broad scope of coverage and to clarify the application of title IX of the Education Amendments of 1972, section 504 of the Rehabilitation Act of 1973, the Age Discrimination Act of 1975, and title VI of the Civil Rights Act of 1964. Be it enacted by the Senate and House of Representatives of the United States of America in Congress assembled,

SHORT TITLE

SECTION 1. This Act may be cited as the "Civil Rights Act of 1987."

SEC. 2. The Congress finds that—

(1) certain aspects of recent decisions and opinions of the Supreme Court have unduly narrowed or cast doubt upon the broad application of title IX of the Education Amendments of 1972, section 504 of the Rehabilitation Act of 1973, the Age Discrimination Act of 1975, and title VI of the Civil Rights Act of 1964; and

(2) legislative action is necessary to restore the prior consistent and long-standing executive branch interpretation and broad, institution-wide application of those laws as previously administered.

EDUCATION AMENDMENTS

SEC. 3. (a) Title IX of the Education Amendments of 1972 is amended by adding at the end the following new sections:

"INTERPRETATION OF 'PROGRAM OR ACTIVITY'"

"SEC. 908. For the purposes of this title, the term 'program or activity' and 'program' mean all of the operations of—

"(1) (A) a department, agency, special purpose district, or other instrumentality of a State or of a local government; or

"(B) the entity of such State or local government that distributes such assistance and each such department or agency (and each other State or local government entity) to which the assistance is extended, in the case of assistance to a State or local government;

"(2) (A) a college, university, or other post-secondary institution, or a public system of higher education; or

"(B) a local educational agency (as defined in section 198(a)(10)) of the Elementary and Secondary Education Act of 1965), system of vocational education, or other school system;

"(3) (A) an entire corporation, partnership, or other private organization, or an entire sole proprietorship—

"(i) if assistance is extended to such corporation, partnership, private organization, or sole proprietorship as a whole; or

"(ii) which is principally engaged in the business of providing education, health care, housing, social services, or parks and recreation; or

"(B) the entire plant or other comparable, geographically separate facility to which Federal financial assistance is extended, in the case of any other corporation, partnership, private organization, or sole proprietorship; or

"(4) any other entity which is established by two or more of the entities described in paragraph (1), (2), or (3); any part of which is extended Federal financial assistance, except that such term does not include any operation of an entity which is controlled by a religious organization if the application of section 901 to such operation would not be consistent with the religious tenets of such organization."

2. In *Choike v. Slippery Rock University of Pennsylvania of State System of Higher Educ.*, 2006 WL 2060576 (W.D. Pa. July 21, 2006), Slippery Rock announced it would eliminate eight sports, men's and women's swimming, men's and women's water polo, women's field hockey, men's golf, men's wrestling, and men's tennis for budgetary reasons. Twelve female student-athletes requested a preliminary injunction claiming that Slippery Rock had violated Title IX's equal participation requirement and that it had failed to treat female athletes substantially equal. In 2000, a firm retained by Slippery Rock determined that it was noncompliant with Title IX in all respects and recommended Slippery Rock offer another women's sport. Slippery Rock refused the advice. In determining what teams to cut, the President of Slippery Rock used a system that was determined to be facially discriminatory by requiring women's teams to have a higher GPA than men's teams to be graded exceptional in his system. To become compliant with Title IX's participation proportionality requirements, Slippery Rock announced plans to use roster limits. The court determined that the proposed limits were artificially meant to be based on the amount of male participants and subsequently enjoined the elimination of the women's swimming and water polo teams.

3. In *Miller v. University of Cincinnati*, 2008 WL 203025 (S.D. Ohio 2008), the court granted the University of Cincinnati's motion for summary judgment after members of the women's rowing team claimed the school violated Title IX and the 14th Amendment by failing to provide adequate facilities, equipment, coaching, or scholarship opportunities and then deciding to eliminate the program in favor of a women's lacrosse team. Using the three-prong compliance test, the court ruled that Cincinnati was in compliance, citing the fact that the duplicated number of intercollegiate athletic participants was 51.1% male and 48.9% female, while only 47.5% of the undergraduate student population was female.

4. In *Pederson v. Louisiana State University*, 213 F.3d 858 (5th Cir. 2000), female student-athletes sued Louisiana State University (LSU) for Title IX violations, alleging that LSU denied them equal opportunity to participate in intercollegiate athletics, LSU denied them the opportunity to compete for athletic scholarships, and LSU denied them equal access to benefits and services. Females made up only 29% of LSU's student-athletes but made up 49% of the student population. The court ruled that LSU did not have a history of expanding women's athletic programs and did not accommodate the interests and abilities of females. In addition, the court stated, "If an institution makes a decision not to provide equal athletic opportunities for its female students because of paternalism and stereotypical assumptions about their interests and abilities, that institution intended to treat women differently because of their sex." Therefore the discrimination was intentional. This determination that the discrimination was intentional opened the door for monetary damages. The parties settled for $1.2 million in damages in 2001.

5. In *Horner v. Kentucky High School Athletic Ass'n*, 206 F.3d 685 (6th Cir. 2000), a group of female student-athletes sued the Kentucky High School Athletic Association for

its failure to sanction fast-pitch softball, claiming that it was a violation of Title IX. Plaintiff failed to establish an intentional violation as necessary to obtain monetary damages for Title IX violations. The case was dismissed in favor of the defendants.

6. In *Boucher v. Syracuse University*, 164 F.3d 113 (2d Cir. 1999), a group of female students interested in competing in softball and lacrosse at the varsity level sued Syracuse University on Title IX grounds. Plaintiffs argued that Syracuse did not effectively accommodate the interests and abilities of its female students. Importantly, the court indicated that Syracuse *would* be able to take refuge in a Title IX "safe harbor"—that is, it had showed a plan that demonstrated the university's attempts to increase athletic opportunities for women over a period of time. Although Syracuse had not added a new women's varsity sport in 14 years at the time of the lawsuit, the university had installed a plan to add three new women's varsity sports in the near future. The court never reached the merits of the claim because Syracuse added women's lacrosse as a varsity sport after the commencement of the lawsuit and planned to introduce women's softball as a varsity sport. Therefore the court ruled that the issue was moot.

7. In *Kelley v. Board of Trustees University*, 35 F.3d 265 (7th Cir. 1994), members of the men's swimming team sued the university on Title IX and equal protection grounds after it eliminated the team along with three other varsity sports. The court held that termination of the men's program "was a reasonable response to the requirements of [Title IX]." Also, the court ruled that the university did not violate equal protection because gender equity was an important objective and eliminating the men's swimming team was substantially related to that objective. "Title IX's stated objective is not to ensure that the athletic opportunities available to women increase. Rather its avowed purpose is to prohibit educational institutions from discriminating on the basis of sex."

8. In *Roberts v. Colorado State University*, 814 F.Supp. 1507 (D. Colo. 1993), plaintiffs contended that a violation of Title IX occurred and/or had been occurring at Colorado State University after the women's softball team was terminated on June 1, 1992. The court used the same three-part "effective accommodation" test used in the *Brown* and *Favia* cases. The court stated that the plaintiffs had the burden of proving the first prong, that participation opportunities for male and female students are not proportionate to their respective enrollments. Once the plaintiffs established this lack of proportionality, then the defendants had the burden of proving either the second prong, that the institution could show a history and continuing practice of program expansion, or the third prong, that the institution can demonstrate that the interests and abilities of the underrepresented gender have been accommodated. After the termination of the women's softball team, women athletes made up approximately 38% of the athletes, while enrollment of women at Colorado State University was 48% of the undergraduate student population. The court found that the percentage of female athletes was not substantially proportionate to the undergraduate enrollment percentage of females and that the defendant could not show evidence of program expansion so that the interests and abilities of the female students were being effectively accommodated. The court, therefore, found a violation of Title IX and ordered Colorado State University to reinstate the women's softball team.

9. In *Favia v. Indiana University of Pennsylvania*, 7 F.3d 332 (3d. Cir. 1993), Indiana University of Pennsylvania (IUP) announced in August 1991 that the women's gymnastics and field hockey teams, along with the men's soccer and tennis teams, would be eliminated as a result of a reduction in the athletic department's budget. IUP had an undergraduate enrollment of 44% men compared to 56% women, while the athletic department comprised 62% men and 38% women. After the elimination of these four teams, the percentage of male and female athletes would not change. Women students brought a lawsuit arguing violation of Title IX and sought the reinstatement of the two women's teams. In ruling in favor of the plaintiffs, the court applied the three-part test contained in the policy interpretation: comparison of athletic participation opportunities for each gender proportionate to their respective enrollments; whether the institution can show a history and continuing practice of program expansion; and whether the interests and abilities of the members are met by

the present program. The court found that IUP had failed to override the proportionality requirement of the test by failing to show a history of expanding the number of athletic opportunities for women or demonstrating that it had fully and effectively accommodated the interests and abilities of women students. The court ordered the immediate restoration of the two women's teams to their former status, with university backing and funding equivalent to that furnished during their last year as a varsity team.

10. In *Franklin v. Gwinnett County Public Schools*, 503 U.S. 60 (1992), a female high school student sued her school district for the continued sexual harassment she suffered from a male teacher. Plaintiff claimed that the school district knew of the sexual harassment but did nothing, in violation of Title IX. The defendant claimed that Title IX does not authorize monetary damages as a remedy. The Supreme Court disagreed with the defendant, stating, "We conclude that a damages remedy is available for an action brought to enforce Title IX." The Supreme Court held, however, that damages are only available when the plaintiff in a Title IX claim can prove that the violation was intentional. There was no question in this case that the sexual harassment was an intentional violation.

8.3. GENDER DISCRIMINATION CASES INVOLVING INDIVIDUAL ATHLETES

The subsections and cases that follow are discussed in terms of the presence or absence of teams available to either gender. Within each category, the subsections and cases are further divided into those dealing with contact sports and those dealing with non-contact sports. This was done because the approach taken—and sometimes the results reached—by the courts differ due to more important factors.

The division of subsections and cases is not by legal theory since very often the litigant makes use of one, two, or even three prominent theories—for example, equal protection, Title IX, and state Equal Rights Amendments (in certain states). The courts view contact sports and noncontact sports differently. Thus, in cases involving gender discrimination in athletics, the arguments used will vary depending on whether or not the particular sport is designated a contact sport.

Under Title IX, contact sports include boxing, wrestling, rugby, ice hockey, football, basketball, and other sports in which the purpose or major activity involves bodily contact. In some jurisdictions, baseball and soccer have also been labeled contact sports.

In a sport designated as contact, certain arguments are commonly propounded. The most frequent argument raised by defendants is that women, as a group, lack the physical qualifications necessary for safe and reasonable competition against men in a sport in which bodily contact is expected to occur. It is argued that women are more susceptible to injury because they have a higher percentage of adipose (fatty) tissues and a lighter bone structure. Because of these differences, the argument goes, contact sports are dangerous for all women. Physiological differences between the genders have generally been found to be a valid reason for the exclusion of one sex from a contact sport.

Plaintiffs counter this argument by insisting that determinations of physical capability should be made on a case-by-case basis. When there is no other opportunity for participation in a certain sport, a blanket prohibition is over-inclusive and violates equal protection by assuming that all women have identical physical structures and that all men are stronger and more athletically capable than women. Indeed, the health and safety rationale behind such total exclusion may fail a court challenge, as has been demonstrated in some cases. In one case, a woman who was five feet, nine inches tall and weighed over 200 pounds was denied a chance to play football because her supposedly lighter bone structure would render her more susceptible to injury. There were, however, no height or weight requirements for men, and the court thus found exclusion from participation to be unacceptable.

Although the most important consideration used to substantiate separate teams for contact sports is the health and safety of the participants, this argument does not apply to noncontact sports. Since there is no legitimate and important state interest for allowing exclusion from noncontact sports, citing gender as the sole exclusionary factor would constitute a violation of the U.S. constitutional guarantees of the equal protection clause. Thus the arguments made by defendants in noncontact sports gender discrimination cases are different.

One argument is that if men and women are allowed to compete together and/ or against each other, the psychological development of both would be impaired. This stance is generally based on a variation of the "tradition" argument, which says that allowing men and women to compete as equals will irreparably disturb the innate nature of relationships between the genders.

Another argument is that if men and women are allowed to compete together, men will dominate the coed teams. The underlying rationale here is that since men are inherently stronger and more physically capable than women, coed teams will actually limit opportunities for women. Plaintiffs argue that a justification of this sort does not take into account individual differences among participants. It also does not recognize the argument that if women are given opportunities to compete against men from the beginning of their athletic careers, their capabilities will improve and men may not be able to totally dominate the athletic field.

8.3.1. Men's Team, No Women's Team

The general rule in both contact and noncontact sports is that when only a men's team is available, both genders must be allowed to try out for and play on that team. In contact sports under Title IX, females do not have to be allowed to try out for male teams. However, if the institution does not allow a woman or girl to try out, it must then conduct the tryouts in a nondiscriminatory manner (see note 1). In ERA and equal protection cases, courts are split on the issue of allowing females to participate on male teams in contact sports when there are no teams in the same sport. Determination as to the student-athlete's capability and risk of injury should be made on an individual basis, with the recognition that the contact or noncontact sports designation makes a difference only if there is opportunity for athletes of both genders to compete. If there is ample opportunity for women to compete on their own, courts appear to be less apt to allow women to compete with men in contact sports.

8.3.1.1. Contact Sports

In cases where contact sports are involved and there is no women's team, there is a split in decisions as to whether to allow a female to play on the men's team. In some cases, as represented by *Lantz v. Ambach*, 620 F. Supp. 663 (S.D.N.Y. 1985), and *Saint v. U. Nebraska School Activities Ass'n*, 684 F. Supp. 626 (D. Neb. 1988) (see notes 5 and 6), the courts have upheld the plaintiff's gender discrimination claim and have allowed participation on the men's team.

In other cases, the plaintiff female has been unsuccessful because she has not been able to prove that she has a right to participation (see note 2) or that her arguments fall under the auspices of Title IX (see note 4). While most recent court cases have generally held that women do not possess a right to participate on all-male teams, in *Mercer v. Duke University*, 190 F.3d 643 (4th Cir. 1999), the federal appellate court ruled that Duke had the right to prevent a female from trying out for an all-male contact sport. However, once Duke allowed a female to try out for the team, she had to be afforded the same treatment as all other players (see note 1).

Owing to various factors, including the evolution of women's sport opportunities, an increased use of coed sports teams, and the willingness to settle cases before litigation arises, the volume of these types of cases has decreased in recent years. Although recent cases have generally been decided against female plaintiffs, a split still remains.

NOTES

1. In *Mansourian v. Regents of University of California*, 602 F.3d 957 (9th Cir. 2010), Female wrestlers brought a class action suit against UC-Davis alleging that their exclusion from the wrestling team violated Title IX and their equal protection rights where there was no women's wrestling team. In reversing summary judgment for the defendants, the Ninth Circuit stated that an institution may violate Title IX solely by failing to accommodate effectively the interests and abilities of student athletes of both sexes, even if the benefits provided to the athletes of both sexes are equivalent.

2. In *Mercer v. Duke University*, 190 F.3d 643 (4th Cir. 1999), female plaintiff sued Duke University for Title IX violations. Plaintiff was a kicker for her high school football team and tried out for Duke's football team. While she did not make the team, she did attend practices and participated in conditioning drills. Plaintiff was allowed to participate in an intrasquad game. After that game, the head football coach told the media that plaintiff was on the team. In addition, Duke's sports information director asked plaintiff to participate in several interviews. Plaintiff did not play in any games her second year; however, she was on the roster that was submitted to the NCAA and her picture appeared in Duke's football yearbook. At the beginning of plaintiff's third year, the coach informed her that she was being dropped from the team. At the trial court level, the plaintiff's claim was dismissed because the court reasoned that Title IX provided a blanket exemption for contact sports. However, the appeals court noted that while generally the school could exclude plaintiff from the team because football is a contact sport, Duke violated Title IX once it let her on the team and then removed her because of her gender. The appeals court stated, "We hold that where a university has allowed a member of the opposite sex to try out for a single-sex team in a contact sport, the university is . . . subject to Title IX and therefore prohibited from discriminatory action against that individual on the basis of his or her sex." Although Duke had no obligation to allow Mercer to try out for the team, once it allowed her to try out, it could not discriminate against her based on her gender. Therefore schools can avoid Title IX claims for equal participation in contact sports simply by refusing to allow members of the excluded sex to try out for the team. The decision of the trial court was overturned upon appeal by the plaintiff. In assessing damages, Mercer received $2 million in punitive damages and $1 million in compensatory damages.

3. In *Barnett v. Texas Wrestling Ass'n*, 16 F.Supp. 2d 690 (N.D. Tex. 1998), two female high school athletes wanted to participate on the all-boys wrestling team and there was no corresponding female wrestling team at the school. The court dismissed their Title IX

claim against the association rule forbidding female wrestlers to compete against boys in the North Texas Open Wrestling Tournament. The court reasoned that because wrestling was a contact sport, the females did not have a right to participate on the team.

4. In *Adams v. Baker*, 919 F.Supp. 1496 (D. Kan. 1996), female plaintiff was not allowed to compete on her high school wrestling team. Plaintiff alleged Title IX violations in her action for a preliminary injunction. The court noted, "Because wrestling is a contact sport, Title IX does not require that Valley Center High School allow a female to try out for the boys' wrestling team." The court ruled that plaintiff was not likely to succeed on the merits of her Title IX claim, and therefore an injunction was not warranted.

5. In *Libby v. South Inter-Conference Ass'n*, 728 F.Supp. 504 (N.D. Ill. 1990), a female high school student brought a civil rights action against a high school athletic association, challenging a rule prohibiting her from playing interscholastic soccer on the boys' team, where a girls' team did not exist. After a series of temporary restraining orders, which allowed her to compete in the state tournament, the case was dismissed as moot because the season had ended. Plaintiff was not awarded attorney's fees because she was not the prevailing party.

6. In *Saint v. Nebraska School Activities Ass'n*, 684 F.Supp 626 (D. Neb. 1988), a female high school sophomore sought a temporary restraining order to restrain the Nebraska School Activities Association from refusing to permit her to wrestle on the high school boys' wrestling team while trial was pending. The high school did not have a girls' wrestling team. A U.S. District Court judge ruled in favor of plaintiff, granting a temporary restraining order. The judge reasoned that plaintiff showed a reasonable probability of success on the merits in the claim, and the plaintiff would suffer irreparable harm if the restraining order were denied.

7. In *Lantz v. Ambach*, 620 F.Supp. 663 (S.D.N.Y. 1985), the court prohibited enforcement of a New York public high school regulation that prohibited mixed gender competition in football as a violation of the 14th Amendment and permitted a 16-year-old healthy female student to try out for junior varsity football. Although the court acknowledged an important governmental objective in protecting the health and safety of female high school students, it found the regulation was overbroad and lacked reasonable relation to the objective.

8. In *Leffel v. Wisconsin Interscholastic Athletic Ass'n*, 444 F.Supp. 1117 (E.D. Wis. 1978), plaintiff brought a class action suit charging that an interscholastic athletic association's rule limiting coeducational athletics violated her civil rights as guaranteed under the equal protection clause. The court granted summary judgment for the plaintiff, finding that exclusion of girls from all contact sports in order to protect female high school athletes from unreasonable risk of injury was not fairly or substantially related to a justifiable government objective in the context of the 14th Amendment, where demand for relief by plaintiffs would be met by establishing separate girls' teams with comparable programs. The plaintiffs were granted the right to participate in a varsity interscholastic program in any sport in which only a boys' team was provided.

9. In *Hoover v. Meiklejohn*, 430 F.Supp. 164 (D. Colo. 1977), an action was brought by plaintiff Hoover, who wanted to play on her high school soccer team. The Colorado High School Athletic Association limited interscholastic soccer team membership to boys. The district court held for Hoover, based on an equal protection analysis. The court held that the appropriate analysis required a triangular balancing of the importance of the opportunities being unequally burdened or denied against the strength of the state's interests and the character of the group being denied the opportunity. The court found that a complete denial, as in this case, violated Hoover's rights to equal protection. The court determined that the school had three options. It could allow coed teams, it could discontinue the sport for males, or it could field a second all-female team.

10. In *Muscare v. O'Malley*, Civil No. 76-C-3729 (N.D. Ill. 1977), an action was brought by a 12-year-old girl who wanted to play tackle football in Chicago Park District football games. There was a touch football program available for girls. In ruling for the girl, the court reasoned that offering a sport for males, yet not to females, is a violation of equal opportunity rights under the 14th Amendment.

11. In *Lavin v. Chicago Board of Education*, 73 F.R.D. 438 (N.D. Ill. 1975), *Lavin v. Illinois High School Ass'n*, 527 F.2d 58 (7th Cir. 1977), a class action lawsuit for declaratory, injunctive, and monetary relief against the Chicago Board of Education was instituted because plaintiff Lavin was denied participation in interscholastic athletics based on her gender. Lavin and another classmate tried out for the varsity basketball team at their high school and were denied positions on the squad because of Illinois State High School Association rules. Lavin contended that the 14th Amendment guarantee of equal protection had been violated. The appeals court reversed and remanded the trial court's summary judgment for the board of education and awarded monetary damages to the athletes. On remand, the trial court denied the class action claim; Lavin was no longer a member of the "class" because of graduation. In addition, the trial court reasoned that she did not present an argument that showed she was qualified enough to make the boys' squad and therefore was not a member of that particular "class" of girls either. The trial court allowed Lavin's individual claim for damages.

12. See section 5.2.4, "Injunctive Relief," for an explanation of the standards required for an injunction.

13. See section 4.10, "Waiver and Release of Liability," for a discussion of waivers and releases of liability. The plaintiff in *Clinton v. Nagy* (see note 11) signed one before being allowed to participate.

For more information on the contact sports exemption, see the following law review articles:

1. Blake J. Furman, "Gender Equality in High School Sports: Why There Is a Contact Sports Exemption to Title IX, Eliminating It, and a Proposal for the Future," 17 *Fordham Intellectual Property, Media and Entertainment Law Journal* 1169 (2007).

2. Jamal Greene, "Hands Off Policy: Equal Protection and the Contact Sports Exemption of Title IX," 11 *Michigan Journal of Gender and Law* 133 (2005).

3. Abigail Crouse, "Comment: Equal Athletic Opportunity: An Analysis of *Mercer v. Duke University* and a Proposal to Amend the Contact Sport Exception to Title IX," 84 *Minnesota Law Review* 1655 (2000).

4. James Puszczewicz, "Chalk Talk: The Fourth Circuit Kicks a Hole through Contact Sport Exemption," 29 *Journal of Law and Education* 107 (2000).

5. Suzanne Sangree, "Title IX and the Contact Sports Exception: Gender Stereotypes in a Civil Rights Statute," 32 *Connecticut Law Review* 381 (2000).

8.3.1.2. Noncontact Sports

In cases in which noncontact sports are involved and there is a men's team and no women's team, the majority of cases allow the women to participate on the men's team. Specifically, women have been allowed to participate on men's teams in cross-country (see notes 3, 4, and 9), baseball (see note 1), golf (see notes 7 and 8), and tennis (see notes 6 and 10) where there were no women's teams. Few courts have prevented women from participating on the men's teams.

In cases where private organizations are involved, the plaintiff women must also prove state action (see note 11), which cannot always be demonstrated. One area of athletics where the separation between genders became controversial was in Little League Baseball. It was not until after a series of lawsuits in the mid-1970s that Little League Baseball began to allow girls to participate in official competition (see note 11).

Litigation in this area of gender discrimination has decreased due to increased opportunities for women's teams in interscholastic athletics as well as an increased acceptance of females participating on traditionally all-male teams. Finally, it is increasingly rare to find interscholastic or intercollegiate athletic programs that do not field teams for both genders in noncontact sports such as tennis, cross-country, golf, and softball/baseball.

NOTES

1. *In Phillips v. Anderson County Board of Education*, 2006 WL 3759893 (E.D.Tenn. Dec. 19, 2006), a female high school student brought suit under Title IX after she was removed from a weightlifting class. The court rejected the Board's argument that weightlifting was a contact sport, but granted the Board summary judgment because no one on the Board had actual knowledge of the discrimination.

2. In *Israel v. West Virginia Secondary Schools Activities Commission*, 388 S.E.2d 480 (W. Va. 1989), a female high school student brought a gender discrimination action against the School Activities Association after she was refused the opportunity to play on the boys' high school baseball team. In reversing the lower court's decision, the appeals court held that the regulation prohibiting girls' participation in baseball violated federal and state equal protection standards, and the games of baseball and softball were not substantially equivalent for purposes of determining whether equal athletic opportunities are provided to boys and girls in high school.

3. In August 1983, Mary Decker, Grete Waitz, and 50 other leading female runners filed a gender discrimination suit against the International Olympic Committee (IOC), the Los Angeles Olympic Organizing Committee, the International Amateur Athletic Federation, and the Athletics Congress, among others (see *Martin v. International Olympic Committee*, 740 F.2d 670 (9th Cir. 1984)). The suit was filed in Los Angeles Superior Court and sought an order that would force the defendants to include 5,000- and 10,000-meter runs for women at the 1984 Olympic Games in Los Angeles. These events were part of the men's events and were historically excluded from the women's program because of the belief that women could not physically handle the distances. The court denied the request for injunctive relief. The IOC added these events to the women's program for the 1988 Olympic Games in Seoul, South Korea.

4. In *Bednar v. Nebraska School Activities Ass'n*, 531 F.2d 922 (8th Cir. 1976), the mother of a high school student brought a civil rights action on behalf of her daughter, who had been denied the opportunity to participate on the boys' cross country team because of her gender. There was no girls' team. The district court issued a preliminary injunction prohibiting the school from excluding Bednar from competition. The school association appealed the decision, but the court of appeals affirmed, finding that since Bednar was one of the top competitors in her event and her qualification for higher levels of competition was likely, she would be subject to irreparable harm if she were not allowed to compete.

5. In *Gilpin v. Kansas State High School Activities Ass'n*, 377 F.Supp. 1233 (D. Kan. 1973), plaintiff, a junior at Southeast High School in Wichita, Kansas, brought a civil rights suit against the Kansas State High School Activities Association (KSHSAA). Gilpin claimed she was deprived of equal protection by a KSHSAA rule that prevented her from participating in interscholastic cross-country competition solely on the basis of her gender. The court held that because Southeast High School offered no cross country program for girls, the KSHSAA rule effectively deprived Gilpin of an opportunity to compete at all. The court held that "although the Association's overall objective is commendable and legitimate, the method employed to accomplish that objective is simply overbroad in its reach. It is precisely this sort of overinclusiveness, which the Equal Protection Clause disdains." The district court determined that the KSHSAA rule prohibiting mixed competition was unconstitutional as applied to Gilpin and accordingly granted her the requested injunctive relief.

6. In *Brenden v. Independent School District*, 342 F.Supp. 1224 (D. Minn. 1972), *aff'd.*, 477 F.2d 1292 (8th Cir. 1973), plaintiff's high school student-athletes brought an action against Independent School District 742, alleging violation of their constitutional rights under the 14th Amendment and Civil Rights Act (42 U.S.C. §1983). The plaintiffs contended that the Minnesota State High School League (MSHSL) rule prohibiting girls from participating in boys' interscholastic athletic competition was arbitrary and unreasonable as applied to their particular situations and thus constituted a violation of their rights under the equal protection clause of the 14th Amendment. Because of the circumstances—the girls were capable of competing on the boys' team, that no girls' team existed at their respective

schools in the sports in which they wished to participate, and that plaintiffs were kept from participation solely on the basis of gender—the court found the application of the rule to be arbitrary and unreasonable. Since the classification by gender had no fair or substantial relation to the objective of the interscholastic league rule, its application to plaintiffs was in violation of the equal protection clause of the 14th Amendment. The district court granted the requested injunctive relief and prohibited the MSHSL from imposing sanctions on the schools or any of their opponents stemming from plaintiffs' participation on boys' interscholastic athletic teams.

7. In *Morris v. Michigan State Board of Education*, 472 F.2d 1207 (6th Cir. 1973), plaintiff Morris brought an action against a state high school athletic association rule barring mixed competition in interscholastic sports. Morris and a female friend wanted to play on the high school boys' tennis team. There was no girls' team. Morris contended a violation of equal protection under the 14th Amendment. The lower court ruled for Morris. The appeals court affirmed the decision but remanded the suit to the lower court to have non-contact sports added to the wording of the order granting the injunction. As a result of the case, Michigan Laws Act 183 was enacted, which permitted women to participate with men on non-contact sports teams.

8. In *Reed v. Nebraska School Activities Ass'n*, 341 F.Supp. 258 (D. Neb. 1972), plaintiff, a student-athlete at Norfolk High School, brought an action that challenged a state high school athletic association's practice of providing a public school golf program for boys while providing none for girls and prohibiting girls from interscholastic participation with or against boys. Reed sought a preliminary injunction prohibiting the Nebraska School Activities Association and school officials from denying her membership on the boys' golf team. The court held for Reed, stating that Reed would lose the benefits of participation when the season expired and that the loss would be irretrievable.

9. In *Haas v. South Bend Community School Corp.*, 289 N.E.2d 495 (Ind. 1972), a female who was seeking injunctive relief from a state high school athletic association rule barring mixed competition on sports teams brought a suit. Plaintiff Haas had made the "B" golf team but was denied the opportunity to play with the "A" team because of the association's rule. The lower court held for the association. The decision was later reversed by the appellate court, which held that the rule was a violation of equal protection under the 14th Amendment and the Civil Rights Act. The court found the association's arguments to be insufficient justification for barring girls from noncontact sports or from denying girls the chance to qualify.

10. In *Hollander v. Connecticut Interscholastic Athletic Conference, Inc.*, 164 Conn. 654 (Conn. Super. Ct.), *appeal dismissed*, 295 A.2d 671 (Conn. Ct. App. 1972), an action was brought by plaintiff Hollander, who wanted to run on the boys' cross-country team at her high school. The Connecticut Intercollegiate Athletic Association barred mixed competition. The court worked out an agreement with the association to allow girls to compete on boys' teams in noncontact sports. Despite that, the court held for the defendant association based on 14th Amendment equal protection arguments. The court expressed the opinion that allowing girls to compete on the same teams with boys would bring into question the physical safeguard for girls and the "removal of challenge and incentive for boys to win."

The following cases involve suits against Little League and noninterscholastic youth teams:

1. In *Perkins v. Londonderry Basketball Club*, 196 F.3d 13 (1st Cir. 1999), a 10-year-old female basketball player on a mixed-gender team brought suit against a voluntary tax-exempt organization formed by several community groups. The organization sponsored a tournament with separate brackets for boys and girls teams, but no bracket for mixed-gender teams. As a result, the organization told the plaintiff's town that she could not play with its All-Star team in the tournament. The plaintiff's town did not have an all-girls team. Owing to the fact that the hosting organization was private, the U.S. First Circuit Court of Appeals affirmed the lower court's decision that the organization's conduct did not amount to state action, thereby dismissing the plaintiff's suit.

2. In *Rappaport v. Little League Baseball, Inc.*, 65 F.R.D. 545 (D. Del. 1975), a group of parents and plaintiff girl filed suit against the Little League because of its policy of excluding girls from participation. The Little League changed its policy after the complaint was filed. The court ruled the case moot.

3. In *McGill v. Avonworth Baseball Conference*, 516 F.2d 1328 (3d Cir. 1975), the court of appeals affirmed the trial court's decision for the conference because the girl had failed to show significant state involvement in the league's discrimination. The court reasoned that the waiver of a $25 fee for use of the public playing field was de minimus; that analysis of nature, value, and proportion of state aid to the conference did not end the court's inquiry; and that the nexus between the state's and the conference's allegedly offensive policy was not sufficiently close so that the conference's action could be fairly treated as state action in that the conference was granted nonexclusive scheduled use of four public playing fields, school buildings were used only for once-a-year registration purposes, and no government officials were involved in determining eligibility requirements.

4. In *Fortin v. Darlington Little League, Inc.*, 376 F.Supp. 473 (D.R.I. 1974), *rev'd.*, 514 F.2d 344 (1st Cir. 1975), an action was brought by a 10-year-old girl who was denied the opportunity to try out for Little League baseball solely because of her gender. Plaintiff Fortin argued that the baseball park where the team played was public property, a fact that supplied sufficient proof to find the required state action. The appeals court ruled for the girl, reversing the lower court's decision. The appeals court found that the league's preferred dependency on city baseball diamonds introduced significant state involvement to find state action. The appeals court also rejected the league's argument that the discrimination was appropriate because females would injure more easily than males, because it was not supported by the facts.

5. In *King v. Little League Baseball, Inc.*, 505 F.2d 264 (6th Cir. 1974), an action was brought by a 12-year-old girl who wanted to play on a Little League team. The national Little League Baseball rules excluded girls from competing. However, the Little League Regional Board permitted plaintiff King to try out, and she made the team on the basis of her ability. The team was notified by the National Little League Association that if King continued to play or practice with the team, the team would lose its charter. King was dropped from the roster. The town revoked the team's privilege to use the municipal field for games. King was then put back on the roster, and the team lost its charter. The case was dismissed and affirmed on appeal. The courts held that there was not sufficient state action involved in the defendant's enforcement of the "no girls" rule to bring it under the color of state law. The courts agreed that they did not have jurisdiction over the subject matter in the case.

6. In *National Organization for Women, Essex County Chapter v. Little League Baseball, Inc.*, 318 A.2d 33 (N.J. Super. Ct. App. Div. 1974), the Essex County chapter of the National Organization for Women (NOW) filed suit on behalf of 8- to 12-year-old girls who wanted to play Little League Baseball. NOW contended this discrimination against girls was a violation of New Jersey's antidiscrimination laws. In affirming a lower court order for the girls, the superior court held that the evidence permitted the finding that girls of the particular age concerned were not subject to greater hazard of injury while playing baseball than boys of the same age group and that the Little League did not fall within any statutory exemptions.

8.3.2. Women's Team, No Men's Team

In most cases where an athletic program sponsors women's teams but no corresponding men's teams, the sport is noncontact. Unlike the situations contained in the previous section, where a men's team but not a women's team was provided in a noncontact sport, men are generally not allowed to play on all-female teams. However, there have been exceptions.

One sport that has recently tested the above doctrine is interscholastic field hockey. A sport that is played by both genders on the international level, field hockey is considered in most areas of the United States to be a women's sport on the high school level. Courts are split over whether field hockey should be considered a contact sport or not. If field hockey is construed as a contact sport, exclusion of males would be permitted under Title IX without any inquiry into purposes or motives for the exclusion (see note 2). However, if field hockey is found to be a noncontact sport, the plaintiff could proceed on a Title IX claim.

In 2001, Massachusetts, California, and Maine were the only three states that allowed boys to play on high school field hockey teams. In Massachusetts, six of the state's high school field hockey teams had boys on their rosters, including the two Division I state champion teams from the two previous years (see note 4). While several parents and opposing coaches have called for a ban on male players, or a realigned league for males only, such action would violate the Massachusetts Interscholastic Athletic Association's (MIAA) rule 43, which states, "No student shall be denied in any implied or explicit manner the opportunity to participate in any interscholastic activity because of his or her gender." In the 1970s, the MIAA had a rule explicitly excluding boys from girls' teams, but that rule was found invalid by the Supreme Judicial Court of Massachusetts based on equal protection laws and Massachusetts' ERA in *Attorney General v. Massachusetts Interscholastic Athletic Ass'n*, 393 N.E.2d 284 (Mass. 1979).

If field hockey gains popularity among high school age boys, it is likely that court cases over male inclusion in the sport will increase. A similar trend occurred with volleyball (see notes 4, 6, 8, 9, and 10), which began in the United States as a traditionally female sport but saw a rise in male participation in the 1990s.

Male plaintiffs that bring claims of discrimination for exclusion from female teams generally use the same legal theories that females use in bringing claims of discrimination for not being allowed participation on men's teams. The two most common theories used by plaintiffs are equal protection and Title IX. Most courts will not uphold a Title IX claim unless the plaintiffs can show that opportunities for males have been limited (see notes 3, 7, and 8). Similarly, equal protection arguments have often been denied because courts have held that athletic associations have a rational reason for separating men's and women's athletic teams or allowing women to field single-sex squads (see notes 6 and 9).

In cases in which there is a women's team and no men's team for noncontact sports, the majority of decisions have not allowed the male to participate on the women's team. Only in *Gomes v. Rhode Island Interscholastic League* (see note 10) did the court uphold the male's gender discrimination claim and allow him to play on the women's volleyball team. The *Gomes* case, however, is not a very strong precedent. In this situation, Gomes received a judgment for an injunction in the middle of the season. The appellate court was going to attempt immediate review of the issue, but the league persuaded the court to wait until the end of the team's schedule so that the season would not be disrupted. The merits of the case were never evaluated since the court deemed the case moot because Gomes had graduated.

The majority of the decisions in this area are similar to *Clark v. Arizona Interscholastic Ass'n* (see note 6), with the court refusing to allow boys to compete on the girls' volleyball team. The plaintiff male has been successful for a variety of reasons, including lack of state action when a private organization is involved (see note 11), prohibition of males on women's teams to redress disparate treatment of females in scholastic athletic programs (see note 4), promotion of athletic opportunities for females (see note 9), and the fact that males already have more athletic opportunities than females (see note 7). In addition, there has been some litigation on what types of sports constitute "contact sports." For instance, the argument has now arisen over whether field hockey should be considered a contact sport (see notes 2 and 3). As with the previous sections concerning discrimination against individual athletes, the number of these types of cases has decreased in recent years due to increased opportunities and lack of willingness to enter into costly litigation.

NOTES

1. In *Maine Human Rights Commission v. Maine Principals Ass'n*, No. CV-97–599 1999 Me. Super. LEXIS 23 (Me. Super. Ct. Jan. 21, 1999), two male high school students in Maine brought a case alleging that they were being discriminated against under the Maine Human Rights Act. The court commented on the peculiarity of the fact that the students did not bring a Title IX or equal protection claim but did not enter into analysis on those issues. The Maine Human Rights Act declares it "unlawful to deny any person equal opportunity in athletic programs on the basis of sex." The court believed that the plaintiffs had to show that the defendant had deprived them of their right to overall athletic opportunities, and not just participation in field hockey. In its conclusion, the court summarized the general doctrine used by most courts, stating, "There is a substantial relationship between excluding boys from playing field hockey and providing equal opportunities for girls in athletics. Conversely, the evidence also establishes that permitting boys to compete with girls in field hockey will likely result in an overall lessening of equal opportunities for girls in athletics." The court, therefore, found for the defendant school association.

2. In *Williams v. School District*, 998 F.2d 168 (3d Cir. 1993), male plaintiff tried out for the girls' field hockey team. Plaintiff made the team and was even given a uniform. School officials then said that plaintiff could not play on the team. The district court granted plaintiff's motion for summary judgment, stating that field hockey is not a contact sport and therefore plaintiff should be allowed to participate on the girls' field hockey team. However, the court of appeals reversed the district court's decision by concluding that field hockey is a contact sport. A contact sport is one in which "the purpose or major activity...involves bodily contact." Title IX provides that "exclusion is permitted if the sport involved is a contact sport."

3. In *Kleczek v. Rhode Island Interscholastic League, Inc.*, 768 F.Supp. 951 (D.R.I. 1991), male plaintiff sought to participate on his high school girls' field hockey team because there was no boys' field hockey team. The Rhode Island Interscholastic League (RIIL) refused to let the boy participate on the girls' team. RIIL was a private entity, but it got funds from member schools. South Kingstown High School, the plaintiff's high school, did receive federal funds. However, these funds were "restrictive" in that they were specifically earmarked for particular programs (math, science, etc.). The court held that plaintiff had not shown that he was likely to succeed on the merits of his "Title IX claim for three reasons: (1) the programs and activities of the defendants in question do not receive federal funds; (2) the overall athletic opportunities for males at South Kingstown High School have not been limited; and (3) the evidence indicates that field hockey is not a 'noncontact sport.'"

4. For more information on boys playing Massachusetts field hockey cases, see Mike Wise, "In Field Hockey, a Twist on Title IX," *New York Times* (October 18, 2001).

5. In *Clark v. Arizona Interscholastic Ass'n*, 886 F.2d 1191 (9th Cir. 1989), the brother of plaintiff in *Clark v. Arizona Interscholastic Ass'n* (see note 6) brought a civil rights action challenging a rule of the association prohibiting him from competing on the girls' high school volleyball team. The appeals court affirmed the lower court's decision in favor of the association. As in the earlier *Clark* case, the judge reasoned that the rule was substantially related to the goal of redressing past discrimination and promoting equality of athletic opportunity between the sexes.

6. In *Clark v. Arizona Interscholastic Ass'n*, 695 F.2d 1126 (9th Cir. 1982), *cert. denied*, 464 U.S. 818 (1983), plaintiffs were Arizona high school students who demonstrated their prowess in volleyball by participating on national championship teams sponsored

by the Amateur Athletic Union. The student-athletes were not, however, able to partici-pate on their high school volleyball teams. Their schools sponsored interscholastic volley-ball teams only for girls, and a policy of the Arizona Interscholastic Association (AIA) had been interpreted to preclude boys from playing on girls' teams, even though girls were permitted to participate on boys' athletic teams. The trial court found that the rules and regulations of the AIA do not violate the equal protection clause of the 14th Amendment. It held that the maintenance of a girls only volleyball team "is substantially related to and serves the achievement of the important governmental objective" of (1) promoting equal athletic opportunities for females in interscholastic sports and (2) redressing the effects of past discrimination. On appeal, the trial court decision was affirmed, upholding the rule prohibiting boys from playing on the girls' volleyball team.

7. In *B.C. v Cumberland Regional School District*, 531 A.2d 1059 (N.J. Super. A.D. 1987), a male high school student challenged an athletic association rule prohibiting him from competing on the girls' field hockey team. In affirming the lower court's decision, the court held that a rule prohibiting boys from playing on the girls' field hockey team is per-missible under both the state and the federal Constitution. The court reasoned that were plaintiff permitted to compete on the girls' team, his personal interest would be gained at the cost of denying females the right to have equality of athletic opportunities with their male counterparts.

8. In *Mularadelis v. Haldane Central School Board*, 427 N.Y.S.2d 458 (N.Y. App. Div. 1980), plaintiff Mularadelis, a member of his high school's girls' tennis team, who was told by the school board that he could no longer play on the team, brought a lawsuit. The appeals court reversed a lower court decision and held for the school board on the basis that Title IX allowed for the exclusion of boys from the girls' team when there were, overall, more athletic opportunities for boys in the community.

9. In *Forte v. Board of Education, North Babylon Union Free School District*, 431 N.Y.S.2d 321 (N.Y. Sup. 1980), an action was brought by plaintiff Forte on behalf of his son, a 17-year-old high school student who wanted to play on the North Babylon High School volleyball team, which was all female. The court held for the school district. The court rea-soned that the rule the school district had enacted was a discernible and permissible means of redressing disparate treatment of females in interscholastic athletic programs.

10. In *Petrie v. Illinois High School Ass'n*, 394 N.E.2d 855 (Ill. 1979), an action was brought by plaintiff Petrie, who wanted to play on the girls' high school volleyball team since the school had no boys' team. The appeals court affirmed a lower court decision, which up-held the association's rule. The court found no violation of state law and reasoned that the association's rule "substantially related to and served the achievement of the governmental objective of maintaining, fostering, and promoting athletic opportunities for girls."

11. In *Gomes v. Rhode Island Interscholastic League*, 469 F.Supp. 659 (D.R.I. 1979), *vacated as moot*, 604 F.2d 733 (1st Cir. 1979), plaintiff Gomes, a senior at Rogers High School in Newport, Rhode Island, brought an action under the federal civil rights statute. He sought preliminary injunctive relief prohibiting school officials from preventing his par-ticipation on the girls' volleyball team since the school offered no separate male squad in this sport. Rogers High allowed Gomes to join the all-female team but did not use him in Rhode Island Interscholastic League competition for fear of league disqualification. Consequently, Gomes brought suit against the league at the start of the volleyball season. He alleged that the rule against male participation in volleyball competition violated both the 14th Amend-ment and Title IX. Without reaching the constitutional issues, the district court ruled in Gomes's favor. The district court found that the exception for separate-gender teams under Title IX was not applicable since defendants sponsored no men's volleyball teams and op-portunities for boys to play the sport previously had been nonexistent. Since the district court decision was rendered in the middle of the volleyball season, the league persuaded the appeals court that implementation of the district court's order would disrupt the remainder of the season. The appeals court stopped the implementation of the order pending review. The merits of the case were never reached on appeal since the case was dismissed as moot because the season had ended and Gomes was graduating.

12. In *White v. Corpus Christi Little Misses Kickball Ass'n*, 526 S.W.2d 766 (Tex. Civ. App. 1975), an action was brought by plaintiff White, a 10-year-old boy who was not allowed to register to play in the girls' kickball association because of his gender. The district court held for the association, and the boy appealed. On appeal, the boy argued that denial of right to play because of his gender was a denial of equal protection under both federal and state constitutions. The appeals court denied his claim because he had failed to establish the requisite state action. His participation was denied by a private organization acting without any connection to government except that the games were played in a public park.

8.3.3. Women's Teams and Men's Teams

Four different types of legal arguments are raised in cases in which there are teams for both genders. The first type is in cases in which the plaintiff women argue that "separate but equal is not equal." In these situations, the women sue to participate on the men's team because the competition may be better and the women are far superior to the participants on the women's teams. As *O'Connor v. Board of Education of School District No. 23* (see note 2 in section 8.3.3.2, "Contact Sports") illustrates, the court will generally approve "separate but equal" teams and rule against plaintiff females who want to play on boys' teams based on playing ability arguments.

The second type of argument is that the separate teams are not equal, especially with respect to the benefits and opportunities provided to the teams. In *Aiken v. Lieuallen* (see note 5 in section 8.3.3.2, "Contact Sports"), plaintiff female athletes contended that they were discriminated against in the areas of transportation, officiating, coaching, and the school's commitment to competitive programs.

The third type of case occurs when two teams exist but the women compete under different rules than the men (see section 8.3.4, "Same Sport, Different Rules"). These situations, challenged on equal protection grounds, have produced mixed results. The trend recently does not allow different rules to exist when those rules are based purely on the gender of the athletes, especially when those rules place those who play under them at a disadvantage if they want to continue in the sport.

The fourth type of case involves different seasons for the same men's and women's sport (see section 8.3.5, "Same Sport, Different Seasons"). The courts have historically held that separate seasons of play are not a denial of equal protection of the law; however, the sentiment within the court system is changing, as evidenced by the decision in *Communities for Equity v. Michigan High School Athletic Ass'n* and in *Alston v. Virginia High School League, Inc.* (see notes 2 and 3 in section 8.3.5, "Same Sport, Different Seasons").

8.3.3.1. Separate but Equal

When there are both men's and women's teams in the same sport, challenges for participation on the other team have been unsuccessful. The doctrine of "separate but equal" remains applicable to gender distinctions, even though it has been rejected for distinctions based on race. Thus if separate teams exist for men and women, there may be a prohibition against coed teams or against women competing against men. The doctrine of "separate but equal" raises the critical question of whether such separate teams are substantially equal.

The fact that two teams exist does not necessarily satisfy the doctrine. "Separate but equal" is based on the concept that the exclusion of a group is not unconstitutional if the excluded group is provided with comparable opportunities. If women are excluded from the men's basketball team but are provided with an equal team of their own, the school district will not be in violation of the Title IX under the "separate but equal" theory. When the genders are segregated in athletics, there must be an overall equality of expenditures (see note 1), coaching, and access to facilities. Without this substantial equality, the existence of separate teams and the prohibition of women competing with men may be unconstitutional.

Apart from these circumstances, the segregation of the genders in athletics is generally upheld, although the court is careful to examine the specific circumstances in each case before making a determination. The court usually considers whether or not the particular sport in question is considered to be a contact or a noncontact sport. Physiological differences between the genders have been found to be a valid reason for the exclusion of one gender from a contact sport.

Contact sports include boxing, wrestling, rugby, ice hockey, football, basketball, and other sports in which the major activity involves bodily contact. As the rights of female athletes have increasingly been served in recent years, the number of cases in this area has decreased. The quality of competition has increased in women's sports, making females less likely to demand an opportunity to play on men's teams. Furthermore, the treatment of female athletic teams has begun to equal the support that male teams receive on the interscholastic and intercollegiate levels, leading to a decrease in "separate but equal" cases.

NOTE

1. In 2002, the Hampton, Virginia, City Council was scrutinized by press reports, such as one in *USA Today*, because it had spent $7,000 on rings for Phoebus High's 2001 state champion boys' football team but gave no money to championship girls' teams. Because the school receives federal funds, this may have been a Title IX violation. The boys and girls track teams at another Hampton high school also won state titles. The city manager pointed out in his defense to the media that neither of these two other teams requested ring money. For more information, see Dan Cronin, "Kournikova Wins, Faces V. Williams," *USA Today* (February 13, 2002).

8.3.3.2. Contact Sports

In cases in which there are both women's and men's teams in contact sports, the courts have generally not allowed a female to participate on the men's team. In *O'Connor v. Board of Education of School District No. 23* (see note 2), the court denied the gender discrimination allegation of a female who wanted to participate in better competition by playing on the men's team. The other issue that may be raised is whether the separate men's and women's teams are in fact equal. For example, in *Aiken v. Lieuallen* (see note 5), members of the female basketball team at the University of Oregon argued that they did not receive the same treatment as the men's basketball team at the university. The school was found to be in violation because it discriminated against the female players in the areas of transportation, coaching, and officiating.

NOTES

1. In *Michigan Department of Civil Rights, ex rel. Forton v. Waterford Township Department of Parks and Recreation*, 387 N.W.2d 281 (Mich. 1986), plaintiff brought a Civil Rights Act claim based on defendant's policy of maintaining a gender-based elementary level basketball program. The appeals court reversed the district court's decision and ruled

in favor of the plaintiff. The court reasoned that (1) separate leagues involved were not equal and could not withstand equal protection analysis, and consequently violated the Civil Rights Act and that (2) subsequent modification of policy to allow up to two girls to participate on each boys' basketball team and two boys on each girls' basketball team did not cure the statutory violation.

2. In *O'Connor v. Board of Education*, 645 F.2d 578 (7th Cir. 1981), *cert. denied*, 454 U.S. 1084 (1981), an appeal was instituted in response to a district court order granting a preliminary injunction to restrain defendant school board from refusing to permit female plaintiff from trying out for the boys' sixth grade basketball team. The plaintiff argued that the school board's policy of maximizing participation in sports by providing for separate but equal boys' and girls' interscholastic sports teams violated Title IX. The appellate court held that the trial court abused its discretion in granting a preliminary injunction restraining the school board because the plaintiff failed to show a reasonable likelihood of success on the merits.

3. In *Lafler v. Athletic Board of Control*, 536 F.Supp. 104 (W.D. Mich. 1982), the court upheld the denial of a woman's application to box in the flyweight division of the Golden Gloves boxing competition under the 14th Amendment, the state public accommodation statute, and the state Equal Rights Amendment. The court cited Title IX regulations permitting establishment of separate male-female teams in contact sports and the Amateur Sports Act provisions providing for separate programs for females and males.

4. Two student-athletes filed a complaint with the Oregon Board of Education, alleging that Oregon State University (OSU) offered athletic programs of lesser quality to female student-athletes than were offered to their male counterparts. A settlement reached in July 1980, titled "OSU Conciliation Agreement for Sex Equality in Intercollegiate Athletics," implemented a five-year plan at OSU designed to put the men's and women's athletic programs on an equal competitive basis.

5. In *Aiken v. Lieuallen*, 593 P.2d 1243 (Or. Ct. App. 1978), an action was brought by plaintiff taxpayers and parents of student-athletes on the University of Oregon's women's varsity basketball team who appealed a determination by the chancellor of the State Board of Higher Education that the university was not violating state statute ORS 659.150, which prohibited discrimination on the basis of gender in state-financed education programs. The plaintiffs filed a complaint in March 1977, alleging that the following four areas of Oregon's athletic program were in violation of ORS 659.150: transportation, officiating, coaching, and commitment to competitive programs. A contested case hearing was held in October 1977, in which the hearing officer determined that the university was in violation of ORS 659.150. The findings and recommendations were issued in March 1978 and were submitted to the Oregon chancellor of higher education for review and entry of an order. The chancellor reversed the hearing officer's decision and found that the university was not in violation of the statute. The appeals court reversed the chancellor's order and sent the case back for further proceedings. The court, after reviewing the plaintiffs' allegations of discrimination in the areas of transportation, officiating, coaching, and university commitment, stated that upon the second hearing, the chancellor should address these allegations to determine whether the university's actions have led to "unreasonable differentiation of treatment" under ORS 659.150. Determinations of the unreasonableness of actions should include evaluations of whether the action by the university had a disparate effect on the opportunity for women to participate in athletics.

6. In *Hutchins v. Board of Trustees of Michigan State University*, 705 F.2d 454 (6th Cir. 1982), the women's basketball team from the East Lansing campus of Michigan State brought a Title IX complaint against Michigan State University and the board of trustees, alleging that the men's team was receiving better treatment. The alleged better treatment included more money for traveling and better facilities. The court held for the women's basketball team and issued a temporary restraining order disallowing the better treatment of the men's team.

8.3.3.3. Noncontact Sports

In cases in which there are both women's and men's teams in noncontact sports, the courts have generally not allowed the female to participate on the men's team. The rationale is that separate but equal is equal since this enhances athletic opportunities for females. As mentioned previously, as the quality of female athletics has grown since the 1980s, the demand by women to participate on men's teams for increased competition has decreased sharply. This trend is evidenced in the notes, with few cases being heard since the inception of Title IX in 1972.

NOTES

1. In *Ruman v. Eskew*, 343 N.E.2d 806 (Ind. Ct. App. 1975), an action was brought by plaintiff Ruman, who wanted to play on the high school boys' tennis team even though there was a girls' team at her school. The Indiana High School Athletic Association prohibited girls from playing on boys' teams if girls' teams in the same sport existed. The court held for the defendant and upheld the rule since it was reasonably related to the objective of providing athletic opportunities for both males and females. The court of appeals affirmed the judgment of the trial court.

2. In *Ritacco v. Norwin School District*, 361 F.Supp. 930 (W.D. Pa. 1973), a high school graduate and her mother filed a class action challenging a Pennsylvania Interscholastic Athletic Association (PIAA) rule that in effect required separate girls' and boys' teams for interscholastic noncontact sports. The district court ruled in favor of the defendant school district. It held that since the school district had not deprived Ritacco of her constitutional rights in violation of the Civil Rights Act, 42 U.S.C. §1983, she was entitled to neither declaratory judgment nor injunctive relief. The court held that "separate but equal" in the realm of athletic competition is justifiable and permissible when a rational basis for the rule exists, and that gender, unlike race, is not an inherently suspect classification for purposes of determining a denial of equal protection. The court concluded that the PIAA rule forbidding coeducational noncontact sports teams did not invalidly and unfairly discriminate against females.

3. In *Gregoria v. Board of Education*, No. A-1277–70 (N.J. Super. Ct. App. Div. 1971) (unreported), the trial court refused to prohibit enforcement of the New Jersey Athletic Association's rule prohibiting coed interscholastic sports, including noncontact sports such as tennis. Among the rational bases for the policy, the court cited the psychological impact on males, the need for additional female trainers, and the possibility of insufficient bathroom facilities. The appeals court affirmed the lower court's ruling that the "psychological well-being of girls is a rational reason for exclusion."

8.3.4. Same Sport, Different Rules

Cases and issues in this section have traditionally arisen in basketball because women's basketball is often played under different rules than men's basketball. As evidenced by *Dodson v. Arkansas Activities Ass'n* (see note 1), the cases have evolved from a generally disparate treatment of student-athletes rather than from different rules of a sport. However, the use of different rules for male and female teams in the same sport has declined.

8.3.4.1. Contact Sports

In cases in which there are different playing rules for women's and men's teams in contact sports, there is a split in decisions as to whether the women's rules should be changed to conform with the men's. The plaintiff women in these cases generally have alleged gender discrimination based on the rule differences with men's sports and also the reduced opportunity to compete against other women (who had the advantage of playing under men's rules) for college scholarships.

In *Dodson v. Arkansas Activities Ass'n* (note 1), the court ruled for the plaintiff, stating that no valid reason exists for women to have to use different rules than men in playing basketball. However, in *Jones v. Oklahoma Secondary School Activities Ass'n* (note 2) and *Cape v. Tennessee Secondary School Athletic Ass'n* (note 3), the courts ruled for the defendant athletic associations, mostly for administrative reasons. Owing to the growth of women's sports on the national level, the use of different rules for men and women has become an antiquated practice. Therefore, since the 1980s, this type of litigation has not arisen frequently.

NOTES

1. In *Dodson v. Arkansas Activities Ass'n*, 468 F.Supp. 394 (E.D. Ark. 1979), plaintiff Dodson, a female junior high school basketball player in the Arkadelphia, Arkansas, public school system, brought an action in January 1977 against three defendants: the school district, the superintendent, and the Arkansas Activities Association. Her suit challenged the constitutionality of rules for girls' junior and senior high school basketball, which in Arkansas differed from those under which boys played. The court held that "none of the reasons proffered [for the rule differentiation] are at all relevant to a gender-based classification." The defendant stated that "no physiological differences between males and females…prohibit females from playing five-on-five basketball." And the primary justification given for the gender-based distinction between rules was simply that of tradition. The court ordered that the defendants be permanently prohibited and restrained from enforcing different rules for girls and boys playing junior and senior high school basketball in Arkansas.

2. In *Jones v. Oklahoma Secondary School Activities Ass'n*, 453 F.Supp. 150 (W.D. Okla. 1977), plaintiff Jones sought an injunction to suspend the association's split-court basketball rules, arguing that they created an arbitrary and unreasonable distinction between boys and girls that violated her right to equal protection. The court held for the athletic association. Jones's Title IX arguments were dismissed because she did not follow administrative procedures. Her 14th Amendment argument was seen as faulty because her allegations concerning her reduced opportunity to compete in the future and a reduced likelihood for college scholarships did not rise to the level of an equal protection interest. Her claims that such rules interfered with her enjoyment of the game as well as her physical development also did not establish a cognizable equal protection claim.

3. In *Cape v. Tennessee Secondary School Athletic Ass'n*, 424 F.Supp. 732 (E.D. Tenn. 1976), *rev'd. per curiam*, 563 F.2d 793 (6th Cir. 1977), plaintiff Cape, a high school student, challenged the "split-court" rules used in women's basketball. These rules, she claimed, denied her the full benefits of the game as well as an athletic scholarship to college. The court held for the athletic association and dismissed Cape's arguments, which were based on a private right of action under Title IX and the 14th Amendment. The court held that Cape, who sought to challenge the regulations, must first exhaust all administrative remedies with the Department of Health, Education and Welfare under Title IX before her suit could be addressed in federal court.

8.3.4.2. Noncontact Sports

The courts have allowed different rules for men and women's noncontact sports. The courts can apply a rational relationship test and find that the physical and psychological differences between male and female athletes justify different rules (see note 1). Cases of this type have not arisen recently, however, and if a court were to try a case involving similar facts, the decision might be different from the verdict in *Bucha* (note 1). owing to the increased uniformity of men's and women's rules in all sports, cases such as this have not arisen in recent years.

NOTE _____

1. In *Bucha v. Illinois High School Ass'n*, 351 F.Supp. 69 (N.D. Ill. 1972), plaintiffs, two female students at Hinsdale Center Township High School, brought a class action challenging the Illinois High School Association (IHSA) bylaws placing limitations on girls' athletic contests that were not applicable to boys' athletics. The girls sought to have the court declare the IHSA rules in violation of the equal protection clause of the 14th Amendment and to prohibit the enforcement of the bylaws. They also sought a judgment against all defendants in the amount of $25,000. The defendants—IHSA, its directors, and the Board of Education of Hinsdale Township—based their motions to dismiss on three arguments: (1) the IHSA and the board of education were not persons within the meaning of 42 USC §1983 (1970); (2) the challenged discrimination was not an action under color of state statute, ordinance, regulation, custom, or usage; and (3) the challenged discrimination did not constitute a deprivation of a right guaranteed by the U.S. Constitution and laws.

Concerning the defendants' first argument, the court held that "all defendants may properly be prohibited as persons under §1983, but only the individual defendants can be liable for the damages sought." On the second argument, the court rejected defendants' contention that the acts of the IHSA did not amount to state action and therefore could not be reached under §1983.

On the third and final argument, the court reviewed the girls' complaint that the athletic association denied them equal protection, stating that the relevant inquiry was whether the challenged classification based on gender was rational. Because participation in interscholastic athletics is not a constitutionally guaranteed right and the Illinois courts do not interfere with the policies of a voluntary association such as the IHSA unless it acts "unreasonably, arbitrarily, or capriciously," the girls had asserted their claims based on an equal educational opportunity argument and not the right to interscholastic athletic participation.

The court found a factual basis for defendants' claim that the physical and psychological differences between male and female student-athletes would lead to male domination of coed interscholastic sports and result in decreased female athletic participation, should unrestricted competition between the genders be permitted. It held that "the uncontroverted existence of a bona fide athletic program for girls coupled with the physical and psychological differences...also support the rationality of the IHSA's decision to conduct girls' interscholastic sports programs different from boys.'"

The district court entered summary judgment in favor of all defendants on the basis that the traditional equal protection standard "requires this court to defer to the judgment of the physical educators of the IHSA once a rational relationship has been shown to exist between their actions and the goals of interscholastic athletic competition."

8.3.5. Same Sport, Different Seasons

Until the decision of *Alston v. Virginia High School League, Inc.*, 108 F.Supp. 2d 543 (W.D. Va. 2000), the courts had allowed different seasons for men and women in the same sport as long as there was a rational basis for the difference. For example, in one case, an athletic association scheduled men's swimming in a different season (fall) than the women's season (winter) and was challenged on gender discrimination grounds. The athletic association's decisions were upheld.

The court reasoned that there was a reasonable basis for the decision: the lack of available pool time for both women's and men's teams to practice during the same season. However, in *Alston*, the association scheduled girls' sports seasons depending on the level of competition but did not use the same method for boys' sports. It is important to note that the plaintiffs in *Alston* were successful using the theory of Title IX in their case. However, the plaintiffs in *Ridgeway v. Montana High School Ass'n*, 633 F.Supp 1564 (D. Mont. 1986) (see note 4), employed Title IX in their arguments and were unsuccessful in their claim. The increased likelihood that plaintiffs will prevail in this type of case is illustrated by these two cases.

NOTES

1. In *Communities for Equity v. Michigan High School Athletic Association*, 459 F.3d 676 (6th Cir. 2006), the plaintiffs alleged that they were discriminated against because female sports were scheduled at less advantageous times than male sports in Michigan. Six girls' sports were played in nontraditional seasons, causing recruiting disadvantages and requiring certain female teams to play outdoor sports in more frequently inclement weather. The association alleged that it needed to have some of the boys' and girls' teams play in different seasons for logistical reasons. The district court responded by saying that if such logistical concerns are valid, the association should "split advantageous and disadvantageous sports equally" between the sexes. On remand from the Supreme Court, the Sixth Circuit held that the MHSAA failed to satisfy its burden of justifying its scheduling practices.

2. In *McCormick ex rel. McCormick v. School Dist. of Mamaroneck*, 370 F.3d 275 (2nd Cir. 2004), parents of female students brought suit for declaratory and injunctive relief that having the soccer season in the spring as opposed to the fall deprived the girls, but not boys, of the opportunity to compete in championship tournaments in violation of Title IX. At the time of the lawsuit, 714 schools in New York offered girls soccer, 643 of them in the fall, when the state championship is determined. Noting the conflicts with recruiting and nonscholastic soccer teams, the court ruled that the school districts failed to effectively accommodate the female soccer players.

3. In *Alston v. Virginia High School League, Inc.*, 108 F.Supp. 2d 543 (W.D. Va. 2000), female high school students brought suit alleging violations of Title IX and equal protection. The Virginia High School League (VHSL) scheduled girls' sports for different seasons, depending on the level of competition for each individual school. Defendant motioned for a dismissal of the case. The court concluded that a Title IX claim does not subsume an equal protection claim, and therefore the defendant's motion to dismiss was denied. After the motion for dismissal was denied, the plaintiff students were successful in their claim, overturning case precedent against females. VHSL was not found to have a legitimate, compelling reason to schedule the girls' seasons differently than the boys.'

4. In *Ridgeway v. Montana High School Ass'n*, 633 F.Supp. 1564 (D. Mont. 1986), the court decided not to overturn the decision of the Montana High School Association (MHSA), which allowed the seasonal placement of girls' basketball (fall) and girls' volleyball (winter) to remain as is, contrary to the prevailing seasonal placement for the sports throughout the rest of the country. The court agreed with the reasoning advanced by the MHSA, which determined that a change in seasonal placement would not facilitate "the goal of maximizing participation in athletics by the most students."

5. In *Striebel v. Minnesota State High School League*, 321 N.W.2d 400 (Minn. 1982), an action was brought by plaintiff female student-athlete against the Minnesota State High School League (MSHSL), challenging the constitutionality of a MSHSL rule that authorized "separate seasons of play for high school athletic teams separated or substantially separated according to gender." The MSHSL had established separate seasons for boys and girls in tennis and swimming. The district court held that the league's policy of establishing separate seasons for boys and girls was constitutional and in compliance with the statute. The court found that under the circumstances presented, separating teams by season was a "reasonable means of achieving maximum participation by both sexes in the high school athletic program." On appeal, the Minnesota Supreme Court held that "where limited athletic facilities make it necessary to schedule high school boys' and girls' athletic teams in

separate seasons and neither was substantially better than the other, that scheduling decision was not a denial of equal protection of the law."

8.3.6. Varsity Sport versus Club Sport

Another trend that has been occurring in recent Title IX litigation involves the argument that a sport that has been operating under "club" status should be raised to "varsity" status when the counterpart gender has a varsity team in that same sport. This argument has been used by women athletes who feel that denial of varsity status to their sport is a violation of Title IX, given that the male student-athletes have a varsity team in the same sport. This argument is based on the Title IX interpretation that calls for proportional ratios of sport participation opportunities offered to men and women student-athletes. The plaintiffs would have to prove initially that the school was out of compliance with Title IX and that adding this particular sport program as a varsity sport would constitute compliance with Title IX. If the school thought it was not in compliance with Title IX, it could raise the women's team to varsity status, thereby increasing participation opportunities.

The plaintiffs could also argue a Title IX complaint based on equal benefits and opportunities provided to the sport programs. The plaintiffs' argument could revolve around the fact that if a school offers a varsity team in a particular sport for men, then it must offer the same sport for women at the varsity level and provide it with the benefits and opportunities that the men's team receives. The plaintiffs would need to prove that student-athletes have the interest and ability to compete on the varsity level and that there is ample competition to sustain a team. This type of argument was used in *Cook et al. v. Colgate University* (see note 2), in which the plaintiff female student-athletes argued that their club sport of women's ice hockey should be raised to varsity status and that failure to do so was a violation of Title IX. This approach to Title IX compliance is relatively new, and the courts have yet to rule on this type of complaint.

NOTES _____

1. In *Bryant v. Colgate University*, 996 F.Supp. 170 (N.D. N.Y. 1998), Colgate University was sued on Title IX grounds for the club status of its women's ice hockey team. The court determined that Colgate was not within the "substantially proportionate" safe harbor provided by the OCR policy interpretations and granted the plaintiffs summary judgment on this issue. However, the court ruled that there were factual disputes as to the other two safe harbors—accommodation of interests and abilities and a continuing practice of increasing women's opportunities—and therefore denied the plaintiffs' motion for summary judgment on these two issues. Colgate subsequently settled the suit and granted women's ice hockey varsity status.

2. In *Cook v. Colgate University*, 802 F.Supp. 737 (N.D. N.Y. 1992), the plaintiff female student-athletes argued that refusal by Colgate University to raise their club ice hockey team to varsity status was a violation of Title IX because they were being denied the benefits and opportunities that were afforded to their male ice hockey–playing counterparts. Shortly after women students were admitted into the university in 1970, a women's ice hockey club team was formed. In 1979, 1983, 1986, and 1988, the women's ice hockey club team applied for varsity status and was denied by the university. Varsity status is important in that it provides the team with full-time coaches, designated schedules, rules and regulations, equipment, practice facilities, travel accommodations, and appropriate budgetary support. Colgate University argued that individual programs should not be examined (a comparison in this instance involving the support received by the men's varsity ice hockey team vs. the women's club ice hockey team) and that no evidence had been presented to show that

Colgate's athletic program discriminates against women. The district court ruled for the plaintiffs and ordered Colgate to grant the women's ice hockey team varsity status and to provide all the amenities that accompany such a designation.

The court ruled that Title IX is designed to protect not only a particular class of persons (women as a whole within the athletic department) but individuals as well. Therefore a separate team comparison is appropriate when analyzing Title IX compliance. The court stated that because Colgate sponsors separate ice hockey teams for each gender, the court has the authority to compare the two programs according to the Title IX equal opportunity and benefit areas.

Colgate University also set forth six reasons why rejection of varsity status for the women's team took place: women's ice hockey is rarely played on the secondary level; championships are not sponsored by the NCAA; the game is played by only approximately 15 colleges in the East; hockey is expensive to fund; there is a lack of general student interest in women's ice hockey; and there is a lack of ability among the members of the women's club team. The court stated that the only real reason why the requests for varsity status were denied was that hockey is expensive to fund and elevating the team to varsity status would have a dramatic financial impact on the university. The court went on to state that financial problems and funding shortfalls are not legitimate excuses for Title IX violations.

Colgate University appealed this decision (*Cook v. Colgate University*, 992 F.2d 17 (2d Cir. 1993)). The U.S. Court of Appeals heard the case and vacated the lower-court decision by ruling that the case was moot because all five of the plaintiffs either had graduated or were scheduled to graduate in May 1993. In August 1993, a new class action suit was filed against Colgate, bringing the same complaint against the institution (see note 1).

Chapter 9

CONTRACT LAW

9.1. Principles of Contract Law

    9.1.1. Formation of a Contract

        9.1.1.1. Offer

        9.1.1.2. Acceptance

        9.1.1.3. Consideration

        9.1.1.4. Legality

        9.1.1.5. Capacity

        9.1.1.6. Drafting a Contract

    9.1.2. Mistakes in Contracts

    9.1.3. Parol Evidence Rule

    9.1.4. Conditions of a Contract

    9.1.5. Statute of Frauds

    9.1.6. Assignment and Delegation of a Contract

    9.1.7. Breach of Contract

    9.1.8. Remedies for a Breach of Contract

9.2. Types of Athletic Contracts

    9.2.1. Standard Player Contract

        9.2.1.1. Reserve or Option Clause

        9.2.1.2. Unique Skill Provisions

        9.2.1.3. Hierarchy of Contracts

        9.2.1.4. Player Exclusivity

        9.2.1.5. Assignability

        9.2.1.6. Bonus Clauses

        9.2.1.7. Health Regulations

        9.2.1.8. Full Performance

        9.2.1.9. Example of a Standard Player Contract: National Football League

    9.2.2. Defenses to Standard Player Contract Breaches

    9.2.3. Tortious Interference with Contractual Relations

    9.2.4. Marketing, Endorsement, and Sponsorship Contracts

        9.2.4.1. Impact of League Rules

        9.2.4.2. Sponsorship Rights

        9.2.4.3. Indemnification

        9.2.4.4. Right to Terminate

        9.2.4.5. Force Majeure and Work Stoppage

        9.2.4.6. Sponsorship Litigation Cases

    9.2.5. Coaches' Contracts: Professional and Collegiate Sports

    9.2.6. Coaches' Contracts: High School

    9.2.7. Physicians' Contracts

    9.2.8. Officials' Contracts

    9.2.9. Facility Contracts

9.1. PRINCIPLES OF CONTRACT LAW

Contract law underlies the daily activities of all facets of every athletic organization. Contracts are formed in order to create and document formal agreements, and are referred to if the terms of such agreements come into dispute. A dispute may involve parties such as television networks, athletes, coaches, teachers, mascots, hot dog vendors, halftime show entertainers, secretaries, insurance companies, and season ticket holders.

Many nonlawyers misunderstand the meaning of the word *contract*. A contract is not necessarily a piece of paper (or several pieces of paper) with multiple parties' signatures at the bottom. With the exception of cases outlined in section 9.1.5, "Statute of Frauds," a handshake deal or a simple quid pro quo promise can be considered a legally binding contract. However, the existence of a written contract helps to prove that an agreement took place, and preserves the details of such an agreement in case a dispute or litigation occurs. Consequently, the chapter will deal primarily with *written* contracts rather than *oral* contracts.

This chapter begins with an introduction to contract law in general, and explores the way in which contracts are formed and enforced. The second part of the chapter focuses more directly on sports law, and examines contracts that professional, intercollegiate, and interscholastic sports organizations encounter.

While the chapter will not discuss every type of athletic contract, it will emphasize the unique characteristics of many of the more common types. It will also emphasize the importance of proper contract drafting and analyze precedent-setting cases. Many of these cases demonstrate the contract disputes that arise in sports. Understanding the facts of these cases, and subsequent judicial decisions, will benefit those who will enter into similar agreements.

NOTES _____

1. There are three major sources of contract law:

   (a) *Common Law*: Common law is based on previous court decisions regarding fact situations not specifically dealt with by statute. These previous court decisions provide guidelines in determining the legality of a contract.

   (b) *Restatement of Contracts*: The American Law Institute (ALI) first published *Restatement of Contracts* in 1932; the most recent (2nd) edition was published in 1981. It has organized and summarized this country's common law concerning contracts. Attorneys and the judiciary rely on it for precedent.

   (c) *Uniform Commercial Code* (U.C.C.): The U.C.C., a uniform statute that every state has enacted, involves commercial transactions (not land or services). Athletic administrators most often would deal with the U.C.C. when dealing with contracts that specifically cover the sale of goods—for example, sporting goods and game tickets. Several educational institutions have been given copyright permission to publish articles of the U.C.C. on the Internet (for limited purposes of study, teaching, and academic research). One such Web site is www.law.cornell.edu/ucc/ucc.table. html.

2. There has been debate over whether a National Collegiate Athletic Association scholarship or letter of intent constitutes a legally binding contract. This issue is addressed in section 6.3.2, "Participation Rules."

3. Television contracts are discussed in section 14.2, "Broadcast Contracts."

4. An example of a standard player contract can be found in section 9.2.1.9, "Example of a Standard Player Contract: National Football League."

5. An example of a college coaches' contract can be found in section 9.2.5, "Coaches' Contracts: Professional and Collegiate Sports."

6. An example of a physician's contract can be found in section 9.2.7, "Physicians' Contracts."

7. An example of an official's contract can be found in section 9.2.8, "Officials' Contracts."

8. Athlete endorsement and international contracts are discussed in section 12.1, "Agency Law."

9.1.1. Formation of a Contract

The major legal concepts involved in the formation of a contract are offer, acceptance, consideration, legality, and capacity.

9.1.1.1. Offer

For a contract to come into existence, the parties involved must agree on the terms of the deal. To reach the stage at which there is mutual assent, the parties must first go through the process of offering and accepting the terms of the contract. The terms of a contract are interpreted objectively, and if necessary, interpretations concerning the terms are answered by determining the intent of the parties forming the contract.

An offer is a conditional promise made by the *offeror* to the *offeree*. The offeror is the party who makes the offer; the offeree is the person(s) to whom an offer is made. The offer is conditional because the offeror will not be bound by the promise unless the offeree responds to the offer in the proper fashion. The *Second Restatement of Contracts* defines an offer as "the manifestation of willingness to enter into a bargain, so made as to justify another person in understanding that his assent to that bargain is invited."

An offer usually includes the following essential terms:

(a) The parties involved

(b) The subject matter

(c) The time (and place) for the subject matter to be performed

(d) The price to be paid.

For example, College A offers to play at College B in football on November 1, 2011, at 2 P.M. for the sum of $1,000 plus complimentary tickets. College B accepts the offer and signs a written contract with College A. In this example, an exchange of promises has been made and the essential terms of parties, time, place, performance, and price have been incorporated. Note, however, that the number of complimentary tickets has not been specified. By itself, this would not void a contract; rather, it would be expected that this number would be the number of tickets usually given to the opposing team as a standard practice for football games.

Most offers contain a pair of promises—a conditional promise made by one party that is premised on the second party's promising to do some act in return. This exchange of promises is categorized as a *bilateral contract*. When an offer is made by one party to a proposed contract to the second party to the contract, it creates a *power of acceptance*, because if the second party accepts the offer, a contract is formed. For example, A promises to pay B $100 if B promises to officiate a basketball game for A. If B accepts, a bilateral contract is formed.

A *unilateral contract* is a contract that does not involve an exchange of promises. It instead involves an exchange of a promise in return for an act by a second party. The second party is not bound to do anything, but if the second party chooses to do the requested act, the first party is bound to the terms of his or her promise. For example, a sporting goods store offers $50 in store credit to anyone who shows up at the store's grand opening. Anyone who shows up has accepted the offer, and the store is bound to deliver on its promise.

An *option contract* involves an offer by one party to keep an offer open exclusively to a second party, for a stated period of time, if the second party agrees to pay a fee (or some other consideration) to the first party for keeping the offer open. For example, a real estate broker offers a basketball team the opportunity to purchase 200 acres of land for $2 million in order to build a playing facility, and also promises that if the basketball team pays a $100,000 security deposit, the $2 million price will remain fixed for six months. This six-month interval can allow the team to obtain zoning approval, league approval, and financing. Although the terms of an option contract are negotiable, the following scenario is typical. If the basketball team takes advantage of this provision in the specified time, the $100,000 will go toward the total asking price of $2 million. If the basketball team pays the $100,000 security deposit, but does not pay the additional $1.9 million within six months, the real seller keeps the $100,000 and the offer of the fixed price is off the table.

In certain contexts, words that might otherwise constitute an offer create no power of acceptance. For example, an offer made in jest is not a valid offer and creates no power of acceptance in the second party. Similarly, an offer is not made if it is just an expression of opinion. It is also important to distinguish preliminary negotiations from offers that create powers of acceptance. Consider the following example: the athletic director of College A calls the athletic director of College B and says College A would be interested in playing College B in men's basketball during the 2011 season. College B's athletic director then sends out a game contract to College A's athletic director that states, "I accept your offer and will play you on February 1, 2011, at 8 P.M. at the Slam-Dunk Center for $10,000." College A has not entered into the contract because its athletic director's call was only a solicitation of a contest and not a firm offer creating the power of acceptance in College B's athletic director. College A was only beginning preliminary negotiations. College A may still agree to the deal, but is under no obligation to do so.

Advertisements are generally not considered offers to sell, but rather are viewed as an invitation to the public to buy. For example, a minor league hockey team advertises an upcoming game in the local newspaper. The game is a sellout, but fans still want to buy tickets to the game. The team is under no obligation to sell more tickets to the game, because the advertisement was just an invitation for the public to buy tickets—not a specific offer to sell tickets to all fans. However, an advertisement that includes the phrase "First come, first served" is considered an offer to enter a unilateral contract. Thus, the first person to respond to the advertisement accepts the offer, creating a binding contract with the advertiser. A valid offer is created only with the first person to respond to the offer, unless the offer specifies a higher number—for example, "The first 1,000 fans to buy tickets will receive one free ticket to a game next season!"

9.1.1.2. Acceptance

An *acceptance* can be made only by the party to whom the offer was made. For example, the women's Olympic lacrosse team offers to buy 20 helmets from Manufacturer A for $100 each. Unknown to the equipment manager of the lacrosse team, Manufacturer B has bought Manufacturer A's business. The equipment manager has dealt with Manufacturer B before, and does not like its warranty policy. Manufacturer B accepts the order from the equipment manager. However, the equipment manager refuses to accept delivery from Manufacturer B and does not have to do so, since the offer to purchase the helmets was made to Manufacturer A and therefore does not create a power of acceptance in Manufacturer B.

The party accepting the offer, the *offeree*, may be required to accept the offer from the party making it, the *offeror*, in a specified manner (e.g., by letter). In some instances, which may depend in part on past practice between the parties, an offer may be accepted by silence (offeree makes no response to offeror). To avoid confusion as to whether an official offer has been made, all contact should be in writing, and the responses should be recorded.

Mutual assent occurs when the offeree clearly accepts the offeror's offer. A problem may result with mutual assent when an acceptance varies in its terms from the initial offer. According to common law, acceptance must be a mirror image of the offer (see note 1). However, the U.C.C. does allow for some exceptions (see note 3).

The offeree's power of acceptance can be terminated in four ways:

1. By rejection or counteroffer by the offeree
2. By a lapse of time
3. By revocation by the offeror
4. By death or incapacity of either party to the contract.

The following examples illustrate these reasons for termination:

- *Rejection or counteroffer*: Notre Dame offers to play Georgia Tech in field hockey on October 15, 2011. Georgia Tech rejects the October 15 date and instead offers to play on October 16. The offer made by Notre Dame was terminated by Georgia Tech's rejection, and the October 16 date is considered a counteroffer. The responsibility would then be placed on Notre Dame either to accept the new date or to reject it and counteroffer.

- *Lapse of time*: The University of Massachusetts sends a letter of intent to a proposed scholarship student-athlete which states that if the letter of intent is not signed by a certain date, it is no longer valid. The student-athlete is considering a number of different scholarship offers and allows the letter of intent to lapse, thus terminating her power of acceptance. After the deadline date, she reconsiders and requests a new letter to be sent. The University of Massachusetts has subsequently offered the scholarship to another individual, and notifies the initial offeree that its offer of a scholarship had lapsed.

- *Revocation*: A promoter in Helsinki, Finland, contacts the Anaheim Ducks and offers to schedule an exhibition game in Helsinki on August 15, 2011, between the Ducks and a Finnish team to take advantage of Anaheim's Teemu Selanne's popularity in his native country. The Ducks say they will think about the offer. Before the Ducks can respond, Selanne decides to retire. Upon hearing of the retirement, the promoter immediately informs the Ducks that its offer is revoked.

- *Death or incapacity*: The New York Knicks, of the National Basketball Association, offer their first round draft pick a three-year deal worth $12 million. Before the draftee can respond, he is fatally injured in a car collision. Therefore, the offer cannot be accepted because the draftee's death makes the performance of a contract impossible.

NOTES

1. In *Los Angeles Rams v. Cannon*, 185 F.Supp. 717 (S.D. Ca. 1960), Billy Cannon signed a contract with the Los Angeles Rams of the National Football League (NFL) for the 1960, 1961, and 1962 seasons. Pursuant to Paragraph 13 of the NFL Constitution, which states that the NFL commissioner needs to sign any player contract before it can become officially recognized, the commissioner signed the 1960 contract. The Houston team from the rival American Football League contacted Cannon prior to the 1960 season, and signed him to a more lucrative deal. Cannon subsequently revoked his contract with the Rams. The Rams attempted to get an injunction barring Cannon from playing for the Houston team, and the court was forced to determine whether a valid contract offer and acceptance had occurred. The court reasoned that Cannon had been offered three years (1960–1962) and that the submission of the signed 1960 contract should be viewed as a counteroffer because the original terms had changed. Thus, Cannon's contract with the Rams was void because the Rams had not accepted the three-year deal, and Cannon had not accepted the one-year deal.

2. In *Detroit Football v. Robinson*, 186 F.Supp. 933 (E.D. La. 1960), Robinson, a college football star, signed a contract with the Detroit Lions of the NFL while he was still in his last year of college. Pursuant to Paragraph 13 of the NFL Constitution, the contract was sent to the commissioner for his approval. Before the commissioner signed the contract, the Dallas Club from the American Football League approached Robinson about securing his services, and did so shortly thereafter, signing him to a lucrative contract. Detroit attempted to get an injunction to stop Robinson from signing with Dallas because he had entered into a binding agreement with them. The court found that the contract Robinson signed with Detroit was really an offer, and that acceptance occurred only when the commissioner signed the contract. Thus, Robinson's contract with Detroit was revoked.

3. Under the U.C.C. provisions for the sale of goods, an acceptance that differs from the offer will be enforceable, as long as the acceptance is not expressly conditioned on the offeror's accepting the new terms. This is provided that one party to the contract is not a merchant. For example, an equipment manager for the Pittsburgh Steelers orders 20 football helmets with face guards and chinstraps for $100 each. The manufacturer accepts the order (offer) but notes on its order acknowledgment form that chin straps are not usually included, but they can be included in this sale for an additional $1 per helmet. This is considered "a proposal for addition to the contract" and will not become part of the contract until the equipment manager agrees to it. If the chinstraps are essential to the formation of the entire contract, then a contract may be deemed not to have come into existence at all.

9.1.1.3. *Consideration*

In the context of contract law, the word *consideration* has a special and uniquely important definition. In addition to mutual assent (offer and acceptance), it is essential for the formation of most contracts that there be some form of consideration—that is, the value that each party to the contract is exchanging. For example, Bob offers Scott his tickets to a boxing match for $25. Scott accepts. This is a binding contract because Bob is giving up his tickets, and Scott is giving up $25. Each party's pledge to give up something of value to the other constitutes consideration. Another example would involve a coach who agrees to work for Team A, to the exclusion of other teams, for a period of two years, at an annual salary of $1 million per year. The coach is giving his services and experience exclusively to Team A, and in return Team A gives the coach a salary, health insurance, and other benefits. Consideration is often the essential element needed in a contract to make it legally enforceable. Without consideration, there may be a promise to do an act, but it may not be legally enforceable as a contract. Consideration can be contrasted to the giving of a gift, which may involve a promise to do something of value but involves no promise in return. For example, A offers to wash B's car as a birthday gift. However, since B is not obligated to do anything for A, there is no consideration, and a binding contract does not exist.

There are three important concepts that can help establish or negate the existence of legal consideration:

1. Preexisting duty rule
2. Mutuality of obligation
3. Promissory estoppel.

The *preexisting duty rule* states that duties imposed by law or by a prior contract will not serve as adequate consideration. Preexisting duties include consideration to earlier contracts, which cannot form the basis for enacting a new, legally binding contract. Past consideration is an act that could have served as consideration if it had been bargained for at the time the contract was formed. Since consideration involves an exchange, parties cannot bargain (or exchange) for something that has already occurred. For example, a baseball team promises to give its bus driver medical benefits if the driver increases his hours. This would be considered inadequate consideration if the team had already promised medical benefits in the bus driver's original contract.

The doctrine of *mutuality of obligation* states that the consideration given by all parties to the contract must be legally sufficient, and $1 is usually sufficient. However, it is important to note that the consideration given by the parties does not need to be equal. For example, assume that a brand new hockey arena contracts to sell in-arena advertising space to a local insurance firm for $10,000. Later, the hockey team discovers that the market value of the advertising space is actually $100,000, and therefore refuses to honor the contract. The insurance firm then sues the hockey team for breach of contract. During trial, the attorney for the hockey team claims that the contract lacks mutuality because it is unequal. The judge in such a trial is likely to reject the hockey team's defense, and will probably allow the transaction to go through. An exception may be made if the insurance company knew of the team's error and sought to exploit the mistake (see section 9.1.2, "Mistakes in Contracts," below). Had the hockey team contracted to sell the ad space to the insurance firm for an "amount to be negotiated later," the judge would likely rule the contract invalid. Such consideration given by the parties lacks mutuality of obligation because it lacks definiteness.

In the professional sports context, the issue of mutuality was predominant in a series of cases in professional baseball in the late 19th century. In *Metropolitan Exhibition Co. v. Ewing*, 42 F. 198 (C.C.D. N.Y. 1890), the defendant had signed a contract with another team after playing the previous season with the plaintiff. The plaintiff claimed that due to the right of reservation, known as the reserve system, the player was not free to sign with any other club. The court found that the terms of the reserve system were not adequately defined in the contract, so it was unclear what the consideration would be for the following season. Thus, Ewing was allowed to sign with another team. In a similar case, *Metropolitan Exhibition Co. v. Ward*, 9. N.Y.S. 779 (N.Y. Sup. Ct. 1890), the court found that the player contract between Ward and the plaintiff was invalid because of lack of mutuality. The court explained that the reserve system allowed the team to keep a player in perpetuity, while also granting the team the opportunity to terminate the contract on 10 days' notice. Because the contract did not express what the teams were obligated to forfeit in exchange for the players' forfeiture of job security and leverage, the contract was revoked. These two cases will be discussed further in section 9.2.2, "Defenses to Standard Player Contract Breaches."

Professional baseball learned something from these cases and altered its player contracts to state that, in exchange for a large salary, the player agreed to the reserve system and the 10-day termination notice. Professional baseball was confident that the new language would satisfy the obligation of mutuality. In *Philadelphia Ball Club, Ltd. v. Lajoie*, 51 A. 973 (Pa. 1902), the court granted an injunction to the Philadelphia club barring Lajoie from playing for any other team. On the issue of mutuality, the court reasoned:

> The defendant has the possibility of enforcing all the rights for which he stipulated in the agreement, which is all that he can reasonably ask; furthermore, owing to the peculiar nature and circumstances of the business, the reservation upon the part of the plaintiff to terminate upon short notice, does not make the whole contract inequitable.

These early cases enforce the rule that contracts need not be equitable to be enforced, but within the contract itself, there does need to be a stipulation that clearly identifies what each party to the contract is giving and receiving as consideration (see notes 2 and 3). In many such cases, including *Lajoie*, players' irreplaceable skills are central issues. See section 9.2.1.2. The significance of reserve clauses in the history of major league sports will be closely examined in Chapter 10.

The doctrine of *promissory estoppel* allows the occasional enforcement of a contract that is not supported by consideration. Under this doctrine, a court will enforce a contract with inadequate consideration if a promise is made that the promisor should reasonably expect would, and which in fact does, induce forbearance or reliance on the part of the promisee. For example, assume that an athletic director tells an employee that since she has been a dedicated and hard worker, when she retires, the athletic department will give her $500 per month for the rest of her life. Relying on this statement, the employee does not purchase an additional retirement plan. While there is no valid consideration given, the court may choose to enforce a contract here because the employee reasonably relied on the statement of the athletic director (see note 2).

NOTES

1. In *Blackmon v. Iverson*, 324 F.Supp.2d 602 (E.D.Pa. 2003), Jamil Blackmon, a family friend of basketball star Allen Iverson claimed that Iverson agreed to give him 25% of all profits that incorporated Iverson's nickname "The Answer," that Blackmon claimed to have created. When the slogan was later used in a Reebok campaign with Iverson and Iverson refused to compensate him, Blackmon claimed breach of contract. Blackmon claimed that the consideration given to Iverson were (1) Blackmon's idea to use "The Answer" as a nickname to sell athletic apparel; (2) Blackmon's assistance to Iverson and his family; and (3) Blackmon's move to Philadelphia to be near Iverson. The court disagreed and invalidated the contract as not supported by adequate consideration.

2. In 2001, Florida Marlins outfielder Cliff Floyd claimed that National League manager Bobby Valentine promised him a spot on the National League All-Star team. Based on

this, Floyd claims that he bought $16,000 in nonrefundable plane tickets so that his family could watch him play the All-Star Game in Seattle. Valentine did *not* name Floyd to the All-Star team, and denies that he ever made such a promise to Floyd. Hypothetically, if Floyd could have proven to a judge that Valentine promised him an All-Star spot, it is possible that the judge would have invoked the doctrine of promissory estoppel and forced Valentine to name Floyd to the All-Star team or make him whole (pay him $16,000). Floyd never threatened action over the matter, and the matter was rendered moot when another player's last-minute injury opened up a spot for Floyd on the All-Star team.

3. In the *Matter of Arbitration Between Phoenix Suns and Athletic Union of Constantinople* (1997), the Phoenix Suns sought the services of a basketball player, Iakovos "Jake" Tsakalidis, who was under contract to play for the Greek professional team, AEK, through the 2000 season. Phoenix argued that the contract was null and void for various reasons, including the lack of mutuality, and therefore Tsakalidis should be allowed to exit his contract without penalty, to play in the NBA. In arbitration, the claimant Suns were successful. The arbitrator ruled that the contract was invalid under Greek law because the penalty clause within the contract was illegally severe and was an excessive curtailment of Tsakalidis's freedom to pursue his basketball career. The Suns were therefore able to sign Tsakalidis because the Greek contract had been nullified. AEK subsequently challenged the arbitrator's decision in an English court, but the court upheld the arbitrator's decision to allow Tsakalidis out of his contract.

4. In the *Matter of Arbitration Between Toronto Raptors and Budocnost* (1997), the Toronto Raptors, in a case similar to the *Tsakalidis* case, sought to gain the services of Aleksandar Radojevic, who was under contract to play for Budocnost of the Yugoslavian Basketball League through the 2000–2001 season. The arbitrator decided that Radojevic's contract with Budocnost was not a valid contract because it did not specify the compensation that would be awarded Radojevic for the final three years of his contract with the team.

9.1.1.4. Legality

Another requirement for an enforceable contract is the *legality* of the underlying agreement. Courts will not enforce a contract that is illegal. The courts are concerned with two types of illegalities: statutory violations and violations of public policy not expressly declared illegal by statute. Statutory violations include gambling contracts, contracts with unlicensed professionals (doctors, lawyers, accountants), and contracts that violate laws regulating consumer credit transactions (loan sharks).

Contracts that may violate public policy include contracts that waive tort liability and contracts that interfere with family relationships. With these contracts, no general rule for determining their legality can be given, except to say that the more egregious the provisions, the less likely that they will withstand judicial scrutiny. For example, courts would not be likely to uphold a contract of a bungee-jumping company that waives tort liability in the event that the company provides a bungee cord that is too long, and the customer dies (see section 4.10, "Waiver and Release of Liability"). Another contract clause that might violate public policy is an egregious *covenant not to compete*. A covenant not to compete is a contractual agreement where an employee promises not to work in a similar job in the same industry for a certain period of time after his or her term of employment is completed. Covenants not to compete are frequently contained in coach's contracts (see note 3).

A court or arbitrator's decision to uphold a covenant not to compete also depends on the reasonableness of the geographic scope, the kind of work covered, and length of time. For example, former Indiana University basketball coach Bobby Knight had a noncompete clause in his 1982 contract saying that he would forfeit his deferred pay if he joined another Big Ten conference team, a state of Indiana team, or a state of Kentucky team after leaving his job at Indiana University.

There was some debate about the legality of this clause when Knight was terminated in 2000. While the clause was clear about geographic scope (Big Ten, Indiana, Kentucky), a court or arbitrator might have found that region to be excessively large. Also, the noncompete pact did not dictate any time period, though many such pacts do. This absence, which may have created a perpetual covenant not to compete, could also have been found excessive. The Knight noncompete clause was rendered moot when he accepted a job at Texas Tech University in 2001, since the Big Ten and states of Indiana and Kentucky were not involved. For more information on Bobby Knight's contract at Indiana University, see section 9.2.5, "Coaches' Contracts: Professional and Collegiate Sports."

Although both types of illegal contracts (statutory and public policy) are generally unenforceable, the severity of this approach has led courts to seek ways to moderate the impact. The principle of restitution has been used to achieve this moderation. *Restitution* requires that no one who has conferred a benefit or suffered a loss should be unfairly denied compensation. In a case where the underlying bargain is illegal, the court may find it appropriate to reimburse or "make whole" the party who unfairly suffered a loss (see section 9.1.8, "Remedies for a Breach of Contract").

NOTES

1. In *Bires v. WalTom LLC*,662 F.Supp.2d 1019 (N.D.Ill. 2009), a professional racecar driver brought a suit against his former racing team alleging that his employment contract with them was illegal. The contract required the driver to continue to pay WalTom 25% of all future earnings for 10 years after he stopped driving for WalTom. The court ruled that the royalty provision was an illegal restrain of trade because of the effect it would have on Bires' future employment opportunities.

2. In *de la Hoya v. Top Rank, Inc.*, 2001 WL 34624886 (C.D.Cal. February 6, 2001), a promotion and management contract between champion boxer Oscar de la Hoya and Top Rank, Inc. was determined to be illegal and unenforceable because Top Rank was not properly licensed under the California Boxing Act and the Professional Boxing Rules of the California Business and Professional Code. In addition, the contract was illegal for exceeding the seven-year maximum term for a personal services contract under the California Labor Code.

3. In 2000, an independent arbitrator found that the Minnesota Timberwolves had signed a secret contract with Joe Smith in an effort to circumvent the cap. The contract was ruled illegal and an arbitrator upheld Commissioner David Stern's penalty against the Timberwolves of a $3.5 million fine, a loss of five first round draft picks, and a loss of re-signing rights for Smith.

4. After winning the Super Bowl as head coach of the St. Louis Rams in 2000, Dick Vermeil resigned in the middle of his multiyear deal with the team. The team accepted his resignation, and paid him $500,000 to work as a consultant. Later in 2000, Vermeil accepted a three-year, $10 million contract to become head coach of the Kansas City Chiefs. The Rams protested and the matter was arbitrated by NFL Commissioner Paul Tagliabue. Tagliabue who found that "the clear purpose and effect of the agreement... was that Vermeil would remain retired from coaching through the 2001 season." Tagliabue transferred a second round and a third round draft pick and $500,000 from the Chiefs in order to "make the Rams whole."

5. In *Vanderbilt University* v. *DiNardo*, 174 F.3d 751 (6th Cir. 1999), the defendant football coach unsuccessfully argued that his termination clause was actually a noncompete clause, illegal under Tennessee law.

6. For more on the role of noncompete clauses in professional sports, see Jason Gershwin, "Will Professional Athletes Continue to Choose Their Representation Freely? An Examination of the Enforceability of Non-Compete Agreements against Sports Agents," 5 *University of Pennsylvania Journal of Labor and Employment Law* 585 (2003).

7. For more on contracts in sports that may be against public policy, see Sean M. Hanlon, "Athletic Scholarships as Unconscionable Contracts of Adhesion: Has the NCAA Fouled Out?" 13 *Sports Lawyers Journal* 41 (2006).

9.1.1.5. Capacity

In addition to the offer and acceptance, the capacity of a party to make or accept an offer is an important factor in the formation of a valid contract. *Capacity* is defined as the ability to understand the nature and effects of one's acts. If a person lacks capacity at the time a contract is formed, that person (and *only* that person) may later void the contract; the other party cannot. The general rule is that anyone who has reached the age of majority (18 years of age in most states) and is mentally competent has the capacity to enter into a contract. A contract entered into by a minor, or one who has not yet reached the age of majority, is considered voidable, but only by the minor. A minor has the right to disaffirm a contract before reaching the age of majority and for a certain amount of time after reaching the age of majority. Nevertheless, minors remain liable for any tangible benefits they have received or still possess, and may have to pay restitution if they disaffirm a contract.

Similarly, parties who have been adjudicated mentally incompetent may disaffirm prior contractual agreements through court-appointed guardians, but may remain liable for tangible benefits received. Finally, parties who have become extremely intoxicated by drugs or alcohol may lack the capacity to enter an agreement. A nonintoxicated signatory who seeks to take advantage of the situation will generally not be able to enforce the terms of the resulting bargain.

Capacity does not only apply to individuals, as certain members of organizations have the capacity to bind the corporations to contracts. A corporate agent can be a natural person or another corporation that is authorized to act for the corporation in signing off on contracts. For example, an athletic director of a college is authorized to bind the school in certain areas; thus the athletic director has corporate capacity to act on behalf of the athletic department and/or school. Likewise, the president of a professional sports team is authorized to act on the team's behalf and therefore has corporate capacity. However, the same team's assistant general manager may not possess corporate capacity.

NOTE _____

1. For a case involving the capacity of a minor to sign a professional contract, see section 9.2.3, "Tortious Interference with Contractual Relations" for *Central Red Army Club v. Arena Associates*, 952 F.Supp. 181 (S.D.N.Y, 1997).

9.1.1.6. Drafting a Contract

To review the different contracts one may find in the sports industry, it is important to understand the makeup of a contract. The following explanation offers a brief description of sections in a typical contract.

1. *Opening*. Identifies the parties to the agreement, the date of the contract, and its effective date.

2. *Representations and warranties.* Contains information regarding the rights and qualifications of the parties to enter into an agreement, as well as any express or implied warranties regarding the subject matter of the contract.

3. *Operational language.* Contains the subject matter of the contract. The precise rights and duties of the parties under the contract are explained.

4. *Other clauses.* Certain other clauses may be included, depending on the nature of the contract. Compensation, rights to arbitration for any disagreements, and the right to assign the contract are typical examples.

5. *Termination.* Discusses the length of the contract and the means of ending the contract.

6. *Entire agreement and amendments.* Details the comprehensiveness of the contract and its relation to other agreements, as well as the methods by which the contract can be amended.

7. *Closing.* Contains the signatures of the parties to the contract, any acknowledgments, and the signatures of any witnesses.

9.1.2. Mistakes in Contracts

Mistakes frequently occur in the contracting process. The claim of a mistake may be raised by one seeking to rescind the contract or to avoid liability under it. Courts will adjudicate such claims differently depending on whether a contractual mistake is unilateral or mutual. *Unilateral mistakes* are those made by only one party as to a basic assumption at the time the contract was formed, and have an adverse material effect on the agreed exchange. The contract may be voidable by the adversely affected party only if the other party actually knew or had reason to know of the mistake at the time the contract was made and sought to take advantage of the error, or where his or her fault caused the mistake. For example, if the Rogers Centre in Toronto contracts with the NFL for an exhibition game, the Rogers Centre may assume that the selected teams' starting players will play in the game. If the NFL knows the Rogers Centre has made this assumption, but accepts the deal knowing that the participating teams will send only reserve players, the Rogers Centre's mistake may allow it to escape liability. Another example would be if one professional team knowingly traded a player who was injured to another team without disclosing the injuries. In this example, there is a possibility the trade could be voided, but there is also the possibility that the team receiving the injured player would have to follow the caveat emptor (buyer beware) rule. To protect themselves from this type of situation, teams typically make the trades conditional upon the passing of a physical examination (see note 1).

On the other hand, a *mutual mistake* occurs when both parties make a mistake about a basic assumption of the contract. The contract is voidable by the party that is adversely affected. For example, Wahoo University entered into an agreement to purchase 125 football helmets made of a compound called "plastex" from Tribex Corporation. Unknown to both the buyer and the seller, two different compounds called plastex could be used to make football helmets, but they did not cost the same. Wahoo University thought it was ordering the less expensive form of the compound, while Tribex used the more expensive form. Courts would void the contract upon the discovery of the mutual mistake at the request of either party, since neither party was aware of the ambiguity and both could be adversely affected due to the cost difference.

NOTES

1. When trades occur in professional sports, it is difficult for one team to prove that another team misrepresented the health of a traded player. Teams must generally abide by the principle of caveat emptor (buyer beware). In 2001, the Toronto Blue Jays sought relief from Major League Baseball Commissioner Bud Selig after at least one of the players received in a six-player trade turned out to be seriously injured. The players had passed an initial physical, but pitcher Mike Sirotka (the key player in the trade from the Chicago White Sox) showed a season-ending shoulder injury in a subsequent physical. The Blue Jays hoped that Selig would rescind the trade, in which they had relinquished star pitcher David Wells. Selig refused to grant the Blue Jays relief, citing the caveat emptor rule: "Although there is a dispute about whether certain facts about Sirotka's condition were disclosed before the clubs agreed to the trade, the Toronto club . . . had the opportunity to make the trade conditional [on the passing of a second physical examination]."

2. Melvin Aron Eisenberg, "The Role of Fault in Contract Law: Unconscionability, Unexpected Circumstances, Interpretation, Mistake, and Nonperformance," 107 *Michigan law Review* 1413 (2009).

9.1.3. Parol Evidence Rule

When a written contract is finalized and the parties agree that it represents the final expression of their agreement, the contract may be described as an *integration of agreement*. Often a contract will contain an integration clause that stipulates that the written document represents the total agreement between the parties. When this occurs, the contract is considered the *total expression of the agreement*.

The *parol evidence rule* prohibits the admission of oral statements, preliminary agreements, or other writings made prior to or at the time of signing that would in any way alter, contradict, or change the meaning of the written contract. Such evidence may be used only to show the intention of the parties if the objective of the contract cannot be ascertained from its language. But when the meaning is clear and the contract was considered integrated at its signing, the parol evidence rule bars the introduction into evidence of any noncontractual understandings between the parties.

For example, at some point in negotiations over a professional athlete's player contract, there may have been discussion between the agent and the team over performance bonuses for the player. Due to the evolving nature of negotiations, the agent dropped the request. Under the parol evidence rule, the player cannot later introduce evidence of the bonuses that were discussed in negotiations. However, if the player and his agent believe that they did indeed negotiate the bonuses but that they were unintentionally omitted, the player may have the option of using an internal resolution mechanism (grievance procedure) or an external mechanism (court). Also, if the parties' intent is not clear from the contract language, for example if the contract mentions bonuses but not their amount, parol evidence may be considered.

9.1.4. Conditions of a Contract

For a contract to be binding, one or more conditions must be met by each of the parties. The nonoccurrence of a condition, or the failure of one party to comply with a condition, operates to void the contractual duty by the other party. Conditions may be expressed (stated directly in the agreement), implied (tacitly understood between the parties as part of the agreement), or constructive (not agreed upon at all by the parties but imposed by a court to ensure fairness).

Generally there are two types of conditions: a condition precedent and a condition subsequent. A *condition precedent* is one that must occur before a contract will be considered binding on the parties. For example, before a Major League Baseball player's contract is official, the commissioner of Major League Baseball must sign the contract. Without the commissioner's signature, the condition is not met and the contract is void. Another example would be if two NCAA basketball schools entered into a regular season game contract for the 2011–2012 season, but with the condition precedent that the contract would only apply if the two teams make the NCAA basketball tournament in the 2010–2011 season.

A *condition subsequent* occurs when the parties condition a contract on an event's nonoccurrence. For example, assume that a college has decided to open a training facility on campus and has contracted with a company to provide exercise equipment on the condition that the company can deliver the equipment one week before the facility's opening. If it occurs that the company does not have the equipment on the date designated for delivery, then the contract is void.

9.1.5. Statute of Frauds

Certain types of contracts are unenforceable under the *statute of frauds* unless they are in writing. This statute, which has its roots in English common law, is designed to prevent injustices resulting from fraudulent claims or promises that were not kept. The exact rules vary from state to state. However, most states require that the following contracts must be in writing:

- Contracts for goods over $500

- Any agreement made upon consideration of marriage

- Agreements for the sale of land or of interests in land; an interest in land includes the sale or mortgaging and leasing of real property and the creation of easements

- Contracts lasting at least one year

- Suretyship agreements (when one party guarantees another's debts)

- Promises of executors and administrators to answer out of their own will for the debts or damage caused by the estates that they administer

NOTES

1. In *Holloway v. King*, 361 F.Supp.2d 351 (S.D.N.Y. 2005), two former managers of boxer Mike Tyson sued promoter Don King, alleging that he breached an oral agreement to give each of them 10% of all of King's earnings resulting from Tyson's fights. The court granted King's motion to dismiss because the agreement was of an indefinite duration and there was a superseding written agreement that contained a valid integration clause of any prior oral contracts.

2. In *Yocca v. Pittsburgh Steelers Sports, Inc.*, 578 Pa. 479 (Pa. 2004), season ticket holders who had purchased Stadium Builder Licenses (SBLs) sued the Steelers claiming, among other things, that the team had breached the season ticket contract because their seats were not as they thought they would be, according to an SBL brochure. Specifically, one fan was upset that his tickets were on the 18-yard line instead of the 20-yard line. The court ruled that the subsequent SBL contract entered into represented the parties' entire contract and the parol evidence rule barred the admission of the SBL brochure.

3. In *Price v. University of Alabama*, 318 F.Supp.2d 1084 (N.D. Ala. 2003), Mike Price sued the University of Alabama and the university's president and athletic director, Robert

Witt, after he was fired in early May 2003 as head coach of the football team before ever coaching a game. Price was fired for allegations of improper behavior, including being heavily intoxicated at a strip club while attending a charitable golf tournament in Florida not associated with the University of Alabama. Along with a constitutional due process claim for being fired without a chance to refute the allegations, Price alleged breach of contract, wrongful termination and fraud, misrepresentation and deceit. In dismissing the case, the District Court ruled that the Eleventh Amendment barred suit against the university and that Witt also had qualified immunity. In addition, Price had never signed his contract as certain terms were still being negotiated. A draft of the contract included liquidated damages in the event that Price was fired without cause. The court held that pursuant to the Alabama Statute of Frauds, the alleged contract was void.

4. Jonathan Fineman, "The Inevitable Decline of the Implied Employment Contract," 29 *Berkeley Journal of Employment and Labor Law* 345 (2008).

9.1.6. Assignment and Delegation of a Contract

Rights and obligations of a contract may be assigned and duties under a contract may be delegated without nullifying the contract. Generally all rights under a contract may be assigned to another party. When one assigns a contract to another party, he or she transfers all obligations under the contract as well. For example, when a professional sports team trades a player to another team, it is assigning that player's contract to a team that did not originally enter into the contract. The player's original team is no longer liable under the contract. However, the new team must abide by the player's contract, unless both sides agree to begin negotiations on a new contract. Potential difficulties arising from assignment and delegation of a contract are averted if a player possesses a nonassignment clause or no-trade clause.

Delegation of duties under a contract does not create a transfer in the same sense as an assignment, because the original party is not relieved of all obligations under the contract. The delegating party may be held liable for any breaches of the contract even if the breach was caused by the party that accepted the delegation. For example, assume a university has a contract with Supplier A for the purchase of 10 cases of tennis balls. If Supplier A will not be able to fulfill the agreement on time, it may delegate its duties for the supply of tennis balls to Supplier B. While this delegation is valid, Supplier A will still be liable for any breach in the original contract with the university if Supplier B does not properly fulfill the duties under the contract by delivering the goods on time.

9.1.7. Breach of Contract

A *breach of contract* can be broadly defined as a failure to perform a duty imposed under a contract. A contract may be either totally or partially breached by any party that has entered into it. A *total* breach of contract occurs when one of the parties has not fully engaged in the specific performance that is outlined in the contract. If one of the parties has engaged in the specific performance outlined in the contract, but not to the exact extent as outlined, there may be a *partial* breach.

Example 1: Total Breach of Contract

- Team A and Team B agree to play a total of two basketball games (the first game at Team A's home venue and the second at Team B's home venue).

- The contract states that the home team must pay the visiting team $100,000 within one week after each event.
- A day *before* the first game, Team B informs Team A that it will not play the games as agreed upon in the contract.

Example 2: Partial Breach of Contract

- Team A and Team B agree to play a total of two basketball games (the first game at Team A's home venue and the second at Team B's home venue).
- The contract states that the home team must pay the visiting team $100,000 within one week after each event.
- A day *after* the first game is played, Team B informs Team A that it will not play the second game as agreed upon in the contract.

The distinction between total and partial breach of contract is important because of the burden placed on the aggrieved party. A total breach (example 1) discharges the aggrieved party of any duty to perform, and that party may immediately file suit. Therefore, in example 1, Team A becomes released from its obligations in the contract. It may immediately sue Team B to recover damages for such things as travel, advertising, and lost concession revenues for the canceled event (see subsection 9.1.8, "Remedies for a Breach of Contract"), and it is not obligated to travel to Team B's arena for the second game. A partial breach (example 2) may not discharge the aggrieved party from a duty to perform, but the aggrieved party may file suit immediately to collect any damages that are due. In other words, Team A may still have to pay Team B its $100,000 guarantee for the first game, despite the breach of contract. However, it may file suit for damages suffered due to the partial breach by Team B (lost television revenue, etc.). According to *Restatement of Contracts*, a party cannot simultaneously sue for total and partial breach. Litigation for breach of contract often occurs relative to players' or coaches' contracts such as in *Alabama Football Inc. v. Stabler* (see note 5).

To avoid damages in a breach of contract case, the defense may attempt to show that a contract never truly existed. To do so, the defendant may *attack the elements* of a contract to show that one or more of them was missing. Concerning the element of offer, the defense in a breach of contract case may argue that the offer was a solicitation and should be considered preliminary negotiation rather than a legal contract offer. Regarding the element of acceptance, the defense may argue that the contract in question is not whole because the proper acceptance was not achieved. For example, a party may contend that it did not accept an offer merely by indicating that its terms were fair, but meant instead to seek further negotiations.

If a party cannot successfully attack the validity of the contract, there are other defenses to a breach of contract suit: *impossibility of performance*, *frustration of purpose*, and *impracticability*. *Impossibility of performance* occurs when a party to the contract promises something that becomes impossible to perform through no fault of his or her own. This defense is used when the subject matter is destroyed, the action required under the contract becomes illegal under newly approved laws, or there is death or incapacity of one of the parties to the contract. For example, if a facility has a contract to host a tennis tournament, but the facility is destroyed by a tornado, it is impossible for the facility to host the event. Even if the event has to be canceled due to rain, a court may accept the defense of impossibility of performance, although this issue is usually addressed in the contract.

The defense of *frustration of purpose* is used when the value of performance to be obtained becomes useless to a party because of an unforeseen change in the circumstances. For example, a college signs a contract with a landscaping company to landscape the college's golf course. However, if the state government passed a conservation law banning significant alterations to the land including the golf course, the purpose for which the university contracted would be frustrated.

The final defense for a breach of contract suit is *impracticability*. This defense can be used when the cost of performance is greatly increased due to an unforeseen occurrence. This is a narrowly interpreted defense and is rarely used in the sports context. Courts have allowed performance to be excused under this defense in cases of war, embargo, or crop failure, among other circumstances.

NOTES

1. In 2009 and 2010 several prominent college football and basketball coaches were fired during the terms of their contracts and responded by filing suit for breach of contract. The coaches and firing institutions included Billy Gillispie and Kentucky who settled for approximately $3 million; Mike Leach and Texas Tech; Jim Leavitt and South Florida; and Bobby Gonzalez and Seton Hall.

2. In *Rocchigiani v. World Boxing Council, Inc.*, 131 F.Supp.2d 527 (S.D.N.Y. 2001), light heavyweight boxer Garciano Rocchigiani claimed the World Boxing Council (WBC) breached its contract by only declaring him "interim" champion after beating Michael Nunn in a fight touted as the WBC Light Heavyweight Championship. Nunn had been slated to fight current WBC Light Heavyweight Champion Roy Jones, Jr., but Jones chose not to participate. The result of the interim designation was a reduced share of the purse in future fights. The court ruled that the WBC did breach its contract with Rocchigiani because the word *interim* was nowhere to be found in the fight contract and that the contract specifically stated that the fight was for the "WBC World Championship." Rocchigiani was awarded $30 million in damages but settled the dispute out of court when the WBC was faced with bankruptcy.

3. Temple University and the University of Cincinnati's men's basketball teams scheduled a pair of basketball games, one to be played on Cincinnati's home court in 1999–2000 and one to be played on Temple's home court in 2000–2001. The two teams played the game in the 1999–2000 season, as scheduled. However, Cincinnati canceled the 2000–2001 game when it learned that it had mistakenly scheduled too many regular season games according to NCAA rules. Temple's athletic department did not have time to find another opponent for a makeup home game. Temple estimated that it lost $100,000 in expected revenue. The schools then entered into a handshake agreement whereby the schools would play two games on Temple's home court in future seasons and Cincinnati would reimburse Temple for reasonable expenses from the canceled game (e.g., reprinting schedule cards). While Cincinnati offered to make up the game in a future season, Temple still sent an $85,000 bill to Cincinnati, contending that a makeup game would not be sufficient to make it whole. Cincinnati found that amount to exceed reasonable reimbursement costs. Cincinnati grudgingly paid the $85,000 bill, but athletic director Bob Goin canceled the future games, vowing to never play Temple again during his tenure.

4. In *Rayle v. Bowling Green State University*, 739 N.E. 2d 1260 (Ct. Cl. Ohio 2000), a seat license/season ticket holder brought a breach of contract suit against a university after the university refunded his deposit when he refused to pay an increased annual service charge on his seats. The court held that the university did not breach contract by refunding the plaintiff's money, but instead that the plaintiff had breached contract by refusing to pay the annual service charge on his seats after he was notified that the fee would increase. The court also held that the university may reasonably increase the value of its seats, and reallocate seats when customers refuse to pay the charges.

5. In *Alabama Football Inc. v Stabler*, 319 So.2d 678 (Ala. 1975), Ken Stabler, a successful quarterback with the Oakland Raiders, sought damages after his contract with the World

Football League's Alabama franchise was breached. In 1973, he signed a lucrative deal with Alabama that included a signing bonus of $100,000 to be distributed in $50,000 increments in 1973 and 1974. The team paid the first $50,000, and then paid the next $20,000, but failed to pay the remaining $30,000. Stabler filed suit claiming breach of contract, and was declared a free agent. The court held that financial condition was not an excuse for non-performance of a contract, therefore the Alabama franchise's inability to pay Stabler constituted a breach of contract.

6. For information pertaining to international breach of contract issues in sports, see Lewis Kurlantzick, "The Tampering Prohibition and Agreements Between American and Foreign Sports Leagues," 32 *Columbia Journal of Law & the Arts* 271 (2009).

9.1.8. Remedies for a Breach of Contract

There are three primary remedies for a breach of contract: monetary damages, specific performance, and negative injunction.

Monetary damages fall into three different categories:

- *expectation* interest
- *reliance* interest
- *restitution*

For reasons described later, courts normally prefer to implement the first of these three remedies.

An *expectation* interest is the benefit that a party expects to get as the direct result of a contract; a *reliance* interest is the loss suffered by a party when it makes expenditure decisions while reasonably relying on another party's contractual promise; and *restitution* is the restoration of any benefits the nonbreaching party has conferred on the other party.

To illustrate the way in which the remedies may be distributed in a particular case, consider the following hypothetical example. The International Olympic Committee (IOC) chooses Toronto, Canada, to host the 2018 winter Olympics. In preparation for the event, $25 million is spent renovating existing buildings and constructing a needed short-track speed skating facility. In addition, $10 million is spent advertising the Olympics, and $5 million is spent luring advertisers to the project. Financial officers from the Toronto group complete a detailed analysis predicting that profits from the event will surpass $25 million. But a year before the Olympics in Toronto, a scandal is discovered that links the Toronto delegation to fraud. In response, the IOC strips the Games from Toronto and awards them to Stockholm, Sweden. The Toronto group files suit against the IOC for breach of contract. Assume that the case is decided in favor of Toronto, with a finding that there was no fraudulent behavior by the Toronto delegation.

The court's monetary damage award would contemplate expectation interest, reliance interest, and restitution. Under *expectation* interest, the court could force the IOC to reimburse Toronto for any profit it might reasonably have expected to derive directly from the games, in this case $25 million. Under *reliance* theory, the court could hold the IOC responsible for all the costs Toronto incurred in reliance on the contract—in this case $25 million spent on construction, $10 million spent on advertising, and $5 million spent luring advertisers. Under *restitution*, the court could require the IOC to reimburse to the Toronto party for any payments made to the IOC in connection with securing the Olympic bid. If the court finds that the

IOC breached its contract with the Toronto group, the latter could recover all of the damages outlined above.

One difficulty with monetary damages is that the aggrieved party must be able to translate the injury into a financial sum and be able to justify that amount to the court. Also, there are times when monetary damages are inadequate compensation for the breach of contract. Thus, a second type of remedy for breach of contract is equitable relief. One type of equitable relief is *specific performance*, which requires the performance of a contract in the specific form called for in the agreement. For example, if a contract for the sale of land is breached, the court could require the seller to give up the land as stipulated in the contract. A sport-related example might concern sports memorabilia.

For example, a fan catches a historic home-run ball and decides to sell the ball to a collector for $20,000. The next day, the fan hears that the ball could be worth up to a million dollars, so he decides not to follow through with the original contract with the collector, and instead seeks other offers. The court could order specific performance and require the fan to sell the ball to the collector for $20,000, because of the uniqueness of the item and the inability of the collector to go out and buy a replacement.

It is important to note that courts rarely require a contract for personal services, like a coach or player's contract, to be specifically performed. The courts usually reason that this would be a form of indentured servitude, in that the employee would be forced against his or her will to work for a certain employer. The Thirteenth Amendment to the U.S. Constitution prohibits indentured servitude and slavery. Therefore, in cases where monetary damages would be insufficient, aggrieved parties commonly appeal to the courts for a *negative injunction*. This second type of equitable relief forbids a party from providing services for parties other than the aggrieved party. For example, if a player leaves a team midway through a contract and signs with a team in another league, the team that held the original contract could attempt to get an injunction stopping the player from playing for the other team. Most sports leagues have systems of arbitration in place in their collective bargaining agreements to prevent such litigation between members. However, if one of the aggrieved parties is not covered by the arbitration agreement, or if a party believes that the arbitrators failed to follow proper procedure (see section 11.3.13, "Arbitration"), the issue may end up in court.

It may also wind up in court if teams from different leagues are involved. For example, in *Boston Celtics Limited Partnership v. Shaw*, 908 F.2d 1041 (1st Cir. 1990), basketball player Brian Shaw signed a two-year contract with Il Messaggero Rona (Italian League team) in 1989, with the second year voidable if he decided to play in the NBA. If such a decision was made, he would have to inform Il Messaggero between June 20 and July 20, 1990. In January 1990, Shaw signed a five-year contract with the NBA's Boston Celtics, to begin after he had rescinded his contract with Il Messaggero during the designated period. However, on June 6, 1990, Shaw informed the Celtics that he would play out his contract with Il Messaggero and would join the Celtics one year later than the contract stated. The Celtics took the matter to arbitration, arguing that Shaw was not abiding by the terms of his contract with them. The arbitrator ruled in favor of the Celtics, but Shaw defied the ruling and prepared to play in Italy. The Celtics requested relief from federal district court, and won a negative injunction to keep Shaw from playing with Il Messaggero for the 1990–1991 season. Shaw appealed the decision, claiming that the arbitrator had failed to follow proper procedure; that he had signed the contract in a weak moment while he was homesick (lack of mental capacity); and that he was not represented by an agent during negotiations with the Celtics. The court disagreed on all points, finding that that the arbitrator did follow proper procedures, and that Shaw was a "college graduate" and veteran player of proper mental capacity to understand the standard player contract.

9.2. TYPES OF ATHLETIC CONTRACTS

The previous sections of this chapter showed how contract law, in general, applies to the business of sports. The remainder of this chapter deals with contract issues that are more specific to the sports world. In the sports industry, officials, administrators, players, and companies will be involved in a wide variety of contractual agreements: coaches' contracts, players' contracts, facility contracts, licensing contracts, physicians' contracts, officials' contracts, equipment contracts, and others. The following sections include examples of contracts at the interscholastic, collegiate, professional, and Olympic levels. While this section will by no means cover every type of athletic contract, it will provide various different contracts and precedent setting cases in various segments of the sports industry.

9.2.1. Standard Player Contract

A standard player contract or uniform player contract contains many unique provisions that separate it from other employment contracts, due to the unique nature of sport. Most professional sports leagues require that teams use standard player contracts exclusively when they employ a player. In other words, even prior to the advent of collective bargaining in sports (see section 11.2, "Collective Bargaining"), teams were not allowed to hire players in a handshake deal, and written contracts had to conform to certain uniform criteria.

Historically, certain items in uniform contracts benefited teams to the detriment of players (e.g., the reserve clause). However, some items in the standard contract are beneficial to players. For example, in most leagues the collective bargaining agreement prevents teams from requiring a player to pay for his or her own lodging and travel expenses. In fact, it can be argued that some type of uniformity is advantageous to all parties involved—players, agents, teams, and the league. While uniformity reduces the total number of contract items that either party may attempt to negotiate to seek advantage, it also reduces transaction costs and enhances each group's ability to carry out business effectively.

While player contracts are "standard" or "uniform," that does not mean they are entirely inflexible. Salaries remain negotiable within the collectively bargained framework. If allowed by existing agreements (league bylaws, collective bargaining agreements), parties may negotiate player bonuses or perquisites (perks) for players, as well as restrictions. These perks may include the use of private planes or larger hotel rooms. Sometimes teams may attempt to negotiate a clause allowing a team to terminate the contract of a player with a history of drug abuse in the event that the player suffers a relapse (see section 7.2.4.1, "National Football League").

The following sections illustrate some of the provisions found in player contracts in the major professional leagues.

9.2.1.1. *Reserve or Option Clause*

The player contract has changed significantly since it was introduced in professional baseball in the early 1880s. At that time, the contract was a one-page document which simply stated that the player would play for the designated club for a period of one year. At first, the contracts were interpreted to mean that after a year, the player had the choice of signing a new contract with another team. However, when competitive bidding for players caused salaries to increase, owners initiated the "reserve system." This system allowed each team to designate five players that no other team could sign. Soon after, the reserve system was expanded to include the entire team, and the standard player contract was modified to include a statement that gave the team an "option" on the players' services in the year following the expiration of the contract. Players signed a contract each year, effectively giving the team the right to that player in perpetuity until it no longer wanted the player.

Players fought this restriction in the courts, using contract law as the basis for their arguments. Initially, courts were sympathetic to the players, and ruled that the one-sided contracts were not enforceable. However, in the 12 years that elapsed between the *Ewing* and *Ward* decisions and the *Lajoie* decision, the owners modified the language in the player contract so that mutuality of obligation was explicitly stated (see section 9.1.1.3, "Consideration"). When they signed their contracts, the players were, in effect, agreeing to abide by the restrictive reserve system in exchange for higher salaries.

Due to the success of the MLB Player Contract in curtailing players' salaries, other professional sport leagues, including the National Hockey League (NHL), NBA, and NFL, employed the use of the standard player contract. Each league's reserve clause withstood legal scrutiny until players began challenging their respective systems under *antitrust* theory instead of under *contract* law (see section 10.2, "Application of Antitrust Law to Professional Sports"). In 1976, the "option" in Major League Baseball's Standard Player Contract was deemed by an arbitrator to be valid only for one year, and not to bind a player to a team in perpetuity. In *Messersmith/McNally* (see note 1), an arbitration panel ruled that when a player plays out the option year of his contract, he becomes a free agent. Since the successful challenges of reserve systems, teams must negotiate with players' unions in order to install very limited versions of reserve clauses into a player contract and/or collective bargaining agreement. Therefore, a standard player contract may bind a player to a team for a period of years, but *not* in perpetuity.

NOTES _____

1. *Messersmith/McNally* is the shorthand name of the case for *In re Twelve Clubs Comprising National League of Professional Baseball Clubs and Twelve Clubs Comprising American League of Professional Baseball Clubs, Los Angeles and Montreal Clubs and Major League Baseball Players Association, Grievance Nos. 75–27 and 75–23, Seitz, Chairman of Arbitration Panel, December 23, 1975.* It is the case that paved the way for free agency in baseball. (For more, see Chapter 11, "Labor Law.")

2. In April 2005, at the start of his 11th season with the Boston Red Sox and 13th overall, pitcher Tim Wakefield agreed to a $4 million contract extension for the 2006 season with a perpetual team option. The option allowed the Red Sox to renew Wakefield's contract at the same terms, including performance bonuses, for as long as they choose. The bonuses include an additional $50,000 for each start between 11 and 20, and $75,000 for each start between 21 and 30. If the Red Sox choose not to pick up the option, no buyout is owed to Wakefield. The contract created a similar situation to the reserve clause, which allowed

teams to retain the rights of a player after his contract expired, challenged unsuccessfully by Curt Flood, see *Flood v. Kuhn*, 401 U.S. 258 (1972). Entering the 2010 season, his 16th with the team, Wakefield ranked third all-time in Red Sox wins and innings and second in strikeouts.

3. For more on players not accepting the highest valued deal, See Michael A. McCann, "It's Not About the Money: The Role of Preferences, Cognitive Biases and Heuristics among Professional Athletes," 71 *Brooklyn Law Review* 1459 (2006).

9.2.1.2. *Unique Skill Provisions*

Unique skill provisions are contained not only in the standard player contracts of professional athletes, but also in the contracts of many coaches and entertainers. Understanding these provisions requires an understanding of *remedies for a breach of contract* (see section 9.1.8). As previously discussed, plaintiffs may seek three remedies for breach of contract: monetary damages, specific performance, and negative injunctions. As a general rule, the more unique the skill involved, the more difficult it is for a court to award monetary damages. For example, if a carpenter or telephone operator signs an employment contract, and then quits his or her job before completing the term of the contract, his or her skills can be replaced. It may cost the employer a significant amount of money to replace the employee (advertising the position, training the replacement employee), but courts can remedy such a breach with monetary damages. However, if Alex Rodriguez were to breach his contract with the New York Yankees in order to play for an upstart rival baseball league, it would be virtually impossible for the Yankees to replace him. Even if the courts forced Rodriguez and the rival baseball league to pay the Yankees $1 billion in monetary damages, the team would not be able to use that money to replace Rodriguez since there are no comparable third basemen on the open market. Thus the Yankees could not be made whole by monetary damages.

In 1902, Napoleon Lajoie was analogous to Alex Rodriguez—a leading slugger at an infield position; baseball's most coveted and unique commodity at the time (see note 1). Consequently, when Lajoie jumped from the National League to the rival American League, it was relatively easy for the team's attorneys to convince the court that he possessed *unique skills* that could not be replaced by money.

In the years since *Lajoie*, professional sport leagues have drafted the standard player contract so that the unique skills provision applies to all players, not just the superstars. For example, the NHL player contract states:

> Section 6: The player represents and agrees that he has exceptional and unique knowledge, skill and ability as a hockey player, the loss of which cannot be estimated with certainty and cannot be fairly or adequately compensated by damages. The Player therefore agrees that the Club shall have the right, in addition to any other rights which the Club may possess, to enjoin him by appropriate injunctive proceedings without first exhausting any other remedy which may be available to the Club, from playing hockey for any other team and/or for any breach of any of the other provisions of this contract (2005 NHL Collective Bargaining Agreement).

In other words, by signing the standard player contract, the player is allowing the league to seek a negative injunction rather than monetary damages. This provision has been put to the test in cases such as *Shaw* (see section 9.1.8, "Remedies for a

Breach of Contract," and *Central New York Basketball, Inc. v. Barnett* (see note 2). Unlike Napoleon Lajoie, neither of the players at issue in these cases was a superstar of his respective era. Nevertheless, the holdings in both cases suggest that courts will consider all players, even "role" players, unique and indispensable to a club. Courts will therefore issue negative injunctions to prevent such players from breaching their contracts and playing for teams in other leagues.

NOTES

1. In 1901, Lajoie won the American League triple crown and had the highest fielding average of any second baseman. He ranks third, trailing only Babe Ruth and Willie Mays, on the list of the top players in the history of baseball, according to John Thorn, Pete Palmer, and Michael Gershman, *Total Baseball*, 7th ed. (Kingston, N.Y.: Total Sports Publishing, 2001).

2. In *Central New York Basketball, Inc. v. Barnett*, 19 Ohio Op.2d 130, 181 N.E. 2d 506 (Ohio C.P. 1961), the Syracuse NBA franchise filed a breach of contract suit against player Richard Barnett, after Barnett signed a contract with the Cleveland franchise in the rival ABL. The Syracuse team contended that (1) Barnett had entered into a verbal contract to return to Syracuse and (2) even if Barnett did *not* enter into a verbal contract (as Barnett claimed), the Syracuse team held a legally binding renewal clause that allowed the club to retain his services. The court agreed, and enjoined Barnett from playing for Cleveland (negative injunction), adding that basketball players' unique skills make them more difficult to replace than employees in other industries. "Whether Barnett ranks with the top basketball players or not . . . he is of peculiar and particular value for plaintiff."

9.2.1.3. Hierarchy of Contracts

What separates a professional athlete's employment contract from many other employment contracts is the fact that professional athletes are bound by several other agreements, including a collective bargaining agreement. To address the fact that athletes in professional sports leagues play under an individual contract and a collective bargaining agreement, the standard player contract may include a provision that deals with this issue. Section 18 of the NHL Standard Player Contract reads:

> The Club and the Player severally and mutually promise and agree to be legally bound by the League Rules and by any Collective Bargaining Agreement that has been or may be entered into between the member clubs of the League and the NHLPA, and by all of the terms and provisions thereof, copies of which shall be open and available for inspection by the Club, its directors and officers, and the Player, at the main office of the League, the main office of the Club and the main office of the NHLPA. This Contract is entered into subject to the Collective Bargaining Agreement between the NHL and the NHLPA and any provisions of this Contract inconsistent with such Collective Bargaining Agreement are superseded by the provisions of the Collective Bargaining Agreement.

Therefore, the player contract cannot contain language that is contradictory to the collective bargaining agreement between the players' union and the league, or to the league's constitution and bylaws. For example, a baseball player and MLB team could not draw up a contract for the player to play for $100 per game (even if the player was willing to do so) if the collective bargaining agreement stipulates that teams must pay players a salary of at least $400,000 per season.

9.2.1.4. Player Exclusivity

Because owners pay millions of dollars to field a team, they want certain assurances that the players they sign to multimillion-dollar deals will not risk injury in an activity that is not related to that athlete's primary sport. To address this issue, uniform player contracts contain player exclusivity clauses, which allow teams to limit a player's physical activity during the off-season or his participating in activities that may cause injury, such as beach volleyball, in-line skating, or skydiving. For example, Section 7 of the NHL Standard Player Contract reads:

> The Player and the Club recognize and agree that the Players' participation in other sports may impair or destroy his ability and skill as a hockey player. Accordingly the Player agrees that he will not during the period of this contract or during any period when he is obligated under this Contract to enter into further contract with the Club engage or participate in football, baseball, softball, hockey, lacrosse, boxing, wrestling or other athletic sport without the written consent of the Club, which consent will not be unreasonably withheld.

Occasionally, players get permission to play in two different professional sports leagues. Deion Sanders, Bo Jackson, and Brian Jordan all played simultaneously in the NFL and MLB. Multiple-sport players are the exception, but those who do play two sports professionally will have language written into their respective player contracts that address the situation.

NOTES _____

1. New England Patriots running back Robert Edwards was seriously injured during a beach football game during Pro Bowl weekend in 1999. The Patriots initially claimed Edwards had violated his player contract, and thus was not entitled to compensation. Edwards contended that the event was league-sponsored because it was part of Pro Bowl weekend, a league-sanctioned event. The situation was further complicated by the fact that participants in the beach football game had signed waivers absolving the NFL of any liability. However, the Patriots and the NFL did eventually agree to compensate Edwards for the $3 million that remained on his five-year $5.75 million contract.

2. Players have been terminated with cause due to injuries sustained in forbidden activities. In 2004 the New York Yankees cut third baseman Aaron Boone after he tore a knee ligament in a pick-up basketball game. Months earlier Boone hit a dramatic Game 7 home run to advance the Yankees to the World Series. Releasing Boone caused the Yankees to pursue Alex Rodriguez. In 2003 after his first season in the NBA, Chicago Bull point guard Jay Williams was in a debilitating motorcycle accident. Rather than simply terminate the remaining two years and $7.7 million of Williams's contract, the Bulls bought it out for $3 million. Cleveland Brown tight end Kellen Winslow and Pittsburgh Steeler quarterback Ben Roethlisberger both suffered serious injuries as a result of motorcycle accidents in 2005 and 2006, respectively, but neither organization attempted to terminate the players' contracts or recoup any portion of money already paid. In 1994, the Atlanta Braves terminated the guaranteed contract of outfielder Ron Gant after he broke his leg in an off-season motorcycle accident.

9.2.1.5. Assignability

In professional sports, players are often traded during the course of their contract. The standard player contract details what rights the player has if a trade occurs. Paragraph 17 of the NFL Standard Player Contract clearly states that, during the term of a contract, a player may be traded and must report to his new team or risk suspension or fine:

Unless this contract specifically provides otherwise, Club may assign this contract and Player's services under this contract to any successor to Club's franchise or to any other Club in the League. Player will report to the assignee Club promptly upon being informed of the assignment of his contract and will faithfully perform his services under this contract. The assignee Club will pay Players necessary traveling expenses in reporting to it and will faithfully perform this contract with Player.

The Major League Baseball contract goes into more detail in outlining the method of payment. According to the MLB Standard Player Contract, the team that trades the player is known as the assignor, and the team that traded for the player is the assignee. MLB has the following language in the standard player contract that outlines the obligations of the assignor and assignee in the case of a trade:

Upon and after such assignment, all rights and obligations of the assignor Club hereunder shall become the rights and obligations of the assignee Club; provided, however, that
  (1) The assignee Club shall be liable to the Player for payments accruing only from the date of assignment and shall not be liable (but the assignor Club shall remain liable) for payments accrued prior to that date.
  (2) If at any time the assignee is a Major League Club, it shall be liable to pay the Player at the full rate stipulated in paragraph 2 hereof for the remainder of the period stated in paragraph 1 hereof and all prior assignors and assignees shall be relieved of liability for any payment for such period.
  (3) Unless the assignor and assignee Clubs agree otherwise, if the assignee Club is a Minor League Baseball Club, the assignee Club shall be liable only to pay the Player at the rate usually paid by said assignee Club to other Players of similar skill and ability in its classification and the assignor Club shall be liable to pay the difference for the remainder of the period stated in paragraph 1 hereof between an amount computed at the rate stipulated in paragraph 2 hereof and the amount so payable by the assignee Club.

If a player refuses to report to the new team he has been traded to, the team may go to arbitration to enforce the contract with the player. If the player continues to withhold his services, the team may seek damages, and will continue to hold the contract until its expiration. Finally, it is important to note that players may negotiate full or limited no-trade clauses depending on the specifics of their league's collective bargaining agreement.

9.2.1.6. Bonus Clauses

Bonus provisions are often used in player contracts, especially for players in the "skilled" positions, but bonus clauses are not a required feature of a standard player contract. There have been many instances where bonus clauses have been written in an ambiguous manner, which has led to disputes over whether the bonus provision has been met or fulfilled. For example in *In the Matter of Arbitration Between Alan Page and the Minnesota Vikings, July 23, 1973*, Page, a member of the Minnesota Vikings, signed a contract in 1972 that read "shall receive a bonus in the amount of $2,500 if he is selected 'All-Pro' by any of the following: AP, UPI, PFW, or *The Sporting News*." Page was named to the second team All-NFL squad by the AP and was chosen as a defensive tackle on the All-NFC team, as selected by *The

Sporting News. Page sought to claim his bonus, and the Vikings refused, claiming he had not made "All-Pro" status. The arbitrator found that because the player had received the highest award possible by the AP, he was entitled to his bonus.

Therefore, to alleviate the potential for litigation or arbitration, bonus provisions must be written in a specific and comprehensive manner. For example, the following example is not specific enough:

> Said player shall receive a bonus in the amount of $250,000 if he is one of the top three kickers in the National Football League.

This language does not indicate what type of kicker this provision is for (i.e., punter, field goal kicker, combined punter/field goal kicker) nor what statistical category would be used (i.e., total versus average yards, field goal percentage). A more detailed provision might read:

> Said player, a punter, shall receive a bonus in the amount of $250,000 if he finishes in the top three punters for total yards (average yards punted) for the 2010 regular season National Football League schedule.

This more detailed language will protect the interests of both the team and the player, and will reduce the likelihood of litigation.

NOTES ———————————————————————————

1. In *White v. National Football League*, 533 F.Supp.2d 929 (D.Minn. 2008), relying on the Lelie ruling, the Minnesota District Court reversed an arbitration ruling of Burbank that stated the Atlanta Falcons could recover $19.97 million of bonus money paid to imprisoned former quarterback Michael Vick. Judge Doty, who has presided over all disputes arising out of the NFL Collective Bargaining Agreement since its inception in 1993, ruled that the Vick roster bonuses were "other salary escalators" under article XXIV, §7(b)(iv)(3), subject to the "already earned" test used in *Lelie*. Once Vick met the requirements of the roster bonus, that of being on the 80-Man Roster of the fifth day of the league year, the bonus became "already earned" and could not be forfeited.

2. In *White v. National Football League (In re Ashley Lelie)*, 2007 WL 939560 (D.Minn. March 26, 2007), the Minnesota District Court affirmed the arbitration decision of Special Master Stephen Burbank forcing the Denver Broncos to repay wide receiver Ashley Lelie $220,000. When Lelie refused to report to training camp in the summer of 2006, the Broncos agreed to trade him so long as Lelie agreed to repay $220,000 of a $1.1 million option bonus paid prior to the 2003 season. Burbank ruled that Lelie's forfeiture was forbidden under §9(c) of the 1993 Stipulation and Settlement Agreement that stated "No forfeitures permitted (current and future contracts) for signing bonus allocations for years already performed, or for other salary escalators or performance bonuses already earned."

3. Following the 2004 season, in which he rushed for 1,372 yards, running back Ricky Williams abruptly retired from the Miami Dolphins after it was revealed he had violated the NFL's substance abuse policy for a third time and faced a four-game suspension. The Dolphins filed a grievance to recover $8.6 million paid to Williams in a signing bonus and incentives. In September 2005, arbitrator Richard Bloch ordered Williams to repay the money. In February 2005, Judge James Cohn of Southern District of Florida upheld the arbitration award. See *Miami Dolphins Ltd. v. Williams*, 356 F.Supp.2d 1301 (S.D. Fla. 2005).

4. For more on the cases mentioned in footnotes 1–3 and the interpretation of forfeiture agreements in NFL contracts, see Chris Deubert and Glenn M. Wong, "Understanding

the Evolution of Signing Bonuses and Guaranteed Money in the National Football League: Preparing for the 2011 Collective Bargaining Negotiations," 16 *UCLA Entertainment Law Review* 179 (Summer 2009).

5. In *Arbitration Between Patrick Ewing and the New York Knickerbockers (Collins, 1991)*, the issue revolved around a provision in Ewing's contract that stated he would be able to void the 1991 year from his contract if four other players earned more "salary compensation" than Ewing. Prior to the 1991 season, it was clear that three others would make more than Ewing, but there was a dispute concerning Larry Bird's contract. Bird had signed a one-year contract for $2,200,000 plus a $4,870,000 bonus. Ewing calculated Bird's salary compensation at $7,070,000 rather than $2,200,000 (as the Knicks contended). The arbitrator found in favor of the Knicks, reasoning that there was no definition of "salary compensation" in Ewing's contract. Therefore, Ewing was behind only three other players in terms of salary and was not entitled to terminate the final year of his contract.

6. In the *Matter of Arbitration Between Major League Baseball Players Association (Dennis Lamp) and The Toronto Blue Jays* (1987), the issue was whether Blue Jays relief pitcher Dennis Lamp was intentionally held out of games during the final weeks of the season in an effort to deter him from reaching the requisite number of appearances in his contract to guarantee a contract extension. Arbitrator George Nicolau ruled for the Blue Jays, stating that the decision on whether to pitch Lamp was one for the field manager, and that there was no evidence that the decision not to pitch Lamp was based on any directive from the Blue Jay front office in an effort to deny Lamp his contract extension.

9.2.1.7. Health Regulations

Because the threat of injury in professional sports is pervasive, both owners and players want to ensure that in the event of injury, each side is protected in various ways. Collective bargaining agreements (CBAs) contain provisions that stipulate what remedies are available in the case of injury, either temporary or career ending. The standard player contract also may contain language that protects the clubs from paying large salaries to unhealthy players. Consequently, contracts often require a player to adhere to a team's medical advice, and allow the team to penalize him (or in some cases terminate him) if he refuses to do so (see note 1). However, unions have negotiated clauses into CBAs allowing a player to seek a second medical opinion if a team doctor makes a decision regarding surgery or other invasive procedure. The MLB Standard Player Contract contains the following language:

> Regulation 2. The Player, when requested by the Club, must submit to a complete physical examination at the expense of the Club, and if necessary to treatment by a regular physician or dentist in good standing. Upon refusal of the Player to submit to a complete medical or dental examination, the Club may consider such refusal a violation of this regulation and may take such action as it deems advisable under regulation 5 [fine/suspension] of this contract (2007 MLB Collective Bargaining Agreement).

There is a clause in the Major League Baseball Collective Bargaining Agreement which allows the player to seek a second medical opinion. The club must pay the cost for the second evaluation if the physician is on the accepted list of medical specialists chosen by the clubs. Expenses for second evaluations by medical specialists who are not on the list will be authorized and paid only by prior mutual agreement between the player and the club (see 2007 MLB Collective Bargaining Agreement Article XIII D).

NOTES

1. Los Angeles Clippers player Rodney Rogers filed a grievance, claiming that the team had improperly fined him for being overweight. Rogers's contract contained a weight clause requiring his weight to be checked twice per month from July, and also allowing the club to fine him for being overweight. Rogers returned to training camp after the prolonged NBA lockout of 1998–1999 at 33 pounds over his promised weight. The team assumed that he was also overweight during the lockout, even though the twice-monthly weigh-ins never occurred. Arbitrator Roger Kaplan ruled in 2000 that the Clippers had no right to fine Rogers for being overweight during the lockout, and required the team to return to him $716,464 in improper fines. However, Kaplan ruled that Rogers *was* liable for the $197,560 in fines for the time it took for him to reach his contracted weight after the first weigh-in.

2. The NBA Uniform Player Contract has a provision that waives the player's right to sue an NBA team for the violent actions of one of its players. Paragraph 19 requires the player to waive any claims he may have as a result of violent conduct that occurs during an exhibition, practice, or game. It is important to note that this provision does not stop the player from filing suit against the player who acted in a violent way (see section 3.3, "Intentional Torts"). The need for this provision arose out of a suit filed by Houston Rocket coach Rudy Tomjanovich against the Los Angeles Lakers. In *Tomjanovich v. California Sports Inc.*, No. H-78-243, 1979 U.S. Dist. LEXIS 9282 (S.D. Tex. Oct. 10, 1979), the plaintiff alleged that Laker forward Kermit Washington punched Tomjanovich in the face, causing fractures of the nose, jaw, and skull, facial lacerations, and a brain concussion. Instead of suing Washington for an intentional tort, Tomjanovich sued the Lakers under respondeat superior (vicarious liability). The jury in the case awarded Tomjanovich $3.6 million. Tomjanovich settled out of court with the Lakers after the decision was appealed. The Houston Rockets sued the Lakers for the loss of Tomjanovich's services, and settled out of court.

9.2.1.8. Full Performance

The matter of whether a contract tolls during player holdouts or retirements is addressed in certain standard player contracts. The absence of such a clause might result in litigation or arbitration, as occurred between the NHL's Ottawa Senators and Alexi Yashin. The Senators filed a breach of contract complaint against their star player Yashin, after he held out for increased salary during the entire 1999–2000 season. Since the season would have been the last of Yashin's multiyear contract, he demanded to be granted free agency after the 1999–2000 season. However, the Senators believed that Yashin owed the team another year, since he did not play for the Senators in the final year specified by the contract. This matter of whether a contract tolls during player holdouts had been addressed in the NFL and NBA collective bargaining agreements (a standard player contract does not expire until "full performance" is given). However, the matter was not addressed in any previous NHL collective bargaining document.

When the matter went to arbitration, arbitrator Lawrence Holden ruled that Yashin could not become a free agent until he honored the last year of his contract, even though the player's association (NHLPA) had explicitly rejected the NHL's attempts to insert a "full performance" clause in the previous collective bargaining agreement (CBA). Holden was compelled by the NHL's argument that the league was merely attempting to codify the "full performance" provision, and that its absence from the CBA did not mean that it was not implied.

Yashin honored the arbitrator's decision and returned to the Senators for the 2000–2001 season (see note 3). The precedent in the *Yashin* case means that teams currently hold a player's "full performance" rights in the NHL, NBA, and NFL until the player finishes the contracted number of years. There is currently no precedent-setting case or explicit standard player contract clause governing the issue in Major League Baseball (see note 4). Certain legal scholars may argue that the "full performance" rule is implied. However, the *Yashin* arbitration decision is not a precedent for Major League Baseball.

NOTES

1. In *Kaiser v. Bowlen*, 200 P.3d 1098 (Colo.App. 2008), Edgar Kaiser, the former majority owner of the Denver Broncos sued Pat Bowlen to whom he sold the team. Kaiser sought to enforce a Right of First Refusal (ROFR) in the contract to repurchase the team. Bowlen had shifted legal ownership of the team between entities over the years to comply with NFL Rules and for tax purposes but always retained the same interest and never offered it for sale. The court granted Bowlen summary judgment finding that the shifting of ownership did not trigger the ROFR.

2. In June 2004, the Pittsburgh Penguins selected center Evgeni Malkin with the second overall pick in the NHL entry draft. Malkin had just finished his first season playing for Metallurg Magnitogorsk in the Russian Super League. Metallurg refused a $200,000 transfer payment that would have allowed Malkin to join the Penguins in 2005–2006. Instead, Malkin signed a deal that would have kept him in Russia through the 2006–2007 season. There were suggestions that the contract was forced on Malkin under duress during a negotiating session that did not end until 3 A.M. In August 2006, while Metallurg began training camp in Helsinki, Finland, Malkin disappeared, apparently heading for Canada and ultimately Pittsburgh. Although Malkin had a contract with Metallurg, Russian law allows any employee to leave a job so long as they give two weeks' written notice, even if under contract. While in hiding, Malkin filed the requisite letter of resignation with Metallurg. Malkin reappeared about a week later and soon thereafter signed a three-year deal worth up to $3.8 million per year.

Not surprisingly, a tribunal of the Russian Ice Hockey Federation voted to ban Malkin from playing anywhere but for Metallurg. In an attempt to have the arbitration ruling enforced, Metallurg sued the NHL and the Penguins in U.S. District Court in the Southern District of New York in October 2006, alleging intentional interference with contractual relations and antitrust violations. In 2005, the NHL agreed to transfer agreements with the International Ice Hockey Federation (IIHF) that includes Finland, Germany, Slovakia, Sweden, the Czech Republic, and Switzerland. However, Russia refused the terms, which called for the NHL to pay a development fee of $200,000 for each player drafted into the NHL who ultimately signs with their NHL club. About 30% of NHL players come from IIHF countries. In November 2006, the court denied Metallurg's request for an injunction, and the entire lawsuit was dismissed in February 2007. Malkin won the Calder Trophy as the NHL Rookie of the Year in 2006–2007 with 33 goals and 52 assists.

3. In 2002, the Washington Capitals drafted Alexander Semin with the 13th overall pick. Semin, a Russian citizen subsequently agreed to a three-year contract starting in the 2003–2004 season. Semin played the first year of the contract without incident, but when the NHL and NHLPA could not reach an agreement on a new CBA before the start of the 2004–2005 season, Semin was assigned to the Capitals' minor league team, the Portland Pirates, as they had authority to do. Semin instead traveled to Russia to play for a private, commercial team known as Lada Togliatta. In September 2004, when the Capitals began fining Semin $1,000 a day for his failure to report to Portland, Semin said he was preparing to report to Portland but had been conscripted in the Russian military. Semin said he negotiated a deal whereby he could perform his military service by playing for Lada Togliatta. When the lockout ended, the Capitals requested that Semin return for the start of training camp in September. Semin contended that he had one more year of requisite military service and resumed playing for Lada Togliatta. The Capitals then filed for a preliminary injunction, but the injunction was denied because the NHL Collective Bargaining Agreement stipulated that the dispute should be arbitrated and that Semin had a potentially valid

impossibility defense based upon his Russian military conscription. In April 2006, Semin agreed to a two-year deal with the Capitals and returned for the 2006–2007 season and was 13th in the league in goals scored with 38. See *Lincoln Hockey Ltd. Liability Co. v. Semin*, 2005 WL 3294008 (D.D.C. 2005).

4. After Yashin returned to the Senators for the 2000–2001 season, Senators owner Rod Bryden wanted to sue Yashin for $930,000, for damages that resulted from Yashin's holdout. Bryden arrived at the $930,000 figure by arguing that if Yashin had not held out during the 1999–2000 season, the club would have reached the second round of the playoffs. Bryden agreed to drop the suit when Yashin agreed to make a charitable contribution of more than $100,000 (Canadian) to the Ottawa Hospital.

9.2.1.9. Example of a Standard Player Contract: National Football League

The standard player contract has evolved over the last century and is now a complex and cohesive document that clearly spells out the obligations of the parties involved (see exhibit 9.1).

9.2.2. Defenses to Standard Player Contract Breaches

Since the inception of professional baseball in the 1880s, there has been a significant amount of litigation surrounding the validity of the standard player contract (see exhibit 9.1). It is important to note that with the advent of collective bargaining in professional sports, very few contractual cases now go to court; rather, such disputes are more likely to be handled by an independent arbitrator or settled before litigation. Players' unions have bargained over the basic structure of the standard player contract and have ensured that if a dispute does arise, it is dealt with by the grievance procedures outlined in the collective bargaining agreement. However, if a player jumps from one league to another, neither league's grievance procedure will apply and the judicial system may be used.

Before collective bargaining agreements established required internal mechanisms for resolving contract disputes, conflicts were decided in the courts. The most common disputes arose when a player decided to join another team in the same league, or jump to another league, before his initial contract had expired. It is important to remember that prior to the 1970s, player contracts were understood to run in perpetuity, so that a player did not have the option of free agency at some point in his career (see section 10.3.1.1, "History of the Reserve System"). Due to the appearance of rival leagues in all sports, players in the traditional leagues were wooed away from their existing contracts to participate in the upstart leagues. If a player walked out on a contract, the original team with which the player had a contract often claimed a breach of contract and used the courts to enforce the original contract.

One of the first cases to deal with this issue was the aforementioned *Metropolitan Exhibition Company v. Ewing*, 42 F. 198 (C.C.D. N.Y 1890). In this case, the defendant ballplayer attempted to sign a contract with the Players' League, a rival league established by disenchanted players, while he was still arguably under contract to his team in the National League. That club attempted to get an injunction stopping Ewing from signing a contract with the new team. In order to succeed, the team was required to show that each of the following applied:

Exhibit 9.1
National Football League Player Contract

THIS CONTRACT is between _____
_____, hereinafter "Player," and _____
_____, a _____
_____corporation (limited partnership) (partnership), hereinafter "Club," operating under the name of the _____
_____ as a member of the National Football League, hereinafter "League." In consideration of the promises made by each to the other, Player and Club agree as follows:

1. TERM. This contract covers _____ football season(s), and will begin on the date of execution or March 1, _____, whichever is later, and end on February 28 or 29, _____, unless extended, terminated, or renewed as specified elsewhere in this contract.

2. EMPLOYMENT AND SERVICES. Club employs Player as a skilled football player. Player accepts such employment. He agrees to give his best efforts and loyalty to the Club, and to conduct himself on and off the field with appropriate recognition of the fact that the success of professional football depends largely on public respect for and approval of those associated with the game. Player will report promptly for and participate fully in Club's official mandatory minicamp(s), official preseason training camp, all Club meetings and practice sessions, and all preseason, regular season and postseason football games scheduled for or by Club. If invited, Player will practice for and play in any all-star football game sponsored by the League. Player will not participate in any football game not sponsored by the League unless the game is first approved by the League.

3. OTHER ACTIVITIES. Without prior written consent of the Club, Player will not play football or engage in activities related to football otherwise than for Club or engage in any activity other than football which may involve a significant risk of personal injury. Player represents that he has special, exceptional and unique knowledge, skill, ability, and experience as a football player, the loss of which cannot be estimated with any certainty and cannot be fairly or adequately compensated by damages. Player therefore agrees that Club will have the right, in addition to any other right which Club may possess, to enjoin Player by appropriate proceedings from playing football or engaging in football-related activities other than for Club or from engaging in any activity other than football which may involve a significant risk of personal injury.

4. PUBLICITY AND NFLPA GROUP LICENSING PROGRAM.

    (a) Player grants to Club and the League, separately and together, the authority to use his name and picture for publicity and the promotion of NFL Football, the League or any of its member clubs in newspapers, magazines, motion pictures, game programs and roster manuals, broadcasts and telecasts, and all other publicity and advertising media, provided such publicity and promotion does not constitute an endorsement by Player of a commercial product. Player will cooperate with the news media, and will participate upon request in reasonable activities to promote the Club and the League. Player and National Football League Players Association, hereinafter "NFLPA," will not contest the rights of the League and its member clubs to

Exhibit 9.1
(continued)

telecast, broadcast, or otherwise transmit NFL Football or the right of NFL Films to produce, sell, market, or distribute football game film footage, except insofar as such broadcast, telecast, or transmission of footage is used in any commercially marketable game or interactive use. The League and its member clubs, and Player and the NFLPA, reserve their respective rights as to the use of such broadcasts, telecasts or transmissions of footage in such games or interactive uses, which shall be unaffected by this subparagraph.

(b) Player hereby assigns to the NFLPA and its licensing affiliates, if any, the exclusive right to use and to grant to persons, firms, or corporations (collectively "licensees") the right to use his name, signature facsimile, voice, picture, photograph, likeness, and/or biographical information (collectively "image") in group licensing programs. Group licensing programs are defined as those licensing programs in which a licensee utilizes a total of six (6) or more NFL player images on or in conjunction with products (including, but not limited to, trading cards, clothing, videogames, computer games, collectibles, internet sites, fantasy games, etc.) that are sold at retail or used as promotional or premium items. Player retains the right to grant permission to a licensee to utilize his image if that licensee is not concurrently utilizing the images of five (5) or more other NFL players on products that are sold at retail or are used as promotional or premium items. If Player's inclusion in a particular NFLPA program is precluded by an individual exclusive endorsement agreement, and Player provides the NFLPA with timely written notice of that preclusion, the NFLPA will exclude Player from that particular program. In consideration for this assignment of rights, the NFLPA will use the revenues it receives from group licensing programs to support the objectives as set forth in the Bylaws of the NFLPA. The NFLPA will use its best efforts to promote the use of NFL player images in group licensing programs, to provide group licensing opportunities to all NFL players, and to ensure that no entity utilizes the group licensing rights granted to the NFLPA without first obtaining a license from the NFLPA. This paragraph shall be construed under New York law without reference to conflicts of law principles. The assignment in this paragraph shall expire on December 31 of the later of (a) the third year following the execution of this contract, or (b) the year in which this contract expires. Neither Club nor the League is a party to the terms of this paragraph, which is included herein solely for the administrative convenience and benefit of Player and the NFLPA. The terms of this subparagraph apply unless, at the time of execution of this contract, Player indicates by striking out this subparagraph (b) and marking his initials adjacent to the stricken language his intention to not participate in the NFLPA Group Licensing Program. Nothing in this subparagraph shall be construed to supersede or any way broaden, expand, detract from, or otherwise alter in any way whatsoever, the rights of NFL Properties, Inc. as permitted under Article V (Union Security), Section 4 of the 1993 Collective Bargaining Agreement ("CBA").

5. COMPENSATION. For performance of Player's services and all other promises of Player, Club will pay Player a yearly salary as follows:

$_____ for the 20_____ season;

$_____ for the 20_____ season;

Exhibit 9.1
(continued)

$_____ for the 20_____ season;

$_____ for the 20_____ season;

$_____ for the 20_____ season.

In addition, Club will pay Player such earned performance bonuses as may be called for in this contract; Player's necessary traveling expenses from his residence to training camp; Player's reasonable board and lodging expenses during preseason training and in connection with playing preseason, regular season, and postseason football games outside Club's home city; Player's necessary traveling expenses to and from preseason, regular season, and postseason football games outside Club's home city; Player's necessary traveling expenses to his residence if this contract is terminated by Club; and such additional compensation, benefits and reimbursement of expenses as may be called for in any collective bargaining agreement in existence during the term of this contract. (For purposes of this contract, a collective bargaining agreement will be deemed to be "in existence" during its stated term or during any period for which the parties to that agreement agree to extend it.)

6. PAYMENT. Unless this contract or any collective bargaining agreement in existence during the term of this contract specifically provides otherwise, Player will be paid 100% of his yearly salary under this contract in equal weekly or biweekly installments over the course of the applicable regular season period, commencing with the first regular season game played by Club in each season. Unless this contract specifically provides otherwise, if this contract is executed or Player is activated after the beginning of the regular season, the yearly salary payable to Player will be reduced proportionately and Player will be paid the weekly or biweekly portions of his yearly salary becoming due and payable after he is activated. Unless this contract specifically provides otherwise, if this contract is terminated after the beginning of the regular season, the yearly salary payable to Player will be reduced proportionately and Player will be paid the weekly or bi weekly portions of his yearly salary having become due and payable up to the time of termination.

7. DEDUCTIONS. Any advance made to Player will be repaid to Club, and any properly levied Club fine or Commissioner fine against Player will be paid, in cash on demand or by means of deductions from payments coming due to the Player under this contract, the amount of such deductions to be determined by Club unless this contract or any collective bargaining agreement in existence during the term of this contract specifically provides otherwise. physical condition. Player will undergo a complete physical examination by the Club physician upon Club request, during which physical examination Player agrees to make full and complete disclosure of any physical or mental condition known to him which might impair his performance under this contract and to respond fully and in good faith when questioned by the Club physician about such condition. If Player fails to establish or maintain his excellent physical condition to the satisfaction of the Club physician, or make the required full and complete disclosure and good faith responses to the Club physician, then Club may terminate this contract.

9. INJURY. Unless this contract specifically provides otherwise, if Player is injured in the performance of his services under this contract and promptly

Exhibit 9.1
(continued)

reports such injury to the Club physician or trainer, then Player will receive such medical and hospital care during the term of this contract as the Club physician may deem necessary, and will continue to receive his yearly salary for so long, during the season of injury only and for no subsequent period covered by this contract, as Player is physically unable to perform the services required of him by this contract because of such injury. If Player's injury in the performance of his services under this contract results in his death, the unpaid balance of his yearly salary for the season of injury will be paid to his stated beneficiary, or in the absence of a stated beneficiary, to his estate.

10. WORKERS' COMPENSATION. Any compensation paid to Player under this contract or under any collective bargaining agreement in existence during the term of this contract for a period during which he is entitled to workers' compensation benefits by reason of temporary total, permanent total, temporary partial, or permanent partial disability will be deemed an advance payment of workers' compensation benefits due Player, and Club will be entitled to be reimbursed the amount of such payment out of any award of workers' compensation.

11. SKILL, PERFORMANCE AND CONDUCT. Player understands that he is competing with other players for a position on Club's roster within the applicable player limits. If at any time, in the sole judgment of Club, Player's skill or performance has been unsatisfactory as compared with that of other players competing for positions on Club's roster, or if Player has engaged in personal conduct reasonably judged by Club to adversely affect or reflect on Club, then Club may terminate this contract. In addition, during the period any salary cap is legally in effect, this contract may be terminated if, in Club's opinion, Player is anticipated to make less of a contribution to Club's ability to compete on the playing field than another player or players whom Club intends to sign or attempts to sign, or another player or players who is or are already on Club's roster, and for whom Club needs room.

12. TERMINATION. The rights of termination set forth in this contract will be in addition to any other rights of termination allowed either party by law. Termination will be effective upon the giving of written notice, except that Player's death, other than as a result of injury incurred in the performance of his services under this contract, will automatically terminate this contract. If this contract is terminated by Club and either Player or Club so requests, Player will promptly undergo a complete physical examination by the Club physician.

13. INJURY GRIEVANCE. Unless a collective bargaining agreement in existence at the time of termination of this contract by Club provides otherwise, the following injury grievance procedure will apply: If Player believes that at the time of termination of this contract by Club he was physically unable to perform the services required of him by this contract because of an injury incurred in the performance of his services under this contract, Player may, within 60 days after examination by the Club physician, submit at his own expense to examination by a physician of his choice. If the opinion of Player's physician with respect to his physical ability to perform the services required of him by this contract is contrary to that of the Club's physician, the dispute will be submitted within a reasonable time to final and binding arbitration by an arbitrator selected by Club and Player or, if they are unable to agree, one

**Exhibit 9.1
(continued)**

selected in accordance with the procedures of the American Arbitration Association on application by either party.

14. RULES. Player will comply with and be bound by all reasonable Club rules and regulations in effect during the term of this contract which are not inconsistent with the provisions of this contract or of any collective bargaining agreement in existence during the term of this contract. Player's attention is also called to the fact that the League functions with certain rules and procedures expressive of its operation as a joint venture among its member clubs and that these rules and practices may affect Player's relationship to the League and its member clubs independently of the provisions of this contract.

15. INTEGRITY OF GAME. Player recognizes the detriment to the League and professional football that would result from impairment of public confidence in the honest and orderly conduct of NFL games or the integrity and good character of NFL players. Player therefore acknowledges his awareness that if he accepts a bribe or agrees to throw or fix an NFL game; fails to promptly report a bribe offer or an attempt to throw or fix an NFL game; bets on an NFL game; knowingly associates with gamblers or gambling activity; uses or provides other players with stimulants or other drugs for the purpose of attempting to enhance on-field performance; or is guilty of any other form of conduct reasonably judged by the League Commissioner to be detrimental to the League or professional football, the Commissioner will have the right, but only after giving Player the opportunity for a hearing at which he may be represented by counsel of his choice, to fine Player in a reasonable amount; to suspend Player for a period certain or indefinitely; and/or to terminate this contract.

16. EXTENSION. Unless this contract specifically provides otherwise, if Player becomes a member of the Armed Forces of the United States or any other country, or retires from professional football as an active player, or otherwise fails or refuses to perform his services under this contract, then this contract will be tolled between the date of Player's induction into the Armed Forces, or his retirement, or his failure or refusal to perform, and the later date of his return to professional football. During the period this contract is tolled, Player will not be entitled to any compensation or benefits. On Player's return to professional football, the term of this contract will be extended for a period of time equal to the number of seasons (to the nearest multiple of one) remaining at the time the contract was tolled. The right of renewal, if any, contained in this contract will remain in effect until the end of any such extended term.

17. ASSIGNMENT. Unless this contract specifically provides otherwise, Club may assign this contract and Player's services under this contract to any successor to Club's franchise or to any other Club in the League. Player will report to the assignee Club promptly upon being informed of the assignment of his contract and will faithfully perform his services under this contract. The assignee club will pay Player's necessary traveling expenses in reporting to it and will faithfully perform this contract with Player.

18. FILING. This contract will be valid and binding upon Player and Club immediately upon execution. A copy of this contract, including any attachment to it, will be filed by Club with the League Commissioner within 10 days after execution. The Commissioner will have the right to disapprove this contract on reasonable

Exhibit 9.1
(continued)

grounds, including but not limited to an attempt by the parties to abridge or impair the rights of any other club, uncertainty or incompleteness in expression of the parties' respective rights and obligations, or conflict between the terms of this contract and any collective bargaining agreement then in existence. Approval will be automatic unless, within 10 days after receipt of this contract in his office, the Commissioner notifies the parties either of disapproval or of extension of this 10-day period for purposes of investigation or clarification pending his decision. On the receipt of notice of disapproval and termination, both parties will be relieved of their respective rights and obligations under this contract.

19. DISPUTES. During the term of any collective bargaining agreement, any dispute between Player and Club involving the interpretation or application of any provision of this contract will be submitted to final and binding arbitration in accordance with the procedure called for in any collective bargaining agreement in existence at the time the event giving rise to any such dispute occurs.

20. NOTICE. Any notice, request, approval or consent under this contract will be sufficiently given if in writing and delivered in person or mailed (certified or first class) by one party to the other at the address set forth in this contract or to such other address as the recipient may subsequently have furnished in writing to the sender.

21. OTHER AGREEMENTS. This contract, including any attachment to it, sets forth the entire agreement between Player and Club and cannot be modified or supplemented orally. Player and Club represent that no other agreement, oral or written, except as attached to or specifically incorporated in this contract, exists are conflicting provisions in any collective bargaining agreement in existence during the term of this contract, in which case the provisions of the collective bargaining agreement will take precedence over conflicting provisions of this contract relating to the rights or obligations of either party.

22. LAW. This contract is made under and shall be governed by the laws of the State of _____.

23. WAIVER AND RELEASE. Player waives and releases any claims that he may have arising out of, related to, or asserted in the lawsuit entitled *White v. National Football League*, including, but not limited to, any such claim regarding past NFL Rules, the College Draft, Plan B, the first refusal/compensation system, the NFL Player Contract, preseason compensation, or any other term or condition of employment, except any claims asserted in *Brown v. Pro Football, Inc.* This waiver and release also extends to any conduct engaged in pursuant to the Stipulation and Settlement Agreement in *White* ("Settlement Agreement") during the express term of that Settlement Agreement or any portion thereof. This waiver and release shall not limit any rights Player may have to performance by the Club under this Contract or Player's rights as a member of the *White* class to object to the Settlement Agreement during its review by the court in Minnesota. This waiver and release is subject to Article XIV (NFL Player Contract), Section 3(c) of the CBA.

24. OTHER PROVISIONS.

   (a) Each of the undersigned hereby confirms that (i) this contract, renegotiation, extension or amendment sets forth all components of the player's remuneration for playing professional football (whether such compensation is being furnished directly by the Club or by a related or affiliated entity); and (ii) there are not undisclosed agreements of any kind, whether express

**Exhibit 9.1
(continued)**

or implied, oral or written, and there are no promises, undertakings, representations, commitments, inducements, assurances of intent, or understandings of any kind that have not been disclosed to the NFL involving consideration of any kind to be paid, furnished or made available to Player or any entity or person owned or controlled by, affiliated with, or related to Player, either during the term of this contract or thereafter. (b) Each of the undersigned further confirms that, except insofar as any of the undersigned may describe in an addendum to this contract, to the best of their knowledge, no conduct in violation of the Anti-Collusion rules of the Settlement Agreement took place with respect to this contract. Each of the undersigned further confirms that nothing in this contract is designed or intended to defeat or circumvent any provisions of the Settlement Agreement, including but not limited to the Rookie Pool and Salary Cap provisions; however, any conduct permitted by the CBA and/or the Settlement Agreement shall not be considered a violation of this confirmation. (c) The Club further confirms that any information regarding the negotiation of this contract that it provided to the Neutral Verifier was, at the time the information was provided, true and correct in all material respects.

25. SPECIAL PROVISIONS.

THIS CONTRACT is executed in six (6) copies. Player acknowledges that before signing this contract he was given the opportunity to seek advice from or be represented by persons of his own selection.

_____	_____
PLAYER	CLUB
_____	_____
Home Address	By
_____	_____
Telephone Number	Club Address
_____	_____
Date	Date

_____
PLAYER'S CERTIFIED AGENT

_____
Address

_____
Telephone Number

_____
Date

Copy Distribution: White-League Office   Yellow-Player

Green-Member Club   Blue-Management Council

Gold-NFLPA   Pink-Player Agent

1. The breach must be one for which monetary damages would be inadequate compensation.

2. The party seeking the injunction must not have "unclean hands" (any underhanded or devious past behavior employed by a party that is seeking an injunction—courts do not wish to endorse this type of behavior, and will deny relief to such parties).

3. The injunction sought must not be unduly oppressive to the defendant.

4. The contract must have mutuality or be founded on adequate consideration.

5. The terms of the contract must be definite.

The court found that the contract between the club and Ewing did not satisfy the fifth requirement, since the right of reservation was not adequately defined, and therefore the other terms of the contract were ambiguous. The same issue was raised in the same year in *Metropolitan Exhibition Company v. Ward*, N.Y.S. 779 (N.Y. Sup. Ct. 1890). In this case, the plaintiff attempted to obtain an injunction stopping the defendant from playing for anyone but the plaintiff, in accordance with the reserve clause and the standard player contract. Like the *Ewing* court, the court in *Ward* found for the defendant because the contract was lacking in mutuality or definiteness. The court stated that a written agreement containing a reserve clause is not really a contract, but instead "is merely a contract to make a contract if the parties can agree." As noted in section 9.1.1.3, concerning the lack of mutuality, the court found that the club had an unfair advantage over the player because the club could reserve the player in perpetuity (conceivably for the rest of that player's career); in contrast, the player could be terminated on 10 days' notice.

But in *Philadelphia Ball Club, Ltd. v. Lajoie*, 51 A. 973 (Pa. 1902), a case decided 12 years after *Ewing* and *Ward*, a new precedent was set. The court found that the standard player contract could be enforced when the club specifically stated in the contract that the right of reservation, in conjunction with the right to terminate with 10 days' notice, was in exchange for the salary to be paid to the player. It is important to emphasize that mutuality is not synonymous with equality; the club may have the upper hand in the contractual relationship. But since the consideration was explicitly stated and the contract was negotiated without coercion, the contract was upheld. The Philadelphia Phillies were granted a negative injunction, preventing Lajoie from playing in the rival American League.

Over the course of the 20th century, players used five defenses against breach of contract claims:

1. Unclean hands: occurs when the party seeking equitable relief has acted improperly, so that the court does not wish to endorse its behavior. This behavior does not have to be illegal or coercive (see defense 3), but only questionable enough for an injunction not to be granted.

2. Lack of mutuality: occurs when one party to the contract does not receive adequate consideration. For example, a professional player contract must state the length of the contract, in addition to what the player receives (salary) for his services.

3. Illegality and unfair bargaining position: occurs when one party to a contract uses illegal or coercive means to create the contract.

4. Lack of commissioner's approval: occurs when the commissioner has not officially signed a player contract, and such act is required under the terms of league bylaws or a collective bargaining agreement.

5. Collusion: occurs when two or more employers (teams) engage in concerted activity whereby the result is detrimental to the employee (player). For example, in the mid-1980s, Major League Baseball owners engaged in collusion when they agreed, en masse, not to sign any free agents during the off-season (see section 11.3.7.1.4, "Baseball Collusion Cases Charge").

It is important to note that many claims of breach of contract have occurred when ballplayers moved from one team to a team in a rival league. During periods when there was no rival league, there are usually fewer breach of contract claims. After the *Lajoie* decision, players turned from contract law to antitrust law and arbitration in order to challenge their restrictive player contracts (see section 10.3.1, "The Baseball Exemption").

NOTES _____

1. In 2001, the Major League Baseball Players Association (MLBPA) filed a grievance with the commissioner's office against the New York Yankees, claiming that the Yankees refused to pay a portion of a prorated signing bonus to Cuban defector Andy Morales. Morales allegedly had lied about his age in order to increase the value of his contract (four years and $4.5 million), claiming to have been born in 1974 when he was allegedly born in 1971. However, the MLBPA contended that the Yankees could not terminate the contract. The Yankees, on the other hand, hoped to recoup their entire investment in Morales. This case is pending. See Ken Davidoff, "Yankees Notebook," *New York Newsday*, July 16, 2001, p. A41. Also see www.espn.go.com/mlb/news/2001/0717/1227355.html

2. For the use of the "unclean hands" defense, see *Boston Celtics Ltd. Partnership v. Shaw*, 908 F.2d 1041 (1st Cir. 1990); *Washington Capitols Basketball Club Inc. v. Barry*, 304 F.Supp. 1193 (N.D.Cal. 1969); and *Weegham v. Killefer*, 215 F.168 (W.D. Mich.) *aff'd.*, 215 F. 289 (6th Cir. 1914).

3. The "lack of mutuality" defense was used in *American League Baseball Club of Chicago v. Chase* (N.Y. Sup. Ct. 1914); *Philadelphia Ball Club, Limited v. Lajoie*, 202 Pa. 210, 51 A. 973 (Pa. 1902); and *Connecticut Professional Sports Corp. v. Heyman*, 276 F.Supp. 618 (S.D.N.Y. 1967).

4. The illegality defense was used by an owner, although unsuccessfully, to avoid adherence to a standard player contract. Star pitcher James "Catfish" Hunter signed a two-year contract with the Oakland Athletics in 1974. Included in his contract was a special covenant that deferred half of his $100,000 salary to the designees of his choice, in this case, to a life insurance provider. Charles Finley, owner of the Oakland club, agreed to this provision. In July, Hunter contacted the Internal Revenue Service (IRS) and submitted to it an agreement for a deferred payment compensation investment account. Under such a plan, Hunter would avoid tax liability on the $50,000. On August 1, Hunter delivered the IRS/life insurance agreement to Finley; his signing it would make the contract complete. Finley stalled in signing the papers when he discovered that the tax liability was shifted to himself and, soon after, refused outright to transfer the $50,000 to the life insurance provider. In October, the players association filed two grievances on Hunter's behalf: (a) to reimburse the $50,000 payment and (b) to make Hunter a free agent. The players association argued that the failure to make the deferred payment constituted a breach of contract and allowed the pitcher to exercise his rights to terminate the contract and become a free agent. The arbitration panel found that Finley had breached the club's duty outlined in the contract, and therefore the pitcher had the right to terminate his agreement with the Athletics. Finley appealed the decision of the arbitrator in *American and National League of Professional Baseball Clubs*

v. Major League Baseball Players Ass'n, 130 Cal. Rptr. 626 (Ct. App. 1976), claiming that his signature on the life insurance document would have been illegal (assisting Hunter in "tax evasion") and that the arbitrator exceeded the scope of his authority in making Hunter a free agent. Courts generally will not overturn arbitration decisions (see section 11.3.13, "Arbitration"), but Finley claimed that court should overturn the Hunter decision because "the 'reserve clause' is not subject to arbitration." The court rejected both of Finley's allegations, citing a recent court decision which stated that the reserve clause was subject to arbitration: *Kansas City Royals Baseball Corp. v. Major League Baseball Players Ass'n.*, 532 F.2d 615 (8th Cir. 1976). That court case stemmed from MLB's appeal of the *Messersmith/ McNally* decisions that resulted in baseball players gaining free agency rights (see section 11.3.9, "Free Agency").

5. The "commissioner's approval" defense is still applicable in some professional leagues. In Major League Baseball, the commissioner must sign the contract before it is considered valid. However, in the National Football League, there is a clause in the standard player contract that enforces the validity of the contract prior to the commissioner's signature.

9.2.3. Tortious Interference with Contractual Relations

Tortious interference with contractual relations occurs when a third party knowingly interferes in a contract already in place between two parties. Not only can this occur between players and agents, but also with coaches who are pursued by potential employers (see note 5), as well as with sponsors and other sports organizations (see note 6). To prove a claim of tortious interference the plaintiff will have to show the following:

1. A binding contract existed.
2. The third party had knowledge of the contract's existence.
3. The third party intended to interfere with the contract.
4. The plaintiff suffered actual damages.
5. Interference by the third party was the proximate cause of the damages.

One case involving the doctrine of tortious interference is *Central Red Army Club v. Arena Associates, Inc.*, 952 F.Supp. 181 (S.D.N.Y. 1997), in which a hockey player attempted to leave his contract with a team in Russia to play hockey in the United States. Sergei Samsonov had played with the Central Sports Army Club (CSKA) since 1986, and had developed into a dominant player by the mid-1990s. At the end of the 1995–1996 season, the CSKA signed Samsonov to a new one-year contract, but because of a power struggle in Russian hockey at the time, the terms of Samsonov's deal could not be met. Samsonov left Russia and signed a contract with the Detroit Vipers of the International Hockey League. Detroit officials believed Samsonov was free to contract with them because his Russian contract had been breached, and also because he had signed the Russian contract when he was under the age of 18 with no parent acting as guardian. Nonetheless, the CSKA informed Vipers management that Samsonov was still under contract in Russia, and included in its correspondence a copy of the contract.

The CSKA filed a lawsuit against the Vipers, alleging tortious interference with the contractual relationship between Samsonov and the CSKA. The court was first faced with the decision of whether to grant an injunction preventing Samsonov from playing hockey for the Vipers. The court considered CSKA's likelihood of success on the merits, and concluded that it would not succeed. Concerning the claim of tortious interference, the court ruled that the CSKA contract was void because Samsonov had signed the contract while a minor. However, the court noted that even if a legitimate contract had existed, CSKA would still lose the case because it had not been able to prove (a) that there had been inducement by the defendant, (b) that the defendant was aware of the contract between CSKA and Samsonov, and (c) that the defendant had an improper motive. Samsonov continued to play for the Vipers, and was subsequently drafted by the Boston Bruins of the NHL.

NOTES

1. In *Harrick v. NCAA*, 454 F.Supp.2d 1255 (N.D.Ga. 2006), former University of Georgia basketball coach Jim Harrick sued the NCAA for tortious interference with contract, after Harrick was fired for violating numerous NCAA rules. The court granted the NCAA's summary judgment motion, stating "that the NCAA was not a "third party" or "stranger" to the contract with which the NCAA allegedly interfered. In order to be liable for tortious interference, one must be a stranger to both the contract at issue and the business relationship giving rise to and underpinning the contract." However, Harrick's contract specifically stated that it was dependent on his compliance with NCAA policies.

2. In 2004 UMass hired Don Brown as its new head football coach, even though Brown was under contract with Northeastern and had not received permission to speak with UMass. Northeastern sued Brown and UMass alleging breach of contract and tortious interference. The case was settled when UMass agreed to hold Brown out for the first three games of the season and pay $150,000.

3. A trading card company brought a tortious interference claim against a major professional league players union in *Cardtoons, L.C. v. Major League Baseball Players Ass'n*, 208 F.3d 885 (10th Cir. 2000), *cert. denied*, 531 U.S. 873 (2000). The plaintiff had contracted with a manufacturing company to produce humorous trading cards featuring satirical caricatures of active baseball players. When the MLPBA heard about this plan, it sent a "cease and desist" letter threatening to sue both Cardtoons and the manufacturing company for copyright infringement. As a result of this threat, the manufacturing company backed out of the deal to produce the cards. Cardtoons then sued the MLPBA for tortious interference. The MLBPA defended itself by claiming that "threatening to sue" does not constitute tortious interference. The U.S. Appeals Court disagreed, remanding the case to a federal trial judge after the U.S. Supreme Court denied certiorari. The trial judge must determine whether *state* law protection exists for the players union's threatening letter. The case of *Cardtoons, L.C. v. Major League Baseball Players Association*, 199 F.R.D. 677 (N.D. Okla. 2001) is pending.

4. In *Omnipoint Communications Inc. v. New York Yankee Partnership and Bell Atlantic Nynex Mobile*, Index No. 601910/97, Seq. Nos.: 001, 002 (N.Y. Sup. Ct. 1999) the plaintiff sued the Yankees for breach of contract and Bell Atlantic for tortious interference. Omnipoint entered into an agreement with Sports Advertising Network, Inc. (SANI), a Yankee agent, to display advertisements in the bullpen at Yankee Stadium. Omnipoint was informed that the Yankees would not honor the contract because it had signed a contract with Bell to use the space for signage. Omnipoint filed suit. The Yankees contended that SANI did not possess the authority to enter into such an agreement on the team's behalf, and thus the claim was unwarranted. The court found that Bell had not tortiously interfered because the original contract between Omnipoint and SANI was not valid due to the fact that neither actual nor apparent authority could be established. The court granted summary judgment to both the Yankees and Bell, and dismissed the charges.

5. In 1996, one month after winning the Stanley Cup as coach of the New York Rangers, Mike Keenan announced he was leaving New York to sign as coach of the St. Louis Blues even though he had completed only the first year of his five-year contract. Keenan claimed a material breach of his contract had occurred when he was not given his bonus by the Rangers in a timely fashion. The Rangers filed suit to get a declaratory judgment as to

the validity of Keenan's contract. Before the matter was argued in court, the Blues and the Rangers came to an agreement to trade several players to the Rangers in exchange for the services of Keenan. After a hearing with Commissioner Gary Bettman, Keenan was suspended for 60 days and fined $100,000 for "conduct detrimental to the league." The Blues were fined $250,000 for negotiating with Keenan while he was still under contract to coach the Rangers.

6. For tortious interference in sponsorship agreements, see *National Football League Properties v. Dallas Cowboys Inc., Texas Stadium Corporation and Jerral W. Jones*, F. 922 Supp. 849 (S.D.N.Y. 1996). It is described further in section 9.2.4.6, "Sponsorship Litigation Cases."

7. Footwear company Reebok sued its former track and field chief, Mark Bossardet, for $2 million in U.S. District Court in Boston in 1995, after Bossardet allegedly lured the popular marathon runner Uta Pippig to his new company, Nike. Reebok also sued Nike for interfering with its contract with Pippig. The case was settled prior to trial.

8. A case that closely resembles *Central Sports Army Club* is *Professional Hockey Club Central Sports v. Detroit Red Wings*, 787 F.Supp. 706 (E.D. Mich. 1992). In this case, Viacheslav Kozlov had entered into a contractual agreement with CSKA, but was subsequently injured and hospitalized for two months. Kozlov was released from military service and dismissed from the hockey team. The Red Wings asked CSKA about Kozlov, but were told he was still under contract. The Reds Wings then approached Kozlov independently and signed him to a contract. The Red Wings were subsequently charged with tortious interference and accused of "abducting" Kozlov. However, Circuit Court justice Sharon Tevis Finch held that "Kozlov had demonstrated a substantial likelihood of success on the merits of his claim that his alleged contract with the Hockey Club is void."

9. In *Cincinnati Bengals Inc. v. Bergey*, 453 F.Supp. 129 (S.D. Ohio 1974), an NFL team attempted to obtain an injunction to prevent the defendant from playing in the new rival league, the World Football League (WFL). The case was unique because, although Bergey signed his WFL contract while he was under contract in the NFL, the WFL contract was not scheduled to commence until *after* he fulfilled his contract with the NFL. The court ruled in favor of the defendant, stating "It was not unlawful...during the time when Bergey was under a valid contract with the Bengals, to negotiate and enter into a contract for Bergey's personal services, the performance of which was not to commence until after the expiration of Bergey's contract with the Bengals...Plaintiff [did not establish] a likelihood of success in its claim that it suffered a tortious interference with its right to full performance under Bergey's contract."

9.2.4. Marketing, Endorsement, and Sponsorship Contracts

Marketing in professional sports has grown dramatically since the 1980s, and now constitutes more than a billion-dollar industry. Corporations pay large sums of money to sponsor tennis or golf tournaments, merchandising companies compete to get contracts with the major professional sport leagues, and companies pay athletes millions to endorse products ranging from deodorants to credit cards. Because these agreements often involve large sums of money and involve obligations that impact many different parties, the written contracts are usually complex and lengthy in nature. It is important that those who draft sponsorship contracts have a clear understanding not just of their client's desires and of marketing principles, but also of the applicable legal issues.

Marketing, endorsement, and sponsorship contracts are similar to other contracts in that they identify the parties, set time limits, list the obligations of the parties, and set forth provisions in case one party cannot carry out its contractual obligations. The companies that sponsor a player, league, or event want to ensure that their investment will offer a healthy return in the form of increased exposure and sales for their products or services. However, industry professionals are not always able to control the actions of their contracted partners. It is common for top talent not to show up for events or for leagues to breach terms of agreements.

In contracts signed between sponsors and the hired talent/league/event, there are a few stipulations that promotion specialists should include to ensure their financial well-being in case of unexpected events. Stipulations such as indemnification, force majeure, and liability insurance help protect sponsors when events occur that are out of their control (see below).

A sponsorship contract, whether between a company and a player, or between a company and a sporting event, is a legally binding agreement that ensures each party will fulfill obligations in its part of the agreement. Situations like those described above often arise where there is controversy surrounding particular terms of the agreement and/or where one party does not feel the agreement is being carried out according to these terms. Consequently, the contract language will attempt to make clear what the obligations of each party are in the event of unforeseen circumstances, such as a labor dispute, a natural disaster, player injury, or company (sponsor) bankruptcy. Several such provisions are discussed below.

To avoid unnecessary litigation, marketing contracts are written comprehensively in an attempt to cover all eventualities. Therefore, player endorsement contracts are very detailed when it comes to the obligations of the endorsing athlete. The following is an example of a typical section in a player endorsement contract that outlines the obligations of the player:

> Athlete agrees during the term of this Agreement, or any extension thereof, to: (a) Permit Company to use his photograph in connection with the advertising and promotion of football merchandise whether or not bearing his name, facsimile signature, or nickname; (b) Demonstrate, discuss, and emphasize the newest features of Company's football products at every opportunity; (c) Lend himself to such press interviews, radio, and/or TV appearances arranged for him by Company as are compatible with his own practice and play requirements; (d) Cooperate to the maximum extent possible, compatible with his practice and play requirements, in effective Company promotional and public relations activities by endeavoring to become acquainted with Company dealers and their sales personnel in each market area; (e) Cooperate with Company in giving advice, suggestions, and recommendations concerning the acceptability and playability of current Company football lines, the development of new Company football lines, and information about significant football product and football market trends; (f) Cooperate to the maximum extent possible in making publicized personal appearances in store promotion events significant to general speaking invitations; (g) In connection with such promotion, it is agreed that Company shall pay to Athlete all basic traveling expenses such as transportation, hotel, meals, and the like, incurred by Athlete relative to such promotion, if specifically requested by Company.

In the event of a legal dispute, the contract clearly indicates what terms the athlete is forced to abide by. For example, if the promoted athlete refused to make public appearances on behalf of the sponsor, there would be a violation of (f) in the athlete's obligations as outlined above. However, the language is ambiguous enough to allow for some disagreement: Are four appearances enough to satisfy the contract language?

9.2.4.1. Impact of League Rules

When these contracts concern athletes from professional sports leagues, it is important to know whether the leagues have policies surrounding the marketing of their athletes. Whereas the NFL addresses this issue in Paragraph 4 of the Standard Player Contract, the NHL has taken a more specific approach in its collective bargaining agreement:

25.1. No player shall be involved in any endorsement of alcoholic beverage and/or tobacco products.

25.2. When a player enters into an endorsement, sponsorship or licensing arrangement for himself, he may mention the name of his Club for identification purposes without needing the consent of his Club or paying for its use. A Player shall not use the Club insignia without the consent of the Club which shall not be unreasonably withheld.

25.3. In the case of a League or Club endorsement or sponsorship or licensing arrangement, the League or Club shall not use the individual personality, including his name and/or likeness, of any Player without his consent. This provision shall not be interpreted to prohibit the League or an individual Club from utilizing "game action" images or footage in League or Club endorsement or sponsorship arrangement, provided the focus of the image or footage is not on an individual player.

25.4. Nothing contained in this Arrangement or in any SPC shall preclude the NHLPA from entering into any endorsement, sponsorship or licensing arrangements provided the NHLPA may not use the insignia of the League or any Club without consent. (2005 NHL Collective Bargaining Agreement, Article 25.)

Prior to any negotiation over a sponsorship contract, the sponsor and its attorneys must be aware of the applicable provisions in the relevant collective bargaining agreement.

9.2.4.2. Sponsorship Rights

Professional sports leagues and other athletic associations usually have a small number of primary sponsors that give the league or association a set amount of money and/or products and services in exchange for sponsorship rights. This means that the company sponsoring the league or association has the right to use the league's or association's logo(s) while promoting its product. For example, MasterCard has been an official sponsor of Major League Baseball, and has certain rights related to this status outlined in its contract. One of those rights is that MasterCard can use the following statements when promoting its credit cards:

a. "Official Card of Major League Baseball"
b. "Major League Baseball Prefers MasterCard"
c. "Preferred Card of Major League Baseball"
d. "Major League Baseball Preferred Card."

Sponsors of professional leagues also usually have the right to use league logos in programs, advertising campaigns, promotional events, and publications. The contract will clearly identify what logos the company is allowed to use when promoting the league. For example, Major League Baseball's agreement with MasterCard allows the credit card company to use the MLB logo, the logos of the American and National Leagues, and the logos for the All-Star Game and postseason series. However, some restrictions do apply. In the MLB-MasterCard agreement there is a provision that limits MasterCard's rights to use the likeness of players, because the collective bargaining agreement between MLB and the MLBPA assigns those rights to the players association.

When a sponsor decides to commit millions of dollars to sponsoring an event, the sponsor wants to be certain that its financial commitment will result in increased publicity. In addition, the sponsor of the event wants to ensure that similar products do not gain publicity through the event. For example, a credit card company sponsoring a golf tournament will want to make sure that rival credit card companies are not also publicized as sponsors. The following language has been used to clarify the sponsor's rights at the tournament:

> **Golf Tournament** hereby grants to **Sponsor** the right for the 2007 through 2010 Tournaments, to be the exclusive sponsor of the Tournaments within the payment services product category (the "Product Category") defined as follows: (1) all card-based payment and/or account access devices (including without limitation, credit cards, charge cards, automated teller machine (ATM) cards, prepaid cards, smart cards, telephone calling cards, electronic benefits transfer cards, travel and entertainment cards, on-line and off-line point-of-sale debit cards, cheque guarantee cards, and cards that combine two or more of the foregoing functions; (2) travelers cheques and travel vouchers; (3) ATMs and ATM networks; and (4) money wire transfers.

When a company sponsors an athlete to market a product, the sponsor wants to be sure that said athlete will be a visible presence in his/her respective sport. For example, if a company is sponsoring a professional golfer, it may include the following language in the agreement to ensure that the golfer is playing in high profile tournaments and a specific number of tournaments.

> Provided **Spokesman** is physically capable of tournament play, **Spokesman** shall enter/participate in not less than 22 official PGA TOUR events per year, which shall include the Masters, US Open, British Open, PGA Championship and other PGA Tour events. As a part of such minimum appearance commitment, **Spokesman** shall, subject to qualification, appear in all 4 "major" golf tournaments, the Players Championship, the Ryder Cup, the Presidents Cup, and other prominent golf events as the parties may agree. In the event **Spokesman** cannot participate in at least four (4) such tournaments in any calendar year, the Term of this agreement shall be extended for an additional one-year period upon the terms and for the fees set forth for the year in which the **Spokesman** fails to play such minimum number of tournaments.

The sponsor of an event, league, association, or athlete must clearly state the obligations of the contracting party so as to avoid unnecessary litigation.

9.2.4.3. Indemnification

An indemnification clause in a sponsorship contract is used to protect the investment the sponsor is making, whether in a league sponsorship agreement or a player endorsement contract. This clause is especially important because it pertains to the endorsement contracts professional athletes enter into. In the wake of increased publicity surrounding athletes' arrests for violent behavior and for drug-related charges, many athlete endorsement contracts have indemnification clauses that protect the company from liability for a player's actions. The following is an example of one.

> The Parties agree that **Spokesman** is not an employee of **Sponsor,** but is in an independent contractor relationship to **Sponsor,** at all times. Pursuant to such relationship, **Spokesman** agrees to indemnify, defend, and hold harmless **Sponsor,** its agents and employees, from and against any and all claims, damages, liabilities, losses, costs or expenses, including reasonable attorney fees, arising out of the breach of any obligation hereunder or any alleged act or omission of **Spokesman,** and **Sponsor** agrees to indemnify, defend and hold harmless **Spokesman** from and against any and all claims, damages, liabilities, losses, costs or expenses, including reasonable attorney fees, arising out of the breach of any obligation hereunder or an alleged act or omission of **Spokesman**. In the event of a claim of indemnification, the party being indemnified shall give the party providing the indemnification prompt notice of such event and shall cooperate in the provision of such indemnification.

9.2.4.4. *Right to Terminate*

A company makes the decision to sponsor an athlete because it feels that the athlete will represent its product well to the public. However, to protect itself from athletes that get into legal trouble or no longer represent the "values" of the sponsor, a sponsorship agreement will often include "right to terminate" language. Here is an example.

> **Sponsor** may terminate this agreement at any time with no further obligation to pay **Spokesman** any amount thereafter otherwise owing should **Spokesman,** at any time during the term of this agreement: (1) die or become unable to perform his obligations hereunder in a competent and professional manner; (2) become the subject of or cause adverse publicity, shame, scandal, or embarrassment to himself or to **Sponsor** through any statement, action, association or otherwise; or (3) make any statement or take any action which **Sponsor** believes could or would disparage any **Sponsor** product, service trademark, or service mark.

9.2.4.5. Force Majeure *and Work Stoppage*

A *force majeure*, or work stoppage, provision is normally associated with facility or event contracts, but has recently become increasingly common in athletic sponsorship contracts, especially those between a manufacturer and a league or association. The term *force majeure* means "superior force," and, in the context of a professional sports contract, the term refers to unforeseeable natural or human events that are beyond the control of the parties to the contract, and that render performance of the contract impossible. A work stoppage provision protects one or both parties in the event of either a strike or a lockout. Only recently have licensing agreements begun to include force majeure clauses, due in part to the increase in work stoppages in professional sports.

To deal specifically with the issue of labor disputes, many sponsorship contracts now have provisions that specifically identify protection against work stoppages. In the Major League Baseball agreement with a sponsor, there is a clause that identifies the remedy should a work stoppage occur:

Notwithstanding anything contained in this agreement to the contrary, in the event that during the Term as a result of a labor dispute between the MAJOR LEAGUE BASEBALL owners and the Major League Baseball Players Association a MAJOR LEAGUE BASEBALL regular season or post-season is delayed or interrupted for fifteen (15) days or more, the rights fee and spending commitment payable by Sponsor in the year during which such delay or interruption occurs shall be reduced hereunder on a percentage basis, the numerator of which shall be the number of dates during the regular and post-season in that year on which at least one MAJOR LEAGUE BASEBALL game was scheduled to be played (collectively "Game Days") and because of such labor dispute was not played, and the denominator of which shall be the total number of Game Days in that year.

9.2.4.6. Sponsorship Litigation Cases

Most sponsorship contracts are carried out successfully, and no contractual disputes arise between the parties. In the event of disputes, some contracts have mechanisms, such as binding arbitration, to avoid lengthy controversies in the courts. However, in the absence of such mechanisms, the courts are called upon to render decisions.

An example of a conflict in the area of sponsorship is the case of *National Football League Properties v. Dallas Cowboys Football Club*, 922 F. Supp. 849 (S.D.N.Y. 1996). The NFL created the Properties Division in 1982, and the exclusive club marks (logo, name, insignia) of each team were transferred there.

The Properties Division negotiates contracts with companies to act as sponsors of the NFL. The revenue generated from these leaguewide licensing contracts is evenly distributed among the teams in the league, consistent with the belief in the NFL that revenue sharing helps maintain competitive balance and a strong league. As a condition for these leaguewide exclusive agreements, individual teams are not permitted to enter into similar agreements on their own. At the time of this case, the NFL had Coca-Cola as the official soft drink of the NFL, and Visa as the league's official credit card. Dallas owner Jerry Jones entered into agreements with various competitors, including Dr. Pepper, Pepsi-Cola Company, Nike, and American Express, thus undermining the investment of the NFL's official sponsors.

For purposes of contract law, the important facet of this case is that Jones claimed it was not the Cowboys that had the sponsorship agreements with rival companies, but rather Texas Stadium Corporation (TSC), which was independent of the NFL. Jones also argued that, as part of the agreements with TSC, the sponsors did not have the right to use marks of the Cowboys for commercial use, thus avoiding any conflict with the NFL Properties Division. The league argued that the defendants had breached the implied covenant of good faith dealing in contract; breached the Cowboys' obligations as a recipient of the NFL trust; breached their fiduciary duty to the other member clubs of the NFL; and tortiously interfered with the property rights granted by NFL Properties to its licensees. The main issue in this case was whether the agreements between the TSC and the sponsors would trick the public into thinking those sponsors were official sponsors of the NFL. The case was dropped and a settlement reached, although details of the settlement were not released to the public.

The *Cowboys* case clearly illustrates the conflicts that may arise in the arena of sponsorship. Several important legal issues raised by this case are dealt with in this chapter, as well as other chapters in the book, including: the legal theories of breach of contract, tortious interference, and the relationship between competing contracts.

NOTES _____

1. Toronto Raptor star Vince Carter was ordered to pay $13.5 million plus attorneys' fees in 2000, after an arbitrator ruled that he breached his contract with Puma. Carter had claimed that he stopped wearing Puma shoes because the shoes did not fit him properly, and because Puma had not fulfilled its promise to create a Vince Carter "signature shoe." In addition to the financial penalty, the arbitrator issued an injunction barring Carter from endorsing a competitor's shoe for three years. Carter subsequently paid additional money to Puma (a settlement), allowing him to endorse a competitor's shoe before the three-year injunction expired.

2. In *TYR Sport, Inc. v. Warnaco Swimwear, Inc.*, 2010 WL 1192438 (C.D.Cal. March 16, 2010) TYR, designer and manufacturer of high-end swimwear sued a competitor for, among other things, tortious interference with contract after American swimmer Erik Vendt switched swimsuits to the the Speedo LZR Racer despite an endorsement deal with TYR. Warnaco does business as Speedo. In granting summary judgment on the claim, the court found that Vendt switched suits because he was dissatisfied with TYR's suits, not because Speedo induced him to do so.

3. In *Adidas America Inc. v. NCAA*, 40 F.Supp.2d 1275 (D. Kan. 1999), the shoe manufacturer brought suit against the NCAA concerning the NCAA's Bylaw 12.5.5, which limited the size of commercial logos that may appear on student-athletes' uniforms and apparel. This case arose out of the fact that the uniforms Adidas supplied to certain schools had three long stripes down the sleeve or pant leg, which were larger than the allowable logo according to Bylaw 12.5.5. The court reasoned that the NCAA and its member institutions did not realize any economic or competitive advantage because of the rule, that the rule was consistent with the NCAA's policy of limiting commercialization in intercollegiate athletics, and that Adidas failed to prove that a preliminary injunction was necessary. The court found in favor of the NCAA.

9.2.5. Coaches' Contracts: Professional and Collegiate Sports

A coach's contract is similar to most other employment contracts. Unlike a standard player contract for athletes, the coaching contract is usually individually drafted for star coaches, with more items independently negotiated. A coaching contract sets forth the nature and duration of the employment, the compensation to be paid to the employee, and other terms and conditions of employment. The employer-employee relationship between the team or institution and the coach is similar to the typical employer-employee relationship in the business world. A coach's contract can contain distinctive clauses, such as provisions for a percentage of gate receipts at certain events, unique provisions for termination, bonuses for high graduation rates, bonuses for remaining with the institution for a number of years, and covenants not to compete.

The standard evaluative measure of a coach is his or her ability to produce a winning team. A coach who is not successful in producing a winning program is a possible candidate for termination. The termination of a coaching contract may constitute a breach, for which the team or institution will be held liable for damages. Sometimes, this liability has been avoided by either making a lump-sum payment based on the dollar value of the remaining years of the contract to the coach or continuing periodic payments to the coach for the remaining term of his or her contract, as if the coach were still employed (see note 8).

A 1983 decision, *Rodgers v. Georgia Tech Athletic Ass'n.*, 303 S.E. 2d 467 (Ga. Ct. App. 1983), suggests that a college institution or professional sports team may be liable to its former coach for more than the salary stated in the contract. Pepper Rodgers, the head coach of the Georgia Tech football program at the time he was fired, sued the school for damages relating to the perquisites (fringe benefits) he had lost as a result of his termination. The parties settled out of court prior to trial on the issue after the Georgia court ruled that the inclusion of the word "perquisite" in Rodgers's contract might permit a jury to award Rodgers some of the damages he was claiming. In light of the *Rodgers* case, institutions now sometimes construct a "Pepper Rodgers clause" to limit the amount of fringe benefits that the school must pay in the event that the coach is terminated.

At the collegiate level, even if an institution is willing to pay for the damages associated with termination, it may encounter procedural problems. In *Yukica v. Leland*, No. 85-E-191 (N.H. Super. Ct. 1985), the New Hampshire Superior Court granted the Dartmouth College head football coach an order restraining the college's athletic director from terminating his coaching contract, which, as interpreted by the court, provided that notice of termination was to be given 12 months prior to actual termination. Termination of a coaching contract may not necessarily occur due to the actions of an institution or team. A coach may wish to leave the organization before his or her contract expires, so as to move to a higher-profile job that offers higher pay, increased exposure, and greater benefits. As these positions become available, a coach may leave his or her current position to assume similar responsibilities with another team or institution. Absent a valid escape or buyout clause (see exhibit 9.2), this departure before the end of the contract term constitutes a breach for which a coach can be held liable (see note 6).

If a coach is performing well or has an excellent track record, teams and institutions can take proactive contractual steps to retain him or her. One such method is a loyalty bonus. For example, Rick Pitino signed a contract to become men's basketball coach at the University of Louisville in 2001. Pitino's contract called for a $5 million bonus if he completed the six years of the deal. However, several options remain open to a team or institution if a coach departs before the expiration of the coaching contract. For one, the team or institution may attempt to block the move of the coach and force him or her to work out the present contract. In *New England Patriots Football Club Inc. v. University of Colorado*, 592 F.2d 1196 (1st Cir. 1979), the U.S. Court of Appeals held that a clause in Chuck Fairbanks's coaching contract with the Patriots, which required him to refrain from contracting elsewhere for his coaching services, was a proper basis for a preliminary injunction to enjoin the University of Colorado from employing Fairbanks while he was under contract with the Patriots.

Another potential solution to either party's prospective desire for early termination is to provide for a buyout clause at an agreed amount. Under a mutual buyout clause, either the institution or the coach may unilaterally and prematurely terminate the contract during its term and be responsible only for damages in the agreed amount. This is also referred to as *liquidated damages*.

However, while it might appear that such a provision in a contract would leave little room for controversy, sometimes problems do arise. For example, in *Vanderbilt University v. DiNardo*, 174 F.3d 751 (6th Cir. 1999), the defendant signed a five-year contract in 1990 to coach the Vanderbilt football team and was offered an extension of that contract in 1994, one year before the original contract was to expire. After negotiations, it appeared the two sides had reached an agreement on a two-year extension. Later that same year, DiNardo accepted the head coaching position with Louisiana State University. Vanderbilt demanded three years in liquidated damages (for the final year of the five-year agreement, plus the two years from the recently negotiated extension) from DiNardo, pursuant to the original

Exhibit 9.2
John Calipari's Coaching Contract

EMPLOYMENT AGREEMENT

THIS EMPLOYMENT AGREEMENT (herein this "Agreement"), is made and entered into as of March 31, 2009, by and between the UNIVERSITY OF KENTUCKY (hereinafter the "University"), and John Vincent Calipari (hereinafter "Coach" or "Employee").

1. <u>Term.</u> This Agreement shall be for eight (8) years beginning March 31, 2009 and ending March 30, 2017 (the "Term"), unless terminated at an earlier date as provided herein. As used herein, "Contract Year" shall be any twelve month period during the Term beginning on March 31 and ending March 30.

2. <u>Duties and Authority.</u> Coach is hereby employed by the University as the Head Men's Basketball Coach. Coach will report directly to the Director of Athletics, who will be primarily responsible for day-to-day supervision of Coach. Coach's duties, responsibilities and obligations shall be those normally associated with the position of head men's basketball coach at a National Collegiate Athletic Association (hereinafter "NCAA") Division I university, such as the University of Kentucky. Coach shall devote such time and attention necessary to satisfy the responsibilities for the position of head men's basketball coach, which shall include, in addition to the usual and customary activities associated with head coaching, the authority and responsibility for the following:

   (a) The employment, supervision, and discharge—subject to the reasonable approval of the Director of Athletics which will be withheld only if the Director of Athletics, in good faith, believes that any such proposed action of Coach will reasonably conflict with the University's policies and/or stated principals of which Coach has been advised—of personnel associated with or related to the men's basketball program at the University including, but not limited to, the following:

      (i) Assistant basketball coaches;

      (ii) Administrative aides;

      (iii) Strength/conditioning coaches;

      (iv) Administrative assistants;

      (v) Team trainers and managers; and

      (vi) Video personnel.

   The employment and discharge of personnel mentioned in subparagraphs (i) through (vi) above shall also be subject to the reasonable approval of the Associate Vice President of Human Resources in accordance with University's Human Resources Policy and Procedures, Administrative Regulations, and any applicable provisions of the NCAA Manual and the Southeastern Conference (hereinafter "SEC") and Commissioner's Regulations Manual, as amended. Notwithstanding the foregoing obligation to obtain reasonable approval of personnel actions, Coach retains responsibility for employment decisions.

   (b) In consultation with the Director of Athletics, the scheduling (including dates, places and times) of all University men's basketball games and the selection of the opponent for each such game, the means of travel to be

Exhibit 9.2
(continued)

employed, hotel accommodations and food service, size and content of the traveling squad and party, and all other matters pertaining to the operation of the University's men's basketball program.

(c) All matters concerning the recruiting of prospective basketball players for the University, including compliance with NCAA and SEC bylaws governing same.

(d) Preparation of a recommended budget for the men's basketball program for submission to the Director of Athletics. Upon approval of the budget for the basketball program (consistent with comparable NCAA Division I basketball programs), Coach shall administer that budget in accordance with applicable and appropriate regulations and policies of the University of which Coach has been advised.

(e) Cooperation with and fulfillment of the requirements and commitments of the University in any of its athletically related agreements including, but not limited to, any agreements for radio and television broadcasting, athletic footwear, apparel, sports/performance beverages, equipment, or other commercial endorsements so long as such cooperation does not adversely affect his coaching duties.

3. <u>Reporting Relationship.</u> The Coach's day-to-day supervisor, for purposes of this Agreement, shall be the Director of Athletics for the University, and all matters pertaining to the operation of the University's men's basketball program shall be subject to the ultimate direction and control of the Director of Athletics. All on court matters shall remain the exclusive province of the Coach, provided Coach's conduct is not in violation of NCAA, SEC, or University bylaws, rules, regulations or policies.

4. <u>University Policy.</u>

(a) The establishment of policies for the entire athletic program shall remain the exclusive prerogative of the University. The Coach shall administer the daily routine and organization of the men's basketball program as he deems necessary to effectuate its success, provided such administration shall be in accordance with policies established by the Director of Athletics and the University of which Coach has been advised. The terms and provisions of the University's Human Resources Policy and Procedure Administrative Regulations, as currently published and as may hereafter be revised or amended, are hereby incorporated herein by reference and made a part of this Agreement as though written herein. To the extent, however, that an actual conflict exists between the terms and provisions of said Regulations and this Agreement, this Agreement shall prevail as it affects the Coach, and no other person.

(b) Coach agrees to conduct the University's basketball program in accordance with the bylaws and regulations of the University, NCAA and SEC and any subsequent amendments thereto, including but not limited to the duty to report known and suspected violations thereof to the University Compliance Director or to the Director of Athletics. Pursuant to NCAA Bylaw 11.2.1, it is stipulated by the parties that if Coach is found in violation of NCAA regulations, he shall be subject to disciplinary or

Exhibit 9.2
(continued)

corrective action as set forth in the provisions of the NCAA enforcement procedures.

5. <u>Compensation.</u> In consideration of Coach's obligations hereunder, the University guarantees to pay Coach as follows:

(a) <u>Signing Payment.</u> Upon execution of this Agreement, a signing payment of $200,000.00 payable directly to the University of Memphis. Coach shall be solely responsible for any and all other expenses associated with resignation of his current employment.

(b) <u>Salary.</u> For each Contract Year during the term hereof, a base salary of Four Hundred Thousand Dollars ($400,000), payable in equal monthly installments, in conformity with the payroll procedures of the University.

(c) <u>Broadcasting and Endorsements.</u> It is understood that the University has entered into an exclusive radio and television broadcasting contract and a contract with a supplier of athletic footwear, sports/performance beverages, apparel and equipment (collectively, the "University Agreements"). In consideration of the compensation set forth below in this Paragraph 5(c), Coach hereby exclusively grants to the University his rights of endorsement, together with the exclusive right, license and privilege of soliciting, securing and/or authorizing all endorsements, publications and/or radio and television performance opportunities for or featuring Coach with respect to the University Agreements only. For purposes of clarification, the foregoing specifically includes any charitable or non-profit activity which involves any form of endorsement or third party promotion and which offers payments of any type whether called an "honorarium" or other similar title. Any endorsements/promotions by the Coach for third parties will be pursuant to the terms and conditions of the University Agreements. Coach acknowledges that the University Agreements provide substantial value to him, and that he may not engage in outside activities that conflict with or infringe upon the rights granted under the University Agreements.

(i) In compensation for Coach's participation in the University Agreements, the University will pay to Coach the sums set forth below for each Contract Year, payable in equal quarterly installments on July 1, October 1, January 1 and March 30 of each Contract Year. All monies received under University Agreements shall be paid directly to University. The University will make Broadcasting and Endorsement payments to Coach as follows:

March 31, 2009 – March 30, 2010	$3,300,000
March 31, 2010 – March 30, 2011	$3,400,000
March 31, 2011 – March 30, 2012	$3,400,000
March 31, 2012 – March 30, 2013	$3,400,000
March 31, 2013 – March 30, 2014	$3,400,000
March 31, 2014 – March 30, 2015	$2,850,000
March 31, 2015 – March 30, 2016	$2,850,000
March 31, 2016 – March 30, 2017	$2,850,000

Exhibit 9.2
(continued)

(ii) The professional and commercial activities required of Coach pursuant to the University Agreements shall be performed at a time and in a way which will not interfere with the duties of the Coach's position as head men's basketball coach and due care shall be taken by the University to assure that the name of the University is used properly in relation to such professional activities.

(iv) Coach may conduct one or more basketball camps, using University athletic facilities and equipment, and retain all income therefrom after payment of appropriate but reasonable expenses (to be mutually agreed upon in advance between Coach and the University) incurred by the University and others.

Such camps will be conducted in accordance with general University policies. Rates for rooms and meals shall not exceed those rates (on a Most Favored Nations basis) charged by the University's Housing and Dining System for any other major sports camps.

(v) In accordance with NCAA Bylaw 11.2.2 regarding athletically related income, Coach agrees to provide a written detailed account to the Director of Athletics and the President of the University at least once annually, or more frequently upon written request (but not to exceed twice per Contract Year unless required by the NCAA), for all athletically related income, compensation, gratuities or benefits from any and all sources outside the institution.

(d) <u>Incentive Compensation</u>.

(i) In the event the University's men's basketball team wins the SEC Regular Season Championship, Coach will, in any year in which the aforementioned event occurs, receive, in addition to the payments due under Paragraphs 5(b) and (c)(i), an additional performance supplement of Fifty Thousand Dollars ($50,000);

(ii) In the event the University's men's basketball team wins the SEC Tournament Championship, Coach will, in any year in which the aforementioned event occurs, receive, in addition to the payments due under Paragraphs 5(b), 5(c)(i), and 5(d)(i), an additional performance supplement of Fifty Thousand Dollars ($50,000);

(iii) In the event the University's men's basketball team qualifies for an NCAA Tournament Sweet 16 Appearance, Coach will, in any year in which the aforementioned event occurs, receive, in addition to the payments due under Paragraphs 5(b), 5(c)(i), 5(d)(i), (ii) and (iii), an additional performance supplement of One Hundred Thousand Dollars ($100,000);

(iv) In the event the University's men's basketball team qualifies for a NCAA Tournament Final Four Appearance, Coach will, in any year in which the aforementioned event occurs, receive, in addition to the payments due under Paragraphs 5(b), 5(c)(i), 5(d)(i), (ii), (iii) and (iv), an additional performance supplement of One Hundred Seventy-Five Thousand Dollars ($175,000);

Exhibit 9.2
(continued)

(v) In the event the University's men's basketball team wins the NCAA Championship, Coach will, in any year in which the aforementioned event occurs, receive, in addition to the payment due under Paragraphs 5(b), 5(c)(i), 5(d)(i), (ii), (iii), (iv) and (v), an additional performance supplement of Three Hundred Seventy-Five Thousand Dollars ($375,000);

(vi) In the event the men's basketball team achieves a .950 Academic Progress Rate for men's basketball student athletes in any academic year, Coach will, in any year in which the aforementioned event occurs, receive, in addition to the base salary, broadcast and endorsement supplemental salary and tournament incentive compensation, a performance supplement of Fifty Thousand Dollars ($50,000);

(vii) In the event the men's basketball team achieves a seventy-five percent (75%) Graduation Rate or better for men's basketball student athletes in each class, the Coach will, in any year in which the aforementioned event occurs, receive, in addition to the base salary, broadcast and endorsement supplement and tournament incentive compensation, and Academic Progress Rate incentive compensation, a performance supplement of Fifty Thousand Dollars ($50,000).

These incentives are intended to reward the achievement of each event in turn and are cumulative. All payments due under this Paragraph 5(d) shall be due and payable to Coach within thirty (30) days from the date the achievement has been reached.

(e) Retention Incentive. In addition to the above stated competitive and academic-based incentives, a retention incentive to encourage Coach to remain with the University shall be provided. University agrees to pay Coach a retention incentive if Coach remains in the employment of the University on each of the following dates: March 31, 2014 (Bonus = $750,000), March 31, 2015 (Bonus = $1,000,000) and March 31, 2016 (Bonus = $1,250,000). Said bonuses to be paid within ten (10) days of the achievement of the applicable bonus.

6. Additional Obligations of the University. In the discharge of Coach's obligations hereunder, the University may require Coach's reasonable participation to promote and enhance University's athletic program. In this regard and for the University's convenience during the term of this Agreement, the University agrees to provide Coach as follows:

(a) Automobiles. Coach shall be provided with the use of two (2) late-model, quality automobiles for his official and personal use. In addition, the University shall reimburse Coach for all business related automobile mileage.

(b) Expense Account. The University shall fully and promptly reimburse Coach for all reasonable and necessary expenses on behalf of the University in connection with the performance of his duties and in accordance with the University's customary expense practices. Transportation expenses for a guest of the Coach to occasionally travel to regular season and post season away games may be approved by the Director of Athletics

Exhibit 9.2
(continued)

upon receipt of Coach's request. Post season travel for Coach's guests may be approved by the Director of Athletics upon receipt of Coach's request. Certain of these guest expenses may be considered a taxable fringe benefit to the Coach in accordance with state and federal Internal Revenue Code and Regulations.

(c) <u>Benefits.</u> During the term of this Agreement, University agrees to offer to Coach and his eligible dependents the standard employee benefits offered to University administrative staff and other head coaches at the University. Standard benefits include, but are not limited to, health plan, life insurance, dental insurance, accidental death and dismemberment insurance, and long term disability. The base salary as provided in Paragraph 5(b) shall determine benefits that are based upon salary.

(d) <u>Tickets.</u> Coach shall receive, without charge, twenty (20) prime, lower level basketball tickets for each University men's home basketball game, each away basketball game and each post season tournament game and the option to purchase up to 20 additional tickets. Eight (8) football tickets, without charge, will also be made available to Coach for each University home football game. Such tickets may not be resold or exchanged for anything of value by Coach. Coach shall be allowed to request additional tickets, if he deems it necessary, and such request shall be fulfilled, if possible.

(e) <u>Retirement.</u> It is agreed that the funded retirement benefits usually paid to University administrative staff and other head coaches will apply to the employment of Coach under this Agreement, as follows: The University will contribute an amount equal to ten percent (10%) of the annual base salary compensation stipulated in Paragraph 5(b) hereof and the Coach will contribute five percent (5%) of said annual base salary compensation for this purpose. The Coach may, at his election, contribute additional amounts to the University retirement plans subject to Internal Revenue Service and University limitations.

(f) <u>Vacation.</u> Coach shall be entitled to one (1) month (i.e., twenty (20) working days) of paid vacation leave each Contract Year, subject to approval of the Director of Athletics. Vacation leave does not accrue.

(g) The University agrees to reimburse Coach and his family for all reasonable and legitimate relocation expenses.

(h) The University agrees to provide Coach a membership in a local golf and country club of his choice and pay monthly dues and initiation fees associated therewith.

7. <u>Termination by University.</u>

(a) If the University terminates this Agreement for "Cause," as defined in Paragraph 7(b) below, University shall be obligated to pay Coach all amounts owing up to the date of such termination only. Coach shall not be entitled to receive any benefits or payments that become due after the date of such termination. Health insurance however shall continue in full force and effect at University's expense for ninety (90) days thereafter or until Coach becomes employed, whichever occurs first.

Exhibit 9.2
(continued)

(b) The University shall have the right at any time to terminate this Agreement without Cause and for its convenience prior to its natural expiration. Termination by the University without Cause shall be effectuated by delivering written notice not less than thirty days prior to the effective date of said termination. Termination shall be effective upon the date specified in the notice. If the University terminates this Agreement any time, without Cause (which shall mean any termination other than a for-Cause termination), the University shall pay, and Coach agrees to accept as liquidated damages, Three Million Dollars ($3,000,000) per year for each Contract Year remaining on this Agreement. The liquidated damages are to be paid over the remainder of the scheduled term of this Agreement. Coach will be entitled to continue such benefits at Coach's own expense as required or permitted by law, but Coach will not otherwise be entitled to any employment or other benefit described herein. Health insurance however shall continue in full force and effect at University's expense for ninety (90) days after date of termination or until Coach is employed, whichever occurs first. The parties have bargained for and agreed to the foregoing liquidated damages provision, giving consideration to the fact that termination of this Agreement by the University without Cause prior to its expiration may cause the Coach to lose certain benefits and incentives, supplemental compensation, or other athletically-related compensation associated with Coach's employment at the University, which damages are extremely difficult to determine with certainty or fairly or adequately. The parties further agree that the payment of such liquidated damages by the University and acceptance thereof by the Coach shall constitute adequate and reasonable compensation to the Coach for the damages and injuries suffered by the Coach because of such termination by the University. The foregoing shall not be, nor construed to be, a penalty. Notwithstanding any other provisions contained in this Agreement, Coach agrees to reasonably mitigate the University's obligation to pay liquidated damages under this Agreement and to make reasonable and diligent efforts to obtain employment as soon as possible after termination of this Agreement by the University. Upon Coach's acceptance of any employment while liquidated damages are still being paid to Coach hereunder, the University's obligation to pay the full amount of liquidated damages shall be reduced by the amount of the minimum guaranteed annual compensation package of Coach's new position. Coach agrees to notify the University within fourteen (14) days of the date Coach accepts new employment and the minimum salary of the new employment.

The word "Cause," as used in this Paragraph 7 shall mean the occurrence of any of the following:

(i) Refusal or failure to furnish information relevant to an investigation of a possible men's basketball program violation or an NCAA or SEC bylaw or regulation;

(ii) Refusal to cooperate with the NCAA, SEC or University staff in the investigation of possible men's basketball program violations of NCAA or SEC bylaws or regulations;

Exhibit 9.2
(continued)

(iii) Knowing involvement in arranging for academic fraud by or for prospective or enrolled student-athletes;

(iv) Knowing involvement in offering or providing prospective or enrolled student athletes improper inducements or extra benefits;

(v) Knowingly furnishing the NCAA, SEC or the University false or misleading information concerning the Coach or any staff member's or athletics' involvement in or knowledge of a violation of an NCAA or SEC bylaw or regulation;

(vi) Knowingly providing information concerning intercollegiate athletics to individuals involved in organized gambling activities;

(vii) Knowingly soliciting a bet on any inter-collegiate team or accepting a bet on any team representing the University;

(viii) Knowingly participating in any gambling activity that involves intercollegiate athletics through a bookmaker, a parlay card or any other method employed by organized gambling;

(ix) Receiving benefits for facilitating or arranging a meeting between a student athlete and an agent or a financial advisor or a known representative of an agent or financial advisor.

(x) Failure to follow written Athletics Department policies or other University policies and procedures (of which Coach has been advised); and of any criminal violation (excluding minor traffic offenses or non-criminal offenses);

(xi) Coach's acts of significant misconduct including, but not limited to, conviction of any criminal violation (excluding minor traffic offenses or non-criminal offenses); and/or

(xii) Major violations of NCAA or University rules or policies in connection with the men's basketball program if committed by any personnel described in Paragraph 2(a)(i)-(vi) or by any student athlete or other "representative of the University's athletic interests" (as defined by the NCAA), whereby, in all of the foregoing, the Coach knew of or should have known of such violation, had prior knowledge of the violation and did not prevent or try to prevent the violation, and/or concealed or failed to report the violation.

It is not the intention or desire of the University that this Agreement be terminable for minor, technical or otherwise insignificant acts of misconduct by Coach or for minor, technical or otherwise insignificant University regulations or NCAA or SEC violations which do not entail the risk of major institutional penalties. It is not the intention or desire of the University that this Agreement be terminable if "secondary violations" occur after Coach has properly exercised institutional control under the Principles of Institutional Control as prepared by the NCAA Committee on Infractions. In order to properly maintain institutional control, Coach shall be notified by the Compliance Office of any and all alleged "secondary violations" committed by Coach, any assistant men's basketball coach or any men's basketball staff member for whom Coach is responsible. Coach

Exhibit 9.2
(continued)

shall then report to the Director of Athletics any corrective or disciplinary action taken to remediate the alleged violations.

However, a "major violation" by Coach or any staff member listed in Paragraph 2(a)(i), Paragraph 2(a)(iii) and/or Paragraph 2(a)(v) above or by a student athlete or representative of the University's athletic interests where the Coach knew or should have known of the major violation of said bylaws of either the NCAA or SEC would entitle the University to terminate this Agreement for "Cause". Anything in this Agreement to the contrary notwithstanding, it is hereby stipulated pursuant to NCAA Bylaw 11.2.1 that the Coach may be suspended for a period of time, without pay, or that the Coach's employment may be terminated if the Coach is found to be involved in deliberate and serious violations of NCAA or SEC bylaws or regulations as defined therein. It is further stipulated that pursuant to NCAA Bylaw 11.2.1 that if the Coach is found to be in violation of NCAA regulations, then the Coach shall be subject to disciplinary or corrective action as set forth in the provisions of the NCAA enforcement procedures.

(c) In the event of Coach's death, the University shall produce a final payment for the appropriate rate of pay in accordance with the number of days the Coach actually worked. Dependents' continued eligibility for benefits shall be in accordance with the standard eligibility of dependents of administrative staff. All deferred compensation money set forth in the Deferred Compensation Agreement shall accelerate and immediately vest and become payable to the designated beneficiaries.

(d) In the event Coach shall become disabled during the term of this Agreement, the University shall continue to provide all salary and benefits to Coach provided for pursuant to Paragraphs 5(b) and (c) and 6(a), (c), (d) and (e) of this Agreement as if Coach were fully performing such duties for a six month period beginning on the date of the disability, and upon such expiration date this Agreement shall terminate; provided, however, if by reason of Coach's disability, Coach shall receive disability insurance payments from any disability insurance policy paid for by the University, the University's obligations to Coach to pay salary pursuant to Paragraph 5(b) and (c) shall be reduced by the amount of disability payments received by Coach; and provided further that any such termination of this Agreement shall not effect Coach's right to continue to receive all disability insurance payments provided pursuant to the disability insurance policy referenced in Paragraph 6(c). The definition set forth in the University's group disability insurance policy (under which Coach shall be covered) for "disability" shall govern the determination of disability for purposes of this subparagraph. In addition, all deferred compensation money set forth in the Deferred Compensation Agreement shall accelerate and immediately vest and become payable to Coach.

8. <u>Termination by Coach.</u> In the event Coach terminates this Agreement (unless such termination results from University's material breach of this Agreement),

**Exhibit 9.2
(continued)**

Coach shall make the payment of liquidated damages within ninety (90) days as follows:

(a) Three Million Dollars ($3,000,000) if the termination occurs any time within the first (1st) year of this Agreement;

(b) Two Million Dollars ($2,000,000) if the termination occurs any time within the second (2nd) year of this Agreement;

(c) One Million Dollars ($1,000,000) if the termination occurs anytime within the third (3rd) year of this Agreement;

(d) Five Hundred Thousand Dollars ($500,000) if the termination occurs anytime within the fourth (4th) year of this Agreement;

(e) If the termination occurs anytime during the fifth (5th) year of this Agreement or thereafter, Coach will not be required to pay the University any liquidated damages.

The parties have bargained for and agreed to the foregoing liquidated damages provision, giving consideration to the fact that the termination by Coach of this Agreement without good cause (material breach by University) prior to the expiration may cause the University to incur programmatic and financial harm, damages which are extremely difficult to determine with certainty or fairly or adequately. The parties further agree that the payment of such liquidated damages by the Coach and acceptance thereof by the University shall constitute adequate and reasonable compensation to the University for all damages and harm suffered by the University because of such termination by the Coach. The foregoing shall not be, nor be construed to be, a penalty.

9. <u>Notices.</u> All notices, claims, requests, demands and other communications hereunder shall be made in writing and shall be deemed given if delivered or mailed (registered or certified mail, postage prepaid, return receipt requested) as follows:

To Coach:	John Vincent Calipari
	Joe Craft Center
	University of Kentucky
	Lexington, Kentucky 40506-0019
With a Copy to:	CAA Sports LLC
	4300 Haddonfield Road
	Suite 309
	Pennsauken, New Jersey 08109
	Attention: Leon Rose
With a Copy to:	CAA Sports LLC
	162 Fifth Avenue
	6th Floor
	New York, New York 10010
	Attention: Terence B. Prince, Esq.

Exhibit 9.2
(continued)

To the University:	Mitch Barnhart
	Director of Athletics
	Joe Craft Center
	University of Kentucky
	Lexington, Kentucky 40506-0019
With a copy to:	President Lee T. Todd, Jr.
	Office of the President
	University of Kentucky
	Room 101, Main Building
	Lexington, Kentucky 40506-0032

10. <u>Severability.</u> If any term, clause or provision of this Agreement shall be deemed to be illegal, invalid or unenforceable by a court of competent jurisdiction, such determination shall not affect the legality, validity or enforceability or any other term, clause or provision of this Agreement, and this Agreement shall be construed and enforced as if such term, clause or provision had not been included.

11. <u>Governing Law and Venue.</u> This Agreement shall be governed by, construed and enforced under the laws of the Commonwealth of Kentucky. Any action arising from or relating to this Agreement shall only be brought in the Franklin Circuit Court of the Commonwealth of Kentucky.

12. <u>Binding Effect.</u> This Agreement binds and is for the benefit of the University and its successors, assignees and legal representatives and of the Coach and his heirs, assignees, administrators and personal representatives.

13. <u>Amendment.</u> No amendment, change, waiver, discharge, or modification of any provision of this Agreement shall be valid unless it is evidenced by a written instrument signed by both parties hereto.

14. <u>Waiver.</u> The failure of either party to require strict performance by the other party of any provision of this Agreement shall not be deemed to affect that party's right to subsequently enforce a provision hereof. A waiver of a breach of any provision of this Agreement is not a waiver of any other breach or a waiver of the provision.

15. <u>Headings.</u> The paragraph headings contained in this Agreement are for reference purposes only and shall not affect in any way the meaning or interpretations of this Agreement.

16. <u>Assignment.</u> Neither party may assign this Agreement (including, without limitation, its respective duties or obligations hereunder), in whole or in part, without the prior express written agreement of the other party.

17. <u>Entire Agreement.</u> This Agreement incorporates any and all prior oral agreements and understandings of the parties with respect to its subject matter and supersedes all prior written contracts between the parties.

**Exhibit 9.2
(continued)**

18. <u>Authority.</u> Each party warrants and represents that it has the full right, power and authority to enter into and perform this Agreement and to make the covenants set forth herein.

IN WITNESS WHEREOF, the parties hereto have duly executed this Agreement as of the date first above written.

THE UNIVERSITY OF KENTUCKY

By: _____
Lee T. Todd, Jr.
President

By: _____
Mitch Barnhart
Director of Athletics

COACH

_____   _____
Witness   John Vincent Calipari

five-year contract signed in 1990. Vanderbilt charged DiNardo with breach of contract after he did not reply to their request. The district court found in favor of Vanderbilt, and the matter was brought to the Sixth Circuit Court of Appeals for review. DiNardo argued that the clause in his Vanderbilt contract was not a liquidated damages clause but rather a "noncompete" clause, which is unenforceable under Tennessee law (see section 9.1.1.4, "Legality"). The court found that the clause was for liquidated damages, and therefore legal, since it reasonably anticipated monetary damages for breach, measured prospectively at the time the contract was entered into, and did not call for compensation grossly disproportionate to the actual damages. The court reasoned:

> Vanderbilt hired DiNardo for a unique and specialized position, and the parties understood that the amount of damages could be easily ascertained should a breach occur. Contrary to DiNardo's suggestion, Vanderbilt did not need to undertake an

analysis to determine actual damages…the fact that liquidated damages declined each year DiNardo remained under contract, is directly tied to the parties' express understanding of the importance of a long-term commitment from DiNardo. Furthermore, the liquidated damages provision was reciprocal.

Therefore, the court determined that the liquidated damages provision was enforceable.

NOTES

1. In recent years, several high-profile college coaches have sued their former employers after they were terminated. Former University of Kentucky men's basketball coach Billy Gillispie sued alleging breach of contract following his termination, and the case was settled for close to $3 million. In 2010, former Texas Tech football coach Mike Leach sued for wrongful termination, and former South Florida football coach Jim Leavitt sued for breach of contract. Both cases are pending. For more on the issues in college coaching contracts, see Richard T. Karcher, "The Coaching Carousel in Big-Time Intercollegiate Athletics: Economic Implications and Legal Considerations," 20 *Fordham Intellectual Property Media & Entertainment Law Journal* 1 (2009).

2. In 2008, West Virginia University sued former head football coach Rich Rodriguez for breach of contract when he left West Virginia to coach the University of Michigan. After Rodriguez had flirted with other college teams in prior seasons, West Virginia renegotiated Rodriguez's contract prior to the 2007 season, increased Rodriguez's salary to $1.8 million, and also included a "buyout" clause of $4 million in the event Rodriguez voluntarily left the university. West Virginia rejected Rodriguez's offer of $1.5 million, the same amount former West Virginia basketball coach John Beilein paid in a buyout when he also left for Michigan. Eventually Rodriguez agreed to pay the $4 million buyout, with Michigan paying $2.5 million of it.

3. After leading his team to the 2008 NCAA Men's Basketball Championship Game, University of Memphis extended the contract of head coach John Calipari through the 2012–2013 season while raising his salary to $2.35 million per year. As an incentive to Calipari to adhere to the terms of the contract, Calipari would receive a $5 million bonus if he stayed at Memphis for the duration of the contract, which he did not.

4. In *O'Brien v. The Ohio State Univ.*, 2006 WL 571043 (Ohio Ct.Cl. February 15, 2006), Jim O'Brien sued The Ohio State University after it fired him as the men's head basketball coach in June 2004. O'Brien admitted giving $6,000 in cash in late 1998 or early 1999 to Alex Radojevic, a recruit who had signed a national letter of intent to attend Ohio State. Having been paid to play in Yugoslavia, Radojevic was ineligible under NCAA rules, a fact discovered by the university and the NCAA in February 1999. O'Brien contended that the money was a loan and that he knew that Radojevic was ineligible and gave him the money to aid Radojevic's family in war-torn Serbia. Following the 1999 season in which O'Brien led Ohio State to the Final Four, he agreed to a contract extension through the 2007 season. In April 2004, O'Brien told Ohio State athletic director, Andy Geiger, about the 1999 loan, who reported the violation to the NCAA. When O'Brien was subsequently fired, he brought suit alleging breach of contract. Although the court found that O'Brien had reasonable cause to believe that he had committed an NCAA infraction, in breach of his contract, the court ruled that O'Brien's failure to report the infraction was not a material breach that would give Ohio State cause for termination. O'Brien was ultimately awarded about $2.5 million in damages.

5. In June 2003, University of Washington football coach Rick Neuheisel was fired one season after signing a contract extension through 2007 that would have paid him as much as $1.8 million annually. Neuheisel was fired after it was revealed that he and three friends had participated in past NCAA men's basketball tournament pools and won over $12,000. NCAA rules do not allow coaches, athletes, or staff members to gamble on college sports,

although the rules do not specifically address such pools. Neuheisel said he was given permission from the Washington athletic department to participate in the pool. Neuheisel sued the university for breach of contract, claiming he was fired without cause. Neuheisel also sued the NCAA, claiming that NCAA investigators interviewed Neuheisel about the gambling accusations without being given proper notification of the purpose of the interview, as required by the NCAA bylaws. After five weeks of trial, in March 2005, the university and the NCAA settled the lawsuit for approximately $4.5 million.

6. In *Northeastern University v. Brown*, 2004 WL 616225 (Mass.Super. March 11, 2004), Northeastern sued to prevent former head football coach Don Brown from coaching at the University of Massachusetts. Northeastern had rejected UMass's request to interview Brown about its head coaching vacancy, but nevertheless UMass hired Brown away from Northeastern. The court granted Northeastern's request for a preliminary injunction because UMass and Northeastern are in the same conference and state and as a result Northeastern would suffer irreparable harm from Brown's willful and intentional breach. UMass and Northeastern settled the matter out of court for a reported $150,000.

7. In 2001, Utah State University reached a settlement with football coach Dave Arslanian, after he contended that an administrator had secretly hired a new coach five weeks before he was fired. Arslanian was fired in the middle of a multiyear contract. The university had originally contended that Arslanian was entitled only to his salary. However, to avoid litigation, the university agreed to continue paying the coach's benefits.

8. In 1998, basketball coach Larry Shyatt agreed to pay $286,000 to the University of Wyoming to settle a lawsuit stemming from his breaching his contract in order to become head coach of Clemson University. Shyatt claimed that he had an unwritten agreement with Wyoming that allowed him to leave in the event of a head coaching vacancy at Clemson (Shyatt was once an assistant coach at Clemson). However, Wyoming denied this claim. According to University of Wyoming officials, the settlement amount was equal to what Shyatt would have made if he had continued to be Wyoming's head coach, plus $40,000 in legal costs.

9. For further information about termination settlements and other issues regarding college coaches, see Martin J. Greenberg, "Representation of College Coaches in Contract Negotiations," 3 *Marquette Sports Law Journal* 101 (1992). Greenberg, who has been an attorney for several college coaches, addresses the issue of reassignment clauses. Sometimes a contract will not allow a university to fire a coach, but it can reassign the coach to a lesser position. He states: "[A reassignment clause] states that a coach can be assigned to a new position, such as head of the gym or head of the latrine committee.... This situation actually arose with Don Morton [former University of Wisconsin football coach]. Because he had no other job, Morton decided to take the latrine job. He thought, 'I'll get my salary, my fringe benefits, my car and my country club membership....' Morton essentially said, 'I'll be happy to clean toilets for the remaining three years for the total package.' What ultimately happens when a situation like this arises? There is some type of financial settlement, because [colleges will not usually] hang out their dirty laundry in public." Also see Martin J. Greenberg and Jay S. Smith, "A Study of Division I Assistant Football and Men's Basketball Coaches' Contracts," 18 *Marquette Sports Law Review* 25 (2007).

10. Occasionally institutions hire coaches as "at-will" employees, where no contract exists. In these cases, the courts have given the institutions complete discretion to terminate contracts at will. *Frazier v. University of District of Columbia*, 742 F.Supp. 28 (D.D.C. 1990) is an example of an at-will employee who unsuccessfully challenged his dismissal. However, at-will coaches are protected by the doctrine of wrongful termination (see section 15.3.1, "Employment-at-Will Contracts").

11. In *Earl Bruce v. The Ohio State University*, No. 87-CV11–7430 (Franklin County, Ohio, 1987), a coach brought a $7.45 million breach of contract suit after his termination over alleged recruiting violations. The plaintiff also raised the issues of slander and wrongful discharge. The case was settled for $471,000.

12. In *Parker v. Graves*, 340 F.Supp. 586 (D.C. Fla. 1972), a coach was dismissed for conduct that he claimed was protected under the First Amendment. The coach sued the

University of Florida for wrongful discharge. In denying the plaintiff's First Amendment claim, the court balanced the coach's rights against his responsibility as a public school employee to provide orderly administration.

9.2.6. Coaches' Contracts: High School

High school coaches are generally teachers first and coaches second. High school coaches are given either a *divisible contract* or an *indivisible contract*. To have a divisible contract means that an individual will have separate coaching and teaching contracts. This can cause problems if one of the individual's contracts is terminated. A teacher in high school is usually eligible for tenure after a specified number of years of teaching. For a coach, however, this is not usually the case. A practical problem arises when a coach is dismissed from his or her job as coach but has tenure as a teacher and decides to remain at the school in that capacity. If the teacher/coach has a divisible contract, a dispute is generally avoided. However, indivisible contracts for teacher/coaches have led to litigation.

The same issue arises when a coach resigns from a coaching position but chooses to keep his or her teaching position. The courts have taken different views of whether a contract is divisible, with the facts of the particular case, the language of the contract, and the specifics of the collective bargaining agreement being important factors.

In *Brown v. Board of Education*, the court ruled that the plaintiff was hired as a teacher and coach. Therefore, the plaintiff could not resign from one post without resigning from the other (see note 11). However, in *Swager v. Board of Education*, the court ruled that the plaintiff could resign from his coaching duties without affecting his position as a math teacher (see note 9).

To address the problem of divisible teacher-coaching contracts, some school districts require the individual to sign an indivisible contract. Under this type of contract, the loss of either position results in the loss of both positions. High school teachers and coaches are often unionized, and therefore, their contracts are governed by a collective bargaining agreement. Consequently, coaches must follow the grievance arbitration procedure rather than go through the court system. Grievance arbitration is the submission of the parties' grievance to a private arbitrator or arbitrators who listen to the disputed question and give a binding decision regarding the dispute (see Chapter 11, "Labor Law"). It is important to note that some cases still go to court, because not all teachers are unionized, and a few decisions made by arbitrators are challenged.

In cases where the interpretation of an employment contract is questioned, the court or arbitrator must carefully scrutinize the wording of the contract to determine its precise meaning. Most disputes involving high school coaches revolve around the issue of dismissal. There are two general types of dismissal cases: procedural and substantive.

In *procedural* dismissal cases, the reason for dismissal is not challenged, but the procedure followed by the employer to dismiss the employee is challenged. Cases are often brought by a coach who claims that he/she was dismissed without proper notice or hearing. In *Bell v. Vista Unified School District*, 92 Cal. Rptr.2d 263 (Cal. Ct. App. 2000), a high school football coach filed suit claiming that the school district violated the state's open-meeting law by firing him without giving him 24 hours' notice of the meeting. The appellate court agreed, ordering the district to reinstate the plaintiff as football coach. The California

Supreme Court refused to hear the district's appeal. The coach and the district also settled allegations of wrongful termination, with the district agreeing to pay Bell $125,000.

In *substantive* dismissal cases, the court must assess whether the reason for the dismissal is valid under the terms of the contract. For example, in *McLaughlin v. Machias School Committee*, 385 A. 2d 53 (Me. 1978), a teacher who struck a student in the face during a pickup basketball game was dismissed as "unfit to teach." The teacher challenged the dismissal, and the Maine Supreme Court ruled that the school committee was acting within its rights when it dismissed the teacher. In substantive dismissal cases, courts must determine whether there is just cause for termination according to the contract terms.

NOTES

1. In *Board of Directors of Ames Community School District v. Cullinan*, 745 N.W.2d 487 (Iowa 2008), former Ames High School basketball coach Dennis Cullinan was fired after a history of threatening and intimidating treatment of student-athletes. Cullinan claimed that there was insufficient evidence to satisfy the just-cause requirement for Cullinan's termination; however, the Supreme Court of Iowa determined that the school board properly considered Cullinan's entire history in making its decision. In addition, the court ruled that the hearsay evidence from student-athletes and their parents bore sufficient indication of reliability to be properly considered.

2. In *Gary Community School Corp. v. Powell*, 881 N.E.2d 57 (Ind.App. 2008), a full-time teacher and part-time football coach sued under the Family and Medical Leave Act (FMLA) after he was not reinstated to his coaching position after returning from a medical leave of absence. The court determined that because Powell's coaching contract was separate from his teaching contract and because Powell did not work at least 1,250 hours as a part-time football coach, he could not be covered by the FMLA, which only protects full-time employees.

3. In *Mullen v. Parchment School District Board of Education*, 2007 WL 1932031 (Mich.App. 2007), an elementary school teacher who also served as the district's head cross country coach and head women's track coach claimed that the board of education violated the teacher–board of education collective bargaining agreement by failing to renew plaintiff's coaching contracts without just cause. The court granted summary judgment for the board of education because the coaching contracts were for a definite period of time, only the sports season of that particular school year. As a result, the school was under no obligation to continue Mullen's contract, rendering the just cause provision irrelevant.

4. A school district can be sued for wrongful termination by a teacher/coach, even if the employee's contract does not mention coaching responsibilities. In the case of *Kingsford v. Salt Lake City School District*, 247 F.3d 1123 (10th Cir. 2001), a high school math teacher brought suit after his termination as football coach. He had been hired more than a decade earlier as a teacher only, but had subsequently taken on coaching responsibilities in several sports. The district court determined that the plaintiff had obtained a property interest in his position as head football coach (see section 6.1, "Athletic Associations and Constitutional Issues"). The school district used an immunity defense in order to avoid having to demonstrate cause for the coach's termination. That defense was rejected, and the case was remanded.

5. In *Cruciotti v. McNeel*, 396 S.E.2d 191 (W. Va. 1990), an unsuccessful applicant for the position of physical education teacher brought action against the school district, alleging that the job posting, which described the opening as "physical education teacher and athletic trainer," constituted an improper joining of employment positions. In affirming the lower court's decision, the Supreme Court of Appeals held that the position of athletic trainer was "extra-curricular" and therefore required a separate contract for employment.

6. In *State ex. rel. Dennis v. Board of Education*, 529 N.E. 2d. 1248 (Ohio 1988), a substitute teacher, who was also a football, basketball, and track coach, was given written notice that his contracts to coach football and basketball would not be renewed. He was not, however, given notice that his substitute teaching and track coaching contracts would not be renewed (though they, too, were not). The coach brought action claiming a procedural violation against the board of education for not giving him notice of nonrenewal of his contracts as substitute teacher and track coach. The court of appeals ruled that the coach was to be reinstated as track coach and substitute teacher.

7. In *Matter of Hahn*, 386 N.W. 2d 789 (Minn. Ct. App. 1986), a girls' basketball coach challenged the hearing officers' conclusion that the school board properly refused to renew her coaching contract. The court of appeals held that the school board established adequate reasons for not renewing the coaching contract.

8. In *Smith v. Board of Education*, 341 S.E. 2d 685 (W.Va. 1985), a teacher and football coach was dismissed from his coaching duties without prior notice and without explanation. The issue before the court was whether a coach was entitled to the same procedural rights that a teacher has under the West Virginia code. The court concluded that a coach was entitled to the same procedural rights, and Smith was reinstated.

9. In *Swager v. Board of Education*, 688 P.2d 270 (Kan. Ct. App. 1984), a teacher brought an action against the board of education to reinstate him as a math teacher after the board had misinterpreted his resignation as basketball coach as a resignation from teaching *and* coaching. In ruling for the teacher, the appellate court reasoned that were his position as teacher not renewed, he would be entitled to certain due process requirements, including a hearing that the board never provided.

10. In *Board of Education v. Youel*, 282 N.W. 2d 677 (Iowa 1979), the court found that the plaintiff's conduct as football coach amounted to just cause for termination despite the fact that most of his salary came from his position as mathematics teacher. The question of partial termination was not at issue in the case, and the court expressed "no opinion as to whether Youel, had he requested, was entitled to stay on as mathematics teacher."

11. In *Brown v. Board of Education*, 560 P.2d 1129 (Utah 1977), a teacher who was also a coach resigned from his coaching duties. The school district, claiming that he could not resign from his coaching duties without also resigning from his teaching duties because they were not separate contracts, treated the resignation as a resignation from both duties. The issue in this case was whether the contract to coach and teach was a divisible contract, thus permitting the teacher to resign from one of his duties without affecting the other. The court ruled that the contract was not divisible, and thus the plaintiff's resignation was a resignation from both duties.

12. In *Stang v. Independent School District*, 256 N.W. 2d 82 (Minn. 1977), a high school basketball coach brought action against a school district, alleging it had failed to give him proper written notice and a hearing prior to his dismissal as coach. In ruling for the school district, the court held that the coach was not a teacher within the meaning of the Teacher Tenure Act, and thus was not entitled to written notice and a hearing.

9.2.7. Physicians' Contracts

There is a need to have a physician available for athletic activities, on the professional, college, and high school level. Injuries are a possibility in all athletic contests, and immediate diagnosis and treatment by a qualified doctor are desirable and often critical. The presence of a physician at certain athletic contests may be a requirement of most teams' or schools' insurance policies.

Some college and university team doctors are actual employees of the institution. However, this is the exception rather than the rule. Physicians are normally signed as independent contractors, and as a result, the hiring party avoids liability under the doctrine of vicarious liability. (See sections 3.6.1. and 4.6.) The following is an example of what might appear in a college physician's contract:

It is understood and agreed that Physician is an independent contractor with regard to all consulting services to be rendered hereunder, and is not acting as College's agent, employee, or servant. It is also understood that Physician is not an insurer of results in any medical treatment rendered under the terms of agreement.

The key difference between an employee and an independent contractor is the degree of control and direction the institution or team exercises over the physician's work. An employee is subject to a much higher degree of control than an independent contractor. Most physicians at the collegiate and professional levels have their own practices or are employees of health maintenance organization and work with teams or schools on a part-time basis, thus classifying themselves as independent contractors. A physician's contract is a basic employment contract with terms and conditions of employment listed within the contract (see exhibit 9.3).

9.2.8. Officials' Contracts

Officials are generally hired by a league or conference, or in some intercollegiate or interscholastic cases, by an institution. Cases have been litigated over the years as to whether officials are employees or independent contractors. This issue has arisen in the area of torts (see Chapter 3, "Legal Principles in Tort Law") and workers' compensation. Like a physician's, an official's actions may make the hiring party liable for any damages if an employer-employee relationship is established. To ensure that they are not held vicariously liable in such situations, many hiring parties will draft contracts that define officials as independent contractors (see exhibit 9.4).

While the courts have generally agreed that decisions made by officials are not subject to court examination, officials may find themselves in court as the plaintiff in a breach of contract case (see section 4.7, "Liability of Officials, Referees, and Umpires"). For example, in *Clemons* v. *Big Ten Conference*, No. 96 (N.D. Ill. 1997), the plaintiff, a football official for the Big Ten, had his contract canceled prior to the 1994 season. Clemons challenged his termination by claiming that it was due to his weight, and he had thus been discriminated against under the Americans with Disabilities Act and Title VII. Clemons's work performance had come under review in 1993 when he placed poorly on the Big Ten's officials rating system. Clemons was placed on probation and told to lose weight, which the conference believed had affected his ratings in a negative way. When Clemons reported to the officials' clinic in August 1994, he had gained more weight and was subsequently terminated. The court concluded that it was not unreasonable for the conference to demand that its officials maintain an acceptable weight insofar as that their weight may interfere with their officiating duties. The court also found that Clemons had been given sufficient notice after the 1993 season to deal with his weight problem, and since he had not, the conference was justified in taking the actions it did. The court granted summary judgment to the Big Ten Conference.

9.2.9. Facility Contracts

When an institution in amateur athletics, or a team in a professional league, does not own an arena or stadium, it becomes necessary to enter into an agreement for the use of such a facility. In addition to the use of the facility (games, practices,

Exhibit 9.3
Physician's Contract

AGREEMENT

STATE _____

COUNTY _____

THIS AGREEMENT made and entered into the _____ day of
_____, 20xx, by and between _____, a college
having its principal place of business in _____ (hereinafter referred to as "College"), and DR. _____, a citizen and resident of
_____, (hereinafter referred to as "Physician").

WITNESSETH:

WHEREAS, College is desirous of obtaining the services of Physician in connection with its intercollegiate sports program, and

WHEREAS, Physician is skilled in the practice of medicine and is willing to assist College with its medical programs in its intercollegiate sports program,

NOW THEREFORE, in consideration of the covenants and promises contained herein, the parties agree as follows:

1. College hereby retains and Physician agrees to be retained by College as College's consultant in College's intercollegiate sports program for the school year
   2010–11.

2. Physician will act as a consultant with the College's coaches, trainers, athletes
   and other personnel with regard to medical problems incurred by athletes in
   the College's intercollegiate sports program. Physician's consulting services shall
   include attendance at home football games whenever possible. In Physician's
   absence, he will attempt to find qualified medical help to attend. Physician will
   be available for consultation one day per week.

3. Physician agrees to review participation medical records on a yearly basis.

4. Physician shall make recommendations to the coaching staff, trainers, and
   other personnel as to the handling of all medical matters with regards to the
   athletes in the College's intercollegiate sports program. Such recommendations shall include prescribing treatment for injuries and other medical problems, and recommendations for surgical and other hospital procedures when
   necessary. All physician charges for such surgery and other hospital procedures are not covered under the terms of this agreement.

5. Physician shall make decisions on athletes practicing, returning to practice or
   playing in athletic contests. In absence of Physician, he will delegate authority
   to another physician, head trainer or sports medicine coordinator.

6. Physician will supervise student trainers and graduate assistants through the
   head athletic trainer and sports medicine coordinator.

7. Physician will make the decision to send an athlete to another physician or delegate that decision to another individual.

8. If an athlete seeks a second opinion without consent of team physician, payment is not guaranteed.

Exhibit 9.3
(continued)

9. As compensation for all consulting services rendered hereunder, College agrees to pay to Physician the sum of $_____ to be paid upon execution of this agreement.

10. It is understood and agreed that Physician is an independent contractor with regard to all consulting services to be rendered hereunder, and is not acting as College's agent, employee or servant. It is also understood that Physician is not an insurer of results in any medical treatment rendered under the terms of this agreement.

11. This agreement is to be construed under and governed by the laws of the State of _____ .

IN WITNESS WHEREOF, the parties hereto have executed this agreement in duplicate originals on the day and year first above written.

_____COLLEGE   DR: _____

By: _____   By: _____

locker rooms, etc.), as well as control of parking, sponsorship, advertising, and signage revenue, consideration should be given to the amount of rent charged, the method of payment, and the specific services provided for the facility owner. The responsibility for the promotion of the event, and the provision of personnel to run the arena (security personnel, concessions, ticket takers, work crews, etc.) also need to be addressed in the contract. The time of the event(s) and the availability of the arena for warm-ups before the event should also be explicitly stated. In addition, any potential schedule conflicts between multiple parties leasing the facilities should be addressed in the drawing of an agreement. Many facility-team contracts have explicit sections titled "Obligations of the (Team or League)" and "Obligations of the (Facility)" (see exhibit 9.5).

Third-party agreements, such as radio or television contracts between the institution and the media, should also be considered in the drafting of facility contracts in case certain accommodations are necessary. Moreover, insurance requirements must be considered. Generally, a facility requires specific types of insurance coverage to be carried by the institution or team before it will allow the use of the facility for a particular event.

Most facility or game contracts have a provision that strikes liability from both parties in the event of an unforeseen circumstance. For example:

> In the event that said exhibition game shall not be played on the said date or some postponed date mutually agreeable to both parties by reason of war, insurrection, strikes, riots, destruction of stadium, act of God, or other force majeure beyond the control of contracting parties, then an exhibition game will be played at said location at a time and date agreed upon by both parties within one year of canceled date.

When complex contracts worth millions of dollars are being brokered, there is always the potential for conflict between the contracting parties. To deal with these

Exhibit 9.4
An Official's Contract

MODEL CONTRACT BETWEEN SCHOOLS
AND SPORTS OFFICIALS

Please note that this is a "Model" and may have to be modified to fit the particular circumstances of your local association and/or schools at which you officiate. Also, it is based upon general principles of law; therefore, you should review it with a local attorney prior to using it due to differences of state law.

The _____ (home school) [hereinafter "School"] of _____ (city and state) and _____ (official's name) of _____ (official's address) [hereinafter "Official"] enter into the following Agreement:

1. **CONTEST.** The Official agrees to officiate a _____ (level) _____ (sport) contest between _____ (home school) and _____ (visitor school) at _____ (place) _____ (city and state) on _____ (date) at _____ (time). The other official(s) is/are _____.

2. **PAYMENT.** In consideration of such services, the _____ (home school) will pay the Official within _____ days of the game date a fee of _____ (amount), plus mileage at the rate of 50 cents/mile for _____ miles, in the amount of $_____.

3. **OFFICIAL'S STATUS.** The Official agrees to work this game as an independent contractor.

4. **OFFICIAL'S REPRESENTATION.** The Official represents that he/she is, or will be by the date of the contest, a duly licensed official in this state authorized to officiate this contest. If it is found to be otherwise, this Agreement shall become null and void.

5. **INTERPRETATION.** The Constitution, By-Laws and rules and regulations of the _____ (state association) and of the _____ (local association) are considered a part of this Agreement and shall govern, except as modified by this Agreement, any disputes arising out of this Agreement. Both parties to this Agreement agree to be so bound.

6. **VOIDING OF CONTRACT.** This contract shall become null and void upon probation or suspension of either the School or the Official by the _____ (state association).

7. **CANCELLATION/POSTPONEMENT.** This contract may be canceled at any time by the mutual written consent of both parties. This contract is voidable if either party cannot comply with its terms for any sufficient reason.

   A. **Sufficient Reason.** If the contest is canceled by mutual written consent or for sufficient reason (including, but not limited to, unfavorable weather, illness, accident, or injury) and the Official is not notified in time to prevent travel to the game site, the Official shall be paid the round-trip mileage at the rate of 20 cents/mile. If the contest begins, but is then canceled

Exhibit 9.4
(continued)

due to unfavorable weather, the Official shall be paid the fee and mileage expenses set forth in Paragraph 2.

B. Insufficient Reason. If the game is canceled for any insufficient reason, or if either school participating in the contest no longer desires the Official to officiate, the Official shall be paid the fee.

C. Rescheduling. If the contest is postponed and rescheduled, the Official shall be paid the fee set forth in Paragraph 2. If the agreed time of the contest is changed, the Official will be given the first opportunity to officiate at the new time, but if the Official is unable to do so, the Official shall be paid the fee set forth in Paragraph 2.

D. Official's Failure To Officiate. If the Official fails to officiate the game for a reason other than a sufficient reason, then the Official shall pay the school an amount equal to the fee within _____ days of the game date.

E. Payment. Payment of the fee and/or mileage as a result of cancellation, rescheduling, or postponement shall be made by the School and received by the Official within _____ days after the original date set for the game.

problems or disagreements outside of the court system, many contracts will have arbitration clauses. This allows potential disagreements to be settled by an independent arbitrator. For example:

Any dispute, controversy, or claim arising out of, or relating to this agreement, or breach, or termination, shall be settled by binding arbitration in accordance with the rules of the American Arbitration Association. The parties hereby expressly and knowingly agree that judgment upon award rendered in such arbitration shall be binding on the parties and may be entered in any court having jurisdiction thereof.

NOTES _____

1. Prior to the 2005 season, Angels Baseball L.P. (ABLP) purchased the Anaheim Angels and changed their name to the Los Angeles Angels of Anaheim, who had spent the previous eight seasons, a period that included their first World Series victory, as the Anaheim Angels. Prior to that, they had been the California Angels for 32 years although were known as the Los Angeles Angels for the first four years of the organization before moving to Anaheim in 1966. The 2005 change was made in hopes of portraying the Angels as a "major market" team. In 1996 the Walt Disney Company purchased the Angels and agreed to lease Anaheim Stadium from the city of Anaheim. The terms of the lease called for the team to include "Anaheim" in the team name, prompting the change from the California Angels.

Upon announcement of the change to Los Angeles Angels of Anaheim, the city of Anaheim filed suit seeking injunctive and declaratory relief, alleging breach of the lease and the implied covenant of good faith and fair dealing. The trial court denied Anaheim's request for a temporary restraining order. The city of Anaheim contended that a strict interpretation of the lease agreement would permit ABLP to change the team name to any of the following: "The Angels Who Are Embarrassed To Be Associated with Anaheim," "The Angels of the Disgusting City of Anaheim," "The Angels Formerly Known

Exhibit 9.5
Facility Contract

THIS AGREEMENT is made this 28th day of February 2010 between *(Conference)* and *(Facility Operator)*.

WHEREAS, the *(conference)* is a collegiate athletic conference comprised of institutions which have Division 1 men's and Women's intercollegiate basketball programs; and

WHEREAS, *(Facility Operator)* is the operator and/or manager of a multi-purpose sports and entertainment arena located in *(city, state)*, known as *(facility name)*: and

WHEREAS, the *(Conference)* desires to hold its 2011 men's and women's basketball tournaments at the arena pursuant to the terms of this Agreement; and

WHEREAS *(Facility Operator)* desires to make the Arena available to the *(Conference)* for the holding of its 2011 men's and women's basketball tournaments pursuant to the terms of this Agreement;

NOW, THEREFORE, in consideration of the mutual promises exchanged below, the parties agree as follows:

1. **(Conference) 2011 Tournaments.** The *(Conference)* will hold its 2010 men's and women's basketball tournaments *(Tournament)* at the Arena pursuant to the terms of this Agreement. The term of this Agreement shall expire on June 30, 2011, except for those provisions that extend beyond the terms of this Agreement. *(Facility Operator)* agrees that it shall not schedule any events of any type in the Arena during the Tournament, including the day and night prior to the first game.

2. **Tournament Dates.** The dates for the tournament are as follows:

    March _____, 2011

    Game times will be mutually agreed upon by the parties. This schedule may be changed upon mutual written agreement of the parties and is subject to change should the NCAA change its schedule.

3. **Lump Sum Payment to *(Conference)***

4. **Net Revenue Payment to** *(Facility Operator)* *(Conference)* agrees to pay the *(Facility Operator)* 60% of all net revenue from the Tournament within 60 days following the end of the Tournament. "Gross Revenue" shall consist of all revenue derived from the sale of tickets in connection with the Tournament, revenue from sponsorships sold in connection with the Tournament (net of implementation costs and commissions) (except to the extent provided in paragraph 25 and not including title sponsorship revenue which shall be divided as provided in paragraph 14), Net Merchandise and Program Revenue (as defined in paragraph 23), and any other items mutually agreed upon in writing. "Net revenue" is defined as gross revenue less Tournament expenses approved in writing by the *(Conference)* and *(Facility Operator)* which are incurred by *(Conference)* or *(Facility Operator)* including the $_____ annual guaranteed payment identified in Paragraph 3 and less all applicable taxes.

Exhibit 9.5
(continued)

(Conference) and the *(Facility Operator)* agree to settle the finances relating to the Tournament within 60 days following the end of the Tournament.

5. **Ticket Promotion and Sales.** Ticket prices shall be mutually agreed upon by the parties. **They shall not be less than the prices set forth in Exhibit A.** *(Conference)* and *(Facility Operator)* will make reasonable efforts to produce promotional mailing materials and ticket order forms and have these materials mailed to all institutions' alumni as identified by the *(Conference)* and to cause all-session brochures to be available for distribution by November 1 of the year proceeding the Tournament. These expenses shall be a Tournament expense. *(Facility Operator)* agrees to include the Tournament as part of the **usual** package purchased by its suite holders for events at the **Arena** and the income from **(1) the value of the tickets for each seat in each suite used, with the value to be $_____ per seat per session or $_____ for all sessions and (2) with the full regular ticket value** four seats in each of the suites, **which may be separately sold, _____** to be included in Gross Revenue **for the Tournament.**

6. **Tournament Expenses.** In addition to all other terms of this Agreement, *(Facility Operator)* shall be responsible for the following items and services related to the operation of the Tournament which shall be Tournament expenses: Jumbotron presentations, court set-up and tear down, building security, telephone line installation, police, EMT, utilities, post-event cleaning, public address announcers, ticket sellers and takers, house electricians, hospitality areas, mutually agreed upon marketing materials, press room meals and refreshments, computerized ticket printing, sound technicians, table rentals, pipe and drape rentals, office equipment rentals for *(Conference)* office, program printing and group sales expenses. The *(Conference)* shall be responsible for the following which shall be a Tournament expense: game officials, statisticians, scorekeepers. Tournament expenses shall included the foregoing as well as any other expenses designated as Tournament expenses in this Agreement and any other expenses mutually agreed upon in writing by the parties as Tournament expenses.

7. **Tournament Suite/Parking.**

8. **Tournament Title Sponsor Suite.** *(Facility Operator)* shall provide the Tournament's title sponsor with a suite for the duration of the Tournament. *(Facility Operator)* shall provide the usual and customary suite services to the title sponsor suite including food and beverage services at in-house catered rates. This suite is in addition, at the option of the title sponsor, to any other suite the Tournament title sponsor may generally have and use in the Arena.

9. **(Conference) Office Space.** *(Facility Operator)* shall provide the *(Conference)* office space with out charge for the *(Conference)* exclusive use beginning at 8:00 A.M. on the Wednesday preceding the Tournament and continuing to 12:00 noon on the day following the day of the championship game of the Tournament. This office space will serve as the Tournament headquarters and the administrative office for all Tournament-related events. The office shall be located in a place to be mutually agreed upon at least 180 days prior to the start of the Tournament. The office shall be equipped with the following with out charge to the *(Conference)* for the equipment or lines: two fax machines with

Exhibit 9.5
(continued)

capability to send to 48 recipients and telephone lines, high speed photocopier with collator, stapler and four direct outside telephones and telephone lines. Telephone charges, including long distance calls, supplies and related items will be a Tournament expense or may be provided as a trade sponsorship.

10. **Media Relations.**

11. **Locker and Training Room Facilities.** *(Facility Operator)* shall provide four locker rooms for use by participating institutions in the Tournament. Each locker room shall include at least 15 separate lockers/stalls for the players, training table and chalkboard or marker board with chalk, markers, erasers and prepared to accommodate both men's and women's teams and readied and available in accordance with daily Tournament schedule. *(Facility Operator)* shall provide use of the *(Facility)* and other **team** training rooms **and equipment therein** for use throughout the Tournament without any charge to the *(Conference)*. *(Facility Operator)* shall secure and have sufficient security personnel available to guard all locker rooms and officials' dressing rooms before, during and after game competition. All persons who use the locker rooms shall conduct themselves and treat the facilities in an appropriate manner for the use of such facilities.

12. **Practice Schedule/Facilities.** *(Facility Operator)*, without charge to the *(Conference)* and the _____ shall jointly develop a practice schedule and secure convenient practice sites and times in the Arena and/ or off-site for all institutions participating in the Tournament. The practice schedule shall be mutually agreed upon in writing at least 30 days prior to the first game of the Tournament. The *(Facility Operator)* shall cause the host institution, _____ University, to make its on-campus practice facilities available for use during the Tournament and to coordinate such use with *(Conference's)* operations personnel.

13. **Title Sponsorship.** *(Conference)* shall use its best efforts to secure a title sponsor for the Tournament and if *(Conference)* so secures it shall provide 60% of the gross sponsorship fee to the *(Facility Operator)*, which amount shall be in addition to the $_____ payment in Paragraph 3. The other 40% shall belong solely to *(Conference)*. No commission shall be charged by *(Facility Operator)* relating to procurement of a title sponsor. The *(Conference)* current Tournament title sponsor, *(Sponsor)* shall have the right to sponsor this Tournament and *(Conference)* agrees that this in no way violates any agreement it has with any other bank. If *(Sponsor)*, the current title sponsor of the *(Conference)* Tournament, decides to sponsor this Tournament or the *(Conference)* secures a new title sponsor, then that sponsorship fee shall be likewise split as set forth earlier in this paragraph.

14. **Associate, Trade and Other Sponsorships.**

15. **Banners and Signage.** *(Facility Operator)* shall design and produce, subject to prior written approval of the designs and materials by the *(Conference)*, which shall not be unreasonably withheld, an inventory of banners and signage for use before and/or during the Tournament. Except as otherwise provided below, the costs of design, production, installation and removal shall be a Tournament expense. A schedule of required banners and signage is set

Exhibit 9.5
(continued)

forth below and shall be in place at all locations, not including the inside of the Arena, at least 3 days prior to the day of the Tip-Off Banquet and remain through the evening of the day after the Tournament championship game, unless otherwise mutually agreed to in writing. All in-Arena banners and signage shall be in place by the morning of the evening of the Tip-off Banquet.

(1) two "Welcome *(Conference)* Tournament" banners containing the *(Conference)* color logo at each hotel hosting *(Conference)* teams;

(2) four "Welcome *(Conference)* Tournament" banners containing the *(Conference)* color logo at _____ Airport.

(3) three 3' by 8' "*(Conference)* Tournament" banners containing the *(Conference)* color logo and dates of the Tournament on exterior of the Arena and regular announcement of the Tournament on the outside Arena electronic signboard at least 21 days prior to the start date of the Tournament up until and during the Tournament;

(4) two 4' by 25' "*(Conference)* Tournament" banners containing the *(Conference)* color logo and dates of the Tournament suspended across streets surrounding the Arena subject to local law permitting this to be done;

(5) ten 8' by 15' *(Conference)* individual member institution banners to be hung from the rafters of the Arena during the Tournament.

(6) vertical "Welcome Fans" banners containing the *(Conference)* color logo hung from light poles surrounding the Arena and headquarters hotel subject to local law permitting this to be done and with the number and placement of banners to be mutually agreed upon by the _____ and _____; the light poles in and around the Arena parking lots have banners that are in place pursuant to a contract between *(Conference)* and the sponsor.

_____ acknowledges that the banners provided for in item (5) above may be re-used in connection with possible future tournaments, and shall be stores by _____ until such time as mutually agreed to in writing.

16. **Signage/Logos.**

17. **Additional Signage/Logos.**

18. **NCAA Floor Markings.**

19. **Arena Marks.**

20. **In-Arena Advertising.** *(Facility Operator)* shall advertise the *(Conference)* Tournament throughout the term of this Agreement on Arena inside and outside message boards, the Jumbotron and other marketing mediums within *(Facility Operator's)* control, including but not limited to, event schedules, public address announcements, media ads, *(Three Teams that Play in Facility)* and other commercial means in a manner and in such frequency as is mutually agreed upon in writing and in a manner to highly promote the Tournament. With regard to the aforementioned three teams, *(Facility Operator)* will use its best efforts and assist the *(Conference)* in

Exhibit 9.5
(continued)

so obtaining, but *(Facility Operator)* **may not be able to do so** since it does not own or manage these three teams. The *(Conference)* may, at its own option and expense, develop high quality supplemental graphics or in-arena television produced features for use by *(Facility Operator)* in the Arena if such are approved by *(Facility Operator)*, to advertise the *(Conference)* Tournament throughout the term of this Agreement without charge to the *(Facility Operator)* or such advertising and in a manner and in such frequency as mutually agreed upon in writing and in a manner to promote the Tournament.

21. **Tournament Promotions.** *(Conference)* and *(Facility Operator)* shall develop a mutually agreed upon schedule of marketing promotions to be conducted during pre-game, half-time, and between game segments of Tournament games. These costs, if any, of these promotions above the amounts paid for by sponsorships, shall be a Tournament expense and shall be mutually agreed upon in writing in advance. The promotions shall include those conducted on behalf of Tournament and the *(Conference)* broadcast network sponsors. The *(Conference)* broadcast network Tournament promotions will be scheduled and supervised by representatives of the *(Marketing Company)* marketing firm. A list of the *(Marketing Company)* people and their addresses, telephone and fax numbers is attached as **Exhibit D.**

22. **Tournament Programs and Other Merchandise.**

23. **Official Ball.**

24. **Awards.**

25. **Tournament Staffing.**

26. **Medical Services.** *(Facility Operator)* shall arrange for a certified EMT unit to be on-site with an ambulance during all Tournament games. This is a Tournament expense. *(Facility Operator)* shall identify a local hospital that shall handle all emergencies involving the *(Conference)* Tournament and provide the *(Conference)* with its name, address, and telephone number 30 days prior to the Tournament.

27. **Security/Radio Units.**

28. **Tip-Off banquet and Men's Championship Pre-Game Reception.**

29. *(Conference)* **Administrators/VIP Reception.**

30. **Hotels.**

31. **Hotel Rooms.**

32. **Marketing Services.**

33. **NCAA Championships.**

34. *(Conference)* **and Member Institutions' Names**

35. **Confidential Information.**

36. *(Facility Operator)* **Insurance.** *(Facility Operator)* agrees to obtain and maintain in effect policies of insurance with carriers licensed to do business in the State of _____ which shall include at least general liability,

Exhibit 9.5
(continued)

workers' compensation, property damage and products liability insurance. The general liability, products liability and property damage coverages shall contain coverage amounts of no less than $1,000,000 per occurrence with at least $2,000,000 annual aggregate limit. *(Facility Operator)* shall provide *(Conference)* with these Certificates of Insurance confirming the existence of these insurance policies and naming the *(Conference)* and its member institutions as additional insureds on the general liability policy, but solely with respect to the operations of *(Facility)*. This Certificate of Insurance shall be provided to the *(Conference)* at least 60 days prior to the start of the Tournament.

37. ***(Conference)* Insurance.** *(Conference)* agrees to obtain and maintain in effect policies of insurance with carriers licensed to do business in the state of _____ which shall include at least general liability, property damage and workers' compensation coverage. The general liability policy shall contain a coverage amount of no less than $1,000,000 per occurrence and shall, in addition, provide by endorsement or otherwise coverage with respect to athletic participants in the Tournament. The *(Conference)* agrees to provide *(Facility Operator)* with a Certificate of Insurance confirming the existence of the foregoing insurance and naming *(facility)*. County of _____ and the _____ County _____ Authority, and their respective related and affiliated entities, as additional insureds on the general liability policy, and shall provide this to *(Facility Operator)* at least 60 days prior to the start of the Tournament.

38. **Copyright and Trademark Notices and Registrations.** *(Facility Operator)* agrees that the vendor(s) selected to sell *(Conference)* Tournament licensed products shall be required to agree in writing that in any instance where the *(Conference)* and/or member institutions' marks or logos are used, in conjunction with or related to the Tournament, the following general notice shall be prominently attached (i.e. on the product, on a label, on the packaging material or on a separate slip of paper attached to the product): "This is an officially licensed product of the *(Conference)*. The insignias and names depicted on this product are marks which are the exclusive property of the *(Conference)* and/or its member institutions and shall not be reproduced or used in any manner without the *(Conference)* prior written consent." *(Facility Operator)* shall have any licensee agree in writing that it acknowledges and agrees that it shall not have nor acquire any right, title or interest in or to the name, marks or logos of the *(Conference)* and/or its member institutions by virtue of this Agreement or any other agreement.

39. ***(Facility Operator)* Indemnification.** The *(Conference)* shall at all times defend (if *(Facility Operator)* so requests in writing), indemnify and hold harmless *(Facility Operator)*, its affiliates, employees, agents and licensees, from and against any and all claims, actions, liabilities, losses, damages, costs and expenses including, without limitation, reasonable attorney's fees and disbursements, arising out of or relating to: (1) any breach or alleged breach of any representation, warranty, covenant or agreement of the *(Conference)*

Exhibit 9.5
(continued)

or (2) any injury sustained by any person or damage to property as a result of any claimed negligent, grossly negligent or reckless act or omission or intentional wrongdoing of the *(Conference)*, its agents or employees and its member institutions and their respective agents or employees. This paragraph shall survive the termination of this Agreement and shall be effective even after this Agreement ends for any reason, voluntary or involuntary.

40. ***(Conference)* indemnification.** *(Facility Operator)* shall at all times defend (if the *(Conference)* so requests in writing), indemnify, and hold harmless the *(Conference)*, its employees, agents, independent contractors and member institutions, from and against any and all claims, actions, liabilities, losses, damages, costs and expenses including, without limitation, reasonable attorney's fees and disbursements, arising out of or relating to: (1) any breach or alleged breach of any representation, warranty, covenant or agreement of *(Facility Operator)* or (2) any injury sustained by any person or to property as a result of any claimed negligent, grossly negligent or reckless act or omission or intentional wrongdoing of *(Facility Operator)* its agents or employees. This Paragraph shall survive the termination of this Agreement and shall be effective even after this Agreement ends for any reason, voluntary or involuntary. With respect to the indemnification of this and the immediately preceding paragraph and upon the written request of any indemnitee to be requested as soon as practicable after learning of a claim demand or action, the indemnitor will assume the defense of any claim, demand or action against such indemnitee and will, upon request by the indemnitee, allow the indemnitee (to the extent permitted by the indemnitor's insurer in the case of insured claims) to participate in the defense thereof, such participation to be subject to the control of the indemnitor and at the expense of the indemnitee. Settlement by the indemnitee without the indemnitor's prior written consent shall release the indemnitor from the indemnity as to the claim, demand or action so settled. All provisions of this Paragraph shall apply to any claim of any nature that may be made by any person or entity against *(Facility Operator)* related to *(Facility)*, the parking lots or areas and their adjacent walkways **under *(Facility Operator's)* control or supervision** and used by persons attending the Tournament and any related events. All provisions of this Paragraph shall also apply to any claim of any nature that may be made by any person or entity against any person or entity that acts as a vendor, concessionaire or otherwise provides any goods, services, equipment or anything else to the Arena related to the Tournament and any related events.

41. **Defense/Settlement of Claim.**

42. **Status of** _____

43. **Waiver.**

44. ***(Conference)* Warranty / *(Facility Operator)* Warranty.**

45. **Non-Assignability.** This Agreement is not assignable without the written mutual agreement of the parties, except that _____ may

Exhibit 9.5
(continued)

assign this Agreement, or any part of this Agreement, to an affiliate or any entity that acquires all or the majority of the assets.

46. **Renewal.**

47. **Arbitration.** Any controversy or claim arising out of or relating to this Agreement or the breach thereof, shall be submitted to a single arbitrator, to be privately mutually agreed upon by the parties prior to the private arbitration in _____ but shall be conducted in accordance with the regular Commercial Arbitration Rules of the American Arbitration Association as if the arbitration were to be held under the auspices of the American Arbitration Association. A Final Judgement upon the Award rendered by the arbitrator, which may include, without limitation, interest, filing fees, costs and expenses, but not attorney's fees, may be entered in any court having jurisdiction over the party found responsible. Each party is responsible for its own attorney's fees. The parties consent to the jurisdiction of the State of _____ and the state and federal courts located in _____ for the purpose of any action of any type arising out of or relating to this arbitration or Agreement or any terms of this Agreement for any issue that may be outside the scope of arbitration, including but not limited to the vacation, modification or confirmation of the arbitrators Award. The parties agree that the law of the State of _____ shall govern any action that is filed in court arising out of or relating to this arbitration proceeding or Agreement.

48. **Entire Agreement.** This Agreement constitutes the full and complete understanding of the parties related to the Tournament and related events covered by this Agreement. This Agreement may not be modified except by a single writing signed by both parties.

49. **Signing Authority.**

50. **Force Majure.** If either party is unable to perform due to national, regional or local disaster or emergency, labor dispute, fire, accident or other event beyond such party's reasonable control, then such party that is unable to perform as a consequence thereof shall not be deemed in breach of this Agreement.

51. **Compliance with Rules.**

52. **Compliance with Laws.**

53. **Control of Facility.**

54. **Defacement of Property.**

55. **Evacuation of the Arena.**

56. **Interruption or Termination of Event.** *(Facility Operator)* and the *(Conference)* jointly retain the right to cause an event not to take place or the interruption of any event in the interest of public safety and when *(Facility Operator)* and the *(Conference)* agree such act is necessary.

57. **Rules and Regulations.**

58. **Non-Discrimination.**

Exhibit 9.5
(continued)

IN WITNESS WHEREOF, the parties have executed this Agreement as of the date set forth on the first page of this Agreement.

BY:_____

      (*Conference*)
      TITLE: PRESIDENT

BY:_____

      (*Facility Operator*)
      TITLE:

Date:_____

as the Team Identified with Anaheim," "The Angels Who Vastly Prefer Los Angeles to Anaheim," or "The Angels of Bush League Anaheim." However, the trial and appeals court disagreed, stating that the change to the current name was made in good faith for marketing purposes; the other possible names would not have been. In *City of Anaheim v. Superior Court*, 2005 WL 1523338 (Cal. App.4 Dist. June 27, 2005), the appeals court denied the city of Anaheim's request for an extraordinary writ granting the preliminary injunction.

In February 2006, a jury found in favor of the team, determining that the new name complied with the lease agreement. The city of Los Angeles supported Anaheim's position and filed an amicus curiae brief prior to the trial. After the verdict, the Los Angeles Dodgers responded to the Angels' new Los Angeles–based marketing schemes with some of their own, including the slogans "LA Baseball" and "Los Angeles Dodgers of Los Angeles."

2. In *Metropolitan Sports Facilities Commission v. Minnesota Twins Partnership*, 2002 Minn. LEXIS 73 (Minn. Feb. 4, 2002), Major League Baseball in 2001 planned to buy and then eliminate the Minnesota Twins (as well as the Montreal Expos) before the 2002 season began. In response, the Metropolitan Sports Facilities Commission (owners and operators of the Hubert H. Humphrey Metrodome) alleged a breach of contract claim against the Minnesota Twins and requested a temporary injunction to keep the Twins at the Metrodome. In addition, the group also sued Major League Baseball for interference with contractual relations and prospective advantage. The court ordered the Twins to play their entire 2002 major league home baseball schedule in the Hubert H. Humphrey Metrodome and ordered Major League Baseball not to interfere "in any way" with the Twins doing so. The court stated, "based on the irreparable harm that will result if the commission does not receive the benefit of its bargain—which will occur if the Twins breach their promise to play their 2002 home games at the Metrodome—as well as the interests in maintaining the status quo pending resolution on the merits, the possibility of success on the merits, the public policy concerns, and the minimal administrative burdens on the district court, we hold that appellants failed to show that the district court abused its discretion in issuing the temporary injunction."

3. In December 2000, the city of Pontiac, Michigan, filed a breach of contract suit against the Detroit Lions, charging that although the Lions were planning on playing in newly built

Ford Field starting in 2002, the team was under contract to play at the Silverdome until their lease expired in 2006. Silverdome officials also claimed that the move would cause city residents and businesses significant economic harm. The city claimed it would lose between $50 million and $112 million in lost parking and concession revenue over the four years the Lions would have played at the Silverdome. The two sides reached an agreement in November 2001, one week before the matter was to go to trial. The Lions agreed to pay the city of Pontiac $26.25 million in damages to settle the breach of contract claim.

Chapter 10

ANTITRUST LAW

10.1. Overview of Antitrust Law

    10.1.1. Sherman Act, Section 1: Restraint of Trade

    10.1.2. Sherman Act, Section 2: Monopolization

    10.1.3. Clayton Act

        10.1.3.1. Treble Damages

        10.1.3.2. Statutory Labor Exemption

10.2. Application of Antitrust Law to Professional Sports

    10.2.1. Player Restraints and Antitrust Theory

        10.2.1.1. Football

        10.2.1.2. Hockey

        10.2.1.3. Basketball

    10.2.2. Ownership Restraints and Antitrust Theory

        10.2.2.1. Existing Owners v. Existing Owners: *Raiders v. NFL*

        10.2.2.2. *Raiders v. NFL* Revisited

        10.2.2.3. Prospective Owners versus Existing Owners

            10.2.2.3.1. *Piazza v. MLB*

            10.2.2.3.2. *Morsani v. MLB*

            10.2.2.3.3. *MLB v. Crist*

    10.2.3. Interleague Antitrust Challenges

        10.2.3.1. *USFL v. NFL*

        10.2.3.2. *NASL v. NFL*

    10.2.4. Antitrust Litigation in Professional Tennis and Golf

        10.2.4.1. Age Restrictions

        10.2.4.2. Equipment Rules

        10.2.4.3. Blacklisting: *Blalock v. LPGA*

        10.2.4.4. Hosting Tournaments and Conflicts of Interest

10.3. Defenses to Antitrust Challenges

    10.3.1. The Baseball Exemption

        10.3.1.1. History of the Reserve System

        10.3.1.2. Creation of the Baseball Exemption: *Federal Baseball*

        10.3.1.3. Baseball Exemption Reaffirmed: *Toolson*

        10.3.1.4. Baseball Anomaly Upheld: *Flood*

        10.3.1.5. The Curt Flood Act

    10.3.2. The Nonstatutory Labor Exemption

10.3.3. Early Uses of the Nonstatutory Labor Exemption: *Philadelphia, Mackey*, and *McCourt*

10.3.4. Exemption after Expiration of Collective Bargaining Agreement: *Bridgeman* and *Powell*

10.3.5. Exemption after Decertification: *McNeil*

10.3.6. Nonstatutory Labor Exemption after *White: Brown*

10.3.7. The Nonstatutory Labor Exemption in *Clarett*

10.3.8. Single-Entity Defense by the Big Four

10.3.9. Single-Entity Leagues: *Fraser v. MLS*

10.4. Antitrust Law and International Soccer: *Bosman*

10.5. Antitrust Law and the National Collegiate Athletic Association (NCAA)

10.5.1. Decisions before *Board of Regents* (1984)

10.5.2. The NCAA's Reduced Power over Television: *Board of Regents*

10.5.3. Coaches Salaries: *Law v. NCAA*

10.5.4. Tournaments: *MIBA v. NCAA*

10.5.5. The Bowl Championship Series

10.5.6. Other Decisions after *Board of Regents*

INTRODUCTION

Since the 1970s, antitrust litigation has played an important role in influencing the business of the major professional sports leagues in North America. For years, professional sports leagues in the United States and Canada believed that they were protected from antitrust challenges under the broad antitrust immunity afforded professional baseball. However, players and their unions have challenged restrictive player rules since the late 1960s—in particular, the draft, the reserve system, the commissioner's powers, and free agent compensation systems. In addition, new competing leagues have challenged established leagues' monopoly power, and owners have challenged league rules restricting expansion and relocation of franchises. To challenge restrictive league policies, players, owners, and competing leagues have relied on antitrust theory.

Antitrust litigation has also played an important role at the intercollegiate level. Member universities, coaches, athletes, and shoe companies have all brought suit against the National Collegiate Athletic Association (NCAA) in order to recover damages resulting from the NCAA's perceived monopoly power. With varying degrees of success, these plaintiffs have used antitrust theory against the NCAA for its restrictions regarding issues such as broadcasting, coach's earnings, athlete eligibility, and commercialism.

This chapter will briefly discuss the history of antitrust law in the United States, and then its history in the sports industry. Finally, it will chronicle the most important sports antitrust cases and discuss their relevance to the industry. Understanding antitrust law is crucial before persons in the sports industry can ascertain the rationale behind many rules and structures of organizations such as the NCAA, Major League Baseball (MLB), and Major League Soccer (MLS).

10.1. OVERVIEW OF ANTITRUST LAW

Beginning in the late 1880s, the federal government, in conjunction with the states, developed legislation to promote competition and prevent monopolies that might lead to the suppression of competition. A monopoly is defined as exclusive control by one group of the means of producing or selling a product. To monopolize is to dominate by excluding others. In 1890, the Sherman Act was passed by Congress to put an end to unfair monopolization and to protect U.S. consumers by promoting free and open market competition. Since 1890, each state has also passed legislation that has mirrored the Sherman Act. With regard to the sports industry, it is usually the Sherman Act that is applicable, not the state antitrust acts, due to the interstate travel by teams and television and radio broadcasting across state lines. However, if a sport league operates solely within a particular state's borders, then the state antitrust laws will be applicable.

The antitrust provisions most relevant to professional sports are Sections 1 and 2 of the Sherman Act and Section 3 of the Clayton Act:

10.1.1. Sherman Act, Section 1: Restraint of Trade

Section 1: This section proscribes contracts or agreements in restraint of trade:

Every contract, combination in the form of trust or otherwise, or conspiracy, in restraint of trade or commerce among the several States, or with foreign nations, is declared to be illegal. Every person who shall make any contract or engage in any combination or conspiracy hereby declared to be illegal shall be deemed guilty of a felony, and, on conviction thereof, shall be punished by fine not exceeding $10,000,000 if a corporation, or if any other person, $350,000, or by imprisonment not exceeding three years or by both said punishments, in the discretion of the court.

A Section 1 violation requires proof of three elements:

1. The existence of an agreement among two or more distinct persons or entities
2. The activity unreasonably restrains trade
3. The activity affects interstate commerce.

To prove that an agreement is a restraint of trade, the plaintiff must show that the agreement is between two separate entities, rather than between different units in a single entity. To prove this, the plaintiff must show that there was a *combination* between parties, that the two parties acted in *concert*, and that they engaged in a *conspiracy*. The plaintiff must also demonstrate that the challenged agreement *unreasonably restrains trade*; that is, that the challenged conduct's anticompetitive results outweigh the conduct's procompetitive results. Finally, the plaintiff must prove that *interstate commerce* has been affected. This last element is especially important to professional sport leagues, because judicial decisions concerning this issue early in the 20th century concluded that interstate commerce did not exist in relation to professional sports. This issue will be explored in more detail later in the chapter.

Proof that the challenged agreement constitutes an unreasonable restraint on trade depends upon the nature of the challenged conduct. Therefore, two methods of analysis may apply: the *per se rule* and the *rule of reason*. Practices that are deemed illegal per se are those that fall within a division of conduct that is inherently anticompetitive, like price-fixing, horizontal agreements, and group boycotts. If the conduct is found to be illegal per se, the court will not inquire into the business purpose or the actual effect of the offending practice. For example, one of the Sherman Act's aims is to promote price competition. Therefore, agreements that fix, control, raise, lower, maintain, or stabilize the prices charged for products or services have long been viewed to be so destructive to competition that they are automatically considered in violation of the act, without the need to prove the harm. Therefore, horizontal market agreements among competitors that restrict their competition at the same level of the market have traditionally been viewed as a per se violation of the Sherman Act. In addition, any agreement between two separate entities that allocates territories or divides customers is considered a violation. The Supreme Court stated in *Northern Pacific v. United States*, 356 U.S. 1 (1958):

> There are certain agreements or practices which because of their pernicious effect on competition and lack of any redeeming virtue are conclusively presumed to be unreasonable and therefore illegal without elaborate inquiry as to the precise harm they have caused or the business excuse for their use.

In cases where the per se analysis is used, the defense does not have an opportunity to defend the offending agreement; the defense's emphasis is on requesting that the rule of reason analysis be applied instead.

The rule of reason analysis applies to conduct that is not manifestly anticompetitive. The relevant inquiry is whether the challenged conduct unreasonably restrains competition. The principal purpose of the rule of reason standard is to determine whether the challenged conduct has procompetitive results or anticompetitive results. To successfully prove an antitrust violation using the rule of reason standard, the plaintiff must prove three things:

1. There is an agreement between two separate entities.
2. The agreement adversely affects competition in a relevant market.
3. The anticompetitive effects of the agreement outweigh the procompetitive effects.

The rule of reason doctrine allows the defendant to legitimize or argue its reasons for the agreement. To be considered lawful, the action taken must be found to be no more restrictive than necessary to achieve a legitimate business purpose. Therefore, a defendant using this standard will attempt to prove that there is a legitimate business reason for the restraint, and that the restraint in question is in its least restrictive form. The defense will argue that without such restrictions, the business will be adversely affected and there will be a negative impact on the welfare of the consumer.

In *Smith v. Pro Football Inc.*, 593 F.2d 1173 (D.C. Cir. 1978), the court was forced to determine whether the National Football League (NFL) draft was a per se violation of the antitrust laws. Smith argued that the draft was comparable to a group boycott, which was considered a per se violation of the Sherman Act. A group boycott is a concerted refusal to do business with horizontal competitors. Smith argued that the draft did not allow football players to do business (i.e., sign player contracts) with horizontal competitors (teams other than the one that drafted the player). The court found that the draft was not a group boycott because the NFL clubs were not competitors in an economic sense, and the draft did have *some* procompetitive effects. However, under the rule of reason standard, the court found that the draft was anticompetitive:

> The draft is anti-competitive in its effect on the market for players' services, because it virtually eliminates economic competition among buyers for the service of sellers. The draft is allegedly "pro-competitive" in its effect on the playing field; but the NFL teams are not economic competitors on the playing field, and the draft, while it may heighten athletic competition and thus improve the entertainment product offered to the public, does not increase competition in the economic sense of encouraging others to enter the market and to offer the product at a lower cost.... The draft's "anti-competitive evils," in other words, cannot be balanced against its "pro-competitive virtues" and the draft be upheld if the latter outweigh the former. In strict economic terms, the draft's demonstrated pro-competitive effects are nil.

NOTE

1. Smith was a defensive back selected in the first round, 12th overall, by the Washington Redskins in the 1968 NFL draft. Smith played one season for the Redskins before suffering a career-ending neck injury in the final game of the 1968 season. When Smith was drafted in 1968, there were 26 teams drafting for a total of 17 rounds. At the time the draft was initiated through the NFL's "no-tampering" rule, which prohibited teams from negotiating with players prior to the draft and with any player whom had been drafted by another team. The rule was unilaterally implemented by the NFL—that is, there was no collective bargaining agreement. In 1981, on remand to the district court, Smith's damages were calculated at $4,000 and trebled to a $12,000 award. However, by the conclusion of the suit, the NFL draft was now firmly within the collective bargaining agreement and therefore subject to the nonstatutory labor exemption (see section 10.3.2, "The Nonstatutory Labor Exemption").

10.1.2. Sherman Act, Section 2: Monopolization

Whereas Section 1 of the Sherman Act is aimed at multiple parties acting in concert, Section 2 prohibits *unilateral* monopolization and attempted monopolization.

> Section 2: This section proscribes monopolization or attempt to monopolize. Every person who shall monopolize, or attempt to monopolize, or combine or conspire with any other person or persons, to monopolize any part of the trade or commerce among the several states, or with foreign nations, shall be deemed guilty of a felony, and, on conviction thereof, shall be punished by fine not exceeding $10,000,000 if a corporation, or if any other person, $350,000, or by imprisonment not exceeding three years, or by both said punishments, in the discretion of the court.

To prove that a monopoly exists, two elements must be present: the possession of monopoly market power and the use of unacceptable means to acquire, entrench, or maintain that market power. It is important to note that monopoly market power is different from market share. A product may be superior to its competition and, for good reason, would hold a larger market share. As a hypothetical example, imagine that a product holds 80% of a relevant market share. A competitor might then challenge the way in which that product gained or maintained that market share. Assume that Product A holds 80% of the market share in New England, and Product B holds 20%. Product B may challenge Product A by claiming that Product A attempted to keep Product B from gaining increased market share through the use of predatory or exclusionary tactics (see notes 1 and 2). In its defense, Product A will claim a larger relevant market (i.e., the relevant market is the entire United States, not just New England), and claim natural monopoly (better product). Product A will also attempt to show that it does not have the power to control prices or exclude competition.

The objective of antitrust legislation, as it pertains to monopolization, is to ensure that companies which hold a natural monopoly in a given market do not actively discourage the rise of similar products in that market. For example, in *AFL v. NFL*, 323 F.2d 124 (4th Cir. 1963), the newly formed American Football League (AFL) argued that the established National Football League possessed monopoly status in the area of professional football (the product) throughout the 17 cities in which the NFL currently had teams (the relevant market), and attempted to use its monopoly power to keep the AFL from maintaining stability or success in those regions (see note 4). The appeals court found that the relevant market was not restricted to 17 cities but, rather, was nationwide and encompassed over 30 viable sites for professional football. The court ruled against the AFL on the monopolization charge because the plaintiff was not able to show that the NFL was exercising monopoly power in the relevant market.

NOTES

1. It is important to reiterate that the example of Product A and Product B and the "80%" figure is merely a hypothetical example. In many cases, a much smaller market share would be considered anticompetitive by federal authorities. For example, the Federal Trade Commission considers any market with a Herfindahl-Hirschman Index (HHI) of more than 1,800 to "have adverse competitive consequences [that] ordinarily require no further analysis." HHI is calculated by summing the squares of the top four firms. In this hypothetical market, the HHI is $80^2 + 20^2 = 6,800$, well above the HHI threshold for a monopoly. Mathematically, the top firm should always have less than 42.43% of market share in an *ordinary* relevant market—usually much less. For more information, consult the Federal Trade Commission's Web site, and specifically its *1992 Horizontal Merger Guidelines* (revised in 1997), at http://www.ftc.gov/bc/docs/horizmer.htm

2. Examples of predatory or exclusionary tactics in a professional sport context are (1) an established league expands into the territory of a new rival league, thus pitting the established league team against the new team with respect to competing for the support of local fans, media, and marketing; (2) an established league increases its roster size when a rival league forms.

3. In *Tanaka v. University of Southern California*, 252 F.3d 1059 (9th Cir. 2001), the court rejected a student-athlete's Section 1 claim based on the failure to identify a proper relevant antitrust market. The college soccer player had brought suit against her former university after the university allegedly retaliated against her for transferring to a rival school within the same athletic conference. The former school "retaliated" by invoking a never-before-invoked conference rule that would require the student to relinquish a year of financial aid and athletic eligibility at the new institution. Though the student-athlete had been recruited by schools across the country (a national market), the schools involved in the complaint were both in the Los Angeles area. Hence, according to the court, the plaintiff "failed to allege that the transfer rule has had significant anticompetitive effects within a relevant market."

4. The American Football League was created in 1960 by Lamar Hunt, who had attempted to obtain an NFL team in Dallas, and included teams in Houston (Oilers), Denver (Broncos), Oakland (Raiders), Dallas (Texans), Los Angeles (Chargers), Buffalo (Bills), Boston (Patriots), and New York (Titans). By 1968, the Miami (Dolphins) and Cincinnati (Bengals) had joined the new league. The AFL was able to secure a television contract with

ABC, and pooled its television revenues to ensure equal shares to all teams. The NFL would later initiate a similar policy.

10.1.3. Clayton Act

10.1.3.1. Treble Damages

The Clayton Act (1914) states that when a breach of the Sherman Act has been proven, the monetary damages awarded are to be trebled (tripled). The Clayton Act states:

> [A]ny person who shall be injured in his business or property by reason of anything forbidden in the antitrust laws may sue therefore in any district court in the United States in the district in which the defendant resides or is found or has an agent, without respect to the amount in controversy, and shall recover threefold the damages by him sustained, and the cost of suit, including a reasonable attorney's fee.

Therefore, if a company is found to have violated the antitrust laws, the damages stipulated by the court are trebled. This can result in very large damage awards, especially in the sports industry. For example, when Al Davis won his antitrust suit against the NFL in *Los Angeles Memorial Coliseum Commission v. NFL*, 726 F.2d 1381 (9th Cir. 1984), the trebled damages amounted to more than $30 million. The NFL settled with Davis by paying $18 million and allowing the Raiders to move from Oakland to Los Angeles. More recently, the successful antitrust suit against the National Collegiate Athletic Association by coaches whose maximum earnings had been limited by NCAA rules, *Law v. NCAA*, 134 F.3d 1010 (10th Cir. 1998), resulted in a $54.5 million damages settlement. With regard to the *Law* decision, each Division I institution was forced to pay a prorated share of the damages award. The threat of trebled damages, and the fact that winning an antitrust case is weighted in favor of the plaintiff, acts as a deterrent to companies, or leagues, from violating the antitrust laws.

10.1.3.2. Statutory Labor Exemption

Congress also passed the Clayton Act to offer protection to labor unions whose legitimacy was being challenged by employers. Between 1890 and 1914, with the support of the courts, employers had successfully challenged a union's right to organize collectively as a violation of the antitrust laws, specifically that unions acted in concert, combination, and conspiracy, and therefore restrained trade. Employers argued that workers were conspiring against both their employers and the consumers by organizing unions, and by participating in work stoppages.

Section 6 of the Clayton Act provides the first source of an exemption for labor-related activity:

> The labor of a human being is not a commodity or article of commerce. Nothing contained in the antitrust laws shall be construed to forbid the existence and operation of labor...organizations from lawfully carrying out the legitimate objects thereof; nor shall such organizations, or the members thereof, be held or construed to be illegal combinations or conspiracies in restraint of trade, under antitrust laws.

The statutory exemption declares that labor unions are not combinations or conspiracies in restraint of trade, and therefore insulates them from retribution for certain labor practices, such as striking or picketing. Professional sports leagues have not often raised the statutory exemption as a defense because the common interpretation of Section 6 of the Clayton Act is that the law was enacted solely for the benefit of labor unions.

10.2. APPLICATION OF ANTITRUST LAW TO PROFESSIONAL SPORTS

Antitrust law has impacted professional sports in a dramatic way, especially since the 1970s. The National Football League alone has been involved in over 70 antitrust cases in its history. Interpretation of the antitrust laws has defined the nature and structure of professional sports leagues, from player mobility restrictions to franchise relocation regulations. When antitrust challenges were first made against professional sports leagues, in the early 20th century, the courts determined that professional sports were not a business, and therefore could not be subject to antitrust legislation. That judicial viewpoint has changed dramatically since the 1970s, and with new interpretations of the antitrust laws in the professional sports context, the leagues therefore have been forced to change to comply with the law.

In this section, we will look at two types of antitrust cases: challenges against a league by its players, or owners, and challenges against an established league by a rival league. This examination is often organized sport-by-sport, rather than chronologically. However, the reader can refer to exhibit 10.1 in order to ascertain the context of certain litigation in relation to litigation in other sports.

10.2.1. Player Restraints and Antitrust Theory

In 1922, in the case of *Federal Baseball Club of Baltimore, Inc. v. National League of Professional Baseball Clubs*, 259 U.S. 200 (1922) (see note 1), the Supreme Court ruled that the professional sport of baseball was not a business involved in interstate commerce, and therefore was not in violation of the antitrust laws. After the *Federal Baseball* decision, other professional sports leagues may have assumed that they, too, were immune from antitrust challenges. However, beginning in the 1950s and peaking in the 1970s and 1980s, players began to use the antitrust laws again to challenge restrictive league rules that prevented players from earning market value, or even having the choice of where to play. After *Federal Baseball*, several decisions changed the way in which the judiciary examined antitrust cases involving professional sports. In *United States v. Shubert*, 348 U.S. 222 (1955), the Supreme Court found that the antitrust laws extended to both the production and the operation of theatrical productions across the United States. In that same year, in *United States v. International Boxing Club*, 348 U.S. 236 (1955), the Supreme Court determined that the defendant's promotion of boxing across state lines constituted trade or commerce among several states, as outlined in the Sherman Act. The Court ruled against the defendant and opened up the possibility that antitrust laws could indeed apply to the sports industry, contrary to the rulings involving professional baseball.

Why did the courts suddenly shift away from the belief that professional sports should not be considered a business? For one thing, professional sports leagues were run as a business: players signed employment contracts and were forced to abide by the labor laws of the time; owners of clubs entered into employment contracts with concession workers, security personnel, and medical personnel; the leagues entered into radio and television broadcasting contracts with national and local broadcasters; and, most important, owners ran their leagues with the goal of making a profit. In addition, it was very clear that professional sports leagues conducted business across state lines, with the significant addition of radio and then television broadcasts across state lines. For these reasons, the courts decided that professional sports leagues were in fact businesses, and therefore subject to the federal antitrust laws.

It is also important to understand why professional athletes were able to challenge the leagues' restrictive regulations using antitrust law. Each team in a league was viewed as a separate business entity, with separate ownership. Therefore, if two or more teams decided to enact and follow certain rules, such as a college draft, they would be acting in *concert, combination,* and *conspiracy*—the very things prohibited by Section 1 of the Sherman Act. It is also important to keep in mind that for an agreement between two business entities to be considered an antitrust violation, it must have *anticompetitive* consequences and be an *unreasonable* restraint on trade.

Players, represented by the "Players Associations" (see note 2), began to actively challenge particular rules that specifically limited a player's mobility (see sections 10.2.1.1, "Football"; 10.2.1.2, "Hockey"; and 10.2.1.3, "Basketball"). Players argued that rules or regulations which restricted their ability to put their skills on the open market for bidding, violated Section 1 of the Sherman Act, in that the players' ability to demand market value were restrained by league rules.

From their inception, professional sports leagues have used various devices to bind players to specific teams and limit player mobility. Some of these devices include the following:

1 The "reserve clause," found in player contracts until the mid-1970s, gave teams the unilateral right to renew a player's contract in perpetuity. Some standard player contracts still give teams the unilateral right to renew a player's contract, but *not* for a player's entire career.

2 The "draft," which allows only one professional team to draft an eligible player, allows the selected player to negotiate solely with the team that selected him.

3 The "compensation system," still in effect in several leagues, requires a team signing a free agent player to compensate the player's former team by giving up draft picks, players, and/or money.

4 The "right of first refusal" allows a player's prior team to match any competing offer and retain the player's services. This rule still exists in more moderate forms.

Each of these mechanisms allows (or allowed) the original team of a player to restrict or impede that player's ability to offer his services to the highest bidder. The reserve system, which was the most restrictive form because it had the potential to bind a player to a single team over that player's entire career, resulted in a loss of bargaining power on the part of the player, which in turn depressed his salary. More important, from a legal standpoint, the above-mentioned restrictions imposed upon professional athletes violated antitrust laws. A player's ability to earn a fair market salary was artificially stifled by league owners who illegally acted in concert, combination, and conspiracy by maintaining unreasonably restrictive league regulations (see exhibit 10.1).

Exhibit 10.1
Antitrust Litigation and Legislation Relevant to Big Four Sports

Year	Major League Baseball	National Football League	National Basketball Association	National Hockey League
1890	**Sherman Act:** Made illegal unfair monopolization and promoted free market competition			
1914	**Clayton Act:** Damages from Sherman Act violations are tripled; unions do not violate the Sherman Act			
1922	***Federal Baseball***: Baseball is exempt from antitrust laws			
1953	***Toolson***: Affirmed baseball's antitrust exemption			
1955		***Shubert*** and ***United States Boxing***: Antitrust laws apply to sports besides baseball		
1957		***Radovich***: Antitrust laws apply to sports besides baseball		
1961	**Sports Broadcasting Act:** Collective selling of TV rights of Big Four leagues and teams exempt from antitrust law			
1963		***AFL v. NFL***: NFL is not yet a nationwide monopoly		
1970–1972	***Flood***: Affirmed baseball's antitrust exemption		***Haywood***: Eligibility rule unreasonably restrictive	***Philadelphia***: Reserve clause an unreasonable restraint of trade
1974–1975		***Kapp***: Draft and standard player contract unreasonably restrain trade	***Robertson***: Draft and reserve system unreasonably restrain trade	
1976		***Mackey***: Free agency compensation system unreasonably restrictive		
1978–1979		***Smith***: Anticompetitive restraints of draft outweigh procompetitive benefits		***McCourt***: NHL arbitration system protected by labor exemption
1982		***NASL***: NFL cannot prevent owners from owning teams in other leagues		

Exhibit 10.1
(continued)

Year	Major League Baseball	National Football League	National Basketball Association	National Hockey League
1984		***Raiders I***: NFL cannot prohibit franchise relocations	***Wood***: College players cannot bring suit challenging restrictions agreed to in collective bargaining agreement	
1987		***USFL***: NFL did not use predatory tactics against USFL; USFL awarded $3	***Bridgeman***: Labor exemption remains in effect after expiration of collective bargaining agreement	
1989		***Powell***: Labor exemption remains in effect after bargaining to impasse		
1992–1993	***Piazza***: Baseball's antitrust exemption only applies to reserve clause, not franchise relocation	***McNeil***: Labor exemption no longer applicable if union decertifies		
1996–1998	**Curt Flood Act:** Antitrust exemption does not apply to matters directly affecting players	***Brown***: Labor exemption defense can apply even if challenged matter was not collectively bargained		
2003–2004	***Crist***: Baseball exemption applies broadly to business of baseball	***Clarett***: Draft eligibility rules were collectively bargained and therefore exempt		
2008–2010		***American Needle***: For licensing purposes, the NFL is not a single entity		***Dewey Ranch***: Leagues have the right to approve owners and locations of member teams

In their defense, leagues and owners have asserted that restrictive policies such as the college draft, salary cap, and restrictions on free agency are essential to maintaining a competitive league, and thus are *reasonable* restraints on trade. By "reasonable," they mean that the procompetitive effects of the rules outweigh the anticompetitive effects. For example, owners contend that the purpose of the college draft is to give struggling teams a chance to compete with the better teams in the league by giving them first choice from the pool of eligible players. Owners also maintain that league rules restricting the ability of players to move from team to team are necessary to build fan loyalty and to prohibit one team from signing all the quality players. Owners state that these rules are reasonable because the viability of the leagues depends on evenly balanced teams that are able to compete every time on the field, court, or ice. In addition, owners have maintained that such regulations allow teams to remain financially solvent, and that the abolition of these regulations would result in bankruptcy.

Players whose salaries had been kept artificially low due to the restrictive rules of the leagues challenged those restrictive rules using antitrust theory. They focused their attention on two types of common player restraints: (1) those restricting a player's ability to sign with another team and (2) those requiring compensation to be given to the former team by the team acquiring the player. It is the first, a restriction on freedom of movement, that has caused the greatest amount of litigation in this area. The following is a brief explanation of the antitrust challenges in professional football, hockey, and basketball that relate specifically to player restraints.

NOTES

1. The lawsuit was originally brought in 1915 in the Northern District of Illinois and argued in front of Judge Kennesaw Mountain Landis. Landis had been known to strictly apply antitrust scrutiny, but was also an avid baseball fan. During the trial, the Major League Baseball owners agreed to buy out many of the owners of Federal League teams. However, when the owners of the Baltimore and Chicago franchises received nothing, they brought the suit that eventually reached the Supreme Court. Landis officially became the first commissioner of Major League Baseball in 1920, after he oversaw the permanent banishment of eight players following the 1919 Black Sox scandal.

2. The MLBPA formed in 1953, the NBPA in 1954, the NFLPA in 1956, and the NHLPA in 1967. Although the unions attempted to fight player mobility restrictions via antitrust laws, their existence turned out to be a bar to such suits (see section 10.3.4, "Exemption after Expiration of Collective Bargaining Agreement: *Bridgeman* and *Powell*").

10.2.1.1. Football

The first case to challenge a sports league following the *International Boxing* decision was *Radovich v. NFL*, 231 F.2d 620 (9th Cir. 1956). In this case a former Detroit Lion challenged a league decision to blacklist him after he had played two seasons in the rival All American Football Conference, following his Lions career. The challenge was under Sections 1 and 2 of the Sherman Act. The district court and the appeals court determined that football was similar to baseball in its operation, and therefore should be granted the immunity from the antitrust laws that professional baseball enjoyed. The Supreme Court, however, reversed the lower court decisions and found that the business of football was clearly engaged in interstate commerce, and was therefore subject to antitrust laws. In addition, the Court noted "that were we considering the question of baseball for the first time upon a clean slate we would have no doubts that baseball should be subject to antitrust laws" (see *Radovich v. NFL*, 352 U.S. 445 (1957)). The significance of this case is that it clearly illustrated that the antitrust immunity afforded baseball should not apply to other professional sports leagues, a view that would be echoed in *Flood v. Kuhn* (see section 10.3.1.4, "Baseball Anomaly Upheld: *Flood*").

In *Kapp v. NFL*, 390 F.Supp. 73 (N.D. Cal. 1974), the plaintiff was able to prove that NFL player restrictions, including the college draft, the standard player contract "reserve clause," and the option clause were restraints of trade. Using the rule of reason analysis, the court found the challenged restrictions "so patently unreasonable" and that they went "far beyond any possible need." The court decided in favor of Kapp. As a result, the NFL modified its draft so as to appear to be in a less restrictive form.

In *Mackey v. NFL*, 543 F.2d 606 (8th Cir. 1976), the plaintiff challenged the "Rozelle Rule," whereby a team signing a player from another team was required to pay compensation in the form of draft picks, players, or money. The court found for the plaintiff, using the rule of reason analysis. Following the decision, the NFL Players Association negotiated a new collective bargaining agreement that eliminated the Rozelle Rule and in its place created the right of first refusal/compensation system (see note 2).

The college draft was challenged in *Smith v. Pro Football Inc.*, 593 F.2d 1173 (D.C. Cir. 1978). The district court applied the per se doctrine and ruled in favor of the plaintiff. The D.C. Court of Appeals also ruled in favor of the plaintiff, but rejected the per se rule, instead applying the rule of reason.

The right of first refusal/compensation system was challenged unsuccessfully in *Powell v. NFL*, and successfully in *McNeil v. NFL* and *Jackson v. NFL*, which are discussed in more detail in section 10.3.5, "Exemption after Decertification: *McNeil*."

NOTES

1. Former Ohio State running back Maurice Clarett challenged the NFL's eligibility rule in the fall of 2002. Clarett challenged the NFL's rule that a player must be three years removed from his high school graduation to be eligible for the NFL. Clarett was initially granted summary judgment on antitrust grounds (see *Clarett v. NFL*, 306 F.Supp.2d 379 (S.D.N.Y. 2004), but the suit was ultimately overturned citing the procompetitive effects of the NFL's eligibility requirements (see *Clarett v. NFL*, 369 F.3d 124 (2nd Cir. 2004). For more on this case, see section 10.3.7, "Nonstatutory Labor Exemption Today: *Clarett*."

2. The right of first refusal/compensation system still exists today with regard to restricted free agents (a player with more than three but less than four accrued seasons) and Franchise and Transition Players (see Articles XIX and XX of the NFL Collective Bargaining Agreement available at www.nflpa.org).

10.2.1.2. Hockey

In *Philadelphia World Hockey Club, Inc. v. Philadelphia Hockey Club, Inc.*, 351 F.Supp. 462 (E.D. Pa. 1972), the plaintiff was a competing league which argued that the "reserve system" used by the National Hockey League (NHL) clubs, which bound a player to a team in perpetuity, was a violation of Section 1 of the Sherman Act. The plaintiff wanted the per se doctrine applied, but the court refused, citing the "relative paucity of litigation on this type of reserve clause." Using the rule of reason, the court found that some type of reserve system was necessary:

> For maximum customer receptivity and profit it is in the best interest of any club that its opponents not generally be viewed by the public as totally incompetent and utterly

unable to compete effectively.... Thus, if it is not possible to keep the competitive challenge of all teams within some reasonable parameters, some type of intraleague reserve clause may be desirable and in fact necessary.

The case was settled out of court when several teams from the World Hockey Association were merged into the NHL.

The reserve system was again challenged in *McCourt v. California Sports Inc.*, 460 F.Supp. 904 (E.D. Mich. 1978). In this case, a National Hockey League player challenged the decision that he was to be compensated for his team's signing of a free agent. He challenged the decision using antitrust theory against the league's compensation system. He won a preliminary injunction because he was able to convince the court that he had a likelihood of success on the merits:

> Like the "Rozelle Rule," bylaw 9A applies to all players without regard to status or ability; it applies to the average player and to the superstar alike; it is unlimited in duration and acts as a perpetual restriction upon a player's ability to freely contract for his services. Bylaw 9A cannot be justified by any legitimate business purpose and is more restrictive than necessary to achieve the NHL's announced goal of maintaining competitive balance. It inhibits and deters teams from signing free agents, decreases a player's bargaining power in negotiations, denies players the right to sell their services in a free and open market, and it depresses salaries more than if competitive bidding were allowed.

The case was later decided on appeal, *Dale McCourt v. California Sports Inc.*, 600 F.2d 1193 (6th Cir. 1979), in favor of the NHL due to the nonstatutory labor exemption (discussed in detail later in this chapter).

The NHL has long had three main sources of players: the Canadian Hockey League (CHL), consisting of three professional and amateur leagues; European amateur and professional leagues; and U.S. high school and college players. In June 1998, the New Jersey Devils of the NHL drafted Mike Van Ryn from the University of Michigan and subsequently held exclusive rights to him for one year. Van Ryn chose to return to Michigan, extending the Devils' rights to him for one more year, through June 2000. However, in the summer of 1999, Van Ryn signed with the Sarnia Sting of the OHL, a league within the CHL. Having not signed Van Ryn by June 1, 2000, the Devils' rights to Van Ryn expired. Van Ryn, believing himself to be an unrestricted free agent, signed a three-year contract with the San Jose Sharks of the NHL. In a grievance proceeding, the Devils and the NHL unsuccessfully attempted to declare Van Ryn a "defected" player, a status that would have stripped him of his free agency.

As a result of this free agency loophole, the Ontario Hockey League (OHL), as part of the CHL, created a rule that a player over 20 years old, or an "overage" player cannot play in the OHL unless he was previously registered with either the CHL or USA Hockey. Meanwhile, the NCAA bars any player with either of those registrations. As a result of the two rules, the OHL would not be able to sign any NCAA player 20 years or older.

In March 2001, the NHLPA filed suit against the OHL, claiming the "Van Ryn" rule was an unreasonable restraint of trade, illegal under Section 1 of the Sherman Act. The district court ruled in favor the plaintiffs and granted a preliminary injunction against the rule. However, in *NHL Players Ass'n v. Plymouth Whalers Hockey Club*, 325 F.3d 712 (6th Cir. 2003), the court of appeals overturned the ruling, stating that there was no showing of anticompetitive effect in a relevant market.

NOTES

1. The World Hockey Association (WHA) was formed in 1971 and signed a number of NHL stars, including Bobby Hull, Gerry Cheevers, and J. C. Tremblay. The WHA operated for a number of seasons before merging several teams with the NHL. For more information on the WHA, WFL, and ABA, see Gary Davidson, *Breaking the Game Wide Open* (New York: Atheneum, 1974). For historical information about the ABA specifically, see Terry Pluto, *Loose Balls* (New York: Simon & Schuster, 1990).

2. For information about the history of the USFL (United States Football League), see Jim Byrne, *The 1 Dollar League: The Rise and Fall of the USFL* (New York: Prentice Hall, 1986).

10.2.1.3. Basketball

The first successful antitrust case against player restrictions in the National Basketball Association (NBA) was *Denver Rockets v. All-Pro Management*, 325 F.Supp. 1049 (C.D. Cal. 1971). Basketball player Spencer Haywood successfully challenged the NBA's age restrictions for entry into the league, which stated persons were ineligible to play in the NBA, under any circumstances, until four years after their original high school class had graduated. After one year in junior college and an additional year at the University of Detroit, Haywood signed a professional contract with a team in the NBA's rival American Basketball Association (ABA). After a highly successful first season, in which Haywood garnered ABA Rookie of the Year honors, Haywood and his team became embroiled in a contract dispute. Consequently, Haywood signed a contract with the NBA's Seattle Supersonics. NBA Commissioner, Walter Kennedy, rejected the contract, claiming that Haywood was not yet eligible to play under NBA Bylaws 2.05 and 6.03, and threatened sanctions if Haywood attempted to play.

Haywood was allowed to play under a preliminary injunction, while the case was being litigated. Haywood argued that the NBA's bylaws constituted a group boycott under Section 1 of the Sherman Act, against persons less than four years out of high school. The district court agreed and granted Haywood partial summary judgment. The court used the per se standard and denied the NBA an opportunity to argue any procompetitive effects for the rule. The Ninth Circuit granted the injunction permanently, effectively permitting players from college or high school enter the NBA draft whenever they chose (see note 1).

During the same period as the *Kapp* and *Philadelphia* decisions, present and former NBA players brought a class action suit against the National Basketball Association challenging the college draft, the reserve system, and compensation practices. In *Robertson v. NBA*, 389 F.Supp. 867 (S.D.N.Y. 1975), as in the previous two cases, the plaintiffs attempted to prove that the restrictive measures taken by the NBA were violations of antitrust law. The court agreed, and found the restrictions to be a per se violation of the Sherman Act:

> It is difficult for me to conceive of any theory or set of circumstances pursuant to which the college draft, blacklisting, boycotts, and refusals to deal could be saved from Sherman Act condemnation, even if defendants were able to prove at trial their highly dubious contention that these restraints were adopted at the behest of the Players Association.

The next antitrust challenge to the NBA occurred in 1984, after the NBA and the NBA Players Association had come to an agreement on a new collective bargaining agreement that included a salary cap. In *Wood v. NBA*, 602 F.Supp. 525

(S.D.N.Y. 1984), a rookie challenged the salary cap as an unreasonable restraint on trade. The court found against the plaintiff because of the nonstatutory labor exemption defense (see section 10.3.2, "The Nonstatutory Labor Exemption"). NBA players challenged the NBA's restrictive rules when the 1983 agreement expired in 1987, in *Bridgeman v. NBA*, 675 F.Supp. 960 (D.N.J. 1987), but were unsuccessful because the court found the labor exemption to remain in effect even when a collective bargaining agreement had expired.

NOTE _____

1. In July 2005, the NBA and NBPA reached a collective bargaining agreement that included restrictions on player eligibility. To be eligible for the NBA draft, a U.S. player must be at least 19 years old, and one NBA season must have passed since his high school graduation. An international player must simply be 19. See Article 10 of the NBA-NBPA Collective Bargaining Agreement available at www.nbpa.org (For more on the legality of the rule see section 10.3.2, "The Nonstatutory Labor Exemption").

10.2.2. Ownership Restraints and Antitrust Theory

Similar to player restraints, professional sports leagues have rules and regulations that govern the actions of the particular league's owners. What is different about the rules that govern owners, compared to the rules that restrict players, is that ownership standards are predetermined by the league (see note 1), whereas player restrictions are promoted by the ownership and carried out by the league. Leagues have attempted to regulate the actions of owners and potential owners so as to maintain financial stability for the league, and to improve or maintain the league's image. Each league has rules that prohibit owners from criticizing game officials meant to maintain the integrity of the officials. All professional sports leagues have rules that make it difficult for new franchises to be established in the same geographic area as an existing franchise. This rule is in place to allow the established team to maintain its fan base and not have it eroded by a new team a few miles away (see note 1). Owners accepted these rules because they understood that they were in place for the best interests of the game and, more important, because these rules did not financially hurt them.

One rule that has financially hurt the owners is franchise relocation restrictions. Beginning in the late 1960s, owners of professional sports teams began to lobby their local governments for public money to be used for new stadium construction. Several teams received new stadiums, including the Houston Astros, whose new stadium was the then state-of-the-art Astrodome. Owners have realized that increased profits could be obtained by getting a publicly financed stadium with luxury seating and increased capacity. If the local government refuses to publicly support arena/stadium construction, the owner can threaten to move to a city or region that is willing to support the franchise. However, league rules dictate that owners cannot relocate a franchise to another city or region unless other owners unanimously—or in other leagues nearly unanimously—consent to the relocation (see note 2). Each professional sports league has rules pertaining to this issue, and although they vary slightly, each league's policies have the same effect: franchise relocation is kept to an absolute minimum.

From a legal standpoint these restrictions clearly impede an owner's right to increase the profitability of his team by relocating to a city or region that is willing to publicly finance a stadium or arena. According to antitrust theory, to prove a

Section 1 violation, there must be interstate commerce, an unreasonable restraint of trade, and an agreement between at least two entities. Owners who were denied the right to relocate their franchise have argued that their ability to increase profits was restrained by league rules, and that the league owners acted in concert, combination, and conspiracy with each other. The leagues have argued that the rules are a reasonable restraint on trade because they had procompetitive effects. It is in the league's best interest to have a strong and loyal fan base, because such loyalty resulted in league stability and easier marketability.

Leagues were able to maintain a high level of control over the franchises in this area until one owner challenged the right of the league to restrain an owner's ability to relocate a franchise. For more on this, see section 10.2.2.1, "Existing Owners versus Existing Owners: *Raiders v. NFL*" and 10.2.2.2, "*Raiders v. NFL* Revisited."

As television revenues have become an increasingly important financial factor in professional sports, owners attempting to capitalize on this market have occasionally come in conflict with the league, other owners, or television companies. Teams want to be able to sell as many of their games to local networks for as much as possible, but the league may have an interest in limiting these sorts of deals. The leagues sell the collective rights to a network for the right to televise a certain portion of the league's games, typically focusing on the playoffs (see note 3). The network games are usually meant to be marquee matchups that often include games that the individual teams would have liked to sell as part of their cable packages. Chapter 14, "Broadcasting and Multimedia," outlines the relationship teams and leagues have developed with broadcasting companies, specifically Section 14.2.2, "Broadcast Rights of a Professional League."

Owners and leagues have also faced antitrust challenges regarding discipline. In *Molinas v. NBA*, 190 F.Supp. 241 (S.D.N.Y. 1961), a player who had been suspended indefinitely for gambling sued the NBA for entering into a conspiracy with its member teams in restraint of trade. The court of appeals found that Molinas was not able to prove a conspiracy and that the charges did not fall under the Sherman Act. In modern collective bargaining agreements, disciplinary procedures and regulations are often included. As a result, owners and the league are protected from antitrust lawsuits by the nonstatutory labor exemption (see Section 10.3.2, "The Nonstatutory Labor Exemption"). Players are subject to these regulations and can be punished by the league for on- and off-field problems, legal or otherwise, as well as behaviors and practices the league has deemed inappropriate such as gambling or alcohol or drug use. For more information concerning athletes and gambling, see Section 16.2, "Illegal Gambling."

NOTES

1. Following the 2002 season, the other 29 owners of Major League Baseball teams bought the Montreal Expos from Jeffrey Loria for $120 million. With the team clearly floundering in the Montreal market, MLB desired to move the team and voted 28–1 prior to the 2005 season to move the team to Washington, D.C., and rename the team the Nationals. The lone dissenting vote was cast by Baltimore Orioles owner Peter Angelos, who felt that the Nationals would be infringing on Orioles' territory. A deal was reached whereby the other owners would make up the difference between $365 million and a lesser offer if Angelos desired to sell the Orioles. In addition, the Orioles were given control of production and broadcasting of Nationals games on the Orioles Mid-Atlantic Sports Network.

2. Depending on the league, team owners might have varying levels of influence on the decisions of the league office. For example, MLB owners can prevent the league from

allowing the relocation of an American League team if at least 25% of AL owners and more than 50% of NL owners oppose the relocation. Furthermore, any MLB ownership group can prevent the league office from forcing its team to switch leagues. In the NFL, 75% of owners must approve relocation for a team to move.

3. In 2002, the NBA negotiated a six-year, $4.6 billion TV deal with ESPN/ABC and TNT that placed conference final games on cable for the first time ever. Likewise, starting in the 2007 postseason, TBS, a cable network, agreed to a seven-year deal worth $45 million annually to broadcast one of the two MLB League Championship Series. Following the 2004–2005 lockout, ESPN turned down a $60 million option to the NHL's TV rights, and the NHL instead reached a two-year deal worth $135 million with the fledgling Outdoor Life Network (OLN). The deal gave OLN 58 regular season games and the right to playoff games through game 2 of the Stanley Cup Finals.

10.2.2.1. *Existing Owners v. Existing Owners:* Raiders v. NFL

By the mid-1970s the National Football League could claim to have developed the most extensive fan base and achieved the highest level of stability of all the professional sports leagues, based on the fact that the NFL had not had a franchise relocation since the Chicago Cardinals moved to St. Louis in 1960. One reason for this was the fact that a unanimous vote by the NFL's Board of Governors was needed to allow such a move. This rule was put under scrutiny when owner Carroll Rosenbloom moved the Los Angeles Rams from the Los Angeles Memorial Coliseum in Los Angeles County, California, to Anaheim Stadium in Orange County, California. The Governors approved the move, and the Rams moved after the 1976 season. The Los Angeles Memorial Coliseum Commission, the body that administered the Coliseum, immediately began to seek a replacement for the Rams, either an expansion franchise or a current NFL team willing to relocate. Al Davis, owner of the Oakland Raiders, had reached an impasse with the Oakland Coliseum over a new lease, and decided to relocate the Raiders to Los Angeles and play out of the Memorial Coliseum in 1980. Rule 4.3 of the NFL Constitution stated that a unanimous vote was required to move a franchise into the home territory of another team. Since the Raiders would be within 75 miles of Orange County (Rams), unanimous consent was required by the owners. In March 1980, the NFL owners voted 22–0 against the proposed relocation.

The result was *Los Angeles Memorial Coliseum Commission v. NFL*, 726 F.2d 1381 (9th Cir.), *cert. denied*, 469 U.S. 990 (1984), commonly referred to as *Raiders*. The issue before the district court was whether the rule, which stated that unanimous approval of the relocation of a franchise was required by the ownership, was in violation of antitrust laws. The trial court found the antitrust laws had been violated and ruled against the NFL.

The Ninth Circuit upheld the district court's decision. Using the *rule of reason* standard, the court found that the restriction on franchise movement was anticompetitive because it perpetuated local monopolies. The court argued that the move to Los Angeles would promote competition rather than stifle it, stating the following:

> [The] NFL made no showing that the transfer of the Raiders to Los Angeles would have any harmful effect on the League. Los Angeles is a market large enough for the successful operation of two teams, there would be no scheduling difficulties, facilities at the L.A. Coliseum are more than adequate, and no loss of future television revenue was foreseen. Also, the NFL offered no evidence that its interest in maintaining

regional balance would be adversely affected by a move of a northern California team to southern California.

The court awarded damages of $4.6 million to the Coliseum, and $11.5 million to the Raiders, both of which were trebled. The NFL settled by paying out a total of $18 million and granting the franchise move.

The impact of this decision on professional sports is important to consider. While the ruling of the Ninth Circuit is not binding authority on all jurisdictions in the United States, the *Raiders* decision suggested that professional sports leagues do not have the authority to dictate to its members whether or not they can relocate their franchise. Movement of franchises in the NFL, NBA, and NHL since the *Raiders* decision illustrates that these leagues must have reasonable franchise relocation policies (see note 3). The right of leagues to control franchise movement gained some ground in *In re Dewey Ranch Hockey, LLC* 406 B.R. 30 (Bkrtcy.D.Ariz. 2009). In that case, the owner of the bankrupt Phoenix Coyotes attempted to sell the team to Ontario businessman Jim Balsillie without the NHL's permission. The court ruled that the sale could not proceed without being subject to the NHL's relocation restrictions and other requirements of ownership (see *In re Dewey Ranch Hockey, LLC* 414 B.R. 577 (Bkrtcy.D.Ariz. 2009).

It is also important to recall that Major League Baseball is protected under its antitrust exemption from challenges to league ownership issues. The Curt Flood Act of 1998, which will be discussed later in this chapter, altered the exemption only in that players are now allowed to sue using antitrust theory. Prior to the passage of the Curt Flood Act, prospective owners had tested whether MLB's antitrust exemption applied to franchise ownership (see note 1). But in light of the Curt Flood Act, owners, prospective owners, and competitor leagues are explicitly precluded from using antitrust theory against MLB.

10.2.2.2. Raiders v. NFL *Revisited*

In a more recent and separate case, Al Davis again brought suit against the NFL for alleged interference in his attempt to relocate the franchise. Davis claimed that he tried to move the Raiders from the Los Angeles Coliseum to a proposed new site in Hollywood Park in 1994. He accused the NFL of sabotaging the deal by pushing for a second team to play in the Los Angeles market, and asked the jury for $1.2 million in damages. The league countered that Davis was never serious about moving to Hollywood Park, but was merely using the site as leverage in order to get a better stadium deal in Oakland. In fact, Davis did accept a deal to move the Raiders back to Oakland in 1995. The deal included $63 million in loans, payments, and benefits. A federal jury voted 9–3 in favor of the NFL after a six-week trial in 2001.

It is important to point out that Davis's legal theories in the 2001 case were not overtly based on antitrust, but instead on the theories of breach of contract, "unjust enrichment," and fraud. Ironic in light of the original *Raiders* case, Davis's 2001 lawsuit stemmed from the NFL's alleged decision *not* to enforce his monopoly power over the Los Angeles market. Nevertheless, because the 2001 case centered on a league's ability to dictate franchise movement, it is notable in the context of sports antitrust cases.

In September 2003, the Los Angeles Superior Court ordered the case to be retried when it was revealed that two jurors possibly engaged in juror misconduct by stating their dislike for Davis and the Raiders to other jurors during the trial. However, in February 2003, the California Court of Appeals in Los Angeles reinstated the jury verdict by stating that the juror misconduct was not serious enough to overturn the verdict in *Oakland Raiders v. NFL*, 126 Cal.App.4th 1497, 25 Cal. Rptr.3d 141 (Cal. App. 2nd Dist. 2005). Affirmed in *Oakland Raiders v. National Football League (NFL)*, 161 P.3d 151 (Cal. 2007).

The court also upheld the dismissal of the Raiders' claim that they should not have to share revenues from personal seat licenses because Oakland and Alameda County received the revenues, not the Raiders. Two final claims dismissed by the court were the Raiders' objection to the Tampa Bay Buccaneers and Carolina Panthers wearing certain uniforms in California. The Raiders unsuccessfully claimed the Buccaneers' logo was too similar to the Raiders' and that the Panthers' alternate black and silver uniforms violated the Raiders' trademarks.

NOTES

1. For a history of the Raiders' lawsuits and their application today, see Brett Gibbs, "Antitrust and Sports League Franchise Relocation: Bringing Raiders I Into the Modern Era of Antitrust Law," 29 *Hastings Communications and Entertainment Law Journal* 217 (2007).

2. In *NBA v. SDC Basketball Club Inc.*, 815 F.2d 562 (9th Cir), *cert. denied*, 484 U.S. 960 (1987), the San Diego Clippers attempted to move to Los Angeles, but the NBA blocked the move. On summary judgment, the district court said the NBA would lose according to the precedent set forth in *Raiders*. The Ninth Circuit disagreed with the district court's ruling on summary judgment and stated that *Raiders* did not lay down a ban on any rule involving the issue of franchise relocation. Thus the case deserved a full trial, where its merits would be decided. The NBA subsequently altered its franchise relocation rules to include objective standards as outlined by the court in *Raiders*.

3. The following franchise relocations have occurred in Big Four sports since the *Raiders* decision. NHL: the Minnesota North Stars relocated to Dallas (Stars); the Quebec Nordiques to Colorado (Avalanche); the Hartford Whalers to North Carolina (Hurricanes); the Winnipeg Jets to Phoenix (Coyotes). NFL: Baltimore Colts to Indianapolis (Colts); St. Louis Cardinals to Phoenix (Cardinals); Los Angeles Raiders back to Oakland (Raiders); Los Angeles Rams to St. Louis (Rams); Cleveland Browns to Baltimore (Ravens); Houston Oilers to Tennessee (Titans). NBA: Kansas City Kings to Sacramento; San Diego Clippers to Los Angeles; Vancouver Grizzlies to Memphis; Charlotte Hornets to New Orleans; Seattle SuperSonics to Oklahoma City (Thunder). MLB: Montreal Expos to Washington, D.C. (Nationals).

4. Franchise applicants have also used the antitrust laws to challenge denied franchise applications. In *Levin v. NBA*, 385 F.Supp. 149 (S.D.N.Y. 1974), Levin, a prospective buyer of the Boston Celtics, was denied the franchise because of what some owners referred to as a "shady" background. Levin sued, using antitrust theory. The court found that the denial of Levin's application was not an antitrust violation because the rejection did not have an anticompetitive impact: Levin still had the opportunity to compete with the league and was not excluded from that. A similar case is *Mid-South Grizzlies v. NFL*, 720 F.2d 772 (3rd Cir. 1983). The appeals court found that the challenge was unsubstantiated because the plaintiff still had the capacity to compete against the NFL and was not being denied that right even though the team was denied entry into the league.

5. One of the first cases to deal with the issue of franchise relocation was *San Francisco Seals Ltd. v. National Hockey League*, 379 F.Supp. 966 (C.D. Cal. 1974), which concerned denial by the league of a proposed move for the NHL team from San Francisco to

Vancouver. In granting summary judgment for the NHL, the court found there was no restraint of trade or commerce in the relevant market.

10.2.2.3. Prospective Owners versus Existing Owners

Major League Baseball consists of 30 franchises, all individually owned and operated. Through collective bargaining, MLB, like the other three major professional sports, retains the rights to make decisions not affecting the terms and conditions of employment (see Chapter 11, "Labor Law," and section 10.3.2, "The Nonstatutory Labor Exemption"). However, the collective bargaining agreements of the NBA, NFL, and MLB do address expansion and the rights of the league and owners therein. Nevertheless, the leagues and the owners have faced litigation over whether they have the power to determine whether to approve a new franchise or to approve the sale of an existing franchise to a particular prospective owner.

10.2.2.3.1. Piazza v. MLB

In *Piazza v. MLB*, 831 F.Supp. 420 (E.D. Pa. 1993), a potential ownership group, attempting to bring baseball to the Tampa area, brought a Sherman Act Section 1 antitrust claim against MLB and its teams for prohibiting their purchase of the San Francisco Giants. The plaintiffs also alleged that the defendants had discriminated against them due to their Italian American heritage and had unfairly associated them with the Mafia. Despite offering $15 million more than any other ownership group, their offer was denied in favor of a group that would keep the team in San Francisco. The court rejected MLB's argument that its antitrust immunity applied in this case, favoring the plaintiff's arguments that the antitrust exemption was limited to the reserve clause. The Federal Appellate Court agreed with this decision by rejecting MLB's appeal. This led to an estimated $6 million cash settlement for the plaintiffs. These types of suits are less likely to occur again in MLB due to the Curt Flood Act of 1998.

10.2.2.3.2. Morsani v. MLB

In the early 1980s, Frank Morsani unsuccessfully attempted to buy the Minnesota Twins and relocate them to St. Petersburg, Florida. Morsani continued to try and purchase a team, expansion or otherwise, with the intentions of moving them to the Tampa Bay area. Furthermore, Morsani claimed that MLB told him on three separate occasions that he would be able to own a team in the Tampa Bay area. When MLB granted an expansion team in the Tampa Bay area in the early 1990s to a competing group, Morsani and his Tampa Bay Baseball Group filed an antitrust suit, claiming that key officials within MLB conspired to keep Morsani and his group from obtaining a team in *Morsani v. MLB*, 79 F. Supp.2d 1331 (M.D. Fla. 1999). The suit was settled out of court in October 2003 through mediation after over a decade of litigation.

10.2.2.3.3. MLB v. Crist

Following alleged poor financial performance by many of the league's clubs, Major League Baseball began discussing the possibility of contracting or eliminating two teams prior to the 2002 collective bargaining agreement. Amid rumors that the Florida Marlins and/or Tampa Bay Devil Rays may be contracted, Florida Attorney General Robert Butterworth issued civil investigative demands to MLB inquiring as to MLB's intentions. MLB claimed they did not have to answer these demands because the business of baseball is exempt from any antitrust allegation or investigation. The court upheld MLB's longstanding and controversial antitrust exemption discussed later in this chapter; see *Major League Baseball v Crist*, 331 F.3d 1177 (11th Cir. 2003). For more on this case, see M. K. Braza, "Antitrust and Major League Baseball: The MLB v. Crist Antitrust Preemption Case," 23 *Entertainment and Sports Lawyer* 1 (Fall 2005).

10.2.3. Interleague Antitrust Challenges

This section focuses on antitrust litigation that originated from the competition between rival leagues. Competition between competing leagues originates from the time baseball began gaining widespread popularity at the end of the 19th century. The first such litigation surrounding competing leagues was the 1922 *Federal Baseball* decision that created the "baseball exemption" from antitrust laws. The litigation from that case, as well as others that followed, centered on the theory that established leagues, like Major League Baseball and the National Football League, held a monopoly over that particular industry and used anticompetitive measures to maintain that monopoly.

It is important to remember that to prove that a Section 1 antitrust violation exists, the plaintiff must show that there is an agreement between two or more entities, that the agreement adversely affects competition in a relevant market, and that the anticompetitive effects outweigh the procompetitive effects. The professional sports league that has had the most litigation in this area is the NFL.

In *American Football League v. National Football League*, 323 F.2d 124 (4th Cir. 1963), the AFL sued the NFL under the Sherman Antitrust Act. While the plaintiffs filed Section 1, 2, and 3 claims, the case primarily focused on the Section 2 claim that the NFL was using its monopoly status to put the AFL out of business. The court was forced to determine whether the NFL enjoyed monopoly power, and, if so, whether it using its monopoly power to undermine the fledgling AFL. To determine this, the court was forced to judge what the "relevant market" was. The AFL argued that the relevant market was the 17 cities where the NFL had franchises. The NFL argued that the relevant market was the entire country, and when put in that context, it was clear the NFL did not hold monopoly status, since many cities were available.

The court found that a relevant market for antitrust analysis was the national market for players, television rights, and spectators. The court determined that there were approximately 30 areas in the country that could maintain a professional football team. The appeals court affirmed the district court and noted:

> The District Court's finding that [the NFL] did not have the power to monopolize the relevant market appears plainly correct. In 1959, it occupied eleven of the thirty-one apparently desirable sites for team locations, but its occupancy of some of them, such as New York and San Francisco-Oakland was not exclusive, for those metropolitan areas were capable of supporting more than one team.

The court concluded that the NFL had a natural monopoly in the cities where franchises already existed and was not using predatory tactics against the AFL. Soon after the appeals court decision, the American Football League and the National Football League merged into a single league for the purposes of maintaining player salaries and ending further legal skirmishes. The merger itself was anticompetitive and violated the antitrust laws, because the only two leagues in an industry were merging, thus taking away all competition in a single industry, the business of professional football. Congress allowed the merger to take place after the 1961 Sports Broadcast Act was amended. The amendments allowed "a joint agreement by which the members of two or more football leagues combine their operations in expanded single leagues…if such agreement increases rather than decreases the number of professional football clubs to operate." With congressional approval, the two leagues merged in 1970 and immediately began a series of expansions.

NOTES

1. Major League Baseball has not faced a competitor league since 1914, when the Federal League folded. The National Hockey League formed in 1917 and did not face a competitor professional hockey league until the emergence of the World Hockey Association (1973–1979). The National Basketball Association has faced two challenges to its stature as the predominant pro basketball league: the American Basketball League (1961–1962) and the American Basketball Association (1967–1976). The National Football League has had several competitor leagues: the All-American Football Conference (1946–1949), the American Football League (1960–1966), the World Football League (1974–1975), the United States Football League (1983–1985), and the XFL (2001). In addition, the United Football League planned to begin play in the fall of 2008. In women's sports, competition from the WNBA caused the ABL to fold in December 1998. In 1996–1997, the ABL was the best-attended women's professional team sports league in the United States.

2. For more information on Piazza and its relationship to the Curt Flood Act, see John Wolohan, "The Curt Flood Act of 1998 and Major League Baseball's Federal Antitrust Exemption," 9 *Marquette Sports Law Review* 347 (Spring 1999) or Lacie L. Kaiser, "Revisiting the Impact of the Curt Flood Act of 1998 on the Bargaining Relationship between Players and Management in Major League Baseball," 2 *DePaul Journal of Sports Law and Contemporary Problems* 230 (Fall 2004).

3. The AFL began play in 1960 and consisted of teams in Boston, Buffalo, Houston, New York, Dallas, Denver, Los Angeles, and Oakland. The league had a broadcast contract with ABC until 1965, when NBC took over the contract. Dallas moved to Kansas City in 1963 and became the Chiefs. These eight franchises, plus two expansion teams (Miami and Cincinnati) joined the NFL in the merger of 1970.

10.2.3.1. USFL v. NFL

In *United States Football League v. NFL*, 842 F.2d 1335 (2d. Cir. 1988), the upstart United States Football League sued the NFL for allegedly monopolizing professional football and using predatory tactics to limit the growth of the USFL. The USFL, which chose to play in several of the same markets as the NFL, had decided to move its season schedule from the spring (when it did not compete with the NFL playing season) to the fall (in direct competition with the NFL) but was unable to secure a television deal that would broadcast its games. The USFL argued that the NFL had used predatory tactics against it by securing television deals with the three major networks at that time—CBS, ABC, and NBC. The fact that the NFL rotated the Super Bowl among the three networks gave the NFL the leverage it needed to ensure that none of the networks carried USFL games. Without a television contract, the USFL had no way of competing against the NFL. The USFL also argued that the NFL was clearly trying to put the rival league out of business by expanding into USFL geographic areas and increasing rosters.

For example, the USFL alleged that the NFL and the city of Oakland conspired to destroy the USFL's Oakland Invaders in exchange for the NFL's promise that

Oakland would receive an NFL team. The city of Oakland had already lost the NFL Raiders to Los Angeles (see section 10.2.2.1, "Existing Owners versus Existing Owners: *Raiders v. NFL*"), when Raiders' owner Al Davis moved the team over the objections of NFL owners and citizens of Oakland. In fact, the USFL used Davis's testimony in this case to supplement its argument that the NFL was using predatory tactics, as Davis had admitted under oath that he "sensed" the NFL wanted to "destroy" the Invaders. The USFL further alleged that the NFL attempted to "co-opt" its players with a supplemental draft of USFL players and with a roster increase.

The jury found in favor of the USFL insofar as it was able to prove that the NFL did indeed enjoy a monopoly, which was in clear violation of Section 2 of the Sherman Act. The jury did not find that the NFL used predatory tactics to sabotage the USFL. The jury awarded the USFL $1 in damages, which was trebled to $3, pursuant to the Clayton Act. There are two primary reasons why the USFL received such a small damage award. First of all, the jury "expressly rejected" the USFL's television claim, which had alleged that the NFL had used its monopoly power with the networks to keep the USFL from procuring lucrative contracts. While the USFL alleged various counts of anticompetitive behavior, the television accusation was the "heart of this case" by the USFL's own admission. Second, the jury believed that the USFL itself was largely responsible for its unappealing product:

> [T]here was evidence that the USFL abandoned its original strategy of patiently building up fan loyalty and public recognition by playing in the spring. The original plan to contain costs by adherence to team salary guidelines was discarded from the start. Faced with rising costs and some new team owners impatient for immediate parity with the NFL, the idea of spring play itself was abandoned even though network and cable contracts were available. Plans for a fall season were therefore announced, thereby making 1985 spring play a "lame-duck" season. These actions were taken in the hope of forcing a merger with the NFL through the threat of competition and this litigation. The merger strategy, however, required that USFL franchises move out of large television markets and into likely NFL expansion cities. Because these moves further eroded fan loyalty and reduced the value of USFL games to television, the USFL thereby ended by its own hand any chance of a network contract.... The Sherman Act does not outlaw an industry structure simply because it prevents competitors from achieving immediate parity. This is particularly so in the case of major-league professional football because Congress authorized a merger of the two leagues existing in 1966 and thus created the industry structure in question.

The USFL attempted to obtain injunctive relief against the NFL based on the jury's finding of monopolization. The USFL sought one of three possible reliefs: (1) USFL teams were to be merged into the NFL; (2) the NFL was to be split into two separate leagues; or (3) the NFL would be forced to give up one of its three television contracts. The injunctive relief was denied due to an unlikelihood of success on the merits, and the USFL subsequently folded.

10.2.3.2. NASL v. NFL

The main issue at stake in *North American Soccer League v. NFL*, 670 F.2d 1249 (2d Cir.) *cert. denied*, 459 U.S. 1074 (1982) was whether NFL rules that banned "cross-ownership"—that is, ownership of a team in another professional sports league—were in violation of antitrust laws. The North American Soccer League contended that the ban monopolized the pool of potential owners. Cross-ownership had long been a contentious issue between NFL owners, who had an informal policy in place prohibiting NFL owners from owning controlling interest in franchises in other professional sports leagues. In 1978 the cross-ownership policy was strengthened by imposing substantial fines on teams that did not divest their ownership holdings in other professional sports leagues. After the stricter guidelines were initiated, the North American Soccer League (NASL) filed its suit.

At the district court level, the court found in favor of the NFL, relying on the league's "single-entity" defense that the league was protected against the antitrust laws because a single corporation cannot act in concert with itself. (For more on the single-entity defense, see section 10.3.8, "Single-Entity Defense by the Big Four"). The district court noted that the ban was indeed anticompetitive, but the single-entity defense protected the league against prosecution.

On appeal, the United States Court of Appeals, Second Circuit, denied the NFL's argument of the single-entity defense. The court relied on the *rule of reason* standard to weigh the procompetitive effects against the anticompetitive effects of the cross-ownership ban. The NFL argued that the ban "assures it of the undivided loyalty of its teams' owners in competing effectively against the NASL in the sale of tickets, and broadcasting rights." Despite the league's contention, the court found that the NFL was unable to provide any evidence of procompetitive effects of the ban. The court stated:

> [In] the undisputed circumstances here the enormous financial success of the NFL league despite long existing cross-ownership by some members of NASL teams demonstrates that there is no market necessity or threat of disloyalty by cross-owners that would justify the ban. Moreover, the NFL was required to come forward with proof that any legitimate purposes could not be achieved through less restrictive means. This it has failed to do.

The appellate court reversed the ruling of the lower court, entering a permanent injunction to prohibit the NFL's ban on cross-ownership. The U.S. Supreme Court subsequently denied the NFL's request for *certiorari*. Two years later, a jury reached a verdict on the remanded damages question, awarding the NASL $1 in punitive damages. The league, already in financial distress and hoping for a multimillion-dollar damage award, folded that same year.

NOTES

1. Since the NASL decision, several NFL owners have had ownership stakes in other professional sports teams: Wayne Huizenga, former owner of the Miami Dolphins, was also the original owner of MLB's Florida Marlins and the NHL's Florida Panthers; the DeBartolo family, former owners of the San Francisco 49ers, owned the NHL's Pittsburgh Penguins; Paul Allen, owner of the Seattle Seahawks, also owns the NBA's Portland Trailblazers; Malcolm Glazer, owner of the Tampa Bay Buccaneers, also owns the Manchester United of the English Premier League; and Jerry Jones, owner of the Dallas Cowboys, owns the Dallas Desperados of the Arena Football League. However, the NFL does maintain a policy prohibiting public ownership of franchises, except for the Green Bay Packers.

2. The case of *Robertson v. NBA*, 389 F.Supp. 867 (S.D.N.Y. 1975) focused on the ABA-NBA merger and its anticompetitive nature. The players in the class action suit argued that the merger would depress salaries due to the lack of competition. In addition, the merger

between two pro leagues was anticompetitive by nature. The court agreed that the merger would eliminate all competition and that Congress would have to grant the league an exemption. The merger was part of the *Robertson* settlement, which included a system of free agency beginning in 1976.

3. In *Philadelphia World Hockey Club, Inc. v. Philadelphia Hockey Club Inc.*, 351 F.Supp. 462 (E.D. Pa. 1972), the Philadelphia team in the World Hockey Association, a rival professional hockey league to the established National Hockey League, sued the NHL under Sections 1 and 2 of the Sherman Act because of the reserve clause, the NHL's affiliations with minor leagues, and its monopoly power. On a motion for a preliminary injunction, the court found it likely that the reserve clause violated Section 2 by preventing players from joining WHA teams, and that the NHL did indeed have monopoly power and overwhelming control over the supply of players who could play pro hockey. The case was settled out of court when four WHA teams (Edmonton Oilers, New England Whalers, Quebec Nordiques, and Winnipeg Jets) were admitted into the NHL, while the Birmingham Bulls and Cincinnati Stingers were paid to fold.

10.2.4. Antitrust Litigation in Professional Tennis and Golf

Several decades after *United States v. Boxing Club of New York* (see section 10.2.1, "Player Restraints and Antitrust Theory"), individual sports continued to undergo antitrust scrutiny. While the majority of sports antitrust litigation has involved team sports, the concepts of antitrust law are still crucial to professionals in all areas of the sports industry. Governing bodies of individual sports such as the Professional Golfers' Association or the Women's Tennis Association (WTA) unite the most outstanding performers in their respective fields. If an athlete, agent, or equipment manufacturer is excluded by such organizations, there are no alternatives within the sport's market that are financially equivalent. Trade is inherently restrained and markets are inherently monopolized. The question then becomes whether there is a legitimate business reason to restrain trade or to monopolize. In short, is the apparent illegal activity good for the sport and/or the sport's consumers?

10.2.4.1. Age Restrictions

In 1995, the Women's Tennis Association enacted rules that prohibited tournament participation by players younger than 14 and limited participation by players aged 14 to 18 (see note 3). This rule was adopted after certain high-profile women's tennis players suffered physical and emotional difficulties after achieving success at a young age (see note 1). Hence, the age eligibility rule was designed to phase in younger players rather than overwhelm them with constant tournaments. Players such as Anna Kournikova and Serena Williams openly complained that the rule restrained their earning power.

The WTA's rule has not been successfully challenged in the courts. In 1998 Mirjana Lucic of Croatia unsuccessfully petitioned for an injunction in an Australia court in order to play in the Australian Open (see note 3). However, also in 1998, the parents of 14-year-old Monique Viele threatened to sue unless their child was allowed to participate in a WTA event. To avoid litigation, the WTA modified its rules to allow 14-year-olds to enter one WTA tournament that season.

It is unclear whether the tournament's age eligibility requirement would withstand antitrust scrutiny in the United States. But if it were tested, the WTA would likely invoke at least one rule-of-reason defense. As former WTA Tour CEO Bart McGuire stated, "the [age eligibility] rule helps to foster a better game, better competition, and ultimately, that helps the players make more [money] and stay in the game longer" (see note 2).

There is a tennis precedent for successful application of rule-of-reason defense of eligibility rules against antitrust claims. In *Heldman v. United States Lawn Tennis Ass'n*, 354 F.Supp. 1241 (S.D.N.Y. 1973), the plaintiff claimed that the United States Lawn Tennis Association (USLTA) violated the Sherman Act by blacklisting players who participated in the plaintiff's tennis tour from entry into USLTA-sanctioned events. The court denied the plaintiff's motion, saying that the eligibility provisions could be permitted because they helped ensure the uniformity of rules for player rankings and the orderly scheduling of tournaments. The plaintiff appealed this decision, but the case was settled prior to the appeal being heard.

NOTES

1. For instance, Jennifer Capriati was arrested on shoplifting and drug charges in years following her Olympic (1992) and French Open (1993) successes.

2. For more on age restrictions in women's professional tennis, see Bartlett H. McGuire, "Women's Professional Tennis: A Case Study of Procompetitive Restraints of Trade," *Journal of International Media & Entertainment Law* (2007) and Ryan Rodenberg, "Age Eligibility Rules in Women's Professional Tennis," 7 *Sport Lawyer's Journal* 183 (Spring 2000).

3. The WTA age eligibility rule prohibits a player who has not reached her 14th birthday from participating in any professional tournament on the WTA tour. Players between the ages of 14 and 15 are allowed to participate in a maximum of seven "minor league" circuit events. Players age 15 to 16 are allowed to compete in a maximum of 10 professional tournaments' while players between the ages of 16 and 17 and between the ages of 17 and 18 may participate in a maximum of 13 and 17 tournaments, respectively. Eighteen-year-olds are allowed to enter an unlimited number of tournaments on the WTA tour. For more information, the Official Rulebook is available at http://www.sonyericssonwtatour.com.

10.2.4.2. Equipment Rules

A racket manufacturer filed suit in *Gunter Harz Sports, Inc. v. United States Tennis Ass'n*, 665 F.2d 222 (8th Cir. 1981), after the USTA prohibited the use of a tennis racket with double strings in tournaments. A double-strung racket manufacturer cited Section 1 of the Sherman Act, alleging that the USTA's prohibition amounted to a group boycott. The court ruled in favor of the USTA, determining that double-strung rackets harmed the essence of the game by excessively altering the spin on the ball.

As a result of rapidly improving technology, golf's ruling bodies, the PGA, USGA and Royal & Ancient Golf Club, have been forced to place restrictions on clubs, balls, and other equipment. In 1991 several professional golfers, along with the makers of Ping clubs, sued the PGA for banning square grooves on the face of a club. The PGA contended that the square grooves imparted excessive spin on the ball as compared to the standard V-shaped grooves. The complaint alleged both Section 1 and Section 2 violations. The District Court granted an injunction prohibiting enforcement of the rule, stating that the balance of hardships favored the plaintiff players, who would have to abandon clubs that they were comfortable using. The Court of Appeals affirmed in Gilden v. PGA Tour, 936 F.2d 417 (9th Cir. 1991). The ruling effectively created an exemption for square grooved clubs made before April 1990. The controversy continued into 2010 when Phil Mickelson and several other golfers continued using the 20-year old clubs until the PGA Tour and Ping reached an agreement to ban the clubs.

10.2.4.3. Blacklisting: **Blalock v. LPGA**

As in tennis, golf associations have been forced to defend their restraints on trade as legitimate business practices essential to their sport. One type of restraint on trade claim occurred when an association imposed discipline on its members. In *Blalock v. Ladies Professional Golf Association*, 359 F.Supp. 1260 (N.D. Ga. 1973), a golfer was suspended for one year by the LPGA's executive board after discovering that she had illegally moved her ball during tournament play on several occasions. The court held that the exclusion of Blalock constituted a group boycott, and was thus a per se violation of Section 1 of the Sherman Act. Since the LPGA did not allow LPGA members, such as the plaintiff, to compete in other tournaments, the court determined that excluding the plaintiff from the LPGA tour had, in effect, excluded her from the entire market. Just as the court in *Volvo North American* treated the WIPTC as a "joint venture," so the court in *Blalock* treated the LPGA as a "collective action." This designation might have made the single-entity defense difficult, had rule-of-reason been allowed by the court.

While the Federal District Court in *Blalock* felt that the PGA unreasonably restrained trade, a Federal Appellate Court ruled differently in *Deesen v. Professional Golfers' Ass'n*, 358 F.2d 165 (9th Cir.), *cert. denied*, 385 U.S. 846 (1966). A professional golfer brought a Section 1 claim after being denied entrance to PGA events due to his repeated poor performance. The plaintiff alleged that the PGA's eligibility rule unreasonably restrained trade and had the effect of a group boycott. The court rejected the Section 1 claim using the rule of reason standard finding that the PGA's requirement for performance standards was indeed reasonable.

10.2.4.4. Hosting Tournaments and Conflicts of Interest

The ability for agency firms to host tournaments was tested in *Volvo North American Corp v. Men's International Professional Tennis Council*, 857 F.2d 55 (2d Cir.), *cert. denied* 487 U.S. 1219 (1988). Prior to the suit, the defendant Men's International Professional Tennis Council (MIPTC) took issue with the fact that agency firms Pro Serv and IMG were allowed to represent tennis players and also run major tennis tournaments. The MIPTC felt that it was a conflict of interest and therefore proposed the conflicts of interest rule, which would require that any player-agent involved in producing an MIPTC-sanctioned event must obtain MIPTC approval before awarding any player a wild card position in the event. Wild card positions are those offered to players without regard to their rankings and are usually awarded independently by the owners and producers of an event.

But agency firms, along with Volvo, alleged conspiracy against the MIPTC for proposing this and other restrictions. Specifically, the plaintiffs accused the MIPTC of using its power over men tennis players "to impose restrictions...which hamper the ability of actual and potential competitors...to conduct competing tennis events." Although this case was settled, it is interesting to note that the court first rejected the MIPTC's single-entity defense, stating that it was indeed capable of conspiracy as a "joint venture."

In February 2003, the Washington Tennis and Education Foundation (WTEF) along with the Indianapolis Tennis Championships (RCA Championships) filed an antitrust lawsuit against the Association of Tennis Professionals (ATP) claiming both Section 1—restraint of trade and Section 2—monopolization violations by unfairly manipulating the schedule to benefit its better tournaments, the Tennis

Master Series, at the expense of the RCA and Legg Mason tournaments. WTEF and RCA alleged that the ATP forced their better players to sign agreements limiting their play in weeks of Tennis Master events. As a result, the RCA and Legg Mason tournaments could not draw better players, badly hurting attendance. A settlement was reached in November 2003 scaling down the size of the RCA Championship while granting it tournament exclusivity from July 21 to July 27.

The inconsistency and unpredictability of court holdings in seemingly similar cases makes antitrust law in individual sports particularly complicated. Nevertheless, the above cases should provide some benchmarks for practitioners in these areas. Finally, it should be noted that individual sports are normally devoid of players unions in the usual sense. Because of this, collective bargaining does not occur between athletes and governing bodies. When the nonstatutory labor exemption is discussed later in the chapter, readers should keep in mind that individual sports organizations (like the USTA and LPGA) cannot gain antitrust immunity by bargaining with their players.

NOTES

1. In *Deutscher Tennis Bund v. ATP Tour, Inc.*, 2008 WL 2520809 (D.Del. June 23, 2008), the operators of the ATP Tour event in Hamburg, Germany, brought suit against the ATP after it proposed a restructured schedule. The proposed format relegated the Hamburg event to a second-tier status, worth fewer points in the ATP rankings. The organizers alleged the ATP violated antitrust laws by entering into a contract or conspiracy to harm competition and attempted to monopolize the market for professional tennis tournaments. In August 2008, a jury unanimously decided in the ATP's favor and an appeal is pending before the Third Circuit.

2. In *Kentucky Speedway, LLC v. National Association of Stock Car Auto Racing, Inc. (NASCAR)*, 588 F.3d 908 (6th Cir. 2009), Kentucky Speedway sued NASCAR alleging antitrust violations after it had been excluded from NASCAR's Sprint Cup series. NASCAR is affiliated with International Speedway Corporation (ISC), which owns about 55% of the tracks that NASCAR Sprint Cup races are held on. The courts granted NASCAR summary judgment, finding that Kentucky Speedway was unable to define the relevant markets.

10.3. DEFENSES TO ANTITRUST CHALLENGES

10.3.1. The Baseball Exemption

10.3.1.1. History of the Reserve System

The first antitrust challenges against professional sports leagues occurred in the early 20th century. Professional baseball, the oldest professional team sport in the United States, was established in 1869 when Harry Wright created the first salaried team, the Cincinnati Red Stockings. In 1876 the National League was created, and was considered the principal professional baseball league. The National League clubs signed each player to a one-year contract, later referred to as the standard player contract. An element of that contract was the "reserve clause," which prohibited any player from negotiating with any team other than the one with which the player had originally signed. In addition, the contract stipulated that each year the team could exercise an "option" on the player's services for the following season. Thus, a player was bound to a team in perpetuity, or until he was traded, released, or retired. Players initially used contract law to challenge the restrictive standard player contracts, but quickly turned to antitrust law when professional baseball revised the contracts to protect themselves from challenges under contract law (see note 1).

Plaintiffs first used antitrust law to challenge the reserve clause in 1914, in *American League Baseball Club v. Chase*, 149 N.Y.S. 6 (N.Y. Sup. Ct. 1914). While antitrust theory was not the main legal theory being used to challenge the league, the Sherman Act was introduced as possibly applicable to a professional sports league. However, the court found that the Sherman Act did not apply because baseball was not engaged in interstate commerce.

> Baseball is an amusement, a sport, a game that comes clearly within the civil and criminal law of the state, and it is not a commodity or an article of merchandise subject to the regulation of Congress on the theory that it is interstate commerce.

Therefore, the third element needed to prove a restraint of trade could not be satisfied.

NOTE

1. In *Metropolitan Exhibition Co. v. Ewing*, 42 F. 198 (S.D.N.Y. 1890), the court ruled that the plaintiff could not force the defendant to play for them because the terms of the standard player contract were not definite, and therefore the right of reservation could not be enforced. In *Metropolitan Exhibition Co. v. Ward*, 9 N.Y.S. 779 (N.Y. Sup. Ct. 1890), the court denied an injunction to the plaintiff because the standard player contract lacked both definiteness and mutuality, and the plaintiff was unlikely to win a case on the merits. In *Philadelphia Ball Club Limited v. Lajoie*, 51 A. 973 (Pa. 1902), the court found in favor of the plaintiff because mutuality and definiteness were found to exist in the contract. The court stated, "The mere difference in the rights stipulated for, does not destroy mutuality or remedy."

10.3.1.2. *Creation of the Baseball Exemption:* Federal Baseball

In 1915, many of the teams from the failed Federal League were compensated in a variety of ways by the other leagues. The owner of the Baltimore franchise rejected a monetary settlement and accused the National League and the American League of illegally conspiring to monopolize the business of baseball. The case was decided in favor of the plaintiff at the district court level, and treble damages were awarded but the court of appeals reversed the decision. The case ultimately went before the Supreme Court, which issued a decision in 1922 (see exhibit 10.2). The Court, presided over by Justice Oliver Wendell Holmes, determined that the Sherman Act could not be used successfully against Major League Baseball. The Court cited three relevant reasons:

1. That "the business is giving exhibitions of baseball which are purely state affairs," and therefore, no interstate commerce exists
2. That just because there was travel from state to state, "the travel is a mere incident, not the essential thing"
3. That players were not a commodity, and thus "not related to production."

This precedent-setting case held that baseball was not engaged in interstate commerce, meaning that Sections 1 and 2 of the Sherman Act had not been violated. The "baseball exemption," which was to last for over 75 years, and in some respects continues today, gave the professional sport of baseball blanket protection against antitrust challenges from players, maverick owners, and competitor leagues. The significance of this ruling is that it allowed the owners to authoritatively maintain the reserve clause, control franchise location, and maintain the subordinate structure of the minor leagues, without fear of a reprisal in the form of an antitrust challenge.

Exhibit 10.2

FEDERAL BASEBALL CLUB OF BALTIMORE, INC. v. NATIONAL LEAGUE OF PROFESSIONAL BASEBALL CLUBS, ET AL.
No. 204.
SUPREME COURT OF THE UNITED STATES 259 U.S. 200; 42 5. Ct. 465; 1922 U.S. LEXIS 2475; 66 L. Ed. 898; 26 A.L.R. 357

Argued April 19, 1922.
May 29, 1922, Decided

ERROR TO THE COURT OF APPEALS OF THE DISTRICT OF COLUMBIA.

ERROR to a judgment of the Court of Appeals of the District of Columbia reversing a judgment for triple damages under the Anti-Trust Acts recovered by the plaintiff in error in the Supreme Court of the District and directing that judgment be entered for the defendants.

SYLLABUS: 1. The business of providing public baseball games for profit between clubs of professional baseball players in a league and between clubs of rival leagues, although necessarily involving the constantly repeated traveling of the players from one State to another, provided for, controlled and disciplined by the organizations employing them, is not interstate commerce. P. 208.

2. Held that an action for triple damages under the Anti-Trust Acts could not be maintained by a baseball club against baseball leagues and their constituent clubs, joined with individuals, for an alleged conspiracy to monopolize the baseball business resulting injuriously to the plaintiff. P. 209. 269 Fed. 681; 50 App. D.C. 165, affirmed.

COUNSEL: Mr. Charles A. Douglas and Mr. William L. Marbury, with whom Mr. L. Edwin Goldman and Mr. William L. Rawls were on the briefs, for plaintiff in error.

Defendants are voluntary associations and corporations engaged upon a vast scale, involving the investment of millions of dollars, in the business of providing, by the transportation from State to State of baseball teams and their necessary attendants and equipment, exhibitions of professional baseball. The court is not concerned with whether the mere playing of baseball, that is the act of the individual player, upon a baseball field in a particular city, is by itself interstate commerce. That act, it is true, is related to the business of the defendants, but it can no more be said to be the business than can any other single act in any other business forming a part of interstate commerce.

Exhibit 10.2
(continued)

The question with which the court is here concerned is whether the business in which the defendants were engaged when the wrongs complained of occurred, taken as an entirety, was interstate commerce, or more accurately, whether the monopoly which they had established or attempted to establish was a monopoly of any part of interstate commerce.

At the foundation of the business of one of these leagues—in its primary conception—is a circuit embracing seven different States. No single club in that circuit could operate without the other members of the circuit, and accordingly in the very beginning of its business the matter of interstate relationship is not only important but predominant and indispensable.

Each game symbolizes a contest of skill between the two cities that have been brought together by means of interstate communication and travel. Each team of each club in the league carries with it, and it is essential to the profit of the enterprise that it should carry with it, its representative character; it symbolizes the great city that it represents to those assembled to witness the contest.

In addition to this representative city and state aspect, there is also the element of intersectional rivalry. Experience has shown that the game is most largely patronized when clubs are so located as to provide a contest for supremacy between the Eastern and Western sections of the country.

It is necessary to distinguish between baseball as a sport, that is, where it is played merely as a means of physical exercise and diversion, and this business of providing exhibitions of professional baseball. The business of Organized Baseball represents and has represented for many years, an investment of colossal wealth. Defendants who dominate Organized Baseball are not engaged in a sport. They are engaged in a moneymaking business enterprise in which all of the features of any large commercial undertaking are to be found. When the teams of the National or American Leagues or of any other league are sent around the circuit of the league, they go at the direction of employers whose business it is to send them, and whose profits are made as a result of that business operation.

When the profit-making aspect of the business is examined, it will be found that the interstate element is still further magnified. The vast investment of capital which has been made in it is required, among other things, in order to provide a place at which the teams in the league may play their contests. Each club has a ball park, with stands erected upon them, sometimes, as in the case of a major league club, costing several millions of dollars. Every club in the league earns its profit not only by the drawing capacity of its team at home, but also by that of the teams of the clubs which its team visits in the various cities in the league. The gate receipts in all of the cities in which the clubs are located are divided according to a definite proportion, fixed by agreement between the club of the city in which the game is played and the club employing the visiting team.

In no other business that can now be recalled is there such a close interrelationship and interdependence between persons in one State and persons in another.

**Exhibit 10.2
(continued)**

The personality, so to speak, of each club in a league is actually projected over state lines and becomes mingled with that of the clubs in all the other States The continuous interstate activity of each is essential to all the others. The clubs of each league constitute a business unit embracing territorially a number of different States. While each club has, of course, a local legal habitat, yet from a practical business standpoint it is primarily an ambulatory organization.

It is difficult to perceive the relevancy of any discussion about an article of commerce in this case. Commerce may be carried on in one of its forms by traffic in articles of merchandise, but there are countless forms in which it may be carried on without traffic in such articles. *Gibbons v. Ogden,* 9 Wheat. 189.

It is also difficult to discern the relevancy of the contention that personal effort is not an article of commerce. Personal effort, while it may not be an article of commerce, is often commerce itself, but we are not concerned with any such question here. It may be passed by saying that it has been adjudicated by this court in the Hoke case, 227 U.S. 308, that interstate commerce may be created by the mere act of a person in allowing himself to be transported from one State to another, without any personal effort; and further that it is very difficult to see how *International Textbook Co. v. Pigg,* 217 U.S. 91, could have been decided as it was, except upon the principle that the mere exchange of instruction and information, which is about as purely a matter of personal effort as anything that can be imagined, may be a subject of interstate commerce.

If transactions in interstate commerce were to be judged by their isolated ultimate results, as the defendants seek to separate the act of a player in throwing a ball upon a ball field from all the steps which are taken to bring the ball player in the due course of business from other States, of course their interstate character could be plausibly argued away. By such a process of reasoning the American Tobacco Company, for instance, might have removed its gigantic monopoly from the operation of the Sherman Act. See *United States v. American Tobacco Co.,* 221 U.S. 106, 184: *Standard Oil Co. v. United States,* 221 U.S. 1,68; *Swift & Co. v. United States,* 196 U.S. 375.

In the business now under consideration throughout the playing season the ball teams, their attendants and paraphernalia, are in constant revolution around a pre-established circuit. Their movement is only interrupted to the extent of permitting exhibitions of baseball to be given in the various cities. When exhibitions in one city are completed the clubs resume, according to the agreement made, and plan of business long established, their course of travel on to another city, and thus on and on until the schedule of exhibitions is completed. The interruption in interstate movement is nothing like as great as that in the Swift Case, supra. The constant movement of the teams from State to State during a period of over five months each year, is under a single direction and control and in pursuance of one object.

See *Champion v. Ames,* 188 U.S. 321; *Pensacola Telegraph Co. v. Western Union Telegraph Co.,* 96 U.S. 1; *United States v, Patten,* 226 U.S. 525; *Loewe v. Lawlor,* 208 U.S. 274: *Western Union Telegraph Co. v. Foster,* 247 U.S. 105. See particularly

Exhibit 10.2
(continued)

Marienelli v. United Booking Offices, 227 Fed. 165, where the question was presented as to whether a company engaged in booking vaudeville performers for a circuit embracing theatres in cities in different States was engaged in interstate commerce within the Sherman Act. Also, *Motion Picture Patents Co. v. Universal Film Mfg. Co.,* 235 Fed. 401.

It is common knowledge that baseball is the preeminent American sport. Millions of people follow the daily reports of the results of the games in the press, and in the large cities gather in the afternoons around the newspaper offices to see the bulletin reports of the scores. Not only so, but vast numbers of people travel from one city to another for the purpose of witnessing the games. Telegraph facilities are installed at all the ball parks in the Major Leagues, and in those of the more important Minor Leagues, where reports of the games are sent out and are received throughout the country.

Each league contracts for a uniform type of baseball, which is used in tremendous numbers and shipped by the manufacturer from time to time as they are needed by the various clubs.

These incidents, while in themselves not determinative of the question of whether or not the business is interstate in character, yet, when considered in connection with its main features, emphasize the truth of what has before been said, that there is scarcely any business which can be named in which the element of interstate commerce is as predominant as that in which defendants are engaged.

The agreement and combination entered into and maintained by defendants whereby the entire business in the United States of providing exhibitions of professional baseball was brought under the control of defendants and their confederates in Organized Baseball, amounted in law to a conspiracy in restraint of trade among the several States and a monopoly or an attempt to monopolize a part of commerce among the several States within the meaning of the Sherman Act.

There is no testimony in this case legally sufficient to show that the plaintiff has waived its right to recover damages under the Sherman Act.

Mr. George Wharton Pepper, with whom Mr. Benjamin S. Minor and Mr. Samuel M. Clement, Jr., were on the brief, for defendants in error.

Organized Baseball is not interstate commerce and does not constitute an attempt to monopolize within the Sherman Act.

Personal effort, not related to production, is not a subject of commerce; and the attempt to secure all the skilled service needed for professional baseball contests is not an attempt to monopolize commerce or any part of it. Clayton Act, § 8; *Paul v. Virginia,* 8 Wall. 168; *Hooper v. California,* 155 U.S. 648; *Metropolitan Opera Co. v Hammerstein,* 147 N.Y.S. 532; In re Duff, 4 Fed. 519, In re Oriental Society, 104 Fed. 975; *People v. KIaw,* 106 N.YS. 341. The Department of Justice has

Exhibit 10.2
(continued)

ruled that the business conducted by Organized Baseball was not in violation of the Sherman Act; and also that the business of presenting theatrical entertainments is not commerce. Distinguishing: *International Textbook Co. v. Pigg*, 217 US. 91; and *Marienelli v. United Booking Offices*, 227 Fed. 165. The only case in which the question whether Organized Baseball is within the Sherman Act has been directly passed upon is that of *American Baseball Club of Chicago v Chase*, 149 N.Y.S, 6; in which the court answered the question in the negative.

Congress has not imposed a penalty upon the transportation of players for baseball purposes, and therefore *Hoke v. United States*, 227 U.S. 308, is not point. While Congress may regulate the movement of persons in interstate commerce, when it has not regulated movement as such, the doing of an act essentially local is not converted into an interstate act merely because people came from another State to do it.

OPINION BY: HOLMES

OPINION: MR. JUSTICE HOLMES delivered the opinion of the court.

This is a suit for threefold damages brought by the plaintiff in error under the Anti-Trust Acts of July 2, 1890, c. 847, § 7, 26 Stat. 209, 210, and of October 15, 1914, c, 323, § 4, 38 Stat. 730, 731. The defendants are The National League of Professional Base Ball Clubs and The American League of Professional Base Ball Clubs, unincorporated associations, composed respectively of groups of eight incorporated base ball clubs, joined as defendants; the presidents of the two Leagues and a third person, constituting what is known as the National Commission, having considerable powers in carrying out an agreement between the two Leagues; and three other persons having powers in the Federal League of Professional Base Ball Clubs, the relation of which to this case will be explained. It is alleged that these defendants conspired to monopolize the base ball business, the means adopted being set forth with a detail which, in the view that we take, it is unnecessary to repeat.

The plaintiff is a base ball club incorporated in Maryland, and with seven other corporations was a member of the Federal League of Professional Base Ball Clubs, a corporation under the laws of Indiana, that attempted to compete with the combined defendants. It alleges that the defendants destroyed the Federal League by buying up some of the constituent clubs and in one way or another inducing all those clubs except the plaintiff to leave their League, and that the three persons connected with the Federal League and named as defendants, one of them being the President of the League, took part in the conspiracy. Great damage to the plaintiff is alleged. The plaintiff obtained a verdict for $80,000 in the Supreme Court and a judgment for treble the amount was entered, but the Court of Appeals, after an elaborate discussion, held that the defendants were not within the Sherman Act. The appellee, the plaintiff, elected to stand on the record in order to bring the case to this Court at once, and thereupon judgment was ordered for the defendants. 50 App. D.C. 165; 269 Fed. 681, 688. It is not argued that the plaintiff waived any rights by its course. *Thomsen v. Cayser*, 243 U.S. 66.

Exhibit 10.2
(continued)

The decision of the Court of Appeals went to the root of the case and if correct makes it unnecessary to consider other serious difficulties in the way of the plaintiff's recovery. A summary statement of the nature of the business involved will be enough to present the point. The clubs composing the Leagues are in different cities and for the most part in different States. The end of the elaborate organizations and sub-organizations that are described in the pleadings and evidence is that these clubs shall play against one another in public exhibitions for money, one or the other club crossing a state line in order to make the meeting possible. When as the result of these contests one club has won the pennant of its League and another club has won the pennant of the other League, there is a final competition for the world's championship between these two. Of course the scheme requires constantly repeated travelling on the part of the clubs, which is provided for, controlled ant disciplined by the organizations, and this it is said means commerce among the States, But we are of opinion that the Court of Appeals was right.

The business is giving exhibitions of base ball, which are purely state affairs. It is true that, in order to attain for these exhibitions the great popularity that they have achieved, competitions must be arranged between clubs from different cities and States. But the fact that in order to give the exhibitions the Leagues must induce free persons to cross state lines and must arrange and pay for their doing so is not enough to change the character of the business. According to the distinction insisted upon in *Hooper v. California,* 155 U.S. 648, 655, the transport is a mere incident, not the essential thing. That to which it is incident, the exhibition, although made for money would not be called trade or commerce in the commonly accepted use of those words. As it is put by the defendants, personal effort, not related to production, is not a subject of commerce. That which in its consummation is not commerce does not become commerce among the States because the transportation that we have mentioned takes place. To repeat the illustrations given by the Court below, a firm of lawyers sending out a member to argue a case, or the Chautauqua lecture bureau sending out lecturers, does not engage in such commerce because the lawyer or lecturer goes to another State.

If we are right the plaintiffs business is to be described in the same way and the restrictions by contract that prevented the plaintiff from getting players to break their bargains and the other conduct charged against the defendants were not an interference with commerce among the States.

Judgment affirmed.

10.3.1.3. *Baseball Exemption Reaffirmed:* **Toolson**

Players continued to challenge the reserve clause using antitrust theory, and two such cases reached the Supreme Court. In *Toolson v. New York Yankees*, 346 U.S. 356 (1953), a professional baseball player challenged the reserve system. The Supreme Court affirmed the district court's determination that upheld the exemption because Congress had not attempted to change the decision created by *Federal Baseball*. The Court based its decision on four factors:

1. Congressional awareness for three decades of the Court's ruling in *Federal Baseball*, coupled with congressional inaction

2. The fact that baseball was left alone to develop for that period upon the understanding that the reserve system was not subject to federal antitrust laws

3. A reluctance to overrule *Federal Baseball* with consequent retroactive effect

4. A professed desire that any needed remedy be provided by legislation rather than by court decree.

Justices Burton and Reed dissented, claiming that the sport of baseball was clearly interstate commerce, and therefore the exemption should be lifted. Justice Burton wrote:

> Congress, however, has enacted no express exemption of organized baseball from the Sherman Act, and no court has demonstrated the existence of an implied exemption from the Act of any sport that is so highly organized as to amount to an interstate monopoly or which restrains interstate trade or commerce.

10.3.1.4. Baseball Anomaly Upheld: **Flood**

The Supreme Court was forced to make another determination over the validity of the professional baseball antitrust exemption in *Flood v. Kuhn*, 316 F. Supp. 271 (S.D.N.Y. 1970). Curt Flood, a player with the St. Louis Cardinals, was traded to the Philadelphia Phillies after playing with the Cardinals for 12 seasons. He appealed to Commissioner Bowie Kuhn to reject the trade, based on the fact the Philadelphia organization had a history of acute racism. The request was denied by the commissioner. Flood then brought suit against Kuhn and Major League Baseball for violating antitrust laws and sought a preliminary injunction against the trade. The district court cited *Federal Baseball* and *Toolson*, ruling against Flood. The appeals court affirmed.

The Supreme Court granted *certiorari* because of the apparent confusion in this area of the law. Much of the confusion arose out of the fact that other professional sports leagues did not enjoy an antitrust exemption even though the league structure in other sports and professional baseball was almost identical. The contradictions within the Supreme Court forced Justice Blackmun to outline an eight-point decision in *Flood v. Kuhn*, 407 U.S. 258 (1972):

1. Professional baseball is a business and is engaged in interstate commerce.

2. With its reserve system enjoying an exemption from the federal antitrust laws, baseball is an anomaly. *Federal Baseball* and *Toolson* are an aberration confined to baseball.

3. This anomaly has been affirmed in *Shubert, International Boxing, Radovich*, and other cases.

4. Other professional sports operating interstate are not so exempt.

5. The advent of radio and television has not occasioned an overruling of *Federal Baseball* and *Toolson*.

6. Congress has remained inactive in overruling the exemption, or making the reserve system subject to antitrust laws. Thus, this has been deemed to be something other than mere congressional silence and passivity.

7. The Court has expressed concern about the retroactivity of a court decision as compared with a legislative decision that is only prospective in operation.

8. The court noted in *Radovich* that the slate is not clean and has not been for half a century.

Blackmun ended his decision with, "the remedy, if any indicated, is for congressional, and not judicial, action." As a result of this decision, baseball's blanket antitrust exemption was affirmed. However, for the other professional sports leagues, there is no exemption. As discussed in section 10.2.1, "Player Restraints and Antitrust Theory," players and the players' associations in football, hockey, and basketball have challenged their respective leagues' reserve system using antitrust theory.

10.3.1.5. *The Curt Flood Act*

The Curt Flood Act of 1998 is the culmination of three Supreme Court decisions, dozens of unsuccessful congressional acts, and hundreds of law review articles. Following the Court's recommendation that professional baseball's antitrust exemption be remedied by Congress, several members of the House of Representatives and the Senate lobbied successfully to pass the new act, which does not completely erase baseball's exemption, but does limit it significantly. The purpose of the act is stated thus:

> Sec. 2 Purpose. It is the purpose of this legislation to state that Major League Baseball players are covered under the antitrust laws (i.e. that major league baseball players will have the same rights under the antitrust laws as do other professional athletes, e.g. football and basketball players), along with a provision that makes it clear that the passage of this Act does not change the application of the antitrust laws in any other context or with respect to any other person or entity.

Specifically, the act gives Major League Baseball players the same antitrust rights that other professional athletes enjoy; namely, the right to sue their employers under the Sherman Act if an antitrust violation has occurred.

> Sec. 3. Application of the Antitrust Laws to Professional Major League Baseball. The Clayton Act (15 U.S.C. 12 et seq) is amended by adding at the end of the following new section: Sec. 27. (a) Subject to subsections (b) through (d), the conduct, acts, practices, or agreements of persons in the business of organized professional major league baseball directly relating to or affecting employment of major league baseball players to play baseball at the major league level are subject to the antitrust laws if engaged in by persons in any other professional sports business affecting interstate commerce.

However, the act does not completely remove baseball's exemption; the following section clearly states that baseball's antitrust exemption still applies to all nonplayer areas:

> any conduct, acts, practices, or agreements of persons engaging in, conducting, or participating in the business of organized professional baseball relating to or affecting franchise expansion, location or relocation, franchise ownership issues, including ownership transfers, the relationship between the Office of the Commissioner and

franchise owners, the marketing or sales of the entertainment product of organized professional baseball and the licensing of intellectual property rights owned or held by organized professional baseball teams individually or collectively.

Therefore, Major League Baseball players now have the ability to use the Sherman Act, whereas owners upset over a franchise relocation decision, as in *Piazza* (see section 10.2.2.3.1, "*Piazza v. MLB*"), do not enjoy that same right.

Both the Major League Baseball Players Association and MLB management lobbied for this legislation. The rationale for the MLB players' support is clear—they gained the right to sue the league on antitrust grounds. The rationale for MLB management support is more elusive. Some experts contend that management was pressured into supporting the act during collective bargaining. However, there is another school of thought which says that MLB benefited from the act (see note 1). Since the language of the amendment explicitly states that *major league* baseball players may use the Sherman Act, MLB continues to be shielded from antitrust lawsuits filed by minor league and amateur players. Second, even if MLB players do sue on antitrust grounds, their likelihood of success is poor unless they first decertify their union. The concepts of decertification and the nonstatutory labor exemption will become more clear to the reader after reading sections 10.3.2. through 10.3.5.—"The Nonstatutory Labor Exemption," "Early Uses of the Nonstatutory Labor Exemption," "Exemption after Expiration of Collective Bargaining Agreement," and "Exemption after Decertification"—where the precedents in other sports are discussed. Moreover, as mentioned previously, the Curt Flood Act restores MLB autonomy over decisions regarding franchise relocations. Thus, MLB need not fear another legal battle and settlement as seen in *Piazza*.

NOTES

1. The Curt Flood Act has sparked numerous articles. At first, articles such as John Wolohan, "The Curt Flood Act of 1998 and Major League Baseball's Federal Antitrust Exemption," 9 *Marquette Sports Law Journal* 347 (Spring 1999) argued that the passage of the Curt Flood Act would have a positive effect on the business of baseball. However, since then articles such as Mitchell Nathanson, "The Irrelevance of Baseball's Antitrust Exemption: A Historical Review," 58 *Rutgers Law Review* 1 (Fall 2005) argue that nothing substantially has changed. Yet, since the passage of the Act MLB has not had a work stoppage, a fact some commentators attribute to the Act, see Nathaniel Grow, "Reevaluating the Curt Flood Act of 1998," 87 *Nebraska Law Review* 747 (2009).

2. In *Minnesota Twins Partnership v. State of Minnesota*, 592 N.W.2d 847 (Minn. 1999), the Minnesota Supreme Court ruled that the state could not force the MLB team to turn over its financial records in an investigation of an alleged antitrust violation. In overturning the lower court's ruling, the Supreme Court stated, "The business of professional baseball is exempt from federal and state antitrust laws; therefore, Minnesota's Attorney General may not enforce compliance with civil investigative demands served on appellants pursuant to an investigation of potential violations of Minnesota's antitrust laws based on a proposed sale and relocation of the Minnesota Twins baseball team."

10.3.2. The Nonstatutory Labor Exemption

Section 10.1.3, "Clayton Act," discussed the *statutory* labor exemption. This section and several subsequent sections refer to the *nonstatutory* labor exemption. To avoid confusion, the nonlawyer should understand that it is accepted practice to refer to the nonstatutory labor exemption as simply "the labor exemption." Likewise, when the reader sees "the labor exemption" mentioned anywhere in this text, he or she should assume that the author is referring to the nonstatutory labor exemption.

The nonstatutory labor exemption is the result of three Supreme Court decisions that relate to antitrust challenges against joint actions taken by employers acting in concert with unions. In *Allen Bradley Co. v. Local Union No. 3, International Brotherhood of Electrical Workers*, 325 U.S. 797 (1945), *Amalgamated Meat Cutters & Butcher Workmen of North America v. Jewel Tea Co.*, 381 U.S. 676 (1965), *United Mine Workers v. Pennington*, 381 U.S. 657 (1965), the courts found that unions have:

1. An implied labor exemption from antitrust laws to enter into contracts with multiemployer bargaining units
2. The right to advance legitimate employee goals that restrain trade no more than is necessary to achieve those goals.

Therefore, a collective bargaining agreement between a union and employers is exempt from antitrust challenges unless it violates certain criteria. For example, the court found in *Bradley* that a union and its employer could not combine to dominate a market to exclude outside competitors:

> We know that Congress feared the concentrated power of business organizations to dominate markets and prices. It intended to outlaw business monopolies. A business monopoly is no less such because a union participates, and such participation is a violation of the Act.

In *Jewel Tea*, the court found that the subject which allegedly violates antitrust legislation must be a mandatory subject of bargaining. The court stated, "Employers and unions are required to bargain about wages, hours and working conditions, and this fact weighs heavily in favor of antitrust exemption for agreements on these subjects." The court also maintained that the product of the collective bargaining agreement needed to be made through arm's-length bargaining. Ten years later, in *Connell Construction Co. v. Plumbers and Steam Fitters Local Union*, 421 U.S. 616 (1974), the court interpreted the goals of the exemption:

> The Court has recognized...that a proper accommodation between the congressional policy favoring collective bargaining under the NLRA and the free competition in the business markets requires that some union-employer agreements be accorded a limited non-statutory exemption from antitrust sanctions.

These judicial decisions concluded that a union-employer collective bargaining agreement does not constitute a conspiracy, combination, or concerted activity, and thus does not violate antitrust laws. In the sports industry, the nonstatutory labor exemption would become the owners' chief defense against antitrust challenges brought by players or their unions.

10.3.3. Early Uses of the Nonstatutory Labor Exemption: *Philadelphia*, *Mackey*, and *McCourt*

The issue of the labor exemption in the professional sports context was first addressed in *Philadelphia World Hockey Club, Inc. v. Philadelphia Hockey Club,*

Inc., 351 F.Supp. 462 (E.D. Pa. 1972). The World Hockey Association (WHA), a rival professional hockey league, challenged the NHL's "reserve system" using antitrust law, and argued that the league's monopoly over the available hockey player talent pool clearly handicapped the new league from getting top-quality players. The NHL used the labor exemption defense, claiming that the rule in question was part of the collective bargaining agreement between the NHL and the National Hockey League Players Association (NHLPA), and therefore, had been agreed to by the union. The district court found that the reserve clause that was the subject of the challenge had predated the first collective bargaining agreement, and therefore had not been the result of serious, intensive, arms-length bargaining. The court stated:

> Here there is no evidence that the NHLPA was a joint conspirator with the NHL in creating and retaining the reserve clause. The evidence establishes the NHLPA's persistent opposition to the present reserve system. The reserve clause was more than a sturdy teenager when the NHLPA was born.

It is important to recall the precedents set forth by the nonsport cases concerning the labor exemption. In the preceding case, the plaintiff was able to prove that the rule was not the result of arm's-length bargaining, and therefore, the labor exemption should not apply. The case went to trial on the merits, and after several decisions for the plaintiff, the case was settled with the merger of several WHA teams into the NHL.

The most significant case concerning antitrust laws and the applicability of the nonstatutory labor exemption in professional sports is *Mackey v. NFL*, 543 F.2d 606 (8th Cir. 1976). In this case, the plaintiff, a group of present and former professional football players, challenged the "Rozelle Rule," which required a team that signed a veteran free agent to compensate the player's former team with cash, a draft choice, or other players. The compensation award was determined by the commissioner. The plaintiff argued that the compensation system, if not agreed to by the teams, was a restraint on trade, because the threat of losing players, draft choices, and/or money deterred most teams from taking advantage of the system. Therefore, there existed a restriction on player movement, the "market" was restrained, and the result was lower player salaries. The NFL raised the labor exemption defense, claiming the system was a condition of the collective bargaining agreement that had been negotiated collectively by the league and the NFL Players Association, and therefore the league was exempt from antitrust challenges.

The court ruled against the NFL and offered the following analysis:

> Under the general principles surrounding the labor exemption, the availability of the non-statutory exemption for a particular agreement turns upon whether the relevant federal labor policy is deserving of preeminence over federal antitrust policy under the circumstances of the particular case. Although the cases giving rise to the non-statutory exemption are factually dissimilar from the present case, certain principles can be deduced from those decisions governing the proper accommodation of the competing labor and antitrust interests here.

The court in *Mackey* then looked at the three primary nonsport cases, *Jewel Tea*, *Bradley*, and *Pennington*, and proceeded to set up a three-pronged test to determine when a professional sports league could use the labor exemption against antitrust challenges.

1. The restraint on trade must primarily affect only the parties to the collective bargaining agreement

2. The issue must concern a mandatory subject of bargaining

3. The issue must have been achieved through arm's-length bargaining.

In *Mackey*, the plaintiffs were not able to establish all three elements. Concerning the third element, the court found that, even though the compensation system had indeed been bargained over and included in the 1970 collective bargaining agreement, it had not been accomplished through arm's-length bargaining. The court reasoned that the players association had had little bargaining power and was not in a position to negotiate it out of the agreement. The court determined that the league could not use the labor exemption. The court then looked at whether the Rozelle Rule did indeed have anticompetitive results, and whether it was in its least restrictive form. The court concluded:

> [We] agree with the district court's conclusion that the Rozelle Rule is significantly more restrictive than necessary to serve any legitimate purposes it might have in this regard. First, little concern was manifested at trial over the free movement of average or below average players. Only the movement of better players was urged as being detrimental to football. Yet, the Rozelle Rule applies to every NFL player regardless of his status or ability. Second, the Rozelle Rule is unlimited in duration. It operates as a perpetual restriction on a player's ability to sell his services in an open market throughout his career.

The appeals court affirmed the conclusions reached by the district court and remanded the case back to that court for further proceedings. The NFL avoided the trial by dismantling the Rozelle Rule and replacing it with the right of first refusal/ compensation system as outlined in a new collective bargaining agreement with the NFL Players Association (see note 2).

The "Mackey test," as it came to be known, became the marker against which other antitrust cases in professional sports would be compared. There was now a discernible test that could accurately determine whether the labor exemption could be used as a defense by professional sports leagues against antitrust challenges.

One of the first cases to apply the three-pronged test was *McCourt v. California Sports Inc.*, 600 F.2d 1193 (6th Cir. 1979). The plaintiff in this case challenged the reserve system used by the National Hockey League, which severely limited player mobility. It is important to recall that the WHA challenge against the NHL in 1972 had not been decided on the merits, so there had been no official court decision on whether the NHL's reserve system in fact violated Section 1 of the Sherman Act. In 1978, Dale McCourt, a member of the Los Angeles Kings, was awarded to the Detroit Red Wings as compensation for a Los Angeles signing of a free agent. McCourt immediately filed suit against the National Hockey League, claiming the league's free agent compensation system was in violation of federal antitrust laws. The court applied the three-pronged test to determine whether the defense was able to use the labor exemption. As in *Mackey*, the court found that the plaintiff met the first two requirements. However, the *McCourt* court differed in its interpretation of the final element: whether the issue had been a result of arm's-length bargaining. The court in *McCourt* found that the NHLPA's failed attempt to get the reserve system provision out of the agreement did not indicate that arm's-length bargaining had not occurred. The court reasoned that "what the trial court saw as a failure to negotiate was in fact simply the failure to succeed, after the most intensive negotiations, in keeping an unwanted provision out of the contract." Therefore, the labor exemption defense was available for the league to use.

The significance of the *Mackey* decision and the subsequent rulings is that provisions in a collective bargaining agreement that allow for player restraints (i.e., draft or free agent compensation) are protected by the nonstatutory labor exemption, as long as they meet the required three-pronged test as outlined in *Mackey*.

NOTES

1. The Mackey test was further tested in *Wood v. NBA*, 809 F.2d 954 (2nd Cir. 1987). In 1984, a rookie challenged the salary cap that had just been negotiated between the league and the NBA Players Association. The court ruled against the plaintiff because the salary cap had been negotiated in good faith between the two parties, and therefore the league was protected by the labor exemption, even though the plaintiff player and others similarly situated were not yet in the league or the union.

2. The right of first refusal/compensation system still exists in the NFL today. See Article XIX, Veteran Free Agency, §2. Restricted Free Agents in the NFL-NFLPA collective bargaining agreement, available at www.nflpa.org. The compensatory level of draft pick varies depending on the contract offer tendered to the restricted free agent, a player with more than three but fewer than four accrued seasons.

3. In *Zimmerman v. NFL*, 632 F.Supp. 398 (D.D.C. 1986), a potential NFL player brought suit against the league and challenged the supplemental draft system that had been instituted to allow NFL teams to draft former USFL players after the USFL had gone out of business. The plaintiff claimed the draft was in violation of federal antitrust laws because players were restricted from bargaining with more than one team and this restriction impeded their earning potential. The court applied the Mackey test and found that the draft had been a result of bona fide arm's-length negotiations between the NFL and the NFLPA. It further stated:

> It is not the Court's function in the context of the labor exemption to evaluate the relative bargaining process and strategy of the parties, to determine who secured the better deal or whether there was adequate consideration exchanged.

10.3.4. Exemption after Expiration of Collective Bargaining Agreement: *Bridgeman* and *Powell*

After *Mackey*, the important question in this area of the law became: Does the nonstatutory labor exemption continue beyond the expiration of a collective bargaining agreement, and if so, for how long?

The first case that challenged the courts to make a decision on this matter was *Bridgeman v. NBA*, 675 F.Supp. 960 (D.N.J. 1987). This case was a class action suit filed by NBA players in 1983 that challenged the continued imposition by the NBA of the salary cap, college draft, and right of first refusal, after the collective bargaining agreement between the NBA and the National Basketball Players Association had expired in 1982. The plaintiffs claimed that the labor exemption was void because the collective bargaining agreement had expired, and therefore the restrictive measures that were protected before were now in violation of antitrust laws as covered under the Sherman Act.

The *Bridgeman* court was forced to decide whether the NBA maintained its labor exemption after the collective bargaining agreement between itself and the players association had expired. The court came to three conclusions:

1. It rejected the players' assertion that the labor exemption ended immediately after the agreement expired.
2. It stated that the labor exemption was not indefinite after a collective bargaining agreement expired.
3. The labor exemption was still applicable even after impasse had been reached, but not indefinitely.

The *Bridgeman* court had not answered an important question: When, exactly, did the labor exemption end, if it could not be used indefinitely? The ambiguous nature of the *Bridgeman* decision, which allowed the NBA to continue using the labor exemption as a defense against antitrust challenges, ensured that the question would be raised again.

The question was raised again in *Powell v. NFL*, 678 F.Supp. 777 (D. Minn. 1988). Following the expiration of the collective bargaining agreement in August 1987, the NFL Players Association unsuccessfully attempted to strike. After the aborted strike, a group of NFL players filed a class action suit against the NFL that challenged the right of first refusal/compensation system on the fact that the system was in violation of Section 1 of the Sherman Act because it restrained player movement. The NFL moved for summary judgment based on the labor exemption. The players association argued that the exemption was no longer applicable because the collective bargaining agreement had expired and impasse had been reached. The court agreed with the NFL's assertion that the labor exemption should be maintained for some period of time after the agreement had expired because the terms and conditions of that agreement would still be in effect. However, the court concluded that the impasse would mark the point at which the labor exemption ceased to exist, and therefore the trial could move forward based on the merits.

The appeals court reversed the district court's ruling in a 2–1 decision in *Powell v. NFL*, 930 F.2d 1293 (8th Cir. 1989). The court felt the exemption should continue even after impasse had been reached. Said the appeals court: "We believe, however, that the non-statutory labor exemption protects agreements conceived in an ongoing collective bargaining relationship from challenges under the anti-trust laws." In essence, the court stated that as long as the conditions imposed by the league resulted from good faith bargaining during the collective bargaining process, the exemption continued after expiration of the collective bargaining agreement and after impasse. This decision is important because as long as the NFL and the NFLPA maintained a continuing bargaining relationship, and as long as the NFL maintained the status quo, the contract provisions in the agreement were exempt from antitrust litigation, regardless of the fact the collective bargaining agreement had expired.

In dissenting, Judge Lay stated that the only alternative now available to unions would be decertification. He stated:

> The only labor policy of which I am aware that is accommodated by exempting the laws protective of free competition is bona fide collective bargaining. Yet this court's unprecedented decision leads to the ineluctable result of union decertification in order to invoke rights to which the players are clearly entitled under the antitrust

laws. The plain and simple truth of the matter is that the union should not be compelled, short of self-destruction, to accept illegal restraints it deems undesirable. Union decertification is hardly a worthy goal to pursue in balancing labor policy with the antitrust laws.

10.3.5. Exemption after Decertification: *McNeil*

As a result of the *Powell* decision, NFL players voted to decertify the NFLPA as their bargaining representative in order to allow individual players to challenge the NFL's restrictive practices using antitrust theory. After decertification, there would be no bargaining relationship between the players and the NFL, which meant that the league would not be able to use the labor exemption as a defense. Without the labor exemption, the case could then go to trial on the merits.

A new lawsuit, brought forward by a group of players, challenged the NFL's "Plan B" free agency under the antitrust laws. The league had altered its right of first refusal/compensation system prior to the lawsuit in hopes that it would be able to prove, under the rule of reason analysis, that the right of first refusal/compensation system was a necessity for the survival of the league, and was in its least restrictive form. Plan B free agency allowed unrestricted free agency status to any player who was not protected by his team. Each team was permitted to protect 36 players; those 36 players would be subject to the right of first refusal/compensation system.

In *McNeil v. NFL*, 790 F.Supp. 871 (D. Minn. 1992), New York Jets running back Freeman McNeil and other NFL players argued that Plan B free agency restrained players' ability to offer their services on the open market because the compensation deterred other teams from pursuing restricted free agents. The players argued that this violated Section 1 of the Sherman Act. The court rejected the NFL's request for summary judgment based on the labor exemption, and allowed the case to go to trial on the merits. In the trial, the court reasoned that because the players were not represented by a union, no bargaining relationship existed between the players and the league, and thus the first prong of the Mackey test could not be met. The players successfully argued that Plan B was an unreasonable restraint on trade, and was not in its least restrictive form.

Immediately after the *McNeil* decision, Keith Jackson and nine other NFL players filed a lawsuit against the NFL and sought an injunction from the court to make the 10 players unrestricted free agents. In *Jackson v. NFL*, 802 F.Supp. 226 (D.Minn. 1992), the plaintiffs used the doctrine of collateral estoppel to demonstrate a likelihood of success on the merits. The doctrine of collateral estoppel is appropriate where

1. The issue is identical to one raised in a prior adjudication.
2. There is a final judgment on the merits.
3. The estopped party was a party or in privity with a party to the prior adjudication.
4. The estopped party was given a full and fair opportunity to be heard on the adjudicated issue.

The court determined that, based on the *McNeil* decision, the outcome was likely to be the same, and therefore the injunction should be granted. The court ordered:

> All defendants are temporarily enjoined, for a period of five days from the date of this order, from enforcing the Right of First Refusal/Compensation Rules of Plan B against plaintiffs Keith Jackson, Webster Slaughter, D. J. Dozier, and Garin Veris.

Following the *McNeil* and *Jackson* decision, a class action suit was filed against the NFL on behalf of current or former NFL players (*White v. NFL*, 836 F. Supp. 1458 (D. Minn. 1993)).

> All players who have been, and are now or will be under contract to play professional football for an NFL club at any time from August 31, 1987, to the date of final judgment in this action and the determination of any appeal therefrom, have been, are now, or will be eligible to play football as a rookie for an NFL team.

With these court victories, the players and the owners reached a tentative agreement on January 6, 1993, which came to be referred to as the *White* settlement. The players immediately recertified the NFLPA as their official bargaining representative, and incorporated the *White* settlement into a new collective bargaining agreement (1993–2000, extended in 1998, 2001, and again in 2006 through 2012) that gave NFL players a system of free agency in exchange for a salary cap.

10.3.6. Nonstatutory Labor Exemption after *White*: *Brown*

Even though it appeared clear that the labor exemption defense would be upheld in a court of law when a collective bargaining agreement existed between the league and the players association, individual players continued to challenge leagues using antitrust theory. In *Brown v. Pro Football, Inc,* 782 F.Supp. 125 (D.D.C. 1991), the plaintiffs, NFL developmental squad members, filed a class action suit against the NFL, challenging the league's restriction on their earnings. The players argued that during the period when the NFL Players Association had decertified, the league had instituted a new rule that placed a cap on the earnings of practice squad members. When NFL players recertified the players association after the *White* settlement, the new rule was made a part of the collective bargaining agreement. The practice squad players argued that the rule had not been the result of negotiations, and thus it had not been reached through arm's-length bargaining, the third prong of the Mackey test. Thus, the players argued, the labor exemption should not apply and the case against the NFL should move forward on the merits.

The district court in *Brown* concluded:

1. The labor exemption should end immediately after the expiration of a collective bargaining agreement.
2. The standard set in *Powell* hindered, rather than facilitated, the execution of a collective bargaining agreement.
3. If an exemption were to apply after expiration, it should end at impasse.
4. If the challenged restraint had not been part of the expired agreement, the exemption could not apply.

The fourth conclusion of the court meant that the case could move forward on the merits because the new rule had not been part of the old collective bargaining agreement. However, the district court's decision was overturned by the D.C. Circuit Court of Appeals in *Brown v. Pro Football Inc.*, 50 F.3d 1041 (D.D.C. 1995).

In a 2–1 decision, the court found that unionized employees do not have the right to challenge their employer under antitrust laws. The court remarked that "injecting the Sherman Act into the collective bargaining process would disrupt the balance by giving unions a powerful new weapon, one not contemplated by the federal labor laws." Therefore, the appeals court concluded that the labor exemption was applicable regardless of whether a collective bargaining agreement was in place, whether it had expired, or whether impasse had been reached, and passed.

The U.S. Supreme Court reviewed the decisions of the district and appeals courts in *Brown v. Pro Football Inc.*, 518 U.S. 231 (1996) and issued a definitive answer on the topic. The Court found that the labor exemption was applicable even though the restrictive actions were not included in the collective bargaining agreement. The Supreme Court laid out a new four-pronged test for antitrust immunity, requiring that the challenged conduct:

1. Took place during and immediately after a collective bargaining negotiation
2. Grew out of, and was directly related to, the lawful operation of the bargaining process
3. Involved a matter that the parties were required to negotiate collectively
4. Concerned only the parties to the collective bargaining relationship.

The decision by the Supreme Court is vague enough to invite further legal challenges surrounding the labor exemption issue. However, the decertification route appears to be the most viable option for players associations that want to challenge league rules or policies that restrict trade and violate the Sherman Act, after the expiration of a collective bargaining agreement. In the 1998–1999 NBA lockout, several players voiced the opinion that the players should decertify the National Basketball Players Association and challenge the league on antitrust grounds. This can be an effective strategy, because leagues are fearful of having a court decide that their draft, salary cap, or free agency is too restrictive and violates the Sherman Act. However, it can also have negative consequences for players, because without a union, the league can decide to unilaterally implement new rules without having to bargain over them. The NBPA ultimately decided not to decertify.

The NFLPA and the NFL went to the extraordinary step of including a provision in their agreement that deals specifically with the nonstatutory labor exemption.

10.3.7. The Nonstatutory Labor Exemption in *Clarett*

In September 2003, former Ohio State running back Maurice Clarett sued the NFL for not allowing him to enter the NFL draft after what would have been his sophomore season had he not been suspended by the NCAA for the entire season. The NFL's bylaws require that a player must be three years removed from his high school graduation to be eligible for the NFL draft.

Clarett argued that the NFL's eligibility rule constituted a "group boycott" and unreasonably restrained trade in violation of Section 1 of the Sherman Antitrust Act. The NFL countered that the rule was protected under the nonstatutory labor exemption because it was the result of arm's-length bargaining between the NFL and the NFLPA, even though the issue is never actually addressed in the collective bargaining agreement.

The Southern District of New York ruled in favor of Clarett, ordering that the NFL accept Clarett into the 2004 NFL draft (see *Clarett v. NFL*, 306 F.Supp.2d

379 (S.D. N.Y. 2004). The judge ruled that the rule was not a mandatory subject of collective bargaining, that the nonstatutory labor exemption could not apply to someone who was not a member of the bargaining unit, and that the rule was not the result of arm's-length negotiations. The court rejected the NFL's procompetitive justifications, stating that there were less restrictive alternatives to the rule. The NFL contended that the rule (1) protected younger and less experienced players from risk of injury; (2) protected the NFL's entertainment product from the adverse consequences associated with such injuries; (3) protected the NFL clubs from the costs of such injuries; and (4) protected from injury that would result from younger athletes overtraining or using steroids in hopes of reaching the NFL earlier. The judge noted that Clarett, at six feet tall and 230 pounds, was larger than some who are considered to be the best running backs in NFL history—including Walter Payton, Barry Sanders, and Emmitt Smith—and therefore capable of playing in the NFL.

The NFL's motion for a stay was denied in February 2004, when the court rejected the NFL's claim that they would suffer irreparable harm by allowing Clarett and anyone else formerly ineligible to enter the draft, now less than three months away, see *Clarett v. NFL*, 306 F Supp.2d 411 (S.D.N.Y. 2004). The court cited that the harm done to players such as Clarett would be far worse than any minor organizational or financial burden suffered by the league and teams.

The United States Court of Appeals for the Second Circuit reversed the ruling, preventing Clarett from entering the draft and upholding the NFL's eligibility requirements for their necessary procompetitive effects, see *Clarett v. NFL* 369 F.3d 124 (2nd Cir. 2004). The Court of Appeals stated the eligibility rule was in fact protected by the nonstatutory labor exemption, thus barring Clarett from the 2004 NFL draft. In addition, even though the NFL and NFLPA had never bargained over the rule, it was not excluded from the scope of the nonstatutory exemption because similar eligibility rules and the powers of the commissioner relating to such rules were collectively bargained for.

10.3.8. Single-Entity Defense by the Big Four

The single-entity defense is relevant in two areas of professional sports: traditional leagues using the defense against specific antitrust challenges and new leagues structuring themselves as a single entity so as to avoid antitrust challenges. The single-entity defense, which was used as early as the 1970s, defends against Section 1 challenges because it attacks the first element needed to prove a violation: a plurality of actors. It strikes at the heart of this element: a single entity is incapable of contract, combination, or conspiracy. If there is no contract, combination, or conspiracy, then there can be no Section 1 violation.

Traditional leagues have used the defense in an attempt to block challenges against restrictive league rules, such as the college draft, salary cap, and restrictions on free agency. These leagues, specifically the NFL, NHL, and NBA, have all argued in different lawsuits that they are structured as single entities because they share broadcast revenue and licensing revenue, they advertise collectively, and all the teams in the leagues fall under a single administrative body (Commissioner's Office). Overall, this argument has not proven to be successful.

The NFL has used the single-entity defense more than any other professional sports league. It first used the single-entity defense against the North American Soccer League when the soccer league sued the NFL for violating Section 1 of the Sherman Act because of the NFL's rules concerning cross-ownership of a franchise. In *NASL v. NFL*, 670 F.2d 1249 (2nd Cir. 1982), the NASL argued that the rule was a group boycott, subject to per se analysis, and that the soccer league had been unjustly injured by the cross-ownership rule because it unreasonably restricted the pool of experienced capital investors (for more on this case, see Section 10.2.3.2, "*NASL v. NFL*").

In the Second Circuit, the court rejected the NFL's use of the single-entity defense. The court concluded that the teams comprising the NFL were separate economic entities working together in a "joint venture" rather than as a single entity. The court explained:

> Although NFL members thus participate jointly in many of the operations conducted by it on their behalf, each member is a separately owned, discrete entity which does not share its expenses, capital expenditures or profits with other members. Each also derives separate revenues from certain lesser sources, which are not shared with other members, including revenues from local TV and radio, parking and concessions.

The court concluded that, although cooperation existed, there was no evidence to suggest that the NFL was a single corporation.

The NFL raised the single-entity defense again in *Los Angeles Memorial Coliseum Commission v. NFL*, 726 F.2d 1381 (9th Cir.) *cert. denied*, 469 U.S. 990 (1984). Both the district court and the Second Circuit rejected the defense. The Second Circuit stated that what the NFL sought was blanket protection from the antitrust laws even though it had been found guilty of breaking antitrust laws on previous occasions: *Mackey*, *Kapp*, *NASL*, and *Smith*. The court also looked at the way in which profits and losses were distributed in the league, and found that each individual team was responsible for its own losses, and alone reaped the rewards of profit. In addition, the court noted that each team in the NFL had an individual identity. Concerning this issue, the court stated:

> These attributes operate to make each team an entity in large part distinct from the NFL. It is true that cooperation is necessary to produce a football game. However, as the district court concluded, this does not mean that "each club can produce football games only as an NFL member." This is especially evident in light of the emergence of the United States Football League.

As in *NASL v. NFL*, the court found that the NFL was composed of a plurality of actors instead of one single actor and, therefore, rejected the single entity defense. The NFL had initiated the single-entity defense on each occasion it was challenged with an antitrust lawsuit, and in each circumstance the defense was denied by the courts. Based on the court determinations of the 1970s and 1980s, the single-entity defense has generally not been a viable one for traditionally structured leagues like the NFL, NBA, and NHL when it came to issues such as competing leagues and league rules, such as the college draft, salary cap, and restrictions on free agency (MLB was protected by the "baseball exemption," discussed earlier, and did not fear antitrust suits by opposing leagues). However, in *American Needle v. NFL*, 538 F.3d 736 (7th Cir. 2008), the courts ruled that the NFL was a singleentity for purposes of licensing. American Needle designed, manufactured, and sold products incorporating names and logos of various professional athletic teams and leagues, including those in the NFL. When the NFL refused to renew American Needle's license, opting instead for an exclusive relationship with Reebok, American Needle sued, claiming the arrangement violated §1 of the Sherman Act. The 7th Circuit affirmed the NFL's motion for summary judgment, finding that since the creation of NFL Properties in 1963, NFL teams have served as a single entity in licensing their intellectual property.

The Supreme Court unanimously reversed the 7th Circuit's decision (560 U.S. (2010)), holding that the NFL's licensing activities constituted concerted action that is not categorically beyond the coverage of Section 1. The court remanded the case back to the district court to examine the relationship and decisions of the NFL teams and NFL Properties under the rule of reason. While the court noted that NFL clubs "depend upon a degree of cooperation for economic survival," the necessity of cooperation does not transform concerted action into the independent action of a single-entity. Furthermore, that "even if league-wide agreements are necessary to produce football, it does not follow that concerted activity in marketing intellectual property is necessary to produce football." The court found that NFL Properties was merely an "instrumentality" of the teams and that competitors cannot avoid antitrust liability by acting through a third-party intermediary or joint venture.

The court stressed that NFL teams do in fact compete in the market for intellectual property, not just on the playing field. When licensing its intellectual property, the court stated, "teams are acting as separate economic actors pursuing separate economic interests and each team therefore is a potential independent center of decision making." If on remand the district court finds that the NFL Properties structure and agreement with Reebok does not unreasonably restrain trade, then the existing mechanisms by which leagues license their intellectual property through a combined entity such as NFL Properties will remain intact and business will be relatively unchanged. However, if the district court rules that the agreement with Reebok is an unreasonable restraint of trade, the permissible use of joint licensing entities could be in doubt and at a minimum, they would probably be prohibited from agreeing to lucrative exclusive licensing arrangements.

Another significant issue regarding the single-entity defense concerns broadcasting rights. For a further discussion of these issues, see Chapter 14, "Broadcasting and Multimedia."

10.3.9. Single-Entity Leagues: *Fraser v. MLS*

The most recent case to involve the single-entity defense was *Fraser v. MLS*, 97 F.Supp.2d 130 (D. Mass. 2000), *Aff'd by*, 284 F.3d 47 (1st Cir. 2002). MLS soccer players decided to bypass the unionization process so that they could challenge the league's restrictive player restraints using antitrust theory. Had the players unionized first, the league would have been protected by the labor exemption. The players argued that the system MLS employs to restrain player mobility violated the antitrust laws because player salaries are unilaterally determined by a single person, Deputy Commissioner Sunil Gulati. In addition, the MLS enforces a salary cap, the rules of which are known only to MLS and kept secret from the players.

Furthermore, MLS, U.S. Soccer, and the world governing body, FIFA, inserted a system of "transfer fees" into the standard player contract that can prevent MLS players from signing with teams in other countries, even after their MLS contracts have expired. The players argued that the standard player agreement denies players a fair share of group licensing rights while containing a reserve clause, struck down in other sports, giving teams unilateral rights to renew their players' contracts.

The players made two claims of a Section 1 violation of the Sherman Act: first, that because players are forced to contract their player services directly with the MLS rather than member teams, the MLS had unlawfully combined to restrain trade. Their second Section 1 claim was that the transfer fees had the effect of restricting player movement and harming competition for player services throughout the world. The players also made a Section 2 claim: that the MLS was illegally exercising monopoly power.

MLS argued that it was a single entity, and was therefore exempt from Section 1 challenges because it was not acting in combination, concert, or conspiracy with anyone. In contrast to previous cases such as *NASL* and *Smith*, MLS was able to cite more specific evidence that it was indeed a single entity. For example:

1. Profits and losses are shared in a manner similar to a corporation rather than like a traditional sports league.

2. All players are employees of MLS, rather than employees of the individual teams. Players receive paychecks from the league rather than from individual teams.

3. MLS has the right to assign marquee players to certain teams. While teams may make some transactions (e.g., trades), MLS must approve all such transactions.

4. Individual teams do not own the right to their logos.

The players argued that the MLS structure was merely a "sham," concocted by owners in order to avoid antitrust scrutiny. Nevertheless, the district court was compelled by MLS's argument, and ruled in 2000 that MLS is indeed a single entity incapable of conspiracy. This did not vindicate MLS on all counts. For example, the issue of transfer fees was later settled by a jury, although again in favor of MLS (see note 2). The plaintiffs quickly appealed the district court's decisions. In 2002, the 1st U.S. Circuit Court of Appeals affirmed the district court's verdict, agreeing that players failed to show that MLS is not a single entity, in that the league not only owns the teams themselves, but also all intellectual property related to the teams. The court also found that the players failed to prove that the United States was the relevant geographic market and that the relevant product market was limited to Division I professional players.

Even though the district court's single-entity opinion on *Fraser* was affirmed, the case represents somewhat of a panacea for start-up leagues. Even before the *Fraser* decision in 2002, three prominent leagues were created on the MLS model (see note 4). The *Fraser* decision is significant because it implies that leagues structured like MLS are exempt from Sherman Act Section 1 antitrust claims. An appeal to the United States Supreme Court was denied, 537 U.S. 885 (2002).

NOTES

1. For a more detailed analysis of the use of the single-entity defense in professional sports, particularly as it relates to the *American Needle* decision see Michael A. McCann, "American Needle v. NFL: An Opportunity to Reshape American Sports Law," 119 *Yale Law Journal* 726 (2010) and Gabriel Feldman, "The Puzzling Persistence of the Single-Entity Argument for Sports Leagues: American Needle and the Supreme Court's Opportunity to Reject a Flawed Defense," 2009 *Wisconsin Law Review* 835 (2009).

2. For a more detailed analysis of the Fraser case, see Glenn Wong and John Shukie, "All for One: MLS Players Fail To Take Down the League's Single Entity Structure," 28, no. 8 *Athletic Business* 18 (August 2000) and "MLS Scores against Its Players: Fraser v. Major League Soccer, LLC," 1 *DePaul Journal of Sports Law and Contemporary Problems* 76 (Spring 2003).

3. The district court in *Fraser* rejected the plaintiff's claim that transfer fees were illegal on a per se basis. A federal jury in Boston then rejected the claim that MLS and FIFA (Fédération Internationale de Football Association) conspired to impose the fees. However, if MLS ever enforces transfer fees (it has never done so to date), those fees could be susceptible to rule of reason scrutiny. The topic of transfer fees is discussed further in section 10.4, "Antitrust Law and International Soccer: *Bosman*."

4. The district court in *Fraser* also rejected the plaintiff's Section 2 monopolization claim. At the time of MLS's inception in 1996, there was no "Division I" professional soccer in the United States. Therefore, the creation of MLS expanded earning opportunities for players rather than restricting them. Judge George A. O'Toole rejected notions that either consumers were harmed or MLS had behaved as a monopoly, stating: "There was no substantial basis in the evidence for concluding that MLS, if it was a monopsonist, behaved in the way monopsonists do when they abuse their market power" (see *Fraser*).

5. Leagues that have used the single-entity structure included NASL (created 1968, folded 1984), American Professional Soccer League (1990–1996), Continental Indoor Soccer League (1993–1997), National Professional Soccer League (1984–2001), U.S. Interregional Soccer League (1986–1999), Major Indoor Lacrosse League (1986–present), Roller Hockey International Hockey League (1993–1997), World League of American Football (1990–1992), American Basketball League (1996–1998), Major League Soccer (1994–present), Women's National Basketball Association (1996–present), Women's United Soccer Association (2000–2003), and the XFL (2001).

6. Interestingly, in 2007 the Women's United Soccer Association and related entities announced a plan to launch a new women's professional soccer league not as a single-entity but instead with individual team owners. For more on this plan see Marc Edelman and Elizabeth Masterson, "Could the New Women's Professional Soccer League Survive in America? How Adopting a Traditional Legal Structure May Save More than Just a Game," 19 *Seton Hall Journal of Sports and Entertainment Law* 283 (2009).

7. The Supreme Court rejected the claim that joint ventures are protected against antitrust challenges in *United States v. General Motors Corp.*, 121 F.2d 376 (7th Cir.), *cert. denied*, 314 U.S. 618 (1941).

8. In addition to *American Needle*, the NFL attempted to use the single-entity defense in *McNeil* and *Sullivan*. In both cases, the defense was rejected.

9. In the broadcasting arena, professional sports leagues are protected from antitrust challenges under the Sports Broadcast Act of 1961, which states:

> The antitrust laws...shall not apply to any joint agreement by or among persons engaged in conducting the organized professional team sports of football, baseball, basketball or hockey, by which any league of clubs participating in professional football, baseball, basketball or hockey contests sells or otherwise transfers all or any part of the rights of such league's member clubs in the sponsored telecasting of the games of football, baseball, basketball or hockey, as the case may be, engaged in or conducted by such clubs.

10.4. ANTITRUST LAW AND INTERNATIONAL SOCCER: *BOSMAN*

Antitrust laws in Europe are very similar to those in the United States: Article 81 of the European Community Treaty resembles Section 1 of the Sherman Act in that it prohibits "concerted practices" that have the effect of restraining trade. In addition, Article 82 of the EC Treaty outlaws the acquisition and maintenance of monopoly power, similar to Article 2 of the Sherman Act. These laws are monitored by the European Union's Competition Commission.

This chapter's discussion of *Fraser v. Major League Soccer* in the previous paragraphs mentioned "transfer fees." Transfer fees are monies that can be demanded by a player's former team *after* expiration of that player's contract, in the event that the player signs with a different team. The rationale behind transfer fees is that the new team should compensate the old team for the player's training and development.

However, as seen in the NFL during the Rozelle Rule and right of first refusal/compensation system, threats of compensation can effectively deter new teams from courting free agent players in the first place. However, the difference between transfer fees and systems such as the Rozelle Rule is that transfer fees affect players wishing to move from one country to another. In other words, a soccer player could fulfill his contract in Spain, and then be unable to play soccer in Brazil if the Brazilian team was unwilling to pay a transfer fee.

FIFA, the international governing association for soccer, created this rule. Moreover, FIFA rules are incorporated into the standard player contracts or league documents of various soccer leagues worldwide—including MLS.

Jean-Marc Bosman was a Belgian national who played for RC Lie'ge, a Belgian Division I soccer team. His five-year contract was due to expire at the end of June 1990. RC Lie'ge made him an offer to extend his contract for one year, at one-quarter of his current salary. Bosman refused those terms, and then negotiated a contract with a French team. The French team then negotiated a transfer fee with RC Lie'ge "for a one year temporary transfer, and adjusted upward if the French club decided to make the transfer permanent" (see note 3). RC Lie'ge, concerned about the French club's financial position, voided the deal, leaving Bosman unemployed at the start of the 1990–1991 season. Bosman sued RC Lie'ge in a Belgian court, arguing that the transfer fee rule violated Article 48 of the Treaty of Rome, which governs the free movement of workers (see note 3).

This case, *Union Royale Belge des Sociétés de Football Association ASBL v. Bosman*, eventually reached the European Court of Justice (ECJ). In 1995, the ECJ ruling had two effects on European soccer (see notes 2 and 3). First, the ruling eliminated the "non-nationals" rule, which had limited the number of foreign players that could be employed in a UEFA (Union of European Football Associations) soccer match. These rules have had the effect of forcing some of the better U.S. players to play in the MLS as opposed to Europe. More important, the ECJ held that the application of transfer fees was a violation of European law. Hence, if a player completes his contract with a team of one nation, he is free to sign with the team of another nation. European teams grudgingly accepted the *Bosman* decision after the European Commission threatened fines for noncompliance. The teams claimed that the non-nationals rule and transfer fees were both essential to maintain the integrity of soccer, very much as Major League Baseball claimed that the reserve clause was essential to baseball in *Flood* and other cases.

The *Bosman* ruling is significant to sports law in the United States because of the growth of soccer in the United States. While the court that ruled in *Bosman* has no jurisdiction in the United States, appellate court judges are likely to look at the reasoning presented by the European Court of Justice. So far, MLS has not imposed transfer fees, although it has sold players to other teams during the term of the players' contracts. Nevertheless, it is important to point out that the scope of the ECJ decision was limited to transfer fees involving two different teams in the European Union.

In 2009, the Spanish soccer club Real Madrid set a record when it paid 93 million euros (about $131 million at the time) to obtain foward Cristiano Ronaldo from Manchester United. In recent years, high-profile European soccer leagues such as the Premiership, have expressed that escalating transfer fees were causing significant financial harm to its clubs, in much the same way that the Big Four long argued that free agency would lead to their financial ruin.

NOTES

1. In December 2009, British cyclist Bradley Wiggins left his American-based team Garmin-Slipstream for new British team, Team Sky despite being under contract with Garmin. Wiggins finished fourth in the Tour de France only months earlier. Garmin considered legal action but ultimately settled the issue in part because of they did not anticipate a favorable outcome due to the *Bosman* ruling.

2. For more on the implications of *Bosman* in European soccer, see Thomas M. Schiera, Balancing Act: Will the European Commission Allow European Football To Reestablish the Competitive Balance That It Helped Destroy?" 32 *Brooklyn Journal of International Law* 709 (2007); Stratis Camatsos, "European Sports, the Transfer System and Competition Law: Will They Ever Find a Competitive Balance?" 12 *Sports Lawyers Journal* 155 (Spring 2005); Patrick Closson, "Penalty Shot: The European Union's Application of Competition Law to the *Bosman* Ruling," 21 *Boston College International and Comparative Law Review* 167 (Winter 1998); and Rachel B. Arnedt, "European Union Law and Football Nationality Restrictions," 12 *Emory International Law Review* 109 (Spring 1998).

3. In September 1998, the television network BSkyB purchased the British soccer team Manchester United for approximately $1 billion. However, in 1999 the British government's Monopolies and Mergers Commission voided the sale on antitrust grounds. Because BSkyB owned exclusive rights to televise Premiere League games live, the government contended that the media company would thwart competition and harm the quality of British soccer. BSkyB is a subsidiary of News Corporation, which owns the Fox Entertainment Group in the United States.

4. The *Bosman* ruling outlawed intra-Europe transfer fees *after* the expiration of a player's contract. However, it is important to emphasize that transfer fees may still be invoked *while* a player is under contract. In other words, player contracts can be sold from one team to another for cash.

10.5. ANTITRUST LAW AND THE NATIONAL COLLEGIATE ATHLETIC ASSOCIATION (NCAA)

In the past, amateur athletic organizations have not been subject to the type of antitrust litigation faced by the professional sports industry. However, with the increased prominence of amateur athletics and the money now involved, organizations such as the NCAA are increasingly subject to antitrust litigation. While the NCAA is not the only amateur organization that has faced antitrust challenges, this section will focus mostly on the NCAA and its member conferences, institutions, coaches, and athletes.

Historically, defendant college athletic organizations have been successful in arguing that the antitrust laws were not applicable to them because college athletics are not "trade" or "commerce" as defined by the Sherman Act. College organizations have traditionally argued that since their athletic associations are nonprofit organizations, their primary purpose is educational and noncommercial in nature, and hence cannot be defined as trade or commerce. However, beginning in the early 1970s, successful suits were filed against college athletic organizations other than the NCAA, and it was found that these organizations were indeed involved in trade and commerce. By 1984, the Supreme Court would determine that even the NCAA was involved in trade and commerce.

10.5.1. Decisions before *Board of Regents* (1984)

In 1972, the federal antitrust laws were first applied to amateur athletics in *Amateur Softball Ass'n. v. United States*, 467 F.2d 312 (10th Cir. 1972). In this case, the governing organization for softball in the United States was deemed not to be exempt from antitrust laws. The court reasoned that even though the primary purpose of the association was noncommercial, subsequent actions or operations of an amateur athletic association could trigger application of the Sherman Act. A similar result occurred in *Tondas v. Amateur Hockey Ass'n. of the United States*, 438 F.Supp. 310 (W.D.N.Y. 1977). The court held in this case that the amateur hockey association had significant market and economic power to trigger possible antitrust applications.

The NCAA faced several antitrust challenges in the late 1970s and early 1980s. In *College Athletic Placement Services, Inc. v. NCAA*, No. 74–1144, 1974 U.S. Dist. LEXIS 7050 (D. N.J. Aug. 22, 1974), the court found no violations of the Sherman Act for an amendment by the NCAA to its constitution that would render students who obtained information from services such as the plaintiff's ineligible for intercollegiate competition. The court applied the rule of reason test and found that the NCAA amendment was neither anticompetitive nor intended to damage the plaintiff. Instead, the amendment was consistent with the NCAA objective of preserving amateurism in sports.

In *Hennessey v. NCAA*, 564 F.2d 1136 (5th Cir. 1977), the district court found that NCAA Bylaw 12-1, which put a limitation on a school coaching staff, had sufficient impact on interstate commerce (it curtailed the interstate flow of assistant coaching services) to fall within the Sherman Act. The court, however, ruled that the bylaw's fundamental objective was to preserve and foster competition in intercollegiate athletics, and that it was thus permissible under the rule of reason and was not a violation of the Sherman Act.

In *English v. NCAA*, 439 So. 2d 1218 (La. Ct. App. 1983), a college football player, after transferring twice from a four-year college to a two-year college, was declared ineligible for another season of competition because of an NCAA transfer rule. The plaintiff's challenge to the NCAA transfer rule was based on Louisiana antitrust laws. The court held that Louisiana antitrust laws were inapplicable to the NCAA, because the NCAA is engaged in interstate commerce and therefore subject only to federal antitrust law. The court also ruled, however, that if the Louisiana antitrust laws were applicable to the NCAA, the court would still rule for the defendant, because the NCAA rules were reasonable and not a violation of the state antitrust laws.

In *Association for Intercollegiate Athletics for Women v. NCAA*, 558 F.Supp. 487 (D.D.C. 1983), *Aff'd by*, 735 F.2d 577 (D.C. Cir. 1984), the courts held that the NCAA's dominance of the amateur sports television market does not by itself create a monopolistic practice against a rival association, since no illegal tying arrangement existed.

10.5.2. The NCAA's Reduced Power over Television: *NCAA v. Board of Regents*

While the NCAA was successful in defending antitrust cases between 1972 and 1984, it was successfully challenged in *NCAA v. Board of Regents*, 468 U.S. 85 (1984). The NCAA operated a college football television plan that limited the number of televised Division I college football games. The University of

Oklahoma and the University of Georgia were members of the College Football Association, which negotiated an independent television contract allowing for a larger number of appearances on television. When the NCAA announced that it would take disciplinary action in response to this independent contract, the University of Oklahoma and the University of Georgia filed suit, claiming that (1) by fixing the price of broadcasts and threatening to boycott potential advertisers, the NCAA had violated Section 1 of the Sherman Act; and (2) by monopolizing the market of televised college football, the NCAA had violated Section 2 of the Sherman Act.

The district court ruled against the NCAA on both Section 1 and Section 2 counts, going so far as to call the NCAA a "classic cartel." The 10th Circuit Court of Appeals later rejected the plaintiff's Section 2 claim, but upheld the Section 1 claim on a per se basis. Finally, the Supreme Court affirmed the decision of the appellate court in a 7–2 decision, holding that the NCAA television plan violated antitrust laws through an unreasonable restraint on trade and also illegal price fixing. While dissenting Justice White argued that the NCAA's television policy was reasonable because it "foster[ed] the goal of amateurism by spreading revenues among various schools," the majority of justices felt that the harm to the consumer (fewer televised games) outweighed the benefits gained by the NCAA (see note 3 in next section).

This decision was important for three reasons: (1) it was the first successful challenge of the NCAA based on antitrust theory; (2) it had a significant impact on the NCAA and intercollegiate athletic departments by reducing television revenues for most institutions; and (3) the U.S. Supreme Court rendered the decision, and thus it has served as a precedent for future cases.

The precedent set by the Supreme Court has prompted other judges to consider the NCAA differently, depending on whether it acts as a regulator of amateur athletic competition (scholarship limits, grade eligibility) or as a regulator of commerce (televised game limits, limiting coaches' salaries). While the former behavior is generally allowed by the courts, the latter may be punishable under antitrust laws. For more on antitrust issues in broadcasting of college athletics, see section 14.2.4.1. "Antitrust Issues in Broadcasting for Colleges."

10.5.3. Coaches' Salaries: *Law v. NCAA*

A crucial round of antitrust litigation against the NCAA occurred in the class action suit *Law v. NCAA*, 134 F.3d 1010 (10th Cir. 1998). Effective in August 1992, NCAA Bylaw 11.02.3 limited the earnings of certain Division I assistant coaches to $16,000. The plaintiffs, known as "restricted-earnings" coaches (REC), challenged the NCAA rule as a violation of Section 1 of the Sherman Act. The district court granted summary judgment in favor of the coaches and issued a permanent injunction restraining the NCAA from initiating any restrictions on coaches' earnings. The 10th Circuit affirmed the district court's decision and stated, "Because the REC Rule was successful in artificially lowering the price of coaching services, no further evidence or analysis is required to find market power to set prices." The NCAA argued that the procompetitive effects of the rule outweighed the anticompetitive effects and offered three justifications: (a) retention of entry-level coaches; (b) reduction of costs; (c) maintenance of competitive equity. After considering the defendant's justifications, the court concluded:

Thus, on its face, the REC Rule is not directed towards competitive balance nor is the nexus between the rule and a compelling need to maintain competitive balance sufficiently clear on this record to withstand a motion of summary judgment.

The damage issue was remanded to jury, which returned a verdict in favor of the plaintiffs for $22.3 million in April 1998. With trebling, this would have resulted in an award of $66.9 million—the largest judgment ever levied against the NCAA. Instead of appealing the damages verdict, the NCAA agreed to a $54.5 million settlement.

The holding of *Law* was consistent with *Board of Regents*, in the sense that the NCAA's antitrust immunity ceased to exist once the NCAA acted in a commercial capacity (restricting coaches' salaries; limiting the supply of televised games) rather than as a regulator of amateur athletic competition (enforcing academic eligibility standards, etc.). However, the *Board of Regents* precedent was tested in the case of *Adidas Am., Inc. v. NCAA*, 64 F.Supp.2d 1097 (D. Kan. 1999). The plaintiffs alleged that NCAA limits on the size of advertising logos on player uniforms constituted an illegal restraint of trade. However, the court determined that the logo size rule was consistent with the NCAA's objective of limiting commercialization in intercollegiate athletics. The court granted the NCAA's motion to dismiss the complaint, and then rejected Adidas's motion to amend judgment (see note 2).

10.5.4. Tournaments: *MIBA v. NCAA*

In late 2000 and early 2001, the NCAA became the target of multiple antitrust lawsuits regarding the decision to change the limits on the number of basketball games played by its member institutions. Prior rules allowed Division I men's teams to play in 28 regular season games. However, certain "exempt" tournaments, such as the Maui Invitational, Great Alaska Shootout, and Preseason NIT, counted as only one game toward the 28-game limit, even if the schools played more than one game in these tournaments. Effective in 2001, teams would have been allowed 29 regular season games, but would not be given exemptions for the aforementioned tournaments. Sponsors and promoters of such tournaments filed separate lawsuits in Ohio and New York, fearing that the proposed changes would put them out of business.

The NCAA and its members claim that the changes are necessary to reduce travel and reduce the number of classes missed by student-athletes. However, critics contend that the rule change is a ploy to allow schools to have extra home games and increase ticket revenue. In 2001, fearing an expensive legal battle, the NCAA tabled its efforts to reduce or end tournament exemptions in either 2001 or 2002. However, the association has not ruled out abolishing the exemptions in subsequent years.

In 1999, the NCAA established a "two-in-four" rule, limiting a team to playing in only two exempt tournaments in four seasons to help students in the areas mentioned above while also helping give lesser known teams more exposure and quality competition. As a result of this rule, the amount of exempt tournaments decreased, which actually had an adverse effect on smaller schools now that there were fewer spots available in tournaments. In *Worldwide Basketball and Sports Tours, Inc. v. NCAA*, 273 F.Supp.2d 933 (S.D. Ohio 2003), the court ruled that the rule had an adverse competitive effect and ordered a permanent injunction against the rule in September 2003. In 2004, the United States Court of Appeals for the

Sixth Circuit reversed the district court's decision. It ruled that the rule did not prevent the promoters who brought the suit from competing in the relevant market, that of college basketball games, see *Worldwide Basketball and Sports Tours, Inc. v. NCAA*, 388 F.3d 955 (6th Cir. 2004).

In *Metropolitan Intercollegiate Basketball Ass'n. v. NCAA*, 337 F.Supp.2d 563 (S.D.N.Y. 2004), MIBA, the promoter/organizer of the postseason men's basketball National Invitation Tournament (NIT), claimed that the NCAA's rule forbidding a Division I member invited to participate in the NCAA tournament from participating in any other postseason event was in effect a boycott of the only competing postseason men's college basketball tournament. The district court ruled that this claim must be evaluated at a trial under the rule of reason, rather than dismissed as a per se violation.

The case was settled out of court in August 2005, when the NCAA agreed to pay the five members of the MIBA—Fordham University, Manhattan College, New York University, St. John's University, and Wagner College—$56.5 million for the rights to operate the preseason and postseason NIT tournaments while keeping the tournaments in New York City for at least five seasons. For more on the antitrust implications of this settlement, see Lindsay A. Oliver, "NCAA: A Lesson in Cartel Behavior and Antitrust Regulation," 8 *Transactions: The Tennessee Journal of Business Law* 7 (Fall 2006).

10.5.5. The Bowl Championship Series

In an attempt to establish a clearly definitive national champion in college football, the six largest conferences, the ACC, SEC, Big 12, Big Ten, Big East and Pac-10, along with the non–conference-affiliated University of Notre Dame, created the Bowl Championship Series in 1998. The champions of these conferences, along with a top-10 ranked Notre Dame team, are guaranteed spots in the four largest and highest-revenue-producing bowl games: the Rose, Orange, Sugar, and Fiesta bowls. Since then, the National Championship Game has also been added as a separate bowl game. Each season, one of these games is designated as the National Championship game and will host the two top-ranked teams according to the complicated and controversial BCS ranking system. Opponents of the BCS system contend that the ranking system is constructed to favor the BCS teams. This agreement greatly limits the chances of teams from the other five Division 1-A football conferences gaining access to these major bowl games. Presently, each BCS conference is guaranteed $17 million in revenue while only $9 million from BCS revenue is guaranteed to be distributed among the five remaining Division 1-A conferences.

As a result of this agreement, the possibility exists that the BCS and its members may face an antitrust suit. Section 1 of the Sherman Antitrust Act, which addresses parties working in concert for the purposes of restraining trade, is the area of antitrust legislation that would most likely apply. Although the BCS is a nonprofit organization, its purpose is to maximize profits for its members, in part by creating barriers to entry. The BCS would likely contend that the procompetitive effects of its arrangement outweigh the anticompetitive effects, because interest and overall revenue in college football has increased as a result of the BCS and, in its opinion, the establishment of a true national championship game. However, in the same way that many teams within the Big Four have argued at times that increasing financial gaps between clubs is hurting competitive balance, so too have the non-BCS conferences.

Opponents argue that there are less restrictive alternatives, such as the playoff system that determines national champions in every other NCAA sport. However, bowl games have existed as an important part of the college football landscape since 1902. No lawsuits have yet been filed, but the controversy continues as Division 1-A college football searches for a fair and profitable way to determine a national champion.

NOTE

1. The BCS system has caused both criticism and legal debate. Articles such as Jude D. Schmit, "A Fresh Set of Downs? Why Recent Modifications to the Bowl Championship Series Still Draw a Flag under the Sherman Act," 14 *Sports Lawyers Journal* 219 (Spring 2007) and Katherine McClelland, "Should College Football's Currency Read 'In BCS We Trust' or Is It Just Monopoly Money?: Antitrust Implications of the Bowl Championship Series," 37 *Texas Tech Law Review* 167 (Winter 2004) argue that it is an illegal restraint of trade, while articles such as Christopher Pruitt, "Debunknig a Popular Antitrust Myth: The Single-Entity Rule and Why College Football's Bowl Championship Series Does Not Violate the Sherman Antitrust Act," 11 *Texas Review of Entertainment & Sports Law* 125 (2009) and David Scott Moreland, "The Antitrust Implications of the Bowl Championship Series: Analysis through Analogous Reasoning," 21 *Georgia State University Law Review* 721 (Spring 2005) argue that the BCS system's procompetitive features outweigh the alleged anticompetitive effects.

10.5.6. Other Decisions after *Board of Regents*

Following the *Board of Regents* decision, several athletes filed antitrust challenges against the NCAA, but were unsuccessful. In *McCormack v. National Collegiate Athletic Ass'n*, 845 F.2d 1338 (5th Cir. 1988), the court decided that the NCAA's eligibility rules placing restrictions on student-athletes' compensation did not constitute illegal price-fixing and were not in violation of the Sherman Act. In *Banks v. NCAA*, 746 F.Supp. 850 (N.D. Ind. 1990) and *Gaines v. NCAA*, 746 F.Supp. 738 (M.D. Tenn. 1990), football players unsuccessfully challenged the NCAA on antitrust theory with regard to eligibility rules. The Indiana federal district court in *Banks* ruled that the NCAA eligibility rules in question were subject to scrutiny under the Sherman Act, but concluded that the rules were procompetitive and, using the rule of reason test, were reasonable on the basis of their intentions. In *Gaines*, the Tennessee federal district court ruled that the NCAA eligibility rules were not subject to scrutiny under the Sherman Act. However, the court went on to state that, assuming the antitrust laws did apply to the NCAA eligibility rules, the rules were reasonable under the rule of reason test.

In *White v. NCAA*, CV06–0999 (C.D. Cal. January 29, 2008), three former student-athletes filed a class action lawsuit alleging that NCAA bylaws that capped the amount of financial aid a student-athlete may receive constituted an unlawful agreement in restraint of trade in violation of Section 1 of the Sherman Act.

NCAA bylaw 15.02.5 defines "grant-in-aid" to a student-athlete as "financial aid that consists of tuition and fees, room and board, and required course-related books." The "cost of attendance" is more broadly defined in bylaw 15.02.2 as "an amount calculated by an institutional financial aid office, using federal regulations, that includes the total cost of tuition and fees, room and board, books and supplies, transportation, and other expenses related to attendance at the institution." The plaintiffs alleged that the NCAA created a "grant-in-aid" cap that violates Section 1 by restricting schools from competing against one another to offer more financial aid. The suit was settled in January 2008, when the NCAA agreed to make an additional $10 million available to qualifying student-athletes to reimburse them for "bona fide educational expenses hereafter incurred, such as tuition, fees, books, supplies and equipment."

NOTES

1. For more on the application of antitrust laws to NCAA rules, see Bradley S. Pensyl, "Whistling a Foul on the NCAA: How NCAA Recruiting Bylaws Violate the Sherman Antitrust Act," 58 *Syracuse Law Review* 397 (2008), Christian Dennie, "White Out Full Grant-In-Aid: An Antitrust Action the NCAA Cannot Afford to Lose," 7 *Virginia Sports & Entertainment Law Journal* 97 (2007), Peter Kreher, "Antitrust Theory, College Sports, and Interleague Rulemaking: A New Critique of the NCAA's Amateurism Rules," 6 *Virginia Sports and Entertainment Law Journal* 51 (Fall 2006) and Michael B. Licalsi, "The Whole Situation Is a Sham, Baby!-NCAA Self-Regulations Categorize as Horizontal Combinations under the Sherman Act's Rule of Reason Standard: Unreasonable Restraints of Trade or an Unfair Judicial Test?" 12 *George Mason Law Review* 831 (Spring 2004).

2. In the case of *Baum Research & Development v. Hillerich & Bradsby Co.*, 31 F.Supp.2d 1016 (E.D. Mich. 1998), a baseball bat manufacturer brought a Section 1 complaint, alleging that the NCAA and several other bat manufacturers conspired to keep other bat manufacturers out of amateur baseball. The court concluded that the NCAA's rules and actions did not violate or deter competition. On the contrary, the court stated that the plaintiff's lack of success in the market stemmed from competition itself. In a separate case in 1998, Easton Sports Inc. sued the NCAA for $267 million in damages after the Rules Committee suggested changes in aluminum bats. The NCAA suggested the changes in order to reduce injuries caused by lively bats. However, Easton called the rule change an illegal restraint of trade that would render $140 million worth of bats obsolete. In effect, outlawing lively bats would constitute a group boycott by NCAA members. The case was settled in 1999 when the NCAA adopted bat standards that were not as restrictive as the ones that Easton protested.

3. In *Board of Regents v. NCAA*, 561 P.2d 499 (Okla. 1977), University of Oklahoma assistant football coaches asserted that an NCAA bylaw limiting the number of coaches a Division I school might employ was a violation of the Sherman Act by preventing coaches from practicing their lawful profession. The appellate court overruled the decision of the trial court, stating that the NCAA rule appeared to be a reasonable one, rationally related to its announced objective of curtailing costs of NCAA members. The court concluded that the restraint did not prevent coaches from exercising their lawful profession, but merely limited the number of coaches any given school could employ.

4. In *Jones v. NCAA*, 392 F.Supp. 295 (D. Mass. 1975), the plaintiff was a U.S. ice hockey player who was compensated for five years while playing junior hockey in Canada prior to entering Northeastern University. Because he had received compensation for playing, Jones was declared ineligible to compete at Northeastern. Jones argued that the NCAA violated the antitrust laws by declaring him ineligible to compete. With respect to the antitrust allegations, the court held that the Sherman Act does not apply to the NCAA or its members in the setting of eligibility standards for intercollegiate athletics.

CONCLUSION

Antitrust law is particularly complicated in the sports industry because both amateur and professional sports leagues often claim a legitimate business purpose for engaging in activity that would be considered illegal in other industries. Professional leagues claim a legitimate business purpose because of the unique nature of sport and their atypical business models. The cases in this chapter were discussed in order to bridge this complexity, and to highlight the common themes of sports antitrust law. The holdings of these cases have especially impacted labor (see Chapter 11) and broadcasting (see Chapter 14). Consequently, the reader may refer back to this chapter if aspects of such topics require clarification.

Chapter 11

LABOR LAW

11.1. Development of Labor Law

11.1.1. History of Labor Law

11.1.2. National Labor Relations Act (as Amended in 1947)

11.1.3. National Labor Relations Act, Section 7

11.1.4. National Labor Relations Act, Section 8

11.1.5. Unfair Labor Practice Procedures

11.1.5.1. Interference with Organizing or Bargaining Collectively

11.1.5.2. Domination and Assistance

11.1.5.3. Discrimination

11.1.5.4. Retaliation

11.1.5.5. Duty to Bargain in Good Faith

11.1.5.6. Protection from Unions

11.1.6. National Labor Relations Board

11.1.7. Certification of a Union

11.2. Collective Bargaining

11.2.1. The Collective Bargaining Process

11.2.2. Mandatory and Permissive Subjects of Bargaining

11.2.3. Ratification

11.2.4. Decertification

11.3. Collective Bargaining in Professional Sports

11.3.1. The Players Associations in Professional Sports

11.3.2. National Hockey League Players Association

11.3.3. National Football League Players Association

11.3.4. National Basketball Players Association

11.3.5. Major League Baseball Players Association

11.3.6. Other Players Associations in North America

11.3.6.1. Women's National Basketball Association

11.3.6.2. Major League Soccer

11.3.6.3. Arena Football League

11.3.6.4. Canadian Football League Players Association

11.3.6.5. Potential Unionization of Minor League Baseball and College Athletics

11.3.7. Collective Bargaining
Agreements in Professional
Sports
11.3.7.1. Labor Disputes in
Professional Sports
11.3.7.1.1. Strikes
11.3.7.1.2. Lockouts
11.3.7.1.3. Impasse
11.3.7.1.4. Baseball
Col-
lusion
Cases
11.3.8. Outline of a Professional
Sports Collective
Bargaining Agreement

11.3.9. Free Agency
11.3.10. Salary Caps
11.3.11. Calculation of Salary
Cap
11.3.12. Hard Cap versus Soft
Cap
11.3.13. Arbitration
11.3.14. Grievance Procedures
in Professional
Sports
11.3.14.1. Unlawful
Discharge
11.3.15. Salary Arbitration

INTRODUCTION

The difference between a college athlete and a professional athlete is that a professional athlete is considered by the courts to be an employee, whereas the courts have determined a college athlete to be primarily a student. Therefore, as employees, professional athletes are covered under state and federal labor laws. College athletes, on the other hand, do not have the protection of the labor laws; instead, they are protected by school, conference, and league rules, in addition to constitutional laws and applicable athletics-related legislation. Nevertheless, while administrators of intercollegiate and interscholastic athletics need not deal with *players* insofar as labor law, they often must deal with unionized employees such as clerical workers and groundskeepers. Furthermore, many high school coaches are members of teachers' unions. Consequently, it is beneficial for such individuals to understand the rights and expectations that labor law bestows upon employers and employees.

Labor law was designed to protect both employees and employers from the sometimes antagonistic relationship that may develop between the two parties. Labor law is a set of rules that govern the workplace, and affect both employees and employers. Labor law outlines what rights employees have and what rights their employers have. One of the cornerstones of modern U.S. labor law is the right of employees to choose to join or assist a labor union. A union is a trade organization that represents employees in a particular work site, with its primary responsibility to negotiate and administer a collective bargaining agreement (CBA) for its employees (see note 2). A collective bargaining agreement is a contract between an employer and a union that sets minimum standards in areas such as wages, benefits, health and safety, and vacation time, and usually contains a dispute resolution mechanism, commonly referred to as a grievance procedure.

Professional athletes were first organized into unions as far back as the 1950s, in an effort to wrest increased salary, job security, pensions, and player mobility from the leagues. Unionization in the National Hockey League (NHL), National Basketball Association (NBA), Major League Baseball (MLB), and the National Football League (NFL), along with more recent unionization efforts in the Women's National Basketball Association (WNBA) and Major League Soccer (MLS), has had a tremendous impact on professional athletes and professional sports leagues. As the business of professional sports grew tremendously in the 1980s and 1990s, so did the power of the professional sports players associations (see note 1).

What makes professional sports labor relations so complex and unique is the fact that players in professional sports leagues are covered under a collective bargaining agreement between the union (or players association) and the employer (league), in addition to being covered under an individually negotiated contract (see note 3). Players are also bound by the rules and regulations of the league, or league bylaws, which in some circumstances may contradict the interpretations of a collective bargaining agreement or players contract, and in that case, a court may be called in to settle the dispute. Therefore, in professional sports, there is a combination of labor law and contract law at work.

This chapter will offer an introductory look at the relevant labor laws that affect professional sports, including an examination of the National Labor Relations Act (NLRA), the National Labor Relations Board (NLRB), and case law surrounding unfair labor practices and collective bargaining. In addition, this chapter will analyze the development of unionization in professional sports and scrutinize several provisions in current collective bargaining agreements from the NHL, NFL, MLB, and NBA. Finally, this chapter will briefly discuss the often stormy relationship that exists between the leagues and the various players associations by examining work stoppages and other legal issues.

NOTES

1. For a description of how the business of professional sports has changed, refer to Chapter 1.

2. While a union is sometimes confined to one particular work site, the National Labor Relations Board can approve or order multiple work site bargaining units. For example, NFL players work at multiple work sites (e.g., Soldier Field in Chicago, Raymond James Stadium in Tampa) on teams with different ownership. However, all NFL players are represented by the NFLPA. The NLRB is likely to order/approve multiple work site units if there is a centralization of management or significant interchange of employees among the work sites, or if all employers and employees agree on such an arrangement. While multiple work site and multiple employer units are the norm in pro sports, the case of *North American Soccer League v. National Labor Relations Board*, 613 F.2d 1379 (5th Cir. 1980) tested this concept. In this case, the NASL claimed that players should be required to bargain with each individual team, not the league as a whole. The court denied this claim, because the NASL, not individual teams, exercised "a significant degree of control over...selection, retention, and termination of the players, the terms of individual player contracts, dispute resolution, and player discipline."

3. In this chapter, "employer" refers to owners, leagues, and particular management groups, such as Major League Baseball's Labor Relations Department (formerly the Player Relations Committee) and the NFL Management Council. An "employee," in this chapter, is a professional athlete playing for a professional sports league. The unions that are referred to in this text are the National Hockey League Players Association (NHLPA), the National Basketball Players Association (NBPA), the Major League Baseball Players Association (MLBPA), the National Football League Players Association (NFLPA), and the Women's National Basketball Players Association (WNBPA).

11.1. DEVELOPMENT OF LABOR LAW

Labor relations law is derived from statutory law, judicial decisions and interpretations, constitutional rights, and administrative decisions by agencies of the U.S. government. Statutory law can be created or amended by legislation at the federal, state, or local level of government. Examples of statutory labor laws include the Clayton Act, the Norris-LaGuardia Act, and the National Labor Relations Act. Judicial decisions and interpretations occur when a court issues a decision or interpretation that creates a change in existing legislation, or sets a precedent interpreting an existing law differently. For example, in *Federal Baseball Club v. National League of Professional Baseball Clubs,* 259 U.S. 200 (1922), the court ruled that the sport of baseball was not subject to antitrust laws because it was not engaged in interstate commerce. That decision set a precedent that was affirmed in two later judicial decisions involving professional baseball (see section 10.3.1.3, "Baseball Exemption Reaffirmed: *Toolson*"). Had the court in *Federal Baseball,* or subsequent decisions, interpreted the law differently and not given professional baseball an antitrust exemption, then a different precedent would have been established. It is important to note that if a legislature is dissatisfied with a court's interpretation of a statute, the legislature has the power to amend or override the court's interpretation. An example of this is the Curt Flood Act of 1998, which Congress passed to limit the antitrust exemption professional baseball had held since the *Federal Baseball* decision.

11.1.1. History of Labor Law

In the early 1800s, there was an absence of legislative direction as it pertained to labor law, and thus the judicial system not only controlled the relationships between labor unions and employers, but also played a key role in limiting the rights of unions until the 1930s. During this period, workers began to organize into guilds or unions in an attempt to "bargain" with their employers for a fair wage. Workers realized that employers were more likely to respond to groups than to individuals, and therefore began a process of bargaining for groups of employees rather than individuals. If the employer refused, workers would "strike" at their work site as a sign of protest, and not return to work until the particular issue had been resolved. Employers, who frequently did not know the trade themselves, found themselves losing money, and customers, during these labor battles. They turned to the courts for a remedy.

The earliest and most important case in early labor law history is the Philadelphia *Cordwainers'* decision in *Commonwealth v. Pullis* (Phila. Mayor's Ct. 1806), which declared that collective organizing was a "criminal conspiracy." The trial judge stated:

> Our position is that no man is at liberty to combine, conspire, confederate and unlawfully agree to regulate the whole body of workmen in the city. The defendants are not indicted for regulating their own individual wages but for undertaking by a combination, to regulate the price of labor of others as well as their own.

The court found that workers acting in concert with each other were acting in a conspiracy (similar to actions forbade by Section 1 of the Sherman Antitrust Act, see Chapter 10). Therefore, all actions by groups of employees—picketing, striking, holding union meetings—could be considered a conspiracy and were punishable by fine or imprisonment. This decision aroused much protest from workers and was finally overturned by the 1842 decision in *Commonwealth v. Hunt,* 4 Met. 111 (1842). This case established that if the collective action in question was beneficial to the worker, or group of workers, then conspiracy charges could not apply.

In the wake of *Commonwealth v. Hunt*, employers turned to the civil courts as a means to protect themselves from union organizing and work stoppages in their workplaces. More and more workers were protesting unsafe working conditions, squalid housing, and poverty wages. During the latter half of the 1800s and the beginning of the 1900s, labor battles were fought both in the courts and on the picket line. As union-employer violence escalated at the turn of the 20th century, Congress was forced to rethink the labor laws that were governing workers throughout the country. Between 1914 and 1947, Congress passed and amended several pieces of legislation that would shape labor relations for the rest of the 20th century:

1. Clayton Act (1914). This act, signed in 1914, was seen as a victory for the labor movement because it stated that "the labor of a human being is not a commodity or article of commerce." This ensured that unions would not be subject to the Sherman Antitrust Act of 1890. In addition, the Clayton Act restricted the rights of employers to use injunctions against its employees: "no…injunction shall be granted in any case between an employer and employees…growing out of a dispute concerning terms or conditions of work." However, many employers were still able to receive injunctions by proving the threat of violence on the picket line.

2. Norris-LaGuardia Act (1932). This act, often referred to as the Federal Anti-Injunction Act, limited the power of the federal government to issue injunctions and limit union activity. The Norris-LaGuardia Act stated that when a labor dispute was found, federal courts were forbidden to issue any injunction that forbade either the refusal to work or peaceful picketing. However, this act could not limit or stop state courts from issuing injunctions.

3. The Wagner Act (1935). Officially referred to as the National Labor Relations Act (described further below), this piece of legislation gave workers the right to join or assist unions, without fear of employer retribution. This statute was the first piece of legislation that gave workers the right to freely pursue unionization. The Wagner Act covers all areas of labor law, including representation elections, unfair labor practice charges, and duties of representation.

4. Taft-Hartley Act (1947). Officially referred to as the Labor Management Relations Act, this legislation was an amendment to the Wagner Act in the face of increased union unrest and employer pressure. The main change to the Wagner Act was the addition and explanation of what would constitute unfair labor practices by unions, which prohibited unions from pressuring employees to join or assist a union or a unionization drive.

11.1.2. National Labor Relations Act (as Amended in 1947)

Most employees working in private firms are covered by the NLRA. It is important to note that not all employees are covered by the act, however. The following is a list of employees who are excluded from coverage by the NLRA:

1. Employees of federal, state, and local governments

2. Airline and railroad employees

3. Spouses and children of employees

4. Independent contractors

5. Domestic servants

6. Agricultural workers

7. Supervisors and managers.

Some of the workers in these industries are protected under other pieces of legislation. For example, rail and air transportation workers are covered under the Railway Labor Act of 1926.

11.1.3. National Labor Relations Act, Section 7

One of the most important sections in the NLRA is Section 7:

Employees shall have the right to self-organization, to form, join, assist, labor organizations, to bargain collectively through representatives of their own choosing, and to engage in other concerted activities for the purpose of collective bargaining or other mutual aid or protection, and shall also have the right to refrain from any or all of such activities except to the extent that such right may be affected by this agreement requiring membership in a labor organization as a condition of employment as authorized in section 8(a)(3).

Congress created this right because it recognized that workers have more power, or bargaining strength, as a group rather than as individuals. Section 7 assures workers of certain rights:

1. The right to form and organize labor organizations

2. The right to become members of labor unions or to refuse to join

3. The right to bargain collectively through representatives of their own choosing

4. The right to engage in other concerted activity for the purpose of collective bargaining, such as strikes, boycotts, and picketing.

11.1.4. National Labor Relations Act, Section 8

Section 8 of the NLRA protects the rights workers are entitled to under Section 7. If an employer violates a worker's right under Section 7, it is called an *unfair labor practice*. Section 8 outlines what constitutes an unfair labor practice:

1. 8(a)(1) An employer is forbidden from interfering, restraining, or coercing its employees from exercising their rights under Section 7.

2. 8(a)(2) Attempting to dominate, interfere with the formation of, and finance and support a labor union are all prohibited.

3. 8(a)(3) Employers are forbidden to discriminate against employees on account of their union relationship.

4. 8(a)(4) Employers are forbidden to fire, discipline, or lay off an employee because he or she has filed an unfair labor practice.

5. 8(a)(5) Employers must bargain in good faith over wages, hours, terms of employment.

If an employer is found to have breached any Section 8(a) articles, there are six possible remedies: (1) back pay; (2) reinstatement; (3) bargaining order; (4) rerun election; (5) cease and desist order; (6) injunctive relief. Back pay and reinstatement are two remedies that are commonly utilized if an employee wins a Section 8(a) unfair labor practice charge. This is because many employees are terminated for engaging in union organizing and other union activities. Rerun elections are initiated if it is found that the employer has interfered with the formation of a union, and such interference resulted in a negative certification vote.

Section 8 also identifies *unfair union activities:*

1. 8(b)(1) Unions are prohibited from coercing or restraining employees as stated under the rights of the Act.

2. 8(b)(2) Actions that cause an employer to discriminate against an employee for the purpose of encouraging or discouraging union membership are prohibited.

3. 8(b)(3) The union must bargain in good faith.

If a labor organization is found to have breached any of the articles in Section 8, there are five possible remedies: (1) injunctive relief; (2) bargaining order; (3) cease and desist order; (4) damages; (5) disestablishment of the union or withdrawal of recognition. In most cases, the employer will seek an injunction against the union if Section 8(b) violations occur, although the issuance of a bargaining order is also an effective means to ensure that a collective bargaining agreement is negotiated in good faith.

NOTES

1. The constitutionality of the Wagner Act was tested in *National Labor Relations Board v. Jones and Laughlin Steel Corp.*, 301 U.S. 1 (1937). The NLRB found Jones and Laughlin Steel Corp. in violation of the National Labor Relations Act, Section 8(a), after the company was found to have coerced and intimidated employees in order to stop them from organizing a union. The NLRB then petitioned the Circuit Court of Appeals to enforce the order, which was subsequently denied, because the court believed the order lay beyond the range of federal power. The case was sent to the Supreme Court, which concluded that the act was valid as applied in *Jones and Laughlin Steel Corp.*, and reversed the circuit court's decision.

2. The NLRA gives employees the right to strike, but there are certain limitations on this right. If a collective bargaining agreement exists in which the employer has agreed to binding arbitration in place of a no-strike clause, the employer may seek an injunction to stop a strike or walkout. Employees engaging in an economic strike may be permanently replaced, whereas in an unfair labor practice strike, they may not.

3. A clear violation of Section 8(a)(1) would occur if a high school athletic association transferred the contract of its football referees, after those referees formed a union. Other Section 8(a)(1) violations are not so clear-cut. For example, during the NFL-NFLPA CBA negotiations of 2010, the Department of Labor began investigating whether the NFL violated the law by meeting directly with NFL players. Those meetings could have had the effect of coercing players not to exercise certain rights, most notably the right to decertify the union and sue on antitrust grounds. While no lawsuits were filed, these comments constituted coercion and a Section 8(a)(1) violation, according to John Croke in "An Examination of the Antitrust Issues Surrounding the NBA Decertification Crisis," 5 *Sports Lawyers Journal* 163 (Spring 1998).

11.1.5. Unfair Labor Practice Procedures

When an employee's rights have been violated, as outlined in the National Labor Relations Act, that employee has the ability to file an unfair labor practice charge. The NLRA was created to protect the rights of employees, and the NLRB was created to administer and enforce the NLRA. The filing of an unfair labor practice charge illustrates how the NLRA and the NLRB are interconnected. The following is the process that the charging party needs to go through when filing an unfair labor practice charge:

1. *Filing the Charge.* An unfair labor practice charge must be filed within six months of the conduct that gave rise to the allegations. Any person may file a charge with the NLRB, at the closest NLRB regional office.

2. *Investigation.* The NLRB regional director will conduct an investigation to determine whether the charge has merit and should advance through the process. This process is similar to "discovery." If the charge is found to have merit, the regional director will file a complaint. If the charge does not have merit, it is dismissed, but may be appealed through the Office of Appeals, a division of the NLRB.

3. *Hearing.* When a complaint is issued, the charging party is represented by the General Counsel's Office and the hearing is set before an administrative law judge. The hearing is similar to a formal trial, but without the jury.

4. *Decision.* The administrative law judge will render a decision, which may be appealed by either party to the NLRB or to the appropriate court of appeals.

11.1.5.1. Interference with Organizing or Bargaining Collectively

The goal of Section 8(a)(1) is to stop employers from interfering with employees' right to join a labor union. Examples of this interference include threats of bankruptcy, firing, or layoff; interrogations of union members or organizers; offering rewards to employees who go against the union; or spying on union meetings (see note 1).

11.1.5.2. Domination and Assistance

The goal of Section 8(a)(2) is to prohibit the use of company unions, favoritism of one union over another, or endangering the independence of a union. Employers are prohibited from exercising control over the operations of a union, including having undue influence in the decision-making process. Company unions are unions that purport to be independent organizations, but are not certified by the NLRB and are, in act uality, instruments of the employer. An example of this on the pro sport level would be the early years of the MLBPA, which had its executive director picked by MLB, and also was financed and controlled by the league. Section 8(a)(2) prohibits this type of arrangement, although no suit was ever filed by the MLBPA with the NLRB over this issue. In 2001, the NLRB accused Arena Football League owners of coercing players into joining a company union (AFLPOC) by using offers of financial assistance and threats of job loss. The league denied these claims, and its involvement with the AFLPOC, before settling this issue with the players in 2001.

NOTE _____

1. Players of the Philadelphia Eagles filed an unfair labor practice charge in 1993, charging that the collective bargaining agreement reached by the NFL-NFLPA after the *White* settlement was invalid because the NFLPA had not yet recertified its union status. The players claimed that the agreement was therefore a violation of Section 8(a)(2) and possibly of 8(b)(1)(A). The charge was eventually dropped after an ownership change, but there remains a question as to whether the deal reached in 1993 between the NFL and NFLPA rests on solid legal ground. For more on the *White* settlement, see section 10.3.5, "Exemption after Decertification: *McNeil.*"

11.1.5.3. Discrimination

The purpose of Section 8(a)(3) is to eliminate discriminatory behavior by employers against employees due to their relationship with a union. Some forms of discrimination include demotion, discharge, reduction in pay, change in job classification, and change in work site. In these circumstances, the union must prove that the employer acted with malice because of union affiliation (see note 1).

NOTE _____

1. A violation of 8(a)(3) in professional sports usually occurs when a player is traded, reassigned, or waived due to his or her union activities. See *In re: Nordstrom*, 292 NLRB 899 (1989). In this case, Seahawk player Sam McCullum was allegedly released from the team because of his union affiliation. For the subsequent case on the amount of back pay owed to McCullum, see *National Football League and the National Football League Player Association*, 309 NLRB 78 (1992).

11.1.5.4. Retaliation

The aim of Section 8(a)(4) is to protect employees who file unfair labor practice charges against their employer with the NLRB. Employees who either initiate charges or offer testimony during an NLRB unfair labor practice hearing are protected against employer retaliation (actions similar to those that are relevant to Section 8(a)(3)).

11.1.5.5. Duty to Bargain in Good Faith

When a union is recognized by the NLRB, the employer of the unionized employees is required to bargain in good faith with the union representing those employees. Refusal to bargain is a violation of Section 8(a)(5). Case law surrounding Section 8(a)(5) has focused on what, beyond the mere willingness to sign an agreement, is necessary in order to establish good faith bargaining. Simply put, a party that makes no concessions and rejects the other side's proposals outright has, for all intents and purposes, refused to bargain in good faith. For example, if the WNBA bargaining representatives went into negotiations offering a scant increase in salary to the players and refused to discuss any other issues, it could be argued that they were bargaining in bad faith. In addition, an employer that refuses to give the union information that is relevant to negotiations may be in violation of 8(a)(5) (see notes 1 and 2).

NOTES _____

1. An example of a violation of 8(a)(5) of the NLRA occurred when members of the U.S. Men's National Soccer Team, initially recognized by the U.S. Soccer Federation, were unable

to bargain a contract because of the USSF's refusal to bargain. See *USSF, Inc. and the United States Men's National Soccer Team Players*, Case 5-CA-26593 (May 30, 1997). The NLRB issued a complaint against the USSF and ordered it to bargain with the players union. See also *Morio v. North American Soccer League*, 501 F. Supp. 633 (S.D.N.Y. 1980), where the NASL unilaterally changed the conditions of employment without negotiating with the players. The players union successfully won an injunction that rendered the changes voidable.

2. If impasse has not been reached, good faith bargaining must occur on all mandatory subjects of bargaining. In both *Silverman v. Major League Baseball Player Relations Committee, Inc.*, 516 F. Supp. 588 (S.D.N.Y. 1981) and *NFL Management Council and NFLPA*, NLRB case No. 2-CA-13379 (June 30, 1976), the players filed suit against management for failing to provide relevant information during bargaining. This constituted an NLRA Section (8)(a)(5) violation.

11.1.5.6. Protection from Unions

Section 8(b)(1) prohibits unions from forcing its members to engage in a concerted activity (e.g., strikes). This means that a union cannot discipline a member who does not agree to strike with the rest of the union. Section 8(b) of the NLRA also includes rules that prohibit a union from encouraging any individual employed by a person engaged in commerce or in an industry affecting commerce to engage in a strike. This section of the NLRA has not traditionally applied to the realm of sports. Section 8(b)(1) also prevents a union from restraining its members from engaging in concerted activity. Furthermore, a union cannot coerce management during its selection of representatives for collective bargaining. Some states have extended additional protection to workers from unions in the form of "right to work" laws (see note 1).

NOTE _____

1. In 1993, members of the Washington Redskins, unhappy with the collective bargaining agreement that came out of *White v. NFL*, 41 F.3d 402 (8th Cir. 1994), withheld their union dues, $5,000 for the season. The NFLPA sought to have the players suspended after an arbitrator ruled in favor of the union. However, at both the federal level, *NFLPA v. Pro-Football Inc.*, 857 F. Supp. 71 (D.D.C. 1994), and the state level, *Orr v. National Football League Players Ass'n*, 147 LRRM 2845 (Va. 1994), decisions were rendered in favor of the players. The players claimed that they worked in a right to work state, and therefore were not required to join the union or pay dues. The players were able to make this assertion because their practice facilities were located in Virginia, and they convinced the court that their time spent in Virginia outweighed their affiliation with the District of Columbia.

The following are unfair labor practice cases in professional sports:

1. On March 27, 2005, approximately five months into a lockout that cancelled the 2004–2005 National Hockey League season, the NHL filed an unfair labor practice with the NLRB against the National Hockey League Players Association. The NHL alleged that an NHLPA policy punishing would-be replacement players was coercive and exceeded the NHLPA's rights. During the lockout, players received between $5,000 and $10,000 per month, but, according to the NHL, these payments were based upon the condition that the players not return to the NHL without a new collective bargaining agreement. The charges were ultimately deemed moot when the NHL and NHLPA reached a settlement in July 2005.

2. With an August 12 strike deadline looming, MLB owners skipped a pension payment on August 1, 1994. The National Labor Relations Board subsequently filed unfair labor practice charges against MLB that were ultimately withdrawn when a new CBA was reached and the owners agreed to make the payment with back interest. However, with the current CBA already expired on December 31, 1993, MLB owners planned to unilaterally

implement a salary cap and do away with salary arbitration. In March 1995, the NLRB filed unfair labor practice charges against the owners that forced the owners to restore the old work rules for players. This decision allowed the strike to end and the 1995 season to begin without a CBA as the owners chose not to lock the players out. An appeal by the owners was denied and all charges became moot when a new collective bargaining agreement was finally reached on May 19, 1995.

3. Following the expiration of the collective bargaining agreement on August 31, 1987, the National Football League Players Association went on strike September 21, 1987. The NFL and its clubs responded by immediately hiring replacement players. Soon many players began to cross the picket line and the strike was officially ended on October 15, 1987. The NFLPA then filed an antitrust lawsuit against the NFL in *Powell v. NFL*, 930 F.2d 1293 (8th Cir. 1989), mainly over the issue of free agency. The NFL Management Council Executive Committee responded by refusing to allow the returning strikers to play in that week's games and collect their paychecks. The NFLPA appealed to the National Labor Relations Board in cases 5-CA-19170, 5-CA-19508, 5-CA-19559, 5-CA-19415, and 5-CA-19773, which ordered the NFL to allow returning strikers to play and not be discriminated against. Ultimately, the Eighth Circuit Court of Appeals ruled that the players could not sue on antitrust grounds as long as they were part of a union. Shortly thereafter, in November 1989, the players voted to dissolve the NFLPA and once again sued in *McNeil v. NFL*. In March 1990, the NLRB ruled that the owners owed roughly 1,400 players almost $19 million total for refusing to let them return to work in October 1987. McNeil and the players eventually won their case versus the NFL in 1992, and resulting settlement talks produced the first form of free agency in NFL history.

11.1.6. National Labor Relations Board

The National Labor Relations Board is a federal administrative agency that was established to administer and enforce the National Labor Relations Act. The first board took office on August 27, 1935, after Congress had passed the Wagner Act. The board has two primary responsibilities:

1. Supervising and conducting representation elections
2. Adjudicating employer and union unfair labor practices.

The NLRB is located in Washington, D.C., and is made up of two branches: (1) the board itself, made up of five members, and (2) the general counsel, an independent officer who is responsible for prosecuting unfair labor practice cases. It has divided the country into several regions, with each region having an office, a director, staff, attorneys, and agents. Appeals of decisions made at the regional level go to the federal NLRB or the general counsel.

The general counsel has two primary functions:

1. To determine whether, when, and upon what basis unfair labor practice charges shall be prosecuted. The general counsel has the exclusive authority to prosecute a complaint; his determination not to issue a complaint is not subject to board or court review.
2. To supervise all employees in the regional offices and all attorneys (except those serving as administrative law judges or legal assistants to board members). But the appointment, transfer, demotion, or discharge of any regional director or of any officer in charge of a subregional office must have prior approval of the board.

The board has five main functions, as outlined in the NLRA:

1. To prevent and remedy unfair labor practices committed by employers or labor organizations
2. To determine representatives (i.e., to select a union) for purposes of collective bargaining
3. To determine the authority of representatives to have union shop provisions in their collective bargaining agreement (see note 1)
4. To determine jurisdictional disputes that have led to the filing of unfair labor practice charges
5. To poll employees on their employer's last offer in "national emergency" situations.

NOTE

1. A "union shop" is a place of employment where nonunion workers may be hired but must join the union within a certain period of time or lose their jobs. In an "agency shop," a worker is not required to join the union but must pay initiation fees and union dues because that worker will benefit from the union's collective bargaining accomplishments.

11.1.7. Certification of a Union

Before an employer and the union representing a unit of workers meet to negotiate a contract, the affected employees need to go through a process to be properly recognized as a union. There are three ways for a union to be certified:

1. NLRB election
2. Voluntary recognition
3. Board-ordered recognition without election.

Typically, an employer will voluntarily recognize a group of workers as a union only if the union has a particularly high level of bargaining power over the employer, or if the employer feels that most employees support unionization. The NHL, NBA, MLB, and NFL all voluntarily recognize the respective players associations (see note 2). If not voluntarily recognized by management, workers need to get 30% of the workers at a work site to sign a card declaring they would like to unionize. The NLRB will then hold an election at the work site and the employees will vote by secret ballot on whether to join the union. If more than 50% of the workers vote in favor of unionization, a union has been created and management will be required, under the NLRA, to negotiate a contract with that union. If an employer believes there was a problem with the certification election, it may refuse to bargain with that union, although the courts and the NLRB have not looked favorably upon this tactic, and it usually results in a violation of Section 8(a)(5).

NOTES

1. In *North American Soccer League v. NLRB*, 613 F.2d 1379 (5th Cir. 1980), the NLRB made a decision on representation in unionized sports. In *NASL*, the appeals court found that a leaguewide bargaining unit was the most practical unit structure, opposing the argument made by the league, which asserted a team-by-team unit structure. In the other

professional leagues, units are also structured on a leaguewide basis rather than by team or by position.

2. In the NFL, NBA, NHL, and MLB, players associations are "voluntarily" recognized in the sense that there was no NLRB election or board-ordered recognition. This does not necessarily mean that the leagues recognized the unions willingly. For example, the NBPA claims that the NBA refused to recognize the union at its inception in 1954, and did not do so until the players' threatened boycott of the 1964 All-Star Game. For more information, see www.nbpa.com

11.2. COLLECTIVE BARGAINING

Collective bargaining is an activity whereby two groups, union and management representatives, attempt to resolve conflicting interests by exchanging commitments pertaining to the terms and conditions of employment. Normally, employees are looking to secure better wages, job protection, health benefits, health and safety regulations, and a say in the practices that affect their daily work lives. Employers, on the other hand, want to maintain control of the workplace and make decisions they feel are in the best interests of the company or business. The collective bargaining process is designed to come to a compromise between these stands and to reach a contract.

11.2.1. The Collective Bargaining Process

A typical collective bargaining agreement is a complex document that deals with a broad range of diverse issues. A professional sport collective bargaining agreement is no different. It may establish a detailed wage scheduling system while others have different levels of minimum pay according to seniority. It contains a job classification system, a pension plan, and a clause determining how seniority or service is calculated. It also contains management promises of safe working conditions, no discrimination, and union recognition. It may also include articles that are specific to professional sports, such as salary arbitration, free agency, the college draft, and salary cap. More recent agreements have included maternity leave, drug policies, and counseling programs. A typical agreement also contains disciplinary measures and a definition of "just cause." Thus, collective bargaining agreements cover a wide range of issues and may be lengthy documents that affect most aspects of an employee's job.

The negotiating process actually begins before each side sits down at a table to negotiate. Prior to this stage, each set of representatives must determine what the important issues are. For the union, a bargaining committee is appointed or elected by the membership to represent the union in negotiations with management. The bargaining committee will determine, through surveys, meetings, or one-on-one discussions, what issues the union members feel strongly about. The bargaining committee will rely on reports from its representatives on each team. If the union is in its infancy, or bargaining its first contract, its demands will, in all likelihood, revolve around benefits, a minimum salary, and a pension plan. If the union has been in existence for many years, its demands will be more complex and may include increased free agency, salary arbitration, and an injury grievance procedure.

There are three factors that impact what a union will ask for in negotiations:

1. Maturity of the union

2. Bargaining power and leverage

3. Company/league stability.

The *maturity of the union* may play an important role in determining what a union will ask for in negotiations. If a union is negotiating its first contract, the power is on the side of management because the union, in all likelihood, lacks bargaining power, and is content to set minimum standards for wages, benefits, and a pension plan. Many unions negotiating their first contract are content with those items, and pursue items like player mobility or salary arbitration in subsequent negotiations (see note 1).

On the other hand, an established union has experience, public awareness, and many years of negotiations under its belt. Established unions like the United Auto Workers (UAW) and the Major League Baseball Players Association (MLBPA) have comprehensive contracts that are the result of decades of negotiations and renegotiations. The MLBPA is viewed by many to be the most successful labor union in sports. In fact, it is considered by some to be the nation's strongest trade union of *any* kind.

Bargaining power is another important factor a union needs to address. Bargaining power is the power a union brings with it to the negotiating table. UAW workers have a high level of bargaining power because a strike could cost auto companies billions of dollars in lost revenue. In addition, many established unions have funds set aside in the event of a strike/lockout that can be distributed to members during a work stoppage. With respect to professional athletes, their bargaining power can be high because of the popularity of the respective sport or stars in the sport and the lack of public acceptance for replacement players. Another important factor is the importance of sporting events to television networks and advertisers. However, in recent years, public opinion is no longer guaranteed to be in favor of the athletes in the case of a strike. The baseball strike in 1994–1995 and the lockout in the NBA in 1998 are two examples of public support being split between the owners and the players. Therefore, unions need to find their source of bargaining power and determine how it can best be applied. If it is high, and the threat of a strike is great, it is more likely that the union's demands will be met. However, if management believes public opinion will be in its favor in the event of a strike, it will have this in its favor in negotiations. Public perception of work stoppages in sports is a difficult subject as the public often fails to grasp players' rights under federal labor law in the face of multimillion-dollar contracts.

Company stability is another factor that can seriously affect negotiations. If a company is suffering because of a recession or a downturn in the economy, its negotiating team may ask for concessions or a wage rollback. In professional sports, during the 1982 NBA negotiations, the league claimed that it could not afford to maintain operations unless a salary cap was instituted. The NBPA audited the league's financial records and agreed that a cap was necessary. Much of the dissension between labor and management in the NBA in the 1990s was due to the fact that the league became extremely profitable and teams in the league were no longer in fear of insolvency. However, in the agreement that came out of the lockout during the 1998–1999 season, the NBA's salary cap provisions were in fact strengthened, a significant plus for the owners. In 2005, The NBA and NBPA negotiated a CBA very similar to the agreement first reached in 1999, but the salary cap was raised while the maximum length of contracts was reduced.

Following an owner's lockout that cancelled the 2004–2005 season, the NHL and NHLPA agreed to a collective bargaining agreement that included a salary cap. Prior to the negotiations, the NHL hired former Securities and Exchange Commission Chair Arthur Levitt to conduct a report on the finances of the NHL and its teams. The Levitt Report concluded that 19 of the 30 teams lost money during the 2002–2003 season for a total of $273 million. The owners in Major League Baseball have argued for a salary cap but thus far have only been able to influence salaries through the use of a luxury tax system in which teams are fined a certain percentage for every dollar of payroll over a certain threshold. The percentage charged increases for each instance a team exceeds the threshold, while at the same time the threshold increases annually.

NOTE

1. In the first MLS-MLSU CBA (2004-2010), the players focused on minimum salaries ($28,000 in 2005 rising to $34,000 in 2009), insurance benefits and a retirement plan. After contentious negotiations that threatened the 2010 season, a new deal was reached in May 2010 which provided more guaranteed contracts, increased compensation and a re-entry draft which should increase player mobility at the end of their contracts.

11.2.2. Mandatory and Permissive Subjects of Bargaining

When two parties sit down at the negotiating table, they are required to negotiate certain items. Mandatory subjects, as outlined in the NLRA, are wages, hours, and terms and conditions of employment. One side may threaten a strike or lockout potentially causing significant financial harm to force the other party to agree to a proposal on a mandatory subject. However, such a tactic cannot be legally used to force the other party to an agreement on a subject that is permissive but not mandatory. Permissive subjects are topics that may be bargained at the table if both sides are willing to do so, but if one side does not want to discuss a permissive topic, it is not required to do so. Exhibit 11.1 illustrates some examples of each category.

For example, in the professional sports industry, mandatory subjects of bargaining would include the college draft, the salary cap, a limitation on roster size, and health and safety issues because these issues directly affect the players' or employees' rate and methods of pay, work rules, and safety as outlined in exhibit 11.1. An example of a permissive subject of bargaining would be regulation of tickets for players. Permissive subjects of bargaining are included in collective bargaining agreements based on the willingness of both parties to negotiate over the issue. If a union is strong, it will be able to negotiate permissive subjects.

Exhibit 11.1
Mandatory and Permissive Subjects of Bargaining

Mandatory	Permissive
Rate and method of pay	Change in the bargaining unit
Work rules, discipline, drug testing	Identity of the bargaining agent
Safety	Status of supervisors
Grievance and arbitration procedures	Settlement of unfair labor practice charges
Health insurance, pensions, and layoff compensation	Internal union or company affairs

Conversely, if the union is weak, it will likely be unable to bargain these permissive subjects. Often permissive subjects of bargaining are not as important as the mandatory issues and are unlikely to make headlines, but one side may find them particularly important for various reasons. For example, the 2002 Major League Baseball Collective Bargaining Agreement outlined an agreement to print the new CBA in Spanish as well as English. In that case, the growing percentage of Spanish-speaking players felt it was very important that they be able to read and understand the agreement.

After the parties have come to an agreement on an item, they may "sign off" on it. That usually means that each chief negotiator, often the commissioner of the league and the executive director of the players association, initials the written language, and that particular item cannot be bargained over during that round of negotiations unless consented to by both sides. After each item has been agreed to or dropped, negotiations have finished. The length of collective bargaining agreements varies considerably, depending on the size and power of the union, the present financial health of the league, and the amount of changes to be made. The NHL-NHLPA 2005–2011 agreement is over 450 pages as the league adopted an entirely new financial structure by instituting a salary cap. It is important to remember that relevant issues will change depending on the industry and the different sports. For example, what may be important to steelworkers will be different in many respects from those working as bus drivers, secretaries, graduate student employees, or professional athletes. Similarly, the important issues for professional basketball players may be different from those of professional hockey players.

11.2.3. Ratification

Once an agreement has been reached on a tentative contract, the union must take it back to its membership for ratification. Ratification occurs when a vote is accepted by the membership. In most cases, the union needs 50% plus one of its membership to vote in favor of the contract for it to be ratified. Some unions have stipulations in their constitutions that dictate that 60% or 75% or more of the membership needs to vote in favor of the agreement for the ratification to be legitimate. If a union does not think the majority of its members support the agreement, it will return to the table for further negotiations. The negotiating team for management must present the contract to the owners and, depending upon the management structure, there also may need to be a vote. If the contract is ratified by both parties, the agreement will be implemented for the period that was agreed to in negotiations. The next round of bargaining can begin at any time before the agreement expires and may depend on either party's right to opt out of the agreement.

11.2.4. Decertification

If a union member or group of members decides they are unhappy with the way their union is being run or maintained, they have several options with which to initiate changes. There are internal remedies in the union's bylaws or constitution that may include disciplinary measures and other such avenues. Another option that is available is decertification. To decertify a union is to break all formal ties with the union and give up the right for that union to collectively bargain a collective bargaining agreement. After a petition is sent to the NLRB calling for a *decertification election*, an NLRB representative will conduct the election and the employees will vote, by secret ballot, whether to stay in the union or to decertify. As in a certification election, 50% plus one need to vote in favor of decertification for it to pass. If it does pass, all the employees who had been represented by a union would no longer have any affiliation with the union and no collective bargaining agreement would be in place. Players would no longer have a grievance procedure, a minimum salary, or health care/insurance. The league would also have the right to implement any new rules it deemed necessary (e.g., hard salary cap). When a union decertifies, its members lose all rights they had in the collective bargaining agreement. Union decertification has been uncommon to this point in professional sports due to the potential negative consequences it can have on a players union.

As discussed in section 11.3.3, "National Football League Players Association," there has been only one example of a decertification in professional sports, and it was due not to player unrest but rather to union leadership strategy. In 1992, NFL players voted to decertify the NFLPA as their exclusive bargaining representative, so that they could sue the NFL on antitrust grounds, which they did. The NFL owners were protected from antitrust litigation when a collective bargaining agreement was in place, but without one, there was no legal way of legitimizing several of their restrictive policies, mainly the right of first refusal system, which limited player mobility. Following decertification, NFL players won a series of class action lawsuits against the league and finally settled in 1993, in what became known as the *White* settlement. The settlement became part of a new collective bargaining agreement, and the NFLPA was again certified as the official bargaining representative of professional football players. The NFL claimed that the decertification was a sham and that the NFLPA never actually ceased to represent the players. In Article LVII, Mutual Reservation of Rights: Labor Exemption of the current NFL CBA, the NFL and its clubs waived the right to make any claim that any future decertification of the NFLPA "would be a sham, pretext, ineffective, requires additional steps, or has not in fact occurred." For more on the *White* settlement, see section 10.3.5, "Exemption after Decertification: *McNeil*."

11.3. COLLECTIVE BARGAINING IN PROFESSIONAL SPORTS

Professional athletes began seeking union representation over 100 years ago, but there was not an official players' union until the mid-1950s. Since that time, professional sports has been subject to continued labor conflict, especially since the 1970s. Each players association has been involved in at least one work stoppage, and thousands of games have been lost due to strikes and lockouts. Labor conflict in professional sports will be examined in greater detail in section 11.3.7.1, "Labor Disputes in Professional Sports." It is important to understand the history behind the unionization efforts of professional athletes, and to see what gains have been made since the 1970s.

Contracts in professional sports are different from *most* other forms of unionized employment, in that employees can negotiate their own contracts (see section 9.2.1.3, "Hierarchy of Contracts"). For example, it is typical that a union of butchers, teachers, or grocery workers will negotiate salaries into the collective bargaining agreement. Butchers with two years of seniority will get "x" dollars, butchers with five years of seniority will get "y" dollars, and so on. Therefore, such butchers will not be required (or allowed) to individually negotiate their salaries with their employer. In most professional sports leagues, the collective bargaining agreement sets a minimum salary and perhaps a maximum salary (a cap), but players and their agents are free to negotiate within such parameters. One notable exception is the WNBA, which has a salary scale based on seniority and draft position.

11.3.1. The Players Associations in Professional Sports

Most professional team sports athletes in the United States and Canada are represented by a labor union, more commonly referred to in the sports industry as a players association. These associations grew out of player frustrations with the way they were being treated by the league they played in and by the owners of their team. Many of these associations began as unofficial guilds started by players who had been adversely affected by a league or owner decision. By the 1960s, players in the NHL, NFL, MLB, and NBA had all been officially unionized and had begun collective bargaining negotiations with their respective leagues. Today, with the addition of the unionized athletes in the WNBA, players associations have become a powerful tool for the players, and may also be involved in licensing, marketing, representing players in disputes, and certifying player agents.

11.3.2. National Hockey League Players Association

National Hockey League players actively pursued unionization in the early 1950s, and by 1957, with Red Wing star Ted Lindsay as president, the NHL Players Association (NHLPA) was born. When the association was initially formed, it had not been legally recognized as a union by the league, but was still able to negotiate with the owners that a percentage of the money from a new television deal was to go directly into the players' pension fund. When the NHL expanded in 1967 from 6 to 12 teams, the players were officially certified as a union and made Alan Eagleson, an agent and lawyer, the NHLPA's first executive director (see note 1). Between 1967 and 1991, there were no work stoppages in the NHL. In 1991, Bob Goodenow became executive director after the players had become dissatisfied with Eagleson's leadership and concerned about allegations of embezzlement and fraud surrounding his tenure as executive director (see note 2). Under Goodenow, the NHLPA engaged in three work stoppages (1992, 1994–1995 and 2004–2005). Following the cancellation of the 2004–2005 season, Goodenow and the NHLPA ultimately accepted an agreement with a hard salary cap while also accepting significant salary rollbacks on July 21, 2005. Less than a week later, Goodenow resigned and then Senior Director of Business Affairs and Licensing Ted Saskin took over duties as the NHLPA's executive director. Saskin was fired in a unanimous vote by player representatives in May 2007, when it was determined that Saskin attempted to access player e-mail accounts without permission. Paul Kelly, a former assistant U.S. attorney for the District of Massachusetts, was hired as the new NHLPA executive director in October 2007 but then was fired in August 2009 for indefinite reasons. NHLPA executive Ian Penny took over as interim director. The 2004–2005 agreement runs until September 15, 2011, and remains in effect from year to year unless and until either party gives at least 120 days' notice of termination. The NHLPA also has an option to extend the agreement through September 15, 2012.

NOTES

1. Further information on the NHLPA is available at their Web site: www.nhlpa.com/.

2. In 1995, former NHL players filed a class action lawsuit against Alan Eagleson and all individual NHL teams. Among the claims made by the players: Eagleson accepted the reserve system that limited player mobility, to the detriment of the players; he urged players to approve the NHL-WHA merger without demanding concessions; he agreed to remove player representatives from the player pension fund, which gave control over the fund to the owners; and he cooperated with the NHL to maintain a union dominated by the interests of the NHL, to the detriment of the players. The conspiracy case was decided against the players in 1998 because they had waited too long to sue (statute of limitations). The U.S. Supreme Court upheld the decision in 2001 by refusing to hear the players' appeal. However, in 1997 Eagleson pled guilty to fraud and theft charges stemming from his actions as executive director of the NHLPA, spent six months in prison, and faced more than $1 million in fines.

3. For more on the NHL lockout and the resulting CBA, see Joshua M. Liebman, "Tip Your 'Cap' to the Players: 2007-2008 Off-Season Reveals NHL's Salary Cap Benefits On Players," 16 *Sports Lawyers Journal* 81 (2009).

11.3.3. National Football League Players Association

The NFL Players Association was formed in 1956, although between 1956 and 1967 little progress was made for the players, except for a small increase in their pension fund. However, beginning in the early 1970s, NFL players fought for increased benefits and increased player mobility in the courts and on the picket line. The first work stoppage in professional sports occurred in 1968, when NFL players boycotted the league's preseason games, and were subsequently locked out by the owners at the beginning of the regular season. Another short conflict occurred in 1970, during the merger of the AFL and the NFL, followed by a failed strike attempt in 1974, after the expiration of the agreement signed in 1970. Under the leadership of Executive Director Ed Garvey, a former attorney and player advocate, the NFLPA won two court decisions, *Smith v. Pro Football Inc.*, 528 F. Supp. 1266 (D.D.C. 1981) and *Mackey v. National Football League*, 543 F.2d 606 (8th Cir. 1976). These victories provided the players with leverage to negotiate new agreements. The *Mackey* decision abolished the Rozelle Rule, which severely limited player mobility.

However, in the 1977 and 1982 negotiations, the NFLPA gave up its fight for less restriction of player mobility in favor of increased minimum salaries, increased benefits, and an increased contribution to the pension fund, with the 1982 agreement coming after a 57-day strike. After an aborted strike in 1987, the NFLPA challenged the league's restrictive rules and regulations, using antitrust theory, in the court system. The NFLPA was decertified after not finding success in *Powell v. the NFL*, which allowed the players to successfully sue the NFL on antitrust grounds. After the successful *McNeil* verdict, the NFLPA was re-recognized, and subsequently signed a long-term collective bargaining agreement with the NFL in 1993 (see notes 3 and 4). The agreement granted players unrestricted free agency following their fourth accrued season in the league while subjecting teams to a salary cap based upon defined gross revenue (DGR) of the league and its teams. The agreement has been extended four times, most recently through 2012, as the league has experienced enormous financial growth: in 2006 the total value of NFL television contracts reached $3.1 billion annually. However, during the last extension there was some acrimony over the distribution of football-related revenue that would be a sign of things to come (see note 5). Gene Upshaw, a Hall of Fame guard with the Oakland Raiders served as executive director of the NFLPA from 1983 until his death in 2008. In 2009, the NFLPA elected Washington, D.C., attorney DeMaurice Smith as its new executive director.

In May 2008, NFL owners opted out of the agreement unanimously. As a result, 2010 became the final season of the agreement and was played without a salary cap pursuant to the agreement. The agreement had been crafted with "poison pills" meant to encourage both sides to extend the agreement before its expiration and avoid a work stoppage. For the NFLPA, its poison was that in the final league year, to be an unrestricted free agent, a player required six accrued seasons instead of four. For the NFL clubs, their poison was that there would be no salary cap, leading to the possibility that large revenue teams like the Redskins and Cowboys would outspend everyone and parity would be ruined. However, in addition to no salary cap in the final league year, there is also no salary floor, allowing cheaper terms to make tremendous cost savings at the players' expense.

The owners felt that the players received too large a share of revenues in the previous extension and wanted the proportions corrected. However, there remained many other substantive issues on which the parties were having difficult agreeing, including commissioner discipline, rookie compensation, player health and benefits, signing bonus forfeitures, and drug testing (see note 2).

NOTES

1. The NFL Collective Bargaining Agreement can be viewed at www.nflpa.org.

2. The NFL wants to add testing for human growth hormone to its Performance Enhancing Drug Policy. However, presently there is only a blood test available and the NFLPA has resisted subjecting its players to such tests (for more on the NFL's drug testing policy and commissioner discipline, see section 7.2.4.1, "National Football League," and section 16.1.5, "Off-the-Field Criminal Conduct"). For more on signing bonus forfeitures, see section 9.2.1.6, "Bonus Clauses." For more information on the health of NFL players, current and retired, see Brett Edwin LoVellette, "'Mortal [K]ombat in Cleats': An Examination of the Effectiveness of the National Football League's Disability Plan and Its Impact on Retired Players," 36 *Pepperdine Law Review* 1101 (2009); A. Jason Huebinger, "Beyond the Injured Reserve: The Struggle Facing Former NFL Players in Obtaining Much Needed Disability Assistance," 16 *Sports Lawyers Journal* 279 (2009); and Bryan Lipsky, "Dealing with the NFL's Concussion Problems of Yesterday, Today, and Tomorrow," 18 *Fordham Intellectual Property, Media and Entertainment Law Journal* 959 (2008).

3. In *Powell v. NFL*, 678 F. Supp. 777 (D. Minn. 1988), NFL players challenged the NFL's restrictions on free agency, specifically the right of first refusal/compensation system under antitrust law. The case went to the appeals court, *Powell v. National Football League*, 930 F.2d 1293 (8th Cir. 1989), where the court found that the NFL was protected against antitrust litigation due to the labor exemption. The Supreme Court denied *certiorari*.

4. *McNeil v. NFL*, 777 F. Supp. 1475 (D. Minn. 1991) occurred after the National Football League Players Association decertified so that players could sue the league, using antitrust theory. The labor exemption, which protects leagues from antitrust challenges when there is a collective bargaining agreement in place, is no longer applicable when a union has decertified. In *McNeil*, the players challenged Plan B free agency (the owners' response to the challenge against right of first refusal), and were successful. Following *McNeil*, another lawsuit was filed, *White v. NFL*, 41 F.3d 402 (8th Cir. 1994), which culminated in the "White settlement," the basis for a new collective bargaining agreement between the players and the league.

5. The 2006 extension changed DGR to total revenue (TR) to better account for all football-related income, particularly revenues from stadiums owned by NFL franchises, an increasing trend. Players received a smaller percentage of TR as compared previously to DGR, but the end result was a higher salary cap. Cincinnati Bengals owner Mike Brown and Buffalo Bills owner Ralph Wilson were the only owners to vote against the extension of the CBA, fearing it provided insufficient cost controls to smaller franchises such as theirs.

6. Prior to the 2010 season, an arbitrator ruled that the NFL clubs could not discontinue a supplemental revenue sharing program during the uncapped year. The NFLPA filed the grievance fearing that in the absence of this source of revenue, player salaries would be negatively effected.

11.3.4. National Basketball Players Association

The National Basketball Players Association came into existence in 1954, with Boston Celtics' superstar Bob Cousy as its first president, at a time when player unrest in professional basketball was reaching a very high level due to owner ambivalence toward player demands. However, it was not until 1964, after NBA players threatened to boycott the All-Star Game, that the NBA formally recognized the NBPA and agreed to a pension plan. The league then entered into the first collective bargaining agreement in professional sports in 1967. The first executive director of the NBPA was Larry Fleischer, who maintained a low profile and allowed NBA players like Oscar Robertson, Paul Silas, and John Havlicek to help keep the players union in operation during its formative years. In the early 1980s, the NBA and team owners asked the players to accept a salary cap due to the precarious financial position of the NBA and its teams. The NBPA accepted, but only after reviewing the financial records of the teams. With the sport achieving great levels of financial success and popular acceptance by the 1990s, the players, under the leadership of Executive Director Billy Hunter, demanded that the salary cap be dismantled. In 1998 the NBA encountered its first significant work stoppage when the owners locked out their players prior to the beginning of the 1998 season. In January 1999, the NBA season was salvaged when the players agreed to further limits on the salary cap and new minimums for rookies, in exchange for minor concessions. That collective bargaining agreement was extended through the 2004–2005 season. A new CBA was reached July 1, 2005, that resulted in the reduction of the maximum length of a contract to six years from seven, a minimum age requirement, and an increased salary cap. The current agreement expires June 30, 2011, and revenue distribution between the owners and the players, as always, will be a major issue.

NOTES _____

1. The NBA Collective Bargaining Agreement can be viewed on the NBPA website: www.nbpa.com.

2. Commissioner discipline has long been a major issue for the NBA. In January 2010, NBA Commissioner David Stern suspended Washington Wizards guard Gilbert Arenas indefinitely after it was revealed he brandished a firearm in the locker room. Arenas admitted to storing firearms in his locker and pled guilty to carrying an unlicensed pistol. There was discussion that the Wizards could attempt to void the remaining three and a half years on Arenas's six-year $111 million contract. However, the Wizards were considered to be constrained by precedent (see section 11.3.14, "Grievance Procedures in Professional Sports"). See also section 16.1, "Athletes, Violence, and Criminal Law."

11.3.5. Major League Baseball Players Association

The first players association of any kind was the Brotherhood of Professional Baseball Players, formed in 1887, in response to the National League's initiation of the reserve clause in the player contract (see section 10.3.1.1, "History of the Reserve System"). The brotherhood, led by its first president, New York Giant John Montgomery Ward, battled the reserve clause and other contractual issues through the court system. In 1891, the brotherhood was dissolved due to financial reasons, then reemerged in 1900 for two years. The next attempt at organizing a players union came in 1946, when members of the Pittsburgh Pirates formed the American Baseball Guild and attempted to bargain with Pirates management (see note 2). This effort failed, but it motivated the players to stand up for their rights and benefits. In 1953, the Major League Baseball Players Association was formed after player representatives were barred from meetings with the owners. The MLBPA, under the leadership of Marvin Miller (1967–1993), enjoyed considerable success at the bargaining table and became the model for all other players' associations. However, this success came at a price: Major League Baseball experienced seven major work stoppages between 1972 and 1994, including the cancellation of the 1994 World Series. Under the leadership of Donald Fehr (1994–2009) and Michael Weiner (2009–present), the MLBPA is one of the strongest unions in the United States. The 2002 collective bargaining agreement was the first one in Major League Baseball reached without a work stoppage of some kind. The MLBPA was forced by congressional pressure to accept the introduction of steroid testing but withstood the pressure of MLB to accept a salary cap. In 2005, after increasing government scrutiny, MLB and the MLBPA reopened the CBA to alter the drug testing policy. The new policy included a 50-game suspension for a first positive test, 100 games for a second positive test, and a lifetime ban for a third positive test (for more on MLB's drug testing issues and policy, see section 7.2.4.3, "Major League Baseball"). Without much notice, MLB and the MLBPA negotiated an extension to the CBA prior to the 2006 World Series that would run through the 2011 season. No significant changes were made, though the luxury tax or "competitive balance tax" thresholds were raised and draft pick compensation for free agent signings was reduced.

NOTES _____

1. The MLB Collective Bargaining Agreement and the Joint Drug Agreement can be viewed and downloaded through the MLBPA website: http://mlb.mlb.com/pa/.

2. While there were no prominent efforts to form a players' union between 1900 and 1946, the Federal League of 1914–1915 was very much an outgrowth of player discontent with the National and American Leagues. Some major stars jumped to the Federal League, including Joe Tinker, Three Finger Brown, and Hal Chase. This league had the impact of a players association, because player salaries increased in the National and American Leagues due to the rival league's presence. The three leagues negotiated a settlement prior to the 1916 season, and the Federal League agreed to disband. The Baltimore franchise was unhappy with this settlement, and brought the *Federal Baseball* case, discussed at length in Chapter 10, particularly in section 10.3.1.2, "Creation of the Baseball Exemption: *Federal Baseball*."

3. For a more detailed introduction to unionization in professional baseball, see John Helyar, *Lords of the Realm* (New York: Ballantine Books, 1994); Marvin Miller, *A Whole Different Ballgame: The Sport and Business of Baseball* (New York: Birch Lane Press, 1991); and Roger Abrams, *Legal Bases: Baseball and the Law* (Philadelphia: Temple University Press, 1998).

11.3.6. Other Players Associations in North America

Following are discussions of three other players' associations: the WNBA, the Arena Football League, and the Canadian Football League. In addition, there is a brief discussion on potential player associations.

11.3.6.1. Women's National Basketball Association

In early November 1998, WNBA players chose the NBPA, which represents NBA players, as their representative in collective bargaining with the NBA owners of the women's professional league. The NBPA made an immediate impact; the draft for the 1999 season was delayed in the wake of protracted negotiations with the owners. A final settlement was reached in time to start the season on schedule that provided the players' health benefits, a maternity policy, a restriction on ABL players (see note 2) and increased minimum salaries.

The most recent agreement was reached in 2008 and extends through 2013. Among the key provisions of the newest agreement are:

1. Increased the salary cap to as high as $772,000 in 2008 and $913,000 in 2013.
2. Increased minimum salaries to $34,500 for rookies and $50,000 for veterans.
3. Provided more flexibility for players to move teams: under the previous agreement, teams could designate two "core" players who could not sign with other teams, similar to the franchise tag system in the NFL. Under the new deal, teams could only designate one player as a "core" player.

NOTES _____

1. The WNBA Collective Bargaining Agreement can be viewed on the WNBA website: http://www.wnbpa.com/

2. The ABL was a women's professional basketball league that competed with the WNBA from 1996 to 1999. The 1998 WNBA collective bargaining agreement stipulated that during the 1999 season, WNBA teams could include on their rosters up to three players who last played in the American Basketball League (ABL)—except for the league's two new teams, the Orlando Miracle and the Minnesota Lynx, which could include up to five former ABL players. After the 1999 season, there were restrictions on the number of former ABL players on WNBA rosters. The issue became moot in 1999, when the ABL folded.

11.3.6.2. Major League Soccer

Following the league's inaugural 1996 season, the players of Major League Soccer (MLS) formed the Major League Soccer Players Association (MLSPA) and voted to have the National Football League Players Association (NFLPA) represent them. In February 1997, the MLSPA filed an antitrust lawsuit, *Fraser v. Major League Soccer*, 97 F. Supp. 2d 130 (D. Mass. 2000), *Aff'd by*, 284 F.3d 47 (1st Cir. 2002), against MLS, challenging the league's single-entity structure that prevents free agency. Under the league's structure, players must sign their contracts with the league and are assigned to their respective team. This case is discussed in more detail in section 10.3.9, "Single-Entity Leagues: *Fraser v. MLS*."

Following the league's victory in the lawsuit in 2002, MLS players set out to form a stronger union to collectively bargain the terms of their employment with the league. In May 2003, the Major League Soccer Players Union (MLSPU) was formed, ending the players' relationship with the NFLPA.

Eventually, in November 2004, the MLSPU successfully completed a collective bargaining agreement with MLS running through the 2009 season. The agreement raised minimum salaries, improved health insurance plans, increased the contribution to pension plans, and increased players' share of licensing revenues. The MLSPU failed to gain ground on the issue of free agency, which allows a team to hold exclusive negotiation rights to a player even when his contract expires. A new CBA was struck prior to the 2010 season that provided for more guaranteed contracts, increased compensation and a re-entry draft which should increase player mobility at the end of their contracts.

11.3.6.3. Arena Football League

The circumstances surrounding the unionization of Arena Football League players illustrate the difference between labor relations in the sports industry and in other industries. They also illustrate the confluence of labor and antitrust law in professional sports.

At the end of 1999, AFL players began to reevaluate their relationship with AFL owners. The players believed that AFL owners had joined together to eliminate competition for their services, prohibited injury and other contractual guarantees, and fixed the terms of employment for each player at uncompetitive levels. Then came a rather unique sequence of events:

1. The players voted to be represented by the Arena Football League Players' Organizing Committee (AFLPOC) in 2000.

2. Players then filed a complaint with the NLRB in February 2000, alleging the league's owners forced them to become part of the union.

3. The AFLPOC and Arena Football League negotiated a six-year collective bargaining agreement.

4. In August 2000, the collective bargaining agreement was thrown out and the NLRB moved to have the AFLPOC decertified. This occurred after NLRB officials claimed that owners coerced players into joining the union through offers of financial assistance and threats of job loss—violations of Sections 8(a)(2) and 8(a)(3) of the National Labor Relations Act.

5. The players filed a Sherman Act Section 1 antitrust lawsuit in Federal District Court in New Jersey.

6. In May 2001, owners and players reached a tentative settlement. Players agreed to drop all of their pending NLRB and antitrust claims in exchange for a minimum salary increase from $900 per game to $1,400 per game, and salary guarantees for injured players. The deal also guarantees that the players receive a salary cap share of 63% of the designated gross revenue, which includes money from TV and radio contracts, as well as ticket sales, but not parking and concessions. Under the settlement, if players did not form a union by the end of the 2001 season, owners could break the agreement.

7. In June 2001, players began new certification elections, deciding whether they would be represented by the AFLPOC or the Arena Football League Players' Association (AFLPA). The AFLPA received 77% of the votes and was later certified by the NLRB as the collective bargaining representative for AFL players. The AFLPA is supported by the United Food and Commercial Workers International Union.

In most industries, management would strongly prefer that their employees not unionize. Not so, in many professional team sports. Regardless of whether the AFL players' "company union" accusations are accurate, it is clear that AFL owners want the players to join some type of union. This is because of the antitrust immunity granted to sports leagues by the nonstatutory labor exemption (see section 10.3.2, "The Nonstatutory Labor Exemption").

The AFLPA is represented by the same staff and executives as the NFLPA and in June 2002 negotiated for a collective bargaining agreement through the 2010 season. That agreement was extended through 2015 and included a salary cap based on defined gross revenue, similar to the NFL model at the time. The salary cap was $1,903,418 for the 2007 season and was scheduled to be $2,866,099 for the 2015 season. However, due to economic issues, the AFL was unable to play a season in 2009. The AFL returned for the 2010 season, including teams from the original AFL as well as Arena Football League 2 teams. The AFL agreed to continue providing health insurance for players during 2009 and to work with the AFLPA to create a new collective bargaining agreement when they determined they could financially return to play.

NOTE

1. The AFL Collective Bargaining Agreement can be viewed through the AFLPA website: http://www.aflplayers.org/.

11.3.6.4. Canadian Football League Players Association

The Canadian Football League Players Association (CFLPA), formed in 1965, initially requested a pension plan, revision of the standard player contract, and increased salaries for Grey Cup (Canadian Super Bowl) participants. While the league did address all of these matters in the next few years, and even granted restricted free agency in 1971, relations became more contentious by early 1974. First of all, the CFLPA believed that the league had retaliated against prominent union members. Gary Schreider, the first president of the CFLPA, was traded to three different teams and then released (see note 1). Second, the CFLPA resented that players were not compensated for 10 weeks of training camp and preseason games. In June 1974, the players engaged in a "voluntary retirement" strike during training camp. CFL owners flew replacement players into training camp. The strike ended three weeks later, with the players receiving their requested preseason pay.

Since the mid-1970s, the CFL and CFLPA have maintained relatively amicable relations. This is largely due to the league's precarious financial situation. The CFL nearly folded in the late 1990s, and the CFLPA has recognized all along that it cannot make the demands that are made by some of the other players' unions. A new collective bargaining agreement was reached in 2001 that continued to maintain that players would continue to receive at least 50% of gross revenue and place the "competitive expenditure cap" at $2.6 million in 2005, the last year of the agreement. The cap allows for certain exceptions such as the third highest paid quarterback, the second highest paid designated import player, and players on the "nine game" injury list, which consists of players who are deemed incapable of playing nine games that season and cannot return until they have sat out at least nine games. The CBA was extended in 2006 and again in 2010. The 2010 extension increased the salary cap to $4.2 million although it decreased the player's share of revenue. Also the two sides agreed to the league's first ever drug testing policy.

NOTE

1. CFLPA history is available on its website: www.cflpa.com.

11.3.6.5. Potential Unionization of Minor League Baseball and College Athletics

Minor league baseball players and intercollegiate athletes have not formed players associations. Some of the reasons for this are logistical, but other reasons have a legal basis. In a logistical sense, most minor league and collegiate players are unwilling to make the sacrifices and take the risks necessary for unionization due to their short careers at such levels. In other words, assuming unionization attempts could be successful, the fruits of unionization would probably arrive after the initiators had graduated or moved on to other leagues. Thus, any effort to unionize would be purely altruistic.

In a legal sense, minor league baseball players would be inhibited from unionizing due to the Curt Flood Act of 1998 (see section 10.3.1.5, "The Curt Flood Act"). While the act ended MLB's immunity against antitrust suits from *major* league players, it reaffirmed MLB's antitrust protection from minor league players, umpires, owners, and other groups. Other minor league players who have unionized, such as minor league hockey players, have used the per se Sherman Act violation inherent in their league's reserve clause in order to gain negotiating leverage (see note 1). Because MLB is exempt from Sherman Act scrutiny, minor league baseball players would not have that type of leverage if they unionized.

In revenue-producing intercollegiate sports such as men's Division I Bowl Sub-division football and Division I basketball, the athlete's market value often exceeds the economic value of his scholarship. Furthermore, men's basketball coaches can receive millions of dollars for having their players wear certain brands of shoes, while the players are compensated only with an athletic scholarship (see note 2). Periodically over the years, there have been attempts to unionize college athletes. However, the *Rensing* decision (see note 3) held that intercollegiate athletics are inherent to a student-athlete's educational experience, and therefore, the athletic scholarship does not establish an employment relationship (see section 6.3.2, "Participation Rules"). Because the NLRA's jurisdiction is restricted to employer-employee relationships, unionization would be difficult unless this decision is overturned.

NOTES

1. Because minor league baseball players are not a part of the union, MLB can drug test them without having to collectively bargain the procedure for doing so. For more on this issue, see Jonathan D. Gillerman, "Calling Their Shots: Miffed Minor Leaguers, the Steroid Scandal, and Examining the Use of Section 1 of the Sherman Act to Hold MLB Accountable," 73 *Albany Law Review* 541 (2010).

2. For more information about the hurdles that college athletes would face prior to unionization, see Rohith A. Parasuraman, "Unionizing NCAA Division I Athletics: A Viable Solution?" 57 *Duke Law Journal* 727 (2007) and Jonathan H. Nygren, "Forcing the NCAA to Listen: Using Labor Law to Force the NCAA to Bargain Collectively with Student-Athletes," 2 *Virginia Sports & Entertainment Law Journal* 359 (2003).

3. In *Rensing v. Indiana State University Board of Trustees*, 444 N.E. 2d 1170 (Ind. 1983), the Indiana Supreme Court ruled that a college scholarship is not a contract of

employment, and therefore an athlete who is injured during intercollegiate competition or practice is not eligible for workers' compensation benefits. The court held that there must be a mutual belief that an employer-employee relationship exists, and that it is clear in the NCAA constitution that intercollegiate sports are viewed as part of the educational system, and are therefore distinguishable from the professional sports business.

11.3.7. Collective Bargaining Agreements in Professional Sports

Notwithstanding unique provisos such as salary caps and salary arbitration, collective bargaining agreements (CBAs) between professional leagues and their players associations contain many of the same elements found in the CBAs of other industries. It is important to remember that unionized athletes are actually covered under two contracts: their own standard player contract and the collective bargaining agreement negotiated between the league and the players association. Therefore, when a players association negotiates with a league, it does not bargain over individual player's salaries, but over the "terms and conditions" of employment. For example, rather than negotiate over a player's salary, the NFLPA and the NFL will negotiate over a salary cap that may limit the amount a rookie may make in his first year. However, it will be up to that rookie and his agent to negotiate with the individual club over his contract, within the limits set by the collective bargaining agreement. It is important to remember that an athlete may negotiate anything into the standard player contract as long as it does not violate the collective bargaining agreement in the league, or any other relevant labor laws.

11.3.7.1. Labor Disputes in Professional Sports

Labor disputes in professional sports are now as much a part of the game as franchise relocations and coach firings. The last three decades have produced over a dozen work stoppages in the four major professional leagues, costing teams and players hundreds of millions of dollars and angering millions of fans. It is a reality that where there is collective bargaining, there exists the possibility of a strike by the players, or a lockout initiated by the owners. Below is an outline of the work stoppages each league has participated in, followed by some analysis and explanation on strikes, lockouts, and other notable labor disputes that have arisen in professional sports.

NOTE _____

1. In November 2001, Major League Baseball voted to buy and then eliminate two of the league's lowest revenue producing teams. Although MLB admitted that it considered 18 franchises for possible contraction, it was widely believed that the Minnesota Twins and Montreal Expos franchises were selected for contraction. This situation caused concern for the MLBPA, as the contraction would eliminate at least 50 jobs for MLB players. The MLBPA quickly filed a grievance, contending that the contraction plans were subject to collective bargaining and could not be carried out without the players' consent. The union also contended that the owners violated the labor contract and damaged the free agent market as a result of the contraction issue. The issue was settled in the 2002 collective bargaining agreement with MLB agreeing to "not undertake any centralized effort to reduce

the number of Major League Clubs effective for a season covered by this agreement" (Article XV—Miscellaneous, Section H. Future Contraction). Eventually the Montreal Expos were sold to Major League Baseball, moved to Washington, D.C., and renamed the Nationals, while a legal injunction was granted in the case of the Twins to keep them in Minneapolis (see section 9.2.9, "Facility Contracts").

11.3.7.1.1. Strikes

A strike occurs when a group of employees refuse to work, and vow not to return to work until their demands have been met. The right to strike is regulated by legislation, namely the National Labor Relations Act (as amended in 1947). There are two kinds of strikes: a *primary strike* and a *secondary strike.* A primary strike occurs when employees of a company strike against their employer: Major League Baseball players strike against their employer, Major League Baseball (MLB). A secondary strike, which may be illegal under 8(b)(4)(b) of the National Labor Relations Act, occurs when a group of employees at one company strike their employer to protest a strike happening at another company (see note 3). For example, if MLB players go on strike to support striking professional hockey players, that is a secondary strike. According to labor law, secondary strikes do so at their own risk (i.e., MLB teams could potentially terminate such players, with cause).

There are two kinds of primary strikes: *unfair labor practice strikes* and *economic strikes.* An unfair labor practice strike occurs when a group of employees strike because of an employer's unfair labor practice. For example, if a player in the NFL is discharged because of his union affiliation, NFL players may initiate a strike. Another example of an unfair labor practice strike occurs when employees strike because of their employer's failure to bargain in good faith (e.g., 1994 MLB strike). An economic strike occurs when employees strike over wages, hours, or working conditions, and usually takes place when employees are seeking a new collective bargaining agreement. Debates regarding whether a strike is an unfair labor practice or an economic dispute are determined by the NLRB.

Employees who are engaged in a lawful strike may not be discharged from their jobs because of the strike. However, they may be replaced by replacement workers for the period of their strike, and may be replaced permanently, depending upon the type of strike. If the strike in question is an economic strike, strikers can be permanently replaced, but must be reinstated as vacancies occur. Employees who strike over an unfair labor practice may be temporarily replaced, but with the end of the strike, they have full reinstatement rights, including their seniority and benefits. In addition to players, umpires have also gone on strike (see note 1).

NOTES

1. During the 2009–2010 preseason, the NBA was forced to use replacement referees because it could not come to an agreement with the National Basketball Referees Association on a new labor contract. Just days before the season started the parties reached a two-year deal that provided for a slight raise in referee salaries.

2. Showing solidarity that their big league counterparts had previously lacked, during the 2006 season, the Association of Minor League Umpires (AMLU) went on strike from April 6 until May 31. The 220 umpires were seeking raises from salaries that began at $1,800 per month at the lowest levels and peaked at $17,000 annually in AAA. The umpires

Exhibit 11.2
NHL Salary Arbitration, 2006–2011 Collective Bargaining Agreement
12.1. Eligibility

(a) A player is eligible to elect salary arbitration if the player meets the qualifications set forth in the following chart and in Section 12.1(b) below:

First Standard Player Contract (SPC) Signing Age	Minimum Level Professional Experience Required To Be Eligible for Salary Arbitration
18–20	4 years professional experience
21	3 years professional experience
22–23	2 years professional experience
24 and older	1 year professional experience

A player aged 18 or 19 earns a year of "professional experience" by playing ten (10) or more NHL games in a given season. A player aged 20 or above (or who turns 20 between September 16 and December 31 of the calendar year in which he signs his first SPC) earns a year of professional experience by playing ten (10) or more professional games under an SPC in a given season.

(g) Evidence.

    (i) Subject to the limitations set forth in subsection (iii) below, the parties may present whatever witnesses, affidavits, documents and other relevant evidence they choose to present at the hearing. The Arbitrator, on behalf of any party, or on his own behalf, may call witnesses or request documents or other evidence, as he deems necessary to resolve the dispute. The Arbitrator in his discretion shall be the judge of the relevancy and materiality of the evidence offered and/or the weight, if any, to attach to any evidence and shall not be bound by any formal legal rules of evidence. All evidence shall be presented in the presence of all the parties, unless a party is in default, having failed to appear for the hearing, or has waived his right to be present. Statistical evidence asserted in a party's affirmative case must be included in such party's brief in order to be admissible.

  (ii) The parties may offer evidence of the following:

    (A) the overall performance, including official statistics prepared by the League (both offensive and defensive) of the Player in the previous season or seasons;

    (B) the number of games played by the Player, his injuries or illnesses during the preceding seasons;

    (C) the length of service of the Player in the League and/or with the Club;

    (D) the overall contribution of the Player to the competitive success or failure of his Club in the preceding season;

    (E) any special qualities of leadership or public appeal not inconsistent with the fulfillment of his responsibilities as a playing member of his team;

    (F) the overall performance in the previous season or seasons of any Player(s) who is alleged to be comparable to the party Player whose salary is in dispute; and

Exhibit 11.2
(continued)

(G) The compensation of any Player(s) who is alleged to be comparable to the party player, provided, however, that in applying this or any of the above subparagraphs, the Salary Arbitrator shall not consider a Player(s) to be comparable to the party Player unless a party to the arbitration has contended that the Player(s) is comparable; nor shall the Salary Arbitrator consider the compensation or performance of a Player(s) unless a party to the arbitration has contended that the Player(s) is comparable.

(iii) The following categories of evidence are inadmissible and shall not be considered by the Salary Arbitrator:

(A) Any SPC the term of which began when the Player party to such SPC was not a Group 2 Player;

(B) Any SPC entered into by an Unrestricted Free Agent, including SPCs signed by Players after the Player's Club has exercised a walk-away right pursuant to Section 12.10;

(C) The SPC of any Player who is not being offered as a comparable Player to the party Player;

(D) Qualifying Offers made by the Club pursuant to Section 10.2(b);

(E) Any prior offers or history of negotiations between the Player and the Club;

(F) Testimonials, videotapes, newspaper columns, press game reports or similar materials;

(G) Any reference to actual or potential walk-away rights;

(H) Any award issued by a Salary Arbitrator as to which a Club exercised its walk-away rights pursuant to Section 12.10;

(I) The financial condition of the Club or the League;

(J) References to a Club's Upper or Lower Limit, or to the Players' Share;

(K) Any salary arbitration award issued in 2005–06; or

(L) Any reference to any salary or other compensation information in any salary arbitration opinion that took place prior to the execution of this Agreement. If any salary arbitration opinion issued prior to the execution of this Agreement is cited as precedent, all references to any Player's Player Paragraph 1 Salary or other compensation information will be redacted.

eventually reached a new collective bargaining agreement through the 2011 season with the Professional Baseball Umpiring Corporation that raised salaries by $1,000 per month and $3 per diem.

3. With their collective bargaining agreement set to expire on December 31, 1999, Major League Baseball umpires, under the guidance of union head Richie Phillips, staged a group resignation. They did so because of a no-strike pledge in their collective bargaining agreements. Phillips believed that all 68 umpires were going to resign. However, only 57 did so, and 27 of those 57 quickly rescinded. Major League Baseball accepted the resignation of 22 of the umpires, the majority of whom were shocked that their negotiating ploy had

failed. Phillips filed an unfair labor practice charge, which was rejected by the NLRB. The umpires then voted to decertify in November 1999, and reform without Phillips. The matter went to arbitration, and was eventually decided by arbitrator Alan Symonette in May 2001, *In the Matter of the Arbitration Between the Major League Umpires' Association and the National League of Professional Baseball Clubs & the American League of Professional Baseball Clubs*, Case No. 14 300 1395 99. MLB was ordered to rehire 9 of the 22 umpires who had resigned. Among those not rehired were umpires shown to have deficient skills and those with less than five years of major league experience, who were not protected by "merit" and "skill" provisions. In February 2002, baseball owners agreed to rehire another 5 of the 22 umpires who lost their jobs in the failed mass resignation of 1999 and to allow 4 more of the umps to retire with back pay and benefits.

4. Sympathy strikes are different from secondary strikes in that sympathy strikers are not themselves striking against an employer because of a dispute; rather, they are honoring a picket line that may be in place *at their work site* but manned by another work group. For example, if NBA referees went on strike—and replacement referees were being used—NBA players could decide not to cross the referees' picket line, and engage in a sympathy strike by not playing their games until the referee dispute was settled. It is important to note that sympathy strikers will be classified in the same category as the strikers they are supporting. Therefore, if the sympathy strike is over an economic issue, the sympathy strikers will be considered economic strikers.

11.3.7.1.2. Lockouts

A lockout that is used by an employer to preempt a strike occurs when an employer prohibits its employees from working. There are two types of lockouts: *defensive lockouts* and *offensive lockouts*. A defensive lockout occurs when an employer fears a strike by its employees at a time when it is most vulnerable (e.g., right before the playoffs in sports), and thus initiates a lockout at a time that is more conducive to the company (e.g., during the off-season). An offensive lockout occurs when an employer initiates a lockout in an effort to put economic pressure on its employees, a tactic normally used during negotiations of a new collective bargaining agreement.

A recent offensive lockout in professional sports occurred when the National Basketball Association locked out its players during the summer of 1998 because of stalled negotiations over a new collective bargaining agreement. The owners had initiated the negotiations after voting to reopen the collective bargaining agreement signed in 1996. The lockout began on July 1, 1998, after the union and the league could not come to an agreement on a hard salary cap.

Several important legal issues were addressed during this lockout. The players association filed a grievance with arbitrator John Feerick in an attempt to get players with guaranteed contracts paid during the lockout. On October 20, 1998, Feerick ruled in favor of the league, and announced that owners would not have to pay guaranteed contracts during the work stoppage. The lockout continued, and in early January 1999, Commissioner Stern spoke of the possible use of replacement players for the 1999–2000 season. On January 6, 1999, the NBA and the NBPA reached agreement on a new collective bargaining agreement. It is important to note that had replacement players been used in the lockout, several new legal issues would have been raised. The NBA may not have been able to use replacement players in their Canadian franchises, as the provinces of British Columbia (Vancouver Grizzlies) and Ontario (Toronto Raptors) ban replacement workers. In addition, the question of whether locked out employees can be permanently replaced would have been raised. Both of these questions would have been important legal issues had the lockout continued and if replacement players had been used, and these issues may have been litigated.

NOTES

1. The NBA had locked out its players twice in the 1990s prior to the lockout in 1998. In 1995 the league initiated a one-month lockout after the players refused to ratify a new collective bargaining agreement. No games were lost. The owners again locked the players out in July 1996 after there was disagreement between the league and the union over $50 million in television revenue redistribution. That lockout ended after several hours, after the sides were able to resolve this issue.

2. Unions have argued that an employer lockout is in violation of 8(a)(3) of the NLRA because it discourages an employee from participating in union activity. The courts have not agreed with this argument, and allow both defensive and offensive lockouts, equating the lockout with employees' right to strike. However, a lockout will be considered illegal if it is waged over a *permissible*, rather than a *mandatory*, subject of bargaining. A lockout will also be considered illegal if it is waged to coerce workers into voting against their union in an upcoming election. For more information, see Michael Evan Gold, *An Introduction to Labor Law*, rev. ed. (Ithaca, N.Y.: Cornell University Press, 1998).

11.3.7.1.3. Impasse

Both strikes and lockouts are usually the result of some form of impasse in negotiations over a particularly contentious issue, such as free agency or a salary cap. Impasse occurs when the two sides in negotiations have bargained in good faith but have reached a deadlock position on a particular issue or issues. A number of factors determine whether a good-faith impasse has occurred:

1. Bargaining history
2. The good faith of the parties
3. Length of negotiations
4. Importance of the issues that are in disagreement
5. The understanding of the parties as to the state of negotiations
6. Fluidity of positions
7. Demonstration of willingness by parties to consider a proposal.

At no time before good faith impasse can an employer unilaterally implement a change in wages, hours, or terms and conditions of employment. When a good faith impasse is reached, the employer has the right to implement its "last-best offer," or parts thereof. The employer cannot implement any changes that are worse than what was last proposed to the union. When an impasse has been reached, the union has the choice to accept it, file an unfair labor practice charge arguing impasse had not been reached, or strike over the matter. To ensure that employers are not able to charge impasse after the first bargaining session, 8(a)(5) of the NLRA protects unions against surface bargaining, which occurs when an employer is clearly bargaining in appearance only, with the intention of avoiding an agreement rather than reaching one (see note 3).

An example of a dispute in professional sports that dealt with the issue of impasse, the calling of a strike, and several unfair labor practice charges is the 1994–1995 labor dispute between Major League Baseball and the Major League

Exhibit 11.3
NFL Collective Bargaining Agreement History

Date	Situation	Effective Dates of Agreement	Notes
Fall 1968	Players strike/owners lockout		
Fall 1968	Collective bargaining agreement agreed to	Through December 31, 1970	Pension increased
July 30–August 3, 1970	Players strike/owners lockout		
August 3, 1970	Collective bargaining agreement agreed to	Through December 31, 1974	Increased minimum salaries, pension, and benefits; Rozelle Rule stays
July 1–August 10, 1974	Players strike		Anger of disciplinary rules and "freedom" rules; players lack solidarity, call off strike, and pursue antitrust lawsuits
September 16–18, 1975	Players strike		Jets and Patriots refuse to play game, lack of solidarity
March 1977	Collective bargaining agreement agreed to	February 1, 1974–July 15, 1982	Rozelle Rule eliminated; right of first refusal created with compensation; pension fund increased; increased benefits; right to arbitration
September 21–November 16, 1982	Players strike		Increased leverage following lucrative TV deal and emergence of USFL
December 11, 1982	Collective bargaining agreement agreed to	July 16, 1982–August 31, 1987	Drug testing; increased minimum salary, pension, benefits, per diem allowance; 55% of defined gross revenue set aside for players; revenue sharing
September 22–October 15, 1987	Players strike		Strike ended with NFLPA filing antitrust lawsuit and decertifying in 1989

Exhibit 11.3
(continued)

Date	Situation	Effective Dates of Agreement	Notes
May 6, 1993	Collective bargaining agreement agreed to	May 6, 1993–March 1, 2000	Players finally win free agency on back of McNeil and White's successful antitrust lawsuits; unrestricted free agency after 4 seasons; introduction of franchise players; introduction of salary cap based upon defined gross revenue; increased pension, benefits, and share of licensing
February 25, 1998	Collective bargaining agreement extended	Through March 1, 2003	10-year veterans do not count 100% against salary cap; increased pension contributions
June 6, 2001	Collective bargaining agreement extended	Through March 1, 2008	Player receives remaining year's pay if cut after first game; increase in minimum salaries
March 8, 2006	Collective bargaining agreement extended	Through March 1, 2012	Players receive increased share of total revenues (replacing defined gross revenues) resulting in higher salary cap; increased revenue sharing, limits on "cash over cap"; restrictions on franchise tag use
May 20, 2008	Owners unanimously vote to opt out of collective bargaining agreement	Collective bargaining agreement now expires May 1, 2011	Owners say players' share is too large; want improved rookie salary cap; want adjustment to bonus forfeiture provisions

Exhibit 11.4
MLB Collective Bargaining Agreement History

Date	Situation	Effective Dates of Agreement	Notes
1968	First collective bargaining agreement agreed to	January 1, 1968–December 31, 1969	Minimum salary raised from $6,000 to $10,000; pension fund established
May 21, 1970	Collective bargaining agreement agreed to	January 1, 1970–December 31, 1972	Arbitration established to resolve grievances; termination pay established; creation of 10/5 player
April 2–14, 1972	Strike		Pension fund increased
February 8–25, 1973	Owners lockout		Owners resist salary arbitration
February 25, 1973	Collective bargaining agreement agreed to	January 1, 1973–December 31, 1975	Salary arbitration established; players gain some control over movement
March 1–17, 1976	Owners lockout		Owners refuse to accept free agency following *Messersmith/McNally* ruling of 1975
July 12, 1976	Collective bargaining agreement agreed to	January 1, 1976–December 31, 1979	Free agency established for players with six or more years of service; compensation for lost free agents
March 26–April 3, 1980	Players strike		Issue of free agent compensation tabled until 1981
May 23, 1980	Collective bargaining agreement agreed to	January 1, 1980–December 31, 1983	Two-year service requirement for salary arbitration retained; increased pension fund
June 12–July 31, 1981	Players exercise right to strike		No agreement reached by free agency committee; strike ends when compensation issue is resolved with player pools for team losing player; owners' strike insurance runs out
July 31, 1981	Agreement extended following strike	Through December 31, 1984	
August 6–7, 1985	Players strike		Two-day midseason strike

Exhibit 11.4
(continued)

Date	Situation	Effective Dates of Agreement	Notes
August 7, 1985	Collective bargaining agreement agreed to	January 1, 1985–December 31, 1989	Arbitration experience raised from two to three years; minimum salary raised; player compensation eliminated for free agents
February 14–March 18, 1990	Owners lockout		Owners forced to settle collusion suit for $280 million
March 18, 1990	Collective bargaining agreement agreed to	January 1, 1990–December 31, 1993	17% of players between two and three years of service become arbitration eligible
December 11, 1992	Owners exercise option to reopen collective bargaining agreement		Owners fail to formulate proposal before expiration of agreement
August 12, 1994–March 31, 1995	Players strike		1994 World Series cancelled; owners intend to unilaterally implement salary cap in off-season; 1995 season played without agreement
December 7, 1996	Collective bargaining agreement agreed to	January 1, 1997–October 31, 2000	Luxury tax established; revenue sharing begins; parts of collective bargaining agreement dependent upon Curt Flood Act passing
August 28, 2000	Players extend agreement	Through October 31, 2001	
August 30, 2002	Collective bargaining agreement agreed to	September 30, 2002–December 19, 2006	Increased revenue sharing; more severe luxury tax; random steroid testing; increased minimum salary; no contraction of teams during agreement; debt limits
October 25, 2006	Collective bargaining agreement extended	December 20, 2006–December 11, 2011	Increased luxury tax threshold; increased minimum salary; increased free agent draft pick compensation

Exhibit 11.5
NBA Collective Bargaining Agreement History

Date	Situation	Effective Dates of Agreement	Notes
April 1958	NBA recognizes NBPA and grants concessions		Increase in player pool, per diem allowance, moving expenses if traded
January 1961	Agreement reached		Creation of pension plan
January 1964	Players threaten not to play in first televised All-Star Game		Pension fund increased
Spring 1967	First collective bargaining agreement agreed to	Through 1970 season	Increase in pension, benefits, schedule limits, minimum salaries, exhibition pay
October 1970	Collective bargaining agreement agreed to	Through 1973 season	Increase in minimum salaries, playoff pool, and per diem allowance
April 29, 1976	Collective bargaining agreement agreed to	April 29, 1976–July 1, 1979	Followed Robertson suit and ABA merger—elimination of reserve clause; compensation and right of first refusal on free agents begins
October 10, 1980	Existing agreement extended cooperatively	October 10, 1980–June 1, 1982	Increase in minimum salaries; elimination of no-trade clauses; Larry Bird exemption
April 18, 1983	Collective bargaining agreement agreed to	June 1, 1982–June 15, 1987	Salary cap implemented based on defined gross revenues; minimum guarantee of jobs; increase in benefits
April 26, 1988	Collective bargaining agreement agreed to	June 16, 1987–June 15, 1994	Reduction of draft; elimination of right of first refusal for certain veterans; no strike–no lockout deal reached for 1994–1995 season
July 1–September 15, 1995	Owners lockout		NBPA threatens to decertify

Exhibit 11.5
(continued)

Date	Situation	Effective Dates of Agreement	Notes
September 15, 1995	Collective bargaining agreement agreed to	Through 2001 season	Guarantee of basketball-related income; various exceptions to salary cap; rookie salary cap
July 1, 1996	Owners lockout		Day-long lockout over salary cap and TV revenue dispute ends when collective bargaining agreement is finally signed
July 1, 1998–January 6, 1999	Owners lockout—reopen agreement		Claim financial losses by 13 teams
January 7, 1999	Collective bargaining agreement agreed to	January 20, 1999–June 30, 2004	Escrow account created; stiffer drug program and commissioner discipline; maximum length of contracts and raises
December 8, 2003	NBA extends agreement	Through June 30, 2005	Extended through 2004–2005 season
July 1, 2005	Collective bargaining agreement agreed to	July 1, 2005–June 30, 2011	Reduction of maximum contract length; minimum age requirement; increase in salary cap

Exhibit 11.6
NHL Collective Bargaining Agreement History

Date	Situation	Effective Dates of Agreement	Notes
Spring 1967	NHL recognizes NHLPA and grants concessions		Compensation for exhibition games; increase in per diem expenses
May 4, 1976	First collective bargaining agreement agreed to	September 15, 1975–September 15, 1981	Arbitration; salary arbitration; pension plan; no strike–no lockout agreement; modified free agency
March 30, 1979	Agreement extended	Through September 15, 1984	Following merger with WHA
1981	NHLPA exercises option to reopen agreement		Want less compensation for free agency
August 17, 1982	Collective bargaining agreement agreed to	September 16, 1981–September 15, 1987	Compensation remains ; overtime introduced; increased benefits and minimum salary; introduction of international hockey games into agreement
June 1, 1988	Collective bargaining agreement agreed to	September16, 1987–September 15, 1991	Increased benefits, pension, and minimum salary
April 1–11, 1992	Players strike		
April 11, 1992	Collective bargaining agreement agreed to	September 16, 1991–September 15, 1993	Stricter free agency compensation; Economics of Hockey study; players receive increased share and control of licensing revenues
September 15, 1993	CBA expires		1993–1994 season played without agreement
October 1, 1994–January 11, 1995	Owners lockout		Owners introduce idea of salary cap
January 13, 1995	Collective bargaining agreement signed	September 16, 1993–September 15, 2000	Cap on rookie salaries; increased compensation for free agents; salary cap tabled
1998	Agreement extended	Through September 15, 2004	Expansion issues force league to extend agreement
September 16, 2004–July 13, 2005	Owners lockout		Owners insist on cost certainty after claiming 19 teams lost money; season cancelled
July 21, 2005	Collective bargaining agreement agreed to	September 16, 2004–June 1, 2011	Introduction of salary cap based on defined gross revenues; salary rollbacks; maximum salaries; increased revenue sharing; age of free agency lowered; salary arbitration eligibility raised; steroid testing; significant rule changes

Baseball Players Association. In March 1994, the league and the players association began negotiations on a new collective bargaining agreement, and agreed to continue to work under the terms of the expired agreement (1990–1993). In these negotiations, the owners wanted to negotiate a salary cap similar to the hard cap won by the NFL in its negotiations with the NFLPA in 1993. MLB argued that small market teams such as the Montreal Expos and the San Diego Padres could not afford to pay the high salaries demanded by their star players.

These teams and their fans watched as those stars, through free agency or trades, went to teams that could afford their services such as the New York Yankees or the Atlanta Braves. The league proposed a salary cap of 50% of league revenues. During the previous season, the players had received 58% of revenue.

The players association rejected the league's proposal, arguing that it was not up to the players to solve the revenue distribution problems of the league. The players went on strike on August 11, 1994. Despite a federal mediator, and a plea from U.S. President Bill Clinton, the strike forced the cancellation of the rest of the season and the World Series, and put the 1995 season in jeopardy.

On December 22, 1994, the league declared an impasse in negotiations, unilaterally implemented a salary cap, and abolished salary arbitration. In response, the players association instructed its members not to sign any individual contracts, and then filed unfair labor practice charges against the league for unilaterally changing mandatory subjects of bargaining prior to impasse being reached. The league softened its stance concerning the salary cap, but argued that salary arbitration and free agency were permissive subjects of bargaining (not related to wages, hours, and terms and conditions of employment), and could therefore be changed unilaterally. The NLRB found that the changes made by the league dealt specifically with wages, hours, and terms of employment, and were therefore mandatory subjects of bargaining, not subject to unilateral change. On March 27, 1995, the NLRB filed a petition that sought a temporary injunction, which would return these items to the status quo. The injunction was granted in *Silverman v. Major League Baseball Player Relations Committee, Inc.*, 880 F. Supp. 246 (S.D.N.Y. 1995)—and Major League Baseball unsuccessfully appealed—*Silverman v. Major League Baseball Player Relations Committee, Inc.*, 67 F.3d 1054 (2nd Cir. 1995). Subsequently, the owners and players agreed to begin the 1995 season without a collective bargaining agreement in place, and continued operating under the terms of the 1990–1993 collective bargaining agreement. The league and the players association finalized a new agreement on November 26, 1996, effective from January 1, 1997 until November 2001.

Another important legal issue that was raised during the 1994–1995 strike was the possible use of replacement players. As stated earlier, if the work stoppage is an economic strike, then the striking employees can be permanently replaced, whereas if it is an unfair labor practice strike, only temporary replacements can be used. The Major League Baseball Players Association strike was deemed economic, and the league announced it would use replacements to start the 1995 season. Two problems arose concerning replacement players. In Ontario, Canada, home of the Toronto Blue Jays, legislation banned the use of replacement workers during strikes, which meant that the Blue Jays would not be able to play any home games at the Skydome in Toronto. Second, the state of Maryland passed similar legislation that would effectively stop the Baltimore Orioles from playing in the state of Maryland using replacement players. Replacement players were indeed hired for spring training games, including exhibition games at some major league parks (e.g., the opening of Coors Field in Denver). However, the strike ended before the replacement player issue could be resolved, so the question surrounding the legality of replacement players in certain states and provinces is still open to question.

NOTES

1. Attendance at Major League Baseball games declined from a prestrike average of 31,612 per game in 1994 to 26,889 per game in 1996. Despite ongoing steroid scandals, MLB set total attendance records in consecutively in 2004, 2005, 2006, and 2007 reaching 79.5 million. The global recession caused attendance to dip slightly after 2007.

2. For more on impasse in collective bargaining, see Russell Korobkin, "Bargaining Power as Threat of Impasse," 87 *Marquette Law Review* 867 (2004).

3. The NLRB has identified the following bargaining tactics as evidence of surface bargaining: (1) refusing to meet at reasonable times and places; (2) refusing to give basic information to the union needed for meaningful bargaining; (3) refusing to discuss certain issues with the union at all; (4) agreeing to minor issues but refusing to bargain over economic issues; (5) rejecting union proposals without making counterproposals; (6) stalling negotiations by reintroducing proposals that have previously been withdrawn. For more information, see www.nlrb.gov

11.3.7.1.4. Baseball Collusion Cases

In January 1986, the MLBPA filed a grievance against MLB for boycotting the free agent market after the 1985 season, and violating Article 18 of the Basic Agreement, which stated: "Players shall not act in concert with other Players [see note 1] and Clubs shall not act in concert with other Clubs." In accordance with the grievance arbitration system in baseball, a tripartite panel was assigned, with Thomas Roberts as the impartial chairperson.

The dispute arose out of the fact that during the off-season between the 1985 and 1986 seasons, only 4 of the 33 available free agents changed teams, and all 4 of them were marginal players. In *Major League Baseball Players Association v. Twenty-six Major League Baseball Clubs*, A-123, A-136 (1987) (Roberts), Arbitrator Roberts found that Article 18 had been violated and that clubs had a "common understanding that no club would bid on the services of a free agent until his former club no longer desired to sign him." Therefore, owners acted in concert to deprive players of their right to free agency. In January 1988, Roberts made seven players immediate free agents, and in August 1989, awarded those players $10.5 million in damages.

In 1988, a second collusion suit was filed by the MLBPA against the MLB, again for acting in concert against the players in regard to free agency. During the 1986–1987 off-season, the owners instituted a plan that would allow the free agent's original team to attempt to resign the player before any other team could sign him. The owners established an "information bank" that listed offers to players, amounts of those offers, and when those offers took place. Under this system, no player would receive an offer from a club, other than his original one, until his present team illustrated on the information bank that it was no longer interested in the player.

Arbitrator George Nicolau found that the owners had again violated Article 18, and had acted in concert with each other. In his decision Nicolau stated:

> Thus, participating clubs were acting together so that information to which only one was privy—offers it had made to particular players—could be shared, used, and acted

upon by others for their own benefit to the possible detriment of the club supplying that intelligence.

In August 1988, Nicolau found in favor of the players and granted 12 players free agent status. In 1990, Nicolau presided over a third collusion case, *Major League Baseball Players Association v. Twenty-six Major League Clubs* 1 (1990) (Nicolau, Arb.), pertaining to the 1987–1988 off-season, where the owners again used an information bank. Nicolau again found for the players, and a settlement of $280 million was reached.

To prevent collusion from happening in other sports, anticollusion articles have been included in all collective bargaining agreements. Article 20 of the MLB Collective Bargaining Agreement, which outlines a player's free agency rights, also includes an anticollusion clause (see Exhibit 11.7). In addition, to ensure that collusion does not take place, the collective bargaining agreement contains a letter of good faith from the owner's chief negotiator to the player's chief negotiator. The letter, in Attachment 15 of the agreement, promises that the owners will not operate an information bank during the term of the agreement.

NOTES

1. In 1966 Los Angeles Dodger pitchers Don Drysdale and Sandy Koufax both requested raises that would bring their salaries to $100,000. When they were rebuffed, they staged a spring training holdout, claiming they would not re-sign with the Dodgers unless they were signed as a package. The Dodgers could not tolerate the idea of being without two of their best players. Thus, the holdout proved successful after the Dodgers awarded them a total of $240,000. This group holdout behavior is now prohibited by the collective bargaining agreement in exchange for management's agreement not to collude.

2. In *Major League Baseball Players Ass'n v. Garvey*, 532 U.S. 504 (2001), the Supreme Court rejected Steve Garvey's claim for a larger share of the $280 million settlement, citing an unwillingness to overturn a decision from binding arbitration. For more on this case, see Jeffrey Perron, "Administrative Law—Court's Scope of Review of Arbitration Decisions—Supreme Court Overturns the Ninth Circuit's Rejection of the Arbitration Panel's Decision that Found No Collusion Activities by the Baseball Owners—Major League Baseball Players Association v. Steve Garvey, 121 S.Ct. 1724 (2001)," 12 *Seton Hall Journal of Sports and Entertainment Law* 131 (2002).

Exhibit 11.7
Article 20. (E) Individual Nature of Rights (MLB Collective Bargaining Agreement 2007–2011)

---

(1) The utilization or non-utilization of rights under XIX(A)(2) and Article XX is an individual matter to be determined solely by each Player and each Club for his or its own benefit. Players shall not act in concert with other Players and Clubs shall not act in concert with other Clubs.

(2) Upon any finding of a violation of Section (E)(1) of this Article XX by two or more Clubs, any injured Player (or Players) shall be entitled to recover in monetary damages three times the lost baseball income, he (or they) would have had but for the violation.

3. For more information on the baseball collusion cases, see Marc Edelman, "Moving Past Collusion in Major League Baseball: Healing Old Wounds, and Preventing New Ones," 54 *Wayne Law Review* 601 (2008).

11.3.8. Outline of a Professional Sports Collective Bargaining Agreement

The text below offers a brief introduction to some of the relevant issues that are addressed in collective bargaining agreements in sports. It is important to remember that collective bargaining agreements can be extremely long and complicated. The 2006–2012 agreement between the NFL and NFLPA is 244 pages in length and contains 55 articles and 16 appendixes. The following material is designed to give the reader an idea of some of the issues that are covered in a professional sport's collective bargaining agreement:

1. Union/Management Rights: This section includes a management rights article, which outlines what rights the league may retain in order to run its business. Also in this section is an article detailing union security rights, which includes dues deductions, licensing programs, and meetings.

2. Commissioner Discipline: The commissioner may have rights reserved under the collective bargaining agreements, such as levying fines, being the final signatory on player contracts and trades, imposing disciplinary measures, and acting in the best interests of the game.

3. Standard Player Contract: A standard or uniform player contract is incorporated into the collective bargaining agreement, so that the players association can negotiate any changes to the contract with the league.

4. Grievance Procedure: This gives players the right to challenge decisions that are made by the league or by the owners that may violate the collective bargaining agreement. In addition, the procedure can be used to clarify language in the agreement or in individual contracts that may be vague or ambiguous. An impartial arbitrator is selected to issue decisions on disputes that arise.

5. College Draft: Most aspects of the college draft (also known as the "first year player" draft) are included in this section, including length of draft, number of rounds, assignment of draft rights, and undrafted rookie rights.

6. Salary Cap: This section deals with the implementation of a device to put a ceiling on what total player salaries may be for a club. This section outlines what type of salary cap is being used: a hard cap, which sets a tight limit on what a team may spend on player salaries, or a soft cap, which sets limits but allows for certain exceptions, like the Larry Bird exemption in the NBA (see section 11.3.12, "Hard Cap versus Soft Cap").

7. Free Agency: This article deals with player mobility, and the restrictions on that mobility. It outlines when players are eligible for free agency, whether it is restricted or unrestricted, and what type of compensation may be paid (usually for restricted players).

8. Related Player/Club Issues: This section of a collective bargaining agreement deals with articles relating to squad size, off-season workouts, off-season training camps, preseason training camps, and practice squads. Normally, time

limits and roster limits are established for these areas, in addition to compensation to the players and fines clubs may impose.

9. Salaries/Economics: This section outlines the salaries, and limits thereon, for all players in the league. Formulas may be established to determine what percentage of league club revenue player salaries will comprise, if a salary cap is in place. In addition, this section details what maximum and minimum salaries exist for different player groups (such as rookie minimums).

10. Benefits: Professional athletes have negotiated for many benefits, including pensions; medical, dental, and optical care; insurance packages; disability; and workers' compensation. These sections outline the benefits available to the players, in addition to restrictions, time limits, and possibly limits on use or availability.

11. Incidentals: These include expenses, per diem allocations, meal allowance, moving expenses, and others. The related articles outline when such incidentals are available and what limits there are on their use.

12. There are many other topics and areas that may be part of a collective bargaining agreement, such as anticollusion, agent certification, duration, definitions, league expansion, and others.

NOTE

1. For an example of collective bargaining agreements, see the NBPA's website: www.nbpa.com or the NFLPA's Web site: www.nflpa.org.

11.3.9. Free Agency

One of the most contentious issues between players and owners over the years has been player freedom. Before union representation, players fought for increased mobility and pay (free agency) in the courts, using contract law and, later, antitrust theory. The initial attempts by player associations in the late 1960s and early 1970s to bargain for free agency proved fruitless. However, two major events in the mid-1970s altered player mobility in professional sports, and since that time, free agency has developed differently in all the professional sports leagues.

When baseball was first organized into a league structure in the 1880s, players signed one-year contracts and were deemed free agents after that contract. After each contract, players found themselves on the open market, signing contracts with the team that offered the highest salary. As a result, salaries grew at a rapid pace, which in turn caused owners to claim they were losing money at an astounding rate. In 1886 the league imposed the reserve system, whereby each team would reserve five players whom other teams in the league could not sign. Within 10 years, the number of reserved players went from 5 to 10 per team, and eventually to the entire team. The reserve system tied a player to his original team in perpetuity, or until he was traded or retired. This system relied on the standard player contract, which had a clause that stated the team that the player was signing to play for had an option on that player's services the following year. Each year the player signed the same contract, thus giving the team an "option" year after year after year. When professional football, hockey, and basketball leagues formed, they modeled their reserve systems after baseball's.

Free agency was first established in baseball in 1976 after an arbitrator ruled in the *Messersmith/McNally* arbitration decision (see note 1) that the option year in the MLB Standard Players Contract could be applied for only one year, and was not to be optioned year after year. Therefore, the option clause had a one-year life expectancy if a player decided to play out his option. Arbitrator Peter Sietz ruled that if a player chose not to re-sign with his original club after the option year, he was a free agent. The owners challenged the decision of the arbitrator in *Kansas City Royals Baseball Corp. v. Major League Baseball Players Association*, 532 F.2d 615 (8th Cir. 1976), but the court ruled against the owners, stating that the arbitrator had jurisdiction over the case, and had made an appropriate award. In the wake of this decision, the MLBPA and MLB began negotiating a settlement. The owners were fearful that free agency after two years of service would result in major salary increases and significant player movement. After a series of negotiations, an agreement was eventually reached that allowed unrestricted free agency for professional baseball players after six years of major league service.

The *Messersmith/McNally* decision and the resulting collective bargaining agreement both had a significant impact on the game of baseball. Immediately following the decision, 24 players became free agents and were free to negotiate with any team in the league. The result was that the average player salary rose by 50% in the following year, and several clubs began the practice of offering multi-year deals. Owners, fearful that their star players might "test the market" when they became eligible for free agency, signed these players to rich long-term contracts.

Around the time of the *Messersmith/McNally* ruling, the other professional sports leagues began negotiations with their respective players associations to come to an agreement on the issue of free agency. The NFL was using the Rozelle Rule, which forced a team signing a free agent to compensate the player's original team. For all intents and purposes, this rule restricted any player movement, because the high price of signing a free agent player (draft pick, active player, cash) was too costly. The 1976 *Mackey* decision held that the Rozelle Rule was too restrictive under antitrust laws, and the NFL was forced to negotiate with the NFLPA over a new player mobility policy. The NFLPA, with the support of its members, agreed to a right of first refusal (ROFR)/compensation system in exchange for increased benefits, increased minimum salaries, and increased funding of the pension plan. The ROFR/compensation system was almost as restrictive as the Rozelle Rule, and it was not until the early 1990s that the players association, after the favorable decisions in the *McNeil* and *White* cases, was able to negotiate a less restrictive free agency system into the collective bargaining agreement.

At present, the NHL, NBA, NFL, and MLB all have some form of free agency. All leagues have some form of unrestricted, or nearly unrestricted, free agency. It is unrestricted in that once a player has reached a negotiated time limit (six years of service in the MLB), he can sign with any team that makes an offer (see note 2). Restricted free agents are players who have reached a certain service level and may entertain offers from other clubs; however, if a club signs a restricted free agent, it must compensate the player's original team. The restricted free agent status is different in each league. Below is an example of the NFL's free agency system for veterans from the 1993–2012 agreements (see exhibit 11.8).

NOTES

1. In 1975, Andy Messersmith (Los Angeles Dodgers) and Dave McNally (Montreal Expos) challenged baseball's reserve clause by playing out the season without signing new contracts. Both contended that the reserve clause only allowed a team to renew a player's contract for one year, while the team owners contended that the clause could be invoked

Exhibit 11.8
NFL Collective Bargaining Agreement, Article 19 Veteran Free Agency

Section 1. **Unrestricted Free Agents:**

(a) Subject to the provisions of Article XX (Franchise and Transition Players), any player with five or more Accrued Seasons, or with four or more Accrued Seasons in any Capped Year, shall, at the expiration of his Player Contract, become an Unrestricted Free Agent. Such player shall be completely free to negotiate and sign a Player Contract with any Club, and any Club shall be completely free to negotiate and sign a Player Contract with such player, without penalty or restriction, including, but not limited to, Draft Choice Compensation between Clubs or First Refusal Rights of any kind, subject to the signing period set forth below.

Section 2. **Restricted Free Agents:**

(a) Any Veteran player with three or more Accrued Seasons, but less than five Accrued Seasons (or less than four Accrued Seasons in any Capped Year), shall, at the expiration of his last Player Contract during such period, become a Restricted Free Agent. Any such player shall be completely free to negotiate and sign a Player Contract with any Club, and any Club shall be completely free to negotiate and sign a Player Contract with any such player, subject to the restrictions set forth in this Article.

(b) In order to receive the following specified Rights of First Refusal and/or Draft Choice Compensation with respect to a Restricted Free Agent, the Prior Club of a Restricted Free Agent must tender the player a Qualifying Offer on or before the first date of the Restricted Free Agent Signing Period, as follows:

    (i) For Restricted Free Agents with three Accrued Seasons:

        (1) Right of First Refusal: one year Player Contract with Paragraph 5 Salary of at least $721,600 for the 2006 League Year, $850,000 for the 2007 League Year, $927,000 for the 2008 League Year, $1,010,000 for the 2009 League Year, $1,101,000 for the 2010 League Year, $1,200,000 for the 2011 League Year, or $1,308,000 for the 2012 League Year, as applicable;

        (2) Right of First Refusal and Draft Selection at Player's Original Draft Round: one year Player Contract with a Paragraph 5 Salary of at least (a) the amount set forth in Subsection (b)(i)(1) above, or (b) 110% of the player's prior year's Paragraph 5 Salary, whichever is greater; in addition, if option (b) applies, all other terms of the player's prior year contract are carried forward unchanged (this Subsection is subject to the rules of Subsection (c) below);

        (3) Right of First Refusal, One Second Round Draft Selection: one year Player Contract with a Paragraph 5 Salary of at least (a) $1,300,000 in the 2007 League Year, $1,417,000 in the 2008 League Year, $1,545,000 in the 2009 League Year, $1,684,000 in the 2010 League Year, $1,835,000 in the 2011 League Year, or $2,000,000 in the 2012 League Year, as applicable, or (b) 110% of the player's prior

year's Paragraph 5 Salary, whichever is greater; in addition, if option (b) applies, all other terms of the player's prior year contract are carried forward unchanged;

(4) Right of First Refusal and One First Round Draft Selection: one year Player Contract with a Paragraph 5 Salary of at least (a) $1,573,000 for the 2006 League Year, $1,850,000 for the 2007 League Year, $2,017,000 for the 2008 League Year, $2,198,000 for the 2009 League Year, $2,396,000 for the 2010 League Year, $2,611,000 for the 2011 League Year, or $2,846,000 for the 2012 League Year, as applicable, or (b) 110% of the player's prior year's Paragraph 5 Salary, whichever is greater; in addition, if option (b) applies, all other terms of the player's prior year contract are carried forward unchanged;

(5) Right of First Refusal, One First Round Draft Selection, and One Third Round Draft Selection: one year Player Contract with a Paragraph 5 Salary of at least (a) $2,096,600 for the 2006 League Year, $2,350,000 for the 2007 League Year, $2,562,000 for the 2008 League Year, $2,792,000 for the 2009 League Year, $3,043,000 for the 2010 League Year, $3,317,000 for the 2011 League Year, or $3,616,000 for the 2012 League Year, as applicable, or (b) 110% of the player's prior year's Paragraph 5 Salary, whichever is greater; in addition, if option (b) applies, all other terms of the player's prior year contract are carried forward unchanged;

year after year. Messersmith and McNally did not sign their contracts in 1975 because they wanted higher salaries than their owners were willing to give. After the season, they argued that they had played out their option year and were free agents capable of selling their services to the highest bidder. The dispute went to arbitration. In what was considered the biggest victory for the players in baseball history, arbitrator Peter Seitz found that the reserve clause merely gave the owners an additional option year, thus leaving Messersmith and McNally, free agents, free to sign with another team. After an unsuccessful appeal of Seitz's decision, Major League Baseball negotiated a collective bargaining agreement with the players, giving them many new rights and freedoms. This decision began the modern era of free agency, which was reflected in the rapid increase in player salaries.

2. Under the collective bargaining agreement set to expire in 2011, MLB's free agency is not truly "unrestricted." Teams signing free agents are required to provide a draft pick to the team that loses the free agent. However, it should be noted than between 1987 and 1996 more than 35% of players drafted in the *first* round of the MLB draft failed to ever reach the major leagues. Consequently, few see draft pick compensation in baseball as a deterrent to free agent signings.

11.3.10. Salary Caps

The salary cap—a restriction or limit on the amount of money that may be made available by the league to pay player salaries—has been the center of considerable labor unrest since the 1980s. The first salary cap in professional sports was initiated by the NBA in 1982, and was included in that year's collective bargaining agreement. The second league of the Big Four to adopt a salary cap was the National Football League, which implemented one as part of the *White* settlement, in 1993, while exchanging increased free agency rights and increased salary minimums. The

National Hockey League instituted one in its 2005 CBA following the cancellation of the 2004–2005 season. The Major League Baseball Players Association thus far has successfully resisted a salary cap, accepting instead a luxury tax system. Yet, owners claim one is necessary to stop the upward spiral of player salaries and the disparity between small and large market teams.

The salary cap does have a noticeable impact on player salaries. As part of the 1993–2001 NFL collective bargaining agreement, the salary cap was not to be initiated until the second year of the agreement (1994–1995). Therefore, the 1993–1994 season would be the first season in which players enjoyed free agency rights and were not restrained by a salary cap. During the 1993–1994 season, the average team salary was $42.9 million, an increase of 51% over 1992–1993, as players tested the free agency market and signed large contracts. For the 1994–1995 season, the salary cap was initiated, and according to the defined gross revenue formula (DGR is explained in section 11.3.11, "Calculation of Salary Cap"), the cap was set at $34.6 million, almost $9 million less than the average a year before. Thus teams were faced with having to drop almost $9 million from their payrolls. They accomplished this by waiving more expensive veteran players and signing rookies to less expensive contracts. Star players and first round draft picks continue to sign lucrative deals, but the salary cap has hurt the salaries of veteran players who are past their prime.

NOTES

1. Owners often cite increasing player salaries as the reason for salary cap restrictions. Even with a salary cap, the average NFL salary has increased from $816,000 in 1994 to $1.8 million in 2009. Over the same period, the average NBA salary has gone from $1.47 million to $5.85 million.

2. Team attempts to circumvent the cap have led to various litigation: (a) In 2000, an independent arbitrator found that the Minnesota Timberwolves had signed a secret contract with Joe Smith in an effort to circumvent the cap. The arbitrator upheld Commissioner David Stern's penalty of a $3.5 million fine, a loss of five first round draft picks (one pick was later reinstated) and a denial of the Larry Bird exemption for Smith. (b) Also in 2000, the San Francisco 49ers organization was cited for several cap violations by NFL Commissioner Paul Tagliabue. Former 49ers executive Carmen Policy and General Manager Dwight Clark were fined a total of $500,000. The 49ers did not lose any draft picks or have any contracts voided. (c) In *Matter of NBA*, 630 F. Supp. 136 (S.D.N.Y. 1986), the New York Knicks attempted to circumvent the cap by paying Albert King a large signing bonus, which, according to the NBA salary cap provisions, was spread evenly over the contract. The NBA argued that the Knicks were attempting to circumvent the cap by offering the large bonus, in place of regular salary that would go against the cap. The district court found in favor of the league. See also *Bridgeman v. NBA In re: Chris Dudley*, 838 F. Supp. 172 (D.N.J. 1993), which focused on the "one year opt out" provision, which allowed players to terminate their deals after one year. The NBA accused Chris Dudley of signing a contract with the Portland Trail Blazers, which included the opt out provision, with the intention of opting out after one year, and then re-signing with them using the Larry Bird exemption (meaning his salary would not count against the team's salary cap). The special master and the district court found in favor of Dudley and the Trail Blazers.

3. The NBA attempted to unilaterally implement a salary cap in 1982, which was successfully challenged in *Lanier v. NBA*, 82 Civ. 4935 (S.D.N.Y. 1982). A special master (the "judge" who oversees all litigation surrounding a particular dispute; in this case, the *Robertson* settlement) ruled in favor of the players, on the grounds that the salary cap violated the provisions of the *Robertson* settlement. The players association and the league agreed to include a salary cap in the 1983 collective bargaining agreement. The salary cap was later revised, after the *Bridgeman* settlement, in 1988.

11.3.11. Calculation of Salary Cap

Salary caps in professional sports have been designed as a percentage of certain league revenues. Therefore, there must be agreement between the league and the player association as to what revenues will be included. The NHL uses the term "hockey-related revenues," while the NBA uses the term "basketball-related income," and the NFL uses "total revenues" to describe these revenues. The calculated revenues usually consist of gate receipts, local and national television and radio broadcast revenue, and a percentage of income from luxury suites, licensing income, concessions, and merchandising. The 2006–2012 NFL-NFLPA agreement states:

> (i) "Total Revenues" ("TR") means the aggregate revenues received or to be received on an accrual basis, for or with respect to a League Year during the term of this Agreement, by the NFL and all NFL Teams (and their designees), from all sources, whether known or unknown, derived from, relating to or arising out of the performance of players in NFL football games, with only the specific exceptions set forth below. (Article 24)

NOTE

1. The NFL-NFLPA agreement also outlines what is not to be included in the calculation of total revenues: proceeds from the assignment, sale, or trade of a player's contract; proceeds from the sale of an existing franchise or the grant of an NFL expansion franchise; dues or capital contributions received by the NFL; fines; revenue sharing among NFL teams; interest income; insurance recoveries; sales of interests in real estate and other property; revenues generated from stadium events unrelated to NFL football; the value of promotional sports; revenues derived from NFL Attractions; the value of complimentary tickets; specifically designated day-of-game expense reimbursements received from a governmental entity; investments in the purchase of concession equipment and the value of luxury boxes used by the club owner provided to stadium authorities or government officials, owner of the visiting team, or the head coach (Article 24).

11.3.12. Hard Cap versus Soft Cap

The NFL salary cap is often referred to as a hard salary cap—a cap that cannot be exceeded. In 2005, the NHL adopted a salary cap similar to the NFL's in rigidity. On the other hand, the NBA salary cap is often referred to as a soft cap, one that has exceptions and that may allow teams to sign players to contracts that put them over the cap limit. For example, if the salary cap in the NFL is $109 million (2007), then no team is able to spend more than $109 million on player salaries. In the NBA, by contrast, several exemptions allow teams to go over the cap. One of these is called the "Larry Bird exemption," which was created so that teams would not lose established hometown players due to salary cap limits. In other words, a team can exceed its salary cap in order to sign one of its own free agent players, as long as he has played for the team for three years. Following a lockout that delayed the start of the 1998–99 season, the NBA and NBPA reached a collective bargaining agreement for 1999 through 2004. That agreement provided greater salary cap flexibility to teams, a system that was tweaked slightly in the NBA's 2005–2011 agreement. Among the important features of the NBA salary cap system are:

1. Players are guaranteed at least 57% of BRI in total salary and benefits. In addition, teams must spend at least 75% of the salary cap.

2. If a team's salary costs exceed 61% of an equal share of "Basketball Related Income", known as the "Tax Level" or "luxury tax", they are required to pay a $1 tax for every dollar they exceed the Tax Level.

3. The Mid-Level Salary Exception allows teams to sign a player to a contract not exceeding five seasons in length where the first year salary does not exceed 108% of the average NBA player salary for the prior season.

4. "Larry Bird" players can earn 25–35% of the salary cap depending on their level of experience and can sign contracts up to six years in length. If a player signs with a new team, his contract is limited to five years.

5. Rookie contracts are limited to two years with team options for a third and fourth season and the salary is based on an agreed upon scale.

Entering negotiations for a new collective bargaining agreement during a global recession the NBA made clear that its biggest point of contention was to adjust the players' share of revenue. Following the NHL's successful effort to institute a hard salary cap in 2005, the NBA has also talked repeatedly about closing many of the exceptions to the salary cap which can allow teams to dramatically exceed the salary cap. For example, the 2009–10 NBA Champion Los Angeles Lakers had the highest payroll in the NBA at $93.1 million, well above the $57.7 million salary cap.

11.3.13. Arbitration

In professional sports, conflicts regularly arise over the rights of players as outlined in the terms of the collective bargaining agreement, standard player contract, and league/governing body documents. Before unionization in professional sports, the commissioner of each sport had the final say in handling disputes, grievances, or other conflicts. While the commissioner still enjoys considerable power—such as the ability to veto a trade, approve or disapprove a contract, or implement a fine—the commissioner's power in the grievance procedure has been greatly diminished (see note 2).

When unionization occurred on a wide scale in professional sports, one of the first demands that the players associations made was for the implementation of a grievance procedure that was not controlled by the league. The intent of the grievance procedure is twofold: first, to keep litigation outside of the formal court system (the arbitration process is quicker, cheaper, and private); and, second, to give players *due process* rights. A grievance is an alleged wrong that is contrary to the written language or the intent of the written language in a collective bargaining agreement or, by implication, a league bylaw and/or standard player contract. The NFL-NFLPA 2006–2012 agreement defines a grievance in the following manner:

Article IX. Non-Injury Grievance. Section 1. Definition. Any dispute (hereinafter referred to as a grievance) arising after the execution of this Agreement and involving the interpretation of, application of, or compliance with, any provision of this Agreement, the NFL Player Contract, or any other applicable provision of the NFL Constitution or Bylaws pertaining to terms and conditions of employment of NFL players, will be resolved exclusively in accordance with the procedure set forth in this Article, except wherever another method of dispute resolution is set forth else-where in this Agreement, and except wherever the Settlement Agreement provides that the Special Master, Impartial Arbitrator, the Federal District Court or the Accountants shall resolve a dispute.

Players associations argued for an independent arbitrator to preside over grievances because they identified a conflict of interest in the commissioner acting as arbitrator. First, players asserted the commissioner would not be able to remain impartial if the grievance was against a decision he himself had made. Second, the players claimed that the commissioner of a professional sports league is hired and fired by the owners of that league, and therefore is not an impartial entity but may have a bias for the owners. Players demanded a system whereby an independent party would act as final arbitrator. What eventually emerged was a grievance procedure for certain disputes that contained numerous steps, including a hearing with the commissioner, and ended with a final and binding decision made by an impartial arbitrator. As mentioned previously, the commissioner retained jurisdiction for some disputes.

It is important to note that the basic grievance procedure is used for violations of the collective bargaining agreement, and also of any contracts and/or rules and regulations that are referred to in the contract. Therefore, a violation of the standard player contract is handled through the grievance procedure. In addition to the basic grievance procedure, players have negotiated a salary arbitration process (NHL, MLB) and an injury grievance process (NFL). Below is a brief outline of the grievance procedures as found in the collective bargaining agreements in the National Football League and Major League Baseball.

MLB Procedure (Article XI, Basic Agreement)

a) Grievant makes a verbal complaint to club or player representative, followed by discussion. If matter is not resolved, a written grievance is filed. A representative issues an opinion to player and MLBPA.

b) Grievant appeals decision to a representative of the Players Relations Committee, followed by discussion. Written opinion is issued.

c) Grievant appeals decision further to a tripartite arbitration panel, consisting of a representative of management, a representative of the MLBPA, and an impartial chairperson of the panel.

°Not included in this procedure; salary, benefits, commissioner matters (matters that deal with the integrity of baseball).

NFL Procedure (Article IX and X, Basic Agreement)

a) Noninjury. This procedure pertains to the terms and conditions of employment and applies to all noninjury disputes that result from a violation of the collective bargaining agreement, players' contract, and all other documents listed in the agreement. The grievance goes through a joint panel made up of NFLPA representatives and management council representatives. If appealed, the grievance goes to the Player Club Relations Committee, and if still not resolved, goes to a notice arbitrator who submits a list of arbitrators, one of which must be chosen. Decision by arbitrator is final and binding. It should be noted that if the grievance involves a suspension, the player or the NFLPA has the right to appeal directly to the notice arbitrator.

b) Injury. This type of grievance occurs when a player's contract is terminated due to an injury sustained while working for the team. The player must file a written grievance within 20 days, specifying injury, time of injury, and activity involved. The club may claim several defenses, including (a) player did not pass preseason test, (b) player did not disclose injury, (c) injury occurred before preseason and player signed a waiver, (d) injury was non–football-related. A neutral physician will examine the player and submit a report. If report is appealed, the procedure is the same as for a noninjury grievance.

NOTES _____

1. The courts will almost always respect the decision of binding arbitration unless they uncover an egregious procedural error or if the decision is inconsistent with the National Labor Relations Act. The sanctity of arbitration was affirmed by the U.S. Supreme Court in *Major League Baseball Players Ass'n v. Garvey*, 532 U.S. 504 (2001). When arbitrators penalized MLB teams $280 million for their collusion in the 1980s (see section 11.3.7.1.4, "Baseball Collusion Cases"), the arbitrators ruled that the MLBPA would have authority to divide the money. Former San Diego Padre Steve Garvey was unhappy with his share of the settlement, and sued the MLBPA. The district court awarded Garvey his requested $3 million. However, the Supreme Court overruled the lower court in an 8–1 decision, stating: "In discussing the courts' limited role in reviewing the merits of arbitration awards, we have stated that 'courts…have no business weighing the merits of the grievance [or] considering whether there is equity in a particular claim.' When the judiciary does so, it usurps a function which…is entrusted to the arbitration tribunal."

2. The commissioner's power to veto a trade is seldom used. However, there are cases where the commissioner will veto a trade in the best interests of the game. After the 1998–1999 regular season, the New York Islanders attempted to trade star forward Ziggy Pallfy to the New York Rangers for players and cash. Commissioner Gary Bettman, afraid the small-market Islanders were selling off their high-priced talent, vetoed the deal and said that any trade the Islanders made could not involve cash. Pallfy was later traded to the Los Angeles Kings. In 1976, Oakland Athletics owner Charlie Finley sold players Rollie Fingers, Joe Rudi, and Vida Blue for a total of $3.5 million to the Boston Red Sox and New York Yankees. MLB Commissioner Bowie Kuhn voided the deals, citing his "best interests of baseball" powers.

11.3.14. Grievance Procedures in Professional Sports

Exhibit 11.9 outlines the types of grievance procedures that apply for each of the four major professional sports leagues.

Before grievance arbitration is initiated, a procedure exists to determine whether cases can be decided without going to arbitration. For example, if a provision in a collective bargaining agreement has been accidentally violated, management will, in all likelihood, attempt to settle the dispute outside of the formal process. This could also be the case if a provision has been so obviously violated that going through the procedure would be sure to result in a loss. An impartial arbitrator is retained when both parties feel correct in their interpretation of the case and believe an impartial arbitrator would agree with their explanation.

Earlier, this chapter discussed the *Messersmith/McNally* arbitration decision that paved the way for free agency in professional baseball. This case is significant because it illustrates the importance that the grievance procedure can have. Baseball players had challenged the use of the reserve system, using antitrust theory in the court system, but had been unsuccessful in all those cases because of the antitrust immunity enjoyed by professional baseball. The players next turned to the grievance procedure as a mechanism to settle the dispute. The MLB Players Association believed that the option clause, which was part of the standard player contract, was applicable for only one year after the initial contract expired. The league contended that the option clause gave it the right to renew a player's contract year after year, as had been done since the 1880s. The league attempted

Exhibit 11.9
Player Grievance and Arbitration Rights

League	Grievance Procedure	Injury Grievance	Salary Arbitration
Major League Baseball	×		×
National Football League	×	×	
National Hockey League	×	×	×
National Basketball Association	×		
Women's National Basketball Association	×		

to argue that the arbitrator did not have jurisdiction over the case, but the arbitrator, Peter Seitz, dismissed this defense. Seitz found in favor of the players and granted them the right to unrestricted free agency. More important, the decision confirmed that the option on a contract was valid for one year only.

It is important to remember that the purpose of grievance arbitration is to limit the amount of litigation that enters the formal court system. The courts have increasingly yielded to the decisions made by arbitrators, and have also been reluctant to interpret grievance arbitration clauses. Only when there is a clear breach of the purpose of the procedure will the court system intervene.

A decision made by an arbitrator will usually serve as a precedent only *within* that particular sport. For example, an NBA arbitration hearing reduced the suspension of Latrell Sprewell for the 1997 assault on his coach P. J. Carlesimo (see note 2b). However, if identical circumstances were to occur with an NHL player and his coach, the arbitrator would *not* be compelled to consider the facts of the Sprewell case. On the other hand, arbitrators must consider past decisions and practices of commissioners, clubs, and arbitrators *within* the same sport. For example, when an MLB arbitration panel reduced the suspension of John Rocker for his "sexist, racist, homophobic and xenophobic" remarks, it did so in part because of baseball's historical indifference and lack of clear policy regarding similar incidents (see note 2a).

In February 2008, District Court Judge David Doty for the District of Minnesota overruled and reversed arbitrator Stephen Burbank's ruling that former Atlanta Falcons quarterback Michael Vick must return almost $20 million in bonus money after Vick was sentenced to prison for dog fighting, see *White v. NFL*, 2008 WL 304885 (D. Minn. February 4, 2008). Doty presided over the original *White v. NFL*, 41 F.3d 402 (8th Cir. 1994) lawsuit and the resulting stipulation and settlement agreement that created the current NFL Collective Bargaining Agreement. Doty presided over all subsequent litigation regarding the NFL CBA. Unhappy with the reversal, the NFL filed an unsuccessful motion for the decision to be vacated and for Doty to remove himself from any future disputes involving the NFL CBA, claiming that he was biased against the league.

NOTES

1. Three cases in 1960 illustrated that the Supreme Court was inclined to favor arbitration as a dispute mechanism: *Steelworkers v. American Mfg. Co.*, 363 U.S. 564 (1960); *Steelworkers v. Warrior & Gulf Navigation Co.*, 363 U.S. 574 (1960); and *Steelworkers v.*

Enterprise Wheel and Car Corp., 363 U.S. 593 (1960). In these cases, the Supreme Court upheld the decisions of arbitrators, sending a clear message that if an arbitration procedure exists in a collective bargaining agreement, and the arbitrator rules in a professional manner, then the arbitrator's decision will be upheld. These cases are often referred to as the Steelworker Trilogy.

2. According to Article 12, Section A, of the 2007–2011 MLB-MLBPA Collective Bargaining Agreement, an independent arbitrator has the ability to overturn discipline imposed on players by the commissioner if the arbitrator finds no just cause for the discipline given. Article XXXI, Section 8, of the 2005–2011 NBA-NBPA Collective Bargaining Agreement gives an independent arbitrator the ability to overturn discipline imposed on a player if the financial impact on that player exceeds $50,000.

(a) In *In the Matter of the Arbitration Between Major League Baseball Players Association and the Commissioner of Major League Baseball*, Grievance No. 00-3; John Rocker; Das, Chairman of Arbitration Panel, March 1, 2000, Atlanta Braves pitcher John Rocker saw his disciplinary sentence reduced by the arbitration panel. Commissioner Bud Selig had suspended Rocker with pay for all of spring training and nearly a month of the regular season, and also fined Rocker $20,000, after Rocker made disparaging remarks in a *Sports Illustrated* interview. In those remarks, Rocker denigrated "Japanese woman" drivers; referred to an African American teammate as a "fat monkey"; bemoaned the presence of "queer[s] with AIDS" on New York City subways; and admitted that he was "not a very big fan of foreigners." The commissioner urged the panel to uphold the sentence, arguing that Rocker's comments insulted numerous members of MLB's fan base, damaged the business of the Braves and Major League Baseball, endangered the safety of those on the field, and increased security costs during Braves games. The MLBPA argued that Rocker should receive no punishment because (1) Rocker was not "under contract" at the time of his remarks (claiming the uniform contract runs only from spring training until the World Series); (2) the collective bargaining agreement does not allow discipline for speech; (3) MLB and the Braves encouraged Rocker to cooperate with the media, and he was merely complying; and (4) previous incidents of "politically incorrect" speech had gone unpunished. Arbitrator Shyam Das rescinded Rocker's spring training suspension, reduced his regular season suspension by 13 days, and reduced his fine to $500. Das cited an absence of specific rules about speech by players, noting that pitcher Bob Knepper had not been disciplined after he made sexist comments in the 1980s. Das also noted that Rocker's punishment for speech was more severe than that imposed on baseball's drug offenders. Das justified the reduction in Rocker's fine due to the limit specified by Article 1, Section 3 (a), of the Major League Agreement for fines imposed by the commissioner on a player for conduct not in the best interest of baseball. For more information on this case, see Roger Abrams, "Off His Rocker: Sports Discipline and Labor Arbitration," 11 *Marquette Sports Law Review* 167 (Spring 2001).

(b) In *Arbitrator's Decision and Award Involving Latrell Sprewell, the National Basketball Players Association, the Golden State Warriors, and the National Basketball Association*, John D. Feerick, Grievance Arbitrator, March 4, 1998, NBA player Latrell Sprewell saw his punishment reduced by the arbitrator. Sprewell had attacked his coach, P. J. Carlesimo, during practice on December 1, 1997. In that attack, "between seven and ten seconds elapsed during which the Grievant had his hands around the Coach's neck." Carlesimo was not injured. Sprewell then left the court for "between ten and 20 minutes," before returning for an apparent second attempted attack of Carlesimo. However, he was restrained before reaching the coach. The Warriors terminated Sprewell's contract and the nearly $25 million remaining on it, claiming they had "cause" to do so because of the assault. Commissioner David Stern suspended Sprewell from the NBA for one year, emphasizing the "premeditated nature" of the second incident. The NBPA appealed, calling the sanctions against Sprewell "arbitrary and capricious" and lacking "just cause." Arbitrator Feerick overruled the Warriors and the NBA, holding that the Warriors must honor the final two years of Sprewell's contract or trade him. Feerick did, however, uphold the suspension for the remainder of the season (not the full calendar year Stern had imposed) and the player's resulting loss of $6.5 million in salary. He reasoned that the team's and league's dual penalties violated the principle of double jeopardy, and that league sanctions against more harmful player violence had been less severe in the past. Specifically, assaults resulting in serious injuries had produced suspensions no longer than 26 games. Sprewell subsequently filed suit against the NBA and the Warriors in federal district court, seeking the $6.4 million in salary that he lost during his suspension. Sprewell was denied relief in *Sprewell v. Golden State Warriors*, 231 F.3d 520 (U.S. App. 2000). For more information, see Roger A. Javier, "You Cannot Choke Your Boss and Hold Your Job Unless You Play in the NBA: The Latrell Sprewell Incident Undermines Disciplinary Authority in the NBA," 7 *Villanova Sports and Entertainment Law Journal* 2 (2000).

(c) In *In the Matter of the Arbitration Between Major League Baseball Players Association and the Commissioner of Major League Baseball*, Grievance No. 92-7, Suspension of Steven Howe; Nicolau, Chairman of Arbitration Panel, November 12, 1992, Commissioner Fay Vincent banned New York Yankee pitcher Steve Howe from baseball for life, for violating the terms of his reinstatement in 1990 after being suspended during the 1988 and 1989 seasons. Between 1982 and 1988 Howe was hospitalized for drug-related treatment six times, and was reinstated in 1990 on the condition that he refrain from using or selling drugs. However, the arbitrator found that there was no just cause for the lifetime ban because Vincent did not do all that was contractually required for Howe (periodic drug tests) prior to the total ban. For more information, see section 7.2.4.3, "Major League Baseball."

3. In *Kansas City Royals Baseball Corp. v. Major League Baseball Players Ass'n*, 532 F.2d 615 (8th Cir. 1976), Judge Heaney upheld the arbitration decision in the *Messersmith/McNally* arbitration case (see section 11.3.9, "Free Agency") and noted that "the arbitration panel did nothing more than to interpret certain provisions of the Uniform Player's Contract and the Major League Rules. Accordingly, the award must be sustained."

4. Fred Dryer, of the Los Angeles Rams of the NFL, attempted to bypass the usual contract dispute resolution plan as outlined in the collective bargaining agreement between the NFL and NFLPA, and have his matter decided by a California state court in *Dryer v. Los Angeles Rams*, 709 P.2d 826 (Cal. 1985). The Rams petitioned to have the court compel arbitration as outlined in the collective bargaining agreement. The court denied the petition by the Rams because it felt that since all contract disputes could go before the commissioner, it failed to meet the "minimum levels of integrity" required. The California Supreme Court reversed the decision, and found that since an arbitration system that covered the dispute was in place, the court would not interfere.

11.3.14.1 Unlawful Discharge

One area in which grievances are commonly filed pertains to unlawful discharge or termination. While this issue is not as pervasive in professional sports as it is in other industries (due in part to the high number of guaranteed professional sports contracts), there have been several cases where players feel they have been unjustly terminated or discharged. The collective bargaining agreements in the NBA, NFL, and MLB all have language that allows a team to lawfully discharge a player when he fails to exhibit sufficient skill.

NFL: Player understands that he is competing with other players for a position on Club's roster within the applicable player limits. If at any time, in the judgment of the Club, Player's skill or performance has been unsatisfactory as compared with that of other players competing for positions on Club, or if Player has engaged in personal conduct reasonably judged by Club to adversely affect or reflect on Club, then Club may terminate his contract (Article 2 of the NFL's Uniform Player Contract).

MLB: The Club may terminate this contract upon written notice to the Player (but only after requesting and obtaining waivers of this contract from all other Major League Clubs). If the Player at any time...fails, in the opinion of the Club's management, to exhibit sufficient skill or competitive ability to qualify or continue as a member of the Club's team (MLB's Uniform Player Contract, Article 7(b)).

NBA: The Club may terminate this contract upon written notice to the Player (but only after complying with the waiver procedure) if the Player shall at any time: Fail in the sole opinion of management to exhibit sufficient skill or competitive ability to qualify to continue as a member of the Club's team (NBA Uniform Player Contract, Article 20 (b)(2)).

When players file grievances over what they feel is an unfair discharge, arbitrators must determine whether that player lacks the necessary skill to compete at the professional level, or whether that player acted in a way that violated his contract. If neither is found, the player wins the grievance. Arbitrators have insisted that objective criteria be used by clubs to determine whether a player no longer has the proper skill to play. It is important to note that guaranteed player contracts (contracts that cannot be bought out or terminated for any reason) protect those players whose skill has decreased. The player may be terminated but will be paid.

NOTES

1. Cincinnati Bengals punter Lee Johnson was cut on December 7, 1998, one day after criticizing the team's ownership. The following day, he was fined one game check of more than $20,000 for conduct detrimental to the team. Johnson appealed the decision, stating that timing proved he was cut for his comments and not for his performance. The NFLPA also argued that a player cannot be fined after he is released. The Bengals cited a loyalty clause in Johnson's contract, which they argued allowed them to cut Johnson. The case was settled a year later for $12,000, while Johnson was a member of the New England Patriots.

2. *In the Matter of Arbitration Between NBA (Atlanta Hawks) and NBPA (Ken Charles)*, Seitz, Arbitrator, June 22, 1978. In this case, Charles was released from his three-year contract with the Hawks after only 15 months, and challenged that decision based on the fact that the Hawks did not adequately follow the termination guidelines set forth in the collective bargaining agreement. The Hawks failed to give Charles a written notice of the termination, as was required, and also failed to offer a compelling reason for the termination. The Hawks argued that Charles did not fit into their new style of play, and was therefore expendable. The record shows that Charles started in 21 of the team's first 22 games before his termination. Seitz ruled that the Hawks failed to provide sufficient evidence for the termination, and the club was required to pay Charles his entire salary for the remaining period of his contract.

3. *In the Matter of Arbitration Between Detroit Lions and Mitchell Hoopes*, Searce, Arbitrator, September 2, 1978. In this case, punter Mitchell Hoopes was placed on waivers and released after he had missed an important field goal, and had subsequently been

publicly chastised over the miss by the head coach. The coach claimed Hoopes was placed on waivers because too much pressure was placed on him after the public criticism. Hoopes filed the arbitration claiming that he was released for a reason that was not identified in the collective bargaining agreement. The arbitrator, Searce, acknowledged that a player could be released from his contract based on skill and performance, but concluded that the release was not solely motivated by the skill and performance levels of Hoopes. Searce ordered the Lions to pay the remaining portion of Hoopes's 1977 salary.

11.3.15. Salary Arbitration

Salary arbitration is a process used only in Major League Baseball and the National Hockey League. The basic premise behind the procedure is to give players who have played a certain number of years an opportunity to have their salary set by a neutral third party based on market conditions. In both the baseball and hockey procedures, players present their cases before arbitrators who make decisions based on evidence given by both the team and the player. Players file for arbitration for two reasons: (1) the player believes he can win his case; (2) the player is using the threat of arbitration as a bargaining tool in his negotiations with his team.

John Gaherin, who acted as a labor negotiator for Major League Baseball *owners*, had suggested the idea of salary arbitration for baseball in the 1960s. Gaherin and his successor, Ed Fitzgerald, encouraged the owners and the commissioner to adopt salary arbitration for two reasons: (1) to end player holdouts; and, more important, (2) to dissuade the players in their efforts to end baseball's antitrust exemption and the reserve clause (see section 10.3.1, "The Baseball Exemption"). Fitzgerald convinced the owners to adopt salary arbitration in 1973, three years before free agency. The measure passed the owners by a 22–2 vote, and had the approval of Commissioner Bowie Kuhn.

Major League Baseball uses what is known as final-offer or last-best-offer arbitration. The system is set up so that representatives of the player and the team each submit a figure they believe the player is worth for one season of play. The arbitrators, as per the collective bargaining agreement, will consider: (1) career contribution; (2) quality of previous seasons; (3) player's past compensation; (4) competitive salaries; (5) physical and mental defects; (6) recent performance record of the club. The arbitrators will then pick either the salary given by the player or by the team. The arbitrators must choose one of the two salaries given, and may not select a compromise salary. It is important to remember that neither party knows what the other is going to offer. In Major League Baseball, players are eligible for salary arbitration after their third year of service in the league or if they are a "super-two," meaning that they are in the top 17% of major league service among players with at least two years of service and at least 86 days of service in the immediately preceding season. Service is accrued in terms of days spent on the Major League roster. In Major League Baseball, the arbitrator can only award a one-year contract. The player will go through the arbitration process every year that he is eligible until he becomes a free agent following his sixth season or if he signs a long-term contract with his existing team prior to reaching free agency.

As an example, consider one of the first salary arbitration cases. In 1974, the Minnesota Twins offered pitcher Dick Woodson $23,000 for one year, and Woodson offered to pitch for $30,000. The arbitrator therefore was forced to decide whether Woodson was worth more or less than $26,500 (the midpoint). If the arbitrator felt that Woodson was worth less than $26,500, he would be given $23,000. If the arbitrator felt that Woodson was worth more than $26,500, he would be awarded $30,000. As it turned out, the arbitrator found in favor of Woodson, and he was granted $30,000.

While the Minnesota Twins were quite dismayed at the club's loss in this early hearing, the salary arbitration awards have increased significantly since the mid-1970s. The combination of free agency and arbitration-mandated salaries has produced salary arbitration hearings with millions of dollars at stake, rather than the few thousand that were at stake in the Woodson case. For example, in 2008, Philadelphia Phillies first baseman Ryan Howard offered to play for $10 million. The Phillies offered Howard $7 million, a $6.1 million raise over his previous year's salary of $900,000. The arbitrators found in favor of Howard. Again, this does not necessarily mean that arbitrators felt Howard was worth $10 million, but it does mean that the arbitrators felt that Howard was worth more than $8.5 million (the midpoint between $7 million and $10 million).

As of the 2010 season, the highest arbitration award ever was $10 million, given to Philadelphia Phillies first baseman Ryan Howard. Los Angeles Angels of Anaheim closer Francisco Rodriguez and Washington Nationals outfielder Alfonso Soriano received $10 million in 2008 and 2006, respectively, as well; however, they actually lost their cases. The last-best-offer system of arbitration in Major League Baseball has led to it being used less frequently as teams often sign their players before going to arbitration. According to the MLBPA, from 1990 through 2009, 1,806 cases were filed and only 203, or 11%, actually made it to arbitration.

The National Hockey League's system of salary arbitration is different from that of Major League Baseball. The NHL uses conventional interest arbitration, under which the arbitrator is not forced to pick "either/or," but estimates what the arbitrator believes the player is worth and offers that as the decision. In addition, unlike as in Major League Baseball, the arbitrator may award the player a contract of more than one year. Like the system employed in Major League Baseball, neither party in a salary arbitration dispute knows what the other is going to offer. For example, if the Chicago Blackhawks offered Patrick Kane a $5 million one-year contract and Kane asked for $7 million, the arbitrator could decide Kane is worth $6 million and award that salary.

Salary arbitration eligibility in the NHL varies depending upon the age when the player signs his first contract and his relative professional experience. For example, a player who signed his first contract between ages 18 and 20 needs five years of professional experience while a player 25 years or older only needs one year of professional experience. Prior to the 2005 collective bargaining agreement that ended a 10-month lockout, only players could elect salary arbitration but now the clubs can also with respect to certain classes of players.

The 1993 salary arbitration hearing between the Boston Bruins and Raymond Bourque offers a valuable look into the machinations of the salary arbitration process. Bourque asked for a contract that would pay him approximately $4.25 million per year, and the Bruins offered $1.8 million per year. The arbitrator, Richard Bloch, began his analysis by reviewing Bourque's achievements and contributions to the Bruins over his 14-year career. The arbitrator then compared Bourque's statistics with 23 other top defensive players; in these comparisons, he appeared near or at the top of almost all. Bloch noted in his decision:

> It is fully appropriate, in the course of fashioning the contract award, to place one's self in the parties' position, considering the "market" for a player or given category of

player and attempting to discern, to whatever extent possible, the respective positions and the responses. In this context, even accepting a frame of reference that would accommodate non-defensive players, for comparison purposes, the long-term nature of those arrangements and the impact of salary may simply not be ignored.

The arbitration award was set at $2.25 million per year, based on comparisons with other notable impact players of the time, including Steve Yzerman, Eric Lindros, and Joe Sakic.

If a team feels the player is likely to win a large award in arbitration, the team will do all it can to settle before the case goes to an arbitrator. Even when players lose their arbitration cases, they usually receive an increase in salary over the previous year.

NOTES

1. Salary arbitration has had a tremendous impact on salaries in Major League Baseball. In 1976, the average player salary was $51,501; in 1991, the average salary rose to $891,188; in 2010, the average salary of a baseball player was approximately $3 million.

2. For more information on salary arbitration in baseball, see Ed Edmonds, "A Most Interesting Part of Baseball's Monetary Structure—Salary Arbitration In Its Thirty-Fifth Year," 20 Marquette *Sports Law Review* 1 (2009) and Spencer B. Gordon, "Final Offer Arbitration in the New Era of Major League Baseball," 6 *Journal of American Arbitration* 153 (2007).

3. For more information on salary arbitration in hockey, see Stephen M. Yoost, "The National Hockey League and Salary Arbitration: Time for a Line Change," 21 *Ohio State Journal on Dispute Resolution* 485 (2006) as well as exhibit 11.2.

CONCLUSION

Understanding the development and application of labor law in sports is important for both employers and employees in the world of professional sports. Particularly in professional sports, labor law provides the guideline for the often complex and contentious relationship between players and owners. Issues regarding collective bargaining agreements and labor disputes are among the most pressing and relevant issues in modern professional sports. It is clear that an understanding of these issues, as well as the history, laws, and processes involved in professional sports labor relationships is important for anyone in sports law or in sports. For those not involved in sports where the athletes are unionized, sports managers and sports lawyers may face the possibility that the athletes might want to unionize. In addition, these sports managers and sports lawyers may deal with nonplaying personnel who are unionized. This is particularly true in facilities, such as gyms, as well as colleges and universities.

Chapter 12

AGENCY LAW

12.1. Agency Law

12.2. Player Agents

    12.2.1. Functions of the Player Agent
        12.2.1.1. Negotiating
        12.2.1.2. Counseling
        12.2.1.3. Managing
        12.2.1.4. Marketing
        12.2.1.5. Resolving Disputes
        12.2.1.6. Planning

12.3. Players Associations and Agents

    12.3.1. Salary Information
    12.3.2. Union-Agent Relationships
    12.3.3. Agent-Athlete Agreements
    12.3.4. Agent-Athlete Dispute Resolution
    12.3.5. Agent-Agent Grievance Arbitration

12.4. Agent-Agent Litigation

12.5. Government Regulation

    12.5.1. Uniform Athlete Agent Act
    12.5.2. Sports Agent Responsibility and Trust Act
    12.5.3. State Regulations
    12.5.4. Ethical Constraints
    12.5.5. National Collegiate Athletic Association (NCAA) Regulations

12.6. Team Sports Player Drafts

    12.6.1. National Football League Draft
        12.6.1.1. Draft Eligibility
        12.6.1.2. Draft Retention Rights
        12.6.1.3. Impact on NCAA Eligibility
    12.6.2. Major League Baseball Draft
    12.6.3. National Basketball Association Draft
    12.6.4. National Hockey League Draft
    12.6.5. Single-Entity League Drafts
        12.6.5.1. Major League Soccer
        12.6.5.2. Women's National Basketball Association

12.7. Standard Player Contract

12.8. Endorsement Contracts and Financial Planning

12.9. Individual Performer Sports

12.10. Foreign Leagues

INTRODUCTION

As professional, intercollegiate, and Olympic sports have blossomed into billion-dollar industries since the 1980s, the role of the player agent has grown significantly within the world of sports. The prominence of agents within sports has paralleled the booming economic growth of the sports industry. With millions of dollars on the line in many player contracts, the need for competent representation has increased considerably (see Chapter 1). Though historically many sports contracts were negotiated solely between the player and the organization, it is now rare to find a proven or entry-level professional athlete who does not employ the services of an agent. The need for knowledgeable and capable sports agents within the sports industry continues to be important for athletes.

Representing athletes is more than negotiating contracts. When an agent signs a contract with a client to represent him or her, the parties are entering into a legal relationship that usually encompasses many responsibilities. An agent, in addition to negotiating the contract with a professional team or organization, may also be responsible for marketing the athlete, financial management of the athlete's portfolio, counseling the athlete in times of trouble, dealing with any disputes that may arise involving the player, administering or drafting a player's will or trust, and handling any off-the-field legal issues. In order to negotiate effectively on behalf of his or her client, an agent must be well versed in a league's collective bargaining agreement, standard player contract, salary information, and rules and regulations of the league team and/or organization. Before entering into contract negotiations on behalf of a player, agents must ensure that they are licensed or certified to negotiate with team representatives under either the players association's rules and regulations and/or state legislation governing agents. Agents are both nonlawyers and lawyers, and the use of the word "agent" can apply to both groups. Player associations, in order to protect the best interests of their member-players and assure that agents will represent their clients effectively, require that agents be certified before they can conduct contract negotiations. In reality, a successful sports agent must be knowledgeable about not only contract law (see Chapter 9), but also about how antitrust law affects professional athletes (see Chapter 10), how labor law influences professional sports (see Chapter 11), eligibility issues affecting collegiate athletes (see Chapters 5 and 6), and the intellectual property rights of their client (see Chapter 13).

In addition to representing athletes, agents may handle representation for coaches, managers, and administrators. Individuals in these high-profile positions usually have the same need for representation as the athletes. Some associations do not allow agents to represent both athletes and coaches, citing a potential conflict of interest. With respect to representing coaches, agents do not have the benefit of a collective bargaining agreement or standard player contract to work from in the contract negotiations. The focus of this chapter is on player representation; for more information on coaches' contracts, refer to section 9.2.5, "Coaches' Contracts: Professional and Collegiate Sports."

Although league players associations require certification of player agents, anyone can be a sports agent. The life of an agent, popularized in the movie *Jerry Maguire* and television series *Arliss*, appears to be exciting, fast-paced, and very attractive for a person who wants to work in the field of sports. Also, until the late 1980s and early 1990s, it was an occupation that had managed to avoid significant litigation and legislative scrutiny. This lack of regulation and legislation led to a very competitive atmosphere. With the increased attractiveness of being a sports agent, and the potential money an agent can make, situations have arisen where agents have attempted to circumvent NCAA rules and/or state laws. Therefore, many states have passed legislation to deal with problems that may arise with athlete agents. With the approval and aid of the NCAA, the Uniform Athlete Agent Act of 2000 has been passed in 38 states and the District of Columbia by offering the promise of consistent, widespread regulation of agent activity.

One of the most important duties of a responsible sports agent is to provide sensible, realistic guidance to athletes who are dealing with possible professional career opportunities in sports. However, when dealing with intercollegiate athletes, an agent should be aware of the issues that may affect the eligibility of student-athletes, specifically the payment to or employment of an athlete. These areas are addressed in sections 6.3.3.1 "NCAA Rules Regarding Scholarships, Financial Assistance, and Expenses" and 6.3.3.2, "Employment: NCAA." Due to the extensive regulations placed upon college athletes, it is important that an agent also be aware of NCAA regulations governing contact with agents in order to avoid compromising an athlete's eligibility.

An athlete faces many pressures when deciding whether to turn pro. The money an athlete can earn as a professional may make forfeiting college eligibility a very attractive proposition. The money may be viewed by the athlete as a way of becoming self-supporting and/or helping his or her family. A student-athlete may feel the pressure to secure these considerable financial awards before his or her amateur eligibility ends in order to avoid the risk that a career-threatening injury during his or her amateur career will limit the chances of ever earning the large salary. To deal with the possibility of suffering a career-ending injury during amateur play, many college athletes take out insurance policies prior to returning to playing further seasons in college (see notes 2 and 3).

An agent must be careful not to jeopardize the eligibility status of the athlete by negotiating a contract or representing the athlete. However, the agent may serve as an adviser to the player and his or her family, and can advise on the draft, the industry, the sport, and likely contract offers as long as no agreement for future representation is made between the athlete and agent. While it is true that an athlete may have a difficult time retaining eligibility in the face of attractive offers of a professional contract, some agents have unrealistically boosted the expectations of an athlete who may then be drafted lower than promised. The athlete has subsequently made a bad decision to leave college for a pro career, and in many situations this has not worked out for the athlete.

It is the athletes themselves who must ultimately make the critical decisions impacting their lives. They first must decide, with the knowledgeable input of others, whether they are ready to compete at the professional level. They then must try to establish, with this same input, which round they will be drafted in, approximately how much they will be paid, and, if drafted, whether it will be the right team for them. Professional drafts are very difficult for athletes and agents to predict because the process of drafting is an inexact science, with athletes predicted to be chosen early in a draft sometimes falling a number of rounds. In professional basketball and football, the athletes usually do not have the luxury of picking a desired team. In all professional team sports, however, athletes in certain situations can discourage teams from drafting them. Prospective draftees can make it clear that they will not sign or play for a particular team, announce that they will decide to play a different sport if they are drafted by a particular team, or make it plain that they will play only if given a large signing bonus. Even then, the amount prospective draftees can earn in a signing bonus and in their first contracts is often limited by the league's collective bargaining agreements. Athletes must also decide whether they are physically and mentally prepared for the rigors of the game, both on and off the court or field.

Another consideration is what will happen if they wait to turn pro. By waiting, they may sacrifice a large contract. On the other hand, they may improve their draft status and make more money after another season of collegiate play.

Student-athletes who do not want to employ an agent need to know to whom they can turn for assistance. Will the league office give them some direction? Will the club that is interested in drafting them be helpful in giving some direction? And who from the club is best to talk to? Even before being drafted, the athletes will also want to talk with a representative of the players union to obtain salary information and to find out about other resources the players association can offer.

This chapter will provide a basic foundation of the information and issues that need to be considered and understood before representing clients who are aspiring pros or current professional athletes.

The chapter first examines the basics of agency law in the United States. It then scrutinizes the varying definitions of a player agent. The following three sections deal with the relationship between the agent and the league's entry draft, the league's standard player contract, and the league's players association. The next section discusses the varying functions of an agent. Section 12.5. discusses government and private regulations facing agents, including the Uniform Athlete Agent Act. This section also deals with state athlete-agent legislation and applicable NCAA rules and regulations that have been enacted to protect athletes from unscrupulous agents. The chapter concludes with brief sections on individual sports, the opportunities available to U.S. athletes who want to play in foreign leagues, and endorsement contracts.

NOTES

1. In *Ashby v. Underwriters at Lloyd's*, 2008 WL 667420 (S.D. Cal. March 6, 2008), the court refused Lloyd's motion for summary judgment ruling that there was a material issue of fact as to whether or not Ashby had suffered "permanent, total disablement." Ashby, a 14-year MLB veteran filed his disability claim after he underwent Tommy John surgery (ulnar collateral ligament [UCL] reconstruction) in October 2003.

2. In *Certain Underwriters at Lloyd's London Subscribing to Certificate No. 986557 v. Rychel*, 126 P.3d 234 (Colo. App. 2005), Lloyd's of London, a premier international insurance company, won a declaratory judgment against former Colorado Avalanche left wing Warren Rychel that insurance obtained by Rychel with Lloyd's did not cover an injury sustained in an in-game fight.

See the following books for a discussion of the role and history of athlete agents:

1. Black, William H., *Tanked! Behind the Scenes with the NFL's Biggest Stars by the Game's Most Infamous Super Agent*, (Minneapolis, MN: Creative Publishing, 2009).

2. Jerry Crasnick, *License to Deal: A Season on the Run with a Maverick Baseball Agent* (New York: Rodale Books, 2005).

3. Kenneth L. Shropshire and Timothy Davis, *The Business of Sports Agents* (Philadelphia: University of Pennsylvania Press, 2002).

4. Ronald M. Shapiro, Mark A. Jankowski, James Dale, and Cal Ripken, *The Power of Nice: How to Negotiate So Everyone Wins—Especially You!* Rev. ed. (New York: John Wiley and Sons, 2001).

5. David Allen Smith, *From the Prom to the Pros: The Athlete's, Parent's, and Coach's Guide* (Santa Ana, CA: Seven Locks Printing, 2000).

6. Robert H. Mnookin, Lawrence Susskind, and Pacey C. Foster, eds., *Negotiating on Behalf of Others: Advice to Lawyers, Business Executives, Sports Agents, Diplomats, Politicians and Everybody Else* (Thousand Oaks, CA: Sage, 1999).

7. Marc Roberts and Theresa Foy Digeronimo, *Roberts Rules: Success Secrets from America's Most Trusted Sports Agent* (Franklin Lakes, NJ: Career Press, 1998).

8. Leigh Steinberg and Michael D'Orso, *Winning with Integrity* (New York: Random House, 1998).

9. Robert H. Ruxin and Gary A. Uberstine, *Athlete's Guide to Agents*, 3rd ed. (Boston: Jones and Bartlett, 1993).

10. Ron Simon, *The Game Behind the Game: Negotiating in the Big Leagues* (Stillwater, MN: Voyageur Press, 1993).

11. Kenneth L. Shropshire, *Agents of Opportunity: Sports Agents and Corruption in Collegiate Sports*, 2nd ed. (Philadelphia: University of Pennsylvania Press, 1992).

12. Robert Fisher and William L. Ury, *Getting to Yes: Negotiating Agreement without Giving In* (London: Viking Penguin, 1991).

13. Alexander Wolff and Armen Keteyian, *Raw Recruits* (New York: Pocket Books, 1991).

14. Bob Woolf, *Friendly Persuasion: How to Negotiate and Win* (New York: Berkeley Publishing Group, 1991).

12.1. AGENCY LAW

To gain a complete understanding of the role of a sports agent, it is necessary that the basics of agency law be discussed first. The agency relationship is a fiduciary relationship between one person—the agent—who agrees to act for, and under the direction or control of another—the principal. The principal is the one for whom an action is taken, and the agent is the one who acts. The agent acts on behalf of the principal (in our case, the athlete), is subject to the control of the principal, and can act on the principal's behalf only with his or her consent. A fiduciary relationship implies that an obligation of trust and confidence exists between the principal and agent.

Three elements of an agency relationship are especially important to comprehend: *consent, on behalf of,* and *subject to the control of. Consent,* in agency relationships, does not have to be given in written form. Instead, as long as the relationship is consensual, an agent does not need a contract to work for the principal. In fact, anyone, including children, can be agents even though they do not have the capacity to contract for themselves. Only the principal in the relationship must have capacity, consistent with the basics of contract law (see Chapter 9).

Acting *on behalf of* a principal signifies that an agent is not conducting negotiations for his or her own best interest; rather, they are for the profit of the principal in the relationship. When an agent is *subject to the control of* the principal, the agent must act under the direction of the principal. Also important to an agency relationship is an understanding of the duties owed by a principal to an agent. Under agency law, the principal owes three fiduciary duties to the agent: to compensate, to reimburse, and to indemnify the agent. The principal is also liable on contracts negotiated by the agent where the agent possesses the authority to enter into the contract on the principal's behalf. A principal will not be liable under a contract where an agent has no authority to enter into it.

12.2. PLAYER AGENTS

A player agent, also called a player representative, is a person authorized by a player to act in his or her name. The promise of compensation is not required to establish the relationship, although such compensation is usually presumed. The definition of who and what constitute an agent can differ from organization to organization and from state to state. For example, the definition of an agent by the National Football League may not be the same as the definition used by a particular state agent's legislation.

12.2.1. Functions of the Player Agent

Agents who represent professional athletes are called on to render a wide variety of services for their clients. The diversity of services, in fact, is such that it is unreasonable to expect one individual to master all the knowledge and skills necessary to accomplish the tasks required. Among other realities, this has led to a separation of law and management functions, and player representatives are examining a number of options that would allow them to provide all the services required by today's professional athletes.

The traditional role of the player agent has been to negotiate the player's contract and represent the athlete on any other law-related issues with the club. Representation today may also include marketing of the player's name; arranging and negotiating personal appearances; offering financial and investment advice, tax planning, and tax return preparation; and personal, legal, and financial counseling. An athlete must consider either retaining different advisers for legal, financial, and investment advice, or a small firm that subcontracts and/or coordinates the various services, or a multifaceted management group that can provide all of these services within one company. With demands for the full range of services coming to the fore, pressures are mounting to set up a business organization that will respond to a plethora of needs.

The move in the agency market toward agencies offering a "conglomerate" of services has truly changed the way agents approach signing an athlete. In the National Football League, for example, an agent is allowed to receive a maximum of 3% of his client's total contract. Agents are free, however, to set a higher percentage of compensation on other contracts, such as endorsements. Agents may take anywhere from 10% to 25% of the total compensation for athlete endorsements. This high percentage on endorsement contracts explains why so many people are willing to get into the field of player representation when the maximum commission on a contract is only 3%.

While 3% is a maximum commission, in the competitive world of athlete representation, many agents will work for a lower percentage in an attempt to gain clients. Also, with the introduction of salary caps in the NBA, NFL, and NHL, the amount of money that players are making is not increasing at the same pace it was in the mid-1990s. Also, with salary scales (NBA) or rookie salary maximums (NBA), some superstars have negotiated contracts without an agent. These athletes hire an attorney to review the contract on an hourly basis, and therefore can pay significantly less in fees. NBA players who were known to have done this include Ray Allen and Chris Webber.

Agency conglomerates, which include marketing firms, player agents, and financial advisers, were formed in order to provide the athlete with "total representation," and also provide an agency more avenues to produce revenues. Companies such as IMG, CAA, Wasserman Media Group, BEST, and Octagon have been among the leaders in this consolidation of services under one umbrella organization. While some agents still work alone or in small partnerships (e.g., the Scott Boras Corporation in baseball), the trend in the sports agency business is toward companies that can provide individualized service to players by offering a wide range of functions under one organization.

Some players seek the services of an agent who has a unique specialization that makes him or her especially appealing. For example, Herbert Rudoy, an attorney based in Chicago specialized in representing European basketball players who play in the NBA. His client list has included Tony Kukoc, Arvydis Sabonis, Zydrunas Ilgauskas, and other European players of the NBA. Players may sign with Rudoy because he has knowledge of the unique situations faced by European players in the NBA, and maintains contacts in Europe should the athlete return to Europe to play.

Agents use a variety of methods to charge their clients for services rendered. The most common is for an agent to take a percentage of the total value of the player contract—anywhere from 3% to 10%. Many agents looking to get a start in the business often accept smaller percentages. Some agents will represent a player in contract negotiation for a predetermined fee, regardless of the time spent or the amount of the contract. Agents may also elect to charge an hourly rate—usually between $100 and $300. The other alternative is a combination of a stated percentage (usually less than 7%) and a predetermined or hourly fee, whichever is less.

One disadvantage for the athlete in agreeing to pay an hourly fee to the agent is that the athlete is obligated to that agent even if he or she does not make the team. However, if the athlete makes the team, the fee based on an hourly rate may be less than the contingency fee. If the athlete and agent have agreed to a contingency fee, however, there is no obligation to pay the agent if the athlete does not make the team. On the other hand, the athlete may find paying an hourly fee to the agent a disadvantage if the contract negotiations become protracted. These fees can become enormous in view of the salaries paid to some of today's superstar athletes. The escalation of player salaries has made the percentage method very popular among agents. Because of the tremendous amount of money available, some agents are tempted to lure top athletes illegally, even while they are still in school.

The point to remember is that the player representative is in a business that demands a number of services. Before proceeding with other considerations, such as the legal and ethical constraints placed on player representatives, the functions themselves must be considered. In the following sections, the basic functions of a sports agent will be discussed briefly. As can be seen, negotiating contracts only constitutes one aspect of the sports agent's job.

NOTE

1. For a discussion of limits placed upon fees for sports agents, see Diane Sudia and Rob Remis, "Ethical and Statutory Limitations on Athlete-Agent Income: Fees, Referrals, and Ownership Interests," 27 *Florida State University Law Review* 787 (Summer 2002).

In the following cases, the courts dealt with unethical practices of sports agents:

1. In *Lankford v. Irby*, 2006 WL 2828548 (D.N.J. September 29, 2006), former St. Louis Cardinal outfielder Ray Lankford sued his former agent, E. Albert Irby, after he loaned him $475,000 and Irby failed to repay. Because Irby did not dispute that the loan had occurred nor that he failed to repay, the court granted summary judgment for Lankford.

2. In *Hillard v. Black*, 125 F. Supp. 2d 1071 (2000), agent William Black was found to have illegally taken money from two of his clients, Ike Hilliard and Fred Taylor, both NFL players. Black sold shares in a company of which he was president to these clients at an inflated price, took the money, and deposited it into a sham company, with the money being funneled directly to him. At this level, Black was attempting to have the case dismissed, but his request for dismissal was denied. After Black was suspended for three years, he brought a case against the league, alleging that its conduct was racially motivated (*Black v. National Football League Players Ass'n*, 87 F. Supp. 2d 1 (D.D.C. 2001)).

3. In *Total Economic Athletic Management of America v. Pickens*, 898 S.W.2d 98 (1995), TEAM America had signed a contract to represent Pickens in negotiations with National Football League teams. However, Pickens entered into a contract with another contract adviser prior to the negotiation, and used this adviser for the negotiation. Upon appeal of the district court, the appeals court upheld the ruling, ordering Pickens to pay $20,000 in damages to TEAM America.

4. In *Faigin v. Kelly*, 184 F.3d 67 (1st Cir. 1999), A. J. Faigin, the former agent for Buffalo Bills quarterback Jim Kelly, brought a defamation suit against Kelly because Kelly had made negative comments about Faigin in his autobiography. The appeals court upheld a summary judgment for Kelly on the trial court level. Although the statements from the autobiography were found to be defamatory, the jury at the trial court level decided "that Faigin had failed to prove actual malice and, pursuant to the court's instructions, returned a verdict for the defendant." Because Faigin could not prove that the statements were false, he was unsuccessful in his claim.

5. For a discussion of the ethical issues involved in being an agent, see also Stacey B. Evans, "Sports Agents: Ethical Representatives or Overly Aggressive Adversaries?," 17 *Villanova Sports & Entertainment Law Journal* 91 (2010), Melissa Neiman, "Fair Game: Ethical Considerations in Negotiations by Sports Agents," 9 *Texas Review of Entertainment & Sports Law* 123 (2007) and David S. Caudill, "Revisiting the Ethic of Representing Professional Athletes: Agents, 'Attorney-Agents,' Full-Service Agencies, and the Dream Team Model," 3 *Virginia Sports & Entertainment Law Journal* 31 (2003).

6. The following excerpt is from an information pamphlet that was sent to prospective professional athletes by a sports consulting firm that was attempting to establish itself:

What We Do Contract negotiation: We deal directly with management to obtain the maximum commitment regarding salary, benefits and contract provisions.

Endorsements and appearances: We will seek to supplement our clients' regular income by promoting product endorsements and personal appearances. We will both pursue appearance possibilities and negotiate on our clients' behalf for endorsement fees.

Investments: We will review investment recommendations and proposals with our investment consultants. In addition, we will draw upon investment research from several investment banking and brokerage firms to augment our investment consultants.

Financial planning, insurance, legal and tax matters: We will also:

1. Evaluate our clients' financial condition and establish a proper plan to insure maximum use of present and future earnings.

2. Have outside insurance consultants analyze our clients' insurance programs and make recommendations as to adequacy of individual and group life, health and accident and disability insurance programs. We will make recommendations to our clients according to their needs after reviewing our consultants' proposals.

3. Provide complete legal advice in all areas of general law as they may affect our clients' needs.

4. Prepare personal federal, state and other necessary tax returns—and provide complete professional advice on foreign tax matters, tax-sheltered investments and other areas of tax specialization.

Our policy will be to care for the normal needs of the client and this effort will be incorporated into the negotiation fee.

Our clientele will be normally drawn from those who are not superstars and it is our feeling that we should not charge them excessively. We are sure that our fees are at least 1/2 to 1/3 of those fees charged by other people in the athletic representative field.

We want to establish a feeling of honesty and fairness with our clients. We are sure that from our clients will come superstars with whom we will become more involved. But, we will always maintain a policy of providing low cost and honest service to the average professional athlete.

In most cases, our advice to the athletes will be to let their money grow in savings or in AAA bonds. Then, when they have reached superstar status and/or have a large enough cash base, we will have them diversify their investments.

Outside Consultants Investment advisers. We will receive investment advice from professional investment counselors and investment banking and brokerage firms. Our investment counselors include: Investment Banking and Brokerage Houses. We work closely with several brokerage houses including [names of firms]. Investment research and recommendations which are acted upon by us will realize brokerage commissions to those firms. Therefore, there will be no outside fee expense in conjunction with such investments. *Attorneys and tax specialists.* We receive legal and tax advice from several major law firms. *Insurance, pensions, profit sharing, etc.* Our insurance consultants include representatives and managers of several major insurance companies—to include: [names of firms].

Advertising consultants. Our advertising consultants are creative directors, artists and copywriters at several advertising agencies and provide leads of client firms seeking professional athletes as well as advice on public relations, fee schedules and promotions.

12.2.1.1. Negotiating

The player agent must be able to obtain the necessary background information, map the appropriate strategies, and have the flexibility to counter alternatives in order to represent the client effectively. When entering into contract negotiations for a client, the agent must be prepared, not only in terms of the issues to be brought up, but also in regard to refuting or responding to management's claims.

A good agent will know the market value of his or her client, based on salaries of comparable players (position, ability, service). The agent should also have detailed information about the team with respect to the client's likelihood of success, chances of starting, depth at client's position, and the negotiation history of the club. This type of preparation is of paramount importance if an optimal contract is to be negotiated.

One important point to remember in the sports context is that, in a sense, one rarely stops negotiating. The signed contract is usually only the first step. A number of occurrences during the term of the contract may call for even greater skill on the part of the negotiator, a point emphasized later in the chapter.

A second important point is the interconnections between the negotiating function and the functions described below. One cannot, and should not, attempt to completely isolate one from the others. As noted earlier, a single individual cannot effectively handle all functions, at least not in most situations. So knowing how to deal with the overlaps while dividing the functions efficiently calls for careful thought, planning, and organizational structure.

In the sports of baseball and hockey, an agent may also have to deal with the process of salary arbitration. This process, unique to these sports, may necessitate the agent's employing outside assistance from a person(s) with expertise in this particular field.

NOTES _____

1. In *Buse v. Vanguard Group of Investment Cos.*, No. 91–3560, 1996 U.S. Dist. LEXIS 19033 (E.D. Pa. Dec. 20, 1996), an athlete filed suit against an investment company, after his agent misrepresented his pension and retirement plan. The plaintiff (Buse) argued that the Vanguard Group should be liable for complying with a request from the plaintiff's agent (Skinner) to liquidate one half of his pension plan and mail it to the agent on the behalf of Buse. The court held for the plaintiff, agreeing that these actions constituted a breach of fiduciary duty.

2. In *Pro Tect Management Corp. v. Worley*, No. 89 Civ. 3026, U.S. Dist. LEXIS 14574, (S.D.N.Y. Oct. 30, 1990), an agent whose contract with a player made prior to the NFL draft was terminated in favor for another, sued for breach of contract.

3. *Detroit Lions, Inc. v. Argovitz*, 580 F. Supp. 542 (E.D. Mich. 1984), Detroit Lions free agent running back Billy Sims, under the guidance of his agent, Jerry Argovitz, signed a contract with the Houston Gamblers on July 1, 1983. On December 16, 1983, Sims signed a second contract with Detroit, and filed a complaint in Oakland County Circuit Court seeking a determination that the July 1, 1983, contract between Sims and the Houston Gamblers was invalid because the defendant, Jerry Argovitz, breached his fiduciary duty when negotiating the Gamblers contract. The court concluded that Argovitz breached his duty to Sims by having significant ownership interest in the Houston franchise, and not representing him properly in contract negotiations with Detroit. The contract between Sims and Houston was rescinded by the court.

4. In *Brown v. Woolf*, 554 F. Supp. 1206 (S.D. Ind. 1983), a professional athlete brought action for constructive fraud and breach of fiduciary duty against the defendant agent. The athlete claimed the agent negotiated a contract for him with a new team of the National Hockey League. After reaching an agreement for compensation, the new team began to have financial difficulties and eventually defaulted on their contractual obligations. The plaintiff claimed he was paid only $185,000 of the total $800,000 contract, but the defendant agent received his full $40,000 fee (5% of the contract). The plaintiff also contended the agent breached his fiduciary duty to the plaintiff by failing to conduct any investigation into the financial stability of the new team. The district court denied the defendant's motion for a summary judgment.

5. In *Zinn v. Parrish*, 644 F.2d 360 (7th Cir. 1981), an agent recovered damages after being terminated by a player. Leo Zinn, the agent for Cincinnati Bengals cornerback Lemar Parrish, was successful in recovering after Parrish terminated him in 1974, shortly after Zinn negotiated a four-year contract for Parrish. Zinn sought to recover his 10% commission on the 1974–1977 contracts, and did so. The court ruled that Zinn fulfilled the terms of the contract to use reasonable efforts to procure professional football employment, despite failing to obtain jobs or contracts in many cases, it was not a failure to perform.

12.2.1.2. Counseling

Counseling is an often overlooked function of vital importance, both during negotiations and after the contract is signed. Making certain the client understands what is at stake in a professional sports contract may prevent later misunderstandings or disappointments. It is important the agent provide realistic guidance to his or her players. An agent should be able to clearly understand and convey the player's chances of making the team as well as the player's overall career prospects. Agents must help prepare players for many of the negative issues that can affect their careers, in particular injuries. Lastly, an agent's most valuable role to his or her clients may be in helping with off-the-court or off-the-field issues and preparing the athlete for life after professional sports.

After the contract is signed, other problems call for counseling. For example, the player makes the team but is sitting on the bench. Personal frustrations become predominant. Players may also have family problems that an agent can assuage, or damaging outside influences that an agent can steer his or her client away from. As will be discussed in the following section, agents must also direct their clients in business matters, because these are not generally areas where the athlete has any formal experience. In these and many other contexts, the counseling function is crucial.

12.2.1.3. Managing

Many athletes come out of college with little self-discipline and an almost total lack of knowledge about financial matters. The money soon disappears if the client is left unsupervised.

Not all player representatives get into money management, and those who do not should advise the client as to where such assistance can be obtained. An ongoing relationship between the representative and a firm that deals in management and investments should be explored. Agents who are not experienced in financial matters should be careful when managing their client's money. As evidenced by the case of *People v. Sorkin* (see note 3), it is in the best interests of an agent who is not experienced in financial matters to hire the outside assistance of someone who is experienced.

NOTES _____

1. In January 2002, a federal jury found sports agent William "Tank" Black guilty of fraud, conspiracy, and obstruction of justice in the theft of up to $14 million from professional football players he represented. The case centered on testimony from NFL players who claimed Black used his position as their agent to steal millions from them through bogus investments. Black spent nearly seven years in prison before his release in 2008.

2. In 2007, former NFL player turned agent Sean Jones was indicted on fraud charges related to a mortgage loan scheme. Jones was also sued by several former clients from whom he unlawfully converted funds.

3. In *People v. Sorkin*, 407 N.Y.S.2d 772 (N.Y. App. Div 1978), Richard Sorkin, an agent for several New York Islanders of the NHL, was sentenced to jail for grand larceny. He pleaded guilty to stealing $360,000 from players he represented. He had lost almost $300,000 in the stock market due to poor investments, and also had lost $600,000 to bookmakers. Sorkin was representing over 300 players at the height of his representation career.

12.2.1.4. Marketing

There is a prevailing attitude, although a mistaken one, that most professional athletes do well because of lucrative endorsements and other types of outside income. In truth, such wealth is largely reserved for the top stars. Other athletes do what they can to supplement their income with personal appearances at local clubs, dinners, commercial establishments, and other less-than-top-dollar affairs. Even so, the possibilities for some types of outside income do exist. How aggressively they are sought on behalf of the client varies with the representative, but some willingness of the representative to assist the client in seeking supplementary income is demanded. With that in mind, a few rules and regulations should be noted.

First, chances are that either the player's contract with the club or the league's collective bargaining agreement will have some provisions regarding endorsements. These should be reviewed before any action is taken. Second, the other side of the marketing issue is being vigilant about protecting the player's name and image. These are property rights capable of protection under a variety of legal theories, including rights of publicity and privacy (see Chapter 13). Instances in which athletes have had to resort to the courts over alleged infringements are many, although in more than one case the player was held to have signed away his rights through the broad grant contained in an earlier contract. These cases should be fair warning to the player agent about the careless granting of rights.

Cases in this area continue to appear as athletes are increasingly viewed as celebrities whose names and images have commercial potential. Together with the ever-growing number of cases dealing with the rights of celebrities in other entertainment areas, these cases have brought about a substantial body of law involving rights of privacy and publicity.

12.2.1.5. Resolving Disputes

When things have gone awry under an existing contract, and the other side is believed to have done something that must be redressed legally, the player's representative basically has two possibilities for action: arbitration or litigation. Arbitration has preempted litigation in many situations in professional sports. A player agent must be aware of this because the time period in which arbitration complaints must be filed is often short. Rights are easily waived. The arbitration process, which is usually initiated through the player's association, is specified in the collective bargaining agreement between the association and the league. This document has become indispensable to the player agent. Litigation is a feasible alternative in some situations. Alleged antitrust violations by a league or club, for example, are still the province of the courts, although the leagues have become increasingly insulated from attacks due to their protection under the Sherman Act, Clayton Act, and nonstatutory labor exemption (see section 10.3.2, "The Nonstatutory Labor Exemption"). Even so, the cases still occur (see section 11.3.14, "Grievance Procedures in Professional Sports").

12.2.1.6. Planning

Most athletes' careers last only a short time. The average career for a professional athlete, assuming he or she makes the team in the first place, is four to five years, varying slightly by the sport played. Thus, for many, there is never anything beyond the first contract. For this reason, the player agent must prepare the client for what will occur in the not-too-distant future. Such a task is easy to describe, but difficult to carry out.

Athletes may claim that they realize theirs will not be a long career, but it is hard to grasp just how short a career can be. Most players are not really prepared for the end. Their attitude is invariably "next year, perhaps, but not now."

The player agent may be unable to cushion the psychological blow completely. The hope is that the client has had sufficient time to produce enough income so that at least some preparations can be made for the financial transition. Achieving this goal relates to the managing function, but it also requires the future ingredient of careful planning. The player agent may need to obtain professional help to assist the athlete in planning for a new career. A player agent in this business for any period of time will have to confront this problem.

12.3. PLAYERS ASSOCIATIONS AND AGENTS

The players association for a professional league is the organization that works on the athlete's behalf when negotiating the collective bargaining agreement with league officials (see section 11.3.7, "Collective Bargaining Agreements in Professional Sports"). These associations are recognized by the National Labor Relations Board (see section 11.1.6, "National Labor Relations Board"). However, the responsibilities of a players association go beyond simply negotiating and administering the collective bargaining agreement. Players associations also designate the right to negotiate individual contracts to the agents, while continuing to oversee and monitor the process, and also holding the power to repeal this right. Since functions of players associations were discussed extensively in Chapter 11, this section will focus on the relationship between the players association and the agents who represent players within a league.

Beyond their primary responsibility of negotiating and administering the league collective bargaining agreement, players associations also work with players who have filed for grievance arbitration, as per the collective bargaining agreement, with the league. Players associations utilize a wide variety of resources, including experienced labor attorneys, to work with the agent. However, it is usually the players association attorney who has the primary responsibility during the grievance procedure.

NOTES

1. In the arbitration case of *Rona v. Major League Baseball Players Association*, the MLBPA was trying to prevent Barry Rona from becoming a certified agent for baseball players because he had been deeply involved in a collusion scandal (see section 11.3.7.1.4, "Baseball Collusion Cases") against free agency by owners within the league. Rona was former executive director and general counsel of the player relations committee, the owners' labor unit. The association was attempting to deny Rona certification because its own rules and regulations stated that the association may bar any agent whose conduct "may adversely affect his credibility [or] integrity . . . to serve in a representative and/or fiduciary capacity on behalf of the players." The independent arbitrator, Collins, concluded that the MLBPA did not have any solid evidence of Rona's wrongdoing in the collusion cases, only that he was the legal counsel for some of the figures in the case. Because the MLBPA had denied Rona's certification on these grounds, Collins decided that the MLBPA's ruling was arbitrary and capricious, and ordered that Rona be certified as an agent by the MLBPA.

2. In the case of *Collins v. NBPA*, 850 F. Supp. 1468 (D. Colo. 1991), an agent who had his certification revoked by the National Basketball Players Association sought to regain his certification, claiming that the NBPA certification process broke antitrust laws because it constituted a group boycott, and that the dismissal was unfair because it had been based on Collins's breach of fiduciary duties as a investment agent and money manager, but not as a sports agent. The court concluded that the NBPA was allowed under the labor exemption provided by the Sherman Act to have a certification process. Second, the court decided that, in acting in the best interests of their players, the NBPA could investigate the outside actions of players agents.

3. The registration guidelines for NFL player agents can be found at the NFLPA website: www.nflpa.org, under Member Services > Rules and Regulations.

For more information on the registration guidelines for agent certification in major professional team sports, the players associations can be contacted at the following addresses:

1. Major League Baseball Players Association
   12 East 49th Street 24th Floor
   New York, NY 10017

(212) 655-0808
www.mlbplayers.com

2. National Basketball Players Association
2 Penn Plaza Suite 2430
New York, NY 10121
(212) 655-0880
www.nbpa.com

3. National Hockey League Players Association
20 Bay Street Suite 1700
Toronto, ON
M5J 2N8
www.nhlpa.com

4. National Football League Players Association
1133 20th Street NW
Washington, DC 20036
(800) 372-2000
www.nflpa.org

12.3.1. Salary Information

Although the players associations have many responsibilities, one of their primary functions is to negotiate the collective bargaining agreement with the league, which sets forth the terms and conditions of employment for the players, including minimum salaries and other benefits (see section 11.3.7, "Collective Bargaining Agreements in Professional Sports").

Perhaps the most important aspect of the relationship between the agent and the players association is the association's involvement in negotiating individual contracts. The association actually has the right to negotiate contracts on an individual basis for each of its players, but it generally transfers this right to the agent while still overseeing the entire process. It is in the best interest of the players association to keep a close eye on contract negotiations because bad contracts can cause a ripple effect within the league. If a star player, who theoretically "deserves" to make $2 million, is underpaid due to the incompetence of his or her agent, and receives only $1 million, players with similar abilities and histories may have difficulty arguing that they should make any more than $1 million even if they are worth more. Furthermore, in NHL and MLB salary arbitration (see section 11.3.15, "Salary Arbitration"), arbitrators may be compelled to award a salary arbitration eligible player a lesser amount of money after another player at his position signs for less than his "market value" salary. Both the Major League Baseball Players Association and National Hockey League Players Association are actively involved in the process of salary arbitration between teams and players.

Contracts negotiated by agents can include a variety of salary items, including a base salary, signing bonus, training camp reporting bonuses, and deferred compensation packages. Signing bonuses are popular with draft picks because they give the rookie a nice payout before the first year in the professional league. Signing bonuses are also available in Major League Baseball and the National Hockey League, where many players also have guaranteed contracts. The NFL does not have many guaranteed contracts, which makes signing bonuses very attractive for unproven players, since it is the only guaranteed compensation that they will receive. The National Basketball Association does not employ signing bonuses; however, most contracts in the league are guaranteed.

Comparing the four professional leagues—National Basketball Association, National Football League, National Hockey League, and Major League Baseball—the highest average salary is paid in the sport of basketball (NBA), with Major League Baseball not far behind. Exhibits 12.1 through 12.6 contain information on salaries or team payrolls for each of the Big Four professional sports leagues.

Exhibit 12.1
2010 Major League Baseball Team Payroll

Rank	Team	Total Payroll
1	New York Yankees	$206,333,389
2	Boston Red Sox	$162,447,333
3	Chicago Cubs	$146,609,000
4	Philadelphia Phillies	$141,928,379
5	New York Mets	$134,422,942
6	Detroit Tigers	$122,864,928
7	Chicago White Sox	$105,530,000
8	Los Angeles Angels of Anaheim	$104,963,866
9	San Francisco Giants	$98,641,333
10	Minnesota Twins	$97,559,166
11	Los Angeles Dodgers	$95,358,016
12	St. Louis Cardinals	$93,540,751
13	Houston Astros	$92,355,500
14	Seattle Mariners	$86,510,000
15	Atlanta Braves	$84,423,666
16	Colorado Rockies	$84,227,000
17	Baltimore Orioles	$81,612,500
18	Milwaukee Brewers	$81,108,278
19	Tampa Bay Rays	$71,923,471
20	Cincinnati Reds	$71,761,542
21	Kansas City Royals	$71,405,210
22	Toronto Blue Jays	$62,234,000
23	Washington Nationals	$61,400,000
24	Cleveland Indians	$61,203,966
25	Arizona Diamondbacks	$60,718,166
26	Florida Marlins	$57,034,719
27	Texas Rangers	$55,250,544
28	Oakland Athletics	$51,654,900
29	San Diego Padres	$37,799,300
30	Pittsburgh Pirates	$34,943,000

Exhibit 12.2
2008 National Basketball Association First Round Picks and Contract Status

Pick	Player	From	Drafting Team	Maximum Contract Length	Maximum Salary
1	Derrick Rose	Memphis	Chicago	4	$22,547,148
2	Michael Beasley	Kansas State	Miami	4	$20,156,837
3	OJ Mayo	University of Southern California	Memphis	4	$18,129,437
4	Russell Westbrook	UCLA	Seattle	4	$15,986,990
5	Kevin Love	UCLA	Minnesota	4	$14,812,701
6	Danilo Gallinari	Italy	New York	4	$13,243,902
7	Eric Gordon	Indiana	Clippers	4	$12,230,944
8	Joe Alexander	West Virginia	Milwaukee	4	$11,165,379
9	DJ Augustine	Texas	Charlotte	4	$10,131,328
10	Brook Lopez	Stanford	New Jersey	4	$9,794,744
11	Jerryd Bayless	Arizona	Indiana	4	$8,782,080
12	Jason Thompson	Rider	Sacramento	4	$9,109,044
13	Brandon Rush	Kansas	Portland	4	$8,459,018
14	Anthony Randolph	Louisiana State University	Golden State	4	$8,199,741
15	Robin Lopez	Stanford	Phoenix	4	$7,537,621
16	Marreese Speights	Florida	Philadelphia	4	$7,279,514
17	Roy Hibbert	Georgetown	Toronto	4	$6,807,870
18	JaVale McGee	Nevada	Washington	4	$6,498,520
19	J. J. Hickson	NC State	Cleveland	4	$6,204,458
20	Alexis Ajinca	France	Charlotte	4	$6,114,809
21	Ryan Anderson	California	New Jersey	4	$6,095,961
22	Courtney Lee	Western Kentucky	Orlando	4	$6,018,413
23	Kosta Koufos	Ohio State	Utah	4	$5,845,792
24	Serge Ibaka	Congo	Seattle	Did not sign	
25	Nicolas Batum	France	Houston	4	$5,045,721
26	George Hill	Indiana University-Purdue University of Indianapolis (IUPUI)	San Antonio	4	$4,069,946

Exhibit 12.2
(continued)

Pick	Player	From	Drafting Team	Maximum Contract Length	Maximum Salary
27	Darrell Arthur	Kansas	New Orleans	4	$4,315,266
28	Donte Greene	Syracuse	Memphis	4	$4,289,914
29	D. J. White	Indiana	Detroit	4	$5,010,341
30	J. R. Giddens	New Mexico	Boston	4	$4,901,815

Exhibit 12.3
Major League Baseball Average Player Salaries, 1997–2008

1997	$1,383,578	2003	$2,555,476
1998	$1,441,406	2004	$2,486,609
1999	$1,720,050	2005	$2,632,655
2000	$1,998,034	2006	$2,866,544
2001	$2,264,403	2007	$2,944,556
2002	$2,383,235	2008	$3,154,845

Exhibit 12.4
National Football League Average Player Salaries, 1997–2008

1997	$735,730	2003	$1,259,018
1998	$940,470	2004	$1,295,978
1999	$1,012,690	2005	$1,365,078
2000	$1,160,339	2006	$1,400,000
2001	$1,100,939	2007	$1,750,000
2002	$1,041,396	2008	$2,031,537

Exhibit 12.5
National Basketball Association Average Player Salaries, 1996–2008

1996–1997	$1,981,723	2002–2003	$3,884,682
1997–1998	$2,239,352	2003–2004	$3,893,801
1998–1999	$2,463,058	2004–2005	$3,748,658
1999–2000	$2,919,772	2005–2006	$3,844,820
2000–2001	$2,901,595	2006–2007	$4,119,271
2001–2002	$3,465,175	2007–2008	$4,476,272

Exhibit 12.6
National Hockey League Average Player Salaries, 1996–2008

1996–1997	$984,000	2002–2003	$1,790,209
1997–1998	$1,167,713	2003–2004	$1,830,126
1998–1999	$1,288,974	2004–2005	Lockout
1999–2000	$1,356,380	2005–2006	$1,460,000
2000–2001	$1,434,885	2006–2007	$1,708,607
2001–2002	$1,642,590	2007–2008	$1,906,793

12.3.2. Union-Agent Relationships

Marketing is another area in which players associations are actively involved. Players associations are charged with providing licensing rights for trading cards and other products that bear the likenesses of players within the league (see section 13.1.5, "Trademark Infringement"). Players associations also handle group licensing contracts that provide revenue to the association, which is divided equally among all players in the league.

Another important feature of the relationship between the agent and the players association is the registration and certification process that agents need to undergo to become licensed to represent athletes and negotiate contracts in various professional leagues. These players associations are moving to control the player-representative relationship in order to prevent unprincipled, unintelligent, and unprepared agents from representing clients within their players association.

The National Football League, as a result of provisions inserted into the 1982 Collective Bargaining Agreement, set a precedent for all professional sports leagues. The NFL Players Association, pursuant to those provisions, imposed registration and other requirements, including maximum fee schedules, on all agents acting as contract advisers for NFL players. The following are the requirements for an agent to receive certification from the National Football League:

1. A completed application and a nonrefundable application fee of $1,650.

   a. Thereafter, annual fees are $1,200 if representing less than 10 active players and $1,700 in you represent 10 or more active players

2. An undergraduate degree from an accredited four-year university or college **AND** a postgraduate degree (master's or law) **OR** special permission from the NFLPA

3. Mandatory attendance at a two-day seminar in Washington, DC, annually

4. Successful completion of 60-question multiple-choice written, proctored examination

These regulations are in place in the NFL for any person who wishes to provide representation services to any player in the NFL, including rookies. Other professional sports players associations have followed the NFLPA's lead and established guidelines for the registration and regulation of agents. The National Basketball Association's Collective Bargaining Agreement contains the following restrictions on player agents:

Article XXXVI: Player Agents Section 1. Approval of Player Contracts. The NBA shall not approve any Player Contract between a player and a Team unless such player: (i) is represented in the negotiations with respect to such Player Contract by an agent or representative duly certified by the Players Association in accordance with the Players Association's Agent Regulation Program and authorized to represent him; or (ii) acts on his own behalf in negotiating such Player Contract.

Section 2. Fines. The NBA shall impose a fine of $20,000 upon any Team that negotiates a Player Contract with an agent or representative not certified by the Players Association in accordance with the Players Association's Agent Regulation Program if, at the time of such negotiations, such Team either (i) knows that such agent or representative has not been so certified or (ii) fails to make reasonable inquiry of the NBA as to whether such agent or representative has been so certified. Notwithstanding the preceding sentence, in no event shall any Team be subject to a fine if the Team negotiates a Player Contract with the agent designated as the player's authorized agent on the then-current agent list provided by the Players Association to the NBA in accordance with Section 4 below.

In addition, Section 2.C. of the NFLPA Regulations Governing Contract Advisors outlines that the NFLPA has the right to deny the certification of a potential player agent for a variety of reasons, including but not limited to:

- The applicant has made false or misleading statements of a material nature in his/her application;
- The applicant has misappropriated funds, or engaged in other specific acts such as embezzlement, theft or fraud, which would render him/her unfit to serve in a fiduciary capacity on behalf of players;
- The applicant has engaged in any other conduct that significantly impacts adversely on his/her credibility, integrity or competence to serve in a fiduciary capacity on behalf of all players;
- The applicant is unwilling to swear or affirm that he/she will comply with these Regulations and any amendments hereto and/or that he/she will abide by the fee structure contained in the Standard Representation Agreement incorporated into these Regulations;
- The applicant has been denied certification by another professional sports players association;
- The applicant directly or indirectly solicited a player for representation as a Contract Advisor during the period of time between the filing of his/her Application for Certification and Certification by the NFLPA;
- The applicant has not received a degree from an accredited four year college/university, unless excepted from this requirement pursuant to Section 2(A).

The players association can suspend or revoke the certification of a player agent at any time for any of the above reasons as well. The players association must notify the player agent of its decision by the next day, and then the player agent can challenge the suspension or revocation only through arbitration. In addition, an NFL player agent's certification will expire if the agent fails to sign at least one player to a contract, excluding practice squad contracts, during any three-year period.

NOTES

1. When the NFLPA discovered in January 2004 that agent Carl Poston failed to ensure that a 2006 roster bonus worth $6.5 million negotiated with the Washington Redskins for

linebacker LaVar Arrington was not included in the final contract, it initiated disciplinary proceedings against Poston for negligence. In March 2006, the NFLPA suspended Poston for two years and Poston appealed the suspension. At the same time, Poston filed suit seeking a stay to the enforcement of the arbitration proceeding, claiming that he would seek irreparable harm, but the court disagreed; see *Poston v. NFLPA*, 02249 (S.D.N.Y. May 2, 2006). In December 2007, arbitrator Roger Kaplan upheld the suspension.

At Poston's and the other agent's urging, the Congressional Subcommittee on Commercial and Administrative Law held a hearing in December 2006 on the NFLPA's arbitration procedures. Specifically, Poston and agents complained that the arbitrator was not impartial, but instead an employee of the NFLPA. Poston lost a lawsuit against the NFLPA after being disciplined in 2001 because one of his employees provided airfare to Florida State football players. Poston contended that the NFLPA arbitration system was flawed and fundamentally unfair but the court cited deference to the arbitration process; see *Poston v. NFLPA*, 2002 WL 31190142 (E.D.Va. August 26, 2002).

2. In November 2004, the NFLPA Committee on Agent Regulation and Discipline suspended agent Neil Cornrich for one year for aiding General Motors in a lawsuit brought by the estate of the late Kansas City Chief Derrick Thomas. The lawsuit alleged that the Chevrolet Suburban that Thomas drove was defective. Cornrich was hired at a rate of $1,000 per hour to help determine the earnings potential of an NFL player if GM were found liable. The issue of damages became moot when GM was deemed not liable. Although Cornrich never represented Thomas, arbitrator Roger Kaplan ruled that NFLPA-certified player agents have an obligation to the union and thus all NFL players.

3. In November 2004, the NFLPA Committee on Agent Regulation and Discipline suspended agent Jerome Stanley for one year for failing to notify the Cleveland Browns in 2004 that his client, wide receiver Dennis Northcutt, intended to exercise an option in his contract allowing Northcutt to become a free agent. Stanley was also barred from receiving any fee for the three-year, $9 million renegotiated deal that Stanley subsequently worked out with the Browns. Stanley claims that he did give the necessary notice and there was only a question about whether it was technically deficient, an issue that became moot when the renegotiated deal was reached.

4. In June 2003, federal bankruptcy judge Robert Alberts denied the NFLPA's petition to suspend player agent David Dunn for two years as a certified player contract adviser. Dunn and his agency firm Athletes First lost a $40 million lawsuit brought by Dunn's former employer Leigh Steinberg for breach of contract and unfair business practices. Dunn subsequently filed for Chapter 11 bankruptcy protection and it was on this basis that Judge Alberts ruled in Dunn's favor and District Judge Harry Hupp upheld Judge Albert's decision.

5. In February 2003, the NFLPA decertified player agent Sean Jones for life resulting from financial misleadings in representing NFL players Chris Dishman and Ebenezer Ekuban. Jones was accused of unauthorized stock trading, financial mismanagement, and forgery of documents. Arbitrator Roger Kaplan reduced Jones's suspension to two years when Jones introduced a document showing that he had paid $546,500 that he owed to Dishman. Jones was later indicted on criminal fraud charges as part of a mortgage loan scheme.

6. For more on players association regulation of player agents, see Richard T. Karcher, "Fundamental Fairness in Union Regulation of Sports Agents," 40 *Connecticut Law Review* 355 (2007) and Richard T. Karcher, "Solving Problems in the Player Representation Business: Unions Should Be the 'Exclusive' Representatives of the Players," 42 *Willamette Law Review* 737 (2006).

12.3.3. Agent-Athlete Agreements

The relationships established between the player representative and the client has traditionally varied greatly in terms of the formality of any agreement effectuated between the parties. The agreement has ranged from a handshake to a letter of understanding to a detailed contract. Increasingly, interested parties within professional sports are urging that greater formality and detail be introduced into the relationship in order to safeguard the rights of both parties. Players associations now provide form contracts for agents and players in order to simplify the process, avoid misconduct, and make the process consistent throughout the league. While the players associations maintain jurisdiction over the contracts that are signed between players and agents regarding performance, the associations do not maintain control over the execution of contracts concerning marketing and financial management.

NOTES

1. In the case of *Speakers of Sport v. Pro Serv*, 178 F.3d 862 (7th Cir. 1999), the plaintiff, Speakers of Sport, brought a case against Pro Serv for tortious interference with contractual relations, accusing Pro Serv of illegally taking their client, Ivan Rodriguez, a major league catcher. Pro Serv gave the impression to Rodriguez that he would be able to earn $2 million to $4 million in endorsements if he joined their agency. Speakers of Sport alleged that these statements to Rodriguez were false, and that they constituted tortious interference. On appeal of a summary judgment for Pro Serv on the trial court level, the court affirmed this judgment, stating, "There is in general nothing wrong with one sports agent trying to take a client from another if this can be done without precipitating a breach of contract. That is the process known as competition, which though painful, fierce, frequently ruthless, sometimes Darwinian in its pitilessness, is the cornerstone of our highly successful economic system."

2. In *Gandler v. Nazarov*, No. 94 Civ. 2272, 1995 U.S. Dist. LEXIS 8325 (S.D.N.Y June 15, 1995), Andrei Nazarov was a 17-year-old Russian hockey prospect who met with agent Alexander Berkovich in 1992. Nazarov did not have an attorney or speak English. Berkovich, representing International Sports Advisors Co. (ISAC), did not provide a Russian translation of the representation agreement with ISAC. ISAC contended that Nazarov breached the agreement the two parties had entered, because it claimed that it had not been paid for services it had performed for Nazarov, and that he had prematurely terminated the contract. The case concerned forum selection for the trial, Nazarov arguing that the trial should not be held in the United States. In December 2000, a decision was reserved pending an evidentiary hearing. The case was then settled.

3. For more on the effectiveness of player association regulation of agents, see Chris Deubert, "What's a 'Clean' Agent to Do? The Case for a Cause of Action Against a Players Association," *Villanova Sports & Entertainment Law Journal* (2010). For a discussion of issues concerning jurisdiction over agency contracts made on the Internet, see Margaret Danjhal, Daniel S. Strick, and Mark A. Conrad, "Contracting on the Web: Collegiate Athletes and Sports Agents Confront a New Hurdle in Closing the Deal," 8 *Villanova Sports and Entertainment Law Forum* 37 (2001).

4. All of the Player Associations require agents to use a standard representation agreement for the athlete-agent contract. These standard agreements are put of the Player Association regulations and can be found by visiting the Player Association websites noted in section 12.3 Player Associations and Agents.

12.3.4. Agent-Athlete Dispute Resolution

An important facet of the relationship between the player agent and players associations concerns the role of the players associations in resolving disputes between players and their agents. Players associations have taken the responsibility of settling any disputes that arise over fees or the interpretation of contracts through an arbitration process. The following excerpt is taken from the Major League Baseball Players Association Regulations Governing Player Agents:

Section 5

Introduction

In establishing this new system for regulating Player Agents it is the intention of the MLBPA that the impartial arbitration process shall be the exclusive method for resolving any and all disputes between Players and Player Agents that arise out of agreements or contracts between them. This will insure that all such disputes—which involve essentially internal matters concerning the relationship between individual Players, the MLBPA in its capacity as their exclusive bargaining representative, and Player Agents performing certain specified representative functions—will be handled and resolved expeditiously by the neutral decision-maker established herein, instead of through more costly and time-consuming formal court proceedings.

Specifically, the provisions of this section shall apply with respect to two types of disputes: (a) those between a Player and a Player Agent with respect to the existence, meaning, interpretation, or enforcement of any contract between them; and (b) those between a Player and the MLBPA concerning any action taken by the MLBPA in connection with certification.

(A) Procedure for Resolving Player-Player Agent Disputes

The following procedure shall apply to disputes between a Player and Player Agent with respect to the existence, meaning, interpretation, or enforcement of any contract or agreement between them.

1. *Filing*

   A Player or Player Agent shall initiate the dispute resolution procedure by filing a written grievance setting forth in plain and understandable terms the facts and circumstances giving rise to the grievance, the provision(s) of the agreement(s) alleged to have been violated, and the relief sought. Any such grievance must be timely filed and served on the other party, with copy to the Association, within one hundred eighty (180) days from the later of (a) the date of the occurrence of the event upon which the grievance is based, (b) the date on which the facts became known or reasonably should have become known to the grievant, or (c) the effective date of these Regulations.

   If a *Player* initiates any such grievance, he must serve the written grievance by mail or personal delivery to the Player Agent's official business address and must furnish a copy of the grievance to the Association, in an envelope marked "Attention: Agent Regulation," at the Association's offices located at 805 Third Avenue, New York, NY 10022.

   If the *Player Agent* initiates any such grievance, he must serve the player by mail or personal delivery to the Player at either the Player's permanent or in-season residence and must furnish a copy of the grievance to the Association in the same manner as required in the case of a Player-filing.

2. *Answer*

   The party against whom a grievance has been filed ("the respondent") shall answer the grievance in writing by mail or personal delivery within thirty (30) days of receipt of the grievance. The respondent must also provide a copy of his answer to the Association at the same time. The Answer shall admit or deny the facts alleged in the grievance and shall also set forth briefly the reasons why the respondent believes that the grievance should be denied.

3. *Arbitration*

The MLBPA shall then notify both parties in writing that their disputes will be referred to arbitration.

4. *Arbitrator*

Promptly after the effective date of these Regulations, the MLBPA shall name one or more professional and skilled impartial arbitrators to serve as the Impartial Arbitrator of a dispute subject to this Section 5(A).

5. *Proceedings*

Promptly after the Impartial Arbitrator is notified by the MLBPA of a pending case, he shall schedule a hearing on the dispute in New York City, or in such city as the parties, with the concurrence of the Impartial Arbitrator, may agree upon, or in such city as the Impartial Arbitrator may on his own motion direct. At such hearing, the parties—the Player and the Player Agent—may appear in person or by legal counsel or other representative. The parties to the dispute and the MLBPA, as well, will have the right to present, by testimony or otherwise, any evidence deemed by the Impartial Arbitrator to be relevant to the grievance.

The rules of the procedure hearings shall be established by the Impartial Arbitrator and, to the extent deemed practicable to him, shall conform to the Voluntary Labor Arbitration Rules of the American Arbitration Association.

Upon close of the hearing, the Impartial Arbitrator will advise the parties and the MLBPA whether he desires Briefs to be filed or whether he desires the parties and MLBPA to present their arguments orally. The Impartial Arbitrator shall fix the time Briefs are to be filed or the time and place oral arguments are to be presented.

Within thirty (30) days after the receipt of Briefs or the presentation of oral arguments, the Impartial Arbitrator shall issue a written award, including an appropriate remedy if the grievance is sustained. That award shall constitute a full, final, and complete resolution of the grievance and will be binding on the Player and Player Agent involved.

6. *Costs*

Each party will bear the costs of its own witnesses and counsel. Costs of arbitration, including the fees and expenses of the Impartial Arbitrator, will be borne equally between the two parties to the grievance; provided, however, that if the Arbitrator concludes that a party's case is frivolous, he may assess that party with some or all of the opposing party's costs. If the Impartial Arbitrator grants a money award, it shall be paid within thirty (30) days, or such other period as he may direct.

Hearings ordinarily will be transcribed unless the parties and the MLBPA, with the concurrence of the Impartial Arbitrator, agree otherwise, or unless the Impartial Arbitrator so directs. Costs of the transcript, the making of which will be arranged by the Association, will be divided equally among the parties and MLBPA.

7. *Time Limits*

When a dispute has not yet been noticed to the Impartial Arbitrator, the time limits of this Section 5(A) may be extended by the Association, upon good cause shown by either party. Such requests for an extension of time shall be in writing, and served on the opposing party. When a dispute has been noticed to the Impartial Arbitrator, the time limits of this Section may be extended to the Impartial

Arbitrator, upon good cause shown by either party or the MLBPA. Such requests for an extension of time shall be in writing, and, if filed by a party, served on the opposing party and MLBPA, or, if filed by the MLBPA, served on both parties.

NOTES

1. In November 2004, recently retired NBA player Scottie Pippen won an $11.8 million lawsuit against financial adviser Robert Lunn for negligently investing Pippen's money in 2003 in a real estate venture with a developer who shortly thereafter filed for bankruptcy. In January 2005, Pippen filed a legal malpractice suit in Illinois state court in Cook County against his former law firm of Katten, Muchen, Zavis and Rosenman, and one of its lawyers individually, Sheldon T. Zenner, claiming that Zenner acted negligently and with a conflict of interest when he advised Pippen to hire Lunn, one of Zenner's clients, as Pippen's financial adviser. See Mickey Ciokajlo, "Pippen Sues Law Firm for Millions over Investments," *Chicago Tribune* C4 (January 13, 2005).

2. In November 2004, NBA player Vince Carter was ordered to pay former agent William "Tank" Black $4,674,460.45 in lost commissions and damages. Black was sentenced to 82 months in prison in 2001 for money laundering. Black sued Carter for $9 million in commissions from endorsement deals while he was Carter's agent from 1998 to 2000 as well as $5 million in damages. Carter countersued, demanding Black pay him the $15.9 million that Carter lost when Puma sued him over a lost shoe deal as well as a $3 million penalty for breaking the contract with Puma. The court ruled that Carter breached his contract with Black's company Professional Management Inc. and, although Black and his company were negligent in handling the Pumas contract, Carter was not harmed financially by the negligence. However, the court also ordered Black to repay Carter $800,000 in loans Carter had made to Black. See "V. Carter Ordered To Pay Former Agent Nearly $4.7M," *Washington Post* D08 (November 3, 2004).

3. In *In re Ekuban*, 2004 WL 1088340 (Bkrtcy. N.D. Tex., April 16, 2004), Dallas Cowboy Ebenezer Ekuban was sued for defaulting on loans made in his name by agent Sean Jones. Jones used the loaned money in a failed Houston real estate investment and was subsequently decertified by the NFLPA for financial mismanagement. Ekuban claims that Jones fraudulently induced him into participating in the deal by Jones, the property seller and a vice president of the bank. The court granted Ekuban's motion for summary judgment, finding that Ekuban's signing of guaranty agreements did not comply with the statute of frauds.

4. In the summer of 2003, NBA player agent Bill Duffy, head of BDA Sports, apparently failed to notify the Miami Heat by the contract deadline that his client Anthony Carter was going to exercise an option to extend his contract through the 2003–2004 season for $4.1 million in salary. As a result of this failure, Carter's contract expired and he became a free agent. Duffy eventually negotiated a new contract for Carter with the San Antonio Spurs for roughly $1 million. Duffy agreed to make Carter whole for the difference between the $4.1 million Carter would have made with the Heat and what he earned with the Spurs. See "Show Him the Money," *Chicago Tribune* C8 (August 5, 2003).

5. Prior to the 1999 NFL season, the Seattle Seahawks refused to renegotiate the final year of wide receiver Joey Galloway's contract as his contract advisors Ethan Lock and Eric Metz claimed they promised to do. As a result, Galloway refused to play until the 10th week of the season. The Seahawks unsuccessfully claimed that Galloway did not fulfill his contract and owed them one more season. Upon losing their arbitration hearing on February 10, 2000, the Seahawks franchise tagged Galloway, putting him under contract for at least one more season. Unhappy with the situation in Seattle, Metz and Lock began to explore trade options for Galloway. At the same time, Galloway began to consider new representation and contacted agent Leigh Steinberg. Steinberg informed him that he would not discuss representing Galloway while he was currently under representation. Metz and Lock negotiated an agreement with the Dallas Cowboys very close to the terms Galloway was insisting upon. However, on February 11, Galloway informed

Lock and Metz that he wished to terminate his relationship with them. The representation agreement that Metz and Lock had with Galloway said that the agreement was effective until the Seahawks' original contract expired or could be terminated at any time by either side but would remain in effect for five days following notification of intent to terminate. On February 12, Steinberg helped Galloway sign a contract with the Cowboys very similar to the contract negotiated by Lock and Metz. Arbitrator Roger Kaplan eventually ruled that Steinberg did not interfere with the contractual relationship between Lock, Metz, and Steinberg because Galloway made the initial contact. Also, because Metz and Lock were actually Galloway's contract advisors for another five days following Galloway's notice of intent to terminate, they are entitled to the previously agreed upon percentage of the signing bonus Galloway signed with the Cowboys, 1.25% of $12 million.

6. In 1991 former MLB player Bill Madlock sued former agent Steve Greenberg, alleging that in 1981 Greenberg convinced Madlock to invest about $1 million in a "supposedly revolutionary device known as the Terra-Drill which never made it beyond the drawing board and which the IRS deemed to be a tax avoidance 'sham.'" An arbitrator ruled that Greenberg was guilty of a "failure to exercise proper care and skill on Madlock's behalf" and that Madlock never would have invested in the Terra-Drill without the "counsel and suggestion of Greenberg." However, the arbitrator determined that lawsuit was not within the statute of limitations.

12.3.5. Agent-Agent Grievance Arbitration

Players associations are also voluntarily responsible for disputes between player agents. As with grievance procedures between athletes, teams, agents, the league, or any of the above, the association hopes to avoid lengthy and costly legal proceedings by using a grievance arbitration procedure. The NFLPA Regulations Concerning Contract Advisors requires a player agent to file a grievance notification form. The grievance is sent to both the NFLPA as well as the respondent. The respondent must reply to the grievant with a copy sent to the NFLPA within 20 days. The agents are then required to follow the NFLPA's arbitration procedures as laid out in Section 5 of the regulations.

12.4. AGENT-AGENT LITIGATION

In certain situations, especially those involving greater amounts of money and accusations, some player agents have forgone the players associations grievance procedures in favor of civil lawsuits. Common claims brought by agents are client theft, interference with contractual relations, and misappropriation of trade secrets resulting from one more agents leaving a particular firm either for a competing one or in order to start his/her own. Often following the result of the suit, the respective players association responds with its own complaints and often decertifies or suspends the agent in question. The player agent can then appeal through the grievance arbitration process outlined in the players association's agent regulations.

NOTES

1. In 2010 litigation erupted between possibly the two largest agencies, CAA and IMG. Agent Matthew Baldwin left IMG for CAA in 2009, allegedly in violation of a non-compete clause in his contract. The case could hinge on whether California or Ohio law applies. California, where CAA is based, does not permit non-compete clauses.

2. In 2001, superagent Leigh Steinberg sued former partner David Dunn for breach of contract, misappropriation of trade secrets, and unfair competition. After Dunn's departure from the firm, at least 80% of the firm's 86 NFL clients had left to join Dunn's newly created firm Athletes First. Dunn had worked at the firm for 10 years and had signed an agreement stating that he would not compete against the firm in any way until two years after his contract had ended. In 2001, Steinberg won a court order prohibiting Dunn from taking any more clients of the firm. A jury awarded Steinberg and his firm over $47 million in damages for Dunn's having left the firm and improperly taking several clients with him in contravention of a noncompete clause in Dunn's employment contract. In 2005, an appeals court reversed the decision on the grounds that the trial judge had failed to instruct the jury that the noncompete clause in Dunn's contract was invalid under California law; see *Steinberg, Moorad & Dunn, Inc. v. Dunn*, 136 Fed. Appx. 6 (9th Cir.Cal. 2005). Dunn ultimately filed for bankruptcy and was suspended by the NFLPA for two years before returning to lead Athletes First, now one of the top agency firms in football.

3. In 2003 baseball agency firm Beverly Hills Sports Council (BHSC) sued two former employees, Scott Leventhal and Damon Lapa, and the agency firm of Reich, Katz and Landis for improper solicitation of BHSC's clients. Leventhal and Lapa denied any association with Reich, Katz and Landis. In January 2004, Los Angeles Superior Court Judge Jane Johnson dismissed the claims of conspiracy and breach of good faith and fair dealing, required more specific pleading on three other claims, but denied a motion to dismiss the claims of misappropriation of trade secrets, breach of contract, and interference with contract. The entire case was then dismissed in April 2004 without prejudice on the plaintiff's motion.

4. In *Bauer v. Interpublic Group of Companies, Inc.*, 255 F. Supp. 2d 1086 (N.D. Cal. 2003), the court granted summary judgment for defendants Octagon and agent Mike Sullivan in the case brought against them by agent Frank Bauer for tortious interference with contract and unfair competition. The case arose when, in 2002, the NFL's number one overall draft pick quarterback David Carr of Fresno State signed a representation agreement with Bauer, but then terminated it and signed shortly thereafter with the defendants. The court concluded that there was insufficient evidence to sustain the claim that the defendants actually induced Carr to terminate his contract with Bauer.

5. In October 2002, a New York jury awarded NBA player agent Eric Fleisher a $4.6 million judgment against Andy Miller, his protégé and former partner. Fleisher claimed that Miller engaged in unfair competition when Miller started his own agency and signed a number of Fleisher clients, including Kevin Garnett of the Minnesota Timberwolves. The jury accepted Fleisher's claim that Miller engaged in a "scheme to defraud (Fleisher) out of his agency."

6. For more on agency noncompete clauses, see Jason Gershwin, "Will Professional Athletes Continue To Choose Their Representation Freely? An Examination of the Enforceability of Non-Compete Agreements against Sports Agents," 5 *University of Pennsylvania Journal of Labor and Employment Law* 585 (2003).

12.5. GOVERNMENT REGULATION

12.5.1. Uniform Athlete Agent Act

In 2001, the National Conference of Commissioners on Uniform State Laws approved a draft of legislation entitled the Uniform Athlete Agent Act (UAAA; see note 1). The power of a uniform act is that it creates legislation that is the same across each state in the country. The Uniform Athlete Agent Act was proposed to each state government in the country, and it is then up to the individual states whether the act will be considered and adopted.

As of March 2010, the UAAA had been passed in 38 states, the District of Columbia, and the U.S. Virgin Islands:

- Alabama
- Arizona
- Arkansas
- Colorado
- Connecticut
- Delaware
- District of Columbia
- Florida
- Georgia
- Hawaii
- Idaho
- Indiana
- Iowa
- Kansas
- Kentucky
- Louisiana
- Maryland
- Minnesota
- Mississippi
- Missouri
- Nebraska
- Nevada
- New Hampshire
- New York
- North Carolina
- North Dakota
- Oklahoma
- Oregon
- Pennsylvania
- Rhode Island
- South Carolina
- South Dakota
- Tennessee
- Texas
- Utah
- U.S. Virgin Islands
- Washington

- West Virginia
- Wisconsin
- Wyoming

Three states had active UAAA legislation in their legislative chambers:

- California
- Illinois
- New Jersey

Three states had existing, non-UAAA laws designed to regulate athlete agents:

- California
- Michigan
- Ohio

Nine states and one territory had no existing law regulating athlete agents:

- Alaska
- Illinois
- Maine
- Massachusetts
- Montana
- New Jersey
- New Mexico
- Puerto Rico
- Vermont
- Virginia

Beginning in 1997, the NCAA, in conjunction with the National Conference of Commissioners on Uniform State Laws, sought to draft legislation that would make the athlete agent laws of every state consistent. In 2001, 28 states had athlete agent laws; however, the regulations were often vastly different, complex, and confusing due to their lack of uniformity. The NCAA supported the Uniform Athlete Agent Act in order to supply athletes and agents alike with one set of rules and regulations to follow when conducting business. The act is intended to benefits agents, athletes, and colleges. While agents now have clearer rules and regulations to follow, the administrative hassles have only increased as states have failed to adopt reciprocity agreements regarding agent registration. The athlete will know his or her rights regardless of the state in which he or she attends school. Finally, colleges will be better able to police the actions of athlete agents under this new legislation. However, the UAAA is only as strong as its enforcement, which must come from state administrative agencies and individual affected parties, such as competing agents and educational institutions.

NOTES

1. The following is the legislation approved by the NCAA and the National Conference of Commissioners for Uniform State Laws:
  Uniform Athlete Agents Act (2000)°
  Uniform Athlete Agents Act

SECTION 1. SHORT TITLE. This [Act] may be cited as the Uniform Athlete Agents Act.

SECTION 2. DEFINITIONS. In this [Act]:

- (1) "Agency contract" means an agreement in which a student-athlete authorizes a person to negotiate or solicit on behalf of the student-athlete a professional-sports-services contract or an endorsement contract.

- (2) "Athlete agent" means an individual who enters into an agency contract with a student-athlete or, directly or indirectly, recruits or solicits a student-athlete to enter into an agency contract. The term does not include a spouse, parent, sibling, [or] grand-parent, [or guardian] of the student-athlete or an individual acting solely on behalf of a professional sports team or professional sports organization. The term includes an individual who represents to the public that the individual is an athlete agent.

- (3) "Athlete director" means an individual responsible for administering the overall athletic program of an educational institution or, if an educational institution has sepa-rately administered athletic programs for male students and female students, the athletic program for males or the athletic program for females, as appropriate.

- (4) "Contact" means a communication, direct or indirect, between an athlete agent and a student-athlete, to recruit or solicit the student-athlete to enter into an agency contract.

- (5) "Endorsement contract" means an agreement under which a student-athlete is employed or receives consideration to use on behalf of the other party any value that the student-athlete may have because of publicity, reputation, following, or fame obtained because of athletic ability or performance.

- (6) "Intercollegiate sport" means a sport played at the collegiate level for which eligibility requirements for participation by a student-athlete are established by a national association for the promotion or regulation of collegiate athletics.

- (7) "Person" means an individual, corporation, business trust, estate, trust, partner-ship, limited liability company, association, joint venture, government; governmental subdivision, agency, or instrumentality; public corporation; or any other legal or com-mercial entity.

- (8) "Professional-sports-services contract" means an agreement under which an in-dividual is employed or agrees to render services as a player on a professional sports team, with a professional sports organization, or as a professional athlete.

- (9) "Record" means information that is inscribed on a tangible medium or that is stored in an electronic or other medium and is retrievable in perceivable form.

- (10) "Registration" means registration as an athlete agent pursuant to this [Act].

- (11) "State" means a State of the United States, the District of Columbia, Puerto Rico, the United States Virgin Islands, or any territory or insular possession subject to the jurisdiction of the United States.

- (12) "Student-athlete" means an individual who engages in, is eligible to engage in, or may be eligible in the future to engage in, any intercollegiate sport. If an individ-ual is permanently ineligible to participate in a particular intercollegiate sport, the individual is not a student-athlete for purposes of that sport.

SECTION 3. ADMINISTRATION; SERVICE OF PROCESS; SUBPOENAS.

- (a) The [Secretary of State] shall administer this [Act].

- (b) By engaging in the business of an athlete agent in this State, a nonresident individual appoints the [Secretary of State] as the individual's agent to accept service of process in any civil action related to the individual's business as an athlete agent in this State.

- [(c) The [Secretary of State] may issue subpoenas for any relevant material under this [Act].]

SECTION 4. ATHLETE AGENTS: REGISTRATION REQUIRED.

- (a) Except as otherwise provided in subsection (b), an individual may not act as an athlete agent in this State before being issued a certificate of registration under Section 6 or 8.

- (b) An individual may act as an athlete agent before being issued a certificate of registration for all purposes except signing an agency contract if:
  - (1) a student-athlete or another acting on behalf of the student-athlete initiates communication with the individual; and
  - (2) within seven days after an initial act as an athlete agent, the individual submits an application to register as an athlete agent in this State.

- (c) An agency contract resulting from conduct in violation of this section is void. The athlete agent shall return any consideration received under the contract.

SECTION 5. REGISTRATION AS ATHLETE AGENT; FORM; REQUIREMENTS.

- (a) An applicant for registration shall submit an application for registration to the [Secretary of State] in a form prescribed by the [Secretary of State]. [An application filed under this section is a public record.] Except as otherwise provided in subsection (b), the application must be in the name of an individual and signed by the applicant under penalty of perjury and must state or contain:
  - (1) the name of the applicant and the address of the applicant's principal place of business;
  - (2) the name of the applicant's business or employer, if applicable;
  - (3) any business or occupation engaged in by the applicant for the five years next preceding the date of submission of the application;
  - (4) a description of the applicant's:
    - (A) formal training as an athlete agent;
    - (B) practical experience as an athlete agent; and
    - (C) educational background relating to the applicant's activities as an athlete agent;
  - (5) the names and addresses of three individuals not related to the applicant who are willing to serve as references;
  - (6) the name, sport, and last known team for each individual for whom the applicant provided services as an athlete agent during the five years next preceding the date of submission of the application;
  - (7) the names and addresses of all persons who are:
    - (A) with respect to the athlete agent's business if it is not a corporation, the partners, officers, associates, or profit-sharers; and
    - (B) with respect to a corporation employing the athlete agent, the officers, directors, and any shareholder of the corporation with a 5% or greater interest;
  - (8) whether the applicant or any other person named pursuant to paragraph (7) has been convicted of a crime that, if committed in this State, would be a felony or other crime involving moral turpitude, and identify the crime;
  - (9) whether there has been any administrative or judicial determination that the applicant or any other person named pursuant to paragraph (7) has made a false, misleading, deceptive, or fraudulent representation;
  - (10) any instance in which the conduct of the applicant or any other person named pursuant to paragraph (7) resulted in the imposition of a sanction, suspension,

or declaration of ineligibility to participate in an interscholastic or intercollegiate athletic event on a student-athlete or educational institution;

- (11) any sanction, suspension, or disciplinary action taken against the applicant or any other person named pursuant to paragraph (7) arising out of occupational or professional conduct; and

- (12) whether there has been any denial of an application for, suspension or revocation of, or refusal to renew, the registration or licensure of the applicant or any other person named pursuant to paragraph (7) as an athlete agent in any State.

- (b) An individual who has submitted an application for, and received a certificate of, registration or licensure as an athlete agent in another State, may submit a copy of the application and a valid certificate of registration or licensure from the other State in lieu of submitting an application in the form prescribed pursuant to subsection (a). The [Secretary of State] shall accept the application and the certificate from the other State as an application for registration in this State if the application to the other State:

- (1) was submitted in the other State within the six months next preceding the submission of the application in this State and the applicant certifies the information contained in the application is current;

- (2) contains information substantially similar to or more comprehensive than that required in an application submitted in this State; and

- (3) was signed by the applicant under penalty of perjury.

SECTION 6. CERTIFICATE OF REGISTRATION; ISSUANCE OR DENIAL; RENEWAL.

- (a) Except as otherwise provided in subsection (c), the [Secretary of State] shall issue a certificate of registration to an individual who complies with Section 5(a).

- (b) Except as otherwise provided in subsection (c), the [Secretary of State] shall issue a certificate of registration to an individual whose application has been accepted under Section 5(b).

- (c) The [Secretary of State] may refuse to issue a certificate of registration if the [Secretary of State] determines that the applicant has engaged in conduct that has a significant adverse effect on the applicant's fitness to serve as an athlete agent. In making the determination, the [Secretary of State] may consider whether the applicant has:

- (1) been convicted of a crime that, if committed in this State, would be a felony or other crime involving moral turpitude;

- (2) made a materially false, misleading, deceptive, or fraudulent representation as an athlete agent or in the application;

- (3) engaged in conduct that would disqualify the applicant from serving in a fiduciary capacity;

- (4) engaged in conduct prohibited by Section 14;

- (5) had a registration or licensure as an athlete agent suspended, revoked, or denied or been refused renewal of registration or licensure in any State;

- (6) engaged in conduct or failed to engage in conduct the consequence of which was that a sanction, suspension, or declaration of ineligibility to participate in an interscholastic or intercollegiate athletic event was imposed on a student-athlete or educational institution; or

- (7) engaged in conduct that significantly adversely reflects on the applicant's credibility, honesty, or integrity.

- (d) In making a determination under subsection (c), the [Secretary of State] shall consider:

  - (1) how recently the conduct occurred;

  - (2) the nature of the conduct and the context in which it occurred; and

  - (3) any other relevant conduct of the applicant.

- (e) An athlete agent may apply to renew a registration by submitting an application for renewal in a form prescribed by the [Secretary of State]. [An application filed under this section is a public record.] The application for renewal must be signed by the applicant under penalty of perjury and must contain current information on all matters required in an original registration.

- (f) An individual who has submitted an application for renewal of registration or licensure in another State, in lieu of submitting an application for renewal in the form prescribed pursuant to subsection (e), may file a copy of the application for renewal and a valid certificate of registration from the other State. The [Secretary of State] shall accept the application for renewal from the other State as an application for renewal in this State if the application to the other State:

  - (1) was submitted in the other State within the last six months and the applicant certifies the information contained in the application for renewal is current;

  - (2) contains information substantially similar to or more comprehensive than that required in an application for renewal submitted in this State; and

  - (3) was signed by the applicant under penalty of perjury.

- (g) A certificate of registration or a renewal of a registration is valid for [two] years.

SECTION 7. SUSPENSION, REVOCATION, OR REFUSAL TO RENEW REGISTRATION.

- [(a)] The [Secretary of State] may suspend, revoke, or refuse to renew a registration for conduct that would have justified denial of registration under Section 6(c).

- [(b)] The [Secreatry of State] may deny, suspend, revoke, or refuse to renew a registration only after proper notice and an opportunity for a hearing. The [Administrative Procedures Act] applies to this [Act].

SECTION 8. TEMPORARY REGISTRATION. The [Secretary of State] may issue a temporary certificate of registration while an application for registration or renewal is pending.

SECTION 9. REGISTRATION AND RENEWAL FEE. An application for registration or renewal of registration must be accompanied by a fee in the following amount:

- (1) [$] for an initial application for registration;

- (2) [$] for an application for registration based upon a certificate of registration or licensure issued by another State;

- (3) [$] for an application for renewal of registration; or

- (4) [$] for an application for renewal of registration based upon an application for renewal of registration or licensure submitted in another State.

SECTION 10. FORM OF CONTRACT.

- (a) An agency contract must be in a record, signed by the parties.

- (b) An agency contract must state or contain:

- (1) the amount and method of calculating the consideration to be paid by the student-athlete for services to be provided by the athlete agent under the contract and any other consideration the athlete agent has received or will receive from any other source for entering into the contract or for providing the services;

- (2) the name of any person not listed in the application for registration or renewal who will be compensated because the student-athlete signed the agency contract;

- (3) a description of any expenses that the student-athlete agrees to reimburse;

- (4) a description of the services to be provided to the student-athlete;

- (5) the duration of the contract; and

- (6) the date of execution.

- (c) An agency contract must contain, in close proximity to the signature of the student-athlete, a conspicuous notice in boldface type in capital letters stating:

WARNING TO STUDENT-ATHLETE IF YOU SIGN THIS CONTRACT:

- (1) YOU MAY LOSE YOUR ELIGIBILITY TO COMPETE AS A STUDENT-ATHLETE IN YOUR SPORT;

- (2) BOTH YOU AND YOUR ATHLETE AGENT ARE REQUIRED TO TELL YOUR ATHLETIC DIRECTOR, IF YOU HAVE AN ATHLETIC DIRECTOR, WITHIN 72 HOURS AFTER ENTERING INTO AN AGENCY CONTRACT; AND

- (3) YOU MAY CANCEL THIS CONTRACT WITHIN 14 DAYS AFTER SIGN-ING IT. CANCELLATION OF THE CONTRACT MAY NOT REINSTATE YOUR ELIGIBILITY.

- (d) An agency contract that does not conform to this section is voidable by the student-athlete.

- (e) The athlete agent shall give a copy of the signed agency contract to the student-athlete at the time of signing.

SECTION 11. NOTICE TO EDUCATIONAL INSTITUTION.

- (a) Within 72 hours after entering into an agency contract or before the next sched-uled athletic event in which the student-athlete may participate, whichever occurs first, the athlete agent shall give notice in a record of the existence of the contract to the athletic director of the educational institution at which the student-athlete is enrolled or the athlete agent has reasonable grounds to believe the student-athlete intends to enroll.

- (b) Within 72 hours after entering into an agency contract or before the next athletic event in which the student-athlete may participate, whichever occurs first, the student-athlete shall inform the athletic director of the educational institution at which the student-athlete is enrolled that he or she has entered into an agency contract.

SECTION 12. STUDENT-ATHLETE'S RIGHT TO CANCEL.

- (a) A student-athlete may cancel an agency contract by giving notice in a record to the athlete agent of the cancellation within 14 days after the contract is signed.

- (b) A student-athlete may not waive the right to cancel an agency contract.

- (c) If a student-athlete cancels an agency contract, the student-athlete is not required to pay any consideration under the contract or to return any consideration received from the agent to induce the student-athlete to enter into the contract.

SECTION 13. REQUIRED RECORDS.

- (a) An athlete agent shall retain the following records for a period of five years:
  - (1) the name and address of each individual represented by the athlete agent;
  - (2) any agency contract entered into by the athlete agent; and
  - (3) any direct costs incurred by the athlete agent in the recruitment or solicitation of a student-athlete.
- (b) Records required by subsection (a) to be retained are open to inspection by the [Secretary of State] during normal business hours.

SECTION 14. PROHIBITED ACTS.

- (a) An athlete agent may not do any of the following with the intent to induce a student-athlete to enter into an agency contract:
  - (1) give any materially false or misleading information or make a materially false promise or representation;
  - (2) furnish anything of value to a student-athlete before the student-athlete enters into the agency contract; or
  - (3) furnish anything of value to any individual other than the student-athlete or another registered athlete agent.
- (b) An athlete agent may not intentionally:
  - (1) initiate contact with a student-athlete unless registered under this [Act];
  - (2) refuse or willfully fail to retain or permit inspection of the records required by Section 13;
  - (3) violate Section 4 by failing to register;
  - (4) provide materially false or misleading information in an application for registration or renewal of registration;
  - (5) predate or postdate an agency contract; or
  - (6) fail to notify a student-athlete prior to the student-athlete's signing an agency contract for a particular sport that the signing by the student-athlete may make the student-athlete ineligible to participate as a student-athlete in that sport.

SECTION 15. CRIMINAL PENALTIES. The commission of any act prohibited by Section 14 by an athlete agent is a [misdemeanor] [felony] punishable by [].

SECTION 16. CIVIL REMEDIES.

- (a) An educational institution has a right of action against an athlete agent or a former student-athlete for damages caused by a violation of this [Act]. In an action under this section, the court may award to the prevailing party costs and reasonable attorney's fees.
- (b) Damages of an educational institution under subsection (a) include losses and expenses incurred because, as a result of the activities of an athlete agent or former student-athlete, the educational institution was injured by a violation of this [Act] or was penalized, disqualified, or suspended from participation in athletics by a national association for the promotion and regulation of athletics, by an athletic conference, or by reasonable self-imposed disciplinary action taken to mitigate sanctions.
- (c) A right of action under this section does not accrue until the educational institution discovers or by the exercise of reasonable diligence would have discovered the violation by the athlete agent or former student-athlete.

- (d) Any liability of the athlete agent or the former student-athlete under this section is several and not joint.

- (e) This [Act] does not restrict rights, remedies, or defenses of any person under law or equity.

SECTION 17. ADMINISTRATIVE PENALTY. The [Secretary of State] may assess a civil penalty against an athlete agent not to exceed [$25,000] for a violation of this [Act].

SECTION 18. APPLICATION AND CONSTRUCTION. In applying and construing this Uniform Act, consideration must be given to the need to promote uniformity of the law with respect to its subject matter of this [Act] among States that enact it.

SECTION 19. SEVERABILITY. If any provision of this [Act] or its application to any person or circumstance is held invalid, the invalidity does not affect other provisions or applications of this [Act] which can be given effect without the invalid provision or application, and to this end the provisions of this [Act] are severable.

SECTION 20. REPEALS. The following acts and parts of acts are hereby repealed:

SECTION 21. EFFECTIVE DATE. This [Act] takes effect _____.

2. The following is a sample letter developed by the NCAA to be sent to state legislators by NCAA institutions:

Uniform Athlete Agent Act Sample Letter to Legislator

SAMPLE LETTER

[to be sent after legislation is introduced in your state]

Dear [**Senator**] or [**Representative**] [Last Name]:

After three years of work, The National Conference of Commissioners on Uniform State Laws (NCCUSL) recently approved the Uniform Athlete Agent Act (UAAA), a model state law governing the relationships between student-athletes, athlete agents and academic institutions. The National Collegiate Athletic Association (NCAA) and its member institutions are seeking its adoption in every state, and I am writing to urge your support and co-sponsorship of [S. _____ or H.R. _____], recently introduced in the [your state's] legislature.

The problems associated with illegal athlete agent conduct are far greater than the casual observer might believe. Far too often, the actions of athlete agents engaged in unsavory practices result in the loss of student-athlete eligibility, the imposition of financial penalties on the student-athlete's institution and the taint of a "scandal" on both the institution and the larger intercollegiate sports community. In an effort to address these problems, at least 28 states have enacted statutes regulating athlete agents. However, existing laws vary considerably from state-to-state and many statutes contain provisions that are vague and not enforced by the state. As a result, athlete agents largely ignore existing state registration requirements as well as other provisions contained in current athlete agent laws.

The purpose of the UAAA is to protect the interests of student-athletes and institutions by providing for a uniform regulation of athlete agents. The UAAA provides for:

- Uniformity of state laws. These laws are designed to provide a single set of regulations that will ensure greater compliance among athlete agents.

- A reciprocal registration provision and a reasonable fee schedule making agents more likely to register due to the efficiency of this process and the cost savings it provides for athlete agents.

- Consumer information, both professional and criminal in nature, to enable better evaluation of the athlete agents to provide competent representation.

- Notice to institutions when a student-athlete signs an agency contract.

- The Secretary of State or other appropriate agency to issue subpoenas enabling the state to obtain relevant material that will assist in the enforcement of the act.

- Criminal, civil and administrative penalties that will be enforced at the state level.

On behalf of [name of institution], I urge your support of [S. _____ or H.R. _____] and thank you in advance for your efforts to address this important issue.

3. The following is a fact sheet distributed by the NCAA regarding the positive features of the Uniform Athlete Agent Act:

Uniform Athlete Agent Act Fact Sheet

WHAT IS THE UNIFORM ATHLETE AGENT ACT?

After three years of work, the National Conference of Commissioners on Uniform State Laws recently approved the Uniform Athlete Agent Act (UAAA). The UAAA is designed to provide a single set of state regulations that will govern athlete agent conduct. The UAAA ensures greater protection for student-athletes and educational institutions while providing a more manageable and cost-efficient regulatory scheme for athlete agents and states.

WHY DO WE NEED TO ADOPT THE UNIFORM ATHLETE AGENT ACT?

- Protection for student-athletes: The primary purpose of the UAAA is to protect student-athletes and educational institutions from athlete agents who engage in unsavory and, oftentimes, illegal practices.

- Protection for colleges and universities: The UAAA acts as a strong deterrent against improper athlete agent conduct that often subjects institutions to negative publicity and harsh sanctions, including the forfeiture of games and substantial financial penalties.

- Uniformity of state laws: The UAAA is designed to provide a single set of regulations that will ensure greater compliance among athlete agents.

- Reciprocal agent registration and reasonable fees: Reciprocal registration and a reasonable fee schedule provide a system that allows states to honor the registration of athlete agents from states with similar laws. Agents are more likely to register with states due to the efficiency and cost effectiveness of the UAAA prescribed process.

- Strong penalties for violators: The UAAA provides for criminal, civil and/or administrative penalties to be imposed against violators.

- Additional tools for state law enforcement: The right to exercise subpoena power enables the state to obtain relevant information that assists in the enforcement of the act.

- Important consumer information: It is vital for student-athletes, parents and institutions to have access to information contained in the agent application, both professional and criminal in nature, to ensure that the most informed decisions are made regarding athlete agent representation.

- Widespread support: The UAAA is endorsed by the National Collegiate Athletic Association and its 1,000 member universities and colleges, the National Conference of Commissioners on Uniform State Laws and a number of other organizations.

The following law review articles examine the Uniform Athlete Agents Act:

1. Lloyd Zane Remick and Christopher Joseph Cabott "Keeping out the Little Guy: An Older Contract Advisor's Concern, A Younger Contract Advisors Lament," *12 Villanova Sports and Entertainment Law Journal 1* (2005).

2. R. Michael Rogers, "The Uniform Athlete Agents Act Fails to Fully Protect the College Athlete Who Exhausts His Eligibility Before Turning Professional," *2 Virginia Sports and Entertainment Law Journal 63* (2002).

3. Diane Sudia and Rob Remis, "The History Behind Athlete Agent Regulation and the 'Slam Dunking of Statutory Hurdles,'" *8 Villanova Sports and Entertainment Law Journal 67* (2001).

4. Diane Sudia and Rob Remis, "Athlete Agent Legislation in the New Millennium: State Statutes and the Uniform Athlete Agents Act," *11 Seton Hall Journal of Sports and Entertainment Law 263* (2001).

5. Robert N. Davis, "Exploring the Contours of Agent Regulation: The Uniform Athlete Agents Act," 8 *Villanova Sports and Entertainment Law Journal* 1 (2001).

12.5.2. Sports Agent Responsibility and Trust Act

While the Uniform Athlete Agent Act lists forbidden acts and provides for possible criminal and civil liability for unscrupulous and unethical agents, it is limited by its adoption by each individual state. As a result, the Sports Agent Responsibility and Trust Act (SPARTA), the first piece of federal legislation governing the behavior of athlete agents was passed by Congress and signed into law by President Bush in September 2004. The main architect of SPARTA was Nebraska Congressman Tom Osborne, who coached the University of Nebraska football team from 1973 to 1997 and won three national championships in that time.

The acts prohibited by the UAAA and SPARTA are essentially the same; however, SPARTA brings the acts under the scrutiny of the Federal Trade Commission (FTC). Specifically, the FTC can prosecute agents for violating SPARTA for unfair and deceptive practices. Additionally, SPARTA specifically grants state attorneys general the power to prosecute violating agents in federal court under the jurisdiction of the FTC. The FTC is an independent agency of the government charged with consumer protection and deals largely with antitrust cases. As a result, its willingness and fervor in enforcing SPARTA is questionable.

NOTE _____

1. For more on SPARTA, see John A. Gray "Sports Agent's Liability after SPARTA?" 6 *Virginia Sports and Entertainment Law Journal* 141 (2006) and Melissa Steedle Bogad, "Maybe Jerry Maguire Should Have Stuck with Law School: How the Sports Agent Responsibility and Trust Act Implements Lawyer-Like Rules for Sports Agents," 27 *Cardozo Law Review* 1889 (2006).

12.5.3. State Regulations

While the NCAA is encouraging and supporting each state legislature in the country to pass the Uniform Athlete Agent Act, numerous states have, since the 1980s, enacted legislation to regulate the conduct and practice of sports agents. These state laws are very diverse, but the common legislation followed by most states requires sports agents to register with the state and pay a registration fee. In addition, some states require sports agents to post a surety bond, which may be utilized to satisfy any damages caused to an athlete by the acts of an agent. Specified acts upon which an athlete can receive monetary payment due to the agent's misconduct include intentional misrepresentation, fraud, deceit, or any unlawful or negligent act.

Previously, legislation varied from state to state. The definition of an athlete agent differed from state to state, and the definition of a "gift" from an agent to a student-athlete could differ as well. With the gradual acceptance of the Uniform Athlete Agent Act, the NCAA hopes that all inconsistencies between state legislation will be eradicated, and replaced with a single model.

NOTES _____

1. The definition of agents on the intercollegiate level is discussed in section 12.5.5, "National Collegiate Athletic Association (NCAA) Regulations." Basically, an agent is any

person who represents an athlete in exchange for a fee, whether the fee is paid in the present or the future.

2. For more information on government regulation of athlete agents, see the following:

1. Chris Deubert, "What's a 'Clean' Agent to Do? The Case for a Cause of Action Against a Players Association," Villanova Sports & Entertainment Law Journal (2010).

2. Timothy Davis, "Regulating the Athlete-Agent Industry: Intended and Unintended Consequences," 42 *Willamette Law Review* 781 (2006).

3. Lloyd Zane Remick, "Keeping out the Little Guy: An Older Contract Advisor's Concern, A Younger Contract Advisor's Lament," 12 *Villanova Sports and Entertainment Law Journal* (2005).

4. Eric Willenbacher, "Regulating Sports Agents: Why Current Federal and State Efforts Do Not Deter the Unscrupulous Athlete-Agent and How a National Licensing System May Cure the Problem," 78 *Saint John's Law Review* 1225 (2004).

5. Diane Sudia and Rob Remis, "The History Behind Athlete-Agent Regulation and the 'Slam-Dunking of Statutory Hurdles'," 8 *Villanova Sport and Entertainment Law Forum* 67 (2001).

6. Diane Sudia and Rob Remis, "Statutory Regulation of Agent Gifts to Athletes," 10 *Seton Hall Journal of Sports and Entertainment Law* 265 (2000).

7. Diane Sudia and Rob Remis, "Athlete Agent Contracts: Legislative Regulation," 10 *Seton Hall Journal of Sports and Entertainment Law* 317 (2000).

8. Phillip Closius, "Hell Hath No Fury Like a Fan Scorned: State Regulation of Sports Agents," 30 *University of Toledo Law Review* 511 (Summer 1999).

9. Rob Remis and Diane Sudia, "Escaping Athlete-Agent Statutory Regulation: Loopholes and Constitutional Defectiveness Based on Tri-Parte Classification of Athletes," 9 *Seton Hall Journal of Sports and Entertainment Law* 1 (1999).

12.5.4. Ethical Constraints

The player representative who is also an attorney faces the constraints imposed by the canon of ethics (see note 2). This can be particularly troublesome when competing with nonlawyers who do not face similar requirements (see note 1). Issues relating to solicitation are foremost among these concerns (see note 2).

Another ethical area is somewhat more subtle. This relates to dealing with athletes who have remaining college athletic eligibility. Under the NCAA rules, any number of activities involving the athlete with a prospective representative may cause forfeiture of the athlete's remaining eligibility. While these regulations do not impose restrictions directly on the player representative, they do raise ethical issues for that person. It is also possible that a court might view a representative's activities, whereby the representative causes an athlete to lose eligibility, as constituting "unclean hands." This could affect the representative's legal remedies in certain situations.

It should also be pointed out that attorneys who represent players often face ethical concerns with respect to renegotiation. Many of these agents may advise a client not to renegotiate a contract because they believe in the sanctity of contracts. One way to circumvent this is to include a "reopener clause" in the original contract, which would allow renegotiation to take place if certain stated situations come about.

NOTES _____

1. In the case of *Cuyahoga County Bar Association v. Glenn*, 72 Ohio St.3d 299, 649 N.E.2d 1213 (Ohio 1995), Glenn, the agent for a National Football League player, Richard Dent, was not allowed to practice law in the state of Ohio because he had misrepresented

Dent by committing fraud, and undertaking conduct that led to a failure to properly represent his client, including seizing some of Dent's money without his consent ($20,000) and refusing to give it back.

For more on ethical considerations in sports agency, see:

1. Stacey B. Evans, "Sports Agents: Ethical Representatives or Overly Aggressive Adversaries?," 17 *Villanova Sports & Entertainment Law Journal* 91 (2010).

2. Jeremy J. Geisel, "Disbarring Jerry Maguire: How Broadly Defining 'Unauthorized Practice of Law' Could Take the 'Lawyer' Out Of 'Lawyer-Agent' Despite the Current State of Athlete Agent Legislation," 40 *Connecticut Law Review* 355 (2007).

3. Melissa Neiman, "Fair Game: Ethical Considerations in Negotiation by Sports Agents," 9 *Texas Review of Entertainment and Sports Law* 123 (2007).

4. Scott R. Rosner, "Conflicts of Interest and the Shifting Paradigm of Athlete Representation," 11 *UCLA Entertainment Law Review* (2004).

5. Mark Doman, "Attorneys as Athlete-Agents: Reconciling the ABA Rules of Professional Conduct with the Practice of Athlete Representation," 5 *Texas Review of Entertainment and Sports Law* 37 (2003).

6. Bryan Couch, "How Agent Competition and Corruption Affects Sports and the Athlete-Agent Relationship and What Can Be Done to Control It," 10 *Seton Hall Journal of Sports and Entertainment Law* 111 (2000).

7. Diane Sudia and Rob Remis, "Athlete-Agent Solicitation of Athlete Clients: Statutory Authorization and Prohibition," 10 *Seton Hall Journal of Sports and Entertainment Law* 205 (2000).

8. Stacey M. Nahrwold, "Are Professional Athletes Better Served by a Lawyer-Representative Than an Agent? Ask Grant Hill," 9 *Seton Hall Journal of Sports Law* 431 (1999).

2. The American Bar Association's Ethical Code (EC) of Professional Responsibility states:

[A] lawyer should maintain high standards of professional conduct and should encourage fellow lawyers to do likewise. He should be temperate and dignified, and he should refrain from all illegal and morally reprehensible conduct....

EC 2–3 Advice is proper only if motivated by a desire to protect one who does not recognize that he may have legal problems or who is ignorant of his legal rights or obligations. Hence the advice is improper if motivated by a desire to obtain personal benefit, secure personal publicity, or cause litigation to be brought merely to harass or injure another.

EC 2–4 A lawyer who volunteers advice that one should obtain the services of a lawyer generally should not himself accept employment, compensation or other benefit in connection with that matter.

These considerations should be followed by all American Bar Association members. Nevertheless, the position of player representative allows for opportunities to violate some of these recommendations.

12.5.5. National Collegiate Athletic Association (NCAA) Regulations

The NCAA, in an attempt to maintain its status as an amateur organization, has taken a tough stance on agents and athlete eligibility. The *2009–2010 NCAA Manual* states clearly, "An individual shall be ineligible for participation in an intercollegiate sport if he or she has ever agreed (orally or in writing) to be represented by an agent for the purpose of marketing his or her athletics ability or reputation in that sport. Further, an agency contract not specifically limited in writing to a sport or particular sports shall be deemed applicable to all sports and the individual shall be ineligible to participate in any sport" (Bylaw 12.3.1). However, "securing advice from a lawyer concerning a proposed professional sports contract shall not be considered contracting for representation by an agent under this rule, unless the lawyer represents the student-athlete in negotiations for such a contract" (Bylaw 12.3.2). This second bylaw has not always been enforced, however, especially in the case of baseball players who have been eligible for the professional draft directly out of high school.

In order to build or protect their personal interests, some agents will contact, offer inducements to, and attempt to sign student-athletes with remaining college eligibility. They may also entice athletes to leave college early to join professional teams. Inducements may take the form of cash, loans, and/or the use of a car or other benefits. This transfer to, and acceptance of money or other benefits by, student-athletes are in direct conflict with the principles of amateurism and specifically violate rules related to receiving compensation or pay and limits on the amount and type of acceptable remuneration (Bylaw 12.1).

Because several player agents have represented student-athletes in contract negotiations under the guise of supplying legal advice, the NCAA Council issued a clarification concerning the use of legal counsel by student-athletes. The *2009–2010 NCAA Manual* states, "A lawyer may not be present during discussions of a proposed contract offer with a professional organization or have any direct contact (i.e., in person, by telephone, or by mail) with a professional sports organization on behalf of the student-athlete. A lawyer's presence during such discussions is considered representation by an agent" (Bylaw 12.3.2.1). The council asserted, however, that any student-athlete may retain counsel for the purpose of reviewing a contract offered by a professional team. Nevertheless, the student-athlete who decides to have legal counsel contact a professional team concerning a contract offer has effectively hired counsel as an agent and is no longer eligible. In addition, the NCAA specifies that a contract between an athlete and an agent that does not specifically refer to a particular sport (i.e., simply a general employment contract) will result in the loss of eligibility for the athlete in all sports. The NCAA also prohibits contracts for future service: "An individual shall be ineligible per Bylaw 12.3.1 if he or she enters into a verbal or written agreement with an agent for representation in future professional sports negotiations that are to take place after the individual has completed his or her eligibility in that sport" (Bylaw 12.3.1.1). This rule applies at all times, and therefore includes contracts made prior to matriculation at college.

It is crucial to understand, however, that the NCAA cannot pass any bylaws that punish the agents themselves, because they are not part of the NCAA. Therefore, the NCAA punishes the school or university where a student was found to be in violation of bylaws regarding agents. Several programs, including the University of Alabama, have been penalized because an athlete entered into a professional contract or agreed to be represented by an agent before the expiration of his collegiate eligibility. In the case of the University of Alabama, Derrick McKey and Tony Coner, two star players on the 1986–1987 university basketball team, were found to have received illegal payments from agent Norby Walters. (For more on Walters and fellow agent Lloyd Bloom, see note 1.) McKey lost his senior season of eligibility, and the university had to repay $253,447 in NCAA tournament revenue when the allegations were found to be true (see note 1 for a discussion of other similar cases). Other such cases have resulted in the forfeiture of victories, the disqualification of teams from NCAA tournaments, and teams being forced to return television and/or tournament participation monies.

The offer sheet is one method by which agents may attempt to circumvent NCAA rules. An offer sheet is presented by the player agent to the student-athlete, who often mistakes it for a contract. The student-athlete signs this form prior to the expiration of college eligibility, but the agent will not sign it until after the student-athlete's eligibility has expired. Since most student-athletes are not versed in the technicalities of the requirements for a binding contract, they often believe they have a contract with the agent and will stop dealing with other agents. Agents who use this tactic to reserve players claim the offer sheet is not an agency contract until the representative executes the document at the close of student-athlete's playing season. Since no contract exists, there can be no violation of NCAA rules. The NCAA disagrees, however, believing that the substance of its rules clearly prohibits any agreements to provide future services, even if the agreement does not constitute an enforceable contract.

Currently, the NCAA has a career counseling program in individual institutions to assist student-athletes who are contemplating forgoing their remaining college eligibility to pursue a career in professional sports (*2009–2010 NCAA Manual*, Bylaw 12.3.4; see note 3). The institution organizes the counseling panel, which consists of three people from the institution who will advise the student-athlete. The guidelines by which the panel is selected are left to the discretion of the university. For the most part, it is suggested that the panel consist of employees of the institution. The committee can consist of a member of the bar, a law professor, or a teacher of business law, someone who deals with financial matters, and a person chosen at random. The NCAA also allows one full-time member of the athletic department staff to serve as a panel member. During the actual advising and counseling sessions, no agent or prospective agent may be present.

The institution decides whether to organize such a panel; it is not required by the NCAA. In institutions that have set up counseling panels, the student-athletes are able to utilize the panel's services at any time. They do not have to wait for their eligibility to expire. Some of the responsibilities of the panel are to establish policies that indicate the manner by which an agent can contact a student-athlete, to provide support and guidance during interviews with prospective agents, and to coordinate presentations by speakers for the benefit of the student-athlete. Some state laws and universities have set up "career days" for their athletes in lieu of these career counseling panels. Some universities, including the University of Texas, have made these career days mandatory for their athletes to attend.

NOTES

1. The story of New York agent Norby Walters and his partner, Los Angeles agent Lloyd Bloom, provides a disturbing example of abuse, corruption, and manipulation in the relationship between college athletes and agents. The relationship between Walters, Bloom, and the players they represented led to numerous court cases (see notes a and b below) and ultimately, a federal indictment. In the early to mid-1980s, Walters and Bloom were able to sign many of the nation's top college football players on their way to the pros. Stories began to surface that Walters and Bloom had offered the athletes cash, loans, cars, and introductions to celebrities in an effort to induce the athletes to sign with them, before they had completed their eligibility. Through investigation of this matter, the U.S. Attorney was able to prosecute Walters and Bloom under the RICO (Racketeer Influenced and Corrupt Organizations Act) statutes. Details soon emerged that when the athletes began to ask to be released from their contracts, Walters and Bloom would threaten them with physical harm by organized crime associates. Walters was convicted, but subsequently saw his conviction overturned. A few years later, Lloyd Bloom was found murdered, "gangland style," in his apartment.

a. In *Walters v. Fullwood*, 675 F. Supp. 155 (S.D.N.Y. 1987), two agents, Walters and Bloom, brought a breach of contract claim against Brent Fullwood, a star running back for Auburn University, who had signed a contract with the two agents before his college eligibility had run out. Subsequently, Fullwood signed a contract with Lickliter after he had run out of collegiate eligibility. The agents were also suing Lickliter for tortious interference with contractual relations, for interfering with their contract with Fullwood. The court ruled against the two agents on the breach of contract claim because they had brought a case to court with "dirty hands." This doctrine signifies that someone who has broken the law is prevented recovery for damages arising out of that action.

b. In the case of *United States v. Walters and Bloom*, 913 F.2d 388 (7th Cir. 1990), a criminal case was brought against two agents who had signed contracts with college athletes before their college eligibility had expired, and then allegedly used illegal means to maintain these contracts, such as threatening harm to the players if they broke the contract. The case was dismissed upon appeal due to errors during their initial trial that did not allow the agents to receive a fair trial. Although the case was dismissed, the body of the decision supplies an interesting look at some techniques used by agents to gain the services of collegiate athletes.

2. In 1970, Howard Porter, a star basketball player for NCAA runner-up Villanova, was found to have signed a contract with the American Basketball Association three months before his collegiate eligibility had expired. Porter was stripped of his title as tournament MVP, and Villanova was forced to forfeit its tournament victories as well as its tournament winnings.

3. For a discussion of NCAA rules regarding payment of student-athletes by agents, see Thomas R. Hurst and J. Grier Pressly, "Payment of Student-Athletes: Legal and Practical Obstacles," 7 *Villanova Sports and Entertainment Law Forum* 55 (2000).

4. At its 1984 convention, the NCAA approved a plan, recommended by its Special Committee on Players Agents, under which athletes career counseling panels would be established in individual institutions to assist student-athletes who are contemplating forgoing their remaining college eligibility to pursue a career in professional sports (*2009–2010 NCAA Manual*, Bylaw 12.3.4). In addition, should the athlete opt for a professional career, the panel would assist in the selection of a competent representative or agent.

The NCAA, during the 1980s and 1990s, became more concerned with the actions of player agents, particularly as they relate to on-campus solicitation of student-athletes. Accounts of former college athletes stating that they had received illegal payments from agents while still in school have caused the NCAA to crack down in this area (see section 6.2.2.8, "Pay and Expenses: NCAA").

In 1982, the NCAA prepared a manual called *A Career in Professional Sports: Guidelines That Make Dollars and Sense*. This booklet was designed to help students obtain competent representation. It provided a more general discussion of the NCAA's athlete representation regulations.

During the 1984–1985 academic year, the NCAA initiated two programs designed to increase the information available to student-athletes concerning player agents and the transition from collegiate to professional athletics. The first program permitted an institution to provide counseling on professional careers to student-athletes through a panel appointed by the institution's chief executive officer. The panel would consist of employees of the institution outside of the athletic department. Each institution's panel was allowed to obtain information and expertise from a variety of sources (e.g., lawyers, financial consultants, professional sports teams, player associations, and player agents) in an effort to provide objective information about professional career opportunities and evaluate the various services and proposals extended by player agents.

The second program instituted by the NCAA was a player agent registration program. This was a voluntary program in which the player agent registered with the NCAA by supplying requested educational and professional information. The list of registered player agents was provided to the institutional career counseling panel, which would recommend agents on the list to the student-athlete. By registering, the agent agreed to notify the director of athletics at the institution before the first contact with an enrolled student-athlete with remaining eligibility or with the student-athlete's coach. During 1985–1986, the NCAA had over 400 agents registered in this program. The program was discontinued in August 1989.

12.6. TEAM SPORTS PLAYER DRAFTS

With signing bonuses and first-year contracts reaching millions of dollars for rookies in the NBA, NFL, NHL, and MLB, it is obvious that reaching the professional ranks can be very lucrative for an athlete. The status of being a professional represents a very high level of achievement. It also represents a challenge, for the athlete must maintain this status and avoid an early end to his or her professional sports career. The average time span of a professional career is estimated at three to five years, depending upon the sport, and many athletes achieve their highest skill only to fall from the professional ranks within a short period. To successfully represent an athlete, an agent must become knowledgeable about the league entry draft, and how its rules and regulations can affect his or her client. Due to the uncertainty of success upon reaching the professional ranks, it is imperative that the athlete agent place his or her client in the most favorable draft position (see exhibit 12.2 for a description of the salaries for 2008 NBA first round draft picks).

Agents should be aware of the realistic chances that their clients have in the draft. For example, a player who is projected to be a top five pick in the NBA draft may not have to try out for as many teams as the player who is projected to be a late first round or early second round pick. The two most important legal documents for the agent are the standard player contract and the collective bargaining agreement (see section 12.7, "Standard Player Contract"). The end product of negotiations between an agent and the player's club will be the player's contract, which of course includes the player's compensation. Agents must have an in-depth understanding of the league's Standard Player Contract, applicable bonus clauses, salary comparisons, minimum salary requirements, and other language, such as guarantees, before entering into contract negotiations with the organization (see Chapter 3 and section 12.3.1, "Salary Information").

The draft is used by each professional team sport as a means of distributing new talent among the various teams in the league and helping the weaker teams in the league improve. Generally, each team will make a selection in reverse order of finish from the previous season and can trade to improve its draft position. Another important purpose of the draft is to reduce the number of teams with which an incoming player can negotiate. This, in theory, has the effect of minimizing players' negotiating leverage and thereby reducing player salaries, but also equalizes talent among teams. However, this has not worked to the leagues' complete satisfaction. The leagues have put in other restrictions such as salary caps, salary maximums, and luxury taxes.

Each of the four major professional leagues holds an annual draft. As will be discussed further in the following four sections, the eligibility, duration of eligibility, and signing rules for the drafts vary from one sport to another. For illustration purposes, greater detail will be given to the drafting procedures of the

National Football League. A brief overview of the rules and regulations of entry drafts for Major League Baseball, the National Basketball Association, and the National Hockey League are also provided.

12.6.1. National Football League Draft

12.6.1.1. Draft Eligibility

The NFL has perhaps the most restrictive draft eligibility rules of the four major professional leagues. Only college players who have completed their eligibility or have submitted a letter to the NFL forfeiting their remaining college eligibility may be drafted. All players who have had three NFL regular seasons passed since their high school graduation and wish to be eligible for the NFL draft must submit a letter announcing their intentions to the NFL by the January 12 preceding the draft. In 2010, 53 players were granted this special eligibility in the NFL draft, including the first overall pick, Oklahoma quarterback Sam Bradford. In addition, a player who graduates before his eligibility expires must submit a letter stating his intention to be graduated before the fall semester prior to the draft if he wants to be drafted. In this case, the team that selects this player cannot offer the athlete a contract until it receives word from the NFL office that he has in fact graduated. If the player fails to graduate, the club loses the selection and the player forfeits his college eligibility. The NFL draft usually occurs in the last week of April and, per the league collective bargaining agreement, lasts seven rounds. Beginning with the 2007 college football season, NFLPA-certified agents are forbidden from having any direct contact with players not yet eligible for the NFL draft, typically true juniors or younger, until three days after they officially declare for the NFL draft.

The NFL's eligibility rule was most recently challenged when, following an outstanding freshman season at Ohio State University in the fall of 2002, running back Maurice Clarett was suspended for his entire sophomore season for numerous NCAA violations. Rather than sit out a season, Clarett chose to challenge the NFL's eligibility rule. Eventually the United States Court of Appeals for the Second Circuit prevented Clarett from entering the draft and upheld the NFL's eligibility requirements for their necessary procompetitive effects; see *Clarett v. NFL* 369 F.3d 124 (2nd Cir. 2004). (For more on this case, see section 10.3.7, "Nonstatutory Labor Exemption Today: *Clarett*).

The NFL also has a supplemental draft for players who become eligible after the draft but before the start of the NFL season. Former Cleveland Browns quarterback Bernie Kosar graduated early from college, and therefore became eligible for the supplemental draft. After choosing Kosar in the first round of the supplemental draft, Cleveland had to give up its first round selection in the next NFL draft as compensation in this situation.

12.6.1.2. Draft Retention Rights

Article XVI of the NFL Collective Bargaining Agreement outlines the regulations governing the NFL draft. For example, any player drafted is automatically offered the league minimum salary for a one-year contract. Excerpts from this document are in exhibit 12.7. If a draftee chooses not to sign, he is eligible for the next NFL draft, but once again is limited to one club in negotiations. However, if a drafted player does not play professional football for two years, he may then sign with any team. A player who plays professionally in the Canadian Football League or any other professional football league, and whose rights are held by an NFL club, can

Exhibit 12.7
Article XVI. College Draft (NFL Collective Bargaining Agreement 2006–2012)

Section 1. **Time of Draft:** There shall be an Annual Selection Meeting (the "College Draft" or "Draft") each League Year during the term of this Agreement and in the League Year immediately following the expiration or termination of this Agreement, with respect to which the following rules shall apply:

Section 2. **Number of Choices and Eligibility:**

(a) The Draft shall consist of seven rounds, with each round consisting of the same number of selection choices as there will be Clubs in the NFL the following League Year, plus a maximum number of additional Compensatory Draft Selections equal to the number of Clubs then in the League, with such Compensatory Draft Selections reserved for Clubs losing certain Unrestricted Free Agents. Each Draft shall be held between February 14 and May 2, on a date which shall be determined by the Commissioner.

(b) No player shall be permitted to apply for special eligibility for selection in the Draft, or otherwise be eligible for the Draft, until three NFL regular seasons have begun and ended following either his graduation from high school or graduation of the class with which he entered high school, whichever is earlier. For example, if a player graduated from high school in December 2006, he would not be permitted to apply for special eligibility, and would not otherwise be eligible for selection, until the 2010 Draft.

(c) If a player who was not eligible for the Draft in any League Year becomes eligible after the date of the Draft, he will be eligible to be selected in a supplemental Draft, if the League elects to conduct such a Draft, on or before the seventh calendar day prior to the opening of the first training camp that League Year. No player may elect to bypass a Draft for which he is eligible to apply for selection in a supplemental Draft. Any Club that selects a player in a supplemental Draft must forfeit a choice in the same round in the next succeeding principal Draft.

(d) No player shall be eligible to be employed by an NFL Club until he has been eligible for selection in an NFL Draft.

Section 3. **Required Tender:** A Club that drafts a player shall be deemed to have automatically tendered the player a one year NFL Player Contract for the Minimum Active/Inactive List Salary then applicable to the player pursuant to the terms of this Agreement. The NFL or the Club shall provide the player with notice of such Required Tender before or immediately following the Draft.

Section 4. **Signing of Drafted Rookies:**

(a) A drafted player may accept the Required Tender at any time up to and including the Tuesday following the tenth week of the regular season immediately following the Draft, at 4:00 p.m. New York time. In the event the exclusive negotiating rights to the drafted player are assigned to another Club through the NFL waiver system, the acquiring Club must immediately extend the Required Tender following assignment. If released through waivers, the player shall be treated as an Undrafted Rookie Free Agent, with the right to sign an NFL Player Contract with any Club. If the Club that drafted the player signs the player after he is waived and becomes a Rookie Free Agent, the player's

Exhibit 12.7
(continued)

entire salary shall be counted against the Entering Player Pool, in the manner described in Article XVII (Entering Player Pool).

(b) If a Drafted Rookie has not signed a Player Contract during the period from the date of such Draft to the thirtieth day prior to the first Sunday of the regular season: (i) the Club that drafted the player may not thereafter trade to another Club either its exclusive negotiating rights to such player or any Player Contract that it signs with such player for the player's initial League Year; and (ii) the Club that drafted the player is the only Club with which the player may sign a Player Contract until the day of the Draft in the subsequent League Year, at which time such player is eligible to be drafted in the subsequent League Year's Draft by any Club except the Club that drafted him in the initial Draft. (After the Tuesday following the tenth week of the regular season, the player and the Club may only sign a Player Contract for future League Year(s)).

(c) If a Drafted Rookie has not signed a Player Contract by the Tuesday following the tenth week of the regular season, at 4:00 p.m. New York time, the player shall be prohibited from playing football in the NFL for the remainder of that League Year, absent a showing to the Impartial Arbitrator of extreme Club or extreme personal hardship. The determination of the Impartial Arbitrator shall be made within five days of the application, and shall be based upon all information relating to such hardship submitted by such date. The determination of the Impartial Arbitrator shall be final and binding upon all parties.

Section 5. **Other Professional Teams:**

(a) Notwithstanding Section 4(b) above, if a player is drafted by a Club and, during the period between the Draft and the next annual Draft, signs a contract with, plays for or is employed by a professional football team not in the NFL during all or any part of the 12 month period following the initial Draft, then the drafting Club (or any assignee Club) shall retain the exclusive NFL rights to negotiate for and sign a contract with the player until the day of the Draft three League Years after the initial Draft, and shall thereafter have a Right of First Refusal as described herein, and the player may receive offers from any Club at any time thereafter. The player shall notify the NFLPA and the NFL of his desire to sign a contract with an NFL Club, and of the date on which the player will be free of his other contractual obligations of employment, if any. Within thirty days of receipt of such notice by the NFL or the date of the availability of such player, whichever is later, the NFL Club that drafted the player must tender a one year written Player Contract to the player in order to retain its rights to that player, as detailed below.

(b) For a player to whom the drafting Club retains the exclusive NFL rights to negotiate pursuant to Section 4(a) above, the Club must tender a one year Player Contract with salary of at least the Minimum Active/Inactive List Salary for players with less than one credited season, as defined in Article XXXVIII (Salaries), within the thirty day period specified in Subsection (a) above.

Exhibit 12.7
(continued)

The amount of such tender and/or any Player Contract entered into with the player shall be subject to the Entering Player Pool, as set forth in Article XVII (Entering Player Pool). If the player is released through waivers, the player immediately becomes a Free Agent, with the right to sign an NFL Player Contract with any Club, and any Club is then free to negotiate for and sign a Player Contract with such player, without any Draft Choice Compensation between Clubs or First Refusal Rights of any kind, or any signing period.

(c) For players with respect to whom the drafting Club retains a Right of First Refusal pursuant to this Section 5, during each League Year the player shall be treated as if he were a Restricted Free Agent not subject to Draft Choice Compensation, as described in Article XIX (Veteran Free Agency), Section 2, except as otherwise set forth in this Section 5. For such players subject to a Right of First Refusal, the Club must tender a one year Player Contract with at least the Minimum Active/Inactive List Salary for players with two or more Credited Seasons, as defined in Article XXXVIII (Salaries), within the thirty day period specified in Subsection (a) above. The amount of such tender and/or any Player Contract entered into with the player shall not be subject to the Entering Player Pool. If the Club does not make or withdraws the Required Tender, the player immediately becomes a Rookie Free Agent, with the right to negotiate and sign a Player Contract with any Club, and any Club is then free to negotiate for and sign a Player Contract with such player, without any Draft Choice Compensation between Clubs or First Refusal Rights of any kind, or any signing period.

***Section 6.* Return to College:** If any college football player who becomes eligible for the Draft prior to exhausting his college football eligibility through participation is drafted by an NFL Club, and returns to college, the drafting Club's exclusive right to negotiate and sign a Player Contract with such player shall continue through the date of the Draft that follows the last season in which the player was eligible to participate in college football, and thereafter the player shall be treated and the Club shall have such exclusive rights as if he were drafted in such Draft by such Club (or assignee Club).

***Section 7.* Assignment of Draft Rights:** In the event that the exclusive right to negotiate for a Drafted Rookie under Sections 4, 5 or 6 above is assigned from one Club to another Club, the Club to which such right has been assigned shall have the same, but no greater, right to such player, including the Right of First Refusal described in Section 5, as would the Club assigning such right, and such player shall have the same, but no greater, obligation to the NFL Club to which such right has been assigned as he had to the Club assigning such right.

***Section 8.* Subsequent Draft:** A Club that, in a subsequent Draft, drafts a player who

(a) was selected in an initial Draft, and

(b) did not sign a contract with the NFL Club that drafted him or with any assignee Club during the signing period set forth in Sections 4 through 6 above, shall,

Exhibit 12.7
(continued)

during the period from the date of the subsequent Draft to the date of the Draft held the subsequent League Year, be the only NFL Club that may negotiate with or sign a Player Contract with such player. If such player has not signed a Player Contract within the period beginning on the date of the subsequent Draft and ending on the thirtieth day prior to the beginning of the regular season, the Club loses all rights to trade its exclusive negotiating rights to such player or any Player Contract that it signs with such player for the player's initial League Year. After the Tuesday following the tenth week of the regular season, the player and the Club may only sign a Player Contract for future League Year(s), except as provided in Section 4(c) above. If the player has not signed a Player Contract by the day of the next annual College Draft following the subsequent Draft, the player immediately becomes a Rookie Free Agent, with the right to negotiate and sign a Player Contract with any Club, and any Club is then free to negotiate for and sign a Player Contract with such player, without any Draft Choice Compensation between Clubs or First Refusal Rights of any kind, or any signing period.

Section 9. No Subsequent Draft: If a player is drafted by a Club in an initial Draft and

(a) does not sign a contract with a Club during the signing period set forth in Sections 4 through 6 above, and

(b) is not drafted by any Club in the subsequent Draft, the player immediately becomes an Undrafted Rookie, with the right to negotiate and sign a Player Contract with any Club, and any Club is then free to negotiate for and sign a Player Contract with such player, without any Draft Choice Compensation between Clubs or First Refusal Rights of any kind, or any signing period.

Section 10. Compensatory Draft Selections: The rules and procedures regarding Compensatory Draft Selections set forth in Section 2 above shall be as agreed upon by the NFL and the NFLPA.

Section 11. Undrafted Rookies: Any person who has not been selected by a Club in a College Draft shall be free, after the completion of a College Draft for which he is eligible, to negotiate and sign a Player Contract with any Club, and any Club shall be completely free to negotiate and sign a Player Contract with any such person after such date, without any penalty or restriction, including, but not limited to, Draft Choice, Compensation between Clubs, or First Refusal Rights of any kind.

Section 12. Notice of Signing: Promptly following but no later than two business days after receipt of notice of the signing of any Drafted or Undrafted Rookie, the NFL shall notify the NFLPA of such signing.

negotiate with that club for only two years. After that point the player may negotiate with any NFL team, but the team that held his original rights can match the offer and thereby retain the player. As can be seen in exhibit 12.7, the rules and regulations regarding the NFL draft are complex. It is crucial that an agent for a prospective NFL football player be aware of all of the details of that league's draft. For example, section 5 of exhibit 12.7 outlines the rights of athletes who were originally drafted by NFL teams but have chosen to play professional football elsewhere. This clause is extremely important for an agent who represents a player who was originally drafted in the NFL, chose to play in the Canadian Football League, but then decides to enter the NFL.

12.6.1.3. Impact on NCAA Eligibility

If a college athlete enters the NFL draft, he cannot return to the NCAA in Division I regardless of whether he is drafted (see note 1). Bylaw 12.2.4.2. of the *2009–10 NCAA Manual* states:

> An individual loses amateur status in a particular sport when the individual asks to be placed on the draft list or supplemental draft list of a professional league in that sport, even though:
> (a) The individual asks that his or her name be withdrawn from the draft list prior to the actual draft;
> (b) The individual's name remains on the list but he or she is not drafted; or
> (c) The individual is drafted but does not sign an agreement with any professional athletics team.

There is a different rule for aspiring NBA players. An intercollegiate basketball player can enter the NBA draft and retain eligibility as long as that player does not retain the services of an agent (see section 12.6.3, "National Basketball Association Draft"). The NBA draft is the only draft in which an athlete can ask to be placed on the draft list and not immediately lose his amateur eligibility. In Major League Baseball and the National Hockey League, players are often drafted following their junior year in college even though they did not request to enter the draft.

NOTES _____

1. In the following cases, the NCAA rules not allowing athletes to return to college after entering into the NFL draft were upheld:

a. In *Banks v. NCAA*, 508 U.S. 908 (1993), Braxton Banks, a former Notre Dame football player, decided to enter into the 1990 NFL draft. Banks was not selected in the NFL draft and petitioned the NCAA to return to college to finish the one year of eligibility that he had remaining. Banks was denied, and he brought a claim stating that the NCAA rule violated antitrust statutes. Banks was unsuccessful on both the trial court and appeals court levels because he failed to allege any anticompetitive effect on the market by the employment of these rules.

b. In *Gaines v. NCCA*, 746 F. Supp. 738 (M.D. Tenn. 1990), Bradford Gaines, a college football player for Vanderbilt University, declared himself eligible for the 1990 NFL draft. Gaines was not selected by any NFL team in the draft, and wished to complete his senior season of eligibility at Vanderbilt. Gaines sought a preliminary injunction allowing him to play, and claimed that because he had not signed a contract with an agent or a team, he had retained his amateur status. Gaines was unable to prove likelihood of success on the merits of his case, and the court denied his preliminary injunction request.

c. Following an outstanding sophomore season in 2003 that helped lead the University of Southern California (USC) to a share of the national championship, wide receiver Damian Williams chose to declare for the NFL draft. Williams was following the lead of former Ohio State running back Maurice Clarett, who had seemingly successfully challenged the NFL's restriction that a player must be three years removed from his high school graduation to be eligible for the NFL draft (see section 12.6.1.1, "Draft Eligibility"). About a month before the June 2004 draft, Williams and Clarett were ruled ineligible. In the meantime, Williams had hired an agent, not attended a spring class at USC, signed to the NFL Players Association's Group Licensing Agreement, and entered into agreements with Nike and trading card companies. Following the ruling, Williams cut ties with his agent and promised to return all money and benefits received in order to receive reinstatement of his eligibility. Williams's appeal to the NCAA was denied in August 2004. Subsequently, Williams was forced to sit out a season before entering the NFL draft.

2. The following are cases regarding eligibility in NCAA basketball:

a. Lucca Staiger, a guard on the Iowa State basketball team, was declared ineligible for the 2007-08 season because it was determined that a team he had played on in his native Germany was professional. This is a common occurrence for European transfers.

b. After a successful 2004–2005 basketball season, Kentucky center Randolph Morris declared himself eligible for the NBA draft. Morris went undrafted and petitioned the NCAA for reinstatement, as he is allowed to do. However, the NCAA ruled him ineligible because sports agency SFX released a statement regarding Morris prior to the draft and was listed as a contact for Morris in predraft workouts although SFX and Morris attest there was no explicit written or oral agreement between SFX and Morris. Finally in December 2005, Kentucky coach Tubby Smith found a fax from Morris a month before the June 2005 draft in which Morris expressed his intent not to obtain an agent in order to retain his collegiate eligibility. As a result, the NCAA restricted Morris to only 14 games in the 2005–2006 season and ordered him to repay more than $7,000 in workout-related expenses.

12.6.2. Major League Baseball Draft

Major League Baseball has the most complicated rules of any of the professional drafts and is the only league of the Big Four whose draft is not explicitly discussed in the collective bargaining agreement. Each year Major League Baseball conducts a first-year player draft on or about June 10 (a January amateur free agent draft, as well as "secondary drafts" for previously selected players, was eliminated in 1986). The players eligible for the first-year player draft consist of high school graduating seniors (or those without remaining eligibility); certain four-year college players; junior college players; and all other amateur players not previously selected. It is important to note that Major League Baseball does not conduct a worldwide draft, unlike all other professional team sport leagues. The MLB draft is limited to players from the United States, Canada, and Puerto Rico. Furthermore, players signed outside of the United States, Canada, and Puerto Rico need be only 16 years of age. During the 2002 labor negotiations for a new collective bargaining agreement, the issue of a worldwide draft was considered (see note 1). The Office of the Commissioner of Baseball and the Major League Baseball Players Association agreed that all players entering professional baseball, U.S.-born and foreign, should be subject to the first-year player draft (See Attachment 24 of Major League Baseball's 2002 collective bargaining agreement). However, they also agreed that there was insufficient time to research the issue and agreed that a joint committee would begin examining the issue for discussion in future negotiations. Yet, this attachment was dropped from the 2007–2011 MLB CBA and there is no mention of an international draft in the most recent CBA.

A high school player who is drafted may sign with the professional club if his eligibility has expired prior to his graduation from high school because of (1) the student's age, (2) his completion of the maximum number of semesters in attendance, or (3) the ending of the maximum number seasons in which he is eligible to participate in any major sport. A student who drops out of high school prior to expiration of his athletic eligibility, and remains out for at least one year, may thereafter be signed to a contract for immediate service. If, over the summer, a player does not sign with the club that drafted him, the player will automatically sever his draftee relationship with that particular club by attending his first class at a *four-year college*. The player then cannot be selected in future June first-year player drafts until:

1. The player reaches age 21
2. The player completes his junior year.

Consequently, it is not uncommon for a player to be drafted three times: in the summer he graduates high school, three years later (after his junior year of college), and following his senior year of college. It is common for agents to use the possibility of the player's attending or returning to a four-year college as leverage in negotiating a signing bonus.

A *junior college* player is eligible for selection at any first-year player draft. However, should the player return to junior college, he cannot sign with the team that drafted him until completion of the college baseball season.

Once a player is drafted, it is the team's obligation to begin negotiations within 15 days and offer the player a contract. Drafted players' minor league salaries are capped at $1,100 per month for their first year and increase to a maximum of $2,400 per month at the AAA level so long as they never become a minor league free agent. As a result, the signing bonus is one of the major items of negotiation for selected players, especially those chosen in the earlier rounds.

Other relevant considerations include the following:

1. Foreign players, defined as athletes from outside the United States, Canada, and Puerto Rico, may sign with major league teams when they are 16, with the restriction that they must turn 17 by the end of their first professional season.

2. Draft order is determined in alternating fashion between the American League (AL) and National League (NL) teams, with the NL team with the worst record picking first in even-numbered years and the AL team selecting first in odd-numbered years.

3. College players (excluding junior college players) must turn 21 within 45 days of the draft in order to be eligible for it. All junior college players are eligible for the draft.

4. Drafted players who enter (or return to) junior college remain eligible to sign with the team that drafted them until seven days before the next year's draft.

5. A drafted player cannot be traded until a year after he signs his first pro contract.

A player's NCAA eligibility is not affected when he is drafted by a club. This regulation does not apply to basketball and football, however. A high school athlete in these sports who enters a professional draft automatically forfeits intercollegiate eligibility.

NOTES

1. According to *The Report of the Independent Members of the Commissioner's Blue Ribbon Panel on Baseball Economics*, July 2000, Section IV.5.2, "Currently, forty percent of all players signing first-year contracts are excluded from the draft because they do not reside in the United States, Puerto Rico or Canada. With the recent dramatic escalation of signing bonuses to free agent first-year players from the Far East, the Dominican Republic, Venezuela, Cuba, and Australia, high revenue clubs now sign the majority of talented high-profile foreign players. *The implementation of a worldwide draft would ensure all clubs, regardless of revenue, relatively equal access to the crucial foreign player market*" (emphasis in original).

2. NCAA Bylaw 12.3.2 allows amateur athletes to retain attorneys or advisors while considering whether to turn professional so long as the attorney or advisor does not meet with any professional clubs on the player's behalf. In *Oliver v. NCAA*, 920 N.E.2d 203 (Ohio Com. Pleas 2009), Oklahoma State pitcher Andy Oliver brought suit after he was deemed ineligible for violating the bylaw. While in high school, Oliver and two MLB agents, Robert and Tim Baratta, met with representatives of the Minnesota Twins who were trying to convince Oliver to turn professional. Oliver chose Oklahoma State and never paid the Barattas for their services. Such arrangements are commonplace in NCAA baseball, with a degree of understanding that the agents will represent the player when he finally does turn professional. Late in college, Oliver broke off contact with the Barattas and began to consult with agent Scott Boras instead. The Barattas billed Oliver for $113,000 in services, which Oliver refused to pay, saying he had never agreed to compensate them. Had he compensated them, he would have also been deemed ineligible. The court enjoined the NCAA from issuing any further disciplinary action against Oliver, finding the relevant NCAA bylaw unenforceable as "unreliable...capricious... illogical...and arbitrary."

3. For more on the role of agents in baseball, see Richard T. Karcher, "The NCAA's Regulations Related to the Use of Agents in the Sport of Baseball: Are the Rules Detrimental to the Best Interest of the Amateur Athlete?" 7 *Vanderbilt Journal of Entertainment Law and Practice* 215 (2005).

4. The following are cases regarding the Major League Baseball amateur draft:

a. In the 1997 amateur draft, the Philadelphia Phillies made Florida State outfielder J. D. Drew the second overall draft pick. Drew, along with agent Scott Boras, then began a controversial holdout. The Phillies offered Drew a record $2.6 million signing bonus along with a $200,000 one-year major league contract. Drew requested $11.17 million for four years. Drew instead signed with the St. Paul Saints, an independent league team in Minnesota in hopes of being granted free agency when the Phillies lost the rights to him in the week prior to the 1998 amateur draft. Ultimately, Drew did not win free agency because the Phillies had made an offer to Drew in the time frame required. Drew reentered the draft pool and was drafted fifth overall by the St. Louis Cardinals with whom he promptly signed a $3 million signing bonus and a four-year major league contract worth a potential $8.5 million.

b. In the 1996 MLB amateur draft, agent Scott Boras used loopholes that granted four first round picks free agency, including Travis Lee drafted by the Minnesota Twins, John Patterson drafted by the Montreal Expos, Matt White drafted by the San Francisco Giants, and Bobby Seay drafted by the Chicago White Sox. According to Rule 4(E) of the Professional Baseball Agreement, teams must make a formal contract offer to every pick in the draft within 15 days. Braden Looper of the St. Louis

Cardinals, Eric Milton of the New York Yankees, and A. J. Hinch of the Oakland Athletics were also not offered contracts in the appropriate time period but chose to sign before Major League Baseball reached a decision on the issue. Lee and Patterson signed with the Arizona Diamondbacks, and White and Seay signed with the Tampa Bay Devil Rays. The free agent signing bonuses cost almost $30 million. The rule was changed following the 1996 draft.

c. Georgia Tech catcher Jason Varitek was the 14th overall pick in the 1994 Major League Baseball amateur draft by the Seattle Mariners. However, at the advice of agent Scott Boras, Varitek refused to sign a contract with the Mariners who were offering a signing bonus of $500,000 while Boras was requesting $850,000. While MLB was in the middle of a work stoppage, Varitek signed a contract with the St. Paul Saints, an independent league team in Minnesota. Boras's intention was that because Varitek had signed a professional contract that when the next amateur draft was to be held in June and the Mariners no longer had rights to Varitek, Varitek would become a free agent. Eventually Varitek signed with the Mariners prior to the draft for an undisclosed amount.

d. In 1983 amateur high school pitcher Tim Belcher was drafted first overall by the Minnesota Twins but refused to sign. The Twins offered Belcher a $100,000 signing bonus, an amount equivalent to the amount received by the previous year's number-one pick, Shawon Duston of the Chicago Cubs. Belcher and his agent Scott Boras demanded a $150,000 bonus. Belcher reentered the 1984 draft and was chosen number one overall in the secondary phase of the draft by the New York Yankees.

12.6.3. National Basketball Association Draft

The NBA holds its annual draft in June, after the completion of the playoffs. The draft consists of two rounds, with teams selecting in reverse order of finish in the previous year, except for teams that did not qualify for the playoffs. The NBA developed a lottery system in response to critics who claimed some teams were purposely losing games in order to gain a better draft position. All 14 teams that do not make the playoffs participate to determine their draft order. However, the team with the worst record in the league is guaranteed a pick no worse than the fourth overall, to try to ensure the availability of a quality player for the team that needs such a player most. Also, this lottery is weighted, meaning that teams that finish with a worse win-loss record will have a greater chance to attain high draft picks. In addition, there are rules in place that prevent the worse teams from dropping too much in the lottery. All players whose college eligibility has expired are automatically included in the draft pool. Any other player who wants to enter the draft must notify the NBA.

The participation in the draft effectively renounces the athlete's remaining or future intercollegiate eligibility. If a college player changes his mind, he must rescind his notification before the deadline passes in order to maintain intercollegiate eligibility. Any college undergraduate may ask to be drafted by submitting his name to the NBA at least 45 days prior to the draft. Beginning with the 2006 draft, players must be at least 19 years old to be eligible and international players must have had at least one NBA season pass since their high school graduation or the equivalent thereof (see note 3).

Once the player sends notification to the NBA of his intention to enter the draft, he loses his NCAA eligibility, whether selected by a team or not, unless the player withdraws from the draft by 10 days prior to the draft, and has not signed with a player agent or received any compensation. Under NCAA rules, basketball players can be reinstated if they have not contracted with an agent. An undrafted player is an unrestricted free agent who may sign with any team he chooses or petition the NCAA for reinstatement. These rules do not apply to other sports.

Once a player is drafted, the NBA team must offer him at least a minimum contract by September 5. A rookie pay scale was adopted within the NBA Collective Bargaining Agreement that sets a rookie's salary depending on where the player is picked in the draft order (see exhibit 12.2 and see Article VIII, "Rookie Scale," NBA Collective Bargaining Agreement). If the player declines the offer, his rights are held by the team until the next draft. If a player signs a professional contract with another league (such as the Continental Basketball Association or a European league) after being drafted by an NBA team, the NBA team retains the rights to negotiate with the player within the period ending one year from the earlier of the two following dates: (1) the date the player notifies the NBA team that he is immediately ready to sign a contract or (2) the date of the college draft occurring in the 12-period month from September 1 to August 30 in which the player notifies the NBA team of his availability and intention to play in the NBA during the season immediately following the stated 12-month period (Article X, Section 4, NBA Collective Bargaining Agreement).

NOTES

1. Also see Matthew Epps, "Full Court Press: How Collective Bargaining Weakened the NBA's Competitive Edge in a Globalized Sport," 16 *Villanova Sports & Entertainment Law Journal* 343 (2009).

2. The NBA Collective Bargaining Agreement can be found in its entirety at www.nbpa.com and specifically Article X, Player Eligibility and NBA Draft.

3. For more on the NBA draft age restriction, see Daniel A. Applegate, "The NBA Gets a College Education: An Antitrust and Labor Analysis of the NBA's Minimum Age Limit," 56 *Case Western Reserve Law Review* 825 (2006) and Michael A. McCann, "Illegal Defense: The Irrational Economics of Banning High School Players from the NBA Draft," 3 *Virginia Sports and Entertainment Law Journal* 113 (2004).

12.6.4. National Hockey League Draft

The NHL holds its annual seven-round draft in June on a date determined by the commissioner. Any amateur or junior hockey player who will turn 18 years of age by September 15 is eligible. Any player who has gone undrafted previously may be selected until he is 20 years of age as of the next September 15. If, after 20 years of age, he has not been drafted, he is a free agent able to negotiate with any team.

A drafted player must receive a bona fide offer by the next draft or he is eligible to be drafted again, or if he reaches 20 years of age, he becomes a free agent. There is no maximum age requirement for European players, who must be drafted before they can sign. Finally, any drafted player who remains in college remains the property of the drafting team through the August 15 following the graduation of his college class.

Unlike football and basketball, and similar to baseball, participation in the NHL draft is not detrimental to collegiate or high school eligibility. If a player is selected but decides not to sign, he can still participate on the amateur level (see note 1).

12.6.5. Single-Entity League Drafts

Both Major League Soccer (MLS) and the Women's National Basketball Association (WNBA) are structured as single-entity leagues as opposed to a multiple franchise structure. This structure allows them to avoid many of the antitrust issues that have faced the four major professional leagues. In both the MLS and WNBA, players sign directly with the league and are then distributed among the teams in varying ways.

12.6.5.1. Major League Soccer

There are four ways in which Major League Soccer teams can acquire players new to MLS:

a. Super draft and supplemental draft: Both drafts consist of four rounds that allow teams to select players from college and lower division leagues.

b. Discovery signings: Each team is allowed to make six discovery signings per season. A discovery signing occurs when a team scouts and recruits a particular player not already in the MLS.

c. Developmental roster signings: Teams are permitted unlimited signings to ensure that their developmental roster is full to the 10-player maximum. Developmental players consist of players in youth soccer, not yet ready for the MLS.

d. Lottery: Teams can receive players through a team performance–weighted lottery of players signed after original drafts or players who failed to sign with the league prior to the draft.

A team holds the rights to a drafted college player(s) by placing him on their "College Protected List" but loses rights to the player on the second December 31 following the draft in question. MLS teams also receive "allocation money" in reverse order of the prior season's finish. Therefore, the team with the worst record gets the first chance to use its allocation money to sign a player new to MLS, re-sign an existing MLS player, or exercise an option on an existing MLS player's contract.

12.6.5.2. Women's National Basketball Association

The WNBA draft must be held before May 15 but typically occurs in early April following the NCAA's Women's Basketball National Championship tournament final game. The draft consists of three rounds and is structured in the same way as the NBA draft, with the teams that miss the playoffs entering a weighted lottery to determine their draft position.

Only women who have graduated from a four-year college or university or are scheduled to do so before during the calendar year in which the draft is held are eligible for the draft. International players are eligible if they have played under a professional contract for at least two years and are at least 20 years old or are at least 22 years old during the calendar year in which the draft is being held. No player is eligible for more than two WNBA drafts. A player may rescind her entry into the draft by providing the WNBA with written notification at least five days in advance of the draft.

Teams must make an offer to a drafted player within seven days of her having been drafted to retain their exclusive rights to that player. If the team fails to offer a contract to the player, they become a rookie free agent on the eighth day following the draft and can reenter next year's draft if they are still eligible. If a player fails to sign a contract after two WNBA drafts, she then becomes a rookie free agent and can negotiate with any team.

NOTES _____

1. For more information on NHL draft eligibility, refer to Article 8, "Entry Draft," of the National Hockey League Collective Bargaining Agreement (available at www.nhl.com).

2. For more information on NBA draft eligibility, refer to Article 10, "Player Eligibility and NBA Draft," of the National Basketball League Collective Bargaining Agreement (available at www.nbpa.org).

3. For more information on NFL draft eligibility, refer to Article 16, "College Draft," of the National Football League Collective Bargaining Agreement (available at www.nflpa.org/).

4. Major League Baseball's Collective Bargaining Agreement is available at www.mlbplayers.com.

5. For more information on WNBA draft eligibility, refer to Article 8, "Player Eligibility and WNBA Draft," of the Women's National Basketball Association Collective Bargaining Agreement (available at www.wnbpa.com).

12.7. STANDARD PLAYER CONTRACT

The standard player contract is one of the cornerstones of the collective bargaining agreement negotiated between the players association and league management, and provides the basic guidelines for an agent and the club in their negotiations for a player's contract (see section 11.3.7, "Collective Bargaining Agreements in Professional Sports"). A standard player contract is a form contract used by all players and teams in a league. It has several advantages for teams and agents alike. By employing a standard player contract, agents and organizations avoid the negotiation of language and the potential problems associated with drafting unique contracts for each athlete. The use of a standard player contract ensures that all athletes and teams within a league will work with the same basic rights and privileges, negotiating only salary, possibly a few changes in the standard player contract, and additional bonus clauses. Negotiating individual issues such as preseason compensation and prohibited substances (see Section 3(b) and Section 8), would prove to be a very problematic task for individual cases. Therefore, the language of the standard player contract is decided during negotiations over the collective bargaining agreement and is uniformly applied to all players within the league. Another benefit of the standard player contract is that much of the language has withstood the test of time, and has been interpreted, clarified, and revised through grievances raised by the players associations.

The standard player contract is written in conjunction with the league's collective bargaining agreement. Therefore, all athletes and teams are subject to the clauses and provisions within the collective bargaining agreement (see section 9.2.1.3, "Hierarchy of Contracts").

Although the standard player contract is usually a lengthy document, each clause within it serves a distinct purpose. It is important for an agent to be aware of each clause, and especially some clauses that may be revised during some negotiations. For example, in exhibit 12.9, Section 12 and Section 16 are two unique clauses in the NBA Uniform Player Contract. Section 12, for example, does not allow the player to participate in any other athletic sport that could endanger his health without the consent of his team. This clause is crucial for an agent to be aware of before the agent considers signing their client up to participate in a local charity football game (see section 9.2.1.4, "Player Exclusivity").

Section 16 of the NBA Standard Player Contract is a vital clause because it outlines the acceptable reasons for termination of a player's contract. It is crucial that an agent be aware of these guidelines, especially in a situation where the client may have been wrongfully terminated.

While the standard player contract provides a basis for negotiating contracts, it does not include all possible areas for negotiation. Performance and award bonus clauses are frequent issues for individual negotiations (see section 9.2.1.6, "Bonus Clauses"). For example, a player in Major League Baseball may be awarded a salary bonus if he wins the Cy Young Award or receives a Gold Glove. It is often the desire of the player and his agent to include a bonus clause in the player's contract because it can provide for the contingency that the player will be worth more than the current accomplishments or prospects indicate. In some instances, the bonus clause may be used as an incentive to sign. This signing bonus can serve more than one purpose. It can also provide up-front money that may be the only guaranteed money for a player who does not sign a guaranteed contract. For example, a late-round NFL draft pick may receive a $20,000 signing bonus and still be cut from the team during training camp. If the player is released before the regular season begins because of a failure to make the team, he at least gets to keep the signing bonus, even though the rest of the contract becomes null and void.

Bonus clauses are also used to compensate a player who has exceeded expectations, usually based on performance. It is important to structure the bonus so that the proper salary escalation is allowed if the player fulfills or exceeds expectations. Different leagues attach different names to the same type of bonus clause. Generally, however, bonuses are based on draft position (the signing bonus), statistical performance, volume of play, awards and honors, and other contingencies such as "morals clauses." It is important to note that in Major League Baseball bonuses can be based only upon quantitative, and not qualitative, performances. In the National Football League, contracts can include bonuses that provide money for players who report to preseason camp on time. The use of signing bonuses is also a way that NFL teams can manage the league's salary cap. Signing bonuses can be prorated over the length of the contract to make the salary more cap friendly (see section 11.3.10, "Salary Caps"). The NBA has taken the step of including language in the collective bargaining agreement to cover certain issues that are commonly addressed in the addendum of the contract. Serving the same purpose as the standard player contract, this standardization avoids the potential problems associated with drafting separate, unique bonus clauses for each individual athlete.

Although there is a standard form for the uniform player contract in professional leagues, agents and organizations may make changes to this document to suit their particular needs as long as the clauses do not violate the collective bargaining agreement. The collective bargaining agreement for the NBA includes a section on "allowable amendments" that discusses in what particular ways the agent and the organization can amend certain provisions of the uniform player contract. This section is presented below.

Section 3. Allowable Amendments.

In their individual contract negotiations, a player and a Team may amend the provisions of a Uniform Player Contract, but only in the following respects:

(a) By agreeing upon provisions (to be set forth in Exhibit 1 to a Uniform Player Contract) setting forth the Cash Compensation to be paid or amounts to be loaned to the player for each Season of the Contract for rendering the services described in such Contract.

(b) By agreeing upon provisions (to be set forth in Exhibit 1 to a Uniform Player Contract) setting forth the Non-Cash Compensation to be paid or provided to the player for rendering the services described in such Contract.

(c) By agreeing upon provisions (to be set forth in Exhibit 1 to a Uniform Player Contract) setting forth lump sum bonuses, and the payment schedule therefore, to be paid as a result of:

(i) the player's execution of a Uniform Player Contract or Extension (a "signing bonus"),

(ii) the exercise or non-exercise of an option pursuant to Articles VII and XII,

(iii) the player's achievement of agreed-upon benchmarks relating to his performance as a player or the Team's performance during a particular NBA Season, subject to the limitations imposed by paragraph 3(c) of the Uniform Player Contract, or

(iv) the player's achievement of agreed-upon benchmarks relating to his physical condition or academic achievement, including the player's attendance at and participation in an off-season summer league and/or an off-season skill and conditioning program designated by the Team (subject to the limitations imposed by Section 11(h) below). Any amendment agreed upon pursuant to subsections (iii) or (iv) of this subsection (c) must be structured so as to provide an incentive for positive achievement by the player and/or the Team; and any amendment agreed upon pursuant to subsection (iii) must be based upon specific numerical benchmarks or generally recognized league honors. By way of example and not limitation, an amendment agreed upon pursuant to subsection (iii) may provide for the player to receive a bonus if his free-throw percentage exceeds 80%, but may not provide for the player to receive a bonus if his free-throw percentage improves over his previous season's percentage.

(d) By agreeing upon provisions (to be set forth in Exhibit 1 to a Uniform Player Contract) with respect to extra promotional appearances to be performed by the player (in addition to those required by paragraph 13 of such Contract) and the Compensation therefor.

(e) By agreeing upon a Compensation payment schedule (to be set forth in Exhibit 1 to a Uniform Player Contract) different from that provided for by paragraph 3(a) of the Uniform Player Contract; provided, however, such amendment shall comply with the provisions of Section 11(f) below and that no such amendment shall be permitted with respect to any Season in which the player's Compensation is not greater than the Minimum Player Salary called for with respect to that Season pursuant to Section 6 below.

(f) By agreeing upon provisions (to be set forth in Exhibit 2 to a Uniform Player Contract) stating that the Cash Compensation provided for by a Uniform Player Contract (as described in Exhibit 1 to such Contract) shall be, in whole or in part, and subject to any conditions or limitations, protected or insured (as provided for by, and in accordance with the definitions set forth in, Section 4 below) in the event that such Contract is terminated by the Team by reason of the player's:

    (i) lack of skill;

    (ii) death not covered by an insurance policy procured by a Team for the player's benefit ("non-insured death");

    (iii) death covered by an insurance policy procured by a Team for the player's benefit ("insured death");

    (iv) disability or unfitness to play skilled basketball resulting from a basketball-related injury not covered by an insurance policy procured by a Team for the player's benefit ("non-insured basketball-related injury");

    (v) disability or unfitness to play skilled basketball resulting from any injury or illness not covered by an insurance policy procured by a Team for the player's benefit ("non-insured injury or illness");

    (vi) disability or unfitness to play skilled basketball resulting from an injury or illness covered by an insurance policy procured by a Team for the player's benefit ("insured injury or illness");

    (vii) mental disability not covered by an insurance policy procured by a Team for the player's benefit ("non-insured mental disability"); and/or

    (viii) mental disability covered by an insurance policy procured by a Team for the player's benefit ("insured mental disability").

(g) By agreeing upon provisions (to be set forth in Exhibit 3 to a Uniform Player Contract) limiting or eliminating the player's right to receive his Cash Compensation (in accordance with paragraphs 7(c), 16(a)(iii), and 16(b) of the Uniform Player Contract) when the player's disability or unfitness to play skilled basketball is caused by the re-injury of an injury sustained prior to, or by the aggravation of a condition that existed prior to, the execution of the Uniform Player Contract providing for such Cash Compensation.

(h) By agreeing upon provisions (to be set forth in Exhibit 4 to a Uniform Player Contract)

    (i) entitling a player to earn Cash Compensation upon the assignment of such player's Uniform Player Contract, or

    (ii) prohibiting or limiting the Team's right to assign such player's Contract to another Team, subject, however, in either case (i) or (ii) to the provisions of Article XXIV.

(i) By agreeing upon provisions (to be set forth in Exhibit 5 to a Uniform Player Contract) permitting the player to participate or engage in some or all of the activities otherwise prohibited by paragraph 12 of the Uniform Player Contract; provided, however, that paragraph 12 of the Uniform Player Contract may not be amended to permit a player to participate in any public game or public exhibition of basketball not approved in accordance with Article XXIII of this Agreement.

(j) By agreeing upon provisions (to be set forth in Exhibit 6 to a Uniform Player Contract) establishing the date and time of a physical examination of the player to be performed by a physician designated by the Team within seventy-two (72) hours of the execution of the Contract, the passage of such examination by the player (in the sole discretion of the Team) to be a condition precedent to the validity of the player's Uniform Player Contract.

(k) By agreeing to delete clauses (b)(ii) and/or (b)(iii) of paragraph 5 of the Uniform Player Contract in their entirety.

(l) By agreeing to delete paragraph 7(b) of the Uniform Player Contract in its entirety and substituting therefore the provision set forth in Exhibit 7 to a Uniform Player Contract.

(m) By agreeing either

   (i) to delete paragraph 13(b) of the Uniform Player Contract in its entirety, or

   (ii) to delete the last sixteen words of paragraph 13(b) of such Contract.

(n) By agreeing upon provisions for the purpose of terminating an already-existing Uniform Player Contract prior to the expiration of its stated term, stating as follows:

   (i) that the Team will request waivers on the player in accordance with paragraph 16 of the Contract immediately following the Commissioner's approval of such amendment; and

   (ii) should the player clear waivers and his Contract thereupon be terminated, that the amount of any Cash Compensation protection or insurance contained in the Contract will immediately be reduced or eliminated. In addition to the foregoing, the parties may also agree that (x) as a result of the termination of the Contract, the payment schedule for any Compensation remaining to be paid will be accelerated over a shorter period or stretched over a longer period (subject, however, to Section 11(f) below), and/or (y) that the Team's right of set-off under Article XXVII of this Agreement will be modified or eliminated.

(o) By agreeing upon provisions (to be set forth in Exhibit 8 to a Uniform Player Contract) stating that the Contract will be assigned to another team within forty-eight (48) hours of its execution, such assignment and the consummation of such assignment to be conditions precedent to the validity of the Contract; provided, however, that any such sign-and-trade transaction must comply with Article VII, Section 8(e).

Once an agent representing the player and management reach an agreement on a final contract proposal, it is usually up to the athlete to give his approval to the agent, at which point the contract is formed. After consummation of the contract, the player is legally bound to perform to the best of his abilities during the term of the contract, and management must perform its part by remunerating the athlete as expressed in the agreement.

Although both sides are committed to the agreement legally, a common issue in pro sports has been renegotiation of contracts. The athlete will often initiate renegotiation after a season in which he performed well beyond the expectations at the time of the original agreement, or the market for a player of this caliber has shifted upward. For example, a baseball player who signs a long-term contract early in his career may be well underpaid by the end of his contract due to the rapid salary escalation in Major League Baseball. From a management perspective, the club is not obligated to consider the athlete's request; however, teams are often compelled to do so in order to keep the player happy and motivated. Most clubs have established policies regarding re-negotiation, which vary from firm non-renegotiation to frequent renegotiation. One of the most common alternatives used by many teams is to reward players by adding on years at the end of a contract at an increased salary, and possibly combining this with a signing bonus. Professional basketball contracts are not renegotiable.

A team will normally initiate renegotiation for one of two reasons. First, especially in baseball, a team will decide to "lock up" a player in order to avoid salary arbitration (see section 11.3.15, "Salary Arbitration") or to delay free agency (see section 11.3.9, "Free Agency"). In 2008, the Colorado Rockies were obligated to pay their star third-year shortstop, Troy Tulowitzki, the mini-mum salary of $390,000. However, The Rockies signed Tulowitzki to a six-year, $30 million contract, with a $15 million club option for 2014, prior to the 2008 season. Why would the Rockies agree to this? Because the Rockies were con-cerned that after 2008 (when Tulowitzki may have qualified as a "Super-Two"; as defined in the Major League Baseball Collective Bargaining Agreement, a "Super-Two" player is one who has not yet fulfilled his third year of Major League service but is among the top 17% of Major League players between two and three years of service time.), he would command much more than this amount in salary arbi-tration. In addition, the Rockies then have Tulowitzki signed through his eighth season and potentially his ninth, two years after he would have first been eligible for free agency.

The second reason that teams, especially NFL teams, initiate renegotiation is to fit veteran players under the salary cap or under a team's budgetary constraints. In the NFL, where contracts are not guaranteed, teams may convince a player that if he does not renegotiate his contract, he will be released. In Major League Baseball, where contracts *are* guaranteed, a team may convince certain players to defer money in order to improve the team's cash flow. For example, several Arizona Diamondback veteran players agreed to defer contractual payments prior to the 2001 season. As a result, Commissioner Bud Selig announced in 2002 that he would begin enforcing a rule that had long remained dormant. Teams whose debt, including stadium debt, deferred contracts and other loans, exceeded 40% of their asset value, roughly two times gross revenues, would be subject to fines, loss of shared television revenues, or other penalties if they failed to comply to this rule. The rule intends to ensure that teams are capable of paying their salaries when they are signed.

12.8. ENDORSEMENT CONTRACTS AND FINANCIAL PLANNING

Athletes, because of their talents and wide appeal to the public, can be of great interest to a company wanting to increase its exposure and promote its products. Endorsement contracts are entered into frequently in professional sports; the athlete allows the advertising agency or company to use his or her name and image in product promotional activities. In entering into these endorsement contracts, the player must be careful to understand exactly how his or her name and image will be used. In addition, the professional team and league may have certain restrictions on the use of this athlete in the company's promotional activities (e.g., the athlete could be prohibited from wearing the team's uniform unless an endorsement fee is also paid to the professional league) (see Chapter 9).

In addition, agents and agencies are increasingly offering financial planning and management services to their player clients. An agent is often responsible and must be capable of properly handling and investing the income resulting from the lucrative contracts and endorsement deals negotiated by the agent. If the agent does not have the ability or education necessary to handle the client's finances, it is his/her responsibility to find a person or organization that is capable of properly handling the client's money. Athletes' careers are on average much shorter than that of the average citizen and as a result it is very important for the agent to maximize a client's income while playing and to maximize the potential of that income.

Exhibit 12.8 contains an endorsement contract between a professional athlete and a well-known sporting goods manufacturer.

Exhibit 12.8
An Endorsement Contract between a Professional Athlete and a Well-known Sporting Goods Manufacturer

AGREEMENT

This Agreement, made and entered into this thirteenth day of September 2010, by and between _____ having its principal place of business at

_____, _____
(Company)   (Address)
_____ (hereinafter referred to as "Company"),
and _____ (Player's Company)
(hereinafter referred to as "Enterprises").

WITNESSETH

WHEREAS, Enterprises has the sole and exclusive right to provide the services of _____ (hereinafter referred to as "Athlete") and to license the
(Player)
name _____ for the purposes of this Agreement as hereinafter set forth; and

WHEREAS, Athlete is recognized and widely known throughout the world as an expert basketball player; and

WHEREAS, Athlete's name by virtue of his ability and extensive experience, has acquired secondary meaning in the mind of the purchasing public important to the advertisement, promotion, and sale of Endorsed Product as defined in Paragraph One (1)(d) below and

Exhibit 12.8
(continued)

WHEREAS, Company is engaged in the manufacture, distribution, and sale of Endorsed Products and is desirous of acquiring the exclusive right to utilize Athlete's Endorsement (as defined in paragraph One (1) (a) below) and services in connection with the sale, advertisement, and promotion of Endorsed Products:

NOW THEREFORE, in consideration of the mutual covenants as set forth herein and for other good and valuable consideration, it is agreed as follows:

1. <u>Definitions.</u> As used herein, the terms set forth below shall be defined as follows:

   a. "Athlete's Endorsement" shall include only the right to use the name, nickname, likeness, photograph, signature, initials, statements, facsimile, and endorsement of Athlete;

   b. "Contract Territory" shall mean the world;

   c. "Contract Year" shall mean the twelve (12) month period commencing on each thirteenth day of September during the Term of the Agreement;

   d. "Endorsed Products" shall mean any athletic footwear, athletic apparel, caps, visors, and athletic bags as may now or hereinafter be manufactured, distributed, marketed, licensed, and/or sold by Company or on Company's behalf.

2. <u>Term of Agreement.</u> The Term of this Agreement shall commence September 13, 2010, and shall continue until September 12, 2014.

3. <u>Commercial Materials.</u> In connection with this Agreement "Commercial Materials" shall mean those materials produced pursuant to Paragraphs Six (6) and Fifteen (15) hereof, including, without limitation, radio and television commercials, video tapes, audio tapes, still photographs (including those lifted from television commercials or video tapes), billboards, all forms of print advertising, point-of-purchase materials, posters, product packaging, hang tags, the name(s) of products(s), all collateral materials, Company's Annual Report, materials produced for promotional purposes, materials used for trade contests, trade publications, and all internal and/or external sales and marketing pieces.

4. <u>Grant of Endorsement Rights.</u> Subject to the terms and conditions hereinafter set forth. Enterprises hereby grants to Company the exclusive right and license, within the Contract Territory and during the Term, to utilize the Athlete's Endorsement in connection with the advertisement, promotion, and sale of Endorsed Products.

5. <u>Retention of Endorsement Rights.</u> Subject to the provisions of Paragraph Four (4) above, Company agrees that Enterprises shall retain all rights in and to Athlete's name and endorsement and, whether during the Term or any extension thereof, Enterprises shall not be prevented from using, or permitting and licensing other to use. Athlete's name or endorsement in connection with the advertisement, promotion, or sale of any product or service other than the type of products included in the definition of Endorsed Products within the

Exhibit 12.8
(continued)

Contract Territory. However, Enterprises agrees that Athlete will not endorse any non-athletic footwear or apparel products, which are sold under the trademark or trade name of a competitive manufacturer of performance athletic footwear. Enterprises agrees that it shall consult with Company prior to the grant of the Athlete's Endorsement to any other Company, showing due regard for Company's considerations. Company, however, shall have no specific right of approval over Enterprise's other endorsement opportunities.

Company further agrees that upon the expiration or other termination of this Agreement, for any cause whatsoever, it will immediately cease using the Athlete's Endorsement, the Athlete's name, or any facsimile thereof for advertising, promotional, or any other purpose whatsoever, except pursuant to the following paragraph.

However, Enterprises agrees that the Company shall have the right, for a period not to exceed ninety (90) days following the date of the expiration or earlier termination of this Agreement, to continue to sell and distribute all printed promotional materials and, in the event Enterprises has materially breached this Agreement and Company has purchased media time, broadcast materials featuring Athlete which have been produced by or for the Company and are in inventory prior to the date of such termination ("closing inventory").

6. Use and Ownership of Commercial Materials.

A. Commercials. During the Term of this Agreement, company shall have the exclusive right to broadcast, use, and reuse the television and radio commercial(s) and video and audio materials produced hereunder in the Contract Territory and in any and all media.

B. Print Commercial Materials. During the Term of this Agreement, Company shall have the right to use the Athlete's Endorsement, the Commercial Materials, or any part thereof in print for publication and display in the Contract Territory as Company, subject to the reasonable approval by Enterprises and its business representative, may determine, including all forms of print advertising, cooperative advertising, retail tie-in promotions, point-of-purchase materials, product(s), name(s), billboards, posters, Company's Annual Report, materials produced for promotional purposes, internal and/or external sales and marketing pieces, trade contests, trade publications, hang tags and generally to Company's employees and shareholders.

7. Protecting Athlete's Endorsement. Company agrees that it will take all necessary reasonable steps during the Term and any extension thereof to protect Athlete's Endorsement, the Athlete's name or any facsimile thereof, in connection with the promotion, advertisement, and sale of Endorsed Products.

8. Technical Features. Company acknowledges that for Athlete to successfully compete on a championship level in professional basketball, his shoes may have to incorporate certain technical features that he requires. In this connection, company agrees to consult with Enterprises, its business representatives, Athlete and/or technical advisor of Enterprises' choice, to make any modifications to the particular model of Company product, which he will wear, in competitive play. Enterprises agrees that Athlete and his business representatives and/or technical advisor will cooperate with Company

Exhibit 12.8
(continued)

with respect to design and technical features in order to facilitate and maximize the working relationship between Company and Enterprises. Enterprises further acknowledges the possibility that such modifications may be accomplished through the use of custom designed orthotic insert devices. Company agrees to furnish Enterprises, its business representatives, and/or technical advisor, for their inspection and review, samples of the model of Company shoes Athlete selects to wear in competitive play. Enterprises, its business representatives, and/or technical advisor agree to promptly notify Company of their evaluation of such sample model Endorsed Product submitted to them for review and Company shall use its genuine best efforts to incorporate Enterprises' its business representatives, Athlete's and/or technical advisor's recommendations and suggestions into the final design of said shoes.

9. <u>Direction and Control.</u> Athlete's services, pursuant to the terms and conditions of this Agreement, may be on-camera or off-camera, as Company may select and shall be rendered under Company's direction and control at such times and locations as shall be designated by Company, subject to reasonable prior notice to Enterprises and subject to Athlete's then existing professional commitments. The commercials to be produced hereunder may be taped, filmed, or recorded in such a manner as Company may determine.

10. <u>Premier Spokesman.</u> The parties mutually agree that one of the major inducements for Enterprises to enter into this long-term contract is Company's assurance that Athlete will be advertised and promoted as one of its premier "flagships" in basketball, particularly professional basketball, for as long as he continues to be an All-Star Player. In this connection, Company agrees to utilize Athlete during the Term as one of its spokesmen and ambassadors in the advertising, promotion and sale of Company's basketball products and basketball related products, particularly the articles of Company product contained in the Endorsed Products. In achieving this goal and business purpose, Company agrees to consult with Enterprises and its business representatives, _____, regarding advertising and promotional campaigns and strategy featuring Athlete.

11. <u>Marketing Commitment.</u> The parties acknowledge that the successful introduction to the public and continued profitability of the Company's basketball products and the overall Company-Enterprises relationship mandates an aggressive marketing commitment by Company. It is the specific intent and understanding of the parties that Company will aggressively advertise and promote its relationship with Enterprises and the sale of the Endorsed Products in a manner consistent with Paragraph Six (6) of this Agreement in order to maximize the sales of endorsed products.

12. <u>Use of Endorsed Products.</u> Athlete warrants and represents that he is a user of the Endorsed Products and that, during the Term of this Agreement, he shall continue to use the Endorsed Products exclusively. Enterprises further warrants and represents that all personal endorsements or representations made by or attributed to Athlete with his consent in the Commercial Materials produced hereunder are true and accurate.

Exhibit 12.8
(continued)

13. <u>Athlete to Use Endorsed Products.</u> Enterprises agrees that during the Term and within the Contract Territory Athlete will exclusively wear Company athletic shoes and Company athletic apparel whenever he is playing competitive basketball, posing for basketball photographs, conducting basketball-related promotional interviews, or is otherwise engaged in basketball and athletic-related promotional activities, and shall not wear the athletic shoes and, where appropriate, the athletic apparel of a company competitive with Company.

14. <u>Endorsed Products for Athlete's Use.</u> During the Term, Company shall supply Enterprises, at no charge, with such quantities of Endorsed Products as Athlete may reasonably request for his own personal use and for personal use of his immediate family. In addition, company agrees to supply Enterprises at no charge such quantities of Endorsed Products as Athlete may reasonably request for gifts to others, up to an aggregate wholesale value of Four Thousand U.S. Dollars ($4,000) during each Contract Year.

15. <u>Athlete to Be Available to Company.</u>

   a. If requested by Company, Enterprises agrees to make Athlete available for up to twenty (20) days in each Contract Year, at times and places as designated by the Company, subject to reasonable prior notice to Enterprises and subject to Athlete's then-existing professional commitments, to make personal appearances, pose for photographs, and otherwise assist Company in the preparation of advertising and promotional materials utilizing the Athlete Endorsement; provided, however, that such appearances shall include the production of radio and television commercials. Company and Enterprises agree that the Athlete's obligations for the aforementioned twenty (20) days shall be allocated as follows:

      (i) Up to five (5) consecutive days may take place outside of the United States;

      (ii) Up to nine (9) days may be spent producing television and radio commercials, posing for photographs, and making elite level corporate appearances: and

      (iii) Up to six (6) days may be spent making personal appearances within the United States.

      Each such "day" as used herein, shall be defined as consisting of no more than eight (8) hours per appearance, excluding travel time, for the production of radio and/or television commercials, and no more than four (4) hours excluding travel time, for photography sessions or personal appearances.

   b. Company agrees to reimburse Enterprises for first class, round-trip travel as well as all other reasonable travel, hotel, meals, and expenses incurred by Athlete in connection with such appearances on behalf of the Company. On all appearances, Athlete shall be accompanied by a representative of either Company or Enterprise at Company's expense.

**Exhibit 12.8
(continued)**

16. <u>Optional Appearances.</u> "Optional Appearance" shall mean any appearance by Athlete requested by Company in excess of the twenty (20) appearances per Contract Year, as set forth in Paragraph Fifteen (15) above. For each Optional Appearance, Enterprises shall receive a mutually agreeable fee, payable within ten (10) days following each Optional Appearance. No appearance by Athlete shall be deemed an Optional Appearance unless made upon the prior written request of the Company.

17. <u>Approval of Advertising and Promotional Materials.</u> Company agrees to submit to Enterprises and its business representative _____ for their approval, a copy of all advertising and/or promotional materials utilizing the Athlete's Endorsement at least five (5) working days prior to their release to the general public; and Company further agrees that the same shall not be released without prior written approval of Enterprises or its business representatives. Enterprises and its business representatives agree however, that they shall not unreasonably withhold or delay their approval of said materials and that in the absence of disapproval within five (5) working days of receipt thereof, said advertising and promotional materials shall be deemed approved. Enterprises further agrees that once said materials are deemed approved, Company shall have the right to make multiple uses of said materials without submitting to Enterprises and its business representatives for approval of every such use.

18. <u>Annual Compensation.</u> In consideration for the rights and benefits granted to Company pursuant to this Agreement, Company agrees to pay Enterprises the following amounts as Annual Compensation in each Contract Year

	Contract Year	Annual Compensation
First	September 13, 2010 through	$300,000
	September 12, 2011	(Three Hundred Thousand U.S. Dollars)
Second	September 13, 2011 through	$300,000
	September 12, 2012	(Three Hundred Thousand U.S. Dollars)
Third	September 13, 2012 through	$300,000
	September 12, 2013	(Three Hundred Thousand U.S. Dollars)
Fourth	September 13, 2013 through	$300,000
	September 12, 2014	(Three Hundred Thousand U.S. Dollars)

The annual compensation due and owing Enterprises by Company in each Contract Year shall be paid quarterly on or before January 1, April 1, July 1, and October 1 of each Contract Year except that the initial quarterly payment hereunder shall be made on the first business day of January 2011 (i.e. Enterprises Compensation for the first quarter shall cover the period commencing September 13, 2010 and ending December 31, 2010) and except that the final payment due hereunder shall be made on September 12, 2014, in lieu of the first business day of October 2014 in the amount of a full quarterly payment.

Exhibit 12.8
(continued)

If Company decides, in its sole discretion, to manufacture and market Endorsed Products which bear the name, nickname, likeness and/or initials of Athlete directly on the Product, or by means of decals or labels, or on packaging therefore (such as Endorsed Products to be known as "Signature Products") at any time during the Term, Company agrees to pay Enterprises Royalty Compensation on the net sales of all such Signature Products in an amount to be mutually agreed upon by Company and Enterprises. Such Royalty Compensation shall be deemed to be full consideration for the use by Company of all trademarks owned and registered by Enterprises.

19. Bonus Compensation. In addition to all other Compensation provided for herein, Company agrees to pay Enterprises the following Bonus Compensation in the applicable Bonus Years (as defined below) if the total amount of sales revenues, less returns, accrued by Company from the sale of (i) Company brand men's basketball shoes (as designated in (Company's) product line catalogues, but not including children's basketball shoes); and (ii) fifty percent (50%) of the sales revenues, less returns, of _____ brand women's performance basketball shoes during the applicable Bonus Year equals or exceeds the amounts set forth in the table below, within thirty (30) days of the end of each Bonus Year:

Total Amount of Sales Revenues, Less Returns Accrued by Company from Sale of Products Defined in Paragraph Nineteen (19)	Amount of Bonus For Bonus Years One and Two	Amount of Bonus For Bonus Years Three and Four
$250,000,000 through $349,999,999	$100,000	$150,000
$350,000,000 through $499,999,999	$250,000	$250,000
$500,000,000 and above	$500,000	$500,000

For the purposes of this section only, the First Bonus Year shall begin on March 1, 2011 and continue through February 28, 2012; the Second Bonus Year shall begin on March 1, 2012 and continue through February 28, 2013; the Third Bonus Year shall begin on March 1, 2013 and continue through February 28, 2014; and the Fourth Bonus Year shall begin on March 1, 2014 and continue through February 28, 2015.

20. Reductions.

   a. Company shall have the right to reduce the amount of the Annual Compensation payable to Enterprises in accordance with Paragraph Eighteen (18) hereof in the event Athlete plays in fewer than Seventy-six (76) official NBA regular season games during each Contract Year by an amount equal to Three Thousand Three Hundred Thirty-Three U.S. Dollars ($3,333) for each game missed below Seventy-six (76) games.

   b. Company shall have the right to reduce the amount of Bonus Compensation payable to Enterprises in accordance with Paragraph Nineteen (19)

Exhibit 12.8
(continued)

hereof, in the event Athlete plays in fewer than Fifty (50) official NBA regular season games during any Contract Year, by an amount equal to Fifty Percent (50%) of the Bonus Compensation otherwise payable to Enterprises in such Contract Year. In this connection, it is agreed that each Bonus Year, as described in Paragraph Nineteen (19) above, shall correspond to same ordinal Contract Year, as defined in paragraph 1c. above. For example, the First Bonus Year shall correspond to the First Contract Year.

21. <u>Active Basketball Professional.</u> During the Term of this Agreement, Athlete shall remain active as a National Basketball Association ("NBA") professional basketball player. Company shall have the right, by written notice to Enterprises, to terminate this Agreement and to be relieved of all its obligations hereunder, including without limitation, its obligation to pay any compensation to Enterprises, if for any reason during the Term of this Agreement, Athlete fails to be on either the active or injured reserve list of any NBA Team.

22. <u>Payments to Enterprises.</u> All payments to be made to Enterprises pursuant to this Agreement shall be made by check in U.S. Dollars and made payable to and mailed to it.

23. <u>Time Is of the Essence.</u>

    a. Company acknowledges that time is of the essence in the payment of all compensation due Enterprises and Enterprises acknowledges that time is of the essence in the performance of his obligations. Company hereby agrees that in the event any payment due Enterprises is not received by Enterprises or its business representatives within thirty (30) days of the date set forth in this Agreement for such payment that, in the event written notice has been proved to Company and Company has failed to cure such nonpayment in five (5) days. Enterprises shall be paid interest at the rate of two percent (2%) per month or the maximum interest rate permitted by U.S. law, whichever is less, on the total balance due and owing Enterprises, calculated from the actual payment date set forth herein. In addition, Enterprises shall also have the right and option to terminate this Agreement, effective upon the expiration of thirty (30) days following written notice to Company of his election to so terminate for failure of Company to perform in accordance with the provisions hereof, unless such payment has been received by Enterprises or its business representatives within such thirty (30) day period. The reservation of specific rights by Enterprises herein shall not preclude Athlete from exercising any other remedy it may have at law or in equity to enforce the terms of this Agreement.

    b. Enterprises hereby agrees that if Athlete should fail to appear for the filming of a previously scheduled television commercial without providing Company at least one (1) day's prior notice of his inability to appear, and his failure to appear was not due to a strike, boycott, war, act of God, labor troubles, rift, delay of commercial carriers, restraint of public authority, or for any other reason, similar or dissimilar, he shall reimburse Company for an amount equal to twenty-five percent (25%) of Company's out-of-pocket

Exhibit 12.8
(continued)

production costs, for said commercial, not to exceed Seventy-five Thousand U.S. Dollars ($75,000).

24. <u>Insurance.</u> Company shall have the unrestricted right to obtain disability, life and any other types of insurance policies covering Athlete if Company, in its sole discretion, so chooses, and Enterprises agrees that Company or its designee shall be the beneficiaries of such policies. Promptly following Enterprise's execution of this Agreement, Enterprises agrees that Athlete shall submit to physical examinations, undertake any reasonable actions, and execute all documents required to assist Company in obtaining such insurance.

25. <u>Special Right of Termination by Enterprises.</u> Enterprises shall have the right to terminate this Agreement upon thirty (30) days prior written notice to Company in the event of the occurrence of any of the following:

   a. If Company is adjudicated as insolvent, declares bankruptcy, or fails to continue its business of selling Endorsed Products; or

   b. If Company fails to make payment to Enterprises of any sums pursuant to this Agreement within the thirty (30) days following the receipt by Company of written notice from Enterprises that such payment is past due.

26. <u>Special Right of Termination by Company.</u> Enterprises agrees that Company shall have the right to terminate this Agreement upon written notice to Enterprises:

   a. In the event of Athlete's death during the Term; or

   b. In the event Athlete is convicted of a felony or any other crime involving moral turpitude; or

   c. In the event Athlete is permanently disabled; or

   d. In the event the commercial value of Athlete is substantially impaired by reason of the commission by Athlete of any act or acts.

27. <u>Breach.</u>

   a. <u>By Enterprises:</u> If Enterprises or Athlete at any time commits a material breach of any provision of this Agreement or at any time Enterprises or Athlete fails or refuses to fulfill his obligations hereunder, and fails to remedy the same within thirty (30) days after having received such notice, then Company may, by written notice to Enterprises specifying the default or breach by Enterprises or Athlete, terminate this Agreement forthwith. In the event this Agreement is terminated prior to the expiration of the Term of the Agreement, the Company's sole obligation shall be to pay to Enterprises the compensation that may be due to Enterprises as of the date of termination. Company shall have no further obligation or liability to Enterprises except as to any amount due as a result of the use or reuse of any commercial(s) broadcast pursuant to this Agreement.

   b. <u>By Company:</u> In the Event Company fails to make any payment due pursuant to Paragraphs Eighteen (18) and Nineteen (19) hereof within

Exhibit 12.8
(continued)

thirty (30) days after having received written notice from Enterprises of Enterprises' representative and fails to remedy the same within thirty (30) days after having received such notice, or Company at any time commits a material breach of this Agreement, and fails to remedy the same within thirty (30) days after having received notice from Enterprises specifying the breach, then Enterprises may, in addition to all other remedies available to it in law or equity, terminate this Agreement by written notice to Company specifying the default or breach by Company.

28. <u>Right of First Negotiation.</u> During the Term of this Agreement and for a period of thirty (30) days following the expiration or earlier termination of this Agreement, Enterprises shall negotiate in good faith only with Company and not with any third party or entity concerning Athlete's endorsement of any products which are the same as or similar to or otherwise compete with the Athlete's Endorsed Products. If, at the end of such thirty (30) day period, Enterprises and Company are unable to reach an agreement concerning Athlete's endorsement of the Endorsed Products, Company shall submit to Enterprises, in writing, its last best offer for a new contract. Enterprises shall then be free to negotiate a new contract with any company of its choice. However, Enterprises agrees that Company shall have the right of first refusal to match any offer from a new company which is one hundred twenty-five percent (125%) or less the total guaranteed compensation set forth in Company's last best written offer.

29. <u>No Disparagement.</u> Enterprises agrees that at no time during and after the Term of this Agreement shall Athlete disparage his association with the Company, its product, employees, advertising agencies or other connected with the Company. The provisions of this paragraph shall survive any termination of this Agreement.

30. <u>Trademarks.</u> In the event that Enterprises should desire to obtain at any time during the Term a trademark or trademarks in any part of the Contract Territory which include any part or all of the Athlete's Endorsement, Company, if so requested by Enterprises, shall execute any and all documents which Enterprises reasonably believes to be necessary and/or desirable for successful registration and protection of such trademark or trademarks registered in the name of Enterprises. Upon use of such trademark, if requested by Company, Enterprises agrees to grant Company a license for the exclusive use of such trademark during the Term in connection with the manufacture, advertisement, promotion, distribution, and sale of Endorsed Products which licensee shall be coextensive and coterminous with the endorsement rights granted pursuant to this Agreement with respect tot he Athlete Endorsement. Said licensee shall not require any increase in the Compensation payable to Enterprises hereunder, but shall contain any additional provisions, not inconsistent herewith, which Enterprises reasonably believes are necessary for the protection of such trademark registered in the name of Enterprises. However, it is understood that Enterprises shall acquire no interest whatsoever in the Company trade name.

Exhibit 12.8
(continued)

31. <u>Warranties.</u> Company and Enterprises warrant that they are free to enter into this Agreement and that the rights granted hereunder will not infringe upon the rights of any third party. Enterprises' execution, delivery, and performance of this Agreement shall not violate the rights of any third party or breach any agreement in which Enterprises is a party.

32. <u>Indemnity.</u>

    a. Company agrees to protect, indemnify, and save harmless Enterprises and/or Athlete from and against any and all expenses, damages, claims, suits, actions, judgments, and costs whatsoever, including attorney's fees, arising out of, or in any way connected with, any claim or action including but not limited to personal injury or death resulting from the advertisement, manufacture, distribution, sale or use of any Endorsed Products. The provisions of this paragraph shall survive any termination of this Agreement or any act or omission of Company.

    b. Enterprises and/or Athlete shall at all times indemnify and hold harmless Company and its officers and directors from and against any and all claims, damages, liabilities, costs and expenses, including reasonable attorney's fees, arising out of or related to any breach or alleged breach by Enterprises of any representation, warranty or agreement made by Enterprises herein or any act or omission of Enterprises.

33. <u>Force Majeure.</u> If, for any reason, such as strike, boycott, war, act of God, labor troubles, riot, delay of commercial carriers, restraint of public authority or for any other reason, similar or dissimilar, beyond Company's control, Company shall be unable to use and/or reuse the Commercial Materials or the services of Athlete for any period of time during the Term of this Agreement, then Company shall have the right to extend the Term of this Agreement for an equivalent period thereof, without additional Compensation to Enterprises.

34. <u>Assignment.</u> Neither Enterprises nor Company shall have the right to grant sublicenses hereunder or to otherwise assign, alienate, transfer, encumber, or hypothecate any of its rights or obligations hereunder, except that Enterprises shall have the right to assign the financial benefits hereof and Company hereby consents to such assignment upon receipt by Company of written notice thereof from Enterprises or its business representative.

35. <u>Waiver.</u> The failure of Company and Enterprises at any time to demand strict performance by the other of any of the terms, covenants, or conditions set forth herein shall not be construed as a continuing waiver or relinquishment thereof, and either party may, at any time, demand strict and complete performance by the other of said terms, covenants, and conditions.

36. <u>Employer/Employee Relationship.</u> Enterprises' and/or Athlete's relationship with Company shall be that of an independent contractor, and nothing contained in this Agreement shall be construed as establishing an employer/employee relationship, partnership, or joint venture between Company and Enterprises and/or Athlete. Accordingly, there shall be no

Exhibit 12.8
(continued)

withholding for tax purposes from any payment by Company to Enterprises herein.

37. <u>Notices.</u> All notices and/or submissions hereunder shall be sent via Certified Mail. Return Receipt Requested, to the parties at the following addresses, or such other addresses as may be designated in writing from time to time:

      Company

      Enterprises

Notices shall be deemed given upon deposit of same with the postal authority.

38. <u>Terms of Agreement Confidential.</u> It is hereby agreed that the specific terms and conditions of this Agreement, including, but not limited to, the financial terms and the duration, are strictly confidential, and shall not be divulged to any third parties without the prior written consent of both Company and Enterprises, unless otherwise required by law.

39. <u>Significance of Paragraph Headings.</u> Paragraph headings contained hereunder are solely for the purposes of aiding in speedy location of subject matter and are not in any sense to be given weight in the construction of this Agreement. Accordingly, in case of any question with respect to the construction of this Agreement, it is to be construed as though paragraph headings had been omitted.

40. <u>Governing Law.</u> This Agreement shall be governed by and construed in accordance with the laws of the Commonwealth of Massachusetts regardless of the fact that any of the parties hereto may be or may become a resident of a different state or jurisdiction. Any suit or action arising shall be filed in a court of competent jurisdiction within the Commonwealth of Massachusetts.

The parties hereby consent to the personal jurisdiction of said court within the Commonwealth of Massachusetts.

41. <u>Severability.</u> If any provision of this Agreement or the application thereof shall be invalid or unenforceable to any extent, the remainder of this Agreement or the application thereof shall not be affected, and each remaining provision of this Agreement shall be valid and enforceable to the fullest extent permitted by law.

42. <u>Service Unique.</u> The parties hereto agree that the services to be performed by Athlete and the rights granted to Company hereunder are special, unique, extraordinary, and impossible to replace, which gives them a peculiar value, the loss of which could not reasonably or adequately be compensated in damages in an action at law, and that Athlete's failure or refusal to perform obligations hereunder would cause irreparable loss and damage. Should Athlete fail or refuse to perform such obligations Company shall be entitled, in addition to any other legal remedies Company may have, to <u>ex parte</u> injunctive or other equitable relief against Enterprises to prevent the continuance of such failure or refusal or to prevent Athlete from performing services for, or granting rights to other in violation of this Agreement, and Company's exercise of such right shall not constitute a waiver or any other additional

Exhibit 12.8
(continued)

rights at law or pursuant to the terms of this Agreement, it being understood that all such remedies shall be cumulative.

43. <u>Union Membership.</u> Enterprises warrants and represents that Athlete is, and will remain during the Term of this Agreement, a member in good standing of all unions, guilds, or other organizations having jurisdiction over Athlete's services as rendered under this Agreement. In the event Company is assessed or incurs any expense, including without limitation, any fine or penalty, as a result of Athlete's failure to remain a member in good standing or otherwise comply with the regulations governing members of such union, guild, or other organization, then Enterprise shall immediately pay to such union, guild or other organization any such expense, fine, or penalty assessed against Company as a result thereof, and if Company actually incurs and pays any such expenses, fine, or penalty, Enterprises will reimburse Company the full amount of any such expense, fine, or penalty, including attorneys' fees incurred or paid by Company.

44. <u>Entire Agreement.</u> This Agreement constitutes the entire understanding between Company and Enterprises and cannot be altered or modified except by an agreement in writing signed by both Company and Enterprises. Upon its execution, this Agreement shall supercede all prior negotiations, understandings, and agreements, whether oral or written, and such prior agreements shall thereupon be null and void and without further legal effect.

IN WITNESS WHEREOF, the parties hereto have caused this Agreement to be executed as of the date first above written.

ACCEPTED AND AGREED:

_____   _____
(Company)   (Player)

_____   _____
(Date)   (Date)

ASSENT AND GUARANTEE

In order to induce _____ ("Company") to enter into the Agreement dated September 13, 2010 between Company and _____ ("Athlete"), by his signature below, hereby assents to the execution of the Agreement and agrees to be bound by the terms and conditions thereof relating to the Athlete. Athlete acknowledges, warrants and represents that he has read and understands the Agreement, that he is free to perform the provisions on his part to be performed pursuant thereto, that he shall comply with all of the provisions thereof which refer to him and that he shall not enter into commitments in conflict therewith. Athlete represents that all warranties and representations made by which concern him are true and that he will fully perform all of obligations under the Agreement. Further, Athlete personally guarantees that he will perform all of the terms and conditions of the Agreement on its part to be performed. Finally,

**Exhibit 12.8
(continued)**

Company shall be under no obligation to make any payments whatsoever to Athlete in connection with the services and materials to be provided and/or rendered by Athlete pursuant to the Agreement, except as may be specifically provided in said Agreement.

Date _____

(Athlete)

12.9. INDIVIDUAL PERFORMER SPORTS

Tennis, golf, boxing, track, horse and auto racing, and other sports in which the athlete largely competes as an individual rather than on a team or in a league present far different issues than those which have been considered to this point. A few of the important considerations will be raised here, but a comprehensive review is not provided.

The compensation method and the contracts are much different for individual sports. For example, athletes in individual performer sports do not enjoy the security of a standard player contract or NLRB-recognized collective bargaining (see Chapters 9 and 11). Hence, individual sport organizations do not unilaterally implement a drug policy or code of conduct, or take other legal actions that affect wages, hours, and terms and conditions of employment. In tennis, golf, and cycling, there are players associations or informal unions—perhaps not unions in the full sense, as in team sports, but important in terms of giving their blessings to certain activities, including the types of contracts tendered to players. Thus, when it comes to tournaments and races, the sponsor-athlete obligation assumes great uniformity as to many of the terms.

Endorsement contracts are staples in individual performer sports. These are not discussed here, except to note their prevalence and importance. But they are analogous with league player endorsements.

Finally, for many of the individual performer sports, there are clubs or resorts that wish to have a player's name associated with the facility. Any number of deals are possible, ranging from straight money payments to trade-outs and other enticements.

12.10. FOREIGN LEAGUES

As sports become more international, there are an increasing number, although still relatively small in total, of opportunities for U.S. athletes to play professionally in foreign countries. In football, since the folding of NFL Europe in 2007, there is only the Canadian Football League. For baseball players, Japan, Mexico, and the Far East offer opportunities, generally for marginal Major Leaguers. In basketball and hockey, leagues exist around the world, with the quality of play varying substantially from country to country, and usually below the quality of the United States. This discussion focuses on the Big Four professional team sports. However, one clear exception to this rule is the sport of soccer, where elite U.S. players can make substantially more money by playing abroad against better competition.

Many foreign professional leagues limit the number of noncitizens who can play on any one team. This makes the scramble for spots by U.S. players an intense one, particularly in the better leagues. For example, the Italian basketball league is considered the strongest outside the United States, and top U.S. players can be paid well, even though the league is classified as amateur under international rules. Each Italian team is severely limited as to how many foreign players can make the squad. It takes a top U.S. player, one just below the NBA level, to secure a contract, unless the player can claim Italian citizenship and not count against a team's foreign player quota.

In March 1997, the National Basketball Association and FIBA (Fédération Internationale de Basketball), the international governing body for the sport, reached an agreement to use an independent arbitrator when disputes arise over the transfer of players to and from international teams and the National Basketball Association. The agreement also provides for arbitration for a number of other disputes that could arise in international basketball. The NBA did not wait long to test this new arbitration method, with the Toronto Raptors and Phoenix Suns seeking the services of European athletes who, they contended, were playing abroad under invalid contracts (see notes 1 and 2). The FIBA arbitration system has proven to be very beneficial for handling these types of disputes.

NOTES

1. In *Lincoln Hockey Ltd. Liability Co. v. Semin*, 2005 WL 3294008 (D.D.C. 2005), the Washington Capitals filed for a preliminary injunction against Alexander Semin. In 2002 the Washington Capitals drafted Alexander Semin with the 13th overall pick. Semin, a Russian citizen subsequently agreed to a three-year contract starting in the 2003–2004 season. Semin played the first year of the contract without incident, but when the NHL and NHLPA could not reach an agreement on a new CBA before the start of the 2004–2005 season, Semin was assigned to the Capitals' minor league team, the Portland Pirates, as they had authority to do. Semin instead traveled to Russia to play for a private, commercial team known as Lada Togliatta. In September 2004, the Capitals began fining Semin $1,000 a day for his failure to report to Portland, but Semin said that as he was preparing to report to Portland he had been conscripted in the Russian military. Semin said he negotiated a deal whereby he could perform his military service by playing for Lada Togliatta, a private Russian hockey team. When the lockout ended, the Capitals requested that Semin return for the start of training camp in September. Semin contended that he had one more year of requisite military service and resumed playing for Lada Togliatta. The Capitals' injunction was denied because the NHL collective bargaining agreement stipulated that the dispute should be arbitrated and that Semin had a potentially valid impossibility defense based upon his Russian military conscription. In April 2006, Semin agreed to a two-year deal with the Capitals and returned for the 2006–2007 season and was 13th in the league in goals scored with 38.

2. In *ANO Hockey Club Metallurg Magnitogorsk v. Malkin*, No. 10221 (S.D.N.Y. January 29, 2007), the Metallurg Magnitogorsk, a hockey team in the Russian Super League sued the NHL, the Pittsburgh Penguins, and Evgeni Malkin to enforce an arbitration ruling by the Russian Ice Hockey Federation banning Malkin from playing anywhere but for Metallurg. Metallurg also alleged intentional interference with contractual relations and antitrust violations. The Penguins drafted Malkin in June 2004 with the second overall pick in the NHL entry draft. Malkin had just finished his first season playing for Metallurg Magnitogorsk in the Russian Super League. Metallurg refused

a $200,000 transfer payment that would have allowed Malkin to join the Penguins in 2005–206. Instead Malkin signed a deal that would have kept him in Russia through the 2006–2007 season, allegedly under duress. In August 2006, when Metallurg began training camp in Helsinki, Finland, Malkin disappeared, apparently heading for Canada and ultimately Pittsburgh. Although Malkin had a contract with Metallurg, Russian law allows any employee to leave a job so long as they give two weeks' written notice, even if under contract. While in hiding, Malkin filed the requisite letter of resignation with Metallurg. Malkin reappeared about a week later and soon thereafter signed a three-year deal worth up to $3.8 million per year with the Penguins. The Southern District of New York denied Metallurg's request for an injunction and the entire lawsuit was dismissed in January 2007. Malkin won the Calder Trophy as the NHL Rookie of the Year in 2006–2007 with 33 goals and 52 assists.

3. In the *Matter of Arbitration Between Phoenix Suns and Athletic Union of Constantinople* (1997), the Phoenix Suns sought the services of a basketball player, Iakovos "Jake" Tsakalidis, who was under contract to play for the Greek professional team AEK through the 2000 season. Phoenix argued that the contract was null and void for various reasons, and that Tsakalidis should be allowed to exit his contract without penalty to play in the NBA. In arbitration, the claimant Suns were successful. The arbitrator ruled that the contract was invalid under Greek law because the "penalty clause" within the contract was illegally severe and was an excessive curtailment of Tsakalidis's freedom to pursue his basketball career. The Suns were therefore able to sign Tsakalidis because the Greek contract had been nullified. AEK subsequently challenged the arbitrator's decision in an English court, but the court upheld the arbitrator's decision to allow Tsakalidis out of his contract.

4. In the *Matter of Arbitration Between Toronto Raptors and Budocnost* (1997), the Toronto Raptors, in a case similar to the Tsakalidis case, sought to gain the services of Aleksandar Radojevic, who was under contract to play for Budocnost of the Yugoslavian Basketball League through the 2000–2001 season. The arbitrator decided that Radojevic's contract with Budocnost was not a valid contract because it did not specify the compensation that would be awarded Radojevic for the final three years with the team.

5. In *Behagen v. Amateur Basketball Association*, 884 F.2d 524 (10th Cir. 1989), Ronald Behagen, a former All-American at the University of Kentucky, was not granted a reinstatement of amateur status by the Amateur Basketball Association, the national governing body for amateur basketball in the United States at the time, because he had participated professionally and received compensation for his play in the United States. Due to this lack of reinstatement, Behagen was not able to continue playing basketball in Europe in an amateur league. Behagen settled with FIBA (the international governing body for basketball), but brought a claim of antitrust violations and due process violations against the Amateur Basketball Association. Upon appeal, the court overturned the previous decision and decided for the association on both counts. It said that the actions of the association were not antitrust violations, but that under the Amateur Sports Act, the association had the power to take such actions because it is the sole governing body for a sport within the country. Behagen was not able to prove that the association was a state actor, and therefore was unsuccessful in his lack of due process constitutional claim.

6. In *Ponce v. Basketball Federation*, 760 F.2d 375 (1st Cir. 1985), the federation appealed a district court's decision to grant Ponce an injunction allowing him to continue playing in Puerto Rico despite not achieving the certification requirements of citizenship needed. On appeal, the court decided for the federation, against which Ponce had brought an equal protection claim, claiming his rights had been violated because he was a U.S. citizen, but not from Puerto Rico. The appeals court found that the actions of the federation did not constitute state action, and therefore they could not be held liable for violations of equal protection.

Exhibit 12.9
National Basketball Association Uniform Player Contract

THIS AGREEMENT made this _____ day of _____, is by and between _____ (hereinafter called the "Team"), a member of the National Basketball Association (hereinafter called the "NBA" or "League") and _____, an individual whose address is shown below (hereinafter called the "Player"). In consideration of the mutual promises hereinafter contained, the parties hereto promise and agree as follows:

1. TERM.
The Team hereby employs the Player as a skilled basketball player for a term of _____ year(s) from the 1st day of September _____.

2. SERVICES.
The services to be rendered by the Player pursuant to this Contract shall include:

(a) training camp,

(b) practices, meetings, workouts, and skill or conditioning sessions conducted by the Team during the Season,

(c) games scheduled for the Team during any Regular Season,

(d) Exhibition games scheduled by the Team or the League during and prior to any Regular Season,

(e) if the Player is invited to participate, the NBA's All-Star Game (including the Rookie-Sophomore Game) and every event conducted in association with such All-Star Game, but only in accordance with Article XXI of the Collective Bargaining Agreement currently in effect between the NBA and the National Basketball Players Association (hereinafter the "CBA"),

(f) Playoff games scheduled by the League subsequent to any Regular Season,

(g) promotional and commercial activities of the Team and the League as set forth in this Contract and the CBA, and

(h) any NBADL Work Assignment in accordance with Article XLII of the CBA.

3. COMPENSATION.

(a) Subject to paragraph 3(b) below, the Team agrees to pay the Player for rendering the services and performing the obligations described herein the Compensation described in Exhibit 1 or Exhibit 1A hereto (less all amounts required to be withheld by any governmental authority, and exclusive of any amount(s) which the Player shall be entitled to receive from the Player Playoff Pool). Unless otherwise provided in Exhibit 1, such Compensation shall be paid in twelve (12) equal semi-monthly payments beginning with the first of said payments on November 15th of each year covered by the Contract and continuing with such payments on the first and fifteenth of each month until said Compensation is paid in full.

(b) The Team agrees to pay the Player $1,500 per week, pro rata, less all amounts required to be withheld by any governmental authority, for each week (up to a maximum of four (4) weeks for Veterans and up to a maximum of five (5) weeks for Rookies) prior to the Team's first Regular Season game that the Player is in attendance at training camp or Exhibition games; provided, however, that no

Exhibit 12.9
(continued)

such payments shall be made if, prior to the date on which he is required to attend training camp, the Player has been paid $10,000 or more in Compensation with respect to the NBA Season scheduled to commence immediately following such training camp. Any Compensation paid by the Team pursuant to this subparagraph shall be considered an advance against any Compensation owed to the Player pursuant to paragraph 3(a) above, and the first scheduled payment of such Compensation (or such subsequent payments, if the first scheduled payment is not sufficient) shall be reduced by the amount of such advance.

(c) The Team will not pay and the Player will not accept any bonus or anything of value on account of the Team's winning any particular NBA game or series of games or attaining a certain position in the standings of the League as of a certain date, other than the final standing of the Team.

4. EXPENSES.

The Team agrees to pay all proper and necessary expenses of the Player, including the reasonable lodging expenses of the Player while playing for the Team "on the road" and during the training camp period (defined for this paragraph only to mean the period from the first day of training camp through the day of the Team's first Exhibition game) for as long as the Player is not then living at home. The Player, while "on the road" (and during the training camp period, only if the Player is not then living at home and the Team does not pay for meals directly), shall be paid a meal expense allowance as set forth in the CBA. No deductions from such meal expense allowance shall be made for meals served on an airplane. During the training camp period (and only if the Player is not then living at home and the Team does not pay for meals directly), the meal expense allowance shall be paid in weekly installments commencing with the first week of training camp. For the purposes of this paragraph, the Player shall be considered to be "on the road" from the time the Team leaves its home city until the time the Team arrives back at its home city.

5. CONDUCT.

(a) The Player agrees to observe and comply with all Team rules, as maintained or promulgated in accordance with the CBA, at all times whether on or off the playing floor. Subject to the provisions of the CBA, such rules shall be part of this Contract as fully as if herein written and shall be binding upon the Player.

(b) The Player agrees:

    (i) to give his best services, as well as his loyalty, to the Team, and to play basketball only for the Team and its assignees;

    (ii) to be neatly and fully attired in public;

    (iii) to conduct himself on and off the court according to the highest standards of honesty, citizenship, and sportsmanship; and

    (iv) not to do anything that is materially detrimental or materially prejudicial to the best interests of the Team or the League.

Exhibit 12.9
(continued)

(c) For any violation of Team rules, any breach of any provision of this Contract, or for any conduct impairing the faithful and thorough discharge of the duties incumbent upon the Player, the Team may reasonably impose fines and/or suspensions on the Player in accordance with the terms of the CBA.

(d) The Player agrees to be bound by Article 35 of the NBA Constitution, a copy of which, as in effect on the date of this Contract, is attached hereto. The Player acknowledges that the Commissioner is empowered to impose fines upon and/or suspend the Player for causes and in the manner provided in such Article, provided that such fines and/or suspensions are consistent with the terms of the CBA.

(e) The Player agrees that if the Commissioner, in his sole judgment, shall find that the Player has bet, or has offered or attempted to bet, money or anything of value on the outcome of any game participated in by any team which is a member of the NBA, the Commissioner shall have the power in his sole discretion to suspend the Player indefinitely or to expel him as a player for any member of the NBA, and the Commissioner's finding and decision shall be final, binding, conclusive, and unappealable.

(f) The Player agrees that he will not, during the term of this Contract, directly or indirectly, entice, induce, or persuade, or attempt to entice, induce, or persuade, any player or coach who is under contract to any NBA team to enter into negotiations for or relating to his services as a basketball player or coach, nor shall he negotiate for or contract for such services, except with the prior written consent of such team. Breach of this subparagraph, in addition to the remedies available to the Team, shall be punishable by fine and/or suspension to be imposed by the Commissioner.

(g) When the Player is fined and/or suspended by the Team or the NBA, he shall be given notice in writing (with a copy to the Players Association), stating the amount of the fine or the duration of the suspension and the reasons therefor.

6. WITHHOLDING.

(a) In the event the Player is fined and/or suspended by the Team or the NBA, the Team shall withhold the amount of the fine or, in the case of a suspension, the amount provided in Article VI of the CBA from any Current Base Compensation due or to become due to the Player with respect to the contract year in which the conduct resulting in the fine and/or the suspension occurred (or a subsequent contract year if the Player has received all Current Base Compensation due to him for the then current contract year). If, at the time the Player is fined and/or suspended, the Current Base Compensation remaining to be paid to the Player under this Contract is not sufficient to cover such fine and/or suspension, then the Player agrees promptly to pay the amount directly to the Team. In no case shall the Player permit any such fine and/or suspension to be paid on his behalf by anyone other than himself.

(b) Any Current Base Compensation withheld from or paid by the Player pursuant to this paragraph 6 shall be retained by the Team or the League, as the case may be, unless the Player contests the fine and/or suspension by

Exhibit 12.9
(continued)

initiating a timely Grievance in accordance with the provisions of the CBA. If such Grievance is initiated and it satisfies Article XXXI, Section 13 of the CBA, the amount withheld from the Player shall be placed in an interest-bearing account, pursuant to Article XXXI, Section 9 of such Agreement, pending the resolution of the Grievance.

7. PHYSICAL CONDITION.

(a) The Player agrees to report at the time and place fixed by the Team in good physical condition and to keep himself throughout each NBA Season in good physical condition.

(b) If the Player, in the judgment of the Team's physician, is not in good physical condition at the date of his first scheduled game for the Team, or if, at the beginning of or during any Season, he fails to remain in good physical condition (unless such condition results directly from an injury sustained by the Player as a direct result of participating in any basketball practice or game played for the Team during such Season), so as to render the Player, in the judgment of the Team's physician, unfit to play skilled basketball, the Team shall have the right to suspend such Player until such time as, in the judgment of the Team's physician, the Player is in sufficiently good physical condition to play skilled basketball. In the event of such suspension, the Base Compensation payable to the Player for any Season during such suspension shall be reduced in the same proportion as the length of the period during which, in the judgment of the Team's physician, the Player is unfit to play skilled basketball, bears to the length of such Season. Nothing in this subparagraph shall authorize the Team to suspend the Player solely because the Player is injured or ill.

(c) If, during the term of this Contract, the Player is injured as a direct result of participating in any basketball practice or game played for the Team, the Team will pay the Player's reasonable hospitalization and medical expenses (including doctor's bills), provided that the hospital and doctor are selected by the Team, and provided further that the Team shall be obligated to pay only those expenses incurred as a direct result of medical treatment caused solely by and relating directly to the injury sustained by the Player. Subject to the provisions set forth in Exhibit 3, if in the judgment of the Team's physician, the Player's injuries resulted directly from playing for the Team and render him unfit to play skilled basketball, then, so long as such unfitness continues, but in no event after the Player has received his full Base Compensation for the Season in which the injury was sustained, the Team shall pay to the Player the Base Compensation prescribed in Exhibit 1 to this Contract for such Season. The Team's obligations hereunder shall be reduced by

   (i) any workers' compensation benefits, which, to the extent permitted by law, the Player hereby assigns to the Team, and

   (ii) any insurance provided for by the Team whether paid or payable to the Player.

Exhibit 12.9
(continued)

(d) The Player agrees to provide to the Team's coach, trainer, or physician prompt notice of any injury, illness, or medical condition suffered by him that is likely to affect adversely the Player's ability to render the services required under this Contract, including the time, place, cause, and nature of such injury, illness, or condition.

(e) Should the Player suffer an injury, illness, or medical condition, he will submit himself to a medical examination, appropriate medical treatment by a physician designated by the Team, and such rehabilitation activities as such physician may specify. Such examination when made at the request of the Team shall be at its expense, unless made necessary by some act or conduct of the Player contrary to the terms of this Contract.

(f) The Player agrees

   (i) to submit to a physical examination at the commencement and conclusion of each Contract year hereunder, and at such other times as reasonably determined by the Team to be medically necessary, and

   (ii) at the commencement of this Contract, and upon the request of the Team, to provide a complete prior medical history.

(g) The Player agrees to supply complete and truthful information in connection with any medical examinations or requests for medical information authorized by this Contract.

(h) A Player who consults a physician other than a physician designated by the Team shall give notice of such consultation to the Team and shall authorize and direct such other physician to provide the Team with all information it may request concerning any condition that in the judgment of the Team's physician may affect the Player's ability to play skilled basketball.

(i) If and to the extent necessary to enable or facilitate the disclosure of medical information as provided for by this Contract or Article XXII of the CBA, the Player shall execute such individual authorization(s) as may be requested by the Team or as may be required by health care providers who examine or treat the Player.

8. PROHIBITED SUBSTANCES.

The Player acknowledges that this Contract may be terminated in accordance with the express provisions of Article XXXIII (Anti-Drug Program) of the CBA, and that any such termination will result in the Player's immediate dismissal and disqualification from any employment by the NBA and any of its teams. Notwithstanding any terms or provisions of this Contract (including any amendments hereto), in the event of such termination, all obligations of the Team, including obligations to pay Compensation, shall cease, except the obligation of the Team to pay the Player's earned Compensation (whether Current or Deferred) to the date of termination.

9. UNIQUE SKILLS.

The Player represents and agrees that he has extraordinary and unique skill and ability as a basketball player, that the services to be rendered by him hereunder

Exhibit 12.9
(continued)

cannot be replaced or the loss thereof adequately compensated for in money damages, and that any breach by the Player of this Contract will cause irreparable injury to the Team, and to its assignees. Therefore, it is agreed that in the event it is alleged by the Team that the Player is playing, attempting or threatening to play, or negotiating for the purpose of playing, during the term of this Contract, for any other person, firm, entity, or organization, the Team and its assignees (in addition to any other remedies that may be available to them judicially or by way of arbitration) shall have the right to obtain from any court or arbitrator having jurisdiction such equitable relief as may be appropriate, including a decree enjoining the Player from any further such breach of this Contract, and enjoining the Player from playing basketball for any other person, firm, entity, or organization during the term of this Contract. The Player agrees that this right may be enforced by the Team or the NBA. In any suit, action, or arbitration proceeding brought to obtain such equitable relief, the Player does hereby waive his right, if any, to trial by jury, and does hereby waive his right, if any, to interpose any counterclaim or set-off for any cause whatever.

10. ASSIGNMENT.

(a) The Team shall have the right to assign this Contract to any other NBA team and the Player agrees to accept such assignment and to faithfully perform and carry out this Contract with the same force and effect as if it had been entered into by the Player with the assignee team instead of with the Team.

(b) In the event that this Contract is assigned to any other NBA team, all reasonable expenses incurred by the Player in moving himself and his family to the home territory of the team to which such assignment is made, as a result thereof, shall be paid by the assignee team.

(c) In the event that this Contract is assigned to another NBA team, the Player shall forthwith be provided notice orally or in writing, delivered to the Player personally or delivered or mailed to his last known address, and the Player shall report to the assignee team within forty-eight (48) hours after said notice has been received (if the assignment is made during a Season), within one (1) week after said notice has been received (if the assignment is made between Seasons), or within such longer time for reporting as may be specified in said notice. The NBA shall also promptly notify the Players Association of any such assignment. The Player further agrees that, immediately upon reporting to the assignee team, he will submit upon request to a physical examination conducted by a physician designated by the assignee team.

(d) If the Player, without a reasonable excuse, does not report to the team to which this Contract has been assigned within the time provided in subsection (c) above, then

    (i) upon consummation of the assignment, the Player may be disciplined by the assignee team or, if the assignment is not consummated or is voided as a result of the Player's failure to so report, by the assignor Team, and

    (ii) such conduct shall constitute conduct prejudicial to the NBA under Article 35(d) of the NBA Constitution, and shall therefore subject the Player to discipline from the NBA in accordance with such Article.

Exhibit 12.9
(continued)

11. VALIDITY AND FILING.

(a) This Contract shall be valid and binding upon the Team and the Player immediately upon its execution.

(b) The Team agrees to file a copy of this Contract, and/or any amendment(s) thereto, with the Commissioner of the NBA as soon as practicable by facsimile and overnight mail, but in no event may such filing be made more than forty-eight (48) hours after the execution of this Contract and/or amendment(s).

(c) If pursuant to the NBA Constitution and By-Laws or the CBA, the Commissioner disapproves this Contract (or amendment) within ten (10) days after the receipt thereof in his office by overnight mail, this Contract (or amendment) shall thereupon terminate and be of no further force or effect and the Team and the Player shall thereupon be relieved of their respective rights and liabilities thereunder. If the Commissioner's disapproval is subsequently overturned in any proceeding brought under the arbitration provisions of the CBA (including any appeals), the Contract shall again be valid and binding upon the Team and the Player, and the Commissioner shall be afforded another ten-day period to disapprove the Contract (based on the Team's Room at the time the Commissioner's disapproval is overturned) as set forth in the foregoing sentence. The NBA will promptly inform the Players Association if the Commissioner disapproves this Contract.

12. OTHER ATHLETIC ACTIVITIES.

The Player and the Team acknowledge and agree that the Player's participation in certain other activities may impair or destroy his ability and skill as a basketball player, and the Player's participation in any game or exhibition of basketball other than at the request of the Team may result in injury to him. Accordingly, the Player agrees that he will not, without the written consent of the Team, engage in any activity that a reasonable person would recognize as involving or exposing the participant to a substantial risk of bodily injury including, but not limited to:

(i) sky-diving, hang gliding, snow skiing, rock or mountain climbing (as distinguished from hiking), rappelling, and bungee jumping;

(ii) any fighting, boxing, or wrestling;

(iii) driving or riding on a motorcycle or moped;

(iv) riding in or on any motorized vehicle in any kind of race or racing contest;

(v) operating an aircraft of any kind;

(vi) engaging in any other activity excluded or prohibited by or under any insurance policy which the Team procures against the injury, illness or disability to or of the Player, or death of the Player, for which the Player has received written notice from the Team prior to the execution of this Contract; or

(vii) participating in any game or exhibition of basketball, football, baseball, hockey, lacrosse, or other team sport or competition.

Exhibit 12.9
(continued)

If the Player violates this Paragraph 12, he shall be subject to discipline imposed by the Team and/or the Commissioner of the NBA. Nothing contained herein shall be intended to require the Player to obtain the written consent of the Team in order to enable the Player to participate in, as an amateur, the sports of golf, tennis, handball, swimming, hiking, softball, volleyball, and other similar sports that a reasonable person would not recognize as involving or exposing the participant to a substantial risk of bodily injury.

13. PROMOTIONAL ACTIVITIES.

(a) The Player agrees to allow the Team, the NBA, or a League-related entity to take pictures of the Player, alone or together with others, for still photographs, motion pictures, or television, at such reasonable times as the Team, the NBA or the League-related entity may designate. No matter by whom taken, such pictures may be used in any manner desired by either the Team, the NBA, or the League-related entity for publicity or promotional purposes. The rights in any such pictures taken by the Team, the NBA, or the League-related entity shall belong to the Team, the NBA, or the League-related entity, as their interests may appear.

(b) The Player agrees that, during any year of this Contract, he will not make public appearances, participate in radio or television programs, permit his picture to be taken, write or sponsor newspaper or magazine articles, or sponsor commercial products without the written consent of the Team, which shall not be withheld except in the reasonable interests of the Team or the NBA. The foregoing shall be interpreted in accordance with the decision in *Portland Trail Blazers v. Darnell Valentine and Jim Paxson*, Decision 86-2 (August 13, 1986).

(c) Upon request, the Player shall consent to and make himself available for interviews by representatives of the media conducted at reasonable times.

(d) In addition to the foregoing, and subject to the conditions and limitations set forth in Article II, Section 8 of the CBA, the Player agrees to participate, upon request, in all other reasonable promotional activities of the Team, the NBA, and any League-related entity. For each such promotional appearance made on behalf of a commercial sponsor of the Team, the Team agrees to pay the Player $2,500 or, if the Team agrees, such higher amount that is consistent with the Team's past practice and not otherwise unreasonable.

14. GROUP LICENSE.

(a) The Player hereby grants to NBA Properties, Inc. (and its related entities) the exclusive rights to use the Player's Player Attributes as such term is defined and for such group licensing purposes as are set forth in the Agreement between NBA Properties, Inc. and the National Basketball Players Association, made as of September 18, 1995 and amended January 20, 1999 and July 29, 2005 (the "Group License"), a copy of which will, upon his

Exhibit 12.9
(continued)

request, be furnished to the Player; and the Player agrees to make the appearances called for by such Agreement.

(b) Notwithstanding anything to the contrary contained in the Group License or this Contract, NBA Properties (and its related entities) may use, in connection with League Promotions, the Player's

(i) name or nickname and/or

(ii) the Player's Player Attributes (as defined in the Group License) as such Player Attributes may be captured in game action footage or photographs. NBA Properties (and its related entities) shall be entitled to use the Player's Player Attributes individually pursuant to the preceding sentence and shall not be required to use the Player's Player Attributes in a group or as one of multiple players. As used herein, League Promotion shall mean any advertising, marketing, or collateral materials or marketing programs conducted by the NBA, NBA Properties (and its related entities) or any NBA team that is intended to promote

(A) any game in which an NBA team participates or game telecast, cablecast or broadcast (including Pre-Season, Exhibition, Regular Season, and Playoff games),

(B) the NBA, its teams, or its players, or

(C) the sport of basketball.

15. TEAM DEFAULT.

In the event of an alleged default by the Team in the payments to the Player provided for by this Contract, or in the event of an alleged failure by the Team to perform any other material obligation that it has agreed to perform hereunder, the Player shall notify both the Team and the League in writing of the facts constituting such alleged default or alleged failure. If neither the Team nor the League shall cause such alleged default or alleged failure to be remedied within five (5) days after receipt of such written notice, the National Basketball Players Association shall, on behalf of the Player, have the right to request that the dispute concerning such alleged default or alleged failure be referred immediately to the Grievance Arbitrator in accordance with the provisions of the CBA. If, as a result of such arbitration, an award issues in favor of the Player, and if neither the Team nor the League complies with such award within ten (10) days after the service thereof, the Player shall have the right, by a further written notice to the Team and the League, to terminate this Contract.

16. TERMINATION.

(a) The Team may terminate this Contract upon written notice to the Player if the Player shall:

(i) at any time, fail, refuse, or neglect to conform his personal conduct to standards of good citizenship, good moral character (defined here to mean not engaging in acts of moral turpitude, whether or not such acts would constitute a crime), and good sportsmanship, to keep himself in first class physical condition, or to obey the Team's training rules;

Exhibit 12.9
(continued)

(ii) at any time commit a significant and inexcusable physical attack against any official or employee of the Team or the NBA (other than another player), or any person in attendance at any NBA game or event, considering the totality of the circumstances, including (but not limited to) the degree of provocation (if any) that may have led to the attack, the nature and scope of the attack, the Player's state of mind at the time of the attack, and the extent of any injury resulting from the attack;

(iii) at any time, fail, in the sole opinion of the Team's management, to exhibit sufficient skill or competitive ability to qualify to continue as a member of the Team; provided, however,

(A) that if this Contract is terminated by the Team, in accordance with the provisions of this subparagraph, prior to January 10 of any Season, and the Player, at the time of such termination, is unfit to play skilled basketball as the result of an injury resulting directly from his playing for the Team, the Player shall (subject to the provisions set forth in Exhibit 3) continue to receive his full Base Compensation, less all workers' compensation benefits (which, to the extent permitted by law, and if not deducted from the Player's Compensation by the Team, the Player hereby assigns to the Team) and any insurance provided for by the Team paid or payable to the Player by reason of said injury, until such time as the Player is fit to play skilled basketball, but not beyond the Season during which such termination occurred; and provided, further,

(B) that if this Contract is terminated by the Team, in accordance with the provisions of this subparagraph, during the period from the January 10 of any Season through the end of such Season, the Player shall be entitled to receive his full Base Compensation for said Season; or

(iv) at any time, fail, refuse, or neglect to render his services hereunder or in any other manner materially breach this Contract.

(b) If this Contract is terminated by the Team by reason of the Player's failure to render his services hereunder due to disability caused by an injury to the Player resulting directly from his playing for the Team and rendering him unfit to play skilled basketball, and notice of such injury is given by the Player as provided herein, the Player shall (subject to the provisions set forth in Exhibit 3) be entitled to receive his full Base Compensation for the Season in which the injury was sustained, less all workers' compensation benefits (which, to the extent permitted by law, and if not deducted from the Player's Compensation by the Team, the Player hereby assigns to the Team) and any insurance provided for by the Team paid or payable to the Player by reason of said injury.

(c) Notwithstanding the provisions of paragraph 16(b) above, if this Contract is terminated by the Team prior to the first game of a Regular Season by reason of the Player's failure to render his services hereunder due to an injury or condition sustained or suffered during a preceding Season, or after such Season but prior to the Player's participation in any basketball practice or game played

Exhibit 12.9
(continued)

for the Team, payment by the Team of any Compensation earned through the date of termination under paragraph 3(b) above, payment of the Player's board, lodging, and expense allowance during the training camp period, payment of the reasonable traveling expenses of the Player to his home city, and the expert training and coaching provided by the Team to the Player during the training season shall be full payment to the Player.

(d) If this Contract is terminated by the Team during the period designated by the Team for attendance at training camp, payment by the Team of any Compensation earned through the date of termination under paragraph 3(b) above, payment of the Player's board, lodging, and expense allowance during such period to the date of termination, payment of the reasonable traveling expenses of the Player to his home city, and the expert training and coaching provided by the Team to the Player during the training season shall be full payment to the Player.

(e) If this Contract is terminated by the Team after the first game of a Regular Season, except in the case provided for in subparagraphs (a)(iii) and (b) of this paragraph 16, the Player shall be entitled to receive as full payment hereunder a sum of money which, when added to the salary which he has already received during such Season, will represent the same proportionate amount of the annual sum set forth in Exhibit 1 hereto as the number of days of such Regular Season then past bears to the total number of days of such Regular Season, plus the reasonable traveling expenses of the Player to his home.

(f) If the Team proposes to terminate this Contract in accordance with subparagraph (a) of this paragraph 16, it must first comply with the following waiver procedure:

(i) The Team shall request the NBA Commissioner to request waivers from all other clubs. Such waiver request may not be withdrawn.

(ii) Upon receipt of the waiver request, any other team may claim assignment of this Contract at such waiver price as may be fixed by the League, the priority of claims to be determined in accordance with the NBA Constitution and By-Laws.

(iii) If this Contract is so claimed, the Team agrees that it shall, upon the assignment of this Contract to the claiming team, notify the Player of such assignment as provided in paragraph 10(c) hereof, and the Player agrees he shall report to the assignee team as provided in said paragraph 10(c).

(iv) If the Contract is not claimed prior to the expiration of the waiver period, it shall terminate and the Team shall promptly deliver written notice of termination to the Player.

(v) The NBA shall promptly notify the Players Association of the disposition of any waiver request.

(vi) To the extent not inconsistent with the foregoing provisions of this subparagraph

Exhibit 12.9
(continued)

(g) the waiver procedures set forth in the NBA Constitution and By-Laws, a copy of which, as in effect on the date of this Contract, is attached hereto, shall govern.

(h) Upon any termination of this Contract by the Player, all obligations of the Team to pay Compensation shall cease on the date of termination, except the obligation of the Team to pay the Player's Compensation to said date.

17. DISPUTES.

In the event of any dispute arising between the Player and the Team relating to any matter arising under this Contract, or concerning the performance or interpretation thereof (except for a dispute arising under paragraph 9 hereof), such dispute shall be resolved in accordance with the Grievance and Arbitration Procedure set forth in Article XXXI of the CBA.

18. PLAYER NOT A MEMBER.

Nothing contained in this Contract or in any provision of the NBA Constitution and By-Laws shall be construed to constitute the Player a member of the NBA or to confer upon him any of the rights or privileges of a member thereof.

19. RELEASE.

The Player hereby releases and waives any and all claims he may have, or that may arise during the term of this Contract, against

(a) the NBA and its related entities, the NBADL and its related entities, and every member of the NBA or the NBADL, and every director, officer, owner, stockholder, trustee, partner, and employee of the NBA, NBADL and their respective related entities and/or any member of the NBA or NBADL and their related entities (excluding persons employed as players by any such member), and

(b) any person retained by the NBA and/or the Players Association in connection with the NBA/NBPA Anti-Drug Program, the Grievance Arbitrator, the System Arbitrator, and any other arbitrator or expert retained by the NBA and/or the Players Association under the terms of the CBA, in both cases (a) and (b) above, arising out of, or in connection with, and whether or not by negligence,

  (i) any injury that is subject to the provisions of paragraph 7 hereof,

  (ii) any fighting or other form of violent and/or unsportsmanlike conduct occurring during the course of any practice, any NBADL game, and/or any NBA Exhibition, Regular Season, and/or Playoff game (in all cases on or adjacent to the playing floor or in or adjacent to any facility used for such practices or games),

  (iii) the testing procedures or the imposition of any penalties set forth in paragraph 8 hereof and in the NBA/NBPA Anti-Drug Program, or

Exhibit 12.9
(continued)

    (iv) any injury suffered in the course of his employment as to which he has or would have a claim for workers' compensation benefits. The foregoing shall not apply to any claim of medical malpractice against a Team-affiliated physician or other medical personnel.

20. ENTIRE AGREEMENT.

This Contract (including any Exhibits hereto) contains the entire agreement between the parties and, except as provided in the CBA, sets forth all components of the Player's Compensation from the Team or any Team Affiliate, and there are no other agreements or transactions of any kind (whether disclosed or undisclosed to the NBA), express or implied, oral or written, or promises, undertakings, representations, commitments, inducements, assurances of intent, or understandings of any kind (whether disclosed or undisclosed to the NBA)

(a) concerning any future Renegotiation, Extension, or other amendment of this Contract or the entry into any new Player Contract, or

(b) involving compensation or consideration of any kind (including, without limitation, an investment or business opportunity) to be paid, furnished, or made available to the Player, or any person or entity controlled by, related to, or acting with authority on behalf of the Player, by the Team or any Team Affiliate.

EXAMINE THIS CONTRACT CAREFULLY BEFORE SIGNING IT.
THIS CONTRACT INCLUDES EXHIBITS ____, WHICH ARE
ATTACHED HERETO AND MADE A PART HEREOF.
IN WITNESS WHEREOF the Player has hereunto signed his name
and the Team has caused this Contract to be executed by its duly
authorized officer.

Dated: _____	By: _____
	Title: _____
	Team: _____
Dated: _____	Player: _____
	Player's Address: _____

Chapter 13

INTELLECTUAL PROPERTY LAW

13.1. Trademark Law

    13.1.1. The Lanham Act of 1946

    13.1.2. Service Marks and Collective Marks

    13.1.3. Identification Function of a Trademark

    13.1.4. Secondary Meaning

    13.1.5. Trademark Infringement

    13.1.6. Ambush Marketing

    13.1.7. Licensing Programs for Intercollegiate Athletics

        13.1.7.1. Litigation Involving Intercollegiate Licensing Programs

        13.1.7.2. Trademark Law and Nicknames

    13.1.8. Trademark Law and the Olympics

13.2. Copyright Law

    13.2.1. Copyright Law and the Internet

13.3. Patent Law

13.4. The Right of Publicity

INTRODUCTION

To familiarize the reader with intellectual property law and introduce the concept of intellectual property, this chapter begins with an example of how a typical sporting event intersects with intellectual property. First, the names of the competing teams, their respective uniforms, and other related items should be registered as trademarks (see section 13.1, "Trademark Law"). The owners of the teams have a property interest in all of the merchandise for sale to the general public. This interest ensures that the owners receive revenue when jerseys, hats, socks, T-shirts, or any other piece of apparel is sold to fans.

Once the games start, there is music played. The music is copyrighted and owned by other entities. The owners of the teams must get permission, or a license, to use this music. This music is generally licensed through one of the two leading agencies (ASCAP or BMI) that handle the license for a fee. These licensing agencies represent the musicians and collect licensing fees for all public performances of their music, whether it is on radio, television, or the Internet. After these royalties are collected by the agencies, they are distributed to the writers and copyright holders of the songs. Songs are usually packaged together so that the purchaser gets more than one song for the fee. The fee varies according to such factors as the popularity of the song, the number of times the song is used, and the number of songs purchased at a time.

The home team usually sells a program detailing information about the game and its participants. Some of the information is normally obtainable by the general public, but when it is compiled in this certain way, it becomes copyrightable and a property interest. Additionally, the game will likely be videotaped and broadcast over the radio and/or television. This is significant because once it is broadcast on film, radio, or television, the game itself has created a copyrightable interest; use or broadcast of the game is now a property interest and can be bought and sold. (See Chapter 14.)

The players also have a property interest in their name and likeness (see section 13.4, "The Right of Publicity"). The players are recognized publicly because they compete in a national or local spotlight.

In intercollegiate or Olympic situations, the players do not own their own pictures, but the university or governing body does (see section 13.1.8, "Trademark Law and the Olympics"). This is a significant difference between professional athletes and collegiate and Olympic athletes. The concept of the player's right to publicity has become a major topic of dispute. The right to publicity is the athlete's right to control and profit from the commercial use of his or her name or likeness. Although there has been a demand for a federal law concerning the right to publicity, many states have laws that protect the right to publicity for people who are considered to be celebrities. Laws concerning the right to publicity currently vary from state to state. However, collegiate and Olympic athletes cannot capitalize on their own identity during the games/events. This has caused some conflicts because colleges, schools, and governing bodies can make enormous amounts of money from a player's likeness and affiliation for what is a relatively small investment (e.g., a college scholarship).

One example is a university selling jerseys with a particular player's number. The university, not the player, earns money from this merchandise, even though it may be the player's popularity that is driving the sale (see section 13.1.7, "Licensing Programs for Intercollegiate Athletics"). As demonstrated, many issues of property interest are raised when a sporting event occurs. Whether it is the trademarked logo of a favorite sports team (see section 13.1.2, "Service Marks and Collective Marks"), the copyrighted broadcast of a sporting event (see Chapter 14), or the patent of the sporting equipment used during the game (see section 13.3, "Patent Law"), intellectual property is an important and ever-increasing legal issue in the sports industry. The legal system provides certain rights and protections for owners of property. The kind of property that results from mental labor is called intellectual property. Rights and protections for owners of intellectual property are based on federal, patent, trademark, and copyright laws and state trade secret laws. In general, trademarks protect a name or symbol that identifies the source of goods or services; copyrights protect various forms of written and artistic expression; and patents protect inventions of tangible things.

This chapter first presents the legal principles of intellectual property law, including relevant legislation, terms, and the basics of intellectual property law (sections 13.1.1, "The Lanham Act of 1946," and 13.1.2, "Service Marks and Collective Marks"). The chapter then discusses the functions of trademarks, trademark infringement, and ambush marketing. Some recent cases that have defined the crucial issues involved in the use of sports trademarks are discussed in sections 13.1.3, "Identification Function of a Trademark," 13.1.4, "Secondary Meaning," and 13.1.5, "Trademark Infringement."

Section 13.1.7, "Licensing Program for Intercollegiate Athletics," covers the relationship of intellectual property law to intercollegiate athletics. It discusses licensing programs, the increasing use of licensing agents by colleges and universities for the sale of products bearing school logos, and issues concerning nicknames and trademark laws. Section 13.1.8. discusses trademark law and its application to the Olympic games. The final three sections of the chapter deal with copyright, patent law, and the right to publicity. The sections on copyright law and the right to publicity contain discussions of the growing issues in intellectual property law and the Internet.

NOTE

1. For additional information on licensing and intellectual property in professional sports, see Mark A. Kahn, "May the Best Merchandise Win: The Law of Non-Trademark Uses of Sports Logos," 14 *Marquette Sports Law Review* 283 (2004) and Dannean J. Hetzel, "Professional Athletes and Sports Teams: The Nexus of Their Identity Protection," 11 *Sports Lawyers Journal* 141 (2004).

13.1. TRADEMARK LAW

The names, logos, and symbols associated with sports organizations have become very marketable items. Their primary purpose has historically been to create an identifiable image through which an athletic organization can promote the sale of its product or service. More recently, however, the sale of a name, logo, or symbol in association with caps, pennants, T-shirts, jerseys, and other souvenirs has become a significant revenue generator in and of itself for an athletic organization. As a result, these organizations have fought many legal battles to retain the exclusive right to dictate who will put their name, logo, or symbol on these profitable items.

The licensing of trademarks is big business in sports. In addition to gate receipts, television, and other sources of income, the consumer's appetite for sport-related items with a team affiliation has created a significant revenue stream for many sport organizations. Most professional sports leagues, for example, have developed licensing programs to capitalize on the public demand. College athletic departments, conferences, and the NCAA itself, as well as other organizations such as the U.S. Olympic Committee and the U.S. Tennis Association, have done likewise.

In professional sports leagues, the league has the rights and controls team marks. The leagues (such as Major League Baseball, the National Football League, the National Basketball Association, and the National Hockey League) formed separate entities, often known as a "properties" division, that primarily deal with the licensing of the league and club trademarks (including teams and league names and logos) to vendors who manufacture products featuring these marks and, in turn, sell these products to retailers and to the general public. The merchandising revenue is then divided among the teams, usually on an equal or pro rata basis. A pro rata distribution of licensing revenues helps smaller-market clubs compete with larger-market clubs in their leagues. For example, merchandise with the New York Yankees logo might comprise more than 10% of licensing revenues among clubs for Major League Baseball clubs, yet the Yankees are entitled to only 1/30 of the revenue generated from the licensing of Yankee marks.

Like the leagues, players associations have formed entities that handle licensing issues for athletes. For example, the NFL Players Association (NFLPA) formed Players, Inc., which is the licensing arm of the NFLPA. Players, Inc. provides marketing and licensing services to companies interested in using names and likenesses of current and past NFL players. Any program involving six or more NFL players requires a Players, Inc. license. The revenues received from this licensing are then distributed, pro rata, to the players and used for other association needs. These revenues can be quite significant; for example, it has been reported that the total licensing revenue for the MLBPA exceeds $52 million per year.

Not surprisingly, consumer demand for merchandise associated with professional and amateur athletic organizations has prompted a number of manufacturers to attempt to cash in on this lucrative opportunity by using names, logos, or symbols associated with a team or organization without authorization. Such attempts have, on a number of occasions, resulted in litigation in which the athletic organization sought to protect its exclusive right to its name, logo, or symbol, usually on the basis of trademark laws.

The denial of a license to manufacture sports merchandise has resulted in litigation. American Needle, a headwear manufacturer and previous licensee of NFL Properties (NFLP) and the individual clubs of the NFL, sued when NFLP granted an exclusive merchandising license to Reebok, claiming that the exclusive license violated Section 1 of the Sherman Act. Originally the District Court granted the NFL's motion for summary judgment, see *American Needle, Inc v. New Orleans Saints*, 496 F. Supp. 2d 941 (N.D. Ill., 2007) affirmed in *American Needle v. NFL*, 538 F.3d 736 (7th Cir. 2008). However, the Supreme Court reversed and remanded, ruling that the NFL could not be considered a single entity for licensing purposes . For more on this case and its potential impact on the world of sports, see section 10.3.8, "Single-Entity" Defense by the "Big Four."

NOTE

1. The NFL and NFLPA also reached an exclusive contract with Electronic Arts for the exclusive rights to video games; see Darren Rovell, *All Madden, All the Time*, http:// sports.espn.go.com/espn/sportsbusiness/news/story?id=1945691 (last updated December 14, 2004).

13.1.1. The Lanham Act of 1946

The Federal Trademark Act of 1946, 15 U.S.C. §§ 1051–1127, commonly known as the Lanham Act, governs the law of trademarks, the registration of trademarks, and remedies for the infringement of registered trademarks. Many common law principles governing this area have been incorporated into the Act. The Lanham Act was passed to "simplify trademark practice, secure trademark owners in their good-will which they have built up, and to protect the public from imposition by the use of counterfeit and imitated marks and false descriptions." This act sets trademark guidelines for colleges, universities, corporations, organizations, and individuals. The general purpose of trademark legislation is to protect the owner of the mark, as well as prevent others from using distinctive marks that will confuse people into thinking they are dealing with the owner of the trademark when they are not.

The Lanham Act's definition of *trademark* was distilled from, and is consistent with, definitions appearing in court decisions both under prior trademark laws and the common law. Trademark is defined as "any word, name, symbol, or device or any combination thereof adopted and used by a manufacturer or merchant to identify his goods and distinguish them from those manufactured or sold by others." Trademarks refer to goods and are distinguished from service marks and collective marks.

13.1.2. Service Marks and Collective Marks

The Lanham Act also protects service marks and collective marks. A *service mark* is "a mark used in the sale or advertising of services to identify the services of one person and distinguish them from the services of others." While a trademark identifies and distinguishes the source and quality of a tangible product, a service mark identifies and distinguishes the source and quality of an intangible service. An example of a service mark is "NCAA." This stands for events or products related to the National Collegiate Athletic Association, as differentiated from other sporting bodies and associations. The term *collective mark*, as defined in the Lanham Act, means a trademark or service mark used by the "members of a cooperative, association, or other collective group or organization and includes marks used to indicate membership in a union, an association or other organization." An example of a collective mark in sports is "Major League Baseball."

A trademark serves the following functions:

1. It designates the source of origin of a particular product or service, even though the source is unknown to the consumer.

2. It denotes a particular standard of quality, which is embodied in the product or service.

3. It identifies a product or service and distinguishes it from the products or services of others.

4. It symbolizes the goodwill of its owner and motivates consumers to purchase the trademarked product or service.

5. It represents a substantial advertising investment and is treated as a species of property.

6. It protects the public from confusion and deception, ensures that consumers are able to purchase the products and services they want, and enables the courts to fashion a standard of acceptable business conduct.

League and sports teams' names and logos, when used to identify the activities of leagues and teams, are service marks.

Normally, a mark for goods appears on the product or on its packaging; a service mark appears in advertising for the services. In sports, trademarks are used to promote team loyalty and the sale of licensed merchandise; service marks are used for promoting athletic events. The overall objective behind establishing a trademark is to set one brand apart from another. The registration of a trademark ensures the owner that competitors will not capitalize on the owner's efforts to establish brand loyalty and that they will not profit from confusing consumers through the use of the same mark or a similar mark.

An example of a trademark is "Boston College Eagles." The name of the school and its nickname identify the mark as representing that particular school. In addition, the colors of red and yellow in conjunction with the Boston College logo help consumers identify with that institution.

Common law protection is secured by the use of the trademark and extends only so far as is necessary to prevent consumer confusion. State registration is a quick and inexpensive option for local businesses that cannot qualify for federal registration because the mark is not used in interstate or foreign commerce. State registration is also useful for local anti-infringement and anticounterfeiting efforts.

13.1.3. Identification Function of a Trademark

Although the trademark may not disclose the origin of the goods, it does provide the purchaser with a way of recognizing the goods of a particular seller or manufacturer. When the seller or manufacturer has conveyed origin and authenticity of the goods to the purchaser through the trademark, the seller or manufacturer has something of value. This identification function of the trademark also serves as a symbol of the goodwill established by a business. Trademarks therefore "are symbols by which goodwill is advertised and buying habits established."

Goodwill is a business value that arises from the reputation of a business and its relations with its customers. It is unique to the particular business. Goodwill has also been defined as "buyer momentum" and "the lure to return." Goodwill is an intangible asset of a business. An *intangible asset* exists only in connection with something else. It is an idea or formula, not something that can be touched. A *tangible asset*, on the other hand, is something that can be touched. A pitching machine or hockey puck is a tangible asset.

Trademarks should be *distinctive* and should not be either generic or merely descriptive of the goods or services to which they pertain. Words such as *cola*, *table tennis*, and *photocopier* are examples of nondistinctive or generic terms. Generic names of products and services do not qualify for trademark protection. They represent the actual product and are not associated with the source or manufacturer of the product. This is because the generic word defines only the product or service, not its source. The trademark laws, however, protect terms such as Coca-Cola and Ping-Pong. They clearly are identified with the manufacturer and qualify as being distinctive terms. In many countries, trademarks that comprise only letters and/or numbers (the proposed trademark cannot be pronounced as a word or words or has too few letters) or are surnames are considered indistinct. Nevertheless, these legal flaws in trademarks are not always fatal, and in a number of instances, a trademark registration can still be obtained for trademarks that are arguably (1) descriptive, (2) a surname, (3) geographic, or (4) indistinct. When nondistinctive words become distinctive and qualify for trademark protection, they are said to have acquired secondary meaning.

Trademarks are generally distinctive symbols, pictures, or words that sellers affix to distinguish and identify the origin of their products. Trademark status may also be granted to distinctive and unique packaging, color combinations, building designs, product styles, and overall presentations. Service marks receive the same legal protection as trademarks but are meant to distinguish services rather than products. In the United States, trademarks may be protected by both federal statutes, under the Lanham Act, and by state statute and/or common law.

The United States Congress enacted the Lanham Act under its constitutional grant of authority to regulate interstate and foreign commerce. A trademark registered under the Lanham Act has nationwide protection. However, if a trademark is not registered under the Lanham Act, it still may be protected. Under state common laws, marks are protected as part of the common law of unfair competition, and registration of the mark is not required to prove ownership.

Trademark or service mark rights continue indefinitely, since these marks identify the source of goods or services. A mark can be registered for 10 years and can be renewed for subsequent 10-year periods. This procedure is in contrast to other forms of intellectual property protection, such as patents or copyrights, which have finite terms. Between the fifth and sixth year after the date of initial trademark registration, the registrant must file an affidavit setting forth certain information to keep the registration active. If an affidavit is not filed, the registration is canceled. To maintain rights in the mark, it must be used, must not be abandoned, and must be protected so as not to become generic.

13.1.4. Secondary Meaning

Secondary meaning is a mental recognition in the buyer's mind associating symbols, words, colors, and designs with goods from a single source. Secondary meaning is a very important concept in trademark law. Secondary meaning "tests the connection in the buyer's mind between the product bearing the mark and its source." In a commercial sense, secondary meaning is buyer association, mental association, drawing power, or commercial magnetism. The purpose of the Lanham Act is to prevent consumer confusion as to the source of goods. If a good has acquired secondary meaning, the public associates the product with a certain source and the mark is then afforded greater protection under federal law. For example, the Cleveland Indians' trademarked logo is distinct, unique, and widely associated with Major League Baseball, even though neither the word *Cleveland* nor *Indians* appears anywhere in the design. Due to its widely recognized association with the baseball club, the Lanham Act would likely prevent the unauthorized use of similar images to promote other products. Secondary meaning is particularly important when the trademark is nondistinctive. Nondistinctive marks may not be registered and protected under the Lanham Act as trademarks until they have become distinctive of the goods in commerce. It is also possible to receive trademark status for identification that is not on its face distinct or unique, but developed a secondary meaning over time that identifies it with the product or seller. The owner of a trademark has exclusive right to use it on the product it was intended to identify, and often on related products (for an example of a case involving secondary marks, see note 9).

An example of a nondistinctive mark is a *descriptive mark*. A mark is descriptive if it describes the intended purpose, function, or use of the goods, the size of the goods, the class of users of the goods, a desirable characteristic of the goods, or the end effect upon the user. Some examples of descriptive marks are "Beer Nuts" for salted nuts, "Holiday Inn" for a motel, and "Raisin Bran" for cereal made with raisins and bran. Descriptive marks are considered weak marks and, at most, are given narrow trademark protection. Weak marks, as the name suggests, are marks that only describe the product and are not necessarily a unique or creative name. Descriptive marks are not usually given trademark protection, because they do not adhere to the Lanham Act's distinctiveness requirement. Descriptive marks also lack secondary meaning, since the mark does not cause mental recognition of the product in the buyer's mind.

However, secondary meaning does not have to be demonstrated when the trademark is distinctive. Distinctive marks may be registered and protected under the Lanham Act as trademarks. Some examples of distinctive marks are arbitrary, fanciful, and suggestive marks, which are considered strong marks, and therefore are given strong trademark protection. *Arbitrary marks* are "words, names, symbols, or devices" that are in common linguistic use but that, when used with the goods or services in issue, neither suggest nor describe any ingredient, quality, or characteristic of those goods or services. Some examples of arbitrary marks are "Cobra" golf clubs and "Puma" athletic wear. *Fanciful marks* are coined words that have been invented for the sole purpose of functioning as a trademark. Such marks comprise words that are either totally unknown in the language or are completely out of common usage at the time, as with obsolete or scientific terms. Some examples of fanciful marks are "Clorox" bleach, "Kodak" photographic supplies, and "Polaroid" cameras. *Suggestive marks* are legally indistinguishable from arbitrary marks. An example of a suggestive mark would be "Greyhound" for a bus line, a name that suggests speed and sleekness. Suggestive marks generally imply a characteristic of the product they represent. For example, the name "Harlem Globetrotters" suggests that the team is a group that travels around the world playing basketball.

NOTES

1. In *University of Alabama Bd. of Trustees v. New Life Art Inc.*, 2009 WL 5213713 (N.D. Ala. November 19, 2009), Alabama sued an artist who had been creating paintings of famous Alabama football plays. The parties had a licensing agreement from 1991 to 2000, at which point the defendants claimed that the paintings did not have to be licensed. Alabama brought suit, claiming that the uniforms and colors in the paintings were trade dress on which it had a protectable trademark. The District Court found for the defendants, citing the First Amendment and fair use.

2. In *Dallas Cowboys Football Club, Ltd. v. America's Team Properties, Inc.*, 616 F. Supp. 2d 622 (N.D. Tex. 2009), the Cowboys sued a Minnesota clothing company who registered its name as a trademark and printed the slogan "America's Team" on various shirts sold at sporting events. The court found that the Cowboys' use of "America's Team" extended all the way to 1979, giving it trademark priority over the defendant. Furthermore, the team's use had acquired secondary meaning and thus the defendant infringed on the Cowboys' trademark.

3. In 1997, the University of South Carolina filed for a trademark for an interlocking *S* and *C*. The logo was intended primarily for athletic-related use, specifically the hats of the South Carolina baseball team. The University of Southern California opposed the registration of the South Carolina's mark, alleging priority of use and likelihood of confusion when compared to Southern California's similar logo. In a 2008 ruling, the United States Patent and Trademark Office denied South Carolina's trademark, finding that the South Carolina

logo would create a likelihood of confusion with Southern California's existing trademark. The Federal Circuit affirmed the decision. See *University of South Carolina v. University of Southern California*, 2010 WL 157220 (C.A. Fed. January 19, 2010).

4. In *Intersport, Inc. v. NCAA*, 2008 WL 881295 (Ill. App. 1st Dist. March 26, 2008), a producer of television programming and videos was granted a declaratory judgment that its licensing various programs over Sprint's wireless network did not violate the terms of a licensing agreement with the Illinois State High School Association (IHSA). In 1990, Intersport and the IHSA created March Madness LLC after engaging in a trademark dispute over the use of the term *March Madness*. In 1996, it was determined that the NCAA and the IHSA had a joint right to the trademark; see *Illinois High School Ass'n v. GTE Vantage Inc.*, 99 F.3d 244 (7th Cir. 1996). As a result, the IHSA and the NCAA created the March Madness Athletic Association, which controlled the rights to the term. As part of the new agreement, March Madness LLC dissolved but Intersport retained a perpetual right to license the term in connection with its shows, such as those licensed to Sprint.

5. In *Adidas America, Inc. v. Payless Shoesource, Inc.*, 2008 WL 4279812 (D. Or. September 12, 2008), a jury awarded Adidas $304.6 million after it determined that Payless infringed on and acted willfully, maliciously, or in wanton and reckless disregard of Adidas's trademark and trade dress rights. The jury found that 268 different styles and colors of Payless shoes resembled Adidas's trademarks and created a likelihood of confusion.

6. In *Bouchat v. Baltimore Ravens Football Club, Inc.*, 346 F.3d 514 (4th Cir. 2003), it was determined that one of the Baltimore Ravens' logos infringed on an artist's copyright. The artist created a logo for the Ravens but was never compensated and subsequently registered the trademark in 1997, a year after the Ravens had already begun play. While it was determined by a jury that the Ravens did infringe on Bouchat's copyright, he was denied damages because infringement began before he registered the work and because the team's revenues were not attributable to the use of the team logo. In *Bouchat v. Bon-Ton Dept. Stores, Inc.*, 506 F.3d 315 (4th Cir. 2007), the artist sued several hundred companies that sold items with the logo with a similar result.

7. In May 2007, the NFL withdrew a trademark application for the words "The Big Game." The NFL filed for the trademark to address the concerns of official Super Bowl sponsors whose competitors had been attempting to market their products in association with the Super Bowl by using the term "The Big Game." Among the opponents to the application were the University of California, Berkeley, and Stanford University, whose annual football game has been referred to as "The Big Game" for over 100 years. The NFL stated it did not intend to claim exclusivity over the trademark, but simply to prevent ambush marketing in connection with the Super Bowl.

8. In *GRIDIRON.Com, Inc. v. National Football Players Ass'n* 106 F. Supp. 2d 1309 (S.D. Fla. 2000), plaintiffs sued for a declaration that it did not violate defendant's licensing agreement with NFL players. The defendant has a licensing agreement with 97% of NFL players. The defendant defines a group licensing program as one that utilized six or more NFL players. The plaintiff operates a group of Web sites "devoted to professional football" that utilizes the images of over 150 players. The court held that "plaintiff's contractual agreements with the players violates defendant's proprietary rights in six or more NFL players' images." The court permanently enjoined the plaintiff from using the images of six or more NFL players.

9. In *Resorts of Pinehurst, Inc. v. Pinehurst National Corp.*, 148 F.3d 417 (4th Cir. 1998), the plaintiff sued for trademark infringement of the mark "Pinehurst." The defendant used the mark in association with several golf courses in the same geographic area as the plaintiff's famous Pinehurst golf courses. The court noted that the plaintiff had acquired secondary meaning in the mark so that it was associated with a source rather than a geographic area. Additionally, the court ruled that there was a likelihood of confusion in that both the plaintiff and defendant received mail, deliveries, and phone calls that were actually meant for the other. The court granted the plaintiff's request for an injunction

and directed the district court to immediately and permanently enjoin the defendant from using the mark "Pinehurst."

10. In *Jaguar Cars, Ltd. v. NFL*, 886 F. Supp. 335 (S.D.N.Y. 1995), a suit was brought by Jaguar Cars, Ltd. against the NFL when the NFL franchise in Jacksonville, Florida, decided to use the name "Jaguars" and the image of a sleek jaguar that resembled the emblem serving as hood ornaments on Jaguar automobiles. The case was eventually settled out of court. 8. In *In re National Novice Hockey League, Inc.*, 222 U.S.P.Q. 638 (TTAB 1984), the Trademark Board refused to register the marks *National Novice Hockey League* and *NNHL* because of the likelihood of confusion with the National Hockey League.

13.1.5. Trademark Infringement

An inherent threat to trademark owners of highly visible sporting events, teams, schools, and the Olympics is the pirating of their marks. Capitalizing on the fans' desire to identify with a favorite franchise or athletic organization, numerous businesses have exploited the goodwill and marketability of sports organizations by producing anything from hats to T-shirts to jerseys to pennants that carry a team name, nickname, team player name or number, logo, or symbol of the organization without authorization. This type of exploitation can have damaging consequences. First, the unauthorized use of a mark is injurious, because the market demand for any product or service is finite, and sales of unlicensed merchandise will reduce licensed sales, especially since it can be underpriced.

Second, assuming consumer confusion, if the unlicensed merchandise is of a lesser quality, it will reflect negatively on the quality of the licensed merchandise and also on the organization. Thus the goodwill and the reputation that the trademark owner established would be damaged, resulting in a decreased value of the trademark. Therefore, it is very important for sports organizations to protect their marks. After being made aware of the infringement, the trademark owner can demand that the activity cease. If the demand is ignored, the owner is left with no other recourse but to pursue legal remedies provided under the Lanham Act and common law.

The Lanham Act defines *trademark infringement* as the reproduction, counterfeiting, copying, or imitation in commerce of a registered mark "in connection with the sale, offering for sale, distribution, or advertising of any goods or services on or in connection with which such use is likely to cause confusion or to cause mistake, or to deceive without consent of the registrant." To succeed in a trademark suit, the trademark owner must first establish a protectable property right in the name or mark it seeks to defend. Second, the owner must establish that the infringing party's use of a similar mark is likely to cause confusion, mistake, or deception in the market as to the source, origin, or sponsorship of the products on which the marks are used.

Trademark rights are established by (1) actual use of the mark or (2) the filing of a proper application to register a mark in the United States Patent and Trademark Office (USPTO) stating that the applicant has a bona fide intention to use the mark in commerce regulated by the U.S. Congress. Federal registration is not required to establish rights in a mark, nor is it required to begin use of a mark. However, federal registration can secure benefits beyond those rights acquired by merely using a mark. For example, the owner of a federal registration is presumed to be the owner of the mark for the goods and services specified in the registration, and to be entitled to use the mark nationwide. In addition, under the Lanham Act, the registration of a mark with the USPTO (see note 1) constitutes prima facie evidence that the registrant owns the mark and has the exclusive right to use the mark, and that the registration itself is valid. The burden is then placed on the one challenging the mark to rebut the presumption of validity.

There are two related but distinct types of rights in a mark: the right to register and the right to use. Generally, the first party who either uses a mark in commerce or files an application in the USPTO has the ultimate right to register that mark. The USPTO's authority is limited to determining the right to register. The right to use a mark can be more complicated to determine. This is particularly true when two parties have begun use of the same or similar marks without knowledge of one another and neither has a federal registration. Only a court can render a decision about the right to use, such as issuing an injunction or awarding damages for infringement. When making its decision, the court will attempt to determine factually which party was the first to use the mark in commerce. Second, the court will weigh the positive and negative reasons for allowing each party to use the particular mark.

This issue was highlighted in *Hawaii-Pacific Apparel Group, Inc. v. Cleveland Browns Football Co. LLC,* 418 F. Supp. 2d 501 (S.D.N.Y. 2006) in a dispute over who owned the "Dawg Pound" trademark. The Browns and NFL Properties Inc. (NFLP) had registered the marks "Cleveland Browns Dogs" and "Cleveland Browns Dawgs" with the State of Ohio Trademark Office in 1985 after Browns fans became known as the Dawg Pound. The request was granted in 1988 for a period of 10 years. NFLP and the Browns licensed the trademarks to various apparel and novelty manufacturers. Unaware of the registered trademarks, Hawaii Pacific Apparel Group (HP) started a line of apparel featuring phrases such as "Dawg Pound" in 1986 and attempted to register the phrase in 1994 with the U.S. Patent and Trademark Office. Its request was denied as a result of the opposition from NFLP.

The situation became complicated when the Browns left Cleveland for Baltimore in 1995, thus eliminating the Dawg Pound. HP was able to register the phrase "Lil Dawg Pound" in 1996. When a new Cleveland Browns franchise was created to start play in 1999, the new Cleveland Browns and NFLP attempted to register "Dawg Pound" with the USPTO in 1999, but they were denied due to a likelihood of confusion between the brands. HP sued when the Browns ignored HP's cease and desist order and decided to use the phrase anyway. The district court ruled that despite never registering the mark "Dawg Pound" (an action that is not required by the Lanham Act), NFLP and the Browns had proof of using the mark in licensing agreements since 1989, while HP did not use the phrase until 1994. It was also determined that NFLP never abandoned the mark when the Browns left Cleveland because NFLP had sent cease and desist letters to HP during the time the Browns did not exist.

There are three ways that an organization or individual can lose rights in a mark. First, abandonment of a trademark is stopping the use of it with an intention not to resume its use. The second is by licensing the mark to others without controlling the nature and quality of the licensee's goods or services under the mark. Finally, rights to a mark may be lost when there is misuse of the mark by the organization—or a failure to police against the mark's misuse by others—so that it ceases to indicate source but becomes just another generic word in the language, such as *escalator*, *aspirin*, and *cellophane*.

A defendant in a trademark infringement case, in addition to contending that the "word, name, symbol, or device" is indistinguishable from that of other owners or manufacturers, may contend that the mark is functional and, therefore, not worthy of trademark status. A functional mark can be defined as a mark that does not describe or distinguish the product, but is necessary for the product to exist. This was one of the key issues in *Dallas Cowboys Cheerleaders Inc. v. Pussycat Cinema, Ltd.*, 604 F.2d 200 (2d Cir. 1979), where the defendant alleged that cheerleading uniforms were a purely functional item necessary for the performance of cheerleading routines and, therefore, incapable of becoming the subject of a trademark.

The infringer may also contend that the owner of the mark, though once possessed of a property interest in the mark, had abandoned or relinquished its right. Here, however, rather than relying on the owner's failure to prosecute alleged infringers or allowing the uncontrolled use of the mark for a period of time as evidence of abandonment, the infringer must establish both the intent of the owner to abandon the mark and the loss of all indication as to the source of the mark's origin. Abandonment of a mark is not as simple as stopping the use of a trademark. In *Indianapolis Colts, Inc. v. Metropolitan Baltimore Football Club, L.P.*, 34 F.3d 410 (7th Cir. 1994), a case involving the former Baltimore Colts team that moved to Indianapolis, the Canadian Football League and one of its owners were sued for using the name Baltimore CFL Colts, even though the owner of the Baltimore Colts had moved his franchise to Indianapolis and there were no longer any Baltimore Colts. The court enjoined the CFL team from using the name because it was likely to confuse a substantial number of consumers. The defendant's reliance on *Major League Baseball Properties Inc. v. Sed Non Olet Denarius, Ltd.*, 817 F. Supp. 1103, 1128 (S.D.N.Y. 1993), a case where the Los Angeles Dodgers unsuccessfully challenged a Brooklyn restaurant called the Brooklyn Dodger on trademark infringement grounds, proved to be futile. The Indianapolis Colts court distinguished the case by saying there was no likelihood for confusion because "[n]o one would think the Brooklyn Dodgers baseball team reincarnated in a restaurant."

Even though an alleged infringer may be unable to prove the validity of a mark, this does not settle the infringement issue under the Lanham Act. The owner of the mark still bears the burden of establishing that the infringement is likely to cause confusion, mistake, or deception in the market as to the source, origin, or sponsorship of the products on which the mark is used. One might expect that the similarity or duplication of a registered mark would be sufficient to establish confusion, but such has not been the case. Courts generally have required the production of evidence to establish that individuals make the critical distinction as to sponsorship or endorsement, or direct evidence of actual confusion between the authentic and counterfeit products. The "likely to cause confusion" issue has proven to be the key question in the majority of sports trademark cases. The Ninth Circuit interpreted it thus:

> In order to determine whether there is a likelihood of confusion in a trademark infringement case, the Court must consider numerous factors, including *inter alia*, the strength or weakness of the marks, similarity in appearance, sound, and meaning, the class of goods in question, the marketing channels, evidence of actual confusion, and evidence of the intention of defendant in selecting and using the alleged infringing [mark].

Of paramount concern is whether there is a likelihood of confusion such that the public believes that the goods are endorsed or authorized by someone other than the trademark owner. As can be seen through the Ninth Circuit interpretation of likelihood of confusion, the court must take numerous factors into account when judging whether two marks are likely to be confused (see notes 6, 8, and 13 for cases decided on likelihood of confusion arguments).

An important early case dealing with likelihood of confusion in sports is *National Football League Properties, Inc. v. Wichita Falls Sportswear, Inc.*, 532 F. Supp. 651 (W. D. Wash. 1982) (see note 18). In this case, the defendant company, Wichita Falls Sportswear, was manufacturing and selling NFL football jersey replicas that, due to their similarity to authentic NFL jerseys, created the likelihood of confusion in the minds of the consumer. Wichita Falls manufactured jerseys in the blue and green colors of the Seattle Seahawk uniforms. The court held that NFL Properties had the burden of proving (1) that the secondary meaning of the descriptive term (e.g., Seattle) related the jersey to the NFL team, and (2) that Wichita Falls' activities created a likelihood of confusion. The NFL was able to prove that placing Seattle on the jersey created a likelihood of confusion in the buyer's mind over whether these were authentic, licensed jerseys.

In addition, there are circumstances where products display a disclaimer proclaiming that the trademark owner does not endorse the articles. In *Boston Professional Hockey Ass'n. v. Dallas Cap & Emblem Mfg.*, 510 F.2d 1004 (5th Cir. 1975), the defendant manufactured products that contained registered and unregistered marks of various NHL teams. The defendant included a disclaimer on its products indicating that use of the marks was not authorized. The court concluded that the defendant's use of a disclaimer did not prevent liability under the Lanham Act. The court's conclusion was based on the belief that there would likely be a degree of consumer confusion. The confusion requirement was met since "the defendant duplicated the protected trademarks and sold them to the public knowing that the public would identify them as being the team's trademarks. The certain knowledge of the buyer that the source and origin of the trademark symbols were in [the] plaintiff's satisfies the requirement of the act." In addition, the court found that the team had an interest in its own individualized symbol and was entitled to legal protection against such unauthorized duplication.

In *Major League Baseball Properties, Inc. v. Opening Day Productions, Inc.*, 385 F. Supp. 2d 256, (S.D.N.Y. 2005), Major League Baseball Properties (MLBP) sought a declaration that they were not infringing on an "opening day" trademark held by the defendant. In 1990, the defendant and MLBP discussed a partnership featuring a line of "opening day" merchandise to be sold year-round with nationwide promotions featuring a single corporate sponsor leading up to baseball's opening day, but discussions ended that year with no agreements being made. The defendant claimed that MLBP was infringing on its "opening day" trademark when MLBP began a national promotion with True Value Hardware surrounding MLB's opening day in 1995 (even though no "opening day" merchandise was actually sold during the promotion). Without successfully registering the trademark, the defendant was unable to prove that it had made sufficient use of the mark (it had sold only 360 shirts on a test basis) or that a likelihood of confusion arose by MLBP's usage of the term. Furthermore, it was ruled that "opening day" was a descriptive mark and could not be registered under the Lanham Act unless it had acquired secondary meaning, which it had not for the defendant. Summary judgment was granted for MLBP.

Another issue dealing with licensing is the situation where the permission of two organizations is needed to produce goods or services. In professional sports, the athlete has a right to publicity and desires to have an influence over what products bear his likeness. By the same token, leagues stand to profit from licensing players' names and likenesses to many producers in order to benefit the entire league economically. For example, in *Major League Baseball Properties, Inc. v. Pacific Trading Cards, Inc.*, 150 F.3d 149 (2d Cir. 1998), the Major League Baseball Players Association gave permission to the defendant to produce trading cards; however, the league did not provide its permission. Major League Baseball Properties, Inc., the licensing arm for the Major League clubs, sued the defendant, seeking to block distribution of the company's cards. Major League Baseball Properties, Inc., alleged that the defendant violated the clubs' trademark rights. Specifically, Major League Baseball Properties argued that the team logos and uniforms could not be used without their permission. Pacific had had a licensing agreement with the owners until the previous year. Pacific countered that it was not violating trademark rights because it was not using the owners' pictures of the players and was not marketing the cards as officially owner endorsed. The district court did not issue a preliminary injunction prohibiting distribution of the baseball cards. However, on appeal, the district court's decision was vacated in order for the matter to be settled out of court.

NOTES

1. For more information on how to register a trademark, see the USPTO's Web site at www.uspto.gov/teas/.

2. In *Major League Baseball Properties, Inc. v. Salvino, Inc.*, 420 F. Supp. 2d 212, (S.D.N.Y 2005), MLBP was granted summary judgment against antitrust, unfair competition, and tortious interference claims brought by Salvino. Salvino had manufactured and sold plush bean-filled bears called "Bammers" featuring the logos of various Major League Baseball clubs. However, Salvino had an MLBP license to produce figurines, not the bean-filled bears. Salvino filed an antitrust claim against the plaintiff when they received a cease and desist letter from MLBP regarding the Bammers. In response, MLBP cross-claimed trade dress, breach of contract, and unfair competition claims since the bears featured team colors corresponding with the player name and number on the jersey (Salvino did have a license from the Major League Baseball Players Association). The district court determined that the procompetitive benefits of their licensing business superseded the defendant's claims.

3. Starting in 1984, the phrase "12th man" became a significant part of marketing and fan relations plan for the Seattle Seahawks, but Texas A&M University and its football team had been using the phrase since 1922 and officially trademarked it in 1990. Texas A&M requested that the Seahawks stop using the phrase in 2004 and 2005, but the Seahawks continued, offering Texas A&M $10,000 to use the phrase for 10 years. With the Seahawks making a Super Bowl run and using the phrase more than ever in January 2006, Texas A&M filed for a restraining order on trademark infringement grounds. The suit was resolved in May 2006 when a deal was reached that allows the Seahawks to use the phrase under a license.

4. A fan site for the University of Southern California (USC), trojanwire.com, attempted to trademark the phrase "Three-Pete" as the Pete Carroll–coached Trojans approached a potential third consecutive college football national championship title in January 2006. Its request was denied by the United States Patent Office because long-time NBA head coach Pat Riley owned the trademark for "Three-Peat," which he registered before his Los Angeles Lakers failed to win a third consecutive title in the 1988–1989 season. Attorneys for Riley sent cease and desist letters to the Web site and an individual who had started producing T-shirts with "Three-Pete" on them. Ironically, the Trojans ended up losing the championship game.

5. In *Ignition Athletic Performance Group, LLC v. Hantz Soccer U.S.A., LLC*, 2007 WL 2258839 (6th Cir. August 8, 2007), Ignition, an organizer of soccer camps and the operator of the professional soccer team the Cincinnati Kings, filed for a preliminary injunction against the newly founded Detroit Ignition of the Major Indoor Soccer League. Ignition alleged that the new team's logo was a trademark violation under the Lanham Act. In denying the injunction, the court determined that "because Ignition and Detroit Ignition are in different cities and their goods are substantially different, there is no likelihood of confusion between Ignition and Detroit Ignition."

6. In *International Star Class Yacht Racing Ass'n v. Tommy Hilfiger U.S.A., Inc.*, 146 F.3d 66 (2d Cir. 1998), the plaintiff, the International Star Class Yacht Racing Association (ISCYRA), sued the defendant, a clothing design and marketing company, for trademark infringement of the mark "Star Class." The court held that the defendant had infringed the plaintiff's mark and enjoined the defendant from using the mark. The plaintiff requested an accounting for profits based on the bad faith of the defendant. The plaintiff claimed that the defendant conducted an improper trademark search. The district court denied injunctive relief as to ISCYRA's insignia and an accounting of Hilfiger's profits, actual damages, and attorney fees in finding that Hilfiger had not acted in bad faith. On appeal, the issue of whether Hilfiger acted in bad faith was remanded back to the district court, which later affirmed its decision, stating that, "although there is some evidence that points toward the existence of bad faith, we cannot say, after review of the record, that we are left with [the] definite and firm conviction that a mistake has been committed."

7. In *Pebble Beach Company v. Tour 18 Ltd.*, 155 F.3d 526 (5th Cir. 1998), the defendant owned and operated a public golf course in which several of the golf holes were copied from more famous golf courses, particularly Pinehurst No. 2, Pebble Beach, and Harbour Town owned by Sea Pines, the plaintiffs in this case. None of the courses had a copyright or trademark registration for the specific golf holes that were copied. Therefore, the defendant was successful against the owners of Pinehurst No. 2 and Pebble Beach. However, the suit involving Harbour Town came down to a trade dress issue. Trade dress is defined as the distinctive packaging or design of a product that promotes the product and distinguishes it from other products in the marketplace. The trade dress issue in question was that the defendant copied Harbour Town's most famous golf hole, number 18, which is better known as the "Lighthouse Hole." The court stated:

> For the plaintiffs to prevail on their service-mark and trade dress infringement claims, they must show (1) that the mark or trade dress, as the case may be, qualifies for protection and (2) that Tour 18's use of the mark or trade dress creates a likelihood of confusion in the minds of potential consumers. With trade dress, the question is whether the "combination of features creates a distinctive visual impression, identifying the source of the product."

The court ruled that the Lighthouse Hole had acquired secondary meaning for the plaintiff and, therefore, was worthy of protection. The court also held that consumers were likely to be confused as to the affiliation of the golf course. Therefore, the defendant violated the plaintiff's rights, and the court required the defendant to remove the lighthouse from its golf course.

8. In *Johnny Blastoff, Inc. v. Los Angeles Rams Football Company*, 48 U.S.P.Q. 2d (BNA) 1385 (W.D. Wis. 1998), both plaintiff and defendant claim exclusive rights for the use of the mark "St. Louis Rams." The plaintiff registered the mark in Wisconsin with the intent of using it in conjunction with a fictional cartoon storyline. The defendant registered the mark in Missouri after the announcement that the Los Angeles Rams were moving to St. Louis and would change their name to the St. Louis Rams. The court noted, "As between competing claimants to a trademark, the party who first appropriates the mark through use acquires superior rights." The court held that a substantial portion of the public associated the mark "St. Louis Rams" with the defendant at the time of plaintiff's registration.

The court found that there was a likelihood of confusion by prospective purchasers of the goods and services of the parties. The court disagreed with the plaintiff's argument that the "Rams" mark had become generic and that therefore the defendants lost their rights in the mark. The plaintiff argued that the use of "Rams" by several college football teams made "Rams" generic. The court held that this was irrelevant to a professional football team. Major League Baseball faced a similar issue when the Montreal Expos moved to Washington, D.C. after the 2004 season. Bygone Sports LLC of Atlanta had applied for the trademark "Washington Senators" and "Washington Nationals" in 2002 amid talks of contraction and relocation in baseball. According to Major League Baseball Properties (MLBP), an agreement for the "Nationals" trademark was reached where Bygone Sports would receive $130,000 in cash, a $10,000 credit to the MLB.com store, and four tickets to the Nationals' home opener. However, both parties filed suit when Bygone Sports allegedly reneged on the agreement. MLBP claimed breach of contract, while Bygone Sports claimed trademark infringement. Before the cases went to court, the U.S. Patent and Trademark Office officially granted the trademark to Bygone Sports. The two parties finally reached an agreement that granted the exclusive rights of "Washington Nationals" to MLBP in March 2006, but the terms were not disclosed.

9. In *Dream Team Collectibles, Inc. v. NBA Properties, Inc.*, 958 F. Supp. 1401 (E.D. Missouri 1997), a lawsuit resulted over the rights to the mark "Dream Team." The plaintiff produced "unframed collages of sports trading cards and sports-related merchandise." The defendant held the rights to market and license merchandise associated with the 1992 men's basketball Olympic team, which became known as the Dream Team because the team consisted of NBA stars. The plaintiff claimed "reverse confusion," which occurs when a junior user (the second user of the mark) appears to have superior rights to the mark in the public's eye, so that the senior user (the first user of the mark) actually appears to be the infringer. The court concluded that there was a genuine issue of material fact as to whether the defendant or the media associated the mark "Dream Team" with the basketball team. While both NBA Properties and Dream Team Collectibles made summary judgment motions on this issue, the court granted Dream Team Collectibles' motion. The court held that NBA Properties had cited no authority for the "proposition that cancellation of a mark is warranted when a party demonstrates some unlawful use of a mark by its owner who, for the most part, is using the mark lawfully."

10. *Monster Communications, Inc. v. Turner Broadcasting System, Inc.*, 935 F. Supp. 490 (S.D.N.Y. 1996) deals with film footage of the Muhammad Ali–George Foreman heavyweight title fight that took place in Zaire. The plaintiff "made and owns an 84 minute motion picture called 'When We Were Kings.'" The defendant planned to air a movie on Turner Network Television called *The Whole Story*. The plaintiff claims that the defendant's movie "contains between 41 seconds and 2 minutes" of footage to which the plaintiff owned the rights. The court held that, even if the plaintiff were able to prove protectable rights in the footage, the defendant would prevail because it would be able to prove fair use of the copyrighted material. The plaintiff's injunction request to prevent the defendant's broadcasting of its movie was denied.

11. In *National Basketball Ass'n Properties, Inc. v. YMG, Inc.*, No. 93 C 1533, 1993 U.S. Dist. LEXIS 15864 (N.D. Ill. Nov. 5, 1993), the plaintiff, which holds the exclusive license from the NBA and its member teams to license others to manufacture and sell merchandise bearing NBA trademarks, brought an action for trademark infringement. An investigator employed by the plaintiff ordered merchandise from the defendant that had NBA logos on it. After a determination that the goods were counterfeit, NBA Properties executed a seizure of the goods. Although the merchandise bore NBA registered trademarks and purported to be "officially licensed" merchandise, YMG was not licensed to embroider, distribute, or sell merchandise bearing reproductions of NBA trademarks. Summary judgment was granted to the plaintiff.

12. In *Major League Baseball Players Ass'n v. Dad's Kid Corp.*, 806 F. Supp. 458 (S.D.N.Y. 1992), the defendant manufactured a baseball card, called the Tri-Card, by

using three authentic licensed baseball cards originally made by MLBPA's licensees. The defendant corporation disclaimed any copyright or trademark rights with respect to the baseball cards used to manufacture the Tri-Card. The disclaimer provided that Dad's Kid Corp. disclaimed any proprietary rights to the name and logo of Major League Baseball and of the Major League Baseball Players Association. The district court held that (1) there was no likelihood of confusion as to origin as required for injunction, since genuine cards were used to produce the display item and the manufacturer put the disclaimer on the packaging of its products, and (2) the manufacturer had not misappropriated the publicity rights of major league players. This decision was important because it held that baseball players had little, if any, publicity rights with respect to the use and reuse of their pictures on cards, after the original sale of the card by an official licensee, for which the players received a royalty payment.

13. In *Maryland Stadium Authority v. Becker*, 806 F. Supp. 1236 (D. Md. 1992), the owner of Camden Yards baseball park brought a trademark infringement action against a vendor that used the words "Camden Yards" on T-shirts and other clothing items. The district court held for the plaintiff and reasoned that evidence concerning the owner's promotional efforts and media coverage given to the park was sufficient to establish that the plaintiff had adopted and used the "Camden Yards" mark before the vendor started using the mark. Additionally, the court held that there was enough evidence to establish that the owner's "Camden Yards" mark had acquired secondary meaning and that vendor's action created a likelihood of confusion.

14. In *National Football League Properties, Inc. v. Playoff Corp.*, 808 F. Supp. 1288 (N.D. Tex 1992), NFL Properties, exclusive licensing representative for the NFL asserted claims for trademark infringement and unfair competition under the Lanham Act and state statutes against a company that planned to market football trading cards. On the plaintiff's motion for preliminary injunction, the district court held that, although the plaintiff showed a substantial likelihood of success on the merits, the plaintiff failed to show that irreparable harm would result from failure to issue an injunction. The motion was denied.

15. In *Harlem Globetrotters, Inc. v. Harlem Magicians, Inc.*, 872 F.2d 1025 (6th Cir. 1989), the plaintiff filed suit alleging that the defendant violated the plaintiff's registered trademarks "Harlem Globetrotters" and "Magicians of Basketball" by using the words "Harlem Magicians." In 1964, a consent agreement, which had been approved by the court system, permanently enjoined the defendant from using the terms "Harlem," "Globetrotters," or "Trotters" to promote its basketball team. The court of appeals held that the 1964 consent agreement was valid, and therefore the defendant violated the plaintiff's trademark rights.

16. In *Boston Athletic Association v. Sullivan*, 867 F.2d 22 (1st Cir. 1989), the defendant sold T-shirts with the logos "Boston Marathon" and "B.A.A. Marathon" printed on them. The plaintiff brought action against the defendant for infringement of the plaintiff's trademark. In reversing the lower court's decision, the judge ruled that the shirts infringed on BAA's trademark, and enjoined the defendant from manufacturing and selling the shirts.

17. In *National Football League Properties, Inc. v. New Jersey Giants, Inc.*, 637 F. Supp. 507 (D.N.J. 1986), the defendant company exploited the fact that the New York Giants football team played their home games in New Jersey. The company manufactured and sold T-shirts and other merchandise displaying the name "New Jersey Giants." The New York Giants and NFL Properties, Inc., brought action against the company, alleging infringement of the New York Giants' trademark. In ruling for the plaintiffs, the judge permanently enjoined the defendant from further use of the name "New Jersey Giants" on merchandise and as the company name. The court held that "Giants" and "New York Giants" are valid service marks worthy of protection, and that under the Lanham Act, owners of service marks and owners of trademarks are protected from other marks that are likely to cause consumer confusion. The Giants would only be afforded this protection if their marks possessed secondary meaning at the time the defendant began using them. The court found that there

was strong evidence showing that secondary meaning in the marks "Giants" and "New York Giants" had been proven.

18. In the important sports trademark case *National Football League Properties, Inc. v. Wichita Falls Sportswear, Inc.*, 532 F. Supp. 651 (W.D. Wash. 1982), it was the court's scrutiny of the consumer confusion issue that led to the plaintiff's success in preventing the defendant sportswear company from manufacturing and selling NFL football jersey replicas that created the likelihood of confusion. NFL Properties alleged that its trademark rights were violated when Wichita Falls manufactured jerseys in the blue and green colors of the Seattle Seahawks uniform. The court held that NFL Properties had the burden of proving that (1) the secondary meaning of the descriptive term (i.e., Seattle) related the jersey to the NFL team, and (2) Wichita Falls' activities created a likelihood of confusion. The NFL was able to prove that placing "Seattle" on the jersey created a likelihood of confusion in the buyer's mind over whether these were authentic, licensed jerseys.

13.1.6. Ambush Marketing

Within the sports industry, a recent trend related to trademark law has been ambush marketing, which is defined as the intentional efforts of a company to weaken or "ambush" a competitor's official association with a sports entity that was acquired through the payment of sponsorship fees. The company that is ambushing has not paid any money to the sports organization to affiliate its organization with the event. Companies have undertaken this marketing tactic through many different avenues, including the purchase of advertising time on television before and during an official event. The purchase of commercial time allows the ambushing company to associate itself with a sporting event without having to pay the official sponsor fees.

Another form of ambush marketing is the sponsoring of a contest surrounding a sporting event without using the name of the event in its promotional materials. Ambush marketing may be difficult to challenge legally (see note 4). This is because the ambushing company usually takes steps to avoid creating a "likelihood of confusion," which is prohibited by the Lanham Act. Disclaimers are often used to communicate information to the consumer that the company sponsoring the contest or featured in the commercial is not a sponsor of the sporting event, is not affiliated with any such sponsors, and claims no ownership rights to the sporting event.

Ambush marketing has been costly to sports organizations trying to sell rights to their sporting events to companies for sponsorship revenue. As more and more ambush marketing occurs, the value placed on "official sponsor" language can decrease and the sports organizations lose out financially. It is extremely difficult for the sports organizations to challenge ambush marketing techniques. First, companies have become increasingly sophisticated and creative in their methods of testing the gray area between legal marketing activity, which is covered by the commercial and free speech provisions of the First Amendment and the fair use doctrine and illegal marketing activity that could constitute trademark infringement and unfair competition. Sports organizations need to show that a likelihood of confusion exists in the consumer's mind, a very difficult thing to prove. The following are examples of how ambush marketing can occur in the sports industry. One example of ambush marketing is the purchase of advertising signage around an event where a main competitor is also purchasing signage. This type of ambush marketing is prevalent around major events with multiple promotional and advertising opportunities such as the Olympics or the Super Bowl. Another example is if a competing office supply store sets up a gigantic billboard on the street leading to the Staples Center in Los Angeles. Finally, a company buys advertising on a television show that is sponsored by its main competitor. All of these forms of ambush marketing attempt to weaken the effect of an official sponsorship without spending the money for the sponsorship.

The second reason it is hard to challenge ambush marketing is that few decided cases address the legal parameters of ambush marketing, and fewer still specifically refer to the term *ambush marketing* (see notes 3 and 4). Third, most ambush marketing campaigns last only a brief period of time, making the time and cost of litigation prohibitive. Sports organizations are also fearful of the consequences of a negative ruling on ambush marketing, which could open the floodgates to future problems. However, sports organizations can defend themselves against ambush marketing by planning ahead and anticipating the actions of competitive marketers. One method of defense is to make sure that all potential issues are specifically and precisely addressed in the contract stage. An organization should use the contract to maintain tight reign over elements that are under its control (i.e., trademark registration, names, logos, mascots). Legislation, such as the Ted Stevens Amateur Sports Act (see section 13.1.8, "Trademark Law and the Olympics"), has also helped strengthen the rights of organizations that are battling ambush marketing.

NOTES

1. In *AT&T v. NASCAR*, 494 F.3d 1356 (11th Cir. 2007), AT&T brought suit after NASCAR denied it the right to put its logo on Jeff Burton's car, a driver for Richard Childress Racing. Sprint Nextel became the title sponsor of the NASCAR Nextel Cup in 2004, but grandfathered in existing sponsorship agreements with competing wireless brands. One of the competing companies grandfathered in was Cingular, who had its logo on Burton's car. When AT&T acquired Cingular in 2006, it wanted to swap the Cingular logo with its own, but Sprint Nextel and NASCAR protested, claiming it violated their sponsorship agreement. The 11th Circuit reversed an injunction that would have prevented NASCAR from ordering the AT&T logo removed because it found that AT&T was not a third-party beneficiary to the grandfathering agreement between RCR and NASCAR and therefore lacked standing. Before proceeding on remand, the parties reached a settlement whereby AT&T could keep the logo on Burton's car through the 2008 season.

2. In *Mastercard International Inc. v. FIFA*, 239 Fed. Appx. 625 (2nd Cir. 2007), Mastercard brought suit against soccer's ruling body after a deal to be the exclusive credit card sponsor of the 2010 and 2014 World Cups was surprisingly given to Visa. Mastercard, which had sponsored the previous two World Cups and agreed to pay $100 million over 16 years for in-stadium and broadcasting ads, claimed it had a 90-day period of negotiating exclusivity and a right of first refusal. The District Court agreed that FIFA had breached its contract, but the Second Circuit reversed and remanded after finding a lack of clarity in the district court's conclusions of law and remedy. A settlement was reached whereby FIFA paid Mastercard about $90 million to give up all future sponsorship claims. Shortly thereafter, Visa agreed to a $170 million deal to be the official credit card sponsor of the World Cup.

3. In *Master Card International v. Sprint Communications Co.*, 23 F.3d 397 (2d. Cir. 1994), Master Card had signed an exclusive agreement with the 1994 World Cup organizers to be the sole credit card sponsor for the event. Sprint signed on with the event and proceeded to manufacture cards that bore the World Cup symbol. These cards contained a number that the user either entered into the phone upon hearing a prompt or read to the operator. The cards, however, lacked a magnetic stripe that would permit them to be scanned by a card reader and also lacked any information relating to the cardholder that could be used for making a credit purchase from a vendor. However, because Master Card

was the official credit card sponsor, the court enjoined Sprint from manufacturing these calling cards that bore the name and logo of the World Cup.

4. The following case shows how creative companies can be in marketing, while not violating the law, as well as the difficulty the court has in drawing the line. In *National Hockey League, et al. v. Pepsi-Cola Canada Ltd.*, 42 C.P.R.3d 390 (B.C. 1992), the National Hockey League filed a lawsuit alleging that Pepsi-Cola Canada, a company without rights to NHL trademarks, had engaged in misappropriation and unfair competition by using marks "confusingly similar" to those owned by the NHL. In spring 1990, Pepsi-Cola Canada conducted a consumer contest called the "Diet Pepsi $4,000,000 Pro Hockey Play-off Pool," whereby fans matching information under bottle caps with NHL playoff results became eligible for prizes. In addition, Pepsi-Cola Canada sponsored the broadcasts of the NHL playoff games throughout Canada and used its commercial spots to advertise the promotion. On all promotional materials connected with this contest and at the beginning of all commercials during the playoff games, Pepsi-Cola Canada displayed a disclaimer disassociating Pepsi-Cola Canada and its promotion from the NHL. The NHL claimed that not only was use of these disclaimers an admission by Pepsi-Cola Canada that it was aware of the misrepresentations contained in its advertising, but also that use of the words "National Hockey League" in the disclaimers was itself a trademark infringement. The Supreme Court of British Columbia ruled against the NHL, holding that Pepsi-Cola Canada had used sufficient disclaimers in its promotional announcements and commercial advertising to make consumers aware that it was not officially associated with the NHL. The judge stated that Pepsi's product is soft drinks and the NHL's product is hockey, and therefore there can be no confusion in the consumer's minds as to which product belongs to which company. The judge refused to accept the arguments brought forth by the NHL about the disclaimers used by Pepsi-Cola Canada, stating that a company can use the trademark of another company in its disclaimers because this allows the company to convey its promotional offer to the consumers truthfully and accurately. The use of disclaimers by Pepsi-Cola Canada was found to be sufficient to alleviate any potential confusion among consumers.

5. In *National Football League v. Governor of Delaware* 435 F. Supp. 1372, (D. Del. 1977), the National Football League (NFL) sought to bar the Delaware State Lottery from continuing to produce football-themed lottery games based on trademark laws because the lottery games depended on the outcomes of actual NFL games. Although the lottery games did not use NFL marks, the NFL thought the close relationship to its own games would create the impression that the NFL endorsed gambling. The court ruled that the games merely needed a "conspicuous statement" disclaiming them from any endorsement from the NFL. The court found no evidence that a perceived association with the NFL increased sales of the lottery games.

6. For additional information regarding ambush marketing, see Anita T. Moorman and T. Christopher Greenwell, "Consumer Attitudes of Deception and the Legality of Ambush Marketing Practices," 15 *Journal of Legal Aspects of Sport* 183 (2005).

13.1.7. Licensing Programs for Intercollegiate Athletics

In search of the economic benefits to be reaped from the sale of caps, pennants, T-shirts, jerseys, and souvenirs bearing a school's name or logo, many universities have instituted licensing programs in order to merchandise properties associated with their athletic teams. What is developing is a situation analogous to that in the major professional sport leagues, in that a licensing agent handles the licensing program for one or more university athletic departments. One such agent, the Collegiate Licensing Company (CLC), in 2010 represented nearly 200 colleges and universities, several postseason football bowl games, multiple college conferences, and the Downtown Athletic Club, the presenter of the Heisman Trophy (see note 1).

There are several reasons why a university or bowl game might use a licensing agent. For example, a university may not have the expertise or time to register the marks, negotiate licensing agreements with manufacturers, police mark infringers, and litigate when necessary. Also, a licensing agent often packages marks to manufacturers on a state, regional, or conference basis. For example, a licensing agent will package all of the marks of the Atlantic Coast Conference to one manufacturer. Therefore, a manufacturer who desires to produce Duke University apparel will also acquire the rights to produce apparel for Wake Forest University, another member of the ACC. This may save on costs for the manufacturer, who does not have to negotiate separately with each school.

Along with the advantages of using a licensing agent, there are several potential disadvantages. The university may prefer to control the selection of manufacturers and the quality of products, as well as to maintain flexibility in arranging licensing agreements. For example, universities that handle their own licensing programs may vary fees according to the type of product, the sales volume, whether the item is academically oriented, and other factors. A university that contracts with a licensing agent generally pays 40% to 50% of the royalty revenues generated to the agent, which reduces the university's net royalty revenues to 3% or 4% (instead of 6% to 8%). Also, the university may prefer to retain control of the decision-making authority with respect to enforcement of mark infringement cases.

Universities face a number of decisions and challenges in the area of trademarks and service marks. Initially, there is the decision of whether to begin a licensing program. If the answer is affirmative, the university should consider registering the existing marks on both the state and the federal level. The university may later be faced with the decision of whether to register a new mark—for instance, the phrase "Fab Five" for the University of Michigan basketball team in the early 1990s. The university must weigh the advantages and disadvantages of handling the licensing program itself or contracting with a licensing agent. In either situation, the university must establish public association between the mark, as used on various products, and the university's sponsorship.

The university must decide whether and what collateral marks and products will be sold. Finally, the university must be able to enforce the marks. If the university undertakes its own licensing program, it must police the mark wherever the products are sold. This may be only on a local basis in the state or region of the university, or it may be on a national basis if the school has a national reputation and sells its products nationwide.

Policing marks against infringers is one of the key determinants of long-term success for intercollegiate licensing programs. This is a costly and timely undertaking, and one that may well reduce the profitability of a licensing program for universities that do not realize significant royalty revenues. It remains to be seen whether universities will be able to establish the expertise, allocate the manpower, and spend the dollars necessary for effective enforcement of their marks. This issue alone may be a compelling reason for many universities to contract with a licensing agent, who, with tremendous economies of scale, can police and enforce marks.

Regardless of whether the university decides to handle the licensing program by itself or to contract with a licensing agent, it must make some decisions regarding the distribution of royalty revenues. Among the alternatives to be considered in distributing royalty revenues are appropriating money for athletic scholarships, for the general scholarship fund, for the general university fund, and/or returning the money to the campus bookstore. There is a wide range of ways in which colleges and universities have distributed royalty revenues on campus.

NOTES

1. For more on the CLC, visit its Web site at www.clc.com.

2. Steve McKelvey, Sheranne Fairley and Mark D. Groza, "Caught in the Web?: The Communication of Trademark Rights and Licensing Policy on University Official Athletic Websites," 20 *Journal of Legal Aspects* 1 (2010).

3. Examples of hundreds of different kinds of contracts, including radio licensing and cable broadcast agreements, are available at http://contracts.onecle.com/, specifically under "License Agreements."

4. For an example of an intercollegiate merchandise license agreement, see Alexander Lindey and Michael Landau, *Lindey on Entertainment, Publishing and the Arts*, 3rd ed., chap. 13, § 13:11.50 (Eagan, MN: West, 2008).

13.1.7.1. Litigation Involving Intercollegiate Licensing Programs

The practice of licensing college trademarks is a multimillion-dollar industry. Revenues from the sale of licensed products bearing the logos of popular colleges and universities can bring in millions of dollars annually. Therefore, it is not surprising that litigation has arisen between universities, manufacturers, and retailers over who owns the rights to the marks of the school. Discussed below is an early case that arose when colleges and universities and manufacturers were first beginning to realize the potential revenue from trademarked items.

In *University of Pittsburgh v. Champion Products, Inc.*, 686 F.2d 1040 (3d Cir.), *cert. denied*, 459 U.S. 1087 (1982), the U.S. District Court declined to extend the *Wichita Falls* holding (see section 13.1.5, "Trademark Infringement," note 18) to intercollegiate athletics, thus reversing an appeals court decision that had applied the *Wichita Falls* rationale. The initial decision of the court of appeals had extended the *Wichita Falls* decision by holding that the University of Pittsburgh had a right of relief against a manufacturer that allegedly infringed the university's trademark. This was seen as an especially important development in sports trademark law, because manufacturers/sellers had enjoyed unrestricted use of educational institutions' symbols for years.

However, the district court, on remand from its original decision that dealt with an unrelated question, found that "there is no likelihood of confusion, whether of source, origin, sponsorship, endorsement, or any other nature, between the soft goods of . . . Pitt." Soft goods include such items as T-shirts, hats, and sweatshirts. The court declined to apply the *Wichita Falls* rationale, which the appeals court had suggested might govern. Therefore, Champion was allowed to produce goods bearing the Pittsburgh logo without fear of litigation.

Since the 1930s, the school had goods with its insignia manufactured and sold by one company, initially for the school's athletic department, somewhat later for retail sales in the local area, and eventually for national distribution. In the mid-1970s, the school registered its marks under state and federal trademark laws in order to protect what it believed were valuable rights. This was due to the increasing popularity and national prominence of Pitt's football team. School officials sought to enter into a licensing agreement with Champion for continued use of the insignia. Champion was the premier manufacturer of soft goods imprinted with the insignia of educational institutions and reproduced emblems of more than 10,000 schools, colleges, and universities. At the time, the company reported annual sales in excess of $100 million. Champion had no such licensing agreement with any other schools, and Champion refused to enter into an agreement with Pitt.

Pitt went to court to stop Champion's unauthorized use of the school's insignia. The district court denied Pitt's request for a temporary injunction pending trial due to the doctrine of laches (neglect to take lawful action for an unreasonable time). The court of appeals, however, ruled that Pitt's delay in bringing an infringement action did not prevent its right to future injunctive relief. The case was remanded to the district court.

In the district court, the plaintiff in the case had to prove four elements to be successful in its case. These elements, considered essential for success in any trademark case based on unfair competition, were likelihood of confusion, non-functionality, secondary meaning, and priority of use. In the district court's ruling against Pitt, the court stated that Pitt *did not* "provide any real evidence of confusion." The court held that the university's presentation was very weak, and instead of showing a likelihood of confusion, the university showed little chance of any confusion whatsoever (see note 1). The district court, in discussing the functionality aspect of the case, noted that "the insignia on these soft goods serves a real, albeit aesthetic function for the wearers." Similarly, the court found no likelihood that, in regard to secondary meaning, the university was being associated with the manufacture of the product.

Finally, as to priority of use, Pitt had to show that it had priority "of trademark use in commerce." The district court ruled that the Pitt insignia was an ornament and not eligible for trademark protection. The court noted that Pitt had failed to prove any of the elements necessary to make its case.

An issue not discussed in the Pitt case but a common point of contention in trademark disputes is when each party began using the desired trademark and whether one party has abandoned its claim to the trademark (see notes 2 and 3). While this chapter has focused on the legal issues involved in trademarks, litigation may well be obviated by purely business considerations. On the intercollegiate level, despite its success on the merits in the *University of Pittsburgh* case, Champion Products settled the case and executed a licensing agreement with the university. There are several reasons for the move to licensing agreements and away from litigation. First, the manufacturer that challenges the university faces litigation expenses. Second, a manufacturer may have other business dealings with a university that may be adversely affected by litigation. For example, Champion Products supplied uniforms for intercollegiate athletic programs at many universities, and the loss of this business has been costly. When Champion settled the Pitt case by executing a licensing agreement, many other manufacturers decided to do the same. Universities must make prudent decisions about the products on which they license their marks. In December 2007, the state attorney generals of New York and Florida jointly announced that Student Financial Services, a college student loan company, was "co-branding" its loan offerings with official school insignias and mascots, thus creating the impression that the loans were officially endorsed by the school. In the deal, the school or athletic department received around $15,000 up front and $75 to $100 per applicant. The company accepted a settlement agreement effectively putting it out of business by forcing it to terminate all existing lending agreements, launch an advertising campaign to warn students to protect themselves when looking for loans, and to stop other cash inducements, such as paying students to refer their friends. None of the 63 schools involved (57 were Division I) or the loan company faced a financial penalty from the individual states, but legal action by students is still possible.

NOTES

1. In *Board of Supervisors of the Louisiana State University v. Smack Apparel Co.*, 438 F. Supp. 2d 653 (E.D. La. 2006), major football powers Louisiana State University (LSU), Oklahoma, Ohio State, and the University of Southern California and their licensing agent, Collegiate Licensing Company, sued Smack Apparel Company for trademark infringement. Smack had sold shirts using school colors and obvious references to the schools without a license. For example, one of the LSU shirts (using its official colors) featured "2003 College Football National Champions" on the front and a colored circular depiction of game scores, with "2003 College Football National Champions" and "Sweet as Sugar" on the back, in reference to the 2004 Sugar Bowl, which Louisiana State was set to play in for the national title. The district court found that the marks of the schools had acquired secondary meaning, a likelihood of confusion existed, and that the schools' marks were not functional, and thus granted summary judgment in favor of the plaintiffs.

2. In *Illinois High School Ass'n. v. GTE Vantage, Inc.*, 99 F. 3d. 244 (7th Cir. 1996), the plaintiff brought suit against the defendant to protect its trademark, "March Madness." The defendant holds a license for "March Madness" from the NCAA. The plaintiff began using the term "March Madness" in the 1940s. An announcer first used "March Madness" to describe the NCAA basketball tournament in 1982. Beginning in 1993–1994, the NCAA began licensing the use of the term to producers and suppliers. The court ruled that the Illinois High School Association (IHSA) did not have trademark that the law would protect, so far as the use of the term "March Madness" in connection with the NCAA tournament is concerned. This theory is based on the fact that the term "March Madness" in connection with the NCAA tournament was a term first appropriated to the NCAA by the media, and if the media call the NCAA tournament "March Madness," that is what the public will call it. Because of the free speech clause of the First Amendment, the IHSA could not have stopped the media from calling the NCAA tournament "March Madness," which is what the public now know it as. Therefore, the defendant was not the one responsible for "blotting out" the exclusive association of "March Madness" with the Illinois high school basketball tournament.

3. In *Board of Governors v. Helpingstine*, 714 F. Supp. 167 (M.D.N.C. 1989), the court held that the failure of the University of North Carolina at Chapel Hill to prosecute substantial uncontrolled use of its marks by third parties from its founding in 1795 until the inception of its licensing program in 1982 did not result in abandonment because the university's marks did not lose significance as indications of origin.

4. Other issues in the intercollegiate athletics area are raised in *Texas A&M University System v. University Book Store, Inc.*, 683 S.W.2d 140 (Tex. App. 1984). University Book Store, Inc. (UBC) and four other retail book stores filed suit against Texas A&M in August 1981. UBC operated stores near the university's campus in College Station and wanted to sell goods with the Texas A&M marks on them. Texas A&M refused to allow UBC to do so.

The case was tried without a jury, and a judgment was rendered for UBC; the trial court canceled Texas A&M's marks. The judgment was based on the trial court's finding that Texas A&M "is not the owner of the described marks" because it has not used the marks, and the conclusion that "the certificates of registration should be canceled pursuant to Art. 16.16(a)(4)(B), Tex. Bus. & C. Code."

Texas A&M appealed on two grounds, asserting that (1) the trial court erred in failing to dismiss this suit on its plea of sovereign immunity (see section 4.4.1, for a discussion on sovereign immunity), and (2) the trial court's finding that Texas A&M does not own the service marks because of lack of use is not supported by any evidence. The court of appeals reversed the district court's decision. It based its decision on sovereign immunity and also held:

> We disagree with appellees' contentions that the University is not the owner of the service marks and that the registrations are unlawful or invalid acts. The service marks carried rebuttable presumptions of the validity of the registrations, of the University ownership of the service marks, and of the University's exclusive right to use the mark in connection with higher education services.
>
> The court of appeals reasoned, "There is no evidence rebutting the University's use of the marks in connection with its higher education services."

A number of different considerations were raised in the *Texas A&M University System* case, in contrast to the *University of Pittsburgh* case. First, a retailer was involved instead of a manufacturer. Second, the plaintiff in *Texas A&M University System* challenged the marks and, as a plaintiff, could not successfully raise a laches argument, since laches is generally viewed as a defense. And, third, *Texas A&M University System* involved state institutions, which consequently raised sovereign immunity arguments.

5. For additional information on trademark infringement in collegiate licensing, see C. Knox Withers, "Sine Qua Non: Trademark Infringement, Likelihood of Confusion, and the Business of Collegiate Licensing," 11 *Journal of Intellectual Property Law* 421 (2004).

13.1.7.2. Trademark Law and Nicknames

Intellectual property law affects various aspects of intercollegiate athletics. Universities must be careful to protect their copyrights as well as trademark rights. For example, the Washington Redskins nearly lost federal protection of its trademarks because the term "redskin" was considered disparaging to groups of Native Americans (see note 2). This would not have foreclosed the Washington Redskins from using their logos or names, but it would have denied them federal trademark protection. They could have licensed merchandise with their name and logo and utilized state trademark common law for protection. However, as noted earlier, federal protection is more desirable.

The NCAA took matters into its own hands in August 2005, banning schools that use "hostile or abusive" Native American nicknames, mascots, or imagery from participating in NCAA postseason tournaments and from hosting postseason games. For example, nicknames such as "Braves" and "Indians" were considered to be "hostile and abusive." The Florida State University Seminoles were among five schools that were able to obtain the approval of local tribes, allowing it to keep its nickname without penalty. The University of Illinois officially retired mascot Chief Illiniwek on February 21, 2007, but was allowed to retain the nickname "Fighting Illini." Illinois stopped production of official Illiniwek merchandise in June 2007. The mascot had previously survived a lawsuit which claimed that it was in violation of the Illinois Civil Rights Act of 2003 (see note 1). In addition, the University of North Dakota sued the NCAA in an attempt to keep its "Fighting Sioux" nickname and logo, resulting in a settlement in October 2007. As a result of the settlement, North Dakota was given a three-year window to win the approvals of the local tribes.

Some colleges and universities had already altered their team nicknames or changed some of their practices. St. Johns University and the University of Massachusetts are two examples of schools that have already switched from the nickname Redman. In addition, the University of Oklahoma mascot, "Little Red," no longer performs war dances on the sidelines. Miami University (Ohio) changed its name from the Miami Redskins to the Miami Red Hawks.

NOTES

1. In *Illinois Native American Bar Association v. University of Illinois by its Board of Trustees*, 856 N.E.2d 460 (Ill. Ct. App. 1st Dist. 2006), the Bar Association claimed that the Chief Illiniwek dance was embarrassing and discouraged Native Americans from attending Illinois athletic events. The court disagreed, citing a 1996 amendment to the University of Illinois Act passed by the Illinois state legislature that declared Chief Illiniwek "an honored symbol of a great university." In June 2007, an Illinois court dismissed two lawsuits challenging the university's decision to no longer use Chief Illiniwek as the team mascot. One suit challenged the board of trustees' authority to make the decision, and another was brought by students who had impersonated the mascot at athletic events, claiming that barring them from performing as the chief violated their First Amendment rights. For more on this issue, see Andre Douglas Pond Cummings, "Progress Realized? The Continuing American Indian Mascot Quandry," 18 *Marquette Sports Law Review* 309 (2008) and Kenneth B. Franklin, "A Brave Attempt: Can the National Collegiate Athletic Association Sanction Colleges and Universities with Native American Mascots?" 13 *Journal of Intellectual Property Law* 435 (2006).

2. In *White v. Board of Regents*, 614 N.W.2d 330 (Neb. 2000), the defendant began a line of merchandise called "Huskers Authentic." At about the same time, the plaintiff registered the mark "Husker Authentics" for use in his store where he sold Nebraska merchandise. The court noted that the defendant began use of the mark before the plaintiff. The court stated, "We conclude...that the University had prior common-law rights superior to those of [plaintiff] in the trade name 'Husker Authentics' and that therefore the district court properly canceled [plaintiff's] registration."

3. In *Harjo v. Pro-Football, Inc.*, 50 U.S.P.Q.2d 1705 (T.T.A.B. 1999), a group of Native American rights advocates petitioned the Trademark Trial and Appeal Board of the U.S. Patent and Trademark Office against the Washington Redskins of the NFL. The Redskins had six different marks that contained Native American images or names that were offensive to the petitioners. In June 1999, the Patent and Trademark Office issued an order to cancel the registration of the marks held by the Redskins due to their offensive nature. The Redskins successfully appealed the cancellation of the marks in *Pro Football, Inc. v. Harjo* 284 F. Supp. 2d 96 (D.D.C. 2003), as the district court found that there was not substantial evidence to indicate disparagement and that the suit was barred by the doctrine of laches, which prevents legal action after a certain time period. The decision was affirmed in *Pro Football Inc. v. Harjo*, 565 F.3d 880 (C.A.D.C. 2009). For more information about the impact of this decision, see Mark S. Nagel, "Washington 'Redskins' - Disparaging Term or Valuable Tradition?: Legal and Economic Issues Concernig Harjo v. Pro-Football, Inc." 17 *Fordham Intellectual Property, Media & Entertainment Law Journal* 789 (2007) and Christian Dennie, "Native American Mascots and Team Names: Throw Away the Key; The Lanham Act Is Locked for Future Trademark Challenges," 15 *Seton Hall Journal of Sports and Entertainment Law* 197 (2005).

4. A legal dispute arose between Ohio State University (OSU) and Ohio University (OU) over the use of the word "Ohio." OU registered the mark "Ohio," but OSU objected to the mark's registration in 1997 after it became concerned that names such as Ohio Stadium might be in jeopardy. The issue was ultimately settled out of court. The parties agreed that OU gets to keep the trademark but that OSU gets to use it, too. "In the proposed settlement, Ohio State would drop its challenge of Ohio University's trademark, giving the Athens school the unchallenged trademark. Ohio State would retain some rights to the word Ohio in future marketing and merchandising, when those uses are in keeping with traditional OSU uses. An example would be commemorative OSU track uniforms featuring the Ohio logo, like those worn by track legend Jesse Owens in the 1930s." The Ohio attorney general will mediate any future disputes. "Old Pals Settle OU-OSU Battle over Four-Letter Word," *Columbus Dispatch*, April 29, 1999, Sec. A, p. 1.

5. In the late 1980s, Georgia Tech officials obtained trademarks for the national and international use of the word "Buzz," as it related to sporting events and clothing. In 1998, Georgia Tech filed a trademark suit against the Salt Lake City Buzz minor league baseball team. In its trademark suit, Georgia Tech alleged that the Salt Lake Buzz merchandise confused the buying public into being mistaken for Georgia Tech's. The case was settled and, as a result of the settlement, the Salt Lake City team can no longer use the word "buzz" in its team's name, Web site, or for merchandising purposes.

6. In *Univ. of Georgia Athletic Ass'n v. Laite*, 756 F.2d 1535 (11th Cir. 1985), the Laite Distributing Co., a wholesaler of novelty beers, began marketing "Battlin' Bulldog Beer."

The beer was sold in red and black cans bearing the image of an English bulldog wearing a red sweater emblazoned with a black G. The bulldog had bloodshot eyes, a football tucked under its right "arm," and a frothy beer stein in its left "hand." The Eleventh Circuit held that the University of Georgia's bulldog mascot is not a descriptive mark and is therefore protectable without a showing of secondary meaning. The court reasoned that the selection of an English bulldog as a mascot for its athletic teams is "suggestive, if not downright arbitrary" and the University of Georgia obtained preliminary and permanent injunctive relief in federal district court based on the likelihood of confusion between the Battlin' Bulldog and the University of Georgia Bulldog.

7. In *Board of Trustees v. Professional Therapy Services, Inc.*, 873 F. Supp. 1280 (W.D. Ark. 1995), the University of Arkansas sought to protect its trademarked "Razorback" mascot name from being used in the name of a local clinic. The school filed a federal trademark infringement claim under Section 32 of the Lanham Act against the Razorback Sports and Physical Therapy Clinic in 1989, when two university-associated athletic trainers became clinic consultants and limited partners. For a design logo, the clinic used a red, running razorback hog, and distributed promotional materials emphasizing its relationship with the university. The court granted summary judgment in favor of Arkansas. Chief Judge Waters, in considering the factors relevant to determining the existence of a likelihood of confusion, found in favor of the university, stating:

> The following factual and legal conclusions are undisputed. First, the visual impression created by the dominant elements of the RAZORBACK marks and the Clinic's marks is highly similar. Second, the RAZORBACK marks are strong ones that distinctively identify the University in the public mind. Third, the Clinic's services and the University's are competitive or so closely related as to suggest a common source. And no degree of care on the part of the Clinic customers can remedy any likelihood of confusion that may exist.
>
> These undisputed conclusions demonstrate a likelihood of confusion and a serious risk to the University that it will lose control over its public image as a provider of medical services, if the Clinic continues to use its marks. Also, there is no reasonable expectation that further evidence presented by the Clinic will change the court's mind in respect to the undisputed facts discussed above and the legal results that flow from them, especially since this case is before the court on cross-motions for summary judgment. Summary judgment is therefore granted for the University on the Lanham Act cause of action.

13.1.8. Trademark Law and the Olympics

The Olympic Games also present intellectual property issues. The International Olympic Committee owns the familiar "Olympic Rings," giving it the right to use the mark all over the world. In the United States, the U.S. Olympic Committee (USOC) has pursued violators who tried to use the protected marks and terminology of the USOC (for more on the USOC, see section 5.1.2, "The U.S. Olympic Committee"). In fact, protection has been provided not only through use of trademark law but also through the Ted Stevens Amateur Sports Act (the goal of

690 • ESSENTIALS OF SPORTS LAW

which is to promote and coordinate amateur athletic activity in the United States, to recognize certain rights for U.S. amateur athletes, to provide for the resolution of disputes involving national governing bodies, and for other purposes), which contains a section devoted entirely to the protection of Olympic terminology and symbols (subchapter 1—Corporation):

Excerpts from Ted Stevens Olympic and Amateur Sports Act:
§ 220506. Exclusive right to name, seals, emblems, and badges

(a) EXCLUSIVE RIGHT OF CORPORATION.—Except as provided in subsection (d) of this section, the corporation has the exclusive right to use—

    (1) the name "United States Olympic Committee";

    (2) the symbol of the International Olympic Committee, consisting of 5 interlocking rings, the symbol of the International Paralympic Committee, consisting of 3 TaiGeuks, or the symbol of the Pan-American Sports Organization, consisting of a torch surrounded by concentric rings;

    (3) the emblem of the corporation consisting of an escutcheon having a blue chief and vertically extending red and white bars on the base with 5 interlocking rings displayed on the chief; and

    (4) the words "Olympic", "Olympiad", "Citius Altius Fortius", "Paralympic", "Paralympiad", "Pan-American", "America Espirito Sport Fraternite", or any combination of those words.

(b) CONTRIBUTORS AND SUPPLIERS.—The corporation may authorize contributors and suppliers of goods or services to use the trade name of the corporation or any trademark, symbol, insignia, or emblem of the International Olympic Committee, International Paralympic Committee, the Pan-American Sports Organization, or of the corporation to advertise that the contributions, goods, or services were donated or supplied to, or approved, selected, or used by, the corporation, the United States Olympic team, the Paralympic team, the Pan-American team, or team members.

(c) CIVIL ACTION FOR UNAUTHORIZED USE.—Except as provided in subsection (d) of this section, the corporation may file a civil action against a person for the remedies provided in the Act of July 5, 1946 (15 U.S.C. 1051 et seq.) (popularly known as the Trademark Act of 1946) if the person, without the consent of the corporation, uses for the purpose of trade, to induce the sale of any goods or services, or to promote any theatrical exhibition, athletic performance, or competition—

    (1) the symbol described in subsection (a)(2) of this section;

    (2) the emblem described in subsection (a)(3) of this section;

    (3) the words described in subsection (a)(4) of this section, or any combination or simulation of those words tending to cause confusion or mistake, to deceive, or to falsely suggest a connection with the corporation or any Olympic, Paralympic, or Pan-American Games activity; or

    (4) any trademark, trade name, sign, symbol, or insignia falsely representing association with, or authorization by, the International Olympic Committee, the International Paralympic Committee, the Pan-American Sports Organization, or the corporation.

(d) PRE-EXISTING RIGHTS AND GEOGRAPHIC REFERENCE.—

    (1) A person who actually uses the emblem described in subsection (a)(3) of this section, or the words or any combination of the words described in subsection (a)(4) of this section, for any lawful purpose before September 21, 1950, is not prohibited by this section from continuing the lawful use for the same purpose and for the same goods or services.

    (2) A person who actually used, or whose assignor actually used, the words or any combination of the words described in subsection (a)(4) of this section, or a trademark, trade name, sign, symbol, or insignia described in subsection (c)(4) of this section, for any lawful purpose before September 21, 1950, is not prohibited by this section from continuing the lawful use for the same purpose and for the same goods or services.

    (3) Use of the word "Olympic" to identify a business or goods or services is permitted by this section where—

        (A) such use is not combined with any of the intellectual properties referenced in subsections (a) or (c) of this section;

        (B) it is evident from the circumstances that such use of the word "Olympic" refers to the naturally occurring mountains or geographical region of the same name that were named prior to February 6, 1998, and not to the corporation or any Olympic activity; and

        (C) such business, goods, or services are operated, sold, and marketed in the State of Washington west of the Cascade Mountain range and operations, sales, and marketing outside of this area are not substantial.

The USOC has been involved in several lawsuits against different businesses that attempted to use the words and/or symbols of the Olympics. These cases have generally involved attempts by various companies to use variations on the word "Olympics" in association with their organization, product or event. Organizations frequently try to appropriate the notions of goodwill, purity, competition and ethics from the Olympic Games. The USOC has been largely successful in these cases, as demonstrated by the following notes.

NOTES ⎯⎯⎯⎯⎯⎯⎯⎯⎯⎯⎯⎯⎯⎯⎯⎯⎯⎯⎯⎯⎯⎯⎯⎯⎯⎯⎯⎯⎯⎯⎯

    1. In *U.S. Olympic Committee v. Olympic Supply, Inc.*, 655 F.Supp.2d 599 (D.Md. 2009), the USOC brought an action against the seller of medical, janitorial, and industrial supplies for trademark infringement under the Lanham Act. The court rules that the USOC is entitled to prevent any use of the word "Olympic" in connection with any wholesale or retail business.

    2. In *U.S. Olympic Commitee v. Xclusive Leisure & Hospitality Ltd.*, 2008 WL 3971120 (N.D. Cal. August 25, 2008), the court granted the USOC's request for a preliminary injunction preventing the defendant from continuing to operate several websites whose domain names contained the word "olympic" in them. The defendants were selling tickets to the 2008 Beijing Olympics but the court found their actions to be violative of trademark, anti-cybersquatting and consumer fraud laws.

    3. In *United States Olympic Committee* v. *Toy Truck Lines*, 237 F.3d 1331 (Fed. Cir. 2001), the USOC was successful, upon appeal, against a manufacturer of toy trucks. The manufacturer had applied for a trademark for its trucks that bore the mark "Pan-American" on their side. Initially, the Patent and Trademark Office allowed this registration, even

though the USOC had registered the marks "Pan American Games," "USA Pan Am Team," and "Pan Am Games" for use with selling various goods. The appeals court reversed the decision of the Patent and Trademark Office, stating that the USOC had a legal right to the mark "Pan American." The court reasoned that the protection granted to the USOC's use of the Olympic words and symbols differs from the normal trademark protection in that the USOC did not need to prove that a contested use is likely to cause confusion, and that an unauthorized user of the word does not have available the normal statutory defenses.

4. In *O-M Bread v. United States Olympic Committee*, 65 F.3d 933 (Fed. Cir. 1995), the plaintiff, O-M Bread Company, attempted to register a bread product that would bear the name "Olympic Kids Bread." The USOC opposed the registration of this mark because it holds the rights to the word "Olympic" with the U.S. Patent and Trademark Office. Upon O-M Bread's appeal, the USOC was successful because it had clearly registered the mark in question. The court felt even though the marks "Olympic" and "Olympic Kids" were different, the two marks were still likely to cause confusion. "Further, as in determining likelihood of confusion, it is not relevant whether a portion of the mark is disclaimed or does not have strong trademark significance, such as the word 'kids.' No part of the mark can be ignored in comparing the marks as a whole."

5. In *San Francisco Arts & Athletics, Inc.* v. *United States Olympic Committee*, 483 U.S. 522 (1987), the United States Olympic Committee brought action against San Francisco Arts & Athletics, Inc. (SFAA), for using the word "Olympics" in its promotion of the "Gay Olympic Games." The USOC alleged a trademark violation under the Lanham Act. The court of appeals affirmed the lower court's summary judgment for the USOC and issued a permanent injunction against SFAA from further using the word "Olympics."

6. In *United States Olympic Committee* v. *Interlicense Corp.*, 469 U.S. 982 (1984), the defendant, a Swiss corporation, had a license from the International Olympic Committee to market pictograms bearing the Olympic rings. Because the defendant did not have the consent of the USOC, it was found to be in infringement of the trademark granted by the Amateur Sports Act and was enjoined from all further sales in the United States.

7. In *United States Olympic Committee v. Union Sport Apparel*, 220 U.S.P.Q. 526 (E.D. Va. 1983), the Trademark Board enjoined the defendant sportswear manufacturer from marketing clothing bearing a logo of three interlocking rings and the letters "U.S.A." The court determined that the defendant was trying to take advantage of the goodwill created by the USOC and thus infringed the trademark established in the Amateur Sports Act. The court held that the defendants violated the Amateur Sports Act of 1978 and issued an order awarding the USOC treble damages, its costs and attorney's fees, and defendant's wrongful profits. The awarding of costs, attorney's fees, and wrongful profits represented a first in the USOC's legal battles against trademark exploitation. The court's rationale in the awarding of damages was based upon a finding of deliberate and willful infringement.

8. In *United States Olympic Committee v. International Federation of Bodybuilders*, 219 U.S.P.Q. 353 (D.D.C. 1982), the defendants were enjoined from using a seven-ring symbol, similar to the Olympic interlocking ring symbol, in their magazines or for purposes of advertising various products. This ruling was based on the trademark protection granted through the Amateur Sports Act. The term "Mr. Olympia," used to refer to the winner of a professional bodybuilding contest, was allowed.

9. For more on the Ted Stevens Olympic and Amateur Sports Act, see Noelle K. Nish, "How Far Have We Come? A Look at the Olympic and Amateur Sports Act of 1998, the United States Olympic Committee and the Winter Olympic Games of 2002," 13 *Seton Hall Journal of Sports and Entertainment Law* 53 (2003).

10. For more on ambush marketing during the Olympics, see Patrick Donohue Sheridan, "An Olympic Solution to Ambush Marketing: How the London Olympics Show the Way to More Effective Trademark Law," 17 *Sports Lawyers Journal* 27 (2010) and Doris Estelle Long, "Trademarks and the Beijing Olympics: Gold Medal Challenges," 7 *John Marshall Review of Intellectual Property Law* 433 (2008).

13.2. COPYRIGHT LAW

Copyright law issues are found in television, radio broadcasting, media guides, team or school publications, league or conference publications, music, and the Internet. Copyright law protects the expression of ideas, but not the ideas themselves.

In the sports setting, some examples of copyrighted works include the music played at sporting events, the media guides or programs sold at sporting events, and even the sporting event itself after it has been recorded/broadcast for television or radio. More in-depth discussion of how copyright law impacts broadcasting and sports can be found in Chapter 14. Intangible items cannot be copyrighted because it is virtually impossible to protect an idea, something that exists in the mind only. It is much more practical to protect items that are identifiable on paper, videotape or audiotape, and so on. "Copyright protection subsists…in original works of authorship fixed in any tangible medium of expression, now known or later developed, from which they can be perceived, reproduced, or otherwise communicated, either directly or with the aid of a machine or device." Copyright law protects works such as books, pictorials, graphic and sculptural works, music, photographs, movies, and computer programs (see notes 3 and 5).

The owner of a registered copyright enjoys the ability to block the unauthorized copying or public performance of a work protected by copyright (see note 7). In the United States, the law that governs copyrights is Title 17 of the United States Code (§§ 101–810; 1001–1010). It incorporates the Berne Convention, which is an international treaty regarding copyrights that most countries have signed. Copyright law is often described as a bundle of rights. As established by 17 U.S.C. § 106, "the owner of copyright under this title has the exclusive rights to do and to authorize any of the following:

1. to reproduce the copyrighted work in copies or phonorecords;
2. to prepare derivative works based upon the copyrighted work;
3. to distribute copies or phonorecords of the copyrighted work to the public by sale or other transfer of ownership, or by rental, lease, or lending;
4. in the case of literary, musical, dramatic, and choreographic works, pantomimes, and motion pictures and other audiovisual works, to perform the copyrighted work publicly;
5. in the case of literary, musical, dramatic, and choreographic works, pantomimes, and pictorial, graphic, or sculptural works, including the individual images of a motion picture or other audiovisual work, to display the copyrighted work publicly; and
6. in the case of sound recordings, to perform the copyrighted work publicly by means of a digital studio transmission."

Copyright law arises upon creation and, under current law, endures for the life of the author plus 70 years. Copyright law applies to both unpublished and published works. Registration of a copyrighted work with the Copyright Office in Washington, D.C., is not required for existence of the copyright; however, it is a prerequisite to a lawsuit for copyright infringement and to certain legal remedies (e.g., injunctive relief). The familiar copyright notice is no longer required on copies of works published after March 1, 1989. However, it is still in the copyright owner's interest to place a copyright notice on publicly distributed copies of published works. The notice should include the copyright symbol, ©, or the word "copyright" or its abbreviation, followed by the year of first publication of the work and the name of the copyright owner.

One area where copyright law and sports have intersected concerns the providing of real-time scores of professional sporting events without the consent of the governing leagues. In *NBA v. Motorola, Inc.*, 105 F.3d 841 (2d Cir. 1997), the NBA filed suit against the manufacturer and promoter of handheld pagers that provided real-time information about professional basketball games, alleging copyright infringement. The league also sought to enjoin an online provider, Sports Team Analysis and Tracking Systems (STATS) of the same information. The pager was able to provide (i) the teams playing; (ii) score changes; (iii) the team in possession of the ball; (iv) whether the team was in the free-throw bonus; (v) the quarter of the game; and (vi) time remaining in the quarter. The information was recorded by STATS reporters who watched the games on television or listened to them on the radio. The reporters then entered that information into a computer which was then relayed to STATS host computer from where it was retransmitted to the pagers. The entire process took approximately two to three minutes. The district court found Motorola and STATS liable for misappropriation and granted the NBA's request for a permanent injunction.

While the media has the right to report hot news, it cannot report on information where: (i) a plaintiff generates or gathers information at a cost; (ii) the information is time-sensitive; (iii) a defendant's use of the information constitutes free riding on the plaintiff's efforts; (iv) the defendant is in direct competition with a product or service offered by the plaintiffs; and (v) the ability of other parties to free-ride on the efforts of the plaintiff or others would so reduce the incentive to produce the product or service that its existence or quality would be substantially threatened.

In reversing the injunction, the Second Circuit determined that Motorola and STATS did not meet this test, finding that Motorola's transmission of real-time statistics could not possibly serve as a disincentive for the NBA to continue to produce its primary product, that of professional basketball games. The court of appeals also held that the professional basketball games were not "original works of authorship," and therefore there was no copyright infringement.

A similar issue arose in *Morris Communications Corp. v. PGA Tour, Inc.* 364 F.3d 1288 (11th Cir. Fla. 2004), though the claim was based on alleged antitrust violations as opposed to copyright infringement. In *Morris*, the PGA was granted summary judgment, preventing Morris from providing real-time scoring for professional golf events. The process, known as the Real-Time Scoring System (RTSS) went as follows. The PGA employed "hole reporters" who follow each group of golfers on the golf course and tabulate the scores of each player at the end of each hole of golf played. The scores are then collected by volunteers located at each of the 18 greens on the golf course, who, with the aid of handheld wireless radios, relay the scoring information to a remote production truck staffed by personnel employed by the defendant. The scores of all participating golfers are then processed at the remote production truck and transmitted by the defendant to its Web site, pgatour.com. At the same time, real-time scores are also transmitted to an on-site media center where members of the media are able to access the scores. The PGA did not allow media to release the scores until they were posted on pga tour.com in order to protect its investment in a real-time scoring system. Morris claimed that the PGA was monopolizing the market for real-time golf scores, but the Eleventh Circuit found that the PGA was justified in its restrictions because it wanted to prevent Morris from free-riding on its RTSS technology. In doing so, the Court specifically stated "this case is not about copyright law" and did not address Morris's right of access to real-time golf scores, only its ability to sell them.

In these cases, the courts allowed companies to provide real-time scores through their Web sites and handheld pagers, respectively. Although leagues and organizations own the rights to broadcast games, companies have been allowed to provide real-time scores because they are not rebroadcasts of the game, and are solely providing information, not commentary or detailed information. With the expansion of Internet technology, this area of copyright law has seen more litigation.

Some copyrighted material can, however, be used without the owner's permission in the context that the work is for "fair use." Section 107 of the Copyright Act of 1976 provides that "the fair use of a copyrighted work, including such use by reproduction in copies or phonorecords or by any other means specified by that section, for purposes such as criticism, comment, news reporting, teaching (including multiple copies for classroom use), scholarship, or research, is not an infringement of copyright." Also, according to Section 107, there are several factors that must be considered in making a determination of fair use. Those factors are as follows:

1. The purpose and character of the use, including whether such use is of a commercial nature or is for nonprofit educational purposes
2. The nature of the copyrighted work
3. The amount and substantiality of the portion used in relation to the copyrighted work as a whole
4. The effect of the use upon the potential market for or value of the copyrighted work.

For example, in sports, ABC used a biography about the legendary wrestler Dan Gable without permission from the copyright owner, Iowa State University. ABC argued that it was not subject to copyright infringement because it used a portion of the biography as fair use and that the information was of a public interest; however, the court found that ABC was not exempt because of fair use. The network's use of the film had a profit-making character, and the network usurped an extremely significant market for the film. See *Iowa State University Research Foundation, Inc. v. American Broadcasting Company, Inc.*, 621 F.2d 57 (2d Cir. 1980).

Another questionable area of copyright law and sports is whether specific plays or moves can be copyrighted. While individual plays and moves are generally considered public ideas or facts, scripts and compilations may be subject to copyright law (see notes 6 and 7).

NOTES _____

1. In *Gutkowski v. Steinbrenner*, 680 F.Supp.2d 602 (S.D.N.Y. 2010), a television executive alleged that the very successful Yankees Entertainment and Sports (YES) Network was his idea and unlawfully used by the Yankees. The case was dismissed on contractual grounds. The Baltimore Ravens and former head coach Brian Billick experienced a similar suit in *Davis v. Billick*, 2002 U.S. Dist. LEXIS 11504 (N.D. Tex. June 26, 2002). That case was dismissed on jurisdictional grounds.

2. In *The Football Ass'n of Premier League Ltd. v. YouTube, Inc.*, 633 F.Supp.2d 159 (S.D.N.Y. 2009) the English soccer league brought a class action suit along with several music companies alleging copyright violations against YouTube for allowing copyrighted clips to be posted on the site without permission. The court dismissed any claim for statutory damages based on the plaintiffs' failure to register the foreign works in the United States.

3. In *Jacob Maxwell, Inc. v. Veeck*, 110 F.3d 749 (11th Cir. 1997), the plaintiff composed a song, "Cheer! The Miracle Is Here," for the defendant minor league baseball team, the Miracle. The plaintiff sued for copyright infringement after the defendant failed to pay for the song and allegedly used the song without permission. The defendant was supposed to acknowledge the plaintiff as the writer and producer of the song but failed to do so. The plaintiff apparently gave the defendant permission to use the song even though he had not yet been paid and, in fact, attended many Miracle games and did not complain after failing to hear the requisite acknowledgment. In granting summary judgment, the court held that the plaintiff's conduct indicated a nonexclusive license to make use of the song, and, therefore, there was no copyright infringement.

4. In *Hoopla Sports and Entertainment, Inc. v. Nike, Inc.*, 947 F. Supp. 347 (N.D. Ill. 1996), the organizer of an international high school age all-star basketball game brought action against the shoe manufacturer that sponsored a competing game and the television station that broadcast the game. The plaintiff alleged copyright infringement, among other legal theories. On the defendant's motion to dismiss, the district court held that the idea for the game was not copyrightable. Additionally, even if the basketball game was copyrightable, the organizer failed to comply with the necessary prerequisites to copyright the game.

5. In *NFL v. Cousin Hugo's, Inc.*, 600 F. Supp. 84 (E.D. Missouri 1984), the NFL sued a restaurant for intercepting and broadcasting live telecasts of St. Louis Cardinals football games. The district court held that the NFL was entitled to a temporary restraining order preventing the defendant's actions.

6. In *Open Source Yoga Unity v. Choudhury*, 2005 WL 756558 (N.D. Cal. April 1, 2005), the plaintiff sought a declaration that the copyright for "Bikram yoga" was invalid. Bikram yoga is a yoga sequence developed by the defendant, who sought to have all yoga instructors licensed by him. The court refused summary judgment for either party on the matter, but noted that if the copyright was valid, it was very "thin" and only pertained to the specific sequence.

7. For more information on the copyrighting of specific moves and compilations, see Henry M. Abromson, "The Copyrightability of Sports Celebration Moves: Dance Fever or Just Plain Sick?" 14 *Marquette Sports Law Review* 571 (Spring 2004) and Brent C. Moberg, "Football Play Scripts: A Potential Pitfall for Federal Copyright Law," 14 *Marquette Sports Law Review* 525 (2004).

13.2.1. Copyright Law and the Internet

The Internet is becoming a troublesome area for intellectual property law without clear-cut answers. Internet problems cover several areas, including broadcast rights, the use of sports teams' names and logos, and the use of athletes' names.

Ever-growing technology presents a problem for sports organizations. Right now, fans can listen to games, just as they would the radio, over the Internet. Currently, teams own the rights to broadcast games over the Internet. In the future, we will likely see Internet broadcast rights negotiated the same way we see television and radio rights negotiated today. However, the advent of Internet broadcasting brings about some new potential problem areas and issues, including "policing" and protecting the rights holder across an entity as broad and global as the Internet.

Two federal acts that have been passed to address the ever-changing legal problems of intellectual property and the Internet are the Digital Millennium

Copyright Act (DMCA) and the No Electronic Theft Act (NET Act) (see note 1 and section 14.4, "Internet Rights for Sports Broadcasts"). The DMCA was implemented to ensure that a holder of a copyright cannot have its copyrighted material posted on the Internet without authorization. Among other things, the act allows for penalties for people who attempt to circumvent copyright protection systems or who sell equipment that allows people to avoid these protection systems. The NET Act makes it illegal for someone to willfully infringe a copyright (1) for purposes of commercial advantage or private financial gain, or (2) by the reproduction or distribution, including by electronic means, during any 180-day period of one or more copies of one or more copyrighted works that have a total retail value of more than $1,000. The basic premise behind the NET Act is to punish people who willfully infringe upon copyrighted material on the Internet for financial gain.

Another problem in this area is "cybersquatting." Cybersquatters are people who register sports teams' domain names before the team does. Many of these cybersquatters register the domain names in hopes of later selling the domain names to the named party. The Anticybersquatting Consumer Protection Act (15 U.S.C. § 1125(d)) was enacted to prevent the deliberate and bad-faith registration of Internet domain names in violation of trademark rights. (For a review of the legislation, see note 2.) Cybersquatting is also a problem for athletes. Cybersquatters register the names of famous sports figures, or even potentially famous sports figures, in hopes of later selling the Internet addresses to the athletes at a profit.

The major sports leagues have begun to take a proactive approach to cybersquatters. The four major leagues and the Collegiate Licensing Company formed the Coalition to Advance the Protection of Sports Logos. This group has brought action against two cybersquatters under the Anti-Cybersquatting Protection Act (ACPA) (see note 2). The group brought action in late 1999 against Jeff Burgar, a profile cybersquatter, who registered names such as *chargers1.com*, *redskins1. com*, and *goclippers.com*. The action resulted in the transfer of 175 domain names and a $16,000.00 penalty against Burgar. Although the leagues are attempting to be proactive in protecting their marks on the Internet, cybersquatters are becoming more creative. Cybersquatters are even registering the names of high school athletes who may make it big in the future (see notes 4 through 7 for a discussion of cases involving cybersquatters).

The Anti-Cybersquatting Consumer Protection Act also provides some protection to individual athletes.

> Any person who in good faith registers a domain name that consists of the name of another living person, or a name substantially similar thereto, without that person's consent, with the specific intent to profit from such name by selling the domain name for financial gain to that person or any third party, shall be liable in a civil action by such person.

This section of the act indicates that individual persons will have the ability to bring a civil suit if another uses his or her name. However, the cybersquatter must have the specific intent to profit from the sale of the domain name.

In addition to the ACPA, organizations and individuals can utilize the Uniform Domain Name Dispute Resolution Policy (see note 3) promulgated by the Internet Corporation for Assigned Names and Numbers. This policy provides an arbitration process that offers an alternative to litigation for domain name disputes. The policy requires that the domain name be identical or confusingly similar to the trademark owner's mark. The owner must also demonstrate that the registered domain name was registered in bad faith and that the registrant has no legitimate interest in the domain name.

Even though these methods for domain name resolution have been developed and have proven to be effective in the short term, there is some question as to how effective they can continue to be. Questions exist as to whether the ACPA will be effective as disputes become more international.

NOTES

1. More information on the DMCA and the NET Act can be found from the Library of Congress at http://thomas.loc.gov.
2. The ACPA (also available from the Library of Congress website) provides:

A person shall be liable in a civil action by the owner of a mark, including a personal name which is protected as a mark under [the Lanham Act], if, without regard to the goods or services of the parties, that person
1. has a bad faith intent to profit from that mark, including a personal name which is protected as a mark under [the Lanham Act]; and
2. registers, traffics in, or uses a domain name that

  i. in the case of a mark that is distinctive at the time of registration of the domain name, is identical or confusingly similar to that mark;

  ii. in the case of a famous mark that is famous at the time of registration of the domain name, is identical or confusingly similar to or dilutive of that mark; or

  iii. is a trademark, word, or name protected by reason of section 706 of title 18, United States Code, or section 220506 of title 36, United States Code.

  The section outlines nine factors that may be considered in determining whether the registration took place in bad-faith:

  In determining whether a person has a bad faith intent described under [the section above], a court may consider factors such as, but not limited to:

  iv. the trademark or other intellectual property rights of the person, if any, in the domain name;

  v. the extent to which the domain name consists of the legal name of the person or a name that is otherwise commonly used to identify that person;

  vi. the person's prior use, if any, of the domain name in connection with the bona fide offering of any goods or services;

  vii. the person's bona fide noncommercial or fair use of the mark in a site accessible under the domain name;

  viii. the person's intent to divert consumers from the market owner's online location to a site accessible under the domain name that could harm the goodwill represented by the mark, either for commercial gain or with the intent to tarnish or disparage the mark, by creating a likelihood of confusion as to the source, sponsorship, affiliation, or endorsement of the site;

  ix. the person's offer to transfer, sell, or otherwise assign the domain name to the mark owner or any third party for financial gain without having used, or having an intent to use, the domain name in the bona fide offering of any goods or services, or the person's prior conduct indicating a pattern of such conduct;

  x. the person's provision of material and misleading false contact information when applying for the registration of the domain name, the person's intentional failure to maintain accurate contact information, or the person's prior conduct indicating a pattern of such conduct;

xi. the person's registration or acquisition of multiple domain names which the person knows are identical or confusingly similar to marks of others that are distinctive at the time of registration of such domain names, or dilutive of famous marks of others that are famous at the time of registration of such domain names, without regard to the goods or services of the parties; and

xii. the extent to which the mark incorporated in the person's domain name registration is or is not distinctive and famous within the meaning of subsection (c)(1) of section 43.

3. The Act also provides that bad faith shall not be found when the registrant had reasonable grounds to believe that the use of the domain name was fair and lawful.

4. For more information on the Uniform Domain-Name Dispute-Resolution Policy, see www.icann.org/udrp/.

5. In *March Madness Athletic Association, LLC v. Netfire, Inc.*, 310 F. Supp. 2d 786 (N.D. Tex. 2003), the defendant was determined to have registered the Web site marchmadness.com in bad faith and in violation of the Anti-Cybersquatting Consumer Protection Act. The court ruled that "march madness" was protected under the Lanham Act and ordered the transfer of the domain from the defendant to the plaintiff.

6. In the case of *NBA Properties, Inc. v. Adirondack Software Corporation*, WIPO Arbitration and Mediation Center, Administrative Panel Decision, case no. D2000–1211 (2000), NBA Properties was attempting to claim the Web site www.knicks.com away from Adirondack Software Corporation, which had registered the domain name through Network Solutions, a Web domain name registration company, in 1995. The league attempted to contact Adirondack unsuccessfully over the course of four years, starting in 1996. At one point, Adirondack allegedly sent a letter to Network Solutions transferring the site to the NBA, but Network Solutions deemed the letter insufficient, and no further attempts were made. Network Solutions put the site on "hold," pending a resolution between the two parties, but when none was had by March 30, 2000, Network Solutions informed the NBA that the site would be taken off hold. At that point, the Knicks brought their case to the WIPO Arbitration and Mediation Center. In deciding the case for Adirondack, the court outlined five reasons that Adirondack should maintain its rights over the site:

1. Madison Square Garden is the rightful owner of the Knicks trademark, and therefore NBA Properties does not have the rights to the mark, or standing to bring the case.

2. Adirondack did not register the domain name solely in order to sell the rights, as evidenced by its attempt to transfer the rights to the NBA at one point.

3. Adirondack does not have a pattern of registering domain names that are trademarked items.

4. The domain name was not registered to disrupt the business of the NBA.

5. The domain name was not used to attract users to a Web site other than the site of the owners.

7. In *ISL Marketing and Federation Internationale de Football Association v. Nutt*, Case No. D2000–0363, World Intellectual Property Organization Administrative Panel Decision, July 17, 2000, ISL and FIFA brought a complaint against the respondent who registered fifa-world-cup.com. FIFA has registrations for the following marks internationally and in certain European countries: FIFA World Cup, FIFA, and World Cup. The panel found that the respondent's domain name was confusingly similar to FIFA's marks, that the respondent had no rights in those marks, and that he acted in bad faith in registering the domain name. The panel ordered the domain name to be transferred to the complainant.

8. In *Quokka Sports, Inc. v. Cup Int'l, Ltd.*, 99 F. Supp. 2d 1105 (N.D. Cal. 1999), the plaintiff, holder of the Internet rights to use certain America's Cup trademarks (licensed by

America's Cup Properties, Inc.), filed suit requesting a temporary restraining order based on trademark infringement. The defendant had registered the domain name americascup. com. The court ruled "that the operation of the Web site at www.americascup.com is likely to cause consumer confusion." Additionally, the court stated that "[t]he website appears for all intents and purposes to be masquerading as an official site associated with the America's Cup event." The court further stated that plaintiff suffered irreparable harm in that traffic was being diverted from the official America's Cup Web site. The district court granted the temporary restraining order.

9. For examples of litigation regarding cybersquatting and the NCAA, see Scott A. Bearby, "Marketing, Protection and Enforcement of NCAA Marks," 12 *Marquette Sports Law Review* 543 (2002).

10. For more information on cybersquatting, see Mairead Moore, "Cybersquatting: Prevention Better than Cure?" 17 *International Journal of Law and Information Technology* 220 (2009); Aaron Jay Horowitz, "U.S. Jurisdictional Monopolization of International Cybersquatting Disputes: A Review of Current Inequities and Future Consequences," 11 *Journal of Technology Law and Policy* 191 (2006); and David S. Magier, "Tick, Tock, Time Is Running out to Nab Cybersquatters: The Dwindling Utility of the Anticybersquatting Consumer Protection Act," 46 *Intellectual Property Law Review* 415 (2006).

11. For more information on fantasy sports, Risa J. Weaver, "Online Fantasy Sports Litigation and the Need for a Federal Right of Publicity Statute," 2010 *Duke Law & Technology Review* 2 (2010), Michael Gerton "Kids' Play: Examining the Impact of the CBC Distribution Decision on College Fantasy Sports," 11 *Texas Review of Entertainment & Sports Law* 153 (2009) and Manav K. Bhatnagar, "Fantasy Liability: Publicity Law, The First Amendment, and Fantasy Sports," 119 *Yale Law Journal* 131 (2009).

13.3. PATENT LAW

A patent is a document, issued by the federal government, that grants its owner a legally enforceable right to exclude others from claiming ownership of the invention described and claimed in the document. The Patent Act governs patent protection. It allows an individual to acquire a patent for an invention or discovery of "any new useful process, machine, manufacture, or composition of matter, or any new and useful improvement thereof." There is a further specification that the invention or discovery be nonobvious. The Supreme Court has adopted the view that such patent protection is applicable to "anything under the sun that is made by man." Congress allows this right, through the Patent Act (35 U.S.C. §§ 1–376), for a term ending 20 years from the date of the filing of an application for patent, to encourage the public disclosure of technical advances and as an incentive for investing in their commercialization. Thus, the overall progress of technical innovation is favored, while at the same time inventors are rewarded for their specific contributions. Like other forms of property, the rights symbolized by a patent can be inherited, sold, rented, mortgaged, and even taxed.

When a patent expires, or is held invalid, the right to exclude others from use of a patent ceases. The public is the ultimate beneficiary of the technical advance. Examples of patents that are used in a sports setting include baseball "donuts" (warm-up weights that wrap around a baseball bat), golf swing machines, golf putting machines, and even athletic shoes. The Nike Air shoes and the Reebok Pump were both products used in the sports industry, and their technical innovation was patented to protect the inventor and the company that owned the rights (see note 2). Congress has specified that a patent will be granted if the inventor files a timely application at the U.S. Patent and Trademark Office that adequately describes a new, useful, and unobvious invention of proper subject matter. To be timely, an application must be filed within one year of certain acts (by the inventor or others) that place the invention in the hands of the public (e.g., patented or published anywhere in the world, on sale or in public use in this country). This one-year grace period, however, is not available in most foreign countries. A U.S. inventor who wants to obtain corresponding foreign patents must file an application in the United States before any written or oral public presentation of the invention complete enough to enable others to practice the invention. Moreover, the application must describe the best manner ("best mode") known to the inventor of carrying out the invention.

The proper subject matter of a patent is any product, process, apparatus, or composition, including living matter, such as genetically engineered bacteria or plants. Purely mental processes, newly discovered laws of nature, and methods of doing business are not proper subjects for a patent. Most inventors seek a patent to obtain the actual or potential commercial advantages that go along with the right to exclude others. Given the high cost of research and development, the opportunity to recoup these costs through commercial exploitation of the invention may be the primary justification for undertaking research in the first place.

The described invention must be new. This means that it must not have been invented first by another person or identically known, or used by others in this country, or patented or published anywhere in the world before the actual invention date (not the application filing date). The invention also must be useful. It must serve some disclosed or generally known purpose. Section 103 of the Patent Act has an additional requirement of unobviousness, meaning that the differences between the invention and the prior public knowledge in its technical field must be such that a person having ordinary skill in this field would not have found the invention obvious at the time it was made.

Patent rights can be commercially exploited in two basic ways: (1) directly, by the inventor's practice of the invention to obtain an exclusive marketplace advantage (as where the patent technology results in a better product or produces an old product less expensively) and/or (2) indirectly, by receiving income from the sale or licensing of the patent. It is important to note that a patent does not give the inventor the right to practice the invention. The inventor can practice his or her invention only if by so doing he or she does not also practice the invention of an earlier unexpired patent.

Licenses can be nonexclusive, allowing many parties, including the inventor, to practice the invention simultaneously. An example of a nonexclusive license is a baseball pitching machine. This device to help hitters during practice is used all over the country. A patent allows the inventor and many players to use the machine at the same time. A patent may also provide commercial advantages in addition to the potential for an exclusive market position or licensing income. A patent often lends business credibility to start-up ventures and can open doors to both markets. An improvement patent may also make it possible to cross-license any basic patents held by others that block the path to the market.

NOTES _____

1. Callaway Golf has been very active in trying to protect its patents. In *Callaway Golf Company v. Acushnet Company*, 585 F. Supp. 2d 600 (D. Del. 2008), Callaway sued the parent company of Titleist, alleging that its Pro V1 golf ball infringed on Callaway patents. The court granted Callaway's request for an injunction, finding that a person of ordinary skill in

the art of golf ball making would not have been motivated to create the Pro V1 without prior knowledge of the Callaway ball. Prior to the suit, the Pro V1 ball was the most popular ball on the PGA Tour. In December 2007, Callaway and rival TaylorMade resolved patent claims against each other by allowing usage of specific patents by the other. Also, in December 2007, Callaway received a favorable jury decision which ruled that the top-selling Titleist Pro V1 golf ball made by Acushnet used patents that Callaway owns. Acushnet attempted to declare certain patents invalid, but was unable to do so in *Callaway Golf Co. v. Acushnet Co.*, 2007 U.S. Dist. LEXIS 85599 (D. Del. Nov. 20, 2007). In *Callaway Golf Co. v. Dunlop Slazenger*, 384 F. Supp. 2d 735, (D. Del. 2005), Callaway was awarded $1.1 million when it proved that Dunlop was wrongly advertising that its golf balls travel further. Dunlop countered that Callaway had misappropriated its trade secrets, but a jury ruled that while Callaway improperly acquired the trade secrets, it did not use them. For more on Callaway's efforts to protect its intellectual property, see C. Bradford Jorgensen, "Golf Club Technology: Intellectual Property and the Counterfeiting Epidemic," 13 *Syracuse Science and Technology Law Reporter* 58 (2006).

2. The most recent sneaker invention to spark litigation has been cushioning technology, sometimes known as "Shox" or "Shock" technology. First, in *Nike, Inc. v. Dixon*, 2004 WL 3065757 (D. Or. April 6, 2004), Nike was granted summary judgment against a shoe designer's claim that Nike misappropriated his "Shockee 2000" design. However, Nike was forced to settle a lawsuit with another shoe designer that claimed he had designed the cushioning technology being used by Nike; see *Ian Whatley v. Nike, Inc.*, No. 3:98–963 (D. Or. May 23, 2005). Nike then sued Adidas, claiming that Adidas infringed on Nike's Shox technology patent, but its claims were limited in *Nike, Inc. v. Adidas America Inc.*, 479 F. Supp. 2d 664 (E.D. Tex. 2007). Last, in *Cushion Technologies, LLC v. Adidas Salomon North America, Inc.*, 537 F. Supp. 2d 839 (E.D. Tex. 2008), the court was forced to rule on a dispute over a number of shoe-related terms.

3. In *Antonious v. Spalding & Evenflo Companies, Inc.*, 217 F.3d 849 (Fed. Cir. 1999), the plaintiff filed suit, alleging infringement of a design patent for iron golf clubs. The court, citing a U.S. Supreme Court case, provided that "[i]f, in the eye of an ordinary observer, giving such attention as a purchaser usually gives, two designs are substantially the same, if the resemblance is such as to deceive such an observer, inducing him to purchase one supposing it to be the other, the first one patented is infringed by the other." The court, in affirming the lower court's ruling, held that there was no patent infringement.

4. In the case of *Nike Inc. v. Wal-Mart Stores Inc.*, 138 F.3d 1437 (Fed. Cir. 1998), Wal-Mart was appealing a decision by the trial court to grant Nike $6 million because Wal-Mart and the shoe manufacturer, Hawe Yue Inc., had allegedly infringed upon Nike's patent No. 348,765, which is a particular shoe design. The appeals court remanded the decision for a discussion of whether Nike had met the "marking statute." This marking statute deals with whether the patent holder affixes anything on the product that shows the product is indeed patented.

5. For an idea of what type of sports-related materials can be patented, visit the Web site for the U.S. Patent and Trademark Office at www.uspto.gov/patft. For example, U.S. Patent No. 5,419,561 is a method of miniature golf that is registered as follows:

A method of playing traditional, championship golf using only a putter and a single golf ball, comprising the steps of: a) providing a reduced size golf course including a series of eighteen holes each including a playing surface simulating grass and defining a teeing area and a putting green at opposite ends of a fairway, means for limiting the number of strokes to play said eighteen holes, using only a putter and a single golf ball, to a par 72, the said eighteen holes including four par-3 holes, four par-5 holes, and ten par-4 holes, b) Providing representations of natural hazards along said holes as bunkers and water hazards by selectively colored areas wherein a selected color is employed to represent a particular hazard and any penalty associated therewith, c) providing and indicating maximum distance boundaries across the fairways of said holes in selective manner past which the player must not stroke a ball with the putter without incurring a penalty, and d) said colored areas and boundaries being so arranged that the player may play the reduced area course with only a putter as if it were a full size championship golf course by virtue of the selective stroke distance boundaries and hazard indications and the player is prevented from reaching each of said greens in less strokes than it takes to reach the greens in said full size course using select clubs from a set of clubs.

6. For more information on sports patents, see Derek Bambauer, "Legal Responses to the Challenges of Sports Patents," 18 *Harvard Journal of Law and Technology* 401 (2005).

13.4. THE RIGHT OF PUBLICITY

Individual persons have the right to control and profit from the commercial use of their name, likeness, and persona, generally known as the "right of publicity." Using a person's name, likeness, or persona without his or her permission can amount to misappropriation, a state law tort claim. The right of publicity must be balanced with the First Amendment, which allows for the reporting of newsworthy events or stories of public interest. The right of publicity is different from the right to privacy or the tort of defamation, which holds public figures such as athletes to a higher standard of proof in cases of possible invasion.

Income derived from endorsements and the licensed use of athletes' names and images constitutes an increasingly important stream of income for professional athletes. As the different types and uses of electronic media continue to expand, it is important that athletes, coaches, executives, and other notable people in the world of sports protect their identities against unlicensed and unlawful profiteering. Makers and providers of videos, games, sporting goods, and a vast array of other products and services may attempt to use an athlete's name or picture in conjunction with the product, suggesting the athlete's endorsement. Whether the use of the athlete's identity is for commercial purposes is an important factor. For example, in *ETW Corp. v. Jireh Publishing Inc.*, 99 F. Supp. 2d 829 (N.D. Ohio 2000), *aff'd*, 332 F.3d 915 (6th Cir. 2003), golfer Tiger Woods claimed that an artist's creation and sale of 5,000 limited edition prints commemorating Woods's historic 1997 Masters victory infringed on his trademark and violated his right of publicity. In granting summary judgment for the defendant, the court noted that a certificate of authenticity accompanied the work and that the print's packaging included a statement by the artist expressing his desire to create "serious art" about sports. The court found that the print was not a "mere poster" or item of "sports merchandise" but rather "an artistic creation seeking to express a message" entitled to broad constitutional protection. Accordingly, the court held that the common law right of publicity was superseded by the First Amendment and could not prohibit its sale.

The increasing popularity of fantasy sports has also raised important questions about what information is in the public domain and what rightfully belongs to the athlete (see note 9). In fantasy sports, individuals acting as "owners" form leagues and draft and assemble teams of players to compete, with the winners determined by the statistical performance of real players. In an attempt to capitalize on this growing industry, the interactive arm of Major League Baseball entitled Major League Baseball Advanced Media (MLBAM) signed a five-year, $50 million deal with the Major League Baseball Players Association (MLBPA) in 2005 to acquire the players' online publicity rights, including for use in fantasy sports. MLBAM then licensed fantasy game creators, such as ESPN and Yahoo!, the right to use players' names, likenesses, pictures, and biographical data in conjunction with the games. Prior to 2005, the MLBPA sold these licenses. When MLBAM refused to offer C.B.C. Distribution and Marketing a license in 2005, as the MLBPA previously had, C.B.C. brought suit seeking a declaratory judgment that the players' names and statistics were in the public domain and that unlicensed use of such information in fantasy gaming would not violate the players' right to publicity. In *C.B.C. Distribution and Marketing, Inc. v. Major League Baseball Advanced Media, L.P.*, 443 F. Supp. 2d 1077 (E.D. Mo. 2006), *aff'd*, 505 F.3d 818 (8th Cir. 2007), *cert. denied*, 128 S.Ct. 2872 (2008), the court agreed, ruling that the names and statistics of players lacked the originality required for copyright protection and that the First Amendment rights of C.B.C. took precedence over the players' right to control publicity. As a result of the ruling, ESPN opted out of a seven-year, $140 million licensing deal with MLBAM in January 2008 (see note 2).

NOTES

1. In *Dryer v. National Football League*, 689 F.Supp.2d 1113 (D.Minn. 2010), former NFL players brought a class action suit against the league alleging that league's use of video footage from games in which they played in league's promotional videos violated their common law and statutory rights of publicity. In denying the NFL's motion for judgment on the pleadings, the court held that the right of publicity claim was not preempted by the Copyright Act and that allegations were sufficient to support players' claim that the videos amounted to commercial speech, for First Amendment purposes. The case is ongoing at the time of publication.

2. In *CBS Interactive Inc. v. National Football League Players Association, Inc.*, 259 F.R.D. 398 (D. Minn. 2009), the court granted CBS's request for a declaratory judgment that it could use players' names and statistics for fantasy games without a licensing agreement, based in large part on the *C.B.C.* ruling.

3. In *Facenda v. N.F.L. Films, Inc.*, 488 F. Supp. 2d 491 (E.D. Pa. 2007), the son of the late John Facenda brought suit alleging the licensing of the use of his father's famous voice by NFL Films for use in the video game "Madden NFL 06" was an invasion of privacy, a violation of the Lanham Act, and an unauthorized use of his father's name and likeness. John Facenda was the legendary narrator of NFL Films' game footage and highlight reels from 1965 until his death in 1984. In the months prior to his death, Facenda executed the first ever written agreement for his work, which included a release to NFL Films for the unequivocal rights of audio and video using Facenda's voice so long as such use did not constitute an endorsement of any product or service. The court ruled for the Facenda estate, finding that the use of the voice once described as "the voice of God" constituted an endorsement of the product and was consequently an unauthorized use of Facenda's likeness.

4. In *Doe v. McFarlane*, 207 S.W.3d 52 (Mo. App. E.D. 2006), former St. Louis Blues defenseman Tony Twist won a $15 million verdict against comic book creator Todd MacFarlane. MacFarlane had created a comic book villain with the same name as the plaintiff, which MacFarlane later admitted was to be based on the plaintiff. Twist alleged the misappropriation of his name cost him endorsement opportunities and that he was entitled to royalties from the comic. In 2000, a trial judge threw out a $24.5 million verdict for Twist, claiming MacFarlane's use of his name was protected by the First Amendment. A new trial was ordered by the Missouri Supreme Court in 2003, which determined that, in this instance, Twist's name was not being used with regard to his status as a hockey player but instead for the unprotected commercial purpose of selling comic books. The new trial resulted in the affirmed $15 million verdict.

5. In *Gionfriddo v. Major League Baseball*, 94 Cal. App. 4th 400 (Cal. App. 1 Dist. 2001), the court determined that the dissemination of factual data about baseball players, such as statistics, as well as their photographs and verbal and video descriptions of their play did not violate the players' right to publicity. The court stated that such information was of a

substantial public interest and that the use of the information was merely for historical purposes, as protected by the First Amendment.

6. In *Cardtoons, L.C. v. Major League Baseball Players Association*, 95 F.3d 959 (10th Cir. 1996), the plaintiff "brought this action to obtain a declaratory judgment that its parody trading cards featuring active Major League Baseball players do not infringe on the publicity rights of members of the Major League Baseball Players Association." The plaintiff used the likenesses of Major League players to poke fun at the game of baseball and how much players were paid. The court held that there was no trademark infringement because there was not a likelihood of confusion on the part of the consumer. The court did hold that the plaintiff infringed on MLBPA's publicity rights under state law. "Publicity rights...are a form of property protection that allows people to profit from the full commercial value of their identities." However, the plaintiff's First Amendment rights outweigh MLBPA's publicity rights, and therefore the plaintiff may continue to produce the parody cards.

7. In *Town & Country Properties, Inc. v. Riggins*, 457 S.E.2d 356 (Va. 1995), NFL Hall of Fame running back John Riggins sued a real estate broker who advertised the sale of a house as being "John Riggins' former home." Riggins had conveyed his interest in the house to his wife when they divorced in 1991. A jury found that the broker had misappropriated Riggins's name and reputation without his express written consent and awarded him $25,000 in compensatory damages and $28,608 in punitive damages. At trial, a sports marketing expert testified as to the value of lost endorsement possibilities arising from the misappropriation.

8. In *Zacchini v. Scripps-Howard Broadcasting Co.*, 433 U.S. 562 (1977), the plaintiff, Hugo Zacchini, conducted an act under the moniker "The Human Cannonball," and toured around the country, stopping at fairs and circuses. Zacchini did not charge an admission fee to see his exhibitions. However, without his permission, a reporter from a television station owned by Scripps-Howard taped an entire performance of Zacchini's and aired it on the station's evening newscast. Zacchini sued, stating that he was in the entertainment business, and that the broadcast of his performance on television was an "unlawful appropriation of plaintiff's professional property." In a split decision, the Supreme Court decided in favor of Zacchini, deciding that his right to publicity had been infringed upon.

9. For more on the right of publicity with regard to fantasy sports, see Robert T. Ferguson, Jr., "Extreme Makeover: Redefining Athletes' Identities in a Fantasy World," 14 *Villanova Sports and Entertainment Law Journal* 287 (2007) and Ryan T. Holte, "The Freedom to Imagine Fantasy Sports: Applying New Ideas in Copyright Law to Professional Athletes' Right of Publicity," 54 *Journal of the Copyright Society of the U.S.A.* 771 (2007).

10. For more on the right of publicity in sports, see Abib Tejan Conteh, "The Right of Publicity in Sports: Athletic and Economic Competition," 3 *DePaul Journal of Sports Law and Contemporary Problems* 136 (2006).

Chapter 14

BROADCASTING AND MULTIMEDIA

14.1. Legal Foundation: Establishing the Property Right, History, and Laws

    14.1.1. Case Law

    14.1.2. Copyright Laws

    14.1.3. Federal Communications Commission (FCC) Regulations

    14.1.4. Other Legislation

14.2. Broadcast Contracts

    14.2.1. Rights Granted

    14.2.2. Broadcast Rights of a Professional League

        14.2.2.1. Broadcast Rights of a Professional Team

    14.2.3. Broadcast Rights of the National Collegiate Athletic Association (NCAA)

        14.2.3.1. Broadcast Rights of the NCAA Championships

        14.2.3.2. Broadcast Rights of the Bowl Championship Series

    14.2.4. Broadcast Rights for Conferences and Schools

        14.2.4.1. Antitrust Issues in Broadcasting for Colleges

14.2.5. Broadcast Rights of Individual Sports

14.2.6. Broadcast Rights for the Olympics

14.2.7. Broadcast Rights of Individual Players

14.3. Other Important Issues in Sports Broadcasting

    14.3.1. Restrictions on Sports Broadcasting

        14.3.1.1. Restrictions on the Use of Advertising

        14.3.1.2. Restrictions on the Use of Replays

14.4. Internet Rights for Sports Broadcasts

    14.4.1. Home Recording of Copyrighted Events

    14.4.2. Domestic and International Piracy of Satellite and Cable Transmissions

    14.4.3. Blackouts of Scheduled Programming

    14.4.4. Satellite Distribution

    14.4.5. FCC and Indecency

14.5. A Broadcasting Checklist

INTRODUCTION

All sports entities potentially have a valuable property right in the accounts and descriptions of their games and events, whether these activities are broadcast on radio, television, cable television, the Internet, or via cellular phones. The importance of these contracts cannot be overstated, because they provide enormous amounts of revenue (see section 1.2.2, "Impact of Broadcast Contracts"), more than some organizations can make through all other sources of revenue combined. The value of this property right has led to numerous contentious lawsuits concerning who owns the rights to these broadcasts.

These lawsuits have involved issues of copyright law (see Chapter 13), antitrust law (see Chapter 10), and contract law (see Chapter 9). Copyright law and sports intersect whenever a sports organization broadcasts one of its games. The descriptions and accounts of these games are a copyrightable work, and the team may be entitled to royalty fees if the game is rebroadcast.

Antitrust law and sports broadcasting meet when a sports organization attempts to negotiate broadcasting contracts on the behalf of its member teams. While this is allowed on the professional level as a result of the Sports Broadcast Act of 1961, the pooling of broadcast rights on the intercollegiate level has been the cause of litigation that has reached the Supreme Court. Finally, a holder of property rights will enter into contracts with many different organizations (networks, advertisers, cable companies) when broadcasting a sports contest. It is imperative for the rights holder to be aware of the different clauses and situations that exist in broadcast contracts. It is important for broadcast rights holders at all levels of sport to be aware of these legal considerations when entering into contract negotiations for the rights to their organizations' sporting event.

Chapter 14 begins with a section explaining why sports broadcasts are a protectable property right of the athletic organization owning the event. The history of legislation and evolution of case law is discussed to provide the reader with knowledge of the foundations of the law and sports broadcasting. Its subsections discuss how Congress and the Federal Communications Commission (FCC) further strengthened this legal right with the passage of the Copyright Act of 1976, as well as subsequent cable regulations. The second section of the chapter explores issues that are unique to different constituencies within the sports world, from professional to intercollegiate to Olympic organizations.

The third section discusses restrictions placed on the broadcasting organizations by a league or conference, as well as the restrictions placed upon sports television stations for the replaying of sports highlights. The fourth section concerns other issues in sports broadcasting that have recently emerged in litigation and may have a tremendous impact on the future of sports broadcasting. To describe these legal considerations, some basic terminology relating to the broadcasting industry must be reviewed.

- *Standard Broadcast Television.* This is what most individuals consider "basic television." Local television stations broadcast programming that is received by local home television sets when the antenna picks up transmission signals. Standard broadcast television is broadcast on channels 2 through 69, with channels 2 through 13 known as very high frequency and channels 14 through 69 known as ultra high frequency (UHF). UHF stations may include the local CBS, NBC, ABC, PBS, and FOX affiliates.

- *Cable Television* (formerly known as CATV [community antenna television]). This is a service provided to consumers by which traditional television programming and/or other broadcast signals (e.g., pay cable) are brought into the home of the subscriber via cable transmission (as opposed to over-the-air transmission), usually for an initial installation charge and a monthly subscription fee. Standard broadcast stations can also be brought into a subscriber's home through cable television, in order to receive a clearer picture. The stations that may fall into the cable television category include ESPN, CNN, TNT, FOX Sports Net, USA, and Lifetime.

- *Pay Cable*. This refers to a premium cable television service, which provides special channels to subscribers, for an additional cost, that carry unique programming such as sports. Examples of special channels are Showtime and HBO. These channels may televise sports, and historically have televised boxing matches.

- *Superstations*. These are local, independent, distant signal television stations whose programs, including sports, are carried via satellite to cable systems outside of the station's local broadcast range. Examples are WGN in Chicago, WWOR in New Jersey, and WPIX in New York. These television stations often carry sports programming, such as the Chicago Bulls on WGN. TBS Superstation was the first superstation and aired Atlanta Braves games all across the country for 32 years. TBS cut back on nationally broadcast Braves games in 2007 in preparation for a national deal with Major League Baseball whereby it began broadcasting other teams' regular season games as well as the Division Series and League Championship Series.

- *Satellites*. Satellites provide a space-based distribution system of program services for standard broadcast and cable television. Satellites relay television signals across the world. The use of satellites to carry distant television signals is becoming more prevalent with the emergence of technology such as DSS, which can provide thousands of television stations from around the world to people who subscribe to this "home satellite" service.

- *Earth Station, Uplink, Downlink, and Transponder*. All of these are used in satellite transmissions of broadcast signals. The uplink is the ground-to-satellite transmission of a broadcast signal; a downlink is a satellite-to-earth transmission of a broadcast signal; and an earth station is a ground antenna designed to communicate with a satellite. A transponder is the part of the satellite that consists of a receiver to pick up the signals from the uplink, a processor to convert the signal's frequency and amplify its strength, and a transmitter to rebroadcast the signal on the downlink.

- *Fixation*. Fixation is recording all parts of a broadcast on film, videotape, or replay tape for purposes of protecting the copyright and the manner in which it was recorded.

- *Internet*. This is the worldwide interconnection of computer networks used by the government, academic institutions, businesses, and individuals. The Internet has had a profound impact on sports broadcasting because it has the capability to broadcast events worldwide, regardless of geographic location. Therefore, more people will have access to sports programming than ever before. However, who owns the rights to these Internet broadcasts will undoubtedly continue to be a topic of litigation.

- *Compulsory Licenses*. These are licenses issued by the government that give a broadcasting company the right to use a work or product that is owned by a separate copyright holder. The user of the work must pay a royalty fee for its use. The copyright holder is obligated to grant the license to any organization that agrees to pay the royalty fees.

- *Cellular Phones*. Along with their regular uses, such as making phone calls, receiving text messages, and facilitating contact without grounded telephone lines, these small electronic devices can provide real-time updates of sports scores, Internet access, video highlights, and other content.

- *Multimedia.* Multimedia is media and content that uses a combination of different content forms. Multimedia includes a combination of text, audio, still images, animation, video and interactivity forms. Multimedia rights, typically as they apply to the internet, are an increasingly important part of any broadcasting rights deal.

14.1. LEGAL FOUNDATION: ESTABLISHING THE PROPERTY RIGHT, HISTORY, AND LAWS

In 1939, an intercollegiate baseball game between Columbia University and Princeton University became the first televised sporting event in the United States. While this was the first televised sporting event, issues concerning radio sports broadcasting had arisen for almost two decades prior to the airing of that game. Since 1921, athletic organizations have attempted to claim property rights over the broadcasts of their games and, in turn, charge money for the right to broadcast their sporting events to the public. While sport organizations do not charge money for the print media to write about the games, broadcasters have always been charged for their transmissions.

14.1.1. Case Law

The courts and the government initially had difficulty deciding who owned the property rights to sports broadcasts: the team, the broadcasting station, the players, or the league. The ownership of this property right entitles an organization to fees, royalties, and therefore increased revenues. Generally, it has been decided, through the courts and legislation, that the home team is the owner of the property rights of a game, and therefore is entitled to any benefits, such as broadcasting fees and retransmission royalties. In the 1938 case of *Pittsburgh Athletic Co. v. KQV Broadcasting* (see note 3), the court decided that the home team holds the property rights of the game, and that they also control the right to disseminate these games, as well as the right to license these rights. The opposing clubs (i.e., the visiting team) do have a property right in that they own the rights to rebroadcast the games back to their own home region.

As mentioned above, the early cases in the area of sports broadcasting dealt with unauthorized radio broadcasts of professional sports contests (see notes 1 through 4). In cases of unauthorized use, the courts held that such use was a misappropriation of a club's property right to control "descriptions or accounts" of games, and to allow broadcast stations to do so would be an "unjust enrichment" for a station. For example, in *National Exhibition Co. v. Fass* (see note 2), the court ruled that a broadcaster could not immediately teletype the play-by-play of a baseball game without infringing upon the property rights of the original rights holder. *Property* is generally defined as "That which belongs exclusively to one...the unrestricted and exclusive right to a thing; the right to dispose of a thing in every legal way, to possess it, to use it, and to exclude everyone else from interfering with it" (*Black's Law Dictionary*).

This legal right to the sports broadcast, which was established by the earlier court decisions, was further strengthened when Congress enacted the Copyright Act of 1976. In enacting that law, Congress extended copyright protection to live sports broadcasts. This copyright protection had been established through court decisions, but now the protection was through legislation. Under this act, copyright protection grants the owners of a copyrightable work the exclusive right to "perform the copyrighted work publicly." One of the important results of the Copyright Act was that it established a governmental agency known as the Copyright Royalty Tribunal. The tribunal was charged with deciding disputes over copyrights of broadcasts, collecting royalties for owners of copyrights, and disbursing these royalties to the proper owners.

Until the late 1970s, it was widely believed by broadcast networks that the copyright of a sports broadcast belonged to them. However, in 1978 the Copyright

Royalty Tribunal concluded that, based on the legislative history of the Copyright Act, the copyright of the game being broadcast belonged to the sports entity whose game or event was being telecast. It has been found that the broadcasting company, which pays money for the rights to broadcast an event, does not have this property right.

This holding by the tribunal was a very important one for the holder of broadcast rights. First, it signified that the sports organization or its parent had the ultimate right to decide whether it wants to have its sporting events (property) broadcast on one of the electronic media outlets. Second, it means that for any subsequent rebroadcast of the sports entity's game, the organization can expect to receive compensation.

As mentioned previously, another potential property issue raised in broadcasting revolves around who owns the rights to a game—the home team or the visiting team. Generally, this issue is resolved in the game contract, and such agreements usually give the property right to the home team or host sports entity. The visiting team usually receives a fee that could be from a TV or radio broadcast. An alternative option for the visiting team might be agreeing on no fee from TV and/or radio, but settling on a "home and home" series, where the visiting team hosts the game in the following season. However, one court has ruled that, based on common law, principles of misappropriation, and contractual interference, a visiting team controls the right to broadcast a game back to its home city and surrounding area (see *Wichita State University Intercollegiate Athletic Association v. Swanson Broadcasting Co.*, Case No. 81C130 (Kan. Dist. Ct. 1981).

NOTES _____

1. In *Post-Newsweek Stations-Connecticut Inc. v. Travelers Insurance Co.*, 510 F. Supp. 81 (D. Conn. 1981), the plaintiff television station was attempting to obtain a preliminary injunction to allow it to cover the events, as news, of the International Figure Skating Championships being held in the Hartford Civic Center. The defendants had not allowed the plaintiffs to cover the event at all because ABC had been granted the exclusive broadcasting rights for the event. The contract had stated that ABC had "exclusivity against television news broadcasts of any length which would include video film or videotape coverage of any of the Championships prior to our telecasts." In deciding in favor of the defendants, and not granting the injunction, the court stated, "The plaintiff has no special right of access to this event, and ... the contractual restrictions imposed do not violate the plaintiff's First and Fourteenth Amendment rights." This decision, although involving only a preliminary injunction and restraining order, was an influential decision in strengthening the property and copyright clauses in broadcasting contracts.

2. In *National Exhibition Co. v. Fass*, 143 N.Y.S.2d 767 (N.Y. Sup. Ct. 1955), the defendant, Martin Fass, was an independent sports reporter who would listen to radio broadcasts of the 1953 New York Giants baseball games and then teletype the details of the games to other radio stations, which would immediately rebroadcast the news. Fass argued that the news was "in the public domain," and that he was not rebroadcasting the information, simply teletyping the information. Similar to the decision in *Pittsburgh Athletic Co. v. KQV Broadcasting*, the court found for the owner of the property right to the game, stating, "The aforesaid actions ... have deprived plaintiff of the just benefits of its labors and expenditures in respect of the creation and production of baseball games and public dissemination of descriptions and accounts thereof and will continue so to do and will cause great and irreparable loss, injury and damage to plaintiff unless enjoined."

3. In *Pittsburgh Athletic Co. v. KQV Broadcasting*, 24 F. Supp. 490 (W.D. Pa. 1938), the Pittsburgh Pirates brought a request for an injunction against KQV Broadcasting from broadcasting Pirates' home games without the team's consent. The defendants would place

reporters outside of the stadium, where they still would see the baseball field. The reporters would then provide a play-by-play broadcast of the game to listeners. The court ruled in favor of the Pirates' organization, stating, "The right, title and interest in and to the baseball games played within the parks of members of the National League, including Pittsburgh, including the property right in, and the sole right of, disseminating or publishing or selling, or licensing the right to disseminate, news, reports, descriptions, or accounts of games played in such parks, during the playing thereof, is vested exclusively in such members." It is interesting to note how closely this decision is followed in the message that is broadcast by a broadcast station during every professional sporting event.

4. *In the Matter of A. E. Newton (WOCL)*, 2 FCC 281 (1936), was the first legal case (but not an official court case) that dealt with sports broadcasting. A. E. Newton was applying to the FCC, a government entity, to renew his radio license, a procedure undergone every five to seven years. It was made apparent that Newton, whose radio station, WOCL, originated from his home, had placed a radio in his house that was broadcasting a game of the 1934 World Series on the station WGR. Newton attached earphones to the radio and listened to the account of the game on WGR. After listening to the account of the game, Newton would relate, nearly simultaneously, the account of the game to his listeners. The FCC ruled that "when a station engages in practice here, its conduct is inconsistent with fair dealing, is dishonest in nature, and amounts to unfair utilization of ... another's labor." However, despite its negative view of Newton's conduct, the FCC ruled that, from a strict point of view, Newton's rebroadcasting of the game did not constitute a retransmission of the game, and therefore was not in violation of statutes. No court ruling was ever made, and Newton's license was renewed.

5. In *National Exhibition v. Teleflash*, 24 F. Supp. 488 (S.D.N.Y. 1936), the producers of a baseball radio broadcast were seeking to stop defendants from providing a play-by-play radio broadcast through telephones used inside the stadium. Although the defendants did convey to the listeners what they were seeing in the game, the court did not find that the defendants were violating any rights of the broadcast organization. In his decision, the judge stated, "Even if ticket holders were the source of news about the plays, the tickets themselves are not shown to have contained any notice or statement of objection to the doing of what was done. A ticket was a complete license to see the game. What is there to prevent a man from telling in his own way, what he saw and telling it when and in the form he chose?" The court also said that the failure of the admission ticket to the game to state that the fans could not practice such conduct was another reason that the plaintiff was not successful.

6. For more information on sports broadcasting and its effects upon professional and intercollegiate sports, see Chris Gratton and Harry Arne Solberg, *The Economics of Sports Broadcasting* (New York: Routledge, 2007); Matthew Nicholson, *Sport and the Media: Managing the Nexus* (Atlanta: Elsevier, 2007); and Ronald A. Smith, *Play-By-Play: Radio, Television, and Big-Time College Sport* (Baltimore: Johns Hopkins University Press, 2001).

14.1.2. Copyright Laws

As noted previously, the Copyright Act of 1976 gave sports organizations a right to copyright the broadcast of their games or contests, ensuring a statutory property right. Organizations are most often impacted by the copyright laws in regard to *retransmission* of a broadcast of the organization's games or contests. This rebroadcasting most frequently occurs with cable television—for instance, when a local cable system broadcasts a game by picking up a distant signal television station. Under the 1976 law, cable television companies were granted a compulsory license that exempts them from having to seek permission to retransmit any programming that a standard broadcast television station is originating.

A compulsory license is an agreement that gives a user the unlimited right to use a work or product, and accordingly the user will pay a set fee or royalty at a later time. The holder of the copyright must abide by compulsory licenses, which are issued by the government, and the copyright holder cannot refuse permission to rebroadcast if someone pays the mandatory royalty fees. This means that if a local television station is broadcasting a school's basketball game, and a cable system has the capability to pick up that transmission, the cable company can broadcast it over its cable system without the permission of the school, as long as it pays a fee. This system of compulsory licenses diminishes the value of a copyright holder's property because the license allows a wider distribution of the broadcast, which weakens contracts that the copyright holder might have with network television stations.

The Copyright Royalty Tribunal, as established by the Copyright Act of 1976, initially determined the fee that a user of a broadcast had to pay to the copyright holder. (See note 5 for more information on the Copyright Royalty Tribunal.) Sports organizations were not content with the amount of money that they were receiving from the Copyright Royalty Tribunal, and believed that they would be able to negotiate better arrangements if they could negotiate individually with the cable companies. In 1982, the Big Four (Major League Baseball, the National Basketball Association, the National Football League, and the National Hockey League), other sports entities, and organizations such as the Motion Picture Association of America brought a case against the Copyright Royalty Tribunal, challenging the amount they received from the rebroadcasts of their games and performances (see note 5). However, in a judgment for the tribunal, the court upheld the distribution methods of the organization, stating that "it was impossible to satisfy all the claimants.... The Tribunal's decision has achieved an initial allocation of the Fund that is well within the metes prescribed by Congress." The tribunal, constantly under scrutiny from sports organizations and non-sports copyright holders, was replaced in 1993 by the Copyright Royalty Tribunal Reform Act (see note 6). This act replaced the tribunal with the Copyright Royalty Arbitration Panel, which is directed by the Librarian of Congress. Under this system, the arbitration panel is charged with the same duties as the previous tribunal, deciding who is entitled to royalties and how much they are entitled to. The librarian, however, must approve the determination of these allocations before they are made official.

14.1.3. Federal Communications Commission (FCC) Regulations

Cable is the only communications medium that has been permitted to present the accounts and descriptions of a club's games without individually negotiating for the right to do so. Obviously, this has resulted in a special privilege for cable broadcasters. However, Congress has not shown any willingness to abolish cable's compulsory license. Under existing FCC rules, cable systems may import literally hundreds of sports events (see note 1, section 14.1.3, "Federal Communications Commission (FCC) Regulations," for a discussion of siphoning). Sports teams have been concerned that such lack of restraint adversely affects gate receipts and broadcast revenues. Sports organizations have attempted through litigation and legislation to curb the ability of cable companies to rebroadcast games on a widespread scale (see note 1).

To combat the nearly free rein that cable companies benefit from, the FCC has enacted two rules that are still in effect and provide sports teams with some limited—but nevertheless important—control over cable importation of distant sports events. The first is known as the Sports or Same Game Rule (47 CFR 76.67). Under this rule, a team may require cable systems within 35 miles to delete the distant signal telecast of that team's home game—provided that the home game is not televised locally. For example, assume that the Boston Celtics and the New York Knicks are playing a game in Boston. If the Celtics are not televising the game in Boston, they may request affected cable systems in the Boston area to delete the telecast of the game by the Knicks. A cable system that fails to comply with such a request would be subject to a fine by the FCC, as well as a copyright infringement action, because its compulsory license extends only to programming that is authorized to be carried under FCC rules. The primary effect of the rule is to protect the club's home gate; however, the rule is also important in protecting the club's pay cable or subscription television contracts.

One other set of FCC rules that affords some limited control over the distribution of sports telecasts involves network nonduplication. Professional sports teams, either on their own or through their television flagship station, often establish a network of stations to televise their games. Under the FCC's network nonduplication rules (47 CFR 76.92), the stations in these communities are able to prevent local cable systems from carrying a duplicating telecast. This preserves the local station as the exclusive outlet for the event, and is especially applicable to prevent superstations from broadcasting a duplicating telecast.

NOTE _____

1. In the 1970s and 1980s, as the options of pay television offered on cable systems increased, so did concerns over "siphoning," or the shifting of programs from standard broadcast television to pay cable or subscription television. Originally, the FCC passed regulations that prohibited pay television from televising "specific" events that had been on standard broadcast television in the past five years. However, these regulations were struck down by the U.S. Court of Appeals for the District of Columbia in *Home Box Office, Inc. v. FCC*, 567 F. 2d 9 (D.C. Cir.), *cert. denied*, 434 U.S. 829 (1977). The court ruled that the FCC was violating the First Amendment by making it too hard for pay cable networks to obtain and air sports programming. This court decision allows professional sports teams to put together pay cable packages for their games, which would not have been possible under the FCC rules.

14.1.4. Other Legislation

In professional sports, the major piece of legislation dealing with broadcasting is the Sports Broadcasting Act of 1961 (see note 5). This act immunizes from antitrust liability the pooled sale of telecasting rights by the four major professional sports leagues (MLB, NHL, NFL, and NBA). (See Chapter 10 for a discussion of antitrust law.) Thus, it allows the leagues to negotiate television packages, but it also restricts the ability of the leagues to define the geographical areas into which the pooled telecasts may be broadcast. Satellite television packages have been found not to be "sponsored telecasting" within the protection of the exemption (see note 2). The act also protects college and high school football for Friday and Saturday telecasts within 75 miles.

Professional leagues were eager for Congress to adopt this legislation on behalf of the sports leagues because it allowed a league to pool the television rights of all teams together, giving them added power on their side of the bargaining table. If each team negotiated national contracts separately, it would create less revenue, since competition and nonexclusivity would prevail. This type of situation would also create an atmosphere where more popular teams, or teams in larger markets, would be able to negotiate more lucrative broadcasting contracts, thereby creating a financial gap between the teams within the league (see section 1.2.2, "Impact of

Broadcast Contracts," for a discussion of broadcast revenues). It should be noted that the act does not sanction pooling of rights for intercollegiate athletics. The act's exclusion of intercollegiate athletics led to the landmark case *University of Oklahoma v. NCAA* (see section 14.2.4.1, "Antitrust Issues in Broadcasting for Colleges," for a discussion of this case). The act also does not protect satellite distribution packages. After four years of litigation, the NFL managed to settle a class action lawsuit regarding their "Sunday Ticket" package, which originally required customers to purchase the package for the entire season even if they wanted to watch just one game (see note 2).

NOTES

1. Prior to the 2007 Super Bowl between the Colts and Bears, the NFL issued cease and desist letters to several community groups, including churches, that planned to show the game on projection TVs. Under the Copyright Act, any showing of the game to an audience larger than a person's immediate family and some friends constitutes an unlawful public performance and an infringement of the NFL's copyright in the broadcast. As a result, the groups were forced to cancel their Super Bowl parties.

2. In *Shaw v. Dallas Cowboys Football Club*, 172 F. 3d 299 (3d Cir. 1999), the Third Circuit held that the NFL clubs' agreement to collectively sell their broadcast rights to DirecTV did not constitute "sponsored telecasting" within the exemption of the Sports Broadcasting Act. A "sponsored telecast" is one "which [is] financed by business enterprises (the 'sponsors') in return for advertising time and are therefore provided free to the general public." A settlement was reached in *Schwartz v. Dallas Cowboys Football Club*, 2001 WL 1689714 (E.D. Pa. Nov. 21, 2001), where the NFL agreed to pay the 1.8 million defendants $8.5 million and offer a "Single Sunday Ticket" package which allows customers to purchase the package at a weekly rate. As a result of the settlement, the NFL is also protected from future litigation regarding the matter as long as they continued to offer the weekly package.

3. In *Eastern Microwave Inc. v. Doubleday Sports Inc.*, 691 F.2d 125 (2d Cir. 1982), Doubleday Sports, the owner of the New York Mets baseball team, sued Eastern Microwave (EMI), a common carrier licensed by the FCC, whose services include the retransmission of the television signals of broadcast stations to markets outside the service areas of the broadcast stations. EMI retransmitted the signals of WOR-TV, including baseball games, without altering any of the programs, and had been doing so since 1965 without any complaints from WOR. The Mets sued EMI, charging that the rebroadcast of its games was a copyright infringement even though EMI was simply a passive carrier of the broadcasts, not altering the transmissions. The court decided for EMI, noting that EMI's conduct fell under the auspices of the Copyright Act of 1976, and that by making its royalty payments, as outlined by the act, EMI was not in violation of Doubleday's copyright. The court also held that it would be impossible for each carrier to negotiate with each copyright owner on an individual basis, and would create a situation that was not intended by Congress in the Copyright Act of 1976. However, this decision led to a petition by pro sports leagues and other copyright holders to the Copyright Royalty Tribunal to increase the royalties paid to the rights holders. Subsequently, the CRT imposed restrictions that made it nearly financially impossible for a carrier to import more than two superstations.

4. In *National Ass'n of Broadcasters v. Copyright Royalty Tribunal*, 675 F. 2d 367 (D.C. Cir. 1982), the four major pro sports leagues, along with a number of other copyright holders, including the Motion Picture Association of America, brought action against the Copyright Royalty Tribunal, challenging the first distribution of the cable royalties by the tribunal. The judge stated, "Specific awards [to the plaintiff parties] are reversible only if the agency's [tribunal's] decision is not supported by 'substantial evidence' or is 'arbitrary, capricious, an abuse of discretion or otherwise not in accordance with law' as defined by the Administrative Procedure Act." The judge decided for the defendant tribunal, stating,

"The Tribunal faced a difficult task in conducting the initial distribution of cable royalties because of the number of claimants and the inescapably qualitative problem of evaluating their competing claims. It was impossible to satisfy all the claimants, whose combined requests totaled roughly three times more than the finite amount of the Fund. We are satisfied that the Tribunal's resolution of the problem confronting it was reasonable, that its decisional criteria comported with congressional intent, and that its distribution of royalty shares finds rational support in the administrative record."

5. Under the original Copyright Royalty Tribunal, cable systems had to pay a royalty commission for telecasting the contest to a central fund. The tribunal was established to distribute these royalty payments to deserving sports entities (and non-sports copyright holders). The tribunal was also established so that each cable network and each rights holder would not have to negotiate for the rights to each game. With sports, the tribunal devised a distribution formula that weighed relative marketplace values of the programming retransmitted against the value to the cable system for using the broadcast and the harm inflicted by its broadcast to the copyright holder. The cable companies paid a royalty fee that was based on a sliding scale relative to their overall revenues. When the first royalty fees were divided for the year 1978, it was determined that sports would receive 12% of the total pool, which amounted to $15 million. In 1979 and 1980, the split was 15% of the pool to sports. From 1983 to 1990, the split was 16.35% of the pool.

6. The official legislative citation for the Copyright Royalty Tribunal Reform Act is HR 2840, the Copyright Royalty Tribunal Reform Act of 1993.

7. THE SPORTS BROADCASTING ACT (15 USCA 32):

§ 1291. Exemption from antitrust laws of agreements covering the telecasting of sports contests and the combining of professional football leagues

The antitrust laws, as defined in section 1 of the Act of October 15, 1914, as amended (38 Stat. 730) [15 U.S.C. 12], or in the Federal Trade Commission Act, as amended (38 Stat. 717) [15 U.S.C. 41 et seq.], shall not apply to any joint agreement by or among persons engaging in or conducting the organized professional team sports of football, baseball, basketball, or hockey, by which any league of clubs participating in professional football, baseball, basketball, or hockey contests sells or otherwise transfers all or any part of the rights of such league's member clubs in the sponsored telecasting of the games of football, baseball, basketball, or hockey, as the case may be, engaged in or conducted by such clubs. In addition, such laws shall not apply to a joint agreement by which the member clubs of two or more professional football leagues, which are exempt from income tax under section 501(c)(6) of the Internal Revenue Code of 1986 [26 U.S.C.A. 501(c)(6)], combine their operations in expanded single league so exempt from income tax, if such agreement increases rather than decreases the number of professional football clubs so operating, and the provisions of which are directly relevant thereto.

§ 1292. Area telecasting restriction limitation

Section 1291 of this title shall not apply to any joint agreement described in the first sentence in such section which prohibits any person to whom such rights are sold or transferred from televising any games within any area, except within the home territory of a member club of the league on a day when such club is playing a game at home.

§ 1293. Intercollegiate and interscholastic football contest limitations

The first sentence of section 1291 of this title shall not apply to any joint agreement described in such section which permits the telecasting of all or a substantial part of any professional football game on any Friday after six o'clock postmeridian or on any Saturday during the period beginning on the second Friday in September and ending on the second Saturday in December in any year from any telecasting station located within seventy-five miles of the game site of any intercollegiate or interscholastic football contest scheduled to be played on such a date if—

a. such intercollegiate football contest is between institutions of higher learning both of which confer degrees upon students following completion of sufficient credit hours to equal a four-year course, or

b. in the case of an interscholastic football contest, such contest is between secondary schools, both of which are accredited or certified under the laws of the State or States in which they are situated and offer courses continuing through the twelfth grade of the standard school curriculum, or the equivalent, and

c. such intercollegiate or interscholastic football contest and such game site were announced through publication in a newspaper of general circulation prior to August 1 of such year as being regularly scheduled for such day and place.

§ 1294. Antitrust laws unaffected as regards to other activities of professional sports contests

Nothing contained in this chapter shall be deemed to change, determine, or otherwise affect the applicability or non-applicability of the antitrust laws to any act, contract, agreement, rule, course of conduct, or other activity by, between, or among persons engaging in, conducting, or participating in the organized professional team sports of football, baseball, basketball, or hockey, except the agreements to which section 1291 of this title shall apply.

§ 1295. "Persons" defined

As used in this chapter, "persons" means any individual, partnership, corporation, or unincorporated association or any combination or association thereof.

14.2. BROADCAST CONTRACTS

Copyright laws are just one area of contract language that must be scrutinized by athletic administrators in order to ensure that all the broadcast rights of an athletic organization are protected. A rights holder should be aware of all of the entities that could own rights to a game, and what regulations apply to the contest. For example, a rights holder must be aware that an NFL team cannot negotiate for a Friday night football game due to the provisions in the Sports Broadcast Act, which provide for the protection of high school football games on Friday nights. Rights holders must adhere to rules of their association, conference, or league.

For example, a college athletic department cannot negotiate to telecast an NCAA basketball tournament game or a conference championship game because it does not own the rights to these contests. In fact, universities may not be able to negotiate broadcast contracts for individual regular season games because the rights may have been assigned to the conference. After making sure that no other entity has rights to the contest, the university may then negotiate its contract. Therefore, the basics of contract law, which were covered in Chapter 9, are important. The following sections will focus on contract issues and clauses that are unique to the broadcast business. Whether a rights holder is a member of the NCAA, the NFL, or the United States Olympic Committee, it is imperative that he or she is aware of the unique clauses of the particular broadcast contracts, and how affiliation with certain organization may affect negotiations and the ability to contract with certain television networks. Aside from this knowledge, it is also crucial that a rights holder understand the basic clauses that should be covered in a standard broadcast contract.

14.2.1. Rights Granted

In a broadcast contract, the sports organization grants the rights to broadcast the game in exchange for some specified benefit, generally a rights fee from the broadcast organization. The broadcast organization may be only one station, or it may consist of a number of stations that form a network. Usually, a broadcast organization seeks exclusive rights to telecast a game. *Exclusive rights* are defined as rights granted by the sports organization to one broadcaster for the purpose of setting up a single-station broadcast or an exclusive network, and such rights do not permit any other broadcast organization to broadcast the event. Exclusive rights are the opposite of multi-originations—that is, when many broadcast organizations are given the right to telecast the same event.

Exclusive rights may be granted for different technologies. Therefore, an organization might negotiate exclusive rights contracts for live standard broadcast television, delayed standard broadcast television, cable television, radio, and/or Internet. Often, in intercollegiate athletic broadcast contracts, exceptions are included, even in exclusive arrangements, to allow for an origination by a student radio or television station of a sports broadcast so that the students can gain experience in sports broadcasting. A contract clause with a broadcasting organization might specify as follows: "The parties acknowledge that notwithstanding this agreement, [name] University may grant to University's student-run radio station the right to broadcast any game." In general, any broadcast contract would include at a minimum the following clauses:

1. Term and scope of the contract, including event(s) to be broadcast

   a. Number of years
   b. Number of games
   c. Which type of contests being broadcast

2. Definitions—will elaborate on the important terms within the contract to avoid confusion. For example, terms such as "rights holder," "broadcast," and "termination," may be included in the definitions section.

3. Access and admission to events—outlines what type of access the broadcaster will have to the facilities, including how many people, and what cameras will be allowed.

4. Facilities furnished—the amount and type of facilities that the broadcasting company will have to work in. Can include the booth for broadcasters.

5. Stipulations, requirements, and reservations—any other areas that are not covered in the general contract, or special needs on the part of either party.

6. Rights fee and schedule of payments—outlines the amount of money paid to the rights holder, and how that money will be distributed.

14.2.2. Broadcast Rights of a Professional League

As mentioned earlier, the Sports Broadcast Act of 1961 greatly benefits the four major sports leagues. Each of these leagues is able to negotiate collectively with the television networks without being found in violation of antitrust statutes. One major advantage of this legislative benefit is that if the league divides national broadcasting revenues equally among all of the teams, teams that play in smaller markets receive the same as the largest markets. Another benefit is that it balances out national exposure. However, if teams were negotiating separate local contracts, this would most likely not be the case. For example, in the NFL (where no local television contracts for regular season games exist), the Green Bay Packers' share of the national broadcast revenue is the same as the New York Giants even though the difference in their media markets is millions of people.

Unlike the situation in intercollegiate athletics, most professional leagues have a very organized system of determining who owns the rights to their broadcasts. In a professional league, when no network broadcast is involved, leagues formulate rules that provide for each team to broadcast both its home and away games. Teams in professional leagues do not usually interfere with each other's rights, since each desires to retain exclusivity in its own territory. Also, unlike other sports organizations, the four major sports leagues are able to pool their broadcast rights. For a brief summary of local and national revenue for sports broadcasts in the four major professional sport leagues, see exhibit 14.1. As this exhibit shows, Major League Baseball depends the most on local television broadcast contracts for revenue, while the National Football League relies almost exclusively on its national television contract for income.

A holder of broadcast rights must be aware of the rules that govern the league in which it competes before making any broadcasting decisions. In the four major sports leagues, the national rights fees that are acquired by the league are distributed equally among all of the teams. For example, in the NBA, the large national contracts with ABC/ESPN and TNT produce more revenue for the teams than the smaller local contracts. However, in Major League Baseball, rights from local television contracts tend to produce more revenue for teams than the national contracts. Therefore, there is a larger disparity in broadcasting revenues between teams in large and small markets (see note 1).

Fans who do not live in the market of their hometown team can often purchase an out-of-market package, which allows fans to watch nearly all the teams' games. The NFL has offered its package since 1994 exclusively on DirecTV, a satellite television provider, which requires fans to purchase the DirecTV service if they wish to get the out-of-market package. MLB threatened to move its "Extra Innings" package exclusively to DirecTV before the 2007 season in a seven-year, $700 million

Exhibit 14.1
Shared Television Revenue in the Big Four Professional Sports

League	National Contract	Networks	Annual Revenues	Local Contracts	Comment
National Football League	Yes	CBS, FOX, NBC, ESPN, DirecTV	$3.735 billion	Only preseason games	90% to 95% of revenue is shared equally
National Basketball Association	Yes	ABC, ESPN, TNT	$950 million	Yes	For some, league contract creates more revenue; other teams make more from local contracts
National Hockey League	Yes	Versus, NBC, CBC, TSN	$197 million	Yes	NBC pays no rights fee but NHL gets advertising profits
Major League Baseball	Yes	FOX, TBS, ESPN, DirecTV	$824.6 million	Yes	Local TV contracts provide money for most teams

deal. However, after a public backlash, a Senate Commerce Committee hearing, the willingness of DirecTV to drop its exclusivity clause, and, most importantly, the willingness of cable providers to carry the MLB Network (launched in 2009) on their basic tiers as opposed to their less-viewed premium tiers, the MLB agreed to renew the cable offering of Extra Innings with InDemand, a consortium including cable operators Comcast, Time Warner, and Cox. The NBA faced antitrust claims in *Kingray, Inc. v. NBA, Inc.*, 188 F. Supp. 2d 1177 (S.D. Cal. 2002), for its exclusive agreement with DirecTV and InDemand. The case was dismissed because the evidence was insufficient to allege a price fixing or restriction of output claim. A recent trend among the major sports leagues has been to start cable networks with league-related content. While the MLB appears to have avoided a carriage dispute with cable operators, the NFL has had significant difficulty getting its NFL Network on basic cable tiers, despite carrying eight prime-time games per year (see note 2). The NFL Network has tried encouraging government officials to intervene in the dispute, but Congress has been reluctant to extend the league more power considering its already powerful exemption under the Sports Broadcasting Act. The extent to which leagues use their own television networks to broadcast games and how it will change traditional broadcast relationships will be an evolving topic (see note 3).

NOTES

1. In 2010, Major League Baseball received approximately $800 million annually from FOX, TBS, ESPN, and DirecTV to broadcast regular season and postseason games. The Yankees received an estimated $60 million to $70 million annually for broadcast rights from the YES Network, of which they own a 35% share. At the same time, the Minnesota Twins received around $12 million from FSN North. For more information on this issue, see Jeff Friedman, "The Impact of Major League Baseball's Local Television Contracts," 10 *Sports Lawyers Journal* 1 (2003).

2. In *NFL Enterprises LLC v. Comcast Cable Communications, LLC*, 851 N.Y.S.2d 551 (2008), a New York state appellate court reversed a finding by the lower court that the contract between Comcast and the NFL Network allowed Comcast to restrict distribution of the NFL Network to a sports tier. The court found the agreements ambiguous and held that there was a triable issue of fact as to the parties' intentions and remanded for further consideration. In September 2007, the NFL filed a complaint with the FCC alleging that Comcast's refusal to put the NFL Network on a basic tier constituted unfair discrimination. In May 2009 the parties settled the dispute which included Comcast's agreement to include the Network as part of it's regular package. For more on the issue, see James J. LaRocca, "No Trust at the NFL: League's Network Passes Rule of Reason Analysis," 15 *UCLA Entertainment Law Review* 87 (2008).

3. For more information on the broadcast rights of professional sports leagues, see Lacie L. Kaiser, "Revisiting the Sports Broadcasting Act of 1961: A Call for Equitable Antitrust Immunity from Section One of the Sherman Act for All Professional Sport Leagues," 54 *DePaul Law Review* 1237 (2005); Lacie L. Kaiser, "The Flight from Single-Entity Structured Sport Leagues," 2 *DePaul Journal of Sports Law and Contemporary Problems* 1 (2004); and Ray L. Waters, "21st Century Corporate Mediathletics: How Did We Get to Slamball?" 1 *DePaul Journal of Sports Law and Contemporary Problems* 1 (2003).

4. Examples of hundreds of different kinds of contracts, including radio licensing and cable broadcast agreements, are available at http://contracts.onecle.com/, specifically under "License Agreements."

14.2.2.1. Broadcast Rights of a Professional Team

As mentioned earlier, professional sports teams, depending on their league affiliation, generally have the ability to negotiate contracts with local broadcast stations on top of the leaguewide contract, provided that the contract does not violate the leaguewide agreement. With the exception of the National Football League, all teams in the Big Four leagues are able to negotiate local television contracts for regular season games. The NFL does, however, allow for local radio broadcast agreements.

With the combination of local and national television contracts in the major professional sports, there have been conflicts over who owns the rights to certain games. Due to the large price tag for acquiring national television rights, exclusivity is of growing importance to the networks. The Chicago Bulls, the superstation WGN, and the NBA were involved in such a dispute. The Bulls and WGN sued the NBA, claiming that the agreement between the league and NBC was an impermissible restraint on trade. The Bulls had negotiated a contract with WGN to broadcast 25 Bulls games during the 1991 season, yet NBC claimed this was in violation of its exclusive contract with the league, and WGN should not be allowed to broadcast so many games. The district court sided with the Bulls and WGN, and granted an injunction for the 1991 season; ultimately it made a permanent allowance of the number of games that could be televised by WGN, and declared the NBA's fee for broadcasting these games to be excessive.

However, in *Chicago Professional Sports Limited Partnership v. NBA*, 95 F. 3d 593 (7th Cir. 1996), the court of appeals disagreed and vacated the judgment. Circuit Judge Easterbrook held that: (1) the Sports Broadcasting Act's exemption to antitrust laws was inapplicable to the league's contract to broadcast its teams' games; (2) teams need not have complete unity of interest for the league itself to be treated as a single firm for antitrust purposes; and (3) when acting in the broadcast market, the league was closer to a single firm than to a group of independent firms. This decision is applicable only, however, to conflicts between superstations and network television contracts. NBC thought that 25 games being broadcast by WGN on a national scale infringed on the exclusive rights to broadcast nationally granted to them in its contract. The Bulls, as a member of the NBA, had been part of the negotiations with the network, and therefore were held accountable for upholding the details of the deal.

A trend has emerged in baseball with individual clubs creating their own television channels in order to generate more revenues. Nearly all teams' games were previously broadcast on regional sports networks (RSNs), which deliver sports content relating to a local area. With baseball games filling prime time slots for almost half of the year, the loss of baseball represented a huge loss for the affected RSNs. Therefore, many RSNs have taken legal action to prevent the termination of previous agreements or force their way into negotiations. Fox Sports Net North (FSNN) successfully challenged the Minnesota Twins when the Twins planned on starting their own RSN, Victory Sports, for the 2002 season. FSNN decided to pick up an option in the contract to broadcast the 2002 and 2003 season but the Twins resisted (see note 1). FSNN won the right to broadcast the 2002 and 2003 seasons in court, and the Twins eventually scratched their RSN plans and signed a long-term deal with FSNN.

Other non–team-owned RSNs have not been as fortunate. By contrast, the New York Mets prevailed when Cablevision, the company that previously aired Mets games, was unsuccessful in its attempt to block the Mets from forming their own RSN until the remaining time on their prior agreement expired (see note 2). The Baltimore Orioles successfully started their new RSN, the Mid-Atlantic Sports Network (MASN), after fending off a claim by Comcast SportsNet. Comcast claimed that it was denied its contractual right to match any third-party offers during a specified exclusive bargaining period (see note 3). Both of these cases were examples of non–team-owned RSNs desperately trying to leverage ambiguous contract terms in order to prevent or delay the creation of team-owned RSNs.

Cablevision also wrangled with the New York Yankees' RSN, Yankees Entertainment, and Sports (YES), which was launched in 2002.Cablevision had previously carried Yankees games on one of its channels and decided that it would not carry YES as a cable provider because of the $72 million fee YES demanded. YES filed a lawsuit on antitrust grounds as it initially refused Cablevision's offer to be carried as a premium pay channel (see note 4). The two sides reached a temporary agreement just an hour before the 2003 season began and agreed to reach a long-term deal or settle the dispute through arbitration. The dispute was settled in arbitration in March 2004, as Cablevision was ordered to put YES on the basic tier. As more teams plan to create their own RSNs, in hopes of generating more revenues, the non–team-owned RSNs will continue to press their rights in court.

NOTES

1. In *Fox Sports Net North v. Minnesota Twins Partnership*, 319 F. 3d 329 (8th Cir. 2003), the court of appeals held up a district court ruling that allowed Fox Sports Net North (FSNN) to exercise an option in the broadcast rights contract with the Twins which allowed them to extend its agreement with the Twins for an additional two seasons after 2001. Per the agreement, FSNN could exercise its option if the Twins were able to "secure an acceptable stadium solution, excluding a new stadium" which the court ruled that the team indeed did by extending their lease with the Metrodome.

2. In May 2004, the Mets exercised an option to buy out the remaining five years of their broadcast agreement with Cablevision for $54 million, effective November 1, 2005. The Mets then announced their intention to form an RSN with Time Warner Cable and Comcast. Cablevision sought injunctive relief to stop the Mets from setting up their RSN because Cablevision believed that its first negotiation/first refusal rights were still in effect since the contract stated that the deal did not terminate until November 1, 2005. The case was dismissed in *SportsChannel Associates, v. Sterling Mets, L.P.*, 801 N.Y.S.2d 242 (N.Y.Sup. 2005). The decision hinged on whether the right to broadcast Mets games referred "to all Mets games, whenever played, and accordingly [whether] the Covenant prohibit[ed] Sterling through November 2005 from entering into contracts or taking other actions in connection with licensing the right to broadcast future Mets games to the Mets Network." The court found that the term "Mets games" was ambiguous due to inconsistent usage throughout the contract. As a result, it interpreted the term to include only games up until the termination of the contract; therefore, it allowed the Mets to negotiate for the rights of games after the termination date.

3. A Maryland Circuit Court ruled on July 25, 2005, in *Comcast SportsNet, Inc. v. Baltimore Orioles*, that MASN was actually TCR Sports, an Orioles subsidiary, operating under a new name, and was not a third party. Therefore, the clause in the agreement between Comcast and the Orioles stating that Comcast could match any third-party offers in the negotiations of a new rights deal was not triggered.

4. In *Yankees Entertainment and Sports Network, LLC v. Cablevision Systems Corporation and CSC Holdings, Inc.*, 224 F. Supp. 2d 657 (S.D.N.Y. 2002), YES Network accused Cablevision of trying to monopolize the New York RSN market and engaging in anticompetitive behavior in violation of the Sherman Act and the Clayton Act. YES also alleged Cablevision formed an anticompetitive arrangement in violation of the Donnelly Act, New York State's antitrust act. The sides reached a settlement and agreed to have the matter handled in arbitration if a long-term deal could not be agreed upon. The details of the arbitration deal were not announced due to confidentiality agreements, but while YES Network achieved its goal of being placed on basic cable, the arbitration panel reduced the previous

year's subscription fee from $2.12 to $1.85, and set the following year's rate at $1.93 with 4% annual increases. The president of Cablevision, James Dolan, in voicing his displeasure with the deal, announced that Cablevision was going to raise the subscription fees of all customers by $0.95 a month. For more analysis of this dispute, see "The Advertising Ramifications of the YES Network/Cablevision Lawsuit," 27 *Rutgers Law Record* 2 (2003).

5. For more information, see Diana Moss, "Regional Sports Networks, Competition, and the Consumer," 21 *Loyola Consumer Law Review* 56 (2008).

14.2.3. Broadcast Rights of the National Collegiate Athletic Association (NCAA)

Beyond contractual matters with broadcasters, a broadcast rights holder in intercollegiate athletics must also be concerned about the property rights to a broadcast of competing clubs and institutions, and within a league or conference arrangement.

14.2.3.1. Broadcast Rights of the NCAA Championships

The NCAA exerts a large amount of power over broadcasting when administering its championships. For instance, with any championship sponsored by the NCAA, the association "owns all rights to each and all of its championships…these rights include…rights to television (live and delayed), radio broadcasting, filming, and commercial photography" (*2009–10 NCAA Manual*, Bylaw 31.6.4). The NCAA grants rights to telecast its championships on a sliding scale that in part represents the attractiveness and marketability of the event. The NCAA, in awarding media rights, states that "television," radio and film rights shall be awarded in such a manner as to advance most fully the following interests:

1. gate attendance,
2. promotion of interest in the sport,
3. promotion of intercollegiate athletics as a part of collegiate education, and
4. promotion of the Association and its purposes and fundamental policy (*2009–10 NCAA Manual*, Bylaw 31.6.4.1).

The governing bodies of the NCAA for each championship make the decisions regarding the broadcast policy for the individual championships. For example, the *2009–10 NCAA Manual* states, "Negotiations with respect to the awarding of any such rights shall be conducted by the president, who shall have authority to determine the specific terms and conditions and to execute contracts for the award of such rights in behalf of the Association. Inquiries concerning all such rights should be directed to the president at the national office" (Bylaw 31.6.4.1.1).

The NCAA also maintains the rights over the use of rebroadcasts of NCAA events:

> The Association reserves all rights to the use of still photographs, films and videotapes of its championships.… The filming or videotaping of NCAA championships by parties other than NCAA Productions (i.e., participating institutions or commercial film production companies) for any purpose other than news purposes may be permitted only with the advance written consent of the president (*2009–10 NCAA Manual*, Bylaw 31.6.4.3).

14.2.3.2. Broadcast Rights of the Bowl Championship Series

The Bowl Championship Series (BCS) is not an official NCAA event but is instead managed by the 11 Division I Football Bowl Division conference commissioners, the director of athletics of Notre Dame, and the organizers of the five bowls that comprise the series. Therefore, it is responsible for negotiating its own rights deal. ABC signed a deal for the Rose Bowl and two national championship games for $300 million, running from 2007 to 2014. From 2011 to 2013 the title game is on ESPN as part of a four-year $500 million deal. The BCS has been a controversial system because mathematical formulas determine the participants in the national championship game, so many have called for a playoff system to be implemented instead. However, the BCS and its member schools have been able to command extremely high revenues through broadcasting agreements with the current system, so any plans to change the system are slow in the making. The decision in *NCAA v. Board of Regents*, which ruled that it was an antitrust violation to pool broadcast rights, allowed the conferences to control television rights themselves (see section 14.2.4.1, "Antitrust Issues in Broadcasting for Colleges," for a discussion of this case) and thus create this system.

14.2.4. Broadcast Rights for Conferences and Schools

A conference within the NCAA may also have its own policies for broadcasting. In part, this will reflect how much power the individual conference member institutions have granted the conference to act as an agent for them in seeking broadcast possibilities. An athletic administrator must always be aware of what rights have been granted to a conference and what rights an institution retains. At a minimum, most conferences have the rights to conference championship event broadcasts.

An example of a conference's television policy for NCAA Division I-A football and Division I basketball would be that called for by the Southeastern Conference (SEC) in 2009–2010, a portion of which is reprinted here:

30.21 Television

    30.21.1 Basketball. All television shall conform to current SEC basketball television contracts.

    30.21.2 Football. Football television and recording are governed by the following:

        a. All telecasts of SEC football games are to be conducted in accordance with the current regulations and contracts of the Conference and in keeping with provisions of other entities to whom member institutions assign TV rights, except that no member institution may televise a game selected for a national or Conference syndicated package on an alternative television medium (including pay-per-view) without the approval of the Commissioner; and

        b. No member of the Conference shall make motion pictures of football teams of other members except in games when their own team is participating (*Southeastern Conference Manual & Commissioner's Regulations, 2009–2010*).

A typical conference agreement for delayed football broadcast rights within the conference is that used by the Pac-10 Conference in 2009–2010. It noted the following:

> Delayed Football Television Rights
> The Conference encourages the use of delayed television of football games where possible as a means of promoting Pacific-10 football. The institution should contact the Conference office regarding any questions or interpretations dealing with rights of release and distribution for a delayed telecast. The institution also should refer to the applicable sport-specific television contract(s) regarding said rights of release and distribution (*Pacific-10 Conference, 2009–2010 Handbook*).

To ensure that the above policy was followed, the Pac-10 Conference included the following clauses in its conference television policies:

> 2. Rights of Release.
> If the game is not televised as part of a Conference television program, please contact the Conference office regarding any questions or interpretations dealing with rights of release and distribution. The institution also should refer to the applicable sport-specific television contract(s) regarding said rights of release and distribution. (6/95, 6/07)
> a. Visiting Non-Conference Institution.
> The host Pac-10 institution shall require the visiting non-Conference institution to observe the exclusive time periods and other terms provided the television companies in the applicable Conference media contracts. The host institution should contact the Conference office regarding any questions or interpretations dealing with rights of release and distribution by the visiting non-Conference institution. The host institution should also refer to the applicable sport-specific television contract(s) regarding said rights of release and distribution. (6/95, 6/03, 6/07) (*Pacific-10 Conference, 2009–2010 Handbook*)

Allied conferences also need a policy for distribution of revenues, including broadcast revenue, among member institutions. In 2009–2010, the Southeastern Conference used the following system for distributing television revenue from football:

31.21 Revenue Distribution—Football

31.21.1 Distribution of Bowl Game Receipts. Distribution of revenue (after allowable deductions) generated from member institutions participating in bowl games shall be as follows: [*Revised 6/2/06; effective August 1, 2006; Revised 6/1/95*]

a. For bowl games providing receipts which result in a balance of less than $1,500,000, the participating institution shall retain $840,000 plus a travel allowance as determined by the SEC Executive Committee. The remainder shall be remitted to the Commissioner and shall be divided into 13 equal shares with one share to the Conference and one share to each member institution. [*Revised 6/2/06; effective August 1, 2006; Revised 6/1/02*]

b. For bowl games providing receipts which result in a balance between $1,500,000 and $3,999,999, the participating institution shall retain $1,040,000, plus a travel allowance as determined by the SEC Executive Committee The remainder shall be remitted to the Commissioner and shall be divided into 13 equal shares, with one share to the Conference and one share to each member institution. [*Revised 6/2/06; effective August 1, 2006; Revised 6/1/02*]

c. For bowl games providing receipts which result in a balance between $4,000,000 and $5,999,999, the participating institution shall retain $1,240,000, plus a travel allowance as determined by the SEC Executive Committee. The remainder shall be remitted to the Commissioner and shall be divided into 13 equal shares, with one share to the Conference and one share to each member institution. [*Revised 6/2/06; effective August 1, 2006; Revised 6/1/02*]

d. For bowl games providing receipts which result in a balance of $6,000,000 or more, the participating institution shall receive $1,740,000 ($1,840,000 if the SEC team is a participant in the Bowl Championship Series game which determines the National Championship), plus a travel allowance as determined by the SEC Executive Committee. The remainder shall be remitted to the Commissioner and shall be divided into 13 equal shares, with one share to the Conference and one share to each member institution. [*Revised 6/2/06; effective August 1, 2006; Revised 6/5/99; Revised 6/1/02*]

e. Bowl Revenue Protection Insurance and the cost of unused tickets up to 3,000 tickets, shall be deducted prior to Conference distribution. [*Adopted 6/1/02*]

31.21.2 Distribution of Football Television Receipts. Distribution of revenue generated from football television shall be as follows: (last revised 6/1/96)

a. Network and National Cable Telecast:

1. A member institution appearing in a non-conference game shall receive an appearance fee of $120,000;

2. A member institution appearing in a conference game shall receive an appearance fee of $40,000;

3. A member institution appearing in a non-conference home game or a conference vs. conference game played on a non-traditional playing date to meet contractual commitments or to accommodate a request by the Conference office shall receive an appearance fee of $300,000 as the home team and $200,000 as the visiting team; and [*Revised 6/4/04; Revised 6/1/2007*]

4. All remaining revenue shall be divided into 13 equal shares with one share being distributed to each member institution and one share being distributed to the Conference.

b. Conference Syndicated Program. Revenue from a conference football program shall be divided into 13 equal shares with one share to each member institution and one share to the conference office after home appearance fees and crossover fees have been paid. (revised 6/3/93)

1. Home appearance fees shall be paid as follows:

First Home Appearance—No fee to host institution

Second Home Appearance—$20,000 to host institution

Three or more Home Appearances—$40,000 to host institution for each appearance after second home appearance.

2. Any cross-over fees shall be set by the SEC Executive Committee.

31.21.3 Football Championship Game Revenue. All revenue remaining from the championship game after expenses of planning and conducting the event have been deducted shall be divided as follows: (last revised 6/3/93)

a. Each participating institution shall be reimbursed for the actual cost of transporting an official party of 150 (including student-athletes, coaches, administrators, cheerleaders, etc.) to the site (air or bus travel from campus to the site; local transportation is not included). This amount shall be approved in advance by the conference office and must be supported by actual invoices. In addition, each participating institution shall receive $150,000 to cover all costs associated with institutional lodging, meals and local transportation. Each participating institution will be financially responsible for payment for 150 rooms for two nights at the designated team headquarters hotel. (last revised 6/1/96)

b. Each participating institution shall receive a band travel allowance of $50 per mile, one-way from its campus to the site (according to Rand-McNally Mileage Chart). Each institution shall be financially responsible for 100 rooms for two nights at its designated band hotel; [*Revised 6/1/95; Revised 6/1/96; Revised 6/1/2007*]

c. All remaining revenue shall be divided into 13 equal shares, with one share distributed to each member institution and one share to the Conference office;

d. Institutions may petition to the Executive Committee prior to the game for an increase in the travel allowance only in the event actual expenses exceed the designated amount.

In representing the members of an athletic conference, the conference administration must grant many of the same rights to a broadcast company that an individual institution would usually grant The Pac-10 Conference has a section with information on men's basketball television contracts in its 2009–2010 handbook.

3. Men's Basketball Television Policies.

The Pac-10's men's basketball television program(s) is defined in the contract(s) executed with the Conference's television partner(s) and may be found in that document(s). (revised 6/99)

a. Live Basketball Television Rights.

1. Institutional Telecast.

When not selected for presentation on a Conference television program, each Conference basketball game, or non-Conference game hosted by a Conference member, will be available for live telecasting by the host institution and visiting Conference institution provided such release would be permissible under terms of applicable Conference media contracts and policies, as such policies are set forth herein, and as otherwise provided below. (1/89, 6/95, 6/99, 6/07)

2. Rights of Release.

If the game is not televised as part of a Conference television program, please contact the Conference office regarding any questions or interpretations dealing with rights of release and distribution. The institution also should refer to the applicable sport-specific television contract(s) regarding said rights of release and distribution. (6/95, 6/99, 6/07)

a. Visiting Non-Conference Institution.

The host Pac-10 institution shall require the visiting non-Conference institution to observe the exclusive time periods and other terms provided the television companies in the applicable Conference media contracts. The host institution should contact the Conference office regarding any questions or interpretations dealing with rights of release and distribution by the visiting non-Conference institution. The institution also should refer to the applicable sport-specific television contract(s) regarding said rights of release and distribution. (6/95, 6/03, 6/07) (*Pacific-10 Conference 2009–2010 Handbook*)

Most colleges and universities relinquish their right to negotiate individual game broadcast contracts to their league or conference. With the decision in *NCAA v. Board of Regents*, the trend in intercollegiate sports broadcasting took a major turn (see section 14.2.4.1, "Antitrust Issues in Broadcasting for Colleges," for an in-depth discussion). The current prevalent practice for colleges and universities is to have the conference office negotiate broadcasting contracts on behalf of all conference members. One notable exception to this rule is the negotiation of television contracts by schools with no conference affiliation, such as the University of Notre Dame in football, which negotiated a separate contract with NBC to broadcast its football games. Radio broadcasts are generally left up to the discretion of the participating universities.

In a nonconference game, an institution must also protect its broadcast rights. A typical contract clause would be similar to the one the University of Kentucky used: "Broadcasting rights to UK games are assigned exclusively to Host Creative Communications, Inc., of Lexington. One reciprocal rights fee waiver is guaranteed opponent schools visiting Lexington."

14.2.4.1. Antitrust Issues in Broadcasting for Colleges

As mentioned in the introduction to this chapter, antitrust law can have a major impact upon the broadcasting of sports events. Although basic antitrust law principles are covered in Chapter 10, this section discusses the basic application of antitrust law to sports broadcasting where there is not an antitrust exemption.

For holders of broadcast rights, on all levels of sport, that means being careful not to try to control the overall flow of their sports broadcasts, in a concerted action, such that a monopoly or other antitrust violations develop. It is always important to remember that the antitrust laws were designed to encourage the easy flow of any business activity into the general stream of commerce. In drafting such laws, legislators reasoned that it was important to have open and free market competition.

The best illustration of how antitrust law can affect athletics broadcasting is the case of *NCAA v. Board of Regents of University of Oklahoma*, 468 U.S. 85 (1984). (For more, see section 10.5.2, "The NCAA's Reduced Power over Television: *Board of Regents*"). On June 27, 1984, the Supreme Court of the United States, in a 7–2 decision, struck down the NCAA's 1982–1985 football television plan because it violated federal antitrust law. This section will detail the specifics of the case, and also its effect upon intercollegiate sports.

The ruling in this case immediately impacted networks, producers, syndicators, advertisers, and NCAA member institutions, all of which had to scramble to implement broadcast schedules for the 1984 season. This decision and its ramifications continue to be major factors in the broadcast industry for intercollegiate athletics.

At the time that the lawsuit was brought, an important group in the area of television and intercollegiate athletics was the College Football Association of America (see note 2). Beginning in 1979, the CFA started to believe that its voice in the formulation of football television policy was diluted in the 800-plus institutions of the NCAA membership, and did not reflect its own members' importance in obtaining a national television contract.

The CFA negotiated a contract of its own with the National Broadcasting Company (NBC) for the 1982 and 1983 football seasons. The NBC contract was more attractive to CFA members in terms of rights, fees, and appearances than the 1982–1985 agreements that the NCAA had with ABC and CBS. While CFA member institutions were considering whether to accept the NBC pact, the NCAA indicated that doing so would be in violation of NCAA rules and that disciplinary sanctions would result. This caused many CFA members that originally had approved the CFA-NBC contract to vote against accepting it. As a result of the CFA's failure to contract with NBC and continued dissatisfaction with the NCAA's television policy, the University of Georgia Athletic Association and the University of Oklahoma brought suit in November 1981. They challenged the NCAA's exclusive control over televised football games and contended that the NCAA was violating the Sherman Antitrust Act by its exclusive television contracts with two major networks—ABC and CBS (see note 3 for a brief history of NCAA football policies). The NCAA argued that the television package was beneficial to its membership as a whole and accomplished two important purposes. First, it protected the live gate of college and high school football games, which resulted in a higher attendance at games. In support of this argument, the NCAA pointed to an increase in total attendance for NCAA football games in all but one year during the period 1953 to 1983.

Second, the NCAA contended that its plan had the positive effect of spreading television revenues and exposure to a greater number of member institutions. The NCAA also contended that limitations on the number of television appearances a member institution could make allowed a greater number of institutions to appear on television, which resulted in the schools receiving substantially higher rights fees. In addition to these revenues, these institutions received invaluable television exposure and extensive media attention. As a result, the recruitment efforts of these institutions were enhanced.

The NCAA maintained that uncontrolled televising of football games would result in the creation of a football *super* power group, since a limited number of institutions would be attractive to television broadcasters. With increased revenues and media attention to the super power group, the NCAA predicted that the disparity among the member institutions would be increased. This would be contrary to the policies and purposes of the NCAA, since it would place irresistible temptations for the development of winning teams, thereby threatening the future of the sport.

Judge Burciaga, a federal district court judge, ruled in favor of the University of Oklahoma and the Georgia Athletic Association on September 15, 1982, reasoning that the television contracts between the NCAA and ABC, CBS, and Turner Broadcast System were in violation of the Sherman Antitrust Act, and therefore void. The court held that "[t]he right to telecast college football games is the property of the institutions participating in the games, and that right may be sold or assigned by those institutions to any entity at their discretion." Judge Burciaga found that the NCAA's television football controls constituted price fixing, output restriction, a group boycott, and an exercise of monopoly power over the market of college football television. The court found that the membership of the NCAA agreed to limit production to a level far below what which occurs in a free market situation. In addition, Judge Burciaga was not persuaded that the televising of college football games would have any negative impact on game attendance at nontelevised games. Judge Burciaga disagreed with the NCAA that the television controls helped maintain competitive balance among the football programs of various schools. In his reasoning, he compared the telecasting policies of NCAA football to those of NCAA basketball. The NCAA did not control the televising of regular season basketball games. The arrangements were left to the individual member institutions and conferences that contracted with various national and local television and cable companies. Judge Burciaga rejected the NCAA's contention that televising football was distinguishable from televising basketball; in fact, he held "the market in television basketball to be persuasive evidence of how a free market in television football would operate." Judge Burciaga's decision rendered illegal the NCAA's television contracts with ABC and CBS for $131.75 million each and with Turner Broadcasting System for $18 million. His decision voided a total of $281.5 million in television contracts.

The NCAA appealed the decision to the Court of Appeals for the Tenth Circuit, arguing that Judge Burciaga incorrectly concluded that there was price fixing in the awarding of television contracts, since there was vigorous competition among the networks in bidding for the television contracts. The NCAA further argued that the court erred in its conclusion that the NCAA was not a voluntary association. In May 1983, the court of appeals upheld the district court's ruling.

As noted previously, in *NCAA v. Board of Regents*, the U.S. Supreme Court upheld the decisions of the district court and court of appeals. The Supreme Court summarized its decision by noting:

> The NCAA plays a critical role in the maintenance of a revered tradition of amateurism in college sports. There can be no question but that it needs ample latitude to play that role, or that the preservation of the student-athlete in higher education adds richness and diversity to intercollegiate athletics and is entirely consistent with the goals of the Sherman Act. But consistent with the Sherman Act, the role of the NCAA must be to *preserve* a tradition that might otherwise die; rules that restrict output are hardly consistent with this role. Today we hold only that the record supports the District Court's conclusion that by curtailing output and blunting the ability of member institutions to respond to consumer preference, the NCAA has restricted rather than enhanced the place of intercollegiate athletics in the Nation's life.

In wake of the Court's ruling in this case, a number of lawsuits related to the decision were filed. Unsatisfied with the CFA agreement, which forbade national appearances by member association teams on networks other than ABC or the Entertainment and Sports Programming Network (ESPN), the University of Southern California (USC), the University of California at Los Angeles (UCLA), along with the Pacific-10 Conference and the Big-Ten Conference, brought suit against the ABC-CFA agreement that prevented two games—UCLA against Nebraska and USC against Notre Dame—from being telecast (see *Regents of University of California v. ABC*, 747 F. 2d 511 [9th Cir. 1984]). The suit sought preliminary and permanent injunctions against the defendants because the ABC-CFA exclusive agreement, it was charged, prevented *crossover* games, which are games between CFA member schools and non–CFA member schools. In granting the injunction for UCLA and USC, a federal district court sitting in Los Angeles noted that if the exclusion was allowed to stand, the schools would be harmed by loss of revenue. "By issuance of this order, ABC and ESPN are not measurably harmed, other than by some perceived diminution of their ability quickly to dispatch CBS from the market for nationwide football telecasts." Soon afterward, the parties to the suit settled their differences and dropped any further litigation. In general, such questions of property rights to broadcast ownership are now determined in the game contracts, as was discussed in section 14.2.1, "Rights Granted."

Soon after the decision, the Association of Independent Television Stations (INTV) filed two suits in federal district court aimed at opening the college telecast market further to local broadcast stations (see *Association of Independent Television Stations, Inc. v. College Football Ass'n*, 637 F. Supp. 1289 (1986)). INTV was a coalition of stations not affiliated with the major networks (ABC, CBS, and NBC). The suits sought on antitrust grounds to open *protected* time frames that the major networks have arranged with the different football governing bodies, such as the CFA. INTV's first suit was filed in Los Angeles against CBS and the Big Ten and Pacific-10 Conferences. The second suit was filed in Oklahoma City against ABC, ESPN, the CFA, and the Big Eight Conference.

In March 1986, Judge Burciaga rejected the arguments of INTV and ruled that the CFA's plan granting some networks exclusivity in two time periods was allowable under the antitrust laws. Judge Burciaga noted, "The CFA is a powerful entity.... Nonetheless, it remains to be demonstrated beyond a reasonable factual dispute that the CFA can both control price and restrict entry to the college football television market. The market is a different one than the court analyzed in 1982. Unlike the NCAA, the CFA...have their rivals."

Next, the U.S. government, through the Federal Trade Commission (FTC), scrutinized the CFA television contracts. The FTC has jurisdiction over enforcement of antitrust laws. In September 1990, the FTC filed an administrative complaint against the CFA and Capital Cities-ABC, claiming that their national television contracts were anticompetitive. The complaint alleged that consumers had been deprived of the selection of college football games because of the limitation on teams and games selected to be televised by the CFA-Capital Cities contract. The CFA withstood this challenge when Judge James P. Timony, an administrative law judge, ruled that the FTC has no jurisdiction over the television agreement because colleges and universities are not considered profit-making institutions over which the agency has legal responsibility. The FTC had argued that major college football programs are operated for commercial rather than educational objectives, and therefore are subject to antitrust laws despite the

CFA's nonprofit status. Judge Timony ruled, though, that the proceeds from the CFA's television rights to college football games go to the schools and have a non-profit educational purpose.

The CFA withstood this FTC challenge to its television contract but received a setback when the University of Notre Dame seceded from the CFA television contract with ABC and in January 1990 entered into its own agreement with NBC for $38 million. The original CFA contract was for $210 million, but had to be scaled down by about $25 million when Notre Dame defected and entered into its own agreement. Notre Dame's athletic director, Dick Rosenthal, said the NBC contract was a result of Notre Dame's nonapproval of the ABC contract, which called for regional coverage. Rosenthal believed this would have demoralized the Fighting Irish, hurting their broad appeal. With the NBC contract, Notre Dame's home games are televised nationally. This contract was also more financially lucrative for the Fighting Irish, bringing in $1.2 million per game, which was divided equally between Notre Dame and its opponent. Under the CFA-ABC agreement, Notre Dame was paid $1.53 million during the 1988–1989 season. The CFA had no legal recourse against the University of Notre Dame because of the precedent of free and open competition in the television marketplace that the courts have found since the *NCAA v. Board of Regents* decision.

In comparison to collegiate football television contracts, in which the NCAA is no longer a party, collegiate basketball is another story. The NCAA has a 14-year contract with CBS for the broadcast and multimedia rights to the men's NCAA basketball championship. This contract will bring the NCAA an average of $740 million per year through 2024, which accounts for 90% of NCAA revenue (see section 1.3.2.1, "Revenues"). This contract has not been subject to litigation by the schools or conferences because the NCAA owns the rights to their championship events, but does not control the rights to regular season games and conference playoffs.

The effects of *NCAA v. Board of Regents of University of Oklahoma* are still being felt in intercollegiate football. Now that all universities are able to negotiate contracts on their own, or with their conferences, the differences in revenues between small Division I universities and large Division I universities has increased. In June 2008, Notre Dame and NBC announced an extension of their deal through the 2015 season.

Realizing the power that colleges can have in negotiations, conferences began to realign to bring in traditionally strong football programs. In 1991 Florida State joined the Atlantic Coast Conference and in 1993 Penn State joined the Big Ten in order to strengthen the bargaining power of the conferences. With the power of these big-name universities behind them, conferences were able to negotiate lucrative conferencewide contracts. For example, in 2004 the ACC signed a seven-year football contract with ABC/ESPN worth a total of $258 million.

In a move similar to that of some MLB teams, the Big Ten Conference launched its own television network in 2007. The Big Ten Network (BTN) has also suffered many of the same problems in convincing cable companies to carry the channel on a basic cable package. In August 2008, BTN reached a deal with Comcast whereby BTN would be aired as part of an expanded basic cable package in the eight states with Big Ten universities by 2009.

It is important to remember, however, while many universities have profited from the greater number of games on national television, many other colleges in smaller conferences have lost revenue, and don't have the ability to obtain contracts that provide great amounts of revenue for the institution.

More recently, ESPN faced a U.S. Justice Department inquiry for its exclusive deals with many college conferences. ESPN does not air all of the games it purchases rights for, engaging in the practice of "warehousing," which can be considered to be anticompetitive behavior.

NOTES

1. The reactions to the decision in the *Oklahoma Board of Regents* case were predictably and decidedly mixed: "It's the worst possible thing that could have happened," said former University of Michigan athletic director Don Canham. Pennsylvania State University athletic director Jim Tarman reacted to the decision with concern, stating: "The worst scenario is that everyone is on their own. We don't feel that scenario is in Penn State's best interest or in the best interest of college football." Other parties were delighted by the Supreme Court's decision: "The position of the universities has been vindicated. The property right theory has been upheld," said Chuck Neinas, executive director of the College Football Association (CFA).

2. The CFA was composed of 63 NCAA Division I-A member institutions and included five of the major football-playing conferences—the Big 12, Southeast, Southwest, Atlantic Coast, and Western Athletic Conference—and major independents such as Notre Dame. The only major football-playing schools that were not CFA members were the Pacific-10 and Big Ten Conferences. The CFA was formed to promote the interests of Division I-A member schools within the National Collegiate Athletic Association structure.

3. The NCAA, since it was given authority by a vote of its membership at its annual convention in January 1952, had administered the live telecasting of games for its member institutions. The details of the television plan varied through the years. The plans, however, consistently limited the number of live television appearances an NCAA member institution could make in a year; prevented individual member institutions from contracting on an individual basis with national, local, and cable television companies; fixed revenue amounts for rights fees allocated by the NCAA to member institutions whose teams appeared as part of the network television contract; and allocated a percentage of the total television contract for the NCAA's operating budget.

14.2.5. Broadcast Rights of Individual Sports

Individual sports such as auto racing, golf, and tennis are unique since all of the particular league's action is occurring in one place. NASCAR, the most popular auto racing body in the United States, allowed individual tracks to negotiate their television rights deals until 1999, when NASCAR negotiated a deal with FOX and its cable channel FX, NBC, and TBS that began in 2001 for $2.4 billion over six years. Before NASCAR consolidated its rights, the sport brought in $100 million a year in rights fees with races broadcast on six different channels. NASCAR signed a new, eight-year agreement starting in 2007 with ABC/ESPN, FOX, and TNT worth a total of $4.48 billion.

Like NASCAR, the Professional Golfers' Association (PGA) also sells the rights of its events together as a package. The Golf Channel signed a 15-year agreement that commenced in 2007 to be the exclusive cable home of the PGA tour, carrying the opening rounds on Thursday and Friday for each event of the season. CBS and NBC get the final rounds in a deal that runs until 2012. However, two of golf's biggest events, the U.S. Open and the Masters Tournament are not PGA events, so those events negotiate deals independently.

When the Association of Tennis Professionals (ATP) announced in 2007 that, as part of a new streamlined schedule, the Monte Carlo and Hamburg tournaments would be downgraded in rankings points and prize money, both tournaments filed suit, claiming that the ATP violated antitrust laws. The Monte Carlo tournament settled the suit, whereby top tier players are not required to participate in Monte Carlo like other tournaments in the Masters Series, but the tournament retained its place on the schedule, rankings points, and prize money. Hamburg lost its lawsuit when a jury found in favor of the ATP but an appeal is pending, see *Deutscher Tennis Bund v. ATP Tour, Inc.*, 2008 WL 2520809 (D.Del. June 23, 2008).

Due to the fact that high-interest boxing matches are held only a few times a year, the events lend themselves well to pay-per-view, which allows television viewers to purchase individual events for the private telecasting of that event to their homes. The event subscriptions, typically offered through HBO, usually cost around $50. The fighter's purse is closely tied to the expected amount of subscribers and, with over a million buyers often tuning in for title bouts, fights often bring in many millions of dollars in revenue (see note 1). Illegal pirating of the pay-per-view brings new lawsuits with each new event, as individuals, restaurants, and bars are often sued for violating the Cable Communications Policy Act of 1984, which makes it illegal to "intercept or receive or assist in interception or receiving any communications service offered over a cable system, unless specifically authorized to do so by a cable operator" (see note 2).

NOTES

1. The highest revenue ever for a single pay-per-view event was the bout between Oscar De La Hoya and Floyd Mayweather Jr. on May 5, 2007, in which Mayweather won the WBC junior middleweight title. The event was purchased by 2.4 million households for total revenues of $120 million. De La Hoya earned $58 million for the fight, while Mayweather earned $25 million.

2. See *Kingvision Pay-Per-View Ltd. v. Villalobos*, 2008 WL 1994864 (E.D.N.Y. May 8, 2008), *Garden City Boxing Club, Inc. v. Espinal*, 2008 WL 2078151 (E.D.N.Y. May 15, 2008), *J & J Sports Productions, Inc. v. Meyers*, 2007 WL 2030288 (S.D.N.Y. July 16, 2007), and *National Satellite Sports, Inc. v. J.A. Rocks, Inc.*, 2006 WL 1831332 (E.D.N.Y. June 28, 2006). Damages typically ranged from $2,000 to $15,000.

14.2.6. Broadcast Rights for the Olympics

Broadcast rights for the Olympic Games are similar to those for the NCAA and professional leagues. They bargain for the licensing fee for their television broadcast rights for all of their events. In the end, they sell those rights to broadcast the games to one television network. Broadcast rights for the Olympic Games have become one of the most lucrative sources for revenue of any sporting event in the world. Prices for these rights have escalated over the past two decades, as NBC Sports paid $2.3 billion for the rights to the 2004 Summer Games, 2006 Winter Games, and 2008 Summer Games. NBC also secured the rights for $2.2 billion to the 2010 Winter Games and the 2012 Summer Games.

One area of broadcasting that has increasingly affected the broadcast rights and revenues of the Olympic Games is the attempts of broadcasters to illegally broadcast the games over the Internet. With expanding technology, this practice has become much easier to accomplish without spending exorbitant amounts of money. The International Olympic Committee (IOC) has taken a proactive approach to apprehending these renegade broadcasters. The IOC can intercept illegal satellite transmissions and trace the signals to the illegal broadcaster. Although it is difficult to discover all violators, the IOC is attempting to maintain its relationship with the networks, which have invested millions of dollars for exclusive rights.

NOTE

1. For more information on the Olympic Games and broadcasting, see the following:
   a. The IOC Web site at www.olympic.org. Within the section "Olympic Broadcasting," under the IOC Facts and Figures, the IOC provides a description of Olympic broadcast revenues and coverage.
   b. Jeffrey F. Levine, "A Golden Opportunity for Global Acceptance? How Hosting the Olympic Games Impacts a Nation's Economy and Intellectual Property Rights with a Focus on the Right of Publicity," 15 *Sports Lawyers Journal* 245 (2008).

14.2.7. Broadcast Rights of Individual Players

In some instances, players who participate in an event have argued that they have a right to share in the rights fees for the broadcast. In *Baltimore Orioles, Inc. v. Major League Baseball Players Ass'n*, 805 F. 2d 663 (7th Cir. 1986), players for the Baltimore Orioles argued that they owned a copyright to the telecasts of their games because they were the ones who were playing the game on the field. However, this argument did not succeed because the court found that the clubs, as employers of the players, owned a copyright to the telecasts of baseball games under the "work made for hire" doctrine, and this preempted any publicity right the players had under state law (see note 3). Basically, this means that because the team, which owns the copyright to the broadcast, employs the players, the players are not entitled to share in any of the broadcast fees.

Players who sign endorsement deals must be careful about the statements they make. Former baseball player Steve Garvey was sued by the Federal Trade Commission for making false claims in a pair of infomercials endorsing a weight-loss product. However, Garvey was absolved because he did not know that the statements he made were false (see note 2).

NOTES

1. In *Dryer v. National Football League*, 689 F.Supp.2d 1113 (D.Minn. 2010), former NFL players brought a class action suit against the league alleging that league's use of video footage from games in which they played in league's promotional videos violated their common law and statutory rights of publicity. In denying the NFL's motion for judgment on the pleadings, the court held that the right of publicity claim was not preempted by the Copyright Act and that allegations were sufficient to support players' claim that the videos amounted to commercial speech, for First Amendment purposes. The case is ongoing at the time of publication.

2. In *FTC v. Garvey*, 383 E. 3d 891 (9th Cir. 2004), an appeals court held up a lower court's ruling that Garvey had not violated the Federal Trade Commission Act when he made several false claims in a pair of infomercials while endorsing a weight-loss system. The FTC claimed that Garvey had violated Sections 5(a) and 12 of the FTCA by being either a "direct participant" in the false claims or an "endorser" of the claims. The court ruled that the FTC "failed to show that Garvey was recklessly indifferent to the truth of his statements or was aware that fraud was highly probable and intentionally avoided the truth." Garvey and his wife had in fact used the product and had successful results.

3. Initially, the district court in *Baltimore Orioles, Inc. v. Major League Baseball Players Ass'n*, 1985 WL 1509 (N.D.Ill. May 23, 1985), granted the club summary judgment on the counts of their copyright and "master-servant" claims. Under principles of master-servant law, the employer (Orioles) own all rights in and to Major League Baseball games created at their expense, and pursuant to their direction, supervision, and control, including the right to telecast these games.

14.3. OTHER IMPORTANT ISSUES IN SPORTS BROADCASTING

Several other topics that deal with sports broadcasting will now be covered briefly. An athletic administrator should be aware of each of these issues, which include: (1) restrictions in sports broadcasting; (2) Internet rights for sports broadcasts; (3) siphoning of sport events from network television to pay television; (4) home recording of copyrighted events; (5) domestic and international piracy of satellite and cable transmissions; (6) blackouts of scheduled programs; (7) satellite distribution of sports; and (8) FCC and indecency regulations.

14.3.1. Restrictions on Sports Broadcasting

In many cases, sports organizations, on both the professional and the intercollegiate level, will restrict certain parts of a sports broadcast. The following two sections will focus upon the restriction of advertising in broadcasts on the intercollegiate level, and the restriction on the use of replays on the professional level. Each area of analysis has been marked by a singular, leading case.

14.3.1.1. Restrictions on the Use of Advertising

In addition to restricting the types of advertisements that can be shown on television during intercollegiate athletic contests (including the ability to limit alcohol or tobacco ads), the NCAA restricts the amount of advertising that is allowed on player uniforms. In the case of *Adidas, Inc. v. NCAA*, 40 F. Supp. 2d. 1275 (D. Kan. 1999), sporting goods manufacturer Adidas brought action against the NCAA, alleging that the association's bylaw governing use of commercial logos on student-athletes' uniforms was a restraint of free trade (see note 1) and a violation of the Sherman Act. Adidas was unsuccessful in its claim, the court deciding that the purpose of the bylaw (*2009–10 NCAA Manual*, Bylaw 12.5.4) was to preserve the integrity of college athletics and to avoid the commercial exploitation of student athletes. Furthermore, the bylaw is designed to avoid excessive advertising that could potentially interfere with the basic function of the student-athletes' uniforms, which is to provide immediate identification of the athlete's number and team to his or her teammates and to the referee or umpire officiating the contest. There is no commercial purpose behind the creation and enforcement of Bylaw 12.5.5. Neither the NCAA nor its member institutions realize an economic or competitive advantage through the enforcement of Bylaw 12.5.5 against Adidas or other apparel manufacturers.

NOTE _____

1. The applicable NCAA bylaw states the following: "The student-athlete's institution's official uniform (including numbered racing bibs and warmups) and all other items of apparel (e.g., socks, headbands, T-shirts, wristbands, visors or hats, swim caps, and towels) shall bear only a single manufacturer's or distributor's normal label or trademark (regardless of the visibility of the label or trademark), not to exceed 2 1/4 square inches in area (i.e.,

rectangle, square, parallelogram) including any additional material (e.g., patch) surrounding the normal trademark or logo. The student-athlete's institution's official uniform and all other items of apparel shall not bear a design element similar to the manufacturer's trademark/logo or that is in addition to another trademark/logo that is contrary to the size restriction" (*2009–10 NCAA Manual*, Bylaw 12.5.4).

14.3.1.2. Restrictions on the Use of Replays

Cable television networks such as ESPN and FOX Sports devote much of their programming lineup to shows that provide highlights of the top games in sports. However, these networks do not own a copyright to the games that are being broadcast. The question, then, is how these networks can broadcast highlights without infringing upon copyrights.

In 1981, when ESPN was in its infancy, the Boston Red Sox, Boston Bruins, and WSBK-TV (a local Boston station) brought legal action against ESPN for showing game highlights without their permission. In *New Boston Television v. Entertainment Sports Programming Network, Inc.*, No. 81–1010-Z, 1981 U.S. Dist. LEXIS 15032 (D. Mass. Aug. 3, 1981), the court held that the copyright owner of the telecast has the right to charge a fee and place appropriate restrictions on the showing of highlights. However, the two sides in this case reached an agreement over the use of highlights, because it was advantageous for both. A club may welcome the promotional exposure that results from the showing of highlights in its home territory and may have little interest in deterring this practice by charging a fee.

The ease with which video content can be distributed and hosted on the Internet has complicated this issue. Sports leagues, teams and media outlets are actually competitors on the Internet since they all produce and deliver multimedia content via their respective Web sites. The NFL has taken action to restrict this competition by limiting the length of videos of interviews, press conferences, and practices posted online to just 45 seconds per day, and only allowing the clips to be present on the Web site for 24 hours (see note 1). Furthermore, links to NFL.com and the Web site of the team being covered are required. The 2006 policy that designated NFL.com as the exclusive home of actual game footage (preventing media outlets from hosting any) was also continued. The policy is a blatant attempt by the NFL to capture the sponsorship revenues available for online video content. Many media members derided the policy for its restrictiveness, while others praised the NFL's business acumen (see note 2). In 2008 MLB began to impose similar restrictions on the media. Essentially, the proliferation of information technology has allowed leagues such as the NFL to become media companies themselves, altering the long-standing balance in the symbiotic relationship between the leagues and the traditional media. While the leagues may contend they own the intellectual property in the events of the game, media groups have and will respond that certain amounts of video and photos are necessary for reporting on the game, entitling them to a fair use exception. The league's attempt to control all the media associated with the production of games would effectively result in the league's ability to determine the writing of history.

14.4. INTERNET RIGHTS FOR SPORTS BROADCASTS

The Internet is rapidly changing the way television and sports are marketed and utilized. First, the Internet is used by the sports entities (NFL, NBA, MLB, NHL, Olympics, and NCAA) to help promote their product by establishing Web sites to provide information and recent news related to the respective leagues and sports. In addition, there are individual sites that are utilized by or are about some of the individual players. This is a great marketing tool that the sports leagues do not have to pay for, yet reaches millions of people. In addition to individual sites, the Internet is used as a means to broadcast certain events. For example, MLB allows fans to watch virtually any game through its Web site for a fee, and ESPN launched ESPN360.com, which essentially serves as another ESPN channel by broadcasting live games and archiving past events. However, fans can obtain free live statistical updates for most major professional sports events and even many collegiate and minor league games.

The increase of information technology tools has created many legal issues. In *NBA v. Motorola, Inc.*, 105 F. 3d 841 (2d. Cir. 1997), the NBA brought an action against Motorola, which was manufacturing pagers that provided real-time scoring of NBA basketball games. The NBA argued that Motorola was infringing on its copyright, among other allegations. The circuit judge, on appeal from a lower court, ruled for Motorola, holding that real-time updates of NBA scores were not an infringement upon the copyrights owned by the NBA. This decision has had a significant effect upon the broadcasting of sports on the Internet. With this case as precedent, Internet sports sites are able to provide real-time sports scores for their visitors without fear of infringing upon copyrights.

However, the accounts and descriptions of the game are still protected, and vehemently so in some cases. During the 2007 NCAA College World Series, the NCAA removed a local newspaper reporter and revoked his credential for "blogging" (posting live, journal-like articles on his paper's website) about the game being broadcasted nationally. While it seems unlikely that many would choose to follow written accounts of the game as opposed to watching on television, the NCAA was sending a clear message that it would not tolerate any actions that would challenge the integrity of its broadcast deal with ESPN.

The popular website YouTube.com and other similar Web sites have become an issue for all content providers as they allow users to freely share videos by uploading and viewing content. Many users have posted copyrighted materials such as television shows and sports broadcasts. While YouTube has faced legal action for being unable to remove all of the illegal content, leagues such as the NHL, NBA, and International Fight League have signed agreements with YouTube to post game highlights on the site. These agreements are an example of how the sports industry must find creative ways to protect the integrity of their media content while embracing new technology.

The Digital Millennium Copyright Act (DMCA) criminalizes electronic circumvention and infringement of copyrights (see note 1). However, Title II of the act creates a safe harbor for Web sites by shielding them from liability for copyright infringement if they promptly block access to allegedly infringing material upon notice from the copyright holder. As a result, YouTube and similar file sharing sites are in compliance with the law so long as they remove highlights when asked to by MLB, the NFL, or other leagues, despite the fact that YouTube has the ability to prevent the highlights, and any content it wishes, from ever being posted from the start (for example, you won't find pornography on YouTube). To combat this problem, the leagues have been forced to hire full-time employees to monitor the Internet for unlicensed use of copyrighted materials.

NOTES

1. In *The Football Ass'n of Premier League Ltd. v. YouTube, Inc.*, 633 F.Supp.2d 159 (S.D.N.Y. 2009) the English soccer league brought a class action suit along with several

music companies alleging copyright violations against YouTube for allowing copyrighted clips to be posted on the site without permission. The court dismissed any claim for statutory damages based on the plaintiffs' failure to register the foreign works in the United States.

2. In *Ticketmaster L.L.C. v. RMG Technologies, Inc.*, 507 F. Supp. 2d 1096 (2007) Ticketmaster was granted a preliminary injunction against a maker of an automated device that mined Ticketmaster's Web site, blocked other users, and subsequently made it easier to purchase tickets, in violation of the DMCA and other statutes.

3. In 2007 the English Premier League, one of the top soccer leagues in the world, and Viacom, one of the largest media conglomerates in the world, separately sued YouTube, alleging copyright infringement. In its complaint, Viacom stated that almost 160,000 clips of Viacom's programming had been posted without authorization on YouTube and had been viewed more than 1.5 billion times.

4. For more information on the Internet and broadcasting, see *Twentieth Century Fox Film, Corp. v. ICRAVETV*, Nos. 00–121, 00–120, 2000 U.S. Dist. LEXIS 1013 (W.D. Pa. Jan. 28, 2000). Although not a sports broadcasting case, this case is important because it deals with the ability of Web sites to provide real-time rebroadcasts of copyrighted events. The defendant provided users of his site the opportunity to watch television directly on their personal computers from his site.

5. For more information on issues relating to Internet broadcasting, see Amy R. Mellow, "...And the Ruling on the Field Is Fair: A Fair Use Analysis of Uploading NFL Videos onto YouTube and Why the NFL Should License Its Material to the Website," 17 *Southern California Interdisciplinary Law Journal* 173 (2007) and Gary R. Roberts, "The Scope of the Exclusive Right To Control Dissemination of Real-Time Sports Event Information," 15 *Stanford Law and Policy Review* 167 (2004).

14.4.1. Home Recording of Copyrighted Events

As sports events are being broadcast over the airwaves, viewers are able to record them from their television sets. Although there has not been a case that deals specifically with sports games being taped from television, a landmark case was decided by the Supreme Court concerning copyright infringement by people who use their VCRs to tape copyrighted programs. In *Sony Corporation of America v. Universal City Studios, Inc.*, 464 U.S. 417 (1984), *rehearing denied*, 104 S.Ct. 1619 (1984), the Supreme Court overturned the Ninth Circuit's decision and held that home taping does not constitute copyright infringement. For sports teams, this means that they will probably not be able to gain any royalty fees for the taping of their games from television (see note 2).

VCRs are being increasingly replaced by digital video recorders (DVR) such as TiVo, which allow users to digitally record television programs. Instead of creating a library of video cassettes, users can save programs to their DVR hard drive. TiVo allows users to send programming to up to nine other TiVo boxes or computers. The NFL and MLB opposed the service, but the FCC ruled that it was legal since the distribution is limited. As digital technology reaches more and more consumers, leagues and broadcasters will need to monitor the potential for copyright infringement (see note 1).

NOTES

1. In *Twentieth Century Fox Film Corp. v. Cablevision Systems Corp.*, 478 F. Supp. 2d 607 (S.D.N.Y. 2007), several television networks, including FOX, Turner, Disney, CBS, and NBC, brought suit seeking declaratory judgment that Cablevision's new DVR system would violate their copyrights. The new Remote-Storage DVR System (RS-DVR) would allow customers to record programs on central servers at Cablevision's facilities and then

watch the programs at their home whenever they wanted. In granting summary judgment for the plaintiffs, the court differentiated RS-DVR from existing DVR systems and VCRs because in using the existing systems, the viewer records the program at their own home, whereas the RS-DVR requires Cablevision to make unauthorized copies and transmissions of the programs.

2. In *Sony Corp. of America v. Universal City Studios, Inc.*, 464 U.S. 417 (1984), the Supreme Court reversed the ruling of the Ninth Circuit court, and ruled in a 5–4 split decision that home taping of television broadcasts does not constitute copyright infringement. The Ninth Circuit also held that the manufacturers of the video recorders were responsible for these copyright violations. On overturning the decision of the appellate court, the Supreme Court stated, "The sale of home videotape recorders to the general public did not constitute contributory infringement of copyrights on television programs."

3. For more on these issues, see Shyamkrishna Balganesh, "The Social Costs of Property Rights in Broadcast (and Cable) Signals," 22 *Berkeley Technology Law Journal* 1303 (2007) and Peter S. Menell and David Nimmer, "Legal Realism in Action: Indirect Copyright Liability's Continuing Tort Framework and Sony's De Facto Demise," 55 *UCLA Law Review* 143 (2007).

14.4.2. Domestic and International Piracy of Satellite and Cable Transmissions

Domestic piracy is an increasingly important area of concern for athletic administrators. With the expansion of the availability of satellite technology, anyone with an earth station (see definitions in the introduction to this chapter) is able to intercept, or pirate, sports broadcasts. Some of the most common offenders are bars trying to attract a clientele who otherwise might not be able to view the game. Section 705 of the Communications Act of 1934 prohibits the "unauthorized interception and retransmission of any radio communications that are not broadcast for the use of the general public." For example, the NFL and its clubs have sued bars, restaurants, and hotels for broadcasting home games, via satellite, that are locally blacked out for certain reasons. The courts have consistently found that these establishments are violating copyright infringement law. In *NFL v. The Alley, Inc.*, 624 F. Supp. 6 (S.D. Fla. 1983), the court found that the local games could not be broadcast in this establishment because it used apparatus that is not commonly used in private homes. Even though the law is very clear on this issue, it is hard to enforce due to the large number of such establishments. Therefore, the act authorizes substantial monetary damages and criminal penalties to help deter violations from occurring.

The laws that govern international satellite piracy are much more lenient than the laws that regulate satellite piracy in the United States. In fact, in some situations, some foreign governments have been known to sanction satellite piracy. Sports teams do not have very many alternatives in these situations, because the circumstances are out of their jurisdiction.

Another new technology device that has caused concern to sports leagues is the Slingbox, which allows users to view content from their home television service over the Internet on their personal computer or mobile phone anywhere in the world. Professional sports leagues contend that the service violates their rights agreements because cable and satellite operators pay for "specific geographic locations." George Kliavkoff of Major League Baseball Advanced Media argued that a person from San Francisco who chooses to watch a Giants game on his or her computer while visiting Chicago is actually stealing from the Chicago cable operator who is showing a Cubs or White Sox game. Sling Media, which developed the

Slingbox, argues that if a cable subscriber pays for content, they should be able to view it in any location (see note 3).

NOTES

1. In *N.F.L. v. Insight Telecommunications Corp.*, 158 F. Supp. 2d 124 (D.Mass. 2001) the NFL brought suit against a broadcast retransmitter for violating its copyright by broadcasting seven NFL games in Canada from six Boston television signals through an agreement with a Massachusetts television transmission company. Insight was granted summary judgment when it was determined that it was an exempt "passive carrier" because it had no direct or indirect control over the content or selection of the primary transmission. In *National Football League v. PrimeTime 24 Joint Venture*, 131 F. Supp. 2d 458 (S.D.N.Y. 2001), the NFL won $2.5 million in damages against a satellite carrier that was rebroadcasting NFL games into Canada after first capturing the broadcast signals in the United States without permission.

2. In *NFL v. McBee*, 792 F.2d 726 (8th Cir. 1986), a bar owned by the defendant would intercept live broadcasts of blacked-out football games with a satellite dish, and then provide the game on the television at the bar, while fans would not be able to watch the game at home. The bar, however, did not qualify under any compulsory licenses and was found in violation of copyright infringement by broadcasting the game without the consent of the National Football League. Other similar cases have been decided in favor of the sports organization, unless the defendant can prove that it qualifies under a compulsory license to broadcast the game.

3. For more on the use of the Internet to view sports broadcasts, see Michael J. Mellis, "Internet Piracy of Live Sports Telecasts," 18 *Marquette Sports Law* Review 259 (2008) and Dominic H. Rivers, "Paying for Cable in Boston, Watching It on a Laptop in L.A.: Does Slingbox Violate Federal Copyright Laws?" 41 *Suffolk University Law Review* 159 (2007).

14.4.3. Blackouts of Scheduled Programming

Since the major expansion of television sports broadcasting in the 1950s, blackouts have become common in professional sports. Owners of sports organizations, concerned about protecting their home attendance, have ordered that within a certain radius of the home stadium, games be blacked out to encourage people to watch the game at the stadium instead of staying at home and watching the game on television.

The increase in popularity of football, however, led to the passing of anti-blackout legislation by the FCC in 1973. Even though waiting lists for tickets had reached as long as five years, NFL teams still insisted on maintaining blackouts in their home areas, arguing that there was no right to see sporting events for free on television. Perturbed by these actions, the FCC passed legislation which held that pro teams in the Big Four leagues must lift any blackouts of games if the contest has been sold out 72 hours prior to the start of the game. This legislation effectively got rid of many of the blackouts in the National Football League and allowed more fans to watch the league's games.

NOTES

1. In *Blaich v. NFL*, 212 F. Supp. 319 (S.D.N.Y. 1962), fans of the New York Giants football team brought action against the NFL's policy of blacking out home playoff games within a 75-mile radius of the stadium. The plaintiffs contended that the NFL bylaw concerning blackouts involved only regular season games, and not playoff contests. The NFL bylaw used the generic term "games." The plaintiffs were seeking a preliminary injunction so that they would be able to watch the NFL championship game, which was to air

later that week, in their homes. Although the court noted that the policy may not be a good one for public relations, the NFL's rule concerning blackouts of playoff games was, and the bylaw that used the generic term "game" applied to all games, including playoff contests.

2. In *United States v. NFL*, 116 F. Supp. 319 (E.D.Pa. 1953), the U.S. Department of Justice brought a case attempting to curtail the television blackout policies of the NFL, using antitrust theory. The bylaw for the NFL stated, "No club shall cause or permit a game in which it is engaged to be telecast or broadcast by a station within 75 miles of another League City on the day that the home club of the other city is either playing a game in its home city or is playing away from home and broadcasting or televising its game by use of a station within 75 miles of its home city, unless permission for such broadcast or telecast is obtained from the home club." Such permission was not generally granted by the home club, rendering the game blacked out in certain areas. The court ruled that some of the blackout rules were legal, while others were not. The rules concerning blackouts of home games to protect the gate attendance were seen as reasonable, and were permitted. However, the rule concerning the blackout of all games was considered to be an unreasonable restraint of trade, and the league was ordered to repeal this regulation.

14.4.4. Satellite Distribution

With the emergence of new methods of satellite distribution of television signals, holders of initial broadcast rights have had a difficult time maintaining exclusive control over the dissemination of their broadcasts. Specifically, the emergence of DirecTV, a satellite provider of nationwide sports and entertainment programming, has caused issues to arise among owners of broadcast rights. DirecTV is a digital satellite subscription service that can provide its viewers with the opportunity to receive over 265 channels of movies, sports, and entertainment. Subscribers must purchase a small satellite that receives the signal from DirecTV's satellite. Viewers are able to purchase packages based on their preferences: sports, movies, or entertainment. For example, in 2008, viewers were able to subscribe to NFL Sunday Ticket, a service that provides the subscriber with up to 14 NFL games per weekend for $289. These packages are especially attractive for fans of NFL teams that do not live near their favorite team. Due to the NFL's television package, viewers will see their local team's games on television every week. However, with this technology, fans are able to choose which games they want to watch. While it seems like a blessing for the avid fan, this subscription service has met with some opposition from rights holders. Because of this method of distribution, its impact upon the television market has taken full effect, and cases involving DirecTV have been limited. However, one case, decided by the FCC, could prove to be a foreshadowing of litigation in the future.

In the Matter of DirecTV, Inc. v. Comcast Corporation, CSR 5112-P (1998), Federal Communications Commission, DirecTV claimed that Comcast, an owner of broadcast rights to professional sports teams in the Philadelphia area, was illegally disallowing it from transmitting its signals under Section 628(b) of the Cable Television Consumer Protection and Competition Act of 1992, which states:

> [I]t shall be unlawful for a cable operator, a satellite cable programming vendor in which a cable operator has an attributable interest, or a satellite broadcast programming vendor to engage in unfair methods of competition or unfair or deceptive acts or practices, the purpose or effect of which is to hinder significantly or to prevent

any multichannel video programming distributor from providing satellite cable programming or satellite broadcast programming to subscribers or consumers.

Comcast had bought the rights from the defunct Sports Channel, which had previously negotiated with DirecTV. Comcast created its own unique sports channel, SportsNet, and refused to negotiate with DirecTV for the rights to broadcast its games on DirecTV's system due to what Comcast said were "legitimate business purposes." Comcast delivers its programming only through terrestrial (land-based) distribution, and not satellite distribution, which Sports Channel had employed. Therefore, Comcast argued, it was not susceptible to laws regarding satellite transmissions, and was not obligated to enter into an agreement with DirecTV. The FCC arbitrator decided that Comcast was *not* obligated to negotiate with DirecTV for two reasons. First, its programming was not satellite programming, and therefore not subject to Section 628(b) of the Cable Television Consumer Protection and Competition Act of 1992. Second, it did not find that Comcast had engaged in unfair methods of competition or clearly evaded the rules of the FCC in order to block DirecTV from broadcasting its programming. Due to this decision, fans of the Flyers, Sixers, and Phillies must receive their games over the Comcast cable network, SportsNet, because DirecTV was not able to provide these games. For more on litigation concerning the broadcasting of sports on satellite, see section 14.2.2, "Broadcast Rights of a Professional League."

14.4.5. FCC and Indecency

With essentially all major sports broadcasts aired live, broadcast networks need to be aware of the FCC's indecency standards. CBS was given a record $550,000 fine for the infamous "wardrobe malfunction" incident during the 2004 Super Bowl halftime show, in which performer Janet Jackson's chest was exposed briefly. FOX Sports did not take any chances the following year when incorporating its cable-aired "The Best *Damn* Sports Show Period" into its Super Bowl pregame coverage, renaming the entity "The Best *Darn* Super Bowl Roadshow." Even the opening ceremonies for the 2004 Summer Olympics in Athens drew the ire of the FCC for showing a parade of actors portraying naked statues of ancient Greek Olympians and gods.

The decision in *Fox TV Stations, Inc. v. FCC*, 489 F.3d 444 (2d. Cir. 2007), protects networks from FCC sanctions due to "fleeting expletives." The FCC had long held a policy that "fleeting expletives" were not indecent and recognized that their airing was often unavoidable in live events, but their policy started to change in 2003. The FCC started taking punitive action against networks for isolated usage of profane words, arguing that certain words were inherently indecent. The court found no reason for the FCC to abruptly change its policy without a "reasoned analysis" and found its punitive decisions to be arbitrary and capricious. With advances in features such as in-game audio during live sports telecasts, this decision should protect networks from being fined for errantly allowing inappropriate language to reach the air.

NOTE _____

1. For more on this issue, see Patricia Daza, "FCC Regulation: Indecency by Interest Groups," 2008 *Duke Law and Technology Review* 3 (2008) and Clay Calvert, "Imus,

Indecency, Violence and Vulgarity: Why the FCC Must Not Expand Its Authority over Content," 30 *Hastings Communications and Entertainment Law Journal* 1 (2007).

14.5. A BROADCASTING CHECKLIST

In addition to achieving a basic understanding of sports broadcasting rights within contracts, how sports broadcasts are copyrighted, and how antitrust laws affects sports broadcasting, athletic administrators can minimize legal problems that often accompany television and media broadcasts of athletic events by referring to the following checklist:

1. Establish who has the property right in a broadcast.
2. Make sure the requirements of the 1976 Copyright Act are being followed, especially in regard to "fixing" the broadcast and in filing for any royalty fees due with the Copyright Royalty Arbitration Panel.
3. Include proper broadcast rights clauses in any game or contest contract, including rights of opponents regarding broadcasts into their "home" territory.
4. Review conference or league rights to broadcast applicable championships or individual games or contests.
5. Review all facility lease or rental contracts and facility third-party contracts for possible broadcast rights problems.
6. Review all contracts with television, cable, radio broadcast stations, and the Internet to ensure proper clauses are included to protect the sports entity's property right in a broadcast.
7. Review all conference and league broadcast contracts for possible antitrust monopoly problems.

Chapter 15

BUSINESS LAW: BUSINESS STRUCTURES, TAX LAWS, AND EMPLOYMENT LAW

15.1. Business Structures

    15.1.1. Sole Proprietorships

    15.1.2. Partnerships

    15.1.3. Limited Partnerships

    15.1.4. Corporations

        15.1.4.1. C Corporations

        15.1.4.2. S Corporations

        15.1.4.3. Limited Liability Corporations

        15.1.4.4. Publicly Traded Corporations

15.2. Tax Issues

    15.2.1. Nonprofit Organizations

    15.2.2. Unrelated Business Income

        15.2.2.1. Facility Rentals

        15.2.2.2. Broadcast Receipts

        15.2.2.3. Sponsorship Revenue

    15.2.3. Scholarships

    15.2.4. Charitable Contributions, Luxury Box Rentals, and Entertainment Expenses

    15.2.5. Professional Sport Franchise Tax Issues

    15.2.6. Franchise Depreciation Issues

    15.2.7. State Tax Issues for Player Salaries

15.3. Employment Law

    15.3.1. Employment-at-Will Contracts

    15.3.2. Employment Discrimination Statutes

        15.3.2.1. Equal Pay Act

        15.3.2.2. Equal Employment Opportunity Commission Coaching Pay Guidelines

        15.3.2.3. Title VII of the Civil Rights Act of 1964

        15.3.2.4. Gender Discrimination Cases under Title VII

        15.3.2.5. Gender Discrimination Cases under Title IX

        15.3.2.6. Race Discrimination Cases under Title VII

        15.3.2.7. Age Discrimination in Employment Act of 1967

        15.3.2.8. State Discrimination Laws

    15.3.3. Sexual Harassment

INTRODUCTION

Running any type of business, whether it is sports related or not, requires understanding a number of important legal issues. These issues are both varied and complicated. This chapter offers a general examination of some of the legal issues and basic principles related to the business side of sports. In addition, the chapter tries to identify some other legal issues possibly facing industry professionals who are unclear about tax (section 15.2.), discrimination (section 15.3.2.), and sexual harassment (section 15.3.3.) laws.

The chapter begins by examining some of the most common business structures used by sport organizations. This section examines not only the traditional structures, such as partnerships and corporations, but also less traditional ones, such as limited liability corporations. The section will discuss some of the advantages of various types of business structures for different sport businesses.

Next, the chapter examines the impact of federal, state, and local taxes on the owners of sports organizations. The federal tax laws are an important factor in determining which structure the business should use. The tax law section also examines the tax implications of unrelated business income, luxury box rentals, and stadium construction for both nonprofit organizations, such as universities and colleges, as well as for-profit organizations, such as professional sports teams.

The final section looks at the legal issues governing the employer-employee relationship. The employment law section examines such diverse areas as equal pay, employment discrimination, age discrimination, and sexual harassment litigation. The employment law section also examines the Equal Employment Opportunity Commission (EEOC) guidelines titled "Enforcement Guidance on Sex Discrimination in the Compensation of Sports Coaches in Educational Institutions." The intent of the EEOC guidelines is to illustrate the proper legal analysis of pay disparity cases under both Title VII of the Civil Rights Act of 1964 and the Equal Pay Act. Finally, the chapter examines sexual harassment court decisions that provide guidance for organizations wishing to adopt policies to prevent problems.

15.1. BUSINESS STRUCTURES

Three of the most common business structures in sport are sole proprietorships, partnerships, and corporations. In selecting the appropriate business structure, there are a number of factors to be considered. These factors include limited legal liability, federal tax laws, formality, flexibility, access to capital, cost and ease of formation, and transferability of ownership in the business. The following sections describe various types of business structures and outline some of the advantages and disadvantages of each.

NOTE _____

1. For more information on the business structure of individual teams, see Gabe Feldman, "The Puzzling Persistence of the Single-Entity Argument for Sports Leagues: American Needle and the Supreme Court's Opportunity to Reject a Flawed Defense," 2009 *Wisconsin Law Review* 835 (2009) and Stephen F. Ross and Stefan Szymanski, "Antitrust and Inefficient Joint Ventures: Why Sports Leagues Should Look More Like McDonald's and Less Like the United Nations," 16 *Marquette Sports Law Review* 213 (2006).

15.1.1. Sole Proprietorships

The simplest form of business organization to start and maintain, the sole proprietorship, is an unincorporated business that is owned by one individual. When starting a business, if an individual does not incorporate, the business will be a sole proprietorship by default. A well-known example in the sports industry was the Los Angles Dodgers when they where owned by Walter O'Malley and his family. As the sole proprietor, O'Malley was able to run the Dodgers without any interference from shareholders or partners. Under a sole proprietorship, the business has no existence apart from the owner. The advantages of the sole proprietorship include lower costs, ease of formation, and single taxation. The cost of formation is low because there are no legal papers to file. Therefore no attorneys are needed, making it less expensive. Also, since an owner must include the income and expenses of the business on his or her own tax return, that owner pays no business tax. The disadvantages of the sole proprietorship include the unlimited personal liability for all the financial and legal risks of the business. The business's liabilities (debts) become the owner's personal liabilities. Additionally, the life of the business is limited to the owner, and the business's access to capital is limited to the owner's assets or borrowing power (see exhibit 15.1 for advantages and disadvantages). Borrowing power is particularly important for professional team sports due to increasing costs of owning a franchise. Even a recognized billionaire like Daniel Snyder needed to secure loans in order to purchase the Washington Redskins and FedEx Field for approximately $800 million.

15.1.2. Partnerships

The most common form of business in the Big Four professional leagues is the partnership. This is especially true in the National Football League, which does not allow corporate ownership of teams. A partnership is the relationship existing between two or more persons who carry on a trade or business for profit. Each person contributes money, property, labor, or skill and expects to share in the profits and losses of the business. The rights and obligations of the partners are equal, unless otherwise stated in a partnership agreement. While a written agreement is not required to form a legal partnership, one is recommended to provide protection in the event of disputes, bankruptcy, or termination of the business. A partnership agreement should consist of a written accord outlining the rights and obligations of the partners and how profits and losses should be shared.

The advantages of a partnership include the low cost and ease of formation. As stated above, a partnership does not need a formal or legal agreement to be formed. Also, since the partners do not need to see a lawyer to develop the partnership agreement, the costs can be minimal. (In some cases these agreements are more complex, and partners *will* consult legal counsel.) Another advantage of the partnership is conduit or pass-through taxation. The partnership files an informational tax return only. The partners must then include the income or loss of the partnership in their own personal income tax returns. The informational return shows the results of the operation, allocating the profit or loss among the partners.

Disadvantages include unlimited joint and several liability for the acts of general partners. In a partnership, each partner has a fiduciary duty to the other partners, through which they share in the profits and losses and are legally bound by each other's actions, regardless of whether the partner consented or had notice of the

Exhibit 15.1
Advantages and Disadvantages of Business Structures

Business Structure	Legal Liability	Taxation	Formality	Life of Organization	Access to Capital	Cost of Formation	Transferability
Sole proprietorship	Total	Single taxation	Very informal	Limited	Limited	None	None
Partnership	Total	Pass-through taxation	Informal	Limited	Limited	Minimal	None
Limited Partnership	Total/ Limited	Pass-through taxation	Formal	Limited	Limited	Minimal	None
C Corporation	Limited	Dual taxation	Very formal	Unlimited	Unlimited	High	Unlimited
S Corporation	Limited	Pass-through taxation	Very formal	Unlimited	Unlimited	High	Unlimited
Limited Liability Corporation	Limited	Pass-through taxation	Very formal	Limited	Unlimited	High	Limited
Nonprofit Corporation	Limited	None	Very formal	Unlimited	Unlimited	High	Limited

wrongful action. Because of this unlimited joint and several liability for the acts of the other partners, individuals in a partnership need to trust their partners and be aware of their activities. Another disadvantage of the partnership is that since it is created by a contract, a partner cannot sell or transfer his or her share in the partnership. Also, if a partner dies or wants to dissolve the partnership, the partnership ends. Therefore, the life of the business is limited. Finally, the access to capital is limited to the partners' assets. (See exhibit 15.1.)

15.1.3. Limited Partnerships

"There is nothing quite so limited as being a limited partner of George Steinbrenner's," said New York Yankee limited partner John McMullen in 1979. The limited partnership is a cross between a corporation and a partnership. A limited partnership consists of one or more general partners who retain control over the business operation and one or more limited partners who invest money into the partnership. The limited partners receive profit or loss from the partnership but lack any control over the business. Prior to the formation of YankeeNets LLC in 1999, the New York Yankees were probably the most publicized limited partnership in U.S. sports (see note 1). The general partner, George Steinbrenner, ran the day-to-day operations of the business, and the limited partners had no involvement in the business. When Steinbrenner and his partners bought the Yankees from CBS for $10 million in 1973, they borrowed $6 million. Of the $4 million in equity, only $168,000 was Steinbrenner's (see note 2).

Limited partnerships have the same advantages and disadvantages as a general partnership. These advantages include low cost and ease of formation, no formal or legal agreement to be formed is required, and conduit or pass-through taxation. The disadvantages include unlimited personal liability, unlimited joint and several liability for the acts of the other partners, and the inability to sell or transfer partnership interests.

The major difference between a general partnership and a limited partnership is that the limited partner(s) enjoys limited liability for the debts of the partnership. Since the limited partner has no involvement in the day-to-day operations of the business, his or her liability exposure is limited to the investment. As a result of the limited liability, limited partnerships are able to generate more investments. One disadvantage of the limited partnership is the lack of managerial input that the limited partner has in running the business. Once a limited partner is appointed to the management of the business, he or she becomes a general partner and has unlimited joint and several liability for the acts of the partnership. (See exhibit 15.1)

NOTES

1. YankeeNets LLC was formed through a merger of the Yankees and the New Jersey Nets basketball team. The merger also corresponded with the creation of the YES Network. YankeeNets LLC, who also owned the New Jersey Devils from 2000 to 2004, broke up in 2004 when the Nets were sold to real estate developer Bruce Ratner. The Yankees partnership is now known as Yankee Global Enterprises LLC, whose key properties are the Yankees, the YES Network, and the New Yankee Stadium.

2. For information regarding George Steinbrenner's managing of the Yankees' limited partnership, see Robert Barker, "A Partnership That's Really Limited," *Business Week* (May 23, 2005) and Anthony Bianco, "The Yankees: Steinbrenner's Money Machine," *Business Week* (September 28, 1998).

15.1.4. Corporations

The last business structure this section examines is the corporation. Corporations are different from partnerships and sole proprietorships in that they are generally treated as entities separate from the owners or shareholders. There are a number of different types of corporations. The following sections look at three types of corporations, and the benefits and disadvantages of each.

15.1.4.1. C Corporations

C corporations, or regular corporations, are separate legal entities created under and governed by the laws of the state of incorporation. As a separate legal entity, a corporation has many of the legal rights of an individual. A corporation can sue or be sued, carry on business activities, hire employees, and own tangible and intangible assets. Unlike proprietorships or partnerships, a corporation must pay a separate tax on the business income, rather than it passing through to the owner's personal income tax.

A corporation may have an unlimited number of stockholders who, due to the separate legal nature of the corporation, are protected from the creditors of the business. The shareholders elect a board of directors who have overall responsibility for the management of the corporation. The board of directors elect officers who carry out the wishes of the directors. Thus, a corporation is more complex than a sole proprietorship and a partnership.

One of the biggest advantages to forming a corporation is limited liability. Unlike sole proprietorships and partnerships, where creditors of the business can hold the owner personally liable for all debts, the only personal liability to which a shareholder of a corporation is subject is the money he or she invested into the company. Another advantage of a corporation is that it has unlimited life extending beyond the illness or death of the owners, individual officers, managers, or shareholders. Since a corporation is a separate legal entity, ownership of the business may be transferred through the sale of stock, which makes changes in ownership simple. Finally, it is easier for a corporation to raise capital. This may be accomplished through the sale of stock or bonds. With sole proprietorships and partnerships, investors are much harder to attract because of the personal liability issue.

Some of the disadvantages of incorporating include the cost, the formal legal requirements, state and federal rules and regulations, and double taxation. To form a corporation, articles of incorporation must be filed with the secretary of state in the state of incorporation. Each state has its own legal procedures and regulations for forming and maintaining a corporation in good standing. Therefore, a corporation requires more paperwork and record keeping than a sole proprietorship. Also, unlike other forms of business entities, a corporation must pay taxes on the business income, rather than passing it through to the owner's personal income tax. In addition to the corporation paying tax, individual shareholders must pay taxes on dividends the corporation distributes. As a result, the corporation's profits are taxed doubly: once at the corporate rate and once at the individual shareholder's rate. So, unlike a proprietorship or a partnership, where the owners of the business are able to deduct any losses in the business from their personal income taxes, the profits and losses of the corporation are attributed to the corporation, not the owners/shareholders. (See exhibit 15.1)

While it might appear that the advantages of limited liability are so great that all businesses would want to be incorporated, the decision to incorporate solely for liability purposes should be weighed against the increased cost and complication of the corporate structure, plus taxation disadvantages. As shown in the next section, *every* business in the United States has to pay taxes or file an informational return. However, only businesses that fail can take advantage of unlimited liability protection.

15.1.4.2. S Corporations

The difference between an S corporation and a regular (C) corporation is the special tax designation granted by the IRS to corporations that have already been formed. S corporations are most often used by service-oriented businesses that want the limited liability feature of the corporation but do not want the tax consequences of a C corporation. As stated above, when a general corporation makes a profit, it is required to pay a federal corporate income tax on the profit.

If the company declares a dividend, the shareholders must report the dividend as personal income and pay more taxes. To avoid this double taxation, subchapter S of the Internal Revenue Code allows S corporations to report all income or loss only once, on the personal tax returns of the shareholders.

Therefore, S corporations have the same basic advantages and disadvantages as C corporations, with the added benefit of special tax provisions. There are certain restrictions to forming an S corporation. First, the maximum number of shareholders is 100. Second, stock ownership is limited to individuals, estates, and certain trusts, including small business trusts. Third, all the shareholders must be citizens or residents of the United States. Fourth, S corporations may issue only one class of stock (see exhibit 15.1 for advantages and disadvantages).

15.1.4.3. Limited Liability Corporations

Limited liability corporations (LLCs) were first introduced in the United States in 1977 and authorized for pass-through taxation (similar to partnerships and S corporations) by the IRS in 1988. Viewed by many business planners as the business form of the future, LLCs combine many of the advantages of corporations and partnerships. Under the LLC, investors receive limited liability protection from business debt, as well as the tax advantages of partnerships or S corporations. Also, while similar to S corporations, LLCs do not have as many IRS restrictions. The LLC is so attractive that a number of recent professional sports leagues established themselves as LLCs. These new leagues include: Major League Soccer (MLS), the Women's National Basketball Association (WNBA), the defunct Women's United Soccer Association (WUSA), and NFL Europe. As an LLC, the league owns all the teams. Individuals only "invest" in the league, and there are technically no team owners (see note 1). For example, while Robert Kraft and Clark Hunt own the NFL's New England Patriots and Kansas City Chiefs, respectively, they do not own MLS's New England Revolution or FC Dallas. They are simply the investor/operators in MLS who run the Revolution and FC Dallas, respectively. Some existing leagues have also reorganized as LLCs. For example, in 1999, after Isiah Thomas purchased the entire Continental Basketball League (CBL) for $10 million, one of the first things he did was to reorganize the CBL into an LLC.

LLCs have the same basic advantages as C corporations, such as limited liability, ease of transfer, and the ability to raise capital. The added advantages of the LLC include pass-through taxation, greater flexibility in management of the business, and less restrictive ownership requirements. For example, unlike the S corporation, LLCs can have an unlimited number of shareholders, and the shareholders do not have to be citizens or residents of the United States. Probably the most important difference, however, is that stock ownership is not limited to individuals, estates, and certain trusts; it is open to partnerships and other corporations. Another important advantage for professional sports leagues is that as a single entity structure, LLCs are exempt from federal antitrust law (see section 10.3.8, "Single-Entity Defense by the Big Four").

A major disadvantage of the LLC is the legal uncertainty surrounding the business structure. Due to the newness of the LLC, there is limited case precedent. However, a positive development occurred for proponents of LLCs in sport leagues in *Fraser v. Major League Soccer*, 97 F. Supp. 2d 130 (D. Mass. 2000), *aff'd* 284 F.3d 47 (1st Cir. 2002). Major League Soccer players claimed that the league was using the LLC as a way to circumvent federal antitrust laws. However, the appellate court disagreed by ruling in favor of the league (see exhibit 15.1).

NOTES _____

1. The idea of the league owning all of the teams is not new. In 1901, John Brush, owner of the National League Cincinnati baseball team, proposed that all eight National League teams should merge into a new holding company called the National Baseball Trust. Each team would then receive common stock in the new company. The stock was going to be divided based on each club's value: New York would receive 30%; Cincinnati, 12%; St. Louis, 12%; Boston, 12%; Philadelphia, 10%; Chicago, 10%; Pittsburgh, 8%;

and Brooklyn, 6%. A board of directors, who would appoint managers (at a set salary) for each team and license and assign players wherever the board wanted them, would run the league. Although the idea was criticized by the press, it just barely failed to pass at the 1901 owners' meeting. See Harold Seymour, *Baseball: The Early Years* (New York: Oxford University Press, 1989).

2. For more information on LLCs, see Robert W. Hamilton and Jonathan R. Macey, *Cases and Materials on Corporations: Including Partnerships and Limited Liability Companies* (St. Paul, MN: West Publishing, 2005).

15.1.4.4. Publicly Traded Corporations

With the cost of running a professional sports team increasing, a number of owners have contemplated going public. In 1998, the Cleveland Indians took advantage of a change in Major League Baseball's rules allowing teams to offer stock to the public, and became the third professional sports team in the United States to move into the stock market. The two previous teams were the Boston Celtics of the National Basketball Association and the Orlando Predators of the Arena Football League (see note 4).

Like the other business structures, there are a number of advantages and disadvantages in taking a team public. The first and most important advantage is financial. In 1998, the Cleveland Indians raised $55 million by selling 4 million shares of stock in the team. However, since 1998, the Indians have again become a private company (see note 2). A secondary reason for going public is to increase the visibility of a team and to foster fan loyalty through ownership in the team. Initial public offerings generate a lot of publicity. Also, if a fan is able to purchase a share of the team through stock ownership, he or she may perceive a financial interest in being loyal to the team.

There are a number of disadvantages to going public. First, the organization must comply with all Securities and Exchange Commission rules and regulations. Second, the team must make a full financial disclosure concerning its profits and losses. Third, the team and owner(s) must be accountable to shareholders. As investors in the team, shareholders have certain rights, such as voting on the makeup of the board of directors and attending annual meetings. Finally, there are the added costs to the organization. The team must have annual board of directors' meetings, create and mail annual financial reports, assign staff for investor relations, and pay added legal costs.

Currently, there are no publicly traded sports franchises in the United States. Several major professional teams are owned, at least in part, by larger publicly traded companies. For example, many NHL, NBA, and MLB teams are owned by media companies: Cablevision (New York Knicks, New York Rangers); Comcast (Philadelphia Flyers, Philadelphia 76ers); Gaylord Entertainment (Nashville Predators); and Liberty Media (Atlanta Braves).

The National Football League does not allow public or corporate ownership of its teams, notwithstanding the unusual grandfather exemption it grants to the Green Bay Packers. It is important to point out, however, that while the Packers raised nearly $24 million in a 1997 stock offering, it is not a public company in the traditional sense. While one can own stock in the Green Bay Packers, the team is not publicly traded. In publicly traded companies, the stock is available on officially recognized exchanges. Also, investors in publicly traded companies are able to transfer or sell their shares. Finally, the revenue and profits generated by the team are the primary income sources of the company, and the company is run in order to earn profits for its shareholders. In essence, the stockholders or investors own the company. The Green Bay Packers are a community-owned enterprise and operate on a nonprofit basis. Investors are unable to buy shares in the Packers on an organized exchange, and they receive no dividends, no profits, no discounts, not even a financial report. Investors are able to transfer ownership of their stock only to family members, as gifts.

While it is still relatively uncommon to find publicly traded sports *teams*, it is fairly common for other types of sports businesses to go public. For example, most footwear and apparel companies (Nike, Reebok, Under Armour) are publicly traded, as are many sporting goods companies (e.g., Callaway, Russell). Also, a handful of athletic venues are owned by publicly traded companies, such as Churchill Downs and Madison Square Garden. Even World Wrestling Entertainment became a publicly traded company in 1999 (see note 3).

NOTES

1. For more information on publicly traded sports companies, see Ryan Schaffer, "A Piece of the Rock (or the Rockets): The Viability of Widespread Public Offerings of Professional Sports Franchises," 5 *Virginia Sports & Entertainment Law Journal* 201 (2006); Robert Youngblood, "The Business of Sports: Investors Take to the Field," *International Herald Tribune* (October 11, 2003); and Brian R. Cheffins, "Playing the Stock Market: 'Going Public' and Professional Team Sports," 24 *Journal of Corporate Law* 641 (Spring 1999).

2. In November 1999, Richard Jacobs, the owner of the Cleveland Indians, announced the sale of the team to an investment group headed by an Ohio attorney, Larry Dolan, for $320 million. That $320 million figure included the buying back of stock at a price more than 48% higher than its issued price in the previous year. This sort of return on investment is unusual for a sport franchise stock. Many investors purchase stock in a sport franchise in order to show fan loyalty rather than because of the stock's prospect for growth.

3. World Wrestling Entertainment, Inc. (WWE), sold 10 million shares of stock at $17 each in one of the most highly publicized initial public offerings of 1999. The media company later purchased World Championship Wrestling and created the short-lived XFL. The company is traded under the symbol WWE on the New York Stock Exchange.

4. The Boston Celtics, a limited partnership, began selling stock in 40% of the team on the New York Stock Exchange (NYSE) in 1986. The team's owners used a limited partnership, primarily to take advantage of tax breaks. In 1998, when the tax advantages were no longer available to the limited partnership, the Celtics reorganized into two entities: a public limited partnership, taxable as a corporation, and a private limited partnership. The public limited partnership was the stock listed on the NYSE, until the Celtics bought back all shares of public stock in 2003 after being acquired by a Boston investment group. The team is no longer under partial public ownership.

15.2. TAX ISSUES

Several of the tax issues facing athletic administrators revolve around the tax-exempt status of nonprofit or not-for-profit organizations. Section 501(a) of the Internal Revenue Code governs organizations that seek to obtain an exemption from federal income tax. To qualify for the exemption, the athletic endeavor must be organized for one or more of the purposes set forth in section 501. Section 501(c)(3) of the code designates those organizations, which include religious, charitable, educational, scientific, literary, testing for public safety, fostering national or international amateur sports competition, or the prevention of cruelty to children or animals. State or municipal instrumentalities also fall under 501(c)(3), and these may include high schools and state universities. Therefore, activities such as the Olympics, national sports festivals, and state games may fall in the area of national or international amateur sports competition. Athletic departments may be classified as educational institutions or municipal instrumentalities. Booster clubs, Little Leagues, and Pop Warner Football may be classified as charitable organizations.

15.2.1. Nonprofit Organizations

An organization seeking nonprofit status must file an application with the Internal Revenue Service (IRS). The purposes and proposed activities of the organization must be set forth in the corporate papers. In addition, a classified statement of receipts and expenditures, and a balance sheet for the current year and the three immediate prior years are needed for existing organizations. If a new organization is applying, a proposed budget for two full accounting periods and a current statement of assets and liabilities must be filed. After receipt of the necessary application materials, the IRS will issue a decision in a determination letter.

In making its decision, the IRS examines whether the petitioner has met the three requirements set forth in I.R.C. § 501(c)(3): (1) the corporation must be organized and operated exclusively for exempt purposes; (2) no part of the net earnings of the corporation may inure to the benefit of any shareholder or individual; and (3) the corporation must not engage in political campaigns or, to a substantial extent, in lobbying activities.

The only issue in dispute in most cases is the first requirement: that the corporation must be organized and operated exclusively for exempt purposes. The operational test requires the activities of an organization to be primarily those which accomplish an exempt purpose as described in Section 501(c)(3). A single substantial nonexempt purpose will disqualify an organization despite the importance of its exempt purpose. If an organization serves private rather than public interests, it also will not meet the operational test.

There are three main advantages to an organization that attains nonprofit status. The first and major advantage is the exemption from federal income tax liability. The organization is not subject to any tax on the income it generates as long as it is related to the organization's exempt purpose. The second advantage is that services performed in the employ of a nonprofit organization may be exempted from liability for the Social Security (FICA) taxes. This exemption could lower the operating costs of the organization. The third advantage is that contributions by an individual taxpayer or business to a nonprofit organization qualify as charitable contributions and are deductible by the donor for income tax purposes. This is an obvious incentive for individuals and businesses to contribute to a particular organization.

However, nonprofit status also has its disadvantages. The first is the amount of paperwork that must be filed. The second is that the application for exemption and the supporting documentation are available for public scrutiny. However, there are procedures for withholding the information from the public if the IRS determines that the disclosure would adversely affect the organization.

A variety of other restrictions placed on nonprofit organizations should be considered before applying for the favorable tax treatment. For example, the assets of an organization must be permanently dedicated to the exempt purpose. This means that if the organization is dissolved, the assets must be distributed to another exempt purpose, or to the federal, state, or local government for a public purpose. Therefore, one cannot build profits through a nonprofit organization, then dissolve the business and take the profits. In addition, although employees of a nonprofit organization may be paid a salary, the salary cannot be tied to the profitability of the organization.

A nonprofit organization is often incorrectly interpreted as a business that cannot make money in any tax year. This is untrue; the bottom line for a nonprofit organization may be in the black. However, the profits may not be used to benefit the organizers or employees.

NOTES

1. In *Quad Cities Open, Inc. v. City of Silvis*, 208 Ill. 2d 498 (Ill. 2004), the Supreme Court of Illinois ruled that the Quad Cities Open, a PGA Tour event that was later renamed the John Deere Classic, was exempt from the city's municipal amusement tax because the tournament was operated for a charitable purpose.

2. In *Philadelphia Eagles Football Club, Inc. v. City of Philadelphia*, 573 Pa. 189 (Pa. 2003), the Supreme Court of Pennsylvania ruled that media receipts from television broadcasts of Eagles' games were subject to the business privilege tax, but the amount taxed should be roughly proportional to the amount of games telecast from the Eagles' home stadium.

3. In *Wayne Baseball, Inc. v. Commissioner*, 78 T.C.M. (CCH) 437 (1999), the court held that Wayne Baseball, a nonprofit Delaware corporation whose principal activity is the sponsorship of a highly competitive amateur baseball team, did not qualify as an I.R.C. § 501(c)(3) charitable organization. In distinguishing the case from *Hutchinson* (see note 4), the court concluded that the only activity sponsored by Wayne Baseball was the operation of an adult amateur baseball team, whereas in *Hutchinson* the organization's primary activity was to promote baseball in the surrounding community by maintaining a baseball field for the public and providing coaches for Little League teams and a baseball camp.

4. In *Hutchinson Baseball Enterprises, Inc. v. Commissioner*, 696 F.2d 757 (10th Cir. 1982), the court found that the promotion, advancement, and sponsoring of amateur athletes qualified as an exempt purpose.

5. In *Mobile Arts & Sports Association v. United States*, 148 F. Supp. 311 (S.D. Ala. 1957), the U.S. District Court held that an organization whose purpose was to present an annual senior college bowl football game made substantial civic, educational, and cultural contributions to the community, and therefore qualified for exemption under Section 501(c)(3).

6. For further details on nonprofit organizations, see "Tax-Exempt Status for Your Organization," Internal Revenue Service Publication 557 (2008), available from www.irs. gov/publications/p557/index.html.

15.2.2. Unrelated Business Income

The tax on unrelated business income has become a major issue for tax-exempt athletic organizations, such as colleges and universities. A tax-exempt organization may be held liable for taxes on unrelated business income, which is income from a trade or business, regularly carried on, that is not substantially related to the charitable, educational, or other purpose constituting the basis for its exemption (see I.R.C. § 511–513).

It is important for the college athletics administrator to understand how the structure and function of a college athletics department or program relates to the IRS rules and regulations pertaining to unrelated business income and subsequent taxation. The unrelated business income tax was enacted to accomplish two objectives: (1) to eliminate unfair competition between charitable organizations and the taxed private sector and (2) to increase federal tax revenues. Intercollegiate athletics today have many schools with multimillion-dollar athletic budgets, the desire to win and produce revenue to perpetuate those budgets, and an increasing gap between the goals of the educational institution and the goals of the athletic department. Because of the current climate in intercollegiate athletics, there is an increasing need for athletic administrators to deal intelligently with conflicts that arise from activities that, while within an educational and tax-exempt institution, take on the characteristics and function of an "unrelated business."

Before looking closely at what constitutes unrelated business income according to the IRS definition, here is a general overview of the topic. In 1977, the IRS shocked the college athletics ranks when it issued a tax bill on the broadcast receipts of the Cotton Bowl. The tremendous backlash caused by this action pressured the IRS to reverse its position in 1978, thus creating a de facto exemption for college and university athletic programs. In a report released in 2010, the IRS said it was concerned with large sponsorship deals and the fact that at 43% of large colleges the highest paid employee was a sports coach. Consequently, the IRS said it would continue to examine its position on college athletics and unrelated business income. Decisions such as these raise eyebrows of those who perceive university athletic programs largely as profit-motivated entertainment industries that should be subject to taxation. These critics contend that, by and large, intercollegiate athletic programs are, both financially and philosophically, too far removed from the educational function of the institution to justify charitable, tax-exempt status (see note 5). The critical question in determining whether income is related or unrelated is whether the operation that produces the money—be it a big-time college football game, an on-campus health club, or a summer sports camp—meets the three characteristics of unrelated business income within a charitable institution. An institution's unrelated business taxable income is defined by the IRS as the net income of any

1. trade or business that is
2. "regularly carried on" *and* is
3. "not substantially related (aside from the need of such organization for income of funds or the use it makes of the profits derived) to the exercise or performance" of the college's educational function.

Generally, an unrelated business is not taxable when it (1) fails to meet all three criteria outlined above, (2) is operated entirely by volunteers, or (3) is carried on "primarily for the convenience of the college's members, students, patients, officers, or employees." One also must consider whether the business is "in serious competition" with the private sector. For instance, if a university athletic department managed a money-making tennis facility that competed with a local, privately operated tennis facility, the income from the university tennis facility may be taxable according to IRS rules.

Any activity having these three characteristics is deemed an unrelated business, the income from which, after customary business deductions are taken, is taxed at the regular corporate rates, without regard to whether the entity actually carrying on the business is a charitable corporation. In short, the test of whether an unrelated business is taxable looks to the *source* of the income, irrespective of its use. Proof of the funds' proper use is now irrelevant to the questions of their taxability; instead, the critical question is whether the operation that produces those funds is considered an unrelated business. In addition, any organization whose unrelated activities become predominant in the overall charitable function and goals of the institution risks losing its basic tax exemption. An organization's activities must still be primarily charitable in nature for it to qualify as a tax-exempt organization in the first place.

Of the three characteristics listed above, the most difficult to analyze, because of the broad definition of education, is whether an activity is "substantially related." Hence, the issue of substantial relatedness usually focuses on a more restrictive question: What is the activity's relationship to the exempt purpose? More specifically, does the activity *contribute importantly* to the accomplishment of the exempt purpose of the institution? These judgments are made on a case-by-case basis. For example, a college that uses its tennis facilities in the summer for a public tennis camp may receive unrelated trade or business income (Rev. Rul. 80–297, 1980–2 C.B. 196). Similarly, a university that leases its stadium to a professional football team and provides utilities, grounds maintenance, and se-curity services is engaged in unrelated trade or business, and the income is not excludable as rent from real property (Rev. Rul. 80–298, 1980–2 C.B. 197). On the other hand, operation of a ski facility by an exempt school for its physical education program and also for recreational purposes by students attending the school is substantially related to the school's exempt purpose. Income from the use of the facility by the public, however, is unrelated business income (Rev. Rul. 78–98, 1978–1 C.B. 167).

The question of whether intercollegiate athletics, in general, contributes impor-tantly to the institution's educational mission is a potential area for interpretation. However, until the courts decide otherwise, intercollegiate athletics will remain exempt from taxation as an unrelated business, despite the commercial aspects of these activities. This is because of legislative sympathy toward the educational institution and a hesitancy to tax college sports. However, the increasing commer-cialization and big business of college athletics have caused the government to begin intervening with the NCAA regarding unrelated business income. In 2006 Representative Bill Thomas of the U.S. House of Representative's Committee on Ways and Means and Charles Grassley, the chairman of the Senate Finance Com-mittee requested answers to a variety of questions related to the NCAA's status as a tax-exempt organization from NCAA President Myles Brand. In particular, the committee was concerned with the amateur status of student-athletes, the use of tax-exempt bonds for the purpose of building sports stadiums, and the large sponsorship and rights agreements for NCAA events—in particular, the men's basketball postseason tournament. Brand held off further inquiry by pointing out that, in the 2004–2005 academic year, only 23 of more than 1,000 Division I insti-tutions' athletic departments operated at a profit (see note 2).

NOTES

1. For more guidance as to what constitutes unrelated business income at the university level, see www.tamus.edu/offices/budgets-acct/tax/taxmanual/Ubit.html.

2. Representative Thomas's letter and President Brand's response are both available at http://www.insidehighered.com/news/2006/11/16/ncaa.

3. In 1999, the IRS challenged Rod French's donation to the Iowa State University Foundation as a charitable contribution. French deducted 80% of the gift under Section 170, even though he received the use of a luxury box in the college's football stadium and basket-ball arena in return. In total, French claimed a deduction of $143,584. The IRS claimed that the deduction should be restricted under Section 274(1)(2), which limits such deductions to the sum of the face value of non-luxury box seat tickets for the seats in such box covered by

the lease. The IRS later reversed itself and allowed the deduction under Section 170(1). See "Stadium Sky Boxes Can Be Deducted," *New York Times*, July 16, 1999, p. D7.

4. In *NCAA v. Commissioner*, 914 F.2d 1417 (10th Cir. 1990), the NCAA challenged the IRS determination that the income derived from the sale of advertising space in the programs of the 1982 NCAA men's basketball tournament was taxable as unrelated business income. In reversing the lower court's decision, the court of appeals ruled that the sale of advertising space was not a regularly carried on business, and therefore was not taxable as unrelated business income.

5. See John D. Colombo, "The NCAA, Tax Exemption, and College Athletics," 2010 *University of Illinois Law Review* 109 (2010) and Gabriel A. Morgan, "No More Playing Favorites: Reconsidering the Conclusive Congressional Presumption That Intercollegiate Athletics Are Substantially Related to Educational Purposes," 81 *Southern California Law Review* 149 (2007).

15.2.2.1. Facility Rentals

The use of facilities on campus for university-related activities such as intercollegiate, intramural, and physical education programs clearly qualifies as tax exempt activity. When the university leases a facility to an outside group, however, the income derived may be classified as unrelated business income. For example, a university's rental income from professional sports teams is not tax exempt simply because the university uses the same facility itself at other times. Even when a university leases a facility for an unrelated business, issues may arise with respect to determining the amount of tax. In *Rensselaer Polytechnic Institute v. Commissioner* (see note 4), the method of allocating fixed costs between the unrelated business use of a collegiate facility and the tax-exempt use of the facility is discussed.

NOTES _____

1. In *Connecticut College v. City of London*, 41 Conn. L. Rptr. 635 (Conn.Super. 2006), the court ruled that the college's arena, Dayton Arena, used for the college's ice hockey teams and various other purposes, was tax exempt because the arena is used at least in part for educational purposes. Citing a series of cases in which Yale University argued with the city of New Haven over the same issues, the court stated the relevant question is whether the use of the building "promotes the educational interests of the school, or, on the other hand, merely a commercial relationship."

2. In *Big Ten Conference, Inc. v. Department of Revenue*, 726 N.E.2d 114 (Ill. App. 1 Dist. 2000), property used by the Big Ten for administrative purposes was declared tax exempt because the building was used solely for educational purposes. The court stated that "athletic activities of schools are substantially related to their educational functions."

3. Private athletic facilities may deduct the proportional value of property that is used exclusively for tax-exempt functions. In *Atlanta Athletic Club v. Commissioner*, 980 F.2d 1409 (11th Cir. 1993), a private athletic club successfully argued that a piece of property should be designated as "recreational," and therefore exempt, because it was the site of a number of member activities such as Easter egg hunts, fishing tournaments, kite-flying contests, hot air balloon rides, and organized foot races. Members also jogged on the property and used it for archery practice and flying model airplanes. The court required the club to prove that these noncommercial activities were taking place. Therefore, it behooves an athletic facility to keep detailed records of activities that occur on properties designated tax exempt.

4. In *Rensselaer Polytechnic Institute v. Commissioner*, 732 F.2d 1058 (2d Cir. 1983), a college used its field house for both tax-exempt purposes and unrelated business purposes; therefore, income from the unrelated business use was taxable. However, in this case,

a dispute arose regarding how to allocate the deductible expenses, such as depreciation, between the taxable and tax-exempt uses of the facility. The plaintiff argued that the expenses should be divided in accordance with the relative amount of time the facility was used for each activity. For example, if the facility was used for tax-exempt purposes for five hours and for taxable purposes for five hours, half of the expenses could be used as a deduction for the taxable income. The commissioner, however, argued that the expenses should be allocated proportionally between the amount of time the facility was used for taxable purposes and the amount of time available for use, whether it was actually used or not. Therefore, even if it was used half for tax-exempt purposes and half for taxable purposes, they could not allocate half of the expenses to the taxable purposes because the time that the facility was dormant had to be factored into the equation. The judge ruled for the plaintiff college, holding that their method was "reasonable."

15.2.2.2. Broadcast Receipts

Broadcast receipts of tax-exempt organizations have long been an issue relative to taxes. The simple nature of broadcast receipts seems to imply a profit-making motive. However, this issue was directly addressed by the IRS in 1980 in Revenue Rulings 80-295 and 80-296. In these two rulings, the IRS concluded that revenue received by a tax-exempt athletic organization from the sale of broadcast rights to a radio or television network or to an independent producer does not constitute unrelated business income. This issue came to the forefront when the IRS tried to tax the broadcast receipts of the Cotton Bowl in 1977. The IRS later reversed its decision and subsequently issued the two revenue rulings addressing this issue. It should be noted that while revenue rulings are given some weight by the courts, they are not law.

15.2.2.3. Sponsorship Revenue

The IRS developed regulations (see Internal Revenue Code §513(i)) regarding the circumstances under which payments received by exempt organizations from sponsorship arrangements might result in income from unrelated trade or business. Section 513(i)(2)(a) states that payments to an exempt organization are nontaxable contributions if there "is no arrangement or expectation that such person will receive any substantial return benefit other than the use or acknowledgment of the name or logo (or product lines) of such person's trade or business in connection with the activities of the organization that receives such payments." That is, the mere acknowledgment or recognition of a sponsor as a benefactor normally is incidental to the receipt of a contribution and is not in itself of sufficient benefit to the sponsor to give rise to unrelated trade or business income.

Where an exempt organization performs valuable advertising, marketing, and similar services on a quid pro quo basis for the sponsor, however, the payments are not contributions and questions of unrelated trade or business arise. For example, the payments would be taxable if they were tied to advertising a product or service or if the amount of "payment is contingent upon the level of attendance at one or more events, broadcast ratings, or other factors indicating the degree of public exposure" (I.R.C. § 513(i)(B)(i)). For the purposes of this section, advertising includes any "messages containing qualitative or comparative language, price information, or other indications of savings or value, an endorsement, or an inducement to purchase, sell or use products or services."

The rules regarding sponsorship apply to broadcast as well as nonbroadcast activities. Thus, the guidelines apply uniformly to all sponsorship activities without regard to the local nature of the organization or activities or the amount of the sponsorship payment. For example, an I.R.C. § 501(c)(3) organization conducts an annual college football bowl game. The organization sells to commercial broadcasters the right to broadcast the bowl game on television and radio for $3 million. A major corporation agrees to be the exclusive sponsor of the bowl game and pays the organization $2 million. The organization acknowledges the sponsorship payment by adding the corporation's name to the title of the event. This does not constitute advertising within the meaning of I.R.C. § 1.513–4 because it does not promote the sponsor's service, facility, or product.

In March 2000, the IRS proposed a regulation that "exclusive provider" agreements would be included under this regulation. An exclusive provider agreement is one that "limits the sale, distribution, availability, or use of competing products, services, or facilities in connection with an exempt organization's activity." For example, a university might extend "exclusive pour" rights to a soft drink company. The NCAA and its members would likely push for congressional action if this IRS proposal is codified.

15.2.3. Scholarships

As a general rule, as long as the amount is used for qualified tuition and related expenses, any scholarship received by an individual who is a candidate for a degree at an educational organization is not included in the recipient's gross taxable income. The tax law defines "qualified tuition and related expenses" as tuition and fees required for enrollment, fees, books, supplies, and equipment required for courses of instruction.

The amount for room and board is considered taxable income. Also, any portion of the scholarship or grant representing payment for teaching, research, or other services required as a condition for receiving the scholarship is included in the recipient's gross taxable income. In addition, IRS notice 87-31 urges the grantor to supply the recipient with a calculation of the appropriate amount to be included in his or her gross income.

15.2.4. Charitable Contributions, Luxury Box Rentals, and Entertainment Expenses

Most amateur athletic organizations are set up as nonprofit businesses and do not pay income taxes. However, the tax laws still affect the way they operate. A significant source of funds for many nonprofit athletic organizations is the contributions of individuals and businesses. The attractiveness of these contributions for the contributor directly depends on the tax laws regarding itemized deductions. Since many athletic programs rely heavily on contributions, athletic administrators have kept a close eye on Congress's treatment of certain charitable contributions.

If the luxury box seats are at professional or for-profit sports stadiums, the IRS limits the amount of money businesses can deduct from their taxes as a business entertainment expense. Section 274(1)(2) of the Internal Revenue Code limits the amount of money an individual or business is able to deduct for a luxury box leased for more than one event to "the sum of the face value of non-luxury box seat tickets for the seats in such box covered by the lease."

The issue of whether I.R.C. § 274(1)(2) applies to intercollegiate athletics was not decided until 1999. The IRS has ruled that donors can deduct 80% of their gifts to universities under I.R.C. § 170, which outlines the allowance of deductions even if the donor receives the use of a luxury box in the college's football stadium and basketball arena in return. The ruling was in response to a tax return filed by Iowa State University booster Rod French. French deducted $143,584 of the $200,000 donation he gave the university foundation as a charitable contribution. The IRS, which challenged the deduction because the booster received a 10-year lease on a luxury box and other stadium amenities, claimed that the donation should be covered under I.R.C. § 274(1)(2). The IRS appeals office reversed the decision, concluding that, based on the law's legislative history, Congress did not intend Section 274(1) to preclude an I.R.C. § 170(1) deduction. I.R.C. § 170(1) permits a deduction for amounts paid to an "institution of higher education" in return for the "right to purchase tickets for seating at an athletic event," but limits the deduction to 80%. Since a Section 170 deduction is allowed without regard to a trade or business, the Internal Revenue Service reasoned, I.R.C. § 274 limitations did not apply.

15.2.5. Professional Sport Franchise Tax Issues

It is no secret that professional sports teams are valuable properties. Since the 1980s, franchise prices have skyrocketed worldwide. In 2005, the price for a professional sports franchise soared over $1 billion when U.S. businessman Malcolm Glazer instituted a hostile takeover and secured a majority ownership of the English Premier soccer team Manchester United for $1.47 billion. Given the 2009 sale of baseball's Chicago Cubs for $845 million and Daniel Snyder and others' $800 million purchase of the NFL's Washington Redskins in 1999, it is only a matter of time until there is a purchase of a U.S. sports team for over $1 billion.

With the price of franchises so high, team owners have looked, and continue to look, to state and federal taxpayers for subsidies. The state and local subsidy is typically provided through below-market rents, guarantees, bonds funded by sales taxes, lottery proceeds, and taxes on hotels, parking, and car rentals. A federal subsidy is provided when tax-exempt state or local bonds are used to finance the facility. For example, the new Yankee Stadium originally received $941 million in tax-exempt bonds to finance the construction of the $1.3 billion stadium. The Yankees agreed to make payments in lieu of taxes to the city of New York, but the debt is to be deductible against revenues that are subject to taxes. Citi Field, the new home of the New York Mets, also received an original $632 million in tax-exempt bonds to cover costs of their $700 million to $800 million stadium. In their respective financial agreements with the city and state of New York, the teams agreed to repay the construction bonds and interest on the debt. The two stadiums are also to be supported with taxpayer dollars, as New York City and state residents will pay hundreds of million dollars more to pay for costs with infrastructure, parking, and recreational facilities around the new Yankee Stadium and Citi Field. The tax-exempt bonds will save the teams hundreds of millions in finance charges throughout the debt terms of the stadiums. The teams asked the city to provide additional bonds during the construction process, creating further controversy.

The new Washington Nationals stadium, opened in 2008, was financed entirely with public funds, costing $611 million. The city of Washington, D.C. financed the construction with tax-exempt bonds that the team will pay off with various revenue streams, including ticket sales, concessions, merchandise, and naming rights.

The Baltimore Ravens stadium, M&T Bank Stadium but originally named Ravens Stadium at Camden Yards, was financed with $86 million of tax-exempt bonds. Principal and interest on those bonds are repaid through state lottery funds and the public share of stadium-generated revenue, which could not exceed 10% of the debt service on $86 million. In other situations, taxes on tourism, restaurant sales, car rentals, and other items are also potential sources for funding the municipality's debt obligations.

In 1996, the city of Cincinnati agreed to build Paul Brown Stadium after the Bengals' revised their lease in 1994 to state that if a stadium was not built by 2000, they were free to leave town. The county is paying for the stadium by a sales tax, which it raised by half a cent. The tax was voted on by residents and received 61% of the votes. In total, after calculating construction, land purchases, and other costs, the cost to taxpayers exceeded $400 million. The Bengals' contribution to the stadium was $50 million. States and cities are willing to build these stadiums for team owners because they believe that having a team is good for the local economy. In Cleveland, for example, the cost of the 1999 Cleveland Browns' stadium to taxpayers was over $250 million, but the city predicted that the Browns would generate over $80 million per year for the area's economy.

Some taxpayers, however, have challenged the tax breaks that state and local governments are providing team owners for stadium financing. One such challenge was the case of *Giordano v. Ridge*, 737 A.2d 350 (Pa. Commw. Ct. 1999), in which a taxpayer challenged the constitutionality of the Capital Facilities Debt Enabling Act (CFDEA). The CFDEA authorized the undertaking of debt by the Commonwealth of Pennsylvania for the purpose of making grants to local authorities for the construction, repair, renovation, improvement, or equipment of qualifying capital projects. The taxpayer, Giordano, claimed that CFDEA violated Article VIII, Section 8 of the Pennsylvania State Constitution, which states that "The credit of the Commonwealth shall not be pledged or loaned to any individual, company, corporation or association nor shall the Commonwealth become a joint owner or stockholder in any company, corporation or associations." In rejecting the taxpayer's claim, the court found that acts of the General Assembly have a strong presumption of constitutionality, and that an act of the General Assembly may be declared unconstitutional only when it clearly and plainly violates the state constitution. Citing a Pennsylvania State Supreme Court case, the court held that the language in Article VIII, Section 8, does not prohibit loans from the commonwealth to a municipal authority, even though the ultimate beneficiary of such a loan may be a private entity. Under the CFDEA, the money flows from the commonwealth to a municipality or municipal authority, and not directly to the private entity. Therefore, even assuming that the credit of the commonwealth was being pledged or loaned within the meaning of Article VIII, Section 8, it is to a municipality or authority, and not to any "individual, company, corporation or association."

NOTES

1. In *Moschenross v. St. Louis County*, 188 S.W.3d 13 (Mo. Ct. App. 2006), the appellate court affirmed a declaratory judgment sought by the developers and financiers of the St. Louis Cardinals' new stadium. The court ruled that the recently passed legislation requiring any financial assistance for the development of a professional sports facility to be approved by a majority of voters could not apply retroactively against the county's prior contractual obligation to commit public funds toward the construction of the stadium.

2. In *Friends of the Parks v. Chicago Park District*, 203 Ill. 2d 312 (Ill. 2003), challengers brought suit claiming that the Sports Facilities Authority Act, which would provide public

financing for renovations to Soldier Field, owned by the city but used primarily by the private Chicago Bears, was unconstitutional. The Supreme Court of Illinois determined that the act sufficiently served a public purpose so as not to violate the state constitution.

3. For more information on public financing of sport facilities, see W.S. Miller and Chad LeBlanc, "Bingo?: An Overview of the Potential Issues Arising from the Use of Indian Gaming Revenues to Fund Professional Sports Facilities," 19 *Journal of Legal Aspects of Sport* 121 (2009), Marc Edelman, "Sports and the City: How to Curb Professional Sports Teams' Demands for Free Public Stadiums," 6 *Rutgers Journal of Law & Public Policy* 35 (2008); and Frank A. Mayer, III, "Stadium Financing: Where We Are, How We Got Here, and Where We Are Going," 12 *Villanova Sports & Entertainment Law Journal* 195 (2005).

15.2.6. Franchise Depreciation Issues

A significant tax advantage for ownership of professional sports franchises is the reduction of personal taxes through the depreciation of player contracts. This concept was introduced in the 1950s by Cleveland Indians' owner Bill Veeck. Veeck convinced the IRS that he should be able to treat the player contracts as a "wasting asset," depreciating their contracts over a period of several years as a business would copy machines or personal computers. James Quirk and Rodney Fort's book *Hard Ball* (see note 1) illustrates the power of this tax shelter.

Suppose someone buys an NFL team for $200 million. The new owner assigns 50 percent of the purchase price to player contracts (the maximum allowed under the law)...and then depreciates the contracts over 5 years....Suppose that revenue is $100 million per year and that costs, exclusive of player contract depreciation, are $90 million. Then, for the first five years of operation of the team, the books of the team will look like this:

Revenue	$100 million
Less Costs	$90 million
Less Depreciation	$20 million
Pretax profits	–$10 million

Critics such as Quirk and Fort contend that, not only would the team owners receive a tax break, but the owners also might declare to fans and politicians that the team had suffered a "loss." Various litigation has resulted over the years relative to this tax shelter.

For example, in *Selig v. United States*, 740 F.2d 572 (7th Cir. 1984), Allan "Bud" Selig entered into a contract to purchase the Seattle Pilots baseball team for $10.8 million. The contract between the Pilots and Selig allocated $100,000 of the purchase price to equipment and supplies, $500,000 to the value of the franchise including league membership, and $10.2 million to the player contracts. Selig then attempted to amortize the $10.2 million over the players' five-year useful lives under Section 167(a) of the Internal Revenue Code. The Internal Revenue Service disallowed any allocation of the purchase price to player contracts. The Seventh Circuit Court of Appeals, in upholding the district court, held that Selig properly allocated $10.2 million of the $10.8 million purchase price of the Seattle Pilots to the value of the 149 players he bought. In rejecting the government's claim, the Seventh Circuit held that allocation of $10.2 million to player contracts and $500,000 to the franchise was a reasonable determination of the fair market value of those assets at the time of acquisition. The taxpayer was therefore entitled to depreciation of player contracts on basis of that figure.

Another case involving the depreciation of player salaries is *Laird v. United States*, 556 F.2d 1224 (5th Cir. 1977). Laird bought the Atlanta Falcons of the National Football League for $8.5 million. Laird allocated $7.7 million of the purchase price to the value of the 42 player contracts he acquired. The district court rejected that valuation and allocated only $3.03 million to the player contracts. The Court of Appeals held that, under the purchase agreement, the taxpayer also received the television rights of the club, which were to last as long as the club remained a member of football league, and thus had an unlimited useful life and could not be amortized. The district court concluded that those rights had a present value of $4.3 million, and thus the court calculated that only $3.5 million remained for allocation to the franchise and the player contracts. The court allocated 88% of that amount to the players and 12% to the franchise, noting that it was clear that the players are the primary assets of a professional football club. Without them, there could be no game.

NOTES

1. For more information on taxation in professional sports, see Robert Holo and Jonathan Talansky, "Taxing the Business of Sports," 9 *Florida Tax Review* 161 (2008) and John R. Dorocak, " Tax Advantages of Sports Franchises. Part I: The Stadium," 1 *Law Review of Michigan State University Detroit College of Law* 579 (1999).

2. In *United States v. Cleveland Indians Baseball Co.*, 532 U.S. 200 (2001), with regard to the taxation of back wages awarded to players as a result of baseball's collusion cases, the issue was whether those back wages should be taxed at the tax rates of the 1980s (when the players were wrongly denied wages) or in the 1990s (when the arbitrators ruled in favor of the players and awarded them damages). The court decided that the taxes should be paid at the tax rate when they were actually paid, and not the year when the wages should have been paid.

3. In *P.D.B. Sports, Ltd. v. C.I.R.*, 109 T.C. No. 20 (U.S. Tax. Ct. 1997), Pat Bowlen, the owner of the Denver Broncos, claimed that he was allowed to amortize $1,878,056 and $259,255 in player contracts for the 1989 and 1990 years, respectively. The issue was whether when Bowlen purchased the Broncos he allocated more than a fair market value portion of the purchase price to player contracts. The court agreed with Bowlen, finding that the value given to the contracts was fair, as Bowlen had contacted four NFL general managers to aid in the assessment.

4. In *First Northwest Industries of America, Inc. v. Commissioner*, 649 F.2d 707 (9th Cir. 1981), the issue of tax depreciation of player salaries was brought to the courts by the group involved the 1967 purchase of the Seattle Supersonics expansion franchise in the NBA. The groups' strategy involved using the testimony of sports insiders to establish a valuation of the player contracts. These insiders presented detailed estimates of the value of each of the players acquired by the expansion franchise in the expansion draft. The government argued its mass asset theory and took the position that depreciation could not be allowed on player contracts because they were so intertwined with the other assets, which were acquired, that no amount logically could be allocated to the contracts. They argued that the contracts should account for only $450,000 of the purchase price, rather than the $1.6 million proposed by the owners. The court held that the value of the veteran player contracts was $500,000, or 28.6% of the total acquisition price. The court largely ignored the mass asset arguments as a method of depreciating player contracts.

5. In *Pittsburgh Athletic Co. v. Commissioner*, 27 B.T.A. 1074 (1933), *aff'd.*, 72 F.2d 883 (3d Cir. 1934), one of the first cases to deal with depreciation of player salaries, the IRS challenged the Pittsburgh Pirates' practice of taking a deduction each year for the cost of player contracts acquired and including in gross income any amounts the Pirates received for the sale of their contract players. In *Pittsburgh Athletic*, the court reinstated the practice of permitting current deductions for the cost of acquiring player contracts

15.2.7. State Tax Issues for Player Salaries

Due to their high salaries, professional athletes need to be aware of the state and federal tax laws. For example, in *Hornung v. Commissioner*, 47 T.C. 428 (1967), the court was asked to determine whether the value of prizes that were won by NFL star Paul Hornung should be included in his gross income. During the 1961 National Football League championship game, Hornung won a Corvette from *Sport Magazine* as the outstanding player in the game. The fair market value of the Corvette automobile received was $3,331.04. Hornung failed to include the fair market value of the car in his taxable income in 1962, claiming that the car was a gift. In holding that the value of the Corvette should be included in Hornung's gross income, the court found that had Congress intended to exempt prizes or awards for recognition of athletic prowess or achievement, it could readily and easily have done so. Since it had failed to do so, the value of the Corvette constituted gross income under Section 74, I.R.C. 1954.

Professional athletes must also consider the income tax laws of various U.S. states and Canadian provinces, especially if entering free agency. For example, a $5 million contract offer from a team in a state *without* income tax will be more valuable than a $5.1 million contract offer from a team in a state *with* a 5% state income tax. To complicate matters, many big league cities have begun taxing *visiting* athletes on a pro-rata basis. Cities such as New York and Philadelphia claim that they are entitled to tax income earned for work performed in their jurisdiction even if a player is based elsewhere. For example, if an NBA player for the Seattle Supersonics plays one of his 82 games in New York City, then 1/82 of the player's annual salary is taxable by New York City. It has become common for professional athletes to pay federal income taxes, income taxes in their state of residence, and income taxes in states where they play road games. As a result, professional athletes may have to file as many as 20 tax returns based on their playing schedules. The taxation of athletes by opposing cities began in 1991, when California became the first state to tax opposing athletes after the Los Angeles Lakers lost to the Chicago Bulls in the NBA finals. The state of Illinois the next year instituted its own "jock tax," and today about 20 other states have a similar tax system (see note 1). Cities are also taxing lesser paid members of athletic teams for their hours worked in visiting states such as team trainers, scouts, and front office staff. Some states have tax employees who specifically monitor sports team travel in and out of the state. The jock tax in Illinois is about 3%, while California has one of the highest rates of 9.3%. Illinois has been known to be one of the most aggressive states in taxing visiting athletes (see notes 2 and 3).

There are also issues regarding the taxation of international athletes who play professional sports in the United States and U.S. athletes who play professional sports abroad (see note 5). International tax systems vary by country, so sport managers must be aware of tax residency laws and whether there are tax treaties between the player's home country and country of work. Income tax treaties are one of the only tax law agreements that allow countries to work together to avoid double taxation. The source of the income must also be examined as athletes receive compensation not only for player contracts and salaries, but for endorsements and public appearances.

NOTES _____

1. For issues relating to state tax laws and the taxing of visiting teams, see Nick Hut, "Taxed to the Max," *Northwest Herald*, April 15, 2007.

2. Sammy Sosa of the Chicago Cubs sued the state of Illinois in 2002 for taxing his entire 1998 salary, while rejecting visiting payment deductions of over $38,000. An Illinois state court ruled that it was the state's right to disallow credit from taxes paid in other states.

3. In 1996, Chicago White Sox pitcher Scott Radinsky brought suit against the state of Illinois regarding its visiting player salary tax policy. An Illinois circuit court ruled in favor of Radinsky, and before the Illinois Supreme Court could hear an appeal, the case was settled for an undisclosed amount. However, the Radinsky case allowed about 100 current and former Chicago athletes to receive tax rebates.

4. Section 74 of the Internal Revenue Code—PRIZES AND AWARDS.

    a. General Rule.—Except as provided in subsection (b) and in section 117 (relating to scholarships and fellowship grants), gross income includes amounts received as prizes and awards.

    b. Exception.—Gross income does not include amounts received as prizes and awards made primarily in recognition of religious, charitable, scientific, educational, artistic, literary, or civic achievement, but only if—

        (1) the recipient was selected without any action on his part to enter the contest or proceedings; and

        (2) the recipient is not required to render substantial future services as a condition to receiving the prize or award.

5. For information regarding the taxation of U.S. athletes who play abroad, see Alan Pogroszewski, "When is a CPA as Important as Your ERA? A Comprehensive Evaluation and Examination of State Tax Issues on Professional Athletes," 19 *Marquette Sports Law Review* 395 (2009) and Kara Fratto, "The Taxation of Professional U.S. Athletes in Both the United States and Canada," 14 *Sports Lawyers Journal* 29 (2007).

15.3. EMPLOYMENT LAW

In recent years the courts have begun to pay close attention to employment law issues, particularly in such areas as workplace discrimination, sexual harassment, and equal pay. With all the attention in the courts relative to employment law issues, it is not surprising that some of the practices of athletic departments are starting to come under the review of the courts. This section highlights some of the main legal issues governing the relationship between employers and employees.

It begins by examining the theory of employment-at-will contracts and their impact on the employment relationship. Next is a review of some of the more important federal employment statutes and how the courts have applied these laws. The statutes include the Equal Pay Act, Title VII of the Civil Rights Act, and the Age Discrimination in Employment Act. There is also a review of the Equal Employment Opportunity Commission (EEOC) guidelines on the compensation of sports coaches in educational institutions. The EEOC guidelines are intended to provide guidance for colleges and the courts in addressing pay equity issues among college and university coaches. Title IX issues have also led to retaliation law suits in which the dismissed plaintiffs have claimed they were terminated after questioning their institutions' Title IX policies (see section 15.3.2.5, "Gender Discrimination Cases under Title IX").

15.3.1. Employment-at-Will Contracts

Many employment agreements are considered "at-will." The basic principle of an employment-at-will contract is that an employee who has been hired for an indefinite duration and may be terminated without cause at any time, without the employer incurring liability for breach of contract. Such indefinite employment contracts are deemed terminable-at-will. The classic statement of the at-will rule was that an employer may discharge an employee for "good cause or for no cause."

However, the terminable-at-will doctrine is not absolute. There are some situations when a discharged employee may have some recourse, but as a general rule these arrangements benefit the employer. To balance some of the unfairness of the employment-at-will contract, Congress and some state legislatures, relying on *Restatement (Second) of Contracts* (§ 205) have enacted statutory exceptions to limit the doctrine by imposing an implied covenant of good faith and fair dealing into the employment contract. The *Restatement (Second) of Contracts* (§ 205) states that every contract imposes upon each party a duty of good faith and fair dealing in its performance and enforcement. There is also a trend in some jurisdictions to restrict the employment-at-will doctrine for public policy reasons when, in a narrow class of cases, the discharge is contrary to a clear mandate of public policy as articulated by constitutional, statutory, or case law.

Not every employee is an employment-at-will employee. In athletics, it is common practice for athletic directors and coaches to be under contract for a specific length of time. (For more information, see section 9.2, "Types of Athletic Contracts.")

15.3.2. Employment Discrimination Statutes

In an effort to eliminate discrimination in the workplace, the U.S. Congress has passed a series of laws that prohibit unlawful compensation discrimination and other discriminatory practices. The applicable federal statutes are the Equal Pay Act of 1963, Title VII of the Civil Rights Act of 1964, and the Age Discrimination in Employment Act of 1967, which are all enforced by the Equal Employment Opportunity Commission (EEOC). Another statute that prohibits discrimination based on gender, which is only briefly discussed in this section, because it deals mainly with participation issues and not employment issues, is Title IX of the Education Amendments of 1972. (For more information, see section 8.1.1, "Title IX.")

15.3.2.1. Equal Pay Act

The Equal Pay Act of 1963 (EPA) forbids an employer from paying different salaries to members of the two sexes "for equal work on jobs the performance of which requires equal skill, effort, and responsibility, and which are performed under similar working conditions" (29 U.S.C. § 206(d)(1)). The first step under an EPA analysis is to identify male and female comparators so that their jobs can be analyzed to determine whether they are substantially equal. In selecting comparators, a plaintiff cannot compare herself or himself to a hypothetical man or woman; rather, a plaintiff must show that a specific employee of the opposite sex earned higher wages for a substantially equal job. As in all EPA cases, the skills, efforts, and responsibility required by the positions, as well as the conditions under which the jobs are performed, must be evaluated and compared on a case-by-case basis.

Once the comparators have been identified, the second step outlined under the EEOC guidelines is to determine whether the jobs are substantially equal. The EPA does not require that the jobs in question be identical, only that they are substantially equal. In determining whether two jobs are substantially equal, the courts have developed a two-step analysis. The first step requires the court to determine whether the jobs to be compared have a "common core" of tasks (i.e., a significant portion of the two jobs is identical). For example, the courts have found substantial equality in cases involving women coaches of girls' basketball and men coaches of boys' basketball (*Burkey v. Marshall County Board of Education*, 513 F. Supp. 1084, 1091 [N.D. W. Va. 1981]).

Once an individual has demonstrated that the coaching jobs are substantially equal, the second step of the analysis requires that the employer show that the reason for the unequal pay falls within one of the EPA's four affirmative defenses. These defenses include a seniority system, a merit system, a system that measures earnings by quality or quantity of production, or any other factor based on something other than sex.

A good example of how the courts have interpreted the EPA is *Stanley v. University of Southern California* (see note 4). In this case, Marianne Stanley, the former head coach of the University of Southern California (USC) women's basketball team, sued the university and its athletic director, alleging violations of the Equal Pay Act and the California Fair Employment and Housing Act. Stanley was fired by USC in 1993 after her contract expired and she was unable to renegotiate a new contract. Stanley sought a contract that would have paid her a salary equivalent to that of George Raveling, the USC men's basketball coach. Although finding that the men's and women's coaching jobs share a common core of tasks, the Ninth Circuit Court of Appeals found that Stanley and Raveling had such different levels of experience and qualifications that the university was clearly justified in paying him more, based on his greater experience. Therefore, the court held that since the pay differential between Raveling and Stanley was based on the EPA's affirmative defense of seniority and experience, there was no violation of the EPA.

In reaching the decision, the Ninth Circuit also relied on the EEOC's guidelines on the compensation of sports coaches in educational institutions. (These guidelines are addressed later in this chapter.) The EEOC's guidelines recognize as an affirmative defense that "[s]uperior experience, education, and ability may justify pay disparities if distinctions based on these criteria are not gender based." Stanley appealed her case to the U.S. Supreme Court, but the court denied her petition for a *writ of certiorari* and ended her legal challenge.

NOTES _____

1. Equal Pay Act guidelines are viewable online at www.eeoc.gov/policy/epa.

2. In *Horn v. University of Minnesota*, 362 F.3d 1042 (8th Cir. 2004), the plaintiff, David Horn, claimed wage discrimination, retaliation, and constructive discharge in violation of the Equal Pay Act and Title VII. For the inaugural season of the University of Minnesota women's hockey team, the university hired two assistant coaches and had advertised for the positions with identical job descriptions. The job title and description of the positions were the same, however, the other assistant coach, Elizabeth Witchger made $11,000 more and had one month more of employment on her contract than the plaintiff David Horn. In the suit, the court found that there were differences between the two assistant coach positions, in that Witchger was in charge of recruiting and public relations, while Horn was involved in behind-the-scenes duties.

3. In *Rallins v. Ohio State University*, 191 F. Supp. 2d 920 (S.D. Ohio 2002), a former head coach of women's cross country and track and field teams sued, claiming that her termination violated Title VII and that her lower salary than men coaches had violated the

Equal Pay Act. The court found that most of her claims were barred by the statute of limitations but also stated that the men coaches to whom she sought to compare herself were not similarly situated, that disparities in salaries within athletic departments was not direct evidence of discrimination, and that evidence that she was treated differently than men coaches was not direct evidence of discrimination.

4. In *Stanley v. University of Southern California*, 178 F.3d 1069 (9th Cir. 1999), *cert. denied*, 120 S. Ct. 533 (1999), a Division I women's basketball coach filed suit due to the discrepancy between her salary and that of the men's coach. On April 20, 1993, two months prior to the expiration of Stanley's contract, Stanley and Michael Garrett, the athletic director at USC, met to negotiate a new contract. At the meeting, Stanley asked for a salary equivalent to that of head men's basketball coach George Raveling. Garrett expressly stated that USC could not pay her that salary, but that he would make her a formal offer in writing shortly after that meeting. On April 27, 1993, Garrett offered, in writing, a three-year contract providing $80,000 in year one, $90,000 in year two, and $100,000 in year three, with a $6,000 per year housing allowance for each of the three years. The parties met again on May 27, 1993, but were still unable to reach an agreement. On June 7, 1993, Stanley proposed a three-year contract providing $96,000 per year for the first 18 months, and a salary equivalent to that of Raveling for the remainder of the term. Garrett rejected this offer. Stanley then retained an attorney, who on June 18, 1993, proposed to Garrett a three-year contract with an automatic two-year renewal provision, and total compensation of $88,000 for year one, $97,000 for year two, and $112,000 for year three, plus additional incentives. Garrett rejected this offer and withdrew the April 27 offer. On June 21, 1993, Garrett sent to Stanley's attorney a written offer for a one-year contract for $96,000. Stanley's existing contract expired on June 30, 1993, but Stanley continued to perform her duties. On July 13, while on a recruiting trip, Stanley asked Garrett if he would still offer her a multiyear contract. He indicated that his June 21 one-year contract offer was USC's final offer. On July 15, Garrett revoked the offer, informed Stanley that he was seeking a new coach for the team, and requested that Stanley perform no further services for USC. On August 5, 1993, Stanley initiated this action in Los Angeles County Superior Court, making claims of sex discrimination and retaliatory discharge. On August 6, 1993, the Superior Court granted Stanley's request for a temporary restraining order reinstating her as head coach of the women's team at $96,000 per year, pending the hearing on a preliminary injunction. On that same day, the defendants removed the action to federal court on the ground that the complaint stated claims arising under federal law. On August 30, 1993, the district court denied the motion for a preliminary injunction and Stanley appealed. The Ninth Circuit Court affirmed the denial of the preliminary injunction. On November 29, 1999, the U.S. Supreme Court denied Stanley's petition for a *writ of certiorari*, thus ending her legal challenge.

5. In *Perdue v. City University of New York*, 13 F. Supp. 2d 326 (E.D.N.Y. 1998), the former women's basketball coach sued the university, alleging gender discrimination. Following a trial, a jury returned a verdict in favor of Perdue on her intentional discrimination claim and EPA claim, and awarded damages in excess of $800,000. The district court in approving the award found that the plaintiff's work was equal to that of the men's basketball coach and men's sports administrator, as required to support an employee's EPA claim. The court also found evidence to support the determination that the EPA violation was willful, such as to entitle the employee to liquidated damages under the act. Finally, the court concluded that the evidence also supported Perdue's intentional discrimination claim under Title VII. The evidence, with regard to Perdue's claim of intentional discrimination, showed that Perdue had to do the laundry for the women's team, a task that the male coach of the men's team refused to do. She was also required to clean the gym before and after games played by her team; she had a smaller office, smaller budget, fewer assistant coaches who worked only part-time, no locker room for her team; and she was subjected to sexual slurs and improprieties. The evidence also showed that the university had a defiant attitude toward gender-equity compliance.

6. In *Dugan v. Oregon State University*, No. 95–6250-HO (D. Or. 1998), a former interim softball coach at Oregon State University sued the university when she was fired as coach and excluded from consideration as softball coach. In suing the university, Dugan argued that she was discriminated against and that her team's dismal showing had as much to do with the school's apathy as it did with her coaching abilities. Dugan, who was hired part-time to fill in for the full-time softball coach, only made $9,750 a year. She claimed that she was paid less than men coaches in similar jobs at the school and that the school did not put enough money into the program. The university argued that Dugan's performance was not adequate, and pointed out that the two committees that let her go were made up mostly of women. Dugan's record as a coach at Oregon State University was 64–201. The year she was replaced, the team went 0–24. In November 1997, a jury of all women awarded Dugan $1.275 million—$1.09 million to come from the school and $185,000 to come from Athletic Director Dutch Baughman. The school appealed. The appellate court upheld the jury's verdict, but lowered the damages to $623,000. The state of Oregon also agreed to pay Dugan's legal bills of more than $460,000.

7. In *Bartges v. University of North Carolina-Charlotte*, 908 F. Supp. 1312 (W.D.N.C. 1995), *aff'd*, 94 F.3d 641 (4th Cir. 1996), the court found that the plaintiff, a part-time head softball coach and part-time assistant women's basketball coach, failed to prove that her combined responsibilities were substantially equal to those of several men comparators. The comparators had full-time positions, were responsible for substantially more athletes, and had greater supervisory and other coaching responsibilities.

8. In *Harker v. Utica College of Syracuse University*, 885 F. Supp. 378 (N.D.N.Y. 1995), a former women's college basketball and softball coach claimed that the men's basketball coach was making more money in violation of the EPA; in 1992–1993, he earned $34,814 compared to her $29,916. On the defendant's motion for summary judgment, the district court found that under the EPA, the jobs were substantially equal. While rejecting the defendant's claim that the male coach had more education (master's degree over a bachelor's degree), the court did find the male coach's length of service to be a legitimate reason for the wage differential. The male coach had nine years of experience at the college level at the time the plaintiff was hired. As stated by the court, the defendant was entitled to use individualized qualifications as legitimate grounds for wage differences, provided that such qualifications were not gender based.

9. In *Deli v. University of Minnesota*, 863 F. Supp. 958 (D. Minn. 1994), the former head coach of the university's women's gymnastics team brought action against the university, alleging that it improperly paid her less than the head coaches of the men's football, hockey, and basketball teams. The district court held that Title VII and the Equal Pay Act did not prohibit salary discrimination based on the gender of athletes being coached, and that the coach failed to demonstrate that her position was substantially equal to positions of coaches of men's teams. Deli had less responsibility compared to men comparators, who coached larger teams, supervised more employees, had greater responsibility for public and media relations, and coached teams that generated substantially more spectator interest and revenue.

10. In *EEOC v. Madison Community Unit School District*, 818 F.2d 577 (7th Cir. 1987), the court found equality between the coaches of several like sports (boys' and girls' tennis, boys' and girls' track, and boys' baseball and girls' fast-pitch softball), but set aside the district court's findings of equality between different girls' and boys' sports. The court explained that "there is no objection in principle to comparing different coaching jobs," but concluded that the record before it did not support a finding of cross-sport equality. In particular, the court noted that the men coaches of different boys' sports received different salaries, and one of the women plaintiffs was paid the same wage as one of the men coaches of a boys' team. So long as the evidence does not demonstrate that the differences in salaries are based on discriminatory factors, the situation will not be found in violation of the EPA.

15.3.2.2. Equal Employment Opportunity Commission Coaching Pay Guidelines

On October 29, 1997, the EEOC approved and issued Notice No. 915.002, "Enforcement Guidance on Sex Discrimination in the Compensation of Sports

Coaches in Educational Institutions." The purpose of the EEOC guidelines is to illustrate the proper legal analysis of pay disparity cases under both Title VII of the Civil Rights Act of 1964 and the Equal Pay Act. Citing studies that show substantial differences in salaries paid to coaches of women's and men's teams in educational institutions, the guidelines indicate that while compensation of men's and women's coaches does not have to be the same, any disparity cannot be based on a coach's gender (see notes).

Although the EEOC guidelines address both the EPA and Title VII, the majority of the guidelines examine which factors to use to determine whether certain jobs are substantially equal. The first factor is equal skills. In considering whether two individuals have equal skills, the guidelines look at such factors as experience, training, education, and ability. The second factor is equal effort. To determine whether the coaching jobs require equal effort, the guidelines look at the actual requirements of the jobs being compared, and do not limit analysis to coaches of like sports. Coaches, regardless of the sport, typically are required to perform the following duties at both the high school and the college level: (1) teaching/training; (2) counseling/advising of student-athletes; (3) general program management; (4) budget management; (5) fundraising; (6) public relations; and (7) at the college level, recruiting.

The third factor is equal responsibility. The guidelines require the EEOC to look closely at the actual duties performed by the coaches to assess whether differences in responsibility justify unequal pay. It is important to keep in mind that the jobs need not be identical. In *Brock v. Georgia Southwestern College*, 765 F.2d 1026 (11th Cir. 1985), the employer tried to justify paying the female intramural sports coach less than the male coach of the men's basketball team by arguing that she had less responsibility because she had a smaller budget and did not have to arrange off-campus games. The court, however, recognized that the female coach instead had scheduling and budgetary responsibilities, and found that the two positions were substantially equal.

The fourth element in determining whether the jobs are substantially equal is similar working conditions. The EEOC guidelines note that most coaches work under similar conditions for purposes of the EPA.

After reviewing the factors necessary to determine whether certain jobs are substantially equal, the guidelines review the available affirmative defenses as mentioned in the previous section. The burden of demonstrating that one of the four exceptions to the act applies to the positions in question is on the employer.

While the first three defenses can be applied with little or no confusion, the EEOC guideline pays particular attention to the "factor other than sex" defense because of the particular questions it presents with regard to coaching cases. As a general matter, an employer who uses this defense must show that sex is not an element underlying the wage differential either expressly or by implication. The employer must also show that the wage differential is based on factors related to the performance of the business—in this case, the educational institution. Some of the factors other than sex that have been advanced to justify pay differentials in coaching include revenue production; marketplace; reliance on the employee's prior salary; gender of athletes; experience, education, ability; and other duties.

NOTES ————————————————————————————————

1. The EEOC's "Enforcement Guidance on Sex Discrimination in the Compensation of Sports Coaches in Educational Institutions" is available at www.eeoc.gov/policy/docs/coaches.html.

2. The *2005–2006 NCAA Gender Equity Report* showed that in Division I-A, the proportion of dollars spent on the salaries of head coaches for women's teams was the lowest since 1991–1992 at 31%. The proportion of dollars spent on head coaches of women's teams in all divisions either decreased or remained the same; that is, there were no increases in the amount spent on women's sports coaches' salaries. This report can be viewed online at www.ncaapublications.com.

3. The *2005–2006 NCAA Gender Equity Report* also found that after surveying 119 Football Bowl Subdivisions (FBS) athletic departments, the total average expenditures on men's athletic programs were $16,856,100, while the average expenditures on women's programs were less than half, at $7,055,900.

15.3.2.3. Title VII of the Civil Rights Act of 1964

In addition to the EPA, unequal pay claims can also be brought under Title VII of the Civil Rights Act of 1964, which states that it is unlawful for an employer:

1. to fail or refuse to hire or to discharge any individual, or otherwise to discriminate against any individual with respect to his compensation, terms, conditions, or privileges of employment, because of such individual's race, color, religion, sex, or national origin; or

2. to limit, segregate, or classify his employees or applicants for employment in any way which would deprive or tend to deprive any individual of employment opportunities or otherwise adversely affect his status as an employee, because of such individual's race, color, religion, sex, or national origin. (42 U.S.C. § 2000e-2002)

The burden of proof in a claim of unequal pay is the same in both EPA and Title VII cases. However, if the discrimination is based on more than unequal pay, the employee must satisfy the following four-part test. First, he or she must be a member of a protected class; second, he or she must have qualified for and occupied a particular position; third, despite his or her qualifications, he or she was treated less favorably than a coworker or fellow applicant; and fourth, the circumstances gave rise to an inference of discrimination. Once the plaintiff is able to show that he or she has been discriminated against in violation of Title VII, the employer must demonstrate a legitimate nondiscriminatory reason for the disparate treatment. Title VII allows the same four affirmative defenses as the EPA—seniority system, merit system, system based on quality or quantity of production, or any other factor other than sex.

Although there are some similarities between Title VII and the EPA, they are different in their scope of coverage. Title VII is much broader, covering all aspects of the employment relationship, not just wages (as the EPA does). Title VII also caps the maximum amount of money that can be awarded in damages at $300,000 in compensatory damages plus punitive damages and counsel fees.

15.3.2.4. Gender Discrimination Cases under Title VII

An example of how the courts have applied Title VII to sex discrimination cases is *Ortiz-Del Valle v. NBA*, 42 F. Supp. 2d 334 (S.D.N.Y. 1999). Sandra Ortiz-Del Valle, a basketball referee, sued the NBA, claiming that the league improperly failed to hire her as an NBA referee in violation of Title VII and the state of New York Human Rights Law. At the conclusion of a six-day jury trial, the NBA was found to have intentionally discriminated against Oritz-Del Valle due to her gender. The jury awarded Ortiz-Del Valle $100,000 in damages for lost wages, $750,000 for emotional distress, and $7 million in punitive damages.

After the verdict, the NBA moved for a new trial or, in the alternative, a reduction of damages. The NBA argued that Ortiz-Del Valle did not meet the qualifications. In rejecting the NBA's argument, the district court found that the NBA's requirements for referees were discriminatory. For example, Ortiz-Del Valle was told to upgrade her referee schedule and get an NCAA Division I men's schedule, but she was unable to obtain an NCAA Division I schedule because she is a woman. The NBA also invited various men referees into the NBA training program with less experience than she had and without an NCAA Division I men's schedule. The district court also held that there was enough circumstantial and direct evidence for a reasonable jury to have found a continuous policy barring women from employment as NBA referees. The evidence included the fact that no women were ever hired as NBA referees or invited to the NBA referee training camp until sometime in 1995. Statements were made to the plaintiff that she was "more qualified than some of the men" working for the NBA or the CBA, but that Darrell Garretson, chief of staff of officials, "had a problem with her being female." In addition, the employment form that potential NBA referees filled out had a space to indicate the name of the applicant's wife, but not the name of the applicant's husband.

The appeals court did, however, find that the damages awarded were grossly excessive. The court held that *remittitur*, the process by which a court compels a plaintiff to choose between reduction of an excessive verdict and a new trial, was appropriate in this case. Therefore, although the court found that the NBA violated Title VII and was liable, the damages were reduced to $250,000 in punitive damages, $76,926.20 in lost wages, and $20,000 for emotional distress.

The EEOC has also found that reverse discrimination is a violation of Title VII. For example, in *Medcalf v. University of Pennsylvania*, No. 00–07101, 2001 U.S. Dist. LEXIS 10155 (E.D. Pa. June 19, 2001) *aff'd* 71 Fed. Appx. 924 (3rd Cir. 2003), an EEOC investigation found that Penn officials discriminated against men applicants when hiring the new women's crew coach. The EEOC found that Penn took extraordinary measures to recruit only women candidates and that the university failed to interview Andrew Medcalf, the assistant men's rowing coach at Penn. Medcalf was overlooked even though he was highly recommended by both his immediate supervisor, who said he was highly qualified, and several current male and female rowers at Penn. The case went to federal court, where a jury awarded Medcalf over $115,000 in damages.

NOTES

1. In *Peirick v. Indiana University-Purdue University Indianapolis Athletics Department*, 510 F.3d 681 (7th Cir. 2007), the former head women's tennis coach at IUPUI alleged she was fired from her position based on her gender in violation of Title VII. Peirick was fired in 2003 coming off an undefeated regular season for, according to IUPUI, general insubordination and misconduct. In vacating the district court's grant of summary judgment for IUPUI, the court found that there existed a fact question as to whether IUPUI's stated reasons for firing Peirick were pretext for sex discrimination.

2. In *Fuhr v. School District of Hazel Park*, 364 F.3d 753 (6th Cir. 2004), the plaintiff, Geraldine Fuhr, sued alleging violation of Title VII after she was not hired as the boys' varsity high school basketball coach. After the former boys' varsity coach retired, Geraldine Fuhr

and John Barnett both applied for the job. Fuhr was the women's varsity basketball coach for 10 years, coach of the boys' junior varsity team, and was an assistant coach for the boys' varsity basketball team for 8 years. Barnett, on the other hand, had coached the freshman boys' basketball team for 2 years and received the job because the school board had concerns over a woman coaching the boys' varsity team. Fuhr won damages in a Michigan United States District Court. The case was appealed to the United States Court of Appeals for the Sixth Circuit, where the court affirmed the district court's decision, explaining that intentional gender discrimination could be found due to the comments of the school board and that the district court had not abused its power by forcing the school to hire Fuhr as the boys' varsity coach.

3. In *Lewis v. Smith*, 255 F. Supp. 2d 1054 (D. Ariz. 2003), the plaintiff, Mark Lewis, was an assistant coach for Arizona State University's Women's Basketball Team from 1996 to 2001. Lewis sued both Arizona State University and the women's head basketball coach Sheila Smith on violations of Title VII and the Equal Pay Act. Lewis, an assistant coach, claimed that he was discriminated against due to the hiring of a younger woman assistant who was paid a higher salary than Lewis. The court granted partial summary judgment on behalf of the defendants for the Equal Pay Act violation, as Lewis's coaching duties were different than the female assistant's. However, summary judgment was not granted for the Title VII claim as the university failed to establish why the female assistant was paid a higher salary than Lewis.

4. In *Babyak v. Smith College*, No. 99–204 (Hamden Co., Mass. Dist. Ct. 2001), a jury awarded former Smith College basketball and soccer head coach James Babyak $1.65 million in an age and gender discrimination suit. The court agreed that the all-women's college discriminated against Babyak during his tenure at Smith. Babyak claimed that, in the late 1980s, Smith officials had demoted him from his position as associate athletic director, as the administration allegedly preferred a woman for the position. Babyak, who compiled a 188–216 record in 16 seasons at Smith, claimed he was fired in 1997 because the college wanted a woman and someone younger for his position. Babyak's firing came after his basketball team had established a school record for wins, and his soccer team had won its sixth conference championship. The $1.65 million award to Babyak included $600,000 in lost income, $550,000 for age discrimination, $250,000 for gender discrimination, and $250,000 for retaliation.

5. In *Sobba v. Pratt Community College & Area Vocational School*, 117 F. Supp. 2d 1043 (D. Kan. 2000), the plaintiff tennis coach/dormitory supervisor alleged that Pratt Community College violated the Equal Pay Act by paying her less than male coaches in similar positions, and also engaged in unlawful gender discrimination in violation of Title VII by discriminating in wages. The plaintiff failed to convince the court that her work was "substantially equal" to that of certain men coaches who were paid more by the school to coach other sports. The plaintiff also alleged that the school gave "fluff" jobs to men coaches, while giving more difficult assignments to women coaches, such as assigning women coaches to the most difficult dormitories. This case was unique because Sobba coached both the men's and women's tennis teams. However, the court agreed with the defense's arguments that certain other sports required more skill and/or time to coach effectively. For example, the track coach was responsible for training athletes in multiple events and the softball coach was responsible for supervising more athletes. The softball coach was also responsible for managing a larger budget. The U.S. District Court granted partial summary judgment to the defendant.

6. In *Lowrey v. Texas A&M*, 11 F. Supp.2d 895 (S.D. Tex. 1998), Jan Lowrey, the former women's basketball coach at Tarleton State University (part of the Texas A&M University System), charged that she was illegally discriminated against based upon gender. Specifically, Lowrey alleged that Tarleton demoted her from her position as women's athletic coordinator and refused to promote her to the position of athletic director in retaliation for her role on a gender equity task force that had identified violations of both Title VII and Title IX at Tarleton. In denying summary judgment for the defendant, the court found there was a valid claim for retaliation under Title VII and Title IX, as well as a pay discrimination claim under Title VII and the Equal Pay Act.

7. In *Pitts v. State*, No. CIV-93–1341-A (W.D. Okla. 1994), the coach of the Oklahoma State University women's golf team brought suit under Title IX, Title VII, and the Equal Pay Act.

The men's golf coach received $63,000 in salary, while the plaintiff received approximately $35,712. Although the jury found no violation of the Equal Pay Act, the plaintiff was able to collect $30,000, with $6,000 for emotional distress, on the Title IX and Title VII claims.

8. In *Coble v. Hot Springs School District No. 6*, 682 F.2d 721 (8th Cir. 1982), the school district claimed that men coaches were entitled to higher salaries because of longer-term contracts and higher extra-duty stipends than women coaches. The court rejected this argument by pointing out that "the assignment of extended term contracts and extra duty stipends to particular coaching assignments is itself subject to employer discrimination on the basis of sex."

15.3.2.5. Gender Discrimination Cases under Title IX

Historically Title IX's largest impact has been on the participation levels of male and female student-athletes. However, Title IX is having an increasing importance with regard to employment. Section 106.51(a) of the Title IX Implementing Regulations states:

> No person shall, on the basis of sex, be excluded from participation in, be denied the benefits of, or be subjected to discrimination in employment, or recruitment, consideration, or selection therefor, whether full-time or part-time, under any education program or activity operated by a recipient which receives Federal financial assistance.

The regulations stipulate that all employment decisions should be conducted in a nondiscriminatory manner. Title IX prohibits discrimination or nonequitable treatment in any term, condition or privilege of employment, including recruitment, advertising, hiring, promotions, rates of pay, job assignments, collective bargaining issues, pregnancy issues, fringe benefits, financial assistance, and employee-sponsored activities. According to the implementing regulations, the EEOC is responsible for investigating claims of employment discrimination and not the Office for Civil Rights (OCR).

The OCR is not particularly concerned with the actual claim of employment discrimination; instead the OCR's main concern with regards to employment discrimination under Title IX is the effect such discrimination may have on the student-athletes within the athletic program. Although the OCR recognizes there are numerous legitimate and nondiscriminatory reasons for coaches' pay to be different, the OCR wants to ensure that the school is providing equally qualified and talented coaches.

However, Title IX has been extended to protect coaches of either sex who complain about Title IX violations from retaliatory action by the institution. In *Jackson v. Birmingham Bd. of Educ.*, 544 U.S. 167 (2005), the Court ruled that those who witness and complain about sex discrimination and consequently suffer discrimination on the basis of sex can have a private cause of action under Title IX. Roderick Jackson claimed he was fired from his position as girls' basketball coach at a public high school after he complained that the girls' team was not receiving equal funding and equal access to athletic facilities and equipment. The district court and Eleventh Circuit dismissed the suit, stating that Title IX does not prohibit retaliation. The lower courts also noted that Roderick was not a member of an underrepresented sex, the type of class meant to be protected by Title IX. In a 5–4 decision, the Supreme Court reversed, finding that retaliation is a kind of intentional discrimination on the basis of sex that is protected by Title IX. Title IX also protects those who oppose discrimination and subsequently suffer discrimination, even if they are not the direct victims. On remand, Jackson and the board settled, with Jackson receiving $50,000, his attorneys $340,000, and an agreement by the Board of Education to appoint a Title IX coordinator, adopt Title IX policies and grievance procedures, conduct a review of compliance with Title IX, and provide female athletes with comparable facilities (see note 1).

NOTES

1. For more on the *Jackson v. Birmingham Bd. of Educ.* decision, see Sue Ann Mota, "Title IX after Thirty-Four Years—Retaliation Is Not Allowed According to the Supreme Court in Jackson v. Birmingham Board of Education," 13 *Villanova Sports and Entertainment Law Journal* 245 (2006) and Lindsay C. Ferguson, "Whistle Blowing Is Not Just for Gym Class: Looking into the Past, Present, and Future of Title IX," 39 *Texas Tech Law Review* 167 (2006).

2. In 2007, two California juries awarded two former Fresno State coaches, Lindy Vivas and Stacy Johnson-Klein, $5.85 million and $6.6 million, respectively. Both women claimed to have been fired in retaliation for voicing complaints over issues governed by Title IX. In addition, in 2008, the university settled two suits with similar complaints: former associate athletic director Diane Milutinovich received $3.5 million, and former softball coach Margie Wright received approximately $600,000.

3. In March 2008, the Nevada State Personnel Commission dismissed a claim by former University of Nevada women's soccer coach Terri Patraw that she was fired in retaliation for complaining about Title IX enforcement at the university. The commission found that Patraw's questionable work record, including NCAA violations, failure to follow directions, and unfair threats to the University justified her termination.

4. In *Atkinson v. Lafayette College*, 460 F.3d 447 (3rd Cir. 2006), the plaintiff alleged that she was terminated from her position as director of athletics at Lafayette College as a result of her raising issues of gender equality in the context of submitting various budgetary plans to comply with Title IX. Her suit alleged unlawful employment discrimination and retaliation in violation of Title VII, Title IX, and the Pennsylvania Human Rights Act. The district court granted summary judgment for the defendant, ruling that the plaintiff could not sue for retaliation under Title IX, because individuals do not have standing to sue for enforcement of the antiretaliation regulations. In light of *Jackson v. Birmingham Board of Education*, the circuit court reversed and remanded for further consideration.

5. In *Bowers v. Baylor University*, 862 F. Supp. 142 (W.D. Tex. 1994), a court ruled in one of the first athletic cases resulting from Title IX. This case was also a significant employment law case. Baylor University women's basketball coach Pam Bowers was fired in 1993, allegedly for NCAA violations. Immediately after her termination, Bowers filed a complaint with both the Office of Civil Rights and the Equal Employment Opportunity Commission. Baylor notified Bowers that she would be reinstated under her employment terms that had existed since 1979. Bowers continued her employment complaints with the federal agencies after being reinstated. In 1994, Bowers was terminated because of her unsuccessful win-loss record during her tenure at Baylor. Bowers filed suit, claiming that Baylor retaliated against her for challenging Baylor's allegedly discriminatory conduct. The court denied Baylor's motion to dismiss, stating that Bowers possessed a private cause of action against the school for damages under Title IX. The court granted the individual defendant's motion to dismiss, the administrators and employees of the school, "in and of themselves," were not educational institutions subject to the statute. This case was later settled out of court.

15.3.2.6. Race Discrimination Cases under Title VII

An example of how the courts have applied Title VII to race discrimination cases is *Wallace v. Texas Tech University*, 80 F.3d 1042 (5th Cir. 1996). Phillip Wallace was hired as an assistant basketball coach at Texas Tech University with a one-year contract. Wallace, an African American, had no prior coaching experience, but he had played on the Texas Tech basketball team during his college years. James Dickey, the head coach, also hired another assistant coach for the same period. The other assistant, a white male who had seven years of college coaching experience, was paid $57.83 per month more than Wallace. When Wallace's contract expired, it was not renewed and another African American replaced him.

Wallace sued Texas Tech and Dickey, alleging that they discriminated against him on the basis of his race in violation of Title VII. To succeed on a claim of race discrimination under Title VII, a plaintiff must first prove a prima facie case of discrimination. A plaintiff can prove a prima facie case through a four-element test that allows an inference of discrimination or through direct evidence of discriminatory motive. The four-element test requires that the plaintiff show (1) he or she is a member of a protected class; (2) he or she is qualified for the position; (3) he or she was discharged; and (4) after being discharged, he or she was replaced with a person who is not a member of the protected class.

In upholding the district court's judgment in favor of the university and head coach, the court of appeals held that Wallace failed to establish either that his contract was not renewed based on race or that his receiving a lower salary than a white coach was based on race. Wallace's contract was not renewed, the court concluded, because of poor job performance. Evidence showed that Wallace was unwilling to follow instructions, and that he repeatedly questioned Dickey's coaching judgment. As for the disparity in pay, the white coach had significantly greater college coaching experience. Title VII and the EEOC coaching guidelines state that differences in work experience are a valid nondiscriminatory rationale to justify different salaries for employees performing the same job. Since Texas Tech was able to establish a nondiscriminatory motive for the pay differential, the burden fell to Wallace to show that the articulated reason was only a pretext. Wallace was unable to prove this.

NOTES

1. In *Holcomb v. Iona College*, 521 F.3d 130 (2nd Cir. 2008), a white former men's assistant basketball coach alleged that he was fired because he was married to an African American woman. After the district court granted summary judgment, the Second Circuit vacated and remanded, finding that as a matter of first impression, a claim of adverse action based on an employee's association with a person of another race is cognizable under Title VII.

2. In *Nicholas v. Board of Trustees of University of Alabama*, 251 Fed. Appx. 637 (11th Cir. 2007), an African American who was an assistant women's basketball coach claimed he was treated disparately in violation of Title IX after he was suspended with pay but banned from having contact with the players when it was alleged he made improper sexual advances toward a member of the team. The circuit court affirmed summary judgment for the school, finding that the coach failed to establish a prima facie case of race- or gender-based disparate discipline. The plaintiff failed to show that a similarly situated employee engaged in the same or similar misconduct but did not receive similar discipline.

3. In *Richardson v. Sugg.* 448 F.3d 1046 (8th Cir. 2006), the plaintiff, Nolan Richardson, the former head coach of the University of Arkansas men's basketball team, sued the University of Arkansas president, chancellor, athletic director, and the board of trustees on a Title VII racial discrimination and breach of contract claim. Richardson argued that the University of Arkansas fired him as head coach on the basis of race and because he was outspoken about racial issues at the campus. The university argued that his dismissal was due to Richardson's loss of interest in the basketball program and commitment to the University of Arkansas. The court dismissed the case and the appeals court affirmed the dismissal, stating that, although

there was some evidence of racism on the part of university officials, Richardson did not show that university officials intentionally discriminated against him based on race.

4. In *Cobb v. University of Southern California*, 45 Cal. App. 4th 1140 (Cal. Ct. App. 1996), Marvin Cobb, assistant athletic director for the University of Southern California, filed racial discrimination and breach of contract claims against USC. He charged that he was denied promotions and harassed because of his complaints regarding the academic abilities and preparation of African American student-athletes. Specifically, Cobb alleged that the university failed to afford many of its African American student-athletes an educational opportunity. He also alleged that USC's recruitment of academically underprepared student-athletes, with only a minimal likelihood of succeeding academically, constituted exploitation. The jury awarded Cobb $2.1 million on the breach of contract claim (later reduced to $1.1 million). Cobb's discrimination claims were later dismissed.

15.3.2.7. Age Discrimination in Employment Act of 1967

Section 623 of the Age Discrimination in Employment Act of 1967 (ADEA) states that:

a. it shall be unlawful for an employer

1. to fail or refuse to hire or to discharge any individual or otherwise discriminate against any individual with respect to his compensation, terms, conditions, or privileges of employment, because of such individual's age; or

2. to limit, segregate, or classify his employees in any way which would deprive or tend to deprive any individual of employment opportunities or otherwise adversely affect his status as an employee, because of such individual's age. (29 U.S.C. § 623)

The burden of proof under the ADEA is similar to those for Title VII. To establish a prima facie case of age discrimination under the ADEA, the plaintiff must satisfy four elements: (1) he or she is a member of a protected class; (2) he or she was qualified for the position; (3) he or she was discharged; and (4) he or she was either (a) replaced by someone outside the protected class, (b) replaced by someone younger, or (c) otherwise discharged because of his or her age. The third alternative of the fourth element applies in circumstances where the plaintiff is not replaced.

The ADEA authorizes relief in the form of reinstatement, back pay, injunctive relief, declaratory judgment, and attorney's fees (29 U.S.C. § 626(b)). In addition, in the case of a willful violation of the act, the ADEA authorizes an award of liquidated damages equal to the back pay award (29 U.S.C. § 626(b)).

An example of how the courts have applied the ADEA to age discrimination cases is *Moore v. University of Notre Dame*, 22 F. Supp. 2d 896 (N.D. Ind. 1998). The plaintiff, Joseph Moore, was the offensive line coach for Notre Dame from 1988 until he was fired in 1996. Moore, who claimed that he was fired because he was "too old" and would not be able to continue to coach for another full five-year period, sued the university, alleging age discrimination under ADEA. Notre Dame claimed that Moore was dismissed because he did not measure up to the standards of Notre Dame. The university also claimed that Moore had intimidated, abused, and made offensive remarks to players.

In ruling against Notre Dame, a jury found that the school did in fact fire Moore because of his age, in violation of the ADEA. The district court, however, refused to grant Moore's request for reinstatement to his former coaching position. The court held that, although reinstatement is the preferred remedy in a discrimination case, it is not always an appropriate remedy. Before reinstatement is ordered, the court must consider the hostility in the past employment relationship and the absence of an available position for the plaintiff. In this case, the court found that Moore's reinstatement would cause significant friction as well as disruption of the current football program. Even if Moore's return would not create hostility and undue friction, there was someone else currently occupying Moore's former position. Therefore, there was no available position for Moore.

In lieu of reinstatement, the court granted Moore's request for front pay. Front pay is a lump sum payment representing the difference between the earnings an employee would have received in his old employment and the earnings he can be expected to receive in his present and future (and, by hypothesis, inferior) employment. Although such an award remains discretionary with the court, front pay is an available remedy under ADEA. Its purpose is to ensure that a person who has been discriminated against on the basis of age is made whole, not to guarantee every claimant who cannot mitigate damages by finding comparable work, an annuity to age 70. The court in *Moore* defined front pay as "a lump sum ... representing the discounted present value of the difference between the earnings [an employee] would have received in his old employment and the earnings he can be expected to receive in his present and future, and by hypothesis, inferior, employment."

In determining the amount of front pay to award, the court should consider whether the plaintiff has a reasonable prospect of obtaining comparable employment; whether the time period for the award is relatively short; whether the plaintiff intends to work or is physically capable of working; and whether liquidated damages have been awarded. The final judgment against Notre Dame was $75,577.68 in front pay, $9,672.45 in costs, $394,865.74 in attorney fees and expenses, $42,935.28 in back pay, and an additional $42,935.28 in liquidated damages.

NOTES

1. In *Peirick v. Indiana University-Purdue University Indianapolis Athletics Department*, 510 F.3d 681 (7th Cir. 2007), a former women's tennis coach alleged that she was fired, among other claims, at age 53 in violation of the ADEA. The circuit court affirmed summary judgment on the ADEA claim, because IUPUI is immune from suits under the ADEA because of the Eleventh Amendment.

2. In *Ranieri v. Highland Falls-Fort Montgomery School District*, 198 F. Supp. 2d 542 (S.D.N.Y. 2002), the plaintiff, James Ranieri, brought an ADEA suit against the school district after he was dismissed as high school boys' varsity basketball coach. Ranieri was head coach from 1996 to 2000 and enjoyed some success, winning two section championships and coach of the year honors in 1998. However, he was fired following his 2000 season and replaced by a coach who was 10 years younger and had less recent coaching experience. The district court granted summary judgment on behalf of the defendant since Ranieri could not show a legitimate discriminatory reason for his dismissal.

3. In *Austin v. Cornell University*, 891 F. Supp. 740 (N.D.N.Y. 1995), two former seasonal employees of the university golf course sued Cornell University for age discrimination after they were not rehired. In rejecting Cornell's motion for summary judgment, the district court held that the plaintiffs raised genuine issues of material fact regarding Cornell's refusal to rehire them. In addition, the court held that the head golf professional and associate director of athletics could be individually liable.

4. Also see *Babyak*, section 15.3.2.4, note 4.

5. For more on ADEA and other discrimination issues in athletics, see Diane Heckman, "Educational Athletic Employment and Civil Rights: Examining Discrimination Based on Disability, Age, and Race," 18 *Marquette Sports Law Review* 101 (2007).

15.3.2.8. State Discrimination Laws

Besides federal statutes, discrimination claims may be brought under state laws, which may offer greater protection than the federal statutes. For example, under New Jersey's Law against Discrimination (LAD), an individual is not only entitled to compensatory damages but may also be entitled to punitive damages and attorney's fees. Unlike Title VII, however, the LAD does not contain a damages cap. It is important to note that discrimination laws have different names in each state. For example, Marianne Stanley filed a state discrimination claim under the California Fair Employment and Housing Act. Most often, the state statutes can be found under the state's Human Rights Act.

NOTES ————————————————————————————————

1. In *Seagrave v. Dean*, 908 So. 2d 41 (La. App. 1st Cir. 2005), a Louisiana appellate court reversed a jury verdict of $773,000 for Loren Seagrave against Louisiana State University. Seagrave, a former women's track coach, alleged that race played an unfair factor in his 1989 firing in violation of Louisiana law. Seagrave was fired after he told LSU's head track coach and the LSU athletic director, Joe Dean, that he had an all-night "counseling session" with a female athlete on his team. Seagrave, a white man, maintained that the session was entirely innocent and that he was in fact fired for being married to an African American woman. Seagrave contended that Dean told him in 1987 that he would not be hired for the men's track coaching position because of his engagement to an African American woman. In reversing the jury award, the appellate court ruled that Dean's alleged comments were not sufficient evidence of discrimination in the workplace. In addition, those comments concerned Seagrave's potential promotion, not his termination, the employment decision at issue.

2. In 1995, a District of Columbia Superior Court jury awarded Sanya Tyler, an associate athletic director and the women's basketball coach at Howard University, $2.39 million in a sexual discrimination case against the university. The damages were later reduced to $250,000. The jury found that the university violated the D.C. Human Rights Act as well as Title IX and the Equal Pay Act by discriminating and retaliating against Tyler. While Tyler and her male counterpart had identical job descriptions, Tyler was paid $44,000, and the men's coach was paid $78,000. See *The NCAA News*, October 2, 1995, p. 6.

15.3.3. Sexual Harassment

Sexual harassment, which is a violation of both Title VII and Title IX of the Education Amendments Act of 1972, is an important issue for athletic administrators. It is essential that athletic administrators have a basic knowledge of the legal aspects of sexual harassment, to ensure that their organization policies, procedures, and practices can work toward its prevention. Sexual harassment is a serious offense, and coaches and administrators need to be aware that behavior once seen as merely rude or offensive may now result in legal action. Sexual harassment can be loosely defined as any unwelcome, unsolicited, nonreciprocal, or uninvited behavior of a sexual nature that interferes with a person's work or education. This can include any conduct, including profane language, off-color jokes, leering, or ogling, that refers to sex. Any unwanted touching, patting, hugging, pinching, or request for sexual favors in return for benefits also constitutes sexual harassment.

There are two types of sexual harassment: *quid pro quo* and *hostile environment*. Quid pro quo sexual harassment occurs when an employer or coach grants or withholds benefits, such as pay or scholarship, as a result of an employee's or athlete's willingness or refusal to submit to the employer or coach's sexual demands. The critical point is not whether the victim submits voluntarily, but whether the conduct he or she submits to is unwanted. Hostile environment sexual harassment exists when an employer's or coach's conduct is so severe that it creates an intimidating, hostile, or offensive environment that interferes with the employee's or athlete's ability to perform his or her work. Hostile environment sexual harassment is not necessarily sexual harassment because it involves sexual gestures, language, or activities, but because it is motivated by the victim's sex. The Supreme Court has also determined that the sex of the victim does not have to be different from that of the harasser for there to be sexual harassment (see note 2).

Athletic administrators need to develop comprehensive policies and conduct training sessions in order for their staff and student-athletes to be knowledgeable about sexual harassment issues. The objective should be to ensure a safe environment while also demanding that sexual harassment of any kind will not be tolerated. The standard by which employers are judged is whether they exercised reasonable care to prevent harassing behavior (see notes 3 and 4).

Based on the above decisions, it behooves all athletic organizations to (1) establish a grievance procedure for sexual harassment complaints and (2) publicize the organization's grievance procedure and its sexual harassment policy. It is important to point out that Justice Kennedy's opinion in *Burlington Industries* (note 4) states that an organization *can* be vicariously liable for quid pro quo harassment, even if it possesses a grievance system. Therefore, an athletic organization should make every effort to eliminate an employee's harassing behavior before the behavior escalates to the withholding of benefits or a promotion. The Department of Education Office of Civil Rights defines sexual harassment under Title IX thus:

> unwelcome sexual advances, requests for sexual favors, or other verbal or physical conduct of a sexual nature, imposed on the basis of sex, that could

a. deny, limit, or provide different aids, benefits, services or opportunities,

b. condition the provision of aids, benefits, services or opportunities, or

c. otherwise limit a student's enjoyment of any right, privilege, advantage, or opportunity protected by Title IX.

An example of how the courts have dealt with sexual harassment in federally funded institutions under Title IX is *Franklin v. Gwinnett County Public Schools*, 503 U.S. 60 (1992). The plaintiff, a female high school student, filed suit against the defendant, alleging that she was subjected to continual sexual harassment from Andrew Hill, a coach and teacher at the high school, and that school officials failed to stop Hill's continued harassment (see note 5).

In August 1988, Franklin filed a complaint with the Department of Education's Office of Civil Rights (OCR), alleging that she had been subject to sexual harassment in violation of Title IX. Following a six-month investigation, the OCR found the Gwinnett County School District in violation of Title IX. In particular, the OCR found that the district had violated Franklin's rights by subjecting her to physical and verbal sexual harassment and by interfering with her right to complain about such conduct. The OCR, however, failed to act, and closed its investigation after being assured that the school district would implement a grievance procedure to prevent future violations. Unhappy with the outcome of the OCR's investigation, Franklin filed a Title IX lawsuit seeking damages against the Gwinnett County School District.

The U.S. Supreme Court, in reversing the lower courts, held that "Title IX placed on the Gwinnett County Schools the duty not to discriminate on the basis of sex, and when a supervisor sexually harasses a subordinate because of the subordinate's sex, that supervisor discriminates on the basis of sex." The same rule, the Court held, applies when a teacher or coach "sexually harasses and abuses a student."

Similar circumstances to *Franklin* occurred in *Jennings v. University of North Carolina at Chapel Hill*, 482 F.3d 686 (4th Cir. 2007). The plaintiff was Melissa Jennings, a former player for the UNC women's soccer team, coached by Anson Dorrance, who had led UNC to 18 national championships between 1981 and 2003. Jennings claimed that Dorrance made repeated sexual comments about both her and her teammates and frequently engaged in inappropriate sexual discussions with the team. Dorrance often asked players about their sexual activities, made comments about players' bodies, portrayed them as sexual objects, and voiced sexual fantasies about several players. During her freshman season, Jennings filed a complaint with UNC's legal counsel, who merely insisted that Jennings work out her issues with Dorrance. When Jennings was cut from the team at the end of her sophomore year, her parents submitted numerous complaints to the chancellor's office. After a brief investigation, Athletic Director Richard Baddour sent a letter of apology to Jennings's parents. Still dissatisfied with the response, Jennings and another player, Debbie Keller, brought suit, claiming that UNC discriminated against them in violation of Title IX by subjecting them to severe and pervasive sexual harassment.

The district court stated that Dorrance's conduct was not so severe that it limited Jennings's educational opportunities; however the 4th Circuit *en banc* remanded after stating that Dorrance's actions and behavior, if proven, could constitute a hostile or abusive environment and would be sufficient for liability under Title IX. Prior to a new trial, UNC and Jennings settled the lawsuit for $350,000, which also required the university to revise its sexual harassment policies and Dorrance, who got to keep his job, to write a letter of apology.

NOTES

1. For more information on the prevention of sexual harassment in the workplace, see Michele Paludi and Carmen A. Paludi, eds., *Academic and Workplace Sexual Harassment: A Handbook of Cultural, Social Science, Management, and Legal Perspectives* (Westport, CT: Praeger Publishers, 2003). For more information specific to the sports industry, see Anita M. Moorman and Lisa P. Masteralexis, "An Examination of the Legal Framework between Title VII and Title IX Sexual Harassment Claims in Athletics and Sport Settings: Emerging Challenges for Athletic Personnel and Sport Managers," 18 *Journal of Legal Aspects of Sport* 1 (2008) and Michael E. Buchwald, "Sexual Harassment in Education and Student Athletics: A Case for Why Title IX Sexual Harassment Jurisprudence Should Develop Independently of Title VII," 67 *Maryland Law Review* 672 (2008).

2. Although the issue has not yet been litigated in the context of athletics, discrimination based on sexual orientation has been found to violate Title IX. In *Theno v. Tonganoxie Unified School District*, 377 F. Supp. 3d 952 (D. Kansas 2005), the court ruled that a high school student who was called names and subjected to crude sexual gestures on the basis of his sexual orientation could bring suit under Title IX for sexual harassment. In *Montgomery v. Independent School Dist. No. 709*, 109 F. Supp. 2d 1081 (D. Minn. 2000), the court ruled

that, although Title IX does not prohibit harassment or discrimination based on sexual orientation, it does prohibit harassment based on gender nonconformity.

3. In *Faragher v. Boca Raton*, 524 U.S. 775 (1998), a former lifeguard for the city of Boca Raton sued the city under Title VII for sexual harassment, based on the conduct of her two supervisors. Faragher alleged that her supervisors had created a sexually hostile atmosphere at work by repeatedly subjecting her and other female lifeguards to uninvited and offensive touching, lewd remarks, and offensive references to women. Faragher claimed that this conduct, which went on for five years, constituted discrimination in the terms, conditions, and privileges of her employment, in violation of Title VII. After concluding that the supervisors' conduct was sufficiently serious to alter the conditions of Faragher's employment and constitute an abusive working environment, the U.S. Supreme Court held that the city (employer) could be subject to vicarious liability (see section 3.6, "Vicarious Liability") under Title VII for discrimination caused by a supervisor. The employer, however, may raise an affirmative defense in such a case that looks to the reasonableness of an employer's conduct in preventing and correcting harassing conduct and to the reasonableness of an employee's conduct in seeking to avoid harm. In *Faragher*, the Supreme Court concluded that the city was vicariously liable because of its failure to exercise reasonable care to prevent harassing behavior.

4. The Supreme Court further specified the meaning of "reasonable care" in *Burlington Industries Inc. v. Ellerth*, 524 U.S. 742 (1998). In this hostile environment case, the defendant company argued that it should not be held vicariously liable because it possessed a well-advertised sexual harassment complaint procedure, which the plaintiff had failed to utilize. In offering decision for the court, Justice Kennedy explained that a clear and fair complaint procedure will normally absolve an organization from vicarious liability for hostile environment complaints. An employer is subject to vicarious liability to a victimized employee for an actionable hostile environment created by a supervisor with immediate (or successively higher) authority over the employee. When no tangible employment action is taken, a defending employer may raise an affirmative defense to liability or damages, subject to proof by a preponderance of the evidence.... The defense comprises two necessary elements: (a) that the employer exercised reasonable care to prevent and correct promptly any sexually harassing behavior, and (b) that the plaintiff employee unreasonably failed to take advantage of any preventive or corrective opportunities provided by the employer or to avoid harm otherwise. While proof that an employer had promulgated an anti-harassment policy with a complaint procedure is not necessary in every instance as a matter of law, the need for a stated policy suitable to the employment circumstances may appropriately be addressed in any case when litigating the first element of the defense. And while proof that an employee failed to fulfill the corresponding obligation of reasonable care to avoid harm is not limited to showing any unreasonable failure to use any complaint procedure provided by the employer, *a demonstration of such failure will normally suffice to satisfy the employer's burden under the second element of the defense* [italics added]. No affirmative defense is available, however, when the supervisor's harassment culminates in a tangible employment action.

5. According to the complaint, Hill initiated sexual discussions with Franklin in which Hill asked Franklin about her sexual experiences with her boyfriend and whether she would consider having sexual intercourse with an older man; Hill forcibly kissed Franklin on the school grounds; and, on two or three occasions, Hill interrupted a class, requested that Franklin be excused, and took her to a private office, where he subjected her to coercive intercourse. Franklin further alleged that, even though school officials investigated and knew of Hill's sexual harassment of Franklin and other female students, school administrators took no action to halt Hill's sexual harassment of Franklin and even tried to discourage Franklin from pressing charges against Hill. The principal of the high school closed his investigation into Franklin's allegations when Hill resigned at the end of the school year, on the condition that all matters pending against him would be dropped.

6. In *Simpson v. University of Colorado Boulder*, 500 F.3d 1170 (10th Cir. 2007), the 10th Circuit reversed the district court's dismissal of a sexual harassment suit brought by

a former student. The woman alleged that in 2001 she had been raped at an off-campus party thrown by Colorado football players. She claimed that the university was responsible for condoning an environment in which female students known as "ambassadors" were encouraged to entertain football recruits. The 10th Circuit stated that the evidence created an issue of fact as to whether the risk of an assault during recruiting visits was so obvious that it amounted to deliberate indifference. On remand, Colorado and the woman settled the lawsuit for $2.85 million, and Colorado agreed to hire a Title IX adviser and a part-time employee in the Office of Victim Assistance.

7. In 1999, the University of Alabama at Tuscaloosa paid a university athletic department employee $350,000 to settle a sexual harassment case involving her and the head football coach, Mike DuBose. Alabama fired the athletic director, Bob Bockrath, in the wake of the sexual harassment allegations.

8. In *Davis v. Monroe County Board of Education*, 526 U.S. 629 (1999), a parent, on behalf of a fifth-grade student, sued the school board and officials, alleging that the defendants violated Title IX, and 42 U.S.C. § 1983, by failing to remedy a classmate's sexual harassment of the student. The Supreme Court held that a private action for damages may lie against a school board under Title IX in cases of student-on-student harassment, but only where the school acts with deliberate indifference and the harassment is so severe that it effectively bars the victim's access to an educational opportunity or benefit.

9. In *Gebser v. Lago Vista Independent School District*, 524 U.S. 274 (1998), a student who has been the victim of sexual harassment by an employee of an institution subject to Title IX may not bring a private damages claim against the institution "unless an official of the [institution] who at a minimum has authority to institute corrective measures on the [institution's] behalf has actual notice of, and is deliberately indifferent to, the [employee's] misconduct." This was a 5–4 U.S. Supreme Court decision.

10. In *Klemencic v. Ohio State University*, 10 F. Supp. 2d 911 (S.D. Ohio 1998), a student athlete at Ohio State sued the university and Thomas Ed Crawford, assistant coach of the women's track team, claiming sexual harassment. Klemencic alleged that she was subjected to quid pro quo sexual harassment by Crawford, and as a result of her refusal, was denied access to the team. The district court rejected Klemencic's argument, and found that the coach did not create a hostile educational environment when he asked the student to go out with him or by sending her a sexually suggestive magazine article.

11. In *Rosa H. v. San Elizario Independent School District*, 106 F.3d 648 (5th Cir. 1997), a high school student brought Title IX action against the school district, alleging the district's negligent failure to prevent a teacher of an after-school karate class from committing sexual abuse. The Fifth Circuit Court held that the student who had been sexually abused by her teacher could not recover from the school district under Title IX unless the school district actually knew there was substantial risk that sexual abuse would occur.

12. In *Doe v. Taylor Independent School District*, 15 F.3d 443 (5th Cir. 1994), a high school student brought civil rights action against the school district, superintendent, and principal, alleging sexual molestation by a teacher and coach. The court of appeals held that the student was deprived of her liberty interest recognized under the substantive due process component of the Fourteenth Amendment when her teacher sexually abused her. The court of appeals also held that school officials could be found liable for the actions of school employees when the student can show that the officials, by action or inaction, demonstrate deliberate indifference to the sexual harassment.

13. In *Alexander v. Yale*, 631 F.2d 178 (2d Cir. 1980), the first case to examine whether the scope of Title IX covered sexual harassment, five students sued Yale University, alleging that they were sexually harassed by Yale faculty members and administrators. The plaintiffs further alleged that Yale was in violation of Title IX by refusing to seriously consider the students' complaints of sexual harassment. The court held that a party seeking relief under Title IX must demonstrate a personal "distinct and palpable injury," and the relief requested must "redound to that party's personal benefit." Former students lacked standing to get any relief from sexual harassment charges.

Chapter 16

ADDITIONAL LEGAL CONCERNS

16.1. Athletes, Violence, and Criminal Law

    16.1.1. Defining a Crime

    16.1.2. Player-against-Player Violence

    16.1.3. Player and Fan Violence

    16.1.4. Player-against-Official Violence

    16.1.5. Off-the-Field Criminal Conduct

    16.1.6. Solutions to the Problem of Sports Violence

        16.1.6.1. Governing Body Control

        16.1.6.2. Government Regulation

16.2. Illegal Gambling

    16.2.1. Intercollegiate Athletics and Gambling

    16.2.2. Professional Sports and Gambling

    16.2.3. Internet Gambling

    16.2.4. Fantasy Sports and Office Pools

16.3. Disabilities

    16.3.1. Federal Laws Affecting Persons with Disabilities

        16.3.1.1. The Rehabilitation Act

        16.3.1.2. Individuals with Disabilities Education Act (IDEA)

        16.3.1.3. The Amateur Sports Act

        16.3.1.4. Americans with Disabilities Act (ADA)

            16.3.1.4.1. Title I: Employment

            16.3.1.4.2. Title II: Public Services

            16.3.1.4.3. Title III: Public Accommodations Operated by Private Entities

    16.3.2. Application to Athletic Organizations

        16.3.2.1. Youth Sports

        16.3.2.2. High School

        16.3.2.3. Colleges, Universities, and the National Collegiate Athletic Association

        16.3.2.4. Professional Sports

        16.3.2.5. Sports Facilities

16.4. Athletes with AIDS and Testing for HIV

INTRODUCTION

Athletic administrators and sports lawyers should be aware of and concerned about four additional legal areas: criminal law, illegal gambling, federal disability legislation, and AIDS testing. The four areas covered briefly in Chapter 16 provide an overview and some background information on potential legal problems in these areas.

16.1. ATHLETES, VIOLENCE, AND CRIMINAL LAW

Every year there are an increasing number of incidents, either during an athletic event or off the field, that raise the public's interest and concern about athletes who are charged with criminal law offenses. Violence within the context of sports is a familiar subject to nearly every sports fan. Many of the incidents of violent conduct in sport go beyond the reasonable scope of risks associated with sport. For example, acts that are clearly criminal in the nonsport context seem to be licensed if they take place on the playing field. Many people consider the punishment of fines and suspensions for violent action on the field to be minor when compared with the nature of the conduct. With violent conduct in athletic competition on the rise, the ability of leagues to control violence through league-imposed fines and penalties has been questioned. Many people argue that legislative action is needed to curb the violence (see section 16.1.6, "Solutions to the Problem of Sports Violence"), and others believe that criminal law should be more readily invoked. Both league suspensions and criminal charges were utilized after the brawl on November 19, 2004, between the Detroit Pistons and Indiana Pacers at the Palace of Auburn Hills, Michigan. A fight ensued following a foul on Pistons forward Ben Wallace by the Pacers Ron Artest. Fans began throwing items onto the court, causing Artest to run into the stands to confront the culprits. This sparked a brawl between several Pacers and Pistons players, as well as several fans. Nine players were ultimately suspended, including Artest for the rest of the 2004–2005 season. Twelve were given criminal charges, including five Pacers and seven fans, their charges ranging from felony assault to trespassing. However, only one fan, John Green, served any jail time (see section 16.1.3, "Player and Fan Violence").

Charging athletes with criminal charges for on-field conduct has increased; however, people still question how stringent the courts are toward athletes regarding their criminal behavior. Few athletes have ever been sentenced to jail time for criminal conduct, usually receiving fines or probation. For example, in 2004 NHL player Todd Bertuzzi pled guilty to assault causing bodily harm in a British Columbia court. He received one year of probation after seriously harming NHL player Steve Moore. If Bertuzzi was not an athlete, many argue he would have received prison time since he almost killed another individual (see section 16.1.2, "Player-against-Player Violence").

Athlete violence and crime occurring off the field has also become a heated issue with sports organizations and fans, especially since the O. J. Simpson murder trial in the mid-1990s and the Thomas Junta rink rage case in 2001 (see note 4). However, most of this section will deal with athlete violence occurring *during* a game or practice, or perhaps right before or after the game or practice.

Section 16.1.5, "Off-the-Field Criminal Conduct," briefly addresses the legal issues that arise when crimes are committed outside the scope of athletic competition. Criminal law is based on society's need to be free from harmful conduct.

Criminal law defines criminal conduct and prescribes the punishment to be imposed on a person convicted of engaging in such conduct. In addition to its broad aim of preventing injury to the health, safety, morals, and welfare of the public, criminal law is designed to uphold society's broader notions of morality.

Understanding the basis of criminal law makes it easier to understand why violent and possibly criminal behavior is perceived differently when the violence occurs in a sporting event. All the harm and violence are confined to the participants, who know and assume the risks of the game. The public, while sitting in the stands or watching on television, is not subjected to any risk of physical harm, unless injured by an act of negligence. This may be an underlying reason why society treats sports violence differently from violence in the streets. Yet, what about when the violent actions are upon fans or officials? (See sections 16.1.3, "Player and Fan Violence," and 16.1.4, "Player-against-Official Violence")

Opponents of sports violence argue that this approach overlooks the interests of society as a whole in protecting society's notions of morality. Opponents contend that the incidents just cited evoke a sense of moral outrage and a feeling that some kind of punishment should be exacted. The existence in sporting events of socially unacceptable conduct that is treated with impunity conflicts with society's overall concept of good and bad conduct that has long been usually punishable only by league sanctions that arguably are much less severe than punishment that would be ordered in criminal courts.

To determine whether criminal law sanctions should be imposed for incidents of sports violence, it is useful to examine the rationale behind criminal punishment. Prison terms are imposed for a purpose, and an examination of sports violence situations relative to criminal law may be helpful. A primary rationale for criminal sanctions is the prevention theory—that is, punishment will keep a criminal from becoming a repeat offender. The theory's aim is to rehabilitate the offender in the criminal justice system. In sports, rehabilitation would be a desirable goal if treating the offending athlete as a criminal would actually prevent the repetition of dangerous conduct.

A second theory behind punishment for criminal conduct is the deterrence theory—that exacting punishment for bad conduct deters others from committing applications in the area of sports violence. Athletes would, in theory, be less likely to engage in violent conduct that is outside the scope of the risks of the sport if they feared criminal punishment.

One final theory that is relevant to sports violence is the education theory of punishment, which states that the publicity surrounding a criminal trial and the subsequent punishment of criminals serves to educate the public as to the nature of right and wrong. This theory may be the strongest one for treating sports violence as a criminal act. By failing to treat violent acts as crimes simply because they take place in the limited area of sports, society is sending out a contradictory message and perhaps teaching the public, especially the younger public, that violent acts are permissible under certain circumstances.

NOTES

1. For more information on sports violence and criminal law, see Janine Young Kim and Matthew J. Parlow, "Off-Court Misbehavior: Sports Leagues and Private Punishment," 99 *Journal of Criminal Law and Criminology* 573 (2009) and Jeffrey Standen, "The Manly Sports: The Problematic Use of Criminal Law to Regulate Sports Violence," 99 *Journal of Criminal Law and Criminology* 619 (2009).

2. In 2007, former major leaguer Jose Offerman charged the mound while holding a bat in a minor league game. The pitcher ultimately suffered a broken finger and the catcher a concussion during the melee. Offerman was charged with two counts of assault and eventually give two years of probation. In 2010, while managing in the Dominican Winter League, Offerman punched an umpire. For this incident, Offerman was suspended from the Dominican Winter League for life.

3. In 2000, Marty McSorley of the NHL's Boston Bruins took a two-handed swing with his hockey stick to the right temple of Vancouver Canuck Donald Brashear, causing him to fall and hit his head on the ice. Brashear was carried off on a stretcher, blood flowing from his nose, and taken to a hospital, where he was diagnosed as having a concussion. Such examples of violent conduct might have resulted in prison sentences had they taken place outside the sporting arena. McSorley's criminal trial resulted only in probation.

4. Golden State Warrior Latrell Sprewell attacked his coach, P. J. Carlesimo, during a practice on December 1, 1997. In that attack, "between seven and ten seconds elapsed during which Sprewell had his hands around the Coach's neck." Carlesimo was not injured. Sprewell then left the court for "between ten and 20 minutes" and then returned for an apparent attempted second attack on Carlesimo. However, he was restrained before reaching the coach. The Warriors terminated Sprewell's contract and the nearly $25 million remaining on it, claiming they had "cause" to do so because of the assault. Commissioner David Stern suspended Sprewell from the NBA for one year and the players association appealed, calling the sanctions against Sprewell "arbitrary and capricious" and lacking "just cause." Arbitrator John D. Feerick overruled the Warriors and the NBA, holding that the Warriors must honor the final two years of Sprewell's contract or trade him. Feerick did, however, uphold the suspension for the remainder of the season (not the full calendar year Stern had imposed) and the player's resulting loss of $6.5 million in salary. He reasoned that the team's and league's dual penalties violated the principle of double jeopardy, and that league sanctions against more serious player violence had been less severe in the past. Specifically, assaults resulting in serious injuries had produced suspensions no longer than 26 games. Sprewell subsequently filed suit against the NBA and the Warriors in federal district court, seeking the $6.4 million in salary that he lost during his suspension. Sprewell was denied relief in *Sprewell v. Golden State Warriors*, 231 F.3d 520 (9th Cir. 2000). For more information, see Roger A. Javier, "You Cannot Choke Your Boss and Hold Your Job Unless You Play in the NBA: The Latrell Sprewell Incident Undermines Disciplinary Authority in the NBA," 7 *Villanova Sports and Entertainment Law Journal* 209 (2000). Also see section 11.3.14, "Grievance Procedures in Professional Sports."

5. In *Massachusetts v. Junta* (Middlesex [MA] Superior Court, 2002), a case involving violence between parents of athletes, a Massachusetts jury convicted Thomas Junta of involuntary manslaughter in the death of Michael Costin. In July 2000, the two fathers engaged in an argument during a youth hockey practice involving their 12-year-old sons. Junta alleged that Costin, the boys' coach, was allowing too much rough play. Junta and Costin scuffled on the ice before the fight was broken up and Junta was removed from the arena. However, Junta soon returned to the arena and attacked Costin outside the boys' locker room. In the ensuing brawl, Junta repeatedly punched Costin and slammed his head into the floor. The resulting injuries led to Costin's death. Junta was sentenced to 6 to 10 years in prison.

16.1.1. Defining a Crime

In order to apply criminal law sanctions for undesirable conduct, the act that will incur penalties must first be defined in a way that ensures predictability. This issue is especially difficult in the area of sports violence. Certain sports involve a great deal of physical contact and intimidation. Therefore, a certain amount of physical but legal contact may be considered part of the game. The problem is in drawing a neat and predictable line as to when an act goes beyond the scope of the game and becomes criminal in nature.

The crime of battery is the offense that most often applies to sports violence. Battery can be defined as an unlawful application of force to the person of another, resulting in bodily injury. The requirement that the battery be unlawful is the key to the exemption of sports-related batteries. Although the issue is often couched in such legal terms as "consent" or "assumption of risk," the crux of the problem in distinguishing sports violence from criminal acts is unlawfulness. Society has often exempted sports violence from criminal law by treating it as lawful.

For conduct to be criminal, most offenses require that there be an *actus reus* and a *mens rea*, a guilty act accompanied by a guilty mind. The elements of a criminal battery are (1) a guilty state of mind (*mens rea*), (2) an act (*actus reus*), (3) a physical touching or harming of the victim, and (4) causation—that is, the act must cause the touching or harm. The state of mind for criminal battery does not require actual intent. An extreme conscious disregard of known serious risks, called criminal negligence, will suffice. The criminal statutes in most states define some acts as aggravated battery and punish them as felonies. For example, the use of a deadly weapon or the causing of serious bodily injury is an example of aggravated battery. Interestingly, ordinary objects can qualify as deadly objects if they are used in a way that can cause death. Hockey sticks, baseballs, bats, and football helmets may qualify as deadly objects.

The violence that occurs in sports today clearly meets certain elements of battery in some cases. The unique factor is that the acts occur within the confines of athletics, which underscores the difficult issue of determining when an act within the confines of sports becomes a crime. The problem is that certain sports are extremely physical, and certain violent physical contact is condoned under the rules. Therefore, acts that are crimes on the streets become legal in the arena, because it is difficult to meet the legal definition of criminal battery.

A defendant in a criminal prosecution involving sports violence has two defenses available: consent and self-defense. Consent is not normally a defense to a criminal act. The general rule is that one cannot consent to be the victim of a crime, and this rule is true except for certain specific cases; those exceptions are crimes in which a lack of consent forms one of the elements of the crime.

Sports violence, especially the crime of battery, falls in a more difficult area to define compared with non–sports-related violence. Battery is not a crime that has lack of consent of the victim as an element, but in certain battery cases, the unlawful-application-of-force element is not present because of consent. A consent to application of force is not unlawful. The Model Penal Code (see note 1), Section 2.11, provides:

> When conduct is charged to constitute an offense because it causes or threatens bodily harm, consent to such conduct or to the infliction of such harm is a defense if: (a) the bodily harm consented to is not serious, or (b) the conduct and the harm are *reasonably foreseeable hazards* of joint participation in the *lawful* athletic contest or competitive sport [emphasis added].

The most difficult issue concerning the consent defense is drawing a line between reasonably foreseeable hazards that may be consented to and unforeseeable hazards that are not consented to. One of several different approaches on how to draw the line concerns looking at the normal violence associated with the sport.

This means defining the scope of consented-to physical contact in a particular sport so that a participant in that sport would not be deemed to consent to acts that go beyond the scope.

The rules-of-the-game test is an alternative approach to the consent issue. A participant-victim is not deemed to have consented to acts that are illegal under the rules of the sport. This is a much weaker standard that would reduce the types of violence subject to a successful consent defense. The rules-of-the-game approach is an easier test to apply.

Some courts apply a test that looks toward the seriousness of the injury for a solution. This is a simplistic approach which reasons that the victim cannot be said to have consented to a grave injury. Another approach is the reasonable foreseeability test, which is commonly used in the area of torts. Under this test, a participant would be held to have consented only to those acts of violence which were considered a reasonably foreseeable part of the sport.

Finally, it should be noted that, in addition to the above tests, the *assumption of risk doctrine* of tort law is often discussed in the area of consent to criminal acts. Assumption of risk is very similar to the consent defense. A participant in a contact sport assumes the risk of violent contact and consents to the contact. But any injury that is serious enough to raise the specter of criminal prosecution should exceed the risk assumed by the participant. Therefore, the assumption of risk doctrine does not really add any useful analysis to the problem of the consent defense of battery.

The second major defense to a charge of battery is *self-defense*. The nonaggressor in a violent incident may use a reasonable amount of force against the aggressor when there is reason to believe that immediate danger of harm is imminent and that the use of force is required to avoid this danger. In the area of sports violence, such a defense brings about several considerations. A successful showing of self-defense must prove that the force used by the nonaggressor was no greater than that used against him. Usually, for example, a case will involve escalating violence, such as when a hockey player punches an opponent and the opponent strikes back with his stick. This may cause some difficulty in determining when "reasonable force" has been used. Another problem is the requirement that the defendant have the honest belief that danger of immediate, serious, bodily injury is imminent. In many cases, the possibility of an honest belief is discredited because often the defendant provokes the attack, and this negates a self-defense argument. Finally, some jurisdictions would further limit the defense to those cases in which the defendant had no reasonable means of retreat. Therefore, a player who could have avoided seriously injuring another by breaking off the confrontation would not be able to plead self-defense.

Other factors can relieve a defendant of responsibility for a crime, even though they are not true defenses. Therefore, even though the prosecution proves each and every element of the crime charged, the defendant can escape punishment by showing that he acted in the heat of passion or was intoxicated. A person who acts as the result of an involuntary action may not have the mental element (*mens rea*) that is required under the definition of the crime.

The diminished responsibility theory has been used by the defense in criminal cases involving sports violence. Defense counsels in *Regina v. Maki*, *Regina v. Green*, and *State v. Forbes* raised the defense of involuntary action (see section 16.1.2, "Player-against-Player Violence," and notes). Each defendant argued that players received training in the skills and the mental attitude necessary for a successful hockey player. Because of this training, the defendant's actions were not voluntary but merely instinctual responses or reflex actions. The question in these cases was whether the action causing the injury was a normal or regular part of the game or whether it was an unreasonable response, considering the training each player had received.

NOTE _____

1. The common law system of dividing crimes into felonies and misdemeanors is gradually being replaced with newer systems based on statutes enacted by legislatures. Many of these newer systems are based on a model law called the Model Penal Code. The Model Penal Code recognizes criminal conduct that is considered less serious than crimes that are generally classified as offenses and violations. Although the Model Penal Code has not been widely accepted by all states, it is still the closest thing to a uniform U.S. criminal code. Approximately 22 states have adopted a variant of the Model Penal Code.

16.1.2. Player-against-Player Violence

One of the first incidents of professional sports violence to result in litigation occurred on August 22, 1965, in Candlestick Park, San Francisco. In the third inning, Juan Marichal, a pitcher for the San Francisco Giants, had thrown a pitch at Dodger Maury Wills's head, which caught the attention of the Dodgers' dugout, but nothing had ensued. In the bottom of the third inning, Marichal was at bat against Sandy Koufax of the Dodgers. After the second pitch to Marichal, John Roseboro, the Dodgers catcher, threw the ball back to the pitcher and either nicked Marichal's ear or came close to it. Marichal turned to Roseboro and asked him why he did that. Roseboro came out of his crouch with his fist clenched. Marichal raised his bat and quickly struck Roseboro at least twice on the top and side of the head, opening a two-inch gash. After the incident, National League President Warren Giles fined Marichal $1,750, a record at that time, and suspended him for nine days or eight playing dates. No criminal charges were filed. However, Roseboro filed a $110,000 damage suit against Marichal a week after the incident. After numerous legal delays, the suit finally settled out of court for $7,500 in 1970.

The comparable cases of player-against-player violence that have occurred since *Marichal* have often resulted in larger cash awards, multiple parties being sued, and criminal charges. However, the punishments for such violence, and the resulting awards, have varied drastically, depending on the legal jurisdiction and the league in which the violence occurred.

For example, in 1999 Wichita State University pitcher Ben Christensen noticed that the on-deck batter of the opposing team was "timing" his warm-up pitches, a supposed breach of baseball etiquette. Bothered by this, Christensen threw a ball at the on-deck batter, University of Evansville's Anthony Molina, who was standing 30 feet from home plate in the on-deck circle. The ball fractured Molina's skull, broke three bones in his eye socket, and resulted in lingering vision problems. Molina underwent three operations before playing again for Evansville in 2000. The district attorney's office investigated; however, no criminal charges were filed. Nevertheless, the pitcher's actions resulted in his being suspended for the remainder of the season; his pitching coach being suspended for the remainder of the season; and a $75,000 lawsuit against Christensen, the three umpires who worked the game, and Wichita State University (see section 3.6, "Vicarious Liability").

Football is an extremely physical sport and there are concerns about the violent behavior of its athletes, especially regarding off-the-field behavior (see section 16.1.5, "Off-the-Field Criminal Conduct"). In 2006, the longest suspension for an on-the-field incident in NFL history was given to Albert Haynesworth of the Tennessee Titans. Haynesworth stepped on the helmetless face of Dallas Cowboys center Andre Gurode with his cleat. Gurode suffered 7 lacerations to the face and received 30 stitches to the forehead. Neither criminal charges nor a civil lawsuit were filed against Haynesworth; however, the NFL suspended Haynesworth for five games and he was forced to forfeit more than $190,000 in salary.

Perhaps the most frequent and brutal acts have occurred in hockey, and one of the most infamous of these attacks was the case of *State v. Forbes*. The incident occurred in 1975 during a game between the Minnesota North Stars and the Boston Bruins (see note 7). In a case similar to *Forbes* in its brutality, 19-year-old winger Jesse Boulerice, a fifth-round pick of the Philadelphia Flyers in the 1996 draft, was charged with felony assault by the Wayne County, Michigan, prosecutors after striking another player in the face with his stick. The offense occurred during a first-period incident during game four of the Guelph Storm's sweep of the Whalers in the Ontario Hockey League's semifinals in 1999. The Storm's forward, Andrew Long, checked Boulerice into the boards. After a shoving match, Long skated off to rejoin the play; Boulerice caught up and, with a baseball-style swing of his stick, clubbed Long across the bridge of the nose. Long was knocked unconscious and went into convulsions on the ice. He suffered a broken nose and cheekbone, a 20-stitch gash, and a blood clot on his brain. Boulerice was ejected from the game and given a one-year suspension from the Ontario Hockey League. He eventually pled no contest to a reduced charge of aggravated assault and was sentenced to 90 days' probation. Several other hockey players have also faced criminal charges for their conduct on the ice (see notes 1, 2, 4, 8, and 9).

While it is difficult to convict an athlete for conduct during a game, it is not impossible. Criminal charges were filed against Todd Bertuzzi, a NHL player in 2004; however, the sentence handed out was criticized for its laxness. Vancouver Canucks forward Todd Bertuzzi seriously injured Colorado Avalanche center Steve Moore on March 8, 2004. Moore suffered several fractured vertebrae and facial lacerations after Bertuzzi hit Moore in the side of the head and repeatedly punched Moore in the face after he fell to the ice. The NHL suspended Bertuzzi for the rest of the season and was forbidden to play internationally during the 2004–2005 lockout. Bertuzzi pled guilty to assault causing bodily harm and received one year of probation (see note 1).

NOTES _____

1. Todd Bertuzzi was given one year of probation by a Canadian court after receiving a conditional discharge which stated that he had already received severe penalties by the NHL, after losing over $500,000 in salary. Moore subsequently filed a civil lawsuit against Bertuzzi and the Canucks, but the case was thrown out by the U.S. court, which said that the case should be tried in British Columbia. Another lawsuit has been filed in British Columbia by Moore against Bertuzzi and the Canucks, as well as a civil lawsuit by Moore's parents for infliction of emotional distress. All civil cases are pending.

2. In 2000, a Vancouver, British Columbia, provincial judge found Boston Bruin Marty McSorley guilty of assault with a weapon. Though McSorley avoided prison, he was sentenced to 18 months of probation. Earlier that year, McSorley had taken a two-handed swing with his hockey stick to the right temple of Vancouver Canuck Donald Brashear,

causing him to drop and hit his head on the ice. While McSorley and Brashear had fought earlier in the game, this hit occurred from behind and with less than 10 seconds to go in regulation time. Brashear was carried off on a stretcher, blood flowing from his nose, and taken to a hospital, where he was diagnosed with a concussion. McSorley claimed the hit was accidental. Judge William Kitchen rejected that defense, but justified the lack of a prison sentence by pointing out that McSorley had not earned any income since the incident due to his 23-game suspension and $72,000 fine imposed by the NHL. Kitchen also noted that McSorley had sizable attorney's fees.

3. In 1999 Neal Goss, a 15-year-old Illinois high school hockey player, was sent crashing into the boards at a skating rink by a cross-check from a player at a rival high school. Goss suffered permanent paralysis as a result of the contact. The Lake County state's attorney charged the perpetrator (whose identity was protected due to his age), also 15, with two counts of aggravated battery (both felonies), alleging that the perpetrator caused great bodily harm and that his hockey stick was a deadly weapon. The state's attorney claimed the incident occurred *after* the buzzer sounded to end the game, indicating an intent to harm. In 2000, the defendant entered an Alford plea (similar to a no-contest plea) to a lesser misdemeanor charge, and was sentenced to two years' probation and 120 hours of community service. In justifying the reduced sentence, Associate Judge John Radosevich stated, "11 million people [the population of Illinois] are in part responsible because we promote competitiveness and, frankly, aggressiveness....Everyone loves a winner, unless of course something goes haywire with the winning." Goss also filed a civil complaint—*Goss v. Illinois Hockey Officials Ass'n*, No. 99L-01386 (Ill. Cir. Ct.-Cook County, filed Dec. 8, 1999) against the referees and the league. Goss stated that the officials had ignored his complaints about illegal hits and abusive language from the defendant's team, and that these circumstances had led to the defendant's violent behavior. That civil case is pending.

4. *State of Washington v. Shelley*, Wash. Ct. App. 929 P.2d 489 (1997) is another case that shows how athletes, including amateur athletes, are not immune from criminal sanctions. During an intramural basketball game, Jason Shelley intentionally punched another player and broke his jaw. Shelley argued that the other player, who had a reputation as a rough player, was being physical and rough throughout the game. In upholding Shelley's conviction for assault in the second degree, the court of appeals held that while consent may be a defense to assault in athletic competitions, Shelley had failed to establish a factual basis for that defense. Consent is defined as contact that is contemplated within rules of the game. In this case, Shelley was unable to prove that the victim could consent to an intentional punch to the face, and that the action was, in some way, a natural part and within the rules of the game of basketball. If consent cannot be a defense to assault, then most athletic contests would need to be banned because many involve "invasions of one's physical integrity." However, since society has chosen to foster sports competitions, players necessarily must be able to consent to physical contact and other players must be able to rely on that consent when playing the game. This is the view adopted by the drafters of the Model Penal Code, which states: "[T]here are, however, situations in which consent to bodily injury should be recognized as a defense to crime....There is...the obvious case of participation in an athletic contest or competitive sport, where the nature of the enterprise often involves risk of serious injury. Here, the social judgment that permits the contest to flourish necessarily involves the companion judgment that reasonably foreseeable hazards can be consented to by virtue of participation" (Model Penal Code, supra, § 2.11 cmt. 2, at 396). The court in *Shelley* further held that, while the consent defense is not limited to conduct within the rules of the games, it is limited to conduct and harm that are a reasonably foreseeable hazard of joint participation in an athletic contest. Shelley's punch, the court of appeals concluded, was not a reasonably foreseeable hazard in the game of basketball, or even rugby or hockey. Therefore, Shelley's action was indefensible and constituted assault in the second degree.

5. In a 1997 heavyweight title fight in Las Vegas, boxer Mike Tyson, who was clearly trailing in the fight, made two attempts to bite the ear of his opponent, Evander Holyfield.

Tyson was warned after his first attempt, then disqualified after his second attempt, during which he successfully bit off part of Holyfield's ear. Reconstructive surgery was required following the match. Holyfield declined to file charges against Tyson. However, Tyson was fined $3 million plus legal costs by the Nevada State Athletic Commission, and had his boxing license revoked for one year.

6. In Italy during a hockey game, Jimmy Boni and another player, Miran Schrott, were scuffling in front of the net when Schrott punched Boni. Boni retaliated by slashing Schrott across the chest with his stick. Schrott fell to the ice and died of cardiac arrest. The Italian government charged Boni with manslaughter, which, if he was convicted, would carry a 10- to 18-year prison term. The charges were filed even though the slash did not look very serious and did not even merit a minor penalty during the game. Boni pled guilty to a reduced manslaughter charge and was fined $1,600. *New York Times*, February 17, 1994, p. B16.

7. In *State v. Floyd*, 466 N.W.2d 919 (Iowa Ct. App. 1990), a fight broke out during a basketball game, and the defendant, who was on the sidelines, punched and severely injured several opposing team members. Because neither the defendant nor his victims were voluntarily participating in the game, the consent defense did not apply because the statute "contemplated a person who commits acts during the course of play, and the exception seeks to protect those whose acts otherwise subject to prosecution are committed in furtherance of the object of the sport." The court noted that there is a "continuum, or sliding scale, grounded in the circumstances under which voluntary participants engage in sport...which governs the type of incidents in which an individual volunteers (i.e., consents) to participate."

8. In *People v. Freer*, 381 N.Y.S.2d 976 (N.Y. Dist. Ct. 1976), the victim was punched in the eye during a football game. The incident occurred after the victim had tackled the defendant and the play was over. The court held that, while initially it may be assumed that the first punch thrown by the complainant in the course of the tackle was consented to by the defendant, the act of tackling an opponent in the course of a football game may often involve contact that could easily be interpreted as a punch. The defendant's response cannot be mistaken or accepted. Clearly, the defendant intended to punch the complainant and there was no consent.

9. In *State v. Forbes*, No. 63280 (Minn. Dist. Ct. 1975), in December 1974, an NHL hockey game was played in Minnesota between the Boston Bruins and the Minnesota North Stars. Early in the first period, Henry Boucha, closely followed by David Forbes, chased a loose puck against the boards. Forbes proceeded to check Boucha, using his elbows as offensive weapons, as is commonly done by hockey players. After being elbowed, Boucha turned and knocked Forbes down. The referee penalized both players for a total of seven minutes. Once in their respective penalty boxes, they exchanged threats. Upon their return to the ice, Boucha had started to skate toward the North Stars' bench when Forbes said, "Okay, let's go now," and took a swing at Boucha. Forbes missed him with his hand but connected with his stick, just above Boucha's right eye. Boucha dropped to the ice, covering his injured face. Forbes then discarded his stick and gloves, jumped on top of Boucha, and proceeded to bang Boucha's head on the ice until Boucha was taken from the ice to the hospital, where 25 stitches were required to close the cut beside his right eye. When the patch was removed five days later, Boucha complained of double vision in the injured eye and underwent remedial surgery to repair a small fracture in the floor of the right eye socket. After hearing evidence about the incident, NHL Commissioner Clarence Campbell suspended Forbes for 10 games. Then, on January 15, 1975, Forbes was indicted by a Minnesota grand jury and charged with violating Minnesota statute, section 609.25, aggravated assault, which stated:

Subdivision 1. Whoever assaults another and inflicts great bodily harm may be sentenced to imprisonment for not more than 10 years or to payment of a fine of not more than $10,000.

Subdivision 2. Whoever assaults another with a dangerous weapon but without intent to inflict great bodily harm may be sentenced to imprisonment for not more than five years or to payment of a fine of not more than $5,000 or both.

At trial, the prosecution argued that Forbes had committed an aggravated assault on Boucha. The argument made was that criminal assault was a crime whether it was done in public or under game conditions. The defense argued a variation on the temporary insanity defense, basing its argument on the theory that from the age of four years, hockey players are taught not to let other players intimidate them. Coaches emphasize the need for physical violence against other players, and crowds cheer the sight of fighting and blood. The defense argued that given these circumstances, hockey, and not David Forbes, should be on trial. The trial ended in a nine-to-three hung jury in favor of the assault conviction. The prosecutor decided not to retry the case because he felt that the deep split in public opinion would make a required unanimous verdict virtually impossible.

10. In *Regina v. Maki*, 14 D.L.R.3d 164 (Ont P.C. 1970), Wayne Maki was charged with assault causing bodily harm after hitting Ted Green of the Boston Bruins with his stick during a game. The incident occurred when Maki and Green both went into the corner of the rink, chasing the puck. After some pushing and punching, Maki and Green started swinging their sticks. Green first struck Maki with his stick on the neck and shoulder. Maki then struck Green about the side of the head, causing serious injury. The court dismissed the charges, stating that it could not say beyond any doubt that Maki intended to injure Green, that Maki was not under reasonable apprehension of bodily harm, or that Maki used excessive force under the circumstances. Though it did not enter into the court's decision, the defense of consent was addressed by the court because it had been raised. The court said that no sports league, no matter how well organized or self-policed, could render its players immune from criminal prosecution. The court admitted that all players who step onto a playing field or an ice surface assume certain risks and hazards of the sport, and in most cases the defense of consent (assumption of the risks) would be applicable. However, no athlete should be presumed to accept malicious, unprovoked, or overtly violent attacks as part of playing sport.

11. In *Regina v. Green*, 16 D.L.R.3d 137 (Ont P.C. 1970), a case arose from the same incident as *Regina v. Maki* and involved criminal charges of common assault against Ted Green, who hit Maki with both his gloved hand and his stick. In dismissing the charges, the court found that in the course of a hockey game, a player does not examine each potential action to determine whether it is an assault. The roughness of the game has to permit certain actions that would be considered assault outside the confines of a NHL contest.

12. For additional instances of player-against-player violence, see Chapter 3, "Legal Principles in Tort Law"—in particular, sections 3.2, "The Tort of Reckless Misconduct (Gross Negligence)" and 3.3, "Intentional Torts."

16.1.3. Player and Fan Violence

Another area of concern for professional sport leagues is assaults involving players and fans. Players assaulting fans or fans assaulting players is nothing new. Hall of Fame baseball player Ty Cobb was suspended indefinitely after going into the stands to fight a heckler (who had lost both hands in an industrial accident) in 1912. At a game at Wrigley Field in Chicago in 2000, a Cubs fan grabbed the hat of Los Angeles catcher Chad Kreuter in the Dodgers' bullpen, instigating a wild brawl that spilled into the crowd. While no criminal charges were filed against the players, the incident led to Major League Baseball's suspension of 19 Dodger players, coaches, and officials for a total of 84 games.

A rare occurrence of players facing criminal charges in such circumstances occurred in 1980, when criminal and civil charges were filed against the Boston Bruins when all but two of the Bruins players entered the stands to engage in a general melee with some New York Rangers fans. All criminal and civil charges against the players and the Boston Bruins—*Guttenplan v. Boston Professional Hockey Ass'n., Inc.*, No. 80–415 (1981 U.S. Dist. LEXIS 10434 (S.D.N.Y. Jan. 19, 1981))—were later dropped after an investigation disclosed that the fans had instigated the fight by punching a Bruins player and throwing a stick at him. Criminal and civil charges were also filed in the case regarding the Pacers-Pistons brawl in 2004.

Like the Bruins-Rangers case, fans played a major role in this incident, as several fans fought with Pacers players. John Green, a fan and the only participant to receive jail time for the altercation, was found guilty of assault and battery and served 30 days in jail for throwing a cup at Ron Artest, which sparked Artest, Stephen Jackson, and David Harrison (all Pacers players) to go into the stands to fight with spectators. Nine players were ultimately suspended: Ron Artest (86 games), Stephen Jackson (30 games), Jermaine O'Neal (15 games), Ben Wallace (6 games), Anthony Johnson (5 games); Reggie Miller, Chauncey Billips, Elden Cambell, and Derrick Coleman received one game for leaving their benches. Twelve individuals were criminally charged, with charges ranging from assault and battery, felony assault, and trespassing. Anthony Johnson was given the most stringent penalty of all the athletes: 100 hours of community service, one year of probation, anger management counseling, and a one-year ban on alcohol.

It has been discussed that if athletes commit violent acts on the field, their criminal sentencing usually involves probation, not jail time. Critics argue that preferential treatment is being given to athletes, and had the athlete committed the act outside of the sporting venue, more serious consequences would have resulted. However, in September 2002, fans involved in violence against a coach were only given probation. Kansas City Royals coach Tom Gamboa was assaulted by an intoxicated fan, William Ligue Jr., and his 15-year-old son. Gamboa was tackled and repeatedly punched by the fans and suffered permanent hearing loss after the attack. Ligue Jr. was charged with two counts of aggravated battery and received 30 months' probation. His son was charged with two juvenile counts of assault and battery and received five years' probation. The judge, in arguing for a sentence of probation, said that probation must not be considered only as a slap on the wrist because Ligue Jr. would be labeled as a convicted felon for the rest of his life. Ligue Jr. later violated his parole and is currently serving an undisclosed period in prison.

Famously, the Philadelphia Eagles' former stadium, Veterans Stadium, had a municipal court in the stadium. The court gathered fans who violated the law and were arrested during the game, and had them tried and convicted in Veterans Stadium, all on the same day. Neither the Eagles' or Phillies' new stadiums have a court, and unruly behavior continues to be an issue in the famously fanatical Philadelphia. In 2010, police tasered a 17-year old who ran onto the field during a Phillies game. In another 2010 game, a 21-year old Phillies fan intentionally vomited on an 11-year old girl after a dispute with her father.

NOTES _____

1. Less than one year after the Gamboa attack, in April 2003 a fan tried to tackle umpire Laz Diaz during a game at Chicago's Comiskey Park. The fan, Eric Dybas, was found guilty of aggravated battery and was sentenced to 180 days in jail.

2. With about 3 miles to go in the men's marathon in the 2004 Athens Summer Olympics, a deranged fan grabbed the leader of the race, Vanderlie de Lima of Brazil. The fan pushed de Lima into the crowd until other fans pulled the fan off. An exhausted de Lima strained his right leg in the incident and finished in third.

3. In November 1999, during an NFL game in Denver, a group of fans began pelting the Oakland Raiders players with snowballs. Some of the snowballs were spiked with batteries. Charles Woodson, angry at being attacked, allegedly hurled a snowball that

struck a fan in the face. Another Raiders player, Lincoln Kennedy, went after a fan who had hit him in the face with a snowball. Woodson was charged with misdemeanor assault and Kennedy filed charges against the fan, whom he confronted after the game. In all, 8 people were arrested, 13 others were cited for misdemeanor assault and throwing objects, and 2 people had their season tickets revoked. *New York Times*, December 2, 1999, p. D6.

4. On September 24, 1999, in Milwaukee, a fan came onto the field and attacked Bill Spiers, the right fielder for the Houston Astros, by jumping Spiers from behind and knocking him to the ground. Spiers was removed from the game after suffering a welt under his left eye, a bloody nose, and whiplash. The fan was charged with two counts of battery (one for attacking Spiers and one for slugging a ground crew member who was defending the player) and one count of disorderly conduct.

5. On February 6, 1995, during a time-out, Vernon Maxwell of the Houston Rocket went up into the stands and punched a fan. Maxwell claimed that the fan used racial slurs and made derogatory remarks about his family, which the fan denied. This misconduct earned Maxwell a 10-game suspension, with a loss of $228,000 in salary plus a $20,000 fine by the NBA. No criminal charges were filed. If they had been, Maxwell could have been charged with simple assault, a misdemeanor punishable by a year in jail and a $2,500 fine.

16.1.4. Player-against-Official Violence

While athletes, coaches, and fans have always disputed calls by officials, there have been a growing number of cases where athletes, coaches, and fans assault officials because of the calls they make on the field. For example, during the 2008 Summer Olympics in Beijing, Cuban Taekwondo champion Angel Matos kicked the referee in the face and shoved a judge before being restrained by security. Matos was furious after being disqualified during the Bronze Medal match for taking too long to tend to an injury. Matos and his coach were both banned for life from the World Taekwondo Federation.

The first athlete to be arrested and charged with battery for striking an official during a professional sporting event in the United States was Allan Leavell, a guard for the Tulsa Fast Breakers of the Continental Basketball Association. According to the police report, the incident occurred on March 30, 1990, after the ball went out of bounds in front of the Tulsa bench. Referee Peter Quinn called the ball out on Tulsa. Leavell, who was in the game, came up to Quinn and began arguing with him. Leavell then struck Quinn on the neck with his left hand, knocking him down. Besides the criminal charges, Leavell was fined $5,000 and suspended by the CBA for two years.

In 1996, a high school wrestler head-butted a wrestling official during a match in Washington. The official was knocked unconscious for about 30 seconds. The wrestler was charged with fourth-degree assault and faced a maximum penalty of two years' probation and 30 days in jail. Also in 1996, a hockey referee was repeatedly punched in the head and body, and speared in the groin with a stick, after allowing a controversial goal that ended the hockey game between the University of Moncton and the University of Prince Edward Island.

Even when the offending players face criminal charges, as described above, the charges are usually minimal or dropped. While the lack of punishment received by the defendants in these cases might be due to their lack of criminal records, some argue that there is a lack of comprehensive and effective laws to take care of these types of situations. In fact, only 22 states have enacted statutes making it a criminal violation to assault a sports official (see note 1). On the professional sports level, leagues and players associations will usually encourage parties to resolve such conduct through their established grievance procedures, rather than allowing a case to proceed to trial (see section 11.3.14, "Grievance Procedures in Professional Sports").

NOTES

1. 22 states currently have legislation making it a criminal violation to assault a sports official. For more information see the National Association of Sports Officials at www.naso.org. The following is an example of a statute protecting sports officials:
Delaware Code Ann. Tit. 11, Section 614 provides:

a. Any person who intentionally causes physical injury to a sports official who is acting in the lawful performance of his duty shall be guilty of a Class A misdemeanor. Upon conviction of a second or subsequent offense under this section, such person shall be guilty of a Class G felony.

b. For the purposes of this section, the words "sports official" shall mean any person who serves as a referee, umpire, linesman, or in any similar capacity in supervising or administering a sports event, and who is registered as a member of a local, state, regional or national organization which provides training or educational opportunities for sports officials.

Other states that have enacted protective legislation for sports officials include: Alabama [Section 13A-11-8], Arkansas [Ann. Section 5-13-209], California [Section 243.8], Delaware [Section 1: 614 Title 11], Florida [Section 784.081], Georgia [Statute 16-5-23], Idaho [State No. 32], Illinois [HB4023 Section 5], Kentucky [1.KRS 508.025], Louisiana [Ann. Section 14-34-4], Minnesota [Charter 128C.08 Subdivision 2], Montana [Ann. Section 45-5-211], Nevada [Bill No. 474], New Jersey [Ann. 2C: 44-1], New Mexico, North Carolina [Section 14-33(b)(9)], Oklahoma [Ann. 21, Section 650.1], Oregon, Pennsylvania [Ann. Section 2712], Texas [H.B. No. 716], Washington [Res. 2003-4636], and West Virginia [Section 61-2-159].

2. In 2000, Carl Everett of the Boston Red Sox was suspended 10 games for head-butting umpire Ron Culpa. Everett had accused Culpa of "showing him up" after Culpa demonstratively told him to keep his feet inside the batter's box.

3. In 1999, during a soccer game in South Africa, a referee shot and killed a player in front of 600 spectators, after the player, angry over a disputed goal, lunged at him with a knife. The shooting happened after some fans ran onto the field to protest the goal, which had cut the home team's lead to 2–1. The manager of the home team attributed the violence that occurs during many games, especially among heavy-drinking spectators, to the gambling on the township teams.

4. A prominent case in the NFL occurred in 1999, when Cleveland Browns' lineman Orlando Brown shoved referee Jeff Triplette to the ground after Triplette accidentally threw a flag into Brown's eye. Brown was suspended from December 1999 until March 2000 for the offense. Subsequently, Brown sued the NFL for $200 million in damages, for negligence in failing "to properly supervise and enforce rules that flags be properly weighted and thrown in a proper fashion." Brown claimed that "he still feels pain in the eye and sees white flashes when he exerts himself." While Brown was one of the highest-paid NFL linemen at the time of the injury, he was unable to find employment or acquire endorsements after the incident.

5. For more information on legal concerns of sports officials, see James A.R. Nafziger, "Avoiding and Resolving Disputes During Sports Competition: Of Cameras and Computers," 15 *Marquette Sports Law Review* 13 (2004) and David Paulo, *Human Rights in Youth Sport* (New York: Greengate Publishing, 2004). Also see section 4.7, "Liability of Officials, Referees, and Umpires."

16.1.5. Off-the-Field Criminal Conduct

The arrest or investigation of an athlete, whether at the high school, collegiate, or professional level, is always a newsworthy event. For example, in 2010 the two-time Super Bowl winning quarterback of the Pittsburgh Steelers, Ben Roethlisberger, was investigated in Milledgeville, Georgia for the possible sexual assault of a 20-year college student. Ultimately the district attorney announced no charges would be filed because he did not believe he had enough evidence to prove guilt beyond a reasonable doubt.

When athletes are arrested for off-the-field conduct, a number of problems arise. For example, can or should an organization punish an athlete before he is convicted of the crime? If it does not punish the athlete, the organization is seen as condoning criminal conduct and just interested in winning games. However, if the athlete is punished and forced to miss games, what does that do to the notion that everyone is innocent until proven guilty? Another problem arises when an organization attempts to keep information from the media; to protect its image, an organization may try to control any information that is released to the public. This sometimes tends to make the organization look like it is hiding information and protecting criminals. Finally, collective bargaining agreements sometimes limit the amount of punishment that a league or team can impose on a player for off-the-field conduct. For example, the maximum penalty that the NFL may impose on a player for his first substance-related guilty or no-contest plea is a four-game suspension without pay.

However, following a 2006 season plagued by off-the-field criminal conduct, a new player conduct policy was implemented by the new commissioner of the NFL, Roger Goodell. Both the NFL Players Association and owners agreed that a new conduct policy was necessary, as the flood of arrests of NFL players led to a tarnished reputation of NFL athletes. During the 2006 season, nine Cincinnati Bengals players were arrested in nine months for charges ranging from drunken driving, resisting arrest, possession of marijuana, and spousal battery. Tennessee Titans defensive back Pacman Jones was also involved with at least 10 criminal incidents while an NFL player and as a result was suspended for the entire 2007 season for his long history of criminal conduct. Since then several players have faced lengthy suspensions (see note 10). However, player conduct for criminal convictions is not specifically outlined in the current NFL collective bargaining agreement (CBA), an issue of significant debate (see note 10).

The NBA, however, does have in place a specific policy in its CBA that outlines the actions of the league if a player is charged with a violent felony. Section 7 of Article VI of the NBA CBA states, "When a player is convicted of (including a plea of guilty, no contest, or no lo contender to) a violent felony, he shall immediately be suspended by the NBA for a minimum of ten (10) games." Section 8 also outlines that if an athlete engages in off-the-court violence, he is required to receive an evaluation by a medical professional and may be recommended for counseling.

NOTES

1. During the 2009–2010 Washington Wizards guard Gilbert Arenas it was discovered that Arenas had kept firearms in his locker at the Verizon Center and brandished a weapon towards teammate Javaris Crittenton after a gambling dispute. Arenas was suspended for the remainder of the season, charged with carrying a pistol without a license and sentenced to two years probation and 30 days in a halfway house.

2. In 2007, Ugueth Urbina, former Major League Baseball pitcher was sentenced to 14 years in prison in Venezuela for the attempted murder of five individuals who worked on his Venezuelan ranch.

3. After pleading no contest to assault and battery charges after the Pistons-Pacers brawl of 2004, Ron Artest was again in legal trouble when he was arrested on charges of four misdemeanor counts after a domestic violence dispute with his wife in March 2006. The charges included battery and corporal injury to a spouse, false imprisonment, and dissuading a witness from reporting a crime. Artest was at first suspended indefinitely by the Sacramento Kings, but only sat out two games. His criminal charges are pending.

4. Stephen Jackson of the Golden State Warriors was found by a judge in January 2007 to be in violation of his parole, after firing a gun outside of an exotic dancing club. His parole violation stemmed from his no-contest plea to misdemeanor assault and battery charges for his conduct during the Pacers-Pistons brawl of 2004. Jackson may face jail time and a suspension by the league. Jackson's court case is still ongoing.

5. Professional coaches have also been involved in criminal misconduct off the field. During the 2006 NFL season, Detroit Lions defensive line coach Joe Cullen was suspended for two games, one game by the Lions and one by the league. His suspension was for Cullen's two arrests during the preseason for drunken driving and nude driving misdemeanor charges. Cullen later pled no contest to disorderly conduct and received a court fine of $1,600. The league's suspension of one game was complemented with a $20,000 fine for "conduct detrimental to the league." The NFL's action shows how leagues can implement even stricter penalties than the court system based conduct articles of the CBA.

6. Eric Musselman, head coach of the NBA's Sacramento Kings, was suspended for two games by the NBA for an October 2006 arrest for driving under the influence. Musselman pled no contest to the charge and was fined $580 by the court.

7. One of the biggest stars in the NBA, Kobe Bryant, was charged with sexual assault in 2001. The accuser, Katelyn Faber, also sued Bryant in civil court for engaging in non-consensual sexual conduct. Criminal charges were dropped against Bryant almost two years later, after the accuser failed to cooperate in the court proceedings. The civil case was settled out of court for an undisclosed amount and Bryant was never suspended by the NBA.

8. In 2000, Rae Carruth a wide receiver with the Carolina Panthers was convicted of conspiracy to commit murder by ordering the 1999 drive-by shooting of his pregnant girlfriend. Carruth was sentenced to a minimum of 18 years and 11 months in prison.

9. A 1998 study estimated that 21% of NFL players have adult criminal records. While the NFL disputes that statistic, it nonetheless contends with negative perceptions due to the publicity of high-profile murder trials such as Rae Carruth's, not to mention numerous sexual assault and drunk driving arrests. To deter player misconduct, the NFL in March 1997 introduced a new violent crime policy as part of a larger plan to prevent criminal behavior. Any athlete charged with a violent crime is required to undergo counseling. If convicted, the player is subject to a fine or suspension without pay. A second conviction mandates a longer suspension and possibly banishment. The amount of the fine and length of suspension are up to the commissioner. The 21% statistic is from Jeff Benedict and Don Yaeger, *Pros and Cons: The Criminals Who Play in the NFL* (New York: Warner Books, 1998).

10. Among the players to be suspended under the NFL's new personal conduct policy are Roethlisberger (6 games), Chris Henry (8 games), Tank Johnson (8 games), Michael Vick (18 games) and Plaxico Burress (indefinite during prison term). For more on this issue, see Matthew J. Parlow, "Professional Sports League Commissioners' Authority and Collective Bargaining," 11 *Texas Review of Entertainment & Sports Law* 179 (2010) and Marc Edelman, "Are Commissioner Suspensions Really Any Different from Illegal Group Boycotts? Analyzing Whether the NFL Personal Conduct Policy Illegally Restrains Trade," 58 *Catholic University Law Review* 631 (2009).

16.1.6. Solutions to the Problem of Sports Violence

There are two general methods for reducing the amount of athlete violence, particularly at the professional sports level: league control and government regulation. The following subsections will examine the advantages and disadvantages of each method.

16.1.6.1. Governing Body Control

While a few courts have prosecuted criminal activity that occurs within the scope of an athletic event, many other violent acts have gone unpunished. Many courts are overburdened and will defer to a league's willingness to handle a matter internally. Likewise, the leagues and players associations will always prefer that matters of player violence be handled internally. For example, after the afore-mentioned McSorley incident, the NHL implored Vancouver authorities to allow the league to handle the matter through its grievance procedure. Nevertheless, Vancouver authorities saw the assault against Brashear as a matter that clearly belonged in the courts. Regarding the Bertuzzi incident, criminal charges and league suspensions were offered to Bertuzzi after he seriously injured Steve Moore.

However, in handing down its decision for only offering Bertuzzi one year of parole, the court cited that the league's suspension of Bertuzzi for the remainder of the 2003–2004 season and barring him from international competition during the 2004–2005 lockout were already serious consequences. Along with Bertuzzi's loss of over $500,000 in salary and endorsements, the Canadian court minimized Bertuzzi's penalty in order to complement it with his league-sponsored discipline. As the following cases demonstrate, there are both advantages and disadvantages when the league or athletic organization acts to control violent behavior internally.

The first advantage of league or athletic sanctions is that the league and its officials are familiar with the rules and customs of their sport. Because of this familiarity, the leagues are better able to determine what types of aggressive behavior or acts are reasonably foreseeable hazards or acceptable conduct and which acts are unreasonable. Another benefit of internal league controls is the speed and certainty with which players are punished. In punishing violent behavior, internal controls are faster (usually within a few days) and more uniform and predictable.

Severe internal league control was coupled with criminal charges in the case of MLB pitcher Kenny Rogers. In 2005, Rogers shoved two cameramen before a Texas Rangers game, causing one to go to the hospital for treatment. Rogers was suspended by MLB for 20 games and was fined $50,000, making it the longest on-field conduct suspension since 1988. Like the Bertuzzi case, the sport league's strict action may have led to more lenient court action, as Rogers's original Class A misdemeanor assault charge was changed to a Class C charge, for which Rogers had to only take anger management classes (see note 1).

Following a 2006 brawl between the University of Miami and Florida International University football teams, no criminal charges were filed. Both benches cleared in the closing seconds of the contest, causing punches to be thrown and a player using his helmet as a weapon to fight an opponent. Thirty-one players were suspended for the incident by their respective schools—13 from Miami and 18 from Florida International University.

NOTES _____

1. Rogers's actions also led to a civil suit by Larry Rodriguez, the cameraman who was sent to the hospital. The personal injury suit was against both Rogers and the Rangers, stating that both parties did nothing to stop Rogers's behavior, as he had a history of anger against the media. The suit was later settled for an undisclosed amount.

16.1.6.2. Government Regulation

Critics of sports violence argue that there is too much violence in sports, and because of the ineffectiveness of both league disciplinary rules and criminal sanctions in preventing needless violence, the best and remaining solution would be to promulgate legislation. In the United States, these proposals have had little success, except in the area of violence against officials (see section 16.1.4, "Player-against-Official Violence"). However, bills to police sport violence have failed at both the federal and state levels (see notes).

NOTES _____

1. In 1991 the state of Massachusetts unsuccessfully tried to establish a law to provide penalties for assault and battery committed by athletes during professional sporting events.

2. The Sports Violence Arbitration Act of 1983 was introduced in the 98th Congress by Congressman Thomas A. Daschle of South Dakota. The bill would have established an arbitration board as an independent disciplinary body to handle sports violence incidents. However, the bill died from lack of support. The bill was intended to allow the professional leagues to control incidents of excessive violence more effectively without direct intervention by the federal government. Instead of a federal criminal statute, such as the proposed Sports Violence Act (see note 3), the Sports Violence Arbitration Act required each professional league to establish an arbitration panel that would have had the power to punish teams and players for conduct found to be inconsistent with the competitive goals of the sports. Proposed sanctions against the guilty player's team included payment of the injured player's salary and medical expenses, payment of compensatory damages if the player's career had ended, and/or payment of damages or relinquishment of a draft choice to the injured player's club for loss of the player's services—as well as fines. The guilty player would have been subjected to a severe fine and lengthy suspension at the discretion of the arbitration board. The act provided for a full evidentiary hearing process. The sponsor of the bill believed that its positive impact on the level of violence in professional sports would have great influence on play at the amateur level.

3. One major proposal in this area was the Sports Violence Act, introduced by Congressman Ronald M. Mottl before the House of Representatives in both 1980 (H.R. 7903) and 1981 (H.R. 2263). The bill never made it to the floor of the house, and Congressman Mottl was not reelected in 1982. The act would have made it a criminal offense for a professional athlete to engage in excessive violence. Under the act, a player who "knowingly uses excessive physical force and thereby causes a risk of significant bodily injury to another person involved in that event" could be punished. Excessive physical force was defined as that which was unreasonably violent, had no reasonable relationship to the game, and could not have been reasonably foreseen or consented to. A federal criminal statute covering sports violence was seen as necessary because of the interstate nature of modern professional sports leagues and the lack of enforcement of criminal statutes by the states where professional athletes were involved in behavior that could be classified as a crime. Local assault and battery prosecutions, based on common-law notions of crime, had no relevance to the issues of sports violence because of the special problems of assumption of risk, consent, and self-defense that are present in sports cases.

16.2. ILLEGAL GAMBLING

The problems associated with illegal gambling and the influence it may exert on sporting events are of special concern for athletic administrators and others, because gambling affects the integrity of the games, the games themselves, and public confidence in athletes and sports. Some argue that betting on games is encouraged by the press, which prints the spread (expected margin of victory for the favored team) of games and the odds in its sports pages, as well as advertisements for weekly tip sheets and betting aids. Although some contend that betting on athletics is enjoyable and is a form of entertainment, others contend that gambling has a negative impact on society and sports For example, a 2003 study conducted by the NCAA's National Study on Collegiate Sports Wagering and Associated Health Risks surveyed 21,000 student-athletes concerning gambling. The research revealed that 35% of men student-athletes had wagered on sports in the past year, and 10% of women student-athletes engaged in similar behavior. The study also stated that Division III athletes are most likely to bet on sports, followed by Division II; Division I athletes were least likely to bet (see note 2). According to a 2000 University of Michigan study of 640 NCAA referees and officials, 40% admitted to gambling on sports, and 2% knew of officials who had called a game inaccurately due to gambling interests (see note 1).

The following sections examine the dangers of illegal gambling on athletics and the steps athletic administrators and organizations have taken to preserve the integrity of their sports. Although illegal gambling is a major problem for both intercollegiate and professional sports, they will be treated separately due to the unique legal problems each area presents.

NOTES

1. Also, according to the 2000 University of Michigan study of 640 NCAA referees and officials, 0.8% were rated as "pathological gamblers" and 2.2% had used a bookie. See Geralda Miller/Associated Press, "Study: NCAA Gambling Officials Admit to Gambling, Using Bookies," *Detroit News*, March 30, 2000.

2. To view the 2003 NCAA study online, see www.ncaapublications.com.

16.2.1. Intercollegiate Athletics and Gambling

Over the years, gambling on intercollegiate athletics has steadily increased, most notably with the significant amount of money that is currently being wagered on the NCAA men's Division I basketball tournament. However, very little of that is *legal* betting, and for every dollar bet legally in the United States, approximately $150 is bet illegally (see note 1). Problems associated with and arising from wagering have continually plagued college athletics. The problem of greatest concern to the NCAA and legal authorities is the practice of point shaving. Point shaving occurs when athletes are paid to score fewer points than they otherwise would, so that the point differential is less than the predicted spread. Less frequently, players are paid to lose a game outright. In 1945, five Brooklyn College basketball players were expelled from school after they admitted to accepting bribes to lose a game. In 1951, 32 players at seven schools were caught shaving points in 86 games. A gambling scandal at Boston College during the 1978–1979 season led to the conviction of the basketball player Rick Kuhn, who was sentenced to 10 years in prison on federal gambling charges (see note 6). In 1985, a gambling and drug scandal was uncovered at Tulane University. That incident, which involved a number of basketball players, led to Tulane President Eamon Kelly's decision to drop the Division I men's basketball program "forever." However, just four years later, in 1989, the program was revived for competition in the Metro Conference. In the 1990s, prominent point-shaving scandals occurred at Arizona State University and Northwestern University (see exhibit 16.1).

The NCAA prohibits the participation in any form of legal or illegal sports gambling because of its potential to undermine the integrity of sports contests and jeopardize the welfare of the student-athlete and the intercollegiate athletics community. The NCAA's disapproval of illegal gambling on intercollegiate athletics is clearly spelled out in the following bylaw:

10.3 GAMBLING ACTIVITIES

Staff members of the athletics department of a member institution and student-athletes shall not knowingly:

a. Provide information to individuals involved in organized gambling activities concerning intercollegiate athletics competition;
b. Solicit a bet on any intercollegiate team;
c. Accept a bet on any team representing the institution;
d. Solicit or accept a bet on any intercollegiate competition for any item (e.g., cash, shirt, dinner) that has tangible value; or
e. Participate in any gambling activity that involves intercollegiate athletics or professional athletics, through a bookmaker, a parlay card, or any other method employed by organized gambling. (*2009–2010 NCAA Manual*, Bylaw 10.3)

The NCAA has continued to add to its investigative staff to keep up with the gambling problem. Many NCAA investigators are former FBI agents who attempt to maintain contacts with bookmakers, both in Nevada, where sports gambling is legal, and in states where it is not. This unorthodox relationship between bookmakers and NCAA investigators is based on mutual concern that sporting events not be rigged to reach a predetermined outcome. The bookmakers cannot afford a rigged game for economic reasons, because their winning percentages and profit margins are based on a point spread, which they formulate on the theory that the game is not rigged. The NCAA and the individual schools' concerns are based on the integrity of the game and on their reputations. The bookmakers usually alert investigators if there is a sizable change in the point spread on a particular game. Such a change is suspicious, and may indicate that bettors have placed large wagers on a team. Of course, heavy betting may occur for other reasons, such as a coach's announcement of an injury to a key player. If no legitimate reasons are found, however, it increases the possibility that gamblers have fixed the game by bribing a coach, player, or official. Remember, bribes are not necessarily made to ensure that a team loses—just that it wins by fewer points than the predicted point spread. Once suspicions are aroused, college officials, such as the president and athletic director, are informed by the NCAA. They may also be notified if investigators hear street talk about suspicious activity taking place in the institution's athletic program.

NOTES _____

1. "In 1996, Congress created a National Gambling Impact Study Commission and asked it to report on the effect of betting on the nation. In November 1998, commissioners were told that illegal sports betting takes in as much as $380 billion annually, dwarfing the $2.4 billion bet legally on sports in Nevada."

Exhibit 16.1
NCAA Gambling Chronology

Year	Institution	Description
1951	Several	Thirty-two players from seven institutions were implicated in a gambling scheme designed to fix 86 games. Co-captains of the Manhattan College basketball team were arrested for attempting to fix a game against DePaul. Three members of the CCNY basketball team that won the National Collegiate Athletic Association (NCAA) and NIT Championships, along with several other individuals, were arrested in a game-fixing scandal that involved a number of teams. In this same year, basketball players from Long Island and Bradley University were caught taking bribes from gamblers.
1961	St. Joseph's University (PA)	The NCAA forced St. Joseph's to relinquish its third place finish in the NCAA basketball tournament because of alleged student-athlete involvement with a gambler.
1962	Several	Thirty-seven players from 22 institutions, including legendary New York playground hero Connie Hawkins, then at the University of Iowa, were implicated in a major gambling scandal that resulted in the arrest and conviction of three gamblers charged with fixing college basketball games. Former Columbia University player Jack Molinas served five years in prison for his role in the scandal.
1981	Boston College	Five basketball players were found guilty of shaving points during the 1978–1979 season. The players, along with organized crime figure Henry Hill and New York gambler Richard "the Fixer" Perry, fixed nine Boston College games. Rick Kuhn, the only player convicted, served two and a half years in prison for his part in the conspiracy.
1985	Tulane University	Four members of the basketball team were accused of shaving points in exchange for cash and cocaine. In the aftermath of the incident, the university suspended the program for five years.
1989	Florida and Arkansas	Four Florida football players were suspended for betting on football games, and nine athletes from four different sports at Arkansas were suspended for betting on college football games.
1990	North Carolina State	It was alleged that four players on the basketball team conspired with bookmakers to shave points. Although the players denied the charges and no charges were filed, the controversy and allegations of academic improprieties led to the dismissal of head coach Jim Valvano.
1992	Maine, Rhode Island, and Bryant College	Nineteen athletes from the Maine football and basketball teams were suspended for their participation in a gambling operation. Rhode Island and Bryant College athletes were also discovered to be involved in gambling operations.
1994	Northwestern University	The starting running back was suspended for gambling, though he denied intentionally fumbling on the goal line in a game against the University of Iowa.

**Exhibit 16.1
(continued)**

Year	Institution	Description
1995	Maryland	Basketball and football players (including the starting quarterback) were suspended for betting on college sports.
1996	Boston College	Thirteen football players were suspended for betting on college football, professional football, and baseball games. Three of those suspended were alleged to have bet against their own team.
1997	Arizona State University	Two former members of the basketball team admitted to shaving points during the 1993–1994 season. According to law enforcement officials, more money was wagered in the Arizona State case than in any point-shaving scam in the history of intercollegiate athletics. Star player Steven "Hedake" Smith was sentenced to a year in prison for his role. Prosecutors claimed Smith fixed games in order to pay off a $10,000 gambling debt to the scheme's master-mind, Benny Silman, who was sentenced to 46 months in prison.
1998	Northwestern University and Notre Dame University	Former basketball players were indicted on charges of shaving points, conspiring to fix games, and accepting bets during the 1994–1995 season. The scheme was masterminded by Notre Dame kicker Kevin Pendergast, who spent two months in prison.
2000		U.S. Representatives Lindsey Graham (South Carolina) and Tim Roemer (Indiana) introduced a bill to ban gambling on college and amateur sporting events. The bill was largely denounced due to legal gambling's small share of the total gambling problem.
2001	Florida	Basketball player Teddy Dupay was declared ineligible for his senior season when he admitted to violating team rules by gambling on college sports.
2003	Washington and Florida State	Football head coach Rick Neuheisel was fired for participating in NCAA March Madness pools. It was determined that a school official told Neuheisel that his participation in the pool was acceptable and Neuheisel won a $4.5 million settlement from Washington. Starting quarterback at Florida State, Adrian McPherson, was charged for gambling on professional and college football games and was sentenced to a work camp.
2007	Toledo	Six former football and basketball players were accused of shaving points in exchange for gifts and cash.

2. For more information on gambling in intercollegiate athletics, Ronald J. Rychlak, "A Bad Bet: Federal Criminalization of Nevada's Collegiate Sports Book," 4 *Nevada Law Journal* 320 (2004) and see Charley Rosen, *Scandals of '51: How the Gamblers Almost Killed College Basketball* (New York: Seven Stories Press, 1999).

3. Pursuant to the passage of the 1992 Professional and Amateur Sports Protection Act (PASPA), 28 USC Sec. 3701, Nevada is the only place in the country where sports betting is

legal. The PASPA did allow for the continuation of a sports lottery in Oregon and a hybrid form of sports betting in Montana and Delaware.

4. Nevada, the only state in the nation to allow legal sports gambling, does not permit betting on college games involving public or private institutions located in the state. The regulation was enacted in 1972 by the Nevada Gaming Control Board.

5. In *United States v. Burke*, 700 F.2d 70 (2d Cir. 1983), Rick Kuhn, a former Boston College basketball player, was charged (along with four codefendants) and convicted of racketeering by conspiring to fix at least six games, of sports bribery, and of violation of the Interstate Travel and Aid to Racketeering statutes. In sentencing Kuhn to a 10- year sentence, the court noted:

> The crimes in this case are especially significant in view of the ramifications which they have had on the world of sports, college basketball in particular. A group of gamblers and career criminals were able to band together and successfully bribe and influence college athletes.
>
> Their motivation was simple and clear—financial gain. The crime, however, reminds millions of sports fans that athletics can be compromised and are not always merely honest competition among dedicated athletes. While it is true that only one or possibly two athletes were compromised, the effect remains basically the same. Every college athlete may now come under suspicion by fans and coaches. This suspicion has existed previously due to earlier scandals dating back several years, and it is now renewed as a result of this offense. This 26-year-old defendant undoubtedly assumed one of the more essential roles in this offense. While it may be true that his performance during games was not particularly pivotal, his actions away from the basketball court are of significant importance. He was a member of the 1978–79 Boston College team who initially agreed to participate and thereafter recruited other players, maintained contact with the gamblers and accepted their payments. It is interesting to note that there was not testimony introduced at the trial which indicated a reluctance on the part of the defendant to participate (in point shaving) or a desire to terminate his involvement. Rather, he emerges as somewhat of a greedy individual who was more interested in collecting money from his criminal associates than he was in winning basketball games. The defendant is a product of a stable and supporting working-class family. From a young age, he developed natural abilities in athletics and was essentially successful in signing a professional baseball contract in 1973 and in attending college on a basketball scholarship three years later. Various individuals who have been [associated] with the defendant in his hometown of Swissville, Pennsylvania, have described him in very positive terms. The reasons therefore as to why he became involved in this offense remain unclear. On final analysis, deterrence emerges as the most important sentencing objective. A strong argument can be offered that the substantial term of incarceration imposed on this defendant will be recalled in the future by another college athlete who may be tempted to compromise his performance.

16.2.2. Professional Sports and Gambling

The success of the professional sports industry hinges on maintaining a high level of integrity so that the viewing public has no doubt about the outcome of the event. If people were to believe that there was a connection between the teams and the players and organized gambling, the integrity of the game could be damaged. Therefore, any connection to gambling raises serious concerns. For example, when Major League Baseball was in the process of approving the Walt Disney Company as the controlling owner of the Anaheim Angels, the league sought and received assurances from Disney that it would not have gambling on its cruise ships.

The connection between gambling and professional sports is not a recent occurrence in the United States. The decision to appoint the first commissioner of baseball, Kennesaw Mountain Landis, was a direct result of the Chicago "Black Sox" fix of the

1919 World Series. *The Imperfect Diamond*, by Lee Lowenfish and Tony Lupien, recalls how Landis was appointed because of the public uproar over the scandal:

> The tale of the "Black Sox" scandal has been memorably told by Eliot Asinof in *Eight Men Out*. Asinof observed how the closing of the racetracks during World War I had led the professional gamblers to flock to the ball parks. The owners did little to watch out for irregularities. Key contacts between gamblers and players were made easily....
>
> In late June 1921, seven of the accused fixers of the 1919 World Series went on trial in a Chicago courtroom. Public sympathy was rising for the players—victims of Charles Comiskey's stinginess. "The magnates led the public to believe that the ballplayers got about $10,000 a year...when they got as little as $2,600," defense attorney Ben Short declared to the jury. "At the end of the season, they have nothing left but a chew of tobacco, a glove, and a few pairs of worn-out socks."
>
> It was a strange trial. The owners recognized that airing the game's dirty linen was not in their best interests. Therefore, they decided to provide good attorneys to aid in the players' defense. Later, baseball would punish its sinners by extralegal weapons in its arsenal.
>
> Powerful New York gambler Arnold Rothstein, deeply implicated in the scandal as the man who gave the go-ahead, greatly helped the owners' strategy by arranging for the theft of the players' confessions from the Chicago district attorney's office. Unable to use its most damning evidence in the trial, the prosecution was doomed. On August 2, 1921, the jury acquitted all the players.
>
> Some of the Black Sox dreamed of reinstatement for the duration of the 1921 season. Commissioner Landis, in office since March, quickly crushed that hope. He pronounced, "Regardless of the verdict of juries, no player that entertains proposals or promises to throw a game; no player that sits in a conference with a bunch of crooked players and gamblers where the ways and means of throwing games are discussed, and does not promptly tell his club about it, will ever play professional baseball" (Lowenfish and Lupien, *The Imperfect Diamond* [New York: Stein & Day, 1980], pp. 96, 103–104).

Ever since the Black Sox scandal, baseball has been extremely sensitive to the issue of gambling. In baseball, the general policy is that baseball owners, officers, directors, and employees cannot own or work for any legalized gambling entities, including casinos and racetracks. However, while the leagues have taken very firm stands against players and their involvement in gambling (see note 2), that has not always been the case with owners. For example, at the same time Bowie Kuhn was banning Willie Mays and Mickey Mantle from baseball (see note 2(c)), George Steinbrenner, owner of the Yankees, was able to keep his interest in the Tampa Downs racetrack in Florida. Baseball has since changed its rules to prohibit its owners from owning any interests in gambling operations, and did suspend Steinbrenner in 1990 for his involvement with former gambler Howard Spira during the 1980s.

A multimillion-dollar sports betting bust involving several high-profile NHL player suspects occurred in 2006, when former player and assistant coach of the Phoenix Coyotes Rick Tocchet and two others were charged with taking millions of dollars in bets on sports. The gambling ring reportedly involved Wayne Gretzky's wife as a potential bettor. Tocchet was immediately put on indefinite leave by the Coyotes and is currently waiting on charges of bookmaking. Two others have pled guilty to bookmaking charges in order to receive reduced sentences for implicating Tocchet. Supposedly, no bets were made on hockey; however, the charges have hurt the NHL's reputation and have put coaches more in the spotlight regarding their off-the-rink behavior.

The NBA, the NFL, and the NHL all allow their owners to own legal gambling operations as long as they are not involved in any activity that includes taking bets on league games. The leagues have no prohibition on their owning racetracks or casinos as long as all league games are removed from the betting boards. For example, the NFL allowed Edward DeBartolo, Jr., then owner of the five-time Super Bowl champion San Francisco 49ers, to pursue gambling licenses even though it bans coaches, players, and other personnel from making promotional appearances involving casinos and gambling cruises. However, in 1997 DeBartolo was forced to give up control of the team after it was discovered that he was the target of an investigation into gambling fraud and extortion. DeBartolo, who paid a $1 million fine for his involvement in the affair, has since given up his stake in the team, and his estranged sister, Denise DeBartolo York, and her husband, John York, have assumed full ownership and control.

While the leagues may have no clear policy concerning the gambling interests of their owners, they have worked hard to keep people from gambling on their games through state lotteries and offshore sports books. The leagues lobbied for the passage of the Professional and Amateur Sports Protection Act of 1992 and for the Internet Gambling Prohibition Act of 1999 (see section 16.2.3, "Internet Gambling"). The Professional and Amateur Sports Protection Act of 1992 (28 U.S.C. § 3701) prohibits state lotteries based on sports events, except in those states where such lotteries already existed.

Besides their lobbying efforts, the leagues have filed lawsuits to prohibit the use of their games in government lotteries. For example, in *OFC Comm Baseball v. Markell*, 579 F.3d 293 (3rd Cir. 2009), MLB, the NFL, the NBA, the NHL, and the NCAA brought suit against the governor and state of Delaware after its legislature proposed to allow gambling on individual games. The Third Circuit found that such a provision would violate PASPA. The case was reminiscent of *NFL v. Governor of Delaware*, 435 F. Supp. 1372 (D. Del. 1977), in which the league sued the governor and the director of the state lottery to bar the state from using a lottery based on the outcome of NFL games. The league argued that such a lottery would harm the image of the league by forcing it into association with gambling. The NFL also claimed trademark violation and misappropriation. The court, in upholding the right of the state to conduct such a lottery, held that the use of NFL schedules, scores, and public popularity in the Delaware lottery did not constitute a misappropriation of the league's property. The court did, however, grant the NFL limited injunctive relief, which required the lottery to employ a disclaimer of association with the NFL on all tickets, advertising, and other materials prepared for public distribution.

NOTES

1. In 2007 former NBA referee Tim Donaghy plead guilty to two federal charges related to his involvement in a gambling operation. Donaghy, a 13-year veteran, was providing information to gamblers and placed tens of thousands of dollars in bets on games he was officiating. Donaghy served 11 months in prison for what NBA Commissioner David Stern insisted was an isolated incident.

2. Examples of league sanctions against athletes for gambling or associating with gamblers include the following:

   a. In November 2009, German police arrested 17 people on suspicion of fixing at least 200 soccer matches in 9 countries. Macedonian club FK Pobeda was given an eight year ban from all European competitions, and club president Aleksandar

Zabrcanec and former captain Nikolce Zdravevski were given lifetime European football bans.

b. In 1989, Pete Rose, the all-time hits leader in Major League Baseball history, was banned from the game for his involvement with illegal gambling. The Dowd Report, the investigation into Rose's wrongdoing, is viewable online and includes a scan of a betting stub and thumbprint that Dowd claims incriminate Rose (see www.dowdreport.com/).

c. Former players and Hall of Famers Willie Mays and Mickey Mantle were both banned from organized baseball in 1983 after accepting jobs with Atlantic City gambling casinos. The players were reinstated in 1985 by the new baseball commissioner, Peter Ueberroth.

d. In 1963, NFL commissioner Pete Rozelle suspended for an entire season Hall of Famer and Heisman Trophy winner Paul Hornung (Green Bay Packers) and Alex Karras (Detroit Lions) for gambling activity, some of which involved their own teams. Five other players were fined $2,000 each for betting on games in which they did not play.

e. In 1921, eight members of the "Black Sox" (the 1919 Chicago White Sox) were banned from baseball for life by Commissioner Kennesaw Mountain Landis for throwing the 1919 World Series.

16.2.3. Internet Gambling

A growing problem involving sports gambling is the Internet, which provides gamblers with the opportunity to place wagers on professional and college sporting events from the privacy of their homes in virtual anonymity. The Internet also makes betting on sports easier. Instead of going through a bookie, all a gambler needs to place a bet are a computer, Internet access, and a credit card. Many of these bets are placed with casinos in off-shore locations in other countries where betting is legal.

However, in 2006 a major piece of legislation greatly affected Internet gambling in the United States. The Unlawful Internet Gambling Enforcement Act of 2006 was passed by Congress and signed by President George W. Bush; it prohibits gambling sites from receiving payments from U.S. financial institutions including credit card, check, or lending companies. The bill has caused major gaming sites to withdraw from the U.S online gambling market, including Partypoker.com.

The act defines a bet or wager as risking something of value on the outcome of a contest. Fantasy leagues are defined as legal, but they are subject to restrictions. Fantasy teams are not "based on the current membership of an actual team," meaning that a fantasy team cannot be simply a current sports franchise with all of its actual players. Prizes for fantasy league winners must also be made in advance of the contest. For more information on fantasy football, see section 16.2.4, "Fantasy Sports and Office Pools."

NOTE _____

1. For more information on Internet gambling, see Kraig P. Grahmann, "Betting on Prohibition: The Federal Government's Approach to Internet Gambling," 7 *Northwestern Journal of Technology & Intellectual Property* 161 (2009).

16.2.4. Fantasy Sports and Office Pools

Much like the issue of gambling over the Internet, gambling in fantasy leagues and office pools (see note 3 for definitions) presents a predicament for legal authorities. From a de jure (valid in law) perspective, such activity is clearly illegal and should be prosecuted in order to uphold respect for existing laws. From a de facto (a situation which is accepted for all practical purposes, but is not strictly legal or correct) perspective, there is far too much activity for authorities to police effectively, and the harm created by such activities is usually minimal or nonexistent. Most fantasy leagues require an entry fee totaling less than $10 per week, and most office pools, such as for the NCAA tournament or Kentucky Derby, require entry fees of $20 or less. While these activities seem to constitute gambling in the legal sense of the word, they do not appear to be much of a threat to either society at large or the integrity of sports. A criticism of gambling from a legal perspective is speculation that compulsive gamblers will commit illegal activity and mistreat their families because of their gambling debts. A criticism of gambling from a sports perspective is the speculation that gambling will lead to the fixing of games. Neither of these concerns appears to be valid in the context of fantasy sports and office pools, due to the small per-person amounts that are wagered.

Furthermore, certain states—such as Indiana, Wisconsin, New Jersey, and New York—have laws which stipulate that gambling is legal if it involves a game of skill rather than of chance (see note 1). For example, it would be legal to create a prize money pool for a chess tournament in such states, but not legal to create a prize money pool for a bingo tournament. One could argue, in these states, that one's ability to evaluate talent (players in fantasy leagues, teams or horses in office pools) is the material factor in the game, rather than luck. There is little case precedent in this area. In *Boardwalk Regency Corp. v. Attorney General of New Jersey*, 457 A.2d 847 (N.J. Super. Ct. Law Div. 1982), the court found that the material factor in the game of backgammon was a dice roll, not skill, and therefore gambling on backgammon was found to be illegal.

Professional sports leagues, players associations, the NCAA, and television networks have all benefited from the enthusiasm over fantasy leagues and office pools Because the Internet has spawned a boom in fantasy leagues, their legal future probably hinges on developments in Internet gambling law. Such laws will have less effect on office pools. While 22.9 million people participated worldwide in online office pools for the 2007 NCAA Division I-A men's basketball tournament, according to the *Bloomington Pantagraph*, the vast majority of office pools are cash enterprises kept within one locale. The *Pantagraph* also estimated that an average of 13.5 minutes are spent each day by employees looking at their NCAA tournament picks and that the 19-day tournament costs employers an estimated $1.2 billion per year. Yet with such a loss in productivity, only 6% of employers said they would not allow office pools in their companies. Consequently, office pools are prosecuted only sporadically by police (see note 2).

NOTES

1. For more information on the legal implications of this issue, see M. Christine Holleman, "Fantasy Football: Illegal Gambling or Legal Game of Skill?" *North Carolina Journal of Law and Technology*, Vol. 8 Issue 1, February 14, 2007.

2. In fantasy leagues, participants usually pay an entry fee (occasionally leagues are free) to draft a set number of players prior to a season. Over the course of a season, participants are awarded a certain number of points based on the statistics generated by their players. The participant with the greatest number of points at the season's end usually wins a cash prize. A 2009 report by the consulting firm Challenger, Gray & Christmas, Inc. estimated that 36.8 million consumers participate in fantasy sports. The report also states that the cost

to employers to pay unproductive workers checking their fantasy teams during the National Football League season could be as high as $1.5 billion for 17 weeks.

In office pools, participants typically contribute $5 to $20 to the pool. Each participant fills out a list of winners (a bracket) in the case of a tournament or a predicted score in the case of an individual game (such as the Super Bowl). The person whose prediction is most accurate wins the entire pot. In some cases, there are second prizes, third prizes, and so on, or the pot is divided accordingly. Resource Management According to a 2010 Society for Human study of human resources managers, 67% of companies either allowed or were not concerned with office pools, while 33% banned them. Only 20% of HR professionals reported seeing an impact in employee attendance after a major televised event. While 55% of HR professionals believe that office pools improved employee morale, 37% felt that they had a negative impact on work productivity. Not surprisingly, the negative effects were more common among male employees than female.

16.3. DISABILITIES

The line between a lawful refusal to extend affirmative action and illegal discrimination against handicapped persons will not always be clear. It is possible to envision situations where an insistence on continuing past requirements and practices might arbitrarily deprive genuinely qualified handicapped persons of the opportunity to participate in a covered program (*Southeastern Community College v. Davis*, 442 U.S. 397 [1979]).

In athletics, the line between lawful refusal to modify existing requirements and illegally discriminating against disabled persons is likely to be interpreted in the future. This is especially true in light of the U.S. Supreme Court's 2001 decision requiring the PGA to permit Casey Martin, a disabled golfer, to use a golf cart in competition. Since 1990, when the Americans with Disabilities Act (ADA) was signed into law, disabled athletes have used the ADA and other federal disability legislation to force high schools, colleges, the NCAA, and professional sports to change their rules to accommodate the individual's disability.

Yet, even with the enactment of the ADA, disabled athletes still face a number of obstacles in their struggle to participate in athletics. In an attempt to protect or shield themselves from liability, as well as to protect the athlete, a number of athletic organizations have developed policies prohibiting athletes with certain medical conditions or disabilities from participating in athletics or other extracurricular activities. This section examines the evolution of disability legislation and the impact the laws have had on athletes with disabilities.

16.3.1. Federal Laws Affecting Persons with Disabilities

As recently as the 1970s, children with learning disabilities were regularly denied access to a number of state public school systems because it was thought that their presence would interfere with the learning environment. In 1973, Congress began enacting legislation designed to increase the educational and social opportunities available to individuals with disabilities. The first law passed by Congress was the Rehabilitation Act of 1973, 29 U.S.C. Section 701 et seq. This was followed by the Education for All Handicapped Children Act of 1975, later renamed the Individuals with Disabilities Education Act (IDEA) in 1990. Congress has also passed the Amateur Sports Act, and most recently the Americans with Disabilities Act (ADA).

16.3.1.1. The Rehabilitation Act

One of the stated intents of the Rehabilitation Act is to provide individuals with disabilities the opportunity to participate in physical education and athletic programs or activities without being discriminated against due to their disability. Section 504 of the Rehabilitation Act states: "No otherwise qualified handicapped individual in the United States...shall solely by reason of his handicap, be excluded from participation in, be denied the benefits of, or be subjected to discrimination under any program or activity receiving Federal financial assistance."

For an individual to establish a claim under Section 504, he or she must successfully meet four requirements. First, the individual must show that he or she is a handicapped individual. The definitions used in the Rehabilitation Act and the ADA are very similar in that they define an individual as having a disability if he or she has:

1. A physical or mental impairment that substantially limits one or more of the major life activities of such individual
2. A record of such an impairment or
3. Being regarded as having such an impairment.

Second, the individual must show that he or she is otherwise qualified for the athletic activity. A person is otherwise qualified if he or she can meet all of a program's requirements despite his or her disability. Third, the individual must show that he or she is being excluded from athletic participation solely by reason of the disability. The fourth and final requirement is that the school or institution is receiving federal financial assistance. The majority of challenges under Section 504 in athletics hinge on the judicial interpretation of the "otherwise qualified" element or the "solely by reason of" element. Therefore, an examination of the meaning of these two elements is important. The U.S. Supreme Court has interpreted the phrase "otherwise qualified person" to mean someone who is able to meet all of a program's requirements despite his or her disability. Therefore, the Rehabilitation Act does not compel an organization to disregard a disabled person's individual impairment. Nor does the act require the organization to make substantial modifications in its programs to accommodate the disabled individual.

However, even though there are no affirmative obligations on recipients of federal funds, there are situations where refusal to modify an existing program might become unreasonable and discriminatory. For example, in *Dennin v. Connecticut Interscholastic Athletic Conference (CIAC)*, 94 F.3d 96 (2nd Cir. 1996), the court was asked to decide whether a 19-year-old high school student suffering from Down syndrome could participate on his high school swim team. The plaintiff, due to his age, was prohibited from participating on his high school swim team by the Connecticut Interscholastic Athletic Conference (CIAC). The court held that Dennin was otherwise qualified to participate on the swim team, and that it would be reasonable for the CIAC to accommodate him by waiving the age requirement. Waiving the rule, the court concluded, would not fundamentally or substantially alter the nature of the program in any way or undermine any of the stated purposes of the rule. Therefore, while an organization is not required to make fundamental or substantial modifications to accommodate the disabled, it may be required to make reasonable ones as long as the accommodations do not impose an undue hardship on the operation of its program. In determining whether an accommodation would impose an undue hardship, the court can consider the nature and cost of the accommodation.

The "excluded solely by reason of the disability" requirement is met if the disabled individual is being excluded due to his or her disability. For example, in *Poole v. South Plainfield Board of Education*, 490 F. Supp. 948 (D.N.J. 1980), the South Plainfield Board of Education refused to let Richard Poole wrestle for his high school because he had only one kidney. Poole, who was born with this condition, sued the school board, claiming that it was violating his rights under Section 504. In allowing Poole to compete, the court held that he was otherwise qualified to participate in high school sports and that he was being excluded from participation solely by reason of the fact that he had one kidney. The court also found that whatever duty the board may have had toward Poole was satisfied once it became clear that Poole and his parents knew of the dangers involved in Poole's participation on the team.

The issue of whether someone is being excluded solely by reason of his or her disability is more difficult when an individual, due to an illness or learning disability, is over the athletic association's maximum age requirement by the time he or she reaches the senior year of high school. For example, in *University Interscholastic League (UIL) v. Buchanan*, 848 S.W.2d 298 (Tex. Ct. App. 1993), two 19-year-old students, who were diagnosed with learning disabilities, sought a permanent injunction against the enforcement of UIL's rule requiring all athletes to be under 19 years old. The UIL argued that the age requirement was necessary to ensure the safety of the participating student-athletes and to ensure the equality of competitors. The UIL also argued that the age rule did not discriminate against the plaintiffs because of their disabilities, but was applied equally against both disabled and nondisabled students. Therefore, the plaintiffs were ineligible due to their ages, not their disabilities. In allowing the athletes to compete, the court of appeals found that, except for their disabilities, the students would have been age-eligible to participate in interscholastic athletics. It was due to their learning disabilities that they were still in school. Therefore, the court of appeals held, the waiver of the age rule would have been a reasonable accommodation by UIL to ensure that athletes with disabilities achieve meaningful access.

16.3.1.2. Individuals with Disabilities Education Act (IDEA)

Enacted as the Education for All Handicapped Children Act of 1975, and amended and renamed the Individuals with Disabilities Education Act (IDEA), 20 U.S.C. Section 1400 et seq., in 1990, IDEA was designed to increase the educational opportunity available to disabled children and to secure the right of all disabled children to a free and appropriate public education that emphasizes special education and related services designed to meet their unique needs. In order to satisfy the goal of Congress, IDEA requires that local educational agencies, together with the disabled student's teacher and parents, develop a written statement or an individualized education program (IEP) outlining achievable educational objectives for the student. Although the regulations adopted under the IDEA are less specific with regard to athletics than those pursuant to Section 504, IDEA does require each public agency to ensure that a variety of educational programs and services, including physical education, available to nondisabled children are available to those covered under the act. Besides providing educational programs and services, each public agency is required to provide nonacademic and extracurricular activities and services, including interscholastic athletics, in such manner as is necessary to afford children with disabilities an equal opportunity for participation in those services and activities (34 C.F.R. Section 300.306(a)). For example, in *Lambert v. West Virginia State Board of Education*, 447 S.E.2d 901 (W. Va. 1994), a high school basketball player, who has been deaf since birth, won the right to require her school to provide her with a sign language interpreter so that she could compete on the girls' basketball team. The student was provided with a signer for her basic courses, but the West Virginia Board of Education refused to provide a signer for her vocational classes or her extracurricular activities. In holding that the board of education was required to provide a signer for the plaintiff, the court found that the assistance of a signer was a reasonable accommodation that provided the plaintiff with equal access to extracurricular activities.

Another example of a student-athlete's successfully using the IDEA to gain participation rights is *Crocker v. Tennessee Secondary School Athletic Ass'n*, 980 F.2d 382 (6th Cir. 1992). In *Crocker*, the plaintiff transferred from a private school to his local public high school so that he could receive the special education he needed, which was not available in the private school. When the plaintiff attempted to participate in interscholastic athletics at his new school, the Tennessee Secondary School Athletic Association (TSSAA) ruled that he was ineligible. According to TSSAA rules, any student who transfers from one TSSAA member school to another is ineligible to participate in interscholastic sports for 12 months. The plaintiff argued that the TSSAA, by enforcing its transfer rule, was depriving him of his rights guaranteed under the IDEA. In ruling for Crocker, the court held that since the plaintiff's transfer was motivated by his disability, TSSAA's refusal to waive its transfer rule violated the IDEA.

In *Crocker*, however, the court failed to address the issue of whether the plaintiff's participation in interscholastic athletics was a related service that should have been incorporated into his individualized education program. The importance of including participation in interscholastic athletics in a student's IEP can be seen in *T.H. v. Montana High School Ass'n*, No. CV 92–150- BLG-JFB, 1992 WL 672982 (D. Mont. Sept. 24, 1992). The plaintiff, after being diagnosed as having a learning disability, was provided with an IEP in accordance with the IDEA. One component of T.H.'s IEP was that he participate in interscholastic athletics as a motivational tool. Before his senior year, the Montana High School Association ruled T.H. ineligible to compete in interscholastic athletics due to his age. In finding for the plaintiff, the court held that while students have no constitutional right to participate in interscholastic sports—it is a privilege that may be withdrawn by the school or a voluntary association—when participation in interscholastic sports is included as a component of the IEP as a related service, the privilege of competing in interscholastic sports is transformed into a federally protected right.

16.3.1.3. The Amateur Sports Act

Another piece of legislation affecting the rights of disabled athletes is the Amateur Sports Act, 36 U.S.C. Section 371–396. The Amateur Sports Act names the U.S. Olympic Committee (USOC) as the coordinator of amateur athletics in the United States. As the coordinator of amateur athletics, one of the goals of the USOC is to "encourage and provide assistance to amateur athletic programs and competition for handicapped individuals, including, where feasible, the expansion of opportunities for meaningful participation by handicapped individuals in programs of athletic competition for able-bodied individuals." In order to accomplish its goal, the USOC established the Committee on Sports for the Disabled. The committee helps disabled athletes by removing unnecessary barriers to competition and supporting organizations that provide sports experiences for disabled individuals.

Under the Amateur Sports Act, amended in 1998, it has become the "first priority" of the USOC to merge Paralympic sports with existing able-bodied national governing bodies (NGBs). Responding to this mandate, the executive committee of the USOC met in December 1999 and promised to find additional funding for disabled athletes. The USOC, which supports about 20,000 elite disabled athletes, increased the funds it provided for games for the disabled from $1.7 million in the 1993–1996 quadrennial to $2,964,031 in 1997–2000. The executive committee also considered whether to transfer elite disabled athletes from the organizations that now govern them (sports organizations for athletes with disabilities) to the NGBs that oversee able-bodied athletes in those sports. The executive committee, however, stopped short of requiring NGBs to embrace disabled programs, and took no official stance on how the 45 NGBs should handle programs for the disabled. In 2005, the Associated Press reported that USOC spokesman Darryl Seibel stated the 2005 Paralympic budget was around $15 million.

NOTES

1. In *Hollenbeck v. U.S. Olympic Committee*, 513 F.3d 1191 (10th Cir. 2008), Paralympic wheelchair athletes brought suit against the United States Olympic Committee (USOC), alleging disability discrimination in USOC's provision of certain athlete-support benefits only to Olympic team members but not to Paralympic team members. The court found for the USOC, ruling that the Amateur Sports Act does not direct how the USOC should use its funding.

2. In 2001, five sports organizations for the disabled sent a formal letter of complaint to USOC President Sandra Baldwin, alleging "separate and unequal treatment" under the Amateur Sports Act Amendments of 1998. Although the act was intended to improve opportunities for the disabled, the protesting sports organizations (including Wheelchair Sports USA) claimed that, due to a segregated governance structure, "athletes with disabilities have been denied effective representation on USOC committees, including the important Athlete's Advisory Committee; cannot obtain services provided to Olympic athletes, such as medical insurance, equal access to training facilities and sports medicine clinics, and participation in the Athletes-in-Residence program."

16.3.1.4. Americans with Disabilities Act (ADA)

While many people predicted that the Americans with Disabilities Act (ADA), 42 U.S.C. Section 12101 et seq., would have a large impact on athletic facilities and how they accommodated spectators with disabilities, the biggest impact the law has had is on athletic participation and coaching opportunities. Signed into law July 26, 1990, the ADA has as its purpose "to provide a clear and comprehensive national mandate for the elimination of discrimination against individuals with disabilities." The ADA focuses on eradicating barriers, by requiring public entities to consider whether reasonable accommodations can be made to remove any barrier created by a person's disability. The three sections that athletic managers and attorneys should be aware of are Title I, which covers employment; Title II, which covers public services; and Title III, which covers public accommodations and services operated by private entities.

16.3.1.4.1. Title I: Employment

Title I (42 U.S.C. Section 12112) provides that "no covered entity shall discriminate against a qualified individual with a disability because of the disability of such individual in regard to job application procedures, the hiring, advancement, or discharge of employees, employee compensation, job training, and other terms, conditions, and privileges of employment." In *Clemons v. Big Ten Conference*, No. 96C0124 1997 U.S. Dist. LEXIS 1939 (N.D. Ill. Feb. 19, 1997), a former employee, who had been terminated from his position as a college football official after he failed to comply with his employer's instructions to lose weight, brought action against the Big Ten Conference under ADA. The district court, in dismissing the case, held that the reason the employee was fired was because he failed to perform his job satisfactorily. The court also noted that the Big Ten Conference did not regard the employee as being disabled under ADA.

16.3.1.4.2. Title II: Public Services

Title II (42 U.S.C. Section 12132), which is based on Section 504 of the Rehabilitation Act, provides that "no qualified individual with a disability shall, by reason of such disability, be excluded from participation in or be denied the benefits of the services, programs, or activities of a public entity, or be subjected to discrimination by any such entity."

In order for an individual to successfully state a claim under the ADA, he or she must establish the following elements. First, an individual must show that he or she is a qualified individual with a disability. The ADA defines a qualified individual with a disability as any physically or mentally disabled individual "who, with or without reasonable modifications...meets the essential eligibility requirements for the receipt of services or the participation in programs or activities provided by a public entity." Second, the individual must show that he or she is otherwise qualified for the athletic activity. Third, an individual must show that he or she is being excluded from athletic participation solely by reason of his or her disability. The fourth element that an individual must show is that he or she is being discriminated against by a public entity.

Even if the plaintiff is able to meet all four elements necessary under Title II, the courts will still uphold as valid any rule, policy, or procedure if waiving it would constitute a fundamental alteration in the nature of the association or impose an undue hardship on the organization or pose a direct threat to the health or safety of others.

An example of how the courts have interpreted Title II of the ADA is *Johnson v. Florida High School Activities Ass'n*, 899 F. Supp. 579 (M.D. Fla. 1995). Dennis Johnson, a 19-year-old student, sought a preliminary injunction allowing him to play high school football and wrestle. At the age of nine months, the plaintiff suffered from meningitis and lost all hearing in one ear and most of his hearing in the other ear. Due to his hearing impairment, Johnson was held out of kindergarten for one year (his parent's decision) and forced to repeat the first grade (the school's decision). Before entering his senior year of high school, Johnson sought a waiver of the Florida High School Activities Association's (FHSAA) age eligibility requirement. The FHSAA refused to waive the age requirement, stating that it was an essential eligibility requirement, and Johnson filed a lawsuit seeking an injunction. The FHSAA, citing the Eighth Circuit Court's decision in *Pottgen v. Missouri State High School Activities Ass'n*, 40 F.3d 926 (8th Cir. 1994), argued that the plaintiff was not otherwise qualified to participate and that no reasonable accommodation could be made so as to make the plaintiff otherwise qualified. The FHSAA also argued that Title II did not apply to it because it was not a public entity as defined by the ADA. In rejecting the FHSAA's argument, the court held that the FHSAA had already been found to be a state actor. It followed, therefore, that the FHSAA was an instrument of the state and a public entity. As for the issue of whether the plaintiff was otherwise qualified to participate in interscholastic athletics—and, if not, whether reasonable accommodations could be made to make him otherwise qualified—the court held that the age requirement serves as a simple threshold standard by which the FHSAA can achieve the desired goals of safety and fairness. Absent of these purposes, the age requirement has no purpose.

Thus, to assert that the age requirement is an absolute, unwaivable rule is to place form over substance. The court also held that waiving the age eligibility requirement did not fundamentally alter the nature or purpose of the program. The court reasoned that allowing the athlete to participate in interscholastic athletics did not undermine the purposes of the age requirement. Furthermore, Johnson was not a star athlete, nor was he more experienced than the other players. Because safety and fairness would not be compromised, the court concluded that waiving the age requirement constituted a reasonable accommodation and had to be undertaken.

In 2004, in *Tennessee v. Lane*, 541 U.S. 509 (2004), a 5–4 ruling by the Supreme Court allows people with disabilities to sue states for monetary damages. The plaintiffs were two Tennessee citizens who could not easily reach the upper floors of a state courthouse. One of the plaintiffs had to crawl up two flights of the courthouse to appear at a criminal hearing and was arrested when he did not appear for a second hearing. The plaintiffs sued under Section II of the ADA, stating that their access to public services was being denied by their disabilities alone. The ruling was a victory for the disabled community and may have opened the door for other individuals with disabilities to sue state facilities under the ADA, despite sovereign immunity.

16.3.1.4.3. Title III: Public Accommodations Operated by Private Entities

Title III provides that "no individual shall be discriminated against on the basis of disability in the full and equal enjoyment of the goods, services, facilities, privileges, advantages, or accommodations of any place of public accommodation by any person who owns, leases, or operates a place of public accommodation" (42 U.S.C. Section 12182).

Under Title III of the ADA, the following private entities are considered public accommodations: motion picture houses, theaters, concert halls, stadiums, other places of exhibition or entertainment, camps, gymnasiums, health spas, bowling alleys, golf courses, or other places of exercise or recreation (42 U.S.C. 12181).

A key element in Title III cases is control. In *Cortez v. NBA*, 960 F. Supp. 113 (W.D. Tex. 1997), the court rejected a claim under Title III of the ADA against the NBA by a group of hearing-impaired spectators who had attended professional basketball games at the Alamodome. The plaintiffs were seeking interpretative and captioning services, as a reasonable accommodation, for deaf and hard-of-hearing individuals who attend NBA games at the Alamodome and other arenas. In dismissing the claim against the league, the court held that the league did not own, lease, or operate a place of public accommodation.

A similar decision was reached in *Shepherd v. U.S. Olympic Committee*, 464.F.Supp.2d 1072 (D.Colo. 2006), where a Colorado District court ruled that Olympic training centers were not places of public accommodation. The suit involved Mark Shepherd, a Paralympic athlete who sued the USOC under Title III of the ADA and the Rehabilitation Act, arguing that the USOC unfairly discriminated against Paralympic athletes by failing to offer Paralympians the same access to facilities and funding as Olympic athletes. The court ruled that Olympic training centers are exclusive training facilities that are not open to the public. The plaintiff made the claim that the training centers fell under the category of "gymnasium, health spa" under the 12 categories of "public accommodations" listed in the ADA.

However, in its decision the court said that the Olympic training centers were not gyms or spas because "there is something fundamentally different about the establishments and 'places of exercise and recreation'…the training facilities operated by the USOC are accessible only to those already selected by the national governing bodies to the Olympic, Pan-American, or Paralympic teams in their individual sports and are identified as elite, world-class athletes." Facilities that can be classified as places of public accommodation must be at times open to the general public.

16.3.2. Application to Athletic Organizations

Most of the remainder of this chapter will chronicle the ways that various courts have interpreted laws that affect persons with disabilities. Though the text is broken down by industry sector, persons in *all* sectors of the sports industry should pay particular attention to the discussion of *PGA Tour v. Casey Martin* in section 16.3.2.4, "Professional Sports." First, as a U.S. Supreme Court decision, the judgment is binding throughout the land. Second, the Court's opinion provides a standard for reasonable accommodation and guidance as to how other courts should interpret what does or does not fundamentally alter a sport or sports organization.

16.3.2.1. Youth Sports

In *Anderson v. Little League Baseball, Inc.*, 794 F. Supp. 342 (D. Ariz. 1992), a youth baseball coach, who was confined to a wheelchair and had coached Little League Baseball for the previous three years as an on-field coach, sued the Little League after it adopted a policy prohibiting coaches in wheelchairs from on-field coaching. In support of the policy, the Little League pointed out that the ADA specifically "does not require a public accommodation to permit an individual to participate…when that individual poses a direct threat to the health or safety of others" (28 C.F.R. Section 36.208). The stated intent of the policy was to protect the players from collisions with the wheelchair during the game.

Whether a person poses a direct threat to the health or safety of others, the court held, may not be based on generalizations or stereotypes about the effects of a particular disability, but must be based on an individual assessment. There was no evidence, the court held, to indicate that the plaintiff posed a direct threat to the health or safety of others. The Little League's policy amounted to an absolute ban on coaches in wheelchairs in the coach's box, regardless of the coach's disability or the field or game conditions involved. Such a policy, the court held, falls markedly short of the requirements of the ADA.

Another case involving the ADA and youth sports was the 1999 conflict between Ryan Taylor and the Lawton Evening Optimist Soccer Association in Lawton, Oklahoma. Taylor, who has cerebral palsy, used a walker to help him get around and play. Fearing another player would trip over the walker and hurt Taylor or other children, the soccer association banned him from playing. The ban was lifted after U.S. District Judge David Russell found "it very remote that there could be some injury [from the walker]." The judge did, however, order that the walker be well padded.

16.3.2.2. High School

The area that has seen the most litigation is high school athletic association eligibility rules. The two eligibility rules that have come under attack the most are the age limit, which prohibits a high school athlete from participation in high school sports after reaching the state athletic association's maximum age requirement, and the eight-semester rule, which prohibits a high school athlete from participating in high school sports if he or she has been enrolled in grades 9 to 12, inclusive, for more than eight semesters. The courts are almost equally divided on whether state high school athletic associations are required under federal disability law to waive an eligibility requirement.

In West Virginia, New York, the Eighth Circuit, and the Sixth Circuit, the courts have held that waiving a state high school athletic association's age requirement was not required under the ADA because it would constitute a fundamental alteration in the nature of the state's interscholastic programs (see note 1). Other jurisdictions, including Connecticut, Oregon, Florida, and the Seventh Circuit, have concluded that the ADA does require high school athletic associations to waive their eligibility requirements (see note 2). It is important to note, however, that while these rules may seem reasonable, it often takes a student with a disability extra time to finish high school. Therefore, when applied to older disabled students, especially in non-contact sports and in sports like wrestling, where competitors are matched by weight, some courts have found them to be unreasonable.

NOTES ───

1. The principal function of a state high school athletic association is to promulgate rules and regulations for its member schools that will promote fair athletic competition. When an athletic association's rule or regulation is challenged in a court of law, the court will generally defer to the judgment of the athletic association on eligibility matters unless there is evidence of fraud, collusion, or lack of jurisdiction, or when the school's actions were arbitrary or capricious. The courts, however, have also recognized the rights of disabled student-athletes to challenge an association's eligibility rules under the Rehabilitation Act and the ADA.

The following cases examine student challenges to state high school athletic association eligibility restriction.

    a. The Colorado High School Activities Association's (CHAA) eight-semester rule was upheld in *Tesmer v. Colorado High School Activities Association* 140 P.3d 249 (Colo. App. 2006). Scott Orth challenged the CHAA's eight semester rule after he was barred from playing high school football in his ninth semester, after having to repeat a grade because of a family divorce and sinus infection. Orth was diagnosed with attention deficit disorder (ADD) at age eight and received treatment until the eighth grade. The Colorado Court of Appeals upheld the district court's decision rejecting Orth's claim since the reason for his failure to play athletics in his fifth year was not a direct result of his disability, but due to other factors. Also the court stated that Orth has stopped taking medication for ADD after the eighth grade and therefore was not eligible for a waiver to the eight-semester rule.

b. In *Kanongata'a v. Washington Interscholastic Activities Association*, 2006 WL 1727891 (W.D.Wash. June 20, 2006) William Kanongata'a sued the WIAA based on its four-year eligibility rule which prohibits athletes from participating in high school athletics after four years of school. Kanongata'a was determined ineligible and appealed, stating that the reason for his fifth year of school was due to a learning disability and extenuating personal hardships. The court refused WIAA's motion for summary judgment, finding the application of its hardship waiver to have been arbitrary, capricious, and contrary to law. The WIAA thereafter permitted Kanongata'a to rejoin his team.

c. In *McPherson v. Michigan High School Athletic Ass'n*, 119 F.3d 453 (6th Cir. 1997), Dion McPherson challenged the validity of the Michigan High School Athletic Association's (MHSAA) eight-semester eligibility rule, contending that the rule violates the Americans with Disabilities Act and Section 504 of the Rehabilitation Act. The Sixth Circuit, in overturning the district court's decision, held that the eight-semester rule was a necessary eligibility requirement, and that waiving it would impose an immense financial and administrative burden on the MSHAA. Therefore, accommodating McPherson would be unreasonable.

d. In *Sandison v. Michigan High School Athletic Ass'n*, 64 F.3d 1026 (6th Cir. 1995), Ronald Sandison and Craig Stanley sought an injunction preventing the MSHAA from enforcing its 19-year age limit against them. The Sixth Circuit found that the plaintiffs had failed to meet two of the four elements necessary to bring a claim under Section 504 and the ADA. First, the court of appeals found that the plaintiffs were not otherwise qualified for participation on their high school track teams. A person is otherwise qualified to participate if, with reasonable accommodations, the individual can meet all the necessary requirements of the program. Waiving the eligibility rule and allowing older and more physically mature students to compete with younger students, the Sixth Circuit held, would be a fundamental alteration of the MSHAA. The Sixth Circuit also held that the plaintiffs failed to show that they were being excluded from participation solely by reason of their disabilities. The reason the plaintiffs were being denied the opportunity to participate in high school athletics, the court of appeals held, was due to their date of birth, not their disabilities.

2. Other cases that have upheld state eligibility requirements include *Hoot v. Milan School District*, 853 F. Supp. 243 (E.D. Mich. 1994); *Landers v. West Virginia Secondary School Activities Commission*, 447 S.E.2d 901 (W.Va. 1994); *Pottgen v. Missouri State High School Athletic Ass'n*, 40 F.3d 926 (8th Cir. 1994); *Reaves v. Mills*, 904 F. Supp. 120 (W.D.N.Y. 1995); *Sadler v. University Interscholastic League*, 1991 WL 633967 (W.D. Tex. 1991).

The following cases have concluded that the Rehabilitation Act and the ADA do require high school athletic associations to waive their eligibility requirement.

a. In *Badgett ex rel. Badgett v. Alabama High School Athletic Association*, 2007 WL 2461928 (N.D. Ala. May 3, 2007), Mallerie Badgett was the only competitor in the wheelchair division of track and field in the entire state. Miss Badgett, a holder of nine Junior National Records for girls with cerebral palsy, wanted her results at the section qualifying to count toward her team's total in the able-bodied competition. The court denied Badgett's request for injunctive relief, finding her request to participate alongside able-bodied athletes to be unreasonable.

b. In *Washington v. Indiana High School Athletic Ass'n*, 181 F.3d 840 (7th Cir. 1999), Eric Washington, a student with a learning disability at Central Catholic High School, obtained a preliminary injunction in the district court enjoining the Indiana High School Athletic Association (IHSAA) from denying him athletic eligibility.

The IHSAA ruled that Washington was ineligible under the eight-semester rule. Washington challenged the IHSSA's policy on the ground that failure to grant a waiver of the eight-semester rule violates Title II of the ADA. The Seventh Circuit Court upheld the injunction, finding such a waiver reasonable. The court rejected IHSAA's claim that granting a waiver would impose an undue hardship because it would be flooded with other cases.

3. Other cases include *Bingham v. Oregon School Activities Ass'n.*, 37 F. Supp. 2d 1189 (D. Or. 1999); *Dennin v. Connecticut Interscholastic Athletic Conference*, 94 F.3d 96 (2nd Cir. Conn. 1996); *Rhodes v. Ohio High School Athletic Ass'n.*, 939 F. Supp. 584 (N.D. Ohio 1996); *Johnson v. Florida High School Activities Association*, 899 F. Supp. 579 (M.D. Fla. 1995); and *Booth v. El Paso Independent School District*, No. A-90-CA-764 (Tex. Dist. Ct. 1990).

16.3.2.3. Colleges, Universities, and the National Collegiate Athletic Association

The federal courts have faced many different issues on how to apply the ADA to intercollegiate athletes. For example, in *Ganden v. NCAA*, the court ruled that waiving the NCAA's core academic requirements would fundamentally alter the nature of college athletics (see note 3). On the other hand, the court in *Butler v. NCAA* found that Title III of the ADA was applicable to the NCAA and ruled that waiving the NCAA's core requirements would not fundamentally alter college athletics (see note 5).

Future issues regarding college athletes with learning disabilities, however, may be reduced. In May 1998, the U.S. Justice Department and the NCAA entered into a consent decree that will allow hundreds of individuals with learning disabilities who do not meet the initial eligibility requirements to keep their fourth year of athletic eligibility. The decree also states that the NCAA will no longer disqualify a course simply because it includes the designations "special needs," "remedial," or "special education." That decree resulted from the lawsuit filed by Michael Bowers (see note 1), who claimed he had been denied an athletic scholarship in 1997 (prior to the decree) due to his learning disability. Bowers's case for damages is pending, but even if he is unable to obtain relief, District Court Judge Stephen Orlafsky has already ruled that the NCAA is subject to the Americans with Disabilities Act because it is a "place of public accommodation." Consequently, the NCAA may be susceptible to increased disability claims.

NOTES

1. In *Bowers v. NCAA*, 130 F. Supp. 2d 610 (D. N.J. 2001), a football player with a learning disability was denied participation in athletics by NCAA rules as a college freshman due to a poor standardized test score. Bowers claimed that colleges refused to recruit him because they knew he would be a nonqualifier under NCAA rules. He therefore brought suit in 1997 under the ADA, the Rehabilitation Act, and the New Jersey Law against Discrimination. Bowers passed away by suicide while the suit was pending, and, even though the case is now moot, the appeals court the case back to the district court to determine whether the NCAA policies violate disability law. The appeals court established that (1) Bowers may recover monetary damages under the Rehabilitation Act if he can prove he was discriminated against intentionally, and (2) the NCAA is a place of public accommodation, and therefore subject to the ADA. In 2008, a jury found that Bowers was not a person with a disability as that term is defined in the Rehabilitation Act.

2. In *Matthews v. NCAA*, 1769 F.Supp.2d 1209 (E.D. Wash. 2001), U.S. Dist., a judge ruled that the NCAA's 75/25 rule may be a violation of the ADA. The rule states that athletes

must earn at least 75% of their credits to be eligible for athletics during the regular collegiate year, and only 25% of credits can be summer school credits. The plaintiff, Anthony Matthews, a football player at Washington State University, graduated before the case went to court; therefore, the case was ruled moot and was discontinued.

3. In *Tatum v. NCAA*, 992 F. Supp. 1114 (E.D. Mo. 1998), a basketball player with generalized anxiety disorder and a specific phobia related to testing brought suit against the NCAA when the NCAA failed to recognize his untimed test scores. According to NCAA Bylaw 14.3.1.4.3, untimed tests are recognized only for persons who are "learning disabled" or "handicapped." The NCAA contended that the plaintiff was neither. The court ruled in favor of the NCAA, refusing to grant injunctive relief due to an unlikelihood of success on the merits of the case.

4. In *Ganden v. NCAA*, No. 96 C 6953, 1996 U.S. Dist. LEXIS 17368 (N.D. Ill. Nov. 19, 1996), a college swimmer who had a learning disability sued the NCAA to permit him to participate in swimming competitions until resolution of his claims against the NCAA under the Americans with Disabilities Act. The district court, in finding for the NCAA, held that the swimmer did not demonstrate reasonable likelihood of success at trial so as to be entitled to a preliminary injunction.

5. In *Butler v. NCAA*, No. C 96–1656 D, 1996 WL 1058233 (W.D. Wash. Nov. 8, 1996), a court found in favor of the student plaintiff Butler, who was offered a full scholarship to attend the University of Washington and play for its football team. However, the NCAA declared the plaintiff academically ineligible to participate in Division I college athletics when he failed meet the NCAA core course requirements. As a result, Butler was removed from the football team and his scholarship was revoked. Butler sued the NCAA, claiming that the academic eligibility requirements discriminated against persons with learning disabilities in violation of Title III of the ADA. In rejecting the NCAA's motion to dismiss, the court found that, even though Butler's likelihood of success on the merits might not be strong, the harm he would suffer if the court refused to issue a preliminary injunction far outweighed that of the NCAA.

6. In *Pahulu v. University of Kansas*, 897 F. Supp. 1387 (D. Kan. 1995), a college student, who was disqualified by the team physician from participation in intercollegiate football, brought suit against the university, alleging violation of the Rehabilitation Act. The district court held that Pahulu, who had been barred from playing football following the discovery that he had a congenitally narrow cervical canal, was not disabled within the meaning of the act, even though intercollegiate football might be part of the major life activity of learning. The court also concluded that, even if Pahulu was disabled, he was not otherwise qualified, given the university physician's conclusion that he was at extremely high risk for subsequent, and potentially permanent, severe neurological injury.

7. In *Knapp v. Northwestern University*, 101 F.3d 473 (7th Cir. 1996), a student who had been barred from participation in intercollegiate basketball because of a heart defect filed action against the university, seeking declaratory relief, preliminary and permanent injunctive relief, and compensatory damages under the Rehabilitation Act. In rejecting the student's claim, the court of appeals held that Knapp was not disabled within the meaning of the Rehabilitation Act because his condition did not affect the major life activity of learning. The court also held that playing intercollegiate basketball was not in and of itself a major life activity, because it was not a basic function of life on the same level as walking, breathing, and speaking. Finally, the court concluded that the existence of substantial risk of future harm and severity of injury risked made Knapp not otherwise qualified within the meaning of the Rehabilitation Act. As a matter of law, the court held that Northwestern University must be allowed to make its own determinations of substantial risk and severity of injury if they are based on reliable evidence.

8. In *Maddox v. University of Tennessee*, 62 F.3d 843 (6th Cir. 1995), a former assistant university football coach sued the university, its board of trustees, and its athletic director for disability discrimination, alleging that he was discharged on the basis of a disability, alcoholism. In granting the university's motion for summary judgment, the court of appeals held that the university did not discharge the coach solely because of a disability.

16.3.2.4. Professional Sports

The sport of golf has served as the primary proving ground for professional athletes to use disability laws in order to challenge organizational rules—in particular the cases of *Martin v. PGA Tour* and *Olinger v. U.S. Golf Association*. The case of *Martin v. PGA* began when Casey Martin, a disabled professional golfer, brought action against the PGA Tour alleging that, by failing to make a golf cart available to him, the PGA failed to make its golf tournaments accessible to disabled individuals in violation of Title III of the ADA. Title III pertains to public accommodations operated by private organizations, and the PGA is a private organization. Martin suffers from Klippel-Trenaunay-Weber syndrome, a degenerative circulatory disorder that prevents him from walking golf courses, and his disorder constitutes a disability under the ADA. In defense, the PGA Tour argued that its walking-only rule was an essential element of professional golf on the PGA and Nike tours, and that waiving the rule would fundamentally alter the nature of the sport. In addition, the PGA disputed that membership on the PGA Tour was public accommodation, a requirement of Title III. The district court in *Martin v. PGA Tour, Inc.*, 994 F. Supp. 1242 (D. Or. 1998), held that use of golf cart, as reasonable modification to accommodate a disabled professional golfer, would not frustrate the purpose of the association's walking rule and would not alter the fundamental nature of professional golf tournament competition. In other words, the fatigue that Martin suffers, even with the aid of a golf cart, is greater than the fatigue his able-bodied competitors face when walking the course. Furthermore, the district court concluded that golf courses *are* places of public accommodation during tournaments. The judgment of the Oregon District Court was affirmed by the Ninth Circuit Court of Appeals in *Martin v. PGA Tour*, 204 F.3d 994 (9th Cir. 2000). One of the arguments raised by the PGA Tour in the *Martin* case was that the court's decision would impose an undue hardship on the organization by forcing it to review numerous appeals by other golfers. As if to validate the PGA concerns, Ford Olinger, another professional golfer whose physical condition (bilateral avascular necrosis) prevented him from playing a full round of golf on foot, sought a court order allowing him to use a golf cart to qualify for and compete in the U.S. Open golf tournament. However, unlike Martin, the court in *Olinger v. U.S. Golf Ass'n.*, 55 F. Supp. 2d 926 (N.D. Ind. 1999), refused to apply the ADA. The district court held that while the USGA was subject to ADA with regard to golf tournaments, the use of golf carts at tournaments would fundamentally change the nature of the activity, and thus was not mandated by ADA. Athletic competition, the court held, presents ADA concerns different from those presented by the workplace. In the workplace, the pertinent inquiry is whether a particular otherwise-qualified individual can perform the job if a reasonable accommodation is made to allow for the person's disability. The point of an athletic competition, in contrast, is to decide who, under conditions that are about the same for everyone, can perform an assigned set of tasks better than (not as well as) any other competitor. The set of tasks assigned to the competitor in the U.S. Open includes not merely striking a golf ball with precision, but doing so under greater than usual mental and physical stress. The accommodation Olinger sought, while reasonable in a general sense, would alter the fundamental nature of that competition.

The lower court verdict was later affirmed by the Seventh U.S. Circuit Court of Appeals in *Olinger v. United States Golf Association*, 205 F.3d 1001 (7th Cir.

2000). The conflicting Ninth and Seventh Circuit rulings on *Martin* and *Olinger* compelled the U.S. Supreme Court to grant *certiorari* of the *Martin* case in 2000. In *PGA Tour Inc. v. Casey Martin*, 532 U.S. 661 (2001), the Court affirmed the lower court ruling in favor of Martin in a 7–2 decision. The Court ordered the PGA Tour to allow Martin to use a cart, rejecting its argument that PGA golfers are not a protected class under Title III. The PGA Tour's argument was particularly invalid, the Court argued, because PGA golfers must pay a $3,000 fee to attend qualifying school before qualifying for the Tour. Consequently, PGA golfers are not different from customers of any other private business.

Within days of the ruling in *Martin*, the U.S. Supreme Court ordered the Seventh U.S. Circuit Court of Appeals to reconsider its ruling in *Olinger*. It remains to be seen how the *Martin* decision will affect other sports and how broadly the ruling will be interpreted. Dissenting Justice Antonin Scalia expressed concern that judges would force Little League baseball umpires to grant children with attention deficit disorder four strikes instead of three. Justice Stevens, presenting the majority opinion, stated that "the waiver of an essential rule of competition for anyone would fundamentally alter the nature of [a] petitioner's tournaments." Consequently, future petitioners in other sports must prove that the rule that they wish to waive is not fundamental.

16.3.2.5. Sports Facilities

In *Paralyzed Veterans of America v. D.C. Arena L.P.*, 117 F.3d 579 (D.C. Cir. 1997), the Paralyzed Veterans of America brought an ADA suit against the owners and operators of an athletic arena under construction (MCI Center) to require that wheelchair seating in the arena provide lines of sight over standing spectators. The district court ruled that most, but not all, wheelchair seating had to have sight lines over standing spectators. The court of appeals, in affirming the decision, held that the guidelines requiring that wheelchair areas in public accommodations covered by ADA provide their users with lines of sight comparable to those of members of the general public was entitled to deference. One of these guidelines, issued by the Public Access Section of the Department of Justice (Standard 4.33.3), states that wheelchair areas shall be an integral part of any fixed seating plan and shall be located so as to provide people with physical disabilities a choice of admission prices and lines of sight comparable with those for members of the general public.

In December 1999, the New York Yankees settled a lawsuit by four disabled fans that alleged the Yankees were in violation of the Americans with Disabilities Act. Under the settlement, which effectively ended a bias lawsuit against the team and the city, the Yankees offered wheelchair users and their companions about 300 pairs of seats in various areas of the old Yankee Stadium, including box seats. People with disabilities also were given improved access to the stadium's concession stands, restaurants, and suites. The team also paid $25,000 to the federal government and contributed $10,000 to charities chosen by the four fans.

NOTE _____

1. In 2008, the University of Michigan was sued by Paralyzed Veterans of America who alleged that Michigan's football stadium, Michigan Stadium, was not compliant with ADA rules. ADA rules require that public venues make one percent of seats wheelchair-accessible and disperse them throughout the venue. The case was settled when Michigan agreed to install more wheelchair accessible seating, reducing the stadium's capacity from 107,501 to

106,201, dropping it behind Penn State's Beaver Stadium as the largest stadium in college football.

16.4. ATHLETES WITH AIDS AND TESTING FOR HIV

Another concern for athletic administrators is whether individuals testing HIV positive or with the AIDS virus should be allowed to participate in athletic competitions. The U.S. Supreme Court, in *School Board of Nassau County v. Arline*, 480 U.S. 273 (1987), held that individuals with contagious diseases could be defined as handicapped persons under the meaning of Section 504 of the Rehabilitation Act.

While the plaintiff in *Arline* had tuberculosis, not HIV or AIDS, and the Supreme Court refused to address whether Section 504 would cover individuals with HIV or AIDS, the issue was addressed in *Doe v. Dolton Elementary School District*, 694 F. Supp. 440 (N.D. Ill. 1988). In that case, a 12-year-old student who was infected with AIDS was excluded from attending school. In ruling for the student, the court, relying on *Nassau County v. Arline*, held that an individual with AIDS was likely to qualify as a handicapped individual under Section 504. Although the court did allow Doe to attend classes, it also placed certain limits on the activities the plaintiff could engage in, one of those activities being contact sports.

With increased public awareness about the transmission of HIV and the AIDS virus, however, administrators may have to address questions involving the participation by individuals testing HIV-positive or with the AIDS virus. For example, should athletes who test HIV-positive be excluded from participation in contact sports, such as football? The issue has yet to be tested in the courts, yet, as illustrated by the situations of Magic Johnson and Tommy Morrison, administrators may need to address the issue.

Although no league requires mandatory or random testing for HIV, the issue came to the forefront in November 1991, when Magic Johnson of the Los Angeles Lakers announced that he had the HIV virus and was retiring from basketball. When Johnson attempted to return to the NBA in 1992, a number of players and owners voiced concern over his playing in the league, and Johnson was compelled to retire again. Due to the reaction of the players and owners, the NBA began an AIDS education program, and in 1996 Johnson returned to the NBA as an active player. One sport that does conduct HIV/AIDS testing is boxing. In 1996, heavyweight boxer Tommy Morrison announced that he had tested positive for HIV in a prefight physical. In 2007, Morrison, after 11 years, was cleared to fight again after passing medical exams showing he was no longer HIV-positive and won his fight against John Castle in the second round. The states that require professional boxers to undergo mandatory HIV testing before they are licensed are Arizona, California, Colorado, Georgia, Indiana, Maryland, Massachusetts, New Mexico, Nevada, New York, Oregon, Pennsylvania, Utah, Washington, and the Commonwealth of Puerto Rico. Several other states have considered making prefight HIV testing mandatory.

GLOSSARY OF LEGAL AND SPORTS TERMS

Acceptance: The offeree's notification to the offeror that he or she agrees to be bound by the terms and conditions of the offer.

Accommodation: Adjustment or settlement.

Accrue: Increase, add to, become due.

ACT: An assessment examination for college admission that consists of English, mathematics, reading, and science reasoning sections.

Addendum: Addition and/or change.

Adjudicate: Have a court make a decision or decide a dispute.

Administrative law: Law that affects private parties and is promulgated by governmental agencies other than courts or legislative bodies. The administrative agencies derive their power from legislative enactments and are subject to judicial review.

Advance: To give or grant funds.

Aff'd. (affirmed): To affirm a judgment, decree, or order is to declare that it is valid and right, and must stand as rendered by the lower court.

Affidavit: A written statement or declaration of facts sworn to by the maker, taken before a person officially permitted by law to administer oaths.

Age Discrimination in Employment Act (ADEA): Federal law passed in 1967 which states that an employer may not fail to hire, refuse to hire, discharge, demote, or discriminate against an employee based on his or her age.

Agent: One who is authorized by the principal to make contracts with third parties on behalf of the principal.

Amateur Athletic Union (AAU): An amateur athletic association dedicated to the development of amateur sports and physical fitness for amateur athletes of all ages.

Amateur Sports Act: Passed by the U.S. Congress in 1978 to reorganize and coordinate amateur athletics in the United States and to encourage and strengthen participation of U.S. amateurs in international competition. The act creates a governing structure for the United States Olympic Committee (USOC) by empowering it to select one governing body for each Olympic or Pan-American sport. Amendments known as the Ted Stevens Olympic and Amateur Sports Act, were made in 1998. Changes include the incorporation of athletes with disabilities into the governance structure by requiring the USOC to serve as the national Paralympic representative to the International Paralympic Committee, and requiring that athletic representatives, elected by fellow athletes, make up at least 20% of the membership and voting power of all USOC legislative bodies.

Ambush marketing: A company's intentional efforts to associate its product with an event, without paying the event sponsor, in an effort to give the consumer the impression that it is actually a sponsor of, or in some way affiliated with, the event. Ambush marketing can provide some, if not most, of the benefits of a legitimate, paid-for sponsorship at a fraction of the cost.

American Bar Association: National association of lawyers in the United States.

American Basketball Association: Professional basketball league that existed from 1967 to 1976.

American Basketball League: Defunct women's professional basketball league that existed from 1996 to 1999.

American Football League: Defunct corporation that operated a professional football league in the United States from 1960 to 1970, when it became the American Football Conference and merged with the National Football League.

Americans with Disabilities Act: A 1990 law created in order to eliminate discrimination against individuals with disabilities, and to mandate reasonable accommodations in order to remove barriers created by persons' disabilities.

Amicus curiae: Friend of the court; a third party who presents a brief to a court on behalf of one of the parties in a case.

Annotations: (1) Statutory: brief summaries of the law and facts of cases interpreting statutes passed by Congress or state legislatures that are included in codes; or (2) textual: expository essays of varying length on significant legal topics chosen from selected cases published with the essays.

Answer: The defendant's initial pleading on the alleged violation of criminal or civil law.

Anticompetitive: That which discourages competition among businesses.

Antitrust law: Legislation designed to promote competition in the business sector through regulation that will control the exercise of private economic power.

Appeal: A request from the losing party in a case that a higher court review the decision. Acceptance of the request and issuance by a writ of appeal is mandatory for the higher court.

Appeal denied: A refusal by the higher (or appellate) court to review a lower court decision for error.

Appeal filed: A request by the higher (or appellate) level court to review a lower court decision for error.

Appellant: The party who appeals a decision from a lower court to a higher court.

Appellate court: Court of appellate jurisdiction.

Appellate jurisdiction: Covers cases tried or reviewed by the individual state's highest court involving federal questions, including those bearing on the U.S. Constitution, congressional acts, or foreign treaties. It also covers cases tried or reviewed by the U.S. courts of appeals or the U.S. district courts.

Appellee: The party against whom an appeal is taken.

Arbitrary marks: Words, names, symbols, or devices used to distinguish one product or service from another. The common definition of such words, names, symbols, or devices neither suggests nor describes any ingredient, quality, or characteristic of those goods or services. Such marks receive a broad scope of protection, such as the Lanham Act of 1946.

Arbitration: The hearing and settlement of a dispute between opposing parties by a neutral third party. This decision is often binding by prior agreement of the parties.

Arena Football League: Fifty-yard indoor football league, generally considered to be the second most elite professional football league in the United States.

Arraignment: The appearance of a defendant to a criminal charge before a judge for the purpose of pleading guilty or not guilty to the indictment.

Assault: An unlawful, intentional show of force or an attempt to do physical harm to another person. Assault can constitute the basis of a civil or a criminal action. *See also* **Battery**.

Assignee: A person to whom a right has been transferred.

Assignor: A person who assigns a right, regardless of whether he or she is the original owner thereof.

Association of Intercollegiate Athletics for Women: Defunct amateur athletic association that governed women's intercollegiate athletics before the National Collegiate Athletic Association assumed those duties in the mid-1980s.

Assumption of the risk: Knowledge by one of the parties to an agreement of the risks to be encountered, and that party's consent to take the chance of injury therefrom.

Athlete-agent laws: State legislatures have passed statutes that regulate the conduct of sports agents within the boundaries of that state. One such law is the Uniform Athlete Agents Act, which is designed to protect student-athletes and universities from unscrupulous agent behavior.

Attorney general opinions: Opinions issued by the government's chief counsel, at the request of a governmental body, which interpret the law for the requesting agency in the same manner as a private attorney would for a client. The opinions are not binding on the courts but are usually accorded some degree of persuasive authority.

Authority: Refers to the precedential value to be accorded an opinion of a judicial or administrative body. A court's opinion is binding authority on other courts directly below it in the judicial hierarchy. Opinions of lower courts or of courts outside the hierarchy are governed by the degree to which they adhere to the doctrine of stare decisis. Authority may be either primary or secondary. Statute law, administrative regulations issued pursuant to enabling legislation, and case law are primary authority and, if applicable, will usually determine the outcome of a case. Other statements of or about law are considered secondary authority and thus are not binding.

Battery: An unlawful use of force against another person resulting in physical contact (a tort); it is commonly used in the phrase "assault and battery," assault being the threat of force and battery the actual use of force. *See also* **Assault**.

Bern Convention of 1886: Modified and amended since 1886 to suit the changing needs of international intellectual property regulation, the convention established a union for the protection of industrial property and guarantees moral and economic rights. It provides that copies which infringe these rights can be seized, and the law of the country in which protection is claimed governs the legal remedies for infringement.

Big Four leagues: Unofficial, colloquial term for the four preeminent North American professional sports leagues: Major League Baseball, the National Basketball Association, the National Football League, and the National Hockey League.

Bill: A proposed law introduced in the legislature. The term distinguishes unfinished legislation from directly enacted law.

Blackout: A policy which states that if a sporting event is not sold out prior to a particular time and date, it may not be televised within a certain radius of a home stadium. This policy is intended to encourage people to buy tickets and attend the event instead of staying at home and watching the game on television.

Bona fide: Real, true, and actual.

Book value: The value at which a security is carried on the bank's balance sheet. Book value is often acquisition cost plus or minus accretion or amortization, which can differ significantly from market value.

Bowl Championship Series: A selection system designed to create five bowl matchups involving 10 of the top-ranked teams in the NCAA Division I Football Bowl Subdivision, including an opportunity for the top two to compete in a national championship game.

Branch banking: The right of banks headquartered in some states to take deposits, cash checks, and make loans at more than one location (branch) in the state. Where branch banking is not allowed, unit banking prevails.

Breach of contract: The failure to perform any of the terms of an agreement.

Brief: In U.S. law practice, a written statement prepared by the counsel arguing a case in court. It contains a summary of the facts of the case, the pertinent laws, and argument of how the law applies to the facts supporting counsel's position.

Buckley Amendment: Federal legislation that regulates the release and review of student-athletes' records concerning academic and financial aid information.

Burden of proof: The necessity or duty of positively proving a fact or facts in a dispute on an issue raised between parties.

Business unit: A part of a bank managed and accounted for as a self-contained, independent business serving customers outside the bank and/or other business units in the bank. These units are encouraged to innovate and contribute to corporate profits, consistent with corporate policies and objectives.

Cable television: A service provided to consumers by which traditional television programming and other broadcast signals (e.g., pay cable) are brought into the home of the subscriber by way of cable transmission (as opposed to over-the-air transmission), usually for an initial installation charge and a monthly subscription fee. Standard broadcast stations can also be brought into a subscriber's home through cable television in order to receive a clearer picture.

Canadian Football League (CFL): 110-yard outdoor professional football league. Currently, all franchises are based in Canada, although the league experimented with expansion into the United States in 1993.

Casebook: A textbook used to instruct law students in a particular area of substantive law. The text consists of a collection of court opinions, usually from appellate courts, and notes by the author(s).

Case law: The law of reported appellate judicial opinions, as distinguished from statutes or administrative law.

Cause of action: A claim in law and in fact sufficient to bring the case to court; the grounds of an action (e.g., breach of contract).

Cert. (certiorari) denied: A decision by an appellate court to refuse to review a lower court decision.

Cert. (certiorari) granted: A decision by an appellate court to grant a hearing to review a lower court decision.

Certification: Process whereby a union becomes officially recognized by the National Labor Relations Board as the exclusive bargaining agent for a particular set of workers.

Certiorari: A writ issued by a superior court to an inferior court that requires the latter to produce the records of a particular case tried therein. It is most commonly used to refer to the U.S. Supreme Court, which uses the writ of certiorari as a discretionary device to choose the cases it wishes to hear. The term's origin is the Latin meaning "to be informed of."

Charitable immunity: Similar to sovereign immunity in that it limits the liabilities of charitable organizations.

Citation: The reference to authority necessary to substantiate the validity of one's argument or position. Citation to authority and supporting reference is both important and extensive in any form of legal writing. Citation form is also given emphasis in legal writing, and the information is found in *A Uniform System of Citation*, 17th ed., published by the Harvard Law Review Association, Cambridge, Massachusetts.

Cited case: A case that is referred to in a court decision.

Civil law: (1) Type of law that is based on the writings of Justinian and his successors in the Roman empire; (2) the law concerning noncriminal matters in a common law jurisdiction; (3) one form of legal action for enforcement or protection of private rights and prevention or redress of private wrongs.

Civil Rights Restoration Act: Legislation enacted by Congress in 1988 that returned Title IX applicability to the "institutional approach"; therefore, in a collegiate setting, athletic departments or any program within an institution that receives federal funding is subject to Title IX legislation.

Claim: (1) The assertion of a right, as to money or property; (2) the accumulation of facts that give rise to a right enforceable in court.

Class action: A lawsuit brought by a representative party on behalf of a group, all of whose members have the same or a similar grievance against the defendant.

Clayton Act: A federal law passed in 1914 which stated that the "labor of a human being is not a commodity or article of commerce." The act also affirmed that no court shall grant an injunction in any case between an employer and employees which resulted from a "dispute concerning the terms and conditions of employment." Also, nothing in antitrust law shall forbid the existence or legitimate activities of nonprofit labor organizations created for self-help (*see* **Statutory labor exemption**).

Code: In popular usage, a compilation or a revised statute. Technically, the laws in force are rewritten and arranged in classified order, with the addition of material having the force of law taken from judicial decrees. The repealed and temporary acts are eliminated and the revision is reenacted.

Collective bargaining: The process by which the terms and conditions of employment are agreed upon through negotiations between the bargaining representative of the employees (union) and the employer (management).

Collective bargaining agreement: An agreement between a union and management that governs various aspects of the employment relationship. It may or may not cover items such as pension, insurance, minimum salary, drug testing, or anything related to wages, hours, and terms and conditions of employment.

Collective mark: A trademark or service mark used by the members of a cooperative association or other collective group or organization; includes marks used to indicate membership in a union, an association, or other organization.

Collusion: A secret agreement between two or more persons for a fraudulent, unlawful, or deceitful purpose. This occurs in professional sports when teams secretly agree not to hire one another's players, secretly agree not to spend more than a certain amount of money on players, and/or secretly share information that they are forbidden to share under the terms of a collective bargaining agreement.

Committee on Infractions (COI): National Collegiate Athletic Association (NCAA) committee consisting of 10 attorneys from NCAA member institutions, conferences, and the general public that is responsible for administration of the NCAA enforcement program. The COI hears cases brought by the NCAA against member institutions or their employees and determines the appropriate penalties. COI decisions are appealable to the Infractions Appeals Committee.

Common law: The origin of the Anglo-American legal systems. English common law was largely customary law, and unwritten, until discovered, applied, and reported by the courts of law. In theory, the common law courts did not create law but discovered it in the customs and habits of the English people. The strength of the judicial system in pre-parliamentary days is one reason for the continued emphasis on case law in common law systems. In a narrow sense, common law is the phrase still used to distinguish case law from statutory law.

Comparative negligence: Doctrine in the law of negligence by which the negligence of the parties is compared, and a recovery is permitted when the negligence of the plaintiff was less than the negligence of the defendant.

Compensatory damages: A money award equivalent to the actual injury or loss sustained by the plaintiff.

Complaint: The plaintiff's initial pleading and, according to the Federal Rules of Civil Procedure, no longer full of technicalities demanded by the common law. A complaint need only contain a short and plain statement of the claim upon which relief is sought, an indication of the type of relief requested, and an indication that the court has jurisdiction to hear the case.

Compromise: An agreement reached by each party's giving up part of its claim(s), right(s), or property.

Compulsory license: A license issued by the government that gives a broadcasting company the right to use a work or product that is owned by a copyright holder. The user of the work or product must pay a royalty fee for its use. The copyright holder is obligated to grant the license to any organization that agrees to pay the royalty fee.

Condition precedent: A condition that must occur before a contract will be considered binding on the parties.

Condition subsequent: When parties condition a contract on an event's non-occurrence.

Conferences: Subset of larger amateur sports associations, usually consisting of a number of schools that have similar institutional goals and interests. These schools compete against each other in a number of sports and often compete for conference championships in each of the sports.

Congressional documents: Important sources for legislative histories, which are often necessary for proper interpretation of statute law. Congressional documents are most accessible through specialized indexes and include hearings before congressional committees, reports by or to House of Representatives or Senate committees, and special studies conducted under congressional authority.

Consideration: Something to be done or abstained from by one party to a contract in order to induce another party to enter into a contract.

Constitution: Contains the fundamental law of any organization possessing one. Most national constitutions are written; the English and Israeli constitutions are unwritten.

Continental Basketball Association: A professional second-tier basketball league in the United States from 1978 until 2001.

Contract: An agreement between two or more parties. A preliminary step in making a contract is an offer by one party and acceptance by the other, in which the minds of the parties meet and concur in the understanding of terms. The elements of an enforceable contract are competent parties, a proper subject matter, consideration, and mutuality of agreement and obligation.

Contributory negligence: The negligence of a plaintiff that contributes to or enhances the complaining party's injuries. Contributory negligence is a bar to recovery at common law in some jurisdictions.

Copyright: A protection that covers published and unpublished literary, scientific, and artistic works, in every form of expression, provided that such works are fixed in a tangible or material form. Copyright laws give the creator the exclusive right to reproduce, prepare derivative works, distribute, display, and perform the work publicly. This protection is for a limited period of time.

Copyright Act of 1976: Legislation that extended copyright protection to live sports broadcasts and granted the owners of a copyrightable work the exclusive right to perform the copyrighted work publicly. One of the most important results of the Copyright Act was that it established a governmental agency known as the Copyright Royalty Tribunal.

Copyright Royalty Arbitration Panel: The organization that replaced the Copyright Royalty Tribunal. Under this system, the panel is charged with the same duties as the tribunal: deciding who is entitled to royalties and how much they are entitled to. The Librarian of Congress must approve the determination of these allocations before they are made official.

Copyright Royalty Tribunal: A governmental agency that was charged with deciding disputes over copyrights of broadcasts, collecting royalties for owners of copyrights, and disbursing these royalties to the proper owners.

Corporation: A business that is its own legal entity, separate from its owners. For example, owners, also known as stockholders, cannot be held personally liable for a corporation's debts.

Counterclaim: A claim made by the defendant against the plaintiff in a civil lawsuit; it constitutes a separate cause of action.

Counteroffer: The offeree's response to an offer, in which the offeree proposes different or additional terms than were contained in the original offer. A counteroffer is construed as a rejection of the original offer, and a new offer by the original offeree.

Court of Arbitration for Sport: International court that deals exclusively with international sports-related disputes; created by former International Olympic Committee President Juan Antonio Samaranch.

Covenant: An agreement or promise involving two or more parties.

Covenant not to compete: Also called a noncompete pact, it is a contractual agreement in which an employee promises not to work for certain rival companies for a certain period of time after his or her term of employment is completed.

Criminal law: One form (division) of legal action by which the government treats crimes and their punishments, usually by imprisonment, fine, or both.

Cross-examination: The examination of a witness in a trial or hearing, or in taking a deposition, by the party opposed to the one who produced the witness.

Curt Flood Act: 1998 law that gave Major League Baseball players the right to sue under antitrust laws, but reaffirmed Major League Baseball's immunity from antitrust law in other cases, such as the sale of franchises.

Cybersquatters: People who register sports teams' domain names before the team does. Many of these people register the domain names in hopes of later selling them to the named party. This term also applies to people who register domain names of other famous persons or organizations.

Damages: Monetary compensation awarded by a court for an injury caused by the act of another. Damages may be *actual* or *compensatory* (equal to the amount of loss shown), *exemplary* or *punitive* (in excess of the actual loss and awarded to punish the person for the malicious conduct that caused the injury), or *nominal* (less than the actual loss—often a trivial amount; awarded because the injury is slight or because the exact amount of the injury has not been determined satisfactorily).

Database: The accumulation of textual or other material available to the user of an online computerized information service.

Decertification: Process whereby a union is no longer officially recognized by the National Labor Relations Board as the exclusive bargaining agent for a particular set of workers. Normally, this occurs after a majority of workers vote to dissolve, or decertify, the union.

Defamation: Anything published (libel) or publicly spoken (slander) that injuries a person's character, fame, or reputation by false and malicious statements.

Defendant: The party against whom legal action is taken; particularly, a person accused or convicted of a criminal offense.

Demurrer: A formal objection attacking the legal sufficiency of an opponent's pleadings. It is an assertion, made without disputing the facts, that the pleading does not state a cause of action and that the demurring party is entitled to judgment.

Deposition: The testimony of a witness, taken out of court before a court reporter and under oath.

Descriptive marks: These marks describe the intended purpose, function, use, or size of the goods. They also describe the class of users of the goods, a desirable characteristic of the goods, or the end effect upon the user.

Digital Millennium Copyright Act: Law implemented to ensure that copyrighted material cannot be posted on the Internet without authorization.

The act allows for the imposition of penalties upon persons who attempt to circumvent copyright protection systems or sell equipment that allows people to avoid these protective systems.

Direct examination: The first interrogation or examination of a witness, on the merits, by the party on whose behalf the witness is called.

Direct Payment License: Program administered by USA Track and Field in which licensed athletes can receive endorsement fees, sponsorship monies, and so on directly and still maintain amateur eligibility.

Discharge: To release, usually from an obligation.

Disclosure: An argument that certain information possessed by associations, or meetings held by organizations, should be a matter of public record and, therefore, open to the public. The general meaning of disclosure is "to reveal facts."

Discovery: A method by which opposing parties may obtain information from each other, to prepare for trial and to narrow the issues to be presented at trial.

Distinctive marks: Marks that clearly are identified with the manufacturer of the product and cannot be considered generic.

Diversity jurisdiction: That aspect of the jurisdiction of the federal courts which applies to suits between residents of different states.

Docket number: A number sequentially assigned by the clerk at the beginning of a lawsuit brought to a court for adjudication.

Doping: An athlete's use of drugs that enhance his or her performance, thereby providing advantage over competitors. The term typically refers to intentional users; however, the penalty for unintentional users is the same.

Draft: System commonly used in professional sports whereby a first-year player is selected by a particular team, and that team is granted exclusive bargaining rights with that player for a period of time.

Due care: The legal duty one owes to another according to the circumstances of a particular case.

Due process of law: A term found in the Fifth and Fourteenth Amendments of the U.S. Constitution and also in many states' constitutions. Its exact meaning varies from one situation to another and from one era to the next, but basically it is concerned with the guarantee of every person's enjoyment of his or her rights (e.g., the right to a fair hearing in any legal dispute).

Duty of care: An obligation, recognized by law, that requires an individual or a group to conform to a particular standard of conduct toward another.

Employment-at-will contract: An explicit or implicit agreement that allows an employer to fire an employee at any time, without cause. The employer cannot fire an employee for an illegal cause (e.g., retaliation, discrimination).

Endorse: (1) To sign; (2) to give testimony for, or associate one's self with, a particular product or service (e.g., an athlete "endorses" a restaurant).

Equal Pay Act: This law, passed in 1963, stipulates that an employer must pay equal salaries to men and women holding jobs that require equal skill, effort, and responsibility and that are performed under similar working conditions.

Equal protection: The constitutional guarantee that no person shall be unreasonably discriminated against.

Equal Rights Amendment: A proposed amendment to the U.S. Constitution to guarantee equal rights to women that was not ratified in the early 1980s but that certain states have adopted.

Equitable: Just; fair; reasonable.

Equity: Legal rules, remedies, customs, practices, and principles devised by courts of law to supplement those of the common law.

Et al.: And another; and others.

Evidence: Any form of proof presented at trial through the use of eyewitness testimony, records, documents, and concrete objects, and used to assist the trier of fact in making his or her determination of the case.

Exclusive rights: Rights granted by a sports organization to one broadcaster for the purpose of setting up a single-station broadcast or an exclusive network. Such rights do not permit any other broadcast organization to broadcast the event.

Ex parte: A hearing or examination in the presence of only one of the parties to a case.

Ex rel.: On behalf of, in the name of; a legal proceeding instituted by a state on behalf of an individual who has a private interest in the matter.

Fair Use Doctrine: Section 107 of the Copyright Act of 1976 provides that "the fair use of a copyrighted work, including such use by reproduction in copies or phonorecords or by any other means specified by that section, for purposes such as criticism, comment, news reporting, teaching (including multiple copies for classroom use), scholarship, or research, is not an infringement of copyright."

Fanciful marks: Coined words that have been invented for the sole purpose of functioning as a trademark. Such marks comprise words that are either totally unknown in the language or are completely out of common usage, such as obsolete or scientific terms.

Federal question: A case that contains a major issue involving the U.S. Constitution or a provision of an act of Congress or a U.S. treaty. The jurisdiction of the federal courts is governed in part by the existence of a federal question.

Felony: A serious criminal offense, as distinct from a misdemeanor. Typically, crimes for which the punishment may exceed one year in jail.

Fixation: Recording all parts of a broadcast on film, videotape, or replay tape for purposes of protecting the copyright and the manner in which it was recorded.

Forbearance: Refraining from doing something that one has a legal right to do.

Force majeure: A legal provision that protects a person or organization from the inability to fulfill a contractual obligation as the result of causes outside the control of the parties to a contract that could not be avoided by the exercise of due care—in sports, force majeure usually protects against a strike or lockout.

Free agency: A system generally agreed to in a collective bargaining agreement that allows professional athletes to accept offers from all teams in a professional sports league upon the expiration of their contract, provided they have a played an agreed-upon amount of time in that professional league.

General partner(s): Individual(s) with unlimited responsibility for the operations and debts of a partnership.

Goodwill: A business value that arises from the reputation of a business and its relations with its customers and is unique to the particular business. It has also been defined as "buyer momentum" and "the lure to return." It is an intangible asset of a business.

Governmental activity: An activity that can be performed only by the state.

Grievance arbitration: The submission of the parties' grievance to a private, unofficial person(s) who listens to the disputed question and contentions, then gives a decision regarding the dispute.

Health, Education and Welfare Department: A former cabinet department in the federal government that oversaw Title IX compliance.

Hearings: Extensively employed by both legislative and administrative agencies; they can be adjudicative or investigatory. Adjudicative hearings can be appealed in a court of law. Congressional committees often hold hearings prior to the enactment of legislation; these hearings are then important sources of legislative history.

Hearsay evidence: Evidence not based on the personal knowledge of the witness but on repeating what he or she has heard another say.

Holding: The declaration of the conclusion of law reached by the court regarding the legal effect of the facts of the case.

Holdout: A professional athlete who has contracted or has been compelled to play for a team, but refuses to play until the terms of his or her contract are renegotiated. It can also be used as a verb—to hold out from one's contract.

Hostile environment sexual harassment: Unwelcome sexual advances, requests for sexual favors, and other verbal or physical conduct of a sexual nature constitute hostile environment sexual harassment when such conduct has the purpose or effect of unreasonably interfering with an individual's work performance or creating an intimidating, hostile, or offensive working environment.

Immunity: A condition that protects against liability (tort) or prosecution (criminal law).

Impasse: A condition that exists when the parties to collective bargaining negotiations have bargained in good faith but have reached a deadlock position on a particular issue or issues.

Incur: To take on or accept.

Indemnification: A legal provision that protects and/or reimburses, in whole or in part, a person or organization in the event of a loss, damage, or penalty.

Independent contractor: One who contracts to perform work according to his or her own methods and without being subject to the control of the employer except for the result of the contractor's work.

Indictment: A formal accusation of a crime made by a grand jury at the request of a prosecuting attorney.

Individuals with Disabilities Education Act: A 1990 amendment to the Education for All Handicapped Children Act of 1975, designed to secure the right of children with disabilities to appropriate and cost-free education-related services.

Induce: To urge on or to lead into.

Infractions Appeals Committee: National Collegiate Athletic Association (NCAA) committee consisting of five attorneys from NCAA member institutions, conferences, and the general public that hears and acts upon appeals of the findings of the Committee on Infractions involving member institutions.

Initial eligibility requirements: Regulations formulated by college athletic associations to ensure that entering student-athletes are qualified for college.

Injunction: A judge's order that a person do or, more commonly, refrain from doing a certain act. An injunction may be preliminary or temporary, pending trial of the issue presented, or it may be final if the issue has already been decided in court.

In loco parentis: Placed in the position of the parents of the child, such as a coach or teacher given this status within a relationship with the student-athlete.

In personam: Against a person. A legal proceeding instituted to obtain decrees or judgments against a person.

In re: In the matter of, concerning; usual method of titling a judicial proceeding in which there are no adversary parties.

Instructions to the jury: A judge's statement to a jury of the applicable law.

Instrument: Usually a document, such as a contract.

Intangible asset: An asset that exists only in connection with something else. It is an idea or formula, not something that can be touched. Goodwill is an example of an intangible asset of a business.

Interlocutory relief: Relief, usually an injunction, that lasts only during the course of a trial.

International Federations: An International Olympic Committee–recognized body for each sport; it sets its own rules and regulations governing eligibility of athletes for international competitions.

International Olympic Committee: World sanctioning body for the Olympic Games; it is located in Switzerland.

Internet: Worldwide interconnection of computer networks used by the government, academic institutions, businesses, and individuals. Each site on the Internet has its own "address," and users are able to access these sites for various reasons.

Interrogatories: Return questions directed to a party or witness, who must serve return answers to the questions under oath.

Jurisdiction: The power of a court to hear and determine a given class of cases; the power to act or a particular action.

Jurisprudence: (1) The science or philosophy of law; (2) a collective term for case law as opposed to legislation.

Knight Commission: Created in 1989 by the John and James L. Knight Foundation (a charitable organization) in order to reform college sports. The 2000–2001 commission consisted of National Collegiate Athletic Association representatives, university presidents, a trustee board chair, faculty, conference commissioners, athletic directors, coaches, athletes, authors, professional sports executives, television officials, a sports apparel representative, a gambling lobbyist, leaders of national higher education associations, and a U.S. senator.

Labor exemption: Created under the Clayton Act of 1914 to shield unions from antitrust liability. There are two types of labor exemptions: statutory and non-statutory. The modern use of the term describes nonstatutory labor exemption. *See also* **Nonstatutory labor exemption** and **Statutory labor exemption**.

Laches: Wrongful or unwarranted delay.

Ladies Professional Golf Association: Organization dedicated to the promotion of golf worldwide and claiming to be the largest women's sport organization in the world. The association is best known for a professional tour of elite women golfers. Affiliated with the Professional Golfers' Association.

Lanham Act of 1946: Governs the law of trademarks, the registration of trademarks, and remedies for the infringement of registered trademarks.

Legislative history: Provides the meanings and interpretations (intent) of a statute as embodied in legislative documents. Also, citations and dates to legislative enactments, amendments, and repeals of statutes are sometimes imprecisely identified as legislative histories. More accurate designations of the citations of legislative changes, as included in codes, are historical notes or amendatory histories.

Lexis-Nexis: The pioneering computerized full-text legal research system, which is a division of Reed Elsevier, Inc. The database organizes documents into "libraries" and "files." Documents include court decisions, law reviews, and statutory or administrative provisions.

Liability: The condition of being responsible either for damages resulting from an injurious act or for discharging an obligation or debt.

Libel: Written defamation of a person's character.

Licensing: The sale of an organization's logo or symbol to another organization that will use the logo or symbol for profit on "licensed" materials, such as apparel or trading cards.

Licensing agent: Person who oversees the licensing of the marks of an organization or a group of organizations. Often an agent will package the marks of several organizations to sell to manufacturers. Generally the agent receives a percentage of the profits from such licensing agreements.

Likelihood of confusion: A measure used by courts to determine whether the use of an organization's marks has reached a level such that the public believes that the goods are endorsed or authorized by someone other than the trademark owner.

Limited judicial review: Derives from a theory that courts should not review every legislative judgment of an organization, but rather defer to the organization's decisions. As a general rule, the legal system intervenes through judicial review only when legislative actions violate rights guaranteed by the Constitution, rights granted by the institution concerned, or basic notions of fairness.

Limited liability: An investment in which a partner cannot legally lose more than he or she invested.

Limited liability corporation: A business structure, legal in some states, in which owners receive the limited liability of a corporation (an S corporation) without having to adhere to S corporation restrictions. For example, an limited liability corporation can have more than 75 owner/investors, but an S corporation cannot.

Limited partnership: An unincorporated business owned by two or more individuals, in which one or more partners retains control over the business and assumes legal debts (general partners), and one or more other partners simply invests money in the business but relinquishes both control of the business and responsibility for debts (limited partners).

Lockout: An employer's withholding of work and closing of a business because of a labor dispute, as opposed to a strike. Can occur in professional sports upon the expiration of the collective bargaining agreement.

Longevity rules: Regulations of an amateur athletic association that govern the maximum age or number of semesters for which athletes can participate in athletics in that particular athletic association.

Luxury suites: Also referred to as luxury boxes. Premiere seating with amenities sold by sports franchises, athletic departments, or arena owners—often to corporate clientele. Normally, corporations lease a particular suite for a season.

Major Indoor Soccer League: Defunct corporation that operated professional indoor soccer in the United States from 1978 to 1992.

Majority opinion: An appellate court decision in which the holding of the court is not unanimous.

Major League Baseball: Corporation that operates professional baseball in the United States and Canada; it is located in New York City.

Major League Baseball Players Association: A union that represents professional players in Major League Baseball.

Major League Soccer: The only premiere soccer league in the United States. It is structured in the single-entity/limited liability corporation model.

Malfeasance: The doing of an act that is wrong and unlawful.

Malpractice: Professional misconduct or unreasonable lack of skill. This term is usually applied to such conduct by doctors and lawyers.

Misdemeanor: Offense lower than felony and generally punishable by fine or imprisonment of up to one year.

Misfeasance: Performance of a legal act in an illegal manner.

Mitigation of damages: A requirement in contract law that a plaintiff alleviate the damages of the one who has breached a contract.

Modified: Changed; a decision altered by the introduction of new elements or the cancellation of existing elements.

Monopoly: The market condition existing when only one economic entity produces a particular product or provides a particular service.

Moot question: A case that, because of changed circumstances or conditions after the litigation was begun, no longer contains a justiciable question.

Motion: A formal request made to a judge pertaining to any issue arising while a lawsuit is pending.

Naming rights fee: A fee that a company pays to place its name on a facility or, in the case of certain international sports, on a team.

National Association for Intercollegiate Athletics: An amateur intercollegiate athletic association for small four-year colleges; it is located in Olathe, Kansas.

National Basketball Association: Corporation that operates professional basketball in the United States; it is located in New York City.

National Basketball Players Association: A union that represents professional players in the National Basketball Association and the Women's National Basketball Association.

National Collegiate Athletic Association: The major intercollegiate athletic association for men and women in the United States; it is located in Indianapolis, Indiana.

National Federation of State High School Associations: Amateur athletic association for interscholastic athletics in the United States; its headquarters are located in Indianapolis, Indiana.

National Football League: Corporation that operates professional football in the United States; it is located in New York City.

National Football League Players Association: A union that represents professional players in the National Football League.

National governing bodies: Governing bodies for individual sports sanctioned by the U.S. Olympic Committee. *See also* **USA Track and Field**.

National Hockey League: Corporation that operates professional hockey in the United States and Canada; it is located in New York City.

National Hockey League Players Association: A union that represents professional players in the National Hockey League.

National Junior College Athletic Association: Amateur intercollegiate athletic association for two-year colleges in the United States; it is located in Colorado Springs, Colorado.

National Labor Relations Act: A federal law which mandates that private employers bargain with certified unions and prohibits discrimination against workers who join a union. It also protects both workers and management from unfair labor practices.

National Labor Relations Board: Federal administrative agency that was established to administer and enforce the National Labor Relations Act. The board has two primary responsibilities: supervising and conducting representation elections and adjudicating employer and union unfair labor practices.

National reporter system: The network of reporters published by West Publishing Company; these reporters attempt to publish all cases of precedential value from all state and federal courts.

National Small College Athletic Association: An amateur intercollegiate athletic association for small four-year institutions; it is located in Warners, New York.

Negative covenant: An understanding in a deed or contract whereby a party obliges himself or herself to refrain from doing or performing some act.

Negligence: The failure to exercise due care.

Negotiation: The deliberation, settling, or arranging of the terms and conditions of a possible transaction.

No Electronic Theft Act: A law that makes it illegal for someone to willfully infringe upon a copyright (1) for purposes of commercial advantage or private financial gain or (2) via reproduction or distribution, including electronic means. The basic purpose of the act is to punish people who willfully infringe upon copyrighted material on the Internet for financial gain.

Noncompete pact: *See* **Covenant not to compete**.

Nonfeasance: In tort law, this term applies to nonperformance of some act that ought to be performed, omission to perform a required duty at all, or total neglect of duty.

Nonstatutory labor exemption: A judicially derived expansion of the labor exemption that is based on the policy that favors collective bargaining and gives it preference over the antitrust laws. Therefore, union-management collective bargaining agreements that are the result of a good faith negotiation will be protected from antitrust laws. The provisions of the agreement usually cannot be successfully attacked as collusive or anticompetitive. The modern use of the term *labor exemption* is applied to the nonstatutory labor exemption.

North American Soccer League: Defunct corporation that operated professional soccer in the United States from 1968 to 1985.

Obligation: Debt or duty.

Offer: An act by one person giving another person the legal power to create the obligation called a contract.

Offeree: One to whom a contract offer is made.

Offeror: One who makes a contract offer.

Office for Civil Rights: A governmental agency that is charged with providing an interpretation of Title IX and how it should be applied to programs that receive federal funding.

Opinion: An expression of the reasons why a certain decision (the judgment) was reached in a case. A *majority opinion* is usually written by one judge and represents the principles of law that a majority of the judge's colleagues on the court deem operative in a given decision; it has more precedential value than any of the following. A *separate opinion* may be written by one or more judges who concur in or dissent from the majority opinion. A *concurring opinion* agrees with the result reached by the majority but disagrees with the precise reasoning leading to that result. A *dissenting opinion* disagrees with the result reached by the majority and thus disagrees with the reason and/or principles of law used by the majority in deciding the case. A *plurality opinion* (called a judgment by the Supreme Court) is agreed to by less than a majority as to the reasoning, but is agreed to by a majority as the result. A *per curiam opinion* is an opinion by the court that expresses its decision in a case but does not identify the author. A *memorandum opinion* is a holding of the whole court in which the opinion is very concise.

Option clause: In sports law, the club's right to renew a contract for a one-year period under the same terms and conditions as the previous year of the contract, including another option year, except that the option year of the contract will not contain an option clause. The only term that may differ in the option year is the salary, which varies from league to league, according to the provisions set forth in the contract and/or collective bargaining agreement.

Option contract: A contract that binds the offeror to hold the offer open for a specified period of time, during which the offeree must give consideration to the option.

Ordinance: The equivalent of a municipal statute, passed by the city council and governing matters not already covered by a federal or state law.

Original jurisdiction: Jurisdiction to take cognizance of a cause at its inception, try it, and pass judgment upon the law and fact. It covers two types of cases: those involving ambassadors, ministers, and consuls and those involving a state as one of the parties to a lawsuit.

Parallel citation: A citation reference to the same case printed in two or more different reports.

Parol evidence rule: Prohibits the admission of oral statements, preliminary agreements, or writings made prior to or at the time of signing that would in any way alter, contradict, or change the written contract.

Partnership: An unincorporated business owned by two or more individuals.

Patent: A document issued by the federal government that grants its owner a legally enforceable right to exclude others from making, using, or selling the invention described and claimed in the document for a limited period of time without the permission of the inventor. Patents are property that can be bought, sold, hired, or rented. In addition, there are territorial rights (the holder of the patent has rights as it pertains to the product within the United States).

Pay cable: Refers to a premium cable television service, by which special channels are provided to subscribers for an additional cost. It is usually used for unique programming, such as movies or sporting events, unavailable on standard broadcast television or more basic cable television channels.

Per annum: Per year.

Per curiam: By the court. An opinion of the Supreme Court that is authored by the justices collectively.

Per diem: Per day.

Performance-enhancing drug: A substance used by athletes to improve their performances in the sports in which they engage.

Permanent injunction: An injunction intended to remain in force until the termination of the particular suit.

Per se: By itself; inherently; in isolation.

Personal seat license: A license sold by a facility that gives a patron exclusive right to purchase tickets for a particular seat for all or most of the facility's events. Terms of a personal seat license can be one year, several years, or the life of the facility. Personal seat licenses are commonly used to finance new arenas and stadiums of professional and intercollegiate athletic teams.

Petitioner: The party who brings an action; the party who seeks a writ of certiorari.

Piracy: The interception of broadcasts (including sports broadcasts) by satellite technology without consent of the rights holder.

Plaintiff: The party who brings an action; the complainant.

Players association: The organization that works on the athletes' behalf when negotiating the collective bargaining agreement with league officials. The players associations of the Big Four include the Major League Baseball Players Association, the National Football League Players Association, the National Basketball Players Association, and the National Hockey League Players Association.

Precedent: A case that furnishes an example or authority for deciding subsequent cases in which identical or similar facts are present.

Preliminary injunction: An injunction granted at the institution of a suit to restrain the defendant from doing or continuing some act; it may be discharged or made perpetual as soon as the rights of the parties are determined.

Presidents Commission of the National Collegiate Athletic Association: An advisory body comprised of university presidents within the NCAA's governing structure; it can propose legislation to be voted upon by the NCAA membership.

Prima facie: At first sight; on the face of it; presumability; a fact presumed to be true unless disproved by some evidence to the contrary.

Procompetitive: That which encourages competition among businesses.

Professional Golfers' Association: A 26,000-member organization dedicated to the promotion of golf worldwide. The association is best known for having a professional tour of elite men golfers. Affiliated with the Ladies Professional Golf Association.

Property: Tangible or intangible item or items that a person, group, or corporation has exclusive right to possess. That person, group, or corporation is called the owner and may legally exclude others from using or possessing its property.

Proprietary activity: An activity that is done by the state but could be undertaken by the private sector.

Proximate cause: The act that is the natural and reasonably foreseeable cause of the harm or agent that injures the plaintiff.

Publicly traded: Denotes that a company's stock is available for purchase in a market that is widely accessible to all investors or consumers (such as the New York Stock Exchange or NASDAQ).

Punitive damages: Compensation in excess of actual or consequential damages. They are awarded to punish the wrongdoer, but only in cases involving willful or malicious misconduct.

Quid pro quo: This for that. Something given in exchange for something else.

Quid pro quo sexual harassment: Unwelcome sexual advances, requests for sexual favors, and other verbal or physical conduct of a sexual nature constitute quid pro quo sexual harassment when (1) submission to such conduct is made either explicitly or implicitly a term or condition of an individual's employment, or (2) submission to or rejection of such conduct by an individual is used as the basis for employment decisions affecting such individual.

Racketeer Influenced Corrupt Organization Statute: A federal law that makes it a crime for organized criminal conspiracies to operate legitimate businesses.

Ratification: The adopting or confirming of an act that was previously executed without authority or of an act that was voidable.

Reckless misconduct: An action that falls between the unintentional tort of negligence and the intentional torts of assault and battery. Behavior characterized by intent on the part of the defendant to commit the act but no intent to harm the plaintiff by the act.

Redshirting: To extend the playing career of a student-athlete by postponing or passing over a year of intercollegiate athletic participation while not affecting the student-athlete's maximum allowable time for participating. The term is used in both college and high school athletics.

Regional reporter: A unit of the National Reporter System that reports state court decisions within a defined geographical area.

Regional sports network: A cable television station that presents sports programming, most importantly live broadcasts of sporting events, to a local network. Examples of regional sports networks include the YES Network in New York City and NESN in Boston.

Regulations: Orders issued by various governmental departments to carry out the intent of the law. Agencies issue regulations to guide the activity of their employees and to ensure uniform application of the law. Regulations are not the work of the legislature and in theory do not have the effect of law. In practice, however, because of the intricacies of judicial review of administrative action, regulations can have an important effect in determining the outcome of cases involving regulatory activity. U.S. government regulations appear first in the *Federal Register*, published five days a week, and are subsequently arranged by subject in the *Code of Federal Regulations*.

Relinquish: To give up, surrender, or turn over.

Reports: (1) *Court reports* are published judicial cases arranged according to some grouping, such as jurisdiction, court, period of time, subject matter, or case significance; (2) *administrative reports or decisions* are published decisions of an administrative agency; (3) *annual statements of progress, activities, or policy* are reports issued by an administrative agency or an association.

Rescission: Canceling, annulling, voiding.

Reserve clause: In sports law, the club's right to renew a contract for a one-year period under the same terms and conditions as the previous year of the contract; the only term that may differ in the option year is the salary, which varies from league to league according to provisions set forth in the contract and/or collective bargaining agreement.

Res ipsa loquitur: A method of rebuttal to the presumption that a defendant was negligent. It arises upon proof that the instrumentality causing the injury was not under the defendant's exclusive control and that the extent of injury was one that ordinarily does not happen in the absence of negligence.

Res judicata: An adjudicated matter; a legal issue that has been decided by a court.

Respondent: The party against whom legal action is taken; the party against whom a writ of certiorari is sought.

Rev'd. (reversed): A decision by an appellate court that voids a lower court decision based on some error made in the lower court. Often the case is remanded (sent back) to the lower court with instruction.

Right: That which a person is entitled to keep and enjoy, and to be protected by law in its enjoyment. A right constitutes a claim when it is not in one's possession. The word *right* also signifies an interest when used in regard to property—in this sense, entitling a person to hold or convey his or her property at pleasure.

Right of publicity: An individual person's right to control and profit from the commercial use of his or her name, likeness, and persona.

Rozelle Rule: In effect from 1963 to 1976, generally required a team signing a contract with a player formerly employed by another team to pay compensation to that team. If the two teams could not agree, the commissioner would determine compensation.

Rule of reason: The judicial doctrine holding that a trade practice violates the Sherman Act only if the practice is an unreasonable restraint of trade, based on economic factors.

Salary cap: A league's limit on a particular player's and/or team's total salary expenditure.

SAT: A scholastic achievement test that measures intellectual ability in math and English.

Satellites: A space-based distribution system of program services for standard broadcast and cable television. Satellites relay television signals across the world.

S corporation: A corporation with 75 or fewer shareholders, enjoying the benefits of a corporation (limited liability) and the tax advantages of a partnership.

Secondary meaning: A mental recognition in the buyer's mind associating symbols, words, colors, and designs with goods from a single source. It tests the connection in the buyer's mind between the product bearing the mark and its source. In a commercial sense, secondary meaning is buyer association, mental association, drawing power, or commercial magnetism.

Service mark: A mark used in the sale or advertising of services to identify the services of one person and distinguish them from the services of others. Identifies and distinguishes the source and quality of an intangible service.

Sexual harassment: A form of sex discrimination that violates Title VII of the Civil Rights Act of 1964. Sexual harassment is behavior of a sexual nature that is unwanted or unreciprocated by the recipient. It can take many forms, including but not limited to (1) physical sexual harassment, which includes staring, leering, gestures, and unnecessary touching; (2) verbal harassment, including propositions, demands or requests for sexual favors, suggestive remarks, innuendo, offensive comments about dress or appearance, and jokes of a sexual nature; and (3) visual harassment, including the display of pornographic pictures or other sexually suggestive materials.

Shepardizing: To look up a case citation in *Shepard's Citations*, especially to check the status of the case, parallel citations, or the use of the case in other jurisdictions.

Sherman Act: Federal law passed in 1890 to protect U.S. consumers by controlling unfair monopolization. It serves to promote free and open market competition. Sometimes called the Sherman Antitrust Act.

Single-entity league: A type of sports league governance that evolved in the late 1990s so that the organization is not subject to antitrust law attack. It is a business structure in which one is not allowed to own an individual franchise. Instead, franchises (teams) are owned by the league and controlled by operators/investors.

Siphoning: The shifting of programs from standard broadcast television to pay cable or basic cable television.

Slander: Oral defamation of a person's character.

Sole proprietorship: An unincorporated business owned by one individual.

Sovereign immunity: Certain protections afforded to the state against tort liability, regardless of the circumstances, when the state is engaged in governmental function.

Specific performance: An equitable remedy whereby the court orders one of the parties to a contract to perform his or her duties under the contract. Usually granted when money damages would be an inadequate remedy.

Sports Agent Responsibility and Trust Act: Federal legislation regulating the conduct of athlete agents.

Sports Broadcast Act of 1961: A statutory exemption from antitrust laws that allows the teams in each of the four major professional sports leagues in the United States to negotiate collectively with the television networks.

Standard broadcast television: What most individuals consider basic television. Local television stations broadcast programming that is received by local home television sets when the antenna picks up air transmission signals.

Standard of care: The level of caution that one should exercise.

Standard player contract: Also called a uniform player contract. A form contract that must be signed by all players in a typical professional sports league, as stipulated by a league's bylaws or collective bargaining agreement. Normally, standard player contracts will be virtually identical from one player to another, with the exception of salary consideration, bonus clauses, and additional clauses.

Standing: The qualifications needed to bring legal action. The qualifications relate to the existence of a controversy in which the plaintiff has suffered or is about to suffer an injury or infringement upon a legally protected right that a court is competent to redress.

Stare decisis: To stand on what has been decided; to adhere to the decision of previous cases. It is a rule, sometimes departed from, that a point settled in a previous case becomes a precedent that should be followed in subsequent cases decided by the same court.

State action: Legal principle that the university, association, or governing body is shown to be part of the federal government, state government, or an arm or agency of a state government. State action must be proven to bring a constitutional law challenge.

State Equal Rights Amendments: Legislation passed by certain states that protects women from discrimination on the basis of their gender.

Statute of frauds: Has its roots in English common law and is designed to prevent injustices resulting from fraudulent claims or promises that were never kept. The exact rules vary from state to state.

Statutes: Acts of legislature. Depending upon the context, a statute may mean a single act of a legislature or a body of acts that are collected and arranged according to a scheme or for a session of a legislature or parliament.

Statutes of limitations: Laws setting time periods during which disputes may be taken to court.

Statutory labor exemption: The statutory labor exemption created under the Clayton Act of 1914 allows unions to enter into agreements with management regarding the working conditions of the employees they represent and stipulates that union activity does not constitute a restraint of trade under the Sherman Act.

Strict liability: Liability regardless of fault. Under tort law, strict liability is imposed on any person who introduces into commerce any good that is unreasonably dangerous when in a defective condition.

Strike: A concerted refusal by employees to work for their employer, or to work at their customary rate of speed, until the employer grants the concessions that they seek, as opposed to a lockout. Occurs during a labor dispute over the terms and conditions of the collective bargaining agreement.

Subpoena: A court order compelling a witness to appear and testify in a certain proceeding.

Summary proceeding: A judicial action, usually a judgment or decision, that is taken without benefit of a formal hearing. Summary decisions of the Supreme Court are those made without the Court having heard an oral argument.

Summons: A notice to a person that an action has been commenced against him or her and that he or she is required to appear in court and answer the complaint in such action.

Superstation: A local, independent, distant-signal television station whose programs, including sports, are carried via satellite to cable systems outside of the station's local broadcast range.

Supreme Court: (1) The court of last resort in the federal judicial system. (It also has original jurisdiction in some cases.) (2) In most states, the highest appellate court or court of last resort (but not in New York).

Tangible asset: Something that can be touched. Examples of tangible assets are sports equipment and team apparel.

Tax shelter: A financial arrangement, such as the use of special depletion allowances, that reduces taxes on current earnings.

Ted Stevens Olympic and Amateur Sports Act: *See* **Amateur Sports Act**.

Temporary restraining order: An order of limited duration restricting the defendant from doing a threatened act until the propriety of granting an injunction can be determined.

Terminate: To end or bring to an end.

Third-party beneficiary: Party who is not privy to a contract but for whom the contract is made and will benefit from it.

Title VII: Part of the Civil Rights Act of 1964 focusing on discrimination on the basis of race, color, religion, sex, or national origin in hiring/firing practices and advancement policies within companies.

Title IX: Part of the Educational Amendments of 1972. This law specifically and clearly recognizes the problems of sex discrimination and forbids such discrimination in any program, organization, or agency that receives federal funds.

Tolls: To delay, suspend, or hold off the effect of a statute.

Tort: A civil wrong that does not involve a contractual relationship. The elements of a tort are a duty owed, breach of that duty, and the resultant harm to the one to whom the duty is owed.

Trademark: A name, device, or symbol that has become sufficiently associated with a good or has been registered with a governmental agency; once it is established, the manufacturer has a right to bring legal action against those who infringe upon the protection given the trademark.

Trademark infringement: The reproduction, counterfeiting, copying, or imitation, in commerce, of a registered mark in connection with the sale, offering for sale, distribution, or advertising of any goods or services on or in connection with which such use is likely to cause confusion or to cause mistake, or to deceive, without consent of the registrant.

Trial court: The court before which issues of fact and law are tried and first determined, as distinguished from an appellate court.

Unfair labor practice: Activity by management or union, under the National Labor Relations Act, that the National Labor Relations Board determines to be in violation of the act.

Uniform Athlete Agent Act: Legislation supported by the National Collegiate Athletic Association and passed by the National Conference of Commissioners on Uniform State Laws in 2000. It is designed to provide a single set of state regulations that will govern athlete agent conduct.

Uniform Commercial Code: Code that governs numerous areas of commercial law and has been adopted as statutory law in nearly every state.

Uniform player contract: *See* **Standard player contract**.

United States Anti-Doping Agency: Nongovernmental agency responsible for implementation of the World Anti-Doping Code in the United States, specifically as it applies to U.S. Olympic athletes.

United States Football League: Defunct professional football league that played games in the spring and summer months from 1983 to 1985.

United States Olympic Committee: Amateur athletic association that governs Olympic competition and eligibility in the United States. It is located in Colorado Springs, Colorado.

USA Track and Field: The national governing body for track and field in the United States.

U.S.C.: United States Code. A compilation of congressional statutes and their amendments, organized into 50 subject titles.

U.S.C.A.: United States Code Annotated. A commercially published edition of the United States Code.

Vacated: Annulled, set aside, canceled, or rescinded; the canceling or rescinding of an entry or record or of a judgment.

Vacated case: When a judge sets aside or annuls an order or judgment that he or she finds improper.

Venue: The geographical area where a court with jurisdiction may try a case.

Vicarious liability: Imposes liability for a tortious act upon a person who in not personally negligent but is held liable because of the relationship between the parties (i.e., a school may be held liable for a coach's tortious act because the school is the employer of the coach).

Void: Having no legal effect and not binding on anyone.

Voidable: That which may be legally annulled at the option of one of the parties.

Voluntary organizations: Associations consisting of members who wish to participate in association events, agree to abide by the rules of the association, and meet membership requirements.

Waiver: The voluntary relinquishment of a known right.

Westlaw: A computerized database and legal research system available through West Publishing Company. The database contains statutory material and cases from components of the National Reporter System.

Women's Basketball Association: Defunct corporation that operated a professional women's basketball league in the United States from 1978 to 1982.

Women's National Basketball Association: The preeminent women's professional basketball league in the United States. It is structured in the single-entity model and managed by the National Basketball Association. The league began play in 1997.

Women's United Soccer Association: Defunct women's professional soccer league in the United States. It was structured in the single-entity model and operated from 2001 to 2003.

Workers' compensation: The methods and means created by statutes for giving greater protection and security to workers and their dependents against injury or death occurring in the course of employment.

World Anti-Doping Agency: Independent foundation whose mission is to promote, coordinate, and monitor the fight against the use of performance-enhancing drugs in sports. The agency created and updates the World Anti-Doping Code, which lists prohibited drugs and methods and is used by the International Olympic Committee and many other sports organizations.

World Football League: Defunct corporation that operated a professional football league in the United States in the 1970s.

World Intellectual Property Organization: An international organization that regulates intellectual property. It handles disputes among member countries through mediation, arbitration, and the administration of treaties.

World League of American Football: Original name for NFL Europe, an eight-team league playing American football in Europe.

Writ: A written order, of which there are many types, issued by a court and directed to an official or party, commanding the performance of some act.

Writ of appeal: A suit or action brought before the court that holds a federal act to be unconstitutional or a state action to be constitutional, or that involves a lower federal court deciding against the United States in a criminal case; a suit brought by the United States under the Interstate Commerce Act; or a federal district court hearing a suit involving a restraint on enforcement of a state or federal statute on the grounds that it is unconstitutional.

Writ of certiorari: An appellate court reviewing an action of an inferior court.

XFL: A 100-yard outdoor football league that existed for one season (2001). It was structured in the single-entity model and managed by World Wrestling Federation Entertainment, Inc.

ESSENTIALS OF SPORTS LAW CASE INDEX

(Sorted Alphabetically by Plaintiff)

Acosta v. Unified School District, 37 Cal. Rptr. 2d. 171 (Cal. Ct. App. 1995), p. 126 note 6.

Adams v. Baker, 919 F. Supp. 1496 (D. Kan. 1996), pp. 322; 337 note 2; 352 note 4.

Adidas America Inc. v. National Collegiate Athletic Association, 40 F. Supp. 2d 1275 (D. Kan. 1999), pp. 159; 416 note 3; 507; 736.

Adidas America, Inc. v. Payless Shoesource, Inc., 2008 WL 4279812 (D. Or. September 12, 2008), p. 671 note 5.

Aiken v. Lieuallen, 593 P.2d 1243 (Or. Ct. App. 1978), pp. 360; 361; 362 note 5.

Alabama Football Inc. v. Stabler, 319 So. 2d 678 (Ala. 1975), pp. 384; 385 note 5.

Alabama High School Athletic Association v. Medders, 456 So. 2d 284 (Ala. Sup. Ct. 1984), p. 246 note 3.

Alexander v. Yale University, 631 F.2d 178 (2d Cir. 1980), p. 784 note 13.

Allen Bradley Co. v. Local Union No. 3, International Brotherhood of Electrical Workers, 325 U.S. 797 (1945), p. 490.

Allen v. Dover Co-Recreational Softball League, 807 A.2d 1274 (N.H. 2002), p. 67 note 2.

Alston v. Virginia High School League, Inc., 108 F. Supp. 2d 543 (W.D. Va. 2000), pp. 342; 360; 365; 366 note 3.

Amalgamated Meat Cutters & Butcher Workmen of North America v. Jewel Tea Co., 381 U.S. 676 (1965), p. 490.

Amateur Softball Association v. United States, 467 F.2d 312 (10th Cir. 1972), p. 505.

American and National League of Professional Baseball Clubs v. Major League Baseball Players Association, 130 Cal. Rptr. 626 (Ct. App. 1976), pp. 407–408 note 4.

American Football League v. National Football League, 323 F.2d 124 (4th Cir. 1963), p. 472.

American League Baseball Club of Chicago v. Chase, 149 N.Y.S. 6 (N.Y. Sup. Ct. 1914), p. 407 note 3.

American Needle, Inc v. New Orleans Saints, 496 F. Supp. 2d 941 (N.D. Ill., 2007), p. 666.

American Needle v. NFL, 538 F.3d 736 (7th Cir. 2008), pp. 499; 501; 666.

Anderson v. Little League Baseball, Inc., 794 F. Supp. 342 (D. Ariz. 1992), p. 819.

Angstadt v. Midd-West School District, 377 F.3d 338 (3rd Cir. 2004), p. 224 note 2.

ANO Hockey Club Metallurg Magnitogorsk v. Malkin, No. 10221 (S.D. N.Y. January 29, 2007), p. 648 note 2.

Antonious v. Spalding & Evenflo Companies Inc., 217 F.3d 849 (Fed. Cir. 1999), p. 702 note 3.

Archbishop Walsh High School v. Section VI of the New York State Public High School Athletic Association, Inc., 660 N.E.2d. 521 (N.Y. 1996), p. 178 note 4.

Arlosoroff v. National Collegiate Athletic Association, 746 F.2d 1019 (4th Cir. 1984), pp. 216; 218 note 3.

Ascher v. Scarsdale School District, 700 N.Y.S.2d 210 (N.Y. App. Div. 1999), p. 72 note 2.

Ashby v. Underwriters at Lloyd's, 2008 WL 667420 (S.D. Cal. March 6, 2008), p. 576 note 1.

Associated Students, Inc. v. National Collegiate Athletic Association, 493 F.2d 1251 (9th Cir. 1974), p. 218 note 5.

Association for Intercollegiate Athletics for Women v. National Collegiate Athletic Association, 558 F. Supp. 487 (D.D.C. 1983), *Aff'd by*, 735 F.2d 577 (D.C. Cir. 1984), p. 505.

Association of Independent Television Stations, Inc. v. College Football Association, 637 F. Supp. 1289 (W.D. Okla. 1986), p. 731.

Atkinson v. Lafayette College, No. 01-CV-2141, 2002 U.S. Dist. LEXIS 1432 (E.D. Pa. Jan. 29, 2002), p. 776 note 4.

Atlanta Athletic Club v. Commissioner, 980 F.2d 1409 (11th Cir. 1993), p. 758 note 3.

Atlanta Hawks (by NBA) v. Charles, Ken (by NBPA), Seitz, Arbitrator, 6/22/1978, p. 578 note 2.

Atlanta National League Baseball Club Inc. v. Kuhn, 432 F. Supp. 1213 (N.D. Ga. 1977), p. 15 note 2.

Attorney General (Mass.) v. Massachusetts Interscholastic Athletic Association, 393 N.E.2d 284 (Mass. 1979), p. 332.

AT&T v. NASCAR, 494 F.3d 1356 (11th Cir. 2007), p. 681 note 1.

Austin v. Cornell University, 891 F. Supp. 740 (N.D. N.Y. 1995), p. 779 note 3.

Avila v. Citrus Community College District, 41 Cal. Rptr. 3d 299 (Cal. Ct. App. 2006), p. 77 note 1.

Babyak v. Smith College, No. 99-204 (Hamden Co., Mass. Dist. Ct. 2001), pp. 784 note 4; 774 note 4.

Badgett ex rel. Badgett v. Alabama High School Athletic Association, 2007 WL 2461928 (N.D. Ala. May 3, 2007), p. 821 note 2a.

Baggs v. Little League Baseball, Inc., 840 N.Y.S.2d 529 (N.Y. Sup. 2007), p. 148.

Bain v. Gillespie, 357 N.W.2d 47 (Iowa Ct. App. 1984), p. 145 note 7.

Baisden v. West Virginia Secondary Schools Activities Commission (WVSAC), 568 S.E.2d 32 (W. Va. 2002), pp. 198 note 2; 243 note 1.

Baker v. Briarcliff School Dist., 613 N.Y.S.2d. 660 (N.Y. App. Div. 1994), p. 122 note 4.

Bally v. National Collegiate Athletic Association, 707 F. Supp. 57 (D. Mass. 1988), pp. 289; 291 note 2.

Bally v. Northeastern University, 532 N.E.2d 49 (Mass. 1989), p. 293 note 3.

Baltimore Orioles, Inc. v. Major League Baseball Players Association, 1985 WL 1509 (N.D. Ill. May 23, 1985), p.736 note 3.

Baltimore Orioles, Inc. v. Major League Baseball Players Association, 805 F.2d 663 (7th Cir. 1986), p. 735.

Banks v. National Collegiate Athletic Association, 508 U.S. 908 (1993), p. 621 note 1a.

Banks v. National Collegiate Athletic Association, 746 F. Supp. 850 (N.D. Ind. 1990), p. 509.

Barbay v. National Collegiate Athletic Association, No. 86-5697 1987 U.S. Dist. LEXIS 393 (E.D. La. Jan. 20, 1987), p. 291 note 3.

Barnett v. Texas Wrestling Association, 16 F. Supp. 2d 690 (N.D. Tex. 1998), p. 391 note 3.

Barrett v. West Chester University of Pennsylvania of State System of Higher Educ., 2003 WL 22803477 (E.D. Pa. November 12, 2003), pp. 328 note 7; 345.

Bartges v. University of North Carolina-Charlotte, 908 F. Supp. 1312 (W.D. N.C. 1995), aff'd, 94 F.3d 641 (4th Cir. 1996), p. 770 note 7.

Bauer v. Interpublic Group of Companies, Inc., 255 F. Supp. 2d 1086 (N.D. Cal. 2003), pp. 87 note 1; 598 note 4.

Baum Research & Development v. Hillerich & Bradsby Co., 31 F. Supp. 2d 1016 (E.D. Mich. 1998), p. 510 note 2.

B.C. (a minor) v. Cumberland Regional School District, 531 A.2d 1059 (N.J. Super. A.D. 1987), p. 359 note 7.

Beal v. Midlothian Independent School Dist. 070908 of Ellis County, 2002 WL 1033085 (N.D. Tex. May 21, 2002), p. 328 note 8.

Bearman v. University of Notre Dame, 453 N.E.2d 1196 (Ind. Ct. App. 1983), p. 135 note 9.

Beckett v. Clinton Prairie School Corporation, 504 N.E.2d 552 (Ind. 1987), p. 68 note 3.

Bednar v. Nebraska School Activities Association, 531 F.2d 922 (8th Cir. 1976), p. 354 note 4.

Beeson v. Kiowa County School District, 567 P.2d 801 (Colo. Ct. App. 1977), p. 268 note 1.

Behagen v. Amateur Basketball Association of the United States, 884 F.2d 524 (10th Cir. 1989), pp. 262 note 10; 649 note 5.

Behagen v. Intercollegiate Conference of Faculty Representatives, 346 F.Supp. 602 (D. Minn. 1972), p. 223.

Bell v. Lone Oak Independent School District, 507 S.W.2d 636 (Tex. Ct. App. 1974), p. 268 note 3.

Bell v. Vista Unified School District, 92 Cal. Rptr.2d 263 (Cal. Ct. App. 2000), p. 432.

Benejam v. Detroit Tigers Inc., 635 N.W.2d 219 (Mich. Ct. App. 2001), p. 133 note 6.

Benjamin v. State, 453 N.Y.S.2d 329 (N.Y. Ct. Cl. 1982), p. 133 note 9.

Bennett v. City of New York, 303 A.D.2d 614 (N.Y. App. Div. 2003), p. 76 note 2.

Bennett v. West Texas State University, 525 F. Supp. 77 (N.D. Tex. 1981), rev'd, 698 F. 2d 1215 (5th Cir. 1983), cert. denied, 466 U.S. 903 (1984), p. 338.

Big Ten Conference, Inc. v. Department of Revenue, 726 N.E.2d 114 (Ill. App. 1 Dist. 2000), p. 758 note 2.

Bilney v. Evening Star Newspaper Co., 406 A.2d 652 (Md. Ct. App. 1979), p. 93.

Bingham v. Oregon School Activities Ass'n., 37 F. Supp. 2d 1189 (D. Or. 1999), pp. 246 note 1; 822 note 3.

Bires v. WalTom LLC,662 F.Supp.2d 1019 (N.D. Ill. 2009), p. 378 note 1.

Black v. National Football League Players Association, 87 F. Supp. 2d 1 (D. D.C. 2001), p. 580 note 2.

Blackmon v. Iverson, 324 F. Supp. 2d 602 (E.D. Pa. 2003), p. 376 note 1.

Blaich v. NFL, 212 F. Supp. 319 (S.D. N.Y. 1962), p. 741 note 1.

Blair v. Washington State University, 740 P.2d 1379 (Wash. 1987), pp. 331 note 4; 337 note 3.

Blalock v. Ladies Professional Golf Association, 359 F. Supp. 1260 (N.D. Ga. 1973), p. 478.

Bloom v. NCAA, 93 P.3d 621 (Colo. App. 2004), pp. 19 note 3; 170 note 2.

Board of Directors of Ames Community School District v. Cullinan, 745 N.W.2d 487 (Iowa 2008), p. 433 note 1.

Board of Directors v. Green, 147 N.W.2d 854 (Iowa 1967), p. 268 note 2.

Board of Education of Independent School District No. 92 of Pottawatomie County v. Earls, 536 U.S. 822 (2002), pp. 280 note 2; 287 note 4.

Board of Education v. Youel, 282 N.W. 2d 677 (Iowa 1979), p. 434 note 10.

Board of Governors v. Helpingstine, 714 F. Supp. 167 (M.D. N.C. 1989), p. 686 note 3.

Board of Regents v. National Collegiate Athletic Association, 561 P.2d 499 (Okla. 1977), p. 510 note 3.

Board of Regents v. Roth, 408 U.S. 564 (1972), p. 222.

Board of Supervisors of the Louisiana State University v. Smack Apparel Co., 438 F. Supp. 2d 653 (E.D. La. 2006), p. 686 note 1.

Board of Trustees v. Professional Therapy Services, Inc., 873 F. Supp. 1280 (W.D. Ark. 1995), p. 689 note 7.

Boardwalk Regency Corp. v. Attorney General of New Jersey, 457 A.2d 847 (N.J. Super. Ct. Law Div. 1982), p. 811.

Booth v. El Paso Independent School District, No. A-90-CA-764 (Tex. Dist. Ct. 1990), p. 822 note 3.

Borne v. The Haverhill Golf and Country Club, Inc., No. 96-6511-C, 1999 Mass. Super. LEXIS 523 (Mass. Super. Nov. 19, 1999), p. 37 note 2.

Bostick v. Flex Equipment Company, Inc., 107 Cal. App. 4th 80 (Cal. Ct. App. 2007), p. 147 note 2.

Boston Athletic Association v. International Marathons, Inc., 467 N.E.2d 58 (Mass. 1984), p. 209 note 1.

Boston Athletic Association v. Sullivan, 867 F.2d 22 (1st Cir. 1989), p. 679 note 16.

Boston Celtics Limited Partnership v. Shaw, 908 F.2d 1041 (1st Cir. 1990), pp. 387; 407 note 2.

Boston Professional Hockey Association v. Dallas Cap & Emblem Mfg., 510 F.2d 1004 (5th Cir. 1975), p. 675.

Bouchard v. Smile Bros, 685 N.Y.S.2d 289 (2 N.Y. App. Div. 1999), p. 77 note 5.

Bouchat v. Baltimore Ravens Football Club, Inc., 346 F.3d 514 (4th Cir. 2003), p. 671 note 6.

Bouchat v. Bon-Ton Dept. Stores, Inc., 506 F.3d 315 (4th Cir. 2007), p. 671 note 6.

Boucher v. Syracuse University, 164 F.3d 113 (2d Cir. 1999), pp. 345; 348 note 6.

Boulahanis v. Board of Regents, 198 F.3d 633 (7th Cir. 1999), p. 320 note 6.

Bourne v. Marty Gilman, Inc., 452 F.3d 632 (7th Cir. 20 06), p. 96 note 1.

Bowers v. Baylor University, 862 F. Supp. 142 (W.D. Tex. 1994), p. 776 note 5.

Bowers v. National Collegiate Athletic Association, 130 F. Supp. 2d 610 (D. N.J. 2001), pp. 198 note 1; 822 note 1.

Bowers v. National Collegiate Athletic Association (NCAA), 475 F.3d 524 (2007), p. 238 note 1.

Boyd v. Texas Christian University, Inc., 8 S.W.3d 758 (Tex. App. 1999), p. 67 note 4.

Boyle v. Pennsylvania Athletic Ass'n, 676 A.2d 695 (Pa. Commw. Ct. 1996), p. 225 note 2.

Bradwell v. State, 83 U.S. 130 (1873), p. 334.

Brahatcek v. Millard School District, 273 N.W.2d 680 (Neb. 1979), p. 120 note 10.

Breeden v. Valencia, Inc., 557 So. 2d 302 (La. Ct. App. 1990), p. 148 note 5.

Breighner v. Michigan High School Athletic Association, Inc. (MHSAA), 683 N.W.2d 639 (Mich. 2004), p. 207 note 5.

Brenden v. Independent School District, 342 F. Supp. 1224 (D. Minn. 1972), aff'd., 477 F.2d 1292 (8th Cir. 1973), p. 354 note 6.

Brennan v. Board of Trustees for University of Louisiana Systems, 691 So.2d 324 (La. Ct. App. 1 Cir. 1997), p. 289 note 1.

Brentwood Academy v. Tennessee Secondary School Athletic Association, 531 U.S. 288 (2001), pp. 159; 216–217.

Bridgeman v. National Basketball Association, 675 F. Supp. 960 (D. N.J. 1987), pp. 466; 493.

Bridgeman v. National Basketball Association, 838 F. Supp. 172 (D. N.J. 1993), p. 560.

Brighton School District v. Lyons, 873 P.2d 26 (Colo. Ct. App. 1993), p. 102 note 3.

Brisbin v. Washington Sports and Entertainment, Ltd., 422 F. Supp. 2d 9 (D. D.C. 2006), p. 134 note 3.

Brock v. Georgia Southwestern College, 765 F.2d 1026 (11th Cir. 1985), p. 771.

Brown ex rel. Brown v. Oklahoma Secondary School Activities Ass'n, 125 P.3d 1219 (Okla. 2005), pp. 36 note 2; 176; 184 note 1; 272 note 1.

Brown v. Board of Education, 560 P.2d 1129 (Utah 1977), pp. 432; 434 note 11.

Brown v. Pro Football Inc., 50 F.3d 1041 (D. D.C. 1995), p. 496.

Brown v. Pro Football Inc., 518 U.S. 231 (1996), p. 497.

Brown v. Pro Football, Inc., 782 F. Supp. 125 (D. D.C. 1991), p. 496.

Brown v. Racquetball Centers, Inc., 534 A.2d 842 (Pa. Super. Ct. 1987), p. 152 note 2.

Brown v. Woolf, 554 F. Supp. 1206 (S.D. Ind. 1983), p. 582 note 4.

Bruce v. Ohio State University, No. 87-CV11-7430 (Franklin County, Ohio, 1987), p. 431 note 11.

Bryant v. Colgate University, 996 F. Supp. 170 (N.D. N.Y. 1998), p. 367 note 1.

Bryant v. National Football League, Inc., 2007 WL 3054985 (D. Colo. October 18, 2007), p. 303 note 5.

Bucha v. Illinois High School Association, 351 F. Supp. 69 (N.D. Ill. 1972), p. 365 note 1.

Buckton v. National Collegiate Athletic Association, 366 F. Supp. 1152 (D. Mass. 1973), pp. 217 note 3; 256 note 3; 258.

Bukowski v. Wisconsin Interscholastic Athletic Association (WIAA), 726 N.W.2d 356 (Table) (Wis. App. 2006), pp. 319 note 1; 339 note 2.

Burkart v. Health and Tennis Corporation of America, 730 S.W.2d 367 (Tex. Ct. App. 1987), p. 73 note 11.

Burkey v. Marshall County Board of Education, 513 F. Supp. 1084, 1091 [N.D. W. Va. 1981]), p. 768.

Burlington Industries Inc. v. Ellerth, 524 U.S. 742 (1998), p. 783 note 4.

Burrows et al. v. Ohio High School Athletic Association, 712 F. Supp. 620 (S.D. Ohio 1988), p. 259 note 2.

Burton v. Wilmington Parking Authority, 365 U.S. 715 (1961), p. 217 note 3.

Buse v. Vanguard Group of Investment Cos, No. 91-3560, 1996 U.S. Dist. LEXIS 19033 (E.D. Pa. Dec. 20, 1996), p. 582 note 1.

Butler v. National Collegiate Athletic Association, NCAA, No. C 96-1656 D, 1996 WL 1058233 (W.D. Wash. Nov. 8, 1996), pp. 822; 823 note 5.

Butler v. Oak Creek Franklin School District, 116 F. Supp. 2d 1038 (E.D. Wis. 2000), pp. 221 note 1; 273.

Butts v. National Collegiate Athletic Association, 751 F.2d 609 (3rd Cir. 1984), pp. 247; 247 note 1.

Caldwell v. Griffin Spalding County Bd. Of Ed., 503 S.E.2d 43 (Ga. Ct. App. 1998), p. 125 note 3.

Calhanas v. South Amboy Roller Rink, 679 A.2d 185 (N.J. Super. Ct. App. Div. 1996), p. 79 note 6.

Callaway Golf Company v. Acushnet Company, 585 F. Supp. 2d 600 (D. Del. 2008), p. 701 note 1.

Callaway Golf Co. v. Acushnet Co., 2007 U.S. Dist. LEXIS 85599 (D. Del. Nov. 20, 2007), p. 702 note 1.

Callaway Golf Co. v. Dunlop Slazenger, 384 F. Supp. 2d 735 (D. Del. 2005), p. 702 note 1.

Campbell v. Shelton, 727 N.E.2d 495 (Ind. Ct. App. 2000), p. 140 note 2.

Cañas v. ATP Tour, Matter of Arbitration (2006), CAS 2005/A/951, p. 203 note 4.

Cannon v. University of Chicago, 460 U.S. 1013 (1983), p. 339 note 6.

Cape v. Tennessee Secondary School Athletic Association, 424 F. Supp. 732 (E.D. Tenn. 1976), rev'd. per curiam, 563 F.2d 793 (6th Cir. 1977), p. 364 note 3.

Capello v. Village of Suffern, 648 N.Y.S.2d 699 (N.Y. App. Div. 1996), p. 78 note 10.

Carabba v. Anacortes School District, 435 P.2d 936 (Wash. 1967), p. 120 note 11.

Cardtoons, L.C. v. Major League Baseball Players Association, 95 F.3d 959 (10th Cir. 1996), p. 705 note 6.

Cardtoons, L.C. v. Major League Baseball Players Association, 199 F.R.D. 677 (N.D. Okla. 2001), p. 409 note 3.

Cardtoons, L.C. v. Major League Baseball Players Association, 208 F.3d 885 (10th Cir. 2000), cert. denied, 531 U.S. 873 (2000), p. 409 note 3.

Carroll v. State of Oklahoma, 620 P.2d 416 (Okla. Crim. App. 1980), p. 145 note 10.

Carter v. New Trier High School, 650 N.E.2d 657 (Ill. App. Ct. 1995), p. 126 note 5.

C.B.C. Distribution and Marketing, Inc. v. Major League Baseball Adanced Media, L.P., 443 F. Supp. 2d 1077 (E.D. Mo. 2006), *aff'd*, 505 F.3d 818 (8th Cir. 2007), *cert. denied*, 128 S.Ct. 2872 (2008), p. 704.

CBS Interactive Inc. v. National Football League Players Association, Inc., 259 F.R.D. 398 (D. Minn. 2009), p. 704 note 2.

Central New York Basketball, Inc. v. Barnett, 19 Ohio Op.2d 130, 181 N.E.2d 506 (Ohio C.P. 1961), p. 391 note 2.

Central Red Army Club v. Arena Associates, Inc., 952 F. Supp. 181 (S.D. N.Y, 1997), pp. 379 note 1; 408.

Certain Underwriters at Lloyd's London Subscribing to Certificate No. 986557 v. Rychel, 126 P.3d 234 (Colo. App. 2005), p. 576 note 2.

Chalenor v. University of North Dakota, 291 F.3d 1042 (8th Cir. 2000), p. 320 note 4.

Chandler v. Siegelman, 230 F.3d 1313 (11th Cir. 2000), p. 266 note 4.

Chicago National League Ball Club Inc. v. Vincent, No. 92C 4398, 1992 U.S. Dist. LEXIS 11033 (N.D. Ill. July 23, 1992), p. 15 note 2.

Chicago Professional Sports Limited Partnership v. National Basketball Association, 95 F.3d 593 (7th Cir. 1996), pp. 13 note 2; 721.

Childress v. Madison County, 777 S.W.2d 1 (Tenn. Ct. App. 1989), p. 153 note 7.

Choike v. Slippery Rock University of Pennsylvania of State System of Higher Educ., 2006 WL 2060576 (W.D. Pa. July 21, 2006), p. 347 note 2.

Christ the King Regional High School v. Catholic High Schools Athletic Association, 624 N.Y.S.2d 755 (N.Y. App. Div. 1995), pp. 222 note 2; 272 note 1.

Christian Heritage Academy v. Oklahoma Secondary School Activities Association (OSSAA), 483 F.3d 1025 (10th Cir. 2007), pp. 177 note 2; 228 note 1.

Chuy v. Philadelphia Eagles Football Club, 431 F. Supp. 254 (E.D. Pa. 1977), aff'd, 595 F.2d 1265 (3d Cir. 1979), p. 88.

Cincinnati Bengals Inc. v. Bergey, 453 F. Supp. 129 (S.D. Ohio 1974), p. 410 note 9.

City of Anaheim v. Superior Court, 2005 WL 1523338 (Cal. App. 4 Dist. June 27, 2005), p. 448 note 1.

City of Coral Springs v. Rippe, 743 So. 2d 61 (Fla. Dist. Ct. App. 1999), p. 133 note 7.

City of Miami v. Cisneros, 662 So. 2d 1272 (Fla. Dist. Ct. App. 1997), p. 113 note 5.

Clarett v. NFL, 306 F. Supp. 2d 379 (S.D. N.Y. 2004), pp. 463 note 1; 497–498.

Clarett v. NFL 369 F.3d 124 (2nd Cir. 2004), pp. 49; 463 note 1; 498; 616.

Clark v. Arizona Interscholastic Association, 695 F.2d 1126 (9th Cir. 1982), *cert. denied*, 464 U.S. 818 (1983), pp. 357; 358 note 6.

Clark v. Arizona Interscholastic Association, 886 F.2d 1191 (9th Cir. 1989), p. 358 note 5.

Classen v. Izquierdo, 520 N.Y.S.2d 999 (N.Y. County Sup. Ct. 1987), p. 99 note 3.

Clemons v. Big Ten Conference, No. 96C0124 1997 U.S. Dist. LEXIS 1939 (N.D. Ill. Feb. 19, 1997), pp. 435; 817.

Cobb v. Time, Inc., 278 F.3d 629 (6th Cir. 2002), p. 92 note 2.

Cobb v. University of Southern California, 45 Cal. App. 4th 1140 (Cal. Ct. App. 1996), p. 778 note 4.

Cobb v. U.S. Dept. of Educ. Office for Civil Rights, 2007 WL 951688 (D. Minn. March 27, 2007), p. 328 note 6.

Coble v. Hot Springs School District, No. 6, 682 F.2d 721 (8th Cir. 1982), p. 775 note 8.

Cohane v. NCAA, 215 Fed. Appx. 13 (2nd Cir. 2007), p. 170 note 3.

Cohen v. Brown University, 101 F.3d 155 (1st Cir. 1993), cert. denied, 520 U.S. 1186 (1997), pp. 317; 343.

Cole v. Football Association Premier League (FAPL), Matter of Arbitration (2006), CAS 2005/A/952, p. 204 note 6.

Cole v. National Collegiate Athletic Association, 120 F. Supp. 2d 1060 (N.D. Ga. 2000), p. 338 note 3.

Coleman v. Western Michigan University, 336 N.W.2d 224 (Mich. Ct. App. 1983), p. 103 note 5.

College Athletic Placement Services, Inc. v. National Collegiate Athletic Association, No. 74-1144, 1974 U.S. Dist. LEXIS 7050 (D. N.J. Aug. 22, 1974), p. 505.

Collins v. National Basketball Players Association, 850 F. Supp. 1468 (D. Colo. 1991), p. 585 note 2.

Comcast SportsNet, Inc. v. Baltimore Orioles, Circuit Court for Montgomery County, Case number: 260751V, p. 722 note 3.

Commonwealth (of Massachusetts) v. Hunt, 4 Met. 111 (1842), pp. 516–517.

Commonwealth (of Pennsylvania) v. Pennsylvania Interscholastic Athletic Association, 334 A.2d 839 (Pa. Commw. Ct. 1975), pp. 331; 332 note 7.

Commonwealth (of Pennsylvania) v. Pullis (Phila. Mayor's Ct. 1806), p. 516.

Communities for Equity v. Michigan High School Athletic Association, 459 F.3d 676 (6th Cir. 2006), pp. 360; 366 note 1.

Connecticut College v. City of London, 41 Conn. L. Rptr. 635 (Conn. Super. 2006), p. 758 note 1.

Connecticut Professional Sports Corp. v. Heyman, 276 F. Supp. 618 (S.D. N.Y. 1967), p. 407 note 3.

Connell Construction Co. v. Plumbers and Steam Fitters Local Union, 421 U.S. 616 (1974), p. 490.

Connery v. Liberty Northwest Insurance Corp., 929 P.2d 222 (Mont. 1996), p. 102 note 4.

Cook v. Colgate University, 802 F. Supp. 737 (N.D. N.Y. 1992), p. 367 note 2.

Cook v. Colgate University, 992 F.2d 17 (2d Cir. 1992), pp. 343; 367–368 note 2.

Cortez v. National Basketball Association, 960 F. Supp. 113 (W.D. Tex. 1997), p. 818.

Cottrell v. NCAA, 975 So. 2d 306 (Ala. 2007), p. 187.

Covert v. South Florida Stadium Corp., 762 So. 2d 938 (Fla. App. Ct. 2000), p. 153 note 5.

Craig v. Boren, 429 U.S. 190 (1976), p. 335.

Crespin v. Albuquerque Baseball Club, LLC, 216 P.3d 827 (N.M. App. 2009), p. 132 note 1.

Crocker v. Tennessee Secondary School Athletic Ass'n, 980 F.2d 382 (6th Cir. 1992), p. 815.

Cruciotti v. McNeel, 396 S.E. 2d 191 (W.Va. 1990), p. 433 note 5.

Cruz v. Pennsylvania Interscholastic Athletic Association, 157 F. Supp. 2d 485 (E.D. Pa. 2001), pp. 184 note 3; 198 note 3; 248 note 4.

Cureton v. National Collegiate Athletic Association, 37 F. Supp. 2d 687 (E.D. Pa. 1999), rev'd. 198 F.3d 107 (3rd Cir.1999), pp. 238 note 2; 239 note 4; 239 note 5.

Curtis Publishing Co. v. Butts, 388 U.S. 130 (1967), p. 91.

Cushion Technologies, LLC v. Adidas Salomon North America, Inc., 537 F. Supp. 2d 839 (E.D. Tex. 2008), p. 702 note 2.

Cuyahoga County Bar Association v. Glenn, 72 Ohio St.3d 299, 649 N.E.2d 1213 (Ohio 1995), p. 610 note 1.

D.N. v. Penn Harris Madison School Corp., 2006 LEXIS 70605 (N.D. Ind. September 18, 2006), p. 273 note 1.

Dal Balcon v. Comitato Olimpico Nazionale Italione (CONI) & Federazione Italiana Sport Invernali (FISI), p. 204 note 7.

Dallas Cowboys Cheerleaders Inc. v. Pussycat Cinema, Ltd., 604 F.2d 200 (2d Cir. 1979), p. 674.

Dallas Cowboys Football Club, Ltd. v. America's Team Properties, Inc., 616 F. Supp. 2d 622 (N.D. Tex. 2009), p. 670 note 2.

Dandenault v. Workers' Compensation Appeals Board, 728 A. 2d 1001 (Pa. Commw. 1999), p. 102 note 2.

Daniels v. Atlanta National League Baseball Club, Inc., 524 S.E.2d 801 (Ga. Ct. App. 1999), p. 135 note 7.

Daniels v. School Board, 985 F. Supp. 1458 (M.D. Fla. 1997) and 985 F. Supp. 1394 (M.D. Fla. 1997), p. 329 note 11.

Darrin v. Gould, 540 P.2d 882 (Wash. 1975), p. 332 note 6.

Davenport v. Randolph County Bd. of Education, 730 F.2d 1395 (11th Cir. 1984), p. 267 note 1.

Davidson v. University of North Carolina at Chapel Hill, 543 S.E. 2d 920 (N.C. Ct. App. 2001), p. 67 note 3.

Davis v. Billick, 2002 U.S. Dist. LEXIS 11504 (N.D. Tex. June 26, 2002), pp. 695 note 1.

Davis v. Massachusetts Interscholastic Athletic Association, No. 94-2887, 1995 Mass. Super. LEXIS (Mass. Jan. 18, 1995), p. 177.

Davis v. Monroe County Board of Education, 526 U.S. 629 (1999), p. 784 note 8.

Davis v. Sayona Central School District, 675 N.Y.S.2d 269 (N.Y. App. Div. 1998), p. 77 note 8.

Deesen v. Professional Golfers' Association, 358 F.2d 165 (9th Cir.), cert. denied, 385 U.S. 846 (1966), p. 478.

DeFrantz v. United States Olympic Committee, 492 F. Supp. 1181 (D. 5.1 D.C. 1980), aff'd. without decision, 701 F.2d 221 (D.C. Cir. 1980), pp. 165 note 7; 218 note 5; 262 note 9.

de la Hoya v. Top Rank, Inc., 2001 WL 34624886 (C.D. Cal. February 6, 2001, p. 378 note 2.

DelBuono v. Massachusetts Interscholastic Athletic Association (MIAA), 2006 WL 1345563 (Mass. Super. March 13, 2006), p. 197 note 2.

Deli v. University of Minnesota, 863 F. Supp. 958 (D. Minn. 1994), p. 770 note 9.

DeMauro v. Tusculum College, Inc., 603 S.W.2d 115 (Tenn. 1980), p. 120 note 9.

Dempsey v. State, WL 3933737 (Del. Ch. December 21, 2006), pp. 181 note 1; 248 note 1.

Dennin v. Connecticut Interscholastic Athletic Conference (CIAC), 94 F.3d 96 (2nd Cir. 1996), pp. 813; 822 note 3.

Denver Rockets v. All-Pro Management, 325 F. Supp. 1049 (C.D. Cal. 1971), p. 465.

Detroit Football v. Robinson, 186 F. Supp. 933 (E.D. La. 1960), p. 374 note 2.

Detroit Lions, Inc. v. Argovitz, 580 F. Supp. 542 (E.D. Mich. 1984), p. 582 note 3.

Detroit Lions v. Mitchell Hoopes, Searce, Arbitrator, September 2, 1978, p. 568 note 3.

Deutscher Tennis Bund v. ATP Tour, Inc., 2008 WL 2520809 (June 23, 2008), p. 479 note 1; 734.

Diaz v. Board of Education, 618 N.Y.S.2d 948 (N.Y. Sup. Ct. 1994), pp. 222 note 3; 273 note 2.

Dillman v. Trustees of Indiana University, 848 N.E.2d 348 (Ind. App. 2006), p. 206 note 3.

Dimeo v. Griffin, 721 F. Supp. 958 (N.D. Ill. 1989), pp. 282 note 2.

DirecTV, Inc. v. Comcast Corporation, Matter of Arbitration CSR 5112-P (1998), p. 742.

Dixon v. Ohio High School Athletic Association, No. C-1-99-827, 1999 U.S. Dist. LEXIS 21388 (S.D. Ohio Nov. 4, 1999), p. 198 note 5.

Dodson v. Arkansas Activities Association, 468 F. Supp. 394 (E.D. Ark. 1979), pp. 363; 364 note 1.

Doe v. Dolton Elementary School District, 694 F. Supp. 440 (N.D. Ill. 1988), pp. 826.

Doe v. McFarlane, 207 S.W.3d 52 (Mo. App. E.D. 2006), p. 704 note 4.

Doe v. Taylor Independent School District, 15 F.3d 443 (5th Cir. 1994), pp. 784 note 12.

Doe v. Woodford County Board of Education, 213 F.3d 921 (6th Cir. 2000), p. 211 note 3.

Dolan v. United States Equestrian Team, Inc., 608 A.2d 434 (N.J. Super. Ct. App. Div. 1992), p. 261 note 6.

Dominic J v. Wyoming Valley West High School, 362 F. Supp. 2d 560 (M.D. Pa. 2005), p. 287 note 2.

Dostert v. Berthold Public School Dist., No. 594, 391 F. Supp. 876 (D.N. Dak. 1975), p. 267 note 1.

Doyle v. Bowdoin College and Cooper International, Inc., 403 A.2d 1206 (Me. 1979), p. 153 note 8.

Dozier v. Mid-Del School System, 959 P.2d 604 (Okla. App. Div. 1998), p. 102 note 3.

Dream Team Collectibles v. NBA Properties, Inc., 958 F. Supp. 1401 (E.D. Missouri 1997), p. 678 note 9.

Dryer v. Los Angeles Rams, 709 P.2d 826 (Cal. 1985), p. 567 note 4.

Dryer v. National Football League, 689 F.Supp.2d 1113 (D. Minn. 2010), pp. 704 note 1; 735 note 1.

Dubinsky v. St. Louis Blues Hockey Club, 229 S.W.3d 126 (Mo. App. E.D. 2007), p. 101 note 1.

Dudley Sports Co. v. Schmitt, 279 N.E.2d 266 (Ind. Ct. App. 1972), p. 149 note 9.

Duffy v. Suffolk County High School Hockey League, Inc., 289 A.D.2d 368 (N.Y. App. Div. 2001), p. 119 note 2.

Dugan v. Oregon State University, No. 95-6250-HO (D. Or. 1998), p. 770 note 6.

Eastern Microwave Inc. v. Doubleday Sports Inc., 691 F.2d 125 (2d Cir. 1982), p. 715 note 3.

Eddy v. Syracuse University, 433 N.Y.S.2d 923 (N.Y. App. Div. 1980), p. 137 note 8.

Edelson v. Uniondale Union Free School District, 631 N.Y.S.2d 391 (N.Y. App. Div. 1995), pp. 113 note 7.

EEOC v. Madison Community Unit School District, 818 F.2d 577 (7th Cir. 1987), p. 770 note 10.

Elledge v. Richland/Lexington School District Five, 534 S.E.2d 289 (S.C. Ct. App. 2000), p. 122 note 2.

Eneman v. Richter, 577 N.W.2d 386 (Wisc. Ct. App. 1998), p. 81 note 2.

English v. National Collegiate Athletic Association, 439 So. 2d 1218 (La. Ct. App. 1983), p. 505.

Equity in Athletics, Inc. v. Department of Educ., 504 F. Supp. 2d 88 (W.D. Va. 2007), p. 25 note 2.

Equity in Athletics, Inc. v. U.S. Department of Education, 291 Fed. Appx. 517 (4th Cir. 2008), p. 327 note 4.

Estay v. La Fourche Parish School Board, 230 So.2d 443 (La. Ct. App. 1969), p. 267 note 1.

ETW Corp. v. Jireh Publishing Inc., 99 F. Supp. 2d 829 (N.D. Ohio 2000), *aff'd*, 332 F.3d 915 (6th Cir. 2003), p. 703.

Evans v. Oaks Mission Public School, 945 P.2d 492 (Okla. 1997), p. 81 note 3.

Everett v. Bucky Warren, Inc., 380 N.E.2d 653 (Mass. 1978), p. 148 note 7.

Ewing (Patrick) v. New York Knickerbockers, Collins, arbitrator, 1991, p. 395 note 5.

Facenda v. N.F.L. Films, Inc., 488 F. Supp. 2d 491 (E.D. Pa. 2007), p. 704 note 3.

Faigin v. Kelly, 184 F.3d 67 (1st Cir. 1999), p. 580 note 4.

Faragher v. Boca Raton, 524 U.S. 775 (1998), p. 783 note 3.

Favia v. Indiana University of Pennsylvania, 7 F.3d 332 (3d Cir. 1993), pp. 343; 348 note 9.

Federal Baseball Club of Baltimore, Inc. v. National League of Professional Baseball Clubs, 259 U.S. 200 (1922), pp. 41; 458; 481.

Filler v. Rayex Corp., 435 F.2d 336 (7th Cir. 1970), p. 149 note 10.

Fintzi v. New Jersey YMHA-YWHA Camps, 765 N.E.2d 288 (N.Y. 2001), p. 112 note 3.

First Northwest Industries of America v. Commissioner, 649 F.2d 707 (9th Cir. 1981), p. 764 note 4.

Fish v. L.A. Dodgers Baseball Club, 128 Cal. Rptr. 807 (Cal. Ct. App. 1976), p. 142 note 11.

Fitzergald v. Barnstable, 129 S. Ct. 788 (2009) p. 336.

Flood v. Kuhn, 316 F. Supp. 271 (S.D.N.Y. 1970), pp. 463; 487.

Flood v. Kuhn, 401 U.S. 258 (1972), pp. 389–390 note 2.

Flood v. Kuhn, 407 U.S. 258 (1972), p. 487.

Florida High School Athletic Association (FHSAA) v. Marazzito, 891 So.2d 653 (2005), p. 181 note 2.

Florida High School Athletic Association (FHSAA) v. Melbourne Central Catholic High School, 867 So. 2d 1281 (Fla. App. 5 Dist. 2004), p. 197 note 3.

Florida State University Infractions Appeals Report (January 5, 2010), p. 191 note 1.

Floyd v. United States Olympic Committee, 965 S.W.2d 35 (Tex. Ct. App. 1998), pp. 164 note 4; 261 note 3; 298 note 13.

Ford v. Gouin, 266 Cal. Rptr. 870 (Cal. Ct. App. 1990), p. 78 note 13.

Ford v. Nairn, 717 N.E.2d 525 (Ill. App. Ct. 1999), p. 95 note 1.

Forte v. Board of Education, North Babylon Union Free School District, 431 N.Y.S.2d 321 (N.Y. Sup. Ct. 1980), p. 359 note 9.

Fortier v. Los Rios Community College District, 52 Cal. Rptr. 2d 812 (Cal. Ct. App. 1996), pp. 78 note 12.

Fortin v. Darlington Little League, Inc., 376 F. Supp. 473 (D. R.I. 1974), rev'd., 514 F.2d 344 (1st Cir. 1975), p. 356 note 4.

Foschi v. United States Swimming Inc., 916 F. Supp. 232 (E.D. N.Y. 1996), pp. 165 note 5; 261 note 4; 282 note 1.

Fox Sports Net North v. Minnesota Twins Partnership, 319 F.3d 329 (8th Cir. 2003), p. 722 note 1.

Fox TV Stations, Inc. v. FCC, 489 F.3d 444 (2d. Cir. 2007). p. 743.

Franklin v. Gwinnett County Public Schools, 503 U.S. 60 (1992), pp. 316; 343; 349 note 10; 781.

Fraser v. Major League Soccer, 97 F. Supp. 2d 130 (D. Mass. 2000), *Aff'd by*, 284 F.3d 47 (1st Cir. 2002), pp. 15; 16 note 1; 500–502; 535; 751.

Frazier v. University of District of Columbia, 742 F. Supp. 28 (D. D.C.1990), p. 431 note 10.

Friends of the Parks v. Chicago Park District, 203 Ill. 2d 312 (Ill. 2003), pp. 762–763 note 2.

Frontiero v. Richardson, 411 U.S. 677 (1973), pp. 335; 337 note 6.

Frye v. Michigan High Sch. Athletic Association, No. 95-1266, 1997 U.S. App. LEXIS 21071 (6th Cir. Mich. Aug. 5, 1997), p. 198 note 8.

FTC v. Garvey, 383 F.3d 891 (9th Cir. 2004), p. 735 note 2.

Fuhr v. School District of Hazel Park, 364 F.3d 753 (6th Cir. 2004) p. 773 note 2.

Fusato v. Washington Interscholastic Activities Association, 970 P.2d 774 (Wash. Ct. App. 1999), pp. 229 note 4; 252 note 6.

Gadye v. Bases Loaded Group, LLC 2:2009cv04598 (N.J. 2009), p. 134 note 1.

Gahan v. Mineola Union Free School District, 241 A.D.2d 439, 660 N.Y.S.2d 144 (N.Y. App. Div. 1997), p. 117 note 5.

Gaines v. National Collegiate Athletic Association, 746 F. Supp. 738 (M.D. Tenn. 1990), pp. 509; 621 note 1b.

Gale v. Greater Washington, D.C. Softball Umpires Association, 311 A.2d 817 (Md. Ct. Spec. App. 1973), p. 146 note 12.

Ganden v. National Collegiate Athletic Association, No. 96 C 6953 1996 U.S. Dist. LEXIS 17368 (N.D. Ill. Nov. 21, 1996), pp. 198 note 3; 822; 823 note 4.

Gandler v. Nazarov, No. 94 Civ. 2272, 1995 U.S. Dist. LEXIS 8325 (S.D. N.Y June 15, 1995), p. 593 note 2.

Garden City Boxing Club, Inc. v. Espinal, 2008 WL 2078151 (E.D. N.Y. May 15, 2008), p. 734 note 2.

Gary Community School Corp. v. Powell, 881 N.E.2d 57 (Ind. App. 2008), p. 433 note 2.

Gauvin v. Clark, 537 N.E.2d 94 (Mass. 1989), p. 108 note 5.

Gebser v. Lago Vista Independent School District, 524 U.S. 274 (1998), p. 784 note 9.

Gehling v. St. George University School of Medicine, 705 F. Supp. 761 (E.D. N.Y. 1989), p. 73 note 9.

Georgia High School Association v. Waddell, 285 S.E.2d 7 (Ga. 1981), p. 145 note 9.

Gertz v. United States, 418 U.S. 323 (1974), p. 91.

Gilden v. PGA Tour, 936 F.2d 417 (9th Cir. 1991), p. 477.

Gil-De-Rebollo v. Miami Heat Association, 137 F.3d 56 (1st Cir. 1998), p. 135 note 8.

Gilpin v. Kansas State High School Activities Association, 377 F. Supp. 1233 (D. Kan.1973), p. 354 note 5.

Gionfriddo v. Major League Baseball, 94 Cal. App. 4th 400 (Cal. App. 1 Dist. 2001), p. 704 note 5.

Giordano v. Ridge, 737 A.2d 350 (Pa. Commw. Ct. 1999), p. 762.

Giovinazzo v. Mohawk Valley Community College, 617 N.Y.S.2d 90 (N.Y. App. Div. 1994), p. 119 note 7.

Gomes v. Rhode Island Interscholastic League, 469 F. Supp. 659 (D. R.I. 1979), vacated as moot, 604 F.2d 733 (1st Cir. 1979), pp. 357; 359 note 11.

Gonyo v. Drake University, 879 F. Supp. 1000 (S.D. Iowa 1995), p. 329 note 12.

Goss v. Illinois Hockey Officials Ass'n, No. 99L-01386 (Ill. Cir. Ct.-Cook County, filed Dec. 8, 1999), p. 793 note 3.

Goss v. Lopez, 419 U.S. 565 [1974], p. 223.

Grandson v. University of Minnesota, 272 F.3d 568 (8th Cir. 2001), p. 328 note 9.

Grauer v. State of New York, 181 N.Y.S.2d 994 (N.Y. App. Div. 1959), p. 71 note 2.

Gray v. Girous, 730 N.E.2d 338 (Mass. App. 2000), p. 82 note 1.

Greene v. Athletic Council of Iowa State University, 251 N.W.2d 559 (Iowa 1977), p. 205.

Gregoria v. Board of Education, No. A-1277-70 (N.J. Super. Ct. App. Div. 1971), p. 363 note 3.

GRIDIRON.Com, Inc. v. National Football Players Association, 106 F. Supp. 2d 1309 (S.D. Fla. 2000), p. 671 note 8.

Griggas v. Clauson, 128 N.E.2d 363 (Ill. App. Ct. 1955), p. 109 note 8.

Grove City College v. Bell, 465 U.S. 555 (1984), pp. 316; 323; 339 note 5.

Gutkowski v. Steinbrenner, 680 F.Supp.2d 602 (S.D.N.Y. 2010), p. 695 note 1.

Guttenplan v. Boston Professional Hockey Ass'n., Inc., No. 80–415 (1981 U.S. Dist. LEXIS 10434 (S.D.N.Y. Jan. 19, 1981), pp. 135 note 10; 795.

Haas v. South Bend Community School Corp., 289 N.E.2d 495 (Ind. 1972), p. 355 note 9.

Hackbart v. Cincinnati Bengals, 435 F. Supp. 352 (D. Colo. 1977), rev'd, 601 F.2d 516 (10th Cir. 1979), p. 109 note 2.

Hadley v. Rush Henrietta Central School District, 2007 WL 12321753 (W.D. N.Y. April 25, 2007), p. 224 note 1.

Haffer v. Temple University, 524 F. Supp. 531 (E.D. Pa. 1981), aff'd., 688 F.2d 14 (3d Cir. 1982), pp. 338; 340 note 9; 340 note 10.

Hairston v. National Collegiate Athletic Association, 101 F.3d 1315 (9th Cir. 1997), p. 182 note 2.

Hale v. City of Jefferson, 6 S.W.3d 187 (Mo. Ct. App. 1999), p. 71 note 1.

Hall v. National Collegiate Athletic Association, 985 F. Supp. 782 (N.D. Ill. 1997), pp. 218 note 1; 224 note 1.

Hall v. University of Minnesota, 530 F. Supp. 104 (D. Minn. 1982), pp. 241 note 2; 272 note 1.

Hamilton v. United States Anti-Doping Agency (USADA) & Union Cycliste Internationale (UCI), Matter of Arbitration (2006), CAS 2005/A/884, p. 203 note 1.

Hammond v. Board of Education, 639 A.2d 223 (Md. Ct. Spec. App. 1994), p. 115 note 5.

Hansberry v. Massachusetts Interscholastic Athletic Association, No. 95-6807-B 1998 Mass. Super LEXIS 706 (Mass. Super. Ct. Oct. 21, 1998), p. 206.

Harding v. United States Figure Skating Association, 851 F. Supp. 1476 (D. Or. 1994), pp. 165 note 6; 261 note 5.

Harjo v. Pro-Football, Inc., 50 U.S.P.Q.2d 1705 (T.T.A.B. 1999), p. 688 note 3.

Harker v. Utica College of Syracuse University, 885 F. Supp. 378 (N.D. N.Y. 1995), p. 770 note 8.

Harlem Globetrotters, Inc. v. Harlem Magicians, Inc., 872 F.2d 1025 (6th Cir.1989), p. 679 note 15.

Harrick v. NCAA, 454 F. Supp. 2d 1255 (N.D. Ga. 2006), p. 409 note 1.

Harris v. Cherry Valley-Springfield School District, 760 N.Y.S.2d 768 (N.Y. App. Div. 2003), p. 77 note 2.

Hart v. National Collegiate Athletic Association, 550 S.E.2d 79 (W.Va. 2001), p. 180 note 2.

Harvey v. Ouachita Parish School Board, 545 So. 2d 1241 (La. Ct. App. 1989), pp. 99 note 2; 145 note 6.

Hawaii-Pacific Apparel Group, Inc. v. Cleveland Browns Football Co. LLC, 418 F. Supp. 2d 501 (S.D. N.Y. 2006) p. 673.

Hayden v. University of Notre Dame, 71b N.E.2d 603 (Ind. Ct. App. 1999), p. 135 note 6.

Heldman v. Uniroyal Inc., 371 N.E.2d 557 (Ohio Ct. App. 1977), p. 148 note 8.

Heldman v. United States Lawn Tennis Association, 354 F. Supp. 1241 (S.D. N.Y. 1973), p. 477.

Hemady v. Long Beach Unified School District, 143 Cal. App. 4th 566 (Cal. Ct. App. 2006), p. 118 note 1.

Hennessey v. National Collegiate Athletic Association, 564 F.2d 1136 (5th Cir. 1977), p. 505.

Hertzog v. Harrison Island Shores Inc., 251 N.Y.S.2d 164 (N.Y. App. Div. 1964), p. 154 note 9.

Hiett v. Lake Bancroft Community Association, 418 S.E.2d 894 (Va. 1992), p. 153 note 6.

Hill v. National Collegiate Athletic Association, 865 P.2d 633 (Cal. 1994), pp. 280 note 4; 289; 291 note 1.

Hillard v. Black, 125 F. Supp. 2d 1071 (2000), p. 580 note 2.

Hillsdale College v. Department of Health, Education and Welfare, 696 F.2d 418 (6th Cir. 1982), pp. 338; 340 note 8.

Hispanic College Fund, Inc (HCF). v. NCAA, 826 N.E.2d 652 (Ind. App. 2005), p. 169 note 1.

Holcomb v. Iona College, 521 F.3d 130 (2nd Cir. 2008) p. 777 note 1.

Hollander v. Connecticut Interscholastic Athletic Conference, Inc., 164 Conn. 654 (Conn. Super. Ct.), appeal dismissed, 295 A.2d 671 (Conn. Ct. App. 1972), p. 355 note 10.

Hollenbeck v. U.S. Olympic Committee, 513 F.3d 1191 (10th Cir. 2008), pp. 261 note 1; 816 note 1.

Hollon v. Mathis Independent School District, 358 F. Supp. 1269 (S.D. Tex. 1973), p. 268 note 4.

Holloway v. King, 361 F. Supp. 2d 351 (S.D. N.Y. 2005), p. 382 note 1.

Holmes v. National Football League, 939 F. Supp. 517 (N.D. Tex. 1996), p. 281.

Holzer v. Dakota Speedway, Inc., 610 N.W.2d 787 (S.D. 2000), p. 152 note 3.

Home v. North Kitsap School District, 965 P.2d 1112 (Wash. Ct. App. 1998), p. 81 note 4.

Home Box Office, Inc. v. FCC, 567 F.2d 9 (D.C. Cir.), cert. denied, 434 U.S. 829 (1977), p. 714 note 1.

Hoopla Sports and Entertainment, Inc. v. Nike, Inc., 947 F. Supp. 347 (N.D. Ill. 1996), p. 696 note 3.

Hoot v. Michigan High School Athletic Association, 853 F. Supp. 243 (E.D. Mich. 1994), p. 240 note 1.

Hoot v. Milan School District, 853 F. Supp. 243 (E.D. Mich. 1994), p. 821 note 2.

Hoover v. Meiklejohn, 430 F. Supp. 164 (D. Colo. 1977), p. 352 note 9.

Horn v. University of Minnesota, 362 F.3d 1042 (8th Cir. 2004), p. 768 note 2.

Horner v. Kentucky High School Athletic Association, 206 F.3d 685 (6th Cir. 2000), pp. 347–348 note 5.

Hornung v. Commissioner, 47 T.C. 428 (1967), p. 765.

Howard University v. National Collegiate Athletic Association, 510 F.2d 213 (D.C. Cir. 1975), pp. 219 note 1; 232 note 5.

Hudgens v. NLRB, 424 U.S. 507 (1976), p. 217 note 1.

Hutchinson Baseball Enterprises, Inc. v. Commissioner, 696 F.2d 757 (10th Cir. 1982), p. 755 note 4.

Hutchins v. Board of Trustees of Michigan State University, 705 F.2d. 454 (6th Cir. 1982), p. 362 note 6.

Ian Whatley v. Nike, Inc., No. 3:98-963 (D. Or. May 23, 2005), p. 702 note 2.

Ignition Athletic Performance Group, LLC v. Hantz Soccer U.S.A., LLC, 2007 WL 2258839 (6th Cir. August 8, 2007), p. 677 note 5.

Illinois High School Association v. GTE Vantage, Inc., 99 F.3d. 244 (7th Cir. 1996), pp. 671 note 4; 686 note 2.

Illinois Native American Bar Association v. University of Illinois by Its Board of Trustees, 856 N.E.2d 460 (Ill. Ct. App. 1st Dist. 2006), p. 688 note 1.

Ilott v. University of Utah, 12 P.3d 1011 (Utah Ct. App. 2000), p. 125 note 2.

In Re University Interscholastic League, 20 S.W.3d 690 (Tex. 2000), pp. 221 note 4; 272 note 2.

In the Matter of Kellenberg Memorial High School v. Section VIII of the New York State Public High School Athletic Association, 679 N.Y.S.2d 660 (N.Y. App. Div. 1998), p. 176.

Indiana High School Athletic Association, Inc. (IHSAA) v. Watson, 913 N.E.2d 741 (Ind. App. 2009), p. 251 note 1.

Indiana High School Athletic Association v. Carlsberg, 694 N.E.2d 222 (Ind. Ct. App. 1997), p. 218 note 2.

Indiana High School Athletic Association v. Durham, 748 N.E.2d 404 (Ind. Ct. App. 2001), pp. 180 note 2; 250; 251 note 4.

Indiana High School Athletic Association v. Reyes, 694 N.E.2d 249 (Ind. 1997), p. 218 note 3.

Indiana High School Athletic Association v. Vasario, 726 N.E.2d 325 (Ind. Ct. App. 2000), p. 181 note 3.

Indiana High School Athletics Association v. Raike, 329 N.E.2d 66 (Ind. Ct. App. 1975), p. 268 note 2.

Indianapolis Colts, Inc. v. Metropolitan Baltimore Football Club L.P., L.P., 34 F.3d 410 (7th Cir. 1994), p. 674.

Ingram v. Toledo City School District Board of Education, 339 F. Supp. 2d 998 (N.D. Ohio 2004), p. 243.

International Marathons, Inc. v. Attorney General (Mass.), 467 N.E.2d 55 (Mass. 1984), p. 209 note 2.

International Star Class Yacht Racing Association v. Tommy Hilfiger U.S.A., Inc., 146 F.3d 66 (2d Cir. 1998), p. 677 note 6.

Intersport, Inc. v. NCAA, 2008 WL 881295 (Ill. App. 1st Dist. March 26, 2008), p. 671 note 4.

Iowa State University Research Foundation, Inc. v. American Broadcasting Company, Inc., 621 F.2d 57 (2d Cir. 1980), p. 695.

ISL Marketing and Federation Internationale de Football Association v. Nutt, Arbitration case no. D2000-0363, p. 699 note 7.

Israel v. West Virginia Secondary Schools Activities Commission, 388 S.E.2d 480 (W. Va. 1989), p. 354 note 2.

J & J Sports Productions, Inc. v. Meyers, 2007 WL 2030288 (S.D. N.Y. July 16, 2007), p. 734 note 2.

Jackson v. Birmingham Bd. of Educ., 544 U.S. 167 (2005), pp. 775; 776 note 1; 776 note 4.

Jackson v. National Football League, 802 F. Supp. 226 (D. Minn. 1992), pp. 463; 495.

Jacob Maxwell, Inc. v. Veeck, 110 F.3d 749 (11th Cir. 1997), p. 696.

Jacobs v. USA Track & Field (USATF), 374 F.3d 85 (2nd Cir. 2004), p. 164 note 1.

Jaguar Cars, Ltd. v. National Football League, 886 F. Supp. 335 (S.D. N.Y. 1995), p. 672 note 10.

Jasper v. Chicago National League Ball Club, 722 N.E.2d 731 (Ill. App. Ct. 1999), p. 133 note 8.

Jennings v. University of North Carolina at Chapel Hill, 482 F.3d 686 (4th Cir. 2007), p. 782.

Johnny Blastoff, Inc. v. Los Angeles Rams Football Company, 48 U.S.P.Q. 2d BNA 1385 (W.D. Wis. 1998), p. 677 note 8.

Johnny's Icehouse, Inc. v. Amateur Hockey Ass'n of Illinois, Inc., 134 F. Supp. 2d 965 (N.D. Ill. 2001), p. 339 note 4.

Johnson v. Florida High School Activities Ass'n, 899 F. Supp. 579 (M.D. Fla. 1995), pp. 817; 822 note 3.

Johnson v. Florida High School Activities Association, 102 F.3d 1172 (11th Cir. 1997), p. 198 note 7.

Johnson's Adm'x v. Rich Danville R.R. Co., 11 S.E. 829 (Va. 1890), p. 153 note 6.

Jones v. National Collegiate Athletic Association, 392 F. Supp. 295 (D. Mass. 1975), pp. 256 note 2; 510 note 4.

Jones v. National Collegiate Athletic Association, 679 So.2d 1337 (La. 1996), p. 246 note 2.

Jones v. Oklahoma Secondary School Activities Association, 453 F. Supp. 150 (W.D. Okla. 1977), pp. 364; 364 note 2.

Jones v. West Virginia State Board of Education, 622 S.E.2d 289 (W.Va. 2005), p. 228 note 3.

Jordan v. Indiana High School Athletic Association, 16 F.3d 785 (7th Cir. 1994), p. 243 note 2.

Joye v. Hunterdon Cent. Regional High School Bd. of Educ., 176 N.J. 568 (N.J. 2003), p. 287 note 3.

Kaiser v. Bowlen, 200 P.3d 1098 (Colo. App. 2008), p. 397 note 1.

Kane v. North Colonie Central School District, 708 N.Y.S.2d 203 (N.Y. App. Div. 2000), pp. 79 note 3; 119 note 3.

Kanongata'a v. Washington Interscholastic Activities Association, 2006 WL 1727891 (W.D. Wash. June 20, 2006), pp. 198 note 1; 248 note 2; 821 note 1b.

Kansas City Royals Baseball Corp. v. Major League Baseball Players Association, 532 F.2d 615 (8th Cir. 1976), pp. 407–408 note 4; 557; 567 note 3.

Kansas v. Colorado, 533 U.S. 1 (2001), p. 41.

Kapp v. National Football League, 390 F. Supp. 73 (N.D. Cal. 1974), p. 463.

Karas v. Strevell, 860 N.E.2d 1163 (Ill. App. Ct. 2006), p. 114 note 1.

Kavanagh v. Trustees of Boston University, 795 N.E.2d 1170 (Mass. 2003), p. 66 note 1.

Kelley v. Board of Trustees University, 35 F.3d 265 (7th Cir. 1994), pp. 320 note 7; 348 note 7.

Kelly v. McCarrick, 841 A.2d 869 (Md. Ct. Spec. App. 2004), pp. 122 note 1; 139 note 1.

Kemether v. Pennsylvania Interscholastic Athletic Association, Inc., 1999 WL 1012948 (E.D. Pa. November 8, 1999), p. 331 note 3.

Kentucky High School Athletic Association v. Hopkins County Board of Education, 552 S.W.2d 685 (Ky. Ct. App. 1977), p. 252 note 7.

Kentucky Speedway, LLC v. National Association of Stock Car Auto Racing, Inc. (NASCAR), 588 F.3d 908 (6th Cir. 2009), p. 479 note 2.

Kevan v. Manesiotis, 728 A.2d 1006 (Pa. Commw. 1999), p. 79 note 4.

Kiley v. Patterson, 763 A.2d 583 (R.I. 2000), p. 108 note 4.

King v. Kayak Manufacturing Corp., 387 S.E.2d 511 (W.Va. 1989), p. 148 note 6.

King v. Little League Baseball, Inc., 505 F.2d 264 (6th Cir. 1974), p. 356 note 5.

Kingray, Inc. v. NBA, Inc., 188 F. Supp. 2d 1177 (S.D. Cal. 2002), p. 720.

Kingsford v. Salt Lake City School District, 247 F.3d 1123 (10th Cir. 2001), p. 433 note 4.

Kingvision Pay-Per-View Ltd. v. Villalobos, 2008 WL 1994864 (E.D. N.Y. May 8, 2008), p. 734 note 2.

Kirwan v. The Diamondback, 721 A.2d 196 (Md. Ct. App. 1998), p. 208 note 9.

Kite v. Marshall, 661 F.2d 1027 (5th Cir. 1981), p. 258.

Kleczek v. Rhode Island Interscholastic League, Inc., 768 F. Supp. 951 (D. R.I. 1991), p. 358 note 3.

Kleinknecht v. Gettysburg College, 989 F.2d 1360 (3rd Cir. 1993), pp. 67 note 5; 117 note 6; 121 note 3.

Klemencic v. Ohio State University, 10 F. Supp. 2d 911 (S.D. Ohio 1998), p. 784 note 10.

Kling v. Mentor Public School District, 136 F. Supp. 2d 744 (N.D. Ohio 2001), p. 248 note 3.

Knapp v. Northwestern University, 101 F.3d 473 (7th Cir. 1996), p. 823 note 7.

Knapp v. Northwestern University, No. 95-C-6454 1996 U.S. Dist. LEXIS 12463 (N.D. Ill. Aug. 23, 1996), p. 224 note 2.

Kneeland v. National Collegiate Athletic Association, 850 F.2d 224 (5th Cir. 1988), p. 206.

Knievel v. ESPN, 393 F.3d 1068 (9th Cir. 2005), p. 92 note 1.

Koffman v. Garnett, 265 Va. 12 (Va. 2003), p. 112 note 2.

Krueger v. San Francisco Forty-Niners, 234 Cal. Rptr. 579 (Cal. Ct. App. 1987), p. 141 note 6.

Lackner v. North, 135 Cal. App. 4th 1188 (Cal. Ct. App. 2006), p. 123 note 1.

Lafler v. Athletic Board of Control, 536 F. Supp. 104 (W.D. Mich. 1982), p. 362 note 3.

Laird v. United States, 556 F.2d 1224 (5th Cir. 1977), p. 764.

Lambert v. West Virginia State Board of Education, 447 S.E.2d 901 (W.Va. 1994), p. 815.

Landers v. West Virginia Secondary School Activities Commission, 447 S.E.2d 901 (W. Va. 1994), p. 821 note 2.

Landow v. School Bd. of Brevard County, 132 F. Supp. 2d 958 (M.D. Fla. 2000), p. 329 note 10.

Lanier v. National Basketball Association, 82 Civ. 4935 (S.D. N.Y. 1982), p. 560 note 3.

Lankford v. Irby, 2006 WL 2828548 (D. N.J. September 29, 2006), p. 579 note 1.

Lantz v. Ambach, 620 F. Supp. 663 (S.D. N.Y. 1985), pp. 350; 352 note 7.

Lasege v. National Collegiate Athletic Association, 53 S.W.3d 77 (Ky. 2001), p. 234 note 1.

Lavin v. Chicago Board of Education, 73 F.R.D. 438 (N.D. Ill. 1975), p. 353 note 11.

Lavin v. Illinois High School Association, 527 F.2d 58 (7th Cir. 1977), p. 353 note 11.

Law v. National Collegiate Athletic Association, 134 F.3d 1010 10th Cir. (1998), pp. 19 note 4; 159; 457; 506.

Lee v. Maloney, 704 N.Y.S.2d 729 (3 N.Y. App. Div. 2000), p. 77 note 4.

Leffel v. Wisconsin Interscholastic Athletic Association, 444 F. Supp. 1117 (E.D. Wis. 1978), p. 352 note 8.

Lesser v. Neosho County Community College, 741 F. Supp. 854 (D. Kan. 1990), p. 226 note 3.

Lester v. Public Building Authority of County of Knox, No. 78491 (1983), p. 208.

Lestina v. West Bend Mutual Insurance, 501 N.W.2d 28 (Wis. 1993), p. 82 note 2.

Letendre ex rel. Letendre v. Missouri State High School Activities Association, 86 S.W.3d 63 (Mo. App. E.D. 2002), p. 259 note 1.

Levin v. National Basketball Association, 385 F. Supp. 149 (S.D. N.Y. 1974), p. 470 note 4.

Lewis v. Smith, 255 F. Supp. 2d 1054 (D. Ariz. 2003), p. 774 note 3.

Libby v. South Inter-Conference Association, 728 F. Supp. 504 (N.D. Ill. 1990), p. 352 note 5.

Lincoln Hockey Ltd. Liability Co. v. Semin, 2005 WL 3294008 (D. D.C. 2005), pp. 398 note 3; 648 note 1.

Lindland v. U.S. Wrestling Ass'n Inc. (USAW), 227 F.3d 1000 (7th Cir. 2000), p. 164 note 3.

Livshitz v. United State Tennis Association National Tennis Center, 761 N.Y.S.2d 825 (N.Y. Civ. Ct. 2003), pp. 79–80 note 2.

Locilento v. Coleman Catholic High School, 523 N.Y.S.2d 198 (N.Y. App. 1987), p. 67 note 10; p. 73 note 10.

Long v. National Football League, 66 F.3d 311 (3rd Cir. 1994), p. 304.

Long v. National Football League, 870 F. Supp. 101 (U.S. Dist. 1994), p. 278.

Long v. Zopp, 476 F.2d 180 (4th Cir. 1973), p. 267 note 2.

Los Angeles Memorial Coliseum Commission v. National Football League, 726 F.2d 1381 (9th Cir.) cert. denied, 469 U.S. 990 (1984), pp. 457; 468; 499.

Los Angeles Rams v. Cannon, 185 F. Supp. 717 (S.D. Ca. 1960), p. 374 note 1.

Lowery v. Euverard, 2007 WL 2213215 (6th Cir. August 3, 2007), p. 265 note 1.

Lowrey v. Texas A&M, 11 F. Supp. 2d 895 (S.D. Tex. 1998), p. 774 note 6.

L.P.M. and D.J.T. v. School Board, 753 So. 2d 130 (Fla. Dist. Ct. App. 2000), pp. 221 note 3; 274 note 3.

Lund v. Bally's Aerobic Plus, Inc., 93 Cal. Rptr. 2d 169 (Cal. App. Ct. 2000), p. 153 note 4.

Lynch v. Board of Education of Collingsville Community School District, 390 N.E.2d 526 (Ill. App. Ct. 1979), p. 113 note 8.

Mackey v. National Football League, 543 F.2d 606 (8th Cir. 1976), pp. 463; 491; 531.

MacLean v. First Northwest Industries of America, 600 P.2d 1027 (Wash. Ct. App. 1979), p. 332 note 5.

Maddox v. City of New York, 455 N.Y.S.2d 102 (N.Y. App. Div. 1982), 487 N.Y.S.2d 354 (N.Y. App. Div. 1985), p. 137 note 6.

Maddox v. University of Tennessee, 62 F.3d 843 (6th Cir. 1995), p. 823 note 8.

Maine Human Rights Commission v. Maine Principals Association, No. CV-97-599 1999 Me. Super. LEXIS 23 (Me. Super. Ct. Jan. 21, 1999), p. 358 note 1.

Maisonave v. Newark Bears Professional Baseball Club, Inc., 881 A.2d 700 (N.J. 2005), p. 132 note 3.

Major League Baseball Players Association and Howe v. Commissioner of Major League Baseball, No. 92-7, Suspension of Steven Howe, Nicolau, Chairman of Arbitration Panel, November 12, 1992, pp. 307 note 7; 567 note 2c.

Major League Baseball Players Association and Lamp v. Toronto Blue Jays, Matter of Arbitration, Dennis Lamp (1987), p. 395 note 6.

Major League Baseball Players Association and Rocker v. Commissioner of Major League Baseball, Grievance No. 00-3; John Rocker; Das, chairman of Arbitration Panel, March 1, 2000, p. 566 note 2a.

Major League Baseball Players Association v. Dad's Kid Corp., 806 F. Supp. 458 (S.D. N.Y. 1992), pp. 678–679 note 12.

Major League Baseball Players Association v. Garvey, 532 U.S. 504 (2001), pp. 554 note 2; 564 note 1.

Major League Baseball Players Association v. Steve Garvey, 121 S. Ct. 1724 (2001), p. 554 note 2.

Major League Baseball Players Association v. Twenty-six Major League Baseball Clubs, A-123, A-136 (1987) (Roberts), p. 553.

Major League Baseball Players Association v. Twenty-six Major League Clubs, 1 (1990) (Nicolau, Arb.), p. 554.

Major League Baseball Properties, Inc. v. Opening Day Productions, Inc., 385 F. Supp. 2d 256, (S.D. N.Y. 2005), p. 675.

Major League Baseball Properties, Inc. v. Pacific Trading Cards, Inc., 150 F.3d 149 (2d Cir. 1998), p. 676.

Major League Baseball Properties, Inc. v. Salvino, Inc., 420 F. Supp. 2d 212 (S.D. N.Y 2005), p. 676 note 2.

Major League Baseball Properties, Inc. v. Sed Non Olet Denarius, Ltd., 817 F. Supp. 1103, 1128 (S.D. N.Y. 1993), p. 674.

Major League Baseball v. Crist, 331 F.3d 1177 (11th Cir. 2003), p. 472.

Major League Umpires' Association v. National League of Professional Baseball Clubs & the American League of Professional Baseball Clubs, Case No. 14 300 1395 99, p. 543 note 3.

Mansourian v. Regents of University of California, 602 F.3d 957 (9th Cir. 2010), p. 351 note 1.

Manuel v. National Association of Intercollegiate Athletics, 833 P.2d 288 (Okla. Ct. App. 1992), p. 172 note 1.

March Madness Athletic Association, LLC v. Netfire, Inc., 310 F. Supp. 2d 786 (N.D. Tex. 2003), p. 699 note 5.

Mark v. Moser, 746 N.E.2d 410 (Ind. Ct. App. 2001), p. 108 note 3.

Marsh v. Alabama, 326 U.S. 501 (1946), p. 217 note 5.

Marsh v. Delaware State University, WL 141680 (D. Del. January 19, 2006), p. 221 note 1.

Marshall v. Heartland Park Topeka, 49 P.3d 501 (Kan. 2002), p. 132 note 5.

Martin v. International Olympic Committee, 740 F.2d 670 (9th Cir. 1984), pp. 262 note 7; 354 note 3.

Martin v. PGA Tour, Inc., 204 F.3d 994 (9th Cir. 2000), p. 824.

Martin v. PGA Tour, Inc., 532 U.S. 661 (2001), pp. 43; 824.

Martin v. PGA Tour, Inc., 994 F.Supp. 1242 (D. Or. 1998), p. 824.

Maryland Stadium Authority v. Becker, 806 F. Supp. 1236 (D. Md. 1992), p. 673 note 13.

Massachusetts v. Junta (Middlesex [MA] Superior Court, 2002), p. 788 note 5.

Master Card International v. Sprint Communications Co., 23 F.3d 397 (2d. Cir. 1994), p. 681 note 3.

Mastercard International Inc. v. FIFA, 239 Fed. Appx. 625 (2nd Cir. 2007), p. 681 note 2.

Mathews v. Eldridge, 424 U.S. 319 [1976], p. 220.

Matthews v. National Collegiate Athletic Association, 79 F. Supp. 2d 1199 (E.D. Wash. 1999), pp. 198 note 2; 241 note 1.

Matthews v. NCAA, 1769 F.Supp.2d 1209 (E.D. Wash. 2001), p. 822 note 2.

Mazevski v. Horseheads Central School District, 950 F. Supp. 69 (W.D. N.Y. 1997), pp. 221 note 5; 272 note 3.

McCarthy v. Quest International Co., 667 A.2d 379 (N.J. Super. Ct. App. Div. 1995), p. 102 note 5.

McCormack v. National Collegiate Athletic Association, 845 F.2d 1338 (5th Cir. 1988), p. 509.

McCormick ex rel. McCormick v. School Dist. of Mamaroneck, 370 F.3d 275 (2nd Cir. 2004), p. 366 note 2.

McCourt v. California Sports Inc., 460 F.Supp. 904 (E.D. Mich. 1978), p. 464.

McCourt v. California Sports Inc., 600 F.2d 1193 (6th Cir. 1979), pp. 464; 492.

McDonald v. National Collegiate Athletic Association, 370 F. Supp. 625 (C.D. Calif. 1974), p. 218 note 2.

McGill v. Avonworth Baseball Conference, 516 F.2d 1328 (3d Cir. 1975), p. 356 note 3.

McHugh v. Hackensack Public Schools, 483 A.2d 148 (N.J. 1984), p. 145 note 8.

McKichan v. St. Louis Hockey Club, 967 S.W.2d. 209 (Mo. Ct. App. 1998), p. 109 note 1.

McLaughlin v. Machias School Committee, 385 A.2d 53 (Me. 1978), p. 433.

McNeil v. National Football League, 777 F. Supp. 1475 (D. Minn. 1991), pp. 463; 523 note 3; 532 note 4.

McNeil v. National Football League, 790 F. Supp. 871 (D. Minn. 1992), pp. 463; 495; 523 note 3.

McPherson v. Michigan High School Athletic Association, 119 F.3d 453 (6th Cir. 1997), pp. 198 note 6; 249 note 6; 821 note 1c.

Medcalf v. University of Pennsylvania, No. 00-07101, 2001 U.S. Dist. LEXIS 10155 (E.D. Pa. June 19, 2001), p. 773.

Menora v. Illinois High School Association, 527 F. Supp. 637 (N.D. Ill. 1981), vacated, 683 F.2d 1030 (7th Cir. 1982), cert. denied, 103 S. Ct. 801 (1983), p. 267 note 7.

Mercer v. Duke University, 190 F.3d 643 (4th Cir. 1999), pp. 336; 351 note 2; 353 note 3.

Merrill v. Birhanzel, 310 N.W.2d 522 (S.D. 1981), p. 126 note 2.

Metropolitan Exhibition Co. v. Ewing, 42 F. 198 (C.C.D. N.Y. 1890), pp. 375; 398; 480 note 1.

Metropolitan Exhibition Co. v. Ward, 9 N.Y.S. 779 (N.Y. Sup. Ct. 1890), pp. 375; 406; 480 note 1.

Metropolitan Intercollegiate Basketball Association (MIBA) v. NCAA, 339 F. Supp. 2d 545 (S.D. N.Y. 2004), p. 22.

Metropolitan Intercollegiate Basketball Association v. NCAA, 337 F. Supp. 2d 563 (S.D. N.Y. 2004), p. 508.

Metropolitan Sports Facilities Commission v. Minnesota Twins Partnership, No. C2-01-2010, 2002 Minn. LEXIS 73 (Minn. Feb. 4, 2002), p. 448 note 2.

M.G. v. Time Warner, Inc., 89 Cal. App. 4th 623 (Cal. Ct. App. 2001), p. 207 note 7.

Miami Dolphins Ltd. v. Williams, 356 F. Supp. 2d 1301 (S.D. Fla. 2005), p. 394 note 3.

Miami University Wrestling Club v. Miami University, 302 F.3d 608 (6th Cir. 2002), p. 320 note 3.

Michels v. United States Olympic Committee, 741 F.2d 155 (7th Cir. 1984), p. 262 note 8.

Michigan Department of Civil Rights, ex rel. Forton v. Waterford Township Department of Parks and Recreation, 387 N.W.2d 281 (Mich. 1986), p. 361 note 1.

Mid-South Grizzlies v. National Football League, 720 F.2d 772 (3rd Cir. 1983), p. 470 note 4.

Miller v. University of Cincinnati, 2008 WL 203025 (S.D. Ohio 2008), pp. 328 note 5; 347 note 3.

Minnesota Twins Partnership v. State of Minnesota, 592 N.W.2d 847 (Minn. 1999), p. 489 note 2.

Mira v. National Collegiate Athletic Association, No. 87-55213 (Fla. Dist. Ct. 1988), p. 291 note 4.

Mississippi University for Women v. Hogan, 458 U.S. 718 (1982), p. 335.

Missouri State High School Activities Association v. Romines, 37 S.W.3d 421 (Mo. Ct. App. 2001), p. 251 note 5.

Mobile Arts & Sports Association v. United States, 148 F. Supp. 311 (S.D. Ala.1957), p. 755 note 5.

Mogabgab v. Orleans Parish School Board, 239 So. 2d 456 (La. Ct. App. 1970), p. 117 note 8.

Molinas v. National Basketball Association, 190 F. Supp. 241 (S.D. N.Y. 1961), p. 467.

Monster Communications, Inc. v. Turner Broadcasting System, Inc., 935 F. Supp. 490 (S.D. N.Y. 1996), p. 678 note 10.

Montgomery v. City of Detroit, 448 N.W.2d 822 (Mich. Ct. App. 1989), p. 126 note 7.

Montgomery v. Independent School Dist No. 709, 109 F. Supp. 2d 1081 (D. Minn. 2000), p. 782 note 2.

Moore v. University of Notre Dame, 22 F. Supp. 2d 896 (N.D. Ind. 1998), p. 778.

Moore v. University of Notre Dame, 968 F. Supp. 1330 (N.D. Ind. 1997), p. 92 note 4.

Moose v. Massachusetts Institute of Technology, 683 N.E.2d 706 (Mass. App. Ct. 1997), p. 119 note 6.

Moran v. School District #7, Yellowstone County, 350 F. Supp. 1180 (D. Mont. 1972), p. 268 note 5.

Morgan v. State, 685 N.E.2d 202 (N.Y. 1997), p. 78 note 9.

Morio v. North American Soccer League, 501 F. Supp. 633 (S.D. N.Y. 1980), p. 522 note 1.

Morris Communications Corporation v. PGA Tour, 117 F. Supp. 2d 1322 (M.D. Fla. 2000), p. 694.

Morris v. Michigan State Board of Education, 472 F.2d 1207 (6th Cir. 1973), p. 355 note 7.

Morsani v. MLB, 79 F. Supp. 2d 1331 (M.D. Fla. 1999), p. 471.

Moschenross v. St. Louis County, 188 S.W.3d 13 (Mo. Ct. App. 2006), pp. 208 note 1; 762 note 1.

Moulas v. PBC Productions, Inc., 570 N.W.2d 739 (Wis. Ct. App. 1997), p. 68 note 2.

Mularadelis v. Haldane Central School Board, 427 N.Y.S.2d 458 (N.Y. App. Div. 1980), p. 359 note 8.

Mullen v. Parchment School District Board of Education, 2007 WL 1932031 (Mich. App. 2007), p. 433 note 3.

Muller v. Oregon, 208 U.S. 412 (1908), p. 334.

Muscare v. O'Malley, Civil No. 76-C-3729 (N.D. Ill. 1977), p. 352 note 10.

Myers v. Friends of Shenendehowa Crew, Inc., 31 A.D.3d 853 (N.Y. App. Div. 2006), p. 116 note 4.

Myricks v. Lynwood Unified School District, 74 Cal. App. 4th 231 (1999), p. 98 note 1.

Nabozny v. Barnhill, 334 N.E.2d 258 (Ill. App. Ct. 1975), pp. 83 note 3; 106; 108 note 7.

National Association of Broadcasters v. Copyright Royalty Tribunal, 675 F.2d 367 (D.C. Cir. 1982), pp. 715–716 note 4.

National Basketball Ass'n Properties, Inc. v. YMG, Inc., No. 93 C 1533, 1993 U.S. Dist. LEXIS 15864 (N.D. Ill. Nov. 5, 1993), p. 678 note 11.

National Basketball Association v. Motorola, Inc., 105 F.3d 841 (2d Cir. 1997), pp. 694; 738.

National Basketball Association v. SDC Basketball Club Inc., 815 F.2d 562 (9th Cir), cert. denied, 484 U.S.960 (1987), p. 470 note 2.

National Collegiate Athletic Association v. Board of Regents of University of Oklahoma and University of Georgia, 468 U.S. 85 (1984), pp. 159; 505; 728; 729; 730; 732.

National Collegiate Athletic Association v. Brinkworth, 680 So. 2d 1081 (Fla. Dist. Ct. App. 1996), p. 245 note 1.

National Collegiate Athletic Association v. Califano, 444 F. Supp. 425 (D. Kan. 1978), rev'd., 622 F.2d 1382 (10th Cir. 1980), p. 338.

National Collegiate Athletic Association v. Commissioner, 914 F.2d 1417 (10th Cir. 1990), p. 758 note 4.

National Collegiate Athletic Association v. Gillard, 352 So. 2d 1072 (Miss. 1977), p. 271 note 1.

National Collegiate Athletic Association v. Tarkanian, 488 U.S. 179 (1988), pp. 159; 190.

National Collegiate Athletic Association v. Yeo, 171 S.W.3d 863 (Tex. 2005), pp. 184 note 2; 249.

National Exhibition Co. v. Fass, 143 N.Y.S.2d 767 (N.Y. Sup. Ct. 1955), pp. 710; 711 note 2.

National Exhibition v. Teleflash, 24 F. Supp. 488 (S.D. N.Y. 1936), p. 712 note 5.

National Football League Players Association v. Pro-Football Inc., 857 F. Supp. 71 (D. D.C. 1994), p. 522 note 1.

National Football League Properties, Inc. v. New Jersey Giants, Inc., 637 F. Supp. 507 (D. N.J. 1986), p. 679 note 17.

National Football League Properties, Inc. v. Playoff Corp., 808 F. Supp. 1288 (N.D. Tex 1992), p. 679 note 14.

National Football League Properties, Inc. v. Wichita Falls Sportswear, Inc., 532 F. Supp. 651 (W.D. Wash. 1982), pp. 675; 680 note 18.

National Football League Properties v. Dallas Cowboys Inc., Texas Stadium Corporation and Jerral W. Jones, F. 922 Supp. 849 (S.D. N.Y. 1996), pp. 11; 410 note 6; 415.

National Football League v. Cousin Hugo's, Inc., 600 F. Supp. 84 (E.D. Missouri 1984), p. 696 note 5.

National Football League v. Governor of Delaware, 435 F. Supp. 1372 (D. Del. 1977), pp. 682 note 5; 809.

National Football League v. Insight Telecommunications Corp., 158 F.Supp.2d 124 (D. Mass. 2001), p. 741 note 1.

National Football League v. McBee, 792 F.2d 726 (8th Cir. 1986), p. 741 note 2.

National Football League v. PrimeTime 24 Joint Venture, 131 F. Supp. 2d 458 (S.D. N.Y. 2001), p. 741 note 1.

National Football League v. The Alley, Inc., 624 F. Supp. 6 (S.D. Fla. 1983), p. 740.

National Hockey League, et al. v. Pepsi-Cola Canada Ltd., 42 C.P.R.3d 390 (B.C. 1992), p. 682 note 4.

National Labor Relations Board v. Jones and Laughlin Steel Corp., 301 U.S. 1 (1937), p. 519 note 1.

National Organization for Women, Essex County Chapter v. Little League Baseball, Inc., 318 A.2d 33 (N.J. Super. Ct. App. Div. 1974), p. 356 note 6.

National Satellite Sports, Inc. v. J.A. Rocks, Inc., 2006 WL 1831332 (E.D. N.Y. June 28, 2006), p. 734 note 2.

National Treasury Employees Union v. Von Raab, 489 U.S. 656 (1989), pp. 279; 281 note 5.

National Wrestling Coaches Ass'n v. U.S. Dept. of Educ., 263 F. Supp. 2d 82 (D. D.C. 2003), p. 320 note 2.

NBA Properties, Inc. v. Adirondack Software Corporation, case no. D2000-1211 (2000), p. 699 note 6.

NCAA v. Tarkanian, 109 S. Ct. 454 (1988), p. 216.

Neal v. Board of Trustees, 198 F.3d 763 (9th Cir. 1999), p. 320 note 5.

New Boston Television v. Entertainment Sports Programming Network, Inc., No. 81-1010-Z, 1981 U.S. Dist. LEXIS 15032 (D. Mass. Aug. 3, 1981), p. 737.

New England Patriots Football Club, Inc. v. University of Colorado, 592 F. 2d 1196 (1st Cir. 1979), pp. 418 note 5; 417.

New York Times Company v. Sullivan, 376 U.S. 254 (1964), p. 91.

NFL Enterprises LLC v. Comcast Cable Communications, LLC, 851 N.Y.S.2d 551 (2008), p. 720 note 2.

NHL Players Association v. Plymouth Whalers Hockey Club, 325 F.3d 712 (6th Cir. 2003), p. 464.

Nicholas v. Board of Trustees of University of Alabama, 251 Fed. Appx. 637 (11th Cir. 2007), p. 777 note 2.

Nike, Inc. v. Adidas America Inc., 479 F. Supp. 2d 664 (E.D. Tex. 2007), p. 702 note 2.

Nike, Inc. v. Dixon, 2004 WL 3065757 (D. Or. April 6, 2004), p. 702 note 2.

Nike, Inc. v. Wal-Mart Stores Inc., 138 F.3d 1437 (Fed. Cir. 1998), p. 702 note 4.

Noffke ex. rel Swenson v. Bakke, 760 N.W.2d 156 (Wis. 2009), pp. 107–108 note 1.

North American Soccer League v. National Football League, 670 F.2d 1249 (2d Cir.) cert. denied, 459 U.S. 1074 (1982), pp. 474; 498.

North American Soccer League v. National Labor Relations Board, 613 F.2d 1379 (5th Cir. 1980), pp. 515 note 2; 524 note 1.

Northeastern University v. Brown, 2004 WL 616225 (Mass. Super. March 11, 2004), p. 431 note 6.

Northern Pacific v. United States, 356 U.S. 1 (1958), p. 454.

Novak v. Lamar Insurance Co., 488 So. 2d 739 (La. Ct. App. 1986), pp. 78 note 15; 108 note 6.

Nunez v. Recreation Rooms and Settlement, Inc., 645 N.Y.S.2d 789 (N.Y. App. Div. 1996), p. 76 note 2.

Oakland Raiders v. National Football League (NFL), 161 P.3d 151 (Cal. 2007), p. 470.

O'Brien v. The Ohio State Univ., 2006 WL 571043 (Ohio Ct. Cl. February 15, 2006), *aff'd*, 2007 WL 2729077 (Ohio App. 10 Dist. Sep 20, 2007), pp. 191 note 2; 430 note 4.

O'Connor v. Board of Education, 645 F.2d 578 (7th Cir. 1981), cert. denied, 454 U.S. 1084 (1981), pp. 336; 360; 361; 362 note 2.

OFC Comm Baseball v. Markell, 579 F.3d 293 (3rd Cir. 2009), p. 809.

O'Halloran v. University of Washington, 679 F. Supp. 997 (W.D. Wash. 1988), p. 293 note 4.

Olinger v. U.S. Golf Association, 55 F. Supp. 2d 926 (N.D. Ind. 1999), p. 824.

Olinger v. United States Golf Association, 205 F.3d 1001 (7th Cir. 2000), pp. 824–825.

Oliver v. NCAA, 920 N.E.2d 203 (Ohio Com. Pleas 2009), p. 624 note 2.

O-M Bread v. United States Olympic Committee, 65 F.3d 933 (Fed. Cir. 1995), p. 692 note 4.

Omnipoint Communications Inc. v. New York Yankee Partnership and Bell Atlantic Nynex Mobile, Index No. 601910/97, Seq. Nos.: 001, 002 (N.Y. Sup. Ct. 1999), p. 409 note 4.

Open Source Yoga Unity v. Choudhury, 2005 WL 756558 (N.D. Cal. April 1, 2005), p. 696 note 6.

Orr v. Brigham Young University, 960 F. Supp. 1522 (D. Utah 1994), p. 121 note 2.

Orr v. National Football League Players Association, 147 LRRM 2845 (Va. 1994), p. 522 note 1.

Ortiz-Del Valle v. National Basketball Association, 42 F. Supp. 2d 334 (S.D. N.Y. 1999), p. 772.

Othen v. Ann Arbor School Board, 507 F. Supp. 1376 (E.D. Mich. 1981), *aff'd.*, 699 F.2d 309 (6th Cir. 1983), pp. 338; 339 note 7.

Page, Alan v. Minnesota Vikings, In the Matter of arbitration (July 23, 1973), p. 393.

Pagnotta v. Pennsylvania Interscholastic Athletic Association, 681 A.2d 235 (Pa. Commw. Ct. 1996), p. 183.

Pahulu v. University of Kansas, 897 F. Supp. 1387 (D. Kan. 1995), p. 823 note 6.

Palmer v. Mount Vernon Township High School District 201, 169 Ill.2d 55, 662 N.E.2d 1260 (Ill. 1996), p. 122 note 3.

Pantalone v. Lenape Valley Regional High School, Docket No. L-40828-26, Sussex Co. (N.J. Sup. Ct. 1976), p. 146 note 11.

Paralyzed Veterans of America v. D.C. Arena L.P., 117 F.3d 579 (D.C. Cir. 1997), p. 825.

Parish v. NCAA, 361 F. Supp. 1220 (W.D. La. 1973), *aff'd.*, 506 F.2d 1028 (5th Cir. 1975), p. 217 note 2.

Parker ex rel. Parker v. Arizona Interscholastic Association, Inc. (AIA), 59 P.3d 806 (Ariz. App. Div. 1 2002), p. 251 note 3.

Parker v. Graves, 340 F. Supp. 586 (D.C. Fla. 1972), pp. 431–432 note 12.

Patton v. United States of America Rugby Football, Union, Ltd., 851 A.2d 566 (Md. 2004), p. 144 note 1.

P.D.B. Sports, Ltd. v. C.I.R., 109 T.C. No. 20 (U.S. Tax Ct. 1997), p. 764 note 3.

Pebble Beach Company v. Tour 18 Ltd., 155 F.3d 526 (5th Cir. 1998), p. 677 note 7.

Pederson v. Louisiana State University, 213 F.3d 858 (5th Cir. 2000), pp. 345; 347 note 4.

Pegram v. Nelson, 469 F. Supp. 1134 [M.D. N.C. 1979], p. 223.

Peirick v. Indiana University-Purdue University Indianapolis Athletics Department, 510 F.3d 681 (7th Cir. 2007), p. 779 note 1.

Pelletier v. Maine Principals' Association (MPA), 261 F. Supp. 2d 10 (D. Me. 2003), pp. 182 note 1; 224 note 3.

Pennoyer v. Neff, 95 U.S. 714 [1877], p. 219.

People v. Freer, 381 N.Y.S.2d 976 (N.Y. Dist. Ct. 1976), p. 794 note 8.

People v. Sorkin, 407 N.Y.S.2d 772 (N.Y. App. Div 1978), p. 583 note 3.

Perdue v. City University of New York, 13 F. Supp. 2d 326 (E.D. N.Y. 1998), p. 769 note 5.

Perkins v. Londonderry Basketball Club, 196 F.3d 13 (1st Cir. 1999), p. 335 note 1.

Perry v. Ohio High School Athletic Association (OHSAA), 2006 WL 2927260 (S.D. Ohio October 11, 2006), pp. 36 note 1; 225 note 2; 251 note 2.

Petrie v. Illinois High School Association, 394 N.E.2d 855 (Ill. 1979), p. 359 note 10.

PGA Tour, Inc. v. Casey Martin, 532 U.S. 661 (2001), pp. 37 note 1; 241 note 1; 311; 819; 825.

Philadelphia Ball Club, Ltd. v. Lajoie, 51 A. 973 (Pa. 1902), pp. 376; 406; 407 note 3; 480 note 1.

Philadelphia Eagles Football Club, Inc. v. City of Philadelphia, 573 Pa. 189 (Pa. 2003), p. 755 note 2.

Philadelphia World Hockey Club, Inc. v. Philadelphia Hockey Club, 351 F. Supp. 462 (E.D. Pa. 1972), pp. 463; 476 note 3; 490.

Phillip v. Fairfield University and National Collegiate Athletic Association, 118 F.3d 131 (2nd Cir. 1997), p. 180 note 3.

Phillipe v. City of New York Board of Education, 678 N.Y.S.2d 662 (N.Y. App. Div. 1998), p. 119 note 5.

Phillips v. Anderson County Board of Education, 2006 WL 3759893 (E.D. Tenn. Dec. 19, 2006), p. 354 note 1.

Phoenix Suns and Tsakalidis v. Athletic Union of Constantinople, In the Matter of Arbitration (1997), pp. 377 note 3; 649 note 3.

Piazza v. Major League Baseball, 831 F. Supp. 420 (E.D. Pa. 1993), p. 471.

Pirkle v. Oakdale Union Grammer School Dist., 253 P.2d 1 (Cal. Sup. Ct. 1953), p. 115 note 8.

Pitts v. State, No. CIV-93-1341-A (W.D. Okla. 1994), p. 774 note 7.

Pittsburgh Athletic Co. v. Commissioner, 27 B.T.A. 1074 (1933), *aff'd.*, 72 F.2d 883 (3d Cir. 1934), p. 764 note 5.

Pittsburgh Athletic Co. v. KQV Broadcasting, 24 F. Supp. 490 (W.D. Pa. 1938), p. 711 notes 2 and 3.

Plotsker v. Whitey Ford's Grand Slam, Inc., 693 N.Y.S.2d 219 (N.Y. App. Div. 1999), p. 137 note 5.

Ponce v. Basketball Federation, 760 F.2d 375 (1st Cir. 1985), p. 649 note 6.

Poole v. South Plainfield Board of Education, 490 F. Supp. 948 (D. N.J. 1980), p. 814.

Post-Newsweek Stations-Connecticut Inc. v. Travelers Insurance Co., 510 F. Supp. 81 (D. Conn. 1981), p. 711 note 1.

Poston v. NFLPA, 02249 (S.D. N.Y. May 2, 2006), p. 592 note 1.

Poston v. NFLPA, 2002 WL 31190142 (E.D. Va. August 26, 2002), p. 592 note 1.

Pottgen v. Missouri State High School Activities Ass'n, 40 F.3d 926 (8th Cir. 1994), pp. 817; 821 note 2.

Powell v. National Football League, 678 F. Supp. 777 (D. Minn.1988), pp. 463; 494; 531; 532 note 3.

Powell v. National Football League, 930 F.2d 1293 (8th Cir. 1989), pp. 494; 523 note 3; 532 note 3.

Prejean v. East Baton Rouge Parish School Board, 729 So. 2d 686 (La. Ct. App. 1999), p. 112 note 4.

Premock v. Montana, No. 74947/40 (Mont. Dist. Ct. 1991), pp. 289; 290 note 2.

Price v. University of Alabama, 318 F. Supp. 2d 1084 (N.D. Ala. 2003), p. 382 note 3.

Pro-Football, Inc. v. Harjo, 284 F. Supp. 2d 96 (D. D.C. 2003), p. 688 note 3.

Pro-Football Inc. v. Harjo, 565 F.3d 880 (C.A. D.C. 2009), p. 688 note 3.

Pro-Football, Inc. v. Paul, 569 S.E.2d 66 (Va. Ct. App. 2002), p. 102 note 2.

Pro Tect Management Corp. v. Worley, No. 89 Civ. 3026, U.S. Dist. LEXIS 14574 at °1 (S.D. N.Y. Oct. 30, 1990), p. 582 note 2.

Professional Hockey Club Central Sports v. Detroit Red Wings, 787 F. Supp. 706 (E.D. Mich. 1992), p. 410 note 8.

Pryor v. NCAA, 288 F.3d 548 (3rd Cir. 2002), p. 238 note 2.

Puchalski v. School District of Springfield, 161 F. Supp. 2d 395 (E.D. Pa. 2001), p. 225 note 1.

Quad Cities Open, Inc. v. City of Silvis, 208 Ill.2d 498 (Ill. 2004), p. 755 note 1.

Quokka Sports, Inc. v. Cup Int'l, Ltd., 99 F. Supp. 2d 1105 (N.D. Cal. 1999), p. 699 note 8.

Radovich v. National Football League, 231 F.2d 620 (9th Cir. 1956), p. 462.

Radovich v. National Football League, 352 U.S. 445 (1957), p. 463.

Raducan, Andrea v. International Olympic Committee, Matter of Arbitration (2000), CAS 2000/011, p. 204 note 9.

Rallins v. Ohio State University, 191 F. Supp. 2d 920 (S.D. Ohio 2002), pp. 768–769 note 3.

Ranieri v. Highland Falls-Fort Montgomery School District, 198 F. Supp. 2d 542 (S.D. N.Y. 2002), p. 779 note 2.

Rappaport v. Little League Baseball, Inc., 65 F.R.D. 545 (D. Del. 1975), p. 356 note 2.

Rayle v. Bowling Green State University, 739 N.E.2d 1260 (Ct. Cl. Ohio 2000), p. 385 note 4.

Reagan v. State of New York, 654 N.Y.S. 2d 488 (N.Y. App. Div. 1997), p. 72 note 3.

Reaves v. Mills, 904 F. Supp. 120 (W.D. N.Y. 1995), p. 821 note 2.

Reed v. Nebraska School Activities Association, 341 F. Supp. 258 (D. Neb. 1972), p. 355 note 8.

Reed v. Reed, 404 U.S. 71 (1971), p. 335.

Regents of University of California v. ABC, 747 F.2d 511 [9th Cir. 1984]), p. 731.

Regents of University of Minnesota v. National Collegiate Athletic Association, 422 F. Supp. 1158 (D. Minn. 1976), p. 269.

Regents of University of Minnesota v. National Collegiate Athletic Association, 560 F.2d 352 (8th Cir. 1977), p. 270.

Regina v. Green, 16 D.L.R.3d 137 (Ont P.C. 1970), pp. 790; 795 note 11.

Regina v. Maki, 14 D.L.R.3d 164 (Ont P.C. 1970), pp. 790; 795 notes 10 and 11.

Rendell-Baker v. Kohn, 457 U.S. 830 (1982), p. 217 note 1.

Rensing v. Indiana State University Board of Trustees, 444 N.E.2d 1170 (Ind. 1983), pp. 100; 102 note 4; 538–539 note 3.

Rensselaer Polytechnic Institute v. Commissioner, 732 F.2d 1058 (2d Cir. 1983), p. 758 note 4.

Repka v. Arctic Cat, Inc., 20 A.D.3d 916 (N.Y. App. Div. 2005), p. 147 note 3.

Resorts of Pinehurst, Inc. v. Pinehurst National Corp., 148 F.3d 417 (4th Cir. 1998), p. 671 note 9.

Reynolds v. International Amateur Athletic Federation, 23 F.3d 1110 (6th Cir. 1994), p. 299 note 14.

Reynolds v. International Amateur Athletic Federation, 505 U.S. 1301 (1992), p. 163.

Reynolds v. International Amateur Athletic Federation, 841 F. Supp. 1444 (S.D. Ohio 1992), p. 299 note 14.

Rhodes v. Ohio High School Athletic Association, 939 F. Supp. 584 (N.D. Ohio 1996), pp. 198 note 9; 246 note 2; 822 note 3.

Richard v. Perkins, 373 F. Supp. 2d 1211 (D. Kan. 2005), p. 221 note 2.

Richards v. United States Tennis Association, 400 N.Y.S.2d 267 (N.Y. Sup. Ct. 1977), p. 337 note 5.

Richardson v. Sugg., 448 F. 3d 1046 (8th Cir. 2006), p. 777 note 3.

Ridgefield Women's Political Caucus, Inc. v. Fossi, 458 F. Supp. 117 (D. Conn. 1978), p. 337 note 4.

Ridgeway v. Montana High School Association, 633 F. Supp. 1564 (D. Mont. 1986), p. 366 note 4.

Riggs v. Clark County School District, 19 F. Supp. 2d 1177 (D. Nev. 1998), p. 92 note 3.

Ritacco v. Norwin School District, 361 F. Supp. 930 (W.D. Pa. 1973), p. 363 note 2.

Roane v. Greenwich Swim Committee, 330 F. Supp. 2d 306 (S.D. N.Y. 2004), p. 152 note 2.

Roberts v. Colorado State University, 814 F. Supp. 1507 (D. Colo. 1993), pp. 349; 348 note 8.

Roberts v. Timber Birch-Broadmoore Athletic Association, 852 A.2d 271 (N.J. Super. Ct. App. Div. 2004), p. 127 note 2.

Robertson v. National Basketball Association, 389 F. Supp. 867 (S.D. N.Y. 1975), p. 475 note 2.

Robitaille v. Vancouver Hockey Club, 3 W.W.R. 481 (Ct. App. B.C. 1981), p. 141 note 9.

Rocchigiani v. World Boxing Council, Inc., 131 F. Supp. 2d 527 (S.D. N.Y. 2001), p. 385 note 2.

Rodgers v. Georgia Tech Athletic Association, 303 S.E. 2d 467 (Ga. Ct. App. 1983), p. 416.

Rodriguez v. New York State Public High School Athletic Association, 809 N.Y.S.2d 483 (Table) (2005), p. 180 note 1.

Rodriquez v. Topps Co., 104 F. Supp. 2d 1224 (S.D. Cal. 2000), p. 62.

Roe ex rel. Callahan v. Gustine Unified School District, 678 F.Supp.2d 1008 (E.D. Cal. 2009), p. 338 note 1.

Rogers v. Professional Golfers Association of America, 28 S.W.3d 869 (Ky. Ct. App. 2000), p. 135 note 5.

Rolison v. City of Meridian, 691 So. 2d 440 (Miss. 1997), p. 144 note 4.

Romanowski v. Township of Washington, 2006 WL 1650967 (N.J. Super. A.D. June 16, 2006), p. 127 note 1.

Rona v. Major League Baseball Players Association, Matter of Arbitration, p. 585 note 1.

Rosa H. v. San Elizario Independent School District, 106 F.3d 648 (5th Cir. 1997), p. 784 note 11.

Rose v. Diocese of Bridgeport, No. CV92-0293727, 1993 Conn. Super. LEXIS 880 (Apr. 16, 1993), pp. 69–70 note 1.

Rostai v. Neste Enterprises, 138 Cal. App. 4th 326 (Cal. Ct. App. 2006), p. 99 note 1.

Rottmann v. Pennsylvania Interscholastic Athletic Association, Inc. (PIAA), 349 F. Supp. 2d 922 (W.D. Pa. 2004), p. 265 note 2.

Ruiz v. Massachusetts Interscholastic Athletic Association, No. CV00-68, 2000 Mass. Super LEXIS 213 (Mass. Feb. 7, 2000), p. 198 note 5.

Ruman v. Eskew, 343 N.E.2d 806 (Ind. Ct. App. 1975), p. 363 note 1.

Ryan v. California Interscholastic Federation, 94 Cal. App. 4th 1048 (Cal. Ct. App. 2001), p. 225 note 4.

Sadler v. University Interscholastic League, 1991 WL 633967 (W.D. Tex. 1991), p. 821 note 2.

Saint v. Nebraska School Activities Association, 684 F. Supp. 626 (D. Neb. 1988), pp. 357; 352 note 6.

St. Patrick High School v. New Jersey Interscholastic Athletic Association, 2010 WL 715826 (D.N.J. March 1, 2010), pp. 197 note 1; 225 note 1.

Salte v. YMCA of Metropolitan Chicago Foundation, 814 N.E.2d 610 (Ill. App. Ct. 2004), p. 136 note 4.

Samara v. National Collegiate Athletic Association, 1973 Trade Cases (CCH) 74,536 (E.D. Va.), p. 272 note 2.

San Antonio Independent School District v. Rodriguez, 411 U.S. 1 [1973], p. 223.

San Francisco Arts & Athletics, Inc. v. United States Olympic Committee, 483 U.S. 522 (1987), p. 692 note 3.

San Francisco Seals Ltd. v. National Hockey League, 379 F. Supp. 966 (C.D. Cal. 1974), pp. 470–480 note 5.

Sanders v. Kuna Joint School District, 876 P.2d 154 (Idaho Ct. App. 1994), p. 73 note 7.

Sandison v. Michigan High School Athletic Ass'n, 64 F.3d 1026 (6th Cir. 1995), p. 821 note 1d.

Sandler v. Half Hollow Hills West High School, 672 N.Y.S.2d 120 (N.Y. App. Div. 1998), p. 77 note 7.

Santa Fe Independent School District v. Doe, 530 U.S. 290 (2000), pp. 264; 265 note 3; 266 note 4.

Santho v. Boy Scouts of America, 857 N.E.2d 1255 (Ohio Ct. App. 2006), p. 112 note 1.

Santopietro v. City of New Haven, 682 A.2d 106 (Conn. 1996), p. 145 note 5.

Sauray v. City of New York, 690 N.Y.S.2d 716 (N.Y. App. Div. 1999), p. 79 note 5.

Schiffman v. Spring, 609 N.Y.S.2d 482 (N.Y. App. Div. 1994), p. 120 note 8.

School Board of Nassau County v. Arline, 480 U.S. 273 (1987), p. 826.

Schultz v. Foster-Glocester Reg'l School Dist., 755 A.2d 153 (R.I. 2000), p. 114 note 3.

Schwartz v. Dallas Cowboys Football Club, 2001 WL 1689714 (E.D. Pa. Nov. 21, 2001), p. 715 note 2.

Scott v. Rapides Sch. Bd., 732 So.2d 749 (La. Ct. App. 1999), p. 119 note 4.

Seagrave v. Dean, 908 So.2d 41 (La. App. 1st Cir. 2005), p. 780 note 1.

Searles v. Trustees of St. Joseph's College, 695 A. 2d. 1206 (Me. 1997), p. 113 note 6.

Segura, Bernardo v. International Amateur Athletic Federation, Matter of Arbitration, CAS OG 00/013, p. 204 note 10.

Selig v. United States, 740 F.2d 572 (7th Cir. 1984), p. 763.

Shaw v. Dallas Cowboys Football Club, 172 F.3d 299 (3d Cir. 1999), p. 715 note 2.

Shelley v. Kraemer, 334 U.S. 1 (1948), p. 217.

Shelly v. Stepp, 73 Cal. Rptr. 2d 323 (Cal. Ct. App., 1998), p. 77 note 6.

Shelton v. National Collegiate Athletic Association, 539 F.2d 1197 (9th Cir. 1976), p. 256 note 1.

Shepherd v. U.S. Olympic Committee, 464 F.Supp.2d 1072 (D. Colo. 2006), p. 819.

Shin v. Ahn, 141 Cal. App. 4th 726 (Cal. Ct. App. 2006) p. 78 note 1.

Shoemaker v. Handel, 795 F.2d 1136 (3rd Cir. 1986), p. 282 note 3.

Shorten v. City of White Plains, 637 N.Y.S.2d 791 (N.Y. App. Div. 1996), p. 73 note 6.

Silverman v. Major League Baseball Player Relations Committee, Inc., 516 F. Supp. 588 (S.D. N.Y. 1981), p. 522 note 2.

Silverman v. Major League Baseball Player Relations Committee, Inc., 880 F. Supp. 246 (S.D. N.Y. 1995), p. 552.

Silverman v. Major League Baseball Player Relations Committee, Inc., 67 F.3d 1054 (2nd Cir. 1995), p. 552.

Simpson v. University of Colorado Boulder, 500 F.3d 1170 (10th Cir. 2007), pp. 783–784 note 6.

Singerman v. Municipal Service Bureau, Inc., 565 N.W.2d 383 (Mich. 1997), pp. 72 note 5; 125 note 4.

Skinner v. Railway Labor Executive Assn., 489 U.S. 602 (1989), pp. 279; 281 note 5.

Slaney v. The International Amateur Athletic Federation and United States Olympic Committee, 244 F 3d 580 (7th Cir. 2001), pp. 164 note 2; 261 note 2; 298 note 12.

Smith v. Allwright, 321 U.S. 649 (1944), p. 217 note 6.

Smith v. Board of Education, 341 S.E. 2d 685 (W.Va. 1985), p. 434 note 8.

Smith v. National Collegiate Athletic Ass'n, 266 F.3d 152 (3rd Cir. 2001), p. 339 note 3.

Smith v. Plati, 56 F. Supp.2d 1195 (D. Co. 1999), p. 207 note 8.

Smith v. Pro Football Inc., 593 F.2d 1173 (D.C. Cir. 1978), pp. 454; 463.

Smith v. Pro Football Inc., 528 F. Supp. 1266 (D.D.C. 1981), p. 531.

Sobba v. Pratt Community College & Area Vocational School, 117 F. Supp. 2d 1043 (D. Kan. 2000), p. 774 note 5.

Somerville School Committee v. Massachusetts Interscholastic Athletic Association, No. 00-01042B, 2000 Mass. Super. LEXIS 109 (Mass. Mar. 15, 2000), p. 197 note 4.

Sony Corp. of America v. Universal City Studios, Inc., 464 U.S. 417 (1984), p. 740 note 2.

Southeastern Community College v. Davis, 442 U.S. 397 [1979], p. 812.

Souza v. Squaw Valley Ski Corporation, 138 Cal. App. 4th 262 (Cal. Ct. App. 2006), p. 136 note 3.

Spath v. National Collegiate Athletic Association, 728 F.2d 25 (1st. Cir. 1984), p. 248 note 2.

Speakers of Sport v. Pro Serv, 178 F.3d 862 (7th Cir. 1999), p. 593 note 1.

SportsChannel Associates, v. Sterling Mets, L.P., 801 N.Y.S.2d 242 (N.Y. Sup. 2005), p. 722 note 2.

Sprewell v. Golden State Warriors and National Basketball Association, John D. Feerick, Grievance Arbitrator, March 4, 1998, pp. 567 note 2b; 788 note 4.

Stang v. Independent School District, 256 N.W. 2d 82 (Minn. 1977), p. 434 note 12.

Stanley v. University of Southern California, 178 F.3d 1069 (9th Cir. 1999), cert.denied, 120 S. Ct. 533 (1999), pp. 768; 769 note 4.

Starkey v. Board of Education, 381 P.2d 718 (Utah Sup. Ct. 1963), p. 268 note 3.

State, ex rel. Cincinnati Enquirer v. Krings, 758 N.E.2d 1135 (Ohio 2001), p. 207 note 6.

State ex. rel. Dennis v. Board of Education, 529 N.E.2d. 1248 (Ohio 1988), p. 434 note 6.

State ex rel. National Junior College Athletic Ass'n. v. Luten, 492 S.W.2d 404 (Mo. Ct. App. 1973), pp. 171; 172 note 3.

State of Oregon v. Superior Court, 29 Cal. Rptr. 2d 909 (Cal. Ct. App. 1994), p. 140 note 3.

State of Washington v. Shelley, Wash. Ct. App. 929 P.2d 489 (1997), p. 793 note 4.

State v. Floyd, 466 N.W.2d 919 (Iowa Ct. App. 1990), p. 794 note 7.

State v. Forbes, No. 63280 (Minn. Dist. Ct. 1975), pp. 790; 792; 794 note 9.

Steelworkers v. American Mfg. Co., 363 U.S. 564 (1960), p. 565 note 1.

Steelworkers v. Enterprise Wheel and Car Corp., 363 U.S. 593 (1960), p. 566 note 1.

Steelworkers v. Warrior & Gulf Navigation Co., 363 U.S. 574 (1960), p. 565 note 1.

Steinberg, Moorad & Dunn, Inc. v. Dunn, 136 Fed. Appx. 6 (9th Cir. Cal. 2005), p. 598 note 2.

Stelluti v. Casapenn Enterprises, LLC, 975 A.2d 494 (N.J. Super. A.D. 2009), pp. 136 note 1.

Stineman v. Fontbonne College, 664 F.2d 1082 (8th Cir. 1981), p. 117 note 7.

Striebel v. Minnesota State High School League, 321 N.W.2d 400 (Minn. 1982), p. 366 note 5.

Stringer v. Minnesota Viking Football Club, LLC, 705 N.W.2d 746 (Minn. 2005), p. 116 note 2.

Stringer v. National Football League, CV-0065-JDH-MRA (S.D. Ohio July 10, 2009), p. 147 note 1.

Suburban Scholastic Council v. Section 2 of the New York State Public High School Athletic Association (NYSPHSAA), 803 N.Y.S.2d 270 (2005), p. 177 note 2.

Summy v. City of Des Moines, 708 N.W.2d 333 (Iowa 2006), p. 125 note 1.

Swager v. Board of Education, 688 P.2d 270 (Kan. Ct. App. 1984), pp. 432; 434 note 9.

Swan v. Town of Grand Island, 652 N.Y.S.2d 166 (N.Y. App. Div. 1996), p. 78 note 11.

Tanaka v. University of Southern California, 252 F.3d 1059 (9th Cir. 2001), pp. 170 note 4; 250 note 1; 456 note 3.

Tarkanian v. NCAA, 103 Nev. 331 (Nev. 1987), p. 190.

Tarkanian v. National Collegiate Athletic Association, 511 U.S. 1033 (1994), pp. 19 note 5; 174; 193 note 1.

Tatum v. National Collegiate Athletic Association, 992 F. Supp. 1114 (E.D. Mo. 1998), pp. 239 note 5; 823 note 3.

Taylor v. Enumclaw School Dist. No. 216, 133 P.3d 492 (Wash. App. Div. 1 2006), pp. 225 note 3; 274 note 2.

Taylor v. Massapequa International Little League, 689 N.Y.S.2d 523 (N.Y. App. Div. 1999), p. 114 note 4.

Tennessee Secondary School Athletic Association (TSSAA) v. Brentwood Academy, 127 S. Ct. 2489 (2007), p. 218 note 1.

Tennessee v. Lane, 541 U.S. 509 (2004), p. 818.

Tesmer v. Colorado High School Activities Association, 140 P.3d 249 (Colo. App. 2006), p. 820 note 1a.

Texas A&M University System v. University Book Store, Inc., 683 S.W.2d 140 (Tex. App. 1984), p. 686 note 4.

The Football Ass'n of Premier League Ltd. v. YouTube, Inc., 633 F.Supp.2d 159 (S.D.N.Y. 2009), pp. 696 note 2; 738 note 1.

Theno v. Tonganoxie Unified School District, 377 F. Supp. 3d 952 (D. Kansas 2005), p. 782 note 2.

Thomas v. United States Soccer Federation, Inc., 653 N.Y.S.2d 958 (N.Y. App. Div. 1997), p. 72 note 4.

Thomka v. Massachusetts Interscholastic Athletic Association, Inc. (MIAA), 2007 WL 867084 (Mass. Super. February 12, 2007), pp. 179 note 1; 228 note 2; 331 note 2.

Thompson v. Park River Corporation, 830 N.E.2d 1252 (Ohio Ct. App. 2005), p. 108 note 2.

Thompson v. Seattle Public School District (unpublished decision 1985), p. 115 note 6.

Thurmond v. Prince William Professional Baseball Club, 574 S.E.2d 246 (Va. 2003), p. 77 note 3.

T.H. v. Montana High School Ass'n, No. CV 92-150-BLG-JFB, 1992 WL 672982 (D. Mont. September 24, 1992), p. 815.

Ticketmaster L.L.C. v. RMG Technologies, Inc., 507 F. Supp. 2d 1096 (2007), p. 739 note 2.

Time, Inc. v. Hill, 385 U.S. 374 (1967), p. 93.

Tinker v. Des Moines Independent School District, 93 U.S. 503 (1969), p. 267 note 8.

Todd v. Rush County School, 133 F.3d 984 (7th Cir. 1998), p. 287 note 7.

Tomjanovich v. California Sports Inc., No. H-78-243, 1979 U.S. Dist. LEXIS 9282 (S.D. Tex. Oct. 10, 1979), p. 396 note 2.

Tondas v. Amateur Hockey Ass'n. of the United States, 438 F. Supp. 310 (W.D. N.Y. 1977), p. 505.

Toolson v. New York Yankees, 346 U.S. 356 (1953), p. 486.

Toone v. Adams, 137 S.E.2d 132 (N.C. 1964), pp. 123 note 2; 145 note 8.

Toronto Raptors and Radojevic v. Budocnost, In the Matter of Arbitration (1997), pp. 377 note 4; 649 note 4.

Total Economic Athletic Management of America v. Pickens, 898 S.W.2d 98 (Mo. Ct. App. 1995), p. 580 note 3.

Town & Country Properties, Inc. v. Riggins, 457 S.E.2d 356 (Va. 1995), p. 705 note 7.

Townsley v. Cincinnati Gardens, Inc., 314 N.E.2d 409 (Ohio Ct. App. 1974), p. 136 note 12.

Turner v. Mandalay Sports Entertainment, LLC, 180 P.3d 1172 (Nev. 2008), p. 132 note 2.

Twelve Clubs Comprising National League of Professional Baseball Clubs and Twelve Clubs Comprising American League of Professional Baseball Clubs v. Major League Baseball Players Association and Messersmith/McNally, Grievance Nos. 75-27 and 75-23, Seitz, Chairman of Arbitration Panel, December 23, 1975, p. 389 note 1.

Twentieth Century Fox Film Corp. v. Cablevision Systems Corp., 478 F. Supp. 2d 607 (S.D. N.Y. 2007), p. 750 note 1.

Twentieth Century Fox Film, Corp. v. ICRAVETV, Nos. 00-121, 00-120, 2000 U.S. Dist. LEXIS 1013 (W.D. Pa. Jan. 28, 2000), p. 739 note 5.

TYR Sport, Inc. v. Warnaco Swimwear, Inc., 2010 WL 1192438 (C.D. Cal. March 16, 2010), p. 416 note 2.

Unincorporated Operating Div. of Indiana Newspapers, Inc. v. Trustees of Indiana, 787 N.E.2d 893 (Ind. App. 2003), p. 210 note 2.

Union Royale Belge des Sociétés de Football Association ASBL v. Bosman, Court of Justice of the European Communities, C-415/93, award of December 15, 1995, p. 503.

United Mine Workers v. Pennington, 381 U.S. 657 (1965), p. 490.

United States Anti-Doping Agency (USADA) v. Montgomery, Matter of Arbitration (2005), CAS 2004/O/645, p. 203 note 3.

United States Dept. of Educ. v. NCAA, 481 F.3d 936 (7th Cir. 2007), p. 206 note 2.

United States Football League v. National Football League, 842 F.2d 1335 (2d Cir. 1988), p. 473.

United States Olympic Committee and USA Canoe and Kayak v. International Olympic Committee, CAS arbitration case, p. 204 note 8.

United States Olympic Committee v. Interlicense Corp., 469 U.S. 982 (1984), p. 692 note 4.

United States Olympic Committee v. Interlicense Corporation, 737 F.2d 263 (2nd Cir. 1984), p. 262.

United States Olympic Committee v. International Federation of Bodybuilders, 219 U.S.P.Q. 353 (D. D.C. 1982), p. 692 note 8.

United States Olympic Committee v. Toy Truck Lines, 237 F.3d 1331 (Fed. Cir. 2001), p. 691 note 1.

United States Olympic Committee v. Union Sport Apparel, 220 U.S.P.Q. 526 (E.D. Va. 1983), p. 692 note 7.

United States v. Burke, 700 F.2d 70 (2d Cir.), aff'd., 464 U.S. 816 (1983), p. 807 note 5.

United States v. Cleveland Indians Baseball Co., 532 U.S. 200 (2001), p. 764 note 2.

United States v. General Motors Corp., 121 F.2d 376 (7th Cir.), cert. denied, 314 U.S. 618 (1941), p. 502 note 7.

United States v. International Boxing Club, 348 U.S. 236 (1955), p. 458.

United States v. NFL, 116 F. Supp. 319 (E.D. Pa. 1953), p. 742 note 2.

United States v. Shubert, 348 U.S. 222 (1955), p. 458.

United States v. Walters and Bloom, 913 F.2d 388 (7th Cir. 1990), p. 614 note 1b.

United States v. Wrestling Division of the AAU, 545 F. Supp. 1053 (N.D. Ohio 1982), p. 262 note 1.

United States Wrestling Federation v. United States Olympic Committee, Civil Action No. 13460-78, Superior Court, District of Columbia (1978), p. 262 note 1.

Univ. of Georgia Athletic Association v. Laite, 756 F.2d 1535 (11th Cir. 1985), p. 689 note 6.

University Interscholastic League (UIL) v. Buchanan, 848 S.W.2d 298 (Tex. Ct. App. 1993), p. 814.

University of Alabama Bd. of Trustees v. New Life Art Inc., 2009 WL 5213713 (N.D. Ala. November 19, 2009), p. 670 note 1.

University of Alabama, Tuscaloosa Infractions Appeals Report (September 17, 2002), p. 191 note 4.

University of Colorado v. Derdeyn, 863 P.2d 929 (Colo. 1993), p. 293 note 2.

University of Denver v. Nemeth, 257 P.2d 423 (Colo. 1953), pp. 100; 102 note 6.

University of Kentucky Infractions Appeals Report (September 17, 2002), p. 191 note 5.

University of Michigan Infractions Appeals Report (September 25, 2003), p. 191 note 3.

University of Minnesota v. Haskins, File No. 00-12750 (2002), p. 189 note 7.

University of Pittsburgh v. Champion Products, Inc., 686 F.2d 1040 (3d Cir.) cert. denied, 459 U.S. 1087 (1982), p. 684.

University of South Carolina v. University of Southern California, 2010 WL 157220 (C.A. Fed. January 19, 2010), pp. 670–671 note 3.

University System of Maryland v. Baltimore Sun Co., 847 A.2d 427 (Md. 2004), p. 207 note 4.

U.S. v. Comprehensive Drug Testing, Inc., 473 F.3d 915 (9th Cir. 2006), p. 308 note 2.

U.S. Dept. of Educ.v. NCAA, 481 F.3d 936 (7th Cir. 2007), p. 206 note 2.

Vaillancourt v. Latifi, 840 A.2d 1209 (Ct. App. Ct. 2004), p. 72 note 1.

Vanderbilt University v. DiNardo, 174 F.3d 751 (6th Cir. 1999), pp. 378 note 5; 7.

Vendrell v. School District, No. 26C, Malheur County, P.2d 406 (Or. 1961), p. 115 note 7.

Verni v. Harry M. Stevens, Inc., 903 A.2d 475 (N.J. Super. Ct. App. Div. 2006), p. 134 note 2.

Vernonia School District v. Acton, 515 U.S. 646 (1995), pp. 280 note 3; 283.

Volvo North American Corp v. Men's International Professional Tennis Council, 857 F.2d 55 2d Cir.), cert. denied 487 U.S. 1219 (1988), p. 478.

Wagner v. SFX Motor Sports, Inc., 460 F. Supp. 2d 1263 (D. Kan. 2006), p. 152 note 1.

Waldrep v. Texas Employers Insurance Association, No. 03-98-00053, 2000 Tex. Ct. App. LEXIS 4023 (Tex. Nov. 16, 2000), p. 102 note 1.

Walker v. National Collegiate Athletic Association, No. El-C-916 (W.D. Wis. 1981), p. 270.

Wallace v. Texas Tech University, 80 F.3d 1042 (5th Cir. 1996), p. 776.

Walsh v. Louisiana High School Athletic Association, 616 F.2d 152 [5th Cir. 1980], p. 223.

Walters v. Fullwood, 675 F. Supp. 155 (S.D. N.Y. 1987), p. 614 note 1a.

Walton v. Cook, Civil Case No. A8003-0165 (Or. 1981), p. 142 note 10.

Washington Capitols Basketball Club Inc. v. Barry, 304 F. Supp. 1193 (N.D. Cal. 1969), p. 407 note 2.

Washington v. Indiana High School Athletic Association, 181 F.3d 840 (7th Cir. 1999), pp. 198 note 4; 248 note 5; 821 note 2b.

Wayne Baseball, Inc. v. Commissioner, 78 T.C.M. (CCH) 437 (1999), p. 755 note 3.

Weegham v. Killefer, 215 F.168 (W.D. Mich.) aff'd., 215 F. 289 (6th Cir. 1914), p. 407 note 2.

Weinstein v. Evanston Township Community, 351 N.E.2d 236 (Ill. App. Ct. 1976), p. 126 note 1.

Wertheim v. U.S. Tennis Association, 540 N.Y.S.2d 443 (N.Y. App. Div. 1989), pp. 73 note 8; 78 note 14.

White v. Board of Regents, 614 N.W.2d 330 (Neb. 2000), p. 688 note 2.

White v. Corpus Christi Little Misses Kickball Association, 526 S.W.2d 766 (Tex. Civ. App. 1975), p. 360 note 12.

White v. National Collegiate Athletic Association, CV06-0999 (C.D. Cal. January 29, 2008), p. 509.

White v. National Football League (In re Ashley Lelie), 2007 WL 939560 (D. Minn. March 26, 2007), p. 394 note 2.

White v. National Football League, 41 F.3d 402 (8th Cir. 1994), pp. 522 note 1; 532 note 4; 565.

White v. National Football League, 533 F. Supp. 2d 929 (D. Minn. 2008), pp. 394 note 1; 565.

White v. National Football League, 836 F. Supp. 1458 (D. Minn. 1993), p. 496.

Whooley v. Commonwealth, 783 N.E.2d 461 (Mass. App. Ct. 2003), p. 128 note 1.

Wichita State University Intercollegiate Athletic v. Swanson Broadcasting Co., Case No. 81C130 (Kan. Dist. Ct. 1981), p. 711.

Wildman ex rel. Wildman v. Marshalltown School Dist., 249 F.3d 768 (8th Cir. 2001), p. 264.

Wiley v. National Collegiate Athletic Association, 612 F.2d 473 (10th Cir. 1979), cert. denied, 446 U.S. 943 (1980), p. 254.

Wilkinson v. Hartford Accident and Indemnity Co., 411 So. 2d 22 (La. 1982), p. 137 note 7.

Williams v. Eaton, 468 F.2d 1079 (10th Cir. 1972), p. 266 note 6.

Williams v. Hamilton, 497 F. Supp. 641 (D. N.H. 1980), p. 171.

Williams v. National Football League, 582 F.3d 863 (8th Cir. 2009), p. 301.

Williams v. School District, 998 F.2d 168 (3d Cir. 1993), p. 358 note 2.

Wilson v. Vancouver Hockey Club (1983), 5 D.L.R. (4th) 282, p. 141 note 8.

Withers v. Bogus Basin Recreational Association, Inc., 156 P.3d 579 (Idaho 2007), p. 136 note 2.

Wood v. National Basketball Association, 602 F. Supp. 525 (S.D. N.Y. 1984), p. 465

Wood v. National Basketball Association, 809 F.2d 954 (2nd Cir. 1987), p. 493 note 1.

Woodring v. Board of Education of Manhasset, 435 N.Y.S.2d 52 (N.Y. App. Div. 1981), p. 136 note 11.

Wooten v. Pleasant Hope School Dist., 139 F. Supp. 2d 835 (W.D. Mo. 2000), p. 269.

World Anti-Doping Agency (WADA) v. United States Anti-Doping Agency (USADA), United States Bobsled & Skeleton Fed'n (USBSF) & Lund, Matter of Arbitration (2006), CAS 06/001, p. 203 note 2.

Worldwide Basketball and Sports Tours, Inc. v. NCAA, 273 F. Supp. 2d 933 (S.D. Ohio 2003), p. 507.

Worldwide Basketball and Sports Tours, Inc. v. NCAA, 388 F.3d 955 (6th Cir. 2004), p. 508.

Wu v. Shattuck-St. Mary's School, 393 F. Supp. 2d 831 (D. Minn. 2005), p. 114 note 2.

Yanero v. Davis, 65 S.W.2d 510 (Ky. 2002), p. 81 note 1.

Yang and Korean Olympic Committee v. International Gymnastics Federation (FIG), Matter of Arbitration (2004), CAS 2004/A/704, p. 203 note 5.

Yankees Entertainment and Sports Network, LLC v. Cablevision Systems Corporation and CSC Holdings, Inc., 224 F. Supp. 2d 657 (S.D. N.Y. 2002), p. 722 note 4.

Yellow Springs Exempted School District v. Ohio High School Athletic Association, 443 F. Supp. 753 (S.D. Ohio 1978), rev.'d, 647 F.2d 651 (6th Cir. 1981), p. 342 note 11.

Yocca v. Pittsburgh Steelers Sports, Inc., 578 Pa. 479 (Pa. 2004), p. 382 note 2.

York v. Wahkiakum School Dist. No. 200, 163 Wash.2d 297 (Wash. 2008), pp. 280 note 1; 292 note 1.

Yukica v. Leland, No. 85-E-191 (N.H. Super. Ct. 1985), p. 417.

Zacchini v. Scripps-Howard Broadcasting Co., 433 U.S. 562 (1977), p. 705 note 8.

Zehner v. Central Berkshire Regional School District, 921 F. Supp. 850 (D. Mass. 1996), p. 274 note 4.

Zeller v. Donegal School District, 517 F.2d 600 (3rd Cir. 1975), p. 267 note 2.

Zimmerman v. National Football League, 632 F. Supp. 398 (D. D.C. 1986), p. 493 note 3.

Zinn v. Parrish, 644 F.2d 360 (7th Cir. 1981), p. 582 note 5.

Zuments v. Colorado High School Activities Association, 737 P.2d 1113 (Colo. Ct. App. 1987), p. 259 note 3.

INDEX

Academic eligibility rules: academic progress (high school), 242–44; academic progress (NCAA), 240–42; grade point average (high school), 239–40; initial eligibility (NCAA), 236–39

Acting on behalf of, in agency relationships, 577

Administrative Procedure Act, 47

Administrators, schools, athletic organizations, liability of, 117–24; failure to hire qualified personnel, 118–20; failure to provide proper medical assistance, 120–21; failure to provide safe equipment, 121–23; failure to provide supervision of athletic activities, 118–20; vicarious liability for actions of fans, players, 123. *See also* Coaches and teachers, liability of

Age Discrimination in Employment Act (ADEA, 1967), 766, 778–80

Agency law: agent-agent litigation, 597–98; described, 577; endorsement contracts/financial planning, 633–47; foreign leagues, 647–49; government regulation, 598–615; individual performer sports, 647; player agents, 578–84; players associations and agents, 585–97; standard player contracts, 628–33; team sports player drafts, 615–28

Agency law, government regulation of: ethical constraints, 610–11; NCAA regulations, 611–15; state regulations, 609–10;

Uniform Athlete Agent Act, 59, 575, 598–609

Agents. *See* Player agents; Player agents and players associations

Age restrictions (antitrust litigation), 476–77

AIDS, athletes with/testing for, 826

Alcohol: ban at NCAA tournaments, 131; challenge of rules by athletes, 273–74

Amateur athletic associations, enforcement authority: background information, 184–85; NCAA procedures, 185–93

Amateur athletic associations, legal principles pertaining to: background information, 178; injunctive relief, 182–84; judicial review, 178–82; standing, 182

Amateur Athletic Union (AAU), 163

Amateurism rules, 252–63; employment (NCAA), 257; scholarships, financial assistance, expenses (NCAA), 252–57; summer camps/independent teams, 258–60

Amateur Sports Act (ASA) (1978), 30, 161–62, 163, 815–16

Ambush marketing, 680–82

American Arbitration Association, 595

American Basketball Association (ABA), 465

American Law Reports (ALB), 54

Americans with Disabilities Act (ADA): Title I: Employment, 817; Title II: Public Accommodations Operated by

Private Entities, 818–19; Title II: Public Services, 817–18

Annotated law reports, 54

Anti-Cybersquatting Protection Act (ACPA), 697–98

Antitrust law, 452–511; application to professional sports, 458–72; and broadcasting/multimedia, 716–17; Clayton Act, 457–58; coaches salaries (NCAA), 506–7; interleague challenges to, 472–76; and international soccer, 502–4; issues with college broadcasting, 728–33; legislation relevant to Big Four sports, 460–61; litigation in professional tennis and golf, 476–79; and the NCAA, 504–10; reduced power over television (NCAA), 505–6; Sherman Act, 453–57; and tournaments (NCAA), 507–8; violations, 22. *See also* Ownership restraints and antitrust theory; Player restraints and antitrust theory

Antitrust law, defenses to challenges of, 479–502; baseball exemption, 479–88; early use of nonstatutory labor exemption, 490–93; exemption after decertification, 495–96, 504; exemption after expiration of collective bargaining, 493–95; nonstatutory labor exemptions, 489–93, 496–98; single-entity defense by Big Four, 498–500; single-entity leagues, 500–502

Appeals process (of civil legal process), 52

Appearances, and agency law, 580

Arbitrary marks, 670

Arbitration procedures: agent-agent grievances, 597; agent-athlete dispute resolution, 593–97; and collective bargaining, 562–64; of NOCs, 199–201

Arbitration procedures of NOCs, 199–201

Arena Football League, 520; and collective bargaining, 536–37

Assault and battery, defenses for: consent, 85–86; privilege, 86–87

Assets, intangible/tangible, 668

Assignment/delegation of contracts (contract law), 383

Association of Tennis Professionals (ATP), 2; antitrust litigation, 476–79, 477; broadcast rights of, 734

Athletes: agreements with agents, 592–92; broadcast rights of, 735–36; challenge of rules by, 263–74; off-the-field criminal conduct, 799–800; player and fan violence, 795–97; player vs. official

violence, 797–98; player vs. player violence, 791–95; resolution of disputes with agents, 593–97. *See also* Student-athletes

Athletes in Action, 32

Athletic associations, constitutional issues, 215–29; due process, 219–26; equal protection, 226–29; state action requirement, 215–17

Athletic associations, public responsibility of, 205–11; Buckley Amendment, 209–12; disclosure, 205–8; funding of public facilities, 208–9

Athletic contracts, types of: defenses to standards player breaches, 398, 406–8; standard player contract, 388–98; tortuous interference with contractual relations, 408–10. *See also* Coaches' contracts; Officials' contracts; Physicians' contracts; Sample contracts; Standard player contracts

Athletics Investigator's Manual (Title IX), 324–26

Atlantic Coast Conference (college football), 167

Attendance: revenue streams, 9

Automated external defibrillators (AEDs), 130

Banned substances. *See* Drug testing, legal principles

Baseball Act, 134

Baseball exemption (to antitrust challenges), 479–88; creation of (Federal baseball), 480–86; Curt Flood Act, 461, 469, 488–89; reaffirmation of, 486–87; reserve system history, 479–80; upholding of anomaly, 487–88

Basketball Travelers, Inc., 32

Battery (tort), 84–85. *See also* Assault and battery, defenses for

Bettman, Gary (NHL commissioner), 14

Big East Conference (college football), 167

Big Four Leagues, 2; baseball contract salaries, 8; basic agreements of, 4; and blackout legislation, 741; collective bargaining agreements, 14; and copyright law, 714–17; player's associations, 14; single-entity defenses by, 498–500; television broadcast contracts, 6–7; ticket-revenues, 9. *See also* Major League Baseball; National Basketball Association; National Football League; National Hockey League

Big Ten Network (BTN), 732
Bill of Rights, 263–64
Blackouts of scheduled programming, 741–42
Blood doping, 289, 293
Blue Book: A Uniform System of Citation, 60
Bowl Championship Series, antitrust litigation, 508–9
Bowl Coalition Series (BCS), 21
Breach of contract (contract law), 383–86; partial, 384; remedies for, 386–88; total, 383–84
Broadcast contracts: administrative agencies, 47; antitrust issues for colleges, 728–33; case law, 710–12; copyright laws, 712–13; FCC regulations, 713–14; impact on professional sports, 6–7; rights for conferences and schools, 724–33; rights granted, 717–18; rights of a professional league, 718–23; rights of a professional team, 720–23; rights of individual players, 735–36; rights of individual sports, 733–34; rights of the Bowl championship series, 724; rights of the NCAA championships, 723–24; rights of the Olympics, 734–35; types of, 708–9
Broadcasting: advertising restrictions, 736–37; checklist for minimizing problems, 744; home recording of copyrighted events, 739–40; and Internet rights, 737–44; piracy of satellite/cable transmissions, 740–41; programming blackouts, 741–42; replay usage restrictions, 737; satellite distribution, 742–43
Brotherhood of Professional Baseball Players, 534
Buckley Amendment, 209–11
Business invitees, 129
Business law: business structures, 746–53; employment law, 766–84; tax issues, 753–66
Business structures: corporations, 749–53; limited partnerships, 748–49; partnerships, 747–48; sole proprietorships, 747

Cable Communications Policy Act (1984), 733
Cable television, 708–9, 740–41
Cable Television Consumer Protection and Competition Act (1992), 743
California Interscholastic Federation (CIF), 160, 161, 173, 175–77; on eligibility, 230; student eligibility appeals procedures, 195–98; student eligibility review procedures, 196–98
A Call to Action: Reconnecting Sports to Higher Education (Knight Commission), 193–95
Canadian Football League Players Association (CFLPA): and collective bargaining, 537
Capital Facilities Debt Enabling Act (CFDEA), 762
CAS. See Court of Arbitration for Sport
Case law: Courts of Appeals, 60–61; District Courts, 61–62; State Courts, 62; Supreme Court, 60
Catastrophic injury protection insurance plan (NCAA), 101, 151
C corporation, 749–50
Cellular phones, 709
Central Sports Army Club (CSKA), 408–9
Charitable immunity, 79–81, 126–27
Civil Legal Process: the answer, 49–50; the appeals process, 52; the complaint, 48–49; court jurisdiction, 49; discovery, 50; the judgment, 52; the parties, 49; pretrial motions, 50; the summons, 49; the trial, 51; types of court, 50–51
Civil liability immunity legislation, 127–28
Civil Rights Act (Title VII), 766
Clayton Act (antitrust law), 516; described, 517; statutory labor exemption, 457–58; treble damages, 457
Coaches and teachers, liability of, 110–17; failure to provide adequate supervision, 111–12; failure to provide prompt and capable medical assistance, 115–17; failure to provide proper instruction and training, 113–15; reasonable care standard expectations, 116; sovereign immunity defense, 110. *See also* Administrators, schools, athletic organizations, liability of
Coaches' contracts: Employment Agreement sample, 418–32; high school, 432–34; professional/collegiate sports, 416–17; salary/antitrust litigation, 506–7
Code of Sports-Related Arbitration, 202
Collective Bargaining Agreements (CBAs), 14; arbitration, 562–64; Arena Football League and, 536–37; baseball collusion cases, 553–54; Canadian Football League Players Association and, 537; decertification, 528–29; and drug use testing, 281; free agency, 556–59; grievance procedures, 564–67; impasse,

543–44, 552–53; labor disputes, 539–40; lockouts, 543–44; Major League Baseball Players Association and, 528, 534; Major League Soccer Players Association and, 535–36; mandatory/permissive subjects, 527–28; minor league baseball/college athletics and, 538–39; National Basketball Players Association and, 533; National Football League Players Association and, 301, 531–33; National Hockey League Players Association and, 528, 530–31, 541–43; process (description), 525–27; ratification, 528; salary arbitration, 569–71; salary caps, 559–61; strikes, 540; text of, 555–56; unlawful discharge, 567–69; Women's National Basketball Association and, 535

Collective marks, 667–68

College and high school eligibility requirements, 234–63; academic eligibility rules, 236–39; amateurism rules, 257–67; employment rules, 257; participation rules, 244–52; rules challenged by athletes, 263–74

College Football Association (CFA), 729–32

Commissioners, 13–14

Commission on Intercollegiate Athletics, 193

Committee on Infractions (COI) of NCAA, 186–89, 190, 192

Computer services, 57

Concurring opinion, 43

Condition precedent, 382

Condition subsequent, 382

Conduct rules, athlete challenge of, 273–74

Congressional enactments: Administrative Procedure Act, 47; Amateur Sports Act, 30, 161–62; Family Educational Rights and Privacy Act, 209; Title IX, Education Amendments (1972), 59–60

Connecticut Interscholastic Athletic Conference (CIAC), 176

Consent, 85–86; in agency relationships, 577

Constitution (U.S.): Fifth Amendment, 219, 226, 344; First Amendment, 263–64; Fourteenth Amendment, 226, 278–79; Fourth Amendment, 278–79. See also Rules challenged by athletes

Constitutional issues of athletic associations, 215–29; due process, 219–26; equal protection, 226–29; state action requirement, 217–21

Constitutional issues of drug testing, 278–81

Constitutions, 58; Pac-10, 169; Southeastern conference, 168

Consultants, and agency law, 580

Continental Basketball League (CBL), 751

Contract law, principles, 151, 378–96; assignment/delegation of contracts, 383; breach of contract, 383–86; conditions of contract, 381–82; mistakes in contracts, 380–81; parol evidence rule, 381; remedies for breach of contract, 386–88; statute of frauds, 382–83. See also Contracts, formation of

Contracts, formation of, 371–80; acceptance, 373–74; capacity, 379; consideration, 374–77; drafting of a contract, 379–80; endorsement contracts, 633–47; legality, 377–79; offer, 371–72. See also Athletic contracts, types of; Standard player contracts

Contractual relations, tortious interference with, 87

Copyright Act (1976), 695, 710, 712

Copyright law, 693–700; and broadcasting/multimedia, 712–13; and the Internet, 696–700; legislation, 697–98, 707–8

Copyright Royalty Arbitration Panel, 713, 744

Copyright Royalty Tribunal Reform Act, 713

Corporations: C, 749–50; limited liability, 751–52; publicly traded, 752–53; S, 750–51

Counseling, and agency law, 582–83

Country clubs, 3

Court and legal system (U.S.): civil legal process, 48; Federal Court system, 41–47; legal information sources, 53–62; State Court system, 47–48

Court of Arbitration for Sport (CAS), 34–35, 201–5, 294

Courts of Appeals: jurisdiction, types of, 43; locations, 44; publications, 60–61

Creative Artists Agency (CAA), 37

Criminal law. See Violence in sports

Curt Flood Act (1998), 461, 469, 496–97, 538

Damages for intentional torts, 89

Defamation laws: libel, 90; slander, 90–92

Defects of equipment, 147–50

Defense of sovereign immunity, 110, 114, 118

Defensive lockouts, 543–44

Descriptive marks, 669–70

Dictionaries, 53

Digital Millennium Copyright Act (DMCA), 696–97, 738

DirecTV, 47

Disabilities legislation: AIDS, athletes with/testing for, 826; Amateur Sports Act, 30, 161–62, 815–16; Americans with Disabilities Act, 816–19; Individuals with Disabilities Education Act, 814–15; Rehabilitation Act, 813–14

Disabilities legislation, application to athletic organizations: colleges, universities, NCAA, 822–23; high school, 820–22; professional sports, 824–25; sports facilities, 825; youth sports, 819–20

Discipline, 268–73; athlete's violation of rights, 274; disputes with institutions/governing associations, 275; for recruiting violations, 275–77

Disclosure cases, 205–8

Dismissal cases, procedural/substantive, 432–33

Dispute resolution procedures: and agency law, 584; between agent-athlete, 593–97; California Interscholastic Federation, 195–98; International Olympic Committee, 201–4

Dissenting opinion, 43

District Courts, 44, 45–46, 61–62; publications of, 61–62

Divisible contracts (high school coaches), 432

Doping. See Blood doping

Draft regulations: Major League Baseball, 622–25; Major League Soccer, 627; National Basketball Association, 625–26; National Football League, 616–62; National Hockey League, 626; Women's National Basketball Association, 627–28

Drug testing, legal principles: challenge of rules by athletes, 273–74; college conferences/schools, 291–93; Constitutional law, 278–82; due process, 278; equal protection, 278–79; and NCAA, 287–93; Olympics and international sports, 293–300; policies and legal challenges, 282–93; professional sports, 300–313; WADA prohibited list, 294–95

Due process, 219–26; analysis by athlete, 214–15; case against the NCAA, 159; described/defined, 179, 219; doping issue, 35; and drug testing, 278; and IOC, 199; and nonrenewal of scholarships, 259; procedural, 220–22; substantive, 222–26; and Title V (Education Code), 196; transfer rules and, 254

Economic overview: of intercollegiate athletics, 19–22; of Olympic bodies, 33–34; of professional sports leagues, 4, 6

Education Amendments Act (1972), 60

Education for All Handicapped Children Act (1975). See Individuals with Disabilities Education Act (IDEA)

Eligibility: amateurism rules, 252–63; athlete's challenge of rules, 263–74; definitions of, 229–34; IOC on, 230; participation rules, 244–52. See also College and high school eligibility requirements

Employment (NCAA rules), 257

Employment discrimination statutes: Age Discrimination in Employment Act, 778–80; EEOC coaching pay guidelines, 770–72; Equal Pay Act, 317, 766, 767–70; gender discrimination cases (under Title IX), 775–76; gender discrimination cases (under Title VII), 772–75; race discrimination cases (under Title VII), 776–78; state discrimination laws, 780; Title VII (Civil Rights Act of 1964), 766, 772

Employment law, 766–84; employment-at-will contracts, 766–67; employment discrimination statutes, 767; sexual harassment, 780–84

Endorsements: and agency law, 578, 580, 633–47; contracts, and financial planning, 633–47; Knight's Commission recommendations, 26–27; and marketing/sponsorship contracts, 410–16, 583–84; and Olympic medals, 293

Enforcement authority of National Collegiate Athletic Association (NCAA): Committee on Infractions, 186–89; Infractions Appeals Committee, 189–92; infractions process, 192–93

Entanglement theory, 216

Entertainment and Sports Programming Network (ESPN), 731

Equal Employment Opportunity Commission (EEOC), 766

Equal Pay Act (EPA), 317, 767–70

Equal protection, 36, 215, 226–29; described, 179; and drug testing, 278–79; and high school transfer rules, 254;

intermediate scrutiny test, 227; and marital classifications, 265; rational basis test, 227, 262; strict scrutiny test, 226–29, 258, 335; and summer camp rules, 258

Equal protection laws, 334–37

Equal Rights Amendment (ERA), 316, 330–34

Equipment: defects, 147–50; rules (antitrust litigation), 477

Equitable subrogation, 150

Ethics Commission (of the IOC), 198–99

European Community (EC) Treaty, 502

European Union Competition Commission, 502

Exculpatory agreements, 151

Exemptions to antitrust law: after decertification, 495–96; after expiration of collective bargaining, 493–95; baseball exemption, 479–88; early use of nonstatutory labor exemption, 490–92; nonstatutory labor exemption, 489–93, 496–98

Expectation interest, 386

Expenses: of intercollegiate athletics, 21–22

Express warranty, 97

Facility contract, 435, 437; sample, 440–49

Family Educational Rights and Privacy Act (1974), 209

Fanciful marks, 670

Fantasy sports gambling, 810–12

Federal Anti-Injunction Act. *See* Norris-LaGuardia Act

Federal Baseball Club of Baltimore, Inc. v. National League of Professional Baseball Clubs, 41

Federal Communications Commission (FCC), 47; and blackout legislation, 741–42; copyright regulations, 713–14; and indecency, 743

Federal Court System: administrative agencies, 44, 47; Courts of Appeals, 43–44, 60–61; District Courts, 44, 45–46, 61–62; Supreme Court, 41, 43, 60

Federal Reporter (appeals courts decisions), 60–61

Federal Supplement (District Court decisions), 61–62

Federal Trade Act (1946). *See* Lanham Act (1946)

Federal Trade Commission (FTC), 44, 609

Federal Trade Commission Act, 716

Fédération Internationale de Basketball (FIBA), 29–30, 31

FIFA (international soccer governing association), 503

Fifth Amendment (U.S. Constitution), 219, 226, 344. *See also* Due process

Financial matters, and agency law, 580

First Amendment rights, 263–64

Fitness clubs, 3

Fixation (broadcast recording), 709

Florida High School Activities Association (FHSAA), 817

Force majeure and work stoppage (athletic contract), 414–15

Fourteenth Amendment (U.S. Constitution), 226, 278–279

Fourth Amendment (U.S. Constitution), 227–79

Free agency, 556–59

Freedom of expression, challenge by athletes, 263–68

Freedom of Information Act, 206

Funding of public facilities, 208–9

Gambling. *See* Illegal gambling

Gender discrimination cases, involving individual athletes, 349–68; men's teams, no women's teams, 350–56; same sport, different rules, 363–65; same sport, different seasons, 365–67; varsity sport vs. club sport, 367–68; women's teams, no men's teams, 356–60; women's teams and men's teams, 360–63

Gender discrimination cases, legal theories, 321–37; equal protection laws, 334–37; Equal Rights Amendment, 316, 330–34; Title IX of the Education Amendments Act, 60, 316–18, 323–30

Goodell, Roger (NFL commissioner), 14

Good Samaritan statutes, 79–81

Goodwill, 668

Governmental activity, 124

Grievance procedures, 564–67

Harlem Globetrotters, 32

Harm to economic/dignitary interests (tort), 90–94; defamation law, 90–92; invasion of privacy, 93–94

High school athletic associations, 172–78; coaches' contracts, 432–34. *See also* California Interscholastic Federation

High school eligibility requirements. *See* College and high school eligibility requirements

Hunter, Billy (NBPA), 14

Illegal gambling: fantasy sports/office pools, 810–12; in intercollegiate athletics, 803–7; Internet gambling, 810; in professional sports, 807–10

Immunity and Good Samaritan statutes, 79–81

Immunity defense, 124–28; charitable immunity, 126–27; civil liability immunity legislation, 127–28; sovereign immunity, 124–26; vs. privilege, 124

Impartial Arbitrator, 595

Impasse, 544, 552–53

Implied warranty, 97

Indecency, and the Federal Communications Commission (FCC), 743

Indemnification, 413–14

Independent contractors exception (vicarious liability), 98–99

Individuals with Disabilities Education Act (IDEA), 814–8155

Indivisible contracts (high school coaches), 432

Infractions Appeals Committee (IAC) of NCAA, 189–92

Infractions process (of NCAA), 192–93

Injunctive relief, 182–84

Injury Surveillance System 2004-2005 survey (NCAA), 107

Institutional control principle (NCAA), 235

Intangible assets, 668

Integration of agreement, 389

Intellectual property law: and copyright law, 693–700; and patent law, 700–703; and right of publicity, 703–5; and trademark law, 665–92

Intentional infliction of emotional distress (tort), 88–89

Intentional torts: assault, 83–84; battery, 84–85; damages for, 89; defenses for assault and battery, 85–87

Intercollegiate athletics, 2, 16–27; broadcasting limitations, 716–17; coaches' contract sample, 418–32; economic overview, 19–22; and illegal gambling, 803–7; Knight Foundation Commission on, 25–27; liabilities of coaches and teachers, 110–17; licensing programs for, 682–89; member institutions, 22–23; NCAA Injury Surveillance System survey, 107; organizational structure, 17–19; University of Michigan case study, 23–25; women's, 316–17

Interleague antitrust challenges, 472–76; NASL vs. NFL, 474–76; USFL vs. NFL, 473–74

Intermediate scrutiny test, 227

Internal Revenue Service, 44

International Council of Arbitration for Sport (ICAS), 202

International Equestrian Federation (FEI), 202

International Federations (IFs), 29–30, 202; and drug testing, 295; economic overview of, 33–34; on eligibility, 230; responsibilities of, 31–33; support of CAS, 204

International Hockey League, 408

International Management Group (IMG), 37

International Olympic Committee (IOC): administrative structure, 29; advertising rules imposed by, 30; amateur designation modification, 214; by-laws/charter of, 28; Court of Arbitration for Support, 201–5; and due process, 202; duties of, 27; economic overview of, 33–34; on eligibility, 230; enforcement procedures, 198–201; Ethics Commission, 198–99; hosting decisions by, 31; responses to prevailing legal issues, 27, 34–35; WADA Code, 295

International Paralympic Committee, 163

International Sports Federations (ISFs), 202

Internet, 709; and copyright law, 696–700; and gambling, 810; and intellectual property law, 664–65; and legal research, 56–57; and rights for sports broadcast, 708–9, 718, 734, 737–44

Internet Gambling Prohibition Act (1999), 809

Interscholastic athletics, 2, 35–36; contact sports, 350–51; and disabled students, 248, 814–15; drug testing programs, 283–84, 285–87; eligibility rules, 206, 817; and gender discrimination, 350; and GPA, 245; and home-schooling, 177; and labor law, 517; noncontact sports, 353–56; performance enhancing drug policies, 285; privilege vs. right of participation, 173, 223, 365

Invasion of privacy (tort), 93–94

Investments, and agency law, 580

Invitees, 128

John and James L. Knight Foundation, 193–95. *See also* Knight Foundation Commission on Intercollegiate Athletics

Jurisdiction, types of: appellate jurisdiction, 41; original jurisdiction, 41; personal jurisdiction, 49; subject matter jurisdiction, 49

Kerry, John, 47

Knight Foundation Commission on Intercollegiate Athletics, 193–95

Labor law: domination and assistance, 520–21; history of, 516–17; interference with organizing/collective bargaining, 520; National Labor Relations Act, 517–19; unfair labor practice procedures, 520–23

Labor Management Relations Act. *See* Taft-Hartley Act (1947)

Ladies Professional Golf Association (LPGA), 2; advocacy issues, 36; black-listing, 478

Lanham Act (1946), 667; and ambush marketing, 680–82; described, 667, 669, 672; and descriptive marks, 667–68, 669–70, 674–75. *See also* Trademark infringement; Trademark law

Latent defects, 129

Law reports, annotated, 54

Law review articles, 55–56

Legal information sources, 53–62; case law, 60–62; constitutions, 58; Federal administrative rules/regulations, 59–60; legislation, 59; reference materials, 53–58

Legal theories in gender discrimination cases. *See* Gender discrimination cases, legal theories

Legislation, 59; against assault of game officials, 148; of civil liability immunity, 128–29; described/examples, 59; limited liability, 134; by NASO, 148; by NCAA, 18–19, 171, 186–89; Olympics-based, 30; sources of, 54, 57. *See also* individual acts throughout the index

Levitt Report, 527

Liability: of administrators, schools, athletic organizations, 117–23; of coaches/teachers, 110–17; of facility owners/possessors liability, 128–39; of medical personnel, 138–42; of officials, referees, umpires, 142–47; of participants, 106–10; waiver and release of, 151–55. *See also* Vicarious liability

Liability insurance, 80, 131, 150–51, 453

Libel, 90

Licensing/licensees, 11–12, 129

Licensing programs for intercollegiate athletics, 682–89; litigation, 682–89; trademark law and nicknames, 687–89

Limited liability corporations, 751–52

Limited partnerships, 748–49

Little League baseball, 2

Local organizing committees (LOCs), 31

Lockouts, 543–44

Luxury suites, 10

Major League Baseball (MLB), 2; antitrust exemption protection, 469; broadcast contracts, 6–7; Collective Bargaining Agreement, 281; Collective Bargaining Agreement (2002), 528; collective marks, 667–68; collusion cases, 553–54; and copyright law, 714–17; and corporate law, 752; DirecTV and, 47; draft regulations, 622–25; and drug testing, 306–10; exemptions to antitrust challenges, 479–88; force majeure/work stoppage provisions, 414–15; and gambling, 807–8; labor law and, 520–21; ownership restraints cases, 471–72; personal seat licenses, 10; player contract provisions, 389, 393; player's contracts, 382; right of publicity and, 703–4; salaries by position, 8–9; salary data, 4; single-entity defenses by, 498–500; sponsoring restrictions, 11; sponsorship agreements, 413; ticket revenue, 9; and trademark infringement, 674–76. *See also* Baseball exemption (to antitrust challenges)

Major League Baseball Players Association (MLBPA), 306; and collective bargaining, 534; contract negotiations, 526; labor law and, 520–21; regulating player agents by, 593–94; right of publicity and, 703–4; sponsorship agreements, 413

Major League Soccer (MLS), 2, 3, 15; draft regulations, 627; and limited liability corporations, 751–52; single-entity defense, 500–502

Major League Soccer Players Association, 535–36

Major League Soccer Players Union, 535–36

Managing, and agency law, 583

Marketing, endorsement, and sponsorship contracts, 410–16; and agency law,

583–84; force majeure/work stoppage, 414–15; impact of league rules, 412; indemnification, 413–14; right to terminate, 414; sponsorship litigation cases, 415–16; sponsorship rights, 412–13

Marriage rules, 265

Martin, Casey, 36

Massachusetts Interscholastic Athletic Association (MIAA), 2, 35, 177, 206

McCormack, Mark, 37

Media. *See* Broadcasting; Cable television; Satellite television

Medical assistance: administrative rules establishment for, 118; failure to provide, 115–17, 120–22; and Good Samaritan statutes, 79–81; and lawsuits against coaches or teachers, 111; and reasonable care, 66

Medical personnel liability, 138–42

Melpomene Institute report (1995), 316–17

Men's teams, no women's teams (gender discrimination cases): contact sports, 350–51; noncontact sports, 353–56

Merchandising, 11–12

Metropolitan Intercollegiate Basketball Association (MIBA) v. NCAA, 22

Miller Lite Report (1985), 316–17

Minor League Baseball, 307

Monopolization (Sherman Act), 455–57

Montreal Olympic Games, 277

NASCAR: broadcast rights of, 733

National Association of Intercollegiate Athletics (NAIA), 33, 170–71

National Association of Intercollegiate Basketball. *See* National Association of Intercollegiate Athletics

National Basketball Association (NBA), 2; advocacy issues, 36–37; Collective Bargaining Agreement, 281; and copyright law, 714–17; and corporate law, 752; draft regulations, 625–26; and drug testing, 304–6; and gambling, 809; labor/management dispute, 526; personal seat licenses, 10; player restraints and antitrust theory, 465–66; salary scales, 578; single-entity defenses by, 498–500; strike (1994-1995)/lockout (1998), 526; ticket revenue, 9; Uniform Player Contract, 650–62; and violent player felonies, 799

National Basketball Players Association (NBPA), 304, 533

National Christian College Athletic Association (NCCAA), 171

National Collegiate Athletic Association (NCAA), 2, 160, 165–70; academic eligibility rules, 236–44, 243–45; and agency law, 611–15; and antitrust law, 504–10; ban on alcoholic beverages at tournaments, 131; and broadcast law, 730–33; catastrophic injury protection insurance plan (NCAA), 101, 151; conference structure of, 167–69; decisions before *Board of Regents*, 505–6; drug testing plan, 287–93; eligibility Bylaws, 230; employment rules, 257; expenses, 21–22; and illegal gambling, 811; initial eligibility, 236–39; Injury Surveillance System survey, 107; institutional control principle, 235; member institutions, 22–23; organizational structure, 17–19; overseeing function of, 161; public responsibilities of, 205; purpose of, 166–69; reduced power over television, 505–6; revenue generation, 19–21; rules and regulations of, 166; scholarships, financial assistance, expense rules, 252–57; and service/collective marks, 667–68; and state regulations/agency law, 609–10; student information access limitations, 209; summer camps/independent teams rules, 258–60; and trademark law/nicknames, 687–89; University of Michigan case study, 23–25; women's intercollegiate athletics, 316. *See also* National Collegiate Athletic Association (NCAA), enforcement authority

National Collegiate Athletic Association (NCAA), enforcement authority: Committee on Infractions, 186–89; Infractions Appeals Committee, 189–92; infractions process, 192–93; Knight Commission report recommendations, 193–95. *See also NCAA Manual*

National Federation of State High School Associations (NFSHSA), 2, 152–53, 160, 173

National Football League (NFL), 2; and agents, 578; coaches' contracts, 437–38; and collective bargaining, 529; Collective Bargaining Agreement, 281; and copyright law, 714–17; and corporate ownership, 752; draft regulations, 616–22; and drug testing, 301–4; and gambling, 809; interleague antitrust challenges, 472–76; and limited liability

corporations, 751–52; ownership restraints case, 468–71; personal seat
licenses, 10; piracy of broadcast transmissions, 740–41; player contract, sample, 399–408; player contract provisions,
391–93; player restraints and antitrust
theory, 462; and satellite broadcast distribution, 742–43; single-entity defense,
475; single-entity defenses by, 498–500;
sponsorship litigation cases, 415–16;
ticket revenue, 9; and trademark infringement, 675

National Football League Players Association, 529; and collective bargaining,
531–33; Regulations Concerning Contract Advisors, 597; and violent player
felonies, 799

National Governing Bodies (NGBs), 201;
by-laws/charter of, 28; and drug testing,
295; economic overview of, 33–34; responsibilities of, 31–33; of U.S. basketball, 29–30. *See also* USA Basketball

National Hockey League (NHL), 2; Collective Bargaining Agreement (2005-
2011), 528, 541–43; and copyright law,
714–17; and corporate law, 752; draft
regulations, 626; and drug testing, 310–
11; and gambling, 809; personal seat licenses, 10; player contract provisions,
391, 412; player restraints and antitrust
theory, 463–65; single-entity defenses
by, 498–500; tortious interference with
contractual relations, 408–10; and trademark infringement, 675

National Hockey League Players Association, 310; and collective bargaining,
530–31

National Junior College Athletic Association (NJCAA), 158, 171

National Labor Relations Act (NLRA), 300,
517–19; 1947 Amendment, 517–18; certification of unions, 524–25; and drug
testing, 277–78; right to strike, 540; Section 7 (workers' rights), 518; Section 8
(unfair labor practice), 518–19. *See also*
Clayton Act; Norris-LaGuardia Act;
Taft-Hartley Act; Wagner Act

National Labor Relations Board (NLRB),
44, 520, 523–24, 585

National Olympic Committees (NOCs), 29–
30, 198; arbitration procedures, 202–3;
economic overview of, 33–34; on eligibility status decisions, 230–33; responsibilities of, 202; support of CAS, 201

National Operating Committee on Standards for Athletic Equipment (NOC-
SAE), 122

National Reporter System (State Court decisions), 62

National sports governing body (NSGB),
230

NCAA Division I Manual (2009-2010), 611

NCAA Manual (of conference rules), 169,
188

Negative injunction, 387

Negligence (tort): actual/proximate causation, 71–72; breach of duty owed,
69–71; damages, 73–74; defenses
for, 74–81; duty of care owed, 65–69;
wrongful death statutes, 81. *See also*
Reckless misconduct (gross negligence)
tort

Negotiation, and agency law, 581–82

Newsletters, sports law, 57–58

New York State Public High School Athletic Association, 176

Nicknames, and trademark law, 687–89

No Electronic Theft Act (NET Act), 697

Noncontact sports (gender discrimination
cases), 364–65

Nonstatutory labor exemptions, 489–93;
after *White*, 496–97; early use of, 490–
93; in modern times, 497–98

Norris-LaGuardia Act (1932), 517

North American Soccer League (NASL),
474–76

Offensive lockouts, 543–44

Office of Civil Rights (OCR) policy: analy-
sis/method of enforcement, 326–30; interpretation of Title IX, 323–26

Office pools gambling, 811

Officials (referees, umpires): contracts, 435,
438–39; liability issues, 142–47; player
vs. official violence, 797–98

Olympic Games, 27–35; broadcast rights
of, 734–35; and drug testing, 293–300;
economic overview, 33–34; eligibility
requirements, 260–63; full-scale testing program, 277; international federa-
tions/national governing bodies, 31–33;
IOC responses to prevailing issues, 27,
34–35; organizational structure, 27–31;
trademark law and, 689–92. *See also*
U.S. Olympic Committee

Olympic Partners (TOP) program, 34

Opinion of the court, 43

Oral contracts, 370

Organizational structure: of the NCAA, 17–19; of the Olympic Games, 27–31

Organizing Committees of Olympic Games (OCOG), 29

Original jurisdiction, 41

Overinclusiveness, 227

Ownership restraints and antitrust theory, 466–72; existing owners vs. existing owners, 468–69; Major League Baseball cases, 471–72; NFL cases, 468–71; prospective owners vs. existing owners, 471

Pac-10 conference (college football), 158, 167, 168

Pan American Games, 29, 163

Parol evidence rule (contract law), 381

Participant liability, 106–10

Participation rules, 244–52; longevity, 247–49; redshirting, 244–46; transfer rules, 249–52

Patent defects, 129

Patent law, 700–703

Pay cable television, 709

Pennsylvania State Equal Rights Amendment, 331

Performance-enhancing drug policies, 285

Performance-Enhancing Substances Program (NHL/NHLPA), 310

Permanent injunctions, 183

Per se rule, 453

Personal Conduct Policy: National Football League, 302; National Hockey League, 310

Personal seat licenses (PSLs), 10

Physicians' contracts, 434–35

Piracy of satellite/cable transmissions, 740–41

Planning, and agency law, 584

Player agents: agent-agent litigation, 597–98; contract negotiation by, 581–82; counseling, 582–83; dispute resolution, 584; functions, 578–81; managing, 583; marketing, 583–84; negotiating, 581–82; planning, 584

Player agents and players associations, 585–97; agent-agent grievance arbitration, 597; agent-athlete agreements, 592–93; agent-athlete dispute resolution, 593–97; salary information, 578–81, 586–90; union-agent relationships, 590–92

Player contracts. See Standard player contracts

Player restraints and antitrust theory, 458–66; basketball, 465–66; football, 462; hockey, 463–65

Player's associations (PAs), 14; and collective bargaining, 530–37. See also individual player's associations

Pop Warner football, 2

Posttrial components (of civil legal process), 48

Preliminary injunctions, 183

Pretrial components (of civil legal process), 48–50

Privacy. See Invasion of privacy (tort)

Privilege, 86–87

Procedural dismissal cases, 432

Procedural due process, 220–22

Products liability law: implied/express warranties-based, 97; intent-based, 94; negligence-based, 94–95; strict-tort liability-based, 95–96

Professional and Amateur Sports Protection Act (1992), 809

Professional Golf Association (PGA), 2; antitrust litigation, 476–79, 478–79; broadcast rights of, 733; and drug testing, 277, 311–12; legal battle with Casey Martin, 36; sponsorship agreements, 412–13

Proprietary activity, 124

Public facilities, funding of, 208–9

Public function theory, 216

Publicity, right of, 703–5

Publicly traded corporations, 752–53

Public/private athletic associations, 2–3

Public responsibility of athletic associations, 205–11; Buckley Amendment, 209–12; disclosure, 205–8; funding of public facilities, 208–9

Punitive damages, 89

Railway Labor Act (1926), 518

Rational basis test, 227, 262

Reason, rule of, 453

Reckless misconduct (gross negligence) tort, 82–83

Recreation centers, 3

REC Rule, 515

Referee liability, 142–47

Reference materials (legal): annotated law reports, 54; computer services, 57; dictionaries, 53; encyclopedias, 54; indexes, 55; law review articles, 55–56; research guides, 53; restatements of the law, 54; *Restatements of the Law*, 54; sports law newsletters, 57–58; sports law Web sites, 58; treatises, 54–55

Rehabilitation Act, 813–14

Release of liability, 153–57

Reliance interest, 386

Research guides, 53

Respondeat superior doctrine (vicarious liability), 110

Respondent superior doctrine (vicarious liability), 97–99

Restatement (Second) of Torts, 87, 93

Restatement (Third) of Torts, 94

Restatements of the Law, 54

Restitution of benefits, 386

Restraining orders, 183

Restraint of trade (Sherman Act), 453–55

Right of publicity, 703–5

Right to terminate (athletic contract), 414

Rodriguez, Alex, 4

Rozelle Rule, 503

Rule of reason defense, 453–55, 454, 463, 475

Rules challenged by athletes, 263–74; alcohol, drug, conduct rules (high school), 273–74; discipline, 268–73; freedom of expression, 263–68

Salaries: Big Four agreements, 4; calculation of cap, 559–61; and collective bargaining, 569–71; and player agents, 578–81, 586–90

Same sport, different rules (gender discrimination cases): contact sports, 363–64; noncontact sports, 364–65

Same sport, different seasons (gender discrimination cases), 365–67

Sample contracts: coaches, 418–32; facilities, 440–49; officials, 438–39; physicians, 434–35; players, NFL, 399–408

Satellite television, 709, 740–41

School liability. *See* Administrators, schools, athletic organizations, liability of

S corporations, 750–51

Seat licenses, personal use, 10

Secondary meaning, 669–70

Self-defense, 86

Selig, Bud (MLB commissioner), 14

Service marks, 667–68

Session laws, 59

Sexual harassment, 780–84

Shepard's Citations, 53, 56

Sherman Antitrust Act (antitrust law): blacklisting challenge (football), 462–63; "concerted practices" prohibition, 503; monopolization, 455–57; prohibitions of, 459; reduced power over television (NCAA), 506; "reserve system" challenge (hockey), 463–64; restraint of trade, 453–55; and tournaments (NCAA), 508; "trade"/"commerce" (definitions), 505

Single-entity defense, 475; by the Big Four, 498–500; Major League Soccer, 500–502

Single-entity leagues, 2. *See also* Major League Soccer; Women's National Basketball Association

Siphoning (of TV programs), 709

Slander, 90–92

Slip law, 59

Smith, DeMaurice (NFLPA), 14

Sole proprietorships, 747

Southeastern Conference (SEC), 168

Sovereign immunity defense, 106, 110–11, 114, 118, 124–26

Specific performance, 387

Sponsorship contracts, 410–16; litigation cases, 415–16; tax issues, 759–60. *See also* Marketing, endorsement, and sponsorship contracts

Sports Agent Responsibility and Trust Act (SPARTA), 609

Sports Broadcasting Act (1961), 460, 714

Sports leagues, professional, 3–16; attendance revenue streams, 9; broadcast contracts impact, 6–7; commissioners, 13–15; economic overview, 4, 6; industry share data, 3; legal issues, 5; licensing, 11–12; luxury suites, 10; merchandising, 11–12; personal seat licenses, 10; single-entity leagues, 15–16; sponsorships, 11–12; stadium naming rights deals, 13. *See also* individual leagues

Sports or Same Game Rule, 713

Sports Tours International, Inc., 32

Stadium naming rights, 13

Standard player contracts, 388–98, 628–33; allowable amendments, 629–33; assignability, 392–93; bonus clauses, 393–95; full performance, 396–98; health regulations, 395–96; hierarchy of contracts, 391; player exclusivity, 392; reserve/option clause, 389–90; unique skill provisions, 390–91

State action requirement, 215–18

State Courts: jurisdiction, types of, 47–48; publications of, 62; structure exhibit, 46

State equal rights amendments, 330–34

Statute of frauds (contract law), 382–83
Statute of limitations, 79
Statutory labor exemption (Clayton Act), 465–66
Steroid use. *See* Drug testing, legal principles
Strict scrutiny, 226–29, 258, 335
Strikes: and collective bargaining, 494, 526–27, 530–32, 535–36, 538, 540; National Labor Relations Act and, 518, 522; role of commissioners, 14; types of, 540; and work stoppage provision (of contracts), 414
Student-athletes: amateurism rules, 252–63; Buckley Amendment and, 209–12; and due process, 220, 222–26; eligibility requirements, 234–63; and equal protection, 226–29; graduation rate issues, 26; and injunctive relief, 185–87; instruction/training for, 114; and intentional infliction of emotional distress, 89; judicial review for, 179; Knight Commission and, 193–95; liability insurance for, 152–53; liability of coaches/teachers for, 110–11; medical assistance issues, 115–17, 120–22; and NCAA infractions process, 192; NCAA involvement in violations, 166; participation rules, 244–52; as plaintiffs in lawsuits, 49; provision of adequate supervision for, 111–12; sponsorship/rights agreement concerns, 20; sport-related risk data, 107; state enforcement procedures, 196; worker's compensation issues, 100–101. *See also* College and high school eligibility requirements; High school athletic associations
Subject to the control of, in agency law, 577
Subrogation, 150
Substance Abuse and Behavioral Health Program (NHL), 310
Substantive dismissal cases, 433
Substantive due process, 222–26
Suggestive marks, 670
Summer camps/independent teams (NCAA rules), 258–60
Summer Olympics (Montreal, 1976), 277
"Sunshine laws," 206
Super Bowl: broadcast contracts, 6; sponsoring restrictions, 11
Superstation television, 709
Supreme Court: and due process, 220; and equal protection, 226; jurisdiction, types of, 41, 43; print/online publications, 60

Taft-Hartley Act (1947), 517
Tangible assets, 668
Tax issues: charitable contributions, 760–61; entertainment expenses, 760–61; franchise depreciation issues, 763–64; luxury box rentals, 760–61; nonprofit organizations, 754–55; professional sport franchise tax issues, 761–63; scholarships, 760; state tax issues for player salaries, 765–66; unrelated business income, 755–58
Teachers liability. *See* Coaches and teachers, liability of
Team sports player drafts, 615–28; Major League Baseball, 622–25; Major League Soccer, 627; National Basketball Association, 625–26; National Football League, 616–22; National Hockey League, 626; Women's National Basketball Association, 627–28
Ted Stevens Olympic and Amateur Sports Act, 59, 163, 681, 689–99, 842
Television: and antitrust law, 505–6; broadcasts by Big Four Leagues, 6–7; cable television, 708–9, 740–41; pay cable television, 709; satellite television, 709, 740–41. *See also* Broadcasting
Temporary restraining orders, 183
Tennis. *See* Association of Tennis Professionals (ATP)
Termination rights (athletic contract), 414
Texas Open Records Act, 206
Title I: Employment (ADA), 817
Title II: Public Accommodations Operated by Private Entities (ADA), 818–19
Title II: Public Services (ADA), 817–18
Title IX of the Education Amendments Act (1972), 60, 316–18; gender discrimination cases, 775–76; legality and scope of, 337–42; legislative history of, 323; OCR analysis/method of enforcement, 326–30; OCR policy interpretation, 323–26; post-Civil Rights Restoration Act litigation, 342–49
Title VII (Civil Rights Act of 1964), 766, 772; gender discrimination cases, 772–75; race discrimination cases, 776–78
Tortious interference with contractual relations, 65, 87, 408–10
Tort law, 63–103, 151; harm to economic/dignitary interests, 89–94; intentional torts, 83–89; negligence, 65–82; products liability, 94–97; reckless con-

duct, 82–83; vicarious liability, 97–99; worker's compensation, 99–102

Tort law, applications of, 105–57; administrators, schools, athletic organization liabilities, 117–24; coaches/teachers liability, 110–17; defects in equipment, 147–50; defense of immunity, 124–28; facility owners/possessors liability, 128–39; liability insurance, 152–53; medical personnel liability, 138–42; officials, referees, umpire liabilities, 142–47; participant liability, 106–10; waiver and release of liability, 153–57

Tour de France, 293

Tournaments, antitrust litigation, 507–8

Trademark infringement, 672–80; and Major League Baseball, 674–76; and National Hockey League, 675

Trademark law: ambush marketing, 680–82; described, 665–66; identification function of trademarks, 668–69; licensing programs for intercollegiate athletics, 682–89; and nicknames, 687–89; and the Olympics, 689–92; secondary meaning, 669–70; service marks/collective marks, 667–68; trademark infringement, 672–80. *See also* Lanham Act (1946)

Transfer rules, 249–52

Treatises, 54–55

Treble damages (Clayton Act), 457

Trial components (of civil legal process), 48, 50–52

Umpire liability, 142–47

Underinclusiveness, 227–28

Uniform Athlete Agent Act (2000), 59, 575, 598–609; reason for adopting, 608

Uniform Commercial Code, 97

Uniform Domain Dispute Resolution Policy, 697

Uniform Player Contract: National Basketball Association, 650–62

Unilateral monopolization, 463

Union of European Football Associations (UEFA), 503

Unions (associations) of players, 14; certification by NLRA, 524–25; and collective bargaining, 520; relationships with agents, 590–92; and Section 8 (NLRB), 520–21, 520–23

United States Code (U.S.C.), 59

United States Code Annotated (U.S.C.A.), 59

United States Code Service (U.S.C.S.), 59

United States Football League, 473–74

United States Patent and Trademark Office (USPTO), 672–73

University Interscholastic League (UIL/Texas), 176, 262

University of Michigan Athletic Department (case study), 23–25

Unlawful Internet Gambling Enforcement Act (2006), 810

Unrelated business income, 755–58; broadcast receipts, 759; facility rentals, 758–59; sponsorship revenue, 759–60

Urine testing, 279, 282, 287

U.S. Anti-Doping Agency (USADA), 295

USA Basketball, 29–30, 31–33

USA Track and Field, 161

U.S. Collegiate Athletic Association, 173

U.S. Court of Appeals (for the Fifth Circuit), 206

U.S. Olympic Committee (USOC), 2, 161–65; "Arbitration of Challenge" section of constitution, 202–4; areas of focus of, 164; athlete eligibility regulations, 260–63; and drug testing, 295; on eligibility status decisions, 230–33; enforcement procedures, 198–201; formation of, 161; governing structure support by ASA, 162; organizational chart showing regulatory power, 162; organizational structure, 161; and trademark law, 689–92

U.S. Statutes at Large, 59

U.S. Tennis Association (USTA), 233

U.S. Women's National Soccer Team, 317

Varsity sport vs. club sports (gender discrimination cases), 367–68

Vicarious liability (tort), 97–99, 106, 110; for actions of fans and players, 123; of administrators, schools, universities, 118–20; of coaches and teachers, 111; of employers, 140; independent contractor exception, 98–99; of medical personnel, 138; of referees, officials, umpires, 143; use of (described), 65

Vietnam War, drug testing, 275

Violence in sports: crime, defined, 788–91; off-the-field criminal conduct, 799–800; player and fan violence, 795–97; player vs. official violence, 797–98; player vs. player, 791–95; solutions to, 801–2

Voluntary athletic associations: background information, 160–61; California Interscholastic Federation, 158; high school

athletic associations, 172–78; legal challenge parameters, 159; National Association of Intercollegiate Athletics, 170–71; National Christian College Athletic Association, 171; National Collegiate Athletic Association, 167–72; National Junior College Athletic Association, 171; Pac-10, 158; U.S. Olympic Committee, 2, 161–65
Voluntary Labor Arbitration Rules (American Arbitration Association), 595

Wagner Act (1935), 517, 523
Waiver and release of liability, 151–55
Warranties, 97
Washington Tennis and Education Foundation (WTEF), 478–79
Web sites, sports law, 58
Western Athletic Conference (college football), 167
"Women in Intercollegiate Sport" report, 317
Women's National Basketball Association (WNBA), 2, 3, 15–16; and collective bargaining, 535; draft regulations, 627–28; and drug testing, 312–13; and limited liability corporations, 751–52
Women's Sports Foundation, 316–17
Women's teams, no men's teams (gender discrimination cases), 356–60

Women's teams and men's teams (gender discrimination cases): contact sports, 361–62; noncontact sports, 363; separate but equal, 360–61
Women's Tennis Association, 476–77
Women's United Soccer Association (WUSA), 751
Women's World Cup of Soccer, 316
Workers' compensation (tort), 99–103
World Anti-Doping Agency (WADA), 34–35; prohibited list, 294–95
World Conference on Doping, 294
World Series (baseball): sponsoring restrictions, 11
World Wrestling Entertainment, Inc., 16
Writ of appeal, 43
Writ of certiorari, 43
Written contracts, 370
Wrongful death statutes, 81

Yankees Entertainment and Sports (YES) Network, 6
YES (Yankees Entertainment and Sports) Network, 6–7
Youth Sports Volunteer Coalition (YSVC), 35
YouTube.com (Web site), 738

About the Author

GLENN M. WONG is Professor of Sport Management, University of Massachusetts, Amherst. Wong has authored or coauthored four books on sports and the law, including *The Essentials of Amateur Sports Law* and *Law and Business of the Sports Industries.*